THE HEATH INTRODUCTION TO
LITERATURE

THE HEATH INTRODUCTION TO

LITERATURE

FIFTH EDITION

Alice S. Landy

D. C. HEATH AND COMPANY
Lexington, Massachusetts   Toronto

Address editorial correspondence to:

D. C. Heath and Company
125 Spring Street
Lexington, MA 02173

Acquisitions Editor:	Paul A. Smith
Developmental Editor:	Linda Bieze
Production Editor:	Bryan Woodhouse
Designer:	Kenneth Hollman
Photo Researcher:	Anne Barnard
Production Coordinator:	Lisa Merrill
Permissions Editor:	Margaret Roll

Published simultaneously in Canada.

Printed in the United States of America.

Student Edition International Standard Book Number: 0-669-35510-0

Instructor's Edition International Standard Book Number: 0-669-35511-9

Library of Congress Catalog Number: 95-68032

10 9 8 7 6 5 4 3 2 1

TEXT CREDITS

PREFACE

All five editions of *The Heath Introduction to Literature* have been constructed in consultation with hundreds of teachers of literature and writing from all over the country. Although the text has evolved considerably from its first incarnation, our mission continues to be to provide a rich yet inexpensive collection of literature, organized by genre and broken up into useful units that focus upon various literary concepts, techniques, and modes. It is our hope that students will not only "encounter" literature but also learn new ways to experience, interact with, and write critically about literature. The chapter introductions, apparatus, study questions, and composition instruction are all intended to help the different literary texts cohere into both a thorough presentation of the different genres and a thoughtful, challenging, and *complete* course in reading and writing about literature.

Like previous editions, the fifth edition is divided into four parts. The first part supplies a general introduction to the study of literature. Its opening chapter, on reading literature, introduces the student to the basic components of literature—plot, character, and theme—and to basic critical concepts such as unity and inevitability. This chapter also introduces the philosophy of the text: that literature is a dialogue between writer and reader, an art form whose subject is a vision of humanity and the universe. The second chapter, on writing about literature, reiterates these fundamentals and shows how they underlie the skills and techniques of writing about literature. Whereas the first chapter is philosophical in bent, the second is practical. Work plans, lists of questions, and diagrams make the idea of writing both concrete and comprehensible and provide "how-to's" for the assignments in the rest of the book.

Although these introductory chapters precede the structured parts on fiction, poetry, and drama, they need not be read first. The instructor who wishes to begin with short stories or poems can elicit spontaneous student responses, unguided by study questions. The questions raised in the introductory chapters can then be applied to works everyone has recently read, and the focus of the course will be clearly defined as being the reading *of* (rather than *about*) literature.

The first genre offered is fiction. Its presentation is organized around modes of narration and narrative techniques. The interplay of listener and narrator is thus highlighted, and the basic framework of the text is kept simple. Within this framework, other concepts appear as a natural outgrowth of the subject under discussion and easily become a part of the student's critical vocabulary. The presentation provides a variety of critical concepts within a firmly structured framework—a more satisfying organization than the "grasshopper" approach in which each chapter, or each story, heralds a new topic and leaves students and instructors alike negotiating the jumps between topics as best they can. Seventeen stories are new to this edition. Also, four new thematic groups—The Storytellers, The Reporters, Tales Within Tales, and Autobiography—appear in this edition.

Poetry follows fiction, this being the order preferred by most instructors. Throughout the poetry section we use well-known and highly readable works to introduce the student to the technical aspects of poetry, such as rhythm and verse form, and then to the genre's subtler concerns, among them imagery, the use of sound, and the voice of the speaker. This movement allows the student to begin with a general overview of what a poem *is* and then to delve more deeply into the specific characteristics that *make* it a poem. For those instructors who wish to offer their students works free of critical commentary, an anthology of poems completes the part. Sixteen poems have been added to this edition, appearing in both the introductory chapters and the poetry anthology. Also, two new thematic groups, Poetry as Narrative, and Protest and Social Comment, appear in this edition.

Drama receives strong, chronological coverage in this edition. The section, including works from tragedy, comedy, realism, and contemporary drama, features two plays new to this edition: Shakespeare's *Much Ado About Nothing* and Havel's *Protest*. The chronological organization of this section clearly illustrates the important structural and historical developments of this genre. We are pleased to include G. Blakemore Evans's respected editions of *Hamlet* and *Much Ado About Nothing*.

Within each section there are plentiful study aids: introductory essays, study questions, essay suggestions, and questions for further thought. Objective and subjective responses both have their place as answers to our questions; the emphasis is on knowing the difference and on achieving a judicious balance between the two. In general, questions near the beginning of a section will offer more guidance than those that come later, thus tacitly encouraging students to greater independence as their skills and familiarity with literature grow. Some sets of questions are constructed so that they form an example of how to organize an essay; others concentrate on showing how to follow a theme through a story, poem, or play; still others encourage students to look at a work from as many angles as possible.

We feel that a good textbook, like the literature it contains, must offer variety within unity, and we have done our best to achieve that goal. Our thanks to Skai Ahern, Borough of Manhattan Community College; Michael Anzelone, Nassau Community College; Phillip D. Atteberry, University of Pittsburgh at Titusville; Ethel Bonds, Virginia Western Community College; Thomas Brazie, Glendale Community College; Susan Bullard, Cedar Valley College; Robert

Burke, Joliet Junior College: Adele Carpenter, Lewis and Clark Community College; Sean Clark, Joliet Junior College; Thomas Cody, El Camino College; John Driscoll, Phoenix College; Allan Duane, Ulster County Community College; Lou Ellison, Lurleen B. Wallace State Junior College; Craig Etchison, Allegany Community College; James F. Gordon Jr., Mississippi Delta Junior College; Michael Greene, Wentworth Institute of Technology; Maria Haman, Louisiana Technical University; Julia Jay, San Jacinto College, Central Campus; Jeff Jeske, University of California, Los Angeles; Mary Lund, Henry Ford Community College; J. V. McCrory, William Carey College; Vernon Miles, University of Arkansas; Eileen Neville, Mount Marty College; Don Richardson, Phoenix College; Richard M. Salamas, Henry Ford Community College; Margaret Shepherd, Surry Community College; Rebecca Shuttleworth, Mississippi Delta Junior College; Bev Smith, Lurleen B. Wallace State Junior College; Joel Stancliff, Georgia Institute of Technology; Margaret Stein, University of Notre Dame; Jean Anne Strebinger, University of Notre Dame; Margaret Sullivan, University of California, Los Angeles; Barry Tomkins, Hudson County Community College; John Tucker, Nassau Community College; John A. Weldon, Clinton Community College; and Roger Zimmerman, Lewis and Clark Community College.

We offer a special word of thanks to Rodney Allen for his help with this edition.

Finally, we thank you, the users of this book, who have helped us revise the menu of selections and commentary, and who bring to it your own love of literature and skills in teaching. May you enjoy using this book, and may it serve you well.

ALICE S. LANDY
Editor

PAUL A. SMITH
Senior Editor

D. C. Heath and Company

CONTENTS

❧

Character Study and Social Commentary

AN ANTHOLOGY OF SHORT STORIES

POETRY

Elements of Poetry

The Speaker in the Poem

Imagery

Sound

AN ANTHOLOGY OF POEMS

DRAMA

THE HEATH INTRODUCTION TO
LITERATURE

INTRODUCTION:
ON LITERATURE

1

THE BASES OF LITERATURE

Literature has its roots in one of the most basic human desires—the desire for pleasure. Its writers find one source of pleasure in mastering the difficult demands of their craft. If they do well, they then reap a second delight from witnessing the pleasure their work gives to others. Readers, meanwhile, derive pleasure from literature's power to imitate life. A truly good book can speak of imaginary people so vividly that they seem more alive than people we meet on the street, and can make us care about its characters as if they were close friends.

We are always curious about each other, and usually curious about ourselves as well. Why do we behave as we do? What are the causes of our actions? Literature is far from having all the answers, but it does offer hints, suggestions, and flashes of insight. Moreover, it offers them in such a way as to refresh and encourage our own thinking, and so leads us to insights of our own. Readers have many standards for judging writers. But one enduring standard is the writers' power to interpret us, as humans, to ourselves. The greater the writers' knowledge of people seems to be, the more openly they share their knowledge with us, the higher we rate them. We speak with disdain of shallow or insincere writers; we demand truth and sincerity even in the most fantastic fiction.

Literature, then, exists because it pleases us. And it pleases us by imitating life—or, more precisely, by displaying its writers' visions of life as it is or as the writers think it should be. But how does it contrive its imitation? Its only medium is words; and we know how hard it is to make words say what we want them to say. How do writers handle their words to get such powerful effects from them? What guidelines help them make the million-and-one choices that result in a play, a poem, or a story?

The first necessities for any work of literature—and therefore the first things that writers must consider—are **plot** and **character.** These may occur to a writer in either order. That is, a writer may first imagine some characters, and then decide what actions they are to perform; or a writer may envision some action, and then decide on the people who must perform it. Every work of literature, however, must have both action and characters. It cannot please us, or hold our interest, otherwise.

It may seem that poetry is an exception to this rule. Whereas stories and plays tend to present fully developed plots with sequences of actions with discernible beginnings, middles, and ends, poems more often plunge us into the middle of an event, and may tell us neither what came before the event nor what comes after it. Here, for instance, is a poem with no physical action at all. Yet it shows us one person, at least, and gives us some insight into his actions and feelings.

George Gordon, Lord Byron

(1788–1824)

So We'll Go No More A-Roving

> So we'll go no more a-roving
>   So late into the night,
> Though the heart be still as loving,
>   And the moon be still as bright.
>
> 5 For the sword outwears its sheath,
>   And the soul wears out the breast,
> And the heart must pause to breathe,
>   And Love itself have rest.
>
> Though the night was made for loving,
> 10   And the day returns too soon,
> Yet we'll go no more a-roving
>   By the light of the moon.

We know several things about the speaker of this poem. We know that he has enjoyed "roving," and that he still thinks warmly of it, because he declares that "the night was made for loving, / And the day returns too soon." We know that he feels weary, like a sheath worn out by the motions of the sword within it. We hear him declare that his roving days are done. But we also hear him speak of pausing and resting, verbs that imply an eventual return to action. And so we begin to wonder: is he really finished with love, as he says he is? The action of the poem might thus be described as the act of the lover forswearing love. Its interest arises from our recognition of the complex emotions the renunciation reveals. It is the action, and the emotion, of a moment; but it is none the less real—and none the less action—for its momentary nature.

For now, however, let us return to the more thoroughly developed plots of drama and fiction. These, too, must find some balance between action and emotion, some method of telling us both what the characters do and how they feel. A given story may emphasize action or feeling; that choice, like so many others, is up to its writer. But it must contain some of both. We have no interest in unfeeling characters or in characters who do nothing.

In addition to a plot and to characters who act and feel, a work of literature must have **unity** and **coherence.** It must make us believe that its characters really would have committed the actions it says they commit, and that the actions could really have taken place. At its best, the movement of a play, a poem, or a story must make us feel that the tale could have reached no other end, and that it could have reached it in no other way. When this happens, the story's ending seems inevitable. Its characters and its actions have convinced us wholly. A sense of inevitability is thus another hallmark of a fine work of literature. Works so marked tend to be moving and powerful.

The **language** of a work of literature is also important. Words have so many undercurrents of meaning that the change of one word may change our image of a scene or a character. Consider, for instance, the difference between *a thin, tense man; a thin, nervous man;* and *a thin harried man*—or the difference between *a plump woman, a well-rounded woman,* and *an overweight woman.* A writer's language must be chosen with care. It should carry overtones that enrich our sense of the story, thus adding to the pleasure we get from the tale. And it must avoid all false tones, for those would diminish our pleasure. Again, we demand at least that the words fit the actions and characters of which they tell. And again, we shall find that the best seem almost inevitable. Reading them, we cannot imagine the author having used any other words.

When we read, we don't want to be aware of these choices of words and acts and characters. We don't want to hear the author muttering behind the scenes: "I need this word, not that one. This character must say this; that description must carry this message." Rather, we want to be able to concentrate on the story itself, accepting everything within it as valid and necessary parts of its world. When we discuss and analyze works of literature, however, we do become aware of the choices the writers made in constructing them. We note who the characters are and how they relate to each other. We observe how the action begins, how it ends, and how it is carried from beginning to ending. We study the ways in which the language characterizes people and events and consider the broader or deeper meanings it suggests.

These questions, we may note, are **questions of fact.** Their answers can be found, decided, and agreed upon. We can count the characters in *Hamlet,* and we will learn that Hamlet is a prince of Denmark, that Gertrude is his mother and Claudius his stepfather, and that the ghost who appears from time to time is the ghost of Hamlet's murdered father. Similarly, we learn that eight people are killed during the course of the play (one by stabbing, one by drowning, two by beheading, one by poison, and three by some combination of sword wounds and poison) and that virtually none of the major characters is still alive when the play ends. There is no question about any of these happenings and no reason to argue about them.

Questions of fact, however, are only a beginning in thinking about a work of literature. They tell us certain choices a writer made, but they rarely tell us why the writer made those particular choices. To learn that, we must go on to **questions of interpretation,** questions that deal with the artistic vision underlying the work and thus with such issues as theme, pattern, message, and meaning.

Message and **meaning** are not universal to literature. They belong to one school of literature, the **didactic.** When writers or critics demand that a story carry a message to its readers, that it "mean something" to them, they are saying that literature should teach us something and that it should appeal to our sense of moral values. At its simplest, this approach ends in pat morals: "Always tell the truth; stop beating up on your fellow humans." On a more sophisticated level, however, didacticism becomes what the critic Matthew Arnold called "high seriousness" and produces literature that deals with such complex questions as the value of human life and the sources of human ideals and aspirations.

Not all literature is didactic. Some writers believe that literature does not need to make a moral statement. For these writers, a work of literature is important for its own sake, not for any message it might carry. As one modern poet put it, "A poem should not mean, but be."[1] In works like these, the concept of message does not apply; to impose it upon them is to falsify the intent of the writer.

The questions of **theme** and **pattern,** however, concern all literature. Within any work of literature that strikes us as unified and complete, we will find some sort of pattern into which its parts fit or through which they are perceived. Didactic tales, for example, present acts and people in terms of a moral order. Hence the tales tend to be built around patterns of good and evil, temptation and response. In contrast, a Romantic poem describing a summer day might have sensory impressions of light and shade, coolness and warmth, as its unifying vision.

There may be many patterns—patterns of action, characterization, language, or metaphor—within a single work. Sometimes each will work separately; sometimes several will be intertwined to bear on a single theme. Sometimes, too, several themes will be interwoven within one work to create a complexity of vision that no single theme could contain. But always there will be that sense of a single ordered vision embracing and unifying all the patterns or themes.

When we study literature, we first look at each story as an entity in itself, existing on its own terms. We enter the world of the story and speak of its characters and narrator as though they were living people. Eventually, however, we begin to wonder about the writers of the stories. Why did they choose to create these characters, to have them perform these actions, to tell their tales from this particular point of view?

We can never know exactly what writers had in mind when they were writing their stories. The process of writing is too complex, with too much of it hidden even from the writers themselves, to allow any sure or simple answers to that question. But we should examine our own ideas on the subject—our sense of what the writers seem to consider important and what values or feelings of ours they seem to be invoking because our impression of the writers' values and intentions plays an important part in our response to their work.

Here interpretation becomes most individual and most varied. We all read the same words when we read a story. We observe the same characters acting out the same deeds and passions. But we each interpret them a little differently be-

---

[1] Archibald MacLeish, "Ars Poetica," p. 525.

cause of our individual views of life, our interests, and our experience. Therefore, when we try to explain how the story works, or decide what themes are being emphasized, we read some of our own perceptions into the story.

If we realize that we are interpreting, all is well. Then we can say, "This is how it seems to me." We can look for patterns of language or imagery and details of action or characterization to support our view. We can listen to others who have other views and evaluate the support they bring for their arguments; and, in the end, we can probably come to a pretty fair idea of what the story does have to offer and how it is able to offer it.

On the other hand, if we do not recognize the extent to which we are active interpreters of what we read, we may have trouble when we try to deal with such subjective issues as theme or message. For then we may make the error of saying, "I see this. Therefore the author intended it that way and I have found the only correct interpretation this story can possibly have." Because very few works of literature will not admit some variation in interpretation, definitive statements such as this are wrong more often than not. It is true that there are limits to the range of interpretations we can apply to a work of literature if we are to read it honestly on its own terms. Within those limits, however, we must be willing to acknowledge various ways of looking at it.

We must also be willing to allow our perceptions to change. It often happens that what we notice the first time we read a story is not what seems most important to us later on. Nor would it make sense to talk or write about a poem or a story if our perception of it could not be enriched by the discussion. Too, we must be willing to use our full judgment, to read the story carefully and attentively. We must be sure we are trying to discover what it really does say rather than simply assuming that it says what we want it to say. Once we have done this, however, we should be able to feel comfortable with our judgments and our responses. Above all, we must not undervalue ourselves. We are the people for whom these stories, plays, and poems are written. If we cannot trust ourselves, we will have a hard time trusting them.

2

WRITING ABOUT LITERATURE

Literature allows writers to share their ideas and visions with their readers. Their work is not complete until someone has read it and responded to it.

As readers, we too have something to say. At the very least, we have opinions about the work itself, but we also may have other ideas to express. Perhaps we are moved to compare this story with others, or perhaps it has given us some new ideas that we want to explore further. Sometimes we share our ideas directly with others in face-to-face discussions. At other times, we become writers in order to communicate our thoughts and opinions.

The first part of writing about literature, therefore, is thinking about it. This step is perhaps the most vital part of the process, because we need to know not only what we think but why we think as we do. Which of our thoughts come from the work itself? Which have been inspired by it? Which come from our predispositions and preconceptions about literature?

We enjoy stories for many reasons. Some are intrinsic to the story itself: language artfully used, characters we believe in and care about, actions that carry significant messages for us or give us new insight into ourselves and our society. (Whether the story provides that insight by answering questions for us or by urging us into asking our own questions does not matter here. What *does* matter is that the impetus for question or answer comes from within the story itself.) Other causes of enjoyment are external, coming not from the artistry of the story, but from the fact that the story fits our current notions of what a story should be like or calls forth some pleasant personal memories. In short, the external factors in our response to a story come from things we already think or feel. Intrinsic factors come from the writer's craftsmanship and art.[1]

When we read for pleasure alone, we need not care where our pleasure comes from. Any appeal a story may have will be welcome. When we study literature, however, we want to concentrate on the intrinsic qualities of the works we read, for they can teach us most about the craft and the workings of literature. It is a story's intrinsic qualities, therefore, and our response to them, that we want to write about when we write about literature.

When we rule out external responses to literature and say that we are only going to talk and write about its intrinsic qualities, we are not denying the individuality of our responses. In fact, only when we escape from our prejudices and

---

[1]What is true for stories is true for plays and poems as well. For the rest of this chapter, therefore, I shall use the word *stories* to stand for all types of literature, rather than repeating the more awkward phrases *stories, plays, and poems* and *works of literature.*

9

preconceptions about literature can we respond most freely to the stories we read. Even when we write most directly of the story itself and the art that created it, our writing will contain an emotional component as well as an intellectual one. Emotion and intellect together answer such questions as, Does the hero's death seem inevitable? and How has it been made to seem so?

All analysis ends in judgment. All questions of How is this done? begin or end with Is it a success? It would be useless to ask How has the writer characterized his heroine? if we could not also ask Has he made me care what happens to her? Literature appeals to mind and emotions alike; our response, therefore, must be both analytic and emotional, objective and subjective. Concentrating on those things that are intrinsic to the story does not deny the subjective component of our response. Rather, it frees us for more truly personal reactions, subjective and objective alike, even while it helps us recognize how and why we are responding.

Before we begin to write about a story, therefore, we should ask ourselves some version of the following questions:

1. Which aspects of the story had the greatest impact on me?
2. What did they seem to be saying? How did they say it? (Or what did they make me think that seemed new to me? How did they make me think it?)
3. How did other aspects of the story support or contribute to my response?
4. How did these particular aspects of the story help create the story's total effect?

We start, that is, with our response to the story; we move from there to an analysis of the art that creates the response; and then we return to the overall impression or effect.

When we write, we follow the same pattern of response, analysis, and final judgment. Unless we have unlimited time and paper, however, we will not be able to write down all that we have thought about the story. Choices must be made: What shall I include? What shall I emphasize? To make those choices, we must consider not only the story and our response to it, but the purpose of our paper and the audience for which we are writing it.

Let's look at two extreme examples. Let's imagine, first, that we keep a journal or diary and that we want to record in it the fact that we read and enjoyed a story. In this case, our main interest would be our own reaction to the story; our writing, therefore, would concentrate on our subjective response. We would mention only those incidents or characters that impressed us most strongly; and we could write in whatever style we pleased, for we would be our only audience.

At the other extreme, suppose we were writing a paper for a scholarly journal. In this case, we would write in an objective, balanced style, presenting carefully worked-out analyses of each aspect of the story that related to our topic. We would define our terms carefully and provide adequate illustrations to support our thesis. In fact, we would be writing almost like a debater, trying to make our points as clear, convincing, and firmly based on factual evidence as possible.

Most writing assignments lie somewhere between these extremes. Two we might look at are book reviews and English papers. Let's consider what these types of writing most often say. Then let's look at how they can go about saying it.

Book reviews tend to be frankly subjective, focusing on "what I liked and why I liked it" (or, alternatively, "why you shouldn't waste time or money on this book"). By its very nature, a review commits the reviewer to making judgments: the book may be "one of the year's best," or "not up to this author's usual standards," or simply "a pleasant afternoon's reading." Too, the reviewer may try to judge what type of reader would enjoy the book most: "Readers with a taste for psychological studies will enjoy . . .", or "Mystery fans will welcome the appearance of. . . ."

A brief review may contain little more than these judgments. A more thorough review will usually provide evidence to support them, by discussing some particularly outstanding character or episode or by quoting a few lines of description or dialogue as a sample of the writer's style. Readers of reviews are presumed to be asking themselves, Is this a book I want to read? Through judgments and illustrations supporting the judgments, reviews are designed to help readers answer that question.

A review, therefore, will generally begin in one of two ways. It will either start right out with its broadest judgment to show exactly where the reviewer stands, or it will start out with a "teaser," a quote or detail from the book that seems striking enough to catch the readers' attention and "tease" them into reading at least the review, if not the book itself.

Then will come the explanation, details, and analyses. What was it that made the experience of reading the book so enjoyable? Why is the teaser a good sample of what the book has to offer? Reviews may focus on one aspect of a book, such as its characters, or they may glance at many aspects in turn. But they must maintain a balance between the personal interest of the reviewers' subjective comments and the objective analyses with which they try to convince us that they are sound judges of books whose opinions should be respected. And they must bring their comments and analyses together again in a final summary, judgment, or call to action: "Rush right out and buy this book; you won't be disappointed."

Reviewers, then, consider their audience (potential readers of the book being reviewed) and their purpose (telling their readers that the book exists and helping them decide whether or not they want to read it). They offer their own judgments, support them with relevant evidence, and draw all together to a logical conclusion.

English papers demand many of the same techniques as reviews and are often written in similar formats. They vary in scope and purpose, however, more than reviews do. The assignments in this book provide a range of possible types of papers.

Many of the assignments are quite narrowly defined. Their purpose is to make you look closely at some particular technique the writer used—the role of the narrator in a story, for example, or the way a theme is carried through a tale. In this case your writing, too, must be tightly focused, your style almost wholly objective. Your first sentence will probably state your basic theme; and every sentence that follows, down to your final summation, will bear directly on that theme. The particular points you discuss, and the order in which you present them, may be suggested by the questions or instructions of the assignment itself. The evidence with which you support your answers will come from within the story. But the finished product will be very much your own: a tight, coherent piece of writing built on your own handling of the material given to you by the story.

Other assignments are broader or ask that you define your own subject (for example, What do you think is the major theme of this story? How would you support your view?). Now your own judgments must be more boldly expressed. You must decide which aspects of the story should be emphasized, and which are irrelevant to the question at hand. Your responsibility is not only to provide evidence to support a theory you were told to discuss, but first to set up your theory and then to support it.

Again, you will want to write a tightly focused paper, making full use of detailed evidence. But your opening, conclusion, and whatever general statements control your central discussion will be somewhat broader in their implications than those of the earlier assignment, and they will represent your own judgments as to what is most important to the story and to your essay. This essay, too, will follow the general format of initial response → analysis → final summary. But the analysis will be fuller and more complex than is necessary with a more narrowly defined paper.

Rarely, however, do ideas come to us already neatly arranged in these logical progressions. Usually, when we first think of writing an essay, we think of a number of random things. If we are clever about such things, we jot those down. Later, more ideas will arrive—some of them outgrowths of our first ideas, some of them totally new ideas; jot those down, also.

The way to deal with this process is as follows:

1. Write down each idea as you get it. You can write them down as a numbered list on a sheet of paper, or you can write each on a separate card (a real 3″ × 5″ or 4″ × 6″ card, or a computer-software "card").
2. When you have collected a fair number of ideas, look them over. Look for ideas that fall together into groups, ideas that relate to each other. If you are using cards, create physical groups of cards from these logical connections (see Figure 1). If you are using a numbered list, write your groups of numbers down on a new sheet of paper (see Figure 2). Note that some ideas may not fit neatly into groups. These will be left over, by themselves.
3. Look at your various groups. What is your main topic for each? You may find your general topic already declared as one of your original ideas, or you

may have to create it now. In any event, create and mark "major topic" cards or list entries to go at the head of each group.

4. Now look at your major topics, and at your "left over" ideas. Which groups and singletons fit together well into a paper of the sort you want to write? Are there any "holes" in your paper, now that you see it starting to take shape? If so, fill them in now, creating cards or entries for them. Do some ideas, or groups of ideas, not fit into the paper as you now see it? If so, leave them out. Even professional writers often throw away much of their early work, and this "gathering, grouping, and arranging" process is one that many professional writers use when they are working on explanatory books and articles.

5. Arrange your chosen major topics, with the ideas that support them, in the order you think will make the strongest paper. If you need new entries for introductory and closing statements, sketch those out now and put them in place. You now have the outline for the first draft of your paper. In fact, if you wrote out your ideas very fully, your first draft may be half written already!

It is possible that, as you work, you will become dissatisfied with your first outline and will modify it. Ideas you first included may end up omitted; ideas that were rejected early on may come back in. Papers and essays are often dynamic things, changing as they go along. Sometimes, indeed, it's not till you've sketched out your first draft that you realize what it was that you *really* wanted to write—and it's not this at all.

The act of writing about literature, by forcing us to look closely at what we have read and to analyze both the work and our own responses to it, can thus be seen as the final step in the act of reading. Now we are not only enjoying the words by which someone else speaks to us but also stretching our own minds to the task of communicating with others. In reading and writing, we take an active role and thus reassert ourselves as active, thinking, feeling beings. The opportunity to make that reassertion may well represent one of the deepest values of literature. It is certainly an opportunity well worth responding to.

FIGURE 1

Step 1.   Ideas sketched out on cards, in no special order.

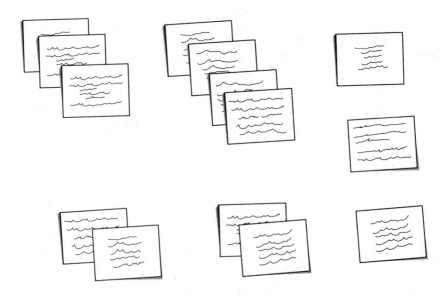

Step 2.   Group by relevance to each other.

Step 3.   Add headings, where you don't already have them.

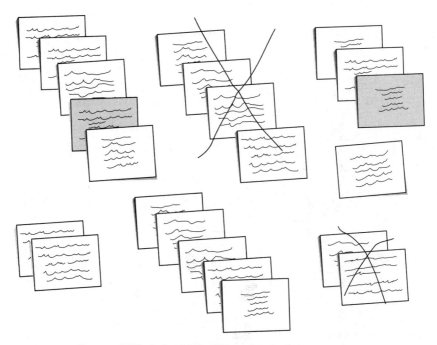

Step 4.   Fill in holes. Discard ideas that don't fit this paper.

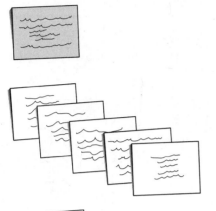

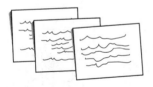

Step 5.   Arrange chosen entries in outline
order. Add introduction, closing, if needed.

FIGURE 2

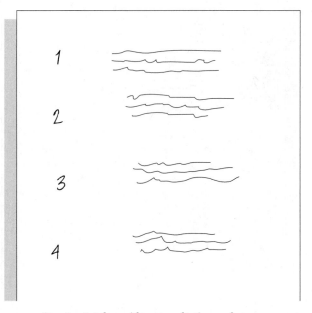

Step 1. Jot down ideas, numbering each one.

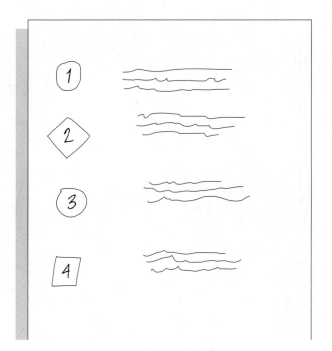

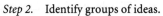

Step 2. Identify groups of ideas.

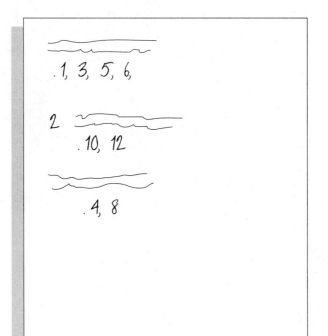

Step 3.   List groups. Add headings (topic sentences) if needed.

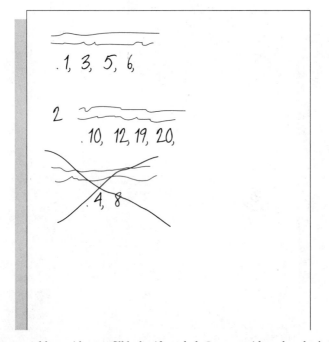

Step 4.   Add new ideas to fill holes if needed. Cross out ideas that don't fit.

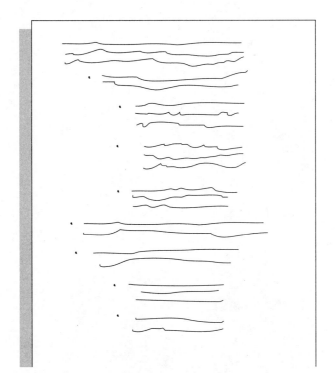

Step 5.   Recopy in outline form. Add introduction, closing, if needed.

FICTION

Fiction as Narrative

3

THE ART OF NARRATION:
GIVING MEANING TO ACTION

Fiction is the art of the storyteller. Not only are writers of fiction storytellers themselves, but within every story they create a new storyteller, the narrator of the tale. It is the narrator's voice we hear speaking as we read a novel or short story. The narrator introduces the tale to us, keeps us amused during its telling, and dismisses us at its end. The narrator describes scenes and characters, relates events, sets the tone of the tale, and supplies whatever meanings or explanations the author sees fit to provide.

Reader and story are thus brought together by the narrator. For this reason, the study of fiction usually begins with a study of types of narrators and narrations. Let us now look at two very brief stories: first a folk tale from one of the oldest traditions of storytelling and then a more modern tale. Notice in each case the simplicity of the action and the sharp contrasts drawn among the few characters. Listen to the voices of the storytellers as they build their tales.

Clever Manka (Czechoslovakia)

Anonymous

There was once a rich farmer who was as grasping and unscrupulous as he was rich. He was always driving a hard bargain and always getting the better of his poor neighbors. One of these neighbors was a humble shepherd who, in return for service, was to receive from the farmer a heifer. When the time of payment came, the farmer refused to give the shepherd the heifer, and the shepherd was forced to lay the matter before the burgomaster.

The burgomaster, who was a young man and as yet not very experienced, listened to both sides, and when he had deliberated, he said:

"Instead of deciding this case, I will put a riddle to you both, and the man who makes the best answer shall have the heifer. Are you agreed?"

The farmer and the shepherd accepted this proposal and the burgomaster said:

"Well, then, here is my riddle: What is the swiftest thing in the world? What is the sweetest thing? What is the richest? Think out your answers and bring them to me at this same hour tomorrow."

The farmer went home in a temper.

"What kind of burgomaster is this young fellow!" he growled. "If he had let me keep the heifer, I'd have sent him a bushel of pears. But now I'm in a fair way of losing the heifer, for I can't think of any answer to his foolish riddle."

"What is the matter, husband?" his wife asked.

"It's that new burgomaster. The old one would have given me the heifer without any argument, but this young man thinks to decide the case by asking us riddles."

When he told his wife what the riddle was, she cheered him greatly by telling him that she knew the answers at once.

"Why, husband," said she, "our gray mare must be the swiftest thing in the world. You know yourself nothing ever passes us on the road. As for the sweetest, did you ever taste honey any sweeter than ours? And I'm sure there's nothing richer than our chest of golden ducats that we've been laying by these forty years."

The farmer was delighted.

"You're right, wife, you're right! That heifer remains ours!"

The shepherd, when he got home, was downcast and sad. He had a daughter, a clever girl named Manka, who met him at the door of his cottage and asked:

"What is it, father? What did the burgomaster say?"

The shepherd sighed.

"I'm afraid I've lost the heifer. The burgomaster set us a riddle, and I know I shall never guess it."

"Perhaps I can help you," Manka said. "What is it?"

The shepherd gave her the riddle, and the next day, as he was setting out for the burgomaster's, Manka told him what answers to make.

When he reached the burgomaster's house, the farmer was already there rubbing his hands and beaming with self-importance.

The burgomaster again propounded the riddle and then asked the farmer his answers.

The farmer cleared his throat and with a pompous air began:

"The swiftest thing in the world? Why, my dear sir, that's my gray mare, of course, for no other horse ever passes us on the road. The sweetest? Honey from my beehives, to be sure. The richest? What can be richer than my chest of golden ducats!"

And the farmer squared his shoulders and smiled triumphantly.

"H'm," said the young burgomaster dryly. Then he asked:

"What answers does the shepherd make?"

The shepherd bowed politely and said:

"The swiftest thing in the world is thought, for thought can run any distance in the twinkling of an eye. The sweetest thing of all is sleep, for when a man is tired and sad, what can be sweeter? The richest thing is the earth, for out of the earth come all the riches of the world."

"Good!" the burgomaster cried. "Good! The heifer goes to the shepherd!"

Later the burgomaster said to the shepherd:

"Tell me now, who gave you those answers? I'm sure they never came out of your own head."

At first the shepherd tried not to tell, but when the burgomaster pressed him, he confessed that they came from his daughter, Manka. The burgomaster, who thought he would like to make another test of Manka's cleverness, sent for ten eggs. He gave them to the shepherd and said:

"Take these eggs to Manka and tell her to have them hatched out by tomorrow and to bring me the chicks."

When the shepherd reached home and gave Manka the burgomaster's message, Manka laughed and said: "Take a handful of millet and go right back to the burgomaster. Say to him: 'My daughter sends you this millet. She says that if you plant it, grow it, and have it harvested by tomorrow, she'll bring you the ten chicks and you can feed them the ripe grain.'"

When the burgomaster heard this, he laughed heartily.

"That's a clever girl of yours," he told the shepherd. "If she's as comely as she is clever, I think I'd like to marry her. Tell her to come to see me, but she must come neither by day nor by night, neither riding nor walking, neither dressed nor undressed."

When Manka received this message, she waited until the next dawn when night was gone and day not yet arrived. Then she wrapped herself in a fish net and, throwing one leg over a goat's back and keeping one foot on the ground, she went to the burgomaster's house.

Now I ask you: did she go dressed? No, she wasn't dressed. A fish net isn't clothing. Did she go undressed? Of course not, for wasn't she covered with a fish net? Did she walk to the burgomaster's? No, she didn't walk, for she went with one leg thrown over a goat. Then did she ride? Of course she didn't ride, for wasn't she walking on one foot?

When she reached the burgomaster's house, she called out:

"Here I am, Mr. Burgomaster, and I've come neither by day nor by night, neither riding nor walking, neither dressed nor undressed."

The young burgomaster was so delighted with Manka's cleverness and so pleased with her comely looks that he proposed to her at once and in a short time married her.

"But understand, my dear Manka," he said, "you are not to use that cleverness of yours at my expense. I won't have you interfering in any of my cases. In fact, if ever you give advice to anyone who comes to me for judgment, I'll turn you out of my house at once and send you home to your father."

All went well for a time. Manka busied herself in her housekeeping and was careful not to interfere in any of the burgomaster's cases.

Then one day two farmers came to the burgomaster to have a dispute settled. One of the farmers owned a mare that had foaled in the marketplace. The colt had run under the wagon of the other farmer, and thereupon the owner of the wagon claimed the colt as his property.

The burgomaster, who was thinking of something else while the case was being presented, said carelessly:

"The man who found the colt under his wagon is, of course, the owner of the colt."

As the owner of the mare was leaving the burgomaster's house, he met Manka and stopped to tell her about the case. Manka was ashamed of her husband for making so foolish a decision, and she said to the farmer:

"Come back this afternoon with a fishing net and stretch it across the dusty road. When the burgomaster sees you, he will come out and ask you what you are doing. Say to him that you're catching fish. When he asks you how you can expect to catch fish in a dusty road, tell him it's just as easy for you to catch fish in a dusty road as it is for a wagon to foal. Then he'll see the injustice of his decision and have the colt returned to you. But remember one thing: you mustn't let him find out that it was I who told you to do this."

That afternoon, when the burgomaster chanced to look out the window, he saw a man stretching a fish net across the dusty road. He went out to him and asked:

"What are you doing?"

"Fishing."

"Fishing in a dusty road? Are you daft?"

"Well," the man said, "it's just as easy for me to catch fish in a dusty road as it is for a wagon to foal."

Then the burgomaster recognized the man as the owner of the mare, and he had to confess that what he said was true.

"Of course the colt belongs to your mare and must be returned to you. But tell me," he said, "who put you up to this? You didn't think of it yourself."

The farmer tried not to tell, but the burgomaster questioned him until he found out that Manka was at the bottom of it. This made him very angry. He went into the house and called his wife.

"Manka," he said, "did you forget what I told you would happen if you went interfering in any of my cases? Home you go this very day. I don't care to hear any excuses. The matter is settled. You may take with you the one thing you like best in my house, for I won't have people saying that I treated you shabbily."

Manka made no outcry.

"Very well, my dear husband, I shall do as you say: I shall go home to my father's cottage and take with me the one thing I like best in your house. But don't make me go until after supper. We have been very happy together and I should like to eat one last meal with you. Let us have no more words but be kind to each other as we've always been and then part as friends."

The burgomaster agreed to this, and Manka prepared a fine supper of all the dishes of which her husband was particularly fond. The burgomaster opened his choicest wine and pledged Manka's health. Then he set to, and the supper was so good that he ate and ate and ate. And the more he ate, the more he drank until at last he grew drowsy and fell sound asleep in his chair. Then without awakening him, Manka had him carried out to the wagon that was waiting to take her home to her father.

The next morning, when the burgomaster opened his eyes, he found himself lying in the shepherd's cottage.

"What does this mean?" he roared out.

"Nothing, dear husband, nothing!" Manka said. "You know you told me I might take with me the one thing I liked best in your house, so of course I took you! That's all."

For a moment the burgomaster rubbed his eyes in amazement. Then he laughed loud and heartily to think how Manka had outwitted him.

"Manka," he said, "you're too clever for me. Come on, my dear, let's go home."

So, they climbed back into the wagon and drove home.

The burgomaster never again scolded his wife, but thereafter whenever a very difficult case came up, he always said:

"I think we had better consult my wife. You know she's a very clever woman."

The Story of an Hour

Kate Chopin (1851–1904)

Knowing that Mrs. Mallard was afflicted with a heart trouble, great care was taken to break to her as gently as possible the news of her husband's death.

It was her sister Josephine who told her, in broken sentences; veiled hints that revealed in half concealing. Her husband's friend Richards was there, too, near her. It was he who had been in the newspaper office when intelligence of the railroad disaster was received, with Brently Mallard's name leading the list of "killed." He had only taken the time to assure himself of its truth by a second telegram, and had hastened to forestall any less careful, less tender friend in bearing the sad message.

She did not hear the story as many women have heard the same, with a paralyzed inability to accept its significance. She wept at once, with sudden, wild abandonment, in her sister's arms. When the storm of grief had spent itself she went away to her room alone. She would have no one follow her.

There stood, facing the open window, a comfortable, roomy armchair. Into this she sank, pressed down by a physical exhaustion that haunted her body and seemed to reach into her soul.

She could see in the open square before her house the tops of trees that were all aquiver with the new spring life. The delicious breath of rain was in the air. In the street below a peddler was crying his wares. The notes of a distant song which some one was singing reached her faintly, and countless sparrows were twittering in the eaves.

There were patches of blue sky showing here and there through the clouds that had met and piled one above the other in the west facing her window.

She sat with her head thrown back upon the cushion of the chair, quite motionless, except when a sob came up into her throat and shook her, as a child who has cried itself to sleep continues to sob in its dreams.

She was young, with a fair, calm face, whose lines bespoke repression and even a certain strength. But now there was a dull stare in her eyes, whose gaze was fixed away off yonder on one of those patches of blue sky. It was not a glance of reflection, but rather indicated a suspension of intelligent thought.

There was something coming to her and she was waiting for it, fearfully. What was it? She did not know; it was too subtle and elusive to name. But she felt it, creeping out of the sky, reaching toward her through the sounds, the scents, the color that filled the air.

Now her bosom rose and fell tumultuously. She was beginning to recognize this thing that was approaching to possess her, and she was striving to beat it back with her will—as powerless as her two white slender hands would have been.

When she abandoned herself a little whispered word escaped her slightly parted lips. She said it over and over under her breath: "free, free, free!" The vacant stare and the look of terror that had followed it went from her eyes. They stayed keen and bright. Her pulses beat fast, and the coursing blood warmed and relaxed every inch of her body.

She did not stop to ask if it were or were not a monstrous joy that held her. A clear and exalted perception enabled her to dismiss the suggestion as trivial.

She knew that she would weep again when she saw the kind, tender hands folded in death; the face that had never looked save with love upon her, fixed and gray and dead. But she saw beyond that bitter moment a long procession of years to come that would belong to her absolutely. And she opened and spread her arms out to them in welcome.

There would be no one to live for her during those coming years; she would live for herself. There would be no powerful will bending hers in that blind persistence with which men and women believe they have a right to impose a private will upon a fellow-creature. A kind intention or a cruel intention made the act seem no less a crime as she looked upon it in that brief moment of illumination.

And yet she had loved him—sometimes. Often she had not. What did it matter! What could love, the unsolved mystery, count for in face of this possession of self-assertion which she suddenly recognized as the strongest impulse of her being!

"Free! Body and soul free!" she kept whispering.

Josephine was kneeling before the closed door with her lips to the keyhole, imploring for admission. "Louise, open the door! I beg; open the door—you will make yourself ill. What are you doing, Louise? For heaven's sake open the door."

"Go away. I am not making myself ill." No; she was drinking in a very elixir of life through that open window.

Her fancy was running riot along those days ahead of her. Spring days, and summer days, and all sorts of days that would be her own. She breathed a quick prayer that life might be long. It was only yesterday she had thought with a shudder that life might be long.

She arose at length and opened the door to her sister's importunities. There was a feverish triumph in her eyes, and she carried herself unwittingly like a goddess of Victory. She clasped her sister's waist, and together they descended the stairs. Richards stood waiting for them at the bottom.

Some one was opening the front door with a latchkey. It was Brently Mallard who entered, a little travel-stained, composedly carrying his grip-sack and umbrella. He had been far from the scene of accident, and did not even know there had been one. He stood amazed at Josephine's piercing cry; at Richards' quick motion to screen him from the view of his wife.

But Richards was too late.

When the doctors came they said she had died of heart disease—of joy that kills.

THINKING ABOUT WHAT WE'VE READ

How can we compare these two stories we have just read? What can we say about them?

We can begin by noticing some things the two stories have in common. For instance, both are quite short. Both have women as their main characters (or protagonists); both women are loved by those who know them, and each one's marriage is an important element in her story.

Next, we can look at the ways in which the two stories differ. Before you read further, make a list—by yourselves or as a group—of the differences you notice between the two stories. Then, as we consider what steps one should take when thinking about a story in order to discuss it (either by itself or in comparison with some other story), and how we can apply these steps to "Clever Manka" and

"The Story of an Hour," you can find out how many of the ideas in the essay you yourselves discovered.

Let's return now to our questions: What steps should one take when thinking about a story, in order to discuss it and write about it? How can we apply these steps to "Clever Manka" and "The Story of an Hour"?

STEP 1.   Begin with your initial impressions.

The first thing to do is to jot down whatever points or features about the story (or stories) strike you as being most noticeable—the ideas that affect you most strongly. For example, the most striking difference I notice between these two stories is that Manka, because of her cleverness, is always triumphant—a victor—while Louise Mallard seems destined to be a victim. Manka's story ends happily, with its heroine and her husband living happily ever after, whereas Mrs. Mallard's tale ends, surprisingly and grimly, with her misunderstood death. I notice, too, that my mood after ending each story varies accordingly. You probably had other "first impressions," or more of them; but these will do for a sample.

STEP 2.   Consider the structure of the story.

The ordering of incidents within a story may be spoken of as its **structure.** Traditionally, a story's structure has been said to consist of four basic parts:

1. The **exposition**—the beginning of the story, which introduces the reader to the tale's setting (time and place) and to some or all of its characters.
2. The **conflict.** Every story centers on a conflict of some sort: one person, or group of people, against another; people against nature; an individual against some rule or custom of society. Generally, the conflict increases in tension or in complexity until it reaches a climax.
3. The **climax**—the point of greatest tension, at which the turning point or breaking point is reached.
4. The **denouement** or **resolution**—the ending, which brings the tale to a close, picking up the pieces of the action and reordering the lives left disordered by the conflict and its climax.

Of these four parts, only 2 and 3, the conflict and the climax, are essential. You don't have to begin with an exposition; your first sentence can show your characters already embroiled in their conflict. You don't have to end with a resolution; you can stop your tale short at its climactic moment. But you must have some sort of conflict in your action, and it must rise to some peak of intensity somewhere between the middle and end of your story.

How can we apply this theory to our two stories? Let's find out.

> There was once a rich farmer who was as grasping and unscrupulous as he was rich. He was always driving a hard bargain and always getting the better of his poor neighbors. One of these neighbors was a humble shepherd who, in return for service, was to receive from the farmer a heifer. When the time of payment came, the farmer refused to give the shepherd the heifer, and the shepherd was forced to lay the matter before the burgomaster.

This is obviously an exposition. The opening words, "There was once," tell us immediately that this will be a "tall tale," not a realistic story. The rich farmer—"as grasping and unscrupulous as he was rich"—and the "humble shepherd" in danger of being cheated by the rich man reinforce this idea, and alert us to the coming conflict as well, setting out its themes of rich versus poor and justice versus injustice. The burgomaster—young and inexperienced—does not promise to be much help. What will happen?

The conflict develops as we hear the rich man's wife and the poor man's daughter ponder the burgomaster's riddle. The wife, like her husband, thinks of their property: "our gray mare," "our honey," "our chest of golden ducats." The shepherd's daughter thinks of essential things, in which all humans share: thought, sleep, the earth. And so, of course, the underdogs win in the first round of the conflict.

But it is only the first round. The burgomaster now challenges Manka directly: he "thought he would like to make another test of Manka's cleverness." Manka wins this round as well. The burgomaster begins to think of marriage, and sets a third riddling test. Manka triumphs again, and is married. But now the burgomaster sets limits to Manka's use of her wits:

> "But understand, my dear Manka," he said, "you are not to use that cleverness of yours at my expense. I won't have you interfering in any of my cases. In fact, if ever you give advice to anyone who comes to me for judgment, I'll turn you out of my house at once and send you home to your father."

Do we hear a husband-wife conflict starting here? We certainly do. Once again, Manka sees an injustice about to happen; once again, she prevents the injustice. But the burgomaster, holding to his warning, exiles her, allowing her only to "take with you the one thing you like best in my house." This, of course, is all Manka needs. As the climax of the story, she kidnaps her own husband, once again asserting the claim of the essential over that of mere property: "You know you told me I might take with me the one thing I liked best in your house, so of course I took you! That's all."

The resolution, of course, is reconciliation, happiness, and the firm establishment of Manka's right to use her cleverness for the general good: "I think we had better consult my wife. You know she's a very clever woman."

"The Story of an Hour" begins even more directly: "Knowing that Mrs. Mallard was afflicted with a heart trouble, great care was taken to break to her as gently as possible the news of her husband's death." We are told that there has been a death, and that the dead man's widow is herself in danger from the strain the bad news may place on her weak heart. No conflict between people here: rather, a conflict of caring people against uncaring nature and disease.

As the story develops, a second conflict grows clear: a conflict between grief and joy, between expected and actual emotions. The marriage, loving though it was, has not been happy for her: in the freedom of her widowhood, Louise expects to find happiness.

At the tale's climax, Louise emerges "like a goddess of Victory" to rejoin her sister and friend, only to die from shock at the sight, not of a dead husband, but of a live one. The kindly plan has backfired; the new shock, with its reversal of already-strong emotion, is deadlier than the originally feared shock would have been.

The tale's last sentence provides its resolution: "When the doctors came, they said she had died of heart disease—of joy that kills." Nature and illness have defeated care; and no one is left within the tale who can realize the gap between the expected emotion and the true one. Only we, the readers, know whether or not it was "joy" that killed Louise Mallard.

STEP 3.   Consider the major aspects of each story.

As Chapter 1, "The Bases of Literature," suggested, each work of fiction involves four key elements: action, or plot; character; setting; and language, or voice. When considering a work of fiction, we look at these various aspects; we note how they're presented and what is the balance among them. What do we find in this case?

Action, or plot: We notice substantial differences between the plots of the two tales. The action of "Clever Manka" consists of a number of brief episodes, each of which shows the heroine acting cleverly, so that she moves from triumph to triumph toward the successful climax and resolution. In "The Story of an Hour" we have a single, more fully developed episode, in which the heroine *reacts* first to a piece of news, then to her own emotions, finally to the sight of a man believed dead. The climax of this tale represents a complete reversal of everything expected by characters and readers alike, and thus presents a classic "surprise ending", while the resolution, with its irony, underscores the reversals that distinguish this tale.

Character: Manka is a clever, active, resourceful character; she judges situations correctly and acts decisively. Louise reacts, rather than acts; she is defined by her emotions and her illness rather than by her more active attributes. Manka is worth reading about because she does something praiseworthy; Louise is worth reading about because she is the victim of such a remarkable chain of accidents.

Setting: "Clever Manka" has almost a fairy-tale setting, with its burgomaster who wields absolute power but can yield to a wise peasant girl; "The Story of an Hour" is set in its author's own social setting.

Language, or voice: The language of "Clever Manka" is that of the traditional storyteller. Direct and to the point, it spends little time on description, but concentrates instead on the tale's action. "The Story of an Hour," in contrast, uses much more sophisticated language and takes considerable care to describe and comment upon its characters' thoughts and sensations, as when describing "a physical exhaustion that haunted her body and seemed to reach into her soul" or telling how the heroine "carried herself unwittingly like a goddess of Victory."

STEP 4.   Create a synthesis.

Now we've gathered our data. We've noted our initial reactions, and we've filled those out by checking each of the major aspects and structural elements of the stories under discussion, noting key aspects of each and strengthening our understanding of how the story creates those effects we first noted. Now it's time to put together the information thus gathered to arrive at an overall picture of the stories: a sense of the vision that informs each one, and of your interpretation of that vision. If you write a formal essay on a story, this is the point at which you write it. Even if you write only on a single theme out of the number you've noticed, it's best to have this balanced study behind you so that you're working from a firm foundation.

If I were writing an essay on these two tales, for example, I would probably choose to write on one of my first ideas. I'd call the paper something like "Victors and Victims," and concentrate on the character and fortune of the two protagonists. I'd bring in ideas from my study of action, character, setting, and conflict, to show how Manka uses her cleverness to succeed in a world in which people have only other individuals as adversaries, and individual wisdom and honesty are important and valid weapons in the perpetual combat against injustice; and I'd say that Manka's success leaves me, as a reader, feeling good about the possibility of taking action in my own world to make good things happen. Then I'd show, in contrast, how Kate Chopin's tale depicts people as well-meaning, caring creatures (in contrast to the combative types that people Manka's world), but also as creatures whose power is severely limited by the dangers inherent in living in a "real world" in which physical limitations and accidents can overturn whatever people plan. I'd show how Louise Mallard is victim to all these types of dangers. And I'd admit that—although I enjoyed the story, with its study of hidden feelings—it left me less cheerful than did "Clever Manka," and did nothing to increase my sense of my own potential powers.

In doing such an essay, I'd think that I had covered some of the important points about the two stories, and particularly the key difference between the two. But many other, equally valid essays could be written, stressing other themes and ideas about the stories. Perhaps you have already thought of some such ideas. If you were to write an essay on one or both of these tales, what would you want to write?

4

THE STORYTELLERS

We have said that fiction has its roots in the art of the storyteller. It is with the storytellers, therefore, that we shall begin. This chapter provides three tales, from three storytelling traditions.

The first tale, "High Horse's Courting," comes from the oral storytelling tradition. It is a Native American tale, handed down from one storyteller to another, until it was written down by a scholar to whom a Sioux holy man, Black Elk, told it. Speaking to the scholar, Black Elk recalled that "[Watanye] liked to tell me stories, mostly funny ones. . . . I still remember one story he told me about a young Lakota called High Horse, and what a hard time he had getting the girl he wanted. Watanye said the story happened just as he told it, and maybe it did. If it did not, it could have, just as well as not. I will tell that story now." The second tale, "If Not Higher," comes from the Yiddish tradition. This tradition began in the villages and ghettos of Eastern Europe, then migrated, with its tellers, to this country. This particular tale is set in Russia. The third tale, "And He Built a Crooked House," combines the American comic storytelling tradition with a twentieth-century genre, science fiction. The result of the combination is a type of comic tale often called a "tall tale." It is written by Robert Heinlein, who was a master storyteller within the science-fiction genre. The three tales thus come from different traditions, and from different times, as well. Yet as you read these stories, you may notice a number of similarities among them. First, they all deal with relatively simple, straightforward characters. The actions of which they tell tend to be straightforward, as well, with clearly defined purposes. All use a conversational style, derived from oral storytelling, that draws the audience into the world of the tale. All are told with verve, with the storyteller enjoying the act of telling the tale. And, finally, all deal, to some extent, with extremes or exaggeration. As you read these stories, you should note the differences in narrative style and tone among them, but notice also their similarities; as a foundation for studying fiction, it's good to get a firm sense of the methods used by the first masters of the field, the tellers of tales.

Note: Identical Study Questions are given for all stories in this chapter to make it easier to compare and contrast the stories.

High Horse's Courting

Black Elk (1863–?)

You know, in the old days, it was not so very easy to get a girl when you wanted to be married. Sometimes it was hard work for a young man and he had to stand a great deal. Say I am a young man and I have seen a young girl who looks so beautiful to me that I feel all sick when I think about her. I can not just go and tell her about it and then get married if she is willing. I have to be a very sneaky fellow to talk to her at all, and after I have managed to talk to her, that is only the beginning.

Probably for a long time I have been feeling sick about a certain girl because I love her so much, but she will not even look at me, and her parents keep a good watch over her. But I keep feeling worse and worse all the time; so maybe I sneak up to her tepee in the dark and wait until she comes out. Maybe I just wait there all night and don't get any sleep at all and she does not come out. Then I feel sicker than ever about her.

Maybe I hide in the brush by a spring where she sometimes goes to get water, and when she comes by, if nobody is looking, then I jump out and hold her and just make her listen to me. If she likes me too, I can tell that from the way she acts, for she is very bashful and maybe will not say a word or even look at me the first time. So I let her go, and then maybe I sneak around until I can see her father alone, and I tell him how many horses I can give him for his beautiful girl, and by now I am feeling so sick that maybe I would give him all the horses in the world if I had them.

Well, this young man I am telling about was called High Horse, and there was a girl in the village who looked so beautiful to him that he was just sick all over from thinking about her so much and he was getting sicker all the time. The girl was very shy, and her parents thought a great deal of her because they were not young any more and this was the only child they had. So they watched her all day long, and they fixed it so that she would be safe at night too when they were asleep. They thought so much of her that they had made a rawhide bed for her to sleep in, and after they knew that High Horse was sneaking around after her, they took rawhide thongs and tied the girl in bed at night so that nobody could steal her when they were asleep, for they were not sure but that their girl might really want to be stolen.

Well, after High Horse had been sneaking around a good while and hiding and waiting for the girl and getting sicker all the time, he finally caught her alone and made her talk to him. Then he found out that she liked him maybe a little. Of course this did not make him feel well. It made him sicker than ever, but now he felt as brave as a bison bull, and so he went right to her father and said he loved the girl so much that he would give two good horses for her—one of them young and the other one not so very old.

But the old man just waved his hand, meaning for High Horse to go away and quit talking foolishness like that.

High Horse was feeling sicker than ever about it; but there was another young fellow who said he would loan High Horse two ponies and when he got some more horses, why, he could just give them back for the ones he had borrowed.

Then High Horse went back to the old man and said he would give four horses for the girl—two of them young and the other two not hardly old at all. But the old man just waved his hand and would not say anything.

So High Horse sneaked around until he could talk to the girl again, and he asked her to run away with him. He told her he thought he would just fall over and die if she did not. But she said she would not do that; she wanted to be bought like a fine woman. You see she thought a great deal of herself too.

That made High Horse feel so very sick that he could not eat a bite, and he went around with his head hanging down as though he might just fall down and die any time.

Red Deer was another young fellow, and he and High Horse were great comrades, always doing things together. Red Deer saw how High Horse was acting, and he said: "Cousin, what is the matter? Are you sick in the belly? You look as though you were going to die."

Then High Horse told Red Deer how it was, and said he thought he could not stay alive much longer if he could not marry the girl pretty quick.

Red Deer thought awhile about it, and then he said: "Cousin, I have a plan, and if you are man enough to do as I tell you, then everything will be all right. She will not run away with you; her old man will not take four horses; and four horses are all you can get. You must steal her and run away with her. Then afterwhile you can come back and the old man cannot do anything because she will be your woman. Probably she wants you to steal her anyway."

So they planned what High Horse had to do, and he said he loved the girl so much that he was man enough to do anything Red Deer or anybody else could think up.

So this is what they did.

That night late they sneaked up to the girl's tepee and waited until it sounded inside as though the old man and the old woman and the girl were sound asleep. Then High Horse crawled under the tepee with a knife. He had to cut the rawhide thongs first, and then Red Deer, who was pulling up the stakes around that side of the tepee, was going to help drag the girl outside and gag her. After that, High Horse could put her across his pony in front of him and hurry out of there and be happy all the rest of his life.

When High Horse had crawled inside, he felt so nervous that he could hear his heart drumming, and it seemed so loud he felt sure it would 'waken the old folks. But it did not, and afterwhile he began cutting the thongs. Every time he cut one it made a pop and nearly scared him to death. But he was getting along all right and all the thongs were cut down as far as the girl's thighs, when he became so nervous that his knife slipped and stuck the girl. She gave a big, loud yell. Then the old folks jumped up and yelled too. By this time High Horse was outside, and he and Red Deer were running away like antelope. The old man and some other people chased the young men but they got away in the dark and nobody knew who it was.

Well, if you ever wanted a beautiful girl you will know how sick High Horse was now. It was very bad the way he felt, and it looked as though he would starve even if he did not drop over dead sometime.

Red Deer kept thinking about this, and after a few days he went to High Horse and said: "Cousin, take courage! I have another plan, and I am sure, if you are man enough, we can steal her this time." And High Horse said: "I am man enough to do anything anybody can think up, if I can only get that girl."

So this is what they did.

They went away from the village alone, and Red Deer made High Horse strip naked. Then he painted High Horse solid white all over, and after that he painted black stripes all over the white and put black rings around High Horse's eyes. High Horse looked terrible. He looked so terrible that when Red Deer was through painting and took a good look at what he had done, he said it scared even him a little.

"Now," Red Deer said, "if you get caught again, everybody will be so scared they will think you are a bad spirit and will be afraid to chase you."

So when the night was getting old and everybody was sound asleep, they sneaked back to the girl's tepee. High Horse crawled in with his knife, as before, and Red Deer waited outside, ready to drag the girl out and gag her when High Horse had all the thongs cut.

High Horse crept up by the girl's bed and began cutting at the thongs. But he kept thinking, "If they see me they will shoot me because I look so terrible." The girl was restless and kept squirming around in bed, and when a thong was cut, it popped. So High Horse worked very slowly and carefully.

But he must have made some noise, for suddenly the old woman awoke and said to her old man: "Old Man, wake up! There is somebody in this tepee!" But the old man was sleepy and didn't want to be bothered. He said: "Of course there is somebody in this tepee. Go to sleep and don't bother me." Then he snored some more.

But High Horse was so scared by now that he lay very still and as flat to the ground as he could. Now, you see, he had not been sleeping very well for a long time because he was so sick about the girl. And while he was lying there waiting for the old woman to snore, he just forgot everything, even how beautiful the girl was. Red Deer who was lying outside ready to do his part, wondered and wondered what had happened in there, but he did not dare call out to High Horse.

Afterwhile the day began to break and Red Deer had to leave with the two ponies he had staked there for his comrade and girl, or somebody would see him.

So he left.

Now when it was getting light in the tepee, the girl awoke and the first thing she saw was a terrible animal, all white with black stripes on it, lying asleep beside her bed. So she screamed, and then the old woman screamed and the old man yelled. High Horse jumped up, scared almost to death, and he nearly knocked the tepee down getting out of there.

People were coming running from all over the village with guns and bows and axes, and everybody was yelling.

By now High Horse was running so fast that he hardly touched the ground at all, and he looked so terrible that the people fled from him and let him run. Some braves wanted to shoot at him, but the others said he might be some sacred being and it would bring bad trouble to kill him.

High Horse made for the river that was near, and in among the brush he found a hollow tree and dived into it. Afterwhile some braves came there and he could hear them saying that it was some bad spirit that had come out of the water and gone back in again.

That morning the people were ordered to break camp and move away from there. So they did, while High Horse was hiding in his hollow tree.

Now Red Deer had been watching all this from his own tepee and trying to look as though he were as much surprised and scared as all the others. So when the camp moved, he sneaked back to where he had seen his comrade disappear. When he was down there in the brush, he called, and High Horse answered, because he knew his friend's voice. They washed off the paint from High Horse and sat down on the river bank to talk about their troubles.

High Horse said he never would go back to the village as long as he lived and he did not care what happened to him now. He said he was going to go on the war-path all by himself. Red Deer said: "No, cousin, you are not going on the war-path alone, because I am going with you."

So Red Deer got everything ready, and at night they started out on the war-path all alone. After several days they came to a Crow camp just about sundown, and when it was dark they sneaked up to where the Crow horses were grazing, killed the horse guard, who was not thinking about enemies because he thought all the Lakotas were far away, and drove off about a hundred horses.

They got a big start because all the Crow horses stampeded and it was probably morning before the Crow warriors could catch any horses to ride. Red Deer and High Horse fled with their herd three days and nights before they reached the village of their people. Then they drove the whole herd right into the village and up in front of the girl's tepee. The old man was there, and High Horse called out to him and asked if he thought maybe that would be enough horses for his girl. The old man did not wave him away that time. It was not the horses that he wanted. What he wanted was a son who was a real man and good for something.

So High Horse got his girl after all, and I think he deserved her.

STUDY QUESTIONS

1. How does the narrator introduce the story?
2. Describe the main characters in the story. How does the narrator depict these characters? How do you respond to the depictions?
3. What goal does each of these characters have? What conflicts or frustrations does each meet with in trying to attain his goal? How does he respond to these challenges? How do you react to the character's endeavors and setbacks?
4. Discuss the ending of the story. On what does the narrator focus? On your first reading, how did you respond to the ending?

If Not Higher

I. L. Peretz (1851–1915)

Early every Friday morning, at the time of the Penitential Prayers, the Rabbi of Nemirov would vanish.

He was nowhere to be seen—neither in the synagogue nor in the two Houses of Study nor at a *minyan*. And he was certainly not at home. His door stood open; whoever wished could go in and out; no one would steal from the rabbi. But not a living creature was within.

Where could the rabbi be? Where should he be? In heaven, no doubt. A rabbi has plenty of business to take care of just before the Days of Awe. Jews, God bless them, need livelihood, peace, health, and good matches. They want to be pious and good, but our sins are so great, and Satan of the thousand eyes watches the whole earth from one end to the other. What he sees he reports; he denounces, informs. Who can help us if not the rabbi!

That's what the people thought.

But once a Litvak came, and he laughed. You know the Litvaks. They think little of the Holy Books but stuff themselves with Talmud and law. So this Litvak points to a passage in the *Gemarah*—it sticks in your eyes—where it is written that even Moses, our Teacher, did not ascend to heaven during his lifetime but remained suspended two and a half feet below. Go argue with a Litvak!

So where can the rabbi be?

"That's not my business," said the Litvak, shrugging. Yet all the while—what a Litvak can do!—he is scheming to find out.

That same night, right after the evening prayers, the Litvak steals into the rabbi's room, slides under the rabbi's bed, and waits. He'll watch all night and discover where the rabbi vanishes and what he does during the Penitential Prayers.

Someone else might have got drowsy and fallen asleep, but a Litvak is never at a loss; he recites a whole tractate of the Talmud by heart.

At dawn he hears the call to prayers.

The rabbi has already been awake for a long time. The Litvak has heard him groaning for a whole hour.

Whoever has heard the Rabbi of Nemirov groan knows how much sorrow for all Israel, how much suffering, lies in each groan. A man's heart might break, hearing it. But a Litvak is made of iron; he listens and remains where he is. The rabbi, long life to him, lies on the bed, and the Litvak under the bed.

Then the Litvak hears the beds in the house begin to creak; he hears people jumping out of their beds, mumbling a few Jewish words, pouring water on their fingernails, banging doors. Everyone has left. It is again quiet and dark; a bit of light from the moon shines through the shutters.

(Afterward the Litvak admitted that when he found himself alone with the rabbi a great fear took hold of him. Goose pimples spread across his skin, and the roots of his earlocks pricked him like needles. A trifle: to be alone with the rabbi at the time of the Penitential Prayers! But a Litvak is stubborn. So he quivered like a fish in water and remained where he was.)

Finally the rabbi, long life to him, arises. First he does what befits a Jew. Then he goes to the clothes closet and takes out a bundle of peasant clothes: linen trousers, high boots, a coat, a big felt hat, and a long wide leather belt studded with brass nails. The rabbi gets dressed. From his coat pocket dangles the end of a heavy peasant rope.

The rabbi goes out, and the Litvak follows him.

On the way the rabbi stops in the kitchen, bends down, takes an ax from under the bed, puts it in his belt, and leaves the house. The Litvak trembles but continues to follow.

The hushed dread of the Days of Awe hangs over the dark streets. Every once in a while a cry rises from some *minyan* reciting the Penitential Prayers, or from a sickbed. The rabbi hugs the sides of the streets, keeping to the shade of the houses. He glides from house to house, and the Litvak after him. The Litvak hears the sound of his heartbeats mingling with the sound of the rabbi's heavy steps. But he keeps on going and follows the rabbi to the outskirts of the town.

A small wood stands behind the town.

The rabbi, long life to him, enters the wood. He takes thirty or forty steps and stops by a small tree. The Litvak, overcome with amazement, watches the rabbi take the ax out of his belt and strike the tree. He hears the tree creak and fall. The rabbi chops the tree into logs and the logs into sticks. Then he makes a bundle of the wood and ties it with the rope in his pocket. He puts the bundle of wood on his back, shoves the ax back into his belt, and returns to the town.

He stops at a back street beside a small broken-down shack and knocks at the window.

"Who is there?" asks a frightened voice. The Litvak recognizes it as the voice of a sick Jewish woman.

"I," answers the rabbi in the accent of a peasant.

"Who is I?"

Again the rabbi answers in Russian. "Vassil."

"Who is Vassil, and what do you want?"

"I have wood to sell, very cheap." And, not waiting for the woman's reply, he goes into the house.

The Litvak steals in after him. In the gray light of early morning he sees a poor room with broken, miserable furnishings. A sick woman, wrapped in rags, lies on the bed. She complains bitterly, "Buy? How can I buy? Where will a poor widow get money?"

"I'll lend it to you," answers the supposed Vassil. "It's only six cents."

"And how will I ever pay you back?" said the poor woman, groaning.

"Foolish one," says the rabbi reproachfully. "See, you are a poor sick Jew, and I am ready to trust you with a little wood. I am sure you'll pay. While you, you have such a great and mighty God and you don't trust him for six cents."

"And who will kindle the fire?" said the widow. "Have I the strength to get up? My son is at work."

"I'll kindle the fire," answers the rabbi.

As the rabbi put the wood into the oven he recited, in a groan, the first portion of the Penitential Prayers.

As he kindled the fire and the wood burned brightly, he recited, a bit more joyously, the second portion of the Penitential Prayers. When the fire was set he recited the third portion, and then he shut the stove.

The Litvak who saw all this became a disciple of the rabbi.

And ever after, when another disciple tells how the Rabbi of Nemirov ascends to heaven at the time of the Penitential Prayers, the Litvak does not laugh. He only adds quietly, "If not higher."

"Early every Friday morning . . . the Rabbi of Nemirov would vanish." The statement is blunt and surprising. Rabbis do not usually vanish. We read on, expecting some explanation for the rabbi's behavior. But we find only more mystery. First the narrator tells us where the rabbi isn't. Then he tells us where the townspeople think he is; then he introduces the Litvak who argues that the rabbi can't be there, either. "So where can the rabbi be?" By the time the Litvak sets out to discover the answer, we may be pardoned for being curious ourselves. The narrator has certainly done his best to catch our interest and make us curious.

We notice, meanwhile, that the narrator is not unbiased. Although he takes no direct part in the tale, he does identify himself somewhat with the townspeople, slipping from the statement that "*they* want to be pious and good" to the recognition that "*our* sins are so great. . . . Who can help us if not the rabbi!" He pulls back in the next sentence: "That's what the people thought"; but the identification remains in our minds.

That "our" and "us," in fact, might almost include us, the readers. Certainly the narrator treats us as people who share with him knowledge of rabbis and religious matters and Litvaks—especially Litvaks. "You know the Litvaks. . . . Go argue with a Litvak!" The Litvak has an important role in the story. In contrast to the townspeople, who are ready to spread and believe miraculous rumors, the Litvak is a sceptic. He is a well-read man, so studied in law and religious books that he can keep himself awake all night by reciting Biblical commentaries; but he is a sceptic, nonetheless. It is precisely because he is sceptical, however, that the Litvak becomes curious enough to find out the real answer to the mystery; and it is he who has the final word at the end of the tale.

The Litvak is almost a type or symbol of the person with more knowledge than faith. The narrator, in fact, insists on seeing him as a type—"the Litvak" rather than a man with a name. At the same time, his prejudice characterizes the narrator. We feel that he'd like to see the Litvak shown up, the rabbi and townsfolk triumphant; we feel he himself has a stake in the outcome of the tale.

As the tale continues, the suspense builds. The narrator helps it along by his talk of "groaning" and "hushed dread," his relation of how even the Litvak suffers "goose pimples" and "a great fear," how he "trembles" and quivers "like a fish in water."

Finally, the mystery is revealed. Now, for the first time, we hear voices other than the narrator's. We hear the rabbi (the only words we do hear from him) and the sick woman (the only characterization we have of her; and it's enough). We see what the Litvak sees, hear what he hears; and we are not told what to think about any of it. The narrator, who heretofore has been generous with his comments, is now letting actions and characters speak for themselves.

Even the conclusion is restrained. We learn that "the Litvak who saw all this became a disciple of the rabbi," and we learn his new attitude toward the tale that the rabbi ascends to heaven on Fridays. Note that this is the Litvak's attitude; it is he, not the narrator, who says, "If not higher," and so makes the final judgment on the rabbi's actions. Note, too, that we are told nothing else of how the Litvak's life may have changed. What does becoming the rabbi's disciple mean for him? That we must figure out for ourselves.

The tale is rich in interpretive value. There is no need for the narrator to characterize the rabbi's actions; we can all supply our own view of their significance. Similarly, we can all tell what the Litvak means by his comment, "If not higher," though we might each phrase the meaning somewhat differently. At the start of the story, the Litvak was looking for something. At the end, he has found it, and we feel the value to him of the discovery. Yet even this is lightly handled, in keeping with the slightly humorous tone of the story. The narrator continues to focus on his one question, "Where does the rabbi go early Friday mornings?" It is the solution of that mystery, the resolution of that conflict between Litvak and the townspeople, that he presents as the "quietly" triumphant ending of his story. Anything else we choose to read into it is our own affair.

"If Not Higher," then, is a tale (almost a "tall tale") told by a narrator who takes no direct part in the action, but who has some concern that the story come out well. His voice is a speaking voice, sometimes humorous, sometimes emphatic, sometimes exasperated. Clearly, this is a practiced speaker, a man who enjoys telling stories. We sense his enjoyment in every line of the tale.

In contrast, look at this next story. It too is told by a narrator who remains outside the action; it too is a tale that lends itself to symbolic interpretation. But notice the differences in tone and technique. What attitudes does this narrator convey? How far does she go in interpreting actions and characters for us?

STUDY QUESTIONS

1. How does the narrator introduce the story?
2. Describe the main characters in the story. How does the narrator depict these characters? How do you respond to the depictions?
3. What goal does each of these characters have? What conflicts or frustrations does each meet with in trying to attain his or her goal? How does he or she respond to these challenges? How do you react to the character's endeavors and setbacks?
4. Discuss the ending of the story. On what does the narrator focus? On your first reading, how did you respond to the ending?

"—And He Built a Crooked House—"

Robert Heinlein (1907–1988)

Americans are considered crazy anywhere in the world.

They will usually concede a basis for the accusation but point to California as the focus of the infection. Californians stoutly maintain that their bad reputation is derived solely from the acts of the inhabitants of Los Angeles County. Angelenos will, when pressed, admit the charge but explain hastily, "It's Hollywood. It's not our fault—we didn't ask for it; Hollywood just grew."

The people in Hollywood don't care; they glory in it. If you are interested, they will drive you up Laurel Canyon "—where we keep the violent cases." The Canyonites—the brown-legged women, the trunks-clad men constantly busy building and rebuilding their slap-happy unfinished houses—regard with faint contempt the dull creatures who live down in the flats, and treasure in their hearts the secret knowledge that they, and only they, know how to live.

Lookout Mountain Avenue is the name of a side canyon which twists up from Laurel Canyon. The other Canyonites don't like to have it mentioned; after all, one must draw the line somewhere!

High up on Lookout Mountain at number 8775, across the street from the Hermit—the original Hermit of Hollywood—lived Quintus Teal, graduate architect.

Even the architecture of southern California is different. Hot dogs are sold from a structure built like and designated "The Pup." Ice cream cones come from a giant stucco ice cream cone, and neon proclaims "Get the Chili Bowl Habit!" from the roofs of buildings which are indisputably chili bowls. Gasoline, oil, and free road maps are dispensed beneath the wings of tri-motored transport planes, while the certified rest rooms, inspected hourly for your comfort, are located in the cabin of the plane itself. These things may surprise, or amuse, the tourist, but the local residents, who walk bareheaded in the famous California noonday sun, take them as a matter of course.

Quintus Teal regarded the efforts of his colleagues in architecture as faint-hearted, fumbling, and timid.

"What is a house?" Teal demanded of his friend, Homer Bailey.

"Well—" Bailey admitted cautiously, "speaking in broad terms, I've always regarded a house as a gadget to keep off the rain."

"Nuts! You're as bad as the rest of them."

"I didn't say the definition was complete—"

"Complete! It isn't even in the right direction. From that point of view we might just as well be squatting in caves. But I don't blame you," Teal went on magnanimously, "you're no worse than the lugs you find practicing architecture. Even the Moderns—all they've done is to abandon the Wedding Cake School in favor of the Service Station School, chucked away the gingerbread and slapped on some chromium, but at heart they are as conservative and traditional as a county courthouse. Neutra! Schindler! What have those bums got? What's Frank Lloyd Wright got that I haven't got?"

"Commissions," his friend answered succinctly.

"Huh? Wha' d'ju say?" Teal stumbled slightly in his flow of words, did a slight double take, and recovered himself. "Commissions. Correct. And why? Because I don't think of a house as an upholstered cave; I think of it as a machine for living, a vital process, a live dynamic thing, changing with the mood of the dweller—not a dead, static, oversized coffin. Why should we be held down by the frozen concepts of our ancestors? Any fool with a little smattering of descriptive geometry can design a house in the ordinary way. Is the static geometry of Euclid the only mathematics? Are we to completely disregard the Picard-Vessiot theory? How about modular systems?—to say nothing of the rich suggestions of stereochemistry. Isn't there a place in architecture for transformation, for homomorphology, for actional structures?"

"Blessed if I know," answered Bailey. "You might just as well be talking about the fourth dimension for all it means to me."

"And why not? Why should we limit ourselves to the— Say!" He interrupted himself and stared into distances. "Homer, I think you've really got something. After all, why not? Think of the infinite richness of articulation and relationship in four dimensions. What a house, what a house—" He stood quite still, his pale bulging eyes blinking thoughtfully.

Bailey reached up and shook his arm. "Snap out of it. What the hell are you talking about, four dimensions? Time is the fourth dimension; you can't drive nails into *that*."

Teal shrugged him off. "Sure. Sure. Time is *a* fourth dimension, but I'm thinking about a fourth spatial dimension, like length, breadth and thickness. For economy of materials and convenience of arrangement you couldn't beat it. To say nothing of the saving of ground space—you could put an eight-room house on the land now occupied by a one-room house. Like a tesseract—"

"What's a tesseract?"

"Didn't you go to school? A tesseract is a hypercube, a square figure with four dimensions to it, like a cube has three, and a square has two. Here, I'll show you." Teal dashed out into the kitchen of his apartment and returned with a box of toothpicks which he spilled on the table between them, brushing glasses and a nearly empty Holland gin bottle carelessly aside. "I'll need some plasticine. I had some around here last week." He burrowed into a drawer of the littered desk which crowded one corner of his dining room and emerged with a lump of oily sculptor's clay. "Here's some."

"What are you going to do?"

"I'll show you." Teal rapidly pinched off small masses of the clay and rolled them into pea-sized balls. He stuck toothpicks into four of these and hooked them together into a square. "There! That's a square."

"Obviously."

"Another one like it, four more toothpicks, and we make a cube." The toothpicks were now arranged in the framework of a square box, a cube, with the pellets of clay holding the corners together. "Now we make another cube just like the first one, and the two of them will be two sides of the tesseract."

Bailey started to help him roll the little balls of clay for the second cube, but became diverted by the sensuous feel of the docile clay and started working and shaping it with his fingers.

"Look," he said, holding up his effort, a tiny figurine, "Gypsy Rose Lee."

"Looks more like Gargantua; she ought to sue you. Now pay attention. You open up one corner of the first cube, interlock the second cube at the corner, and then close the corner. Then take eight more toothpicks and join the bottom of the first cube to the bottom of the second, on a slant, and the top of the first to the top of the second, the same way." This he did rapidly, while he talked.

"What's that supposed to be?" Bailey demanded suspiciously.

"That's a tesseract, eight cubes forming the sides of a hypercube in four dimensions."

"It looks more like a cat's cradle to me. You've only got two cubes there anyhow. Where are the other six?"

"Use your imagination, man. Consider the top of the first cube in relation to the top of the second; that's cube number three. Then the two bottom squares, then the front faces of each cube, the back faces, the right hand, the left hand—eight cubes." He pointed them out.

"Yeah, I see 'em. But they still aren't cubes; they're whatchamucallems—prisms. They are not square, they slant."

"That's just the way you look at it, in perspective. If you drew a picture of a cube on a piece of paper, the side squares would be slaunchwise, wouldn't they? That's perspective. When you look at a four-dimensional figure in three dimensions, naturally it looks crooked. But those are all cubes just the same."

"Maybe they are to you, brother, but they still look crooked to me."

Teal ignored the objections and went on. "Now consider this as the framework of an eight-room house; there's one room on the ground floor—that's for service, utilities, and garage. There are six rooms opening off it on the next floor, living room, dining room, bath, bedrooms, and so forth. And up at the top, completely enclosed and with windows on four sides, is your study. There! How do you like it?"

"Seems to me you have the bathtub hanging out of the living room ceiling. Those rooms are interlaced like an octopus."

"Only in perspective, only in perspective. Here, I'll do it another way so you can see it." This time Teal made a cube of toothpicks, then made a second of halves of toothpicks, and set it exactly in the center of the first by attaching the corners of the small cube to the large cube by short lengths of toothpick. "Now—the big cube is your ground floor, the little cube inside is your study on the top floor. The six cubes joining them are the living rooms. See?"

Bailey studied the figure, then shook his head. "I still don't see but two cubes, a big one and a little one. Those other six things, they look like pyramids this time instead of prisms, but they still aren't cubes."

"Certainly, certainly, you are seeing them in different perspective. Can't you see that?"

"Well, maybe. But that room on the inside, there. It's completely surrounded by the thingamujigs. I thought you said it had windows on four sides."

"It has—it just looks like it was surrounded. That's the grand feature about a tesseract house, complete outside exposure for every room, yet every wall serves two rooms and an eight-room house requires only a one-room foundation. It's revolutionary."

"That's putting it mildly. You're crazy, bud; you can't build a house like that. That inside room is on the inside, and there she stays."

Teal looked at his friend in controlled exasperation. "It's guys like you that keep architecture in its infancy. How many square sides has a cube?"

"Six."

"How many of them are inside?"

"Why, none of 'em. They're all on the outside."

"All right. Now listen—a tesseract has eight cubical sides, *all on the outside*. Now watch me. I'm going to open up this tesseract like you can open up a cubical pasteboard box, until it's flat. That way you'll be able to see all eight of the cubes." Working very rapidly he constructed four cubes, piling one on top of the other in an unsteady tower. He then built out four more cubes from the four exposed faces of the second cube in the pile. The structure swayed a little under the loose coupling of the clay pellets, but it stood, eight cubes in an inverted cross, a double cross, as the four additional cubes stuck out in four directions. "Do you see it now? It rests on the ground floor room, the next six cubes are the living rooms, and there is your study, up at the top."

Bailey regarded it with more approval than he had the other figures. "At least I can understand it. You say that is a tesseract, too?"

"That is a tesseract unfolded in three dimensions. To put it back together you tuck the top cube onto the bottom cube, fold those side cubes in till they meet the top cube and there you are. You do all this folding through a fourth dimension of course; you don't distort any of the cubes, or fold them into each other."

Bailey studied the wobbly framework further. "Look here," he said at last, "why don't you forget about folding this thing up through a fourth dimension— you can't anyway—and build a house like this?"

"What do you mean, I can't? It's a simple mathematical problem—"

"Take it easy, son. It may be simple in mathematics, but you could never get your plans approved for construction. There isn't any fourth dimension; forget it. But this kind of a house—it might have some advantages."

Checked, Teal studied the model. "Hm-m-m—Maybe you got something. We could have the same number of rooms, and we'd save the same amount of ground space. Yes, and we would set that middle cross-shaped floor northeast, southwest, and so forth, so that every room would get sunlight all day long. That central axis lends itself nicely to central heating. We'll put the dining room on the northeast and the kitchen on the southeast, with big view windows in every room. O.K., Homer, I'll do it! Where do you want it built?"

"Wait a minute! Wait a minute! I didn't say you were going to build it for me—"

"Of course I am. Who else? Your wife wants a new house; this is it."

"But Mrs. Bailey wants a Georgian house—"

"Just an idea she has. Women don't know what they want—"

"Mrs. Bailey does."

"Just some idea an out-of-date architect has put in her head. She drives a new car, doesn't she? She wears the very latest styles—why should she live in an eighteenth century house? This house will be even later than this year's model; it's years in the future. She'll be the talk of the town."

"Well—I'll have to talk to her."

"Nothing of the sort. We'll surprise her with it. Have another drink."

"Anyhow, we can't do anything about it now. Mrs. Bailey and I are driving up to Bakersfield tomorrow. The company's bringing in a couple of wells tomorrow."

"Nonsense. That's just the opportunity we want. It will be a surprise for her when you get back. You can just write me a check right now, and your worries are over."

"I oughtn't to do anything like this without consulting her. She won't like it."

"Say, who wears the pants in your family anyhow?"

The check was signed about halfway down the second bottle.

Things are done fast in southern California. Ordinary houses there are usually built in a month's time. Under Teal's impassioned heckling the tesseract house climbed dizzily skyward in days rather than weeks, and its cross-shaped second story came jutting out at the four corners of the world. He had some trouble at first with the inspectors over these four projecting rooms but by using strong girders and folding money he had been able to convince them of the soundness of his engineering.

By arrangement, Teal drove up in front of the Bailey residence the morning after their return to town. He improvised on his two-tone horn. Bailey stuck his head out the front door. "Why don't you use the bell?"

"Too slow," answered Teal cheerfully. "I'm a man of action. Is Mrs. Bailey ready? Ah, there you are, Mrs. Bailey! Welcome home, welcome home. Jump in, we've got a surprise for you!"

"You know Teal, my dear," Bailey put in uncomfortably.

Mrs. Bailey sniffed. "I know him. We'll go in our own car, Homer."

"Certainly, my dear."

"Good idea," Teal agreed; " 'sgot more power than mine; we'll get there faster. I'll drive, I know the way." He took the keys from Bailey, slid into the driver's seat, and had the engine started before Mrs. Bailey could rally her forces.

"Never have to worry about my driving," he assured Mrs. Bailey, turning his head as he did so, while he shot the powerful car down the avenue and swung onto Sunset Boulevard, "it's a matter of power and control, a dynamic process, just my meat—I've never had a serious accident."

"You won't have but one," she said bitingly. "Will you *please* keep your eyes on the traffic?"

He attempted to explain to her that a traffic situation was a matter, not of eyesight, but intuitive integration of courses, speeds, and probabilities, but Bailey cut him short. "Where is the house, Quintus?"

"House?" asked Mrs. Bailey suspiciously. "What's this about a house, Homer? Have you been up to something without telling me?"

Teal cut in with his best diplomatic manner. "It certainly is a house, Mrs. Bailey. And what a house! It's a surprise for you from a devoted husband. Just wait till you see it—"

"I shall," she agreed grimly. "What style is it?"

"This house sets a new style. It's later than television, newer than next week. It must be seen to be appreciated. By the way," he went on rapidly, heading off any retort, "did you folks feel the earthquake last night?"

"Earthquake? What earthquake? Homer, was there an earthquake?"

"Just a little one," Teal continued, "about two A.M. If I hadn't been awake, I wouldn't have noticed it."

Mrs. Bailey shuddered. "Oh, this awful country! Do you hear that, Homer? We might have been killed in our beds and never have known it. Why did I ever let you persuade me to leave Iowa?"

"But my dear," he protested hopelessly, "you wanted to come out to California; you didn't like Des Moines."

"We needn't go into that," she said firmly. "You are a man; you should anticipate such things. Earthquakes!"

"That's one thing you needn't fear in your new home, Mrs. Bailey," Teal told her. "It's absolutely earthquake-proof; every part is in perfect dynamic balance with every other part."

"Well, I hope so. Where is this house?"

"Just around this bend. There's the sign now." A large arrow sign, of the sort favored by real estate promoters, proclaimed in letters that were large and bright even for southern California:

THE HOUSE OF THE FUTURE!!!

COLOSSAL—AMAZING—
REVOLUTIONARY

*See How Your Grandchildren
Will Live!*

Q. Teal, Architect

"Of course that will be taken down," he added hastily, noting her expression, "as soon as you take possession." He slued around the corner and brought the car to a squealing halt in front of the House of the Future. "*Voilà!*" He watched their faces for response.

Bailey stared unbelievingly, Mrs. Bailey in open dislike. They saw a simple cubical mass, possessing doors and windows, but no other architectural features, save that it was decorated in intricate mathematical designs. "Teal," Bailey asked slowly, "what have you been up to?"

Teal turned from their faces to the house. Gone was the crazy tower with its jutting second-story rooms. No trace remained of the seven rooms above ground floor level. Nothing remained but the single room that rested on the foundations. "Great jumping cats!" he yelled, "I've been robbed!"

He broke into a run.

But it did him no good. Front or back, the story was the same: the other seven rooms had disappeared, vanished completely. Bailey caught up with him, and took his arm. "Explain yourself. What is this about being robbed? How come you built anything like this—it's not according to agreement."

"But I didn't. I built just what we had planned to build, an eight-room house in the form of a developed tesseract. I've been sabotaged; that's what it is! Jealousy! The other architects in town didn't dare let me finish this job; they knew they'd be washed up if I did."

"When were you last here?"

"Yesterday afternoon."

"Everything all right then?"

"Yes. The gardners were just finishing up."

Bailey glanced around at the faultlessly manicured landscaping. "I don't see how seven rooms could have been dismantled and carted away from here in a single night without wrecking this garden."

Teal looked around, too. "It doesn't look it. I don't understand it."

Mrs. Bailey joined them. "Well? Well? Am I to be left to amuse myself? We might as well look it over as long as we are here, though I'm warning you, Homer, I'm not going to like it."

"We might as well," agreed Teal, and drew a key from his pocket with which he let them in the front door. "We may pick up some clues."

The entrance hall was in perfect order, the sliding screens that separated it from the garage space were back, permitting them to see the entire compartment. "This looks all right," observed Bailey. "Let's go up on the roof and try to figure out what happened. Where's the staircase? Have they stolen that, too?"

"Oh, no," Teal denied, "look—" He pressed a button below the light switch; a panel in the ceiling fell away and a light, graceful flight of stairs swung noiselessly down. Its strength members were the frosty silver of duralumin, its treads and risers transparent plastic. Teal wriggled like a boy who has successfully performed a card trick, while Mrs. Bailey thawed perceptibly.

It was beautiful.

"Pretty slick," Bailey admitted. "Howsomever it doesn't seem to go any place—"

"Oh, that—" Teal followed his gaze. "The cover lifts up as you approach the top. Open stair wells are anachronisms. Come on." As predicted, the lid of the staircase got out of their way as they climbed the flight and permitted them to debouch at the top, but not, as they had expected, on the roof of the single room. They found themselves standing in the middle one of the five rooms which constituted the second floor of the original structure.

For the first time on record Teal had nothing to say. Bailey echoed him, chewing on his cigar. Everything was in perfect order. Before them, through open doorway and translucent partition lay the kitchen, a chef's dream of up-to-the-minute domestic engineering, monel metal, continuous counter space, concealed lighting, functional arrangement. On the left the formal, yet gracious and hospitable dining room awaited guests, its furniture in parade-ground alignment.

Teal knew before he turned his head that the drawing room and lounge would be found in equally substantial and impossible existence.

"Well, I must admit this *is* charming," Mrs. Bailey approved, "and the kitchen is just *too* quaint for words—though I would never have guessed from the exterior that this house had so much room upstairs. Of course *some* changes will have to be made. That secretary now—if we moved it over *here* and put the settle over *there*—"

"Stow it, Matilda," Bailey cut in brusquely. "What'd' yuh make of it, Teal?"

"Why, Homer Bailey! The very id—"

"Stow it, I said. Well, Teal?"

The architect shuffled his rambling body. "I'm afraid to say. Let's go on up."

"How?"

"Like this." He touched another button; a mate, in deeper colors, to the fairy bridge that had let them up from below offered them access to the next floor. They climbed it, Mrs. Bailey expostulating in the rear, and found themselves in the master bedroom. Its shades were drawn, as had been those on the level below, but the mellow lighting came on automatically. Teal at once activated the switch which controlled still another flight of stairs, and they hurried up into the top floor study.

"Look, Teal," suggested Bailey when he had caught his breath, "can we get to the roof above this room? Then we could look around."

"Sure, it's an observatory platform." They climbed a fourth flight of stairs, but when the cover at the top lifted to let them reach the level above, they found themselves, not on the roof, but *standing in the ground floor room where they had entered the house.*

Mr. Bailey turned a sickly gray. "Angels, in heaven," he cried, "this place is haunted. We're getting out of here." Grabbing his wife he threw open the front door and plunged out.

Teal was too much preoccupied to bother with their departure. There was an answer to all this, an answer that he did not believe. But he was forced to break off considering it because of hoarse shouts from somewhere above him. He lowered the staircase and rushed upstairs. Bailey was in the central room leaning over Mrs. Bailey, who had fainted. Teal took in the situation, went to the bar built into the lounge, and poured three fingers of brandy, which he returned with and handed to Bailey. "Here—this'll fix her up."

Bailey drank it.

"That was for Mrs. Bailey," said Teal.

"Don't quibble," snapped Bailey. "Get her another." Teal took the precaution of taking one himself before returning with a dose earmarked for his client's wife. He found her just opening her eyes.

"Here, Mrs. Bailey," he soothed, "this will make you feel better."

"I never touch spirits," she protested, and gulped it.

"Now tell me what happened," suggested Teal. "I thought you two had left."

"But we did—we walked out the front door and found ourselves up here, in the lounge."

"The hell you say! Hm-m-m—wait a minute." Teal went into the lounge. There he found that the big view window at the end of the room was open. He peered cautiously through it. He stared, not out at the California countryside, but into the ground floor room—or a reasonable facsimile thereof. He said nothing, but went back to the stair well which he had left open and looked down it. The ground floor room was still in place. Somehow, it managed to be in two different places at once, on different levels.

He came back into the central room and seated himself opposite Bailey in a deep, low chair, and sighted him past his upthrust bony knees. "Homer," he said impressively, "do you know what has happened?"

"No, I don't—but if I don't find out pretty soon, something is going to happen and pretty drastic, too!"

"Homer, this is a vindication of my theories. This house is a real tesseract."

"What's he talking about, Homer?"

"Wait, Matilda—now Teal, that's ridiculous. You've pulled some hanky-panky here and I won't have it—scaring Mrs. Bailey half to death, and making me nervous. All I want is to get out of here, with no more of your trapdoors and silly practical jokes."

"Speak for yourself, Homer," Mrs. Bailey interrupted, "I was *not* frightened; I was just took all over queer for a moment. It's my heart; all of my people are delicate and highstrung. Now about this tessy thing—explain yourself, Mr. Teal. Speak up."

He told her as well as he could in the face of numerous interruptions the theory back of the house. "Now as I see it, Mrs. Bailey," he concluded, "this house, while perfectly stable in three dimensions, was not stable in four dimensions. I had built a house in the shape of an unfolded tesseract; something happened to it, some jar or side thrust, and it collapsed into its normal shape—it folded up." He snapped his fingers suddenly. "I've got it! The earthquake!"

"Earthquake?"

"Yes, yes, the little shake we had last night. From a four-dimensional standpoint this house was like a plane balanced on edge. One little push and it fell over, collapsed along its natural joints into a stable four-dimensional figure."

"I thought you boasted about how safe this house was."

"It *is* safe—three-dimensionally."

"I don't call a house safe," commented Bailey edgily, "that collapses at the first little temblor."

"But look around you, man!" Teal protested. "Nothing has been disturbed, not a piece of glassware cracked. Rotation through a fourth dimension can't effect a three-dimensional figure any more than you can shake letters off a printed page. If you had been sleeping in here last night, you would never have awakened."

"That's just what I'm afraid of. Incidentally, has your great genius figured out any way for us to get out of this booby trap?"

"Huh? Oh, yes, you and Mrs. Bailey started to leave and landed back up here, didn't you? But I'm sure there is no real difficulty—we came in, we can go out. I'll try it." He was up and hurrying downstairs before he had finished talking. He flung open the front door, stepped through, and found himself staring at his companions, down the length of the second floor lounge. "Well, there does seem to be some slight problem," he admitted blandly. "A mere technicality, though—we can always go out a window." He jerked aside the long drapes that covered the deep French windows set in one side wall of the lounge. He stopped suddenly.

"Hm-m-m," he said, "this is interesting—very."

"What is?" asked Bailey, joining him.

"This." The window stared directly into the dining room, instead of looking outdoors. Bailey stepped back to the corner where the lounge and the dining room joined the central room at ninety degrees.

"But that can't be," he protested, "that window is maybe fifteen, twenty feet from the dining room."

"Not in a tesseract," corrected Teal. "Watch." He opened the window and stepped through, talking back over his shoulder as he did so.

From the point of view of the Baileys he simply disappeared.

But not from his own viewpoint. It took him some seconds to catch his breath. Then he cautiously disentangled himself from the rosebush to which he had become almost irrevocably wedded, making a mental note the while never again to order landscaping which involved plants with thorns, and looked around him.

He was outside the house. The massive bulk of the ground floor room thrust up beside him. Apparently he had fallen off the roof.

He dashed around the corner of the house, flung open the front door and hurried up the stairs. "Homer!" he called out, "Mrs. Bailey! I've found a way out!"

Bailey looked annoyed rather than pleased to see him. "What happened to you?"

"I fell out. I've been outside the house. You can do it just as easily—just step through those French windows. Mind the rosebush, though—we may have to build another stairway."

"How did you get back in?"

"Through the front door."

"Then we shall leave the same way. Come, my dear." Bailey set his hat firmly on his head and marched down the stairs, his wife on his arm.

Teal met them in the lounge. "I could have told you that wouldn't work," he announced. "Now here's what we have to do: As I see it, in a four-dimensional figure a three-dimensional man has two choices every time he crosses a line of juncture, like a wall or a threshold. Ordinarily he will make a ninety-degree turn through the fourth dimension, only he doesn't feel it with his three dimensions. Look." He stepped through the very window that he had fallen out of a moment before. Stepped through and arrived in the dining room, where he stood, still talking.

"I watched where I was going and arrived where I intended to." He stepped back into the lounge. "The time before I didn't watch and I moved on through normal space and fell out of the house. It must be a matter of subconscious orientation."

"I'd hate to depend on subconscious orientation when I step out for the morning paper."

"You won't have to; it'll become automatic. Now to get out of the house this time—Mrs. Bailey, if you will stand here with your back to the window, and jump backward, I'm pretty sure you will land in the garden."

Mrs. Bailey's face expressed her opinion of Teal and his ideas. "Homer Bailey," she said shrilly, "are you going to stand there and let him suggest such—"

"But Mrs. Bailey," Teal attempted to explain, "we can tie a rope on you and lower you down eas—"

"Forget it, Teal," Bailey cut him off brusquely. "We'll have to find a better way than that. Neither Mrs. Bailey nor I are fitted for jumping."

Teal was temporarily nonplused; there ensued a short silence. Bailey broke it with, "Did you hear that, Teal?"

"Hear what?"

"Someone talking off in the distance. D'you s'pose there could be someone else in the house, playing tricks on us, maybe?"

"Oh, not a chance. I've got the only key."

"But I'm sure of it," Mrs. Bailey confirmed. "I've heard them ever since we came in. Voices. Homer, I can't stand much more of this. Do something."

"Now, now, Mrs. Bailey," Teal soothed, "don't get upset. There can't be anyone else in the house, but I'll explore and make sure. Homer, you stay here with Mrs. Bailey and keep an eye on the rooms on this floor." He passed from the lounge into the ground floor room and from there to the kitchen and on into the bedroom. This led him back to the lounge by a straight-line route, that is to say, by going straight ahead on the entire trip he returned to the place from which he started.

"Nobody around," he reported. "I opened all of the doors and windows as I went—all except this one." He stepped to the window opposite the one through which he had recently fallen and thrust back the drapes.

He saw a man with his back toward him, four rooms away. Teal snatched open the French window and dived through it, shouting, "There he goes now! Stop thief!"

The figure evidently heard him; it fled precipitately. Teal pursued, his gangling limbs stirred to unanimous activity, through drawing room, kitchen, dining room, lounge—room after room, yet in spite of Teal's best efforts he could not seem to cut down the four-room lead that the interloper had started with.

He saw the pursued jump awkwardly but actively over the low sill of a French window and in so doing knock off the hat. When he came up to the point where his quarry had lost his headgear, he stopped and picked it up, glad of an excuse to stop and catch his breath. He was back in the lounge.

"I guess he got away from me," he admitted. "Anyhow, here's his hat. Maybe we can identify him."

Bailey took the hat, looked at it, then snorted, and slapped it on Teal's head. It fitted perfectly. Teal looked puzzled, took the hat off, and examined it. On the sweat band were the initials "Q.T." It was his own.

Slowly comprehension filtered through Teal's features. He went back to the French window and gazed down the series of rooms through which he had pursued the mysterious stranger. They saw him wave his arms semaphore fashion. "What are you doing?" asked Bailey.

"Come see." The two joined him and followed his stare with their own. Four rooms away they saw the backs of three figures, two male and one female. The taller, thinner of the men was waving his arms in a silly fashion.

Mrs. Bailey screamed and fainted again.

Some minutes later, when Mrs. Bailey had been resuscitated and somewhat composed, Bailey and Teal took stock. "Teal," said Bailey, "I won't waste any time blaming you; recriminations are useless and I'm sure you didn't plan for this to happen, but I suppose you realize we are in a pretty serious predicament. How are we going to get out of here? It looks now as if we would stay until we starve; every room leads into another room."

"Oh, it's not that bad. I got out once, you know."

"Yes, but you can't repeat it—you tried."

"Anyhow we haven't tried all the rooms. There's still the study."

"Oh, yes, the study. We went through there when we first came in, and didn't stop. Is it your idea that we might get out through its windows?"

"Don't get your hopes up. Mathematically, it ought to look into the four side rooms on this floor. Still we never opened the blinds; maybe we ought to look."

" 'Twon't do any harm anyhow. Dear, I think you had best just stay here and rest—"

"Be left alone in this horrible place? I should say not!" Mrs. Bailey was up off the couch where she had been recuperating even as she spoke.

They went upstairs. "This is the inside room, isn't it, Teal?" Bailey inquired as they passed through the master bedroom and climbed on up toward the study. "I mean it was the little cube in your diagram that was in the middle of the big cube, and completely surrounded."

"That's right," agreed Teal. "Well, let's have a look. I figure this window ought to give into the kitchen." He grasped the cords of Venetian blinds and pulled them.

It did not. Waves of vertigo shook them. Involuntarily they fell to the floor and grasped helplessly at the pattern on the rug to keep from falling. "Close it! Close it!" moaned Bailey.

Mastering in part a primitive atavistic fear, Teal worked his way back to the window and managed to release the screen. The window had looked *down* instead of *out,* down from a terrifying height.

Mrs. Bailey had fainted again.

Teal went back after more brandy while Bailey chafed her wrists. When she had recovered, Teal went cautiously to the window and raised the screen a crack. Bracing his knees, he studied the scene. He turned to Bailey. "Come look at this, Homer. See if you recognize it."

"You stay away from there, Homer Bailey!"

"Now, Matilda, I'll be careful." Bailey joined him and peered out.

"See up there? That's the Chrysler Building, sure as shooting. And there's the East River, and Brooklyn." They gazed straight down the sheer face of an enormously tall building. More than a thousand feet away a toy city, very much alive, was spread out before them. "As near as I can figure it out, we are looking down the side of the Empire State Building from a point just above its tower."

"I don't think so—it's too perfect. I think space is folded over through the fourth dimension here and we are looking past the fold."

"You mean we aren't really seeing it?"

"No, we're seeing it all right. I don't know what would happen if we climbed out this window, but I for one don't want to try. But what a view! Oh, boy, what a view! Let's try the other windows."

They approached the next window more cautiously, and it was well that they did, for it was even more disconcerting, more reason-shaking, than the one looking down the gasping height of the skyscraper. It was a simple seascape, open ocean and blue sky—but the ocean was where the sky should have been, and contrariwise. This time they were somewhat braced for it, but they both felt seasickness about to overcome them at the sight of waves rolling overhead; they lowered the blind quickly without giving Mrs. Bailey a chance to be disturbed by it.

Teal looked at the third window. "Game to try it, Homer?"

"Hrrumph—well, we won't be satisfied if we don't. Take it easy." Teal lifted the blind a few inches. He saw nothing, and raised it a little more—still nothing. Slowly he raised it until the window was fully exposed. They gazed out at— nothing.

Nothing, nothing at all. What color is nothing? Don't be silly! What shape is it? Shape is an attribute of *something.* It had neither depth nor form. It had not even blackness. It was *nothing.*

Bailey chewed at his cigar. "Teal, what do you make of that?"

Teal's insouciance was shaken for the first time. "I don't know, Homer, I don't rightly know—but I think that window ought to be walled up." He stared at the lowered blind for a moment. "I think maybe we looked at a place where space *isn't*. We looked around a fourth-dimensional corner and there wasn't anything there." He rubbed his eyes. "I've got a headache."

They waited for a while before tackling the fourth window. Like an unopened letter, it might *not* contain bad news. The doubt left hope. Finally the suspense stretched too thin and Bailey pulled the cord himself, in the face of his wife's protests.

It was not so bad. A landscape stretched away from them, right side up, and on such a level that the study appeared to be a ground floor room. But it was distinctly unfriendly.

A hot, hot sun beat down from lemon-colored sky. The flat ground seemed burned a sterile, bleached brown and incapable of supporting life. Life there was, strange stunted trees that lifted knotted, twisted arms to the sky. Little clumps of spiky leaves grew on the outer extremities of these misshapen growths.

"Heavenly day," breathed Bailey. "Where is that?"

Teal shook his head, his eyes troubled. "It beats me."

"It doesn't look like anything on Earth. It looks more like another planet—Mars, maybe."

"I wouldn't know. But, do you know, Homer, it might be worse than that, worse than another planet, I mean."

"Huh? What's that you say?"

"It might be clear out of space entirely. I'm not sure that that is our sun at all. It seems too bright."

Mrs. Bailey had somewhat timidly joined them and now gazed out at the outré scene. "Homer," she said in a subdued voice, "those hideous trees—they frighten me."

He patted her hand.

Teal fumbled with the window catch.

"What are you doing?" Bailey demanded.

"I thought if I stuck my head out the window I might be able to look around and tell a bit more."

"Well—all right," Bailey grudged, "but be careful."

"I will." He opened the window a crack and sniffed. "The air is all right, at least." He threw it open wide.

His attention was diverted before he could carry out his plan. An uneasy tremor, like the first intimation of nausea, shivered the entire building for a long second, and was gone.

"Earthquake!" They all said it at once. Mrs. Bailey flung her arms around her husband's neck.

Teal gulped and recovered himself, saying:

"It's all right, Mrs. Bailey. This house is perfectly safe. You know you can expect settling tremors after a shock like last night." He had just settled his features into an expression of reassurance when the second shock came. This one was no mild shimmy but the real seasick roll.

In every Californian, native born or grafted, there is a deep-rooted, primitive reflex. An earthquake fills him with soul-shaking claustrophobia which impels him blindly to *get outdoors!* Model Boy Scouts will push aged grandmothers aside to obey it. It is a matter of record that Teal and Bailey landed on top of Mrs. Bailey. Therefore, she must have jumped through the window first. The order of precedence cannot be attributed to chivalry; it must be assumed that she was in readier position to spring.

They pulled themselves together, collected their wits a little, and rubbed sand from their eyes. Their first sensations were relief at feeling the solid sand of the desert land under them. Then Bailey noticed something that brought them to their feet and checked Mrs. Bailey from bursting into the speech that she had ready.

"Where's the house?"

It was gone. There was no sign of it at all. They stood in the center of flat desolation, the landscape they had seen from the window. But, aside from the tortured, twisted trees there was nothing to be seen but the yellow sky and the luminary overhead, whose furnacelike glare was already almost insufferable.

Bailey looked slowly around, then turned to the architect. "Well, Teal?" His voice was ominous.

Teal shrugged helplessly. "I wish I knew. I wish I could even be sure that we were on Earth."

"Well, we can't stand here. It's sure death if we do. Which direction?"

"Any, I guess. Let's keep a bearing on the sun."

They had trudged on for an undetermined distance when Mrs. Bailey demanded a rest. They stopped. Teal said in an aside to Bailey, "Any ideas?"

"No . . . no, none. Say, do you hear anything?"

Teal listened. "Maybe—unless it's my imagination."

"Sounds like an automobile. Say, it *is* an automobile!"

They came to the highway in less than another hundred yards. The automobile, when it arrived, proved to be an elderly, puffing light truck, driven by a rancher. He crunched to a stop at their hail. "We're stranded. Can you help us out?"

"Sure. Pile in."

"Where are you headed?"

"Los Angeles."

"Los Angeles? Say, where is this place?"

"Well, you're right in the middle of the Joshua-Tree National Forest."

The return was as dispiriting as the Retreat from Moscow. Mr. and Mrs. Bailey sat up in front with the driver while Teal bumped along in the body of the truck, and tried to protect his head from the sun. Bailey subsidized the friendly rancher to detour to the tesseract house, not because they wanted to see it again, but in order to pick up their car.

At last the rancher turned the corner that brought them back to where they had started. But the house was no longer there.

There was not even the ground-floor room. It had vanished. The Baileys, interested in spite of themselves, poked around the foundations with Teal.

"Got any answers for this one, Teal?" asked Bailey.

"It must be that on that last shock it simply fell through into another section of space. I can see now that I should have anchored it at the foundations."

"That's not all you should have done."

"Well, I don't see that there is anything to get downhearted about. The house was insured, and we've learned an amazing lot. There are possibilities, man, possibilities! Why, right now I've got a great new revolutionary idea for a house—"

Teal ducked in time. He was always a man of action.

STUDY QUESTIONS

1. How does the narrator introduce the story?
2. Describe the main characters in the story. How does the narrator depict these characters? How do you respond to the depictions?
3. What goal does each of these characters have? What conflicts or frustrations does each meet with in trying to attain his or her goal? How does he or she respond to these challenges? How do you react to the character's endeavors and setbacks?
4. Discuss the ending of the story. On what does the narrator focus? On your first reading, how did you respond to the ending?

5

THE REPORTERS

The stories we have read so far, and those we will read in this chapter, are all related by omniscient narrators. As the term implies, these narrators "know all" about the characters and events of which they tell. Somewhat distanced by their greater knowledge from action and actors alike, omniscient narrators project an air of authority over their material. Their relationship to their readers is also variable.

Storytellers, such as those we met in the last chapter, and the teller of "Clever Manka" in the first chapter, treat us as a present and welcome audience. Often they may speak to us directly, either asking us questions ("Now I ask you: did she go dressed?") or by making sure that we understand what we need to know in order to appreciate their stories ("You know, in the old days, it was not so very easy to get a girl when you wanted to be married").

Storytellers often seem to care about their protagonists as well. We sense that Black Elk wants High Horse to win his girl, that Peretz's narrator wants the Litvak to understand the rabbi and be satisfied. All in all, there is frequently a strong push for closure in many of the tales told by storytellers: some triumph of action or learning must be achieved within the tale, and some benefit of entertainment or learning must come to the audience in the process.

Reporters, in contrast, hold themselves more aloof from characters and audience alike. For instance, Chopin's narrator, in the first chapter, keeps us at the same distance that she keeps her material. She tells us of her protagonist's thoughts and feelings, so that we see the contrast between the private thoughts and the public image; but she does so with the objectivity of a reporter. Her prose carries no awareness of its audience. Whereas the storyteller seems actively interested in sharing some knowledge or enjoyment with us, the reporter's stance is much more "take it or leave it." "Here is a story: something I have observed, imagined, created; make of it what you will, whoever you are."

This chapter contains four stories told by omniscient reporters. Read each story through once, as you would any story, and note your reactions to its plot, characters, and style. Then read and answer the questions that follow the story, rereading the story as necessary while you consider your answers. Note, throughout, how the narrator's voice helps shape your view of the story's action and characters.

Hills like White Elephants

Ernest Hemingway (1898–1961)

The hills across the valley of the Ebro were long and white. On this side there was no shade and no trees and the station was between two lines of rails in the sun. Close against the side of the station there was the warm shadow of the building and a curtain, made of strings of bamboo beads, hung across the open door into the bar, to keep out flies. The American and the girl with him sat at a table in the shade, outside the building. It was very hot and the express from Barcelona would come in forty minutes. It stopped at this junction for two minutes and went on to Madrid.[1]

"What should we drink?" the girl asked. She had taken off her hat and put it on the table.

"It's pretty hot," the man said.

"Let's drink beer."

"Dos cervezas," the man said into the curtain.

"Big ones?" a woman asked from the doorway.

"Yes. Two big ones."

The woman brought two glasses of beer and two felt pads. She put the felt pads and the beer glasses on the table and looked at the man and the girl. The girl was looking off at the line of hills. They were white in the sun and the country was brown and dry.

"They look like white elephants," she said.

"I've never seen one," the man drank his beer.

"No, you wouldn't have."

"I might have," the man said. "Just because you say I wouldn't have doesn't prove anything."

The girl looked at the bead curtain. "They've painted something on it," she said. "What does it say?"

"Anis del Toro. It's a drink."

"Could we try it?"

The man called "Listen" through the curtain. The woman came out from the bar.

"Four reales."[2]

"We want two Anis del Toro."

"With water?"

"Do you want it with water?"

---

[1]The references to the Ebro River and the cities of Barcelona and Madrid identify the setting as Spain.

[2]Spanish coins

"All right. But you've got to realize—"

"I realize," the girl said. "Can't we maybe stop talking?"

They sat down at the table and the girl looked across at the hills on the dry side of the valley and the man looked at her and at the table.

"You've got to realize," he said, "that I don't want you to do it if you don't want to. I'm perfectly willing to go through with it if it means anything to you."

"Doesn't it mean anything to you? We could get along."

"Of course it does. But I don't want anybody but you. I don't want any one else. And I know it's perfectly simple."

"Yes, you know it's perfectly simple."

"It's all right for you to say that, but I do know it."

"Would you do something for me now?"

"I'd do anything for you."

"Would you please please please please please please please stop talking?"

He did not say anything but looked at the bags against the wall of the station. There were labels on them from all the hotels where they had spent nights.

"But I don't want you to," he said. "I don't care anything about it."

"I'll scream," the girl said.

The woman came out through the curtains with two glasses of beer and put them down on the damp felt pads. "The train comes in five minutes," she said.

"What did she say?" asked the girl.

"That the train is coming in five minutes."

The girl smiled brightly at the woman, to thank her.

"I'd better take the bags over to the other side of the station," the man said. She smiled at him.

"All right. Then come back and we'll finish the beer."

He picked up the two heavy bags and carried them around the station to the other tracks. He looked up the tracks but could not see the train. Coming back, he walked through the barroom, where people waiting for the train were drinking. He drank an Anis at the bar and looked at the people. They were all waiting reasonably for the train. He went out through the bead curtain. She was sitting at the table and smiled at him.

"Do you feel better?" he asked.

"I feel fine," she said. "There's nothing wrong with me. I feel fine."

STUDY QUESTIONS

1. In contrast to the vivid action of "High Horse's Courting" and "If Not Higher," "Hills like White Elephants" seems to contain almost no action whatever. Nor do the characters at its end seem to have changed, or been changed, from what they were at its beginning. For many years, in fact, critics questioned whether "static" stories like this one deserved the title of "story" at all. What do you think? "Hills like White Elephants" is generally

regarded as an excellent example of twentieth-century fiction. Do you agree that it merits this regard? If it is a fine example of the art of fiction, in what lies its artistry?

2. Discuss the mechanics of the story.

   a. How are the characters created? Do you find them clearly drawn? recognizable? or not?

   b. By what means is the tale's conflict defined? How completely is it defined? Is it resolved by the tale's end? What sense do you have regarding its ultimate resolution? Why?

   c. How is the setting described? Is it important? Why or why not?

   d. What amount of time does the story cover? How does this affect your perception of characters, conflict, and setting?

3. How do the elements listed in question 2 work together to create coherence and vision within the story?

Miss Brill

Katherine Mansfield (1888–1923)

Although it was so brilliantly fine—the blue sky powdered with gold and great spots of light like white wine splashed over the Jardins Publiques[3]—Miss Brill was glad that she had decided on her fur. The air was motionless, but when you opened your mouth there was just a faint chill, like a chill from a glass of iced water before you sip, and now and again a leaf came drifting—from nowhere, from the sky. Miss Brill put up her hand and touched her fur. Dear little thing! It was nice to feel it again. She had taken it out of its box that afternoon, shaken out the moth powder, given it a good brush, and rubbed the life back into the dim little eyes. "What has been happening to me?" said the sad little eyes. Oh, how sweet it was to see them snap at her again from the red eiderdown![4] . . . But the nose, which was of some black composition, wasn't at all firm. It must have had a knock, somehow. Never mind—a little dab of black sealing-wax when the time came—when it was absolutely necessary . . . Little rogue! Yes, she really felt like that about it. Little rogue biting its tail just by her left ear. She could have taken it off and laid it on her lap and stroked it. She felt a tingling in her hands and arms, but that came from walking, she supposed. And when she breathed, something light and sad—no, not sad, exactly—something gentle seemed to move in her bosom.

---

[3]public gardens
[4]a quilt stuffed with the down of the eider duck

There were a number of people out this afternoon, far more than last Sunday. And the band sounded louder and gayer. That was because the Season had begun. For although the band played all the year round on Sundays, out of season it was never the same. It was like some one playing with only the family to listen; it didn't care how it played if there weren't any strangers present. Wasn't the conductor wearing a new coat, too? She was sure it was new. He scraped with his foot and flapped his arms like a rooster about to crow, and the bandsmen sitting in the green rotunda blew out their cheeks and glared at the music. Now there came a little "flutey" bit—very pretty!—a little chain of bright drops. She was sure it would be repeated. It was; she lifted her head and smiled.

Only two people shared her "special" seat: a fine old man in a velvet coat, his hands clasped over a huge carved walking-stick, and a big old woman, sitting upright, with a roll of knitting on her embroidered apron. They did not speak. This was disappointing, for Miss Brill always looked forward to the conversation. She had become really quite expert, she thought, at listening as though she didn't listen, at sitting in other people's lives just for a minute while they talked round her.

She glanced, sideways, at the old couple. Perhaps they would go soon. Last Sunday, too, hadn't been as interesting as usual. An Englishman and his wife, he wearing a dreadful Panama hat and she button boots. And she'd gone on the whole time about how she ought to wear spectacles; she knew she needed them; but that it was no good getting any; they'd be sure to break and they'd never keep on. And he'd been so patient. He'd suggested everything—gold rims, the kind that curved round your ears, little pads inside the bridge. No, nothing would please her. "They'll always be sliding down my nose!" Miss Brill had wanted to shake her.

The old people sat on the bench, still as statues. Never mind, there was always the crowd to watch. To and fro, in front of the flower beds and the band rotunda, the couples and groups paraded, stopped to talk, to greet, to buy a handful of flowers from the old beggar who had his tray fixed to the railings. Little children ran among them, swooping and laughing; little boys with big white silk bows under their chins, little girls, little French dolls, dressed up in velvet and lace. And sometimes a tiny staggerer came suddenly rocking into the open from under the trees, stopped, stared, as suddenly sat down "flop," until its small high-stepping mother, like a young hen, rushed scolding to its rescue. Other people sat on the benches and green chairs, but they were nearly always the same, Sunday after Sunday, and—Miss Brill had often noticed—there was something funny about nearly all of them. They were odd, silent, nearly all old, and from the way they stared they looked as though they'd just come from dark little rooms or even—even cupboards!

Behind the rotunda the slender trees with yellow leaves down drooping, and through them just a line of sea, and beyond the blue sky with gold-veined clouds.

Tum-tum-tum tiddle-um! tiddle-um! tum tiddley-um tum ta! blew the band.

Two young girls in red came by and two young soldiers in blue met them, and they laughed and paired and went off arm-in-arm. Two peasant women with funny straw hats passed, gravely, leading beautiful smoke-colored donkeys. A cold, pale nun hurried by. A beautiful woman came along and dropped her bunch of violets, and a little boy ran after to hand them to her, and she took them and threw them away as if they'd been poisoned. Dear me! Miss Brill didn't know whether to admire that or not! And now an ermine toque[5] and a gentleman in gray met just in front of her. He was tall, stiff, dignified, and she was wearing the ermine toque she'd bought when her hair was yellow. Now everything, her hair, her face, even her eyes, was the same color as the shabby ermine, and her hand, in its cleaned glove, lifted to dab her lips, was a tiny yellowish paw. Oh, she was so pleased to see him—delighted! She rather thought they were going to meet that afternoon. She described where she'd been—everywhere, here, there, along by the sea. The day was so charming—didn't he agree? And wouldn't he, perhaps? . . . But he shook his head, lighted a cigarette, slowly breathed a great deep puff into her face, and, even while she was still talking and laughing, flicked the match away and walked on. The ermine toque was alone; she smiled more brightly than ever. But even the band seemed to know what she was feeling and played more softly, played tenderly, and the drum beat, "The Brute! The Brute!" over and over. What would she do? What was going to happen now? But as Miss Brill wondered, the ermine toque turned, raised her hand as though she'd seen some one else, much nicer, just over there, and pattered away. And the band changed again and played more quickly, more gayly than ever, and the old couple on Miss Brill's seat got up and marched away, and such a funny old man with long whiskers hobbled along in time to the music and was nearly knocked over by four girls walking abreast.

Oh, how fascinating it was! How she enjoyed it! How she loved sitting here, watching it all! It was like a play. It was exactly like a play. Who could believe the sky at the back wasn't painted? But it wasn't till a little brown dog trotted on solemn and then slowly trotted off, like a little "theater" dog, a little dog that had been drugged, that Miss Brill discovered what it was that made it so exciting. They were all on the stage. They weren't only the audience, not only looking on; they were acting. Even she had a part and came every Sunday. No doubt somebody would have noticed if she hadn't been there; she was a part of the performance after all. How strange she'd never thought of it like that before! And yet it explained why she made such a point of starting from home at just the same time each week—so as not to be late for the performance—and it also explained why she had quite a queer, shy feeling at telling her English pupils how she spent her Sunday afternoons. No wonder! Miss Brill nearly laughed out loud. She was on the stage. She thought of the old invalid gentleman to whom she read the newspaper four afternoons a week while he slept in the garden. She had got quite used to the frail head on the cotton pillow, the hollowed eyes, the open mouth

---

[5]a woman's small, round, close-fitting hat—in this case, such a hat made from the white fur of the ermine

and the high pinched nose. If he'd been dead she mightn't have noticed for weeks; she wouldn't have minded. But suddenly he knew he was having the paper read to him by an actress! "An actress!" The old head lifted; two points of light quivered in the old eyes. "An actress—are ye?" And Miss Brill smoothed the newspaper as though it were the manuscript of her part and said gently: "Yes, I have been an actress for a long time."

The band had been having a rest. Now they started again. And what they played was warm, sunny, yet there was just a faint chill—a something, what was it?—not sadness—no, not sadness—a something that made you want to sing. The tune lifted, lifted, the light shone; and it seemed to Miss Brill that in another moment all of them, all the whole company, would begin singing. The young ones, the laughing ones who were moving together, they would begin, and the men's voices, very resolute and brave, would join them. And then she too, she too, and the others on the benches—they would come in with a kind of accompaniment—something low, that scarcely rose or fell, something so beautiful—moving . . . And Miss Brill's eyes filled with tears and she looked smiling at all the other members of the company. Yes, we understand, we understand, she thought—though what they understood she didn't know.

Just at that moment a boy and a girl came and sat down where the old couple had been. They were beautifully dressed; they were in love. The hero and heroine, of course, just arrived from his father's yacht. And still soundlessly singing, still with that trembling smile, Miss Brill prepared to listen.

"No, not now," said the girl. "Not here, I can't."

"But why? Because of that stupid old thing at the end there?" asked the boy. "Why does she come here at all—who wants her? Why doesn't she keep her silly old mug at home?"

"It's her fu-fur which is so funny," giggled the girl. "It's exactly like a fried whiting."[6]

"Ah, be off with you!" said the boy in an angry whisper. Then: "Tell me, ma petite chère—"[7]

"No, not here," said the girl. "Not *yet*."

On her way home she usually bought a slice of honeycake at the baker's. It was her Sunday treat. Sometimes there was an almond in her slice, sometimes not. It made a great difference. If there was an almond it was like carrying home a tiny present—a surprise—something that might very well not have been there. She hurried on the almond Sundays and struck the match for the kettle in quite a dashing way.

But today she passed the baker's by, climbed the stairs, went into the little dark room—her room like a cupboard—and sat down on the red eiderdown. She sat there for a long time. The box that the fur came out of was on the bed. She unclasped the necklet quickly; quickly, without looking, laid it inside. But when she put the lid on she thought she heard something crying.

---

[6] a food fish related to cod
[7] my dear little one

STUDY QUESTIONS

Katherine Mansfield's style in "Miss Brill" concentrates on details—details seen, heard, and interpreted by her highly observant and imaginative heroine. Note how the story is built and shaped by these details.

1. During the first part of the story, notice how the accumulation of details sets the scene. Note how observation mixes with imagination. For example, how does Miss Brill see or describe her fur piece? the bandmaster? the people on benches? the woman in the ermine toque?

2. The climax of the tale turns on a "discovery" made by Miss Brill, which tries to impose a unity on the scene and its many details. The climax itself, however, builds up in three stages. The first begins with the sentence, "Oh, how fascinating it was!" and ends with the sentence, "Yes, I have been an actress for a long time." The second begins with "The band had been having a rest." and continues through "Yes, we understand, we understand, she thought—though what they understood she didn't know." The third begins with "Just at that moment a boy and girl came" and closes with " 'No, not here,' said the girl. 'Not *yet.*' "

   a. What is the theme of each of these three stages? What part do observation, imagination, and feeling play in each? How fully do you accept each discovery? To what extent do you believe it to be true or feel in sympathy with it?

   b. What progression or contrast is created by the three stages? How do you react to it?

3. What does Mansfield do with her heroine after the climax? How does the story end? Note again the use of details observed and imagined; how does the ending tie in with the story's beginning and climax? How effective a means is this for rounding off the story?

A Worn Path

Eudora Welty (1909–   )

It was December—a bright frozen day in the early morning. Far out in the country there was an old Negro woman with her head tied in a red rag, coming along a path through the pinewoods. Her name was Phoenix Jackson. She was very old and small and she walked slowly in the dark pine shadows, moving a little from side to side in her steps, with the balanced heaviness and lightness of a pendulum in a grandfather clock. She carried a thin, small cane made from an umbrella, and with this she kept tapping the frozen earth in front of her. This made a grave and persistent noise in the still air, that seemed meditative like the chirping of a solitary little bird.

She wore a dark striped dress reaching down to her shoetops, and an equally long apron of bleached sugar sacks, with a full pocket; all neat and tidy, but every time she took a step she might have fallen over her shoe-laces, which dragged from her unlaced shoes. She looked straight ahead. Her eyes were blue with age. Her skin had a pattern all its own of numberless branching wrinkles and as though a whole little tree stood in the middle of her forehead, but a golden color ran underneath, and the two knobs of her cheeks were illuminated by a yellow burning under the dark. Under the red rag her hair came down on her neck in the frailest of ringlets, still black, and with an odor like copper.

Now and then there was a quivering in the thicket. Old Phoenix said, "Out of my way, all you foxes, owls, beetles, jack rabbits, coons, and wild animals! . . . Keep out from under these feet, little bobwhites. . . . Keep the big wild hogs out of my path. Don't let none of those come running my direction. I got a long way." Under her small black-freckled hand her cane, limber as a buggy whip, would switch at the brush as if to rouse up any hiding things.

On she went. The woods were deep and still. The sun made the pine needles almost too bright to look at, up where the wind rocked. The cones dropped as light as feathers. Down in the hollow was the mourning dove—it was not too late for him.

The path ran up a hill. "Seems like there is chains about my feet, time I get this far," she said, in the voice of argument old people keep to use with themselves. "Something always take a hold of his hill—pleads I should stay."

After she got to the top she turned and gave a full, severe look behind her where she had come. "Up through pines," she said at length. "Now down through oaks."

Her eyes opened their widest and she started down gently. But before she got to the bottom of the hill a bush caught her dress.

Her fingers were busy and intent, but her skirts were full and long, so that before she could pull them free in one place they were caught in another. It was not possible to allow the dress to tear. "I in the thorny bush," she said. "Thorns, you doing your appointed work. Never want to let folks pass—no sir. Old eyes thought you was a pretty little green bush."

Finally, trembling all over, she stood free, and after a moment dared to stoop for her cane.

"Sun so high!" she cried, leaning back and looking, while the thick tears went over her eyes. "The time getting all gone here."

At the foot of this hill was a place where a log was laid across the creek.

"Now comes the trial," said Phoenix.

Putting her right foot out, she mounted the log and shut her eyes. Lifting her skirt, levelling her cane fiercely before her, like a festival figure in some parade, she began to march across. Then she opened her eyes and she was safe on the other side.

"I wasn't as old as I thought," she said.

But she sat down to rest. She spread her skirts on the bank around her and folded her hands over her knees. Up above her was a tree in a pearly cloud of mistletoe. She did not dare to close her eyes, and when a little boy brought her a little plate with a slice of marble-cake on it she spoke to him. "That would be acceptable," she said. But when she went to take it there was just her own hand in the air.

So she left that tree, and had to go through a barbed-wire fence. There she had to creep and crawl, spreading her knees and stretching her fingers like a baby trying to climb the steps. But she talked loudly to herself: she could not let her dress be torn now, so late in the day, and she could not pay for having her arm or her leg sawed off if she got caught fast where she was.

At last she was safe through the fence and risen up out in the clearing. Big dead trees, like black men with one arm, were standing in the purple stalks of the withered cotton field. There sat a buzzard.

"Who you watching?"

In the burrow she made her way along.

"Glad this not the season for bulls," she said, looking sideways, "and the good Lord made his snakes to curl up and sleep in the winter. A pleasure I don't see no two-headed snake coming around that tree, where it come once. It took a while to get by him, back in the summer."

She passed through the old cotton and went into a field of dead corn. It whispered and shook, and was taller than her head. "Through the maze now," she said, for there was no path.

Then there was something tall, black, and skinny there, moving before her.

At first she took it for a man. It could have been a man dancing in the field. But she stood still and listened, and it did not make a sound. It was as silent as a ghost.

"Ghost," she said sharply, "who be you the ghost of? For I have heard of nary death close by."

But there was no answer, only the ragged dancing in the wind.

She shut her eyes, reached out her hand, and touched a sleeve. She found a coat and inside that an emptiness, cold as ice.

"You scarecrow," she said. Her face lighted. "I ought to be shut up for good," she said with laughter. "My senses is gone. I too old. I the oldest people I ever know. Dance, old scarecrow," she said, "while I dancing with you."

She kicked her foot over the furrow, and with mouth drawn down shook her head once or twice in a little strutting way. Some husks blew down and whirled in streamers about her skirts.

Then she went on, parting her way from side to side with the cane, through the whispering field. At last she came to the end, to a wagon track, where the silver grass blew between the red ruts. The quail were walking around like pullets, seeming all dainty and unseen.

"Walk pretty," she said. "This the easy place. This the easy going."

She followed the track, swaying through the quiet bare fields, through the little strings of trees silver in their dead leaves, past cabins silver from weather, with the doors and windows boarded shut, all like old women under a spell sitting there. "I walking in their sleep," she said, nodding her head vigorously.

In a ravine she went where a spring was silently flowing through a hollow log. Old Phoenix bent and drank. "Sweetgum makes the water sweet," she said, and drank more. "Nobody knows who made this well, for it was here when I was born."

The track crossed a swampy part where the moss hung as white as lace from every limb. "Sleep on, alligators, and blow your bubbles." Then the track went into the road.

Deep, deep the road went down between the high green-colored banks. Overhead the live-oaks met, and it was as dark as a cave.

A black dog with a lolling tongue came up out of the weeds by the ditch. She was meditating, and not ready, and when he came at her she only hit him a little with her cane. Over she went in the ditch, like a little puff of milk-weed.

Down there, her senses drifted away. A dream visited her, and she reached her hand up, but nothing reached down and gave her a pull. So she lay there and presently went to talking. "Old woman," she said to herself, "that black dog came up out of the weeds to stall you off, and now there he sitting on his fine tail, smiling at you."

A white man finally came along and found her—a hunter, a young man, with his dog on a chain.

"Well, Granny!" he laughed. "What are you doing there?"

"Lying on my back like a June-bug waiting to be turned over, mister," she said, reaching up her hand.

He lifted her up, gave her a swing in the air, and set her down, "Anything broken, Granny?"

"No sir, them old dead weeds is springy enough," said Phoenix, "when she had got her breath. "I thank you for your trouble."

"Where do you live, Granny?" he asked, while the two dogs were growling at each other.

"Away back yonder, sir, behind the ridge. You can't even see it from here."

"On your way home?"

"No, sir, I going to town."

"Why, that's too far! That's as far as I walk when I come out myself, and I get something for my trouble." He patted the stuffed bag he carried, and there hung down a little closed claw. It was one of the bobwhites, with its beak hooked bitterly to show it was dead. "Now you go on home, Granny!"

"I bound to go to town, mister," said Phoenix. "The time come around."

He gave another laugh, filling the whole landscape. "I know you colored people! Wouldn't miss going to town to see Santa Claus!"

But something held Old Phoenix very still. The deep lines in her face went into a fierce and different radiation. Without warning she had seen with her own eyes a flashing nickel fall out of the man's pocket on to the ground.

"How old are you, Granny?" he was saying.

"There is no telling, mister," she said, "no telling."

Then she gave a little cry and clapped her hands, and said, "Git on away from here, dog! Look at that dog!" She laughed as if in admiration. "He ain't scared of nobody. He a big black dog." She whispered, "Sick him!"

"Watch me get rid of that cur," said the man. "Sick him, Pete! Sick him!"

Phoenix heard the dogs fighting and heard the man running and throwing sticks. She even heard a gunshot. But she was slowly bending forward by that time, further and further forward, the lids stretched down over her eyes, as if she were doing this in her sleep. Her chin was lowered almost to her knees. The yellow palm of her hand came out from the fold of her apron. Her fingers slid down and along the ground under the piece of money with the grace and care they would have in lifting an egg from under a sitting hen. Then she slowly straightened up, she stood erect, and the nickel was in her apron pocket. A bird flew by. Her lips moved. "God watching me the whole time. I come to stealing."

The man came back, and his own dog panted about them. "Well, I scared him off that time," he said, and then he laughed and lifted his gun and pointed it at Phoenix.

She stood straight and faced him.

"Doesn't the gun scare you?" he said, still pointing it.

"No, sir, I seen plenty go off closer by, in my day, and for less than what I done," she said, holding utterly still.

He smiled, and shouldered the gun. "Well, Granny, he said, "you must be a hundred years old and scared of nothing. I'd give you a dime if I had any money with me. But you take my advice and stay home, and nothing will happen to you."

"I bound to go on my way, mister," said Phoenix. She inclined her head in the red rag. Then they went in different directions, but she could hear the gun shooting again and again over the hill.

She walked on. The shadows hung from the oak trees to the road like curtains. Then she smelled wood-smoke, and smelled the river, and she saw a steeple and the cabins on their steep steps. Dozens of little black children whirled around her. There ahead was Natchez shining. Bells were ringing. She walked on.

In the paved city it was Christmas time. There were red and green electric lights strung and crisscrossed everywhere, and all turned on in the daytime. Old Phoenix would have been lost if she had not distrusted her eyesight and depended on her feet to know where to take her.

She paused quietly on the sidewalk, where people were passing by. A lady came along in the crowd, carrying an armful of red-, green-, and silver-wrapped presents; she gave off perfume like the red roses in hot summer, and Phoenix stopped her.

"Please, missy, will you lace up my shoe?" She held up her foot.

"What do you want, Grandma?"

"See my shoe," said Phoenix. "Do all right for out in the country, but wouldn't look right to go in a big building."

"Stand still then, Grandma," said the lady. She put her packages down carefully on the sidewalk beside her and laced and tied both shoes tightly.

"Can't lace 'em with a cane," said Phoenix. "Thank you, missy. I doesn't mind asking a nice lady to tie up my shoe when I gets out on the street."

Moving slowly and from side to side, she went into the stone building and into a tower of steps, where she walked up and around and around until her feet knew to stop.

She entered a door, and there she saw nailed up on the wall the document that had been stamped with the gold seal and framed in the gold frame which matched the dream that was hung up in her head.

"Here I be," she said. There was a fixed and ceremonial stiffness over her body.

"A charity case, I suppose," said an attendant who sat at the desk before her.

But Phoenix only looked above her head. There was sweat on her face; the wrinkles shone like a bright net.

"Speak up, Grandma," the woman said. "What's your name? We must have your history, you know. Have you been here before? What seems to be the trouble with you?"

Old Phoenix only gave a twitch to her face as if a fly were bothering her.

"Are you deaf?" cried the attendant.

But then the nurse came in.

"Oh, that's just old Aunt Phoenix," she said. "She doesn't come for herself—she has a little grandson. She makes these trips just as regular as clockwork. She lives away back off the Old Natchez Trace." She bent down. "Well, Aunt Phoenix, why don't you just take a seat? We won't keep you standing after your long trip." She pointed.

The old woman sat down, bolt upright in the chair.

"Now, how is the boy?" asked the nurse.

Old Phoenix did not speak.

"I said, how is the boy?"

But Phoenix only waited and stared straight ahead, her face very solemn and withdrawn into rigidity.

"Is his throat any better?" asked the nurse. "Aunt Phoenix, don't you hear me? Is your grandson's throat any better since the last time you came for the medicine?"

With her hand on her knees, the old woman waited, silent, erect and motionless, just as if she were in armor.

"You mustn't take up our time this way, Aunt Phoenix," the nurse said. "Tell us quickly about your grandson, and get it over. He isn't dead, is he?"

At last there came a flicker and then a flame of comprehension across her face, and she spoke.

"My grandson. It was my memory had left me. There I sat and forgot why I made my long trip."

"Forgot?" The nurse frowned. "After you came so far?"

Then Phoenix was like an old woman begging a dignified forgiveness for waking up frightened in the night. "I never did go to school—I was too old at the Surrender," she said in a soft voice. "I'm an old woman without an education. It was my memory fail me. My little grandson, he is just the same, and I forgot it in the coming."

"Throat never heals, does it?" said the nurse, speaking in a loud, sure voice to Old Phoenix. By now she had a card with something written on it, a little list. "Yes. Swallowed lye. When was it—January—two—three years ago—"

Phoenix spoke unasked now. "No, missy, he not dead, he just the same. Every little while his throat begin to close up again, and he not able to swallow. He not get his breath. He not able to help himself. So the time come around, and I go on another trip for the soothing-medicine."

"All right. The doctor said as long as you came to get it you could have it," said the nurse. "But it's an obstinate case."

"My little grandson, he sit up there in the house all wrapped up, waiting by himself," Phoenix went on. "We is the only two left in the world. He suffer and it don't seem to put him back at all. He got a sweet look. He going to last. He wear a little patch quilt and peep out, holding his mouth open like a little bird. I remembers so plain now. I not going to forget him again, no, the whole enduring time. I could tell him from all the others in creation."

"All right." The nurse was trying to hush her now. She brought her a bottle of medicine. "Charity," she said, making a check mark in a book.

Old Phoenix held the bottle close to her eyes and then carefully put it into her pocket.

"I thank you," she said.

"It's Christmas time, Grandma," said the attendant. "Could I give you a few pennies out of my purse?"

"Five pennies is a nickel," said Phoenix stiffly.

"Here's a nickel," said the attendant.

Phoenix rose carefully and held out her hand. She received the nickel and then fished the other nickel out of her pocket and laid it beside the new one. She stared at her palm closely, with her head on one side.

Then she gave a tap with her cane on the floor.

"This is what come to me to do," she said. "I going to the store and buy my child a little windmill they sells, made out of paper. He going to find it hard to believe there such a thing in the world. I'll march myself back where he waiting, holding it straight up in this hand."

She lifted her free hand, gave a little nod, turned round, and walked out of the doctor's office. Then her slow step began on the stairs, going down.

STUDY QUESTIONS

1. How much of the story takes place with Granny Phoenix as its only character? What happens in this first part of the tale? What effect does it have on you, the reader?
2. Describe Granny's first meeting with another person. What new information do we learn from it?
3. The story's climax is the scene in the clinic. Here we finally learn why Granny has made her long journey. What is your reaction to this scene? How have the story and its narrator brought you to feel as you do?

Where Are You Going, Where Have You Been?

Joyce Carol Oates (1938–   )

For Bob Dylan

Her name was Connie. She was fifteen and she had a quick, nervous giggling habit of craning her neck to glance into mirrors or checking other people's faces to make sure her own was all right. Her mother, who noticed everything and knew everything and who hadn't much reason any longer to look at her own face, always scolded Connie about it. "Stop gawking at yourself. Who are you? You think you're so pretty?" she would say. Connie would raise her eyebrows at these familiar old complaints and look right through her mother, into a shadowy vision of herself as she was right at that moment: she knew she was pretty and that was everything. Her mother had been pretty once too, if you could believe those old snapshots in the album, but now her looks were gone and that was why she was always after Connie.

"Why don't you keep your room clean like your sister? How've you got your hair fixed—what the hell stinks? Hair spray? You don't see your sister using that junk."

Her sister June was twenty-four and still lived at home. She was a secretary in the high school Connie attended, and if that wasn't bad enough—with her in the same building—she was so plain and chunky and steady that Connie had to hear her praised all the time by her mother and her mother's sisters. June did this, June did that, she saved money and helped clean the house and cooked and Connie couldn't do a thing, her mind was all filled with trashy daydreams. Their father was away at work most of the time and when he came home he wanted supper and he read the newspaper at supper and after supper he went to bed. He didn't bother talking much to them, but around his bent head Connie's mother kept picking at her until Connie wished her mother was dead and she herself was dead and it was all over. "She makes me want to throw up sometimes," she complained to her friends. She had a high, breathless, amused voice that made everything she said sound a little forced, whether it was sincere or not.

There was one good thing: June went places with girl friends of hers, girls who were just as plain and steady as she, and so when Connie wanted to do that her mother had no objections. The father of Connie's best girl friend drove the girls the three miles to town and left them at a shopping plaza so they could walk through the stores or go to a movie, and when he came to pick them up again at eleven he never bothered to ask what they had done.

They must have been familiar sights, walking around the shopping plaza in their shorts and flat ballerina slippers that always scuffed on the sidewalk, with charm bracelets jingling on their thin wrists; they would lean together to whisper and laugh secretly if someone passed who amused or interested them. Connie had long dark blond hair that drew anyone's eye to it, and she wore part of it pulled up on her head and puffed out and the rest of it she let fall down her back. She wore a pull-over jersey blouse that looked one way when she was at home and another way when she was away from home. Everything about her had two sides to it, one for home and one for anywhere that was not home: her walk, which could be childlike and bobbing, or languid enough to make anyone think she was hearing music in her head; her mouth, which was pale and smirking most of the time, but bright and pink on these evenings out; her laugh, which was cynical and drawling at home—"Ha, ha, very funny,"—but highpitched and nervous anywhere else, like the jingling of the charms on her bracelet.

Sometimes they did go shopping or to a movie, but sometimes they went across the highway, ducking fast across the busy road, to a drive-in restaurant where older kids hung out. The restaurant was shaped like a big bottle, though squatter than a real bottle, and on its cap was a revolving figure of a grinning boy holding a hamburger aloft. One night in midsummer they ran across, breathless with daring, and right away someone leaned out a car window and invited them over, but it was just a boy from high school they didn't like. It made them feel good to be able to ignore him. They went up through the maze of parked and cruising cars to the bright-lit, fly-infested restaurant, their faces pleased and expectant as if they were entering a sacred building that loomed up out of the night to give them what haven and blessing they yearned for. They sat at the counter and crossed their legs at the ankles, their thin shoulders rigid with excitement, and listened to the music that made everything so good: the music was always in the background, like music at a church service; it was something to depend upon.

A boy named Eddie came in to talk with them. He sat backwards on his stool, turning himself jerkily around in semicircles and then stopping and turning back again, and after a while he asked Connie if she would like something to eat. She said she would and so she tapped her friend's arm on her way out—her friend pulled her face up into a brave, droll look—and Connie said she would meet her at eleven, across the way. "I just hate to leave her like that," Connie said earnestly, but the boy said that she wouldn't be alone for long. So they went out to his car, and on the way Connie couldn't help but let her eyes wander over the windshields and faces all around her, her face gleaming with a joy that had nothing to do with Eddie or even this place; it might have been the music. She drew her shoulders up and sucked in her breath with the pure pleasure of being alive, and just at that moment she happened to glance at a face just a few feet away from hers. It was a boy with shaggy black hair, in a convertible jalopy painted gold. He stared at her and then his lips widened into a grin. Connie slit her eyes at him and turned away, but she couldn't help glancing back and there he was, still watching her. He wagged a finger and laughed and said, "Gonna get you, baby," and Connie turned away again without Eddie noticing anything.

She spent three hours with him, at the restaurant where they ate hamburgers and drank Cokes in wax cups that were always sweating, and then down an alley a mile or so away, and when he left her off at five to eleven only the movie house was still open at the plaza. Her girl friend was there, talking with a boy. When Connie came up, the two girls smiled at each other and Connie said, "How was the movie?" and the girl said, "*You* should know." They rode off with the girl's father, sleepy and pleased, and Connie couldn't help but look back at the darkened shopping plaza with its big empty parking lot and its signs that were faded and ghostly now, and over at the drive-in restaurant where cars were still circling tirelessly. She couldn't hear the music at this distance.

Next morning June asked her how the movie was and Connie said, "So-so."

She and that girl and occasionally another girl went out several times a week, and the rest of the time Connie spent around the house—it was summer vacation—getting in her mother's way and thinking, dreaming about the boys she met. But all the boys fell back and dissolved into a single face that was not even a face but an idea, a feeling, mixed up with the urgent insistent pounding of the music and the humid night air of July. Connie's mother kept dragging her back to the daylight by finding things for her to do or saying suddenly, "What's this about the Pettinger girl?"

And Connie would say nervously, "Oh, her. That dope." She always drew thick clear lines between herself and such girls, and her mother was simple and kind enough to believe it. Her mother was so simple, Connie thought, that it was maybe cruel to fool her so much. Her mother went scuffling around the house in old bedroom slippers and complained over the telephone to one sister about the other, then the other called up and the two of them complained about the third one. If June's name was mentioned her mother's tone was approving, and if Connie's name was mentioned it was disapproving. This did not really mean she disliked Connie, and actually Connie thought that her mother preferred her to June just because she was prettier, but the two of them kept up a pretense of exasperation, a sense that they were tugging and struggling over something of little value to either of them. Sometimes, over coffee, they were almost friends, but something would come up—some vexation that was like a fly buzzing suddenly around their heads—and their faces went hard with contempt.

One Sunday Connie got up at eleven—none of them bothered with church—and washed her hair so that it could dry all day long in the sun. Her parents and sister were going to a barbecue at an aunt's house and Connie said no, she wasn't interested, rolling her eyes to let her mother know just what she thought of it. "Stay home alone then," her mother said sharply. Connie sat out back in a lawn chair and watched them drive away, her father quiet and bald, hunched around so that he could back the car out, her mother with a look that was still angry and not at all softened through the windshield, and in the back seat poor old June, all dressed up as if she didn't know what a barbecue was, with all the running yelling kids and the flies. Connie sat with her eyes closed in the sun, dreaming and dazed with the warmth about her as if this were a kind of love, the caresses of love, and her mind slipped over onto thoughts of the boy she had been with the night before and how nice he had been, how sweet it always was, not the way someone like June would suppose but sweet, gentle, the way it was in movies and promised in songs; and when she opened her eyes she hardly knew where she was, the back yard ran off into weeds and a fence-like line of trees and behind it the sky was perfectly blue and still. The asbestos "ranch house" that was now three years old startled her—it looked small. She shook her head as if to get awake.

It was too hot. She went inside the house and turned on the radio to drown out the quiet. She sat on the edge of her bed, barefoot, and listened for an hour and a half, to a program called XYZ Sunday Jamboree, record after record of hard, fast, shrieking songs she sang along with, interspersed by exclamations from "Bobby King": "An' look here, you girls at Napoleon's—Son and Charley want you to pay real close attention to this song coming up!"

And Connie paid close attention herself, bathed in a glow of slow-pulsed joy that seemed to rise mysteriously out of the music itself and lay languidly about the airless little room, breathed in and breathed out with each gentle rise and fall of her chest.

After a while she heard a car coming up the drive. She sat up at once, startled, because it couldn't be her father so soon. The gravel kept crunching all the way in from the road—the driveway was long—and Connie ran to the window. It was a car she didn't know. It was an open jalopy, painted a bright gold that caught the sunlight opaquely. Her heart began to pound and her fingers snatched at her hair, checking it, and she whispered, "Christ, Christ," wondering how she looked. The car came to a stop at the side door and the horn sounded four short taps, as if this were a signal Connie knew.

She went into the kitchen and approached the door slowly, then hung out the screen door, her bare toes curling down off the step. There were two boys in the car and now she recognized the driver: he had shaggy, shabby black hair that looked crazy as a wig and he was grinning at her.

"I ain't late, am I?" he said.

"Who the hell do you think you are?" Connie said.

"Toldja I'd be out, didn't I?"

"I don't even know who you are."

She spoke sullenly, careful to show no interest or pleasure, and he spoke in a fast, bright monotone. Connie looked past him to the other boy, taking her time. He had fair brown hair, with a lock that fell onto his forehead. His sideburns gave him a fierce, embarrassed look, but so far he hadn't even bothered to glance at her. Both boys wore sunglasses. The driver's glasses were metallic and mirrored everything in miniature.

"You wanta come for a ride?" he said.

Connie smirked and let her hair fall loose over one shoulder.

"Don'tcha like my car? New paint job," he said. "Hey."

"What?"

"You're cute."

She pretended to fidget, chasing flies away from the door.

"Don'tcha believe me, or what?" he said.

"Look, I don't even know who you are," Connie said in disgust.

"Hey, Ellie's got a radio, see. Mine broke down." He lifted his friend's arm and showed her the little transistor radio the boy was holding, and now Connie began to hear the music. It was the same program that was playing inside the house.

"Bobby King?" she said.

"I listen to him all the time. I think he's great."

"He's kind of great," Connie said reluctantly.

"Listen, that guy's *great*. He knows where the action is."

Connie blushed a little, because the glasses made it impossible for her to see just what this boy was looking at. She couldn't decide if she liked him or if he was a jerk, and so she dawdled in the doorway and wouldn't come down or go back inside. She said, "What's all that stuff painted on your car?"

"Can'tcha read it?" He opened the door very carefully, as if he were afraid it might fall off. He slid out just as carefully, planting his feet firmly on the ground, the tiny metallic world in his glasses slowing down like gelatine hardening, and in the midst of it Connie's bright green blouse. "This here is my name, to begin with," he said. ARNOLD FRIEND was written in tarlike black letters on the side, with a drawing of a round, grinning face that reminded Connie of a pumpkin, except it wore sunglasses. "I wanta introduce myself. I'm Arnold Friend and that's my real name and I'm gonna be your friend, honey, and inside the car's Ellie Oscar, he's kinda shy." Ellie brought his transistor radio up to his shoulder and balanced it there. "Now, these numbers are a secret code, honey," Arnold Friend explained. He read off the numbers 33, 19, 17 and raised his eyebrows at her to see what she thought of that, but she didn't think much of it. The left rear fender had been smashed and around it was written, on the gleaming gold background: DONE BY CRAZY WOMAN DRIVER. Connie had to laugh at that. Arnold Friend was pleased at her laughter and looked up at her. "Around the other side's a lot more—you wanta come and see them?"

"No."

"Why not?"

"Why should I?"

"Don'tcha wanta see what's on the car? Don'tcha wanta go for a ride?"

"I don't know."

"Why not?"

"I got things to do."

"Like what?"

"Things."

He laughed as if she had said something funny. He slapped his thighs. He was standing in a strange way, leaning back against the car as if he were balancing himself. He wasn't tall, only an inch or so taller than she would be if she came down to him. Connie liked the way he was dressed, which was the way all of them dressed: tight faded jeans stuffed into black, scuffed boots, a belt that pulled his waist in and showed how lean he was, and a white pull-over shirt that was a little soiled and showed the hard small muscles of his arms and shoulders. He looked as if he probably did hard work, lifting and carrying things. Even his neck looked muscular. And his face was a familiar face, somehow; the jaw and chin and cheeks slightly darkened because he hadn't shaved for a day or two, and the nose long and hawklike, sniffing as if she were a treat he was going to gobble up and it was all a joke.

"Connie, you ain't telling the truth. This is your day set aside for a ride with me and you know it," he said, still laughing. The way he straightened and recovered from his fit of laughing showed that it had been all fake.

"How do you know what my name is?" she said suspiciously.

"It's Connie."

"Maybe and maybe not."

"I know my Connie," he said, wagging his finger. Now she remembered him even better, back at the restaurant, and her cheeks warmed at the thought of how she had sucked in her breath just at the moment she passed him—how she must have looked to him. And he had remembered her. "Ellie and I come out here especially for you," he said. "Ellie can sit in back. How about it?"

"Where?"

"Where what?"

"Where're we going?"

He looked at her. He took off the sunglasses and she saw how pale the skin around his eyes was, like holes that were not in shadow but instead in light. His eyes were like chips of broken glass that catch the light in an amiable way. He smiled. It was as if the idea of going for a ride somewhere, to someplace, was a new idea to him.

"Just for a ride, Connie sweetheart."

"I never said my name was Connie," she said.

"But I know what it is. I know your name and all about you, lots of things," Arnold Friend said. He had not moved yet but stood still leaning back against the side of his jalopy. "I took a special interest in you, such a pretty girl, and found out all about you—like I know your parents and sister are gone somewheres and I know where and how long they're going to be gone, and I know who you were with last night, and your best girl friend's name is Betty. Right?"

He spoke in a simple lilting voice, exactly as if he were reciting the words to a song. His smile assured her that everything was fine. In the car Ellie turned up the volume on his radio and did not bother to look around at them.

"Ellie can sit in the back seat," Arnold Friend said. He indicated his friend with a casual jerk of his chin, as if Ellie did not count and she should not bother with him.

"How'd you find out all that stuff?" Connie said.

"Listen: Betty Schultz and Tony Fitch and Jimmy Pettinger and Nancy Pettinger," he said in a chant. "Raymond Stanley and Bob Hutter—"

"Do you know all those kids?"

"I know everybody."

"Look, you're kidding. You're not from around here."

"Sure."

"But—how come we never saw you before?"

"Sure you saw me before," he said. He looked down at his boots, as if he were a little offended. "You just don't remember."

"I guess I'd remember you," Connie said.

"Yeah?" He looked up at this, beaming. He was pleased. He began to mark time with the music from Ellie's radio, tapping his fists lightly together. Connie looked away from his smile to the car, which was painted so bright it almost hurt her eyes to look at it. She looked at that name, ARNOLD FRIEND. And up at the front fender was an expression that was familiar—MAN THE FLYING SAUCERS. It was an expression kids had used the year before but didn't use this year. She looked at it for a while as if the words meant something to her that she did not yet know.

"What're you thinking about? Huh?" Arnold Friend demanded. "Not worried about your hair blowing around in the car, are you?"

"No."

"Think I maybe can't drive good?"

"How do I know?"

"You're a hard girl to handle. How come?" he said. "Don't you know I'm your friend? Didn't you see me put my sign in the air when you walked by?"

"What sign?"

"My sign." And he drew an X in the air, leaning out toward her. They were maybe ten feet apart. After his hand fell back to his side the X was still in the air, almost visible. Connie let the screen door close and stood perfectly still inside it, listening to the music from her radio and the boy's blend together. She stared at

Arnold Friend. He stood there so stiffly relaxed, pretending to be relaxed, with one hand idly on the door handle as if he were keeping himself up that way and had no intention of ever moving again. She recognized most things about him, the tight jeans that showed his thighs and buttocks and the greasy leather boots and the tight shirt, and even that slippery friendly smile of his, that sleepy dreamy smile that all the boys used to get across ideas they didn't want to put into words. She recognized all this and also the sing-song way he talked, slightly mocking, kidding, but serious and a little melancholy, and she recognized the way he tapped one fist against the other in homage to the perpetual music behind him. But all these things did not come together.

She said suddenly, "Hey, how old are you?"

His smile faded. She could see then that he wasn't a kid, he was much older—thirty, maybe more. At this knowledge her heart began to pound faster.

"That's a crazy thing to ask. Can'tcha see I'm your own age?"

"Like hell you are."

"Or maybe a coupla years older. I'm eighteen."

"Eighteen?" she said doubtfully.

He grinned to reassure her and lines appeared at the corners of his mouth. His teeth were big and white. He grinned so broadly his eyes became slits and she saw how thick the lashes were, thick and black as if painted with a black tar-like material. Then, abruptly, he seemed to become embarrassed and looked over his shoulder at Ellie. "*Him*, he's crazy," he said. "Ain't he a riot? He's a nut, a real character." Ellie was still listening to the music. His sunglasses told nothing about what he was thinking. He wore a bright orange shirt unbuttoned halfway to show his chest, which was a pale, bluish chest and not muscular like Arnold Friend's. His shirt collar was turned up all around and the very tips of the collar pointed out past his chin as if they were protecting him. He was pressing the transistor radio up against his ear and sat there in a kind of daze, right in the sun.

"He's kinda strange," Connie said.

"Hey, she says you're kinda strange! Kinda strange!" Arnold Friend cried. He pounded on the car to get Ellie's attention. Ellie turned for the first time and Connie saw with shock that he wasn't a kid either—he had a fair, hairless face, cheeks reddened slightly as if the veins grew too close to the surface of his skin, the face of a forty-year-old baby. Connie felt a wave of dizziness rise in her at this sight and she stared at him as if waiting for something to change the shock of the moment, make it all right again. Ellie's lips kept shaping words, mumbling along with the words blasting in his ear.

"Maybe you two better go away," Connie said faintly.

"What? How come?" Arnold Friend cried. "We come out here to take you for a ride. It's Sunday." He had the voice of the man on the radio now. It was the same voice, Connie thought. "Don'tcha know it's Sunday all day? And honey, no matter who you were with last night, today you're with Arnold Friend and don't you forget it! Maybe you better step out here," he said, and this last was in a different voice. It was a little flatter, as if the heat was finally getting to him.

"No, I got things to do."

"Hey."

"You two better leave."

"We ain't leaving until you come with us."

"Like hell I am—"

"Connie, don't fool around with me. I mean—I mean, don't fool around," he said, shaking his head. He laughed incredulously. He placed his sunglasses on top of his head, carefully, as if he were indeed wearing a wig, and brought the stems down behind his ears. Connie stared at him, another wave of dizziness and fear rising in her so that for a moment he wasn't even in focus but was just a blur standing there against his gold car, and she had the idea that he had driven up the driveway all right but had come from nowhere before that and belonged nowhere and that everything about him and even about the music that was so familiar to her was only half real.

"If my father comes and sees you—"

"He ain't coming. He's at a barbecue."

"How do you know that?"

"Aunt Tillie's. Right now they're—uh—they're drinking. Sitting around," he said vaguely, squinting as if he were staring all the way to town and over to Aunt Tillie's back yard. Then the vision seemed to get clear and he nodded energetically. "Yeah. Sitting around. There's your sister in a blue dress, huh? And high heels, the poor sad bitch—nothing like you, sweetheart! And your mother's helping some fat woman with the corn, they're cleaning the corn—husking the corn—"

"What fat woman?" Connie cried.

"How do I know what fat woman, I don't know every goddamn fat woman in the world!" Arnold Friend laughed.

"Oh, that's Mrs. Hornsby. . . . Who invited her?" Connie said. She felt a little lightheaded. Her breath was coming quickly.

"She's too fat. I don't like them fat. I like them the way you are, honey," he said, smiling sleepily at her. They stared at each other for a while through the screen door. He said softly, "Now, what you're going to do is this: you're going to come out that door. You're going to sit up front with me and Ellie's going to sit in the back, the hell with Ellie, right? This isn't Ellie's date. You're my date. I'm your lover, honey."

"What? You're crazy—"

"Yes, I'm your lover. You don't know what that is but you will," he said. "I know that too. I know all about you. But look: it's real nice and you couldn't ask for nobody better than me, or more polite. I always keep my word. I'll tell you how it is. I'm always nice at first, the first time. I'll hold you so tight you won't think you have to try to get away or pretend anything because you'll know you can't. And I'll come inside you where it's all secret and you'll give in to me and you'll love me—"

"Shut up! You're crazy!" Connie said. She backed away from the door. She put her hands up against her ears as if she'd heard something terrible, something not meant for her. "People don't talk like that, you're crazy," she muttered. Her heart was almost too big now for her chest and its pumping made sweat break out all over her. She looked out to see Arnold Friend pause and then take a step toward the porch, lurching. He almost fell. But, like a clever drunken man, he managed to catch his balance. He wobbled in his high boots and grabbed hold of one of the porch posts.

"Honey?" he said. "You still listening?"

"Get the hell out of here!"

"Be nice, honey. Listen."

"I'm going to call the police—"

He wobbled again and out of the side of his mouth came a fast spat curse, an aside not meant for her to hear. But even this "Christ!" sounded forced. Then he began to smile again. She watched this smile come, awkward as if he were smiling from inside a mask. His whole face was a mask, she thought wildly, tanned down to his throat but then running out as if he had plastered makeup on his face but had forgotten about his throat.

"Honey—? Listen, here's how it is. I always tell the truth and I promise you this: I ain't coming in that house after you."

"You better not! I'm going to call the police if you—if you don't—"

"Honey," he said, talking right through her voice, "honey. I'm not coming in there but you are coming out here. You know why?"

She was panting. The kitchen looked like a place she had never seen before, some room she had run inside but that wasn't good enough, wasn't going to help her. The kitchen window had never had a curtain, after three years, and there were dishes in the sink for her to do—probably—and if you ran your hand across the table you'd probably feel something stick there.

"You listening, honey? Hey?"

"—going to call the police—"

"Soon as you touch the phone I don't need to keep my promise and can come inside. You won't want that."

She rushed forward and tried to lock the door. Her fingers were shaking. "But why lock it," Arnold Friend said gently, talking right into her face. "It's just a screen door. It's just nothing." One of his boots was at a strange angle, as if his foot wasn't in it. It pointed out to the left, bent at the ankle. "I mean, anybody can break through a screen door and glass and wood and iron or anything else, if he needs to, anybody at all, and especially Arnold Friend. If the place got lit up with a fire, honey, you'd come runnin' out into my arms, right into my arms an' safe at home—like you knew I was your lover and'd stopped fooling around. I don't mind a nice shy girl but I don't like no fooling around." Part of those words were spoken with a slight rhythmic lilt, and Connie somehow recognized them—the echo of a song from last year, about a girl rushing into her boy friend's arms and coming home again—

Connie stood barefoot on the linoleum floor, staring at him. "What do you want?" she whispered.

"I want you," he said.

"What?"

"Seen you that night and thought, that's the one, yes sir. I never needed to look anymore."

"But my father's coming back. He's coming to get me. I had to wash my hair first—" She spoke in a dry, rapid voice, hardly raising it for him to hear. "No, your daddy is not coming and yes, you had to wash your hair and you washed it for me. It's nice and shining and all for me. I thank you sweetheart," he said with a mock bow, but again he almost lost his balance. He had to bend and adjust his boots. Evidently his feet did not go all the way down; the boots must have been stuffed with something so that he would seem taller. Connie stared out at him and behind him at Ellie in the car, who seemed to be looking off toward Connie's right, into nothing. This Ellie said, pulling the words out of the air one after another as if he were just discovering them, "You want me to pull out the phone?"

"Shut your mouth and keep it shut," Arnold Friend said, his face red from bending over or maybe from embarrassment because Connie had seen his boots. "This ain't none of your business."

"What—what are you doing? What do you want?" Connie said. "If I call the police they'll get you, they'll arrest you—"

"Promise was not to come in unless you touch that phone, and I'll keep that promise," he said. He resumed his erect position and tried to force his shoulders back. He sounded like a hero in a movie, declaring something important. But he spoke too loudly and it was as if he were speaking to someone behind Connie. "I ain't made plans for coming in that house where I don't belong but just for you to come out to me, the way you should. Don't you know who I am?"

"You're crazy," she whispered. She backed away from the door but did not want to go into another part of the house, as if this would give him permission to come through the door. "What do you . . . you're crazy, you . . ."

"Huh? What're you saying, honey?"

Her eyes darted everywhere in the kitchen. She could not remember what it was, this room.

"This is how it is, honey: you come out and we'll drive away, have a nice ride. But if you don't come out we're gonna wait till your people come home and then they're all going to get it."

"You want that telephone pulled out?" Ellie said. He held the radio away from his ear and grimaced, as if without the radio the air was too much for him.

"I toldja shut up, Ellie," Arnold Friend said, "you're deaf, get a hearing aid, right? Fix yourself up. This little girl's no trouble and's gonna be nice to me, so Ellie keep to yourself, this ain't your date—right? Don't hem in on me, don't hog, don't crush, don't bird dog, don't trail me," he said in a rapid, meaningless voice, as if he were running through all the expressions he'd learned but was no longer sure which of them was in style, then rushing on to new ones, making them up with his eyes closed. "Don't crawl under my fence, don't squeeze in my chipmunk hole, don't sniff my glue, suck my popsicle, keep your own greasy fingers on yourself!" He shaded his eyes and peered in at Connie, who was backed against the kitchen table. "Don't mind him, honey, he's just a creep. He's a dope. Right? I'm the boy for you and like I said, you come out here nice like a lady and give me your hand, and nobody else gets hurt, I mean, your nice old bald-headed daddy and your mummy and your sister in her high heels. Because listen: why bring them in this?"

"Leave me alone," Connie whispered.

"Hey, you know that old woman down the road, the one with the chickens and stuff—you know her?"

"She's dead!"

"Dead? What? You know her?" Arnold Friend said.

"She's dead—."

"Don't you like her?"

"She's dead—she's—she isn't here any more—"

"But don't you like her, I mean, you got something against her? Some grudge or something?" Then his voice dipped as if he were conscious of a rudeness. He touched the sunglasses perched up on top of his head as if to make sure they were still there. "Now, you be a good girl."

"What are you going to do?"

"Just two things, or maybe three," Arnold Friend said. "But I promise it won't last long and you'll like me the way you get to like people you're close to. You will. It's all over for you here, so come on out. You don't want your people in any trouble, do you?"

She turned and bumped against a chair or something, hurting her leg, but she ran into the back room and picked up the telephone. Something roared in her ear, a tiny roaring, and she was so sick with fear that she could do nothing but listen to it—the telephone was clammy and very heavy and her fingers groped down to the dial but were too weak to touch it. She began to scream into the phone, into the roaring. She cried out, she cried for her mother, she felt her breath start jerking back and forth in her lungs as if it were something Arnold Friend was stabbing her with again and again with no tenderness. A noisy sorrowful wailing rose all about her and she was locked inside it the way she was locked inside this house.

After a while she could hear again. She was sitting on the floor with her wet back against the wall.

Arnold Friend was saying from the door, "That's a good girl. Put the phone back."

She kicked the phone away from her.

"No, honey. Pick it up. Put it back right."

She picked it up and put it back. The dial tone stopped.

"That's a good girl. Now, you come outside."

She was hollow with what had been fear but what was now just an emptiness. All that screaming had blasted it out of her. She sat, one leg cramped under her, and deep inside her brain was something like a pinpoint of light that kept going and would not let her relax. She thought, I'm not going to see my mother again. She thought, I'm not going to sleep in my bed again. Her bright green blouse was all wet.

Arnold Friend said, in a gentle-loud voice that was like a stage voice, "The place where you came from ain't there any more, and where you had in mind to go is cancelled out. This place you are now—inside your daddy's house—is nothing but a cardboard box I can knock down any time. You know that and always did know it. You hear me?"

She thought, I have got to think. I have got to know what to do.

"We'll go out to a nice field, out in the country here where it smells so nice and it's sunny," Arnold Friend said. "I'll have my arms tight around you so you won't need to try to get away and I'll show you what love is like, what it does. The hell with this house! It looks solid all right," he said. He ran his fingernail down the screen and the noise did not make Connie shiver, as it would have the day before. "Now, put your hand on your heart, honey. Feel that? That feels solid too but we know better. Be nice to me, be sweet like you can because what else is there for a girl like you but to be sweet and pretty and give in?—and get away before her people get back?"

She felt her pounding heart. Her hand seemed to enclose it. She thought for the first time in her life that it was nothing that was hers, that belonged to her, but just a pounding, living thing inside this body that wasn't really hers either.

"You don't want them to get hurt," Arnold Friend went on. "Now, get up, honey. Get up all by yourself."

She stood.

"Now, turn this way. That's right. Come over here to me—Ellie, put that away, didn't I tell you? You dope. You miserable creepy dope," Arnold Friend said. His words were not angry but only part of an incantation. The incantation was kindly. "Now, come out through the kitchen to me, honey, and let's see a smile, try it, you're a brave, sweet little girl and now they're eating corn and hot dogs cooked to bursting over an outdoor fire, and they don't know one thing about you and never did and honey, you're better than them because not a one of them would have done this for you."

Connie felt the linoleum under her feet; it was cool. She brushed her hair back out of her eyes. Arnold Friend let go of the post tentatively and opened his arms for her, his elbows pointing in toward each other and his wrists limp, to show that this was an embarrassed embrace and a little mocking, he didn't want to make her self-conscious.

She put out her hand against the screen. She watched herself push the door slowly open as if she were back safe somewhere in the other doorway, watching this body and this head of long hair moving out into the sunlight where Arnold Friend waited.

"My sweet little blue-eyed girl," he said in a half-sung sigh that had nothing to do with her brown eyes but was taken up just the same by the vast sunlit reaches of the land behind him and on all sides of him—so much land that Connie had never seen before and did not recognize except to know that she was going to it.

STUDY QUESTIONS

1. The highly realistic style of this story is built on many mundane details.
   a. List some details that describe Connie. What sense of her do they give you?
   b. List some details that describe Connie's family and friends, home and neighborhood. What sense do these give you of her surroundings, and of the society in which she lives?
   c. List some details that describe Arnold Friend. How does he fit, or *not* fit, into the society you have described above?
2. Consider next the narrator's voice. How would you describe it? Does the narrator give you any hints as to how she feels about Connie? about Connie's family and friends? Can you cite instances in which you think the narrator shows sympathy for the girl? Can you cite any instances in which you think she judges her? In each case, why do you think so?
3. Do the narrator's style and the details of the story as she tells them lead you to feel sympathy for Connie? to judge her? How do you find yourself responding to the characters as the story progresses?
4. Consider the ending of the story. When you first read the story, what was your reaction to the ending?
5. Look again at the story, and at what you have written about it so far. In light of this, to what extent do you think the ending seems inevitable? To what extent is it a surprise or a shock? Has Oates moved from the everyday into the realm of horror, or is she, rather, revealing a horror that can be part of an everyday world?
6. Why do you think Oates ends the story where she does? Do you think the story would be stronger or weaker if Oates continued the tale and told the rest of what happened between Connie and Arnold Friend? Discuss your reasoning.

6

FIRST-PERSON NARRATORS

Omniscient narrators stand somewhat apart from their stories. Having no role in the action themselves, they can interpret its events and characters impartially. Even when an omniscient narrator shows us most of the story through one central character's eyes, he or she can still give us glimpses into minds and actions that the character cannot see, and can still interpret the events from his or her own point of view, even when that point of view conflicts with that of the central character.

First-person narrators, on the other hand, are participants in their own stories. They are telling us of something that happened to them, and are telling their tale from their own point of view. They cannot see into the minds of the other characters; indeed, they may hardly understand their own actions. In contrast to the total knowledge of the omniscient narrator, the first-person narrator's powers of interpretation may be slight indeed.

As the narrator's knowledge shrinks, the reader's role expands. If we cannot trust the narrator as an omniscient, final authority, then our own wisdom and judgment must come into play. We must weigh the narrator's perceptions against our own and so create our own understanding of the actions and characters within the story.

Often, therefore, first-person narratives are rich in **irony,** with the narrators describing what they think they see and the readers interpreting the descriptions to discover what "really" happened. In these stories the relationship between readers and narrators is completely reversed. Now we are the wise ones, the ones with the fullest perception of what's going on. If we could only speak to these narrators, as they seem to be speaking to us, how much we could tell them!

In other stories, however, first-person narrators retain the full authority of the storyteller. Indeed, if the tales they tell are set far enough in their pasts, the narrators may view themselves as nearly omniscient. They know what they were thinking and feeling when the events took place, so they can take us into their major character's mind; they know how events turned out, so they feel that they can interpret the patterns within them. Moreover, they may feel that they have grown considerably wiser since the time of the actions they are relating and can therefore combine past feelings and present understanding to interpret events and emotions as no one else could.

In either case, and in less extreme cases as well, we often feel closer to first-person narrators than we feel either to omniscient narrators or to the characters they describe. The limitations of human knowledge and insight within which the first-person narrators work, the blend of attempted objectivity and personal involvement their voices convey, and their apparent openness in telling their own stories appeal to our sympathy and our sense of fellowship. In telling us, as they often do, of their dreams and desires, first-person narrators speak eloquently of human aspirations; in confessing (consciously or unconsciously) their shortcomings, they speak no less eloquently of human limitations.

The narrators of "Bartleby the Scrivener," "My Man Bovanne," and "Not for Sale" are storytellers in the grand tradition. They catch our attention from the opening sentence, and share with us both facts and feelings as they move from incident to incident toward a well-crafted climax. Their voices, however, are very different. Melville's narrator, deliberately telling a formal tale, sets a leisurely pace. His tale is rich in detail and reflection; his vocabulary and tone attest to his position as a solid and educated citizen; and he is conscientious in telling his story as fully as he can and in admitting the limits of his knowledge. Bambara's narrator, in contrast, seems to be carrying on a conversation with people she already knows. Her tone and opinions are direct, and mix humor with insight and common sense; her pace is relatively rapid, as befits an active woman with a strong sense of her own priorities. In contrast to both, Cofer's narrator speaks in a clean, unadorned, open style. Her tone is reminiscent but direct.

"The Yellow Wall-Paper" represents a second tradition in first-person narrative: the creation of a tale in the shape of a journal or diary. Unlike the first two stories, which claim clear descent from the oral tradition of tale-telling, this story comes from a purely written tradition. You must have journals—and hence writing—before you can create a story that pretends to be a group of entries from somebody's journal.

Stories written in this "diarylike" tradition share several interesting features. First, they allow their narrators to ponder and reveal things the narrators would shrink from saying aloud. As the narrator of "The Yellow Wall-Paper" says, "I would not say it to a living soul, of course, but this is dead paper and a great relief to my mind." We, however, do read this "dead paper"; and we thus gain a closeness to the narrator that his or her closest friends might not have.

Second, the diarylike tale assumes that each event within it is chronicled on the day it occurs. It thus makes possible an immediacy that few other types of writing allow.

Third, there is little room, however, for hindsight in this sort of writing, little chance for the narrator to fit events into a pattern. We, as readers, must provide the pattern ourselves, just as we must come to our own understanding of the narrator by observing how her feelings and perceptions change during the course of the narrative. Caught up in the flow of events, the narrator may or may not be able to interpret them. We, standing outside those events, are challenged to do so.

Each of these stories is well worth reading for its own sake. Taken together, they remind us, once again, of the range of style and effect available to writers, and of the uniqueness of each voice that we hear speaking to us from literature.

Bartleby the Scrivener

Herman Melville (1819–1891)

I am a rather elderly man. The nature of my avocations, for the last thirty years, has brought me into more than ordinary contact with what would seem an interesting and somewhat singular set of men, of whom, as yet, nothing, that I know of, has ever been written—I mean, the law-copyists, or scriveners. I have known very many of them, professionally and privately, and, if I pleased, could relate divers histories, at which good-natured gentlemen might smile, and sentimental souls might weep. But I waive the biographies of all other scriveners, for a few passages in the life of Bartleby, who was a scrivener, the strangest I ever saw, or heard of. While, of other law-copyists, I might write the complete life, of Bartleby nothing of that sort can be done. I believe that no materials exist, for a full and satisfactory biography of this man. It is an irreparable loss to literature. Bartleby was one of those beings of whom nothing is ascertainable, except from the original sources, and, in his case, those are very small. What my own astonished eyes saw of Bartleby, *that* is all I know of him, except, indeed, one vague report, which will appear in the sequel.

Ere introducing the scrivener, as he first appeared to me, it is fit I make some mention of myself, my *employés,* my business, my chambers, and general surroundings; because some such description is indispensable to an adequate understanding of the chief character about to be presented. Imprimis: I am a man who, from his youth upwards, has been filled with a profound conviction that the easiest way of life is the best. Hence, though I belong to a profession proverbially energetic and nervous, even to turbulence, at times, yet nothing of that sort have I ever suffered to invade my peace. I am one of those unambitious lawyers who never addresses a jury, or in any way draws down public applause; but, in the cool tranquillity of a snug retreat, do a snug business among rich men's bonds, and mortgages, and title-deeds. All who know me, consider me an eminently *safe* man. The late John Jacob Astor,[1] a personage little given to poetic enthusiasm, had no hesitation in pronouncing my first grand point to be prudence; my next, method. I do not speak it in vanity, but simply record the fact, that I was not unemployed in my profession by the late John Jacob Astor, a name which, I admit, I love to repeat; for it hath a rounded and orbicular sound to it, and rings like unto bullion. I will freely add, that I was not insensible to the late John Jacob Astor's good opinion.

Some time prior to the period at which this little history begins, my avocations had been largely increased. The good old office, now extinct in the State of New York, of a Master in Chancery, had been conferred upon me. It was not a

---

[1](1763–1848), an American fur trader and financier

very arduous office, but very pleasantly remunerative. I seldom lose my temper; much more seldom indulge in dangerous indignation at wrongs and outrages; but, I must be permitted to be rash here, and declare, that I consider the sudden and violent abrogation of the office of Master in Chancery, by the new Constitution, as a—premature act; inasmuch as I had counted upon a life-lease of the profits, whereas I only received those of a few short years. But this is by the way.

My chambers were up stairs, at No.—Wall Street. At one end, they looked upon the white wall of the interior of a spacious sky-light shaft, penetrating the building from top to bottom.

This view might have been considered rather tame than otherwise, deficient in what landscape painters call "life." But, if so, the view from the other end of my chambers offered, at least, a contrast, if nothing more. In that direction, my windows commanded an unobstructed view of a lofty brick wall, black by age and everlasting shade; which wall required no spy-glass to bring out its lurking beauties, but, for the benefit of all near-sighted spectators, was pushed up to within ten feet of my window panes. Owing to the great height of the surrounding buildings, and my chambers being on the second floor, the interval between this wall and mine not a little resembled a huge square cistern.

At the period just preceding the advent of Bartleby, I had two persons as copyists in my employment, and a promising lad as an office-boy. First, Turkey; second, Nippers; third, Ginger Nut. These may seem names, the like of which are not usually found in the Directory. In truth, they were nicknames, mutually conferred upon each other by my three clerks, and were deemed expressive of their respective persons or characters. Turkey was a short, pursy Englishman, of about my own age—that is, somewhere not far from sixty. In the morning, one might say, his face was of a fine florid hue, but after twelve o'clock, meridian—his dinner hour—it blazed like a grate full of Christmas coals; and continued blazing—but, as it were, with a gradual wane—till six o'clock, P.M., or thereabouts; after which, I saw no more of the proprietor of the face, which, gaining its meridian with the sun, seemed to set with it, to rise, culminate, and decline the following day, with the like regularity and undiminished glory. There are many singular coincidences I have known in the course of my life, not the least among which was the fact, that, exactly when Turkey displayed his fullest beams from his red and radiant countenance, just then, too, at that critical moment, began the daily period when I considered his business capacities as seriously disturbed for the remainder of the twenty-four hours. Not that he was absolutely idle, or averse to business, then; far from it. The difficulty was, he was apt to be altogether too energetic. There was a strange, inflamed, flurried, flighty recklessness of activity about him. He would be incautious in dipping his pen into his inkstand. All his blots upon my documents were dropped there after twelve o'clock, meridian. Indeed, not only would he be reckless, and sadly given to making blots in the afternoon, but, some days, he went further, and was rather noisy. At such times, too, his face flamed with augmented blazonry, as if cannel coal had been heaped on anthracite. He made an unpleasant racket with his chair; spilled his sand-box; in mending his pens, impatiently split them all to pieces, and threw them on the floor in a sudden passion; stood up, and leaned over his table, boxing his papers about in a most indecorous manner, very sad to behold in an elderly man like him. Nevertheless, as he was in many ways a most valuable person to me, and all the time before twelve o'clock, meridian, was the quickest, steadiest creature, too, accomplishing a great deal of work in a style not easily to be matched—for these reasons, I was willing to overlook his eccentricities, though, indeed, occasionally, I remonstrated with him. I did this very gently, however, because, though the civilest, nay, the blandest and most reverential of men in the morning, yet, in the afternoon, he was disposed, upon provocation, to be slightly rash with his tongue—in fact, insolent. Now, valuing his morning services as I did, and resolved not to lose them—yet, at the same time, made uncomfortable by his inflamed ways after twelve o'clock—and being a man of peace, unwilling by my admonitions to call forth unseemly retorts from him, I took upon me, one Saturday noon (he was always worse on Saturdays) to hint to him, very kindly, that, perhaps, now that he was growing old, it might be well to abridge his labors; in short, he need not come to my chambers after twelve o'clock, but, dinner over, had best go home to his lodgings, and rest himself till tea-time. But no; he insisted upon his afternoon devotions. His countenance became intolerably fervid, as he oratorically assured me—gesticulating with a long ruler at the other end of the room—that if his services in the morning were useful, how indispensable, then, in the afternoon?

"With submission, sir," said Turkey, on this occasion, "I consider myself your right-hand man. In the morning I but marshal and deploy my columns; but in the afternoon I put myself at their head, and gallantly charge the foe, thus"—and he made a violent thrust with the ruler.

"But the blots, Turkey," intimated I.

"True; but, with submission, sir, behold these hairs! I am getting old. Surely, sir, a blot or two of a warm afternoon is not to be severely urged against gray hairs. Old age—even if it blot the page—is honorable. With submission, sir, we *both* are getting old."

This appeal to my fellow-feeling was hardly to be resisted. At all events, I saw that go he would not. So, I made up my mind to let him stay, resolving, nevertheless, to see to it that, during the afternoon, he had to do with my less important papers.

Nippers, the second on my list, was a whiskered, sallow, and, upon the whole, rather piratical-looking young man, of about five and twenty. I always deemed him the victim of two evil powers—ambition and indigestion. The ambition was evinced by a certain impatience of the duties of a mere copyist, an unwarrantable usurpation of strictly professional affairs, such as the original drawing up of legal documents. The indigestion seemed betokened in an occasional nervous testiness and grinning irritability, causing the teeth to audibly grind together over mistakes committed in copying; unnecessary maledictions, hissed, rather than spoken, in the heat of business; and especially by a continual discontent with the height of the table where he worked. Though of a very ingenious mechanical turn, Nippers could never get this table to suit him. He put chips under it, blocks of various sorts, bits of pasteboard, and at last went so far as to attempt an exquisite adjustment, by final pieces of folded blotting-paper. But no invention would answer. If, for the sake of easing his back, he brought the table lid at a sharp angle well up towards his chin, and wrote there like a man using the steep roof of a Dutch house for his desk, then he declared that it stopped the circulation in his arms. If now he lowered the table to his waistbands, and stooped over it in writing, then there was a sore aching in his back. In short, the truth of the matter was, Nippers knew not what he wanted. Or, if he wanted anything, it was to be rid of a scrivener's table altogether. Among the manifestations of his diseased ambition was a fondness he had for receiving visits from certain ambiguous-looking fellows in seedy coats, whom he called his clients. Indeed, I was aware that not only was he, at times, considerable of a ward-politician, but he occasionally did a little business at the Justices' courts, and was not unknown on the steps of the Tombs. I have good reason to believe, however, that one individual who called upon him at my chambers, and who, with a grand air, he insisted was his client, was no other than a dun, and the alleged title-deed, a bill. But, with all his failings, and the annoyances he caused me, Nippers, like his compatriot Turkey, was a very useful man to me; wrote a neat, swift hand; and, when he chose, was not deficient in a gentlemanly sort of deportment. Added to this, he always dressed in a gentlemanly sort of way; and so, incidentally, reflected credit upon my chambers. Whereas, with respect to Turkey, I had much ado to keep him from being a reproach to me. His clothes were apt to look oily, and smell of eating-houses. He wore his pantaloons very loose and baggy in summer. His coats were execrable; his hat not to be handled. But while the hat was a thing of indifference to me, inasmuch as his natural civility and deference, as a dependent Englishman, always led him to doff it the moment he entered the room, yet his coat was another matter. Concerning his coats, I reasoned with him; but with no effect. The truth was, I suppose, that a man with so small an income could not afford to sport such a lustrous face and a lustrous coat at one and the same time. As Nippers once observed, Turkey's money went chiefly for red ink. One winter day, I presented Turkey with a highly respectable-looking coat of my own—a padded gray coat, of a most comfortable warmth, and which buttoned straight up from the knee to the neck. I thought Turkey would appreciate the favor, and abate his rashness and obstreperousness of afternoons. But no; I verily believe that buttoning himself up in so downy and blanket-like a coat had a pernicious effect upon him—upon the same principle that too much oats are bad for horses. In fact, precisely as a rash, restive horse is said to feel his oats, so Turkey felt his coat. It made him insolent. He was a man whom prosperity harmed.

Though, concerning the self-indulgent habits of Turkey, I had my own private surmises, yet, touching Nippers, I was well persuaded that, whatever might be his faults in other respects, he was, at least, a temperate young man. But, indeed, nature herself seemed to have been his vintner, and, at his birth, charged him so thoroughly with an irritable, brandy-like disposition, that all subsequent potations were needless. When I consider how, amid the stillness of my chambers, Nippers would sometimes impatiently rise from his seat, and stooping over his table, spread his arms wide apart, seize the whole desk, and move it, and jerk it, with a grim, grinding motion on the floor, as if the table were a perverse voluntary agent, intent on thwarting and vexing him, I plainly perceive that, for Nippers, brandy-and-water were altogether superfluous.

It was fortunate for me that, owing to its peculiar cause—indigestion—the irritability and consequent nervousness of Nippers were mainly observable in the morning, while in the afternoon he was comparatively mild. So that, Turkey's paroxysms only coming on about twelve o'clock, I never had to do with their eccentricities at one time. Their fits relieved each other, like guards. When Nippers' was on, Turkey's was off; and *vice versa*. This was a good natural arrangement, under the circumstances.

Ginger Nut, the third on my list, was a lad, some twelve years old. His father was a car-man, ambitious of seeing his son on the bench instead of a cart, before he died. So he sent him to my office, as student at law, errand-boy, cleaner and sweeper, at the rate of one dollar a week. He had a little desk to himself, but he did not use it much. Upon inspection, the drawer exhibited a great array of the shells of various sorts of nuts. Indeed, to this quick-witted youth, the whole noble science of the law was contained in a nut-shell. Not the least among the employments of Ginger Nut, as well as one which he discharged with the most alacrity, was his duty as cake and apple purveyor for Turkey and Nippers. Copying law-papers being proverbially a dry, husky sort of business, my two scriveners were fain to moisten their mouths very often with Spitzenbergs, to be had at the numerous stalls nigh the Custom House and Post Office. Also, they sent Ginger Nut very frequently for that peculiar cake—small, flat, round, and very spicy—after which he had been named by them. Of a cold morning, when business was but dull, Turkey would gobble up scores of these cakes, as if they were mere wafers—indeed, they sell them at the rate of six or eight for a penny—the scrape of his pen blending with the crunching of the crisp particles in his mouth. Of all the fiery afternoon blunders and flurried rashnesses of Turkey, was his once moistening a ginger-cake between his lips, and clapping it on to a mortgage, for a seal. I came within an ace of dismissing him then. But he mollified me by making an oriental bow, and saying—

"With submission, sir, it was generous of me to find you in stationery on my own account."

Now my original business—that of a conveyancer and title hunter, and drawer-up of recondite documents of all sorts—was considerably increased by receiving the master's office. There was now great work for scriveners. Not only must I push the clerks already with me, but I must have additional help.

In answer to my advertisement, a motionless young man one morning stood upon my office threshold, the door being open, for it was summer. I can see that figure now—pallidly neat, pitiably respectable, incurably forlorn! It was Bartleby.

After a few words touching his qualifications, I engaged him, glad to have among my corps of copyists a man of so singularly sedate an aspect, which I thought might operate beneficially upon the flighty temper of Turkey, and the fiery one of Nippers.

I should have stated before that ground glass folding-doors divided my premises into two parts, one of which was occupied by my scriveners, the other by myself. According to my humor, I threw open these doors, or closed them. I resolved to assign Bartleby a corner by the folding-doors, but on my side of them, so as to have this quiet man within easy call, in case any trifling thing was to be done. I placed his desk close up to a small side-window in that part of the room, a window which originally had afforded a lateral view of certain grimy backyards and bricks, but which, owing to subsequent erections, commanded at present no view at all, though it gave some light. Within three feet of the panes was a wall, and the light came down from far above, between two lofty buildings, as from a very small opening in a dome. Still further to a satisfactory arrangement, I procured a high green folding screen, which might entirely isolate Bartleby from my sight, though not remove him from my voice. And thus, in a manner, privacy and society were conjoined.

At first, Bartleby did an extraordinary quantity of writing. As if long famishing for something to copy, he seemed to gorge himself on my documents. There was no pause for digestion. He ran a day and night line, copying by sunlight and by candle-light. I should have been quite delighted with his application, had he been cheerfully industrious. But he wrote on silently, palely, mechanically.

It is, of course, an indispensable part of a scrivener's business to verify the accuracy of his copy, word by word. Where there are two or more scriveners in an office, they assist each other in this examination, one reading from the copy, the other holding the original. It is a very dull, wearisome, and lethargic affair. I can readily imagine that, to some sanguine temperaments, it would be altogether intolerable. For example, I cannot credit that the mettlesome poet, Byron, would have contentedly sat down with Bartleby to examine a law document of, say five hundred pages, closely written in a crimpy hand.

Now and then, in the haste of business, it had been my habit to assist in comparing some brief document myself, calling Turkey or Nippers for this purpose. One object I had, in placing Bartleby so handy to me behind the screen, was, to avail myself of his services on such trivial occasions. It was on the third day, I think, of his being with me, and before any necessity had arisen for having his own writing examined, that, being much hurried to complete a small affair I had in hand, I abruptly called to Bartleby. In my haste and natural expectancy of instant compliance, I sat with my head bent over the original on my desk, and my right hand sideways, and somewhat nervously extended with the copy, so that, immediately upon emerging from his retreat, Bartleby might snatch it and proceed to business without the least delay.

In this very attitude did I sit when I called to him, rapidly stating what it was I wanted him to do—namely, to examine a small paper with me. Imagine my surprise, nay, my consternation, when, without moving from his privacy, Bartleby, in a singularly mild, firm voice, replied, "I would prefer not to."

I sat awhile in perfect silence, rallying my stunned faculties. Immediately it occurred to me that my ears had deceived me, or Bartleby had entirely misunderstood my meaning. I repeated my request in the clearest tone I could assume; but in quite as clear a one came the previous reply, "I would prefer not to."

"Prefer not to," echoed I, rising in high excitement, and crossing the room with a stride. "What do you mean? Are you moon-struck? I want you to help me compare this sheet here—take it," and I thrust it towards him.

"I would prefer not to," said he.

I looked at him steadfastly. His face was leanly composed; his gray eye dimly calm. Not a wrinkle of agitation rippled him. Had there been the least uneasiness, anger, impatience or impertinence in his manner; in other words, had there been any thing ordinarily human about him, doubtless I should have violently dismissed him from the premises. But as it was, I should have as soon thought of turning my pale plaster-of-paris burst of Cicero out of doors. I stood gazing at him awhile, as he went on with his own writing, and then reseated myself at my desk. This is very strange, thought I. What had one best do? But my business hurried me. I concluded to forget the matter for the present, reserving it for my future leisure. So calling Nippers from the other room, the paper was speedily examined.

A few days after this, Bartleby concluded four lengthy documents, being quadruplicates of a week's testimony taken before me in my High Court of Chancery. It became necessary to examine them. It was an important suit, and great accuracy was imperative. Having all things arranged, I called Turkey, Nippers, and Ginger Nut, from the next room, meaning to place the four copies in the hands of my four clerks, while I should read from the original. Accordingly, Turkey, Nippers, and Ginger Nut had taken their seats in a row, each with his document in his hand, when I called to Bartleby to join this interesting group.

"Bartleby! quick, I am waiting."

I heard a slow scrape of his chair legs on the uncarpeted floor, and soon he appeared standing at the entrance of his hermitage.

"What is wanted?" said he, mildly.

"The copies, the copies," said I, hurriedly. "We are going to examine them. There"—and I held towards him the fourth quadruplicate.

"I would prefer not to," he said, and gently disappeared behind the screen.

For a few moments I was turned into a pillar of salt, standing at the head of my seated column of clerks. Recovering myself, I advanced towards the screen, and demanded the reason for such extraordinary conduct.

"*Why* do you refuse?"

"I would prefer not to."

With any other man I should have flown outright into a dreadful passion, scorned all further words, and thrust him ignominiously from my presence. But there was something about Bartleby that not only strangely disarmed me, but, in a wonderful manner, touched and disconcerted me. I began to reason with him.

"These are your own copies we are about to examine. It is labor saving to you, because one examination will answer for your four papers. It is common usage. Every copyist is bound to help examine his copy. Is it not so? Will you not speak? Answer!"

"I prefer not to," he replied in a flutelike tone. It seemed to me that, while I had been addressing him, he carefully revolved every statement that I made; fully comprehended the meaning; could not gainsay the irresistible conclusion; but, at the same time, some paramount consideration prevailed with him to reply as he did.

"You are decided, then, not to comply with my request—a request made according to common usage and common sense?"

He briefly gave me to understand, that on that point my judgment was sound. Yes: his decision was irreversible.

It is not seldom the case that, when a man is browbeaten in some unprecedented and violently unreasonable way, he begins to stagger in his own plainest faith. He begins, as it were, vaguely to surmise that, wonderful as it may be, all the justice and all the reason is on the other side. Accordingly, if any disinterested persons are present, he turns to them for some reinforcement of his own faltering mind.

"Turkey," said I, "what do you think of this? Am I not right?"

"With submission, sir," said Turkey, in his blandest tone, "I think that you are."

"Nippers," said I, "what do *you* think of it?"

"I think I should kick him out of the office."

(The reader, of nice perceptions, will here perceive that, it being morning, Turkey's answer is couched in polite and tranquil terms, but Nippers' replies in ill-tempered ones. Or, to repeat a previous sentence, Nippers' ugly mood was on duty, and Turkey's off.)

"Ginger Nut," said I, willing to enlist the smallest suffrage in my behalf, "what do *you* think of it?"

"I think, sir, he's a little *luny*," replied Ginger Nut, with a grin.

"You hear what they say," said I, turning towards the screen, "come forth and do your duty."

But he vouchsafed no reply. I pondered a moment in sore perplexity. But once more business hurried me. I determined again to postpone the consideration of this dilemma to my future leisure. With a little trouble we made out to examine the papers without Bartleby, though at every page or two Turkey deferentially dropped his opinion, that this proceeding was quite out of the common; while Nippers, twitching in his chair with a dyspeptic nervousness, ground out, between his set teeth, occasional hissing maledictions against the stubborn oaf behind the screen. And for his (Nippers') part, this was the first and the last time he would do another man's business without pay.

Meanwhile Bartleby sat in his hermitage, oblivious to everything but his own peculiar business there.

Some days passed, the scrivener being employed upon another lengthy work. His late remarkable conduct led me to regard his ways narrowly. I observed that he never went to dinner; indeed, that he never went anywhere. As yet I had never, of my personal knowledge, known him to be outside of my office. He was a perpetual sentry in the corner. At about eleven o'clock though, in the morning, I noticed that Ginger Nut would advance toward the opening in Bartleby's screen, as if silently beckoned thither by a gesture invisible to me where I sat. The boy would then leave the office, jingling a few pence, and reappear with a handful of ginger-nuts, which he delivered in the hermitage, receiving two of the cakes for his trouble.

He lives, then, on ginger-nuts, thought I; never eats a dinner, properly speaking; he must be a vegetarian, then; but no; he never eats even vegetables, he eats nothing but ginger-nuts. My mind then ran on in reveries concerning the probable effects upon the human constitution of living entirely on ginger-nuts. Ginger-nuts are so called, because they contain ginger as one of their peculiar constituents, and the final flavoring one. Now, what was ginger? A hot, spicy thing. Was Bartleby hot and spicy? Not at all. Ginger, then, had no effect upon Bartleby. Probably he preferred it should have none.

Nothing so aggravates an earnest person as a passive resistance. If the individual so resisted be of a not inhumane temper, and the resisting one perfectly harmless in his passivity, then, in the better moods of the former, he will endeavor charitably to construe to his imagination what proves impossible to be solved by his judgment. Even so, for the most part, I regarded Bartleby and his ways. Poor fellow! thought I, he means no mischief; it is plain he intends no insolence; his aspect sufficiently evinces that his eccentricities are involuntary. He is useful to me. I can get along with him. If I turn him away, the chances are he will fall in with some less-indulgent employer, and then he will be rudely treated, and perhaps driven forth miserably to starve. Yes. Here I can cheaply purchase a delicious self-approval. To befriend Bartleby; to humor him in his strange willfulness, will cost me little or nothing, while I lay up in my soul what will eventually prove a sweet morsel for my conscience. But this mood was not invariable with me. The passiveness of Bartleby sometimes irritated me. I felt strangely goaded on to encounter him in new opposition—to elicit some angry spark from him answerable to my own. But, indeed, I might as well have essayed to strike fire with my knuckles against a bit of Windsor soap. But one afternoon the evil impulse in me mastered me, and the following little scene ensued:

"Bartleby," said I, "when those papers are all copied, I will compare them with you."

"I would prefer not to."

"How? Surely you do not mean to persist in that mulish vagary?"

No answer.

I threw open the folding-doors near by, and, turning upon Turkey and Nippers, exclaimed:

"Bartleby a second time says, he won't examine his papers. What do you think of it, Turkey?"

It was afternoon, be it remembered. Turkey sat glowing like a brass boiler; his bald head steaming; his hands reeling among his blotted papers.

"Think of it?" roared Turkey; "I think I'll just step behind his screen, and black his eyes for him!"

So saying, Turkey rose to his feet and threw his arms into a pugilistic position. He was hurrying away to make good his promise, when I detained him, alarmed at the effect of incautiously rousing Turkey's combativeness after dinner.

"Sit down, Turkey," said I, "and hear what Nippers has to say. What do you think of it, Nippers? Would I not be justified in immediately dismissing Bartleby?"

"Excuse me, that is for you to decide, sir. I think his conduct quite unusual, and, indeed, unjust, as regards Turkey and myself. But it may only be a passing whim."

"Ah," exclaimed I, "you have strangely changed your mind, then—you speak very gently of him now."

"All beer," cried Turkey; "gentleness is effects of beer—Nippers and I dined together to-day. You see how gentle *I* am, sir. Shall I go and black his eyes?"

"You refer to Bartleby, I suppose. No, not to-day, Turkey," I replied; "pray, put up your fists."

I closed the doors, and again advanced towards Bartleby. I felt additional incentives tempting me to my fate. I burned to be rebelled against again. I remember that Bartleby never left the office.

"Bartleby," said I, "Ginger Nut is away; just step around to the Post Office, won't you? (it was but a three minutes' walk), and see if there is anything for me."

"I would prefer not to."

"You *will* not?"

"I *prefer* not."

I staggered to my desk, and sat there in a deep study. My blind inveteracy returned. Was there any other thing in which I could procure myself to be ignominiously repulsed by this lean, penniless wight?—my hired clerk? What added thing is there, prefectly reasonable, that he will be sure to refuse to do?

"Bartleby!"

No answer.

"Bartleby," in a louder tone.

No answer.

"Bartleby," I roared.

Like a very ghost, agreeably to the laws of magical invocation, at the third summons, he appeared at the entrance of his hermitage.

"Go to the next room, and tell Nippers to come to me."

"I prefer not to," he respectfully and slowly said, and mildly disappeared.

"Very good, Bartleby," said I, in a quiet sort of serenely-severe self-possessed tone, intimating the unalterable purpose of some terrible retribution very close at hand. But upon the whole, as it was drawing towards my dinner-hour, I thought it best to put on my hat and walk home for the day, suffering much from perplexity and distress of mind.

Shall I acknowledge it? The conclusion of this whole business was, that it soon became a fixed fact of my chambers, that a pale young scrivener, by the name of Bartleby, had a desk there; that he copied for me at the usual rate of four cents a folio (one hundred words); but he was permanently exempt from examining the work done by him, that duty being transferred to Turkey and Nippers, out of compliment, doubtless, to their superior acuteness; moreover, said Bartleby was never, on any account, to be dispatched on the most trivial errand of any sort; and that even if entreated to take upon him such a matter, it was generally understood that he would "prefer not to"—in other words, that he would refuse point-blank.

As days passed on, I became considerably reconciled to Bartleby. His steadiness, his freedom from all dissipation, his incessant industry (except when he chose to throw himself into a standing revery behind his screen), his great stillness, his unalterableness of demeanor under all circumstances, made him a valuable acquisition. One prime thing was this—he was always there—first in the morning, continually through the day, and the last at night. I had a singular confidence in his honesty. I felt my most precious papers perfectly safe in his hands. Sometimes, to be sure, I could not, for the very soul of me, avoid falling into sudden spasmodic passions with him. For it was exceeding difficult to bear in mind all the time those strange peculiarities, privileges, and unheard of exemptions, forming the tacit stipulations on Bartleby's part under which he remained in my office. Now and then, in the eagerness of dispatching pressing business, I would inadvertently summon Bartleby, in a short, rapid tone, to put his finger, say, on the incipient tie of a bit of red tape with which I was about compressing some papers. Of course, from behind the screen the usual answer, "I prefer not to," was sure to come; and then, how could a human creature, with the common infirmities of our nature, refrain from bitterly exclaiming upon such perverseness—such unreasonableness. However, every added repulse of this sort which I received only tended to lessen the probability of my repeating the inadvertence.

Here it must be said, that according to the custom of most legal gentlemen occupying chambers in densely-populated law buildings, there were several keys to my door. One was kept by a woman residing in the attic, which person weekly scrubbed and daily swept and dusted my apartments. Another was kept by Turkey for convenience sake. The third I sometimes carried in my own pocket. The fourth I knew not who had.

Now, one Sunday morning I happened to go to Trinity Church, to hear a celebrated preacher, and finding myself rather early on the ground I thought I would walk around to my chambers for a while. Luckily I had my key with me; but upon applying it to the lock, I found it resisted by something inserted from the inside. Quite surprised, I called out; when to my consternation a key was turned from within; and thrusting his lean visage at me, and holding the door ajar, the apparition of Bartleby appeared, in his shirt sleeves, and otherwise in a strangely tattered deshabille, saying quietly that he was sorry, but he was deeply engaged just then, and—preferred not admitting me at present. In a brief word or two, he moreover added, that perhaps I had better walk around the block two or three times, and by that time he would probably have concluded his affairs.

Now, the utterly unsurmised appearance of Bartleby, tenanting my law-chambers of a Sunday morning, with his cadaverously gentlemanly *nonchalance*, yet withal firm and self-possessed, had such a strange effect upon me, that incontinently I slunk away from my own door, and did as desired. But not without sundry twinges of impotent rebellion against the mild effrontery of this unaccountable scrivener. Indeed, it was his wonderful mildness chiefly, which not only disarmed me, but unmanned me as it were. For I consider that one, for the time, is somehow unmanned when he tranquilly permits his hired clerk to dictate to him, and order him away from his own premises. Furthermore, I was full of uneasiness as to what Bartleby could possibly be doing in my office in his shirt sleeves, and in an otherwise dismantled condition of a Sunday morning. Was anything amiss going on? Nay, that was out of the question. It was not to be thought of for a moment that Bartleby was an immoral person. But what could he be doing there?—copying? Nay again, whatever might be his eccentricities, Bartleby was an eminently decorous person. He would be the last man to sit down to his desk in any state approaching to nudity. Besides, it was Sunday; and there was something about Bartleby that forbade the supposition that he would by any secular occupation violate the proprieties of the day.

Nevertheless, my mind was not pacified; and full of a restless curiosity, at last I returned to the door. Without hindrance I inserted my key, opened it, and entered. Bartleby was not to be seen. I looked round anxiously, peeped behind his screen; but it was very plain that he was gone. Upon more closely examining the place, I surmised that for an indefinite period Bartleby must have ate, dressed, and slept in my office, and that, too, without plate, mirror, or bed. The cushioned seat of a rickety old sofa in one corner bore the faint impression of a lean, reclining form. Rolled away under his desk, I found a blanket; under the empty grate, a blacking box and brush; on a chair, a tin basin, with soap and a ragged towel; in a newspaper a few crumbs of ginger-nuts and a morsel of cheese. Yes, thought I, it is evident enough that Bartleby has been making his home here, keeping bachelor's hall all by himself. Immediately then the thought came sweeping across me, what miserable friendlessness and loneliness are here revealed! His poverty is great; but his solitude, how horrible! Think of it. Of a Sunday, Wall Street is deserted as Petra;[2] and every night of every day it is an emptiness. This building, too, which of week-days hums with industry and life, at nightfall echoes with sheer vacancy, and all through Sunday is forlorn. And

---

[2] ancient city in Syria

here Bartleby makes his home; sole spectator of a solitude which he has seen all populous—a sort of innocent and transformed Marius brooding among the ruins of Carthage!

For the first time in my life a feeling of over-powering stinging melancholy seized me. Before, I had never experienced aught but a not unpleasing sadness. The bond of a common humanity now drew me irresistibly to gloom. A fraternal melancholy! For both I and Bartleby were sons of Adam. I remembered the bright silks and sparkling faces I had seen that day, in gala trim, swan-like sailing down the Mississippi of Broadway; and I contrasted them with the pallid copyist, and thought to myself, Ah, happiness courts the light, so we deem the world is gay; but misery hides aloof, so we deem that misery there is none. These sad fancyings—chimeras, doubtless, of a sick and silly brain—led on to other and more special thoughts, concerning the eccentricities of Bartleby. Presentiments of strange discoveries hovered round me. The scrivener's pale form appeared to me laid out, among uncaring strangers, in its shivering winding sheet.

Suddenly I was attracted by Bartleby's closed desk, the key in open sight left in the lock.

I mean no mischief, seek the gratification of no heartless curiosity, thought I; besides, the desk is mine, and its contents, too, so I will make bold to look within. Everything was methodically arranged, the papers smoothly placed. The pigeon holes were deep, and removing the files of documents, I groped into their recesses. Presently I felt something there, and dragged it out. It was an old bandanna handkerchief, heavy and knotted. I opened it, and saw it was a saving's bank.

I now recalled all the quiet mysteries which I had noted in the man. I remembered that he never spoke but to answer; that, though at intervals he had considerable time to himself, yet I had never seen him reading—no, not even a newspaper; that for long periods he would stand looking out, at his pale window behind the screen, upon the dead brick wall; I was quite sure he never visited any refectory or eating house; while his pale face clearly indicated that he never drank beer like Turkey, or tea and coffee even, like other men; that he never went anywhere in particular that I could learn; never went out for a walk, unless, indeed, that was the case at present; that he had declined telling who he was, or whence he came, or whether he had any relatives in the world; that though so thin and pale, he never complained of ill health. And more than all, I remembered a certain unconscious air of pallid—how shall I call it?—of pallid haughtiness, say, or rather an austere reserve about him, which had positively awed me into my tame compliance with his eccentricities, when I had feared to ask him to do the slightest incidental thing for me, even though I might know, from his long-continued motionlessness, that behind his screen he must be standing in one of those dead-wall reveries of his.

Revolving all these things, and coupling them with the recently discovered fact, that he made my office his constant abiding place and home, and not forgetful of his morbid moodiness; revolving all these things, a prudential feeling began to steal over me. My first emotions had been those of pure melancholy and sincerest pity; but just in proportion as the forlornness of Bartleby grew and grew to my imagination, did that same melancholy merge into fear, that pity into repulsion. So true it is, and so terrible, too, that up to a certain point the thought or sight of misery enlists our best affections; but, in certain special cases, beyond that point it does not. They err who would assert that invariably this is owing to the inherent selfishness of the human heart. It rather proceeds from a certain hopelessness of remedying excessive and organic ill. To a sensitive being, pity is not seldom pain. And when at last it is perceived that such pity cannot lead to effectual succor, common sense bids the soul be rid of it. What I saw that morning persuaded me that the scrivener was the victim of inate and incurable disorder. I might give alms to his body; but his body did not pain him; it was his soul that suffered, and his soul I could not reach.

I did not accomplish the purpose of going to Trinity Church that morning. Somehow, the things I had seen disqualified me for the time from church-going. I walked homeward, thinking what I would do with Bartleby. Finally, I resolved upon this—I would put certain calm questions to him the next morning, touching his history, etc., and if he declined to answer them openly and unreservedly (and I supposed he would prefer not), then to give him a twenty dollar bill over and above whatever I might owe him, and tell him his services were no longer required; but that if in any other way I could assist him, I would be happy to do so, especially if he desired to return to his native place, wherever that might be, I would willingly help to defray the expenses. Moreover, if, after reaching home, he found himself at any time in want of aid, a letter from him would be sure of a reply.

The next morning came.

"Bartleby," said I, gently calling to him behind his screen.

No reply.

"Bartleby," said I, in a still gentler tone, "come here; I am not going to ask you to do anything you would prefer not to do—I simply wish to speak to you."

Upon this he noiselessly slid into view.

"Will you tell me, Bartleby, where you were born?"

"I would prefer not to."

"Will you tell me *anything* about yourself?"

"I would prefer not to."

"But what reasonable objection can you have to speak to me? I feel friendly towards you."

He did not look at me while I spoke, but kept his glance fixed upon my bust of Cicero, which, as I then sat, was directly behind me, some six inches above my head.

"What is your answer, Bartleby," said I, after waiting a considerable time for a reply, during which his countenance remained immovable, only there was the faintest conceivable tremor of the white attenuated mouth.

"At present I prefer to give no answer," he said, and retired into his hermitage.

It was rather weak in me I confess, but his manner, on this occasion, nettled me. Not only did there seem to lurk in it a certain calm disdain, but his perverseness seemed ungrateful, considering the undeniable good usage and indulgence he had received from me.

Again I sat ruminating what I should do. Mortified as I was at his behavior, and resolved as I had been to dismiss him when I entered my office, nevertheless I strangely felt something superstitious knocking at my heart, and forbidding me to carry out my purpose, and denouncing me for a villain if I dared to breathe one bitter word against this forlornest of mankind. At last, familiarly drawing my chair behind his screen, I sat down and said: "Bartleby, never mind, then, about revealing your history; but let me entreat you, as a friend, to comply as far as may be with the usages of this office. Say now, you will help to examine papers to-morrow or next day: in short, say now, that in a day or two you will begin to be a little reasonable:—say so, Bartleby."

"At present I would prefer not to be a little reasonable," was his mildly cadaverous reply.

Just then the folding-doors opened, and Nippers approached. He seemed suffering from an unusually bad night's rest, induced by severer indigestion than common. He overheard those final words of Bartleby.

"*Prefer not*, eh?" gritted Nippers—"I'd *prefer* him, if I were you, sir," addressing me—"I'd *prefer* him; I'd give him preferences, the stubborn mule! What is it, sir, pray, that he *prefers* not to do now?"

Bartleby moved not a limb.

"Mr. Nippers," said I, "I'd prefer that you would withdraw for the present."

Somehow, of late, I had got into the way of involuntarily using this word "prefer" upon all sorts of not exactly suitable occasions. And I trembled to think that my contact with the scrivener had already and seriously affected me in a mental way. And what further and deeper aberration might it not yet produce? This apprehension had not been without efficacy in determining me to summary measures.

As Nippers, looking very sour and sulky, was departing, Turkey blandly and deferentially approached.

"With submission, sir," said he, "yesterday I was thinking about Bartleby here, and I think that if he would but prefer to take a quart of good ale every day, it would do much towards mending him, and enabling him to assist in examining his papers."

"So you have got the word, too," said I, slightly excited.

"With submission, what word, sir," asked Turkey, respectfully crowding himself into the contracted space behind the screen, and by so doing, making me jostle the scrivener. "What word, sir?"

"I would prefer to be left alone here," said Bartleby, as if offended at being mobbed in his privacy.

"*That's* the word, Turkey," said I—"*that's* it."

"Oh, *prefer?* oh yes—queer word. I never use it myself. But, sir, as I was saying, if he would but prefer—"

"Turkey," interrupted I, "you will please withdraw."

"Oh, certainly, sir, if you prefer that I should."

As he opened the folding-door to retire, Nippers at his desk caught a glimpse of me, and asked whether I would prefer to have a certain paper copied on blue paper or white. He did not in the least roguishly accent the word prefer. It was plain that it involuntarily rolled from his tongue. I thought to myself, surely I must get rid of a demented man, who already has in some degree turned the tongues, if not the heads of myself and clerks. But I thought it prudent not to break the dismission at once.

The next day I noticed that Bartleby did nothing but stand at his window in his dead-wall revery. Upon asking him why he did not write, he said that he had decided upon doing no more writing.

"Why, how now? what next?" exclaimed I, "do no more writing?"

"No more."

"And what is the reason?"

"Do you not see the reason for yourself," he indifferently replied.

I looked steadfastly at him, and perceived that his eyes looked dull and glazed. Instantly it occurred to me, that his unexampled diligence in copying by his dim window for the first few weeks of his stay with me might have temporarily impaired his vision.

I was touched. I said something in condolence with him. I hinted that of course he did wisely in abstaining from writing for a while; and urged him to embrace that opportunity of taking wholesome exercise in the open air. This, however, he did not do. A few days after this, my other clerks being absent, and being in a great hurry to dispatch certain letters by the mail, I thought that, having nothing else earthly to do, Bartleby would surely be less inflexible than usual, and carry these letters to the post-office. But he blankly declined. So, much to my inconvenience, I went myself.

Still added days went by. Whether Bartleby's eyes improved or not, I could not say. To all appearance, I thought they did. But when I asked him if they did, he vouchsafed no answer. At all events, he would do no copying. At last, in reply to my urgings, he informed me that he had permanently given up copying.

"What!" exclaimed I; "suppose your eyes should get entirely well—better than ever before—would you not copy then?"

"I have given up copying," he answered, and slid aside.

He remained as ever, a fixture in my chamber. Nay—if that were possible—he became still more of a fixture than before. What was to be done? He would do nothing in the office; why should he stay there? In plain fact, he had now become a millstone to me, not only useless as a necklace, but afflictive to bear. Yet I was sorry for him. I speak less than truth when I say that, on his own account, he occasioned me uneasiness. If he would but have named a single relative or friend, I would instantly have written, and urged their taking the poor fellow away to some convenient retreat. But he seemed alone, absolutely alone in the universe. A bit of wreck in the mid Atlantic. At length, necessities connected with my business tyrannized over all other considerations. Decently as I could, I told Bartleby that in six days time he must unconditionally leave the office. I warned him to take measures, in the interval, for procuring some other abode. I offered to assist him in this endeavor, if he himself would but take the first step towards a removal. "And when you finally quit me, Bartleby," added I, "I shall see that you go not away entirely unprovided. Six days from this hour, remember."

At the expiration of that period, I peeped behind the screen, and lo! Bartleby was there.

I buttoned up my coat, balanced myself; advanced slowly towards him, touched his shoulder, and said, "The time has come; you must quit this place; I am sorry for you; here is money; but you must go."

"I would prefer not," he replied, with his back still towards me.

"You *must*."

He remained silent.

Now I had an unbounded confidence in this man's common honesty. He had frequently restored to me sixpences and shillings carelessly dropped upon the floor, for I am apt to be very reckless in such shirt-button affairs. The proceeding, then, which followed will not be deemed extraordinary.

"Bartleby," said I, "I owe you twelve dollars on account; here are thirty-two; the odd twenty are yours—Will you take it?" and I handed the bills towards him.

But he made no motion.

"I will leave them here, then," putting them under a weight on the table. Then taking my hat and cane and going to the door, I tranquilly turned and added—"After you have removed your things from these offices, Bartleby, you will of course lock the door—since every one is now gone for the day but you—and if you please, slip your key underneath the mat, so that I may have it in the morning. I shall not see you again; so good-by to you. If, hereafter, in your new place of abode, I can be of any service to you, do not fail to advise me by letter. Good-by, Bartleby, and fare you well."

But he answered not a word; like the last column of some ruined temple, he remained standing mute and solitary in the middle of the otherwise deserted room.

As I walked home in a pensive mood, my vanity got the better of my pity. I could not but highly plume myself on my masterly management in getting rid of Bartleby. Masterly I call it, and such it must appear to any dispassionate thinker. The beauty of my procedure seemed to consist in its perfect quietness. There was no vulgar bullying, no bravado of any sort, no choleric hectoring, and striding to and fro across the apartment, jerking out vehement commands for Bartleby to bundle himself off with his beggarly traps. Nothing of the kind. Without loudly bidding Bartleby depart—as an inferior genius might have done—I *assumed* the ground that depart he must; and upon that assumption built all I had to say. The more I thought over my procedure, the more I was charmed with it. Nevertheless, next morning, upon awakening, I had my doubts—I had somehow slept off the fumes of vanity. One of the coolest and wisest hours a man has, is just after he awakes in the morning. My procedure seemed as sagacious as ever—but only in theory. How it would prove in practice—there was the rub. It was truly a beautiful thought to have assumed Bartleby's departure; but, after all, that assumption was simply my own, and none of Bartleby's. The great point was, not whether I had assumed that he would quit me, but whether he would prefer so to do. He was more a man of preferences than assumptions.

After breakfast, I walked down town, arguing the probabilities *pro* and *con*. One moment I thought it would prove a miserable failure, and Bartleby would be found all alive at my office as usual; the next moment it seemed certain that I should find his chair empty. And so I kept veering about. At the corner of Broadway and Canal Street, I saw quite an excited group of people standing in earnest conversation.

"I'll take odds he doesn't," said a voice as I passed.

"Doesn't go?—done!" said I, "put up your money."

I was instinctively putting my hand in my pocket to produce my own, when I remembered that this was an election day. The words I had overheard bore no reference to Bartleby, but to the success or nonsuccess of some candidate for the mayoralty. In my intent frame of mind, I had, as it were, imagined that all Broadway shared in my excitement, and were debating the same question with me. I passed on, very thankful that the uproar of the street screened my momentary absent-mindedness.

As I had intended, I was earlier than usual at my office door. I stood listening for a moment. All was still. He must be gone. I tried the knob. The door was locked. Yes, my procedure had worked to a charm; he indeed must be vanished. Yet a certain melancholy mixed with this: I was almost sorry for my brilliant success. I was fumbling under the door mat for the key, which Bartleby was to have left there for me, when accidentally my knee knocked against a panel, producing a summoning sound, and in response a voice came to me from within—"Not yet; I am occupied."

It was Bartleby.

I was thunderstruck. For an instant I stood like the man who, pipe in mouth, was killed one cloudless afternoon long ago in Virginia, by summer lightning; at his own warm open window he was killed, and remained leaning out there upon the dreamy afternoon, till some one touched him, when he fell.

"Not gone!" I murmured at last. But again obeying that wondrous ascendancy which the inscrutable scrivener had over me, and from which ascendancy, for all my chafing, I could not completely escape, I slowly went down stairs and out into the street, and while walking round the block, considered what I should next do in this unheard-of perplexity. Turn the man out by an actual thrusting I could not; to drive him away by calling him hard names would not do; calling in the police was an unpleasant idea; and yet, permit him to enjoy his cadaverous triumph over me—this, too, I could not think of. What was to be done? or, if nothing could be done, was there anything further that I could *assume* in the matter? Yes, as before I had prospectively assumed that Bartleby would depart, so now I might retrospectively assume that departed he was. In the legitimate carrying out of this assumption, I might enter my office in a great hurry, and pretending not to see Bartleby at all, walk straight against him as if he were air. Such a proceeding would in a singular degree have the appearance of a home-thrust. It was hardly possible that Bartleby could withstand such an application of the doctrine of assumptions. But upon second thoughts the success of the plan seemed rather dubious. I resolved to argue the matter over with him again.

"Bartleby," said I, entering the office, with a quietly severe expression, "I am seriously displeased. I am pained, Bartleby. I had thought better of you. I had imagined you of such a gentlemanly organization, that in any delicate dilemma a slight hint would suffice—in short, an assumption. But it appears I am deceived. Why," I added, unaffectedly starting, "you have not even touched that money yet," pointing to it, just where I had left it the evening previous.

He answered nothing.

"Will you, or will you not, quit me?" I now demanded in a sudden passion, advancing close to him.

"I would prefer *not* to quit you," he replied, gently emphasizing the *not*.

"What earthly right have you to stay here? Do you pay any rent? Do you pay my taxes? Or is this property yours?"

He answered nothing.

"Are you ready to go on and write now? Are your eyes recovered? Could you copy a small paper for me this morning? or help examine a few lines? or step round to the post-office? In a word, will you do anything at all, to give a coloring to your refusal to depart the premises?"

He silently retired into his hermitage.

I was now in such a state of nervous resentment that I thought it but prudent to check myself at present from further demonstrations. Bartleby and I were alone. I remembered the tragedy of the unfortunate Adams and the still more unfortunate Colt in the solitary office of the latter; and how poor Colt, being dreadfully incensed by Adams, and imprudently permitting himself to get wildly excited, was at unawares hurried into his fatal act—an act which certainly no man could possibly deplore more than the actor himself. Often it had occurred to me in my ponderings upon the subject, that had that altercation taken place in the public street, or at a private residence, it would not have terminated as it did. It was the circumstance of being alone in a solitary office, up stairs, of a building entirely unhallowed by humanizing domestic associations—an uncarpeted office, doubtless, of a dusty, haggard sort of appearance—this it must have been, which greatly helped to enhance the irritable desperation of the hapless Colt.[3]

---

[3]*Adams . . . Colt,* a widely publicized murder-case in which John C. Colt killed Samuel Adams, in New York City, in January, 1842

But when this old Adam of resentment rose in me and tempted me concerning Bartleby, I grappled him and threw him. How? Why, simply by recalling the divine injunction: "A new commandment give I unto you, that ye love one another." Yes, this it was that saved me. Aside from higher considerations, charity often operates as a vastly wise and prudent principle—a great safeguard to its possessor. Men have committed murder for jealousy's sake, and anger's sake, and hatred's sake, and selfishness' sake, and spiritual pride's sake; but no man, that ever I heard of, ever committed a diabolical murder for sweet charity's sake. Mere self-interest, then, if no better motive can be enlisted, should, especially with high-tempered men, prompt all beings to charity and philanthropy. At any rate, upon the occasion in question, I strove to drown my exasperated feelings towards the scrivener by benevolently construing his conduct. Poor fellow, poor fellow! thought I, he don't mean anything; and besides, he has seen hard times, and ought to be indulged.

I endeavored, also, immediately to occupy myself, and at the same time to comfort my despondency. I tried to fancy, that in the course of the morning, at such time as might prove agreeable to him, Bartleby, of his own free accord, would emerge from his hermitage and take up some decided line of march in the direction of the door. But no. Half-past twelve o'clock came; Turkey began to glow in the face, overturn his inkstand, and become generally obstreperous; Nippers abated down into quietude and courtesy; Ginger Nut munched his noon apple; and Bartleby remained standing at his window in one of his profoundest dead-wall reveries. Will it be credited? Ought I to acknowledge it? That afternoon I left the office without saying one further word to him.

Some days now passed, during which, at leisure intervals I looked a little into "Edwards on the Will," and "Priestly on Necessity." Under the circumstances, those books induced a salutary feeling. Gradually I slid into the persuasion that these troubles of mine, touching the scrivener, had been all predestinated from eternity, and Bartleby was billeted upon me for some mysterious purpose of an allwise Providence, which it was not for a mere mortal like me to fathom. Yes, Bartleby, stay there behind your screen, thought I; I shall persecute you no more; you are harmless and noiseless as any of these old chairs; in short, I never feel so private as when I know you are here. At last I see it, I feel it; I penetrate to the predestinated purpose of my life. I am content. Others may have loftier parts to enact; but my mission in this world, Bartleby, is to furnish you with office-room for such period as you may see fit to remain.

I believe that this wise and blessed frame of mind would have continued with me, had it not been for the unsolicited and uncharitable remarks obtruded upon me by my professional friends who visited the rooms. But thus it often is, that the constant friction of illiberal minds wears out at last the best resolves of the more generous. Though to be sure, when I reflected upon it, it was not strange that people entering my office should be struck by the peculiar aspect of the unaccountable Bartleby, and so be tempted to throw out some sinister observations concerning him. Sometimes an attorney, having business with me, and calling at my office, and finding no one but the scrivener there, would undertake to obtain some sort of precise information from him touching my whereabouts; but without heeding his idle talk, Bartleby would remain standing immovable in the middle of the room. So after contemplating him in that position for a time, the attorney would depart, no wiser than he came.

Also, when a reference was going on, and the room full of lawyers and witnesses, and business driving fast, some deeply-occupied legal gentleman present, seeing Bartleby wholly unemployed, would request him to run round to his (the legal gentleman's) office and fetch some papers for him. Thereupon, Bartleby would tranquilly decline, and yet remain idle as before. Then the lawyer would give a great stare, and turn to me. And what could I say? At last I was made aware that all through the circle of my professional acquaintance, a whisper of wonder was running round, having reference to the strange creature I kept at my office. This worried me very much. And as the idea came upon me of his possibly turning out a long-lived man, and keep occupying my chambers, and denying my authority; and perplexing my visitors; and scandalizing my professional reputation; and casting a general gloom over the premises; keeping soul and body together to the last upon his savings (for doubtless he spent but half a dime a day), and in the end perhaps outlive me, and claim possession of my office by right of his perpetual occupancy: as all these dark anticipations crowded upon me more and more, and my friends continually intruded their relentless remarks upon the apparition in my room; a great change was wrought in me. I resolved to gather all my faculties together, and forever rid me of this intolerable incubus.

Ere revolving any complicated project, however, adapted to this end, I first simply suggested to Bartleby the propriety of his permanent departure. In a calm and serious tone, I commended the idea to his careful and mature consideration. But, having taken three days to meditate upon it, he apprised me, that his original determination remained the same; in short, that he still preferred to abide with me.

What shall I do? I now said to myself, buttoning up my coat to the last button. What shall I do? what ought I to do? what does conscience say I *should* do with this man, or, rather, ghost. Rid myself of him, I must; go, he shall. But how? You will not thrust him, the poor, pale, passive mortal—you will not thrust such a helpless creature out of your door? you will not dishonor yourself by such cruelty? No, I will not, I cannot do that. Rather would I let him live and die here, and then mason up his remains in the wall. What, then, will you do? For all your coaxing, he will not budge. Bribes he leaves under your own paper-weight on your table; in short, it is quite plain that he prefers to cling to you.

Then something severe, something unusual must be done. What! surely you will not have him collared by a constable, and commit his innocent pallor to the common jail? And upon what ground could you procure such a thing to be done?—a vagrant, is he? What! he a vagrant, a wanderer, who refuses to budge? It is because he will *not* be a vagrant, then, that you seek to count him *as* a vagrant. That is too absurd. No visible means of support: there I have him. Wrong again: for indubitably he *does* support himself, and that is the only unanswerable proof that any man can show of his possessing the means so to do. No more, then. Since he will not quit me, I ~~must quit him. I will change my offices;~~ I will move elsewhere, and give him fair notice, that if I find him on my new premises I will then proceed against him as a common trespasser.

Acting accordingly, next day I thus addressed him: "I find these chambers too far from the City Hall; the air is unwholesome. In a word, I propose to re-move my offices next week, and shall no longer require your services. I tell you this now, in order that you may seek another place."

He made no reply, and nothing more was said.

On the appointed day I engaged carts and men, proceeded to my chambers, and, having but little furniture, everything was removed in a few hours. Throughout, the scrivener remained standing behind the screen, which I di-rected to be removed the last thing. It was withdrawn; and, being folded up like a huge folio, left him the motionless occupant of a naked room. I stood in the en-try watching him a moment, while something from within me upbraided me.

I re-entered, with my hand in my pocket—and—and my heart in my mouth.

"Good-by, Bartleby; I am going—good-by, and God some way bless you; and take that," slipping something in his hand. But it dropped upon the floor, and then—strange to say—I tore myself from him whom I had so longed to be rid of.

Established in my new quarters, for a day or two I kept the door locked, and started at every footfall in the passages. When I returned to my rooms, after any little absence, I would pause at the threshold for an instant, and attentively listen, ere applying my key. But these fears were needless. Bartleby never came nigh me.

I thought all was going well, when a perturbed-looking stranger visited me, inquiring whether I was the person who had recently occupied rooms at No.— Wall Street.

Full of forebodings, I replied that I was.

"Then, sir," said the stranger, who proved a lawyer, "you are responsible for the man you left there. He refuses to do any copying; he refuses to do anything; he says he prefers not to; and he refuses to quit the premises."

"I am very sorry, sir," said I, with assumed tranquillity, but an inward tremor, "but, really, the man you allude to is nothing to me—he is no relation or apprentice of mine, that you should hold me responsible for him."

"In mercy's name, who is he?"

"I certainly cannot inform you. I know nothing about him. Formerly I em-ployed him as a copyist; but he has done nothing for me now for some time past."

"I shall settle him, then—good morning, sir."

Several days passed, and I heard nothing more; and, though I often felt a charitable prompting to call at the place and see poor Bartleby, yet a certain squeamishness, of I know not what, withheld me.

All is over with him, by this time, thought I, at last, when, through another week, no further intelligence reached me. But, coming to my room the day after, I found several persons waiting at my door in a high state of nervous excitement.

"That's the man—here he comes," cried the foremost one, whom I recognized as the lawyer who had previously called upon me alone.

"You must take him away, sir, at once," cried a portly person among them, advancing upon me, and whom I knew to be the landlord of No.—Wall Street. "These gentlemen, my tenants, cannot stand it any longer; Mr. B—," pointing to the lawyer, "has turned him out of his room, and he now persists in haunting the building generally, sitting upon the banisters of the stairs by day, and sleeping in the entry by night. Everybody is concerned; clients are leaving the offices; some fears are entertained of a mob; something you must do, and that without delay."

Aghast at this torrent, I fell back before it, and would fain have locked myself in my new quarters. In vain I persisted that Bartleby was nothing to me—no more than to any one else. In vain—I was the last person known to have anything to do with him, and they held me to the terrible account. Fearful, then, of being exposed in the papers (as one person present obscurely threatened), I considered the matter, and, at length, said, that if the lawyer would give me a confidential interview with the scrivener, in his (the lawyer's) own room, I would, that afternoon, strive my best to rid them of the nuisance they complained of.

Going up stairs to my old haunt, there was Bartleby silently sitting upon the banister at the landing.

"What are you doing here, Bartleby?" said I.

"Sitting upon the banister," he mildly replied.

I motioned him into the lawyer's room, who then left us.

"Bartleby," said I, "are you aware that you are the cause of great tribulation to me, by persisting in occupying entry after being dismissed from the office?"

No answer.

"Now one of two things must take place. Either you must do something, or something must be done to you. Now what sort of business would you like to engage in? Would you like to re-engage in copying for some one?"

"No; I would prefer not to make any change."

"Would you like a clerkship in a dry-goods store?"

"There is too much confinement about that. No, I would not like a clerkship; but I am not particular."

"Too much confinement," I cried, "why you keep yourself confined all the time!"

"I would prefer not to take a clerkship," he rejoined, as if to settle that little item at once.

"How would a bar-tender's business suit you? There is no trying of the eyesight in that."

"I would not like it at all; though, as I said before, I am not particular."

His unwonted wordiness inspirited me. I returned to the charge.

"Well, then, would you like to travel through the country collecting bills for the merchants? That would improve your health."

"No, I would prefer to be doing something else."

"How, then, would going as a companion to Europe, to entertain some young gentleman with your conversation—how would that suit you?"

"Not at all. It does not strike me that there is anything definite about that. I like to be stationary. But I am not particular."

"Stationary you shall be, then," I cried, now losing all patience, and, for the first time in all my exasperating connection with him, fairly flying into a passion. "If you do not go away from these premises before night, I shall feel bound—indeed, I *am* bound—*to*—*to*—*to* quit the premises myself!" I rather absurdly concluded, knowing not with what possible threat to try to frighten his immobility into compliance. Despairing of all further efforts, I was precipitately leaving him, when a final thought occurred to me—one which had not been wholly unindulged before.

"Bartleby," said I, in the kindest tone I could assume under such exciting circumstances, "will you go home with me now—not to my office, but my dwelling—and remain there till we can conclude upon some convenient arrangement for you at our leisure? Come, let us start now, right away."

"No: at present I would prefer not to make any change at all."

I answered nothing; but, effectually dodging every one by the suddenness and rapidity of my flight, rushed from the building, ran up Wall Street towards Broadway, and, jumping into the first omnibus, was soon removed from pursuit. As soon as tranquillity returned, I distinctly perceived that I had now done all that I possibly could, both in respect to the demands of the landlord and his tenants, and with regard to my own desire and sense of duty, to benefit Bartleby, and shield him from rude persecution. I now strove to be entirely care-free and quiescent; and my conscience justified me in the attempt; though, indeed, it was not so successful as I could have wished. So fearful was I of being again hunted out by the incensed landlord and his exasperated tenants, that, surrendering my business to Nippers, for a few days, I drove about the upper part of the town and through the suburbs, in my rockaway; crossed over to Jersey City and Hoboken, and paid fugitive visits to Manhattanville and Astoria. In fact, I almost lived in my rockaway for the time.

When again I entered my office, lo, a note from the landlord lay upon the desk. I opened it with trembling hands. It informed me that the writer had sent to the police, and had Bartleby removed to the Tombs as a vagrant. Moreover, since I knew more about him than any one else, he wished me to appear at that place, and make a suitable statement of the facts. These tidings had a conflicting effect upon me. At first I was indignant; but, at last, almost approved. The landlord's energetic, summary disposition, had led him to adopt a procedure which I do not think I would have decided upon myself; and yet, as a last resort, under such peculiar circumstances, it seemed the only plan.

As I afterwards learned, the poor scrivener, when told that he must be conducted to the Tombs, offered not the slightest obstacle, but, in his pale, unmoving way, silently acquiesced.

Some of the compassionate and curious bystanders joined the party; and headed by one of the constables arm in arm with Bartleby, the silent procession filed its way through all the noise, and heat, and joy of the roaring thoroughfares at noon.

The same day I received the note, I went to the Tombs, or, to speak more properly, the Halls of Justice. Seeking the right officer, I stated the purpose of my call, and was informed that the individual I described was, indeed, within. I then assured the functionary that Bartleby was a perfectly honest man, and greatly to be compassionated, however unaccountably eccentric. I narrated all I knew, and closed by suggesting the idea of letting him remain in as indulgent confinement as possible, till something less harsh might be done—though, indeed, I hardly knew what. At all events, if nothing else could be decided upon, the almshouse must receive him. I then begged to have an interview.

Being under no disgraceful charge, and quite serene and harmless in all his ways, they had permitted him freely to wander about the prison, and, especially, in the inclosed grass-platted yards thereof. And so I found him there, standing all alone in the quietest of the yards, his face towards a high wall, while all around, from the narrow slits of the jail windows, I thought I saw peering out upon him the eyes of murderers and thieves.

"Bartleby!"

"I know you," he said without looking round—"and I want nothing to say to you."

"It was not I that brought you here, Bartleby," said I, keenly pained at his implied suspicion. "And to you, this should not be so vile a place. Nothing reproachful attaches to you by being here. And see, it is not so sad a place as one might think. Look, there is the sky, and here is the grass."

"I know where I am," he replied, but would say nothing more, and so I left him.

As I entered the corridor again, a broad meat-like man, in an apron, accosted me, and, jerking his thumb over his shoulder, said—"Is that your friend?"

"Yes."

"Does he want to starve? If he does, let him live on the prison fare, that's all."

"Who are you?" asked I, not knowing what to make of such an unofficially speaking person in such a place.

"I am the grub-man. Such gentlemen as have friends here, hire me to provide them with something good to eat."

"Is this so?" said I, turning to the turnkey.

He said it was.

"Well, then," said I, slipping some silver into the grub-man's hands (for so they called him), "I want you to give particular attention to my friend there; let him have the best dinner you can get. And you must be as polite to him as possible."

"Introduce me, will you?" said the grub-man, looking at me with an expression which seemed to say he was all impatience for an opportunity to give a specimen of his breeding.

Thinking it would prove of benefit to the scrivener, I acquiesced; and, asking the grub-man his name, went up with him to Bartleby.

"Bartleby, this is a friend; you will find him very useful to you."

"Your sarvant, sir, your sarvant," said the grub-man, making a low salutation behind his apron. "Hope you find it pleasant here, sir; nice grounds—cool apartments—hope you'll stay with us some time—try to make it agreeable. What will you have for dinner to-day?"

"I prefer not to dine to-day," said Bartleby, turning away. "It would disagree with me; I am unused to dinners." So saying, he slowly moved to the other side of the inclosure, and took up a position fronting the dead-wall.

"How's this?" said the grub-man, addressing me with a stare of astonishment, "He's odd, ain't he?"

"I think he is a little deranged," said I, sadly.

"Deranged? deranged is it? Well, now, upon my word, I thought that friend of yourn was a gentleman forger; they are always pale and genteel-like, them forgers. I can't help pity 'em—can't help it, sir. Did you know Monroe Edwards?" he added, touchingly, and paused. Then, laying his hand piteously on my shoulder, sighed, "he died of consumption at Sing-Sing. So you weren't acquainted with Monroe?"

"No, I was never socially acquainted with any forgers. But I cannot stop longer. Look to my friend yonder. You will not lose by it. I will see you again."

Some few days after this, I again obtained admission to the Tombs, and went through the corridors in quest of Bartleby; but without finding him.

"I saw him coming from his cell not long ago," said a turnkey, "may be he's gone to loiter in the yards."

So I went in that direction.

"Are you looking for the silent man?" said another turnkey, passing me. "Yonder he lies—sleeping in the yard there. 'Tis not twenty minutes since I saw him lie down."

The yard was entirely quiet. It was not accessible to the common prisoners. The surrounding walls, of amazing thickness, kept off all sounds behind them. The Egyptian character of the masonry weighed upon me with its gloom. But a soft imprisoned turf grew under foot. The heart of the eternal pyramids, it seemed, wherein, by some strange magic, through the clefts, grass-seed, dropped by birds, had sprung.

Strangely huddled at the base of the wall, his knees drawn up, and lying on his side, his head touching the cold stones, I saw the wasted Bartleby. But nothing stirred. I paused; then went close up to him; stooped over, and saw that his dim eyes were open; otherwise he seemed profoundly sleeping. Something prompted me to touch him. I felt his hand, when a tingling shiver ran up my arm and down my spine to my feet.

The round face of the grub-man peered upon me now. "His dinner is ready. Won't he dine to-day, either? Or does he live without dining?"

"Lives without dining," said I, and closed the eyes.

"Eh!—He's asleep, ain't he?"

"With kings and counselors," murmured I.

There would seem little need for proceeding further in this history. Imagination will readily supply the meagre recital of poor Bartleby's interment. But, ere parting with the reader, let me say, that if this little narrative has sufficiently interested him, to awaken curiosity as to who Bartleby was, and what manner of life he led prior to the present narrator's making his acquaintance, I can only reply, that in such curiosity I fully share, but am wholly unable to gratify it. Yet here I hardly know whether I should divulge one little item of rumor, which came to my ear a few months after the scrivener's decease. Upon what basis it rested, I could never ascertain; and hence, how true it is I cannot now tell. But, inasmuch as this vague report has not been without a certain suggestive interest to me, however sad, it may prove the same with some others; and so I will briefly mention it. The report was this: that Bartleby had been a subordinate clerk in the Dead Letter Office at Washington, from which he had been suddenly removed by a change in the administration. When I think over this rumor, hardly can I express the emotions which seize me. Dead letters! does it not sound like dead men? Conceive a man by nature and misfortune prone to a pallid hopelessness, can any business seem more fitted to heighten it than that of continually handling these dead letters, and assorting them for the flames? For by the cartload they are annually burned. Sometimes from out the folded paper the pale clerk takes a ring—the finger it was meant for, perhaps, moulders in the grave; a bank-note sent in swiftest charity—he whom it would relieve, nor eats nor hungers any more; pardon for those who died despairing; hope for those who died unhoping; good tidings for those who died stifled by unrelieved calamities. On errands of life, these letters speed to death.

Ah, Bartleby! Ah, humanity!

STUDY QUESTIONS

1. The narrator of "Bartleby the Scrivener" begins his narration with the word *I* and ends it with the word *humanity*. We may wonder, therefore, if the events that form the conflict and climax of the story have altered the narrator's vision to allow his attention to shift from himself to others. If so, how did this happen? The following questions may help you to develop your answer.

2. The narrator begins his tale by introducing himself. Why does he do so? What does he reveal as his goals? What things does he seem to value most highly?

3. What tone of voice is the narrator using in this early part of the story? (Paragraph five may be especially helpful here.)

4. Look at the lawyer/narrator's introduction of his office and of his first staff member, Turkey. How does he act toward Turkey? What reasons does he give for acting as he does? Do his actions seem to match his reasons? What impression of the lawyer's character do we receive?

5. Analyze his introductions of Nippers and Ginger Nut. How does the narrator's characterization of his three employees, and our impression of his interactions with them, prepare the way for the introduction of Bartleby and for the narrator's response to him and to his behavior?

6. Having examined how the narrator prepares the way for the introduction of his main character, now look at the first episodes involving that character (pp. 98–102). How well does Bartleby fit into our picture of the office? What does this do for our sense of him and of his relationship with his employer?

7. What is the turning-point of the story? How does it change the narrator's view of Bartleby? What emotions does it raise in him? What action does it prompt him to take? What are the results of that action?

8. Examine the story's progress from this turning point to Bartleby's death. What changes are taking place in the tone of the narrative? the actions? the characterizations? Examine your reactions to these changes and developments. Have you been prepared for them? Can you accept them, or do you find them out of character or hard to believe? How do you react to Bartleby's death? Has the death been made to seem inevitable? Does it seem appropriate that the narrator be the one to discover it? How do you feel now about the narrator's relation to Bartleby?

9. Notice the use of walls to set scenes throughout the story. This will let you glance at the whole story once more and will give you a good key for discussing some of the shifts in tone and atmosphere that occur as the story progresses. It will also let you sum up some of your impressions of Bartleby, because he is the character most closely associated with these walls. What is the effect on you of the combination of walls and Bartleby?

10. Similarly, look at mentions of money throughout the story. What character is most closely associated with them? What characterization do you draw from this association?

11. Look as well at the after-note that ends the story, and ask what it adds to your sense of Bartleby, the narrator, and the story.

12. Sum up your thoughts for yourself. Has the narrator changed during the story? And, if he has, what do you make of the change?

13. Another way to approach the story would be to look at the effects of keeping Bartleby so sketchily characterized. How essential is this pared-down characterization to the story? How does the narrator's sense of his own lack of knowledge about Bartleby affect him? How does it affect your feelings toward Bartleby, toward the narrator, and toward the relationship that develops be-

tween the two men? Does the characterization given Bartleby suggest any symbolic values for Bartleby, the narrator, or their relationship? Or do you feel the story is better dealt with as a realistic tale?

The Yellow Wall-Paper

Charlotte Perkins Gilman (1860–1935)

It is very seldom that mere ordinary people like John and myself secure ancestral halls for the summer.

A colonial mansion, a hereditary estate, I would say a haunted house, and reach the height of romantic felicity—but that would be asking too much of fate!

Still I will proudly declare that there is something queer about it.

Else, why should it be let so cheaply? And why have stood so long untenanted?

John laughs at me, of course, but one expects that in marriage.

John is practical in the extreme. He has no patience with faith, an intense horror of superstition, and he scoffs openly at any talk of things not to be felt and seen and put down in figures.

John is a physician, and *perhaps*—(I would not say it to a living soul, of course, but this is dead paper and a great relief to my mind)—*perhaps* that is one reason I do not get well faster.

You see he does not believe I am sick!

And what can one do?

If a physician of high standing, and one's own husband, assures friends and relatives that there is really nothing the matter with one but temporary nervous depression—a slight hysterical tendency—what is one to do?

My brother is also a physician, and also of high standing, and he says the same thing.

So I take phosphates or phosphites—whichever it is, and tonics, and journeys, and air, and exercise, and am absolutely forbidden to "work" until I am well again.

Personally, I disagree with their ideas.

Personally, I believe that congenial work, with excitement and change, would do me good.

But what is one to do?

I did write for a while in spite of them; but it *does* exhaust me a good deal—having to be so sly about it, or else meet with heavy opposition.

I sometimes fancy that in my condition if I had less opposition and more society and stimulus—but John says the very worst thing I can do is to think about my condition, and I confess it always makes me feel bad.

So I will let it alone and talk about the house.

The most beautiful place! It is quite alone, standing well back from the road, quite three miles from the village. It makes me think of English places that you read about, for there are hedges and walls and gates that lock, and lots of separate little houses for the gardeners and people.

There is a *delicious* garden! I never saw such a garden—large and shady, full of box-bordered paths, and lined with long grape-covered arbors with seats under them.

There were greenhouses, too, but they are all broken now.

There was some legal trouble, I believe, something about the heirs and co-heirs; anyhow, the place has been empty for years.

That spoils my ghostliness, I am afraid, but I don't care—there is something strange about the house—I can feel it.

I even said so to John one moonlight evening, but he said what I felt was a *draught,* and shut the window.

I get unreasonably angry with John sometimes. I'm sure I never used to be so sensitive. I think it is due to this nervous condition.

But John says if I feel so, I shall neglect proper self-control; so I take pains to control myself—before him, at least, and that makes me very tired.

I don't like our room a bit. I wanted one downstairs that opened on the piazza and had roses all over the window, and such pretty old-fashioned chintz hangings! but John would not hear of it.

He said there was only one window and not room for two beds, and no near room for him if he took another.

He is very careful and loving, and hardly lets me stir without special direction.

I have a schedule prescription for each hour in the day; he takes all care from me, and so I feel basely ungrateful not to value it more.

He said we came here solely on my account, that I was to have perfect rest and all the air I could get. "Your exercise depends on your strength, my dear," said he, "and your food somewhat on your appetite; but air you can absorb all the time." So we took the nursery at the top of the house.

It is a big, airy room, the whole floor nearly, with windows that look all ways, and air and sunshine galore. It was nursery first and then playroom and gymnasium, I should judge; for the windows are barred for little children, and there are rings and things in the walls.

The paint and paper look as if a boys' school had used it. It is stripped off—the paper—in great patches all around the head of my bed, about as far as I can reach, and in a great place on the other side of the room low down. I never saw a worse paper in my life.

One of those sprawling flamboyant patterns committing every artistic sin.

It is dull enough to confuse the eye in following, pronounced enough to constantly irritate and provoke study, and when you follow the lame uncertain curves for a little distance they suddenly commit suicide—plunge off at outrageous angles, destroy themselves in unheard of contradictions.

The color is repellent, almost revolting; a smouldering unclean yellow, strangely faded by the slow-turning sunlight.

It is a dull yet lurid orange in some places, a sickly sulphur tint in others.

No wonder the children hated it! I should hate it myself if I had to live in this room long.

There comes John, and I must put this away,—he hates to have me write a word.

We have been here two weeks, and I haven't felt like writing before, since that first day.

I am sitting by the window now, up in this atrocious nursery, and there is nothing to hinder my writing as much as I please, save lack of strength.

John is away all day, and even some nights when his cases are serious.

I am glad my case is not serious!

But these nervous troubles are dreadfully depressing.

John does not know how much I really suffer. He knows there is no *reason* to suffer, and that satisfies him.

Of course it is only nervousness. It does weigh on me so not to do my duty in any way!

I meant to be such a help to John, such a real rest and comfort, and here I am a comparative burden already!

Nobody would believe what an effort it is to do what little I am able,—to dress and entertain, and order things.

It is fortunate Mary is so good with the baby. Such a dear baby!

And yet I *cannot* be with him, it makes me so nervous.

I suppose John never was nervous in his life. He laughs at me so about this wall-paper!

At first he meant to repaper the room, but afterwards he said that I was letting it get the better of me, and that nothing was worse for a nervous patient than to give way to such fancies.

He said that after the wall-paper was changed it would be the heavy bedstead, and then the barred windows, and then that gate at the head of the stairs, and so on.

"You know the place is doing you good," he said, "and really, dear, I don't care to renovate the house just for a three months' rental."

"Then do let us go downstairs," I said, "there are such pretty rooms there."

Then he took me in his arms and called me a blessed little goose, and said he would go down to the cellar, if I wished, and have it whitewashed into the bargain.

But he is right enough about the beds and windows and things.

It is an airy and comfortable room as any one need wish, and, of course, I would not be so silly as to make him uncomfortable just for a whim.

I'm really getting quite fond of the big room, all but that horrid paper.

Out of one window I can see the garden, those mysterious deep-shaded arbors, the riotous old-fashioned flowers, and bushes and gnarly trees.

Out of another I get a lovely view of the bay and a little private wharf belonging to the estate. There is a beautiful shaded lane that runs down there from the house. I always fancy I see people walking in these numerous paths and arbors, but John has cautioned me not to give way to fancy in the least. He says that with my imaginative power and habit of story-making, a nervous weakness like mine is sure to lead to all manner of excited fancies, and that I ought to use my will and good sense to check the tendency. So I try.

I think sometimes that if I were only well enough to write a little it would relieve the press of ideas and rest me.

But I find I get pretty tired when I try.

It is so discouraging not to have any advice and companionship about my work. When I get really well, John says we will ask Cousin Henry and Julia down for a long visit; but he says he would as soon put fireworks in my pillow-case as to let me have those stimulating people about now.

I wish I could get well faster.

But I must not think about that. This paper looks to me as if it *knew* what a vicious influence it had!

There is a recurrent spot where the pattern lolls like a broken neck and two bulbous eyes stare at you upside down.

I get positively angry with the impertinence of it and the everlastingness. Up and down and sideways they crawl, and those absurd, unblinking eyes are everywhere. There is one place where two breadths didn't match, and the eyes go all up and down the line, one a little higher than the other.

I never saw so much expression in an inanimate thing before, and we all know how much expression they have! I used to lie awake as a child and get more entertainment and terror out of blank walls and plain furniture than most children could find in a toy-store.

I remember what a kindly wink the knobs of our big, old bureau used to have, and there was one chair that always seemed like a strong friend.

I used to feel that if any of the other things looked too fierce I could always hop into that chair and be safe.

The furniture in this room is no worse than inharmonious, however, for we had to bring it all from downstairs. I suppose when this was used as a playroom they had to take the nursery things out, and no wonder! I never saw such ravages as the children have made here.

The wall-paper, as I said before, is torn off in spots, and it sticketh closer than a brother—they must have had perseverance as well as hatred.

Then the floor is scratched and gouged and splintered, the plaster itself is dug out here and there, and this great heavy bed which is all we found in the room, looks as if it had been through the wars.

But I don't mind it a bit—only the paper.

There comes John's sister. Such a dear girl as she is, and so careful of me! I must not let her find me writing.

She is a perfect and enthusiastic housekeeper, and hopes for no better profession. I verily believe she thinks it is the writing which made me sick!

But I can write when she is out, and see her a long way off from these windows.

There is one that commands the road, a lovely shaded winding road, and one that just looks off over the country. A lovely country, too, full of great elms and velvet meadows.

This wall-paper has a kind of sub-pattern in a different shade, a particularly irritating one, for you can only see it in certain lights, and not clearly then.

But in the places where it isn't faded and where the sun is just so—I can see a strange, provoking, formless sort of figure, that seems to skulk about behind that silly and conspicuous front design.

There's sister on the stairs!

Well, the Fourth of July is over! The people are all gone and I am tired out. John thought it might do me good to see a little company, so we just had mother and Nellie and the children down for a week.

Of course I didn't do a thing. Jennie sees to everything now.

But it tired me all the same.

John says if I don't pick up faster he shall send me to Weir Mitchell in the fall.

But I don't want to go there at all. I had a friend who was in his hands once, and she says he is just like John and my brother, only more so!

Besides, it is such an undertaking to go so far.

I don't feel as if it was worth while to turn my hand over for anything, and I'm getting dreadfully fretful and querulous.

I cry at nothing, and cry most of the time.

Of course I don't when John is here, or anybody else, but when I am alone.

And I am alone a good deal just now. John is kept in town very often by serious cases, and Jennie is good and lets me alone when I want her to.

So I walk a little in the garden or down that lovely lane, sit on the porch under the roses, and lie down up here a good deal.

I'm getting really fond of the room in spite of the wall-paper. Perhaps *because* of the wall-paper.

It dwells in my mind so!

I lie here on this great immovable bed—it is nailed down, I believe—and follow that pattern about by the hour. It is as good as gymnastics, I assure you.

I start, we'll say, at the bottom, down in the corner over there where it has not been touched, and I determine for the thousandth time that I *will* follow that pointless pattern to some sort of a conclusion.

I know a little of the principle of design, and I know this thing was not arranged on any laws of radiation, or alternation, or repetition, or symmetry, or anything else that I ever heard of.

It is repeated, of course, by the breadths, but not otherwise.

Looked at in one way each breadth stands alone, the bloated curves and flourishes—a kind of "debased Romanesque" with *delirium tremens*—go waddling up and down in isolated columns of fatuity.

But, on the other hand, they connect diagonally, and the sprawling outlines run off in great slanting waves of optic horror, like a lot of wallowing seaweeds in full chase.

The whole thing goes horizontally, too, at least it seems so, and I exhaust myself in trying to distinguish the order of its going in that direction.

They have used a horizontal breadth for a frieze, and that adds wonderfully to the confusion.

There is one end of the room where it is almost intact, and there, when the crosslights fade and the low sun shines directly upon it, I can almost fancy radiation after all,—the interminable grotesques seem to form around a common centre and rush off in headlong plunges of equal distraction.

It makes me tired to follow it. I will take a nap I guess.

I don't know why I should write this.

I don't want to.

I don't feel able.

And I know John would think it absurd. But I *must* say what I feel and think in some way—it is such a relief!

But the effort is getting to be greater than the relief.

Half the time now I am awfully lazy, and lie down ever so much.

John says I mustn't lose my strength, and has me take cod liver oil and lots of tonics and things, to say nothing of ale and wine and rare meat.

Dear John! He loves me very dearly, and hates to have me sick. I tried to have a real earnest reasonable talk with him the other day, and tell him how I wish he would let me go and make a visit to Cousin Henry and Julia.

But he said I wasn't able to go, nor able to stand it after I got there; and I did not make out a very good case for myself, for I was crying before I had finished.

It is getting to be a great effort for me to think straight. Just this nervous weakness I suppose.

And dear John gathered me up in his arms, and just carried me upstairs and laid me on the bed, and sat by me and read to me till it tired my head.

He said I was his darling and his comfort and all he had, and that I must take care of myself for his sake, and keep well.

He says no one but myself can help me out of it, that I must use my will and self-control and not let any silly fancies run away with me.

There's one comfort, the baby is well and happy, and does not have to occupy this nursery with the horrid wall-paper.

If we had not used it, that blessed child would have! What a fortunate escape! Why, I wouldn't have a child of mine, an impressionable little thing, live in such a room for worlds.

I never thought of it before, but it is lucky that John kept me here after all, I can stand it so much easier than a baby, you see.

Of course I never mention it to them any more—I am too wise,—but I keep watch of it all the same.

There are things in that paper that nobody knows but me, or ever will.

Behind that outside pattern the dim shapes get clearer every day.

It is always the same shape, only very numerous.

And it is like a woman stooping down and creeping about behind that pattern. I don't like it a bit. I wonder—I begin to think—I wish John would take me away from here!

It is so hard to talk with John about my case, because he is so wise, and because he loves me so.

But I tried it last night.

It was moonlight. The moon shines in all around just as the sun does.

I hate to see it sometimes, it creeps so slowly, and always comes in by one window or another.

John was asleep and I hated to waken him, so I kept still and watched the moonlight on that undulating wall-paper till I felt creepy.

The faint figure behind seemed to shake the pattern, just as if she wanted to get out.

I got up softly and went to feel and see if the paper *did* move, and when I came back John was awake.

"What is it, little girl?" he said. "Don't go walking about like that—you'll get cold."

I thought it was a good time to talk, so I told him that I really was not gaining here, and that I wished he would take me away.

"Why darling!" said he, "our lease will be up in three weeks, and I can't see how to leave before.

"The repairs are not done at home, and I cannot possibly leave town just now. Of course if you were in any danger, I could and would, but you really are better, dear, whether you can see it or not. I am a doctor, dear, and I know. You are gaining flesh and color, your appetite is better, I feel really much easier about you."

"I don't weigh a bit more," said I, "nor as much; and my appetite may be better in the evening when you are here, but it is worse in the morning when you are away!"

"Bless her little heart!" said he with a big hug, "she shall be as sick as she pleases! But now let's improve the shining hours by going to sleep, and talk about it in the morning!"

"And you won't go away?" I asked gloomily.

"Why, how can I, dear? It is only three weeks more and then we will take a nice little trip of a few days while Jennie is getting the house ready. Really dear you are better!"

"Better in body perhaps—" I began, and stopped short, for he sat up straight and looked at me with such a stern, reproachful look that I could not say another word.

"My darling," said he, "I beg of you, for my sake and for our child's sake, as well as for your own, that you will never for one instant let that idea enter your mind! There is nothing so dangerous, so fascinating, to a temperament like yours. It is a false and foolish fancy. Can you not trust me as a physician when I tell you so?"

So of course I said no more on that score, and we went to sleep before long. He thought I was asleep first, but I wasn't, and lay there for hours trying to decide whether that front pattern and the back pattern really did move together or separately.

On a pattern like this, by daylight, there is a lack of sequence, a defiance of law, that is a constant irritant to a normal mind.

The color is hideous enough, and unreliable enough, and infuriating enough, but the pattern is torturing.

You think you have mastered it, but just as you get well underway in following, it turns a back-somersault and there you are. It slaps you in the face, knocks you down, and tramples upon you. It is like a bad dream.

The outside pattern is a florid arabesque, reminding one of a fungus. If you can imagine a toadstool in joints, an interminable string of toadstools, budding and sprouting in endless convolutions—why, that is something like it.

That is, sometimes!

There is one marked peculiarity about this paper, a thing nobody seems to notice but myself, and that is that it changes as the light changes.

When the sun shoots in through the east window—I always watch for that first long, straight ray—it changes so quickly that I never can quite believe it.

That is why I watch it always.

By moonlight—the moon shines in all night when there is a moon—I wouldn't know it was the same paper.

At night in any kind of light, in twilight, candle light, lamplight, and worst of all by moonlight, it becomes bars! The outside pattern I mean, and the woman behind it is as plain as can be.

I didn't realize for a long time what the thing was that showed behind, that dim sub-pattern, but now I am quite sure it is a woman.

By daylight she is subdued, quiet. I fancy it is the pattern that keeps her so still. It is so puzzling. It keeps me quiet by the hour.

I lie down ever so much now. John says it is good for me, and to sleep all I can.

Indeed he started the habit by making me lie down for an hour after each meal.

It is a very bad habit I am convinced, for you see I don't sleep.

And that cultivates deceit, for I don't tell them I'm awake—O no!

The fact is I am getting a little afraid of John.

He seems very queer sometimes, and even Jennie has an inexplicable look.

It strikes me occasionally, just as a scientific hypothesis,—that perhaps it is the paper!

I have watched John when he did not know I was looking, and come into the room suddenly on the most innocent excuses, and I've caught him several times *looking at the paper!* And Jennie too. I caught Jennie with her hand on it once.

She didn't know I was in the room, and when I asked her in a quiet, a very quiet voice, with the most restrained manner possible, what she was doing with the paper—she turned around as if she had been caught stealing, and looked quite angry—asked me why I should frighten her so!

Then she said that the paper stained everything it touched, that she had found yellow smooches on all my clothes and John's, and she wished we would be more careful!

Did not that sound innocent? But I know she was studying that pattern, and I am determined that nobody shall find it out but myself!

Life is very much more exciting now than it used to be. You see I have something more to expect, to look forward to, to watch. I really do eat better, and am more quiet than I was.

John is so pleased to see me improve! He laughed a little the other day, and said I seemed to be flourishing in spite of my wall-paper.

I turned it off with a laugh. I had no intention of telling him it was *because* of the wall-paper—he would make fun of me. He might even want to take me away.

I don't want to leave now until I have found it out. There is a week more, and I think that will be enough.

I'm feeling ever so much better! I don't sleep much at night, for it is so interesting to watch developments; but I sleep a good deal in the daytime.

In the daytime it is tiresome and perplexing.

There are always new shoots on the fungus, and new shades of yellow all over it. I cannot keep count of them, though I have tried conscientiously.

It is the strangest yellow, that wall-paper! It makes me think of all the yellow things I ever saw—not beautiful ones like buttercups, but old foul, bad yellow things.

But there is something else about that paper—the smell! I noticed it the moment we came into the room, but with so much air and sun it was not bad.

Now we have had a week of fog and rain, and whether the windows are open or not, the smell is here.

It creeps all over the house.

I find it hovering in the dining-room, skulking in the parlor, hiding in the hall, lying in wait for me on the stairs.

It gets into my hair.

Even when I go to ride, if I turn my head suddenly and surprise it—there is that smell!

Such a peculiar odor, too! I have spent hours in trying to analyze it, to find what it smelled like.

It is not bad—at first, and very gentle, but quite the subtlest, most enduring odor I ever met.

In this damp weather it is awful, I wake up in the night and find it hanging over me.

It used to disturb me at first. I thought seriously of burning the house—to reach the smell.

But now I am used to it. The only thing I can think of that it is like is the *color* of the paper! A yellow smell.

There is a very funny mark on this wall, low down, near the mopboard. A streak that runs round the room. It goes behind every piece of furniture, except the bed, a long, straight, even *smooch,* as if it had been rubbed over and over.

I wonder how it was done and who did it, and what they did it for. Round and round and round—round and round and round—it makes me dizzy!

I really have discovered something at last.

Through watching so much at night, when it changes so, I have finally found out.

The front pattern *does* move—and no wonder! The woman behind shakes it!

Sometimes I think there are a great many women behind, and sometimes only one, and she crawls around fast, and her crawling shakes it all over.

Then in the very bright spots she keeps still, and in the very shady spots she just takes hold of the bars and shakes them hard.

And she is all the time trying to climb through. But nobody could climb through that pattern—it strangles so; I think that is why it has so many heads.

They get through, and then the pattern strangles them off and turns them upside down, and makes their eyes white!

If those heads were covered or taken off it would not be half so bad.

I think that woman gets out in the daytime!

And I'll tell you why—privately—I've seen her!

I can see her out of every one of my windows!

It is the same woman, I know, for she is always creeping, and most women do not creep by daylight.

I see her on that long road under the trees, creeping along, and when a carriage comes she hides under the blackberry vines.

I don't blame her a bit. It must be very humiliating to be caught creeping by daylight!

I always lock the door when I creep by daylight. I can't do it at night, for I know John would suspect something at once.

And John is so queer now, that I don't want to irritate him. I wish he would take another room! Besides, I don't want anybody to get that woman out at night but myself.

I often wonder if I could see her out of all the windows at once.

But, turn as fast as I can, I can only see out of one at one time.

And though I always see her, she *may* be able to creep faster than I can turn!

I have watched her sometimes away off in the open country, creeping as fast as a cloud shadow in a high wind.

If only that top pattern could be gotten off from the under one! I mean to try it, little by little.

I have found out another funny thing, but I shan't tell it this time! It does not do to trust people too much.

There are only two more days to get this paper off, and I believe John is beginning to notice. I don't like the look in his eyes.

And I heard him ask Jennie a lot of professional questions about me. She had a very good report to give.

She said I slept a good deal in the daytime.

John knows I don't sleep very well at night, for all I'm so quiet!

He asked me all sorts of questions, too, and pretended to be very loving and kind.

As if I couldn't see through him!

Still, I don't wonder he acts so, sleeping under this paper for three months.

It only interests me, but I feel sure John and Jennie are secretly affected by it.

Hurrah! This is the last day, but it is enough. John is to stay in town over night, and won't be out until this evening.

Jennie wanted to sleep with me—the sly thing! but I told her I should undoubtedly rest better for a night all alone.

That was clever, for really I wasn't alone a bit! As soon as it was moonlight and that poor thing began to crawl and shake the pattern, I got up and ran to help her.

I pulled and she shook, I shook and she pulled, and before morning we had peeled off yards of that paper.

A strip about as high as my head and half around the room.

And then when the sun came and that awful pattern began to laugh at me, I declared I would finish it to-day!

We go away to-morrow, and they are moving all my furniture down again to leave things as they were before.

Jennie looked at the wall in amazement, but I told her merrily that I did it out of pure spite at the vicious thing.

She laughed and said she wouldn't mind doing it herself, but I must not get tired.

How she betrayed herself that time!

But I am here, and no person touches this paper but me,—not *alive!*

She tried to get me out of the room—it was too patent! But I said it was so quiet and empty and clean now that I believed I would lie down again and sleep all I could; and not to wake me even for dinner—I would call when I woke.

So now she is gone, and the servants are gone, and the things are gone, and there is nothing left but that great bedstead nailed down, with the canvas mattress we found on it.

We shall sleep downstairs to-night, and take the boat home to-morrow.

I quite enjoy the room, now it is bare again.

How those children did tear about here!

This bedstead is fairly gnawed!

But I must get to work.

I have locked the door and thrown the key down into the front path.

I don't want to go out, and I don't want to have anybody come in, till John comes.

I want to astonish him.

I've got a rope up here that even Jennie did not find. If that woman does get out, and tries to get away, I can tie her!

But I forgot I could not reach far without anything to stand on!

This bed will *not* move!

I tried to lift and push it until I was lame, and then I got so angry I bit off a little piece at one corner—but it hurt my teeth.

Then I peeled off all the paper I could reach standing on the floor. It sticks horribly and the pattern just enjoys it! All those strangled heads and bulbous eyes and waddling fungus growths just shriek with derision!

I am getting angry enough to do something desperate. To jump out of the window would be admirable exercise, but the bars are too strong even to try.

Besides I wouldn't do it. Of course not. I know well enough that a step like that is improper and might be misconstrued.

I don't like to *look* out of the windows even—there are so many of those creeping women, and they creep so fast.

I wonder if they all come out of that wall-paper as I did?

But I am securely fastened now by my well-hidden rope—you don't get *me* out in the road there!

I suppose I shall have to get back behind the pattern when it comes night, and that is hard!

things and the kids like him. Or used to fore Black Power[4] got hold their minds and mess em around till they can't be civil to ole folks. So we at this benefit for my niece's cousin who's runnin for somethin with this Black party somethin or other behind her. And I press up close to dance with Bovanne who blind and I'm hummin and he hummin, chest to chest like talkin. Not jammin my breasts into the man. Wasn't bout tits. Was bout vibrations. And he dug it and asked me what color dress I had on and how my hair was fixed and how I was doin without a man, not nosy but nice-like, and who was at this affair and was the canapés dainty-stingy or healthy enough to get hold of proper. Comfy and cheery is what I'm tryin to get across. Touch talkin like the heel of the hand on the tambourine or on a drum.

But right away Joe Lee come up on us and frown for dancin so close to the man. My own son who knows what kind of warm I am about; and don't grown men call me long distance and in the middle of the night for a little Mama comfort? But he frown. Which ain't right since Bovanne can't see and defend himself. Just a nice old man who fixes toasters and busted irons and bicycles and things and changes the lock on my door when my men friends get messy. Nice man. Which is not why they invited him. Grass roots you see. Me and Sister Taylor and the woman who does heads[5] at Mamies and the man from the barber shop, we all there on account of we grass roots.[6] And I ain't never been souther than Brooklyn Battery[7] and no more country than the window box on my fire escape. And just yesterday my kids tellin me to take them countrified rags off my head and be cool. And now can't get Black enough to suit em. So everybody passin sayin My Man Bovanne. Big deal, keep steppin and don't even stop a minute to get the man a drink or one of them cute sandwiches or tell him what's goin on. And him standin there with a smile ready case someone do speak he want to be ready. So that's how come I pull him on the dance floor and we dance squeezin past the tables and chairs and all them coats and people standin round up in each other face talkin bout this and that but got no use for this blind man who mostly fixed skates and skooters for all these folks when they was just kids. So I'm pressed up close and we touch talkin with the hum. And here come my daughter cuttin her eye at me like she do when she tell me about my "apolitical" self like I got hoof and mouf disease and there ain't no hope at all. And I don't pay her no mind and just look up in Bovanne shadow face and tell him his stomach like a drum and he laugh. Laugh real loud. And here come my youngest, Task, with a tap on my elbow like he the third grade monitor and I'm cuttin up on the line to assembly.

"I was just talkin on the drums," I explained when they hauled me into the kitchen. I figured drums was my best defense. They can get ready for drums

---

[4]Black Power was a slogan of certain Civil Rights groups during the 1960s and 70s.
[5]hairdresser
[6]"Grass roots" refers to the common people.
[7]Brooklyn Battery is a section of Brooklyn, New York.

what with all this heritage business. And Bovanne stomach just like that drum Task give me when he come back from Africa. You just touch it and it hum thizzm, thizzm. So I stuck to the drum story. "Just drummin that's all."

"Mama, what are you talkin about?"

"She had too much to drink," say Elo to Task cause she don't hardly say nuthin to me direct no more since that ugly argument about my wigs.

"Look here Mama," say Task, the gentle one. "We just tryin to pull your coat. You were makin a spectacle of yourself out there dancing like that."

"Dancin like what?"

Task run a hand over his left ear like his father for the world and his father before that.

"Like a bitch in heat," say Elo.

"Well uhh, I was goin to say like one of them sex-starved ladies gettin on in years and not too discriminating. Know what I mean?"

I don't answer cause I'll cry. Terrible thing when your own children talk to you like that. Pullin me out the party and hustlin me into some stranger's kitchen in the back of a bar just like the damn police. And ain't like I'm old old. I can still wear me some sleeveless dresses without the meat hangin off my arm. And I keep up with some thangs through my kids. Who ain't kids no more. To hear them tell it. So I don't say nuthin.

"Dancin with that tom,"[8] say Elo to Joe Lee, who leanin on the folks' freezer. "His feet can smell a cracker a mile away and go into their shuffle number post haste. And them eyes. He could be a little considerate and put on some shades. Who wants to look into them blown-out fuses that—"

"Is this what they call the generation gap?" I say.

"Generation gap," spits Elo, like I suggested castor oil and fricassee possum in the milk-shakes or somethin. "That's a white concept for a white phenomenon. There's no generation gap among Black people. We are a col—"

"Yeh, well never mind," says Joe Lee. "The point is Mama . . . well, it's pride. You embarrass yourself and us too dancin like that."

"I wasn't shame." Then nobody say nuthin. Them standin there in they pretty clothes with drinks in they hands and gangin up on me, and me in the third-degree chair and nary a olive to my name. Felt just like the police got hold to me.

"First of all," Task say, holdin up his hand and tickin off the offenses, "the dress. Now that dress is too short, Mama, and too low-cut for a woman your age. And Tamu's going to make a speech tonight to kick off the campaign and will be introducin you and expecting you to organize the council of elders—"

"Me? Didn nobody ask me nuthin. You mean Nisi? She change her name?"

---

[8] "Tom" is short for "Uncle Tom," the central character in Harriet Beecher Stowe's novel *Uncle Tom's Cabin.* Uncle Tom is a term of derision used against African Americans who act in a subservient manner to whites.

"Well, Norton was supposed to tell you about it. Nisi wants to introduce you and then encourage the older folks to form a Council of the Elders to act as an advisory—"

"And you going to be standing there with your boobs out and that wig on your head and that hem up to your ass. And people'll say, 'Ain't that the horny bitch that was grindin with the blind dude?'"

"Elo, be cool a minute," say Task, gettin to the next finger. "And then there's the drinkin. Mama, you know you can't drink cause next thing you know you be laughin loud and carryin on," and he grab another finger for the loudness. "And then there's the dancin. You been tattooed on the man for four records straight and slow draggin even on the fast numbers. How you think that look for a woman your age?"

"What's my age?"

"What?"

"I'm axin you all a simple question. You keep talkin bout what's proper for a woman my age. How old am I anyhow?" And Joe Lee slams his eyes shut and squinches up his face to figure. And Task run a hand over his ear and stare into his glass like the ice cubes goin calculate for him. And Elo just starin at the top of my head like she goin rip the wig off any minute now.

"Is your hair braided up under that thing? If so, why don't you take it off? You always did do a neat cornroll."

"Uh huh," cause I'm thinkin how she couldn't undo her hair fast enough talking bout cornroll so countrified. None of which was the subject. "How old, I say?"

"Sixtee-one or—"

"You a damn lie Joe Lee Peoples."

"And that's another thing," say Task on the fingers.

"You know what you all can kiss," I say, gettin up and brushin the wrinkles out my lap.

"Oh, Mama," Elo say, puttin a hand on my shoulder like she hasn't done since she left home and the hand landin light and not sure it supposed to be there. Which hurt me to my heart. Cause this was the child in our happiness fore Mr. Peoples die. And I carried that child strapped to my chest till she was nearly two. We was close is what I'm trying to tell you. Cause it was more me in the child than the others. And even after Task it was the girlchild I covered in the night and wept over for no reason at all less it was she was a chub-chub like me and not very pretty, but a warm child. And how did things get to this, that she can't put a sure hand on me and say Mama we love you and care about you and you entitled to enjoy yourself cause you a good woman?

"And then there's Reverend Trent," say Task, glancin from left to right like they hatchin a plot and just now lettin me in on it. "You were suppose to be talkin with him tonight, Mama, about giving us his basement for campaign headquarters and—"

"Didn nobody tell me nuthin. If grass roots mean you kept in the dark I can't use it. I really can't. And Reven Trent a fool anyway the way he tore into the widow man up there on Edgecomb cause he wouldn't take in three of them foster children and the woman not even comfy in the ground yet and the man's mind messed up and—"

"Look here," say Task. "What we need is a family conference so we can get all this stuff cleared up and laid out on the table. In the meantime I think we better get back into the other room and tend to business. And in the meantime, Mama, see if you can't get to Reverend Trent and—"

"You want me to belly rub with the Reven, that it?"

"Oh damn," Elo say and go through the swingin door.

"We'll talk about all this at dinner. How's tomorrow night, Joe Lee?" While Joe Lee being self-important I'm wonderin who's doin the cookin and how come no body ax me if I'm free and do I get a corsage and things like that. Then Joe nod that it's O.K. and he go through the swingin door and just a little hubbub come through from the other room. Then Task smile his smile, lookin just like his daddy and he leave. And it just me in this stranger's kitchen, which was a mess I wouldn't never let my kitchen look like. Poison you just to look at the pots. Then the door swing the other way and it's My Man Bovanne standin there sayin Miss Hazel but lookin at the deep fry and then at the steam table, and most surprised when I come up on him from the other direction and take him on out of there. Pass the folks pushin up towards the stage where Nisi and some other people settin and ready to talk, and folks gettin to the last of the sandwiches and the booze fore they settle down in one spot and listen serious. And I'm thinkin bout tellin Bovanne what a lovely long dress Nisi got on and the earrings and her hair piled up in a cone and the people bout to hear how we all gettin screwed and gotta form our own party[9] and everybody there listenin and lookin. But instead I just haul the man on out of there, and Joe Lee and his wife look at me like I'm terrible, but they ain't said boo to the man yet. Cause he blind and old and don't nobody there need him since they grown up and don't need they skates fixed no more.

"Where we goin, Miss Hazel?" Him knowin all the time.

"First we gonna buy you some dark sunglasses. Then you comin with me to the supermarket so I can pick up tomorrow's dinner, which is goin to be a grand thing proper and you invited. Then we goin to my house."

"That be fine. I surely would like to rest my feet." Bein cute, but you got to let men play out they little show, blind or not. So he chat on bout how tired he is and how he appreciate me takin him in hand this way. And I'm thinkin I'll have him change the lock on my door first thing. Then I'll give the man a nice warm bath with jasmine leaves in the water and a little Epsom salt on the sponge to do his back. And then a good rubdown with rose water and olive oil. Then a cup of

---

[9]political party

lemon tea with a taste in it. And a little talcum, some of that fancy stuff Nisi mother sent over last Christmas. And then a massage, a good face massage round the forehead which is the worryin part. Cause you gots to take care of the older folks. And let them know they still needed to run the mimeo machine and keep the spark plugs clean and fix the mailboxes for folks who might help us get the breakfast program goin, and the school for the little kids and the campaign and all. Cause old folks is the nation. That what Nisi was sayin and I mean to do my part.

"I imagine you are a very pretty woman, Miss Hazel."

"I surely am," I say just like the hussy my daughter always say I was.

STUDY QUESTIONS

The narrator in "Bartleby the Scrivener" is a classic storyteller. The narrator in "The Yellow Wall-Paper" is a diarist. Both speak a careful, polished, "literary" English.

In contrast, the narrator of "My Man Bovanne" is a conversationalist. She speaks to us directly—"if you notice," "mind you"—and she speaks with the words and rhythm of her natural, conversational speech. She is not an uneducated woman: she can use phrases like "generation gap" and "apolitical"; and she is, in her "grass roots" way, one of her community's leaders. But, as her story points out, she insists on recognition for her own and others' individuality: and her voice is an important part of that individuality.

It is an important element in the story as well. Consider:

1. How do the narrator's voice and her idiom lend humor to her portrayal of the benefit evening? How does it help to put her children's concerns in perspective?
2. How does Bambara draw a portrait of this woman who "mean[s] to do [her] part" for the "little kids" and the "old folks"? What elements stand out? How are they blended into a coherent portrait?
3. How do the family conflict and the larger social issues illuminate each other? What ideas and emotions does the narrator bring to each?
4. What are your feelings about the narrator at the different stages of the story?
5. If you were to project this story into the future, would you expect things to work out well? Why or why not?

Not for Sale

Judith Ortiz Cofer (1952–   )

El Árabe was what the Puerto Rican women called him. He sold them beautiful things from his exotic homeland in the afternoons, at that hour when the day's work is done and there is a little time before the evening duties. He did not carry anything men would buy. His merchandise, mostly linens, was impractical but exquisite. The bed covers were gorgeously woven into oriental tales that he narrated to his customers in his halting Spanish. My mother bought the Scheherazade. It was expensive, but she desired it for my bed, since it was the year when I was being denied everything by my father: no dating like other sixteen-year-olds (I was a decent Puerto Rican señorita, not a wild American teenager); no driver's license (the streets of Paterson, New Jersey, were too dangerous for an inexperienced driver—he would take me where I needed to go); no end-of-the-school-year weekend trip with my junior class to Seaside Heights (even though three teachers would be chaperoning us). *No, no, no,* with a short Spanish "o." Final: no lingering vowels in my father's pronouncements.

She knew that I could be brought out of my surliness, my seething anger at my father's constant vigilance, by a visit from the storytelling salesman. On the days when I heard the heavy footfall on the staircase announcing his coming, I would emerge from my room, where I kept company only with my English-language books no one else in the house could read. Since I was not allowed to linger at the drugstore with my high school classmates nor to go out socially—unless my father could be persuaded to let me after interrogations and arguments I had come to dread—I had turned to reading in seclusion. Books kept me from going mad. They allowed me to imagine my circumstances as romantic: some days I was an Indian princess living in a *zenana,* a house of women, keeping myself pure, being trained for a brilliant future. Other days I was a prisoner: Papillon, preparing myself for my great flight to freedom. When El Árabe came to our door, bearing his immense stack of bed linens on his shoulder, I ran to let him in. Mother brought him a glass of cold water as he settled into a rocking chair. I sat on the linoleum floor Indian-style while he spread his merchandise in front of us. Sometimes he brought jewelry too. He carried the rings and bracelets in a little red velvet bag he pulled out of his coat pocket. The day he showed us the Scheherazade bedspread, he emptied the glittering contents of the velvet bag on my lap, then he took my hand and fitted a gold ring with an immense green stone on my finger. It was ornate and covered my finger up to the knuckle, scratching the tender skin in between fingers. Feeling nervous, I laughed and tried to take it off. But he shook his head no. He said that he wanted me to keep the ring on while he told me some of the stories woven on the bedspread. It was a magic ring, he said, that would help me understand. My mother gave me a little frown from the doorway behind El Árabe, meaning *Be polite but give it back soon.* El Árabe settled back to tell his stories. Every so often he would unfold another corner of the bedspread to illustrate a scene.

On a gold background with green threads running through it, glossy like the patina on the dome at city hall, the weavers had put the seated figure of the storytelling woman among the characters she had created. She seemed to be invisible to them. In each panel she sat slightly behind the action in the posture of wisdom, which the salesman demonstrated: mouth parted and arms extended toward her audience, like a Buddha or a sacred dancer. While Sinbad wields his sword at a pirate, Scheherazade sits calmly in between them. She can be found on the street corner, where Aladdin trades his new lamps for old. But he does not see her.

El Árabe spoke deliberately, but his Spanish was still difficult to understand. It was as if his tongue had trouble with certain of our sound combinations. But he was patient. When he saw that one of us had lost the thread of the story, he would begin again, sometimes at the beginning.

This usually drove my mother out of the room, but I understood that these tales were one continuous story to him. If broken, the pattern would be ruined. They had to be told all the way through. I looked at him closely as he spoke. He appeared to be about my father's age, but it was hard to tell, because a thick beard covered most of his face. His eyes revealed his fatigue. He was stooped from carrying his bundles from building to building, I assumed. No one seemed to know where he lived or whether he had a family. But on the day of the Scheherazade stories he told me about his son. The subject seemed to arise naturally out of the last tale. The king who beheaded his brides was captivated by the storytelling woman and spared her life. I felt uneasy with this ending, though I had read it before, not trusting the gluttonous King Shahryar to keep his word. And what would happen to Scheherazade when she ran out of stories? It was always the same with these fairy tales: the plot was fascinating, but the ending was unsatisfactory to me. "Happily ever after" was a loose knot tied on a valuable package.

El Árabe took the first payment on the bedspread from my mother who had, I knew, gotten the dollar bills out of her underwear drawer where she kept her "secret" little stash of money in the foot of a nylon stocking. She probably thought that neither my father nor I would have any reason to look there. But in that year of my seclusion, nothing was safe from my curiosity: if I could not go out and explore the world, I would learn what I could from within the four walls. Sometimes I was Anne Frank, and what little there was to discover from my keepers belonged by rights to me.

She counted out ten dollars slowly into his hand. He opened his little notebook with frayed pages. He wrote with a pencil: the full amount at the top, her name, the date, and "10.00" with a flourish. She winced a little as she followed his numbers. It would take her a long time to pay it off. She asked me if I really wanted it—three times. But she knew what it meant to me.

My mother left with the bedspread, explaining that she wanted to see how it would look on my bed. El Árabe seemed reluctant to leave. He lit a slender, aromatic cigarette he took out of a gold case with a little diamond in the middle. Then he repeated the story of Scheherazade's winning over of her husband. Though I was by now weary of the repetition, I listened politely. It was then that he said that he had a son, a handsome young man who wanted very much to come to America to take over the business. There was much money to be made. I nodded, not really understanding why he was telling me all this.

But I fell under the spell of his words as he described a heroic vision of a handsome man who rode thoroughbreds over a golden desert. Without my being aware of it, the afternoon passed quickly. It caught me entirely by surprise when I heard the key turning in the front door lock. I was really chagrined at being found out of my room by my father.

He walked in on us before I had time to rise from my childish position on the floor at El Árabe's feet.

He came in, smelling strongly of sweat and coffee from the factory where he was the watchman. I never understood why sacks of unprocessed coffee beans had to be watched, but that's all I knew about his job. He walked in, looking annoyed and suspicious. He did not like any interruption of his routines: he wanted to find my mother and me in our places when he came home. If she had a friend drop by, Mother had to make sure the visit ended before he arrived. I had stopped inviting my friends over after a while, since his silent hostility made them uncomfortable. Long ago, when I was a little girl, he had spent hours every evening playing with me and reading to me in Spanish. Now, since those activities no longer appealed to me, since I wanted to spend time with other people, he showed no interest in me, except to say no to my requests for permission to go out.

Mother tried to mediate between us by reminding me often of my father's early affection. She explained that teenage girls in Puerto Rico did not go out without chaperons as I wanted to do. They stayed home and helped their mothers and obeyed their fathers. Didn't he give me everything I needed?

I had felt furious at her absurd statements. They did not apply to me, or to the present reality of my life in Paterson, New Jersey. I would work myself into a shouting frenzy. I would scream out my protests that we were not living in some backward country where women were slaves.

"Look," I would point out of the window of our fifth-story apartment in a building at the core of the city. "Do you see palm trees, any sand or blue water? All I see is concrete. We are in the United States. I am an American citizen. I speak English better than Spanish and I am as old as you were when you got married!" The arguments would end with her in tears and the heavy blanket of angry silence falling over both of us. It was no use talking to him either. He had her to comfort him for the unfairness of twelve-hour days in a factory and for being too tired to do anything else but read *La Prensa* in the evenings. I felt like an exile in the foreign country of my parents' house.

My father walked into the living room and immediately focused his eyes on the immense ring on my finger. Without greeting the salesman, without acknowledging my mother who had just returned to the room, he kept pointing at my hand. El Árabe stood up and bowed his head to my father in a strange formal way. Then he said something very odd—something like *I greet you as a kinsman, the ring is a gift to your daughter from my son.* What followed was utter confusion. My father kept asking what? what? what? I struggled to my feet trying to remove the ring from my finger, but it seemed to be stuck. My mother waved me into the kitchen where we worked soap around the swollen finger. In silence we listened to the shouting match in the living room. Both men seemed to be talking at once.

From what I could make out, El Árabe was proposing to my father that I be sold to him—for a fair price—to be his son's bride. This was necessary, since his son could not immigrate quickly unless he married an American citizen. The old salesman was willing to bargain with my father over what I was worth in this transaction. I heard figures, a listing of merchandise, a certain number of cattle and horses his son could sell in their country for cash if that was what my father preferred.

My father seemed to be choking. He could not break through the expert haggler's multilingual stream of offers and descriptions of family wealth. My mother pulled the ring off my finger, scraping away some of the skin along with it. I tried not to cry out, but something broke in me when I heard my father's anguished scream of *Not for sale! Not for sale!* persisting until the salesman fell silent. My mother rushed the ring out to the living room while I tried to regain my self-control. But my father's hoarse voice repeating the one phrase echoed in my ears; even after there was the sound of a door being shut and the dull, heavy footsteps of a burdened man descending the stairs, I heard the pained protest.

Then my father came into the kitchen, where I was standing at the sink, washing the blood off my fingers. The ring had cut me deeply. He stood in silence and, unmoving in the doorway, looked at me as if he had not seen me in a long time or just then for the first time. Then he asked me in a soft voice if I was all right. I nodded, hiding my hand behind my back.

In the months that followed, my mother paid on her account at the door. El Árabe did not come into our apartment again. My father learned the word "yes" in English and practiced saying it occasionally, though "no" remained NO in both languages and easier to say for a nonnative speaker.

On my bed Scheherazade kept telling her stories, which I came to understand would never end—as I had once feared—since it was in my voice that she spoke to me, placing my dreams among hers, weaving them in.

STUDY QUESTIONS

1. The conflicts in this story involve all four characters: the narrator, her father, her mother, and El Árabe. Discuss these conflicts. How do they shape
the story? How are they resolved?
2. A small number of symbolic items play important roles in this story: the
ring, the bedspread, and the figure of Scheherazade. Discuss how the narrator uses these items to enrich the story, and especially to enrich your sense
of the narrator herself.

7

TALES WITHIN TALES

Sometimes a writer wants to spend extra care setting the focus or background of a story, or wants to tie several lightly related stories together. A technique often used in this case is the "tale within a tale." In this technique, an initial narrator sets the scene within which one or more other narrators tell their stories.

This technique dates back at least to the Middle Ages: probably the best-known group of tales within a tale is Chaucer's *Canterbury Tales*. In this lengthy poetic work, the outer tale (or "frame story") concerns a diverse group of people who have met on the road while making a pilgrimage to the shrine of St. Thomas Becket at Canterbury. To pass the time, each tells a story. The stories they tell vary widely in style and subject. The frame story, which describes each of the pilgrims and details their interactions with each other, provides links between the tales, and turns what otherwise might have been a fairly commonplace collection of short verse tales into a masterpiece.

The benefit of using multiple narrators in this manner is the ability to either present material from multiple points of view or reinforce a single philosophy by giving it multiple spokespersons. The two works presented in this chapter show both of these potential benefits. The first work, Joseph Conrad's "Youth: A Narrative," may be called a long story or a short novel (or "novella"). In this story, both narrators speak in the first person, and both share a common philosophy as men who have worked on the great nineteenth-century sailing vessels (as indeed Conrad had done). The second work, Mark Twain's short story "The Celebrated Jumping Frog of Calaveras County," presents two narrators with opposing points of view. The narrator of the inner tale represents that downside of storytelling, the unmitigated bore. The narrator of the outer tale represents the innocent victim who falls into the bore's clutches and lives to tell about it. (In the process, of course, he repeats every word the bore says—and we may be forgiven for finding those tales more amusing than the narrator pretends to find them.)

These, then, are two contrasting specimens of a venerable technique. May you enjoy them both!

Youth: A Narrative

Joseph Conrad (1857–1924)

This could have occurred nowhere but in England, where men and sea interpenetrate, so to speak—the sea entering into the life of most men, and the men knowing something or everything about the sea, in the way of amusement, of travel, or of breadwinning.

We were sitting round a mahogany table that reflected the bottle, the claret glasses, and our faces as we leaned on our elbows. There was a director of companies, an accountant, a lawyer, Marlow, and myself. The director had been a *Conway* boy, the accountant had served four years at sea, the lawyer—a fine crusted Tory, High Churchman, the best of old fellows, the soul of honour—had been chief officer in the P. & O. service in the good old days when mail boats were square-rigged at least on two masts, and used to come down the China Sea before a fair monsoon with stunsails set alow and aloft. We all began life in the merchant service. Between the five of us there was the strong bond of the sea, and also the fellowship of the craft, which no amount of enthusiasm for yachting, cruising, and so on can give, since one is only the amusement of life and the other is life itself.

Marlow (at least I think that is how he spelt his name) told the story, or rather the chronicle, of a voyage:

"Yes, I have seen a little of the Eastern seas; but what I remember best is my first voyage there. You fellows know there are those voyages that seem ordered for the illustration of life, that might stand for a symbol of existence. You fight, work, sweat, nearly kill yourself, sometimes do kill yourself, trying to accomplish something—and you can't. Not from any fault of yours. You simply can do nothing, neither great nor little—not a thing in the world—not even marry an old maid, or get a wretched 600-ton cargo of coal to its port of destination.

"It was altogether a memorable affair. It was my first voyage to the East, and my first voyage as second mate; it was also my skipper's first command. You'll admit it was time. He was sixty if a day; a little man, with a broad, not very straight back, with bowed shoulders and one leg more bandy than the other, he had a queer twisted-about appearance you see so often in men who work in the fields. He had a nutcracker face—chin and nose trying to come together over a sunken mouth—and it was framed in iron-grey fluffy hair, that looked like a chin strap of cotton wool sprinkled with coal dust. And he had blue eyes in that old face of his, which were amazingly like a boy's, with that candid expression some quite common men preserve to the end of their days by a rare internal gift of simplicity of heart and rectitude of soul. What induced him to accept me was a wonder. I had come out of a crack Australian clipper, where I had been third officer, and he seemed to have a prejudice against crack clippers as aristocratic and high-toned. He said to me, 'You know, in this ship you will have to work.' I said I had to work in every ship I had ever been in. 'Ah, but this is different, and you gentlemen out of them big ships; . . . but there! I dare say you will do. Join tomorrow.'

"I joined tomorrow. It was twenty-two years ago; and I was just twenty. How time passes! It was one of the happiest days of my life. Fancy! Second mate for the first time—a really responsible officer! I wouldn't have thrown up my new billet for a fortune. The mate looked me over carefully. He was also an old chap, but of another stamp. He had a Roman nose, a snow-white, long beard, and his name was Mahon, but he insisted that it should be pronounced Mann. He was well connected; yet there was something wrong with his luck, and he had never got on.

"As to the captain, he had been for years in coasters, then in the Mediterranean, and last in the West Indian trade. He had never been round the Capes. He could just write a kind of sketchy hand, and didn't care for writing at all. Both were thorough good seamen of course, and between those two old chaps I felt like a small boy between two grandfathers.

"The ship also was old. Her name was the *Judea*. Queer name, isn't it? She belonged to a man Wilmer, Wilcox—some name like that; but he has been bankrupt and dead these twenty years or more, and his name don't matter. She had been laid up in Shadwell basin for ever so long. You may imagine her state. She was all rust, dust, grime—soot aloft, dirt on deck. To me it was like coming out of a palace into a ruined cottage. She was about 400 tons, had a primitive windlass, wooden latches to the doors, not a bit of brass about her, and a big square stern. There was on it, below her name in big letters, a lot of scrollwork, with the gilt off, and some sort of a coat of arms, with the motto 'Do or Die' underneath. I remember it took my fancy immensely. There was a touch of romance in it, something that made me love the old thing—something that appealed to my youth!

"We left London in ballast—sand ballast—to load a cargo of coal in a northern port for Bankok. Bankok! I thrilled. I had been six years at sea, but had only seen Melbourne and Sydney, very good places, charming places in their way—but Bankok!

"We worked out of the Thames under canvas, with a North Sea pilot on board. His name was Jermyn, and he dodged all day long about the galley drying his handkerchief before the stove. Apparently he never slept. He was a dismal man, with a perpetual tear sparkling at the end of his nose, who either had been in trouble, or was in trouble, or expected to be in trouble—couldn't be happy unless something went wrong. He mistrusted my youth, my common sense, and my seamanship, and made a point of showing it in a hundred little ways. I dare say he was right. It seems to me I knew very little then, and I know not much more now; but I cherish a hate for that Jermyn to this day.

"We were a week working up as far as Yarmouth Roads, and then we got in a gale—the famous October gale of twenty-two years ago. It was wind, lightning, sleet, snow, and a terrific sea. We were flying light, and you may imagine how bad it was when I tell you we had smashed bulwarks and a flooded deck. On the second night she shifted her ballast into the lee bow, and by that time we had been blown off somewhere on the Dogger Bank. There was nothing for it but go below with shovels and try to right her, and there we were in that vast hold, gloomy like a cavern, the tallow dips stuck and flickering on the beams, the gale howling above, the sea tossing about like mad on her side; there we all were, Jermyn, the captain, everyone, hardly able to keep our feet, engaged on that gravedigger's work, and trying to toss shovelfuls of wet sand up to windward. At every tumble of the ship you could see vaguely in the dim light men falling down with a great flourish of shovels. One of the ship's boys (we had two), impressed by the weirdness of the scene, wept as if his heart would break. We could hear him blubbering somewhere in the shadows.

"On the third day the gale died out, and by and by a north-country tug picked us up. We took sixteen days in all to get from London to Tyne! When we got into dock we had lost our turn for loading, and they hauled us off to a tier where we remained for a month. Mrs. Beard (the captain's name was Beard) came from Colchester to see the old man. She lived on board. The crew of runners had left, and there remained only the officers, one boy, and the steward, a mulatto who answered to the name of Abraham. Mrs. Beard was an old woman, with a face all wrinkled and ruddy like a winter apple, and the figure of a young girl. She caught sight of me once, sewing on a button, and insisted on having my shirts to repair. This was something different from the captains' wives I had known on board crack clippers. When I brought her the shirts, she said: 'And the socks? They want mending, I am sure, and John's—Captain Beard's—things are all in order now. I would be glad of something to do.' Bless the old woman. She overhauled my outfit for me, and meantime I read for the first time *Sartor Resartus* and Burnaby's *Ride to Khiva*. I didn't understand much of the first then; but I remember I preferred the soldier to the philosopher at the time; a preference which life has only confirmed. One was a man, and the other was either more— or less. However, they are both dead and Mrs. Beard is dead, and youth, strength, genius, thoughts, achievements, simple hearts—all die. . . . No matter.

"They loaded us at last. We shipped a crew. Eight able seamen and two boys. We hauled off one evening in the buoys at the dock gates, ready to go out, and with a fair prospect of beginning the voyage next day. Mrs. Beard was to start for home by a late train. When the ship was fast we went to tea. We sat rather silent through the meal—Mahon, the old couple, and I. I finished first, and slipped away for a smoke, my cabin being in a deckhouse just against the poop. It was high water, blowing fresh with a drizzle; the double dock gates were opened, and the steam colliers were going in and out in the darkness with their lights burning bright, a great plashing of propellers, rattling of winches, and a lot of hailing on the pierheads. I watched the procession of headlights gliding high and of green lights gliding low in the night, when suddenly a red gleam flashed at me, vanished, came into view again, and remained. The fore end of a steamer loomed up close. I shouted down the cabin, 'Come up, quick!' and then heard a startled voice saying afar in the dark, 'Stop her, sir.' A bell jingled. Another voice cried warning, 'We are going right into that barque, sir.' The answer to this was a gruff 'All right,' and the next thing was a heavy crash as the steamer struck a glancing blow with a bluff of her bow about our forerigging. There was a moment of confusion, yelling, and running about. Steam roared. Then somebody was heard saying, 'All clear, sir.' . . . 'Are you all right?' asked the gruff voice. I had jumped forward to see the damage, and hailed back, 'I think so.' 'Easy astern,' said the gruff voice. A bell jingled. 'What steamer is that?' screamed Mahon. By that time she was no more to us than a bulky shadow manoeuvring a little way off. They shouted at us some name—a woman's name. Miranda or Melissa—or some such thing. 'This means another month in this beastly hole,' said Mahon to me, as we peered with lamps about the splintered bulwarks and broken braces. 'But where's the captain?'

"We had not heard or seen anything of him all that time. We went aft to look. A doleful voice arose hailing somewhere in the middle of the dock, '*Judea* ahoy!' . . . How the devil did he get there? . . . 'Hallo!' we shouted. 'I am adrift in our boat without oars,' he cried. A belated water-man offered his services, and Mahon struck a bargain with him for half a crown to tow our skipper alongside; but it was Mrs. Beard that came up the ladder first. They had been floating about the dock in that mizzly cold rain for nearly an hour. I was never so surprised in my life.

"It appears that when he heard my shout 'Come up' he understood at once what was the matter, caught up his wife, ran on deck, and across, and down into our boat, which was fast to the ladder. Not bad for a sixty-year-old. Just imagine that old fellow saving heroically in his arms that old woman—the woman of his life. He set her down on a thwart, and was ready to climb back on board when the painter came adrift somehow, and away they went together. Of course in the confusion, we did not hear him shouting. He looked abashed. She said cheerfully, 'I suppose it does not matter my losing the train now?' 'No, Jenny—you go below and get warm,' he growled. Then to us: 'A sailor has no business with a wife—I say. There I was, out of the ship. Well, no harm done this time. Let's go and look at what that fool of a steamer smashed.'

"It wasn't much, but it delayed us three weeks. At the end of that time, the captain being engaged with his agents, I carried Mrs. Beard's bag to the railway station and put her all comfy into a third-class carriage. She lowered the window to say, 'You are a good young man. If you see John—Captain Beard—without his muffler at night, just remind him from me to keep his throat well wrapped up.' 'Certainly, Mrs. Beard,' I said. 'You are a good young man; I noticed how attentive you are to John—to Captain—' The train pulled out suddenly; I took my cap off to the old woman: I never saw her again. . . . Pass the bottle.

"We went to sea next day. When we made that start for Bankok we had been already three months out of London. We had expected to be a fortnight or so—at the outside.

"It was January, and the weather was beautiful—the beautiful sunny winter weather that has more charm than in the summertime, because it is unexpected, and crisp, and you know it won't, it can't last long. It's like a windfall, like a godsend, like an unexpected piece of luck.

"It lasted all down the North Sea, all down Channel; and it lasted till we were three hundred miles or so to the westward of the Lizards; then the wind went round to the sou'west and began to pipe up. In two days it blew a gale. The *Judea*, hove to, wallowed on the Atlantic like an old candle box. It blew day after day: it blew with spite, without interval, without mercy, without rest. The world was nothing but an immensity of great foaming waves rushing at us, under a sky low enough to touch with the hand and dirty like a smoked ceiling. In the stormy space surrounding us there was as much flying spray as air. Day after day and night after night there was nothing round the ship but the howl of the wind, the tumult of the sea, the noise of water pouring over her deck. There was no rest for her and no rest for us. She tossed, she pitched, she stood on her head, she sat on her tail, she rolled, she groaned, and we had to hold on while on deck and cling to our bunks when below, in a constant effort of body and worry of mind.

"One night Mahon spoke through the small window of my berth. It opened right into my very bed, and I was lying there sleepless, in my boots, feeling as though I had not slept for years, and could not if I tried. He said excitedly:

" 'You got the sounding rod in here, Marlow? I can't get the pumps to suck. By God! it's no child's play.'

"I gave him the sounding rod and lay down again, trying to think of various things—but I thought only of the pumps. When I came on deck they were still at it, and my watch relieved at the pumps. By the light of the lantern brought on deck to examine the sounding rod I caught a glimpse of their weary, serious faces. We pumped all the four hours. We pumped all night, all day, all the week—watch and watch. She was working herself loose, and leaked badly—not enough to drown us at once, but enough to kill us with the work at the pumps. And while we pumped the ship was going from us piecemeal: the bulwarks went, the stanchions were torn out, the ventilators smashed, the cabin door burst in. There was not a dry spot in the ship. She was being gutted bit by bit. The longboat changed, as if by magic, into matchwood where she stood in her gripes. I had lashed her myself, and was rather proud of my handiwork, which had withstood so long the malice of the sea. And we pumped. And there was no break in the weather. The sea was white like a sheet of foam, like a cauldron of boiling milk; there was not a break in the clouds, no—not the size of a man's hand—no, not for so much as ten seconds. There was for us no sky, there were for us no stars, no sun, no universe—nothing but angry clouds and an infuriated sea. We pumped watch and watch, for dear life; and it seemed to last for months, for years, for all eternity, as though we had been dead and gone to a hell for sailors. We forgot the day of the week, the name of the month, what year it was, and whether we had ever been ashore. The sails blew away, she lay broadside on under a weather cloth, the ocean poured over her, and we did not care. We turned those handles, and had the eyes of idiots. As soon as we had crawled on deck I used to take a round turn with a rope about the men, the pumps, and the mainmast, and we turned, we turned incessantly, with the water to our waists, to our necks, over our heads. It was all one. We had forgotten how it felt to be dry.

"And there was somewhere in me the thought: By Jove! this is the deuce of an adventure—something you read about; and it is my first voyage as second mate—and I am only twenty—and here I am lasting it out as well as any of these men, and keeping my chaps up to the mark. I was pleased. I would not have given up the experience for worlds. I had moments of exultation. Whenever the old dismantled craft pitched heavily with her counter high in the air, she seemed to me to throw up, like an appeal, like a defiance, like a cry to the clouds without mercy, the words written on her stern: '*Judea*, London. Do or Die.'

"O youth! The strength of it, the faith of it, the imagination of it! To me she was not an old rattletrap carting about the world a lot of coal for a freight—to me she was the endeavour, the test, the trial of life. I think of her with pleasure, with affection, with regret—as you would think of someone dead you have loved. I shall never forget her. . . . Pass the bottle.

"One night when tied to the mast, as I explained, we were pumping on, deafened with the wind, and without spirit enough in us to wish ourselves dead, a heavy sea crashed aboard and swept clean over us. As soon as I got my breath I shouted, as in duty bound, 'Keep on, boys!' when suddenly I felt something hard floating on deck strike the calf of my leg. I made a grab at it and missed. It was so dark we could not see each other's faces within a foot—you understand.

"After that thump the ship kept quiet for a while, and the thing, whatever it was, struck my leg again. This time I caught it—and it was a saucepan. At first, being stupid with fatigue and thinking of nothing but the pumps, I did not understand what I had in my hand. Suddenly it dawned upon me, and I shouted, 'Boys, the house on deck is gone. Leave this, and let's look for the cook.'

"There was a deckhouse forward, which contained the galley, the cook's berth, and the quarters of the crew. As we had expected for days to see it swept away, the hands had been ordered to sleep in the cabin—the only safe place in the ship. The steward, Abraham, however, persisted in clinging to his berth, stupidly, like a mule—from sheer fright I believe, like an animal that won't leave a stable falling in an earthquake. So we went to look for him. It was chancing death, since once out of our lashings we were as exposed as if on a raft. But we went. The house was shattered as if a shell had exploded inside. Most of it had gone overboard—stove, men's quarters, and their property, all was gone; but two posts, holding a portion of the bulkhead to which Abraham's bunk was attached, remained as if by a miracle. We groped in the ruins and came upon this, and there he was, sitting in his bunk, surrounded by foam and wreckage, jabbering cheerfully to himself. He was out of his mind; completely and forever mad, with this sudden shock coming upon the fag end of his endurance. We snatched him up, lugged him aft, and pitched him headfirst down the cabin companion. You understand there was no time to carry him down with infinite precautions and wait to see how he got on. Those below would pick him up at the bottom of the stairs all right. We were in a hurry to go back to the pumps. That business could not wait. A bad leak is an inhuman thing.

"One would think that the sole purpose of that fiendish gale had been to make a lunatic of that poor devil of a mulatto. It eased before morning, and next day the sky cleared, and as the sea went down the leak took up. When it came to bending a fresh set of sails the crew demanded to put back—and really there was nothing else to do. Boats gone, decks swept clean, cabin gutted, men without a stitch but what they stood in, stores spoiled, ship strained. We put her head for home, and—would you believe it? The wind came east right in our teeth. It blew fresh, it blew continuously. We had to beat up every inch of the way, but she did not leak so badly, the water keeping comparatively smooth. Two hours' pumping in every four is no joke—but it kept her afloat as far as Falmouth.

"The good people there live on casualties of the sea, and no doubt were glad to see us. A hungry crew of shipwrights sharpened their chisels at the sight of that carcass of a ship. And, by Jove! they had pretty pickings off us before they were done. I fancy the owner was already in a tight place. There were delays. Then it was decided to take part of the cargo out and caulk her topsides. This was done, the repairs finished, cargo reshipped; a new crew came on board, and we went out—for Bankok. At the end of a week we were back again. The crew said they weren't going to Bankok—a hundred and fifty days' passage—in a something hooker that wanted pumping eight hours out of the twenty-four; and the nautical papers inserted again that little paragraph: '*Judea*. Barque. Tyne to Bankok; coals; put back to Falmouth leaky and with crew refusing duty.'

"There were more delays—more tinkering. The owner came down for a day, and said she was as right as a little fiddle. Poor old Captain Beard looked like the ghost of a Geordie skipper—through the worry and humiliation of it. Remember he was sixty, and it was his first command. Mahon said it was a foolish business, and would end badly. I loved the ship more than ever, and wanted awfully to get to Bankok. To Bankok! Magic name, blessed name. Mesopotamia wasn't a patch on it. Remember I was twenty, and it was my first second-mate's billet, and the East was waiting for me.

"We went out and anchored in the outer roads with a fresh crew—the third. She leaked worse than ever. It was as if those confounded shipwrights had actually made a hole in her. This time we did not even go outside. The crew simply refused to man the windlass.

"They towed us back to the inner harbour, and we became a fixture, a feature, an institution of the place. People pointed us out to visitors as 'That 'ere barque that's going to Bankok—has been here six months—put back three times.' On holidays the small boys pulling about in boats would hail, '*Judea*, ahoy!' and if a head showed above the rail shouted, 'Where you bound to?—Bankok?' and jeered. We were only three on board. The poor old skipper mooned in the cabin. Mahon undertook the cooking, and unexpectedly developed all a Frenchman's genius for preparing nice little messes. I looked languidly after the rigging. We became citizens of Falmouth. Every shopkeeper knew us. At the barber's or tobacconist's they asked familiarly, 'Do you think you will ever get to Bankok?' Meantime the owner, the underwriters, and the charterers squabbled amongst themselves in London, and our pay went on. . . . Pass the bottle.

"It was horrid. Morally it was worse than pumping for life. It seemed as though we had been forgotten by the world, belonged to nobody, would get nowhere; it seemed that, as if bewitched, we would have to live forever and ever in that inner harbour, a derision and a byword to generations of longshore loafers and dishonest boatmen. I obtained three months' pay and a five days' leave, and made a rush for London. It took me a day to get there and pretty well another to come back—but three months' pay went all the same. I don't know what I did with it. I went to a music hall, I believe, lunched, dined, and supped in a swell place in Regent Street, and was back in time, with nothing but a complete set of Byron's works and a new railway rug to show for three months' work. The boatman who pulled me off to the ship said: 'Hallo! I thought you had left the old thing. *She* will never get to Bankok.' 'That's all *you* know about it,' I said scornfully—but I didn't like that prophecy at all.

"Suddenly a man, some kind of agent to somebody, appeared with full powers. He had grog blossoms all over his face, an indomitable energy, and was a jolly soul. We leaped into life again. A hulk came alongside, took our cargo, and then we went into dry dock to get our copper stripped. No wonder she leaked. The poor thing, strained beyond endurance by the gale, had, as if in disgust, spat out all the oakum of her lower seams. She was recaulked, new coppered, and made as tight as a bottle. We went back to the hulk and reshipped our cargo.

"Then, on a fine moonlight night, all the rats left the ship.

"We had been infested with them. They had destroyed our sails, consumed more stores than the crew, affably shared our beds and our dangers, and now, when the ship was made seaworthy, concluded to clear out. I called Mahon to enjoy the spectacle. Rat after rat appeared on our rail, took a last look over his shoulder, and leaped with a hollow thud into the empty hulk. We tried to count them, but soon lost the tale. Mahon said: 'Well, well! don't talk to me about the intelligence of rats. They ought to have left before, when we had that narrow squeak from foundering. There you have the proof how silly is the superstition about them. They leave a good ship for an old rotten hulk, where there is nothing to eat, too, the fools! . . . I don't believe they know what is safe or what is good for them, any more than you or I.'

"And after some more talk, we agreed that the wisdom of rats had been grossly overrated, being in fact no greater than that of men.

"The story of the ship was known, by this, all up the Channel from Land's End to the Forelands, and we could get no crew on the south coast. They sent us one all complete from Liverpool, and we left once more—for Bankok.

"We had fair breezes, smooth water right into the tropics, and the old *Judea* lumbered along in the sunshine. When she went eight knots everything cracked aloft, and we tied our caps to our heads; but mostly she strolled on at the rate of three miles an hour. What could you expect? She was tired—that old ship. Her youth was where mine is—where yours is—you fellows who listen to this yarn; and what friend would throw your years and your weariness in your face? We didn't grumble at her. To us aft, at least, it seemed as though we had been born in her, reared in her, had lived in her for ages, had never known any other ship. I would just as soon have abused the old village church at home for not being a cathedral.

"And for me there was also my youth to make me patient. There was all the East before me, and all life, and the thought that I had been tried in that ship and had come out pretty well. And I thought of men of old who, centuries ago, went that road in ships that sailed no better, to the land of palms, and spices, and yellow sands, and of brown nations ruled by kings more cruel than Nero the Roman, and more splendid than Solomon the Jew. The old bark lumbered on, heavy with her age and the burden of her cargo, while I lived the life of youth in ignorance and hope. She lumbered on through an interminable procession of days; and the fresh gilding flashed back at the setting sun, seemed to cry out over the darkening sea the words painted on her stern, '*Judea*, London. Do or Die.'

"Then we entered the Indian Ocean and steered northerly for Java Head. The winds were light. Weeks slipped by. She crawled on, do or die, and people at home began to think of posting us as overdue.

"One Saturday evening, I being off duty, the men asked me to give them an extra bucket of water or so—for washing clothes. As I did not wish to screw on the fresh-water pump so late, I went forward whistling, and with a key in my hand to unlock the forepeak scuttle, intending to serve the water out of a spare tank we kept there.

"The smell down below was as unexpected as it was frightful. One would have thought hundreds of paraffin lamps had been flaring and smoking in that hole for days. I was glad to get out. The man with me coughed and said, 'Funny smell, sir.' I answered negligently, 'It's good for the health they say,' and walked aft.

"The first thing I did was to put my head down the square of the midship ventilator. As I lifted the lid a visible breath, something like a thin fog, a puff of faint haze, rose from the opening. The ascending air was hot, and had a heavy, sooty, paraffiny smell. I gave one sniff, and put down the lid gently. It was no use choking myself. The cargo was on fire.

"Next day she began to smoke in earnest. You see it was to be expected, for though the coal was of a safe kind, that cargo had been so handled, so broken up with handling, that it looked more like smithy coal than anything else. Then it had been wetted—more than once. It rained all the time we were taking it back from the hulk, and now with this long passage it got heated, and there was another case of spontaneous combustion.

"The captain called us into the cabin. He had a chart spread on the table, and looked unhappy. He said, 'The coast of West Australia is near, but I mean to proceed to our destination. It is the hurricane month, too; but we will just keep her head for Bankok, and fight the fire. No more putting back anywhere, if we all get roasted. We will try to stifle this 'ere damned combustion by want of air.'

"We tried. We battened down everything, and still she smoked. The smoke kept coming through imperceptible crevices; it forced itself through bulkheads and covers; it oozed here and there and everywhere in slender threads, in an invisible film, in an incomprehensible manner. It made its way into the cabin, into the forecastle; it poisoned the sheltered places on the deck, it could be sniffed as high as the mainyard. It was clear that if the smoke came out the air came in. This was disheartening. This combustion refused to be stifled.

"We resolved to try water, and took the hatches off. Enormous volumes of smoke, whitish, yellowish, thick, greasy, misty, choking, ascended as high as the trucks. All hands cleared out aft. Then the poisonous cloud blew away, and we went back to work in a smoke that was no thicker now than that of an ordinary factory chimney.

"We rigged the force-pump, got the hose along, and by and by it burst. Well, it was as old as the ship—a prehistoric hose, and past repair. Then we pumped with the feeble head pump, drew water with buckets, and in this way managed in time to pour lots of Indian Ocean into the main hatch. The bright stream flashed in sunshine, fell into a layor of white crawling smoke, and vanished on the black surface of coal. Steam ascended mingling with the smoke. We poured salt water as into a barrel without a bottom. It was our fate to pump in that ship, to pump out of her, to pump into her; and after keeping water out of her to save ourselves from being drowned, we frantically poured water into her to save ourselves from being burnt.

"And she crawled on, do or die, in the serene weather. The sky was a miracle of purity, a miracle of azure. The sea was polished, was blue, was pellucid, was sparkling like a precious stone, extending on all sides, all round to the horizon— as if the whole terrestrial globe had been one jewel, one colossal sapphire, a single gem fashioned into a planet. And on the lustre of the great calm waters the *Judea* glided imperceptibly, enveloped in languid and unclean vapours, in a lazy cloud that drifted to leeward, light and slow; a pestiferous cloud defiling the splendour of sea and sky.

"All this time of course we saw no fire. The cargo smouldered at the bottom somewhere. Once Mahon, as we were working side by side, said to me with a queer smile: 'Now, if she only would spring a tidy leak—like that time when we first left the Channel—it would put a stopper on this fire. Wouldn't it?' I remarked irrelevantly, 'Do you remember the rats?'

"We fought the fire and sailed the ship too as carefully as though nothing had been the matter. The steward cooked and attended on us. Of the other twelve men, eight worked while four rested. Everyone took his turn, captain included. There was equality, and if not exactly fraternity, then a deal of good feeling. Sometimes a man, as he dashed a bucketful of water down the hatchway, would yell out, 'Hurrah for Bankok!' and the rest laughed. But generally we were taciturn and serious—and thirsty. Oh! how thirsty! And we had to be careful with the water. Strict allowance. The ship smoked, the sun blazed. . . . Pass the bottle.

"We tried everything. We even made an attempt to dig down to the fire. No good, of course. No man could remain more than a minute below. Mahon, who went first, fainted there, and the man who went to fetch him out did likewise. We lugged them out on deck. Then I leaped down to show how easily it could be done. They had learned wisdom by that time, and contented themselves by fishing for me with a chain-hook tied to a broom-handle, I believe. I did not offer to go and fetch up my shovel, which was left down below.

"Things began to look bad. We put the longboat into the water. The second boat was ready to swing out. We had also another, a 14-foot thing, on davits aft, where it was quite safe.

"Then, behold, the smoke suddenly decreased. We redoubled our efforts to flood the bottom of the ship. In two days there was no smoke at all. Everybody was on the broad grin. This was on a Friday. On Saturday no work, but sailing the ship of course, was done. The men washed their clothes and their faces for the first time in a fortnight, and had a special dinner given them. They spoke of spontaneous combustion with contempt, and implied *they* were the boys to put out combustions. Somehow we all felt as though we each had inherited a large fortune. But a beastly smell of burning hung about the ship. Captain Beard had hollow eyes and sunken cheeks. I had never noticed so much before how twisted and bowed he was. He and Mahon prowled soberly about hatches and ventilators, sniffing. It struck me suddenly poor Mahon was a very, very old chap. As to me, I was as pleased and proud as though I had helped to win a great naval battle. O! Youth!

"The night was fine. In the morning a homeward bound ship passed us hull down—the first we had seen for months; but we were nearing the land at last, Java Head being about 190 miles off, and nearly due north.

"Next day it was my watch on deck from eight to twelve. At breakfast the captain observed, 'It's wonderful how that smell hangs about the cabin.' About ten, the mate being on the poop, I stepped down on the main deck for a moment. The carpenter's bench stood abaft the mainmast: I leaned against it sucking at my pipe, and the carpenter, a young chap, came to talk to me. He remarked, 'I think we have done very well, haven't we?' and then I perceived with annoyance the fool was trying to tilt the bench. I said curtly, 'Don't, Chips,' and immediately became aware of a queer sensation, of an absurd delusion—I seemed somehow to be in the air. I heard all round me like a pent-up breath released—as if a thousand giants simultaneously had said Phoo!—and felt a dull concussion which made my ribs ache suddenly. No doubt about it—I was in the air, and my body was describing a short parabola. But short as it was, I had the time to think several thoughts in, as far as I can remember, the following order: 'This can't be the carpenter—What is it?—Some accident—Submarine volcano?

Coals, gas!—By Jove! We are being blown up—Everybody's dead—I am falling into the after hatch—I see fire in it.'

"The coal dust suspended in the air of the hold had glowed dull red at the moment of the explosion. In the twinkling of an eye, in an infinitesimal fraction of a second since the first tilt of the bench, I was sprawling full length on the cargo. I picked myself up and scrambled out. It was quick like a rebound. The deck was a wilderness of smashed timber, lying crosswise like trees in a wood after a hurricane; an immense curtain of soiled rags waved gently before me—it was the mainsail blown to strips. I thought, The masts will be toppling over directly; and to get out of the way bolted on all fours towards the poop ladder. The first person I saw was Mahon, with eyes like saucers, his mouth open, and the long white hair standing straight on end round his head like a silver halo. He was just about to go down when the sight of the main deck stirring, heaving up, and changing into splinters before his eyes, petrified him on the top step. I stared at him in unbelief, and he stared at me with a queer kind of shocked curiosity. I did not know that I had no hair, no eyebrows, no eyelashes, that my young moustache was burnt off, that my face was black, one cheek laid open, my nose cut, and my chin bleeding. I had lost my cap, one of my slippers, and my shirt was torn to rags. Of all this I was not aware. I was amazed to see the ship still afloat, the poop deck whole—and, most of all, to see anybody alive. Also the peace of the sky and the serenity of the sea were distinctly surprising. I suppose I expected to see them convulsed with horror. . . . Pass the bottle.

"There was a voice hailing the ship from somewhere—in the air, in the sky—I couldn't tell. Presently I saw the captain—and he was mad. He asked me eagerly, 'Where's the cabin table?' and to hear such a question was a frightful shock. I had just been blown up, you understand, and vibrated with that experience—I wasn't quite sure whether I was alive. Mahon began to stamp with both feet and yelled at him, 'Good God! don't you see the deck's blown out of her?' I found my voice, and stammered out as if conscious of some gross neglect of duty, 'I don't know where the cabin table is.' It was like an absurd dream.

"Do you know what he wanted next? Well, he wanted to trim the yards. Very placidly, and as if lost in thought, he insisted on having the foreyard squared. 'I don't know if there's anybody alive,' said Mahon, almost tearfully. 'Surely,' he said, gently, 'there will be enough left to square the foreyard.'

"The old chap, it seems, was in his own berth winding up the chronometers, when the shock sent him spinning. Immediately it occurred to him—as he said afterwards—that the ship had struck something, and he ran out into the cabin. There, he saw, the cabin table had vanished somewhere. The deck being blown up, it had fallen down into the lazarette of course. Where we had our breakfast that morning he saw only a great hole in the floor. This appeared to him so awfully mysterious, and impressed him so immensely, that what he saw and heard after he got on deck were mere trifles in comparison. And, mark, he noticed directly the wheel deserted and his barque off her course—and his only thought was to get the miserable, stripped, undecked, smouldering shell of a ship back again with her head pointing at her port of destination. Bankok! That's what he was after. I tell you this quiet, bowed, bandy-legged, almost deformed little man was immense in the singleness of his idea and in his placid ignorance of our agitation. He motioned us forward with a commanding gesture, and went to take the wheel himself.

"Yes; that was the first thing we did—trim the yards of that wreck! No one was killed, or even disabled, but everyone was more or less hurt. You should have seen them! Some were in rags, with black faces, like coal-heavers, like sweeps, and had bullet heads that seemed closely cropped, but were in fact singed to the skin. Others, of the watch below, awakened by being shot out from their collapsing bunks, shivered incessantly, and kept on groaning even as we went about our work. But they all worked. That crew of Liverpool hard cases had in them the right stuff. It's my experience they always have. It is the sea that gives it—the vastness, the loneliness surrounding their dark stolid souls. Ah! Well! we stumbled, we crept, we fell, we barked our shins on the wreckage, we hauled. The masts stood, but we did not know how much they might be charred down below. It was nearly calm, but a long swell ran from the west and made her roll. They might go at any moment. We looked at them with apprehension. One could not foresee which way they would fall.

"Then we retreated aft and looked about us. The deck was a tangle of planks on edge, of planks on end, of splinters, of ruined woodwork. The masts rose from that chaos like big trees above a matted undergrowth. The interstices of that mass of wreckage were full of something whitish, sluggish, stirring—of something that was like a greasy fog. The smoke of the invisible fire was coming up again, was trailing, like a poisonous thick mist in some valley choked with deadwood. Already lazy wisps were beginning to curl upwards amongst the mass of splinters. Here and there a piece of timber, stuck upright, resembled a post. Half of a fife rail had been shot through the foresail, and the sky made a patch of glorious blue in the ignobly soiled canvas. A portion of several boards holding together had fallen across the rail, and one end protruded overboard, like a gangway leading upon nothing, like a gangway leading over the deep sea, leading to death—as if inviting us to walk the plank at once and be done with our ridiculous troubles. And still the air, the sky—a ghost, something invisible was hailing the ship.

"Someone had the sense to look over, and there was the helmsman, who had impulsively jumped overboard, anxious to come back. He yelled and swam lustily like a merman, keeping up with the ship. We threw him a rope, and presently he stood amongst us streaming with water and very crestfallen. The captain had surrendered the wheel, and apart, elbow on rail and chin in hand, gazed at the sea wistfully. We asked ourselves, What next? I thought, Now, this is something like. This is great. I wonder what will happen. O youth!

"Suddenly Mahon sighted a steamer far astern. Captain Beard said, 'We may do something with her yet.' We hoisted two flags, which said in the international language of the sea. 'On fire. Want immediate assistance.' The steamer grew bigger rapidly, and by and by spoke with two flags on her foremast, 'I am coming to your assistance.'

"In half an hour she was abreast, to windward, within hail, and rolling slightly, with her engines stopped. We lost our composure, and yelled all together in excitement, 'We've been blown up'. A man in a white helmet, on the bridge cried, 'Yes! All right! All right!' and he nodded his head, and smiled, and made soothing motions with his hand as though at a lot of frightened children. One of the boats dropped in the water, and walked towards us upon the sea with her long oars. Four Calashes pulled a swinging stroke. This was my first sight of Malay seamen. I've known them since, but what struck me then was their unconcern; they came alongside, and even the bowman standing up and holding up to our main chains with the boathook did not deign to lift his head for a glance. I thought people who had been blown up deserved more attention.

"A little man, dry like a chip and agile like a monkey, clambered up. It was the mate of the steamer. He gave one look, and cried, 'O boys—you had better quit.'

"We were silent. He talked apart with the captain for a time—seemed to argue with him. Then they went away together to the steamer.

"When our skipper came back we learned that the steamer was the *Somerville*, Captain Nash, from West Australia to Singapore via Batavia with mails, and that the agreement was she should tow us to Anjer or Batavia, if possible, where we could extinguish the fire by scuttling, and then proceed on our voyage—to Bankok! The old man seemed excited. 'We will do it yet,' he said to Mahon, fiercely. He shook his fist at the sky. Nobody else said a word.

"At noon the steamer began to tow. She went ahead slim and high, and what was left of the *Judea* followed at the end of seventy fathom of tow-rope—followed her swiftly like a cloud of smoke with mastheads protruding above. We went aloft to furl the sails. We coughed on the yards, and were careful about the bunts. Do you see the lot of us there, putting a neat furl on the sails of that ship doomed to arrive nowhere? There was not a man who didn't think that at any moment the masts would topple over. From aloft we could not see the ship for smoke, and they worked carefully, passing the gaskets with even turns. 'Harbour furl—aloft there!' cried Mahon from below.

"You understand this? I don't think one of those chaps expected to get down in the usual way. When we did I heard them saying to each other, 'Well, I thought we would come down overboard, in a lump—sticks and all—blame me if I didn't.' 'That's what I was thinking to myself,' would answer wearily another battered and bandaged scarecrow. And, mind these were men without the drilled-in habit of obedience. To an onlooker they would be a lot of profane scallywags without a redeeming point. What made them do it—what made them obey me when I, thinking consciously how fine it was, made them drop the bunt of the foresail twice to try and do it better? What? They had no professional reputation—no examples, no praise. It wasn't a sense of duty; they all knew well enough how to shirk, and laze, and dodge—when they had a mind to it—and mostly they had. Was it the two pounds ten a month that sent them there? They didn't think their pay half good enough. No; it was something in them, something inborn and subtle and everlasting. I don't say positively that the crew of a French or German merchantman wouldn't have done it, but I doubt whether it would have been done in the same way. There was a completeness in it, something solid like a principle, and masterful like an instinct—a disclosure of something secret—of that hidden something, that gift of good or evil that makes racial difference, that shapes the fate of nations.

"It was that night at ten that, for the first time since we had been fighting it, we saw the fire. The speed of the towing had fanned the smouldering destruction. A blue gleam appeared forward, shining below the wreck of the deck. It wavered in patches, it seemed to stir and creep like the light of a glowworm. I saw it first, and told Mahon. 'Then the game's up,' he said. 'We had better stop this towing, or she will burst out suddenly fore and aft before we can clear out.' We set up a yell; rang bells to attract their attention; they towed on. At last Mahon and I had to crawl forward and cut the rope with an axe. There was no time to cast off the lashings. Red tongues could be seen licking the wilderness of splinters under our feet as we made our way back to the poop.

"Of course they very soon found out in the steamer that the rope was gone. She gave a loud blast of her whistle, her lights were seen sweeping in a wide circle, she came up ranging close alongside, and stopped. We were all in a tight group on the poop looking at her. Every man had saved a little bundle or a bag. Suddenly a conical flame with a twisted top shot up forward and threw upon the black sea a circle of light, with the two vessels side by side and heaving gently in its centre. Captain Beard had been sitting on the gratings still and mute for hours, but now he rose slowly and advanced in front of us, to the mizzen shrouds. Captain Nash hailed: 'Come along! Look sharp. I have mailbags on board. I will take you and your boats to Singapore.'

" 'Thank you! No!' said our skipper. 'We must see the last of the ship.'

" 'I can't stand by any longer,' shouted the other. 'Mails—you know.'

" 'Aye! aye! We are all right.'

" 'Very well! I'll report you in Singapore. . . . Good-bye!'

"He waved his hand. Our men dropped their bundles quietly. The steamer moved ahead, and passing out of the circle of light, vanished at once from our sight, dazzled by the fire which burned fiercely. And then I knew that I would see the East first as commander of a small boat. I thought it fine; and the fidelity to the old ship was fine. We should see the last of her. Oh, the glamour of youth! Oh, the fire of it, more dazzling than the flames of the burning ship, throwing a magic light on the wide earth, leaping audaciously to the sky, presently to be quenched by time, more cruel, more pitiless, more bitter than the sea—and like the flames on the burning ship surrounded by an impenetrable night.

"The old man warned us in his gentle and inflexible way that it was part of our duty to save for the underwriters as much as we could of the ship's gear. Accordingly we went to work aft, while she blazed forward to give us plenty of light. We lugged out a lot of rubbish. What didn't we save? An old barometer fixed with an absurd quantity of screws nearly cost me my life: a sudden rush of smoke came upon me, and I just got away in time. There were various stores, bolts of canvas, coils of rope; the poop looked like a marine bazaar, and the boats were lumbered to the gunwales. One would have thought the old man wanted to take as much as he could of his first command with him. He was very, very quiet, but off his balance evidently. Would you believe it? He wanted to take a length of old stream cable and a kedge anchor with him in the longboat. We said, 'Aye, aye, sir,' deferentially, and on the quiet let the things slip overboard. The heavy medicine chest went that way, two bags of green coffee, tins of paint—fancy, paint!— a whole lot of things. Then I was ordered with two hands into the boats to make a stowage and get them ready against the time it would be proper for us to leave the ship.

"We put everything straight, stepped the longboat's mast for our skipper, who was to take charge of her, and I was not sorry to sit down for a moment. My face felt raw, every limb ached as if broken, I was aware of all my ribs, and would have sworn to a twist in the backbone. The boats, fast astern, lay in a deep shadow, and all around I could see the circle of the sea lighted by the fire. A gigantic flame arose forward straight and clear. It flared fierce, with noises like the whirr of wings, with rumbles as of thunder. There were cracks, detonations, and from the cone of flame the sparks flew upwards, as man is born to trouble, to leaky ships, and to ships that burn.

"What bothered me was that the ship, lying broadside to the swell and to such wind as there was—a mere breath—the boats would not keep astern where they were safe, but persisted, in a pigheaded way boats have, in getting under the counter and then swinging alongside. They were knocking about dangerously and coming near the flame, while the ship rolled on them, and, of course, there was always the danger of the masts going over the side at any moment. I and my two boat keepers kept them off as best we could, with oars and boathooks; but to be constantly at it became exasperating, since there was no reason why we should not leave at once. We could not see those on board, nor could we imagine what caused the delay. The boatkeepers were swearing feebly, and I had not only my share of work but also had to keep at it two men who showed a constant inclination to lay themselves down and let things slide.

"At last I hailed, 'On deck there,' and someone looked over. 'We're ready here,' I said. The head disappeared, and very soon popped up again. 'The captain says, All right, sir, and to keep the boats well clear of the ship.'

"Half an hour passed. Suddenly there was a frightful racket, rattle, clanking of chain, hiss of water, and millions of sparks flew up into the shivering column of smoke that stood leaning slightly above the ship. The catheads had burned away, and the two red-hot anchors had gone to the bottom, tearing out after them two hundred fathom of red-hot chain. The ship trembled, the mass of flame swayed as if ready to collapse, and the fore topgallant mast fell. It darted down like an arrow of fire, shot under, and instantly leaping up within an oar's length of the boats, floated quietly, very black on the luminous sea. I hailed the deck again. After some time a man in an unexpectedly cheerful but also muffled tone, as though he had been trying to speak with his mouth shut, informed me, 'Coming directly, sir,' and vanished. For a long time I heard nothing but the whirr and roar of the fire. There were also whistling sounds. The boats jumped, tugged at the painters, ran at each other playfully, knocked their sides together, or, do what we would, swung in a bunch against the ship's side. I couldn't stand it any longer, and swarming up a rope, clambered aboard over the stern.

"It was as bright as day. Coming up like this, the sheet of fire facing me was a terrifying sight, and the heat seemed hardly bearable at first. On a settee cushion dragged out of the cabin Captain Beard, his legs drawn up and one arm under his head, slept with the light playing on him. Do you know what the rest were busy about? They were sitting on deck right aft, round an open case, eating bread and cheese and drinking bottled stout.

"On the background of flames twisting in fierce tongues above their heads they seemed at home like salamanders, and looked like a band of desperate pirates. The fire sparkled in the whites of their eyes, gleamed on patches of white skin seen through the torn shirts. Each had the marks as of a battle about him— bandaged heads, tied up arms, a strip of dirty rag round a knee—and each man had a bottle between his legs and a chunk of cheese in his hand. Mahon got up. With his handsome and disreputable head, his hooked profile, his long white beard, and with an uncorked bottle in his hand, he resembled one of those reckless sea robbers of old making merry amidst violence and disaster. 'The last meal on board,' he explained solemnly. 'We had nothing to eat all day, and it was no use leaving all this.' He flourished the bottle and indicated the sleeping skipper. 'He said he couldn't swallow anything, so I got him to lie down,' he went on; and as I stared, 'I don't know whether you are aware, young fellow, the man had no sleep to speak of for days—and there will be dam' little sleep in the boats.' 'There will be no boats by and by if you fool about much longer,' I said, indignantly. I walked up to the skipper and shook him by the shoulder. At last he opened his eyes, but did not move. 'Time to leave her, sir,' I said quietly.

"He got up painfully, looked at the flames, at the sea sparkling round the ship, and black, black as ink farther away; he looked at the stars shining dim through a thin veil of smoke in a sky black, black as Erebus.

" 'Youngest first,' he said.

"And the ordinary seaman, wiping his mouth with the back of his hand, got up, clambered over the taffrail, and vanished. Others followed. One, on the point of going over, stopped short to drain his bottle, and with a great swing of his arm flung it at the fire. 'Take this!' he cried.

"The skipper lingered disconsolately, and we left him to commune alone for a while with his first command. Then I went up again and brought him away at last. It was time. The ironwork on the poop was hot to the touch.

"Then the painter of the longboat was cut, and the three boats, tied together, drifted clear of the ship. It was just sixteen hours after the explosion when we abandoned her. Mahon had charge of the second boat, and I had the smallest—the 14-foot thing. The longboat would have taken the lot of us; but the skipper said we must save as much property as we could—for the underwriters—and so I got my first command. I had two men with me, a bag of biscuits, a few tins of meat, and a beaker of water. I was ordered to keep close to the longboat, that in case of bad weather we might be taken into her.

"And do you know what I thought? I thought I would part company as soon as I could. I wanted to have my first command all to myself. I wasn't going to sail in a squadron if there were a chance for independent cruising. I would make land by myself. I would beat the other boats. Youth! All youth! The silly, charming, beautiful youth.

"But we did not make a start at once. We must see the last of the ship. And so the boats drifted about that night, heaving and setting on the swell. The men dozed, waked, sighed, groaned. I looked at the burning ship.

"Between the darkness of earth and heaven she was burning fiercely upon a disc of purple sea shot by the blood-red play of gleams; upon a disc of water glittering and sinister. A high, clear flame, an immense and lonely flame, ascended from the ocean, and from its summit the black smoke poured continuously at the sky. She burned furiously; mournful and imposing like a funeral pile kindled in the night, surrounded by the sea, watched over by the stars. A magnificent death had come like a grace, like a gift, like a reward to that old ship at the end of her laborious days. The surrender of her weary ghost to the keeping of stars and sea was stirring like the sight of a glorious triumph. The masts fell just before daybreak, and for a moment there was a burst and turmoil of sparks that seemed to fill with flying fire the night patient and watchful, the vast night lying silent upon the sea. At daylight she was only a charred shell, floating still under a cloud of smoke and bearing a glowing mass of coal within.

"Then the oars were got out, and the boats forming in a line moved round her remains as if in procession—the longboat leading. As we pulled across her stern a slim dart of fire shot out viciously at us, and suddenly she went down, head first, in a great hiss of steam. The unconsumed stern was the last to sink; but the paint had gone, had cracked, had peeled off, and there were no letters, there was no word, no stubborn device that was like her soul, to flash at the rising sun her creed and her name.

"We made our way north. A breeze sprang up, and about noon all the boats came together for the last time. I had no mast or sail in mine, but I made a mast out of a spare oar and hoisted a boat awning for a sail, with a boathook for a yard. She was certainly overmasted, but I had the satisfaction of knowing that with the wind aft I could beat the other two. I had to wait for them. Then we all had a look at the captain's chart, and, after a sociable meal of hard bread and water, got our last instructions. These were simple: steer north, and keep together as much as possible. 'Be careful with that jury rig, Marlow,' said the captain; and Mahon, as I sailed proudly past his boat, wrinkled his curved nose and hailed, 'You will sail that ship of yours under water, if you don't look out, young fellow.' He was a malicious old man—and may the deep sea where he sleeps now rock him gently, rock him tenderly to the end of time!

"Before sunset a thick rainsquall passed over the two boats, which were far astern, and that was the last I saw of them for a time. Next day I sat steering my cockleshell—my first command—with nothing but water and sky around me. I did sight in the afternoon the upper sails of a ship far away, but said nothing, and my men did not notice her. You see I was afraid she might be homeward bound, and I had no mind to turn back from the portals of the East. I was steering for Java—another blessed name—like Bankok, you know. I steered many days.

"I need not tell you what it is to be knocking about in an open boat. I remember nights and days of calm, when we pulled, we pulled, and the boat seemed to stand still, as if bewitched within the circle of the sea horizon. I remember the heat, the deluge of rainsqualls that kept us bailing for dear life (but filled our water cask), and I remember sixteen hours on end with a mouth dry as a cinder and a steering oar over the stern to keep my first command head on to a breaking sea. I did not know how good a man I was till then. I remember the drawn faces, the dejected figures of my two men, and I remember my youth and the feeling that will never come back any more—the feeling that I could last forever, outlast the sea, the earth, and all men; the deceitful feeling that lures us on to joys, to perils, to love, to vain effort—to death; the triumphant conviction of strength, the heat of life in the handful of dust, the glow in the heart that with every year grows dim, grows cold, grows small, and expires—and expires, too soon, too soon—before life itself.

"And this is how I see the East. I have seen its secret places and have looked into its very soul; but now I see it always from a small boat, a high outline of mountains, blue and afar in the morning; like faint mist at noon; a jagged wall of purple at sunset. I have the feel of the oar in my hand, the vision of a scorching blue sea in my eyes. And I see a bay, a wide bay, smooth as glass and polished like ice, shimmering in the dark. A red light burns far off upon the gloom of the land, and the night is soft and warm. We drag at the oars with aching arms, and suddenly a puff of wind, a puff faint and tepid and laden with strange odours of blossoms, of aromatic wood, comes out of the still night—the first sigh of the East on my face. That I can never forget. It was impalpable and enslaving, like a charm, like a whispered promise of mysterious delight.

"We had been pulling this finishing spell for eleven hours. Two pulled, and he whose turn it was to rest sat at the tiller. We had made out the red light in that bay and steered for it, guessing it must mark some small coasting port. We passed two vessels, outlandish and high sterned, sleeping at anchor, and, approaching the light, now very dim, ran the boat's nose against the end of a jutting wharf. We were blind with fatigue. My men dropped the oars and fell off the thwarts as if dead. I made fast to a pile. A current rippled softly. The scented obscurity of the shore was grouped into vast masses, a density of colossal clumps of vegetation, probably—mute and fantastic shapes. And at their foot the semicircle of a beach gleamed faintly, like an illusion. There was not a light, not a stir, not a sound. The mysterious East faced me, perfumed like a flower, silent like death, dark like a grave.

"And I sat weary beyond expression, exulting like a conqueror, sleepless and entranced as if before a profound, a fateful enigma.

"A splashing of oars, a measured dip reverberating on the level of water, intensified by the silence of the shore into loud claps, made me jump up. A boat, a European boat, was coming in. I invoked the name of the dead: I hailed: *Judea* ahoy! A thin shout answered.

"It was the captain. I had beaten the flagship by three hours, and I was glad to hear the old man's voice again, tremulous and tired. 'Is it you, Marlow?' 'Mind the end of that jetty, sir,' I cried.

"He approached cautiously, and brought up with the deep sea lead line which we had saved—for the underwriters. I eased my painter and fell alongside. He sat, a broken figure at the stern, wet with dew, his hands clasped in his lap. His men were asleep already. 'I had a terrible time of it,' he murmured. 'Mahon is behind—not very far.' We conversed in whispers, in low whispers, as if afraid to wake up the land. Guns, thunder, earthquakes would not have awakened the men just then.

"Looking round as we talked, I saw away at sea a bright light travelling in the night. 'There's a steamer passing the bay,' I said. She was not passing, she was entering, and she even came close and anchored. 'I wish,' said the old man, 'you would find out whether she is English. Perhaps they could give us passage somewhere.' He seemed nervously anxious. So by dint of punching and kicking I started one of my men into a state of somnambulism, and giving him an oar, took another and pulled towards the lights of the steamer.

"There was a murmur of voices in her, metallic hollow clangs of the engine room, footsteps on the deck. Her ports shone, round like dilated eyes. Shapes moved about, and there was a shadowy man high up on the bridge. He heard my oars.

"And then, before I could open my lips, the East spoke to me, but it was in a Western voice. A torrent of words was poured into the enigmatical, the fateful silence; outlandish, angry words, mixed with words and even whole sentences of good English, less strange but even more surprising. The voice swore and cursed violently; it riddled the solemn peace of the bay by a volley of abuse. It began by calling me Pig, and from that went crescendo into unmentionable adjectives— in English. The man up there raged aloud in two languages, and with a sincerity in his fury that almost convinced me I had, in some way, sinned against the harmony of the universe. I could hardly see him, but began to think he would work himself into a fit.

"Suddenly he ceased, and I could hear him snorting and blowing like a porpoise. I said:

" 'What steamer is this, pray?'

" 'Eh? What's this? And who are you?'

" 'Castaway crew of an English barque burnt at sea. We came here tonight. I am the second mate. The captain is in the longboat, and wishes to know if you would give us a passage somewhere.'

" 'Oh, my goodness! I say. . . . This is the *Celestial* from Singapore on her return trip. I'll arrange with your captain in the morning, . . . and . . . I say . . . did you hear me just now?'

" 'I should think the whole bay heard you.'

" 'I thought you were a shoreboat. Now, look here—this infernal lazy scoundrel of a caretaker has gone to sleep again—curse him. The light is out, and I nearly ran foul of the end of this damned jetty. This is the third time he plays me this trick. Now, I ask you, can anybody stand this kind of thing? It's enough to drive a man out of his mind. I'll report him . . . I'll get the Assistant Resident to give him the sack, by . . . ! See—there's no light. It's out, isn't it? I take you to witness the light's out. There should be a light, you know. A red light on the—'

" 'There was a light,' I said, mildly.

" 'But it's out, man! What's the use of talking like this? You can see for yourself it's out—don't you? If you had to take a valuable steamer along this Godforsaken coast you would want a light, too. I'll kick him from end to end of his miserable wharf. You'll see if I don't. I will—'

" 'So I may tell my captain you'll take us?' I broke in.

" 'Yes, I'll take you. Good-night,' he said, brusquely.

"I pulled back, made fast again to the jetty, and then went to sleep at last. I had faced the silence of the East. I had heard some of its language. But when I opened my eyes again the silence was as complete as though it had never been broken. I was lying in a flood of light, and the sky had never looked so far, so high, before. I opened my eyes and lay without moving.

"And then I saw the men of the East—they were looking at me. The whole length of the jetty was full of people. I saw brown, bronze, yellow faces, the black eyes, the glitter, the colour of an Eastern crowd. And all these beings stared without a murmur, without a sigh, without a movement. They stared down at the boats, at the sleeping men who at night had come to them from the sea. Nothing moved. The fronds of palms stood still against the sky. Not a branch stirred along the shore, and the brown roofs of hidden houses peeped through the green foliage, through the big leaves that hung shining and still like leaves forged of heavy metal. This was the East of the ancient navigators, so old, so mysterious, resplendent and sombre, living and unchanged, full of danger and promise. And these were the men. I sat up suddenly. A wave of movement passed through the crowd from end to end, passed along the heads, swayed the bodies, ran along the jetty like a ripple on the water, a breath of wind on a field—and all was still again. I see it now—the wide sweep of the bay, the glittering sands, the wealth of green infinite and varied, the sea blue like the sea of a dream, the crowd of attentive faces, the blaze of vivid colour—the water reflecting it all, the curve of the shore, the jetty, the high-sterned outlandish craft floating still, and the three boats with the tired men from the West sleeping, unconscious of the land and the people and of the violence of sunshine. They slept thrown across the thwarts, curled on bottom boards, in the careless attitudes of death. The head of the old skipper, leaning back in the stern of the longboat, had fallen on his breast, and he looked as though he would never wake. Farther out old Mahon's face was upturned to the sky, with the long white beard spread out on his breast, as though he had been shot where he sat at the tiller; and a man, all in a heap in the bows of the boat, slept with both arms embracing the steamhead and with his cheek laid on the gunwale. The East looked at them without a sound.

"I have known its fascination since; I have seen the mysterious shores, the still water, the lands of brown nations, where a stealthy Nemesis lies in wait, pursues, overtakes so many of the conquering race, who are proud of their wisdom, of their knowledge, of their strength. But for me all the East is contained in that vision of my youth. It is all in that moment when I opened my young eyes on it. I came upon it from a tussle with the sea—and I was young—and I saw it looking at me. And this is all that is left of it! Only a moment; a moment of strength, of romance, of glamour—of youth! . . . A flick of sunshine upon a strange shore, the time to remember, the time for a sigh, and—good-bye!—Night—Good-bye . . . !"

He drank.

"Ah! The good old time—the good old time. Youth and the sea. Glamour and the sea! The good, strong sea, the salt, bitter sea, that could whisper to you and roar at you and knock your breath out of you!"

He drank again.

"By all that's wonderful it is the sea, I believe, the sea itself—or is it youth alone? Who can tell? But you here—you all had something out of life: money, love—whatever one gets on shore—and, tell me, wasn't that the best time, that time when we were young at sea; young and had nothing, on the sea that gives nothing, except hard knocks—and sometimes a chance to feel your strength—that only—what you all regret?"

And we all nodded at him: the man of finance, the man of accounts, the man of law, we all nodded at him over the polished table that like a still sheet of brown water reflected our faces, lined, wrinkled; our faces marked by toil, by deceptions, by success, by love; our weary eyes looking still, looking always, looking anxiously for something out of life, that while it is expected is already gone—has passed unseen, in a sigh, in a flash—together with the youth, with the strength, with the romance of illusions.

STUDY QUESTIONS

1. What does the use of the frame story, with its dual narrators, add to Conrad's treatment of the theme "youth"?
2. Marlow begins his narration on what seems a somber note, declaring that

> . . . there are those voyages that seem ordered for the illustration of life, that might stand for a symbol of existence. You fight, work, sweat, nearly kill yourself, sometimes do kill yourself, trying to accomplish something—and you can't. Not from any fault of yours. You simply can do nothing. . . .

Yet he ends it with a paean in praise of youth as the best time of life—with the same voyage still serving as example. How does he get from one tone to the other? How does he keep the two outlooks balanced, without letting them contradict each other?

The Celebrated Jumping Frog of Calaveras County

Mark Twain (1835–1910)

In compliance with the request of a friend of mine, who wrote me from the East, I called on good-natured, garrulous old Simon Wheeler, and inquired after my friend's friend, Leonidas W. Smiley, as requested to do, and I hereunto append the result. I have a lurking suspicion that *Leonidas W.* Smiley is a myth; that my friend never knew such a personage; and that he only conjectured that if I asked old Wheeler about him, it would remind him of his infamous *Jim* Smiley, and he would go to work and bore me to death with some exasperating reminiscence of him as long and as tedious as it should be useless to me. If that was the design, it succeeded.

I found Simon Wheeler dozing comfortably by the barroom stove of the dilapidated tavern in the decayed mining camp of Angel's, and I noticed that he was fat and bald-headed, and had an expression of winning gentleness and simplicity upon his tranquil countenance. He roused up, and gave me good-day. I told him a friend of mine had commissioned me to make some inquiries about a cherished companion of his boyhood named *Leonidas W.* Smiley—*Rev. Leonidas W.* Smiley, a young minister of the Gospel, who he had heard was at one time a resident of Angel's Camp. I added that if Mr. Wheeler could tell me anything about this Rev. Leonidas W. Smiley, I would feel under many obligations to him.

Simon Wheeler backed me into a corner and blockaded me there with his chair, and then sat down and reeled off the monotonous narrative which follows this paragraph. He never smiled, he never frowned, he never changed his voice from the gentle-flowing key to which he tuned his initial sentence, he never betrayed the slightest suspicion of enthusiasm; but all through the interminable narrative there ran a vein of impressive earnestness and sincerity, which showed me plainly that, so far from his imagining that there was anything ridiculous or funny about his story, he regarded it as a really important matter, and admired its two heroes as men of transcendent genius in *finesse*. I let him go on in his own way, and never interrupted him once.

"Rev. Leonidas W. H'm, Reverend Le—well, there was a feller here once by the name of *Jim* Smiley, in the winter of '49—or may be it was the spring of '50—I don't recollect exactly, somehow, though what makes me think it was one or the other is because I remember the big flume warn't finished when he first come to the camp; but any way, he was the curiosest man about always betting on anything that turned up you ever see, if he could get anybody to bet on the other side; and if couldn't he'd change sides. Any way that suited the other man would suit *him*—any way just so's he got a bet, *he* was satisfied. But still he was lucky, uncommon lucky; he most always come out winner. He was always ready and laying for a chance; there couldn't be no solit'ry thing mentioned but that feller'd offer to bet on it, and take ary side you please, as I was just telling you. If there was a horse-race, you'd find him flush or you'd find him busted at the end of it; if there was a dog-fight, he'd bet on it; if there was a cat-fight, he'd bet on it; if there was a chicken-fight, he'd bet on it; why, if there was two birds setting on a fence, he would bet you which one would fly first; or if there was a camp-meeting, he would be there reg'lar to bet on Parson Walker, which he judged to be the best exhorter about here, and so he was too, and a good man. If he even see a straddle-bug start to go anywheres, he would bet you how long it would take him to get to—to wherever he was going to, and if you took him up, he would foller that straddle-bug to Mexico but what he would find out where he was bound for and how long he was on the road. Lots of the boys here has seen that Smiley, and can tell you about him. Why, it never made no difference to *him*—he'd bet on *any* thing—the dangest feller. Parson Walker's wife laid very sick once, for a good while, and it seemed as if they warn't going to save her; but one morning he come in, and Smiley up and asked him how she was, and he said she was considerable better—thank the Lord for his inf'nite mercy—and coming on so smart that with the blessing of Prov'dence she'd get well yet; and Smiley, before he thought, says, "Well, I'll resk two-and-a-half she don't anyway."

Thish-yer Smiley had a mare—the boys called her the fifteen-minute nag, but that was only in fun, you know, because of course she was faster than that—and he used to win money on that horse, for all she was so slow and always had the asthma, or the distemper, or the consumption, or something of that kind. They used to give her two or three hundred yards start, and then pass her under way; but always at the fag end of the race she'd get excited and desperate like, and come cavorting and straddling up, and scattering her legs around limber, sometimes in the air, and sometimes out to one side among the fences, and kicking up m-o-r-e dust and raising m-o-r-e racket with her coughing and sneezing and blowing her nose—and *always* fetch up at the stand just about a neck ahead, as near as you could cipher it down.

And he had a little small bull-pup, that to look at him you'd think he warn't worth a cent but to set around and look ornery and lay for a chance to steal something. But as soon as money was up on him he was a different dog; his under-jaw'd begin to stick out like the fo'castle of a steamboat, and his teeth would uncover and shine like the furnaces. And a dog might tackle him and bully-rag him, and bite him, and throw him over his shoulder two or three times, and Andrew Jackson—which was the name of the pup—Andrew Jackson would never let on but what *he* was satisfied, and hadn't expected nothing else—and the bets being doubled and doubled on the other side all the time, till the money was all up; and then all of a sudden he would grab the other dog jest by the j'int of his hind leg and freeze to it—not chaw, you understand, but only just grip and hang on till they throwed up the sponge, if it was a year. Smiley always come out winner on that pup, till he harnessed a dog once that didn't have no hind legs, because they'd been sawed off in a circular saw, and when the thing had gone along far enough, and the money was all up, and he come to make a snatch for his pet holt, he see in a minute how he'd been imposed on, and how the other dog had him in the door, so to speak, and he 'peared surprised, and then he looked sorter discouraged-like, and didn't try no more to win the fight, and so he got shucked out bad. He gave Smiley a look, as much as to say his heart was broke, and it was *his* fault, for putting up a dog that hadn't no hind legs for him to take holt of, which was his main dependence in a fight, and then he limped off a piece and laid down and died. It was a good pup, was that Andrew Jackson, and would have made a name for hisself if he'd lived, for the stuff was in him and he had genius—I know it, because he hadn't no opportunities to speak of, and it don't stand to reason that a dog could make such a fight as he could under them circumstances if he hadn't no talent. It always makes me feel sorry when I think of that last fight of his'n, and the way it turned out.

Well, thish-yer Smiley had rat-tarriers, and chicken cocks, and tomcats and all them kind of things, till you couldn't rest, and you couldn't fetch nothing for him to bet on but he'd match you. He ketched a frog one day, and took him home, and said he cal'lated to educate him; and so he never done nothing for three months but set in his back yard and learn that frog to jump. And you bet you he *did* learn him, too. He'd give him a little pinch behind, and the next minute you'd see that frog whirling in the air like a doughnut—see him turn one summerset, or may be a couple, if he got a good start, and come down flat-footed and all right, like a cat. He got him up so in the matter of ketching flies, and kep' him in practice so constant, that he'd nail a fly every time as fur as he could see him. Smiley said all a frog wanted was education, and he could do 'most anything—and I believe him. Why, I've seen him set Dan'l Webster down here on this floor—Dan'l Webster was the name of the frog—and sing out,

"Flies, Dan'l, flies!" and quicker'n you could wink he'd spring straight up and snake a fly off'n the counter there, and flop down on the floor ag'in as solid as a gob of mud, and fall to scratching the side of his head with his hind foot as indifferent as if he hadn't no idea he'd been doin' any more'n any frog might do. You never see a frog so modest and straightfor'ard as he was, for all he was so gifted. And when it come to fair and square jumping on a dead level, he could get over more ground at one straddle than any animal of his breed you ever see. Jumping on a dead level was his strong suit, you understand; and when it come to that, Smiley would ante up money on him as long as he had a red. Smiley was monstrous proud of his frog, and well he might be, for fellers that had traveled and been everywheres all said he laid over any frog that ever *they* see.

Well, Smiley kep' the beast in a little lattice box, and he used to fetch him down town sometimes and lay for a bet. One day a feller—a stranger in the camp, he was—come acrost him with his box, and says:

"What might it be that you've got in the box?"

And Smiley says, sorter indifferent-like, "It might be a parrot, or it might be a canary, maybe, but it ain't—it's only just a frog."

And the feller took it, and looked at it careful, and turned it round this way and that, and says, "H'm—so 'tis. Well, what's *he* good for?"

"Well," Smiley says, easy and careless, "he's good enough for *one* thing, I should judge—he can outjump any frog in Calaveras county."

The feller took the box again, and took another long, particular look, and give it back to Smiley, and says, very deliberate, "Well," he says, "I don't see no p'ints about that frog that's any better'n any other frog."

"Maybe you don't," Smiley says. "Maybe you understand frogs and maybe you don't understand 'em; maybe you've had experience, and maybe you ain't only a amature, as it were. Anyways, I've got *my* opinion, and I'll resk forty dollars that he can outjump any frog in Calaveras county."

And the feller studied a minute, and then says, kinder sad like, "Well, I'm only a stranger here, and I ain't got no frog; but if I had a frog, I'd bet you."

And then Smiley says, "That's all right—that's all right—if you'll hold my box a minute, I'll go and get you a frog." And so the feller took the box, and put up his forty dollars along with Smiley's, and set down to wait.

So he set there a good while thinking and thinking to hisself, and then he got the frog out and prized his mouth open and took a teaspoon and filled him full of quail shot—filled him pretty near up to his chin—and set him on the floor. Smiley he went to the swamp and slopped around in the mud for a long time, and finally he ketched a frog, and fetched him in, and give him to this feller, and says:

"Now, if you're ready, set him alongside of Dan'l, with his forepaws just even with Dan'l's, and I'll give the word." Then he says, "One—two—three—*git!*" and him and the feller touched up the frogs from behind, and the new frog hopped off lively, but Dan'l give a heave, and hysted up his shoulders—so—like a Frenchman, but it warn't no use—he couldn't budge; he was planted as solid as a church, and he couldn't no more stir than if he was anchored out. Smiley was a good deal surprised, and he was disgusted too, but he didn't have no idea what the matter was, of course.

The feller took the money and started away; and when he was going out at the door, he sorter jerked his thumb over his shoulder—so—at Dan'l, and says again, very deliberate, "Well," he says, "*I* don't see no p'ints about that frog that's any better'n any other frog."

Smiley stood scratching his head and looking down at Dan'l a long time, and at last he says, "I do wonder what in the nation that frog throw'd off for—I wonder if there ain't something the matter with him—he 'pears to look mighty baggy, somehow." And he ketched Dan'l by the nap of the neck, and hefted him, and says, "Why blame my cats if he don't weigh five pound!" and turned him up-side down and he belched out a double handful of shot. And then he see how it was, and he was the maddest man—he set the frog down and took out after that feller, but he never ketched him. And—"

Here Simon Wheeler heard his name called from the front yard, and got up to see what was wanted. And turning to me as he moved away, he said: "Just set where you are, stranger, and rest easy—I ain't going to be gone a second."

But, by your leave, I did not think that a continuation of the history of the enterprising vagabond *Jim* Smiley would likely to afford me much information concerning the Rev. *Leonidas W.* Smiley, and so I started away.

At the door I met the sociable Wheeler returning, and he buttonholed me and re-commenced:

"Well, thish-yer Smiley had a yaller one-eyed cow that didn't have no tail, only just a short stump like a bannanner, and—"

However, lacking both time and inclination, I did not wait to hear about the afflicted cow, but took my leave.

STUDY QUESTIONS

1. During Twain's lifetime, this story appeared in various forms and with vari-ous titles. Do you think the title used here (the one most often used) is a good one for the story? Why or why not?
2. In your opinion, how important is the use of the "frame story" technique for this tale? What does the initial narrator contribute to the story?
3. What are the sources of humor in this story?
4. Compare and contrast the story's two narrators, in terms of their speech patterns, character, and whatever else you'd like to comment upon.

Character Study and Social Commentary

8

LOOKING INWARD
AND OUTWARD

Human beings are both individuals and social beings. Fiction, throughout its history, has concerned itself with that duality. One of fiction's most fascinating characteristics, in fact, is its ability to look in two directions at once. Fictional narrators can look into their characters, revealing their minds and feelings to us, exploring their personalities. And they can look out at the society to which the characters belong. Looking inward, they seem to ask, "What sort of people are these?" Looking outward, they seem to ask, "What has made them that way?"

Writers of fiction have long felt that their form's unique ability to deal with the common reality of everyday life made it an ideal vehicle for examining the interaction of individuals with their society. We find that concern reflected in nearly all forms of fiction, from old and traditional tales such as "Bartleby the Scrivener" to some of the most experimental contemporary works. Many Americans in the latter half of the twentieth century are deeply concerned with questions of society's influence and power over the individual and of the individual's own power to shape his or her own personality and future. Contemporary fiction reflects these concerns.

The four stories that follow are all works that engage our concern for some central character or characters while forcing upon us some realization of or comment on the society in which these characters live. In these stories, as in others we have read, the physical settings often become metaphors for the social settings. The influence of society, and the characters' reactions to it, thus form an important part of each tale.

As you read these stories, therefore, take note of their physical and social settings, and of how these settings are used to define the characters' actions and personalities. Take note, too—as always when dealing with fiction—of the narrators' voices. What tones of voice do you hear in these stories? What attitudes do they convey? How do the narrators blend their stories' dual focus on individual and society into a concern for the fulfillment or happiness of their central characters? What moods do they leave you in at the stories' ends? How do they get you there?

My Kinsman, Major Molineux

Nathaniel Hawthorne (1804–1864)

After the kings of Great Britain had assumed the right of appointing the colonial governors, the measures of the latter seldom met with the ready and general approbation, which had been paid to those of their predecessors, under the original charters. The people looked with most jealous scrutiny to the exercise of power, which did not emanate from themselves, and they usually rewarded the rulers with slender gratitude, for the compliances, by which, in softening their instructions from beyond the sea, they had incurred the reprehension of those who gave them. The annals of Massachusetts Bay will inform us, that of six governors, in the space of about forty years from the surrender of the old charter, under James II., two were imprisoned by a popular insurrection; a third, as Hutchinson inclines to believe, was driven from the province by the whizzing of a musket ball; a fourth, in the opinion of the same historian, was hastened to his grave by continual bickerings with the House of Representatives; and the remaining two, as well as their successors, till the Revolution, were favored with few and brief intervals of peaceful sway. The inferior members of the court party, in times of high political excitement, led scarcely a more desirable life. These remarks may serve as preface to the following adventures, which chanced upon a summer night, not far from a hundred years ago. The reader, in order to avoid a long and dry detail of colonial affairs, is requested to dispense with an account of the train of circumstances, that had caused much temporary inflammation of the popular mind.

It was near nine o'clock of a moonlight evening, when a boat crossed the ferry with a single passenger, who had obtained his conveyance, at that unusual hour, by the promise of an extra fare. While he stood on the landing-place, searching in either pocket for the means of fulfilling his agreement, the ferryman lifted a lantern, by the aid of which, and the newly risen moon, he took a very accurate survey of the stranger's figure. He was a youth of barely eighteen years, evidently countrybred, and now, as it should seem, upon his first visit to town. He was clad in a coarse grey coat, well worn, but in excellent repair; his under garments were durably constructed of leather, and sat tight to a pair of serviceable and well-shaped limbs; his stockings of blue yarn, were the incontrovertible handiwork of a mother or a sister; and on his head was a three-cornered hat, which in its better days had perhaps sheltered the graver brow of the lad's father. Under his left arm was a heavy cudgel, formed of an oak sapling, and retaining a part of the hardened root; and his equipment was completed by a wallet, not so abundantly stocked as to incommode the vigorous shoulders on which it hung. Brown, curly hair, well-shaped features, and bright, cheerful eyes, were nature's gifts, and worth all that art could have done for his adornment.

The youth, one of whose names was Robin, finally drew from his pocket the half of a little province-bill of five shillings, which, in the depreciation of that sort of currency, did but satisfy the ferryman's demand, with the surplus of a sexangular piece of parchment valued at three pence. He then walked forward into the town, with as light a step, as if his day's journey had not already exceeded thirty miles, and with as eager an eye, as if he were entering London city, instead of the little metropolis of a New England colony. Before Robin had proceeded far, however, it occurred to him, that he knew not whither to direct his steps; so he paused, and looked up and down the narrow street, scrutinizing the small and mean wooden buildings, that were scattered on either side.

"This low hovel cannot be my kinsman's dwelling," thought he, "nor yonder old house, where the moonlight enters at the broken casement; and truly I see none hereabouts that might be worthy of him. It would have been wise to inquire my way of the ferryman, and doubtless he would have gone with me, and earned a shilling from the Major for his pains. But the next man I meet will do as well."

He resumed his walk, and was glad to perceive that the street now became wider, and the houses more respectable in their appearance. He soon discerned a figure moving on moderately in advance, and hastened his steps to overtake it. As Robin drew nigh, he saw that the passenger was a man in years, will a full periwig of grey hair, a wide-skirted coat of dark cloth, and silk stockings rolled about his knees. He carried a long and polished cane, which he struck down perpendicularly before him, at every step; and at regular intervals he uttered two successive hems, of a peculiarly solemn and sepulchral intonation. Having made these observations, Robin laid hold of the skirt of the old man's coat, just when the light from the open door and windows of a barber's shop, fell upon both their figures.

"Good evening to you, honored Sir," said he, making a low bow, and still retaining his hold of the skirt. "I pray you to tell me whereabouts is the dwelling of my kinsman, Major Molineux?"

The youth's question was uttered very loudly; and one of the barbers, whose razor was descending on a well-soaped chin, and another who was dressing a Ramillies wig, left their occupations, and came to the door. The citizen, in the meantime, turned a long favored countenance upon Robin, and answered him in a tone of excessive anger and annoyance. His two sepulchral hems, however, broke into the very centre of his rebuke, with most singular effect, like a thought of the cold grave obtruding among wrathful passions.

"Let go my garment, fellow! I tell you, I know not the man you speak of. What! I have authority, I have—hem, hem—authority; and if this be the respect you show your betters, your feet shall be brought acquainted with the stocks, by daylight, tomorrow morning!"

Robin released the old man's shirt, and hastened away, pursued by an ill-mannered roar of laughter from the barber's shop. He was at first considerably surprised by the result of his question, but, being a shrewd youth, soon thought himself able to account for the mystery.

"This is some country representative," was his conclusion, "who has never seen the inside of my kinsman's door, and lacks the breeding to answer a stranger civilly. The man is old, or verily—I might be tempted to turn back and smite him on the nose. Ah, Robin, Robin! even the barber's boys laugh at you, for choosing such a guide! You will be wiser in time, friend Robin."

He now became entangled in a succession of crooked and narrow streets, which crossed each other, and meandered at no great distance from the waterside. The smell of tar was obvious to his nostrils, the masts of vessels pierced the moonlight above the tops of the buildings, and the numerous signs, which Robin paused to read, informed him that he was near the centré of business. But the streets were empty, the shops were closed, and lights were visible only in the second stories of a few dwelling-houses. At length, on the corner of a narrow lane, through which he was passing, he beheld the broad countenance of a British hero swinging before the door of an inn, whence proceeded the voices of many guests. The casement of one of the lower windows was thrown back, and a very thin curtain permitted Robin to distinguish a party at supper, round a well-furnished table. The fragrance of the good cheer steamed forth into the outer air, and the youth could not fail to recollect, that the last remnant of his travelling stock of provision had yielded to his morning appetite, and that noon had found, and left him, dinnerless.

"Oh, that a parchment three-penny might give me a right to sit down at yonder table," said Robin, with a sigh. "But the Major will make me welcome to the best of his victuals; so I will even step boldly in, and inquire my way to his dwelling."

He entered the tavern, and was guided by the murmur of voices, and fumes of tobacco, to the public room. It was a long and low apartment, with oaken walls, grown dark in the continual smoke, and a floor, which was thickly sanded, but of no immaculate purity. A number of persons, the larger part of whom appeared to be mariners, or in some way connected with the sea, occupied the wooden benches, or leather-bottomed chairs, conversing on various matters, and occasionally lending their attention to some topic of general interest. Three or four little groups were draining as many bowls of punch, which the great West India trade had long since made a familiar drink in the colony. Others, who had the aspect of men who lived by regular and laborious handicraft, preferred the insulated bliss of an unshared potation, and became more taciturn under its influence. Nearly all, in short, evinced a predilection for the Good Creature in some of its various shapes, for this is a vice, to which, as the Fast-day sermons of a hundred years ago will testify, we have a long hereditary claim. The only guests to whom Robin's sympathies inclined him, were two or three sheepish countrymen, who were using the inn somewhat after the fashion of a Turkish Caravansary; they had gotten themselves into the darkest corner of the room, and, heedless of the Nicotian atmosphere, were supping on the bread of their own ovens, and the bacon cured in their own chimney-smoke. But though Robin felt a sort of brotherhood with these strangers, his eyes were attracted from them, to a person who stood near the door, holding whispered conversation with a group of ill-dressed associates. His features were separately striking almost to grotesqueness, and the whole face left a deep impression in the memory. The forehead bulged out into a double prominence, with a vale between; the nose came boldly forth in an irregular curve, and its bridge was of more than a finger's breadth; the eyebrows were deep and shaggy, and the eyes glowed beneath them like fire in a cave.

While Robin deliberated of whom to inquire respecting his kinsman's dwelling, he was accosted by the innkeeper, a little man in a stained white apron, who had come to pay his professional welcome to the stranger. Being in the second generation from a French Protestant, he seemed to have inherited the courtesy of his parent nation; but no variety of circumstance was ever known to change his voice from the one shrill note in which he now addressed Robin.

"From the country, I presume, Sir?" said he, with a profound bow. "Beg to congratulate you on your arrival, and trust you intend a long stay with us. Fine town here, Sir, beautiful buildings, and much that may interest a stranger. May I hope for the honor of your commands in respect to supper?"

"The man sees a family likeness! the rogue has guessed that I am related to the Major!" thought Robin, who had hitherto experienced little superfluous civility.

All eyes were now turned on the country lad, standing at the door, in his worn three-cornered hat, grey coat, leather breeches, and blue yarn stockings, leaning on an oaken cudgel, and bearing a wallet on his back.

Robin replied to the courteous innkeeper, with such an assumption of consequence, as befitted the Major's relative.

"My honest friend," he said, "I shall make it a point to patronize your house on some occasion, when—" here he could not help lowering his voice—"I may have more than a parchment three-pence in my pocket. My present business," continued he, speaking with lofty confidence, "is merely to inquire the way to the dwelling of my kinsman, Major Molineux."

There was a sudden and general movement in the room, which Robin interpreted as expressing the eagerness of each individual to become his guide. But the innkeeper turned his eyes to a written paper on the wall, which he read, or seemed to read, with occasional recurrences to the young man's figure.

"What have we here?" said he, breaking his speech into little dry fragments. 'Left the house of the subscriber, bounden servant, Hezekiah Mudge—had on, when he went away, grey coat, leather breeches, master's third best hat. One pound currency reward to whoever shall lodge him in any jail in the province.' Better trudge, boy, better trudge!"

Robin had begun to draw his hand towards the lighter end of the oak cudgel, but a strange hostility in every countenance, induced him to relinquish his purpose of breaking the courteous innkeeper's head. As he turned to leave the room, he encountered a sneering glance from the bold-featured personage whom he had before noticed; and no sooner was he beyond the door, than he heard a general laugh, in which the innkeeper's voice might be distinguished, like the dropping of small stones into a kettle.

"Now is it not strange," thought Robin, with his usual shrewdness, "is it not strange, that the confession of an empty pocket, should outweigh the name of my kinsman, Major Molineux? Oh, if I had one of these grinning rascals in the woods, where I and my oak sapling grew up together, I would teach him that my arm is heavy, though my purse be light!"

On turning the corner of the narrow lane, Robin found himself in a spacious street, with an unbroken line of lofty houses on each side, and a steepled building at the upper end, whence the ringing of a bell announced the hour of nine. The light of the moon, and the lamps from numerous shop windows, discovered people promenading on the pavement, and amongst them, Robin hoped to recognize his hitherto inscrutable relative. The result of his former inquiries made him unwilling to hazard another, in a scene of such publicity, and he determined to walk slowly and silently up the street, thrusting his face close to that of every elderly gentleman, in search of the Major's lineaments. In his progress, Robin encountered many gay and gallant figures. Embroidered garments, of showy colors, enormous periwigs, gold-laced hats, and silver hilted swords, glided past him and dazzled his optics. Travelled youths, imitators of the European fine gentlemen of the period, trod jauntily along, half-dancing to the fashionable tunes which they hummed, and making poor Robin ashamed of his quiet and natural gait. At length, after many pauses to examine the gorgeous display of goods in the shop windows, and after suffering some rebukes for the impertinence of his scrutiny into people's faces, the Major's kinsman found himself near the steepled building, still unsuccessful in his search. As yet, however, he had seen only one side of the thronged street; so Robin crossed, and continued the same sort of inquisition down the opposite pavement, with stronger hopes than the philosopher seeking an honest man, but with no better fortune. He had arrived about midway towards the lower end, from which his course began, when he overheard the approach of some one, who struck down a cane on the flag-stones at every step, uttering, at regular intervals, two sepulchral hems.

"Mercy on us!" quoth Robin, recognizing the sound.

Turning a corner, which chanced to be close at his right hand, he hastened to pursue his researches, in some other part of the town. His patience was now wearing low, and he seemed to feel more fatigue from his rambles since he crossed the ferry, than from his journey of several days on the other side. Hunger also pleaded loudly within him, and Robin began to balance the propriety of demanding, violently and with lifted cudgel, the necessary guidance from the first solitary passenger, whom he should meet. While a resolution to this effect was gaining strength, he entered a street of mean appearance, on either side of which, a row of ill-built houses was straggling towards the harbor. The moonlight fell upon no passenger along the whole extent, but in the third domicile which Robin passed, there was a half-opened door, and his keen glance detected a woman's garment within.

"My luck may be better here," said he to himself.

Accordingly, he approached the door, and beheld it shut closer as he did so; yet an open space remained, sufficing for the fair occupant to observe the stranger, without a corresponding display on her part. All that Robin could discern was a strip of scarlet petticoat, and the occasional sparkle of an eye, as if the moonbeams were trembling on some bright thing.

"Pretty mistress,"—for I may call her so with a good conscience, thought the shrewd youth, since I know nothing to the contrary—"my sweet pretty mistress, will you be kind enough to tell me whereabouts I must seek the dwelling of my kinsman, Major Molineux?"

Robin's voice was plaintive and winning, and the female, seeing nothing to be shunned in the handsome country youth, thrust open the door, and came forth into the moonlight. She was a dainty little figure, with a white neck, round arms, and a slender waist, at the extremity of which her scarlet petticoat jutted out over a hoop, as if she were standing in a balloon. Moreover, her face was oval and pretty, her hair dark beneath the little cap, and her bright eyes possessed a sly freedom, which triumphed over those of Robin.

"Major Molineux dwells here," said this fair woman.

Now her voice was the sweetest Robin had heard that night, the airy counterpart of a stream of melted silver; yet he could not help doubting whether that sweet voice spoke Gospel truth. He looked up and down the mean street, and then surveyed the house before which they stood. It was a small, dark edifice of two stories, the second of which projected over the lower floor; and the front apartment had the aspect of a shop for petty commodities.

"Now truly I am in luck," replied Robin, cunningly, "and so indeed is my kinsman, the Major, in having so pretty a housekeeper. But I prithee trouble him to step to the door; I will deliver him a message from his friends in the country, and then go back to my lodgings at the inn."

"Nay, the Major has been a-bed this hour or more," said the lady of the scarlet petticoat; "and it would be to little purpose to disturb him to-night, seeing his evening draught was of the strongest. But he is a kind-hearted man, and it would be as much as my life's worth, to let a kinsman of his turn away from the door. You are the good old gentleman's very picture, and I could swear that was his rainy-weather hat. Also, he has garments very much resembling those leather—But come in, I pray, for I bid you hearty welcome in his name."

So saying, the fair and hospitable dame took our hero by the hand; and though the touch was light, and the force was gentleness, and though Robin read in her eyes what he did not hear in her words, yet the slender waisted woman, in the scarlet petticoat, proved stronger than the athletic country youth. She had drawn his half-willing footsteps nearly to the threshold, when the opening of a door in the neighborhood, startled the Major's housekeeper, and, leaving the Major's kinsman, she vanished speedily into her own domicile. A heavy yawn preceded the appearance of a man, who, like the Moonshine of Pyramus and Thisbe, carried a lantern, needlessly aiding his sister luminary in the heavens. As he walked sleepily up the street, he turned his broad, dull face on Robin, and displayed a long staff, spiked at the end.

"Home, vagabond, home!" said the watchman, in accents that seemed to fall asleep as soon as they were uttered. "Home, or we'll set you in the stocks by peep of day!"

"This is the second hint of the kind," thought Robin. "I wish they would end my difficulties, by setting me there to-night."

Nevertheless, the youth felt an instinctive antipathy towards the guardian of midnight order, which at first prevented him from asking his usual question. But just when the man was about to vanish behind the corner, Robin resolved not to lose the opportunity, and shouted lustily after him—

"I say, friend! will you guide me to the house of my kinsman, Major Molineux?"

The watchman made no reply, but turned the corner and was gone; yet Robin seemed to hear the sound of drowsy laughter stealing along the solitary street. At that moment, also, a pleasant titter saluted him from the open window above his head; he looked up, and caught the sparkle of a saucy eye; a round arm beckoned to him, and next he heard light footsteps descending the staircase within. But Robin, being of the household of a New England clergyman, was a good youth, as well as a shrewd one; so he resisted temptation, and fled away.

He now roamed desperately, and at random, through the town, almost ready to believe that a spell was on him, like that, by which a wizard of his country, had once kept three pursuers wandering, a whole winter night, within twenty paces of the cottage which they sought. The streets lay before him, strange and desolate, and the lights were extinguished in almost every house. Twice, however, little parties of men, among whom Robin distinguished individuals in outlandish attire, came hurrying along, but though on both occasions they paused to address him, such intercourse did not at all enlighten his perplexity. They did but utter a few words in some language of which Robin knew nothing, and perceiving his inability to answer, bestowed a curse upon him in plain English, and hastened away. Finally, the lad determined to knock at the door of every mansion that might appear worthy to be occupied by his kinsman, trusting that perseverance would overcome the fatality which had hitherto thwarted him. Firm in this resolve, he was passing beneath the walls of a church, which formed the corner of two streets, when, as he turned into the shade of its steeple, he encountered a bulky stranger, muffled in a cloak. The man was proceeding with the speed of earnest business, but Robin planted himself full before him, holding the oak cudgel with both hands across his body, as a bar to further passage.

"Halt, honest man, and answer me a question," said he, very resolutely. "Tell me, this instant, whereabouts is the dwelling of my kinsman, Major Molineux?"

"Keep your tongue between your teeth, fool, and let me pass," said a deep, gruff voice, which Robin partly remembered. "Let me pass, I say, or I'll strike you to the earth!"

"No, no, neighbor!" cried Robin, flourishing his cudgel, and then thrusting its larger end close to the man's muffled face. "No, no, I'm not the fool you take me for, nor do you pass, till I have an answer to my question. Whereabouts is the dwelling of my kinsman, Major Molineux?"

The stranger, instead of attempting to force his passage, stept back into the moonlight, unmuffled his own face and stared full into that of Robin.

"Watch here an hour, and Major Molineux will pass by," said he.

Robin gazed with dismay and astonishment, on the unprecedented physiognomy of the speaker. The forehead with its double prominence, the broad-hooked nose, the shaggy eyebrows, and fiery eyes, were those which he had noticed at the inn, but the man's complexion had undergone a singular, or, more properly, a two-fold change. One side of the face blazed of an intense red, while the other was black as midnight, the division line being in the broad bridge of the nose; and a mouth, which seemed to extend from ear to ear, was black or red, in contrast to the color of the cheek. The effect was as if two individual devils, a fiend of fire and a fiend of darkness, had united themselves to form this infernal visage. The stranger grinned in Robin's face, muffled his parti-colored features, and was out of sight in a moment.

"Strange things we travellers see!" ejaculated Robin.

He seated himself, however, upon the steps of the church-door, resolving to wait the appointed time for his kinsman's appearance. A few moments were consumed in philosophical speculations, upon the species of the *genus homo,* who had just left him, but having settled this point shrewdly, rationally, and satisfactorily, he was compelled to look elsewhere for amusement. And first he threw his eyes along the street; it was of more respectable appearance than most of those into which he had wandered, and the moon, "creating, like the imaginative power, a beautiful strangeness in familiar objects," gave something of romance to a scene, that might not have possessed it in the light of day. The irregular, and often quaint architecture of the houses, some of whose roofs were broken into numerous little peaks; while others ascended, steep and narrow, into a single point; and others again were square; the pure milk-white of some of their complexions, the aged darkness of others, and the thousand sparklings, reflected from bright substances in the plastered walls of many; these matters engaged Robin's attention for awhile, and then began to grow wearisome. Next he endeavored to define the forms of distant objects, starting away with almost ghostly indistinctness, just as his eye appeared to grasp them; and finally he took a minute survey of an edifice, which stood on the opposite side of the street, directly in front of the church-door, where he was stationed. It was a large square mansion, distinguished from its neighbors by a balcony, which rested on tall pillars, and by an elaborate Gothic window, communicating therewith.

"Perhaps this is the very house I have been seeking," thought Robin.

Then he strove to speed away the time, by listening to a murmur, which swept continually along the street, yet was scarcely audible, except to an unaccustomed ear like his; it was a low, dull, dreamy sound, compounded of many noises, each of which was at too great a distance to be separately heard. Robin marvelled at this snore of a sleeping town, and marvelled more, whenever its continuity was broken, by now and then a distant shout, apparently loud where it originated. But altogether it was a sleep-inspiring sound, and to shake off its drowsy influence, Robin arose, and climbed a window-frame, that he might view the interior of the church. There the moonbeams came trembling in, and fell down upon the deserted pews, and extended along the quiet aisles. A fainter, yet more awful radiance, was hovering round the pulpit, and one solitary ray had dared to rest upon the opened page of the great Bible. Had Nature, in that deep hour, become a worshipper in the house, which man had builded? Or was that heavenly light the visible sanctity of the place, visible because no earthly and impure feet were within the walls? The scene made Robin's heart shiver with a sensation of loneliness, stronger than he had ever felt in the remotest depths of his native woods; so he turned away, and sat down again before the door. There were graves around the church, and now an uneasy thought obtruded into Robin's breast. What if the object of his search, which had been so often and so strangely thwarted, were all the time mouldering in his shroud? What if his kinsman should glide through yonder gate, and nod and smile to him in passing dimly by?

"Oh, that any breathing thing were here with me!" said Robin.

Recalling his thoughts from this uncomfortable track, he sent them over forest, hill, and stream, and attempted to imagine how that evening of ambiguity and weariness, had been spent by his father's household. He pictured them assembled at the door, beneath the tree, the great old tree, which had been spared for its huge twisted trunk, and venerable shade, when a thousand leafy brethren fell. There, at the going down of the summer sun, it was his father's custom to perform domestic worship, that the neighbors might come and join with him like brothers of the family, and that the wayfaring man might pause to drink at that fountain, and keep his heart pure by freshening the memory of home. Robin distinguished the seat of every individual of the little audience; he saw the good man in the midst, holding the Scriptures in the golden light that shone from the western clouds; he beheld him close the book, and all rise up to pray. He heard the old thanksgivings for daily mercies, the old supplications for their continuance, to which he had so often listened in weariness, but which were now among his dear remembrances. He perceived the slight inequality of his father's voice when he came to speak of the Absent One; he noted how his mother turned her face to the broad and knotted trunk; how his elder brother scorned, because the beard was rough upon his upper lip, to permit his features to be moved; how his younger sister drew down a low hanging branch before her eyes; and how the little one of all, whose sports had hitherto broken the decorum of the scene, understood the prayer for her playmate, and burst into clamorous grief. Then he saw them go in at the door; and when Robin would have entered also, the latch tinkled into its place, and he was excluded from his home.

"Am I here, or there?" cried Robin, starting; for all at once, when his thoughts had become visible and audible in a dream, the long, wide, solitary street shone out before him.

He aroused himself, and endeavored to fix his attention steadily upon the large edifice which he had surveyed before. But still his mind kept vibrating between fancy and reality; by turns, the pillars of the balcony lengthened into the tall, bare stems of pines, dwindled down to human figures, settled again in their true shape and size, and then commenced a new succession of changes. For a single moment, when he deemed himself awake, he could have sworn that a visage, one which he seemed to remember, yet could not absolutely name as his kinsman's, was looking towards him from the Gothic window. A deeper sleep wrestled with, and nearly overcame him, but fled at the sound of footsteps along the opposite pavement. Robin rubbed his eyes, discerned a man passing at the foot of the balcony, and addressed him in a loud, peevish, and lamentable cry.

"Halloo, friend! must I wait here all night for my kinsman, Major Molineux?"

The sleeping echoes awoke, and answered the voice; and the passenger, barely able to discern a figure sitting in the oblique shade of the steeple, traversed the street to obtain a nearer view. He was himself a gentleman in his prime, of open, intelligent, cheerful, and altogether prepossessing countenance. Perceiving a country youth, apparently homeless and without friends, he accosted him in a tone of real kindness, which had become strange to Robin's ears.

"Well, my good lad, why are you sitting here?" inquired he. "Can I be of service to you in any way?"

"I am afraid not, Sir," replied Robin, despondingly; "yet I shall take it kindly, if you'll answer me a single question. I've been searching half the night for one Major Molineux; now, Sir, is there really such a person in these parts, or am I dreaming?"

"Major Molineux! The name is not altogether strange to me," said the gentleman, smiling. "Have you any objection to telling me the nature of your business with him?"

Then Robin briefly related that his father was a clergyman, settled on a small salary, at a long distance back in the country, and that he and Major Molineux were brothers' children. The Major, having inherited riches, and acquired civil and military rank, had visited his cousin in great pomp a year or two before; had manifested much interest in Robin and an elder brother, and, being childless himself, had thrown out hints respecting the future establishment of one of them in life. The elder brother was destined to succeed to the farm, which his father cultivated, in the interval of sacred duties; it was therefore determined that Robin should profit by his kinsman's generous intentions, especially as he had seemed to be rather the favorite, and was thought to possess other necessary endowments.

"For I have the name of being a shrewd youth," observed Robin, in this part of his story.

"I doubt not you deserve it," replied his new friend, good naturedly; "but pray proceed."

"Well, Sir, being nearly eighteen years old, and well-grown, as you see," continued Robin, raising himself to his full height, "I thought it high time to begin the world. So my mother and sister put me in handsome trim, and my father gave me half the remnant of his last year's salary, and five days ago I started for this place, to pay the Major a visit. But would you believe it, Sir? I crossed the ferry a little after dusk, and have yet found nobody that would show me the way to his dwelling; only an hour or two since, I was told to wait here, and Major Molineux would pass by."

"Can you describe the man who told you this?" inquired the gentleman.

"Oh, he was a very ill-favored fellow, Sir," replied Robin, "with two great bumps on his forehead, a hook nose, fiery eyes, and, what struck me as the strangest, his face was of two different colors. Do you happen to know such a man, Sir?"

"Not intimately," answered the stranger, "but I chanced to meet him a little time previous to your stopping me. I believe you may trust his word, and that the Major will very shortly pass through this street. In the mean time, as I have a singular curiosity to witness your meeting, I will sit down here upon the steps, and bear you company."

He seated himself accordingly, and soon engaged his companion in animated discourse. It was but of brief continuance, however, for a noise of shouting, which had long been remotely audible, drew so much nearer, that Robin inquired its cause.

"What may be the meaning of this uproar?" asked he. "Truly, if your town be always as noisy, I shall find little sleep, while I am an inhabitant."

"Why, indeed, friend Robin, there do appear to be three or four riotous fellows abroad to-night," replied the gentleman. "You must not expect all the stillness of your native woods, here in our streets. But the watch will shortly be at the heels of these lads, and—"

"Aye, and set them in the stocks by peep of day," interrupted Robin, recollecting his own encounter with the drowsy lantern-bearer. "But, dear Sir, if I may trust my ears, an army of watchmen would never make head against such a multitude of rioters. There were at least a thousand voices went to make up that one shout."

"May not one man have several voices, Robin, as well as two complexions?" said his friend.

"Perhaps a man may; but Heaven forbid that a woman should!" responded the shrewd youth, thinking of the seductive tones of the Major's housekeeper.

The sounds of a trumpet in some neighboring street now became so evident and continual, that Robin's curiosity was strongly excited. In addition to the shouts, he heard frequent bursts from many instruments of discord, and a wild and confused laughter filled up the intervals. Robin rose from the steps, and looked wistfully towards a point, whither several people seemed to be hastening.

"Surely some prodigious merrymaking is going on," exclaimed he. "I have laughed very little since I left home, Sir, and should be sorry to lose an opportunity. Shall we just step round the corner by that darkish house, and take our share of the fun?"

"Sit down again, sit down, good Robin," replied the gentleman, laying his hand on the skirt of the grey coat. "You forget that we must wait here for your kinsman; and there is reason to believe that he will pass by, in the course of a very few moments."

The near approach of the uproar had now disturbed the neighborhood; windows flew open on all sides; and many heads, in the attire of the pillow, and confused by sleep suddenly broken, were protruded to the gaze of whoever had leisure to observe them. Eager voices hailed each other from house to house, all demanding the explanation, which not a soul could give. Half-dressed men hurried towards the unknown commotion, stumbling as they went over the stone steps, that thrust themselves into the narrow foot-walk. The shouts, the laughter, and the tuneless bray, the antipodes of music, came onward with increasing din, till scattered individuals, and then denser bodies, began to appear round a corner, at the distance of a hundred yards.

"Will you recognize your kinsman, Robin, if he passes in this crowd?" inquired the gentleman.

"Indeed, I can't warrant it, Sir; but I'll take my stand here, and keep a bright look out," answered Robin, descending to the outer edge of the pavement.

A mighty stream of people now emptied into the street, and came rolling slowly towards the church. A single horseman wheeled the corner in the midst of them, and close behind him came a band of fearful wind-instruments, sending forth a fresher discord, now that no intervening buildings kept it from the ear. Then a redder light disturbed the moonbeams, and a dense multitude of torches shone along the street, concealing by their glare whatever object they illuminated. The single horseman, clad in a military dress, and bearing a drawn sword, rode onward as the leader, and, by his fierce and variegated countenance, appeared like war personified; the red of one cheek was an emblem of fire and sword; the blackness of the other betokened the mourning which attends them. In his train, were wild figures in the Indian dress, and many fantastic shapes without a model, giving the whole march a visionary air, as if a dream had broken forth from some feverish brain, and were sweeping visibly through the midnight streets. A mass of people, inactive, except as applauding spectators, hemmed the procession in, and several women ran along the sidewalks, piercing the confusion of heavier sounds, with their shrill voices of mirth or terror.

"The double-faced fellow has his eye upon me," muttered Robin, with an indefinite but uncomfortable idea, that he was himself to bear a part in the pageantry.

The leader turned himself in the saddle, and fixed his glance full upon the country youth, as the steed went slowly by. When Robin had freed his eyes from those fiery ones, the musicians were passing before him, and the torches were close at hand; but the unsteady brightness of the latter formed a veil which he could not penetrate. The rattling of wheels over the stones sometimes found its way to his ear, and confused traces of a human form appeared at intervals, and then melted into the vivid light. A moment more, and the leader thundered a command to halt; the trumpets vomited a horrid breath, and held their peace; the shouts and laughter of the people died away, and there remained only a universal hum, nearly allied to silence. Right before Robin's eyes was an uncovered cart. There the torches blazed the brightest, there the moon shone out like day, and there, in tar-and-feathery dignity, sate his kinsman, Major Molineux!

He was an elderly man, of large and majestic person, and strong, square features, betokening a steady soul; but steady as it was, his enemies had found the means to shake it. His face was pale as death, and far more ghastly; the broad forehead was contracted in his agony, so that his eyebrows formed one grizzled line; his eyes were red and wild, and the foam hung white upon his quivering lip. His whole frame was agitated by a quick, and continual tremor, which his pride strove to quell, even in those circumstances of overwhelming humiliation. But perhaps the bitterest pang of all was when his eyes met those of Robin; for he evidently knew him on the instant, as the youth stood witnessing the foul disgrace of a head that had grown grey in honor. They stared at each other in silence, and Robin's knees shook, and his hair bristled, with a mixture of pity and terror. Soon, however, a bewildering excitement began to seize upon his mind; the preceding adventures of the night, the unexpected appearance of the crowd, the torches, the confused din, and the hush that followed, the spectre of his kinsman reviled by that great multitude, all this, and more than all, a perception of tremendous ridicule in the whole scene, affected him with a sort of mental inebriety. At that moment a voice of sluggish merriment saluted Robin's ears; he turned instinctively, and just behind the corner of the church stood the lantern-bearer, rubbing his eyes, and drowsily enjoying the lad's amazement. Then he heard a peal of laughter like the ringing of silvery bells; a woman twitched his arm, a saucy eye met his, and he saw the lady of the scarlet petticoat. A sharp, dry cachinnation appealed to his memory, and, standing on tiptoe in the crowd, with his white apron over his head, he beheld the courteous little innkeeper. And lastly, there sailed over the heads of the multitude a great, broad laugh, broken in the midst by two sepulchral hems; thus—

"Haw, haw, haw—hem, hem—haw, haw, haw, haw."

The sound proceeded from the balcony of the opposite edifice, and thither Robin turned his eyes. In front of the Gothic window stood the old citizen, wrapped in a wide gown, his grey periwig exchanged for a nightcap, which was thrust back from his forehead, and his silk stockings hanging down about his legs. He supported himself on his polished cane in a fit of convulsive merriment, which manifested itself on his solemn old features, like a funny inscription on a tombstone. Then Robin seemed to hear the voices of the barbers; of the guests of the inn; and of all who had made sport of him that night. The contagion was spreading among the multitude, when, all at once, it seized upon Robin, and he sent forth a shout of laughter that echoed through the street; every man shook his sides, every man emptied his lungs, but Robin's shout was the loudest there. The cloud-spirits peeped from their silvery islands, as the congregated mirth went roaring up the sky! The Man in the Moon heard the far bellow; "Oho," quoth he, "the old Earth is frolicsome to-night!"

When there was a momentary calm in that tempestuous sea of sound, the leader gave the sign, the procession resumed its march. On they went, like fiends that throng in mockery round some dead potentate, mighty no more, but majestic still in his agony. On they went, in counterfeited pomp, in senseless uproar, in frenzied merriment, trampling all on an old man's heart. On swept the tumult, and left a silent street behind.

"Well, Robin, are you dreaming?" inquired the gentleman, laying his hand on the youth's shoulder.

Robin started, and withdrew his arm from the stone post, to which he had instinctively clung, while the living stream rolled by him. His cheek was somewhat pale, and his eye not quite so lively as in the earlier part of the evening.

"Will you be kind enough to show me the way to the ferry?" said he, after a moment's pause.

"You have then adopted a new subject of inquiry?" observed his companion, with a smile.

"Why, yes, Sir," replied Robin, rather dryly. "Thanks to you, and to my other friends, I have at last met my kinsman, and he will scarce desire to see my face again. I begin to grow weary of a town life, Sir. Will you show me the way to the ferry?"

"No, my good friend Robin, not to-night, at least," said the gentleman. "Some few days hence, if you continue to wish it, I will speed you on your journey. Or, if you prefer to remain with us, perhaps, as you are a shrewd youth, you may rise in the world, without the help of your kinsman, Major Molineux."

STUDY QUESTIONS

1. Why is the historical introduction that Hawthorne provides necessary to appreciate this story? What does it tell you that you need to know? What does Hawthorne mean (and imply) by the phrase "much temporary inflammation of the popular mind"?

2. Why does Hawthorne have his narrator and characters repeat the phrase "a shrewd youth" so often throughout the story?

3. Three major thematic conflicts exist in this story: country life versus city life; religious scenes and language versus political scenes and language; reality versus unreality (manifesting itself as confusion, misconception, fantasy, and disguise). Write an essay discussing one of the three, showing how it is developed throughout the story and how it helps shape the story.

4. Alternatively, write an essay on the "education" that Robin receives on his first night in the city. Include discussion of some or all of the following:

- the first description of Robin
- the series of meetings Robin has with various citizens, his interpretation of what they mean, and your interpretation of them
- Robin's memory of home
- the use of religious language throughout the story
- the growing sense of unreality that the narrator gives to Robin's experiences as the night wears on, and Robin's own changing ability to respond to them
- Robin's meeting with his kinsman
- the final citizen whom Robin meets, and the ending of the story

A Rose for Emily

William Faulkner (1897–1962)

I

When Miss Emily Grierson died, our whole town went to her funeral: the men through a sort of respectful affection for a fallen monument, the women mostly out of curiosity to see the inside of her house, which no one save an old man-servant—a combined gardener and cook—had seen in at least ten years.

It was a big, squarish frame house that had once been white, decorated with cupolas and spires, and scrolled balconies in the heavily lightsome style of the seventies, set on what had once been our most select street. But garages and cotton gins had encroached and obliterated even the august names of that neighborhood; only Miss Emily's house was left, lifting its stubborn and coquettish decay above the cotton wagons and the gasoline pumps—an eyesore among eyesores. And now Miss Emily had gone to join the representatives of those august names where they lay in the cedar-bemused cemetery among the ranked and anonymous graves of Union and Confederate soldiers who fell at the battle of Jefferson.

Alive, Miss Emily had been a tradition, a duty, and a care; a sort of hereditary obligation upon the town, dating from that day in 1894 when Colonel Sartoris, the mayor—he who fathered the edict that no Negro woman should appear on the street without an apron—remitted her taxes, the dispensation dating from the death of her father on into perpetuity. Not that Miss Emily would have accepted charity. Colonel Sartoris invented an involved tale to the effect that Miss Emily's father had loaned money to the town, which the town, as a matter of business, preferred this way of repaying. Only a man of Colonel Sartoris' generation and thought could have invented it, and only a woman could have believed it.

When the next generation, with its more modern ideas, became mayors and aldermen, this arrangement created some little dissatisfaction. On the first of the year they mailed her a tax notice. February came, and there was no reply. They wrote her a formal letter, asking her to call at the sheriff's office at her convenience. A week later the mayor wrote her himself, offering to call or to send his car for her, and received in reply a note on paper of an archaic shape, in a thin, flowing calligraphy in faded ink, to the effect that she no longer went out at all. The tax notice was also enclosed, without comment.

They called a special meeting of the Board of Aldermen. A deputation waited upon her, knocked at the door through which no visitor had passed since she ceased giving china-painting lessons eight or ten years earlier. They were admitted by the old Negro into a dim hall from which a stairway mounted into still more shadow. It smelled of dust and disuse—a close, dank smell. The Negro led them into the parlor. It was furnished in heavy, leather-covered furniture. When the Negro opened the blinds of one window, they could see that the leather was cracked; and when they sat down, a faint dust rose sluggishly about their thighs, spinning with slow motes in the single sun-ray. On a tarnished gilt easel before the fireplace stood a crayon portrait of Miss Emily's father.

They rose when she entered—a small, fat woman in black, with a thin gold chain descending to her waist and vanishing into her belt, leaning on an ebony cane with a tarnished gold head. Her skeleton was small and spare; perhaps that was why what would have been merely plumpness in another was obesity in her. She looked bloated, like a body long submerged in motionless water, and of that pallid hue. Her eyes, lost in the fatty ridges of her face, looked like two small pieces of coal pressed into a lump of dough as they moved from one face to another while the visitors stated their errand.

She did not ask them to sit. She just stood in the door and listened quietly until the spokesman came to a stumbling halt. Then they could hear the invisible watch ticking at the end of the gold chain.

Her voice was dry and cold. "I have no taxes in Jefferson. Colonel Sartoris explained it to me. Perhaps one of you can gain access to the city records and satisfy yourselves."

"But we have. We are the city authorities, Miss Emily. Didn't you get a notice from the sheriff, signed by him?"

"I received a paper, yes," Miss Emily said. "Perhaps he considers himself the sheriff . . . I have no taxes in Jefferson."

"But there is nothing on the books to show that, you see. We must go by the—"

"See Colonel Sartoris. I have no taxes in Jefferson."

"But Miss Emily—"

"See Colonel Sartoris." (Colonel Sartoris had been dead almost ten years.) "I have no taxes in Jefferson. Tobe!" The Negro appeared. "Show these gentlemen out."

II

So she vanquished them, horse and foot, just as she had vanquished their fathers thirty years before about the smell. That was two years after her father's death and a short time after her sweetheart—the one we believed would marry her—had deserted her. After her father's death she went out very little; after her sweetheart went away, people hardly saw her at all. A few of the ladies had the temerity to call, but were not received, and the only sign of life about the place was the Negro man—a young man then—going in and out with a market basket.

"Just as if a man—any man—could keep a kitchen properly," the ladies said; so they were not surprised when the smell developed. It was another link between the gross, teeming world and the high and mighty Griersons.

A neighbor, a woman, complained to the mayor, Judge Stevens, eighty years old.

"But what will you have me do about it, madam?" he said.

"Why, send her word to stop it," the woman said. "Isn't there a law?"

"I'm sure that won't be necessary," Judge Stevens said. "It's probably just a snake or a rat that nigger of hers killed in the yard. I'll speak to him about it."

The next day he received two more complaints, one from a man who came in diffident deprecation. "We really must do something about it, Judge. I'd be the last one in the world to bother Miss Emily, but we've got to do something." That night the Board of Aldermen met—three graybeards and one younger man, a member of the rising generation.

"It's simple enough," he said. "Send her word to have her place cleaned up. Give her a certain time do it in, and if she don't . . ."

"Dammit, sir," Judge Stevens said, "will you accuse a lady to her face of smelling bad?"

So the next night, after midnight, four men crossed Miss Emily's lawn and slunk about the house like burglars, sniffing along the base of the brickwork and at the cellar openings while one of them performed a regular sowing motion with his hand out of a sack slung from his shoulder. They broke open the cellar door and sprinkled lime there, and in all the outbuildings. As they recrossed the lawn, a window that had been dark was lighted and Miss Emily sat in it, the light behind her, and her upright torso motionless as that of an idol. They crept quietly across the lawn and into the shadow of the locusts that lined the street. After a week or two the smell went away.

That was when people had begun to feel really sorry for her. People in our town, remembering how old lady Wyatt, her great-aunt, had gone completely crazy at last, believed that the Griersons held themselves a little too high for what they really were. None of the young men were quite good enough for Miss Emily and such. We had long thought of them as a tableau, Miss Emily a slender figure in white in the background, her father a spraddled silhouette in the foreground, his back to her and clutching a horsewhip, the two of them framed by the backflung front door. When she got to be thirty and was still single, we were not pleased exactly, but vindicated; even with insanity in the family she wouldn't have turned down all of her chances if they had really materialized.

When her father died, it got about that the house was all that was left to her; and in a way, people were glad. At last they could pity Miss Emily. Being left alone, and a pauper, she had become humanized. Now she too would know the old thrill and the old despair of a penny more or less.

The day after his death all the ladies prepared to call at the house and offer condolence and aid, as is our custom. Miss Emily met them at the door, dressed as usual and with no trace of grief on her face. She told them that her father was not dead. She did that for three days, with the ministers calling on her, and the doctors, trying to persuade her to let them dispose of the body. Just as they were about to resort to law and force, she broke down, and they buried her father quickly.

We did not say she was crazy then. We believed she had to do that. We remembered all the young men her father had driven away, and we knew that with nothing left, she would have to cling to that which had robbed her, as people will.

III

She was sick for a long time. When we saw her again, her hair was cut short, making her look like a girl, with a vague resemblance to those angels in colored church windows—sort of tragic and serene.

The town had just let the contracts for paving the sidewalks, and in the summer after her father's death they began the work. The construction company came with niggers and mules and machinery, and a foreman named Homer Barron, a Yankee—a big, dark, ready man, with a big voice and eyes lighter than his face. The little boys would follow in groups to hear him cuss the niggers, and the niggers singing in time to the rise and fall of picks. Pretty soon he knew everybody in town. Whenever you heard a lot of laughing anywhere about the square, Homer Barron would be in the center of the group. Presently we began to see him and Miss Emily on Sunday afternoons driving in the yellow-wheeled buggy and the matched team of bays from the livery stable.

At first we were glad that Miss Emily would have an interest, because the ladies all said, "Of course a Grierson would not think seriously of a Northerner, a day laborer." But there were still others, older people, who said that even grief could not cause a real lady to forget *noblesse oblige*—without calling it *noblesse oblige*. They just said, "Poor Emily. Her kinsfolk should come to her." She had some kin in Alabama; but years ago her father had fallen out with them over the

estate of old Lady Wyatt, the crazy woman, and there was no communication between the two families. They had not even been represented at the funeral.

And as soon as the old people said, "Poor Emily," the whispering began. "Do
you suppose it's really so?" they said to one another. "Of course it is. What else
could . . ." This behind their hands; rustling of craned silk and satin behind
jalousies closed upon the sun of Sunday afternoon as the thin, swift clop-clop-
clop of the matched team passed: "Poor Emily."

She carried her head high enough—even when we believed that she was
fallen. It was as if she demanded more than ever the recognition of her dignity as
the last Grierson; as if it had wanted that touch of earthiness to reaffirm her im-
perviousness. Like when she bought the rat poison, the arsenic. That was over a
year after they had begun to say "Poor Emily," and while the two female cousins
were visiting her.

"I want some poison," she said to the druggist. She was over thirty then, still
a slight woman, though thinner than usual, with cold, haughty black eyes in a
face the flesh of which was strained across the temples and about the eye-sockets
as you imagine a lighthouse-keeper's face ought to look. "I want some poison,"
she said.

"Yes, Miss Emily. What kind? For rats and such? I'd recom—"

"I want the best you have. I don't care what kind."

The druggist named several. "They'll kill anything up to an elephant. But
what you want is—"

"Arsenic," Miss Emily said. "Is that a good one?"

"Is . . . arsenic? Yes, ma'am. But what you want—"

"I want arsenic."

The druggist looked down at her. She looked back at him, erect, her face like
a strained flag. "Why, of course," the druggist said. "If that's what you want. But
the law requires you to tell what you are going to use it for."

Miss Emily just stared at him, her head tilted back in order to look him eye
for eye, until he looked away and went and got the arsenic and wrapped it up.
The Negro delivery boy brought her the package; the druggist didn't come back.
When she opened the package at home there was written on the box, under the
skull and bones: "For rats."

IV

So the next day we all said, "She will kill herself"; and we said it would be
the best thing. When she had first begun to be seen with Homer Barron, we had
said, "She will marry him." Then we said, "She will persuade him yet," because
Homer himself had remarked—he liked men, and it was known that he drank
with the younger men in the Elks' Club—that he was not a marrying man. Later
we said, "Poor Emily" behind the jalousies as they passed on Sunday afternoon
in the glittering buggy, Miss Emily with her head high and Homer Barron with
his hat cocked and cigar in his teeth, reins and whip in a yellow glove.

Then some of the ladies began to say that it was a disgrace to the town and a bad example to the young people. The men did not want to interfere, but at last the ladies forced the Baptist minister—Miss Emily's people were Episcopal—to call upon her. He would never divulge what happened during that interview, but he refused to go back again. The next Sunday they again drove about the streets, and the following day the minister's wife wrote to Miss Emily's relations in Alabama.

So she had blood-kin under her roof again and we sat back to watch developments. At first nothing happened. Then we were sure that they were to be married. We learned that Miss Emily had been to the jeweler's and ordered a man's toilet set in silver, with the letters H. B. on each piece. Two days later we learned that she had bought a complete outfit of men's clothing, including a nightshirt, and we said, "They are married." We were really glad. We were glad because the two female cousins were even more Grierson than Miss Emily had ever been.

So we were not surprised when Homer Barron—the streets had been finished some time since—was gone. We were a little disappointed that there was not a public blowing-off, but we believed that he had gone on to prepare for Miss Emily's coming, or to give her a chance to get rid of the cousins. (By that time it was a cabal, and we were all Miss Emily's allies to help circumvent the cousins.) Sure enough, after another week they departed. And, as we had expected all along, within three days Homer Barron was back in town. A neighbor saw the Negro man admit him at the kitchen door at dusk one evening.

And that was the last we saw of Homer Barron. And of Miss Emily for some time. The Negro man went in and out with the market basket, but the front door remained closed. Now and then we would see her at a window for a moment, as the men did that night when they sprinkled the lime, but for almost six months she did not appear on the streets. Then we knew that this was to be expected too; as if that quality of her father which had thwarted her woman's life so many times had been too virulent and too furious to die.

When we next saw Miss Emily, she had grown fat and her hair was turning gray. During the next few years it grew grayer and grayer until it attained an even pepper-and-salt iron-gray, when it ceased turning. Up to the day of her death at seventy-four it was still that vigorous iron-gray, like the hair of an active man.

From that time on her front door remained closed, save for a period of six or seven years, when she was about forty, during which she gave lessons in china-painting. She fitted up a studio in one of the downstairs rooms, where the daughters and granddaughters of Colonel Sartoris' contemporaries were sent to her with the same regularity and in the same spirit that they were sent to church on Sunday with a twenty-five-cent piece for the collection plate. Meanwhile her taxes had been remitted.

Then the newer generation became the backbone and the spirit of the town, and the painting pupils grew up and fell away and did not send their children to her with boxes of color and tedious brushes and pictures cut from the ladies' magazines. The front door closed upon the last one and remained closed for good. When the town got free postal delivery, Miss Emily alone refused to let them fasten the metal numbers above her door and attach a mailbox to it. She would not listen to them.

Daily, monthly, yearly we watched the Negro grow grayer and more stooped, going in and out with the market basket. Each December we sent her a tax notice, which would be returned by the post office a week later, unclaimed. Now and then we would see her in one of the downstairs windows—she had evidently shut up the top floor of the house—like the carven torso of an idol in a niche, looking or not looking at us, we could never tell which. Thus she passed from generation to generation—dear, inescapable, impervious, tranquil, and perverse.

And so she died. Fell ill in the house filled with dust and shadows, with only a doddering Negro man to wait on her. We did not even know she was sick; we had long since given up trying to get any information from the Negro. He talked to no one, probably not even to her, for his voice had grown harsh and rusty, as if from disuse.

She died in one of the downstairs rooms, in a heavy walnut bed with a curtain, her gray head propped on a pillow yellow and moldy with age and lack of sunlight.

V

The Negro met the first of the ladies at the front door and let them in, with their hushed, sibilant voices and their quick, curious glances, and then he disappeared. He walked right through the house and out the back and was not seen again.

The two female cousins came at once. They held the funeral on the second day, with the town coming to look at Miss Emily beneath a mass of bought flowers, with the crayon face of her father musing profoundly above the bier and the ladies sibilant and macabre; and the very old men—some in their brushed Confederate uniforms—on the porch and the lawn, talking of Miss Emily as if she had been a contemporary of theirs, believing that they had danced with her and courted her perhaps, confusing time with its mathematical progression, as the old do, to whom all the past is not a diminishing road but, instead, a huge meadow which no winter ever quite touches, divided from them now by the narrow bottle-neck of the most recent decade of years.

Already we knew that there was one room in that region above stairs which no one had seen in forty years, and which would have to be forced. They waited until Miss Emily was decently in the ground before they opened it.

The violence of breaking down the door seemed to fill this room with pervading dust. A thin, acrid pall of the tomb seemed to lie everywhere upon this room decked and furnished as for a bridal: upon the valance curtains of faded rose color, upon the rose-shaded lights, upon the dressing table, upon the delicate array of crystal and the man's toilet things backed with tarnished silver, silver so tarnished that the monogram was obscured. Among them lay a collar and tie, as if they had just been removed, which, lifted, left upon the surface a pale crescent in the dust. Upon a chair hung the suit, carefully folded; beneath it the two mute shoes and the discarded socks.

The man himself lay in the bed.

For a long while we just stood there, looking down at the profound and fleshless grin. The body had apparently once lain in the attitude of an embrace, but now the long sleep that outlasts love, that conquers even the grimace of love, had cuckolded him. What was left of him, rotted beneath what was left of the nightshirt, had become inextricable from the bed in which he lay; and upon him and upon the pillow beside him lay that even coating of the patient and biding dust.

Then we noticed that in the second pillow was the indentation of a head. One of us lifted something from it, and leaning forward, that faint and invisible dust dry and acrid in the nostrils, we saw a long strand of iron-gray hair.

STUDY QUESTIONS

1. Part of the effectiveness of "A Rose for Emily" comes from its surprise ending. How effective do you find the ending? Why?
2. How do the narrator and the townsfolk view the young Miss Emily? How does Miss Emily change with time? How does the town? How does the narrator's view of Miss Emily change? How does yours?

Anxiety

Grace Paley (1922–   )

The young fathers are waiting outside the school. What curly heads! Such graceful brown mustaches. They're sitting on their haunches eating pizza and exchanging information. They're waiting for the 3 p.m. bell. It's springtime, the season of first looking out the window. I have a window box of greenhouse marigolds. The young fathers can be seen through the ferny leaves.

The bell rings. The children fall out of school, tumbling through the open door. One of the fathers sees his child. A small girl. Is she Chinese? A little. Up u-u-p, he says, and hoists her to his shoulders. U-u-p, says the second father, and hoists his little boy. The little boy sits on top of his father's head for a couple of seconds before sliding to his shoulders. Very funny, says the father.

They start off down the street, right under and past my window. The two children are still laughing. They try to whisper a secret. The fathers haven't finished their conversation. The frailer father is uncomfortable; his little girl wiggles too much.

Stop it this minute, he says.

Oink oink, says the little girl.

What'd you say?

Oink oink, she says.

The young father says What! three times. Then he seizes the child, raises her high above his head, and sets her hard on her feet.

What'd I do so bad, she says, rubbing her ankle.

Just hold my hand, screams the frail and angry father.

I lean far out the window. Stop! Stop! I cry.

The young father turns, shading his eyes, but sees. What? he says. His friend says, Hey? Who's that? He probably thinks I'm a family friend, a teacher maybe.

Who're you? he says.

I move the pots of marigold aside. Then I'm able to lean on my elbow way out into unshadowed visibility. Once, not too long ago, the tenements were speckled with women like me in every third window up to the fifth story, calling the children from play to receive orders and instruction. This memory enables me to say strictly, Young man, I am an older person who feels free because of that to ask questions and give advice.

Oh? he says, laughs with a little embarrassment, says to his friend, Shoot if you will that old gray head. But he's joking, I know, because he has established himself, legs apart, hands behind his back, his neck arched to see and hear me out.

How old are you? I call. About thirty or so?

Thirty-three.

First I want to say you're about a generation ahead of your father in your attitude and behavior toward your child.

Really? Well? Anything else, ma'am.

Son, I said, leaning another two, three dangerous inches toward him. Son, I must tell you that madmen intend to destroy this beautifully made planet. That the murder of our children by these men has got to become a terror and a sorrow to you, and starting now, it had better interfere with any daily pleasure.

Speech speech, he called.

I waited a minute, but he continued to look up. So, I said, I can tell by your general appearance and loping walk that you agree with me.

I do, he said, winking at his friend; but turning a serious face to mine, he said again, Yes, yes, I do.

Well then, why did you become so angry at that little girl whose future is like a film which suddenly cuts to white. Why did you nearly slam this little doomed person to the ground in your uncontrollable anger.

Let's not go too far, said the young father. She *was* jumping around on my poor back and hollering oink oink.

When were you angriest—when she wiggled and jumped or when she said oink?

He scratched his wonderful head of dark well-cut hair. I guess when she said oink.

Have you ever said oink oink? Think carefully. Years ago, perhaps?

No. Well maybe. Maybe.

Whom did you refer to in this way?

He laughed. He called to his friend, Hey Ken, this old person's got something. The cops. In a demonstration. Oink oink, he said, remembering, laughing.

The little girl smiled and said, Oink oink.

Shut up, he said.

What do you deduce from this?

That I was angry at Rosie because she was dealing with me as though I was a figure of authority, and it's not my thing, never has been, never will be.

I could see his happiness, his nice grin, as he remembered this.

So, I continued, since those children are such lovely examples of what may well be the last generation of humankind, why don't you start all over again, right from the school door, as though none of this had ever happened.

Thank you, said the young father. Thank you. It would be nice to be a horse, he said, grabbing little Rosie's hand. Come on Rosie, let's go. I don't have all day.

U-up, says the first father. U-up, says the second.

Giddap, shout the children, and the fathers yell neigh neigh, as horses do. The children kick their fathers' horsechests, screaming giddap giddap, and they gallop wildly westward.

I lean way out to cry once more, Be careful! Stop! But they've gone too far. Oh, anyone would love to be a fierce fast horse carrying a beloved beautiful rider, but they are galloping toward one of the most dangerous street corners in the world. And they may live beyond that trisection across other dangerous avenues.

So I must shut the window after patting the April-cooled marigolds with their rusty smell of summer. Then I sit in the nice light and wonder how to make sure that they gallop safely home through the airy scary dreams of scientists and the bulky dreams of automakers. I wish I could see just how they sit down at their kitchen tables for a healthy snack (orange juice or milk and cookies) before going out into the new spring afternoon to play.

STUDY QUESTIONS

1. This is a tale of a sidewalk scene and a brief conversation. How does Paley build a story from such commonplace materials?
2. Why is the narrator so concerned about the children's future? What beliefs do she and the young fathers share? (Note particularly the significance of the phrase "Oink oink.")
3. Given this larger concern, why is the narrator's concern for the affairs of the immediate moment so sharp?
4. Does the conversation strike you as something that might really happen or as something that the narrator is imagining, as she imagines the last part of the story? Discuss your reasoning.

CREATIVE WRITING EXERCISE

Have you ever wanted to give someone advice that would make him or her change his or her actions, as Paley's narrator does? Write a brief story or sketch in which you hold this conversation with that person.

Dream-Vision

Tillie Olsen (1913?–   )

In the winter of 1955, in her last weeks of life, my mother—so much of whose waking life had been a nightmare, that common everyday nightmare of hardship, limitation, longing; of baffling struggle to raise six children in a world hostile to human unfolding—my mother, dying of cancer, had beautiful dream-visions—in color.

Already beyond calendar time, she could not have known that the last dream she had breath to tell came to her on Christmas Eve. Nor, conscious, would she have named it so. As a girl in long ago Czarist Russia, she had sternly broken with all observances of organized religion, associating it with pogroms and wars; "mind forg'd manacles"; a repressive state. We did not observe religious holidays in her house.

Perhaps, in her last consciousness, she *did* know that the year was drawing towards that solstice time of the shortest light, the longest dark, the cruelest cold, when—as she had explained to us as children—poorly sheltered ancient peoples in northern climes had summoned their resources to make out of song, light and food, expressions of human love—festivals of courage, hope, warmth, belief.

It seemed to her that there was a knocking at her door. Even as she rose to open it, she guessed who would be there, for she heard the neighing of camels. (I did not say to her: "Ma, camels don't neigh.") Against the frosty lights of a far city she had never seen, "a city holy to three faiths," she said, the three wise men stood: magnificent in jewelled robes of crimson, of gold, of royal blue.

"Have you lost your way?" she asked, "Else, why do you come to me? I am not religious, I am not a believer."

"To talk with *you*, we came," the wise man whose skin was black and robe crimson assured her, "to talk of whys, of wisdom."

"Come in then, come in and be warm—and welcome. I have starved all my life for such talk."

But as they began to talk, she saw that they were not men, but women;

That they were not dressed in jewelled robes, but in the coarse everyday shifts and shawls of the old country women of her childhood, their feet wrapped round and round with rags for lack of boots; snow now sifting into the room;

That their speech was not highflown, but homilies; their bodies not lordly in bearing, magnificent, but stunted, misshapen—used all their lives as beasts of burden are used;

That the camels were not camels, but farm beasts, such as were kept in the house all winter, their white cow breaths steaming into the cold.

And now it was many women, a babble.

One old woman, seamed and bent, began to sing. Swaying, the others joined her, their faces and voices transfiguring as they sang; my mother, through cracked lips, singing too—a lullaby.

For in the shining cloud of their breaths, a baby lay, breathing the universal sounds every human baby makes, sounds out of which are made all the separate languages of the world.

Singing, one by one the women cradled and sheltered the baby.

"The joy, the reason to believe," my mother said, "the hope for the world, the baby, holy with possibility, that is all of us at birth." And she began to cry, out of the dream and its telling now.

"Still I feel the baby in my arms, the human baby," crying now so I could scarcely make out the words, "the human baby before we are misshapen; crucified into a sex, a color, a walk of life, a nationality . . . and the world yet warrings and winter."

I had seen my mother but three times in my adult life, separated as we were by the continent between, by lack of means, by jobs I had to keep and by the needs of my four children. She could scarcely write English—her only education in this country a few months of night school. When at last I flew to her, it was in the last days she had language at all. Too late to talk with her of what was in our hearts; or of harms and crucifying and strengths as she had known and experienced them; or of whys and knowledge, of wisdom. She died a few weeks later.

She, who had no worldly goods to leave, yet left to me an inexhaustible legacy. Inherent in it, this heritage of summoning resources to make out of song, food and warmth, expressions of human love—courage, hope, resistance, belief; this vision of universality, before the lessenings, harms, divisions of the world are visited upon it.

She sheltered and carried that belief, that wisdom—as she sheltered and carried us, and others—throughout a lifetime lived in a world whose season was, as yet it is, a time of winter.

STUDY QUESTIONS

1. This story combines a description of a woman, a description of her daughter's relationship with her, and a "dream-vision" experienced by the older woman. How are the three interwoven in narrative style? thematically?
2. Would you call this story a tale within a tale? Or do you think that the inner and outer stories are too tightly interwoven for this term to apply? Discuss your reasoning.
3. Discuss the dream-vision itself. How does it fit the character of the mother as the narrator depicts her?
4. Discuss the significance of the story's final phrase, "a time of winter."

9

BEYOND REALITY

In the last chapter, we studied stories that dealt in character study and social commentary in realistic styles and settings. In this chapter, we will look at stories that examine individuals and society by going beyond reality, into fantasy or science fiction.

The first story, from a nineteenth-century master of fantasy, takes place in a world that could be our own, were it not populated, in part, by exaggerated, fantastic or supernatural figures. The setting, too, is exaggerated in this and most other fantasy tales: more colorful than usual, more luxurious, more extreme in one way or another. Poe's language, too, insists on these differences, drawing attention to the strangeness of the worlds his stories build. Princes, palaces, and plagues alike were part of the nineteenth-century world (as indeed they are still part of today's world), but Poe makes the ones in this tale unique. This is a tale of fantasy touched with horror, placed within a romanticized version of the world; the emphasis is on the romance, the horror, the unusual.

In contrast, the second story is set thoroughly (indeed, almost depressingly) in the drab world of all-too-real poverty. Into this world of day-to-day crises García Márquez places a single supernatural figure, "a very old man with enormous wings," and then watches the results unfold. The fantasy is thus brought directly into the midst of everyday life. The style, as if to match the setting, is simple and reportorial. All our attention is focused on the characters and their actions.

The third story is science fiction. Vonnegut sets it not in today's world, but in a possible future world. Such future worlds, in science fiction, usually exaggerate one or two traits of today's society, often showing them in an extreme of development. Alternatively, they may show what happens when one form of thinking replaces another, or when some assumption on which we base our society is overturned. The characters, on the other hand, tend to be normal people: the question is, How will people react, how will they behave, in this changed world?

Throughout all three stories we may notice that, regardless of what techniques of romanticization or fantasy or scientific theorizing are being used, the emphasis remains on human behavior. The stories are not simple escapism; rather, they are attempts to apply different techniques to the standard questions, to make us look at ourselves and our societies in a new way. Strange as these tales may be, there is no essence in them that we cannot apply directly to our own society, to people we know, perhaps even to ourselves.

The Masque of the Red Death

Edgar Allan Poe (1809–1849)

The "Red Death" had long devastated the country. No pestilence had ever been so fatal, or so hideous. Blood was its Avator and its seal—the redness and the horror of blood. There were sharp pains, and sudden dizziness, and then profuse bleeding at the pores, with dissolution. The scarlet stains upon the body and especially upon the face of the victim, were the pest ban which shut him out from the aid and from the sympathy of his fellowmen. And the whole seizure, progress and termination of the disease, were the incidents of half an hour.

But the Prince Prospero was happy and dauntless and sagacious. When his dominions were half depopulated, he summoned to his presence a thousand hale and lighthearted friends from among the knights and dames of his court, and with these retired to the deep seclusion of one of his castellated abbeys. This was an extensive and magnificent structure, the creation of the prince's own eccentric yet august taste. A strong and lofty wall girdled it in. This wall had gates of iron. The courtiers, having entered, brought furnaces and massy hammers and welded the bolts. They resolved to leave means neither of ingress or egress to the sudden impulses of despair or of frenzy from within. They abbey was amply provisioned. With such precautions the courtiers might bid defiance to contagion. The external world could take care of itself. In the meantime it was folly to grieve, or to think. The prince had provided all the appliances of pleasure. There were buffoons, there were improvisatori, there were ballet-dancers, there were musicians, there was Beauty, there was wine. All these and security were within. Without was the "Red Death."

It was toward the close of the fifth or sixth month of his seclusion, and while the pestilence raged most furiously abroad, that the Prince Prospero entertained his thousand friends at a masked ball of the most unusual magnificence.

It was a voluptuous scene, that masquerade. But first let me tell of the rooms in which it was held. There were seven—an imperial suite. In many palaces, however, such suites form a long and straight vista, while the folding doors slide back nearly to the walls on either hand, so that the view of the whole extent is scarcely impeded. Here the case was very different; as might have been expected from the duke's love of the *bizarre*. The apartments were so irregularly disposed that the vision embraced but little more than one at a time. There was a sharp turn at every twenty or thirty yards, and at each turn a novel effect. To the right and left, in the middle of each wall, a tall and narrow Gothic window looked out upon a closed corridor which pursued the windings of the suite. These windows were of stained glass whose colored varied in accordance with the prevailing hue of the decorations of the chamber into which it opened. That at the eastern extremity was hung, for example, in blue—and vividly blue were its windows. The second chamber was purple in its ornaments and tapestries, and here the panes were purple. The third was green throughout, and so were the casements. The fourth was furnished and lighted with orange—the fifth with white—the sixth with violet. The seventh apartment was closely shrouded in black velvet tapestries that hung all over the ceiling and down the walls, falling in heavy folds upon a carpet of the same material and hue. But in this chamber only, the color of the windows failed to correspond with the decorations. The panes here were scarlet—a deep blood color. Now in no one of the seven apartments was there any lamp or candelabrum, amid the profusion of golden ornaments that lay scattered to and fro or depended from the roof. There was no light of any kind emanating from lamp or candle within the suite of chambers. But in the corridors that followed the suite, there stood, opposite to each window, a heavy tripod, bearing a brazier of fire that projected its rays through the tinted glass and so glaringly illumined the room. And thus were produced a multitude of gaudy and fantastic appearances. But in the western or black chamber the effect of the fire-light that streamed upon the dark hangings through the blood-tinted panes, was ghastly in the extreme, and produced so wild a look upon the countenances of those who entered, that there were few of the company bold enough to set foot within its precincts at all.

It was in this apartment, also, that there stood against the western wall, a gigantic clock of ebony. Its pendulum swung to and fro with a dull, heavy, monotonous clang; and when the minute-hand made the circuit of the face, and the hour was to be stricken, there came from the brazen lungs of the clock a sound which was clear and loud and deep and exceedingly musical, but of so peculiar a note and emphasis that, at each lapse of an hour, the musicians of the orchestra were constrained to pause, momentarily, in their performance, to hearken to the sound; and thus the waltzers perforce ceased their evolutions; and there was a brief disconcert of the whole gay company; and, while the chimes of the clock yet rang, it was observed that the giddiest grew pale, and the more aged and sedate passed their hands over their brows as if in confused revery or meditation. But when the echoes had fully ceased, a light laughter at once pervaded the assembly; the musicians looked at each other and smiled as if at their own nervousness and folly, and made whispering vows, each to the other, that the next chiming of the clock should produce in them no similar emotion; and then, after the lapse of sixty minutes (which embrace three thousand and six hundred seconds of the Time that flies), there came yet another chiming of the clock, and then were the same disconcert and tremulousness and meditation as before.

But, in spite of these things, it was a gay and magnificent revel. The tastes of the duke were peculiar. He had a fine eye for colors and effects. He disregarded the *decora* of mere fashion. His plans were bold and fiery, and his conceptions glowed with barbaric lustre. There are some who would have thought him mad. His followers felt that he was not. It was necessary to hear and see and touch him to be *sure* that he was not.

He had directed, in great part, the movable embellishments of the seven chambers, upon occasion of this great *fête;* and it was his own guiding taste which had given character to the masqueraders. Be sure they were grotesque. There were much glare and glitter and piquancy and phantasm—much of what has been since seen in "Hernani." There were arabesque figures with unsuited limbs and appointments. There were delirious fancies such as the madman fashions. There was much of the beautiful, much of the wanton, much of the *bizarre,* something of the terrible, and not a little of that which might have excited disgust. To and fro in the seven chambers there stalked, in fact, a multitude of dreams. And these—the dreams—writhed in and about, taking hue from the rooms, and causing the wild music of the orchestra to seem as the echo of their steps. And, anon, there strikes the ebony clock which stands in the hall of the velvet. And then, for a moment, all is still, and all is silent save the voice of the clock. The dreams are stiff-frozen as they stand. But the echoes of the chime die away—they have endured but an instant—and a light, half-subdued laughter floats after them as they depart. And now again the music swells, and the dreams live, and writhe to and fro more merrily than ever, taking hue from the many tinted windows through which stream the rays from the tripods. But to the chamber which lies most westwardly of the seven, there are now none of the maskers who venture, for the night is waning away; and there flows a ruddier light through the blood-colored panes; and the blackness of the sable drapery appalls; and to him whose foot falls upon the sable carpet, there comes from the near clock of ebony a muffled peal more solemnly emphatic than any which reaches *their* ears who indulge in the more remote gayeties of the other apartments.

But these other apartments were densely crowded, and in them beat feverishly the heart of life. And the revel went whirlingly on, until at length there commenced the sounding of midnight upon the clock. And then the music ceased, as I have told; and the evolutions of the waltzers were quieted; and there was an uneasy cessation of all things as before. But now there were twelve strokes to be sounded by the bell of the clock; and thus it happened, perhaps, that before the last echoes of the last chime had utterly sunk into silence, there were many individuals in the crowd who had found leisure to become aware of the presence of a masked figure which had arrested the attention of no single individual before. And the rumor of this new presence having spread itself whisperingly around, there arose at length from the whole company, a buzz, or murmur, expressive of disapprobation and surprise—then, finally, of terror, of horror, and of disgust.

In an assembly of phantasms such as I have painted, it may well be supposed that no ordinary appearance could have excited such sensation. In truth the masquerade license of the night was nearly unlimited; but the figure in question had out-Heroded Herod, and gone beyond the bounds of even the prince's indefinite decorum. There are chords in the hearts of the most reckless which cannot be touched without emotion. Even with the utterly lost, to whom life and death are equally jests, there are matters of which no jest can be made. The whole company, indeed, seemed now deeply to feel that in the costume and bearing of the stranger neither wit nor propriety existed. The figure was tall and gaunt, and shrouded from head to foot in the habiliments of the grave. The mask which concealed the visage was made so nearly to resemble the countenance of a stiffened corpse that the closest scrutiny must have had difficulty in detecting the cheat. And yet all this might have been endured, if not approved, by the mad revellers around. But the mummer had gone so far as to assume the type of the Red Death. His vesture was dabbled in *blood*—and his broad brow, with all the features of the face, was besprinkled with the scarlet horror.

When the eyes of Prince Prospero fell upon this spectral image (which with a slow and solemn movement, as if more fully to sustain its *rôle*, stalked to and fro among the waltzers) he was seen to be convulsed, in the first moment, with a strong shudder, either of terror or distaste; but, in the next, his brow reddened with rage.

"Who dares?" he demanded hoarsely of the courtiers who stood near him— "who dares insult us with this blasphemous mockery? Seize him and unmask him—that we may know whom we have to hang at sunrise, from the battlements!"

It was in the eastern or blue chamber in which stood the Prince Prospero as he uttered these words. They rang throughout the seven rooms loudly and clearly—for the prince was a bold and robust man, and the music had become hushed at the waving of his hand.

It was in the blue room where stood the prince, with a group of pale courtiers by his side. At first, as he spoke, there was a slight rushing movement of this group in the direction of the intruder, who at the moment was also near at hand, and now, with deliberate and stately step, made closer approach to the speaker. But from a certain nameless awe with which the mad assumptions of the mummer had inspired the whole party, there were found none who put forth hand to seize him; so that, unimpeded, he passed within a yard of the prince's person; and, while the vast assembly, as if with one impulse, shrank from the centres of the room to the walls, he made his way uninterruptedly, but with the same solemn and measured step which had distinguished him from the first, through the blue chamber to the purple—through the purple to the green—through the green to the orange—through this again to the white—and even thence to the violet, ere a decided movement had been made to arrest him. It was then, however, that the Prince Prospero, maddening with rage and the shame of his own momentary cowardice, rushed hurriedly through the six chambers, while none followed him on account of a deadly terror that had seized upon all. He bore aloft a drawn dagger, and had approached, in rapid impetuosity, to within three or four feet of the retreating figure, when the latter, having attained the extremity of the velvet apartment, turned suddenly and confronted his pursuer. There was a sharp cry—and the dagger dropped gleaming upon the sable carpet, upon which, instantly afterwards, fell prostrate in death the Prince

Prospero. Then, summoning the wild courage of despair, a throng of the revellers at once threw themselves into the black apartment, and, seizing the mummer, whose tall figure stood erect and motionless within the shadow of the ebony clock, gasped in unutterable horror at finding the grave-cerements and corpse-like mask which they handled with so violent a rudeness, untenanted by any tangible form.

And now was acknowledged the presence of the Red Death. He had come like a thief in the night. And one by one dropped the revellers in the blood-bedewed halls of the revel, and died each in the despairing posture of his fall. And the life of the ebony clock went out with that of the last of the gay. And the flames of the tripods expired. And Darkness and Decay and the Red Death held illimitable dominion over all.

STUDY QUESTIONS

1. The two major characters in this story are Prince Prospero and the Red Death. How does the story's opening divide the story's world between the two of them?
2. What does the description of the palace tell us about Prospero? What does the narrator's direct description of the prince add to our knowledge of him?
3. Note the narrator's insistence on colors and textures. What importance do they have in the story?
4. Discuss the climax, the denouement, of the story. On whose terms is the final challenge played out? With what result? How does the story's title forewarn us of this ending?
5. This story could be called an allegory. The palace can represent any attempt to hide from the problems of the real world (for instance, it could be the equivalent of drug abuse). The Red Death then represents reality, which insists on breaking in. Does the story work for you on this level? Why or why not?

A Very Old Man with Enormous Wings: A Tale for Children

Gabriel García Márquez (1928–   )

On the third day of rain they had killed so many crabs inside the house that Pelayo had to cross his drenched courtyard and throw them into the sea, because the newborn child had a temperature all night and they thought it was due to the stench. The world had been sad since Tuesday. Sea and sky were a single ash-gray thing and the sands of the beach, which on March nights glimmered like powdered light, had become a stew of mud and rotten shellfish. The light was so weak at noon that when Pelayo was coming back to the house after throwing away the crabs, it was hard for him to see what it was that was moving and groaning in the rear of the courtyard. He had to go very close to see that it was an old man, a very old man, lying face down in the mud, who, in spite of his tremendous efforts, couldn't get up, impeded by his enormous wings.

Frightened by that nightmare, Pelayo ran to get Elisenda, his wife, who was putting compresses on the sick child, and he took her to the rear of the court-yard. They both looked at the fallen body with mute stupor. He was dressed like a ragpicker. There were only a few faded hairs left on his bald skull and very few teeth in his mouth, and his pitiful condition of a drenched great-grandfather had taken away any sense of grandeur he might have had. His huge buzzard wings, dirty and half-plucked, were forever entangled in the mud. They looked at him so long and so closely that Pelayo and Elisenda very soon overcame their surprise and in the end found him familiar. Then they dared speak to him, and he answered in an incomprehensible dialect with a strong sailor's voice. That was how they skipped over the inconvenience of the wings and quite intelligently concluded that he was a lonely castaway from some foreign ship wrecked by the storm. And yet, they called in a neighbor woman who knew everything about life and death to see him, and all she needed was one look to show them their mistake.

"He's an angel," she told them. "He must have been coming for the child, but the poor fellow is so old that the rain knocked him down."

On the following day everyone knew that a flesh-and-blood angel was held captive in Pelayo's house. Against the judgment of the wise neighbor woman, for whom angels in those times were the fugitive survivors of a celestial conspiracy, they did not have the heart to club him to death. Pelayo watched over him all af-ternoon from the kitchen, armed with his bailiff's club, and before going to bed dragged him out of the mud and locked him up with the hens in the wire chicken coop. In the middle of the night, when the rain stopped, Pelayo and Elisenda were still killing crabs. A short time afterward the child woke up with-out a fever and with a desire to eat. Then they felt magnanimous and decided to put the angel on a raft with fresh water and provisions for three days and leave him to his fate on the high seas. But when they went out into the courtyard with the first light of dawn, they found the whole neighborhood in front of the chicken coop having fun with the angel, without the slightest reverence, tossing him things to eat through the openings in the wire as if he weren't a supernat-ural creature but a circus animal.

Father Gonzaga arrived before seven o'clock, alarmed at the strange news. By that time onlookers less frivolous than those at dawn had already arrived and they were making all kinds of conjectures concerning the captive's future. The simplest among them thought that he should be named mayor of the world.

Others of sterner mind felt that he should be promoted to the rank of five-star general in order to win all wars. Some visionaries hoped that he could be put to stud in order to implant on earth a race of winged wise men who could take charge of the universe. But Father Gonzaga, before becoming a priest, had been a robust woodcutter. Standing by the wire, he reviewed his catechism in an instant and asked them to open the door so that he could take a close look at that pitiful man who looked more like a huge decrepit hen among the fascinated chickens. He was lying in a corner drying his open wings in the sunlight among the fruit peels and breakfast leftovers that the early risers had thrown him. Alien to the impertinences of the world, he only lifted his antiquarian eyes and murmured something in his dialect when Father Gonzaga went into the chicken coop and said good morning to him in Latin. The parish priest had his first suspicion of an imposter when he saw that he did not understand the language of God or know how to greet His ministers. Then he noticed that seen close up he was much too human: he had an unbearable smell of outdoors, the back side of his wings was strewn with parasites and his main feathers had been mistreated by terrestrial winds, and nothing about him measured up to the proud dignity of angels. Then he came out of the chicken coop and in a brief sermon warned the curious against the risks of being ingenuous. He reminded them that the devil had the bad habit of making use of carnival tricks in order to confuse the unwary. He argued that if wings were not the essential element in determining the difference between a hawk and an airplane, they were even less so in the recognition of angels. Nevertheless, he promised to write a letter to his bishop so that the latter would write to his primate so that the latter would write to the Supreme Pontiff in order to get the final verdict from the highest courts.

His prudence fell on sterile hearts. The news of the captive angel spread with such rapidity that after a few hours the courtyard had the bustle of a marketplace and they had to call in troops with fixed bayonets to disperse the mob that was about to knock the house down. Elisenda, her spine all twisted from sweeping up so much marketplace trash, then got the idea of fencing in the yard and charging five cents admission to see the angel.

The curious came from far away. A traveling carnival arrived with a flying acrobat who buzzed over the crowd several times, but no one paid any attention to him because his wings were not those of an angel but, rather, those of a sidereal bat. The most unfortunate invalids on earth came in search of health: a poor woman who since childhood had been counting her heartbeats and had run out of numbers; a Portuguese man who couldn't sleep because the noise of the stars disturbed him; a sleepwalker who got up at night to undo the things he had done while awake; and many others with less serious ailments. In the midst of that shipwreck disorder that made the earth tremble, Pelayo and Elisenda were happy with fatigue, for in less than a week they had crammed their rooms with money and the line of pilgrims waiting their turn to enter still reached beyond the horizon.

The angel was the only one who took no part in his own act. He spent his time trying to get comfortable in his borrowed nest, befuddled by the hellish heat of the oil lamps and sacramental candles that had been placed along the wire. At first they tried to make him eat some mothballs, which, according to the wisdom of the wise neighbor woman, were the food prescribed for angels. But he turned them down, just as he turned down the papal lunches that the penitents brought him and they never found out whether it was because he was an angel or because he was an old man that in the end he ate nothing but eggplant mush. His only supernatural virtue seemed to be patience. Especially during the first days, when the hens pecked at him, searching for the stellar parasites that proliferated in his wings, and the cripples pulled out feathers to touch their defective parts with, and even the most merciful threw stones at him, trying to get him to rise so they could see him standing. The only time they succeeded in arousing him was when they burned his side with an iron for branding steers, for he had been motionless for so many hours that they thought he was dead. He awoke with a start, ranting in his hermetic language and with tears in his eyes, and he flapped his wings a couple of times, which brought on a whirlwind of chicken dung and lunar dust and a gale of panic that did not seem to be of this world. Although many thought that his reaction had been one not of rage but of pain, from then on they were careful not to annoy him, because the majority understood that his passivity was not that of a hero taking his ease but that of a cataclysm in repose.

Father Gonzaga held back the crowd's frivolity with formulas of maidservant inspiration while awaiting the arrival of a final judgment on the nature of the captive. But the mail from Rome showed no sense of urgency. They spent their time finding out if the prisoner had a navel, if his dialect had any connection with Aramaic, how many times he could fit on the head of a pin, or whether he wasn't just a Norwegian with wings. Those meager letters might have come and gone until the end of time if a providential event had not put an end to the priest's tribulations.

It so happened that during those days, among so many other carnival attractions, there arrived in town the traveling show of the woman who had been changed into a spider for having disobeyed her parents. The admission to see her was not only less than the admission to see the angel, but people were permitted to ask her all manner of questions about her absurd state and to examine her up and down so that no one would ever doubt the truth of her horror. She was a frightful tarantula the size of a ram and with the head of a sad maiden. What was most heart-rending, however, was not her outlandish shape but the sincere affliction with which she recounted the details of her misfortune. While still practically a child she had sneaked out of her parents' house to go to a dance, and while she was coming back through the woods after having danced all night without permission, a fearful thunderclap rent the sky in two and through the crack came the lightning bolt of brimstone that changed her into a spider. Her only nourishment came from the meatballs that charitable souls chose to toss into her mouth. A spectacle like that, full of so much human truth and with such a fearful lesson, was bound to defeat without even trying that of a haughty angel who scarcely deigned to look at mortals. Besides, the few miracles attributed to the angel showed a certain mental disorder, like the blind man who didn't recover his sight but grew three new teeth, or the paralytic who didn't get to walk but almost won the lottery, and the leper whose sores sprouted sunflowers. Those consolation miracles, which were more like mocking fun, had already ruined the angel's reputation when the woman who had been changed into a spider finally crushed him completely. That was how Father Gonzaga was cured forever of his insomnia and Pelayo's courtyard went back to being as empty as during the time it had rained for three days and crabs walked through the bedrooms.

The owners of the house had no reason to lament. With the money they saved they built a two-story mansion with balconies and gardens and high netting so that crabs wouldn't get in during the winter, and with iron bars on the windows so that angels wouldn't get in. Pelayo also set up a rabbit warren close to town and gave up his job as bailiff for good, and Elisenda bought some satin pumps with high heels and many dresses of iridescent silk, the kind worn on Sunday by the most desirable women in those times. The chicken coop was the only thing that didn't receive any attention. If they washed it down with creolin and burned tears of myrrh inside it every so often, it was not in homage to the angel but to drive away the dungheap stench that still hung everywhere like a ghost and was turning the new house into an old one. At first, when the child learned to walk, they were careful that he not get too close to the chicken coop. But then they began to lose their fears and got used to the smell, and before the child got his second teeth he'd gone inside the chicken coop to play, where the wires were falling apart. The angel was no less standoffish with him than with other mortals, but he tolerated the most ingenious infamies with the patience of a dog who had no illusions. They both came down with chicken pox at the same time. The doctor who took care of the child couldn't resist the temptation to listen to the angel's heart, and he found so much whistling in the heart and so many sounds in his kidneys that it seemed impossible for him to be alive. What surprised him most, however, was the logic of his wings. They seemed so natural on that completely human organism that he couldn't understand why other men didn't have them too.

When the child began school it had been some time since the sun and rain had caused the collapse of the chicken coop. The angel went dragging himself about here and there like a stray dying man. They would drive him out of the bedroom with a broom and a moment later find him in the kitchen. He seemed to be in so many places at the same time that they grew to think that he'd been duplicated, that he was reproducing himself all through the house, and the exasperated and unhinged Elisenda shouted that it was awful living in that hell full of angels. He could scarcely eat and his antiquarian eyes had also become so foggy that he went about bumping into posts. All he had left were the bare cannulae of his last feathers. Pelayo threw a blanket over him and extended him the charity of letting him sleep in the shed, and only then did they notice that he had a temperature at night, and was delirious with the tongue twisters of an Old Norwegian. That was one of the few times they became alarmed, for they thought he was going to die and not even the wise neighbor woman had been able to tell them what to do with dead angels.

And yet he not only survived his worst winter, but seemed improved with the first sunny days. He remained motionless for several days in the farthest corner of the courtyard, where no one would see him, and at the beginning of December some large, stiff feathers began to grow on his wings, the feathers of a scarecrow, which looked more like another misfortune of decrepitude. But he must have known the reason for those changes, for he was quite careful that no one should notice them, that no one should hear the sea chanteys that he sometimes sang under the stars. One morning Elisenda was cutting some bunches of onions for lunch when a wind that seemed to come from the high seas blew into the kitchen. Then she went to the window and caught the angel in his first attempts at flight. They were so clumsy that his fingernails opened a furrow in the vegetable patch and he was on the point of knocking the shed down with the ungainly flapping that slipped on the light and couldn't get a grip on the air. But he did manage to gain altitude. Elisenda let out a sigh of relief, for herself and for him, when she saw him pass over the last houses, holding himself up in some way with the risky flapping of a senile vulture. She kept watching him even when she was through cutting the onions and she kept on watching until it was no longer possible for her to see him, because then he was no longer an annoyance in her life but an imaginary dot on the horizon of the sea.

STUDY QUESTIONS

1. A very old man with enormous wings—quite possibly an angel—arrives in a small seaside village. What would you expect to happen? What does happen?

2. Is there any way in which the angel, or his reception, meets your expectations?

3. We have already noted how many stories are built of the careful presentation and accumulation of details. Note the details in this story: the "stellar parasites," the "eggplant mush," the "three extra teeth." What is their cumulative result?

4. What does the story seem to be saying, about the people involved with this supernatural episode, in the way they treat the angel? in the comparison between the angel and the girl who turned into a spider?

5. How much time passes during this story? How does the narrator show its passage?

6. Why might the author call this "a tale for children"?

Harrison Bergeron

Kurt Vonnegut Jr. (1922–   )

The year was 2081, and everybody was finally equal. They weren't only equal before God and the law. They were equal every which way. Nobody was smarter than anybody else. Nobody was better looking than anybody else. Nobody was stronger or quicker than anybody else. All this equality was due to the 211th, 212th, and 213th Amendments to the Constitution, and to the unceasing vigilance of agents of the United States Handicapper General.

Some things about living still weren't quite right, though. April, for instance, still drove people crazy by not being springtime. And it was in that clammy month that the H-G men took George and Hazel Bergeron's fourteen-year-old son, Harrison, away.

It was tragic, all right, but George and Hazel couldn't think about it very hard. Hazel had a perfectly average intelligence, which meant she couldn't think about anything except in short bursts. And George, while his intelligence was way above normal, had a little mental handicap radio in his ear. He was required by law to wear it at all times. It was tuned to a government transmitter. Every twenty seconds or so, the transmitter would send out some sharp noise to keep people like George from taking unfair advantage of their brains.

George and Hazel were watching television. There were tears on Hazel's cheeks, but she'd forgotten for the moment what they were about.

On the television screen were ballerinas.

A buzzer sounded in George's head. His thoughts fled in panic, like bandits from a burglar alarm.

"That was a real pretty dance, that dance they just did," said Hazel.

"Huh?" said George.

"That dance—it was nice," said Hazel.

"Yup," said George. He tried to think a little about the ballerinas. They weren't really very good—no better than anybody else would have been, anyway. They were burdened with sashweights and bags of birdshot, and their faces were masked, so that no one, seeing a free and graceful gesture or a pretty face, would feel like something the cat drug in. George was toying with the vague notion that maybe dancers shouldn't be handicapped. But he didn't get very far with it before another noise in his ear radio scattered his thoughts.

George winced. So did two out of the eight ballerinas.

Hazel saw him wince. Having no mental handicap herself, she had to ask George what the latest sound had been.

"Sounded like somebody hitting a milk bottle with a ball peen hammer," said George.

"I'd think it would be real interesting, hearing all the different sounds," said Hazel, a little envious. "All the things they think up."

"Um," said George.

"Only, if I was Handicapper General, you know what I would do?" said Hazel. Hazel, as a matter of fact, bore a strong resemblance to the Handicapper General, a woman name Diana Moon Glampers. "If I was Diana Moon Glampers," said Hazel, "I'd have chimes on Sunday—just chimes. Kind of in honor of religion."

"I could think, if it was just chimes," said George.

"Well—maybe make 'em real loud," said Hazel. "I think I'd made a good Handicapper General."

"Good as anybody else," said George.

"Who knows better'n I do what normal is?" said Hazel.

"Right," said George. He began to think glimmeringly about his abnormal son who was now in jail, about Harrison, but a twenty-one-gun salute in his head stopped that.

"Boy!" said Hazel, "that was a doozy, wasn't it?"

It was such a doozy that George was white and trembling, and tears stood on the rims of his red eyes. Two of the eight ballerinas had collapsed to the studio floor, were holding their temples.

"All of a sudden you look so tired," said Hazel. "Why don't you stretch out on the sofa, so's you can rest your handicap bag on the pillows, honeybunch." She was referring to the forty-seven pounds of birdshot in a canvas bag, which was padlocked around George's neck. "Go on and rest the bag for a little while," she said. "I don't care if you're not equal to me for a while."

George weighed the bag with his hands. "I don't mind it," he said. "I don't notice it any more. It's just a part of me."

"You been so tired lately—kind of wore out," said Hazel. "If there was just some way we could make a little hole in the bottom of the bag, and just take out a few of them lead balls. Just a few."

"Two years in prison and two thousand dollars fine for every ball I took out," said George. "I don't call that a bargain."

"If you could just take a few out when you came home from work," said Hazel. "I mean—you don't compete with anybody around here. You just set around."

"If I tried to get away with it," said George, "then other people'd get away with it—and pretty soon we'd be right back to the dark ages again, with everybody competing against everybody else. You wouldn't like that, would you?"

"I'd hate it," said Hazel.

"There you are," said George. "The minute people start cheating on laws, what do you think happens to society?"

If Hazel hadn't been able to come up with an answer to this question, George couldn't have supplied one. A siren was going off in his head.

"Reckon it'd fall all apart," said Hazel.

"What would?" said George blankly.

"Society," said Hazel uncertainly. "Wasn't that what you just said?"

"Who knows?" said George.

The television program was suddenly interrupted for a news bulletin. It wasn't clear at first as to what the bulletin was about, since the announcer, like all announcers, had a serious speech impediment. For about half a minute, and in a state of high excitement, the announcer tried to say, "Ladies and gentlemen—"

He finally gave up, handed the bulletin to a ballerina to read.

"That's all right—" Hazel said of the announcer, "he tried. That's the big thing. He tried to do the best he could with what God gave him. He should get a nice raise for trying so hard."

"Ladies and gentlemen—" said the ballerina, reading the bulletin. She must have been extraordinarily beautiful, because the mask she wore was hideous. And it was easy to see that she was the strongest and most graceful of all the dancers, for her handicap bags were as big as those worn by two-hundred-pound men.

And she had to apologize at once for her voice, which was a very unfair voice for a woman to use. Her voice was a warm, luminous, timeless melody. "Excuse me—" she said, and she began again, making her voice absolutely un-competitive.

"Harrison Bergeron, age fourteen," she said in a grackle squawk, "has just escaped from jail, where he was held on suspicion of plotting to overthrow the government. He is a genius and an athlete, is underhandicapped, and should be regarded as extremely dangerous."

A police photograph of Harrison Bergeron was flashed on the screen upside down, then sideways, upside down again, then right side up. The picture showed the full length of Harrison against a background calibrated in feet and inches. He was exactly seven feet tall.

The rest of Harrison's appearance was Halloween and hardware. Nobody had ever borne heavier handicaps. He had outgrown hindrances faster than the H-G men could think them up. Instead of a little ear radio for a mental handicap, he wore a tremendous pair of earphones, and spectacles with thick wavy lenses. The spectacles were intended to make him not only half blind, but to give him whanging headaches besides.

Scrap metal was hung all over him. Ordinarily, there was a certain symmetry, a military neatness to the handicaps issued to strong people, but Harrison looked like a walking junkyard. In the race of life, Harrison carried three hundred pounds.

And to offset his good looks, the H-G men required that he wear at all times a red rubber ball for a nose, keep his eyebrows shaved off, and cover his even white teeth with black caps at snaggle-tooth random.

"If you see this boy," said the ballerina, "do not—I repeat, do not—try to reason with him."

There was the shriek of a door being torn from its hinges.

Screams and barking cries of consternation came from the television set. The photograph of Harrison Bergeron on the screen jumped again and again, as though dancing to the tune of an earthquake.

George Bergeron correctly identified the earthquake, and well he might have—for many was the time his own home had danced to the same crashing tune. "My God—" said George, "that must be Harrison!"

The realization was blasted from his mind instantly by the sound of an automobile collision in his head.

When George could open his eyes again, the photograph of Harrison was gone. A living, breathing Harrison filled the screen.

Clanking, clownish, and huge, Harrison stood in the center of the studio. The knob of the uprooted studio door was still in his hand. Ballerinas, technicians, musicians, and announcers cowered on their knees before him, expecting to die.

"I am the Emperor!" cried Harrison. "Do you hear? I am the Emperor! Everybody must do what I say at once!" He stamped his foot and the studio shook.

"Even as I stand here—" he bellowed, "crippled, hobbled, sickened—I am a greater ruler than any man who ever lived! Now watch me become what I *can* become!"

Harrison tore the straps of his handicap harness like wet tissue paper, tore straps guaranteed to support five thousand pounds.

Harrison's scrap-iron handicaps crashed to the floor.

Harrison thrust his thumbs under the bar of the padlock that secured his head harness. The bar snapped like celery. Harrison smashed his headphones and spectacles against the wall.

He flung away his rubber-ball nose, revealed a man that would have awed Thor, the god of thunder.

"I shall now select my Empress!" he said, looking down on the cowering people. "Let the first woman who dares rise to her feet claim her mate and her throne!"

A moment passed, and then a ballerina arose, swaying like a willow.

Harrison plucked the mental handicap from her ear, snapped off her physical handicaps with marvelous delicacy. Last of all, he removed her mask.

She was blindingly beautiful.

"Now—" said Harrison, taking her hand, "shall we show the people the meaning of the word *dance?* Music!" he commanded.

The musicians scrambled back into their chairs, and Harrison stripped them of their handicaps, too. "Play your best," he told them, "and I'll make you barons and dukes and earls."

The music began. It was normal at first—cheap, silly, false. But Harrison snatched two musicians from their chairs, waved them like batons as he sang the music as he wanted it played. He slammed them back into their chairs.

The music began again and was much improved.

Harrison and his Empress merely listened to the music for a while—listened gravely, as though synchronizing their heartbeats with it.

They shifted their weights to their toes.

Harrison placed his big hands on the girl's tiny waist, letting her sense the weightlessness that would soon be hers.

And then, in an explosion of joy and grace, into the air they sprang!

Not only were the laws of the land abandoned, but the law of gravity and the laws of motion as well.

They reeled, whirled, swiveled, flounced, capered, gamboled, and spun.

They leaped like deer on the moon.

The studio ceiling was thirty feet high, but each leap brought the dancers nearer to it.

It became their obvious intention to kiss the ceiling.

They kissed it.

And then, neutralizing gravity with love and pure will, they remained suspended in air inches below the ceiling, and they kissed each other for a long, long time.

It was then that Diana Moon Glampers, the Handicapper General, came into the studio with a double-barreled ten-gauge shotgun. She fired twice, and the Emperor and the Empress were dead before they hit the floor.

Diana Moon Glampers loaded the gun again. She aimed it at the musicians and told them they had ten seconds to get their handicaps back on.

It was then that the Bergerons' television tube burned out.

Hazel turned to comment about the blackout to George. But George had gone out into the kitchen for a can of beer.

George came back in with the beer, paused while a handicap signal shook him up. And then he sat down again. "You been crying?" he said to Hazel.

"Yup," she said.

"What about?" he said.

"I forget," she said. "Something real sad on television."

"What was it?" he said.

"It's all kind of mixed up in my mind," said Hazel.

"Forget sad things," said George.

"I always do," said Hazel.

STUDY QUESTIONS

1. How is the society depicted in "Harrison Bergeron" comparable to today's society? How does it differ?

2. Do you feel that the differences are true differences, or that they merely make extreme or explicit problems that exist today? Or are both points of view true?

3. Note the story's depiction of two characters' rebellion and escape, and the audience's reaction to it. How does this climactic act fit into your comparison and contrast of this imaginative society to our own society?

4. In both "A Very Old Man with Enormous Wings" and "Harrison Bergeron," something surprising happens, and the onlookers fail to give wholehearted response. In each case, why? What might this suggest about the techniques of the two writers?

10

AUTOBIOGRAPHY

In these chapter introductions, we've talked a great deal about fiction giving us insights into society and individuals. In fact, though, the communities and individuals that we each know best are those with which we grow up and in which we live as adults.

Many authors draw from their own experiences when creating their fiction, disguising it lightly or heavily. Other writers, discarding the masks of fiction, write about their experiences directly, in autobiographies or memoirs. These writers can "name names" and be as open as they like in describing the communities in which they were brought up, the people who influenced them, and their own thoughts, feelings, and actions throughout the various stages of their development. Such writings can be remarkably important, for they give us, as no other writings can, first-hand looks at communities we cannot visit directly.

As to form, the autobiography promises a relatively complete study of the writer's life, from the beginning to the point where the book ends. For this reason, autobiographies are often written in several volumes, with each volume carrying the story over a further span of years. Memoirs are somewhat less formal. They do not promise completeness in discussing the writer's life. Instead, their technique is often aimed at illuminating the high points and passing quickly over the rest. In compensation, they often include fuller discussions of people whom the writer found influential. Their structure may be looser than that of the autobiography, the focus more inclusive of family or community.

This chapter presents three selections from autobiographical works. The works are far too long to be included here in their entirety, so we have chosen samples from each. The first selection comes from three chapters of Mark Twain's *Old Times on the Mississippi* and tells of Twain's training as a riverboat pilot—a tale he wished to tell before those days vanished into history with the steamboats. The second selection is from the Native American writer N. Scott Momaday's memoir, *The Names*. The selection tells of a time when his parents sent him, as a young boy, to live with his grandmother and uncle. More precisely, it tells of his first day with them, and of the feelings that day engendered in him. The third selection comes from *I Know Why the Caged Bird Sings*, the first volume of Maya Angelou's autobiography. This selection describes the revival meetings that came at intervals to the rural Southern community where she and her brother were being brought up by their grandmother, and how those meetings appeared to the young girl.

As you read these selections, you will notice that all the techniques available to fiction writers are equally available to writers of autobiographical material. A writer of autobiography cannot construct a fictional climax for an incident but can direct our attention, by skillful writing, to an actual climax that we might otherwise not have recognized. They can use voices creatively: Twain uses his finest "story-telling" voice throughout, but Momaday and Angelou both use multiple voices in their work. Both slip easily from first person to third person. (Angelou does this within the selection we read.) To this, Momaday adds the use of "stream of consciousness," a twentieth-century technique in which the writer attempts to record someone's thoughts as they occur, with all the illogical shifts of direction that such streams of thought normally contain.

These selections, therefore, are to be enjoyed for their artistry as much as for the illumination they provide. Each shows the writer's ability to focus on sharply remembered moments—on a trick played on one, a new toy, a sermon, a song—and, by brilliantly telling about them, making them illuminate the time, place, and people of which the writers tell.

From Old Times on the Mississippi

Mark Twain (1835–1910)

FROM II. A "CUB" PILOT'S EXPERIENCE; OR, LEARNING THE RIVER.

The *Paul Jones* was now bound for St. Louis. I planned a siege against my pilot, and at the end of three hard days he surrendered. He agreed to teach me the Mississippi River from New Orleans to St. Louis for five hundred dollars, payable out of the first wages I should receive after graduating. I entered upon the small enterprise of "learning" twelve or thirteen hundred miles of the great Mississippi River with the easy confidence of my time of life. If I had really known what I was about to require of my faculties, I should not have had the courage to begin. I supposed that all a pilot had to do was to keep his boat in the river, and I did not consider that that could be much of a trick, since it was so wide.

The boat backed out from New Orleans at four in the afternoon, and it was "our watch" until eight. Mr. Bixby, my chief, "straightened her up," plowed her along past the sterns of the other boats that lay at the Levee, and then said, "Here, take her; shave those steamships as close as you'd peel an apple." I took the wheel and my heart went down into my boots; for it seemed to me that we were about to scrape the side off every ship in the line, we were so close. I held my breath and began to claw the boat away from the danger, and I had my own opinion of the pilot who had known no better than to get us into such peril, but I was too wise to express it. In half a minute I had a wide margin of safety intervening between the *Paul Jones* and the ships, and within ten seconds more I was set aside in disgrace and Mr. Bixby was going into danger again and flaying me alive with abuse of my cowardice. I was stung but I was obliged to admire the easy confidence with which my chief loafed from side to side of his wheel and trimmed the ships so closely that disaster seemed ceaselessly imminent. When he had cooled a little he told me that the easy water was close ashore and the current outside, and therefore we must hug the bank up-stream, to get the benefit of the former, and stay out down-stream, to take advantage of the latter. In my own mind I resolved to be a down-stream pilot and leave the up-streaming to people dead to prudence.

Now and then Mr. Bixby called my attention to certain things. Said he, "This is Six-Mile Point." I assented. It was pleasant enough information but I could not see the bearing of it. I was not conscious that it was a matter of any interest to me. Another time he said, "This is Nine-Mile Point." Later he said, "This is Twelve-Mile Point." They were all about level with the water's edge; they all looked about alike to me; they were monotonously unpicturesque. I hoped Mr. Bixby would change the subject. But no, he would crowd up around a point, hugging the shore with affection, and then say: "The slack water ends here, abreast this bunch of China trees; now we cross over." So he crossed over. He gave me the wheel once or twice but I had no luck. I either came near chipping off the edge of a sugar-plantation, or I yawed too far from shore and so dropped back into disgrace again and got abused. . . .

It was a rather dingy night, although a fair number of stars were out. The big mate was at the wheel and he had the old tub pointed at a star and was holding her straight up the middle of the river. The shores on either hand were not much more than half a mile apart, but they seemed wonderfully far away and ever so vague and indistinct. The mate said:

"We've got to land at Jones's plantation, sir."

The vengeful spirit in me exulted. I said to myself, "I wish you joy of your job, Mr. Bixby; you'll have a good time finding Mr. Jones's plantation such a night as this, and I hope you never *will* find it as long as you live."

Mr. Bixby said to the mate:

"Upper end of the plantation, or the lower?"

"Upper."

"I can't do it. The stumps there are out of water at this stage. It's no great distance to the lower and you'll have to get along with that."

"All right, sir. If Jones don't like it, he'll have to lump it, I reckon."

And then the mate left. My exultation began to cool and my wonder to come up. Here was a man who not only proposed to find this plantation on such a night but to find either end of it you preferred. I dreadfully wanted to ask a question, but I was carrying about as many short answers as my cargo-room would admit of, so I held my peace. All I desired to ask Mr. Bixby was the simple question whether he was ass enough to really imagine he was going to find that plantation on a night when all plantations were exactly alike and all of the same color. But I held in. I used to have fine inspirations of prudence in those days.

Mr. Bixby made for the shore and soon was scraping it, just the same as if it had been daylight. And not only that but singing:

"Father in heaven, the day is declining," etc.

It seemed to me that I had put my life in the keeping of a peculiarly reckless out-cast. Presently he turned on me and said:

"What's the name of the first point above New Orleans?"

I was gratified to be able to answer promptly, and I did. I said I didn't know.

"Don't *know?*"

This manner jolted me. I was down at the foot again, in a moment. But I had to say just what I had said before.

"Well, you're a smart one!" said Mr. Bixby. "What's the name of the *next* point?"

Once more I didn't know.

"Well, this beats anything. Tell me the name of *any* point or place I told you."

I studied awhile and decided that I couldn't.

"Look here! What do you start out from, above Twelve-Mile Point, to cross over?"

"I—I—don't know."

"You—you—don't know?" mimicking my drawling manner of speech. "What *do* you know?"

"I—I—nothing, for certain."

"By the great Caesar's ghost, I believe you! You're the stupidest dunderhead I ever saw or ever heard of, so help me Moses! The idea of *you* being a pilot—*you!* Why, you don't know enough to pilot a cow down a lane."

Oh, but his wrath was up! He was a nervous man, and he shuffled from one side of his wheel to the other as if the floor was hot. He would boil awhile to himself and then overflow and scald me again.

"Look here! What do you suppose I told you the names of those points for?"

I tremblingly considered a moment and then the devil of temptation provoked me to say:

"Well to—to—be entertaining, I thought."

This was a red rag to the bull. He raged and stormed so (he was crossing the river at the time) that I judged it made him blind, because he ran over the steering-oar of a trading-scow. Of course the traders sent up a volley of red-hot profanity. Never was a man so grateful as Mr. Bixby was, because he was brimful and here were subjects who could *talk back*. He threw open a window, thrust his head out, and such an irruption followed as I never had heard before. The fainter and farther away the scowmen's curses drifted, the higher Mr. Bixby lifted his voice and the weightier his adjectives grew. When he closed the window he was empty. You could have drawn a seine through his system and not caught curses enough to disturb your mother with. Presently he said to me in the gentlest way:

"My boy, you must get a little memorandum-book, and every time I tell you a thing, put it down right away. There's only one way to be a pilot and that is to get this entire river by heart. You have to know it just like ABC."

That was a dismal revelation to me, for my memory was never loaded with anything but blank cartridges. However, I did not feel discouraged long. I judged that it was best to make some allowances, for doubtless Mr. Bixby was "stretching". Presently he pulled a rope and struck a few strokes on the big bell. The stars were all gone now and the night was as black as ink. I could hear the wheels churn along the bank but I was not entirely certain that I could see the shore. The voice of the invisible watchman called up from the hurricane-deck:

"What's this, sir?"

"Jones's plantation."

I said to myself, "I wish I might venture to offer a small bet that it isn't." But I did not chirp. I only waited to see. Mr. Bixby handled the engine-bells and in due time the boat's nose came to the land, a torch glowed from the forecastle, a man skipped ashore, a darky's voice on the bank said: "Gimme de k'yarpet-bag, Mass' Jones," and the next moment we were standing up the river again, all serene. I reflected deeply awhile, and then said—but not aloud—"Well, the finding of that plantation was the luckiest accident that ever happened, but it couldn't happen again in a hundred years." And I fully believed it *was* an accident, too.

From iv. Pilot's Education Nearly Completed

I thought I had finished this chapter, but I wish to add a curious thing, while it is in my mind. It is only relevant in that it is connected with piloting. There used to be an excellent pilot on the river, a Mr. X, who was a somnambulist. It was said that if his mind was troubled about a bad piece of river, he was pretty sure to get up and walk in his sleep and do strange things. He was once fellow-pilot for a trip or two with George Ealer, on a great New Orleans passenger-packet. During a considerable part of the first trip George was uneasy but got over it by and by, as X seemed content to stay in his bed when asleep. Late one night the boat was approaching Helena, Ark.; the water was low and the crossing above the town in a very blind and tangled condition. X had seen the crossing since Ealer had and as the night was particularly drizzly, sullen, and dark, Ealer was considering whether he had not better have X called to assist in running the place, when the door opened and X walked in. Now, on very dark nights light is a deadly enemy to piloting; you are aware that if you stand in a lighted room, on such a night, you cannot see things in the street to any purpose, but if you put out the lights and stand in the gloom you can make out objects in the street pretty well. So, on very dark nights pilots do not smoke, they allow no fire in the pilot-house stove if there is a crack which can allow the least ray to escape, they order the furnaces to be curtained with huge tarpaulins and the skylights to be closely blinded. Then no light whatever issues from the boat. The undefinable shape that now entered the pilot-house had Mr. X's voice. This said:

"Let me take her, George; I've seen this place since you have and it is so crooked that I reckon I can run it myself easier than I could tell you how to do it."

"It is kind of you and I swear *I* am willing. I haven't got another drop of perspiration left in me. I have been spinning around and around the wheel like a squirrel. It is so dark I can't tell which way she is swinging till she is coming around like a whirligig."

So Ealer took a seat on the bench, panting and breathless. The black phantom assumed the wheel without saying anything, steadied the waltzing steamer with a turn or two, and then stood at ease, coaxing her a little to this side and then to that, as gently and as sweetly as if the time had been noonday. When Ealer observed this marvel of steering, he wished he had not confessed! He stared and wondered, and finally said:

"Well, I thought I knew how to steer a steamboat but that was another mistake of mine."

X said nothing but went serenely on with his work. He rang for the leads; he rang to slow down the steam; he worked the boat carefully and neatly into invisible marks, then stood at the center of the wheel and peered blandly out into the blackness, fore and aft, to verify his position, as the leads shoaled more and more he stopped the engines entirely, and the dead silence and suspense of "drifting" followed; when the shoalest water was struck, he cracked on the steam, carried her handsomely over, and then began to work her warily into the next system of shoal-marks; the same patient, heedful use of leads and engines followed, the boat slipped through without touching bottom, and entered upon the third and last intricacy of the crossing; imperceptibly she moved through the gloom, crept by inches into her marks, drifted tediously till the shoalest water was cried, and then, under a tremendous head of steam, went swinging over the reef and away into deep water and safety!

Ealer let his long-pent breath pour in a great relieving sigh, and said:

"That's the sweetest piece of piloting that was ever done on the Mississippi River! I wouldn't believe it could be done, if I hadn't seen it."

There was no reply, and he added:

"Just hold her five minutes longer, partner, and let me run down and get a cup of coffee."

A minute later Ealer was biting into a pie, down in the "texas," and comforting himself with coffee. Just then the night watchman happened in, and was about to happen out again when he noticed Ealer and exclaimed:

"Who is at the wheel, sir?"

"X."

"Dart for the pilot-house, quicker than lightning!"

The next moment both men were flying up the pilot-house companionway, three steps at a jump! Nobody there! The great steamer was whistling down the middle of the river at her own sweet will! The watchman shot out of the place again; Ealer seized the wheel, set an engine back with power, and held his breath while the boat reluctantly swung away from a "towhead" which she was about to knock into the middle of the Gulf of Mexico!

By and by the watchman came back and said:

"Didn't that lunatic tell you he was asleep, when he first came up here?"

"No."

"Well, he was. I found him walking along on top of the railings, just as unconcerned as another man would walk a pavement, and I put him to bed; now just this minute there he was again, away astern, going through that sort of tight-rope deviltry the same as before."

"Well, I think I'll stay by next time he has one of those fits. But I hope he'll have them often. You just ought to have seen him take this boat through Helena crossing. *I* never saw anything so gaudy before. And if he can do such gold-leaf, kid-glove, diamond-breastpin piloting when he is sound asleep, what *couldn't* he do if he was dead!"

FROM V. "SOUNDING". FACULTIES PECULIARLY NECESSARY TO A PILOT

A pilot must have a memory, but there are two higher qualities which he must also have. He must have good and quick judgment and decision, and a cool, calm courage that no peril can shake. Give a man the merest trifle of pluck to start with and by the time he has become a pilot he cannot be unmanned by any danger a steamboat can get into, but one cannot quite say the same for judgment. Judgment is a matter of brains and a man must *start* with a good stock of that article or he will never succeed as a pilot.

The growth of courage in the pilot-house is steady all the time but it does not reach a high and satisfactory condition until some time after the young pilot has been "standing his own watch" alone and under the staggering weight of all the responsibilities connected with the position. When the apprentice has become pretty thoroughly acquainted with the river, he goes clattering along so fearlessly with his steamboat, night or day, that he presently begins to imagine that it is *his* courage that animates him, but the first time the pilot steps out and leaves him to his own devices he finds out it was the other man's. He discovers that the article has been left out of his own cargo altogether. The whole river is bristling with exigencies in a moment, he is not prepared for them, he does not know how to meet them; all his knowledge forsakes him, and within fifteen minutes he is as white as a sheet and scared almost to death. Therefore pilots wisely train these cubs by various strategic tricks to look danger in the face a little more calmly. A favorite way of theirs is to play a friendly swindle upon the candidate.

Mr. Bixby served me in this fashion once and for years afterward I used to blush, even in my sleep, when I thought of it. I had become a good steersman; so good, indeed, that I had all the work to do on our watch, night and day. Mr. Bixby seldom made a suggestion to me; all he ever did was to take the wheel on particularly bad nights or in particularly bad crossings, land the boat when she needed to be landed, play gentleman of leisure nine-tenths of the watch, and collect the wages. The lower river was about bank-full and if anybody had questioned my ability to run any crossing between Cairo and New Orleans without help or instruction, I should have felt irreparably hurt. The idea of being afraid of any crossing in the lot, in the *daytime,* was a thing too preposterous for contemplation. Well, one matchless summer's day I was bowling down the bend above Island 66, brimful of self-conceit and carrying my nose as high as a giraffe's, when Mr. Bixby said:

"I am going below awhile. I suppose you know the next crossing?"

This was almost an affront. It was about the plainest and simplest crossing in the whole river. One couldn't come to any harm whether he ran it right or not, and as for depth, there never had been any bottom there. I knew all this, perfectly well.

"Know how to *run* it? Why, I can run it with my eyes shut."

"How much water is there in it?"

"Well, that is an odd question. I couldn't get bottom there with a church steeple."

"You think so, do you?"

The very tone of the question shook my confidence. That was what Mr. Bixby was expecting. He left, without saying anything more. I began to imagine all sorts of things. Mr. Bixby, unknown to me, of course, sent somebody down to the forecastle with some mysterious instructions to the leadsmen, another messenger was sent to whisper among the officers, and then Mr. Bixby went into hiding behind a smoke-stack where he could observe results. Presently the captain stepped out on the hurricane-deck; next the chief mate appeared; then a clerk. Every moment or two a straggler was added to my audience, and before I got to the head of the island I had fifteen or twenty people assembled down there under my nose. I began to wonder what the trouble was. As I started across, the captain glanced aloft at me and said, with a sham uneasiness in his voice:

"Where is Mr. Bixby?"

"Gone below, sir."

But that did the business for me. My imagination began to construct dangers out of nothing, and they multiplied faster than I could keep the run of them. All at once I imagined I saw shoal water ahead! The wave of coward agony that surged through me then came near dislocating every joint in me. All my confidence in that crossing vanished. I seized the bell-rope; dropped it, ashamed; seized it again; dropped it once more; clutched it tremblingly once again, and pulled it so feebly that I could hardly hear the stroke myself. Captain and mate sang out instantly, and both together:

"Starboard lead there! and quick about it!"

This was another shock. I began to climb the wheel like a squirrel, but I would hardly get the boat started to port before I would see new dangers on that side and away I would spin to the other, only to find perils accumulating to starboard and be crazy to get to port again. Then came the leadsman's sepulchral cry:

"D-e-e-p four!"

Deep four in a bottomless crossing! The terror of it took my breath away.

"M-a-r-k three! M-a-r-k three! Quarter-less-three! Half twain!"

This was frightful! I seized the bell-ropes and stopped the engines.

"Quarter twain! Quarter twain! *Mark* twain!"

I was helpless. I did not know what in the world to do. I was quaking from head to foot and I could have hung my hat on my eyes, they stuck out so far.

"Quarter-*less*-twain! Nine-and-a-*half!*"

We were *drawing* nine! My hands were in a nerveless flutter. I could not ring a bell intelligibly with them. I flew to the speaking-tube and shouted to the engineer:

"Oh, Ben, if you love me, *back* her! Quick, Ben! Oh, back the immortal *soul* out of her!"

I heard the door close gently. I looked around, and there stood Mr. Bixby, smiling a bland, sweet smile. Then the audience on the hurricane-deck sent up a thundergust of humiliating laughter. I saw it all, now, and I felt meaner than the meanest man in human history. I laid in the lead, set the boat in her marks, came ahead on the engines, and said:

"It was a fine trick to play on an orphan, *wasn't* it? I suppose I'll never hear the last of how I was ass enough to heave the lead at the head of 66."

"Well, no, you won't, maybe. In fact I hope you won't, for I want you to learn something by that experience. Didn't you *know* there was no bottom in that crossing?"

"Yes, sir, I did."

"Very well, then. You shouldn't have allowed me or anybody else to shake your confidence in that knowledge. Try to remember that. And another thing, when you get into a dangerous place, don't turn coward. That isn't going to help matters any."

It was a good enough lesson but pretty hardly learned. Yet about the hardest part of it was that for months I so often had to hear a phrase which I had conceived a particular distaste for. It was, "Oh, Ben, if you love me, back her!"

STUDY QUESTIONS

1. How does Twain balance teaching, entertainment, and self-revelation in these selections from *Old Times on the Mississippi?* Discuss at least one example of each.
2. Why, in a narrative of his own experiences, does Twain include the tale of the sleepwalking Mr. X? What does this tale add to the narrative?
3. Why does Twain tell the tale on himself that ends Chapter V?

4. Twain is considered one of the masters of the southern United States comic tradition. In your opinion, do the selections chosen here bear this out? Discuss.

5. Discuss the narrator's style and voice. Note, for example, such sentences as "You could have drawn a seine through his system and not caught enough curses to disturb your mother." What do the various elements of style and voice that you have noticed add to your enjoyment of the narrative, or to your perspective on it?

6. How does the narrator's voice in *Old Times on the Mississippi* differ from that of the narrators in "The Celebrated Jumping Frog of Calaveras County"? Why might these differences exist?

7. How does Twain's narrative voice in *Old Times on the Mississippi* compare with other narrative voices you have met in the fiction in Chapters 2 and 5 of this anthology? Discuss some examples of similarities and differences that seem noteworthy to you.

From The Names

N. Scott Momaday (1934–   )

2

The sun was going down, and now the sky was red and purple in the west. For a few minutes the buildings of the town of Mountain View were edged with orange light, especially the underside of a water tank and the white wall of a silo; then the buildings backed off into the dusk and there was a blur upon them. The panes of a window in Mammedaty's house caught the last glare of the sun.

The darkness rose like a flood from the creek, and there was nothing in it, only a kind of long, lateral hush that divided the plain. It rose, but it could not be seen to rise; it could be seen only to hold off. A spotted cat came from under the south porch of Mammedaty's house, regarded something with its head slung low, and returned. The air told time.

James sat at the oval table in the dining room with his young nephew, muttering sometimes under his breath, as he did always and for no apparent reason, and his mother brought a platter of meat and eggs from the kitchen. The light had gone out of the room, and James struck a match and set fire to the wick in the lamp. When the globe was set down upon it the flame grew hard and bright, but for a time it seemed not to make much of a difference in the color—it was one color—of the room.

The boy, whose first home this was, was homesick. He suffered intensely, knowing that his grandmother and his uncle were watching him. They did not want him to cry. He thought it over; he wanted to cry. Earlier, in the afternoon, when he had played out his solitary games and gone almost to sleep while sitting on a log, watching, listening, rather, to his uncle chop wood, he had cried. A loneliness had grown up in him, and he could no longer keep it all to himself. But at the same time he was ashamed to cry, and so he cried in spite of himself, blinking the tears hard from his eyes, giving no more voice to his crying than he could help.

James cut up some meat on the boy's plate and pushed the plate across the table to the boy's place. There was a blue floral design all around the rim of the white plate, and the pieces of meat were nearly black in the lamplight, and the eggs were fried hard and edged with a thin brown crust, and they were shiny with grease. His grandmother poured the boy some milk from a gray metal pitcher into a tumbler of carnival glass; little bunches of grapes were raised in the glass, lightly frosted with blue and purple. Then she sat down between the boy and his uncle and prayed. She ended with the words, "in Jesus' name. Amen." These were the only words the boy understood.

The boy tried to eat, but he had no appetite, and so after a few minutes he could take nothing but the milk. The milk was warm and fresh and very sweet, having come only a little while before from one of the leaseman's cows. The boy had watched the milking, had patted the cow's shoulder as it stood at the trough in Mammedaty's barn, had seen the thin streams of white milk spurting into the pail. He had been fascinated. "Where you from?" the leaseman said. "Shiprock," the boy answered. "Where's that?" But the boy had forgotten where Shiprock was, and he was suddenly, painfully embarrassed. "Texas?" the leaseman offered. "No." "Kansas? Nebraska?" "No." "Illinois, Missouri, Ohio?" "Maybe Missouri," the boy said. He knew that was wrong, but he had to get out of this predicament. "Yes, Missouri," he said absolutely. "Huh. Ain't never been there," the leaseman said.

And the boy had played in Mammedaty's barn, among the stalls in the wet, stinking straw, stirring up the dust, the dry alfalfa dust, until his clothes were full of chaff and manure and dust, and his grandmother had to take his clothes and shake them out and wash them, and he had to sit in an old galvanized washtub in the kitchen in gray, soapy water in which his grandmother poured more and more hot water from a great kettle on the old wood stove. And he had seen a box of bones in the barn and had been afraid to touch them, but he touched them anyway. They were the bones of a horse, *Guadal-tseyu*.

The boy's grandmother leased most of the land out, now that Mammedaty was gone, and the income was substantial. There was a good deal of land, and much of it was clear and fertile. James, too, had good land of his own, some of the richest land in the state. The leasemen were always trying to buy the land, but neither Aho nor James would sell it. James had received some lease money that day. Had his nephew been older and known what money was, James would have given him some, a generous amount, even, as he would do many times in the years to come, for the satisfaction. The man loved the boy.

The boy held the milk up to the lamp and looked through the carnival glass. His grandmother and his uncle scolded him for not eating, but he knew that he could have his way, and he pleaded simply that he was not hungry and went on playing with the glass. He felt better, and he was getting sleepy.

Well anyway I have this gun this real-looking gun black and brown smooth and hard a carbine tomorrow I will shoot an Indian down by the creek he will see me but I will see him first and I will wait until he sees me it has to be that way of course he sees me and of course he is surprised his eyes are big and his mouth is open and he is *ugly* of course he has a knife it is a great big knife and it gleams and flashes in the sunlight it was stolen of course oh I know that good knife it was stolen from my grandfather one night when he left it outside by the arbor where he liked to cut meat he talked about it of course he meant to give it to my father and my father meant to give it to me it is really my knife the ugly Indian sees me and I am looking right at him and I have been looking right at him for a long long time he recognizes me of course it has to be that way he has been afraid of me all these years running and hiding from me and now it has come to this he is famous because of the knife he has of course killed many men women and children with the knife and he is called Knife sometimes Big Knife some-times Knife Thrower then after a moment he smiles and he is even uglier so it is you at last he says and I nod there is a moment between us then he makes his lightning move and the knife is wheeling in the air and of course I shoot him and nimbly nimbly I catch the knife in the stock of my gun over my heart and the ugly Indian staggers and slumps and pitches headfirst into a ravine and I say you're dead and of course it is so

The cow was a pretty thing her shoulders were warm and smooth and so soft to touch the color of moccasins

I saw too a very fat man with no neck just a black line between his head and shoulders his teeth and the nails of his huge hands were the same color what color a pretty little girl yellow and thin a dirty baby waddling linoleum broken somewhere a dead dog grinning on the side of the road the flies all over it rabbits other guns none as good as the carbine a white radio in the window of Crabtree's drugstore the back of the leaseman's red neck silt moving on the creek an anthill the head of Jesus Christ in a cloud a jar of jellybeans many of them black a green tractor my uncle's stomach through his shirt the teats of the moccasin-colored cow

Grandma and Jimmy in the next room talking sometimes funny words I don't know what they are all of them I know one or two words here and there now and then the talk is so slow there are long silences

There are long silences in which dishes rattle, pots and pans ring. Then there is talk, slow, emphatic. I turn over on my stomach, holding the carbine close against me, at the ready. There is a line of light under the door, not a line, really, but a long, thin triangle of light, under the door. The talk is there in that splinter of light, sliding along, now . . . now . . . now, now sharp, now muffled, close, distant, drawing away, and the black at the window going to blue within my reach. Somewhere a syllable draws away, and a breeze slants across the night, and there is nothing else.

James was slouched at the oval table, his right arm lying under his absent gaze on the oilcloth, his right hand hanging down from the edge, the fingers curled slightly, the thumb extended almost to his left thigh, his head hanging. And across the table sat Aho, his mother, composed, her hands interlaced in her lap, her feet crossed. Her eyes, partly closed and downcast, shone in the lamp-light, and she was chewing gum. In her pensive moments she almost always chewed gum, slowly, exactly, as if, with her back teeth, to regulate her thoughts.

James thought of the boy, his nephew. It was his concession to the boy that he had seen him through the day, had led him around the empty spaces of time in the morning and afternoon, especially the late afternoon, when the shadows stood still. They had walked down to the town, had looked into the wide street, had carried out their business like men of the world, in the post office, in the bank, had eaten ice cream, had bought the good toy gun. They had gone along together, or their paths had crossed many times through the day. Through the day. The day had come down to the night, and the boy was asleep, safe and sound. Now:

A knot was being drawn very tight inside the man. The thought, just the thought, of being drunk had a physical effect upon him, a giddiness, a kind of euphoria in which his body seemed to grow lighter and more supple, and at the same time there was a kind of resistance in it, in the flesh and blood, the body's own anticipation of impairment and pain, of dehydration and the sharp contraction of the brain. His eyes went very dry—and his tongue—and sweat broke out at his head and at the palms of his hands.

He saw his mother out of the corner of his eye. Aho did not provoke him, except that the patience in her pressed upon him like a weariness. It lay between them as a long distance or an interval that he could not comprehend. She was entirely composed. A painter should have loved her in her composure then, in the lamplight. Momently the light shivered in her hair, so lowly that it seemed barely to emanate there. Her head, her face, her shoulders, her bosom were ample and round. Nothing, neither the corners of her eyes and mouth, nor the folds of her flesh and the shadows that were set upon her, hardened to an edge or an angle or a flatness anywhere. Her skin was dark, and yet her face was so radiant against the shadows and the deeper darkness of her hair and her dress that her whole expression was laid out and defined there, fashioned upon the broad, round bone of her skull, which was prominent just now in the strange quality of the light. Her eyes were half-closed, and neither did the lamp's reflection which guttered there seem any way hard and precise, but soft and transparent. The painter should have wondered how to indicate such a thing. He should have had to work a great illusion into a single point, something more a matter of texture than of color, perhaps. He should have had to bring his artist's hand and his artist's eye so close together as to be one and the same thing. She seemed very wise and very strong, and her strength seemed to consist in rest. She seemed simply to know how to be comfortable in the world. James had never been able to tell what she was thinking; the painter should not have been able to tell; he should have had to work his brush across a riddle.

When he went out the moon had only just appeared. It was huge and thick and darkly colored at his back, absorbent. He scarcely knew it was there, but he was screwed tight upon his thirst, and he walked again along the highway. He did not hear the crickets that had begun to crackle everywhere.

And later, later, on his way back, the moon was high and colorless, a perfect spot on the murky midnight. He stumbled in his joy and stupor, knowing not yet what he yearned for, knowing only that he was alive to the night and strangely exhilarated.

He saw the dead silver dog, stealthy in death, and he walked a wide way around it. He wanted to say serious things, but laughter grew up in him. His laughter rang out, rolled along the black bank of the creek below, the gray grass, the undulent way to the Wichitas. Oh, God, he thought, the clamorous night! He could hear everything distinctly now, the rasping of the crickets and the frogs, the wind turning, leaves sliding upon leaves, a motor in the far distance, the echo of his laughter dying away, and beyond that the laughter of God, God's laughter. It was all so beautiful to hear. And he opened his eyes wide and looked all around, and everything shone in his sight, and it was all so beautiful to see. He was involved in the light, enchanted. He said God, spoke the name of God, laughing with his teeth clenched, and he felt himself whirling in the light. The light was like frost on the hills; it lay out in the great round hollow of the plains, as far as he could see, shifting and quaking slowly, tumbling like a fog. Then the beauty was too much, and tears came to his eyes, and he kept saying the name God, God, God, until he choked on it. And through his tears he saw the moon, red and blue and green. A shaft of light like a bolt struck down in the meadow, not a stone's throw away, among chinaberry trees. There were deep colors in it, and it was brighter than the moon, and it took his breath away, and he wanted everyone to see it, especially the boy. Look, look, he thought, how God has drawn the sky with light. Light was laced among the willows; it set a brightness like fire upon the grass, and it rose and floated like smoke. It defined clouds in the sky, and it radiated from the clouds like fractures in glass, like spiderwebs. And suddenly he knew how small he was, how little he mattered in the laughter of God, not at all, really. He knew at once that this moment, the blink of an eye, held more beauty and wonder than he could know. He had not enough life to deal with it. He could only suffer the least part of it; he could only open his eyes and see what he could see of the world. And again he laughed together with God. And he thought: Wait a moment, God. Give me a moment. I have a moment, and it is too big for me, and I cannot hold it in my little hands. And you, God, you give me the night and the world. It is a good joke, and, God, we laugh. But I have seen how you draw the sky with light.

STUDY QUESTIONS

Write an essay on one of the following topics:

1. Instead of moving through time (morning to evening to night), this story moves through places, beginning at its central spot (the supper table) and radiating outward from there to all the places visited during the course of the day and night, ending with the vastness of "the night and the world." Discuss how effective this construction is for this story.
2. Discuss the use of the "stream of consciousness" technique to bring the thoughts of the boy and James directly into the story. Explain what this use of multiple voices adds to the story.
3. Discuss the use of light and color in the story.

From I Know Why the Caged Bird Sings

Maya Angelou (1928–   )

18

Another day was over. In the soft dark the cotton truck spilled the pickers out and roared out of the yard with a sound like a giant's fart. The workers stepped around in circles for a few seconds as if they had found themselves unexpectedly in an unfamiliar place. Their minds sagged.

In the Store the men's faces were the most painful to watch, but I seemed to have no choice. When they tried to smile to carry off their tiredness as if it was nothing, the body did nothing to help the mind's attempt at disguise. Their shoulders drooped even as they laughed, and when they put their hands on their hips in a show of jauntiness, the palms slipped the thighs as if the pants were waxed.

"Evening, Sister Henderson. Well, back where we started, huh?"

"Yes, sir, Brother Stewart. Back where you started, bless the Lord." Momma could not take the smallest achievement for granted. People whose history and future were threatened each day by extinction considered that it was only by divine intervention that they were able to live at all. I find it interesting that the meanest life, the poorest existence, is attributed to God's will, but as human beings become more affluent, as their living standard and style begin to ascend the material scale, God descends the scale of responsibility at a commensurate speed.

"That's just who get the credit. Yes, ma'am. The blessed Lord." Their overalls and shirts seemed to be torn on purpose and the cotton lint and dust in their hair gave them the appearance of people who had turned gray in the past few hours.

The women's feet had swollen to fill the discarded men's shoes they wore, and they washed their arms at the well to dislodge dirt and splinters that had accrued to them as part of the day's pickings.

I thought them all hateful to have allowed themselves to be worked like oxen, and even more shameful to try to pretend that things were not as bad as they were. When they leaned too hard on the partly glass candy counter, I wanted to tell them shortly to stand up and "assume the posture of a man," but Momma would have beaten me if I'd opened my mouth. She ignored the creaks of the counter under their weight and moved around filling their orders and keeping up a conversation. "Going to put your dinner on, Sister Williams?" Bailey and I helped Momma, while Uncle Willie sat on the porch and heard the day's account.

"Praise the Lord, no, ma'am. Got enough left over from last night to do us. We going home and get cleaned up to go to the revival meeting."

Go to church in that cloud of weariness? Not go home and lay those tortured bones in a feather bed? The idea came to me that my people may be a race of masochists and that not only was it our fate to live the poorest, roughest life but that we liked it like that.

"I know what you mean, Sister Williams. Got to feed the soul just like you feed the body. I'm taking the children, too, the Lord willing. Good Book say, 'Raise a child in the way he should go and he will not depart from it.'"

"That's what it say. Sure is what it say."

The cloth tent had been set on the flatlands in the middle of a field near the railroad tracks. The earth was carpeted with a silky layer of dried grass and cotton stalks. Collapsible chairs were poked into the still-soft ground and a large wooden cross was hung from the center beam at the rear of the tent. Electric lights had been strung from behind the pulpit to the entrance flap and continued outside on poles made of rough two-by-fours.

Approached in the dark the swaying bulbs looked lonely and purposeless. Not as if they were there to provide light or anything meaningful. And the tent, that blurry bright three-dimensional A, was so foreign to the cotton field, that it might just get up and fly away before my eyes.

People, suddenly visible in the lamplight, streamed toward the temporary church. The adults' voices relayed the serious intent of their mission. Greetings were exchanged, hushed.

"Evening, sister, how you?"

"Bless the Lord, just trying to make it in."

Their minds were concentrated on the coming meeting, soul to soul, with God. This was no time to indulge in human concerns or personal questions.

"The good Lord give me another day, and I'm thankful." Nothing personal in that. The credit was God's, and there was no illusion about the Central Position's shifting or becoming less than Itself.

Teenagers enjoyed revivals as much as adults. They used the night outside meetings to play at courting. The impermanence of a collapsible church added to the frivolity, and their eyes flashed and winked and the girls giggled little silver drops in the dusk while the boys postured and swaggered and pretended not to notice. The nearly grown girls wore skirts as tight as the custom allowed and the young men slicked their hair down with Moroline Hairdressing and water.

To small children, though, the idea of praising God in a tent was confusing, to say the least. It seemed somehow blasphemous. The lights hanging slack overhead, the soft ground underneath and the canvas wall that faintly blew in and out, like cheeks puffed with air, made for the feeling of a country fair. The nudgings and jerks and winks of the bigger children surely didn't belong in a church. But the tension of the elders—their expectation, which weighted like a thick blanket over the crowd—was the most perplexing of all.

Would the gentle Jesus care to enter into that transitory setting? The altar wobbled and threatened to overturn and the collection table sat at a rakish angle. One leg had yielded itself to the loose dirt. Would God the Father allow His only Son to mix with this crowd of cotton pickers and maids, washerwomen and handymen? I knew He sent His spirit on Sundays to the church, but after all that was a church and the people had had all day Saturday to shuffle off the cloak of work and the skin of despair.

Everyone attended the revival meetings. Members of the hoity-toity Mount Zion Baptist Church mingled with the intellectual members of the African Methodist Episcopal and African Methodist Episcopal Zion, and the plain working people of the Christian Methodist Episcopal. These gatherings provided the one time in the year when all of those good village people associated with the followers of the Church of God in Christ. The latter were looked upon with some suspicion because they were so loud and raucous in their services. Their explanation that "the Good Book say, 'Make a joyful noise unto the Lord, and be exceedingly glad'" did not in the least minimize the condescension of their fellow Christians. Their church was far from the others, but they could be heard on Sunday, a half mile away, singing and dancing until they sometimes fell down in a dead faint. Members of the other churches wondered if the Holy Rollers were going to heaven after all their shouting. The suggestion was that they were having their heaven right here on earth.

This was their annual revival.

Mrs. Duncan, a little woman with a bird face, started the service. "I know I'm a witness for my Lord . . . I know I'm a witness for my Lord, I know I'm a witness . . ."

Her voice, a skinny finger, stabbed high up in the air and the church responded. From somewhere down front came the jangling sound of a tambourine. Two beats on "know," two beats on "I'm a" and two beats on the end of "witness."

Other voices joined the near shriek of Mrs. Duncan. They crowded around and tenderized the tone. Handclaps snapped in the roof and solidified the beat. When the song reached its peak in sound and passion, a tall, thin man who had been kneeling behind the altar all the while stood up and sang with the audience for a few bars. He stretched out his long arms and grasped the platform. It took some time for the singers to come off their level of exaltation, but the minister stood resolute until the song unwound like a child's playtoy and lay quieted in the aisles.

"Amen." He looked at the audience.

"Yes, sir, amen." Nearly everyone seconded him.

"I say, Let the Church say 'Amen.'"

Everyone said, "Amen."

"Thank the Lord. Thank the Lord."

"That's right, thank the Lord. Yes, Lord. Amen."

"We will have prayer, led by Brother Bishop."

Another tall, brown-skinned man wearing square glasses walked up to the altar from the front row. The minister knelt at the right and Brother Bishop at the left.

"Our Father"—he was singing—"You who took my feet out the mire and clay—"

The church moaned, "Amen."

"You who saved my soul. One day. Look, sweet Jesus. Look down, on these your suffering children—"

The church begged, "Look down, Lord."

"Build us up where we're torn down . . . Bless the sick and the afflicted . . ."

It was the usual prayer. Only his voice gave it something new. After every two words he gasped and dragged the air over his vocal chords, making a sound like an inverted grunt. "You who"—grunt—"saved my"—gasp—"soul one"—inhalation—"day"—humph.

Then the congregation, led again by Mrs. Duncan, flew into "Precious Lord, take my hand, lead me on, let me stand." It was sung at a faster clip than the usual one in the C.M.E. Church, but at that tempo it worked. There was a joy about the tune that changed the meaning of its sad lyrics. "When the darkness appears, and the night draweth near and my life is almost gone . . ." There seemed to be an abandon which suggested that with all those things it should be a time for great rejoicing.

The serious shouters had already made themselves known, and their fans (cardboard advertisements from Texarkana's largest Negro funeral home) and lacy white handkerchiefs waved high in the air. In their dark hands they looked like small kites without the wooden frames.

The tall minister stood again at the altar. He waited for the song and the revelry to die.

He said, "Amen. Glory."

The church skidded off the song slowly. "Amen. Glory."

He still waited, as the last notes remained in the air, staircased on top of each other. "At the river I stand—" "I stand, guide my feet—" "Guide my feet, take my hand." Sung like the last circle in a round. Then quiet descended.

The Scripture reading was from Matthew, twenty-fifth chapter, thirtieth verse through the forty-sixth.

His text for the sermon was "The least of these."

After reading the verses to the accompaniment of a few Amens he said, "First Corinthians tells me, 'Even if I have the tongue of men and of angels and have not charity, I am as nothing. Even if I give all my clothes to the poor and have not charity, I am as nothing. Even if I give my body to be burned and have not charity it availeth me nothing. Burned, I say, and have not charity, it availeth nothing.' I have to ask myself, what is this thing called Charity? If good deeds are not charity—"

The church gave in quickly. "That's right, Lord."

"—if giving my flesh and blood is not charity?"

"Yes, Lord."

"I have to ask myself what is this charity they talking so much about."

I had never heard a preacher jump into the muscle of his sermon so quickly. Already the humming pitch had risen in the church, and those who knew had popped their eyes in anticipation of the coming excitement. Momma sat tree-trunk still, but she had balled her handkerchief in her hand and only the corner, which I had embroidered, stuck out.

"As I understand it, charity vaunteth not itself. Is not puffed up." He blew himself up with a deep breath to give us the picture of what Charity was not. "Charity don't go around saying 'I give you food and I give you clothes and by rights you ought to thank me.'"

The congregation knew whom he was talking about and voiced agreement with his analysis. "Tell the truth, Lord."

"Charity don't say, 'Because I give you a job, you got to bend your knee to me.'" The church was rocking with each phrase. "It don't say, 'Because I pays you what you due, you got to call me master.' It don't ask me to humble myself and belittle myself. That ain't what Charity is."

Down front to the right, Mr. and Mrs. Stewart, who only a few hours earlier had crumbled in our front yard, defeated by the cotton rows, now sat on the edges of their rickety-rackety chairs. Their faces shone with the delight of their souls. The mean whitefolks was going to get their comeuppance. Wasn't that what the minister said, and wasn't he quoting from the words of God Himself? They had been refreshed with the hope of revenge and the promise of justice.

"Aaagh. Raagh. I said . . . Charity. Wooooo, a Charity. It don't want nothing for itself. It don't want to be bossman . . . Waah . . . It don't want to be headman . . . Waah . . . It don't want to be foreman . . . Waah . . . It . . . I'm talking about Charity . . . It don't want . . . Oh Lord . . . help me tonight . . . It don't want to be bowed to and scraped at . . ."

America's historic bowers and scrapers shifted easily and happily in the makeshift church. Reassured that although they might be the lowest of the low they were at least not uncharitable, and "in that great Gettin' Up Morning, Jesus was going to separate the sheep (them) from the goats (the whitefolks)."

"Charity is simple." The church agreed, vocally.

"Charity is poor." That was us he was talking about.

"Charity is plain." I thought, that's about right. Plain and simple.

"Charity is . . . Oh, Oh, Oh. Cha-ri-ty. Where are you? Wooo . . . Charity . . . Hump."

One chair gave way and the sound of splintering wood split the air in the rear of the church.

"I call you and you don't answer. Woooh, oh Charity."

Another holler went up in front of me, and a large woman flopped over, her arms above her head like a candidate for baptism. The emotional release was contagious. Little screams burst around the room like Fourth of July firecrackers.

The minister's voice was a pendulum. Swinging left and down and right and down and left and—"How can you claim to be my brother, and hate me? Is that Charity? How can you claim to be my sister and despise me? Is that supposed to be Charity? How can you claim to be my friend and misuse and wrongfully abuse me? Is that Charity? Oh, my children, I stopped by here—"

The church swung on the end of his phrases. Punctuating. Confirming. "Stop by here, Lord."

"—to tell you, to open your heart and let Charity reign. Forgive your enemies for His sake. Show the Charity that Jesus was speaking of to this sick old world. It has need of the charitable giver." His voice was falling and the explosions became fewer and quieter.

"And now I repeat the words of the Apostle Paul, and 'now abideth faith, hope and charity, these three; but the greatest of these is charity.'"

The congregation lowed with satisfaction. Even if they were society's pariahs, they were going to be angels in a marble white heaven and sit on the right hand of Jesus, the Son of God. The Lord loved the poor and hated those cast high in the world. Hadn't He Himself said it would be easier for a camel to go through the eye of a needle than for a rich man to enter heaven? They were assured that they were going to be the only inhabitants of that land of milk and honey, except of course a few whitefolks like John Brown who history books said was crazy anyway. All the Negroes had to do generally, and those at the revival especially, was bear up under this life of toil and cares, because a blessed home awaited them in the far-off bye and bye.

"Bye and bye, when the morning come, when all the saints of God's are gathering home, we will tell the story of how we overcome and we'll understand it better bye and bye."

A few people who had fainted were being revived on the side aisles when the evangelist opened the doors of the church. Over the sounds of "Thank you, Jesus," he started a long-meter hymn:

> "I came to Jesus, as I was,
> worried, wounded and sad,
> I found in Him a resting place,
> And He has made me glad."

The old ladies took up the hymn and shared it in tight harmony. The humming crowd began to sound like tired bees, restless and anxious to get home.

"All those under the sound of my voice who have no spiritual home, whose hearts are burdened and heavy-ladened, let them come. Come before it's too late. I don't ask you to join the Church of God in Christ. No. I'm a servant of God, and in this revival, we are out to bring straying souls to Him. So if you join this evening, just say which church you want to be affiliated with, and we will turn you over to a representative of that church body. Will one deacon of the following churches come forward?"

That was revolutionary action. No one had ever heard of a minister taking in members for another church. It was our first look at Charity among preachers. Men from the A.M.E., A.M.E.Z., Baptist and C.M.E. churches went down front and assumed stances a few feet apart. Converted sinners flowed down the aisles to shake hands with the evangelist and stayed at his side or were directed to one of the men in line. Over twenty people were saved that night.

There was nearly as much commotion over the saving of the sinners as there had been during the gratifying melodic sermon.

The Mothers of the Church, old ladies with white lace disks pinned to their thinning hair, had a service all their own. They walked around the new converts singing,

> "Before this time another year,
> I may be gone,
> In some lonesome graveyard,
> Oh, Lord, how long?"

When the collection was taken up and the last hymn given to the praise of God, the evangelist asked that everyone in his presence rededicate his soul to God and his life's work to Charity. Then we were dismissed.

Outside and on the way home, the people played in their magic, as children poke in mud pies, reluctant to tell themselves that the game was over.

"The Lord touched him tonight, didn't He?"

"Surely did. Touched him with a mighty fire."

"Bless the Lord. I'm glad I'm saved."

"That's the truth. It make a whole lot of difference."

"I wish them people I works for could of heard that sermon. They don't know what they letting theyselves in for."

"Bible say, 'He who can hear, let him hear. He who can't, shame on 'em.'"

They basked in the righteousness of the poor and the exclusiveness of the downtrodden. Let the whitefolks have their money and power and segregation and sarcasm and big houses and schools and lawns like carpets, and books, and mostly—mostly—let them have their whiteness. It was better to be meek and lowly, spat upon and abused for this little time than to spend eternity frying in the fires of hell. No one would have admitted that the Christian and charitable people were happy to think of their oppressors' turning forever on the Devil's spit over the flames of fire and brimstone.

But that was what the Bible said and it didn't make mistakes. "Ain't it said somewhere in there that 'before one word of this changes, heaven and earth shall fall away'? Folks going to get what they deserved."

When the main crowd of worshipers reached the short bridge spanning the pond, the ragged sound of honky-tonk music assailed them. A barrelhouse blues was being shouted over the stamping of feet on a wooden floor. Miss Grace, the good-time woman, had her usual Saturday-night customers. The big white house blazed with lights and noise. The people inside had forsaken their own distress for a little while.

Passing near the din, the godly people dropped their heads and conversation ceased. Reality began its tedious crawl back into their reasoning. After all, they were needy and hungry and despised and dispossessed, and sinners the world over were in the driver's seat. How long, merciful Father? How long?

A stranger to the music could not have made a distinction between the songs sung a few minutes before and those being danced to in the gay house by the railroad tracks. All asked the same questions. How long, oh God? How long?

STUDY QUESTION

1. Write an essay discussing how Angelou's narrator describes the revival meeting and how she uses it to illuminate various issues in the daily life of the field hands who make up a large segment of her community.

SUGGESTIONS FOR FURTHER READING AND WRITING

You may wish to read, and write a paper on, an entire book, either an autobiography or a novel, by one of the authors included in this section. You might choose from

1. N. SCOTT MOMADAY. *The Names* (New York: Harper Colophon, 1977); autobiography.
2. N. SCOTT MOMADAY. *House Made of Dawn* (New York: HarperCollins, 1989); fiction.
3. MAYA ANGELOU. *I Know Why the Caged Bird Sings* (New York: Bantam Classics Spectra, 1983); autobiography.
4. JOHN G. NEIHARDT, ed. *Black Elk Speaks* (Lincoln: U. of Nebraska P., 1979); autobiography.
5. MARK TWAIN (Samuel Clemens). *Life on the Mississippi* (1883); autobiography.
6. MARK TWAIN (Samuel Clemens). *Adventures of Huckleberry Finn* (1885); fiction.

An Anthology of Short Stories

Chickamauga[1]

Ambrose Bierce (1842–1914)

One sunny autumn afternoon a child strayed away from its rude home in a small field and entered a forest unobserved. It was happy in a new sense of freedom from control—happy in the opportunity of exploration and adventure; for this child's spirit, in bodies of its ancestors, had for many thousands of years been trained to memorable feats of discovery and conquest—victories in battles whose critical moments were centuries, whose victors' camps were cities of hewn stone. From the cradle of its race it had conquered its way through two continents, and, passing a great sea, had penetrated a third, there to be born to war and dominance as a heritage.

The child was a boy, aged about six years, the son of a poor planter. In his younger manhood the father had been a soldier, had fought against naked savages, and followed the flag of his country into the capital of a civilized race to the far South. In the peaceful life of a planter the warrior-fire survived; once kindled it is never extinguished. The man loved military books and pictures, and the boy had understood enough to make himself a wooden sword, though even the eye of his father would hardly have known it for what it was. This weapon he now bore bravely, as became the son of an heroic race, and pausing now and again in the sunny spaces of the forest, assumed, with some exaggeration, the postures of aggression and defense that he had been taught by the engraver's art. Made reckless by the ease with which he overcame invisible foes attempting to stay his advance, he committed the common enough military error of pushing the pursuit to a dangerous extreme, until he found himself upon the margin of a wide but shallow brook, whose rapid waters barred his direct advance against the flying foe who had crossed with illogical ease. But the intrepid victor was not to be baffled; the spirit of the race which had passed the great sea burned unconquerable in that small breast and would not be denied. Finding a place where some bowlders in the bed of the stream lay but a step apart, he made his way across and fell again upon the rear guard of his imaginary foe, putting all to the sword.

---

[1]The Battle of Chickamauga Creek took place in Tennessee on September 19–20, 1863. Casualties in the first four hours of battle ran to over fifty percent on both sides. There were nearly 40,000 casualties in all, making it one of the most confusing and deadly battles of the Civil War.

Now that the battle had been won, prudence required that he withdraw to his base of operations. Alas! like many a mightier conquerer, and like one, the mightiest, he could not

> curb the lust for war,
> Nor learn that tempted Fate will leave the loftiest star.[2]

Advancing from the bank of the creek, he suddenly found himself confronted with a new and more formidable enemy; in the path that he was following, bolt upright, with ears erect and paws suspended before it, sat a rabbit. With a startled cry the child turned and fled, he knew not in what direction, calling with inarticulate cries for his mother, weeping, stumbling, his tender skin cruelly torn by brambles, his little heart beating hard with terror—breathless, blind with tears—lost in the forest! Then, for more than an hour, he wandered with erring feet through the tangled undergrowth, till at last, overcome with fatigue, he lay down in a narrow space between two rocks, within a few yards of the stream, and, still grasping his toy sword, no longer a weapon but a companion, sobbed himself to sleep. The wood birds sang merrily above his head; the squirrels, whisking their bravery of tail, ran barking from tree to tree, unconscious of the pity of it, and somewhere far away was a strange, muffled thunder, as if the partridges were drumming in celebration of nature's victory over the son of her immemorial enslavers. And back at the little plantation, where white men and black were hastily searching the fields and hedgerows in alarm, a mother's heart was breaking for her missing child.

Hours passed, and then the little sleeper rose to his feet. The chill of the evening was in his limbs, the fear of the gloom in his heart. But he had rested, and he no longer wept. With some blind instinct which impelled to action, he struggled through the undergrowth about him and came to a more open ground—on his right the brook, to the left a gentle acclivity studded with infrequent trees; over all the gathering gloom of twilight. A thin, ghostly mist rose along the water. It frightened and repelled him; instead of recrossing, in the direction whence he had come, he turned his back upon it and went forward toward the dark inclosing wood. Suddenly he saw before him a strange moving object which he took to be some large animal—a dog, a pig—he could not name it; perhaps it was a bear. He had seen pictures of bears, but knew of nothing to their discredit, and had vaguely wished to meet one. But something in form or movement of this object—something in the awkwardness of its approach—told him that it was not a bear, and curiosity was stayed by fear. He stood still, and as it came slowly on, gained courage every moment, for he saw that at least it had not the long, menacing ears of the rabbit. Possibly his impressionable mind was half conscious of something familiar in its shambling, awkward gait. Before it

---

[2]From *Childe Harold's Pilgrimage* by Lord Byron. Byron's "conqueror" is Napoleon.

had approached near enough to resolve his doubts, he saw that it was followed by another and another. To right and to left were many more; the whole open space about him was alive with them—all moving forward toward the brook.

They were men. They crept upon their hands and knees. They used their hands only, dragging their legs. They used their knees only, their arms hanging useless at their sides. They strove to rise to their feet, but fell prone in the attempt. They did nothing naturally, and nothing alike, save only to advance foot by foot in the same direction. Singly, in pairs, and in little groups, they came on through the gloom, some halting now and again while others crept slowly past them, then resuming their movement. They came by dozens and by hundreds; as far on either hand as one could see in the deepening gloom they extended, and the black wood behind them appeared to be inexhaustible. The very ground seemed in motion toward the creek. Occasionally one who had paused did not again go on, but lay motionless. He was dead. Some, pausing, made strange gestures with their hands, erected their arms and lowered them again, clasped their heads; spread their palms upward, as men are sometimes seen to do in public prayer.

Not all of this did the child note; it is what would have been noted by an older observer; he saw little but that these were men, yet crept like babes. Being men, they were not terrible, though some of them were unfamiliarly clad. He moved among them freely, going from one to another and peering into their faces with childish curiosity. All their faces were singularly white and many were streaked and gouted with red. Something in this—something too, perhaps, in their grotesque attitudes and movements—reminded him of the painted clown whom he had seen last summer in the circus, and he laughed as he watched them. But on and ever on they crept, these maimed and bleeding men, as heedless as he of the dramatic contrast between his laughter and their own ghastly gravity. To him it was a merry spectacle. He had seen his father's negroes creep upon their hands and knees for his amusement—had ridden them so, "making believe" they were his horses. He now approached one of these crawling figures from behind and with an agile movement mounted it astride. The man sank upon his breast, recovered, flung the small boy fiercely to the ground as an unbroken colt might have done, then turned upon him a face that lacked a lower jaw—from the upper teeth to the throat was a great red gap fringed with hanging shreds of flesh and splinters of bone. The unnatural prominence of nose, the absence of chin, the fierce eyes, gave this man the appearance of a great bird of prey crimsoned in throat and breast by the blood of its quarry. The man rose to his knees, the child to his feet. The man shook his fist at the child; the child, terrified at last, ran to a tree near by, got upon the farther side of it, and took a more serious view of the situation. And so the uncanny multitude dragged itself slowly and painfully along in hideous pantomime— moved forward down the slope like a swarm of great black beetles, with never a sound of going—in silence profound, absolute.

Instead of darkening, the haunted landscape began to brighten. Through the belt of trees beyond the brook shone a strange red light, the trunks and branches of the trees making a black lacework against it. It struck the creeping figures and gave them monstrous shadows, which caricatured their movements on the lit grass. It fell upon their faces, touching their whiteness with a ruddy tinge, accentuating the stains with which so many of them were freaked and maculated. It sparkled on buttons and bits of metal in their clothing. Instinctively the child turned toward the growing splendor and moved down the slope with his horrible companions; in a few moments had passed the foremost of the throng—not much of a feat, considering his advantages. He placed himself in the lead, his wooden sword still in hand, and solemnly directed the march, conforming his pace to theirs and occasionally turning as if to see that his forces did not straggle. Surely such a leader never before had such a following.

Scattered about upon the ground now slowly narrowing by the encroachment of this awful march to water, were certain articles to which, in the leader's mind, were coupled no significant associations; an occasional blanket, tightly rolled lengthwise, doubled and the ends bound together with a string; a heavy knapsack here, and there a broken musket—such things, in short, as are found in the rear of retreating troops, the "spoor" of men flying from their hunters. Everywhere near the creek, which here had a margin of lowland, the earth was trodden into mud by the feet of men and horses. An observer of better experience in the use of his eyes would have noticed that these footprints pointed in both directions; the ground had been twice passed over—in advance and in retreat. A few hours before, these desperate, stricken men, with their more fortunate and now distant comrades, had penetrated the forest in thousands. Their successive battalions, breaking into swarms and reforming in lines, had passed the child on every side—had almost trodden on him as he slept. The rustle and murmur of their march had not awakened him. Almost within a stone's throw of where he lay they had fought a battle; but all unheard by him were the roar of the musketry, the shock of the cannon, "the thunder of the captains and the shouting."[3] He had slept through it all, grasping his little wooden sword with perhaps a tighter clutch in unconscious sympathy with his martial environment, but as heedless of the grandeur of the struggle as the dead who died to make the glory.

The fire beyond the belt of woods on the farther side of the creek, reflected to earth from the canopy of its own smoke, was now suffusing the whole landscape. It transformed the sinuous line of mist to the vapor of gold. The water gleamed with dashes of red, and red, too, were many of the stones protruding above the surface. But that was blood; the less desperately wounded had stained them in crossing. On them, too, the child now crossed with eager steps; he was going to the fire. As he stood upon the farther bank, he turned about to look at

---

[3]Job 39:25: "He saith among the trumpets, Ha, ha! and he smelleth the battle afar off, the thunder of the captains, and the shouting."

the companions of his march. The advance was arriving at the creek. The stronger had already drawn themselves to the brink and plunged their faces in the flood. Three or four who lay without motion appeared to have no heads. At this the child's eyes expanded with wonder; even his hospitable understanding could not accept a phenomenon implying such vitality as that. After slaking their thirst these men had not the strength to back away from the water, nor to keep their heads above it. They were drowned. In rear of these the open spaces of the forest showed the leader as many formless figures of his grim command as at first; but not nearly so many were in motion. He waved his cap for their encouragement and smilingly pointed with his weapon in the direction of the guiding light—a pillar of fire to this strange exodus.[4]

Confident of the fidelity of his forces, he now entered the belt of woods, passed through it easily in the red illumination, climbed a fence, ran across a field, turning now and again to coquette with his responsive shadow, and so approached the blazing ruin of a dwelling. Desolation everywhere. In all the wide glare not a living thing was visible. He cared nothing for that; the spectacle pleased, and he danced with glee in imitation of the wavering flames. He ran about collecting fuel, but every object that he found was too heavy for him to cast in from the distance to which the heat limited his approach. In despair he flung in his sword—a surrender to the superior forces of nature. His military career was at an end.

Shifting his position, his eyes fell upon some outbuildings which had an oddly familiar appearance, as if he had dreamed of them. He stood considering them with wonder, when suddenly the entire plantation, with its inclosing forest, seemed to turn as if upon a pivot. His little world swung half around; the points of the compass were reversed. He recognized the blazing building as his own home!

For a moment he stood stupefied by the power of the revelation, then ran with stumbling feet, making a half circuit of the ruin. There, conspicuous in the light of the conflagration, lay the dead body of a woman—the white face turned upward, the hands thrown out and clutched full of grass, the clothing deranged, the long dark hair in tangles and full of clotted blood. The greater part of the forehead was torn away, and from the jagged hole the brain protruded, overflowing the temple, a frothy mass of gray, crowned with clusters of crimson bubbles—the work of a shell!

The child moved his little hands, making wild, uncertain gestures. He uttered a series of inarticulate and indescribable cries—something between the chattering of an ape and the gobbling of a turkey—a startling, soulless, unholy sound, the language of a devil. The child was a deaf mute.

Then he stood motionless, with quivering lips, looking down upon the wreck.

---

[4]Exodus 13:21; during the flight from Egypt, God led the Israelites with a pillar of fire lighting the night.

Araby

James Joyce (1882–1941)

North Richmond Street, being blind, was a quiet street except at the hour when the Christian Brothers' School set the boys free. An uninhabited house of two stories stood at the blind end, detached from its neighbours in a square ground. The other houses of the street, conscious of decent lives within them, gazed at one another with brown imperturbable faces.

The former tenant of our house, a priest, had died in the back drawing-room. Air, musty from having been long enclosed, hung in all the rooms, and the waste room behind the kitchen was littered with old useless papers. Among these I found a few paper-covered books, the pages of which were curled and damp: *The Abbot*, by Walter Scott, *The Devout Communicant*, and *The Memoirs of Vidocq*. I liked the last best because its leaves were yellow. The wild garden behind the house contained a central apple tree and a few straggling bushes under one of which I found the late tenant's rusty bicycle pump. He had been a very charitable priest; in his will he had left all his money to institutions and the furniture of his house to his sister.

When the short days of winter came dusk fell before we had well eaten our dinners. When we met in the street the houses had grown sombre. The space of sky above us was the colour of ever-changing violet and towards it the lamps of the street lifted their feeble lanterns. The cold air stung us and we played till our bodies glowed. Our shouts echoed in the silent street. The career of our play brought us through the dark muddy lanes behind the houses where we ran the gauntlet of the rough tribes from the cottages, to the back doors of the dark dripping gardens where odours arose from the ash-pits, to the dark odorous stables where a coachman smoothed and combed the horse or shook music from the buckled harness. When we returned to the street, light from the kitchen windows had filled the areas. If my uncle was seen turning the corner we hid in the shadow until we had seen him safely housed. Or if Mangan's sister came out on the doorstep to call her brother in to his tea we watched her from our shadow peer up and down the street. We waited to see whether she would remain or go in and, if she remained, we left our shadow and walked up to Mangan's steps resignedly. She was waiting for us, her figure defined by the light from the half-opened door. Her brother always teased her before he obeyed and I stood by the railings looking at her. Her dress swung as she moved her body and the soft rope of her hair tossed from side to side.

Every morning I lay on the floor in the front parlour watching her door. The blind was pulled down to within an inch of the sash so that I could not be seen. When she came out on the doorstep my heart leaped. I ran to the hall, seized my books and followed her. I kept her brown figure always in my eye and, when we came near the point at which our ways diverged, I quickened my pace and passed her. This happened morning after morning. I had never spoken to her, except for a few casual words, and yet her name was like a summons to all my foolish blood.

Her image accompanied me even in places the most hostile to romance. On Saturday evenings when my aunt went marketing I had to go to carry some of the parcels. We walked through the flaring streets, jostled by drunken men and bargaining women, amid the curses of labourers, the shrill litanies of shop-boys who stood on guard by the barrels of pigs' cheeks, the nasal chanting of street-singers, who sang a *come-all-you* about O'Donovan Rossa, or a ballad about the troubles in our native land. These noises converged in a single sensation of life for me: I imagined that I bore my chalice safely through a throng of foes. Her name sprang to my lips at moments in strange prayers and praises which I myself did not understand. My eyes were often full of tears (I could not tell why) and at times a flood from my heart seemed to pour itself out into my bosom. I thought little of the future. I did not know whether I would ever speak to her or not or, if I spoke to her, how I could tell her of my confused adoration. But my body was like a harp and her words and gestures were like fingers running upon the wires.

One evening I went into the back drawing-room in which the priest had died. It was a dark rainy evening and there was no sound in the house. Through one of the broken panes I heard the rain impinge upon the earth, the fine incessant needles of water playing in the sodden beds. Some distant lamp or lighted window gleamed below me. I was thankful that I could see so little. All my senses seemed to desire to veil themselves and, feeling that I was about to slip from them, I pressed the palms of my hands together until they trembled, murmuring: "*O love! O love!*" many times.

At last she spoke to me. When she addressed the first words to me I was so confused that I did not know what to answer. She asked me was I going to *Araby*. I forgot whether I answered yes or no. It would be a splendid bazaar, she said she would love to go.

"And why can't you?" I asked.

While she spoke she turned a silver bracelet round and round her wrist. She could not go, she said, because there would be a retreat that week in her convent. Her brother and two other boys were fighting for their caps and I was alone at the railings. She held one of the spikes, bowing her head towards me. The light from the lamp opposite our door caught the white curve of her neck, lit up her hair that rested there and, falling, lit up the hand upon the railing. It fell over one side of her dress and caught the white border of a petticoat, just visible as she stood at ease.

"It's well for you," she said.

"If I go," I said, "I will bring you something."

What innumerable follies laid waste my waking and sleeping thoughts after the evening! I wished to annihilate the tedious intervening days. I chafed against the work of school. At night in my bedroom and by day in the classroom her image came between me and the page I strove to read. The syllables of the word *Araby* were called to me through the silence in which my soul luxuriated and cast an Eastern enchantment over me. I asked for leave to go to the bazaar on Saturday night. My aunt was surprised and hoped it was not some Freemason affair. I answered few questions in class. I watched my master's face pass from amiability to sternness; he hoped I was not beginning to idle, I could not call my wandering thoughts together. I had hardly any patience with the serious work of life which, now that it stood between me and my desire, seemed to me child's play, ugly monotonous child's play.

On Saturday morning I reminded my uncle that I wished to go to the bazaar in the evening. He was fussing at the hall-stand, looking for the hat brush, and answered me curtly:

"Yes, boy, I know."

As he was in the hall I could not go into the front parlour and lie at the window. I left the house in bad humour and walked slowly towards the school. The air was pitilessly raw and already my heart misgave me.

When I came home to dinner my uncle had not yet been home. Still it was early. I sat staring at the clock for some time and, when its ticking began to irritate me, I left the room. I mounted the staircase and gained the upper part of the house. The high cold empty gloomy rooms liberated me and I went from room to room singing. From the front window I saw my companions playing below in the street. Their cries reached me weakened and indistinct and, leaning my forehead against the cool glass, I looked over at the dark house where she lived. I may have stood there for an hour, seeing nothing but the brown-clad figure cast by my imagination, touched discreetly by the lamplight at the curved neck, at the hand upon the railings and at the border below the dress.

When I came downstairs again I found Mrs. Mercer sitting at the fire. She was an old garrulous woman, a pawnbroker's widow, who collected used stamps for some pious purpose. I had to endure the gossip of the tea-table. The meal was prolonged beyond an hour and still my uncle did not come. Mrs. Mercer stood up to go: she was sorry she couldn't wait any longer, but it was after eight o'clock and she did not like to be out late, as the night air was bad for her. When she had gone I began to walk up and down the room, clenching my fists. My aunt said:

"I'm afraid you may put off your bazaar for this night of Our Lord."

At nine o'clock I heard my uncle's latchkey in the hall-door. I heard him talking to himself and heard the hall-stand rocking when it had received the weight of his overcoat. I could interpret these signs. When he was midway through his dinner I asked him to give me the money to go to the bazaar. He had forgotten.

"The people are in bed and after their first sleep now," he said.

I did not smile. My aunt said to him energetically:

"Can't you give him the money and let him go? You've kept him late enough as it is."

My uncle said he was very sorry he had forgotten. He said he believed in the old saying: "All work and no play makes Jack a dull boy." He asked me where I was going and, when I had told him a second time, he asked me did I know *The Arab's Farewell to his Steed*. When I left the kitchen he was about to recite the opening lines of the piece to my aunt.

I held a florin tightly in my hand as I strode down Buckingham Street towards the station. The sight of the streets thronged with buyers and glaring with gas recalled to me the purpose of my journey. I took my seat in a third-class carriage of a deserted train. After an intolerable delay the train moved out of the station slowly. It crept onward among ruinous houses and over the twinkling river. At Westland Row Station a crowd of people pressed to the carriage doors; but the porters moved them back, saying that it was a special train for the bazaar. I remained alone in the bare carriage. In a few minutes the train drew up beside an improvised wooden platform. I passed out on the road and saw by the lighted dial of a clock that it was ten minutes to ten. In front of me was a large building which displayed the magical name.

I could not find any sixpenny entrance and, fearing that the bazaar would be closed, I passed in quickly through a turnstile, handing a shilling to a weary-looking man. I found myself in a big hall girdled at half its height by a gallery. Nearly all the stalls were closed and the greater part of the hall was in darkness. I recognized a silence like that which pervades a church after a service. I walked into the center of the bazaar timidly. A few people were gathered about the stalls which were still open. Before a curtain, over which the words *Café Chantant* were written in coloured lamps, two men were counting money on a salver. I listened to the fall of the coins.

Remembering with difficulty why I had come I went over to one of the stalls and examined porcelain vases and flowered tea-sets. At the door of the stall a young lady was talking and laughing with two young gentlemen. I remarked their English accents and listened vaguely to their conversation.

"O, I never said such a thing!"

"O, but you did!"

"O, but I didn't!"

"Didn't she say that?"

"Yes. I heard her."

"O, there's a . . . fib!"

Observing me, the young lady came over and asked me did I wish to buy anything. The tone of her voice was not encouraging; she seemed to have spoken to me out of a sense of duty. I looked humbly at the great jars that stood like eastern guards at either side of the dark entrance to the stall and murmured:

"No, thank you."

The young lady changed the position of one of the vases and went back to the two young men. They began to talk of the same subject. Once or twice the young lady glanced at me over her shoulder.

I lingered before her stall, though I knew my stay was useless, to make my interest in her wares seem the more real. Then I turned away slowly and walked down the middle of the bazaar. I allowed the two pennies to fall against the six-pence in my pocket. I heard a voice call from one end of the gallery that the light was out. The upper part of the hall was now completely dark.

Gazing up into the darkness I saw myself as a creature driven and derided by vanity; and my eyes burned with anguish and anger.

The Rocking-Horse Winner

D. H. Lawrence (1885–1930)

There was a woman who was beautiful, who started with all the advantages, yet she had no luck. She married for love, and the love turned to dust. She had bonny children, yet she felt they had been thrust upon her, and she could not love them. They looked at her coldly, as if they were finding fault with her. And hurriedly she felt she must cover up some fault in herself. Yet what it was that she must cover up she never knew. Nevertheless, when her children were present, she always felt the centre of her heart go hard. This troubled her, and in her manner she was all the more gentle and anxious for her children, as if she loved them very much. Only she herself knew that at the centre of her heart was a hard little place that could not feel love, no, not for anybody. Everybody else said of her: "She is such a good mother. She adores her children." Only she herself, and her children themselves, knew it was not so. They read it in each other's eyes.

There were a boy and two little girls. They lived in a pleasant house, with a garden, and they had discreet servants, and felt themselves superior to anyone in the neighbourhood.

Although they lived in style, they felt always an anxiety in the house. There was never enough money. The mother had a small income, and the father had a small income, but not nearly enough for the social position which they had to keep up. The father went into town to some office. But though he had good prospects, these prospects never materialized. There was always the grinding sense of the shortage of money, though the style was always kept up.

At last the mother said: "I will see if I can't make something." But she did not know where to begin. She racked her brains, and tried this thing and the other, but could not find anything successful. The failure made deep lines come into her face. Her children were growing up, they would have to go to school. There must be more money, there must be more money. The father, who was always very handsome and expensive in his tastes, seemed as if he never would be able to do anything worth doing. And the mother, who had a great belief in herself, did not succeed any better, and her tastes were just as expensive.

And so the house came to be haunted by the unspoken phrase: There must be more money! There must be more money! The children could hear it all the time, though nobody said it aloud. They heard it at Christmas, when the expensive and splendid toys filled the nursery. Behind the shining modern rocking horse, behind the smart doll's-house, a voice would start whispering: "There must be more money! There must be more money!" And the children would stop playing, to listen for a moment. They would look into each other's eyes, to see if they had all heard. And each one saw in the eyes of the other two that they too had heard. "There must be more money! There must be more money!"

It came whispering from the springs of the still-swaying rocking horse, and even the horse, bending his wooden, champing head, heard it. The big doll, sitting so pink and smirking in her new pram, could hear it quite plainly, and seemed to be smirking all the more self-consciously because of it. The foolish puppy, too, that took the place of the Teddy bear, he was looking so extraordinarily foolish for no other reason but that he heard the secret whisper all over the house: "There must be more money!"

Yet nobody ever said it aloud. The whisper was everywhere, and therefore no one spoke it. Just as no one ever says: "We are breathing!" in spite of the fact that breath is coming and going all the time.

"Mother," said the boy Paul one day, "why don't we keep a car of our own? Why do we always use uncle's, or else a taxi?"

"Because we're the poor members of the family," said the mother.

"But why are we, mother?"

"Well—I suppose," she said slowly and bitterly, "it's because your father has no luck."

The boy was silent for some time.

"Is luck money, mother?" he asked, rather timidly.

"No, Paul. Not quite. It's what causes you to have money."

"Oh!" said Paul vaguely. "I thought when Uncle Oscar said filthy lucker, it meant money."

"Filthy lucre does mean money," said the mother. "But it's lucre, not luck."

"Oh!" said the boy. "Then what is luck, mother?"

"It's what causes you to have money. If you're lucky you have money. That's why it's better to be born lucky than rich. If you're rich, you may lose your money. But if you're lucky, you will always get more money."

"Oh! Will you? And is father not lucky?"

"Very unlucky, I should say," she said bitterly.

The boy watched her with unsure eyes.

"Why?" he asked.

"I don't know. Nobody ever knows why one person is lucky and another unlucky."

"Don't they? Nobody at all? Does nobody know?"

"Perhaps God. But He never tells."

"He ought to, then. And aren't you lucky either, mother?"

"I can't be, if I married an unlucky husband."

"But by yourself, aren't you?"

"I used to think I was, before I married. Now I think I am very unlucky indeed."

"Why?"

"Well—never mind! Perhaps I'm not really," she said.

The child looked at her, to see if she meant it. But he saw, by the lines of her mouth, that she was only trying to hide something from him.

"Well, anyhow," he said stoutly, "I'm a lucky person."

"Why?" said his mother, with a sudden laugh.

He stared at her. He didn't even know why he had said it.

"God told me," he asserted, brazening it out.

"I hope He did, dear!" she said, again with a laugh, but rather bitter.

"He did, mother!"

"Excellent!" said the mother, using one of her husband's exclamations.

The boy saw she did not believe him; or, rather, that she paid no attention to his assertion. This angered him somewhat, and made him want to compel her attention.

He went off by himself, vaguely, in a childish way, seeking for the clue to "luck." Absorbed, taking no heed of other people, he went about with a sort of stealth, seeking inwardly for luck. He wanted luck, he wanted it, he wanted it. When the two girls were playing dolls in the nursery, he would sit on his big rocking horse, charging madly into space, with a frenzy that made the little girls peer at him uneasily. Wildly the horse careered, the waving dark hair of the boy tossed, his eyes had a strange glare in them. The little girls dared not speak to him.

When he had ridden to the end of his mad little journey, he climbed down and stood in front of his rocking horse, staring fixedly into its lowered face. Its red mouth was slightly open, its big eye was wide and glassy-bright.

"Now!" he would silently command the snorting steed. "Now, take me to where there is luck! Now take me!"

And he would slash the horse on the neck with the little whip he had asked Uncle Oscar for. He knew the horse could take him to where there was luck, if only he forced it. So he would mount again, and start on his furious ride, hoping at last to get there. He knew he could get there.

"You'll break your horse, Paul!" said the nurse.

"He's always riding like that! I wish he'd leave off!" said his elder sister Joan.

But he only glared down on them in silence. Nurse gave him up. She could make nothing of him. Anyhow he was growing beyond her.

One day his mother and his Uncle Oscar came in when he was on one of his furious rides. He did not speak to them.

"Hallo, you young jockey! Riding a winner?" said his uncle.

"Aren't you growing too big for a rocking horse? You're not a very little boy any longer, you know," said his mother.

But Paul only gave a blue glare from his big, rather close-set eyes. He would speak to nobody when he was in full tilt. His mother watched him with an anxious expression on her face.

At last he suddenly stopped forcing his horse into the mechanical gallop, and slid down.

"Well, I got there!" he announced fiercely, his blue eyes still flaring, and his sturdy long legs straddling apart.

"Where did you get to?" asked his mother.

"Where I wanted to go," he flared back at her.

"That's right, son!" said Uncle Oscar. "Don't you stop till you get there. What's the horse's name?"

"He doesn't have a name," said the boy.

"Gets on without all right?" asked the uncle.

"Well, he has different names. He was called Sansovino last week."

"Sansovino, eh? Won the Ascot. How did you know his name?"

"He always talks about horse races with Bassett," said Joan.

The uncle was delighted to find that his small nephew was posted with all the racing news. Bassett, the young gardener, who had been wounded in the left foot in the war and had got his present job through Oscar Cresswell, whose batman he had been, was a perfect blade of the "turf." He lived in the racing events, and the small boy lived with him.

Oscar Cresswell got it all from Bassett.

"Master Paul comes and asks me, so I can't do more than tell him, sir," said Bassett, his face terribly serious, as if he were speaking of religious matters.

"And does he ever put anything on a horse he fancies?"

"Well—I don't want to give him away—he's a young sport, a fine sport, sir. Would you mind asking him yourself? He sort of takes a pleasure in it, and perhaps he'd feel I was giving him away, sir, if you don't mind."

Bassett was serious as a church.

The uncle went back to his nephew, and took him off for a ride in the car.

"Say, Paul, old man, do you ever put anything on a horse?" the uncle asked.

The boy watched the handsome man closely.

"Why, do you think I oughtn't to?" he parried.

"Not a bit of it! I thought perhaps you might give me a tip for the Lincoln."

The car sped on into the country, going down to Uncle Oscar's place in Hampshire.

"Honour bright?" said the nephew.

"Honour bright, son!" said the uncle.

"Well, then, Daffodil."

"Daffodil! I doubt it, sonny. What about Mirza?"

"I only know the winner," said the boy. "That's Daffodil."

"Daffodil, eh?"

There was a pause. Daffodil was an obscure horse comparatively.

"Uncle!"

"Yes, son?"

"You won't let it go any further, will you? I promised Bassett."

"Bassett be damned, old man! What's he got to do with it?"

"We're partners. We've been partners from the first. Uncle, he lent me my first five shillings, which I lost. I promised him, honour bright, it was only between me and him; only you gave me that ten-shilling note I started winning with, so I thought you were lucky. You won't let it go any further, will you?"

The boy gazed at his uncle from those big, hot, blue eyes, set rather close together. The uncle stirred and laughed uneasily.

"Right you are, son! I'll keep your tip private. Daffodil, eh? How much are you putting on him?"

"All except twenty pounds," said the boy. "I keep that in reserve."

The uncle thought it a good joke.

"You keep twenty pounds in reserve, do you, you young romancer? What are you betting, then?"

"I'm betting three hundred," said the boy gravely. "But it's between you and me, Uncle Oscar! Honour bright?"

The uncle burst into a roar of laughter.

"It's between you and me all right, you young Nat Gould," he said, laughing. "But where's your three hundred?"

"Bassett keeps it for me. We're partners."

"You are, are you! And what is Bassett putting on Daffodil?"

"He won't go quite as high as I do, I expect. Perhaps he'll go a hundred and fifty."

"What, pennies?" laughed the uncle.

"Pounds," said the child, with a surprised look at his uncle. "Bassett keeps a bigger reserve than I do."

Between wonder and amusement Uncle Oscar was silent. He pursued the matter no further, but he determined to take his nephew with him to the Lincoln races.

"Now, son," he said, "I'm putting twenty on Mirza, and I'll put five for you on any horse you fancy. What's your pick?"

"Daffodil, uncle."

"No, not the fiver on Daffodil!"

"I should if it was my own fiver," said the child.

"Good! Good! Right you are! A fiver for me and a fiver for you on Daffodil."

The child had never been to a race meeting before, and his eyes were blue fire. He pursed his mouth tight, and watched. A Frenchman just in front had put his money on Lancelot. Wild with excitement, he flayed his arms up and down, yelling "Lancelot! Lancelot!" in his French accent.

Daffodil came in first, Lancelot second, Mirza third. The child, flushed and with eyes blazing, was curiously serene. His uncle brought him four five-pound notes, four to one.

"What am I to do with these?" he cried, waving them before the boy's eyes.

"I suppose we'll talk to Bassett," said the boy. "I expect I have fifteen hundred now; and twenty in reserve; and this twenty."

His uncle studied him for some moments.

"Look here, son!" he said. "You're not serious about Bassett and that fifteen hundred, are you?"

"Yes, I am. But it's between you and me, uncle. Honour bright!"

"Honour bright all right, son! But I must talk to Bassett."

"If you'd like to be a partner, uncle, with Bassett and me, we could all be partners. Only, you'd have to promise, honour bright, uncle, not to let it go beyond us three. Bassett and I are lucky, and you must be lucky, because it was your ten shillings I started winning with . . ."

Uncle Oscar took both Bassett and Paul into Richmond Park for an afternoon, and there they talked.

"It's like this, you see, sir," Bassett said. "Master Paul would get me talking about racing events, spinning yarns, you know, sir. And he was always keen on knowing if I'd made or if I'd lost. It's about a year since, now, that I put five shillings on Blush of Dawn for him—and we lost. Then the luck turned, with that ten shillings he had from you, that we put on Singhalese. And since that time, it's been pretty steady, all things considering. What do you say, Master Paul?"

"We're all right when we're sure," said Paul. "It's when we're not quite sure that we go down."

"Oh, but we're careful then," said Bassett.

"But when are you sure?" smiled Uncle Oscar.

"It's Master Paul, sir," said Bassett, in a secret, religious voice. "It's as if he had it from heaven. Like Daffodil, now, for the Lincoln. That was as sure as eggs."

"Did you put anything on Daffodil?" asked Oscar Cresswell.

"Yes, sir, I made my bit."

"And my nephew?"

Bassett was obstinately silent, looking at Paul.

"I made twelve hundred, didn't I, Bassett? I told uncle I was putting three hundred on Daffodil."

"That's right," said Bassett, nodding.

"But where's the money?" asked the uncle.

"I keep it safe locked up, sir. Master Paul he can have it any minute he likes to ask for it."

"What, fifteen hundred pounds?"

"And twenty! and forty, that is, with the twenty he made on the course."

"It's amazing!" said the uncle.

"If Master Paul offers you to be partners, sir, I would, if I were you; if you'll excuse me," said Bassett.

Oscar Cresswell thought about it.

"I'll see the money," he said.

They drove home again, and sure enough, Bassett came round to the garden-house with fifteen hundred pounds in notes. The twenty pounds reserve was left with Joe Glee, in the Turf Commission deposit.

"You see, it's all right, uncle, when I'm sure! Then we go strong, for all we're worth. Don't we, Bassett?"

"We do that, Master Paul."

"And when are you sure?" said the uncle, laughing.

"Oh, well, sometimes I'm absolutely sure, like about Daffodil," said the boy; "and sometimes I have an idea; and sometimes I haven't even an idea, have I, Bassett? Then we're careful, because we mostly go down."

"You do, do you! And when you're sure, like about Daffodil, what makes you sure, sonny?"

"Oh, well, I don't know," said the boy uneasily. "I'm sure, you know, uncle; that's all."

"It's as if he had it from heaven, sir," Bassett reiterated.

"I should say so!" said the uncle.

But he became a partner. And when the Leger was coming on, Paul was "sure" about Lively Spark, which was a quite inconsiderable horse. The boy insisted on putting a thousand on the horse, Bassett went for five hundred, and Oscar Cresswell two hundred. Lively Spark came in first, and the betting had been ten to one against him. Paul had made ten thousand.

"You see," he said, "I was absolutely sure of him."

Even Oscar Cresswell had cleared two thousand.

"Look here, son," he said, "this sort of thing makes me nervous."

"It needn't, uncle! Perhaps I shan't be sure again for a long time."

"But what are you going to do with your money?" asked the uncle.

"Of course," said the boy, "I started it for mother. She said she had no luck, because father is unlucky, so I thought if I was lucky, it might stop whispering."

"What might stop whispering?"

"Our house. I hate our house for whispering."

"What does it whisper?"

"Why—why"—the boy fidgeted—"why, I don't know. But it's always short of money, you know, uncle."

"I know it, son, I know it."

"You know people send mother writs, don't you, uncle?"

"I'm afraid I do," said the uncle.

"And then the house whispers, like people laughing at you behind your back. It's awful, that is! I thought if I was lucky . . ."

"You might stop it," added the uncle.

The boy watched him with big blue eyes that had an uncanny cold fire in them, and he said never a word.

"Well, then!" said the uncle. "What are we doing?"

"I shouldn't like mother to know I was lucky," said the boy.

"Why not, son?"

"She'd stop me."

"I don't think she would."

"Oh!"—and the boy writhed in an odd way—"I don't want her to know, uncle."

"All right, son! We'll manage it without her knowing."

They managed it very easily. Paul, at the other's suggestion, handed over five thousand pounds to his uncle, who deposited it with the family lawyer, who was then to inform Paul's mother that a relative had put five thousand pounds into his hands, which sum was to be paid out a thousand pounds at a time, on the mother's birthday, for the next five years.

"So she'll have a birthday present of a thousand pounds for five successive years," said Uncle Oscar. "I hope it won't make it all the harder for her later."

Paul's mother had her birthday in November. The house had been "whispering" worse than ever lately, and, even in spite of his luck, Paul could not bear up against it. He was very anxious to see the effect of the birthday letter, telling his mother about the thousand pounds.

When there were no visitors, Paul now took his meals with his parents, as he was beyond the nursery control. His mother went into town nearly every day. She had discovered that she had an odd knack of sketching furs and dress materials, so she worked secretly in the studio of a friend who was the chief "artist" for the leading drapers. She drew the figures of ladies in furs and ladies in silk and sequins for the newspaper advertisements. This young woman artist earned several thousand pounds a year, but Paul's mother only made several hundreds, and she was again dissatisfied. She so wanted to be first in something, and she did not succeed, even in making sketches for drapery advertisements.

She was down to breakfast on the morning of her birthday. Paul watched her face as she read her letters. He knew the lawyer's letter. As his mother read it, her face hardened and became more expressionless. Then a cold, determined look came on her mouth. She hid the letter under the pile of others, and said not a word about it.

"Didn't you have anything nice in the post for your birthday, mother?" said Paul.

"Quite moderately nice," she said, her voice cold and absent.

She went away to town without saying more.

But in the afternoon Uncle Oscar appeared. He said Paul's mother had had a long interview with the lawyer, asking if the whole five thousand could be advanced at once, as she was in debt.

"What do you think, uncle?" said the boy.

"I leave it to you, son."

"Oh, let her have it, then! We can get some more with the other," said the boy.

"A bird in the hand is worth two in the bush, laddie!" said Uncle Oscar.

"But I'm sure to know for the Grand National; or the Lincolnshire; or else the Derby. I'm sure to know for one of them," said Paul.

So Uncle Oscar signed the agreement, and Paul's mother touched the whole five thousand. Then something very curious happened. The voices in the house suddenly went mad, like a chorus of frogs on a spring evening. There were certain new furnishings, and Paul had a tutor. He was really going to Eton, his father's school, in the following autumn. There were flowers in the winter, and a blossoming of the luxury Paul's mother had been used to. And yet the voices in the house, behind the sprays of mimosa and almond blossom, and from under the piles of iridescent cushions, simply trilled and screamed in a sort of ecstasy: "There must be more money! Oh-h-h, there must be more money. Oh, now, now-w! Now-w-w—there must be more money—more than ever! More than ever!"

It frightened Paul terribly. He studied away at his Latin and Greek with his tutors. But his intense hours were spent with Bassett. The Grand National had gone by: he had not "known," and had lost a hundred pounds. Summer was at hand. He was in agony for the Lincoln. But even for the Lincoln he didn't "know" and he lost fifty pounds. He became wild-eyed and strange, as if something were going to explode in him.

"Let it alone, son! Don't you bother about it!" urged Uncle Oscar. But it was as if the boy couldn't really hear what his uncle was saying.

"I've got to know for the Derby! I've got to know for the Derby!" the child reiterated, his big blue eyes blazing with a sort of madness.

His mother noticed how overwrought he was.

"You'd better go to the seaside. Wouldn't you like to go now to the seaside, instead of waiting? I think you'd better," she said, looking down at him anxiously, her heart curiously heavy because of him.

But the child lifted his uncanny blue eyes.

"I couldn't possibly go before the Derby, mother!" he said. "I couldn't possibly!"

"Why not?" she said, her voice becoming heavy when she was opposed. "Why not? You can still go from the seaside to see the Derby with your Uncle Oscar, if that's what you wish. No need for you to wait here. Besides, I think you care too much about these races. It's a bad sign. My family has been a gambling family, and you won't know till you grow up how much damage it has done. But it has done damage. I shall have to send Bassett away, and ask Uncle Oscar not to talk racing to you, unless you promise to be reasonable about it; go away to the seaside and forget it. You're all nerves!"

"I'll do what you like, mother, so long as you don't send me away till after the Derby," the boy said.

"Send you away from where? Just from this house?"

"Yes," he said, gazing at her.

"Why, you curious child, what makes you care about this house so much, suddenly? I never knew you loved it."

He gazed at her without speaking. He had a secret within a secret, something he had not divulged, even to Bassett or to his Uncle Oscar.

But his mother, after standing undecided and a little bit sullen for some moments, said:

"Very well, then! Don't go to the seaside till after the Derby, if you don't wish it. But promise me you won't let your nerves go to pieces. Promise you won't think so much about horse racing and events, as you call them!"

"Oh, no," said the boy casually. "I won't think much about them, mother. You needn't worry. I wouldn't worry, mother, if I were you."

"If you were me and I were you," said his mother, "I wonder what we should do!"

"But you know you needn't worry, mother, don't you?" the boy repeated.

"I should be awfully glad to know it," she said wearily.

"Oh, well, you can, you know. I mean, you ought to know you needn't worry," he insisted.

"Ought I? Then I'll see about it," she said.

Paul's secret of secrets was his wooden horse, that which had no name. Since he was emancipated from a nurse and a nursery-governess, he had had his rocking horse removed to his own bedroom at the top of the house.

"Surely, you're too big for a rocking horse!" his mother had remonstrated.

"Well, you see, mother, till I can have a real horse, I like to have some sort of animal about," had been his quaint answer.

"Do you feel he keeps you company?" she laughed.

"Oh, yes! He's very good, he always keeps me company, when I'm there," said Paul.

So the horse, rather shabby, stood in an arrested prance in the boy's bedroom.

The Derby was drawing near, and the boy grew more and more tense. He hardly heard what was spoken to him, he was very frail, and his eyes were really uncanny. His mother had sudden seizures of uneasiness about him. Sometimes, for half-an-hour, she would feel a sudden anxiety about him that was almost anguish. She wanted to rush to him at once, and know he was safe.

Two nights before the Derby, she was at a big party in town, when one of her rushes of anxiety about her boy, her first-born, gripped her heart till she could hardly speak. She fought with the feeling, might and main, for she believed in common sense. But it was too strong. She had to leave the dance and go downstairs to telephone to the country. The children's nursery-governess was terribly surprised and startled at being rung up in the night.

"Are the children all right, Miss Wilmot?"

"Oh, yes, they are quite all right."

"Master Paul? Is he all right?"

"He went to bed as right as a trivet. Shall I run up and look at him?"

"No," said Paul's mother reluctantly. "No! Don't trouble. It's all right. Don't sit up. We shall be home fairly soon." She did not want her son's privacy intruded upon.

"Very good," said the governess.

It was about one o'clock when Paul's mother and father drove up to their house. All was still. Paul's mother went to her room and slipped off her white fur coat. She had told her maid not to wait up for her. She heard her husband downstairs, mixing a whisky-and-soda.

And then, because of the strange anxiety at her heart, she stole upstairs to her son's room. Noiselessly she went along the upper corridor. Was there a faint noise? What was it?

She stood, with arrested muscles, outside his door, listening. There was a strange, heavy, and yet not loud noise. Her heart stood still. It was a soundless noise, yet rushing and powerful. Something huge, in violent, hushed motion. What was it? What in God's name was it? She ought to know. She felt that she knew the noise. She knew what it was.

Yet she could not place it. She couldn't say what it was. And on and on it went, like a madness.

Softly, frozen with anxiety and fear, she turned the door handle.

The room was dark. Yet in the space near the window, she heard and saw something plunging to and fro. She gazed in fear and amazement.

Then suddenly she switched on the light, and saw her son, in his green pyjamas, madly surging on the rocking horse. The blaze of light suddenly lit him up, as he urged the wooden horse, and lit her up, as she stood, blonde, in her dress of pale green and crystal, in the doorway.

"Paul!" she cried. "Whatever are you doing?"

"It's Malabar!" he screamed, in a powerful, strange voice. "It's Malabar."

His eyes blazed at her for one strange and senseless second, as he ceased urging his wooden horse. Then he fell with a crash to the ground, and she, all her tormented motherhood flooding upon her, rushed to gather him up.

But he was unconscious, and unconscious he remained, with some brain-fever. He talked and tossed, and his mother sat stonily by his side.

"Malabar! It's Malabar! Bassett, Bassett, I know it! It's Malabar!"

So the child cried, trying to get up and urge the rocking horse that gave him his inspiration.

"What does he mean by Malabar?" asked the heart-frozen mother.

"I don't know," said the father stonily.

"What does he mean by Malabar?" she asked her brother Oscar.

"It's one of the horses running for the Derby," was the answer.

And, in spite of himself, Oscar Cresswell spoke to Bassett, and himself put a thousand on Malabar: at fourteen to one.

The third day of the illness was critical: they were waiting for a change. The boy, with his rather long, curly hair, was tossing ceaselessly on the pillow. He neither slept nor regained consciousness, and his eyes were like blue stones. His mother sat, feeling her heart had gone, turned actually into a stone.

In the evening, Oscar Cresswell did not come, but Bassett sent a message, saying could he come up for one moment, just one moment? Paul's mother was very angry at the intrusion, but on second thought she agreed. The boy was the same. Perhaps Bassett might bring him to consciousness.

The gardener, a shortish fellow with a little brown moustache, and sharp little brown eyes, tiptoed into the room, touched his imaginary cap to Paul's mother, and stole to the bedside, staring with glittering, smallish eyes, at the tossing, dying child.

"Master Paul!" he whispered. "Master Paul! Malabar come in first all right, a clean win. I did as you told me. You've made over seventy thousand pounds, you have; you've got over eighty thousand. Malabar came in all right, Master Paul."

"Malabar! Malabar! Did I say Malabar, mother? Did I say Malabar? Do you think I'm lucky, mother? I knew Malabar, didn't I? Over eighty thousand pounds! I call that lucky, don't you, mother? Over eighty thousand pounds! I knew, didn't I know I knew? Malabar came in all right. If I ride my horse till I'm sure, then I tell you, Bassett, you can go as high as you like. Did you go for all you were worth, Bassett?"

"I went a thousand on it, Master Paul."

"I never told you, mother that if I can ride my horse, and get there, then I'm absolutely sure—oh, absolutely! Mother, did I ever tell you? I'm lucky."

"No, you never did," said the mother.

But the boy died in the night.

And even as he lay dead, his mother heard her brother's voice saying to her: "My God, Hester, you're eighty-odd thousand to the good and a poor devil of a son to the bad. But, poor devil, poor devil, he's best gone out of a life where he rides his rocking horse to find a winner."

Sonny's Blues

James Baldwin (1924–1987)

I read about it in the paper, in the subway, on my way to work. I read it, and I couldn't believe it, and I read it again. Then perhaps I just stared at it, at the newsprint spelling out his name, spelling out the story. I stared at it in the swinging lights of the subway car, and in the faces and bodies of the people, and in my own face, trapped in the darkness which roared outside.

It was not to be believed and I kept telling myself that as I walked from the subway station to the high school. And at the same time I couldn't doubt it. I was scared, scared for Sonny. He became real to me again. A great block of ice got settled in my belly and kept melting there slowly all day long, while I taught my classes algebra. It was a special kind of ice. It kept melting, sending trickles of ice water all up and down my veins, but it never got less. Sometimes it hardened and seemed to expand until I felt my guts were going to come spilling out or that I was going to choke or scream. This would always be at a moment when I was remembering some specific thing Sonny had once said or done.

When he was about as old as the boys in my classes his face had been bright and open, there was a lot of copper in it; and he'd had wonderfully direct brown eyes, and great gentleness and privacy. I wondered what he looked like now. He had been picked up, the evening before, in a raid on an apartment downtown, for peddling and using heroin.

I couldn't believe it: but what I mean by that is that I couldn't find any room for it anywhere inside me. I had kept it outside me for a long time. I hadn't wanted to know. I had had suspicions, but I didn't name them, I kept putting them away. I told myself that Sonny was wild, but he wasn't crazy. And he'd always been a good boy, he hadn't ever turned hard or evil or disrespectful, the way kids can, so quick, so quick, especially in Harlem. I didn't want to believe that I'd ever see my brother going down, coming to nothing, all that light in his face gone out, in the condition I'd already seen so many others. Yet it had happened and here I was, talking about algebra to a lot of boys who might, every one of them for all I knew, be popping off needles every time they went to the head. Maybe it did more for them than algebra could.

I was sure that the first time Sonny had ever had horse, he couldn't have been much older than these boys were now. These boys, now, were living as we'd been living then, they were growing up with a rush and their heads bumped abruptly against the low ceiling of their actual possibilities. They were filled with rage. All they really knew were two darknesses, the darkness of their lives, which was now closing in on them, and the darkness of the movies, which had blinded them to that other darkness, and in which they now, vindictively, dreamed, at once more together than they were at any other time, and more alone.

When the last bell rang, the last class ended, I let out my breath. It seemed I'd been holding it for all that time. My clothes were wet—I may have looked as though I'd been sitting in a steam bath, all dressed up, all afternoon. I sat alone in the classroom a long time. I listened to the boys outside, downstairs, shouting and cursing and laughing. Their laughter struck me for perhaps the first time. It was not the joyous laughter which—God knows why—one associates with children. It was mocking and insular, its intent was to denigrate. It was disenchanted, and in this, also, lay the authority of their curses. Perhaps I was listening to them because I was thinking about my brother and in them I heard my brother. And myself.

One boy was whistling a tune, at once very complicated and very simple, it seemed to be pouring out of him as though he were a bird, and it sounded very cool and moving through all that harsh, bright air, only just holding its own through all those other sounds.

I stood up and walked over to the window and looked down into the courtyard. It was the beginning of the spring and the sap was rising in the boys. A teacher passed through them every now and again, quickly, as though he or she couldn't wait to get out of that courtyard, to get those boys out of their sight and off their minds. I started collecting my stuff. I thought I'd better get home and talk to Isabel.

The courtyard was almost deserted by the time I got downstairs. I saw this boy standing in the shadow of a doorway, looking just like Sonny. I almost called his name. Then I saw that it wasn't Sonny, but somebody we used to know, a boy from around our block. He'd been Sonny's friend. He'd never been mine, having been too young for me, and, anyway, I'd never liked him. And now, even though he was a grown-up man, he still hung around that block, still spent hours on the street corner, was always high and raggy. I used to run into him from time to time and he'd often work around to asking me for a quarter or fifty cents. He always had some real good excuse, too, and I always gave it to him, I don't know why.

But now, abruptly, I hated him. I couldn't stand the way he looked at me, partly like a dog, partly like a cunning child. I wanted to ask him what the hell he was doing in the school courtyard.

He sort of shuffled over to me, and he said, "I see you got the papers. So you already know about it."

"You mean about Sonny? Yes, I already know about it. How come they didn't get you?"

He grinned. It made him repulsive and it also brought to mind what he'd looked like as a kid. "I wasn't there. I stay away from them people."

"Good for you." I offered him a cigarette and I watched him through the smoke. "You come all the way down here just to tell me about Sonny?"

"That's right." He was sort of shaking his head and his eyes looked strange, as though they were about to cross. The bright sun deadened his damp dark brown skin and it made his eyes look yellow and showed up the dirt in his conked hair. He smelled funky. I moved a little away from him and I said, "Well, thanks. But I already know about it and I got to get home."

"I'll walk you a little ways," he said. We started walking. There were a couple of kids still loitering in the courtyard and one of them said good night to me and looked strangely at the boy beside me.

"What're you going to do?" he asked me. "I mean, about Sonny?"

"Look. I haven't seen Sonny for over a year, I'm not sure I'm going to do anything. Anyway, what the hell *can* I do?"

"That's right," he said quickly, "ain't nothing you can do. Can't much help old Sonny no more, I guess."

It was what I was thinking and so it seemed to me he had no right to say it.

"I'm surprised at Sonny, though," he went on—he had a funny way of talking, he looked straight ahead as though he were talking to himself—"I thought Sonny was a smart boy, I thought he was too smart to get hung."

"I guess he thought so too," I said sharply, "and that's how he got hung. And how about you? You're pretty goddamn smart, I bet."

Then he looked directly at me, just for a minute. "I ain't smart," he said. "If I was smart, I'd have reached for a pistol a long time ago."

"Look. Don't tell *me* your sad story, if it was up to me, I'd give you one." Then I felt guilty—guilty, probably, for never having supposed that the poor bastard *had* a story of his own, much less a sad one, and I asked, quickly, "What's going to happen to him now?"

He didn't answer this. He was off by himself some place. "Funny thing," he said, and from his tone we might have been discussing the quickest way to get to Brooklyn, "when I saw the papers this morning, the first thing I asked myself was if I had anything to do with it. I felt sort of responsible."

I began to listen more carefully. The subway station was on the corner, just before us, and I stopped. He stopped, too. We were in front of a bar and he ducked slightly, peering in, but whoever he was looking for didn't seem to be there. The juke box was blasting away with something black and bouncy and I half watched the barmaid as she danced her way from the juke box to her place behind the bar. And I watched her face as she laughingly responded to something someone said to her, still keeping time to the music. When she smiled one saw the little girl, one sensed the doomed, still-struggling woman beneath the battered face of the semi-whore.

"I never *give* Sonny nothing," the boy said finally, "but a long time ago I come to school high and Sonny asked me how it felt." He paused, I couldn't bear to watch him, I watched the barmaid, and I listened to the music which seemed to be causing the pavement to shake. "I told him it felt great." The music stopped, the barmaid paused and watched the juke box until the music began again. "It did."

All this was carrying me some place I didn't want to go. I certainly didn't want to know how it felt. It filled everything, the people, the houses, the music, the dark, quicksilver barmaid, with menace; and this menace was their reality.

"What's going to happen to him now?" I asked again.

"They'll send him away some place and they'll try to cure him." He shook his head. "Maybe he'll even think he's kicked the habit. Then they'll let him loose"—he gestured, throwing his cigarette into the gutter. "That's all."

"What do you mean, that's *all*?"

But I knew what he meant.

"I *mean*, that's *all*." He turned his head and looked at me, pulling down the corners of his mouth. "Don't you know what I mean?" he asked softly.

"How the hell *would* I know what you mean?" I almost whispered it, I don't know why.

"That's right," he said to the air, "how would *he* know what I mean?" He turned toward me again, patient and calm, and yet I somehow felt him shaking, shaking as though he were going to fall apart. I felt that ice in my guts again, the dread I'd felt all afternoon; and again I watched the barmaid, moving about the bar, washing glasses, and singing. "Listen. They'll let him out and then it'll just start all over again. That's what I mean."

"You mean—they'll let him out. And then he'll just start working his way back in again. You mean he'll never kick the habit. Is that what you mean?"

"That's right," he said, cheerfully. "*You* see what I mean."

"Tell me," I said at last, "why does he want to die? He must want to die, he's killing himself, why does he want to die?"

He looked at me in surprise. He licked his lips. "He don't want to die. He wants to live. Don't nobody want to die, ever."

Then I wanted to ask him—too many things. He could not have answered, or if he had, I could not have borne the answers. I started walking. "Well, I guess it's none of my business."

"It's going to be rough on old Sonny," he said. We reached the subway station. "This is your station?" he asked. I nodded. I took one step down. "Damn!" he said, suddenly. I looked up at him. He grinned again. "Damn if I didn't leave all my money home. You ain't got a dollar on you, have you? Just for a couple of days, is all."

All at once something inside gave and threatened to come pouring out of me. I didn't hate him any more. I felt that in another moment I'd start crying like a child.

"Sure," I said. "Don't sweat." I looked in my wallet and didn't have a dollar, I only had a five. "Here," I said. "That hold you?"

He didn't look at it—he didn't want to look at it. A terrible, closed look came over his face, as though he were keeping the number on the bill a secret from him and me. "Thanks," he said, and now he was dying to see me go. "Don't worry about Sonny. Maybe I'll write him or something."

"Sure," I said. "You do that. So long."

"Be seeing you," he said. I went on down the steps.

And I didn't write Sonny or send him anything for a long time. When I finally did, it was just after my little girl died, he wrote me back a letter which made me feel like a bastard.

Here's what he said:

DEAR BROTHER,

You don't know how much I needed to hear from you. I wanted to write you many a time but I dug how much I must have hurt you and so I didn't write. But now I feel like a man who's been trying to climb up out of some deep, real deep and funky hole and just saw the sun up there, outside. I got to get outside.

I can't tell you much about how I got here. I mean I don't know how to tell you. I guess I was afraid of something or I was trying to escape from something and you know I have never been very strong in the head (smile). I'm glad Mama and Daddy are dead and can't see what's happened to their son and I swear if I'd known what I was doing I would never have hurt you so, you and a lot of other fine people who were nice to me and who believed in me.

I don't want you to think it had anything to do with me being a musician. It's more than that. Or maybe less than that. I can't get anything straight in my head down here and I try not to think about what's going to happen to me when I get outside again. Sometime I think I'm going to flip and *never* get outside and sometime I think I'll come straight back. I tell you one thing, though, I'd rather blow my brains out than go through this again. But that's what they all say, so they tell me. If I tell you when I'm coming to New York and if you could meet me, I sure would appreciate it. Give my love to Isabel and the kids and I was sorry to hear about little Gracie. I wish I could be like Mama and say the Lord's will be done, but I don't know it seems to me that trouble is the one thing that never does get stopped and I don't know what good it does to blame it on the Lord. But maybe it does some good if you believe it.

Your brother,
SONNY

Then I kept in constant touch with him and I sent him whatever I could and I went to meet him when he came back to New York. When I saw him many things I thought I had forgotten came flooding back to me. This was because I had begun, finally, to wonder about Sonny, about the life that Sonny lived inside. This life, whatever it was, had made him older and thinner and it had deepened the distant stillness in which he had always moved. He looked very unlike my baby brother. Yet, when he smiled, when we shook hands, the baby brother I'd never known looked out from the depths of his private life, like an animal waiting to be coaxed into the light.

"How you been keeping?" he asked me.

"All right. And you?"

"Just fine." He was smiling all over his face. "It's good to see you again."

"It's good to see you."

The seven years' difference in our ages lay between us like a chasm: I wondered if these years would ever operate between us as a bridge. I was remembering, and it made it hard to catch my breath, that I had been there when he was born; and I had heard the first words he had ever spoken. When he started to walk, he walked from our mother straight to me. I caught him just before he fell when he took the first steps he ever took in this world.

"How's Isabel?"

"Just fine. She's dying to see you."

"And the boys?"

"They're fine, too. They're anxious to see their uncle."

"Oh, come on. You know they don't remember me."

"Are you kidding? Of course they remember you."

He grinned again. We got into a taxi. We had a lot to say to each other, far too much to know how to begin.

As the taxi began to move, I asked, "You still want to go to India?"

He laughed. "You still remember that. Hell, no. This place is Indian enough for me."

"It used to belong to them," I said.

And he laughed again. "They damn sure knew what they were doing when they got rid of it."

Years ago, when he was around fourteen, he'd been all hipped on the idea of going to India. He read books about people sitting on rocks, naked, in all kinds of weather, but mostly bad, naturally, and walking barefoot through hot coals and arriving at wisdom. I used to say that it sounded to me as though they were getting away from wisdom as fast as they could. I think he sort of looked down on me for that.

"Do you mind," he asked, "if we have the driver drive alongside the park? On the west side—I haven't seen the city in so long."

"Of course not," I said. I was afraid that I might sound as though I were humoring him, but I hoped he wouldn't take it that way.

So we drove along, between the green of the park and the stony, lifeless elegance of hotels and apartment buildings, toward the vivid, killing streets of our childhood. These streets hadn't changed, though housing projects jutted up out of them now like rocks in the middle of a boiling sea. Most of the houses in which we had grown up had vanished, as had the stores from which we had stolen, the basements in which we had first tried sex, the rooftops from which we had hurled tin cans and bricks. But houses exactly like the houses of our past yet dominated the landscape, boys exactly like the boys we once had been found themselves smothering in these houses, came down into the streets for light and air and found themselves encircled by disaster. Some escaped the trap, most didn't. Those who got out always left something of themselves behind, as some animals amputate a leg and leave it in the trap. It might be said, perhaps, that I had escaped, after all, I was a school teacher; or that Sonny had, he hadn't lived in Harlem for years. Yet, as the cab moved uptown through streets which seemed, with a rush, to darken with dark people, and as I covertly studied Sonny's face, it came to me that what we both were seeking through our separate cab windows was that part of ourselves which had been left behind. It's always at the hour of trouble and confrontation that the missing member aches.

We hit 110th Street and started rolling up Lenox Avenue. And I'd known this avenue all my life, but it seemed to me again, as it had seemed on the day I'd first heard about Sonny's trouble, filled with a hidden menace which was its very breath of life.

"We almost there," said Sonny.

"Almost." We were both too nervous to say anything more.

We live in a housing project. It hasn't been up long. A few days after it was up it seemed uninhabitably new, now, of course, it's already run-down. It looks like a parody of the good, clean, faceless life—God knows the people who live in it do their best to make it a parody. The beat-looking grass lying around isn't enough to make their lives green, the hedges will never hold out the streets, and they know it. The big windows fool no one, they aren't big enough to make space out of no space. They don't bother with the windows, they watch the TV screen instead. The playground is most popular with the children who don't play at jacks, or skip rope, or roller skate, or swing, and they can be found in it after dark. We moved in partly because it's not too far from where I teach, and partly for the kids; but it's really just like the houses in which Sonny and I grew up. The same things happen, they'll have the same things to remember. The moment Sonny and I started into the house I had the feeling that I was simply bringing him back into the danger he had almost died trying to escape.

Sonny has never been talkative. So I don't know why I was sure he'd be dying to talk to me when supper was over the first night. Everything went fine, the oldest boy remembered him, and the youngest boy liked him, and Sonny had remembered to bring something for each of them; and Isabel, who is really much nicer than I am, more open and giving, had gone to a lot of trouble about dinner and was genuinely glad to see him. And she's always been able to tease Sonny in a way that I haven't. It was nice to see her face so vivid again and to hear her laugh and watch her make Sonny laugh. She wasn't, or, anyway, she didn't seem to be, at all uneasy or embarrassed. She chatted as though there were no subject which had to be avoided and she got Sonny past his first, faint stiffness. And thank God she was there, for I was filled with that icy dread again. Everything I did seemed awkward to me, and everything I said sounded freighted with hidden meaning. I was trying to remember everything I'd heard about dope addiction and I couldn't help watching Sonny for signs. I wasn't doing it out of malice. I was trying to find out something about my brother. I was dying to hear him tell me he was safe.

"Safe!" my father grunted, whenever Mama suggested trying to move to a neighborhood which might be safer for children. "Safe, hell! Ain't no place safe for kids, nor nobody."

He always went on like this, but he wasn't, ever, really as bad as he sounded, not even on weekends, when he got drunk. As a matter of fact, he was always on the lookout for "something a little better," but he died before he found it. He died suddenly, during a drunken weekend in the middle of the war, when Sonny was fifteen. He and Sonny hadn't ever got on too well. And this was partly because Sonny was the apple of his father's eye. It was because he loved Sonny so much and was frightened for him, that he was always fighting with him. It doesn't do any good to fight with Sonny. Sonny just moves back, inside himself, where he can't be reached. But the principal reason that they never hit it off is that they were so much alike. Daddy was big and rough and loud-talking, just the opposite of Sonny, but they both had—that same privacy.

Mama tried to tell me something about this, just after Daddy died. I was home on leave from the army.

This was the last time I ever saw my mother alive. Just the same, this picture gets all mixed up in my mind with pictures I had of her when she was younger. The way I always see her is the way she used to be on a Sunday afternoon, say, when the old folks were talking after the big Sunday dinner. I always see her wearing pale blue. She'd be sitting on the sofa. And my father would be sitting in the easy chair, not far from her. And the living room would be full of church folks and relatives. There they sit, in chairs all around the living room, and the night is creeping up outside, but nobody knows it yet. You can see the darkness growing against the window-panes and you hear the street noises every now and again, or maybe the jangling beat of a tambourine from one of the churches close by, but it's real quiet in the room. For a moment nobody's talking, but every face looks darkening, like the sky outside. And my mother rocks a little from the waist, and my father's eyes are closed. Everyone is looking at something a child can't see. For a minute they've forgotten the children. Maybe a kid is lying on the rug half asleep. Maybe somebody's got a kid on his lap and is absent-mindedly stroking the kid's head. Maybe there's a kid, quiet and big-eyed, curled up in a big chair in the corner. The silence, the darkness coming, and the darkness in the faces frightens the child obscurely. He hopes that the hand which strokes his forehead will never stop—will never die. He hopes that there will never come a time when the old folks won't be sitting around the living room, talking about where they've come from, and what they've seen, and what's happened to them and their kinfolk.

But something deep and watchful in the child knows that this is bound to end, is already ending. In a moment someone will get up and turn on the light. Then the old folks will remember the children and they won't talk any more that day. And when light fills the room, the child is filled with darkness. He knows that every time this happens he's moved just a little closer to that darkness outside. The darkness outside is what the old folks have been talking about. It's what they've come from. It's what they endure. The child knows that they won't talk any more because if he knows too much about what's happened to *them*, he'll know too much too soon, about what's going to happen to *him*.

The last time I talked to my mother, I remember I was restless. I wanted to get out and see Isabel. We weren't married then and we had a lot to straighten out between us.

There Mama sat, in black, by the window. She was humming an old church song, *Lord, you brought me from a long ways off.* Sonny was out somewhere. Mama kept watching the streets.

"I don't know," she said, "if I'll ever see you again, after you go off from here. But I hope you'll remember the things I tried to teach you."

"Don't talk like that," I said, and smiled. "You'll be here a long time yet."

She smiled, too, but she said nothing. She was quiet for a long time. And I said, "Mama, don't you worry about nothing. I'll be writing all the time, and you be getting the checks. . . ."

"I want to talk to you about your brother," she said, suddenly. "If anything happens to me he ain't going to have nobody to look out for him."

"Mama," I said, "ain't nothing going to happen to you *or* Sonny. Sonny's all right. He's a good boy and he's got good sense."

"It ain't a question of his being a good boy," Mama said, "nor of his having good sense. It ain't only the bad ones, nor yet the dumb ones that gets sucked under." She stopped, looking at me. "Your Daddy once had a brother," she said, and she smiled in a way that made me feel she was in pain. "You didn't never know that, did you?"

"No," I said, "I never knew that," and I watched her face.

"Oh, yes," she said, "your Daddy had a brother." She looked out of the window again. "I know you never saw your Daddy cry. But *I* did—many a time, through all these years."

I asked her, "What happened to his brother? How come nobody's ever talked about him?"

This was the first time I ever saw my mother look old.

"His brother got killed," she said, "when he was just a little younger than you are now. I knew him. He was a fine boy. He was maybe a little full of the devil, but he didn't mean nobody no harm."

Then she stopped and the room was silent, exactly as it had sometimes been on those Sunday afternoons. Mama kept looking out into the streets.

"He used to have a job in the mill," she said, "and, like all young folks, he just liked to perform on Saturday nights. Saturday nights, him and your father would drift around to different places, go to dances and things like that, or just sit around with people they knew, and your father's brother would sing, he had a fine voice, and play along with himself on his guitar. Well, this particular Saturday night, him and your father was coming home from some place, and they were both a little drunk and there was a moon that night, it was bright like day. Your father's brother was feeling kind of good, and he was whistling to himself, and he had his guitar slung over his shoulder. They was coming down a hill and beneath them was a road that turned off from the highway. Well, your father's brother, being always kind of frisky, decided to run down this hill, and he did, with that guitar banging and clanging behind him, and he ran across the road, and he was making water behind a tree. And your father was sort of amused at him and he was still coming down the hill, kind of slow. Then he heard a car motor and that same minute his brother stepped from behind the tree, into the road, in the moonlight. And he started to cross the road. And your father started to run down the hill, he says he don't know why. This car was full of white men. They was all drunk, and when they seen your father's brother they let out a great whoop and holler and they aimed the car straight at him. They was having fun, they just wanted to scare him, the way they do sometimes, you know. But they was drunk. And I guess the boy, being drunk, too, and scared, kind of lost his head. By the time he jumped it was too late. Your father says he heard his brother scream when the car rolled over him, and he heard the wood of that guitar when it give, and he heard them strings go flying, and he heard them white men shouting, and the car kept on a-going and it ain't stopped till this day. And, time your father got down the hill, his brother weren't nothing but blood and pulp."

Tears were gleaming on my mother's face. There wasn't anything I could say.

"He never mentioned it," she said, "because I never let him mention it before you children. Your Daddy was like a crazy man that night and for many a night thereafter. He says he never in his life seen anything as dark as that road after the lights of that car had gone away. Weren't nothing, weren't nobody on that road, just your Daddy and his brother and that busted guitar. Oh, yes. Your Daddy never did really get right again. Till the day he died he weren't sure but that every white man he saw was the man that killed his brother."

She stopped and took out her handkerchief and dried her eyes and looked at me.

"I ain't telling you all this," she said, "to make you scared or bitter or to make you hate nobody. I'm telling you this because you got a brother. And the world ain't changed."

I guess I didn't want to believe this. I guess she saw this in my face. She turned away from me, toward the window again, searching those streets.

"But I praise my Redeemer," she said at last, "that He called your Daddy home before me. I ain't saying it to throw no flowers at myself, but, I declare, it keeps me from feeling too cast down to know I helped your father get safely through this world. Your father always acted like he was the roughest, strongest man on earth. And everybody took him to be like that. But if he hadn't had *me* there—to see his tears!"

She was crying again. Still, I couldn't move. I said, "Lord, Lord, Mama, I didn't know it was like that."

"Oh, honey," she said, "there's a lot that you don't know. But you are going to find it out." She stood up from the window and came over to me. "You got to hold on to your brother," she said, "and don't let him fall, no matter what it looks like is happening to him and no matter how evil you gets with him. You going to be evil with him many a time. But don't you forget what I told you, you hear?"

"I won't forget," I said. "Don't you worry, I won't forget. I won't let nothing happen to Sonny."

My mother smiled as though she were amused at something she saw in my face. Then, "You may not be able to stop nothing from happening. But you got to let him know you's *there*."

Two days later I was married, and then I was gone. And I had a lot of things on my mind and I pretty well forgot my promise to Mama until I got shipped home on a special furlough for her funeral.

And, after the funeral, with just Sonny and me alone in the empty kitchen, I tried to find out something about him.

"What do you want to do?" I asked him.

"I'm going to be a musician," he said.

For he had graduated, in the time I had been away, from dancing to the juke box to finding out who was playing what, and what they were doing with it, and he had bought himself a set of drums.

"You mean, you want to be a drummer?" I somehow had the feeling that being a drummer might be all right for other people but not for my brother Sonny.

"I don't think," he said, looking at me very gravely, "that I'll ever be a good drummer. But I think I can play a piano."

I frowned. I'd never played the role of the older brother quite so seriously before, had scarcely ever, in fact, *asked* Sonny a damn thing. I sensed myself in the presence of something I didn't really know how to handle, didn't understand. So I made my frown a little deeper as I asked: "What kind of musician do you want to be?"

He grinned. "How many kinds do you think there are?"

"Be *serious*," I said.

He laughed, throwing his head back, and then looked at me. "I *am* serious."

"Well, then, for Christ's sake, stop kidding around and answer a serious question. I mean, do you want to be a concert pianist, you want to play classical music and all that, or—or what?" Long before I finished he was laughing again. "For Christ's *sake*, Sonny!"

He sobered, but with difficulty. "I'm sorry. But you sound so—*scared!*" and he was off again.

"Well, you may think it's funny now, baby, but it's not going to be so funny when you have to make your living at it, let me tell you *that*." I was furious because I knew he was laughing at me and I didn't know why.

"No," he said, very sober now, and afraid, perhaps, that he'd hurt me, "I don't want to be a classical pianist. That isn't what interests me. I mean"—he paused, looking hard at me, as though his eyes would help me to understand, and then gestured helplessly, as though perhaps his hand would help—"I mean, I'll have a lot of studying to do, and I'll have to study *everything*, but I mean, I want to play *with*—jazz musicians." He stopped. "I want to play jazz," he said.

Well, the word had never before sounded as heavy, as real, as it sounded that afternoon in Sonny's mouth. I just looked at him and I was probably frowning a real frown by this time. I simply couldn't see why on earth he'd want to spend his time hanging around night clubs, clowning around on bandstands, while people pushed each other around a dance floor. It seemed—beneath him, somehow. I had never thought about it before, had never been forced to, but I suppose I had always put jazz musicians in a class with what Daddy called "good-time people."

"Are you *serious*?"

"Hell, *yes*, I'm serious."

He looked more helpless than ever, and annoyed, and deeply hurt.

I suggested, helpfully: "You mean—like Louis Armstrong?"

His face closed as though I'd struck him. "No. I'm not talking about none of that old-time, down home crap."

"Well, look, Sonny, I'm sorry, don't get mad. I just don't altogether get it, that's all. Name somebody—you know, a jazz musician you admire."

"Bird."

"Who?"

"Bird! Charlie Parker! Don't they teach you nothing in the goddamn army?"

I lit a cigarette. I was surprised and then a little amused to discover that I was trembling. "I've been out of touch," I said. "You'll have to be patient with me. Now. Who's this Parker character?"

"He's just one of the greatest jazz musicians alive," said Sonny, sullenly, his hands in his pockets, his back to me. "Maybe *the* greatest," he added, bitterly, "that's probably why *you* never heard of him."

"All right," I said, "I'm ignorant. I'm sorry. I'll go out and buy all the cat's records right away, all right?"

"It don't," said Sonny, with dignity, "make any difference to me. I don't care what you listen to. Don't do me no favors."

I was beginning to realize that I'd never seen him so upset before. With another part of my mind I was thinking that this would probably turn out to be one of those things kids go through and that I shouldn't make it seem important by pushing it too hard. Still, I didn't think it would do any harm to ask: "Doesn't all this take a lot of time? Can you make a living at it?"

He turned back to me and half leaned, half sat, on the kitchen table. "Everything takes time," he said, "and—well, yes, sure, I can make a living at it. But what I don't seem to be able to make you understand is that it's the only thing I want to do."

"Well Sonny," I said, gently, "you know people can't always do exactly what they *want* to do—"

"*No*, I don't know that," said Sonny, surprising me. "I think people *ought* to do what they want to do, what else are they alive for?"

"You getting to be a big boy," I said desperately, "it's time you started thinking about your future."

"I'm thinking about my future," said Sonny, grimly. "I think about it all the time."

I gave up. I decided, if he didn't change his mind, that we could always talk about it later. "In the meantime," I said, "you got to finish school." We had already decided that he'd have to move in with Isabel and her folks. I knew this wasn't the ideal arrangement because Isabel's folks are inclined to be dicty and they hadn't especially wanted Isabel to marry me. But I didn't know what else to do. "And we have to get you fixed up at Isabel's."

There was a long silence. He moved from the kitchen table to the window. "That's a terrible idea. You know it yourself."

"Do you have a *better* idea?"

He just walked up and down the kitchen for a minute. He was as tall as I was. He had started to shave. I suddenly had the feeling that I didn't know him at all.

He stopped at the kitchen table and picked up my cigarettes. Looking at me with a kind of mocking, amused defiance, he put one between his lips. "You mind?"

"You smoking already?"

He lit the cigarette and nodded, watching me through the smoke. "I just wanted to see if I'd have the courage to smoke in front of you." He grinned and blew a great cloud of smoke to the ceiling. "It was easy." He looked at my face. "Come on, now. I bet you was smoking at my age, tell the truth."

I didn't say anything but the truth was on my face, and he laughed. But now there was something very strained in his laugh. "Sure. And I bet that ain't all you was doing."

He was frightening me a little. "Cut the crap," I said. "We already decided that you was going to go and live at Isabel's. Now what's got into you all of a sudden?"

"*You* decided it," he pointed out. "*I* didn't decide nothing." He stopped in front of me, leaning against the stove, arms loosely folded. "Look, brother. I don't want to stay in Harlem no more, I really don't." He was very earnest. He looked at me, then over toward the kitchen window. There was something in his eyes I'd never seen before, some thoughtfulness, some worry all his own. He rubbed the muscle of one arm. "It's time I was getting out of here."

"Where do you want to *go*, Sonny?"

"I want to join the army. Or the navy, I don't care. If I say I'm old enough they'll believe me."

Then I got mad. It was because I was so scared. "You must be crazy. You god-damn fool, what the hell do you want to go and join the *army* for?"

"I just told you. To get out of Harlem."

"Sonny, you haven't even finished *school*. And if you really want to be a musician, how do you expect to study if you're in the *army?*"

He looked at me, trapped, and in anguish. "There's ways. I might be able to work out some kind of deal. Anyway, I'll have the G.I. Bill when I come out."

"*If* you come out." We stared at each other. "Sonny, please. Be reasonable. I know the setup is far from perfect. But we got to do the best we can."

"I ain't learning nothing in school," he said. "Even when I go." He turned away from me and opened the window and threw his cigarette out into the narrow alley. I watched his back. "At least, I ain't learning nothing you'd want me to learn." He slammed the window so hard I thought the glass would fly out, and turned back to me. "And I'm sick of the stink of these garbage cans!"

"Sonny," I said, "I know how you feel. But if you don't finish school now, you're going to be sorry later that you didn't." I grabbed him by the shoulders. "And you only got another year. It ain't so bad. And I'll come back and I swear I'll help you do *whatever* you want to do. Just try to put up with it till I come back. Will you please do that? For me?"

He didn't answer and he wouldn't look at me.

"Sonny. You hear me?"

He pulled away. "I hear you. But you never hear anything *I* say."

I didn't know what to say to that. He looked out of the window and then back at me. "OK," he said, and sighed. "I'll try."

Then I said, trying to cheer him up a little, "They got a piano at Isabel's. You can practice on it."

And as a matter of fact, it did cheer him up for a minute. "That's right," he said to himself. "I forgot that." His face relaxed a little. But the worry, the thoughtfulness, played on it still, the way shadows play on a face which is staring into the fire.

But I thought I'd never hear the end of that piano. At first, Isabel would write me, saying how nice it was that Sonny was so serious about his music and how, as soon as he came in from school, or wherever he had been when he was supposed to be at school, he went straight to that piano and stayed there until suppertime. And, after supper, he went back to that piano and stayed there until everybody went to bed. He was at the piano all day Saturday and all day Sunday. Then he bought a record player and started playing records. He'd play one record over and over again, all day long sometimes, and he'd improvise along with it on the piano. Or he'd play one section of the record, one chord, one change, one progression, then he'd do it on the piano. Then back to the record. Then back to the piano.

Well, I really don't know how they stood it. Isabel finally confessed that it wasn't like living with a person at all, it was like living with sound. And the sound didn't make any sense to her, didn't make any sense to any of them—naturally. They began, in a way, to be afflicted by this presence that was living in their home. It was as though Sonny were some sort of god, or monster. He moved in an atmosphere which wasn't like theirs at all. They fed him and he ate, he washed himself, he walked in and out of their door; he certainly wasn't nasty or unpleasant or rude, Sonny isn't any of those things; but it was as though he were all wrapped up in some cloud, some fire, some vision all his own; and there wasn't any way to reach him.

At the same time, he wasn't really a man yet, he was still a child, and they had to watch out for him in all kinds of ways. They certainly couldn't throw him out. Neither did they dare to make a great scene about that piano because even they dimly sensed, as I sensed, from so many thousands of miles away, that Sonny was at that piano playing for his life.

But he hadn't been going to school. One day a letter came from the school board and Isabel's mother got it—there had, apparently, been other letters but Sonny had torn them up. This day, when Sonny came in, Isabel's mother showed him the letter and asked where he'd been spending his time. And she finally got it out of him that he'd been down in Greenwich Village, with musicians and other characters, in a white girl's apartment. And this scared her and she started to scream at him and what came up, once she began—though she denies it to this day—was what sacrifices they were making to give Sonny a decent home and how little he appreciated it.

Sonny didn't play the piano that day. By evening, Isabel's mother had calmed down but then there was the old man to deal with, and Isabel herself. Isabel says she did her best to be calm but she broke down and started crying. She says she just watched Sonny's face. She could tell, by watching him, what was happening with him. And what was happening was that they penetrated his cloud, they had reached him. Even if their fingers had been a thousand times more gentle than human fingers ever are, he could hardly help feeling that they had stripped him naked and were spitting on that nakedness. For he also had to see that his presence, that music, which was life or death to him, had been torture for them and that they had endured it, not at all for his sake, but only for mine. And Sonny couldn't take that. He can take it a little better today than he could then but he's still not very good at it and, frankly, I don't know anybody who is.

The silence of the next few days must have been louder than the sound of all the music ever played since time began. One morning, before she went to work, Isabel was in his room for something and she suddenly realized that all of his records were gone. And she knew for certain that he was gone. And he was. He went as far as the navy would carry him. He finally sent me a postcard from some place in Greece and that was the first I knew that Sonny was still alive. I didn't see him any more until we were both back in New York and the war had long been over.

He was a man by then, of course, but I wasn't willing to see it. He came by the house from time to time, but we fought almost every time we met. I didn't like the way he carried himself, loose and dreamlike all the time, and I didn't like his friends, and his music seemed to be merely an excuse for the life he led. It sounded just that weird and disordered.

Then we had a fight, a pretty awful fight, and I didn't see him for months. By and by I looked him up, where he was living, in a furnished room in the Village, and I tried to make it up. But there were lots of other people in the room and Sonny just lay on his bed, and he wouldn't come downstairs with me, and he treated these other people as though they were his family and I weren't. So I got mad and then he got mad, and then I told him that he might just as well be dead as live the way he was living. Then he stood up and he told me not to worry about him any more in life, that he *was* dead as far as I was concerned. Then he pushed me to the door and the other people looked on as though nothing were happening, and he slammed the door behind me. I stood in the hallway, staring at the door. I heard somebody laugh in the room and then the tears came to my eyes. I started down the steps, whistling to keep from crying. I kept whistling to myself, *You going to need me, baby, one of these cold, rainy days.*

I read about Sonny's trouble in the spring. Little Grace died in the fall. She was a beautiful little girl. But she only lived a little over two years. She died of polio and she suffered. She had a slight fever for a couple of days, but it didn't seem like anything and we just kept her in bed. And we would certainly have called the doctor, but the fever dropped, she seemed to be all right. So we thought it had just been a cold. Then, one day, she was up, playing, Isabel was in the kitchen fixing lunch for the two boys when they'd come in from school, and she heard Grace fall down in the living room. When you have a lot of children you don't always start running when one of them falls, unless they start screaming or something. And, this time, Grace was quiet. Yet, Isabel says that when she heard that *thump* and then that silence, something happened in her to make her afraid. And she ran to the living room and there was little Grace on the floor, all twisted up and the reason she hadn't screamed was that she couldn't get her breath. And when she did scream, it was the worst sound, Isabel says, that she'd ever heard in all her life, and she still hears it sometimes in her dreams. Isabel will sometimes wake up with a low, moaning, strangled sound and I have to be quick to awaken her and hold her to me and where Isabel is weeping against me seems a mortal wound.

I think I may have written Sonny the very day that little Grace was buried. I was sitting in the living room in the dark, by myself, and I suddenly thought of Sonny. My trouble made his real.

One Saturday afternoon, when Sonny had been living with us, or, anyway, been in our house, for nearly two weeks, I found myself wandering aimlessly about the living room, drinking from a can of beer, and trying to work up the courage to search Sonny's room. He was out, he was usually out whenever I was home, and Isabel had taken the children to see their grandparents. Suddenly I was standing still in front of the living room window, watching Seventh Avenue. The idea of searching Sonny's room made me still. I scarcely dared to admit to myself what I'd be searching for. I didn't know what I'd do if I found it. Or if I didn't.

On the sidewalk across from me, near the entrance to a barbecue joint, some people were holding an old-fashioned revival meeting. The barbecue cook, wearing a dirty white apron, his conked hair reddish and metallic in the pale sun, and a cigarette between his lips, stood in the doorway, watching them. Kids and older people paused in their errands and stood there, along with some older men and a couple of very tough-looking women who watched everything that happened on the avenue, as though they owned it, or were maybe owned by it. Well, they were watching this, too. The revival was being carried on by three sisters in black, and a brother. All they had were their voices and their Bibles and a tambourine. The brother was testifying and while he testified two of the sisters stood together, seeming to say, Amen, and the third sister walked around with the tambourine outstretched and a couple of people dropped coins into it. Then the brother's testimony ended and the sister who had been taking up the collection dumped the coins into her palm and transferred them to the pocket of her long black robe. Then she raised both hands, striking the tambourine against the air, and then against one hand, and she started to sing. And the two other sisters and the brother joined in.

It was strange, suddenly, to watch, though I had been seeing these street meetings all my life. So, of course, had everybody else down there. Yet, they paused and watched and listened and I stood still at the window. "*Tis the old ship of Zion,*" they sang, and the sister with the tambourine kept a steady, jangling beat, "*It has rescued many a thousand!*" Not a soul under the sound of their voices was hearing this song for the first time, not one of them had been rescued. Nor had they seen much in the way of rescue work being done around them. Neither did they especially believe in the holiness of the three sisters and the brother, they knew too much about them, knew where they lived, and how. The woman with the tambourine, whose voice dominated the air, whose face was bright with joy, was divided by very little from the woman who stood watching her, a cigarette between her heavy, chapped lips, her hair a cuckoo's nest, her face scarred and swollen from many beatings, and her black eyes glittering like coal. Perhaps they both knew this, which was why, when, as rarely, they addressed each other, they addressed each other as Sister. As the singing filled the air the watching, listening faces underwent a change, the eyes focusing on something within; the music seemed to soothe a poison out of them; and time seemed, nearly, to fall away from the sullen, belligerent, battered faces, as though they were fleeing back to their first condition, while dreaming of their last. The barbecue cook half shook his head and smiled, and dropped his cigarette and disappeared into his joint. A man fumbled in his pockets for change and stood holding it in his hand impatiently, as though he had just remembered a pressing appointment further up the avenue. He looked furious. Then I saw Sonny, standing on the edge of the crowd. He was carrying a wide, flat notebook with a green cover, and it made him look, from where I was standing, almost like a school-boy. The coppery sun brought out the copper in his skin, he was very faintly smiling, standing very still. Then the singing stopped, the tambourine turned into a collection plate again. The furious man dropped in his coins and vanished, so did a couple of the women, and Sonny dropped some change in the plate, looking directly at the woman with a little smile. He started across the avenue, toward the house. He has a slow, loping walk, something like the way Harlem hipsters walk, only he's imposed on this his own halfbeat. I had never really noticed it before.

I stayed at the window, both relieved and apprehensive. As Sonny disappeared from my sight, they began singing again. And they were still singing when his key turned in the lock.

"Hey," he said.

"Hey, yourself. You want some beer?"

"No. Well, maybe." But he came up to the window and stood beside me, looking out. "What a warm voice," he said.

They were singing *If I could only hear my mother pray again!*

"Yes," I said, "and she can sure beat that tambourine."

"But what a terrible song," he said, and laughed. He dropped his notebook on the sofa and disappeared into the kitchen. "Where's Isabel and the kids?"

"I think they went to see their grandparents. You hungry?"

"No." He came back into the living room with his can of beer. "You want to come some place with me tonight?"

I sensed, I don't know how, that I couldn't possibly say No. "Sure. Where?"

He sat down on the sofa and picked up his notebook and started leafing through it. "I'm going to sit in with some fellows in a joint in the Village."

"You mean, you're going to play, tonight?"

"That's right." He took a swallow of his beer and moved back to the window. He gave me a sidelong look. "If you can stand it."

"I'll try," I said.

He smiled to himself and we both watched as the meeting across the way broke up. The three sisters and the brother, heads bowed, were singing *God be with you till we meet again*. The faces around them were very quiet. Then the song ended. The small crowd dispersed. We watched the three women and the lone man walk slowly up the avenue.

"When she was singing before," said Sonny, abruptly, "her voice reminded me for a minute of what heroin feels like sometimes—when it's in your veins. It makes you feel sort of warm and cool at the same time. And distant. And—and sure." He sipped his beer, very deliberately not looking at me. I watched his face. "It makes you feel—in control. Sometimes you've got to have that feeling."

"Do you?" I sat down slowly in the easy chair.

"Sometimes." He went to the sofa and picked up his notebook again. "Some people do."

"In order," I asked, "to play?" And my voice was very ugly, full of contempt and anger.

"Well"—he looked at me with great, troubled eyes, as though, in fact, he hoped his eyes would tell me things he could never otherwise say—"they *think* so. And *if* they think so—!"

"And what do *you* think?" I asked.

He sat on the sofa and put his can of beer on the floor. "I don't know," he said, and I couldn't be sure if he were answering my question or pursuing his thoughts. His face didn't tell me. "It's not so much to *play*. It's to *stand* it, to be able to make it at all. On any level." He frowned and smiled: "In order to keep from shaking to pieces."

"But these friends of yours," I said, "they seem to shake themselves to pieces pretty goddamn fast."

"Maybe." He played with the notebook. And something told me that I should curb my tongue, that Sonny was doing his best to talk, that I should listen. "But of course you only know the ones that've gone to pieces. Some don't— or at least they haven't *yet* and that's just about all *any* of us can say." He paused. "And then there are some who just live, really, in hell, and they know it and they see what's happening and they go right on. I don't know." He sighed, dropped the notebook, folded his arms. "Some guys, you can tell from the way they play, they on something *all* the time. And you can see that, well, it makes something real for them. But of course," he picked up his beer from the floor and sipped it and put the can down again, "they *want* to, too, you've got to see that. Even some of them that say they don't—*some*, not all."

"And what about you?" I asked—I couldn't help it. "What about you? Do *you* want to?"

He stood up and walked to the window and remained silent for a long time. Then he sighed. "Me," he said. Then: "While I was downstairs before, on my way here, listening to that woman sing, it struck me all of a sudden how much suffering she must have had to go through—to sing like that. It's *repulsive* to think you have to suffer that much."

I said: "But there's no way not to suffer—is there, Sonny?"

"I believe not," he said, and smiled, "but that's never stopped anyone from trying." He looked at me. "Has it?" I realized, with this mocking look, that there stood between us, forever, beyond the power of time or forgiveness, the fact that I had held silence—so long!—when he had needed human speech to help him. He turned back to the window. "No, there's no way not to suffer. But you try all kinds of ways to keep from drowning in it, to keep on top of it, and to make it seem—well, like *you*. Like you did something, all right, and now you're suffering for it. You know?" I said nothing. "Well you know," he said, impatiently, "why *do* people suffer? Maybe it's better to do something to give it a reason, *any* reason."

"But we just agreed," I said, "that there's no way not to suffer. Isn't it better, then, just to—take it?"

"But nobody just takes it," Sonny cried, "that's what I'm telling you! *Every-body* tries not to. You're just hung up on the *way* some people try—it's not *your* way!"

The hair on my face began to itch, my face felt wet. "That's not true," I said, "that's not true. I don't give a damn what other people do, I don't even care how they suffer. I just care how *you* suffer." And he looked at me. "Please believe me," I said, "I don't want to see you—die—trying not to suffer."

"I won't," he said, flatly, "die trying not to suffer. At least, not any faster than anybody else."

"But there's no need," I said, trying to laugh, "is there? in killing yourself."

I wanted to say more, but I couldn't. I wanted to talk about will power and how life could be—well, beautiful. I wanted to say that it was all within; but was it? or, rather, wasn't that exactly the trouble? And I wanted to promise that I would never fail him again. But it would all have sounded—empty words and lies.

So I made the promise to myself and prayed that I would keep it.

"It's terrible sometimes, inside," he said, "that's what's the trouble. You walk these streets, black and funky and cold, and there's not really a living ass to talk to, and there's nothing shaking, and there's no way of getting it out—that storm inside. You can't talk it and you can't make love with it, and when you finally try to get with it and play it, you realize *nobody's* listening. So *you've* got to listen. You got to find a way to listen."

And then he walked away from the window and sat on the sofa again, as though all the wind had suddenly been knocked out of him. "Sometimes you'll do *anything* to play, even cut your mother's throat." He laughed and looked at me. "Or your brother's." Then he sobered. "Or your own." Then: "Don't worry. I'm all right now and I think I'll *be* all right. But I can't forget—where I've been. I don't mean just the physical place I've been, I mean where I've *been*. And *what* I've been."

"What have you been, Sonny?" I asked.

He smiled—but sat sideways on the sofa, his elbow resting on the back, his fingers playing with his mouth and chin, not looking at me. "I've been something I didn't recognize, didn't know I could be. Didn't know anybody could be." He stopped, looking inward, looking helplessly young, looking old. "I'm not talking about it now because I feel *guilty* or anything like that—maybe it would be better if I did, I don't know. Anyway, I can't really talk about it. Not to you, not to anybody." and now he turned and faced me. "Sometimes, you know, and it was actually when I was most *out* of the world, I felt that I was in it, and that I was *with* it, really, and I could play or I didn't really have to *play*, it just came out of me, it was there. And I don't know how I played, thinking about it now, but I know I did awful things, those times, sometimes, to people. Or it wasn't that I *did* anything to them—it was that they weren't real." He picked up the beer can; it was empty; he rolled it between his palms: "And other times—well, I needed a fix, I needed to find a place to lean, I needed to clear a space to *listen*—and I couldn't find it, and I—went crazy, I did terrible things to *me*, I was terrible *for* me." He began pressing the beer can between his hands, I watched the metal begin to give. It glittered, as he played with it, like a knife, and I was afraid he would cut himself, but I said nothing. "Oh well, I can never tell you. I was all by myself at the bottom of something, stinking and sweating and crying and shaking, and I smelled it, you know? *my* stink, and I thought I'd die if I couldn't get away from it and yet, all the same, I knew that everything I was doing was just locking me in with it. And I didn't know," he paused, still flattening the beer can, "I didn't know, I still *don't* know, something kept telling me that maybe it was good to smell your own stink, but I didn't think that *that* was what I'd been trying to do—and—who can stand it?" and he abruptly dropped the ruined beer can, looking at me with a small, still smile, and then rose, walking to the window as though it were the lodestone rock. I watched his face, he watched the avenue. "I couldn't tell you when Mama died—but the reason I wanted to leave Harlem so bad was to get away from drugs. And then, when I ran away, that's what I was running from—really. When I came back, nothing had changed, *I* hadn't changed, I was just—older." And he stopped, drumming with his fingers on the windowpane. The sun had vanished, soon darkness would fall. I watched his face. "It can come again," he said, almost as though speaking to himself. Then he turned to me. "It can come again," he repeated. "I just want you to know that."

"All right," I said, at last. "So it can come again. All right."

He smiled, but the smile was sorrowful. "I had to try to tell you," he said.

"Yes," I said. "I understand that."

"You're my brother," he said, looking straight at me, and not smiling at all.

"Yes," I repeated, "yes. I understand that."

He turned back to the window, looking out. "All that hatred down there," he said, "all that hatred and misery and love. It's a wonder it doesn't blow the avenue apart."

We went to the only night club on a short, dark street, downtown. We squeezed through the narrow, chattering, jam-packed bar to the entrance of the big room, where the bandstand was. And we stood there for a moment, for the lights were very dim in this room and we couldn't see. Then, "Hello, boy," said a voice and an enormous black man, much older than Sonny or myself, erupted out of all that atmospheric lighting and put an arm around Sonny's shoulder. "I been sitting right here," he said, "waiting for you."

He had a big voice, too, and heads in the darkness turned toward us.

Sonny grinned and pulled a little away, and said, "Creole, this is my brother. I told you about him."

Creole shook my hand. "I'm glad to meet you, son," he said, and it was clear that he was glad to meet me *there*, for Sonny's sake. And he smiled, "You got a real musician in *your* family," and he took his arm from Sonny's shoulder and slapped him, lightly, affectionately, with the back of his hand.

"Well. Now I've heard it all," said a voice behind us. This was another musician, and a friend of Sonny's, a coal-black, cheerful-looking man, built close to the ground. He immediately began confiding to me, at the top of his lungs, the most terrible things about Sonny, his teeth gleaming like a lighthouse and his laugh coming up out of him like the beginning of an earthquake. And it turned out that everyone at the bar knew Sonny, or almost everyone; some were musicians, working there, or nearby, or not working, some were simply hangers-on, and some were there to hear Sonny play. I was introduced to all of them and they were all very polite to me. Yet, it was clear that, for them, I was only Sonny's brother. Here, I was in Sonny's world. Or, rather: his kingdom. Here, it was not even a question that his veins bore royal blood.

They were going to play soon and Creole installed me, by myself, at a table in a dark corner. Then I watched them, Creole, and the little black man, and Sonny, and the others, while they horsed around, standing just below the bandstand. The light from the bandstand spilled just a little short of them and, watching them laughing and gesturing and moving about, I had the feeling that they, nevertheless, were being most careful not to step into that circle of light too suddenly: that if they moved into the light too suddenly, without thinking, they would perish in flame. Then, while I watched, one of them, the small, black man, moved into the light and crossed the bandstand and started fooling around with his drums. Then—being funny and being, also, extremely ceremonious—Creole took Sonny by the arm and led him to the piano. A woman's voice called Sonny's name and a few hands started clapping. And Sonny, also being funny and being ceremonious, and so touched, I think, that he could have cried, but neither hiding it nor showing it, riding it like a man, grinned, and put both hands to his heart and bowed from the waist.

Creole then went to the bass fiddle and a lean, very bright-skinned brown man jumped up on the bandstand and picked up his horn. So there they were, and the atmosphere on the bandstand and in the room began to change and tighten. Someone stepped up to the microphone and announced them. Then there were all kinds of murmurs. Some people at the bar shushed others. The waitress ran around, frantically getting in the last orders, guys and chicks got closer to each other, and the lights on the bandstand, on the quartet, turned to a kind of indigo. Then they all looked different there. Creole looked about him for the last time, as though he were making certain that all his chickens were in the coop, and then he—jumped and struck the fiddle. And there they were.

All I know about music is that not many people ever really hear it. And even then, on the rare occasions when something opens within, and the music enters, what we mainly hear, or hear corroborated, are personal private, vanishing evocations. But the man who creates the music is hearing something else, is dealing with the roar rising from the void and imposing order on it as it hits the air. What is evoked in him, then, is of another order, more terrible because it has no words, and triumphant, too, for that same reason. And his triumph, when he triumphs, is ours. I just watched Sonny's face. His face was troubled, he was working hard, but he wasn't with it. And I had the feeling that, in a way, everyone on the bandstand was waiting for him, both waiting for him and pushing him along. But as I began to watch Creole, I realized that it was Creole who held them all back. He had them on a short rein. Up there, keeping the beat with his whole body, wailing on the fiddle, with his eyes half closed, he was listening to everything, but he was listening to Sonny. He was having a dialogue with Sonny. He wanted Sonny to leave the shore line and strike out for the deep water. He was Sonny's witness that deep water and drowning were not the same thing—he had been there, and he knew. And he wanted Sonny to know. He was waiting for Sonny to do the things on the keys which would let Creole know that Sonny was in the water.

And, while Creole listened, Sonny moved, deep within, exactly like someone in torment. I had never before thought of how awful the relationship must be between the musician and his instrument. He has to fill it, this instrument, with the breath of life, his own. He has to make it do what he wants it to do. And a piano is just a. It's made out of so much wood and wires and little hammers and big ones, and ivory. While there's only so much you can do with it, the only way to find this out is to try and make it do everything.

And Sonny hadn't been near a piano for over a year. And he wasn't on much better terms with his life, not the life that stretched before him now. He and the piano stammered, started one way, got scared, stopped; started another way, panicked, marked time, started again; then seemed to have found a direction, panicked again, got stuck. And the face I saw on Sonny I'd never seen before. Everything had been burned out of it, and, at the same time, things usually hidden were being burned in, by the fire and fury of the battle which was occurring in him up there.

Yet, watching Creole's face as they neared the end of the first set, I had the feeling that something had happened, something I hadn't heard. Then they finished, there was scattered applause, and then, without an instant's warning, Creole started into something else, it was almost sardonic, it was *Am I Blue*. And, as though he commanded, Sonny began to play. Something began to happen. And Creole let out the reins. The dry, low, black man said something awful on the drums, Creole answered, and the drums talked back. Then the horn insisted, sweet and high, slightly detached perhaps, and Creole listened, commenting now and then, dry, and driving, beautiful and calm and old. Then they all came together again, and Sonny was part of the family again. I could tell this from his face. He seemed to have found, right there beneath his fingers, a damn brand-new piano. It seemed that he couldn't get over it. Then, for awhile, just being happy with Sonny, they seemed to be agreeing with him that brand-new pianos certainly were a gas.

Then Creole stepped forward to remind them that what they were playing was the blues. He hit something in all of them, he hit something in me, myself, and the music tightened and deepened, apprehension began to beat the air. Creole began to tell us what the blues were all about. They were not about anything very new. He and his boys up there were keeping it new, at the risk of ruin, destruction, madness, and death, in order to find new ways to make us listen. For, while the tale of how we suffer, and how we are delighted, and how we may triumph is never new, it always must be heard. There isn't any other tale to tell, it's the only light we've got in all this darkness.

And this tale, according to that face, that body, those strong hands on those strings, has another aspect in every country, and a new depth in every generation. Listen, Creole seemed to be saying, listen. Now these are Sonny's blues. He made the little black man on the drums know it, and the bright, brown man on the horn. Creole wasn't trying any longer to get Sonny in the water. He was wishing him Godspeed. Then he stepped back, very slowly, filling the air with the immense suggestion that Sonny speak for himself.

Then they all gathered around Sonny and Sonny played. Every now and again one of them seemed to say, Amen. Sonny's fingers filled the air with life, his life. But that life contained so many others. And Sonny went all the way back, he really began with the spare, flat statement of the opening phrase of the song. Then he began to make it his. It was very beautiful because it wasn't hurried and it was no longer a lament. I seemed to hear with what burning he had made it his, with what burning we had yet to make it ours, how we could cease lamenting. Freedom lurked around us and I understood, at last, that he could help us to be free if we would listen, that he would never be free until we did. Yet, there was no battle in his face now. I heard what he had gone through, and would continue to go through until he came to rest in earth. He had made it his: that long line, of which we knew only Mama and Daddy. And he was giving it back, as everything must be given back, so that, passing through death, it can live forever. I saw my mother's face again, and felt, for the first time, how the stones of the road she had walked on must have bruised her feet. I saw the moonlit road where my father's brother died. And it brought something else back to me, and carried me past it, I saw my little girl again and felt Isabel's tears again, and I felt my own tears begin to rise. And I was yet aware that this was only a moment, that the world waited outside, as hungry as a tiger, and that trouble stretched above us, longer than the sky.

Then it was over. Creole and Sonny let out their breath, both soaking wet, and grinning. There was a lot of applause and some of it was real. In the dark, the girl came by and I asked her to take drinks to the bandstand. There was a long pause, while they talked up there in the indigo light and after awhile I saw the girl put a Scotch and milk on top of the piano for Sonny. He didn't seem to notice it, but just before they started playing again, he sipped from it and looked toward me, and nodded. Then he put it back on top of the piano. For me, then, as they began to play again, it glowed and shook above my brother's head like the very cup of trembling.

The Man Who Was Almost a Man

Richard Wright (1908–1960)

Dave struck out across the fields, looking homeward through paling light. Whut's the use talkin wid em niggers in the field? Anyhow, his mother was putting supper on the table. Them niggers can't understan nothing. One of these days he was going to get a gun and practice shooting, then they couldn't talk to him as though he were a little boy. He slowed, looking at the ground. Shucks, Ah ain scareda them even ef they are biggern me! Aw, Ah know whut Ahma do. Ahm going by ol Joe's sto n git that Sears Roebuck catlog n look at them guns. Mebbe Ma will lemme buy one when she gits mah pay from ol man Hawkins. Ahma beg her t gimme some money. Ahm ol ernough to hava gun. Ahm seventeen. Almost a man. He strode, feeling his long loose-jointed limbs. Shucks, a man oughta hava little gun aftah he done worked hard all day.

He came in sight of Joe's store. A yellow lantern glowed on the front porch. He mounted steps and went through the screen door, hearing it bang behind him. There was a strong smell of coal oil and mackerel fish. He felt very confident until he saw fat Joe walk in through the rear door, then his courage began to ooze.

"Howdy, Dave! Whutcha want?"

"How yuh, Mistah Joe? Aw, Ah don wanna buy nothing. Ah jus wanted t see ef yuhd lemme look at tha catlog erwhile."

"Sure! You wanna see it here?"

"Nawsuh. Ah wans t take it home wid me. Ah'll bring it back termorrow when Ah come in from the fiels."

"You plannin on buying something?"

"Yessuh."

"Your ma lettin you have your own money now?"

"Shucks. Mistah Joe, Ahm gittin t be a man like anybody else!"

Joe laughed and wiped his greasy white face with a red bandanna.

"Whut you plannin on buyin?"

Dave looked at the floor, scratched his head, scratched his thigh, and smiled. Then he looked up shyly.

"Ah'll tell yuh, Mistah Joe, ef yuh promise yuh won't tell."

"I promise."

"Waal, Ahma buy a gun."

"A gun? Whut you want with a gun?"

"Ah wanna keep it."

"You ain't nothing but a boy. You don't need a gun."

"Aw, lemme have the catlog, Mistah Joe. Ah'll bring it back."

Joe walked through the rear door. Dave was elated. He looked around at barrels of sugar and flour. He heard Joe coming back. He craned his neck to see if he were bringing the book. Yeah, he's got it. Gawddog, he's got it!

"Here, but be sure you bring it back. It's the only one I got."

"Sho, Mistah Joe."

"Say, if you wanna buy a gun, why don't you buy one from me? I gotta gun to sell."

"Will it shoot?"

"Sure it'll shoot."

"Whut kind is it?"

"Oh, it's kinda old . . . a left-hand Wheeler. A pistol. A big one."

"Is it got bullets in it?"

"It's loaded."

"Kin Ah see it?"

"Where's your money?"

"Whut yuh wan fer it?"

"I'll let you have it for two dollars."

"Just two dollahs? Shucks, Ah could buy tha when Ah git mah pay."

"I'll have it here when you want it."

"Awright, suh. Ah be in fer it."

He went through the door, hearing it slam again behind him. Ahma git some money from Ma n buy me a gun! Only two dollahs! He tucked the thick catalogue under his arm and hurried.

"Where yuh been, boy?" His mother held a steaming dish of black-eyed peas.

"Aw, Ma, Ah jus stopped down the road t talk wid the boys."

"Yuh know bettah t keep suppah waitin."

He sat down, resting the catalogue on the edge of the table.

"Yuh git up from there and git to the well n wash yoself! Ah ain feedin no hogs in mah house!"

She grabbed his shoulder and pushed him. He stumbled out of the room, then came back to get the catalogue.

"Whut this?"

"Aw, Ma, it's jusa catlog."

"Who yuh git it from?"

"From Joe, down at the sto."

"Waal, thas good. We kin use it in the outhouse."

"Naw, Ma." He grabbed for it. "Gimme ma catlog, Ma."

She held onto it and glared at him.

"Quit hollerin at me! Whut's wrong wid yuh? Yuh crazy?"

"But Ma, please. It ain mine! It's Joe's! He tol me t bring it back t im termorrow."

She gave up the book. He stumbled down the back steps, hugging the thick book under his arm. When he had splashed water on his face and hands, he groped back to the kitchen and fumbled in a corner for the towel. He bumped into a chair; it clattered to the floor. The catalogue sprawled at his feet. When he had dried his eyes he snatched up the book and held it again under his arm. His mother stood watching him.

"Now, ef yuh gonna act a fool over that ol book, Ah'll take it n burn it up."

"Naw, Ma, please."

"Waal, set down n be still!"

He sat down and drew the oil lamp close. He thumbed page after page, unaware of the food his mother set on the table. His father came in. Then his small brother.

"Whutcha got there, Dave?" his father asked.

"Jusa catlog," he answered, not looking up.

"Yeah, here they is!" His eyes glowed at blue-and-black revolvers. He glanced up, feeling sudden guilt. His father was watching him. He eased the book under the table and rested it on his knees. After the blessing was asked, he ate. He scooped up peas and swallowed fat meat without chewing. Buttermilk helped to wash it down. He did not want to mention money before his father. He would do much better by cornering his mother when she was alone. He looked at his father uneasily out of the edge of his eye.

"Boy, how come yuh don quit foolin wid tha book n eat yo suppah?"

"Yessuh."

"How you n ol man Hawkins gitten erlong?"

"Suh?"

"Can't yuh hear? Why don yuh lissen? Ah ast yu how wuz yuh n ol man Hawkins gittin erlong?"

"Oh, swell, Pa. Ah plows mo lan than anybody over there."

'Waal, yuh oughta keep yo mind on whut yuh doin.'"

"Yessuh."

He poured his plate full of molasses and sopped it up slowly with a chunk of cornbread. When his father and brother had left the kitchen, he still sat and looked again at the guns in the catalogue, longing to muster courage enough to present his case to his mother. Lawd, ef Ah only had tha pretty one! He could almost feel the slickness of the weapon with his fingers. If he had a gun like that he would polish it and keep it shining so it would never rust. N Ah'd keep it loaded, by Gawd!

"Ma?" His voice was hesitant.

"Hunh?"

"Ol man Hawkins give yuh mah money yit?"

"Yeah, but ain no usa yuh thinking bout throwin nona it erway. Ahm keepin tha money sos yuh kin have cloes t go to school this winter."

He rose and went to her side with the open catalogue in his palms. She was washing dishes, her head bent low over a pan. Shyly he raised the book. When he spoke, his voice was husky, faint.

"Ma, Gawd knows Ah wans one of these."

"One of whut?" she asked, not raising her eyes.

"One of these," he said again, not daring even to point. She glanced up at the page, then at him with wide eyes.

"Nigger, is yuh gone plumb crazy?"

"Aw, Ma—"

"Git outta here! Don yuh talk t me bout no gun! Yuh a fool!"

"Ma, Ah kin buy one fer two dollahs."

"Not ef Ah knows it, yuh ain!"

"But yuh promised me one—"

"Ah don care whut Ah promised! Yuh ain nothing but a boy yit!"

"Ma, ef yuh lemme buy one Ah'll *never* ast yuh fer nothing no mo."

"Ah tol yuh t git outta here! Yuh ain gonna toucha penny of tha money fer no gun! Thas how come Ah has Mistah Hawkins t pay yo wages t me, cause Ah knows yuh ain got no sense."

"But, Ma, we needa gun. Pa ain got no gun. We needa gun in the house. Yuh kin never tell whut might happen."

"Now don yuh try to maka fool outta me, boy! Ef we did hava gun, yuh wouldn't have it!"

He laid the catalogue down and slipped his arm around her waist.

"Aw, Ma, Ah done worked hard alla summer n ain ast yuh fer nothin, is Ah, now?"

"Thas whut yuh spose t do!"

"But Ma, Ah wans a gun. Yuh kin lemme have two dollahs outta mah money. Please, Ma. I kin give it to Pa . . . Please, Ma! Ah loves yuh, Ma."

When she spoke her voice came soft and low.

"Whut yu wan wida gun, Dave? Yuh don need no gun. You'll git in trouble. N ef yo pa jus thought Ah let yuh have money t buy a gun he'd hava fit."

"Ah'll hide it, Ma. It ain but two dollahs."

"Lawd, chil, whut's wrong wid yuh?"

"Ain nothin wrong, Ma. Ahm almos a man now. Ah wans a gun."

"Who gonna sell yuh a gun?"

"Ol Joe at the sto."

"N it don cos but two dollahs?"

"Thas all, Ma. Jus two dollahs. Please, Ma."

She was stacking the plates away; her hands moved slowly, reflectively. Dave kept an anxious silence. Finally, she turned to him.

"Ah'll let yuh git tha gun ef yuh promise me one thing."

"Whut's tha, Ma?"

"Yuh bring it straight back t me, yuh hear? It be fer Pa."

"Yessum! Lemme go now, Ma."

She stooped, turned slightly to one side, raised the hem of her dress, rolled down the top of her stocking, and came up with a slender wad of bills.

"Here," she said. "Lawd knows yuh don need no gun. But yer pa does. Yuh bring it right back t me, yuh hear? Ahma put it up. Now ef yuh don, Ahma have yuh pa lick yuh so hard yuh won fergit it."

"Yessum."

He took the money, ran down the steps, and across the yard.

"Dave! Yuuuuuh Daaaaave!"

He heard, but he was not going to stop now. "Naw, Lawd!"

The first movement he made the following morning was to reach under his pillow for the gun. In the gray light of dawn he held it loosely, feeling a sense of power. Could kill a man with a gun like this. Kill anybody, black or white. And if he were holding his gun in his hand, nobody could run over him; they would have to respect him. It was a big gun, with a long barrel and a heavy handle. He raised and lowered it in his hand, marveling at its weight.

He had not come straight home with it as his mother had asked; instead he had stayed out in the fields, holding the weapon in his hand, aiming it now and then at some imaginary foe. But he had not fired it; he had been afraid that his father might hear. Also he was not sure he knew how to fire it.

To avoid surrendering the pistol he had not come into the house until he knew that they were all asleep. When his mother had tiptoed to his bedside late that night and demanded the gun, he had first played possum; then he had told her that the gun was hidden outdoors, that he would bring it to her in the morning. Now he lay turning it slowly in his hands. He broke it, took out the cartridges, felt them, and then put them back.

He slid out of bed, got a long strip of old flannel from a trunk, wrapped the gun in it, and tied it to his naked thigh while it was still loaded. He did not go in

to breakfast. Even though it was not yet daylight, he started for Jim Hawkins'
plantation. Just as the sun was rising he reached the barns where the mules and
plows were kept.

"Hey! That you, Dave?"

He turned. Jim Hawkins stood eying him suspiciously.

"What're yuh doing here so early?"

"Ah didn't know Ah wuz gittin up so early, Mistah Hawkins. Ah wuz fixin t
hitch up ol Jenny n take her t the fiels."

"Good. Since you're so early, how about plowing that stretch down by the
woods?"

"Suits me, Mistah Hawkins."

"O.K. Go to it!"

He hitched Jenny to a plow and started across the fields. Hot dog! This was
just what he wanted. If he could get down by the woods, he could shoot his gun
and nobody would hear. He walked behind the plow, hearing the traces creaking, feeling the gun tied tight to his thigh.

When he reached the woods, he plowed two whole rows before he decided
to take out the gun. Finally, he stopped, looked in all directions, then untied the
gun and held it in his hand. He turned to the mule and smiled.

"Know whut this is, Jenny? Naw, yuh wouldn know! Yuhs jusa ol mule! Anyhow, this is a gun, n it kin shoot, by Gawd!"

He held the gun at arm's length. Whut t hell, Ahma shoot this thing! He
looked at Jenny again.

"Lissen here, Jenny! When Ah pull this ol trigger, Ah don wan yuh t run n
acka fool now!"

Jenny stood with head down, her short ears pricked straight. Dave walked
off about twenty feet, held the gun far out from him at arm's length, and turned
his head. Hell, he told himself, Ah ain afraid. The gun felt loose in his fingers; he
waved it wildly for a moment. Then he shut his eyes and tightened his forefinger.
Bloom! A report half deafened him and he thought his right hand was torn from
his arm. He heard Jenny whinnying and galloping over the field, and he found
himself on his knees squeezing his fingers hard between his legs. His hand was
numb; he jammed it into his mouth, trying to warm it, trying to stop the pain.
The gun lay at his feet. He did not quite know what had happened. He stood up
and stared at the gun as though it were a living thing. He gritted his teeth and
kicked the gun. Yuh almos broke mah arm! He turned to look for Jenny; she was
far over the fields, tossing her head and kicking wildly.

"Hol on there, ol mule!"

When he caught up with her she stood trembling, walling her big white eyes
at him. The plow was far away; the traces had broken. Then Dave stopped short,
looking, not believing. Jenny was bleeding. Her left side was red and wet with
blood. He went closer. Lawd, have mercy! Wondah did Ah shoot this mule? He
grabbed for Jenny's mane. She flinched, snorted, whirled, tossing her head.

"Hol on now! Hol on."

Then he saw the hole in Jenny's side, right between the ribs. It was round, wet, red. A crimson stream streaked down the front leg, flowing fast. Good Gawd! Ah wuzn't shootin at tha mule. He felt panic. He knew he had to stop that blood, or Jenny would bleed to death. He had never seen so much blood in all his life. He chased the mule for half a mile, trying to catch her. Finally she stopped, breathing hard, stumpy tail half arched. He caught her mane and led her back to where the plough and gun lay. Then he stooped and grabbed handfuls of damp black earth and tried to plug the bullet hole. Jenny shuddered, whinnied, and broke from him.

"Hol on! Hol on now!"

He tried to plug it again, but blood came anyhow. His fingers were hot and sticky. He rubbed dirt into his palms, trying to dry them. Then again he attempted to plug the bullet hole, but Jenny shied away, kicking her heels high. He stood helpless. He had to do something. He ran at Jenny; she dodged him. He watched a red stream of blood flow down Jenny's leg and form a bright pool at her feet.

"Jenny . . . Jenny," he called weakly.

His lips trembled. She's bleeding t death! He looked in the direction of home, wanting to go back, wanting to get help. But he saw the pistol lying in the damp black clay. He had a queer feeling that if he only did something, this would not be; Jenny would not be there bleeding to death.

When he went to her this time, she did not move. She stood with sleepy, dreamy eyes; and when he touched her she gave a low-pitched whinny and knelt to the ground, her front knees slopping in blood.

"Jenny . . . Jenny . . ." he whispered.

For a long time she held her neck erect; then her head sank, slowly. Her ribs swelled with a mighty heave and she went over.

Dave's stomach felt empty, very empty. He picked up the gun and held it gingerly between his thumb and forefinger. He buried it at the foot of a tree. He took a stick and tried to cover the pool of blood with dirt—but what was the use? There was Jenny lying with her mouth open and her eyes walled and glassy. He could not tell Jim Hawkins he had shot his mule. But he had to tell something. Yeah, Ah'll tell em Jenny started gittin wil n fell on the joint of the plow. . . . But that would hardly happen to a mule. He walked across the field slowly, head down.

It was sunset. Two of Jim Hawkins' men were over near the edge of the woods digging a hole in which to bury Jenny. Dave was surrounded by a knot of people, all of whom were looking down at the dead mule.

"I don't see how in the world it happened," said Jim Hawkins for the tenth time.

The crowd parted and Dave's mother, father, and small brother pushed into the center.

"Where Dave?" his mother called.

"There he is," said Jim Hawkins.

His mother grabbed him.

"Whut happened, Dave? Whut yuh done?"

"Nothin."

"C mon, boy, talk," his father said.

Dave took a deep breath and told the story he knew nobody believed.

"Waal," he drawled. "Ah brung ol Jenny down here sos Ah could do mah plowin. Ah plowed bout two rows, just like yuh see." He stopped and pointed at the long rows of upturned earth. "Then somethin musta been wrong wid ol Jenny. She wouldn ack right a-tall. She started snortin n kickin her heels. Ah tried t hol her, but she pulled erway, rearin n goin in. Then when the point of the plow was stickin up in the air, she swung erroun n twisted herself back on it'. . .She stuck herself n started t bleed. N fo Ah could do anything, she wuz dead."

"Did you ever hear of anything like that in all your life?" asked Jim Hawkins.

There were white and black standing in the crowd. They murmured. Dave's mother came close to him and looked hard into his face. "Tell the truth, Dave," she said.

"Looks like a bullet hole to me," said one man.

"Dave, whut yuh do wid the gun?" his mother asked.

The crowd surged in, looking at him. He jammed his hands into his pockets, shook his head slowly from left to right, and backed away. His eyes were wide and painful.

"Did he hava gun?" asked Jim Hawkins.

"By Gawd, Ah tol him tha wuz a gun wound," said a man, slapping his thigh.

His father caught his shoulders and shook him till his teeth rattled.

"Tell whut happened, yuh rascal! Tell whut . . ."

Dave looked at Jenny's stiff legs and began to cry.

"Whut yuh do wid tha gun?" his mother asked.

"Whut wuz he doin wida gun?" his father asked.

"Come on and tell the truth," said Hawkins. "Ain't nobody going to hurt you . . ."

His mother crowded close to him.

"Did yuh shoot tha mule, Dave?"

Dave cried, seeing blurred white and black faces.

"Ahh ddinn gggo tt sshooot hher . . . Ah ssswear ffo Gawd Ahh ddin . . . Ah wuz a-tryin t sssee ef the old gggun would sshoot—"

"Where yuh git the gun from?" his father asked.

"Ah got it from Joe, at the sto."

"Where yuh git the money?"

"Ma give it t me."

"He kept worryin me, Bob. Ah had t. Ah tol im t bring the gun right back t me . . . It was fer yuh, the gun."

"But how yuh happen to shoot that mule?" asked Jim Hawkins.

"Ah wuzn shootin at the mule, Mistah Hawkins. The gun jumped when Ah pulled the trigger . . . N for Ah knowed anythin Jenny was there a-bleedin."

Somebody in the crowd laughed. Jim Hawkins walked close to Dave and looked into his face.

"Well, looks like you have bought a mule, Dave."

"Ah swear to Gawd, Ah didn go t kill the mule, Mistah Hawkins!"

"But you killed her!"

All the crowd was laughing now. They stood on tiptoe and poked heads over one another's shoulders.

"Well, boy, looks like yuh done bought a dead mule! Hahaha!"

"Ain tha ershame."

"Hohohohoho."

Dave stood, head down, twisting his feet in the dirt.

"Well, you needn't worry about it, Bob," said Jim Hawkins to Dave's father. "Just let the boy keep on working and pay me two dollars a month."

"Whut yuh wan fer yo mule, Mistah Hawkins?"

Jim Hawkins screwed up his eyes.

"Fifty dollars."

"Whut yuh do wid tha gun?" Dave's father demanded.

Dave said nothing.

"Yuh wan me t take a tree n beat yuh till yuh talk!"

"Nawsuh!"

"Whut yuh do wid it?"

"Ah throwed it erway."

"Where?"

"Ah . . . Ah throwed it in the creek."

"Waal, c mon home. N firs thing in the mawnin git to tha creek n fin tha gun."

"Yessuh."

"Whut yuh pay fer it?"

"Two dollahs."

"Take tha gun n git yu money back n carry it t Mistah Hawkins, yuh hear? N don fergit Ahma lam you black bottom good fer this! Now march yosef on home, suh!"

Dave turned and walked slowly. He heard people laughing. Dave glared, his eyes welling with tears. Hot anger bubbled in him. Then he swallowed and stumbled on.

That night Dave did not sleep. He was glad that he had gotten out of killing the mule so easily, but he was hurt. Something hot seemed to turn over inside him each time he remembered how they had laughed. He tossed on his bed, feeling his hard pillow. N Pa says he's gonna beat me . . . He remembered other beatings, and his back quivered. Naw, naw. Ah sho don wan im t beat me tha way no mo. Dam em all! Nobody ever gave him anything. All he did was work. They treat me like a mule, n then they beat me. He gritted his teeth. N Ma had t tell on me.

Well, if he had to, he would take old man Hawkins that two dollars. But that meant selling the gun. And he wanted to keep that gun. Fifty dollars for a dead mule.

He turned over, thinking how he had fired the gun. He had an itch to fire it again. Ef other men kin shoota gun, by Gawd, Ah kin! He was still, listening. Mebbe they all sleepin now. The house was still. He heard the soft breathing of his brother. Yes, now! He would go down and get that gun and see if he could fire it! He eased out of bed and slipped into overalls.

The moon was bright. He ran almost all the way to the edge of the woods. He stumbled over the ground, looking for the spot where he had buried the gun. Yeah, here it is. Like a hungry dog scratching for a bone, he pawed it up. He puffed his black cheeks and blew dirt from the trigger and barrel. He broke it and found four cartridges unshot. He looked around; the fields were filled with silence and moonlight. He clutched the gun stiff and hard in his fingers. But, as soon as he wanted to pull the trigger, he shut his eyes and turned his head. Naw, Ah can't shoot wid mah eyes closed n mah head turned. With effort he held his eyes open; then he squeezed. *Blooooom!* He was stiff, not breathing. The gun was still in his hands. Dammit, he'd done it! He fired again. *Blooooom!* He smiled. *Blooooom! Blooooom! Click, click.* There! It was empty. If anybody could shoot a gun, he could. He put the gun into his hip pocket and started across the fields.

When he reached the top of a ridge he stood straight and proud in the moonlight, looking at Jim Hawkins' big white house, feeling the gun sagging in his pocket. Lawd, ef Ah had just one mo bullet Ah'd taka shot at tha house. Ah'd like t scare ol man Hawkins jusa little . . . Jusa enough t let im know Dave Saunders is a man.

To his left the road curved, running to the tracks of the Illinois Central. He jerked his head, listening. From far off came a faint *hoooof-hoooof; hoooof-hoooof; hoooof-hoooof. . . .* He stood rigid. Two dollahs a mont. Les see now . . . Tha means it'll take bout two years. Shucks! Ah'll be dam!

He started down the road, toward the tracks. Yeah, here she comes! He stood beside the track and held himself stiffly. Here she comes, erroun the ben . . . C mon, yuh slow poke! C mon! He had his hand on his gun; something quivered in his stomach. Then the train thundered past, the gray and brown box cars rumbling and clinking. He gripped the gun tightly; then he jerked his hand out of his pocket. Ah betcha Bill wouldn't do it! Ah-betcha . . . The cars slid past, steel grinding upon steel. Ahm ridin yuh ternight, so hep me Gawd! He was hot all over. He hesitated just a moment; then he grabbed, pulled atop of a car, and lay flat. He felt his pocket; the gun was still there. Ahead the long rails were glinting in the moonlight, stretching away, away to somewhere, somewhere where he could be a man . . .

The Jilting of Granny Weatherall

Katherine Anne Porter (1890–1980)

She flicked her wrist neatly out of Doctor Harry's pudgy careful fingers and pulled the sheet up to her chin. The brat ought to be in knee breeches. Doctoring around the country with spectacles on his nose! "Get along now, take your schoolbooks and go. There's nothing wrong with me."

Doctor Harry spread a warm paw like a cushion on her forehead where the forked green vein danced and made her eyelids twitch. "Now, now, be a good girl, and we'll have you up in no time."

"That's no way to speak to a woman nearly eighty years old just because she's down. I'd have you respect your elders, young man."

"Well, Missy, excuse me." Doctor Harry patted her cheek. "But I've got to warn you, haven't I? You're a marvel, but you must be careful or you're going to be good and sorry."

"Don't tell me what I'm going to be. I'm on my feet now, morally speaking. It's Cornelia. I had to go to bed to get rid of her."

Her bones felt loose, and floated around in her skin, and Doctor Harry floated like a balloon around the foot of the bed. He floated and pulled down his waistcoat and swung his glasses on a cord. "Well, stay where you are, it certainly can't hurt you."

"Get along and doctor your sick," said Granny Weatherall. "Leave a well woman alone. I'll call for you when I want you . . . . Where were you forty years ago when I pulled through milk-leg[5] and double pneumonia? You weren't even born. Don't let Cornelia lead you on," she shouted, because Doctor Harry appeared to float up to the ceiling and out. "I pay my own bills, and I don't throw my money away on nonsense!"

She meant to wave good-by, but it was too much trouble. Her eyes closed of themselves, it was like a dark curtain drawn around the bed. The pillow rose and floated under her, pleasant as a hammock in a light wind. She listened to the leaves rustling outside the window. No, somebody was swishing newspapers: no, Cornelia and Doctor Harry were whispering together. She leaped broad awake, thinking they whispered in her ear.

"She was never like this, *never* like this!" "Well, what can we expect?" "Yes, eighty years old . . ."

Well, and what if she was? She still had ears. It was like Cornelia to whisper around doors. She always kept things secret in such a public way. She was always being tactful and kind. Cornelia was dutiful; that was the trouble with her.

---

[5]a painful swelling of the legs sometimes occurring in women after childbirth

Dutiful and good: "So good and dutiful," said Granny, "that I'd like to spank her." She saw herself spanking Cornelia and making a fine job of it.

"What'd you say, Mother?"

Granny felt her face tying up in hard knots.

"Can't a body think, I'd like to know?"

"I thought you might want something."

"I do. I want a lot of things. First off, go away and don't whisper."

She lay and drowsed, hoping in her sleep that the children would keep out and let her rest a minute. It had been a long day. Not that she was tired. It was always pleasant to snatch a minute now and then. There was always so much to be done, let me see: tomorrow.

Tomorrow was far away and there was nothing to trouble about. Things were finished somehow when the time came; thank God there was always a little margin over for peace: then a person could spread out the plan of life and tuck in the edges orderly. It was good to have everything clean and folded away, with the hair brushes and tonic bottles sitting straight on the white embroidered linen: the day started without fuss and the pantry shelves laid out with rows of jelly glasses and brown jugs and white stone-china jars with blue whirligigs and words painted on them: coffee, tea, sugar, ginger, cinnamon, allspice: and the bronze clock with the lion on top nicely dusted off. The dust that lion could collect in twenty-four hours! The box in the attic with all those letters tied up, well, she'd have to go through that tomorrow. All those letters—George's letters and John's letters and her letters to them both—lying around for the children to find afterwards made her uneasy. Yes, that would be tomorrow's business. No use to let them know how silly she had been once.

While she was rummaging around she found death in her mind and it felt clammy and unfamiliar. She had spent so much time preparing for death there was no need for bringing it up again. Let it take care of itself now. When she was sixty she had felt very old, finished, and went around making farewell trips to see her children and grandchildren, with a secret in her mind: This is the very last of your mother, children! Then she made her will and came down with a long fever. That was all just a notion like a lot of other things, but it was lucky too, for she had once for all got over the idea of dying for a long time. Now she couldn't be worried. She hoped she had better sense now. Her father had lived to be one hundred and two years old and had drunk a noggin[6] of strong hot toddy[7] on his last birthday. He told the reporters it was his daily habit, and he owed his long life to that. He had made quite a scandal and was very pleased about it. She believed she'd just plague Cornelia a little.

"Cornelia! Cornelia!" No footsteps, but a sudden hand on her cheek. "Bless you, where have you been?"

"Here, mother."

---

[6] a small mug

[7] a drink consisting of brandy or other liquor mixed with hot water, lemon, sugar, and spices

"Well, Cornelia, I want a noggin of hot toddy."

"Are you cold, darling?"

"I'm chilly, Cornelia. Lying in bed stops the circulation. I must have told you that a thousand times."

Well, she could just hear Cornelia telling her husband that Mother was getting a little childish and they'd have to humor her. The thing that most annoyed her was that Cornelia thought she was deaf, dumb, and blind. Little hasty glances and tiny gestures tossed around her and over her head saying, "Don't cross her, let her have her way, she's eighty years old," and she sitting there as if she lived in a thin glass cage. Sometimes Granny almost made up her mind to pack up and move back to her own house where nobody could remind her every minute that she was old. Wait, wait, Cornelia, till your own children whisper behind your back!

In her day she had kept a better house and had got more work done. She wasn't too old yet for Lydia to be driving eighty miles for advice when one of the children jumped the track, and Jimmy still dropped in and talked things over: "Now, Mammy, you've a good business head, I want to know what you think of this? . . ." Old. Cornelia couldn't change the furniture around without asking. Little things, little things! They had been so sweet when they were little. Granny wished the old days were back again with the children young and everything to be done over. It had been a hard pull, but not too much for her. When she thought of all the food she had cooked, and all the clothes she had cut and sewed, and all the gardens she had made—well, the children showed it. There they were, made out of her, and they couldn't get away from that. Sometimes she wanted to see John again and point to them and say, Well, I didn't do so badly, did I? But that would have to wait. That was for tomorrow. She used to think of him as a man, but now all the children were older than their father, and he would be a child beside her if she saw him now. It seemed strange and there was something wrong in the idea. Why, he couldn't possibly recognize her. She had fenced in a hundred acres once, digging the post holes herself and clamping the wires with just a Negro boy to help. That changed a woman. John would be looking for a young woman with the peaked Spanish comb in her hair and the painted fan. Digging post holes changed a woman. Riding country roads in the winter when women had their babies was another thing: sitting up nights with sick horses and sick Negroes and sick children and hardly ever losing one. John, I hardly ever lost one of them! John would see that in a minute, that would be something he could understand, she wouldn't have to explain anything!

It made her feel like rolling up her sleeves and putting the whole place to rights again. No matter if Cornelia was determined to be everywhere at once, there were a great many things left undone on this place. She would start tomorrow and do them. It was good to be strong enough for everything, even if all you made melted and changed and slipped under your hands, so that by the time you finished you almost forgot what you were working for. What was it I set out to do? she asked herself intently, but she could not remember. A fog rose over the valley, she saw it marching across the creek swallowing the trees and moving up the hill like an army of ghosts. Soon it would be at the near edge of the orchard, and then it was time to go in and light the lamps. Come in, children, don't stay out in the night air.

Lighting the lamps had been beautiful. The children huddled up to her and breathed like little calves waiting at the bars in the twilight. Their eyes followed the match and watched the flame rise and settle in a blue curve, then they moved away from her. The lamp was lit, they didn't have to be scared and hang on to mother any more. Never, never, never more. God, for all my life I thank Thee. Without Thee, my God, I could never have done it. Hail, Mary, full of grace.

I want you to pick all the fruit this year and see that nothing is wasted. There's always someone who can use it. Don't let good things rot for want of using. You waste life when you waste good food. Don't let things get lost. It's bitter to lose things. Now, don't let me get to thinking, not when I am tired and taking a little nap before supper. . . .

The pillow rose about her shoulders and pressed against her heart and the memory was being squeezed out of it: oh, push down the pillow, somebody: it would smother her if she tried to hold it. Such a fresh breeze blowing and such a green day with no threats in it. But he had not come, just the same. What does a woman do when she has put on the white veil and set out the white cake for a man and he doesn't come? She tried to remember. No, I swear he never harmed me but in that. He never harmed me but in that . . . and what if he did? There was the day, the day, but a whirl of dark smoke rose and covered it, crept up and over into the bright field where everything was planted so carefully in orderly rows. That was hell, she knew hell when she saw it. For sixty years she had prayed against remembering him and against losing her soul in the deep pit of hell, and now the two things were mingled in one and the thought of him was a smoky cloud from hell that moved and crept in her head when she had just got rid of Doctor Harry and was trying to rest a minute. Wounded vanity, Ellen, said a sharp voice in the top of her mind. Don't let your wounded vanity get the upper hand of you. Plenty of girls get jilted. You were jilted, weren't you? Then stand up to it. Her eyelids wavered and let in streamers of blue-gray light like tissue paper over her eyes. She must get up and pull the shades down or she'd never sleep. She was in bed again and the shades were not down. How could that happen? Better turn over, hide from the light, sleeping in the light gave you nightmares. "Mother, how do you feel now?" and a stinging wetness on her forehead. But I don't like having my face washed in cold water!

Hapsy? George? Lydia? Jimmy? No, Cornelia, and her features were swollen and full of little puddles. "They're coming, darling, they'll all be here soon." Go wash your face, child, you look funny.

Instead of obeying, Cornelia knelt down and put her head on the pillow. She seemed to be talking but there was no sound. "Well, are you tongue-tied? Whose birthday is it? Are you going to give a party?"

Cornelia's mouth moved urgently in strange shapes. "Don't do that, you bother me, daughter."

"Oh, no, Mother. Oh, no. . . ."

Nonsense. It was strange about children. They disputed your every word. "No what, Cornelia?"

"Here's Doctor Harry."

"I won't see that boy again. He just left five minutes ago."

"That was this morning, Mother. It's night now. Here's the nurse."

"This is Doctor Harry, Mrs. Weatherall. I never saw you look so young and happy!"

"Ah, I'll never be young again—but I'd be happy if they'd let me lie in peace and get rested."

She thought she spoke up loudly, but no one answered. A warm weight on her forehead, a warm bracelet on her wrist, and a breeze went on whispering, trying to tell her something. A shuffle of leaves in the everlasting hand of God, He blew on them and they danced and rattled. "Mother, don't mind, we're going to give you a little hypodermic." "Look here, daughter, how do ants get in this bed? I saw sugar ants yesterday." Did you send for Hapsy too?

It was Hapsy she really wanted. She had to go a long way back through a great many rooms to find Hapsy standing with a baby on her arm. She seemed to herself to be Hapsy also, and the baby on Hapsy's arm was Hapsy and himself and herself, all at once, and there was no surprise in the meeting. Then Hapsy melted from within and turned flimsy as gray gauze and the baby was a gauzy shadow, and Hapsy came up close and said, "I thought you'd never come," and looked at her very searchingly and said, "You haven't changed a bit!" They leaned forward to kiss, when Cornelia began whispering from a long way off, "Oh, is there anything you want to tell me? Is there anything I can do for you?"

Yes, she had changed her mind after sixty years and she would like to see George. I want you to find George. Find him and be sure to tell him I forgot him. I want him to know I had my husband just the same and my children and my house like any other woman. A good house too and a good husband that I loved and fine children out of him. Better than I hoped for even. Tell him I was given back everything he took away and more. Oh, no, oh, God, no, there was something else besides the house and the man and the children. Oh, surely they were not all? What was it? Something not given back. . . . Her breath crowded down under her ribs and grew into a monstrous frightening shape with cutting edges; it bored up into her head, and the agony was unbelievable: Yes, John, get the Doctor now, no more talk, my time has come.

When this one was born it should be the last. The last. It should have been born first, for it was the one she had truly wanted. Everything came in good time. Nothing left out, left over. She was strong, in three days she would be as well as ever. Better. A woman needed milk in her to have her full health.

"Mother, do you hear me?"

"I've been telling you—"

"Mother, Father Connolly's here."

"I went to Holy Communion only last week. Tell him I'm not so sinful as all that."

"Father just wants to speak to you."

He could speak as much as he pleased. It was like him to drop in and inquire about her soul as if it were a teething baby, and then stay on for a cup of tea and a round of cards and gossip. He always had a funny story of some sort, usually about an Irishman who made his little mistakes and confessed them, and the point lay in some absurd thing he would blurt out in the confessional showing his struggles between native piety and original sin. Granny felt easy about her soul. Cornelia, where are your manners? Give Father Connolly a chair. She had her secret comfortable understanding with a few favorite saints who cleared a straight road to God for her. All as surely signed and sealed as the papers for the new Forty Acres. Forever . . . heirs and assigns forever. Since the day the wedding cake was not cut, but thrown out and wasted. The whole bottom dropped out of the world, and there she was blind and sweating with nothing under her feet and the walls falling away. His hand had caught her under the breast, she had not fallen, there was the freshly polished floor with the green rug on it, just as before. He had cursed like a sailor's parrot and said, "I'll kill him for you." Don't lay a hand on him, for my sake leave something to God. "Now, Ellen, you must believe what I tell you. . . ."

So there was nothing, nothing to worry about any more, except sometimes in the night one of the children screamed in a nightmare, and they both hustled out shaking and hunting for the matches and calling, "There, wait a minute, here we are!" John, get the doctor now, Hapsy's time has come. But there was Hapsy standing by the bed in a white cap. "Cornelia, tell Hapsy to take off her cap. I can't see her plain."

Her eyes opened very wide and the room stood out like a picture she had seen somewhere. Dark colors with the shadows rising towards the ceiling in long angles. The tall black dresser gleamed with nothing on it but John's picture, enlarged from a little one, with John's eyes very black when they should have been blue. You never saw him, so how do you know how he looked? But the man insisted the copy was perfect, it was very rich and handsome. For a picture, yes, but it's not my husband. The table by the bed had a linen cover and a candle and a crucifix. The light was blue from Cornelia's silk lampshades. No sort of light at all, just frippery. You had to live forty years with kerosene lamps to appreciate honest electricity. She felt very strong and she saw Doctor Harry with a rosy nimbus around him.

"You look like a saint, Doctor Harry, and I vow that's as near as you'll ever come to it."

"She's saying something."

"I heard you, Cornelia. What's all this carrying-on?"

"Father Connolly's saying—"

Cornelia's voice staggered and bumped like a cart in a bad road. It rounded corners and turned back again and arrived nowhere. Granny stepped up in the cart very lightly and reached for the reins, but a man sat beside her and she knew him by his hands, driving the cart. She did not look in his face, for she knew without seeing, but looked instead down the road where the trees leaned over and bowed to each other and a thousand birds were singing a Mass. She felt like singing too, but she put her hand in the bosom of her dress and pulled out a rosary, and Father Connolly murmured Latin in a very solemn voice and tickled her feet. My God, will you stop that nonsense? I'm a married woman. What if he did run away and leave me to face the priest by myself? I found another a whole world better. I wouldn't have exchanged my husband for anybody except St. Michael himself, and you may tell him that for me with a thank you in the bargain.

Light flashed on her closed eyelids, and a deep roaring shook her. Cornelia, is that lightning? I hear thunder. There's going to be a storm. Close all the windows. Call the children in. . . . "Mother, here we are, all of us." "Is that you, Hapsy?" "Oh, no, I'm Lydia. We drove as fast as we could." Their faces drifted above her, drifted away. The rosary fell out of her hands and Lydia put it back. Jimmy tried to help, their hands fumbled together, and Granny closed two fingers around Jimmy's thumb. Beads wouldn't do, it must be something alive. She was so amazed her thoughts ran round and round. So, my dear Lord, this is my death and I wasn't even thinking about it. My children have come to see me die. But I can't, it's not time. Oh, I always hated surprises. I wanted to give Cornelia the amethyst set—Cornelia, you're to have the amethyst set, but Hapsy's to wear it when she wants, and, Doctor Harry, do shut up. Nobody sent for you. Oh, my dear Lord, do wait a minute. I meant to do something about the Forty Acres, Jimmy doesn't need it and Lydia will later on, with that worthless husband of hers. I meant to finish the altar cloth and send six bottles of wine to Sister Borgia for the dyspepsia.[8] I want to send six bottles of wine to Sister Borgia, Father Connolly, now don't let me forget.

Cornelia's voice made short turns and tilted over and crashed.

"Oh, Mother, oh, Mother, oh, Mother. . . ."

"I'm not going, Cornelia. I'm taken by surprise. I can't go."

You'll see Hapsy again. What about her? "I thought you'd never come." Granny made a long journey outward, looking for Hapsy. What if I don't find her? What then? Her heart sank down and down, there was no bottom to death, she couldn't come to the end of it. The blue light from Cornelia's lampshade drew into a tiny point in the center of her brain, it flickered and winked like an eye, quietly it fluttered and dwindled. Granny lay curled down within herself, amazed and watchful, staring at the point of light that was herself; her body was now only a deeper mass of shadow in an endless darkness and this darkness would curl around the light and swallow it up. God, give a sign!

For the second time there was no sign. Again no bridegroom and the priest in the house. She could not remember any other sorrow because this grief wiped them all away. Oh, no, there's nothing more cruel than this—I'll never forgive it. She stretched herself with a deep breath and blew out the light.

---

[8]indigestion

The Chrysanthemums

John Steinbeck (1902–1968)

The high gray-flannel fog of winter closed off the Salinas Valley[9] from the sky and from all the rest of the world. On every side it sat like a lid on the mountains and made of the great valley a closed pot. On the broad, level land floor the gang plows bit deep and left the black earth shining like metal where the shares had cut. On the foothill ranches across the Salinas River, the yellow stubble fields seemed to be bathed in pale cold sunshine, but there was no sunshine in the valley now in December. The thick willow scrub along the river flamed with sharp and positive yellow leaves.

It was a time of quiet and of waiting. The air was cold and tender. A light wind blew up from the southwest so that the farmers were mildly hopeful of a good rain before long; but fog and rain do not go together.

Across the river, on Henry Allen's foothill ranch there was little work to be done, for the hay was cut and stored and the orchards were plowed up to receive the rain deeply when it should come. The cattle on the higher slopes were becoming shaggy and rough-coated.

Elisa Allen, working in her flower garden, looked down across the yard and saw Henry, her husband, talking to two men in business suits. The three of them stood by the tractor shed, each man with one foot on the side of the little Fordson.[1] They smoked cigarettes and studied the machine as they talked.

Elisa watched them for a moment and then went back to her work. She was thirty-five. Her face was lean and strong and her eyes were as clear as water. Her figure looked blocked and heavy in her gardening costume, a man's black hat pulled down over her eyes, clodhopper shoes, a figured print dress almost completely covered by a big corduroy apron with four big pockets to hold the snips, the trowel and scratcher, the seeds and the knife she worked with. She wore heavy leather gloves to protect her hands while she worked.

She was cutting down the old year's chrysanthemum stalks with a pair of short and powerful scissors. She looked down toward the men by the tractor shed now and then. Her face was eager and mature and handsome; even her work with the scissors was over-eager, over-powerful. The chrysanthemum stems seemed too small and easy for her energy.

She brushed a cloud of hair out of her eyes with the back of her glove, and left a smudge of earth on her cheek in doing it. Behind her stood the neat white farm house with red geraniums close-banked around it as high as the windows.

---

[9]The Salinas Valley, south of the town of Salinas, in central California, is one of the state's richest agricultural areas.
[1]two-door Ford car, or coupe

It was a hard-swept looking little house, with hard-polished windows, and a clean mud-mat on the front steps.

Elisa cast another glance toward the tractor shed. The strangers were getting into their Ford coupe. She took off a glove and put her strong fingers down into the forest of new green chrysanthemum sprouts that were growing around the old roots. She spread the leaves and looked down among the close-growing stems. No aphids were there, no sow-bugs or snails or cutworms. Her terrier fingers[2] destroyed such pests before they could get started.

Elisa started at the sound of her husband's voice. He had come near quietly, and he leaned over the wire fence that protected her flower garden from cattle and dogs and chickens.

"At it again," he said. "You've got a strong new crop coming."

Elisa straightened her back and pulled on the gardening glove again. "Yes. They'll be strong this coming year." In her tone and on her face there was a little smugness.

"You've got a gift with things," Henry observed. "Some of those yellow chrysanthemums you had this year were ten inches across. I wish you'd work out in the orchard and raise some apples that big."

Her eyes sharpened. "Maybe I could do it, too. I've a gift with things, all right. My mother had it. She could stick anything in the ground and make it grow. She said it was having planters' hands that knew how to do it."

"Well, it sure works with flowers," he said.

"Henry, who were those men you were talking to?"

"Why, sure, that's what I came to tell you. They were from the Western Meat Company. I sold them those thirty head of three-year-old steers. Got nearly my own price, too."

"Good," she said. "Good for you."

"And I thought," he continued, "I thought how it's Saturday afternoon, and we might go into Salinas for dinner at a restaurant, and then to a picture show—to celebrate, you see."

"Good," she repeated. "Oh, yes. That will be good."

Henry put on his joking tone. "There's fights tonight. How'd you like to go to the fights?"

"Oh, no," she said breathlessly. "No, I wouldn't like fights."

"Just fooling, Elisa. We'll go to a movie. Let's see. It's two now. I'm going to take Scotty and bring down those steers from the hill. It'll take us maybe two hours. We'll go in town about five and have dinner at the Cominos Hotel. Like that?"

"Of course I'll like it. It's good to eat away from home."

"All right, then, I'll go get up a couple of horses."

She said, "I'll have plenty of time to transplant some of these sets, I guess."

---

[2]Terriers (which take their name from a word meaning "earth") were originally bred for hunting out animals living under the ground in burrows.

She heard her husband calling Scotty down by the barn. And a little later she saw the two men ride up the pale yellow hillside in search of the steers.

There was a little square sandy bed kept for rooting the chrysanthemums. With her trowel she turned the soil over and over, and smoothed it and patted it firm. Then she dug ten parallel trenches to receive the sets. Back at the chrysanthemum bed she pulled out the little crisp shoots, trimmed off the leaves of each one with her scissors and laid it on a small orderly pile.

A squeak of wheels and plod of hoofs came from the road. Elisa looked up. The country road ran along the dense bank of willows and cottonwoods that bordered the river, and up this road came a curious vehicle, curiously drawn. It was an old spring-wagon, with a round canvas top on it like the cover of a prairie schooner. It was drawn by an old bay horse and a little gray-and-white burro. A big stubble-bearded man sat between the cover flaps and drove the crawling team. Underneath the wagon, between the hind wheels, a lean and rangy mongrel dog walked sedately. Words were painted on the canvas, in clumsy, crooked letters. "Pots, pans, knives, sisors, lawn mores, Fixed." Two rows of articles, and the triumphantly definitive "Fixed" below. The black paint had run down in little sharp points beneath each letter.

Elisa, squatting on the ground, watched to see the crazy, loose-jointed wagon pass by. But it didn't pass. It turned into the farm road in front of her house, crooked old wheels skirling and squeaking. The rangy dog darted from between the wheels and ran ahead. Instantly the two ranch shepherds flew out at him. Then all three stopped and with stiff and quivering tails, with taut straight legs, with ambassadorial dignity, they slowly circled, sniffing daintily. The caravan pulled up to Elisa's wire fence and stopped. Now the newcomer dog, feeling out-numbered, lowered his tail and retired under the wagon with raised hackles and bared teeth.

The man on the wagon seat called out, "That's a bad dog in a fight when he gets started."

Elisa laughed. "I see he is. How soon does he generally get started?"

The man caught up her laughter and echoed it heartily. "Sometimes not for weeks and weeks," he said. He climbed stiffly down, over the wheel. The horse and the donkey drooped like unwatered flowers.

Elisa saw that he was a very big man. Although his hair and beard were graying, he did not look old. His worn black suit was wrinkled and spotted with grease. The laughter had disappeared from his face and eyes the moment his laughing voice ceased. His eyes were dark, and they were full of the brooding that gets in the eyes of teamsters[3] and of sailors. The calloused hands he rested on the wire fence were cracked, and every crack was a black line. He took off his battered hat.

"I'm off my general road, ma'am," he said. "Does this dirt road cut over across the river to the Los Angeles highway?"

---

[3]truckdrivers

Elisa stood up and shoved the thick scissors in her apron pocket. "Well, yes, it does, but it winds around and then fords the river. I don't think your team could pull through the sand."

He replied with some asperity, "It might surprise you what them beasts can pull through."

"When they get started?" she asked.

He smiled for a second. "Yes. When they get started."

"Well," said Elisa, "I think you'll save time if you go back to the Salinas road and pick up the highway there."

He drew a big finger down the chicken wire and made it sing. "I ain't in any hurry, ma'am. I go from Seattle to San Diego and back every year. Takes all my time. About six months each way. I aim to follow nice weather."

Elisa took off her gloves and stuffed them in the apron pocket with the scissors. She touched the under edge of her man's hat, searching for fugitive hairs. "That sounds like a nice kind of way to live," she said.

He leaned confidentially over the fence. "Maybe you noticed the writing on my wagon. I mend pots and sharpen knives and scissors. You got any of them things to do?"

"Oh, no," she said quickly. "Nothing like that." Her eyes hardened with resistance.

"Scissors is the worst thing," he explained. "Most people just ruin scissors trying to sharpen 'em, but I know how. I got a special tool. It's a little bobbit kind of thing, and patented. But it sure does the trick."

"No. My scissors are all sharp."

"All right, then. Take a pot," he continued earnestly, "a bent pot, or a pot with a hole. I can make it like new so you don't have to buy no new ones. That's a saving for you."

"No," she said shortly. "I tell you I have nothing like that for you to do."

His face fell to an exaggerated sadness. His voice took on a whining undertone. "I ain't had a thing to do today. Maybe I won't have no supper tonight. You see I'm off my regular road. I know folks on the highway clear from Seattle to San Diego. They save their things for me to sharpen up because they know I do it so good and save them money."

"I'm sorry," Elisa said irritably. "I haven't anything for you to do."

His eyes left her face and fell to searching the ground. They roamed about until they came to the chrysanthemum bed where she had been working. "What's them plants, ma'am?"

The irritation and resistance melted from Elisa's face. "Oh, those are chrysanthemums, giant whites and yellows. I raise them every year, bigger than anybody around here."

"Kind of a long-stemmed flower? Looks like a quick puff of colored smoke?" he asked.

"That's it. What a nice way to describe them."

"They smell kind of nasty till you get used to them," he said.

"It's a good bitter smell," she retorted, "not nasty at all."

He changed his tone quickly. "I like the smell myself."

"I had ten-inch blooms this year," she said.

The man leaned farther over the fence. "Look. I know a lady down the road a piece, has got the nicest garden you ever seen. Got nearly every kind of flower but no chrysanthemums. Last time I was mending a copper-bottom washtub for her (that's a hard job but I do it good), she said to me, 'If you ever run acrost some nice chrysanthemums I wish you'd try to get me a few seeds.' That's what she told me."

Elisa's eyes grew alert and eager. "She couldn't have known much about chrysanthemums. You *can* raise them from seed, but it's much easier to root the little sprouts you see there."

"Oh," he said, "I s'pose I can't take none to her, then."

"Why yes you can," Elisa cried. "I can put some in damp sand, and you can carry them right along with you. They'll take root in the pot if you keep them damp. And then she can transplant them."

"She'd sure like to have some, ma'am. You say they're nice ones?"

"Beautiful," she said. "Oh, beautiful." Her eyes shone. She tore off the battered hat and shook out her dark pretty hair. "I'll put them in a flower pot, and you can take them right with you. Come into the yard."

While the man came through the picket gate Elisa ran excitedly along the geranium-bordered path to the back of the house. And she returned carrying a big red flower pot. The gloves were forgotten now. She kneeled on the ground by the starting bed and dug up the sandy soil with her fingers and scooped it into the bright new flower pot. Then she picked up the little pile of shoots she had prepared. With her strong fingers she pressed them into the sand and tamped around them with her knuckles. The man stood over her. "I'll tell you what to do," she said. "You remember so you can tell the lady."

"Yes, I'll try to remember."

"Well, look. These will take root in about a month. Then she must set them out, about a foot apart in good rich earth like this, see?" She lifted a handful of dark soil for him to look at. "They'll grow fast and tall. Now remember this: In July tell her to cut them down, about eight inches from the ground."

"Before they bloom?" he asked.

"Yes, before they bloom." Her face was tight with eagerness. "They'll grow right up again. About the last of September the buds will start."

She stopped and seemed perplexed. "It's the budding that takes the most care," she said hesitantly. "I don't know how to tell you." She looked deep into his eyes, searchingly. Her mouth opened a little, and she seemed to be listening. "I'll try to tell you," she said. "Did you ever hear of planting hands?"

"Can't say I have, ma'am."

"Well, I can only tell you what it feels like. It's when you're picking off the buds you don't want. Everything goes right down into your fingertips. You watch your fingers work. They do it themselves. You can feel how it is. They pick and pick the buds. They never make a mistake. They're with the plant. Do you see?

Your fingers and the plant. You can feel that, right up your arm. They know. They never make a mistake. You can feel it. When you're like that you can't do anything wrong. Do you see that? Can you understand that?"

She was kneeling on the ground looking up at him. Her breast swelled passionately.

The man's eyes narrowed. He looked away self-consciously. "Maybe I know," he said. "Sometimes in the night in the wagon there—"

Elisa's voice grew husky. She broke in on him, "I've never lived as you do, but I know what you mean. When the night is dark—why, the stars are sharp-pointed, and there's quiet. Why, you rise up and up! Every pointed star gets driven into your body. It's like that. Hot and sharp and—lovely."

Kneeling there, her hand went out toward his legs in the greasy black trousers. Her hesitant fingers almost touched the cloth. Then her hand dropped to the ground. She crouched low like a fawning dog.

He said, "It's nice, just like you say. Only when you don't have no dinner, it ain't."

She stood up then, very straight, and her face was ashamed. She held the flower pot out to him and placed it gently in his arms. "Here. Put it in your wagon, on the seat, where you can watch it. Maybe I can find something for you to do."

At the back of the house she dug in the can pile and found two old and battered aluminum saucepans. She carried them back and gave them to him. "Here, maybe you can fix these."

His manner changed. He became professional. "Good as new I can fix them." At the back of his wagon he set a little anvil, and out of an oily tool box dug a small machine hammer. Elisa came through the gate to watch him while he pounded out the dents in the kettles. His mouth grew sure and knowing. At a difficult part of the work he sucked his underlip.

"You sleep right in the wagon?" Elisa asked.

"Right in the wagon, ma'am. Rain or shine I'm dry as a cow in there."

"It must be nice," she said. "It must be very nice. I wish women could do such things."

"It ain't the right kind of a life for a woman."

Her upper lip raised a little, showing her teeth. "How do you know? How can you tell?" she said.

"I don't know, ma'am," he protested. "Of course I don't know. Now here's your kettles, done. You don't have to buy no new ones."

"How much?"

"Oh, fifty cents'll do. I keep my prices down and my work good. That's why I have all them satisfied customers up and down the highway."

Elisa brought him a fifty-cent piece from the house and dropped it in his hand. "You might be surprised to have a rival some time. I can sharpen scissors, too. And I can beat the dents out of little pots. I could show you what a woman might do."

He put his hammer back in the oily box and shoved the little anvil out of sight. "It would be a lonely life for a woman, ma'am, and a scarey life, too, with animals creeping under the wagon all night." He climbed over the singletree,[4] steadying himself with a hand on the burro's white rump. He settled himself in the seat, picked up the lines. "Thank you kindly, ma'am," he said. "I'll do like you told me; I'll go back and catch the Salinas road."

"Mind," she called, "if you're long in getting there, keep the sand damp."

"Sand, ma'am? . . . Sand? Oh, sure. You mean around the chrysanthemums. Sure I will." He clucked his tongue. The beasts leaned luxuriously into their collars. The mongrel dog took his place between the back wheels. The wagon turned and crawled out the entrance road and back the way it had come, along the river.

Elisa stood in front of her wire fence watching the slow progress of the caravan. Her shoulders were straight, her head thrown back, her eyes half-closed, so that the scene came vaguely into them. Her lips moved silently, forming the words "Good-bye—good-bye." Then she whispered, "That's a bright direction. There's a glowing there." The sound of her whisper startled her. She shook herself free and looked about to see whether anyone had been listening. Only the dogs had heard. They lifted their heads toward her from their sleeping in the dust, and then stretched out their chins and settled asleep again. Elisa turned and ran hurriedly into the house.

In the kitchen she reached behind the stove and felt the water tank. It was full of hot water from the noonday cooking. In the bathroom she tore off her soiled clothes and flung them into the corner. And then she scrubbed herself with a little block of pumice, legs and thighs, loins and chest and arms, until her skin was scratched and red. When she had dried herself she stood in front of a mirror in her bedroom and looked at her body. She tightened her stomach and threw out her chest. She turned and looked over her shoulder at her back.

After a while she began to dress slowly. She put on her newest underclothing and her nicest stockings and the dress which was the symbol of her prettiness. She worked carefully on her hair, penciled her eyebrows and rouged her lips.

Before she was finished she heard the little thunder of hoofs and the shouts of Henry and his helper as they drove the red steers into the corral. She heard the gate bang shut and set herself for Henry's arrival.

His steps sounded on the porch. He entered the house calling, "Elisa, where are you?"

"In my room dressing. I'm not ready. There's hot water for your bath. Hurry up. It's getting late."

When she heard him splashing in the tub, Elisa laid his dark suit on the bed, and shirt and socks and tie beside it. She stood his polished shoes on the floor beside the bed. Then she went to the porch and sat primly and stiffly down. She looked toward the river road where the willow-line was still yellow with frosted

---

[4]the horizontal crossbar on a wagon to which the draft animals are attached

leaves so that under the high gray fog they seemed a thin band of sunshine. This was the only color in the gray afternoon. She sat unmoved for a long time. Her eyes blinked rarely.

Henry came banging out of the door, shoving his tie inside his vest as he came. Elisa stiffened and her face grew tight. Henry stopped short and looked at her. "Why—why, Elisa. You look so nice!"

"Nice? You think I look nice? What do you mean by 'nice'?"

Henry blundered on. "I don't know. I mean you look different, strong and happy."

"I am strong? Yes, strong. What do you mean 'strong'?"

He looked bewildered. "You're playing some kind of a game," he said helplessly. "It's a kind of a play. You look strong enough to break a calf over your knee, happy enough to eat it like a watermelon."

For a second she lost her rigidity. "Henry! Don't talk like that. You didn't know what you said." She grew complete again. "I'm strong," she boasted. "I never knew before how strong."

Henry looked down toward the tractor shed, and when he brought his eyes back to her, they were his own again. "I'll get out the car. You can put on your coat while I'm starting."

Elisa went into the house. She heard him drive to the gate and idle down his motor, and then she took a long time to put on her hat. She pulled it here and pressed it there. When Henry turned the motor off she slipped into her coat and went out.

The little roadster bounced along on the dirt road by the river, raising the birds and driving the rabbits into the brush. Two cranes flapped heavily over the willow-line and dropped into the riverbed.

Far ahead on the road Elisa saw a dark speck. She knew.

She tried not to look as they passed it, but her eyes would not obey. She whispered to herself sadly, "He might have thrown them off the road. That wouldn't have been much trouble, not very much. But he kept the pot," she explained. "He had to keep the pot. That's why he couldn't get them off the road."

The roadster turned a bend and she saw the caravan ahead. She swung full around toward her husband so she could not see the little covered wagon and the mismatched team as the car passed them.

In a moment it was over. The thing was done. She did not look back.

She said loudly, to be heard above the motor, "It will be good, tonight, a good dinner."

"Now you're changed again," Henry complained. He took one hand from the wheel and patted her knee. "I ought to take you in to dinner oftener. It would be good for both of us. We get so heavy out on the ranch."

"Henry," she asked, "could we have wine at dinner?"

"Sure we could. Say! That will be fine."

She was silent for a while; then she said, "Henry, at those prize fights, do the men hurt each other very much?"

"Sometimes a little, not often. Why?"

"Well, I've read how they break noses, and blood runs down their chests. I've read how the fighting gloves get heavy and soggy with blood."

He looked around at her. "What's the matter, Elisa? I didn't know you read things like that." He brought the car to a stop, then turned to the right over the Salinas River bridge.

"Do any women ever go to the fights?" she asked.

"Oh, sure, some. What's the matter, Elisa? Do you want to go? I don't think you'd like it, but I'll take you if you really want to go."

She relaxed limply in the seat. "Oh, no. No. I don't want to go. I'm sure I don't." Her face was turned away from him. "It will be enough if we can have wine. It will be plenty." She turned up her coat collar so he could not see that she was crying weakly—like an old woman.

A Good Man Is Hard to Find

Flannery O'Connor (1925–1964)

The grandmother didn't want to go to Florida. She wanted to visit some of her connections in east Tennessee and she was seizing at every chance to change Bailey's mind. Bailey was the son she lived with, her only boy. He was sitting on the edge of his chair at the table, bent over the orange sports section of the *Journal.* "Now look here, Bailey," she said, "see here, read this," and she stood with one hand on her thin hip and the other rattling the newspaper at his bald head. "Here this fellow that calls himself The Misfit is aloose from the Federal Pen and headed toward Florida and you read here what it says he did to these people. Just you read it. I wouldn't take my children in any direction with a criminal like that aloose in it. I couldn't answer to my conscience if I did."

Bailey didn't look up from his reading so she wheeled around then and faced the children's mother, a young woman in slacks, whose face was as broad and innocent as a cabbage and was tied round with a green head-kerchief that had two points on the top like rabbit's ears. She was sitting on the sofa, feeding the baby his apricots out of a jar. "The children have been to Florida before," the old lady said. "You all ought to take them somewhere else for a change so they would see different parts of the world and be broad. They never have been to east Tennessee."

The children's mother didn't seem to hear her but the eight-year-old boy, John Wesley, a stocky child with glasses, said, "If you don't want to go to Florida, why dontcha stay at home?" He and the little girl, June Star, were reading the funny papers on the floor.

"She wouldn't stay at home to be queen for a day," June Star said without raising her yellow head.

"Yes and what would you do if this fellow, The Misfit, caught you?" the grandmother asked.

"I'd smack his face," John Wesley said.

"She wouldn't stay at home for a million bucks," June Star said. "Afraid she'd miss something. She has to go everywhere we go."

"All right, Miss," the grandmother said. "Just remember that the next time you want me to curl your hair."

June Star said her hair was naturally curly.

The next morning the grandmother was the first one in the car, ready to go. She had her big black valise that looked like the head of a hippopotamus in one corner, and underneath it she was hiding a basket with Pitty Sing, the cat, in it. She didn't intend for the cat to be left alone in the house for three days because he would miss her too much and she was afraid he might brush against one of the gas burners and accidentally asphyxiate himself. Her son, Bailey, didn't like to arrive at a motel with a cat.

She sat in the middle of the back seat with John Wesley and June Star on either side of her. Bailey and the children's mother and the baby sat in the front and they left Atlanta at eight forty-five with the mileage on the car at 55890. The grandmother wrote this down because she thought it would be interesting to say how many miles they had been when they got back. It took them twenty minutes to reach the outskirts of the city.

The old lady settled herself comfortably, removing her white cotton gloves and putting them up with her purse on the shelf in front of the back window. The children's mother still had on slacks and still had her head tied up in a green kerchief, but the grandmother had on a navy blue straw sailor hat with a bunch of white violets on the brim and a navy blue dress with a small white dot in the print. Her collar and cuffs were white organdy trimmed with lace and at her neckline she had pinned a purple spray of cloth violets containing a sachet. In case of an accident, anyone seeing her dead on the highway would know at once that she was a lady.

She said she thought it was going to be a good day for driving, neither too hot nor too cold, and she cautioned Bailey that the speed limit was fifty-five miles an hour and that the patrolmen hid themselves behind billboards and small clumps of trees and sped out after you before you had a chance to slow down. She pointed out interesting details of the scenery: Stone Mountain; the blue granite that in some places came up to both sides of the highway; the brilliant red clay banks slightly streaked with purple; and the various crops that made rows of green lace-work on the ground. The trees were full of silver-white sunlight and the meanest of them sparkled. The children were reading comic magazines and their mother had gone back to sleep.

"Let's go through Georgia fast so we won't have to look at it much," John Wesley said.

"If I were a little boy," said the grandmother, "I wouldn't talk about my native state that way. Tennessee has the mountains and Georgia has the hills."

"Tennessee is just a hillbilly dumping ground," John Wesley said, "and Georgia is a lousy state too."

"You said it," June Star said.

"In my time," said the grandmother, folding her thin veined fingers, "children were more respectful of their native states and their parents and everything else. People did right then. Oh look at the cute little pickaninny!" she said and pointed to a Negro child standing in the door of a shack. "Wouldn't that make a picture, now?" she asked and they all turned and looked at the little Negro out of the back window. He waved.

"He didn't have any britches on," June said.

"He probably didn't have any," the grandmother explained. "Little niggers in the country don't have things like we do. If I could paint, I'd paint that picture," she said.

The children exchanged comic books.

The grandmother offered to hold the baby and the children's mother passed him over the front seat to her. She set him on her knee and bounced him and told him about the things they were passing. She rolled her eyes and screwed up her mouth and stuck her leathery thin face into his smooth bland one. Occasionally he gave her a faraway smile. They passed a large cotton field with five or six graves fenced in the middle of it, like a small island. "Look at the graveyard!" the grandmother said, pointing it out. "That was the old family burying ground. That belonged to the plantation."

"Where's the plantation?" John Wesley asked.

"Gone With the Wind," said the grandmother. "Ha. Ha."

When the children finished all the comic books they had brought, they opened the lunch and ate it. The grandmother ate a peanut butter sandwich and an olive and would not let the children throw the box and the paper napkins out the window. When there was nothing else to do they played a game by choosing a cloud and making the other two guess what shape it suggested. John Wesley took one the shape of a cow and June Star guessed a cow and John Wesley said, no, an automobile, and June Star said he didn't play fair, and they began to slap each other over the grandmother.

The grandmother said she would tell them a story if they would keep quiet. When she told a story, she rolled her eyes and waved her head and was very dramatic. She said once when she was a maiden lady she had been courted by a Mr. Edgar Atkins Teagarden from Jasper, Georgia. She said he was a very good-looking man and a gentleman and that he brought her a watermelon every Saturday afternoon with his initials cut in it, E. A. T. Well, one Saturday, she said, Mr. Teagarden brought the watermelon and there was nobody at home and he left it on the front porch and returned in his buggy to Jasper, but she never got the watermelon, she said, because a nigger boy ate it when he saw the initials, E. A. T.! This story tickled John Wesley's funny bone and he giggled and giggled but June Star didn't think it was any good. She said she wouldn't marry a man that just brought her a watermelon on Saturday. The grandmother said she would have done well to marry Mr. Teagarden because he was a gentleman and had bought Coca-Cola stock when it first came out and that he had died only a few years ago, a very wealthy man.

They stopped at The Tower for barbecued sandwiches. The Tower was a part stucco and part wood filling station and dance hall set in a clearing outside of Timothy. A fat man named Red Sammy Butts ran it and there were signs stuck here and there on the building and for miles up and down the highway saying, TRY RED SAMMY'S FAMOUS BARBECUE. NONE LIKE FAMOUS RED SAMMY'S! RED SAM! THE FAT BOY WITH THE HAPPY LAUGH. A VETERAN! SAMMY'S YOUR MAN!

Red Sammy was lying on the bare ground outside The Tower with his head under a truck while a gray monkey about a foot high, chained to a small chinaberry tree, chattered nearby. The monkey sprang back into the tree and got on the highest limb as soon as he saw the children jump out of the car and run toward him.

Inside, The Tower was a long dark room with a counter at one end and tables at the other and dancing space in the middle. They all sat down at a broad table next to the nickelodeon and Red Sam's wife, a tall burnt-brown woman with hair and eyes lighter than her skin, came and took their order. The children's mother put a dime in the machine and played "The Tennessee Waltz," and the grandmother said that tune always made her want to dance. She asked Bailey if he would like to dance but he only glared at her. He didn't have a naturally sunny disposition like she did and trips made him nervous. The grandmother's brown eyes were very bright. She swayed her head from side to side and pretended she was dancing in her chair. June Star said play something she could tap to so the children's mother put in another dime and played a fast number and June Star stepped out onto the dance floor and did her tap routine.

"Ain't she cute?" Red Sam's wife said, leaning over the counter. "Would you like to come be my little girl?"

"No I certainly wouldn't," June Star said. "I wouldn't live in a broken-down place like this for a million bucks!" and she ran back to the table.

"Ain't she cute?" the woman repeated, stretching her mouth politely.

"Aren't you ashamed?" hissed the grandmother.

Red Sam came in and told his wife to quit lounging on the counter and hurry with these people's order. His khaki trousers reached just to his hip bones and his stomach hung over them like a sack of meal swaying under his shirt. He came over and sat down at a table nearby and let out a combination sigh and yodel. "You can't win," he said. "You can't win," and he wiped his sweating red face off with a gray handkerchief. "These days you don't know who to trust," he said. "Ain't that the truth?"

"People are certainly not nice like they used to be," said the grandmother.

"Two fellers come in here last week," Red Sammy said, "driving a Chrysler. It was a old beat-up car but it was a good one and these boys looked all right to me. Said they worked at the mill and you know I let them fellers charge the gas they bought? Now why did I do that?"

"Because you're a good man!" the grandmother said at once.

"Yes'm, I suppose so," Red Sam said as if he were struck with the answer.

His wife brought the orders, carrying the five plates all at once without a tray, two in each hand and one balanced on her arm. "It isn't a soul in this green world of God's that you can trust," she said. "And I don't count anybody out of that, not nobody," she repeated, looking at Red Sammy.

"Did you read about that criminal, The Misfit, that's escaped?" asked the grandmother.

"I wouldn't be a bit surprised if he didn't attact this place right here," said the woman. "If he hears about it being here, I wouldn't be none surprised to see him. If he hears it's two cent in the cash register, I wouldn't be a tall surprised if he . . ."

"That'll do," Red Sam said. "Go bring these people their Co'Colas," and the woman went off to get the rest of the order.

"A good man is hard to find," Red Sammy said. "Everything is getting terrible. I remember the day you could go off and leave your screen door unlatched. Not no more."

He and the grandmother discussed better times. The old lady said that in her opinion Europe was entirely to blame for the way things were now. She said the way Europe acted you would think we were made of money and Red Sam said it was no use talking about it, she was exactly right. The children ran outside into the white sunlight and looked at the monkey in the lacy chinaberry tree. He was busy catching fleas on himself and biting each one carefully between his teeth as if it were a delicacy.

They drove off again into the hot afternoon. The grandmother took cat naps and woke up every few minutes with her own snoring. Outside of Toombsboro she woke up and recalled an old plantation that she had visited in this neighborhood once when she was a young lady. She said the house had six white columns across the front and that there was an avenue of oaks leading up to it and two little wooden trellis arbors on either side in front where you sat down with your suitor after a stroll in the garden. She recalled exactly which road to turn off to get to it. She knew that Bailey would not be willing to lose any time looking at an old house, but the more she talked about it, the more she wanted to see it once again and find out if the little twin arbors were still standing. "There was a secret panel in this house," she said craftily, not telling the truth but wishing that she were, "and the story went that all the family silver was hidden in it when Sherman came through but it was never found . . ."

"Hey!" John Wesley said. "Let's go see it! We'll find it! We'll poke all the woodwork and find it! Who lives there? Where do you turn off at? Hey Pop, can't we turn off there?"

"We never have seen a house with a secret panel!" June Star shrieked. "Let's go to the house with the secret panel! Hey, Pop, can't we go see the house with the secret panel!"

"It's not far from here, I know," the grandmother said. "It wouldn't take over twenty minutes."

Bailey was looking straight ahead. His jaw was as rigid as a horseshoe. "No," he said.

The children began to yell and scream that they wanted to see the house with the secret panel. John Wesley kicked the back of the front seat and June Star hung over her mother's shoulder and whined desperately into her ear that they never had any fun even on their vacation, and that they could never do what THEY wanted to do. The baby began to scream and John Wesley kicked the back of the seat so hard that his father could feel the blows in his kidney.

"All right!" he shouted, and drew the car to a stop at the side of the road. "Will you all shut up? Will you all just shut up for one second? If you don't shut up, we won't go anywhere."

"It would be very educational for them," the grandmother murmured.

"All right," Bailey said, "but get this: this is the only time we're going to stop for anything like this. This is the one and only time."

"The dirt road that you have to turn down is about a mile back," the grandmother directed. "I marked it when we passed."

"A dirt road," Bailey groaned.

After they had turned around and were headed toward the dirt road, the grandmother recalled other points about the house, the beautiful glass over the front doorway and the candle-lamp in the hall. John Wesley said that the secret panel was probably in the fireplace.

"You can't go inside this house," Bailey said. "You don't know who lives there."

"While you all talk to the people in front, I'll run around behind and get in a window," John Wesley suggested.

"We'll all stay in the car," his mother said.

They turned onto the dirt road and the car raced roughly along in a swirl of pink dust. The grandmother recalled the times when there were no paved roads and thirty miles was a day's journey. The dirt road was hilly and there were sudden washes in it and sharp curves on dangerous embankments. All at once they would be on a hill, looking down over the blue tops of trees for miles around, then the next minute, they would be in a red depression with the dust-coated trees looking down on them.

"This place had better turn up in a minute," Bailey said, "or I'm going to turn around."

The road looked as if no one had traveled on it in months.

"It's not much farther," the grandmother said and just as she said it, a horrible thought came to her. The thought was so embarrassing that she turned red in the face and her eyes dilated and her feet jumped up, upsetting her valise in the corner. The instant the valise moved, the newspaper top she had over the basket under it rose with a snarl and Pitty Sing, the cat, sprang onto Bailey's shoulder.

The children were thrown to the floor and their mother, clutching the baby, was thrown out the door onto the ground, the old lady was thrown into the front seat. The car turned over once and landed right-side-up in a gulch on the side of the road. Bailey remained in the driver's seat with the cat—gray-striped with a broad white face and an orange nose—clinging to his neck like a caterpillar.

As soon as the children saw they could move their arms and legs, they scrambled out of the car, shouting, "We've had an ACCIDENT!" The grandmother was curled up under the dashboard, hoping she was injured so that Bailey's wrath would not come down on her all at once. The horrible thought she had had before the accident was that the house she had remembered so vividly was not in Georgia but in Tennessee.

Bailey removed the cat from his neck with both hands and flung it out the window against the side of a pine tree. Then he got out of the car and started looking for the children's mother. She was sitting against the side of the red gutted ditch, holding the screaming baby, but she only had a cut down her face and a broken shoulder. "We've had an ACCIDENT!" the children screamed in a frenzy of delight.

"But nobody's killed," June Star said with disappointment as the grandmother limped out of the car, her hat still pinned to her head but the broken front brim standing up at a jaunty angle and the violet spray hanging off the side. They all sat down in the ditch, except the children, to recover from the shock. They were all shaking.

"Maybe a car will come along," said the children's mother hoarsely.

"I believe I have injured an organ," said the grandmother, pressing her side, but no one answered her. Bailey's teeth were clattering. He had on a yellow sport shirt with bright blue parrots designed in it and his face was as yellow as the shirt. The grandmother decided that she would not mention that the house was in Tennessee.

The road was about ten feet above and they could see only the tops of the trees on the other side of it. Behind the ditch they were sitting in there were more woods, tall and dark and deep. In a few minutes they saw a car some distance away on top of a hill, coming slowly as if the occupants were watching them. The grandmother stood up and waved both arms dramatically to attract their attention. The car continued to come on slowly, disappeared around a bend and appeared again, moving even slower, on top of the hill they had gone over. It was a big black battered hearse-like automobile. There were three men in it.

It came to a stop just over them and for some minutes, the driver looked down with a steady expressionless gaze to where they were sitting, and didn't speak. Then he turned his head and muttered something to the other two and they got out. One was a fat boy in black trousers and a red sweat shirt with a silver stallion embossed on the front of it. He moved around on the right side of them and stood staring, his mouth partly open in a kind of loose grin. The other had on khaki pants and a blue striped coat and a gray hat pulled down very low, hiding most of his face. He came around slowly on the left side. Neither spoke.

The driver got out of the car and stood by the side of it, looking down at them. He was an older man than the other two. His hair was just beginning to gray and he wore silver-rimmed spectacles that gave him a scholarly look. He had a long creased face and didn't have on any shirt or undershirt. He had on blue jeans that were too tight for him and was holding a black hat and a gun. The two boys also had guns.

"We've had an ACCIDENT!" the children screamed.

The grandmother had the peculiar feeling that the bespectacled man was someone she knew. His face was as familiar to her as if she had known him all her life but she could not recall who he was. He moved away from the car and began to come down the embankment, placing his feet carefully so that he wouldn't slip. He had on tan and white shoes and no socks, and his ankles were red and thin. "Good afternoon," he said. "I see you all had you a little spill."

"We turned over twice!" said the grandmother.

"Oncet," he corrected. "We seen it happen. Try their car and see will it run, Hiram," he said quietly to the boy with the gray hat.

"What you got that gun for?" John Wesley asked. "Whatcha gonna do with that gun?"

"Lady," the man said to the children's mother, "would you mind calling them children to sit down by you? Children make me nervous. I want all you all to sit down right together there where you're at."

"What are you telling us what to do for?" June Star asked.

Behind them the line of woods gaped like a dark open mouth. "Come here," said their mother.

"Look here now," Bailey began suddenly, "we're in a predicament! We're in . . ."

The grandmother shrieked. She scrambled to her feet and stood staring. "You're The Misfit!" she said. "I recognized you at once."

"Yes'm," the man said, smiling slightly as if he were pleased in spite of himself to be known, "but it would have been better for all of you, lady, if you hadn't of reckernized me."

Bailey turned his head sharply and said something to his mother that shocked even the children. The old lady began to cry and The Misfit reddened.

"Lady," he said, "don't you get upset. Sometimes a man says things he don't mean. I don't reckon he meant to talk to you thataway."

"You wouldn't shoot a lady, would you?" the grandmother said and removed a clean handkerchief from her cuff and began to slap at her eyes with it.

The Misfit pointed the toe of his shoe into the ground and made a little hole and then covered it up again. "I would hate to have to," he said.

"Listen," the grandmother almost screamed, "I know you're a good man. You don't look a bit like you have common blood. I know you must come from nice people!"

"Yes mam," he said, "finest people in the world." When he smiled he showed a row of strong white teeth. "God never made a finer woman than my mother and my daddy's heart was pure gold," he said. The boy with the red sweat shirt had come around behind them and was standing with his gun at his hip. The Misfit squatted down on the ground. "Watch them children, Bobby Lee," he said. "You know they make me nervous." He looked at the six of them huddled together in front of him and he seemed to be embarrassed as if he couldn't think of anything to say. "Ain't a cloud in the sky," he remarked, looking up at it. "Don't see no sun but don't see no cloud neither."

"Yes, it's a beautiful day," said the grandmother. "Listen," she said, "you shouldn't call yourself The Misfit because I know you're a good man at heart. I can just look at you and tell."

"Hush!" Bailey yelled. "Hush! Everybody shut up and let me handle this." He was squatting in the position of a runner about to sprint forward but he didn't move.

"I pre-chate that, lady," The Misfit said and drew a little circle in the ground with the butt of his gun.

"It'll take a half a hour to fix this here car," Hiram called, looking over the raised hood of it.

"Well, first you and Bobby Lee get him and that little boy to step over yonder with you," The Misfit said, pointing to Bailey and John Wesley. "The boys want to ask you something," he said to Bailey. "Would you mind stepping back in them woods there with them?"

"Listen," Bailey began, "we're in a terrible predicament. Nobody realizes what this is," and his voice cracked. His eyes were as blue and intense as the parrots in his shirt and he remained perfectly still.

The grandmother reached up to adjust her hat brim as if she were going to the woods with him but it came off in her hand. She stood staring at it and after a second she let it fall on the ground. Hiram pulled Bailey up by the arm as if he were assisting an old man. John Wesley caught hold of his father's hand and Bobby Lee followed. They went off toward the woods and just as they reached the dark edge, Bailey turned and supporting himself against a gray naked pine trunk, he shouted, "I'll be back in a minute, Mamma, wait on me!"

"Come back this instant!" his mother shrilled but they all disappeared into the woods.

"Bailey Boy!" the grandmother called in a tragic voice but she found she was looking at The Misfit squatting on the ground in front of her. "I just know you're a good man," she said desperately. "You're not a bit common!"

"Nome, I ain't a good man," The Misfit said after a second as if he had considered her statement carefully, "but I ain't the worst in the world neither. My daddy said I was different breed of dog from my brothers and sisters. 'You know,'

Daddy said, 'it's some that can live their whole life out without asking about it and it's others has to know why it is, and this boy is one of the latters. He's going to be into everything!' " He put on his black hat and looked up suddenly and then away deep into the woods as if he were embarrassed again. "I'm sorry I don't have on a shirt before you ladies," he said, hunching his shoulders slightly. "We buried our clothes that we had on when we escaped and we're just making do until we can get better. We borrowed these from some folks we met," he explained.

"That's perfectly all right," the grandmother said. "Maybe Bailey has an extra shirt in his suitcase."

"I'll look and see terrectly," The Misfit said.

"Where are they taking him?" the children's mother screamed.

"Daddy was a card himself," The Misfit said. "You couldn't put anything over on him. He never got in trouble with the Authorities though. Just had the knack of handling them."

"You could be honest too if you'd only try," said the grandmother. "Think how wonderful it would be to settle down and live a comfortable life and not have to think about somebody chasing you all the time."

The Misfit kept scratching in the ground with the butt of his gun as if he were thinking about it. "Yes'm, somebody is always after you," he murmured.

The grandmother noticed how thin his shoulder blades were just behind his hat because she was standing up looking down on him. "Do you ever pray?" she asked.

He shook his head. All she saw was the black hat wiggle between his shoulder blades. "Nome," he said.

There was a pistol shot from the woods, followed closely by another. Then silence. The old lady's head jerked around. She could hear the wind move through the tree tops like a long satisfied insuck of breath. "Bailey Boy!" she called.

"I was a gospel singer for a while," The Misfit said. "I been most everything. Been in the arm service, both land and sea, at home and abroad, been twict married, been an undertaker, been with the railroads, plowed Mother Earth, been in a tornado, seen a man burnt alive oncet," and he looked up at the children's mother and the little girl who were sitting close together, their faces white and their eyes glassy; "I even seen a woman flogged," he said.

"Pray, pray," the grandmother began, "pray, pray . . ."

"I never was a bad boy that I remember of," The Misfit said in an almost dreamy voice, "but somewheres along the line I done something wrong and got sent to the penitentiary. I was buried alive," and he looked up and held her attention to him by a steady stare.

"That's when you should have started to pray," she said. "What did you do to get sent to the penitentiary that first time?"

"Turn to the right, it was a wall," The Misfit said, looking up again at the cloudless sky. "Turn to the left, it was a wall. Look up it was a ceiling, look down it was a floor. I forgot what I done, lady. I set there and set there, trying to re-member what it was I done and I ain't recalled it to this day. Oncet in a while, I would think it was coming to me, but it never come."

"Maybe they put you in by mistake," the old lady said vaguely.

"Nome," he said. "It wasn't no mistake. They had the papers on me."

"You must have stolen something," she said.

The Misfit sneered slightly. "Nobody had nothing I wanted," he said. "It was a head-doctor at the penitentiary said what I had done was kill my daddy but I know that for a lie. My daddy died in nineteen ought nineteen of the epidemic flu and I never had a thing to do with it. He was buried in the Mount Hopewell Baptist churchyard and you can go there and see for yourself."

"If you would pray," the old lady said, "Jesus would help you."

"That's right," The Misfit said.

"Well then, why don't you pray?" she asked trembling with delight suddenly.

"I don't want no hep," he said. "I'm doing all right by myself."

Bobby Lee and Hiram came ambling back from the woods. Bobby Lee was dragging a yellow shirt with bright blue parrots in it.

"Throw me that shirt, Bobby Lee," The Misfit said. The shirt came flying at him and landed on his shoulder and he put it on. The grandmother couldn't name what the shirt reminded her of. "No, lady," The Misfit said while he was buttoning it up. "I found out the crime don't matter. You can do one thing or you can do another, kill a man or take a tire off his car, because sooner or later you're going to forget what it was you done and just be punished for it."

The children's mother had begun to make heaving noises as if she couldn't get her breath. "Lady," he asked, "would you and that little girl like to step off yonder with Bobby Lee and Hiram and join your husband?"

"Yes, thank you," the mother said faintly. Her left arm dangled helplessly and she was holding the baby, who had gone to sleep, in the other. "Hep that lady up, Hiram," The Misfit said as she struggled to climb out of the ditch, "and Bobby Lee, you hold onto that little girl's hand."

"I don't want to hold hands with him," June Star said. "He reminds me of a pig."

The fat boy blushed and laughed and caught her by the arm and pulled her off into the woods after Hiram and her mother.

Alone with The Misfit, the grandmother found that she had lost her voice. There was not a cloud in the sky nor any sun. There was nothing around her but woods. She wanted to tell him that he must pray. She opened and closed her mouth several times before anything came out. Finally she found herself saying, "Jesus, Jesus," meaning Jesus will help you, but the way she was saying it, it sounded as if she might be cursing.

"Yes'm," The Misfit said as if he agreed. "Jesus thown everything off balance. It was the same case with Him as with me except He hadn't committed any crime and they could prove I had committed one because they had the papers on me. Of course," he said, "they never shown me any papers. That's why I sign myself now. I said long ago, you get you a signature and sign everything you do and keep a copy of it. Then you'll know what you done and you can hold up the crime to the punishment and see do they match and in the end you'll have something to prove you ain't been treated right. I call myself The Misfit," he said, "because I can't make what all I done wrong fit what all I gone through in punishment."

There was a piercing scream from the woods, followed closely by a pistol report. "Does it seem right to you, lady, that one is punished a heap and another ain't punished at all?"

"Jesus!" the old lady cried. "You've got good blood! I know you wouldn't shoot a lady! I know you come from nice people! Pray! Jesus, you ought not to shoot a lady. I'll give you all the money I've got!"

"Lady," The Misfit said, looking beyond her far into the woods, "there never was a body that give the undertaker a tip."

There were two more pistol reports and the grandmother raised her head like a parched old turkey hen crying for water and called, "Bailey Boy, Bailey Boy!" as if her heart would break.

"Jesus was the only One that ever raised the dead," The Misfit continued, "and He shouldn't have done it. He thown everything off balance. If He did what He said, then it's nothing for you to do but thow away everything and follow Him, and if He didn't, then it's nothing for you to do but enjoy the few minutes you got left the best way you can—by killing somebody or burning down his house or doing some other meanness to him. No pleasure but meanness," he said and his voice had become almost a snarl.

"Maybe He didn't raise the dead," the old lady mumbled, not knowing what she was saying and feeling so dizzy that she sank down in the ditch with her legs twisted under her.

"I wasn't there so I can't say He didn't," The Misfit said. "I wisht I had of been there," he said, hitting the ground with his fist. "It ain't right I wasn't there because if I had of been there I would of known. Listen lady," he said in a high voice, "if I had of been there I would of known and I wouldn't be like I am now." His voice seemed about to crack and the grandmother's head cleared for an instant. She saw the man's face twisted close to her own as if he were going to cry and she murmured, "Why you're one of my babies. You're one of my own children!" She reached out and touched him on the shoulder. The Misfit sprang back as if a snake had bitten him and shot her three times through the chest. Then he put his gun down on the ground and took off his glasses and began to clean them.

Hiram and Bobby Lee returned from the woods and stood over the ditch, looking down at the grandmother who half sat and half lay in a puddle of blood with her legs crossed under her like a child's and her face smiling up at the cloudless sky.

Without his glasses, The Misfit's eyes were red-rimmed and pale and defenseless-looking. "Take her off and thow her where you thown the others," he said, picking up the cat that was rubbing itself against his leg.

"She was a talker, wasn't she?" Bobby Lee said, sliding down the ditch with a yodel.

"She would of been a good woman," The Misfit said, "if it had been somebody there to shoot her every minute of her life."

"Some fun!" Bobby Lee said.

"Shut up, Bobby Lee," The Misfit said. "It's no real pleasure in life."

POETRY

11

READING POETRY

Poetry may well be the oldest of all literary forms. Certainly, a great deal of the oldest literature of which we have written records is in verse. Yet today poetry is often regarded as the most sophisticated or difficult of literary forms. What has happened to cause the change? Why should something that seems so difficult to us today have seemed so natural to our ancestors? There are two answers to these questions. The first deals with music; the second with memory.

Poetry is musical, or at least rhythmic, speech. It is also usually a harmonious speech, employing words whose sounds echo each other or blend well. It may even be set to music, to be chanted or sung rather than simply spoken.

Because of its musical nature, poetry is easily remembered. Everyone knows how much easier it is to memorize the words to a song than to memorize even a few paragraphs from a newspaper or textbook. Poetry can thus serve as an aid to memory. If you must remember something, and have no written notes to help you, you can make a song of what you need to remember, and your chances of keeping it in your head will improve.

In almost any society, the desire to keep records, remember events, or tell stories precedes the invention of writing. Poetry, being pleasant and memorable, is then the natural first form for histories and tales. Once the art of writing develops, however, poetry is no longer essential. But it is still pleasing and has by now a tradition of use behind it. Prose takes over for record keeping and for transmitting technical information, but poetry keeps its hold on certain important affairs. Songs are still written to celebrate victories and loves, to mourn deaths, and to worship.

The printing of books, which gave so many people access to written words, has been one factor in the promotion of prose in our society. The invention of radio and television—whose announcers universally speak in the blandest, least musical cadences possible—has been another factor. After the age of nursery rhymes, most of us live in a world where the cadences of poetry are no longer part of our everyday life. Moreover, we live in a society where so many written and spoken words bombard us that we learn to skim through them quickly for whatever information they carry. We take no time to look for the beauty of words or for rhythm—neither of which is very likely to be there, anyway.

Poetry, however, cannot be read rapidly. Newspapers can be, and, in fact, are meant to be. Fiction can be. And, again, some of it is meant for the quick, careless reader, though most good fiction improves with slow, thoughtful reading. Drama, in general, must be read more slowly, if we are to catch the sound of the individual speeches. But poetry must be read most slowly of all. It requires not only that we read it silently at the same pace that we would read it aloud, but also that we pause after we read it, to think about it for a few moments at least, to savor the mood the poem has created before we go on to something else.

It is no wonder, then, that poetry sometimes seems strange or difficult. Almost every other influence in our environment is telling us, "Hurry up! Grab the central fact or idea I'm selling and run!" Poetry is saying, "Slow down! Enjoy the music; let yourself become part of the emotion. I have many suggestions to make. Take time to let them unfold for you." In today's rush of prepackaged ideas, the stubborn individualism and refusal to be hurried that poetry represents are indeed unusual.

But anything that lets us think for ourselves, that offers us a chance to find our own feelings, ideas, and emotions, is worth pursuing. And poetry certainly encourages this kind of thinking and reflection. Moreover, once we agree to slow down enough to savor a poem completely, we discover that poetry is very similar to the literature we've been enjoying all along. Like fiction and drama, poetry tells us of people, of what it means to them and to us to be human. And, like the other forms of literature, it relays this information through the sound of human voices.

So closely related are poetry, fiction, and drama, in fact, that it is sometimes hard to tell which is which. Some poetic dramas seem better suited for reading than for performance. Should they be classed as poetry or as plays? Similarly, there are narratives that tell a complete story in verse. Should they be considered fiction as well as poetry? Or shall we simply ignore the classifications and enjoy each work for what we like best in it, whether that be a supposedly "poetic" quality, such as rhythm, or a supposedly "fictional" or "dramatic" one, such as plot, characterization, or dramatic irony?

We must, then, read poetry with the same close attention we give to all our readings in this course. Poetry, too, demands these basic questions:

1. Who is speaking?
2. What kind of person is he or she? In what mood? Thinking what thoughts? Feeling what emotions?
3. Of whom or what is he or she speaking?
4. How is this person or object being described?
5. What attitudes are being projected?
6. Are we led to share the attitudes and emotions in sympathy, or to rebel against them with feelings of anger or irony?

But, because poetry is both the most structured and the most subjective of literary forms, we may also ask questions about its forms and its sounds, to learn how they contribute to the poem's effect on us. In doing this, we may get some sense of which qualities we want to consider poetic.

Because poetry is a genre of great variety, it cannot be easily defined. Only by reading a variety of poems can we create our knowledge of poetry, enhance our enjoyment of it, and gain a sense of what it has to offer us.

This chapter includes several traditional ballads. Ballads are tales told in song. Traditional ballads (or folk ballads) are songs that have been passed from one singer to another, not by having been written down but by having been sung, heard, and resung.[1] Ballads are thus very like folk tales in their mode of creation and in their sense of the audience. So we may expect that the voices within the ballads will be like the voices of those archetypal storytellers we first met when reading fiction. And yet ballads are sung. Their creators are singers, not speakers. How, then, will these tales sung in verse differ from tales told in prose? How will their stories be told? What will we hear that we have not heard before?

Simon Ortiz

(1941–　　)

And there is always one more story

And there is always one more story. My mother was telling this one. It must be an old story but this time she heard a woman telling it at one of those Sunday meetings. The woman was telling about her grandson who was telling the story which was told to him by somebody else. All these voices telling the story, including the voices in the story—yes, it must be an old one.

           One time,
(or like Rainy said, "You're sposed to say, 'Onesa ponsa
time,' Daddy")

there were some Quail Women grinding corn.
Tsuushki—Coyote Lady—was with them.
5   She was
grinding u-uuhshtyah—juniper berries.
I don't know why she wasn't grinding corn too—
that's just in the story.

It was a hot, hot day, very hot,
10 and the Quail Women got thirsty,
and they decided to go get some water to drink.
They said,

---

[1]This oral tradition accounts for the number of variations ballads possess. A singer may repeat a ballad just as he or she first heard it; or he or she may change the ballad slightly, either on purpose or accidentally. A third singer then learns this new version, and either preserves or changes it. Thus a ballad of any great age may exist in many versions, each being sung by a different group of singers.

"Let's go for a drink of water,
and let's take along our beloved comadre."
15 So they said, "Comadre, let's all go
and get some water to drink."
                                "Shrow-uh,"
Coyote said.

The water was in a little cistern
20 at the top of a tall rock pinnacle
which stands southeast of Aacqu.
                                They walked
over there but they had to fly to get to the top.
The Quail Women looked at Tsuushki who couldn't fly
25 to the top because she had no feathers,
                                        and they felt
very sorry and sad for Tsuushki.

So they decided, "Let us give shracomadre
some of our feathers."
30   The Quail Women said that
and they took some feathers out of themselves
and stuck them on Coyote.
                          And then they all flew
to the top of the pinnacle where the water was.
35 They all drank their fill and Coyote
was the last to drink.
                        While she was drinking
from the cistern, on her hands and knees,
the Quail Women decided to play a trick, a joke
40 on Coyote Lady.
                  They said,
"Let's take the feathers from our comadre
and leave her here."
                      "Alright," they all agreed,
45 and they did that, and they all left.

When Tsuushki had drank her fill of water
and was ready to descend the pinnacle,
she found that she could not
because she had no feathers to fly with anymore.
50 She felt very bad,
                    and she sat down,
                                    wondering
what to do.

The rock pinnacle was too high up
55 to jump down from.

But, pretty soon,
                        Kahmaasquu Dya-ow—
Spider Grandmother—came climbing over the edge
of the pinnacle to drink water also.
60 And Coyote thought to herself,
                                    Aha,
I will ask my Grandmother to help me off.
She is always a wonderful helpful person.

So Coyote asked,
65 "Dya-ow Kahmaasquu, do you think you could help me
descend this pinnacle? You are always such
a wonderful helpful person."

And Spider Grandmother said,
                                "Why yes,
70 beloved one, I will help you.
Climb into my basket."
                            She pointed at a basket
tied at the end of her rope.
                                And then
75 she said, "But I must ask you one thing.
While I am letting you down,
you must not look up, not once,
not even just a little bit.
                            For if you do,
80 I will drop you.
And that is quite a long ways down."

"Oh, don't worry about that, Dya-ow,
I won't look up. I'm not that kind of person,"
Coyote promised.
85   "Alright then,"
Spider said, "Climb in
and I will let you down."

The basket began to descend,
                                down
90   and
                                              down,
But on the way down,

Coyote looked up
(At this point, the voice telling the story
95 is that of the boy who said,
"But Tsuushki
looked up and saw her butt!")
and Spider Grandmother dropped the basket
and Coyote went crashing down.

100 Well, at this point, the story ends but,
as you know, it also goes on.
Well, sometime later,
the Shuuwimuu Guiguikuutchah—
Skeleton Fixer—came along.
105 He saw a scatter of bones at the foot of the pinnacle.
Skeleton Fixer said,
"Oh look,
some poor beloved one must have died.
I wonder who it may be?"
110 The bones
were drying white in the sun, lying around.
And Skeleton Fixer said,
"I think I will put
the bones together
115 and find out and he will live again."

And he joined the bones together,
very carefully,
and when he had finished doing that,
he danced around them while he sang,

120 "Shuuwimuu shuuwimuu chuichukuu
Shuuwimuu shuuwimuu chuichukuu
Bah Bah."
(which is to say)
Skeleton skeleton join together
125 Skeleton skeleton join together
Bah Bah.
And the skeleton bones did,
and the skeleton jumped up,
and it was Coyote.

130 "Ah kumeh, Tsuushkitruda," Skeleton Fixer said.
Oh, it's just you Coyote—I thought
it was someone else.
And as Coyote ran away,
Skeleton Fixer called after her,

135   "Nahkeh-eh,
bah aihatih eyownih trudrai-nah!"
Go ahead and go, may you get crushed
by a falling rock somewhere!

STUDY QUESTIONS

1. Ortiz's "And there is always one more story" is not in traditional ballad form, but it clearly looks back to the oral traditions out of which ballads arise. Identify points in the poem where the narrator acknowledges that many voices from the past echo through the narrative.

2. How are these elements from the past juxtaposed with what appear to be contemporary references? What is the thematic effect of having this seemingly ancient folk story about magical animals being told "at one of those Sunday meetings"?

3. In the poem, the Coyote Lady gets feathers from the Quail Women so that she can fly with them up to the cistern to get water, but then the Quail Women take her feathers away. Then the Coyote falls to her death after looking up at the Spider Grandmother, only to be brought back to life by the Skeleton Fixer. How do you interpret these strange events? Why do the Quail Women at first help, then strand the Coyote Woman? What might the Spider Grandmother represent? Finally, why does the Skeleton Fixer, after bringing the Coyote Woman back to life, yell to her: "may you get crushed/by a falling rock somewhere"?

Leslie Marmon Silko

(1948–   )

The Storyteller's Escape

The storyteller keeps the stories
            all the escape stories
                        she says "With these stories of ours
                                    we can escape almost anything
5   with these stories we will survive."

The old teller has been on every journey
and she knows all the escape stories
            even stories told before she was born.
She keeps the stories for those who return
10   but more important
            for the dear ones who do not come back

so that we may remember them
and cry for them with the stories.

15
                          "In this way
                          we hold them
                          and keep them with us forever
                          and in this way
                          we continue."

20
             This story is remembered
             as her best story
             it is the storyteller's own escape.

In those days
the people would leave the village
25   and hurry into the lava flows
where they waited until the enemy had gone.

                    "This time they were close behind us
                    and we could not stop to rest.
                    On the afternoon of the fourth day
30
                    I was wearing the sun
                    for a hat.

                 Always before
                 it was me
            turning around
35
            for the last look
                 at the pregnant woman
                 the crippled boy
                 old man Shio'see
                   slowing up
40
                   lying down
                   never getting up again.

                 Always before
                 I was the one who looked back
                 before the humpback hills
45
                 rose between us
                 so I could tell where these dear ones stopped."

But sooner or later
even a storyteller knows it will happen.
        The only thing was
50
             this time
             she couldn't be sure
             if there would be anyone

to look back
and later tell the others:
55   She stopped on the north side of Dough Mountain
and she said:

"The sun is a shawl on my back
its heat makes tassels that
shimmer down my arms."

60   And then she sat down in the shade
and closed her eyes.

She was thinking
this was how she would want them
to remember her and cry for her
65 If only somebody had looked back
to see her face for the last time

Someone who would know then
and tell the others:

"The black hills rose between us
70   the shady rock was above her head
and she was thinking
There won't be any escape story this time
unless maybe someone tells
how the sweat spilled over the rock
75   making streams in hills
that had no water.

She was thinking
I could die peacefully
if there was just someone to tell
80   how I finally stopped
and where.

She believed
in this kind of situation
you have to do the best you can.

85   So I just might as well think of a story
while I'm waiting to die:

A'moo'ooh, the child looked back.

"Don't wait!
Go on without me!
90   Tell them I said that—
Tell them I'm too old too tired

> I'd rather just die here
> in the shade
> I'd rather just die
> than climb these rocky hills
> in the hot sun.

95

The child turned back for a last look at her
off in the distance leaning against a cool rock
the old teller waiting for the enemy to find her.

100 The child knew

> how she had been on all the escape journeys
> how she hated the enemy.

She knew

> what she was thinking
105 what she was saying to herself:

> > "I'll fix them good!
> > I'll fool them!
> > I'll already be dead
> > when the enemies come."

110 She laughed out loud.

> I'll die just to spite them!

She was resting close to the boulder
hoping the child would tell—
otherwise

115 how could they remember her
how could they cry for her
without this story?

About this time

> the sun lifted off from her shoulders like a butterfly.

120

> > Let the enemy wear it now!
> > Let them see how they like the heat
> > wrapping them in its blanket!

She laughed sitting there
thinking to herself
125 until it got dark.

> They would cry when they were told
> the sun had been her hat
> until she could walk no more
> the sun had been a shawl
130 until she had to sit down in the shade.

This one's the best one yet—
too bad nobody may ever hear it.

She waited all night
but at dawn
135 there was still no sign of the enemy.
So she decided
to go back to the village.

What difference would it make
if she ran into the enemy?
140 She had already waited
all night
for them to come along
and finish her.

But she didn't see anyone
145   no enemy.
Maybe the sun got to be too much for them too

And it was the best escape story she had come up with yet

How four days later when the people came back
from their hide-outs in the lava flow
150   there she was
sitting in front of her house
waiting for them.

This is the story she told,
the child who looked back,
155   the old teller's escape—
the story she was thinking of
her getaway story
how they remembered her
and cried for her
160 Because she always had a way with stories
even on the last day
when she stopped in the shade
on the north side of Dough Mountain.

STUDY QUESTIONS

1. What does "The Storyteller's Escape" say about the importance of the story-teller or poet in a preliterate society?

2. What virtues does the storyteller exhibit and celebrate during her ordeal on Dough Mountain?
3. What is the function of the child in the poem?
4. How do simile and metaphor contribute to the poem?

Anonymous

Sir Patrick Spens

The king sits in Dumferling town,
    Drinking the blude-reid wine:
"O whar will I get guid sailor,
    To sail this ship of mine?"

5 Up and spak an eldern knicht,
    Sat at the king's richt knee:
"Sir Patrick Spens is the best sailor
    That sails upon the sea."

The king has written a braid letter
10   And signed it wi' his hand,
And sent it to Sir Patrick Spens,
    Was walking on the sand.

The first line that Sir Patrick read,
    A loud lauch[2] lauched he;
15 The next line that Sir Patrick read,
    The tear blinded his ee.[3]

"O wha is this has done this deed,
    This ill deed done to me,
To send me out this time o' the year,
20   To sail upon the sea?

"Mak haste, mak haste, my mirry men all,
    Our guid ship sails the morn."
"O say na sae, my master dear,
    For I fear a deadly storm.

25 "Late, late yestre'en I saw the new moon
    Wi' the auld moon in hir arm,
And I fear, I fear, my dear master,
    That we will come to harm."

---

[2]laugh
[3]eye

O our Scots nobles were richt laith[4]
30   To weet[5] their cork-heeled shoon,[6]
But lang or[7] a' the play were played
    Their hats they swam aboon.[8]

O lang, lang may their ladies sit,
    Wi' their fans into their hand,
35 Or ere they see Sir Patrick Spens
    Come sailing to the land.

O lang, lang may the ladies stand
    Wi' their gold kems[9] in their hair,
Waiting for their ain dear lords,
40   For they'll see them na mair.

Half o'er, half o'er to Aberdour[1]
    It's fifty fadom[2] deep,
And there lies guid Sir Patrick Spens
    Wi' the Scots lords at his feet.

Anonymous

The Cherry-Tree Carol

Joseph was an old man,
    and an old man was he,
When he wedded Mary,
    in the land of Galilee.

5 Joseph and Mary walked
    through an orchard good,
Where was cherries and berries,
    so red as any blood.

Joseph and Mary walked
10   through an orchard green,
Where was berries and cherries,
    as thick as might be seen.

---

[4]loath
[5]wet
[6]shoes
[7]before
[8]above
[9]combs
[1]halfway back to Aberdour, on the Firth of Forth
[2]fathoms

O then bespoke Mary,
   so meek and so mild:
15 "Pluck me one cherry, Joseph,
   for I am with child."

O then bespoke Joseph:
   with words most unkind:
"Let him pluck thee a cherry
20   that brought thee with child."

O then bespoke the babe,
   within his mother's womb:
"Bow down then the tallest tree,
   for my mother to have some."

25 Then bowed down the highest tree
   unto his mother's hand;
Then she cried, "See, Joseph,
   I have cherries at command."

O then bespoke Joseph:
30   "I have done Mary wrong;
But cheer up, my dearest,
   and be not cast down."

Then Mary plucked a cherry,
   as red as the blood,
35 Then Mary went home
   with her heavy load.

Then Mary took her babe,
   and sat him on her knee,
Saying, "My dear son, tell me
40   what this world will be."

"O I shall be as dead, mother,
   as the stones in the wall;
O the stones in the streets, mother,
   shall mourn for me all.

45 "Upon Easter-day, mother,
   my uprising shall be;
O the sun and the moon, mother,
   shall both rise with me."

Anonymous

Get Up and Bar the Door

It fell about the Martinmas[3] time,
   And a gay time it was then,
When our good wife got puddings[4] to make,
   And she's boild them in the pan.

5 The wind sae cauld blew south and north,
   And blew into the floor;
Quoth our goodman to our goodwife,
   "Gae out and bar the door."

"My hands is in my hussyfskap,[5]
10   Goodman, as ye may see;
An it shoud nae be barrd this hundred year,
   It's no be barrd for me."

They made a paction tween them twa,
   They made it firm and sure,
15 That the first word whaeer shoud speak,
   Shoud rise and bar the door.

Then by there came two gentlemen,
   At twelve oclock at night,
And they could neither see house nor hall,
20   Nor coal nor candle-light.

"Now whether is this a rich man's house,
   Or whether is it a poor?"
But neer a word wad ane o them speak,
   For barring of the door.

25 And first they ate the white puddings,
   And then they ate the black;
Tho muckle[6] thought the goodwife to hersel,
   Yet neer a word she spake.

Then said the one unto the other,
30   "Here, man, tak ye my knife;
Do ye tak aff the auld man's beard,
   And I'll kiss the goodwife."

---

[3]November 11
[4]sausages
[5]household chores
[6]much

"But there's nae water in the house,
   And what shall we do than?"
35 "What ails ye at the pudding-broo,
   That boils into the pan?"

O up then started our goodman,
   An angry man was he:
"Will ye kiss my wife before my een,
40   And scad me wi pudding-bree?"

Then up and started our goodwife,
   Gied three skips on the floor:
"Goodman, you've spoken the foremost word,
   Get up and bar the door."

STUDY QUESTIONS

1. Because ballads come out of the oral tradition, it is only natural that they would sound different than more "literary" poems composed by a single author. Comment on the effect of the informal diction and dialect words that characterize "Sir Patrick Spens," "The Cherry-Tree Carol," and "Get Up and Bar the Door."
2. Comment on the different tones of the three ballads. Are ballads limited in the range of moods they can convey?
3. Compare these three anonymous ballads with Dudley Randall's modern "Ballad of Birmingham," which follows. What differences in subject matter and tone do you notice?

Dudley Randall

(1914–   )

Ballad of Birmingham

(On the bombing of a church in Birmingham, Alabama, 1963)

"Mother dear, may I go downtown
Instead of out to play,
And march the streets of Birmingham
In a Freedom March today?"

5 "No, baby, no, you may not go,
For the dogs are fierce and wild,
And clubs and hoses, guns and jails
Aren't good for a little child."

"But, mother, I won't be alone.
10 Other children will go with me,
And march the streets of Birmingham
To make our country free."

"No, baby, no, you may not go,
For I fear those guns will fire.
15 But you may go to church instead
And sing in the children's choir."

She has combed and brushed her night-dark hair,
And bathed rose petal sweet,
And drawn white gloves on her small brown hands,
20 And white shoes on her feet.

The mother smiled to know her child
Was in the sacred place,
But that smile was the last smile
To come upon her face.

25 For when she heard the explosion,
Her eyes grew wet and wild.
She raced through the streets of Birmingham
Calling for her child.

She clawed through bits of glass and brick,
30 Then lifted out a shoe.
"O, here's the shoe my baby wore,
But, baby, where are you?"

STUDY QUESTION

Although "Ballad of Birmingham" was written by a twentieth-century poet, both its form and its content qualify it as a true ballad in the folk tradition. Discuss the various elements in the poem that make this so. What special power or perspective does Randall give to his telling of this historical incident by putting it in ballad form?

Edgar Allan Poe

(1809–1849)

Annabel Lee

It was many and many a year ago,
        In a kingdom by the sea,
That a maiden there lived whom you may know
        By the name of Annabel Lee;—
5 And this maiden she lived with no other thought
        Than to love and be loved by me.

She was a child and *I* was a child,
        In this kingdom by the sea,
But we loved with a love that was more than love—
10   I and my Annabel Lee—
With a love that the wingèd seraphs of Heaven
        Coveted her and me.

And this was the reason that, long ago,
        In this kingdom by the sea,
15 A wind blew out of a cloud by night
        Chilling my Annabel Lee;
So that her highborn kinsmen came
        And bore her away from me,
To shut her up in a sepulchre
20   In this kingdom by the sea.

The angels, not half so happy in Heaven,
        Went envying her and me—
Yes!—that was the reason (as all men know,
        In this kingdom by the sea)
25 That the wind came out of the cloud chilling
        And killing my Annabel Lee.

But our love it was stronger by far than the love
        Of those who were older than we—
        Of many far wiser than we—
30 And neither the angels in Heaven above,
        Nor the demons down under the sea,
Can ever dissever my soul from the soul
        Of the beautiful Annabel Lee:—

For the moon never beams without bringing me dreams
35   Of the beautiful Annabel Lee;
And the stars never rise but I see the bright eyes

Of the beautiful Annabel Lee;
And so, all the night-tide, I lie down by the side
Of my darling, my darling, my life and my bride,
40   In her sepulchre there by the sea—
In her tomb by the side of the sea.

STUDY QUESTIONS

1. What elements in "Annabel Lee" come from the ballad tradition? What elements have been added or altered? In developing your answer, consider the basic use of rhythm and rhyme, repetition, refrain, alliteration, vocabulary, and so on.
2. Consider the story told by the poem, and the emotions it evokes. Is the story one that fits well into the ballad form? Again, what elements harmonize well with the ballad tradition? Which suggest a more sophisticated speaker and audience?

Sterling Brown

(1901–1989)

Slim in Hell

I

Slim Greer went to heaven;
   St. Peter said, "Slim,
You been a right good boy."
   An' he winked at him.

5   "You been a travelin' rascal
        In yo' day.
      You kin roam once mo';
        Den you comes to stay.

"Put dese wings on yo' shoulders,
10   An' save yo' feet."
Slim grin, and he speak up
   "Thankye, Pete."

      Den Peter say, "Go
        To Hell an' see,
15   All dat is doing, and
        Report to me.

"Be sure to remember
 How everything go."
Slim say, "I be seein' yuh
20 On de late watch, bo."

  Slim got to cavortin',
   Swell as you choose,
  Like Lindy in de "Spirit
   Of St. Louis Blues!"

25 He flew an' he flew,
 Till at last he hit
A hangar wid de sign readin'
 DIS IS IT.

  Den he parked his wings,
30   An' strolled aroun'
  Gettin' used to his feet
   On de solid ground.

    II

Big bloodhound came aroarin'
 Like Niagry Falls,
35 Sicked on by white devils
 In overhalls.

Now Slim warn't scared,
 Cross my heart, it's a fac',
An' de dog went on a bayin'
40 Some po' devil's track.

  Den Slim saw a mansion
   An' walked right in;
  De Devil looked up
   Wid a sickly grin.

45 "Suttinly didn't look
 Fo' you, Mr. Greer,
How it happen you comes
 To visit here?"

  Slim say—"Oh, jes' thought
50   I'd drap by a spell."
  "Feel at home, seh, an' here's
   De keys to Hell."

Den he took Slim around
 An' showed him people

55 Raisin' hell as high as
    De First Church Steeple.

    Lots of folks fightin'
        At de roulette wheel,
    Like old Rampart Street,
60   Or leastwise Beale.

Showed him bawdy houses
    An' cabarets,
Slim thought of New Orleans
    An' Memphis days.

65   Each devil was busy
        Wid a devilish broad,
    An' Slim cried, "Lawdy,
        Lawd, Lawd, Lawd."

Took him in a room
70   Where Slim see
De preacher wid a brownskin
    On each knee.

    Showed him giant stills,
        Going everywhere
75   Wid a passel of devils,
        Stretched dead drunk there.

Den he took him to de furnace
    Dat some devils was firing,
Hot as hell, an' Slim start
80   A mean presspirin';

    White devils wid pitchforks
        Threw black devils on,
    Slim thought he'd better
        Be gittin' along.

85 An' he say—"Dis makes
    Me think of home—
Vicksburg, Little Rock, Jackson,
    Waco, and Rome."

    Den de devil gave Slim
90   De big Ha-Ha;
    An' turned into a cracker,
        Wid a sheriff's star.

Slim ran fo' his wings,
    Lit out from de groun'
95 Hauled it back to St. Peter,
    Safety boun'.

III

    St. Peter said, "Well,
        You got back quick.
    How's de devil? An' what's
100   His latest trick?"

An' Slim say, "Peter,
    I really cain't tell,
De place was Dixie
    Dat I took for Hell."

105 Then Peter say, "You must
    Be crazy, I vow,
Where'n hell dja think Hell *was*,
    Anyhow?

"Git on back to de yearth,
110   Cause I got de fear,
You'se a leetle too dumb,
    Fo' to stay up here . . ."

STUDY QUESTIONS

1. "Slim in Hell" is based on a simple joke. How would you state this joke in two or three sentences?
2. How does Brown's use of dialect contribute to the humor of the poem?
3. Does the poem merely criticize whites for racism, or does it also find fault with blacks? If so, why?

Elements of Poetry

12

REPETITION AND RHYTHM

Two elements in ballads are **repetition** and **rhythm.** Sometimes single words or phrases are repeated for emphasis, as in Poe's "Annabel Lee": "She was a child and I was a child/In this kingdom by the sea." Sometimes one or more lines, perhaps with slight variations, appear in nearly every verse as a refrain: "I and my Annabel Lee/. . . . In this kingdom by the sea." In each case, the repetition emphasizes both the content and the rhythm of the ballad, calling our attention to the meter (that is, to the rhythmic pattern of each line) or to the grouping of lines into stanzas.

Of the ballads or ballad-influenced poems printed in the previous chapter, "Annabel Lee" is the most repetitive. In fact, it is built on a technique known as **incremental repetition.** Many phrases recur throughout the stanzas, creating a melancholy, hypnotic effect. The subtle changes in the repeated lines develop the narrative of the poem and help convey the narrator's sorrow over the death of his beloved.

Repetition is important not only in ballads, but in lyric poetry in general. It is most pronounced in songs, as in the next example. But it appears frequently (and often quite subtly) in spoken lyrics as well. Let us look at some poems in which repetition plays an important role, and let us see what effects are produced by it.

William Shakespeare

(1564–1616)

It Was a Lover and His Lass

It was a lover and his lass,
    With a hey, and a ho, and hey nonino,
That o'er the green corn-field did pass
    In the spring time, the only pretty ring time,
5 When birds do sing, hey ding a ding, ding:
Sweet lovers love the spring.

Between the acres of the rye,
    With a hey, and a ho, and a hey nonino,
These pretty country folk would lie,
10   In the spring time, the only pretty ring time,

When birds do sing, hey ding a ding, ding:
Sweet lovers love the spring.

This carol they began that hour,
    With a hey, and a ho, and a hey nonino,
15 How that a life was but a flower
    In the spring time, the only pretty ring time,
When birds do sing, hey ding a ding, ding:
Sweet lovers love the spring.

And therefore take the present time,
20   With a hey, and a ho, and a hey nonino,
For love is crownèd with the prime
    In the spring time, the only pretty ring time,
When birds do sing, hey ding a ding, ding:
Sweet lovers love the spring.

STUDY QUESTIONS

1. How would you characterize this song? What is its mood?
2. How does the refrain help set the mood of the song?
3. What other repetitions of sounds do you find in the poem? What do they contribute? (Note: Two important categories here are **rhyme**—the use of words that *end* with the same sound, like *rye* and *lie*—and **alliteration,** the use of words that *begin* with the same sound, like *lover* and *lass; hey, ho,* and *hey.*)
4. Discuss the progression of thought and feeling from the first stanza to the final one. What sense of completeness does the progression impart to Shakespeare's song?

Thomas Hardy

(1840–1928)

The Ruined Maid

"O 'Melia, my dear, this does everything crown!
Who could have supposed I should meet you in Town?
And whence such fair garments, such prosperi-ty?"—
"O didn't you know I'd been ruined?" said she.

5 —"You left us in tatters, without shoes or socks,
Tired of digging potatoes, and spudding up docks;[1]

---

[1] digging up weeds

And now you've gay bracelets and bright feathers three!"—
"Yes: that's how we dress when we're ruined," said she.

—"At home in the barton[2] you said 'thee' and 'thou,'
10 And 'thik oon,' and 'theäs oon,' and 't'other'; but now
Your talking quite fits 'ee for high compa-ny!"—
"Some polish is gained with one's ruin," said she.

—"Your hands were like paws then, you face blue and bleak
But now I'm bewitched by your delicate cheek,
15 And your little gloves fit as on any la-dy!"—
"We never do work when we're ruined," said she.

—"You used to call home-life a hag-ridden dream,
And you'd sign, and you'd sock; but at present you seem
To know not of megrims[3] or melancho-ly!"—
20 "True. One's pretty lively when ruined," said she.

—"I wish I had feathers, a fine sweeping gown,
And a delicate face, and could strut about Town!"—
"My dear—a raw country girl, such as you be,
Cannot quite expect that. You ain't ruined," said she.

STUDY QUESTIONS

1. How does Hardy use question and answer to characterize the two women?
2. What balance exists here between the two sides of the dialogue? What is the effect of the repetitions in the final line of each stanza?
3. What sort of tone or consciousness would you expect to find in a poem about a "ruined maid" that is absent from this poem? What effect does this have on the tone of the poem and on the characterization of the speakers? On the poet's apparent attitude toward them?

E. E. Cummings

(1894–1963)

All in green went my love riding

All in green went my love riding
on a great horse of gold
into the silver dawn.

---

[2]farmyard
[3]low spirits

four lean hounds crouched low and smiling
5   the merry deer ran before.

Fleeter be they than dappled dreams
the swift sweet deer
the red rare deer.

Four red roebuck at a white water
10 the cruel bugle sang before.

Horn at hip went my love riding
riding the echo down
into the silver dawn.

four lean hounds crouched low and smiling
15 the level meadows ran before.

Softer be they than slippered sleep
the lean lithe deer
the fleet flown deer.

Four fleet does at a gold valley
20 the famished arrow sang before.

Bow at belt went my love riding
riding the mountain down
into the silver dawn.

four lean hounds crouched low and smiling
25 the sheer peaks ran before.

Paler be they than daunting death
the sleek slim deer
the tall tense deer.

Four tall stags at a green mountain
30 the lucky hunter sang before.

All in green went my love riding
on a great horse of gold
into the silver dawn.

four lean hounds crouched low and smiling
35 my heart fell dead before.

STUDY QUESTIONS

1. Incremental repetition is used in this modern poem for an almost balladlike
   effect. But how would you describe the way stanzas are linked in this poem?

2. What effects would you say the poem achieves? How would you distinguish between its effects and those of traditional ballads?

N. Scott Momaday

(1934–   )

The Delight Song of Tsoai-talee

I am a feather in the bright sky.
I am the blue horse that runs in the plain.
I am the fish that rolls, shining, in the water.
I am the shadow that follows a child.
5 I am the evening light, the lustre of meadows.
I am an eagle playing with the wind.
I am a cluster of bright beads.
I am the farthest star.
I am the cold of the dawn.
10 I am the roaring of the rain.
I am the glitter on the crust of the snow.
I am the long track of the moon in a lake.
I am a flame of four colors.
I am a deer standing away in the dusk.
15 I am a field of sumac and the pomme blanche.
I am an angle of geese upon the winter sky.
I am the hunger of a young wolf.
I am the whole dream of these things.

You see, I am alive, I am alive.
20 I stand in good relation to the earth.
I stand in good relation to the gods.
I stand in good relation to all that is beautiful.
I stand in good relation to the daughter of Tsen-tainte.
You see, I am alive, I am alive.

STUDY QUESTIONS

1. Why does Momaday use metaphor rather than simile throughout the poem?
2. Are the metaphors random, or do they form a pattern?
3. How is the line "I am the whole dream of these things" radically different from the lines that precede it?
4. What is the effect of the repetition of "I am ..." and "I stand ..." in the poem?

Etheridge Knight

(1931–1991)

Ilu, the Talking Drum

The deadness was threatening us—15 Nigerians and 1 Mississippi nigger.
It hung heavily, like stones around our necks, pulling us down
to the ground, black arms and legs outflung
on the wide green lawn of the big white house
5 near the wide brown beach by the wide blue sea.
The deadness was threatening us, the day
was dying with the sun, the stillness—
unlike the sweet silence after love/making or
the pulsating quietness of a summer night—
10 the stillness was skinny and brittle and wrinkled
by the precise people sitting on the wide white porch
of the big white house. . . .
The darkness was threatening us, menacing . . .
we twisted, turned, shifted positions, picked our noses,
15 stared at our bare toes, hissed air thru our teeth. . . .
Then Tunji, green robes flowing as he rose,
strapped on *Ilu,* the talking drum,
and began:

   kah doom/kah doom-doom/kah doom/kah doom-doom-doom
20 kah doom/kah doom-doom/kah doom/kah doom-doom-doom
   kah doom/kah doom-doom/kah doom/kah doom-doom-doom
   kah doom/kah doom-doom/kah doom/kah doom-doom-doom

   the heart, the heart beats, the heart, the heart beats slow
   the heart beats slowly, the heart beats
25 the blood flows slowly, the blood flows
   the blood, the blood flows, the blood, the blood flows slow

   kah doom/kah doom-doom/kah doom/kah doom-doom-doom
   and the day opened to the sound
   kah doom/kah doom-doom/kah doom/kah doom-doom-doom
30 and our feet moved to the sound of life
   kah doom/kah doom-doom/kah doom/kah doom-doom-doom
   and we rode the rhythms as one
   from Nigeria to Mississippi
   and back
35 kah doom/kah doom-doom/kah doom/kah doom-doom-doom

STUDY QUESTIONS

1. What is the apparent setting in place and time of the poem?
2. Why is the drum called a "talking drum"?
3. Why does Knight increase the amount of repetition as the poem progresses?

13

COMPRESSION AND VERSE FORMS

To write a short story based on the tale told in "Get Up and Bar the Door" would require at least one thousand words. (That would be roughly the length of "Miss Brill"—quite a short story, as stories go.) This ballad, however, has less than five hundred words, including refrains and repetitions. And even though ballads are much shorter than a very short story, they seem long and loosely constructed when they are compared with such tightly written lyrics as "It Was a Lover and His Lass."

Verse, then, is a highly compressed form. Eliminating inessentials, it takes us directly to the heart of a situation, to the one or two moments most highly charged with emotion. In the case of "Get Up and Bar the Door," this technique produces a ballad centering on two episodes: the one that begins the quarrel and the one that ends it.

Time becomes flexible in ballads, as one memorable moment is juxtaposed with the next, ignoring all that may have gone between: "Then by there came two gentlemen,/At twelve oclock at night." We can imagine that the lateness of the hour would have made the silent house seem even stranger than it was to the "gentlemen," and we may also suspect that quite a few hours must have passed since the feuding couple made their pact. But all the singer gives us is the crucial hour—"twelve"—and the number of intruders. The time between incidents is not important. The conflict between the couple is.

Similarly, "The Cherry-Tree Carol" moves with almost no consciousness of elapsed time from the wedding of Joseph and Mary to the scene in the orchard to a final scene between Mary and her infant son. In each case, a simple "then" defines the sequence, whether the incidents follow each other instantly, as in "then bespoke the babe," "then bowed down the highest tree," and "O then bespoke Joseph," or whether a gap of several months is indicated: "Then Mary took her babe." The passage of time, which affects everyone, is of no concern to the singer. The unique situation of parents confronted with their child's divinity engrosses all the attention, linking together the unusual circumstances of Joseph's marriage, the miracle in the orchard, and Christ's prophecy of his death and resurrection. "The Cherry-Tree Carol" assumes that its hearers are all familiar with the story of Christ's birth and death; it therefore feels free to concentrate on those aspects of the legend that bear on its central theme, leaving us to place them in chronological time if we wish.

Poetic form demands **compression**. A line of eight or ten syllables, a stanza of two, four, or six lines will not allow any wasted words. The poet must pare away all the needless background and inessential details in order to fit the essential ones into those brief stanzas.

Yet this strictness of form also helps the hearer to accept the compression it produces. We would not accept so few details as "Get Up and Bar the Door" gives us in a prose account. Nor could the information given in "The Ruined Maid" stand alone as prose. Ballad and lyric alike need the cadence of their verse—the rhyme, the rhythm, the rounded-off pattern formed by the stanzas—to give our ear and mind the sense of completeness and satisfaction that allows us to enjoy the brief, tightly focused statements their poetry makes.

Compression, then, is another technique that allows the material presented and the form of its presentation to reinforce each other, providing for the reader not only a satisfying unity, but also one that seems notably poetic. Let us now examine that technique in action by looking at a few types of poetry that have compression as their most notable feature, beginning with the oldest of these forms, the **epigram**.

Epigrams may be serious or humorous, flattering or insulting. But they are usually descriptive of a person, animal, or object; and they are invariably brief. Probably the most popular type today is the **satiric epigram,** a form that can be described as a description with a sting. Here is an example:

Countee Cullen

(1903–1946)

For a Lady I Know

She even thinks that up in heaven
Her class lies late and snores,
While poor black cherubs rise at seven
To do celestial chores.

STUDY QUESTIONS

1. What single fact do the four lines of this poem tell us about the "Lady" who is their subject?
2. What further facts do they suggest about her?
3. How do words like *her class* and *poor black cherubs* characterize the lady and the attitudes that the poet suggests she holds?
4. What do words like *snores* and *celestial chores* do for the poem? What do they suggest about the poet's attitude?

Ezra Pound

(1885–1972)

In a Station of the Metro

The apparition of these faces in the crowd;
Petals on a wet, black bough.

Amy Lowell

(1874–1925)

Wind and Silver

Greatly shining,
The Autumn moon floats in the thin sky;
And the fish-ponds shake their backs and flash their
　　dragon scales
As she passes over them.

So far, we have looked at poems that achieved effectiveness through spareness, using as few words as possible and choosing very tight verse forms. But compression can also be achieved within other verse forms. Note, for instance, the richness of words and images that William Carlos Williams manages to crowd into "The Dance," so that the poetic form seems almost too small for the magnitude of the sounds and motions it contains. Notice, too, in the poem that follows, the intensity of argument and feeling that William Wordsworth fits gracefully into the fourteen lines of a sonnet.

William Carlos Williams

(1883–1963)

The Dance

In Breughel's[1] great picture, The Kermess,[2]
the dancers go round, they go round and
around, the squeal and the blare and the
tweedle of bagpipes, a bugle and fiddles
5　tipping their bellies (round as the thick-
sided glasses whose wash they impound)

---

[1]Pieter Breughel, or Brueghel (1525?–1569), a Flemish painter
[2]a carnival or fair

their hips and their bellies off balance
to turn them. Kicking and rolling about
the Fair Grounds, swinging their butts, those
10 shanks must be sound to bear up under such
rollicking measures, prance as they dance
in Breughel's great picture, The Kermess.

STUDY QUESTIONS

1. Although you might expect a poem describing a painting to concentrate on color or form, Williams's poem concentrates at least as heavily on motion and sound. What words or phrases describe the sounds of the scene? Which describe shapes or forms? Which describe motion? What sorts of music and dancers does Williams seem to be portraying with these terms?

2. How do the poem's rhythm and shape support the sense of sound and motion? Note particularly the large number of heavily stressed monosyllables. What effect do they provide? How have sentence structure and grammar been reshaped to contribute to the sensation of noise and speed?

3. Note the plays on words within the poem: "bellies" for both fiddles and dancers, legs called "sound" in a poem much concerned with musical sounds. How does such wordplay help unify the scene? Note also the use of repetition: how does it help shape the poem?

4. If you are able to find a print of *The Kermess*, decide how well you think Williams has caught the spirit of the painting. What aspects of the poem stand out for you as being particularly apt?

William Wordsworth

(1770–1850)

The World Is Too Much with Us

The world is too much with us; late and soon,
Getting and spending, we lay waste our powers:
Little we see in Nature that is ours;
We have given our hearts away, a sordid boon!
5 This Sea that bares her bosom to the moon;
The winds that will be howling at all hours,
And are up-gathered now like sleeping flowers;
For this, for everything, we are out of tune;
It moves us not.—Great God! I'd rather be
10 A Pagan suckled in a creed outworn;
So might I, standing on this pleasant lea,

Have glimpses that would make me less forlorn;
Have sight of Proteus rising from the sea;
Or hear old Triton blow his wreathèd horn.[3]

STUDY QUESTIONS

1. What is the argument of this poem?
2. How does Wordsworth's invocation of Triton and Proteus fit in with the argument of the poem?
3. What words or images in the poem do you find most striking? How do they support the poem's argument?
4. Note the poem's movement from "us" and "we" in the first lines to "I" at the end. At what line does the change take place? How is it marked or signaled? What changes of tone of voice and of mood go with it? What change of imagery?
5. What qualities in the poem make it suitable as a study in compression? Alternatively, if you disagree with this classification, why do you challenge the poem's placement in this chapter?

Finally, we will look at some poems by Emily Dickinson. No study of compression in poetry would be complete without a consideration of the work of this American poet, who was far ahead of her time in the concentration and spareness of her verse. Description and argument blend in Dickinson's poetry into a remarkable unity of vision and idea. Notice, in the following two poems, how images of light and motion bridge the gap between the physical and spiritual worlds and between our own physical and spiritual responses to these worlds.

Emily Dickinson

(1830–1886)

There's a Certain Slant of Light (#258)

There's a certain Slant of light,
Winter Afternoons—
That oppresses, like the Heft
Of Cathedral Tunes—

5 Heavenly Hurt, it gives us—
We can find no scar,

---

[3]In Greek mythology Proteus was a prophetic sea god who, when seized, changed shape to try to escape prophesying. Triton, the son of the sea god Poseidon, played a trumpet made of a conch shell.

But internal difference,
Where the Meanings, are—

None may teach it—Any—
10   'Tis the Seal Despair—
An imperial affliction
Sent us of the Air—

When it comes, the Landscape listens—
Shadows—hold their breath—
15   When it goes, 'tis like the Distance
On the look of Death—

Tell All the Truth but Tell It Slant (#1129)

Tell all the Truth but tell it slant—
Success in Circuit lies
Too bright for our infirm Delight
The Truth's superb surprise
5   As Lightning to the Children eased
With explanation kind
The Truth must dazzle gradually
Or every man be blind—

STUDY QUESTIONS

1. Give examples of images of light and motion in these poems. How are the two types of images connected?
2. Give examples of lines or phrases that you think are particularly good examples of compression. How is Dickinson creating this effect? For what purpose is she using it?
3. What does being human seem to mean in these poems? What aspects of our nature are being emphasized? (Note that we as readers are definitely included in these descriptions of what being human entails. How are we brought into them?)

14

WORD CHOICE:
MEANINGS AND SUGGESTIONS

Common Phrases and New Meanings

Our study of ballads gave us insight into the use of repetition and selectivity in poetry, and thus into poetry's balance of narrative and rhythmic patterns. We saw that poetry is based on the combination of satisfying sounds and sharply focused content. And we saw how the pattern of sounds and words created by the skillful use of rhythm, repetition, and word-sound can be used to heighten the effect of compression or to set a mood.

But ballads could not tell us a great deal about word choice in poetry. For ballads, like other oral poetry, tend to rely on a shared vocabulary of predictable phrases and stock epithets. Hearing ballads, we recognize in them traditional terms, pairings, and comparisons: "my true-love," "my hawks and my hounds," "the sun and the moon," "as red as the blood," and "as dead as the stones." We are not meant to linger on any of them, or on any particular line. Rather, we let each recognized phrase add its bit to mood or situation but reserve our main attention for the pattern made by the story as it unfolds.

In written poetry, on the other hand, word choice is all-important. The play on words by which Shakespeare blends spring, songs, and rings to create an atmosphere (p. 349) and the indelicate verb *snores* with which Cullen mocks his "lady's" pretensions to gentility (p. 358) testify to the power of the well-chosen word. The words themselves are not unusual ones; but they surprise us when they appear, nonetheless. They call on us to pay attention and reward us for our attention by bringing their overtones of meaning and suggestion into the poem, enriching our enjoyment and understanding.

The language of poetry, then, is not necessarily composed of strange, unusual, or uniquely "poetic" words. More often, poetry gains its effects through unexpected juxtapositions of common words, bringing new meaning into the ordinary. Look, for instance, at this poem by Emily Dickinson, and consider how the poet gives significance to the simplest language.

The Bustle in a House (#1078)

The Bustle in a House
The Morning after Death
Is solemnest of industries
Enacted upon Earth—

5   The Sweeping up the Heart
And putting Love away
We shall not want to use again
Until Eternity.

The language of the first stanza is almost like prose. A few extra words, and it would be a simple prose statement: The bustle that takes place in a house, the day after someone who lived there has died, represents one of the most solemn tasks on earth. (The word *industries* may seem a bit strange in this context. At the time this poem was written, however, it was used to denote any sort of labor, just as the word *industrious* does today.)

In the second stanza, however, we notice a change. Here the poet is amplifying her first statement. She is explaining that the "bustle" is caused by the housecleaning that takes place between a death and the funeral, and that it is "solemn" because the workers must reconcile themselves to the loss of a loved one. In fact, the workers are coming to grips with their emotions even as they do the chores.

She does not, however, resort to wordy explanations. Rather, she combines housework and emotions in a tightly compressed pair of images. The verbs of the second stanza speak of housecleaning matters; the nouns, of love. It is not dust that is swept up, but "the heart"; not blankets to be put away, but "love." The combination conveys the sense of loss. "The sweeping up the heart," in particular, suggests that the heart is broken, is in pieces; and the thought of a broken heart, in turn, suggests grief.

But the poet also says that the grief and loss are not permanent. "Love" is not thrown away, but rather "put away" to be used again on a future occasion. "Until eternity": the phrase suggests a fearfully long wait, but insists, nonetheless, that the waiting will end. "Eternity" thus balances "earth," tempering the present sense of loss with faith in restoration. And in that balance the poem ends and rests.

Here is another poem by Dickinson that is notable for its unusual use of words. How would you analyze it?

Because I Could Not Stop for Death (#712)

Because I could not stop for Death—
He kindly stopped for me—
The Carriage held but just Ourselves—
And Immortality.

Again, the following poem presents a straightforward statement. But here the language is slightly richer, the play on words is more pronounced, and the words take on more resonance of meaning. Discuss the poem and its language. How does the choice of words give the poem more impact than its main statement, "Many friends of mine have died," would have?

A. E. Housman

(1859–1936)

With Rue My Heart Is Laden

With rue my heart is laden
   For golden friends I had,
For many a rose-lipt maiden
   And many a lightfoot lad.

5 By brooks too broad for leaping
   The lightfoot boys are laid;
The rose-lipt girls are sleeping
   In fields where roses fade.

STUDY QUESTIONS

1. What repetitions do you find in the poem? How does the second stanza develop the images begun in the first stanza?
2. How does the word *golden* in line 2 fit into the mood and imagery?
3. Note the heavy use of "r" and "l" sounds. What effect does the alliteration of these sounds produce? What other examples of alliteration can you find in the poem? How would you summarize your view of Housman's choice of words for sound and sense?

The next poem presents a wish or desire and paints a scene representing the fulfillment of the wish. Note how the poem creates a simple and direct, yet powerful, evocation of scene and mood. Note the use of details, of images that appeal to sight and hearing, touch and motion, and the use of rhyme, rhythm, and alliteration.

Gerard Manley Hopkins

(1844–1889)

Heaven–Haven

A Nun Takes the Veil

I have desired to go
　　Where springs not fail,
To fields where flies no sharp and sided hail
　　And a few lilies blow.

5　　And I have asked to be
　　　　Where no storms come,
Where the green swell is in the havens dumb,
　　And out of the swing of the sea.

STUDY QUESTIONS

1. Can you explain the poem's title? Is the subtitle necessary for an understanding of the poem?
2. Each stanza in this poem describes a different scene, a different location. What links the two together? How do these scenes develop the subject set out in the poem's title?
3. Notice the differences between the structure of these sentences and that of normal English; notice also the spareness of the form and imagery (even down to the "few lilies" in the fourth line) and the relatively heavy use of alliteration. How do these contribute to the poem's effect?

The next two poems are written in **free verse,** a verse form invented in the early twentieth century. Free verse is marked by uneven line lengths and often by the absence of rhyme, as well. Note how these poems mix repetition and compression to create their very different effects.

Carl Sandburg

(1878–1967)

Cool Tombs

When Abraham Lincoln was shoveled into the tombs, he forgot the copperheads and the assassin . . . in the dust, in the cool tombs.
And Ulysses Grant lost all thought of con men and Wall Street, cash and collateral turned ashes . . . in the dust, in the cool tombs.

Pocahontas' body, lovely as a poplar, sweet as a red haw in November or a paw-
paw in May, did she wonder? does she remember? . . . in the dust, in the cool
tombs?

Take any streetful of people buying clothes and groceries, cheering a hero or
throwing confetti and blowing tin horns . . . tell me if the lovers are los-
ers . . . tell me if any get more than the lovers . . . in the dust . . . in the cool
tombs.

STUDY QUESTIONS

1. What images are associated with each person? Why have they been chosen?
   What do they suggest?
2. Is there a message to the poem? If so, what is it? How does the poem travel
   from its opening statements to its final suggestions?
3. How would you describe the sound of this poem? the rhythm? How do
   sound and rhythm fit the meaning of the poem? How do they create its
   mood?

Ezra Pound

(1885–1972)

These Fought in Any Case[3]

These fought in any case,
and some believing,
        pro domo,[4] in any case . . .

Some quick to arm,
5 some for adventure,
some from fear of weakness,
some from fear of censure,
some for love of slaughter, in imagination,
learning later . . .
10 some in fear, learning love of slaughter;

Died some, pro patria,
        non "dulce" non "et decor"[5] . . .
walked eye-deep in hell

---

[3]Section IV from "E. P. Ode pour L'Election de Son Sépulcre" ("E. P. Ode on the Selection of His
Tomb")
[4]"for homeland"
[5]an ironic allusion to Horace's famous line: "Dulce et decorum est pro patria mori" ("It is sweet and
fitting to die for one's country")

believing in old men's lies, then unbelieving
15 came home, home to a lie,
    home to many deceits,
    home to old lies and new infamy;
    usury age-old and age-thick
    and liars in public places.

20 Daring as never before, wastage as never before.
    Young blood and high blood,
    fair cheeks, and fine bodies;

    fortitude as never before

    frankness as never before,
25 disillusions as never told in the old days,
    hysterias, trench confessions,
    laughter out of dead bellies.

STUDY QUESTIONS

1. How would you describe the tone of voice in this poem? What do the repetitions contribute to it? the word choice? Give examples to prove your assertions.
2. What attitude does the poem suggest toward the soldiers of which it speaks? Is the attitude simple or complex? How is it suggested?
3. What of the poem's attitude toward war in general?
4. An **ode** is a poem of irregular form. How does Pound use irregularity of form to reinforce the suggestions his poem makes?
5. Although "Cool Tombs" and "These Fought in Any Case" are both written in free verse and make heavy use of repetition, the **tone** and **pace** of the two poems are completely different. Why?

The words in this final poem deserve special notice. Their underlying tone and syntax are more casual and friendly than any we have met so far. And yet Cummings has taken enormous liberties with words and syntax alike, even to the point of inventing new words and positioning each word individually on the page. To what new responses does the resulting poem seem to invite you?

E. E. Cummings

(1894–1963)

in Just-

in Just-
spring   when the world is mud-
luscious the little
lame balloonman

5 whistles   far   and wee

and eddieandbill come
running from marbles and
piracies and it's
spring

10 when the world is puddle-wonderful

the queer
old balloonman whistles
far   and   wee
and bettyandisbel come dancing

15 from hop-scotch and jump-rope and

it's
spring
and
    the

20   goat-footed

balloonMan   whistles
far
and
wee

STUDY QUESTIONS

1. In analyzing this poem, we may begin with its wordplay. How do compound words such as *mud-luscious* and *puddle-wonderful* affect the sound and meaning of the lines in which they occur? How many meanings does the word *wee* have, and what is the effect of using it? The balloon-man is described through incremental repetition, beginning as "lame" and ending as "goat-footed." Why goat-footed?

2. We may then note two unusual rhythmic devices: the breaking of lines in the middle of words or phrases, and the spacing out or running together of words. And we may ask how these affect the sound and mood of the poem, and our sense of the scene it describes.

3. Then we may put this play with words and rhythms together with the poem's use of names and detail, and ask how Cummings creates and enhances his description. What does the intent of the poem seem to be? What message does it seem to carry? How do the sound and word choices create the tone and the message?

The Speaker in the Poem

15

THE SPEAKER'S VOICE

We have said that ballads, being traditional, oral poetry, rely on common words and images rather than on the unique images of written poetry. We may now make one final distinction by remarking that this stylization of ballads leaves these songs lacking uniquely memorable voices. A deserted lover in one ballad, for instance, sounds much like a deserted lover in any other ballad. They will speak at least some of the same words in the same tones and rhythms. This is not the case in written poetry, where we would take the appearance of a lover who sounds like any other lover as the sign of a second-rate poem. If we read twenty lyrics about love—or even twenty lyrics about lost love—we expect to hear twenty different voices.

This reflection brings us to one of the basic paradoxes of poetry. Because of its use of rhythm and sound patterns, the language of poetry may be the farthest of all literary languages from everyday speech. Yet the voices within poems are the most intimate of literary voices, speaking to us most vividly and directly and conveying to us most openly the speakers' deepest and most immediate emotions. No other form of literature demands so much care and craft in its writing as poetry; yet no other form can seem to present the spontaneous flow of emotion as convincingly as poetry can.

Because poetry can so thoroughly convince us that in responding to it we are sharing a genuine, strongly felt emotion, it can attract our strongest response. Subjectively, this is good; it represents poetry doing what it should do. Objectively, however, poetry's seeming frankness raises the critical danger that we may mistake the voice within the poem for the voice of the poet. The further danger then arises that we may generalize from a single poem, slipping from the critically acceptable statement "Dickinson's *There's a Certain Slant of Light* is a poem about depression" to the unacceptable "as *There's a Certain Slant of Light* shows, Dickinson was always depressed."

We cannot fall into this error so easily in drama or fiction, where the number of characters and the abundance of circumstantial detail continually warn us of the distance between author and work. Poetry, however, often has but one voice in a poem. The voice often speaks in the first person: "Oh, how that glittering taketh me!" And the intensity of emotion that is felt only in the climatic scenes of fiction and drama may illuminate an entire lyric. This combination of single voice, first person, and unflagging intensity of emotion often obliterates the distance between the poet and speaker. If the speaker than gives us the slightest hint that he or she may represent the poet, we become all too willing to make the identification.

But we must not make the identification so simply. We can speak of a poet's voice—can compare Poe's voice to Dickinson's, for example. But when we do this we must compare all the voices from at least a dozen of Poe's poems to all the voices from an equal number of Dickinson's. We can then speak either of a range of voices that seems typical of each poet or of some specific characteristics that remain constant through all their individual voices. Moreover, we may equally well make comparisons between voices belonging to a single poet—comparing the voices of Poe's early poems to those of his later poems, for instance—which we could not do if the voice in each poem were the poet's only voice.

To further emphasize this distance between speaker and poet, we may look again at poems such as *We Real Cool* and *Sir Patrick Spens*. They seem to speak to us as directly and to be as immediately felt as any other poems, but we know no author for *Sir Patrick Spens* and are sure that Gwendolyn Brooks is not seven adolescents in a pool hall.

The poem is the poet's vision, nothing more. Its speakers may be inside the action (as in *Upon Julia's Clothes*) or outside it (as in *The Cherry-Tree Carol*). They may have elements of the poet's own situation or emotions in them, or they may not. But they are speakers and not writers; they are the poet's creations and not the poet's self.

For discussing speakers who *do* seem to mirror their poets, we have the useful critical term **persona**. The speakers of Browning's *My Last Duchess*, of Frost's *Birches*, and of Levertov's *At David's Grave* may be called their poets' personae. Personae represent one aspect of their poet's personality or experience, isolated from the rest of the poet's life, dramatized, and re-created through art. Poets—like all human beings—are complex and changeable. Personae are simpler: fixed, changeless, and slightly exaggerated. Unlike their makers, who must respond to the many demands of the everyday world in which they live, personae exist only within their poems and respond only to the thoughts and sensations that gave the poems birth.

Here, for the further study of speakers in poetry, are eleven poems. Most of these poems employ speakers who might well be spoken of as personae, but at least one has a speaker who cannot be so described. Be aware, as you read these poems, of sound and language and total effect. But pay most attention to the characterization of the speakers and to the varying voices with which they speak.

Theodore Roethke

(1908–1963)

My Papa's Waltz

The whiskey on your breath
Could make a small boy dizzy;
But I hung on like death:
Such waltzing was not easy.

5 We romped until the pans
Slid from the kitchen shelf;
My mother's countenance
Could not unfrown itself.

The hand that held my wrist
10 Was battered on one knuckle;
At every step you missed
My right ear scraped a buckle.

You beat time on my head
With a palm caked hard by dirt,
15 Then waltzed me off to bed
Still clinging to your shirt.

I Knew a Woman

I knew a woman, lovely in her bones,
When small birds sighed, she would sigh back at them;
Ah, when she moved, she moved more ways than one:
The shapes a bright container can contain!
5 Of her choice virtues only gods should speak,
Or English poets who grew up on Greek
(I'd have them sing in chorus, cheek to cheek).

How well her wishes went! She stroked my chin,
She taught me Turn, and Counter-turn, and Stand;[1]
10 She taught me Touch, that undulant white skin;
I nibbled meekly from her proffered hand;
She was the sickle; I, poor I, the rake,
Coming behind her for her pretty sake
(But what prodigious mowing we did make).

15 Love likes a gander, and adores a goose:
Her full lips pursed, the errant note to seize;

---

[1]terms for the three parts of a Pindaric ode

She played it quick, she played it light and loose;
My eyes, they dazzled at her flowing knees;
Her several parts could keep a pure repose,
20 Or one hip quiver with a mobile nose
(She moved in circles, and those circles moved).

Let seed be grass, and grass turn into hay:
I'm martyr to a motion not my own;
What's freedom for? To know eternity.
25 I swear she cast a shadow white as stone.
But who would count eternity in days?
These old bones live to learn her wanton ways:
(I measure time by how a body sways).

STUDY QUESTIONS

1. What is the subject of each of these poems? What is the emotional state of the speaker?
2. How does the language of the two poems compare? What sort of images does each use? How does the language match the subject and mood in each?
3. How would you characterize the speaker of each poem? What would you have to say to move from a characterization of the speakers to a characterization of the poet?

Edna St. Vincent Millay

(1892–1950)

What Lips My Lips Have Kissed, and Where, and Why

What lips my lips have kissed, and where, and why,
I have forgotten, and what arms have lain
Under my head till morning; but the rain
Is full of ghosts tonight, that tap and sigh
5 Upon the glass and listen for reply,
And in my heart there stirs a quiet pain
For unremembered lads that not again
Will turn to me at midnight with a cry.
Thus in the winter stands the lonely tree,
10 Nor knows what birds have vanished one by one,
Yet knows its boughs more silent than before:
I cannot say what loves have come and gone,
I only know that summer sang in me
A little while, that in me sings no more.

Nikki Giovanni

(1943–   )

You Are There

i shall save my poems
for the winter of my dreams
i look forward to huddling
in my rocker with my life
5   i wonder what i'll contemplate
lovers—certainly those

i can remember
and knowing my life
you'll be there

10   you'll be there in the cold
like a Siamese on my knee
proud purring when you let me stroke you

you'll be there in the rain
like an umbrella over my head
15   sheltering me from the damp mist

you'll be there in the dark
like a lighthouse in the fog
seeing me through troubled waters

you'll be there in the sun
20   like coconut oil on my back
to keep me from burning

i shall save a special poem
for you to say
you always made me smile
25   and even though i cried sometimes
you said i will not let you
down

my rocker and i on winter's porch
will never be sad if you're gone
30   the winter's cold has been stored
against
you will always be
there

STUDY QUESTIONS

1. "What My Lips Have Kissed, and Where, and Why" and "You Are There" concern the same subject: a woman remembering her former lovers. The voices of the speakers of the two poems, however, sound decidedly different. Characterize each voice, paying special attention to the figurative language each speaker employs.
2. Does there seem to be much distance between the poets and the voices of their personae in these poems?

John Crowe Ransom

(1888–1974)

Bells for John Whiteside's Daughter

There was such speed in her little body,
And such lightness in her footfall,
It is no wonder her brown study
Astonishes us all.

5 Her wars were bruited in our high window.
We looked among orchard trees and beyond
Where she took arms against her shadow,
Or harried unto the pond

The lazy geese, like a snow cloud
10 Dripping their snow on the green grass,
Tricking and stopping, sleepy and proud,
Who cried in goose, Alas,

For the tireless heart within the little
Lady with rod that made them rise
15 From their noon apple-dreams and scuttle
Goose-fashion under the skies!

But now go the bells, and we are ready,
In one house we are sternly stopped
To say we are vexed at her brown study,
20 Lying so primly propped.

STUDY QUESTIONS

1. What ironies and paradoxes arise in the poem?
2. What is the speaker's tone as he or she notes these ironies and paradoxes?

3. What is the little girl's "brown study"? Why does the narrator employ this unusual euphemism?

Robert Hayden

(1913–1980)

Mourning Poem for the Queen of Sunday

Lord's lost Him His mockingbird,
His fancy warbler;
Satan sweet-talked her,
four bullets hushed her.

5   Who would have thought
she'd end that way?

Four bullets hushed her. And the world a-clang with evil.
Who's going to make old hardened sinner men tremble now
and the righteous rock?
10 Oh who and oh who will sing Jesus down
to help with struggling and doing without and being colored
all through blue Monday?
Till way next Sunday?

All those angels

15   in their cretonne clouds and finery

the true believer saw
when she rared back her head and sang,
all those angels are surely weeping.
Who would have thought

20   she'd end that way?

Four holes in her heart. The gold works wrecked.
But she looks so natural in her big bronze coffin
among the Broken Hearts and Gates-Ajar,
it's as if any moment she'd lift her head
25 from its pillow of chill gardenias
and turn this quiet into shouting Sunday
and make folks forget what she did on Monday.

Oh, Satan sweet-talked her,
and four bullets hushed her.

30   Lord's lost Him His diva,

His fancy warbler's gone.
Who would have thought,
who would have thought she'd end that way?

STUDY QUESTIONS

1. How does "Mourning Poem for the Queen of Sunday" parallel Ransom's "Bells for John Whiteside's Daughter" in terms of situation, irony, paradox, and tone? How does it differ?
2. How does the poem use a balladlike repetition of key phrases and refrain?
3. Speculate on what the Queen of Sunday "did on Monday" to bring about her murder. How do the Queen of Sunday's paradoxical qualities fit into the theology of the poem?

Denise Levertov

(1923–   )

At David's Grave

for B. and H. F.

Yes, he is here in this
open field, in sunlight, among
the few young trees set out
to modify the bare facts—

5 he's here, but only
because we are here.
When we go, he goes with us

to be your hands that never
do violence, your eyes
10 that wonder, your lives

that daily praise life
by living it, by laughter.

He is never alone here,
never cold in the field of graves.

STUDY QUESTIONS

1. Like the previous two poems, "At David's Grave" is an elegy, a lament for one who has died. What compensations for the loss of the loved one does the speaker of the poem find?
2. What is the significance of the phrase "the bare facts"?

William Butler Yeats

(1865–1939)

The Folly of Being Comforted

One that is ever kind said yesterday:
"Your well-belovèd's hair has threads of gray,
And little shadows come about her eyes;
Time can but make it easier to be wise
5 Though now it seem impossible, and so
All that you need is patience."
                           Heart cries, "No,
I have not a crumb of comfort, not a grain.
Time can but make her beauty over again:
Because of that great nobleness of hers
10 The fire that stirs about her, when she stirs,
Burns but more clearly. O she had not these ways
When all the wild summer was in her gaze."

O heart! O heart! if she'd but turn her head,
You'd know the folly of being comforted.

STUDY QUESTIONS

1. To whom does this lover speak?
2. In what situation does he find himself? What is his reaction to the situation? What emotions and/or thoughts does he express?
3. How do the form and language of the poem, together with the emotion and situation represented, create your picture of each of this lover?

The next poem represents a form known as **dramatic monologue.** After you have read the poem, answer the following questions:

1. Who is the speaker?
2. To whom is he speaking? On what occasion?
3. What does the speaker tell you about his own character? How does he do so?
4. What do you think happened to the "last duchess"?
5. If you were the person being addressed, how would you feel at the end of the monologue?

Robert Browning

(1812–1889)

My Last Duchess

Ferrara

That's my last duchess painted on the wall,
Looking as if she were alive. I call
That piece a wonder, now: Frà Pandolf's[2] hands
Worked busily a day, and there she stands.
5 Will't please you sit and look at her? I said
"Frà Pandolf" by design, for never read
Strangers like you that pictured countenance,
The depth and passion of its earnest glance,
But to myself they turned (since none puts by
10 The curtain I have drawn for you, but I)
And seemed as they would ask me, if they durst,
How such a glance came there; so, not the first
Are you to turn and ask thus. Sir, 'twas not
Her husband's presence only, called that spot
15 Of joy into the Duchess' cheek: perhaps
Frà Pandolf chanced to say "Her mantle laps
"Over my lady's wrist too much," or "Paint
"Must never hope to reproduce the faint
"Half-flush that dies along her throat": such stuff
20 Was courtesy, she thought, and cause enough
For calling up that spot of joy. She had
A heart—how shall I say?—too soon made glad,
Too easily impressed; she liked whate'er
She looked on, and her looks went everywhere.
25 Sir, 'twas all one! My favor at her breast,
The dropping of the daylight in the West,
The bough of cherries some officious fool
Broke in the orchard for her, the white mule
She rode with round the terrace—all and each
30 Would draw from her alike the approving speech,
Or blush, at least. She thanked men—good! but thanked
Somehow—I know not how—as if she ranked
My gift of a nine-hundred-years-old name
With anybody's gift. Who'd stoop to blame

---

[2]a fictitious artist, as is Claus of Innsbruck in the last line

35 This sort of trifling? Even had you skill
In speech—which I have not—to make your will
Quite clear to such an one, and say, "Just this
"Or that in you disgusts me; here you miss,
"Or there exceed the mark"—and if she let
40 Herself be lessoned so, nor plainly set
Her wits to yours, forsooth, and made excuse,
—E'en then would be some stooping; and I choose
Never to stoop. Oh sir, she smiled, no doubt,
Whene'er I passed her; but who passed without
45 Much the same smile? This grew; I gave commands;
Then all smiles stopped together. There she stands
As if alive. Will 't please you rise? We'll meet
The company below, then. I repeat,
The Count your master's known munificence
50 Is ample warrant that no just pretense
Of mine for dowry will be disallowed;
Though his fair daughter's self, as I avowed
At starting, is my object. Nay, we'll go
Together down, sir. Notice Neptune, though,
55 Taming a sea-horse, thought a rarity,
Which Claus of Innsbruck cast in bronze for me!

Robert Frost

(1874–1963)

Birches

When I see birches bend to left and right
Across the lines of straighter darker trees,
I like to think some boy's been swinging them.
But swinging doesn't bend them down to stay
5 As ice-storms do. Often you must have seen them
Loaded with ice a sunny winter morning
After a rain. They click upon themselves
As the breeze rises, and turn many-colored
As the stir cracks and crazes their enamel.
10 Soon the sun's warmth makes them shed crystal shells
Shattering and avalanching on the snowcrust—
Such heaps of broken glass to sweep away
You'd think the inner dome of heaven had fallen.
They are dragged to the withered bracken by the load,

15 And they seem not to break; though once they are bowed
    So low for long, they never right themselves:
    You may see their trunks arching in the woods
    Years afterwards, trailing their leaves on the ground
    Like girls on hands and knees that throw their hair
20 Before them over their heads to dry in the sun.
    But I was going to say when Truth broke in
    With all her matter-of-fact about the ice-storm,
    I should prefer to have some boy bend them
    As he went out and in to fetch the cows—
25 Some boy too far from town to learn baseball,
    Whose only play was what he found himself,
    Summer or winter, and could play alone.
    One by one he subdued his father's trees
    By riding them down over and over again
30 Until he took the stiffness out of them,
    And not one but hung limp, not one was left
    For him to conquer. He learned all there was
    To learn about not launching out too soon
    And so not carrying the tree away
35 Clear to the ground. He always kept his poise
    To the top branches, climbing carefully
    With the same pains you use to fill a cup
    Up to the brim, and even above the brim.
    Then he flung outward, feet first, with a swish,
40 Kicking his way down through the air to the ground.
    So was I once myself a swinger of birches.
    And so I dream of going back to be.
    It's when I'm weary of considerations,
    And life is too much like a pathless wood
45 Where your face burns and tickles with the cobwebs
    Broken across it, and one eye is weeping
    From a twig's having lashed across it open.
    I'd like to get away from earth awhile
    And then come back to it and begin over.
50 May no fate willfully misunderstand me
    And half grant what I wish and snatch me away
    Not to return. Earth's the right place for love:
    I don't know where it's likely to go better.
    I'd like to go by climbing a birch tree,
55 And climb black branches up a snow-white trunk,
    Toward heaven, till the tree could bear no more,
    But dipped its top and set me down again.

That would be good both going and coming back.
One could do worse than be a swinger of birches.

STUDY QUESTIONS

1. Frost is famous for creating speakers with apparently simple, plain-spoken, matter-of-fact voices; yet his speakers usually work their way around to thinking about deeply philosophical issues. How is this the case in "Birches"?
2. A clue that Frost hints at an underlying sexual theme in "Birches" is his persona's description of the bent-over trees as looking "Like girls on hands and knees that throw their hair/Before them over their heads to dry in the sun." Discuss how the apparently literal descriptions of the birches take on metaphoric meanings that give the reader a sense of complexity rather than simplicity in the speaker's voice.

Simon Ortiz

(1941–   )

Notes For My Child

July 5, 1973, when she was born

Wake slow this morning.

Hear Joy moan,
stir around,
and get up sometime after five.

5 Bit of morning light.

Get up and wash,
put on two days-old coffee.

Later,
we walk for you
10 over to University Drug.

Sun slants
through trees,
cool morning.

See two cicadas.
15 One is dead,
the other is buzzing

trying to take off
from the sidewalk.

I want to turn back
20 and help it
to fly again,
but I realize
the inevitable.

Yesterday,
25 while chopping weeds,
I uncovered two chrysalis,
the cicadas within them
curled, soft yet.

We get to the hospital.
30 The taxi driver says, "Good luck."
"Okay, thanks." Smiling nervous.

Hospitals are consistent.
Crummy. We wait
for someone to notice us.

35 I tell Joy
to make herself visible.
She can't be anymore visible
she thinks than now,
her belly sticking out.

40 I ask where my wheelchair is
when Joy gets in hers
and is pushed down the hall
and into an elevator
by a fat unsmiling aide
45 who doesn't think
I am funny at all.

Upstairs and down a hall,
and Joy disappears
behind some doors.

50 I squat on the tile floor,
remember a poem Joy has written
about the story teller.

The aide walks by.
She smiles this time

55 and says, "Okay."
I say, "Okay," too.

Seven other people wait
and make small talk.
A couple of women
60 are rolled by.

I smile at the six women
and one guy.
A couple smile back.

When the women roll by
65 everything becomes somber
and slow.

. . . the Wisconsin Horse
is silent, looks through
the chainlink fence,
70 the construction going on
a mile away. . . .

Finally,
I get to join Joy.
She's getting anxious.
75 Can tell in her eyes,
movements, tremble
about her mouth.

A nurse tells me
to go to Admitting.
80 A girl asks me a question.
"Are you the responsible party?"
I say, "Yes."
She means money, of course.
Who's going to pay?
85 I mean I'm the father
of the child bringing life
and continuance.

I go back upstairs.
A woman on the other side
90 of the room moans a bit,
struggles in her sheets.
An older woman holds her hand.

Joy is pretty relaxed,
takes deep breaths
95 to make it easier.
Amazing how anyone can relax
at the eve of birth—
only a step along the way,
of course.
100 I ask Joy if it hurts,
realize it's a dumb
but important question.

A doctor comes along
and puts a plastic machine
105 upon Joy's belly
and flicks it on.
The doctor calls it
a doptone and says,
"Don't ask me why it's called that.
110 I don't know. It runs on batteries."

I call it
steady, gentle beating noises
called flesh, bones, blood,
runs on mysteries, dreams,
115 the coming child.

I am hungry now
but the hospital atmosphere
prevents any real hunger.
The repressiveness of institutions
120 has trained my stomach.
Tell myself to relax and say,
"When you come out, child,
let's go dance in a while, okay?"

Look out the window
125 and see the sun
and the parking lot.

Remember I wanted to write
something about that old dog,
kind of skinny and pathetic,
130 been hanging around our home
for a while, a week or so,
write a story or poem about it.

And then she was born.

. . . I will tell her
135 about the Wisconsin Horse. . . .

She was born then.

"She's as pretty as a silver dollar,"
said Ed Marlow, a miner
in Eastern Kentucky about Caroline Kennedy.
140 "She's just plain folks."

Albermarle County Sheriff says,
"We found nekkid women
with nekkid pubic hair offensive."

July 5, 1973 is now and soon enough

145 You come forth
the color of a stone cliff
at dawn,
changing colors,
blue to red,
150 to all the colors of the earth.

Grandmother Spider speaks
laughter and growing
and weaving things and threading them
together to make life to wear,
155 all these, all these.

You come out, child,
naked as that cliff at sunrise,
shorn of anything
except spots of your mother's blood.
160 You kept blinking your eyes
and trying to catch your breath.

In five more days,
they will come,
singing, dancing,
165 bringing gifts,
the stones with voices,
the plants with bells.
They will come.

Child, they will come.

STUDY QUESTIONS

1. Why does Ortiz make his poem conversational, even prosaic?
2. What tensions arise in the poem between the personal and public spheres, between different cultures, between people in different economic circumstances?
3. What is the mysterious "Wisconsin Horse"? Does the poem tell us enough to know for sure? If not, why?
4. At the end of the poem the speaker assures the newborn child that "they will come." Who are "they"?

16

THE SPEAKER'S VISION

Like other writers, poets find their visions in three basic sources: the world around them, their own experiences, and their inner vision of what is or might be. The speakers of their poems, who are charged with communicating these visions, may therefore be observers, recording scenes and experiences for our mutual pleasure and insight; or they may be visionaries, recasting real or imagined scenes to produce a new vision for our sharing.

We can see the distinction clearly enough in poems we have already read. For instance, we have already seen two types of reporters at work. The speakers in "Get Up and Bar the Door" and "The Cherry-Tree Carol" are most obviously reporters; they simply tell us what occurred and let us draw our own conclusions about it. The speakers of "We Real Cool" and "For a Lady I Know" are also reporters but are less obviously so, because we sense that the poets are not as objective as their speakers. The speakers provide no interpretation and show no emotion. But the poets' attitudes come through, nonetheless. Indeed, much of the effectiveness of these poems comes from the disparity between the speakers' objectivity and the poets' concern, a disparity felt by the reader as irony. But that is a subject we will speak of more thoroughly in the next chapter.

We can also recall poems in which the speaker was primarily a visionary; Dickinson's poems come to mind here. "Tell All the Truth" is pure vision, having no objective scene or experience whatever as its starting point. Another visionary is the speaker of Pound's "These Fought in Any Case," who draws on visions of so many real or imagined soldiers that we soon lose all sense of individuals in the more compelling vision of the war itself. Maya Angelou's "On the Pulse of the Morning" not only briefly encapsulates all of human history but even goes back in geological time to the period of the dinosaurs, "who left dried tokens/Of their sojourn here/On our planet floor. . . ." The poem emphasizes that behind even the simplest act of someone's saying "Good morning" is the whole complex history of life on the planet.

These, then, are poems that mark the two extremes of the speaker's stance: the objective extreme and the visionary extreme. Between them come those poems (probably typical of the majority of poems) in which the speaker is both reporter and interpreter. These poems balance what is seen and what is felt, allowing neither to overwhelm the other. Their speakers report on what is happening while explaining or suggesting its implications. Thus "There's a Certain Slant of Light" conveys its atmospheric sensation most vividly by interpreting its spiritual overtones. And poems such as "in Just-," and "I Knew a Woman" blend recollection and response so perfectly that it's hard to say where one stops and the other begins. Through the speaker's emotional response, the vision is made real for us; reporter, responder, and interpreter are one.

The poems we shall look at in this chapter blend objective and visionary stances, observation and interpretation. Take careful note of the speaker's character and stance within each poem. Before you answer any of the questions, make sure you know what sort of person is speaking, to what the speaker is responding, and how much of the speaker's response is to things outside himself or herself and how much to inner visions or emotions.

William Wordsworth

(1770–1850)

I Wandered Lonely As a Cloud

I wandered lonely as a cloud
That floats on high o'er vales and hills,
When all at once I saw a crowd,
A host, of golden daffodils;
5 Beside the lake, beneath the trees,
Fluttering and dancing in the breeze.

Continuous as the stars that shine
And twinkle on the Milky Way,
They stretched in never-ending line
10 Along the margin of a bay:
Ten thousand saw I at a glance,
Tossing their heads in sprightly dance.

The waves beside them danced; but they
Outdid the sparkling waves in glee;
15 A poet could not but be gay,
In such a jocund company;
I gazed—and gazed—but little thought
What wealth the show to me had brought:

For oft, when on my couch I lie
20 In vacant or in pensive mood,
They flash upon that inward eye
Which is the bliss of solitude;
And then my heart with pleasure fills,
And dances with the daffodils.

STUDY QUESTIONS

1. The major presence in this poem is that of the "host of golden daffodils"
   seen by the poet-speaker. How does the speaker describe and characterize
   the daffodils? What words and images does he use for them? How many of
   these words and images would normally be used for people?

   How active a role do the daffodils play in this vision—in the original
   scene and in their repeated appearances?
2. How does the speaker describe himself? What images does he use? In what
   activities does he depict himself? How active is his role in his relationship
   with the daffodils? in relation to the poem itself?

John Keats

(1795–1821)

When I Have Fears

When I have fears that I may cease to be
  Before my pen has gleaned my teeming brain,
Before high-piled books, in charactery,[1]
  Hold like rich garners the full ripened grain;
5 When I behold, upon the night's starred face,
  Huge cloudy symbols of a high romance,
And think that I may never live to trace
  Their shadows, with the magic hand of chance;
And when I feel, fair creature of an hour,
10   That I shall never look upon thee more,
Never have relish in the faery power
  Of unreflecting love;—then on the shore
Of the wide world I stand alone, and think
Till love and fame to nothingness do sink.

STUDY QUESTIONS

1. Because the whole poem is one sentence, its syntax gets a bit complicated. Let's start, therefore, by examining it clause by clause, beginning with the three "when" clauses that make up the first eleven and a half lines of the poem: What are the first four lines concerned with? the second four? the third? How are the three tied together? (Who is the "fair creature of an hour"? Why might the speaker call her so at this point in the poem?)

2. What overtones do words like *rich, romance, magic,* and *faery* give to the poem? What contrast do they suggest between the poet's wishes and his sense of reality?

3. Then look at the final clause of the sentence—the last two and a half lines. What action does it show the speaker taking? How explicit are his feelings made? What are you left to fill in?

---

[1]characters, writing

Walt Whitman

(1819–1892)

A Noiseless Patient Spider

A noiseless patient spider,
I mark'd where on a little promontory it stood isolated,
Mark'd how to explore the vacant vast surrounding,
It launch'd forth filament, filament, filament, out of itself,
5 Ever unreeling down, ever tirelessly speeding them.

And you O my soul where you stand,
Surrounded, detached, in measureless oceans of space,
Ceaselessly musing, venturing, throwing, seeking the spheres to connect them,
Till the bridge you will need be form'd, till the ductile anchor hold,
10 Till the gossamer thread you fling catch somewhere, O my soul.

STUDY QUESTIONS

1. Note how this poem is balanced between the first stanza, describing the speaker's vision of the spider, and the second stanza, describing his vision of his own soul. What comparison is made between the two? What characteristics and activities do they share?
2. Note that the speaker describes the spider as "isolated" and as needing or wishing "to explore the vacant vast surrounding." How apt is this as a description of an actual spider? How does it prepare the reader for the depiction of the speaker in the second stanza?

   Similarly, how apt or evocative is the description of the spider's activity? How does it complete the picture of the spider and prepare for the speaker's invocation to his soul?
3. With what words, images, and ideas does the speaker extend his vision of the spider so that it becomes a vision of his own soul's needs?
4. The poem's final lines speak of "the bridge you will need" and "the ductile anchor." What do you think these images represent? What is needed? What does the lack of detailed definition here and in the last line's "somewhere" do for your sense of the speaker's vision?

William Butler Yeats

(1865–1939)

An Irish Airman Foresees His Death[2]

I know that I shall meet my fate
Somewhere among the clouds above;
Those that I fight I do not hate,
Those that I guard I do not love;
5   My country is Kiltartan Cross,[3]
My countrymen Kiltartan's poor,
No likely end could bring them loss
Or leave them happier than before.
Nor law, nor duty bade me fight,
10   Nor public men, nor cheering crowds,
A lonely impulse of delight
Drove to this tumult in the clouds;
I balanced all, brought all to mind,
The years to come seemed waste of breath,
15   A waste of breath the years behind
In balance with this life, this death.

STUDY QUESTIONS

1. Yeats's poem is "visionary" in the sense that it foretells an event that has not yet happened. Comment on how this element of precognition adds an eerie power to the speaker's vision of the world.
2. How does the poem contrast the private motives of the speaker with the usual "public" motives for going to war? How are these motives complicated by the speaker's nationality?

Robert Frost

(1874–1963)

Two Tramps in Mud Time

Out of the mud two strangers came
And caught me splitting wood in the yard.

---

[2]Major Robert Gregory, son of Yeats's friend and patroness Lady Augusta Gregory, was killed in action in 1918.
[3]Kiltartan is an Irish village near Coole Park, the estate of the Gregorys.

And one of them put me off my aim
By hailing cheerily "Hit them hard!"
5 I knew pretty well why he dropped behind
And let the other go on a way.
I knew pretty well what he had in mind:
He wanted to take my job for pay.

Good blocks of oak it was I split,
10 As large around as the chopping block;
And every piece I squarely hit
Fell splinterless as a cloven rock.
The blows that a life of self-control
Spares to strike for the common good,
15 That day, giving a loose to my soul,
I spent on the unimportant wood.

The sun was warm but the wind was chill.
You know how it is with an April day
When the sun is out and the wind is still,
20 You're one month on in the middle of May.
But if you so much as dare to speak,
A cloud comes over the sunlit arch,
A wind comes off a frozen peak,
And you're two months back in the middle of March.

25 A bluebird comes tenderly up to alight
And turns to the wind to unruffle a plume,
His song so pitched as not to excite
A single flower as yet to bloom.
It is snowing a flake: and he half knew
30 Winter was only playing possum.
Except in color he isn't blue,
But he wouldn't advise a thing to blossom.

The water for which we may have to look
In summertime with a witching wand,
35 In every wheelrut's now a brook,
In every print of a hoof a pond.
Be glad of water, but don't forget
The lurking frost in the earth beneath
That will steal forth after the sun is set
40 And show on the water its crystal teeth.

The time when most I loved my task
These two must make me love it more
By coming with what they came to ask.

You'd think I never had felt before
45 The weight of an ax-head poised aloft,
The grip on earth of outspread feet,
The life of muscles rocking soft
And smooth and moist in vernal heat.

Out of the woods two hulking tramps
50 (From sleeping God knows where last night,
But not long since in the lumber camps).
They thought all chopping was theirs of right.
Men of the woods and lumberjacks,
They judged me by their appropriate tool.
55 Except as a fellow handled an ax
They had no way of knowing a fool.

Nothing on either side was said.
They knew they had but to stay their stay
And all their logic would fill my head:
60 As that I had no right to play
With that was another man's work for gain.
My right might be love but theirs was need.
And where the two exist in twain
Theirs was the better right—agreed.

65 But yield who will to their separation,
My object in living is to unite
My avocation and my vocation
As my two eyes make one in sight.
Only where love and need are one,
70 And the work is play for mortal stakes,
Is the deed ever really done
For Heaven and the future's sakes.

STUDY QUESTIONS

Frost's poem begins with a detailed description of an incident, and ends with as explicit a vision of the speaker's "goal in living" as we've met yet. How does this final vision grow out of the incident?

1. Consider how the speaker presents the incident: how he describes the physical scene, the tramps, his own emotions and sensations.
2. Notice the particular descriptions of the wood, sun and wind, bluebird, and water, and of the speaker himself in the sixth stanza. How do these create a sense of "love" to buttress the speaker's claim to love in the sixth and final stanzas?

3. Consider the speaker's voice: its rhythms and phrasings, its appeal to common knowledge with its audience, its blend of detailed observation and of interpretation, of seriousness and humor. What role does the voice play in determining your reaction to the poem?

4. Consider the speaker's proclamation in the final verse. How would you paraphrase it? Does it seem a fitting vision to close this poem? Is it a vision with which you yourself might be comfortable? Why or why not?

Garrett Hongo

(1951–   )

Something Whispered in the *Shakuhachi*

No one knew the secret of my flutes,
and I laugh now
because some said
I was enlightened.
5 But the truth is
I'm only a gardener
who before the War
was a dirt farmer and learned
how to grow the bamboo
10 in ditches next to the fields,
how to leave things alone
and let the silt build up
until it was deep enough to stink
bad as night soil, bad
15 as the long, witch-grey
hair of a ghost.

No secret in that.

My land was no good, rocky,
and so dry I had to sneak
20 water from the whites,
hacksaw the locks off the chutes at night,
and blame Mexicans, Filipinos,
or else some wicked spirit
of a migrant, murdered in his sleep
25 by sheriffs and wanting revenge.
Even though they never believed me,
it didn't matter—no witnesses,
and my land was never thick with rice,
only the bamboo

30 growing lush as old melodies
    and whispering like brush strokes
    against the fine scroll of wind.

    I found some string in the shed
    or else took a few stalks
35 and stripped off their skins,
    wove the fibers, the floss,
    into cords I could bind
    around the feet, ankles, and throats
    of only the best bamboos.
40 I used an ice pick for an awl,
    a fish knife to carve finger holes,
    and a scythe to shape the mouthpiece.

    I had my flutes.

    When the War came,
45 I told myself I lost nothing.
    My land, which was barren,
    was not actually mine but leased
    (we could not own property)
    and the shacks didn't matter.

50 What did were the power lines nearby
    and that sabotage was suspected.

    What mattered to me
    were the flutes I burned
    in a small fire
55 by the bath house.

    All through Relocation,
    in the desert where they put us,
    at night when the stars talked
    and the sky came down
60 and drummed against the mesas,
    I could hear my flutes
    wail like fists of wind
    whistling through the barracks.
    I came out of Camp,
65 a blanket slung over my shoulder,
    found land next to this swamp,

planted strawberries and beanplants,
planted the dwarf pines and tended them,
got rich enough to quit
70 and leave things alone,
let the ditches clog with silt again
and the bamboo grow thick as history.

So, when it's bad now,
when I can't remember what's lost
75 and all I have for the world to take
means nothing,
I go out back of the greenhouse
at the far end of my land
where the grasses go wild
80 and the arroyos come up
with cat's-claw and giant dahlias,
where the children of my neighbors
consult with the wise heads
of sunflowers, huge against the sky,
85 where the rivers of weather
and the charred ghosts of old melodies
converge to flood my land
and sustain the one thicket
of memory that calls for me
90 to come and sit
among the tall canes
and shape full-throated songs
out of wind, out of bamboo,
out of a voice
95 that only whispers.

STUDY QUESTIONS

1. Hongo's poem concerns the "relocation" of Japanese Americans to intern-
   ment camps for the duration of World War II when American officials
   feared that Japanese American citizens might commit acts of sabotage in
   support of Japan. Discuss the complex attitude of the speaker of the poem,
   who reflects back on having been in one of the camps.
2. What do his flutes symbolize?
3. What does the poem have to say about the idea of ownership—of one's land,
   one's cultural heritage, of history?

Maya Angelou

(1928–   )

On the Pulse of Morning

A Rock, a River, a Tree
Hosts to species long since departed,
Marked the mastodon,
The dinosaur, who left dried tokens
5 of their sojourn here
On our planet floor,
Any broad alarm of their hastening doom
Is lost in the gloom of dust and ages.

But today, the Rock cries out to us clearly, forcefully,
10 Come, you may stand upon my
Back and face your distant destiny,
But seek no haven in my shadow.
I will give you no hiding place down here.

You, created only a little lower than
15 The angels, have crouched too long in
The bruising darkness
Have lain too long
Face down in ignorance.
Your mouths spilling words

20 Armed for slaughter.
The Rock cries out to us today,
You may stand upon me,
But do not hide your face.

Across the wall of the world,
25 A River sings a beautiful song. It says,
Come, rest here by my side.

Each of you, a bordered country,
Delicate and strangely made proud,
Yet thrusting perpetually under siege.
30 Your armed struggles for profit
Have left collars of waste upon
My shore, currents of debris upon my breast.
Yet, today I call you to my riverside,
If you will study war no more.

35 Come, clad in peace,
And I will sing the songs

The Creator gave to me when I and the
Tree and the Rock were one.
Before cynicism was a bloody sear across your brow
40 And when you yet knew you still knew nothing.
The River sang and sings on.

There is a true yearning to respond to
The singing River and the wise Rock.
So say the Asian, the Hispanic, the Jew
45 The African, the Native American, the Sioux,
The Catholic, the Muslim, the French, the Greek,
The Irish, the Rabbi, the Priest, the Sheik,
The Gay, the Straight, the Preacher,
The privileged, the homeless, the Teacher.
50 They hear. They all hear
The speaking of the Tree.

They hear the first and last of every Tree
Speak to humankind today.
Come to me,
55 Here beside the River.
Plant yourself beside the River.

Each of you, descendant of some passed-
On traveler, has been paid for.
You, who gave me my first name, you,
60 Pawnee, Apache, Seneca, you
Cherokee Nation, who rested with me, then
Forced on bloody feet,
Left me to the employment of
Other seekers—desperate for gain,
65 Starving for gold.

You, the Turk, the Arab, the Swede,
The German, the Eskimo, the Scot,
The Italian, the Hungarian, the Pole,
You the Ashanti, the Yoruba, the Kru, bought,
70 Sold, stolen, arriving on the nightmare
Praying for a dream.

Here, root yourselves beside me.
I am that Tree planted by the River,
Which will not be moved.
75 I, the Rock, I, the River, I, the Tree
I am yours—your passages have been paid.
Lift up your faces, you have a piercing need

For this bright morning dawning for you.
History, despite its wrenching pain,
80 Cannot be unlived, but if faced
With courage, need not be lived again.
Lift up your eyes
Upon this day breaking for you.
Give birth again
85 To the dream.

Women, children, men,
Take it into the palms of your hands,
Mold it into the shape of your most
Private need. Sculpt it into
90 The image of your most public self.
Lift up your hearts
Each new hour holds new chances
For a new beginning.
Do not be wedded forever
95 To fear, yoked eternally
To brutishness.

The horizon leans forward,
Offering you space
To place new steps of change
100 Here, on the pulse of this fine day
You may have the courage
To look up and out and upon me,
The Rock, the River, the Tree, your country.
No less to Midas than the mendicant.
105 No less to you now than the mastodon then.

Here, on the pulse of this new day
You may have the grace to look up and out
And into your sister's eyes,
And into your brother's face,
110 Your country,
And say simply
Very simply
With hope—
Good morning.

STUDY QUESTIONS

1. Angelou read "On the Pulse of the Morning" during the inauguration ceremony for President Bill Clinton. The last poet invited to read at an inauguration had been Robert Frost, who read "The Gift Outright" at John F. Kennedy's swearing in as President. In what sense is "On the Pulse of the Morning" a "public" poem offering a broad vision to a wide audience?

2. How does Angelou use references to the Bible and phrases from black spiritual songs in the poem?

3. What do the rock, the river, and the tree symbolize?

4. In what sense is the poem about evolution? Does this seem odd in a poem full of biblical references?

17

PROTEST AND SOCIAL COMMENT

Protest poems do not celebrate the beautiful; they rage at ugliness—at racial ha-tred, sexual violence, cultural chauvinism, the ultimate hideousness of war. The protest poem is a cry from a wounded heart, an impassioned condemnation of injustices in a particular place and time. The narrator of such a poem is often difficult to distinguish from the author, who usually writes from an openly auto-biographical stance. The poet almost always seems to be saying: "I was there. I saw these terrible things with my own eyes—and they must not continue." This sharp location in place and time, combined with the angry passion of the poet and vivid, often disturbing language, gives poems of protest their special power. Wilfred Owen's "Dulce et Decorum Est" and Cummings's "next to of course god america i" are reactions to World War I, whereas the other poems in this chapter reflect contemporary concerns about racial strife, loss of cultural heritage, and violence against women.

Implicit in poems of protest is the idea of being in some sort of minority: Owen and Cummings were individual soldiers trying to sound warnings to their propagandized countrymen about the madness of mechanized slaughter in the trench warfare of World War I. In Audre Lorde's "Power," the speaker is obvi-ously an African American who is outraged by a white policeman's acquittal in court for shooting a ten-year-old black child to death in Queens. Joy Harjo's "Anchorage" speaks to the plight of another American minority: Native Ameri-cans who must watch Alaska taken over by corporations and all the social ills of contemporary society. Marge Piercy's "Rape Poem" graphically demonstrates that even members of a majority (women outnumber men) may have to use the protest poem as a weapon of self-defense.

Although protest poems may be open to the charge of being didactic—of subverting aesthetics to get a message across—they insist that aestheticism di-vorced from social concerns is empty at best. Moreover, although poems of protest typically sound bleak or even desparing, at the core they carry at least the implicit hope that things can get better if enough people are made aware of an injustice and are motivated to eliminate it.

Audre Lorde

(1934–1992)

Power

The difference between poetry and rhetoric
is being
ready to kill
yourself
5 instead of your children.

I am trapped on a desert of raw gunshot wounds
and a dead child dragging his shattered black
face off the edge of my sleep
blood from his punctured cheeks and shoulders
10 is the only liquid for miles and my stomach
churns at the imagined taste while
my mouth splits into dry lips
without loyalty or reason
thirsting for the wetness of his blood
15 as it sinks into the whiteness
of the desert where I am lost
without imagery or magic
trying to make power out of hatred and destruction
trying to heal my dying son with kisses
20 only the sun will bleach his bones quicker.

The policeman who shot down a 10-year-old in Queens
stood over the boy with his cop shoes in childish blood
and a voice said "Die you little motherfucker" and
there are tapes to prove that. At his trial
25 this policeman said in his own defense
"I didn't notice the size or nothing else
only the color," and
there are tapes to prove that, too.

Today that 37-year-old white man with 13 years of police forcing
30 has been set free
by 11 white men who said they were satisfied
justice had been done
and one black woman who said
"They convinced me" meaning
35 they had dragged her 4′10″ black woman's frame
over the hot coals of four centuries of white male approval
until she let go the first real power she ever had

and lined her own womb with cement
to make a graveyard for our children.

40 I have not been able to touch the destruction within me.
But unless I learn to use
the difference between poetry and rhetoric
my power too will run corrupt as poisonous mold
or lie limp and useless as an unconnected wire
45 and one day I will take my teenaged plug
and connect it to the nearest socket
raping an 85-year-old white woman
who is somebody's mother
and as I beat her senseless and set a torch to her bed
50 a greek chorus will be singing in 3/4 time
"Poor thing. She never hurt a soul. What beasts they are."

STUDY QUESTIONS

1. What does Lorde mean when she defines the difference between poetry and rhetoric as "being ready to kill/yourself/instead of your children"?
2. How does Lorde use a series of numbers to add power to the poem?
3. What does the conclusion of the poem say about how violence and injustice compound themselves—about how one wrong breeds others?

Joy Harjo

(1951–)

Anchorage

for Audre Lorde

This city is made of stone, of blood, and fish.
There are Chugach Mountains[1] to the east
and whale and seal to the west.
It hasn't always been this way, because glaciers
5 who are ice ghosts create oceans, carve earth
and shape this city here, by the sound.
They swim backwards in time.

---

[1]A range extending about 280 miles along the coast of south Alaska just above the panhandle. Chugach Eskimo (Ahtnas) reside there.

Once a storm of boiling earth cracked open
the streets, threw open the town.
10   It's quiet now, but underneath the concrete
is the cooking earth,
                            and above that, air
which is another ocean, where spirits we can't see
are dancing   joking   getting full
15   on roasted caribou, and the praying
goes on, extends out.

Nora and I go walking down 4th Avenue
and know it is all happening.
On a park bench we see someone's Athabascan[2]
20   grandmother, folded up, smelling like 200 years
of blood and piss, her eyes closed against some
unimagined darkness, where she is buried in an ache
in which nothing makes
                            sense.

25   We keep on breathing, walking, but softer now,
the clouds whirling in the air above us.
What can we say that would make us understand
better than we do already?
Except to speak of her home and claim her
30   as our own history, and know that our dreams
don't end here, two blocks away from the ocean
where our hearts still batter away at the muddy shore.

And I think of the 6th Avenue jail, of mostly Native
and Black men, where Henry told about being shot at
35   eight times outside a liquor store in L.A., but when
the car sped away he was surprised he was alive,

no bullet holes, man, and eight cartridges strewn
on the sidewalk
                    all around him.

40   Everyone laughed at the impossibility of it,
but also the truth. Because who would believe
the fantastic and terrible story of all of our survival
those who were never meant
                            to survive?

---

[2]Athabascan is a complicated but widespread Indian language, part of the Na-Dene Indian language superstock of North America. Indians speak Athabascan in the sub-Arctic interior of Alaska, along the Pacific Northwest Coast (Tlingit of Alaska panhandle, Tolowa of Oregon, and Hupa of California), and in the American Southwest (Apache and Navajo).

STUDY QUESTIONS

1. How are Anchorage's past and present contrasted?
2. One line in the poem, "Once a storm of boiling earth cracked open/the streets, threw open the town," refers to the great earthquake that struck Alaska in 1964. Why does Harjo bring in this detail?
3. How does the anecdote about the man who was shot at eight times but not hit by any of the bullets fit into the poem?

Marge Piercy

(1936–   )

Rape Poem

There is no difference between being raped
and being pushed down a flight of cement steps
except that the wounds also bleed inside.

There is no difference between being raped
5   and being run over by a truck
except that afterward men ask if you enjoyed it.

There is no difference between being raped
and being bit on the ankle by a rattlesnake
except that people ask if your skirt was short
10   and why you were out alone anyhow.

There is no difference between being raped
and going head first through a windshield
except that afterward you are afraid
not of cars
15   but half the human race.

The rapist is your boyfriend's brother.
He sits beside you in the movies eating popcorn.
Rape fattens on the fantasies of the normal male
like a maggot in garbage.

20   Fear of rape is a cold wind blowing
all of the time on a woman's hunched back.
Never to stroll alone on a sand road through pine woods,
never to climb a trail across a bald
without that aluminum in the mouth
25   when I see a man climbing toward me.

Never to open the door to a knock
without that razor just grazing the throat.

The fear of the dark side of hedges,
the back seat of the car, the empty house
30 rattling keys like a snake's warning.
The fear of the smiling man
in whose pocket is a knife.
The fear of the serious man
in whose fist is locked hatred.

35 All it takes to cast a rapist to be able to see your body
as jackhammer, as blowtorch, as adding-machine-gun.
All it takes is hating that body
your own, your self, your muscle that softens to flab.

All it takes is to push what you hate,
40 what you fear onto the soft alien flesh.
To bucket out invincible as a tank
armored with treads without senses
to possess and punish in one act,
to rip up pleasure, to murder those who dare
45 live in the leafy flesh open to love.

STUDY QUESTIONS

1. "Rape Poem" is painfully graphic in its images. Does this seem justified, or is the poet simply being excessive?
2. Identify the metaphors and similes in the poem and discuss how they contribute to its theme.

Wilfred Owen

(1893–1918)

Dulce et Decorum Est

Bent double, like old beggars under sacks,
Knock-kneed, coughing like hags, we cursed through sludge,
Till on the haunting flares we turned our backs
And towards our distant rest began to trudge.
5 Men marched asleep. Many had lost their boots
But limped on, blood-shod. All went lame; all blind;
Drunk with fatigue; deaf even to the hoots
Of tired, outstripped Five-Nines that dropped behind.

Gas! Gas! Quick, boys!—An ecstasy of fumbling,
10 Fitting the clumsy helmets just in time;

But someone still was yelling out and stumbling
And flound'ring like a man in fire or lime . . .
Dim, through the misty panes and thick green light,
As under a green sea, I saw him drowning.
15 In all my dreams, before my helpless sight,
He plunges at me, guttering, choking, drowning.

If in some smothering dreams you too could pace
Behind the wagon that we flung him in,
And watch the white eyes writhing in his face,
20 His hanging face, like a devil's sick of sin;
If you could hear, at every jolt, the blood
Come gargling from the froth-corrupted lungs,
Obscene as cancer, bitter as the cud
Of vile, incurable sores on innocent tongues,—
25 My friend, you would not tell with such high zest
To children ardent for some desperate glory,
The old Lie: Dulce et decorum est
Pro patria mori.

STUDY QUESTIONS

1. How does the poem systematically undercut traditional heroic images of war?
2. Why does Owen directly address the reader as "you" and "my friend" in the poem's last stanza?
3. What is the meaning of the Latin quotation? Why do you think Owen did not translate it for the reader?

E. E. Cummings

(1894–1963)

"next to of course god america i

"next to of course god america i
love you land of the pilgrims' and so forth oh
say can you see by the dawn's early my
country 'tis of centuries come and go
5 and are no more what of it we should worry
in every language even deafanddumb
thy sons acclaim your glorious name by gorry
by jingo by gee by gosh by gum

why talk of beauty what could be more beaut-
10 iful than these heroic happy dead
who rushed like lions to the roaring slaughter
they did not stop to think they died instead
then shall the voice of liberty be mute?"

He spoke. And drank rapidly a glass of water

STUDY QUESTIONS

1. Collage is a visual art form combing bits of newspaper, photos, and small "found objects." What does Cummings's poem have in common with collage?
2. How might you punctuate the poem to clarify its meaning?

18

BEYOND THE SPEAKER: THE DOUBLE VISION OF IRONY

Irony exists whenever we say one thing and mean the opposite. "An exam? What fun!" is an ironic statement. More generally, irony exists whenever we feel a disparity between what someone says or thinks and what we know to be the truth. Irony can be intentional or unintentional, depending on whether the speaker means the statement to be ironic or not. A student who says, "A test today? What fun!" is almost certainly indulging in deliberate irony: he or she neither thinks of the test as fun nor expects others to think of it in that manner.

Suppose, however, that we are fellow students; suppose that you know (but I don't) that an English test has been scheduled for today; and suppose that I now say something like, "Boy, am I tired! I think I'll sleep through English class today!" This is unintentional irony. I am seriously planning to sleep. You know, however, that I will *not* be sleeping through English class. Instead, I will be cudgeling my tired brain, trying to pass an unexpected exam. In this case, it is your perception (as audience) that creates the irony. You know (as I, the innocent speaker, cannot know) how far from reality my words and expectations are.

The emotions of irony arise from our perceptions of a conflict between intent or ideal and reality. The technique of irony consists of creating a parallel disparity in words, by creating an opposition between the apparent meaning of the words and their ironic significance. Always there is some hint of pain in irony, some overtone of pity or anger. And always the emotion is a shared one: shared between reader and speaker if the irony is intentional, shared between reader and writer if it is not.

In responding to irony, then, we are aligning ourselves with someone whose perceptions we share, having been invited—as one right-thinking person by another—to share both the ironist's view of the subject and the emotions of scorn or pity or rage that go with it. Always, therefore, there will be some hint of argument (implicit or explicit) in an ironic poem. And always, the use of irony will produce some distancing of effect, as we stand back and judge the presented disparity.

Beyond these basic facts, however, we will see that irony is a technique that allows many variations of meaning, tone, and effect. As with most definitions, when we have defined a poem as ironic, we have only begun to talk about its construction, its meaning, and its power to touch us.

When you have read the poems that follow, review them in order to answer the following questions:

1. What disparity is being highlighted?
2. What ideals or beliefs that you hold are being appealed to? Is the appeal explicit or implicit?
3. Is the speaker conscious or unconscious of the irony of his or her speech?
4. If there is more than one voice in the poem, how are they contrasted? What part does the contrast play in your sense of the poem's irony?
5. What range of feelings does the poem suggest?

Then discuss each poem more fully, making whatever points you think are most helpful in deciding what role the irony plays in your appreciation of the poem as a whole.

Adrienne Rich

(1929–   )

Aunt Jennifer's Tigers

Aunt Jennifer's tigers prance across a screen,
Bright topaz denizens of a world of green.
They do not fear the men beneath the tree;
They pace in sleek chivalric certainty.

5　Aunt Jennifer's fingers fluttering through her wool
Find even the ivory needle hard to pull.
The massive weight of Uncle's wedding band
Sits heavily upon Aunt Jennifer's hand.

When Aunt is dead, her terrified hands will lie
10　Still ringed with ordeals she was mastered by.
The tigers in the panel that she made
Will go on prancing, proud and unafraid.

A. E. Housman

(1859–1936)

From **A Shropshire Lad**

When I Was One-and-Twenty

When I was one-and-twenty
　　I heard a wise man say,
"Give crowns and pounds and guineas
　　But not your heart away;

5　Give pearls away and rubies
　　But keep you fancy free."
But I was one-and-twenty,
　　No use to talk to me.

When I was one-and-twenty
10　　I heard him say again,
"The heart out of the bosom
　　Was never given in vain;

'Tis paid with sighs a plenty
　　And sold for endless rue."
15　And I am two-and-twenty,
　　And oh, 'tis true, 'tis true.

Dorothy Parker

(1893–1967)

Résumé

Razors pain you;
Rivers are damp;
Acids stain you;
And drugs cause cramp.
5 Guns aren't lawful;
Nooses give;
Gas smells awful;
You might as well live.

Percy Bysshe Shelley

(1792–1822)

Ozymandias

I met a traveler from an antique land
Who said: Two vast and trunkless legs of stone
Stand in the desert . . . Near them, on the sand,
Half sunk, a shattered visage lies, whose frown,
5 And wrinkled lip, and sneer of cold command,
Tell that its sculptor well those passions read
Which yet survive, stamped on these lifeless things,
The hand that mocked them, and the heart that fed:
And on the pedestal these words appear:
10 "My name is Ozymandias, king of kings:
Look on my works, ye Mighty, and despair!"
Nothing beside remains. Round the decay
Of that colossal wreck, boundless and bare
The lone and level sands stretch far away.

W. H. Auden

(1907–1973)

The Unknown Citizen

(To JS/07/M/378
This Marble Monument
Is Erected by the State)

He was found by the Bureau of Statistics to be
One against whom there was no official complaint,
And all the reports on his conduct agree
That, in the modern sense of an old-fashioned word, he was a saint,
5 For in everything he did he served the Greater Community.
Except for the War till the day he retired
He worked in a factory and never got fired,
But satisfied his employers, Fudge Motors Inc.
Yet he wasn't a scab or odd in his views,
10 For his Union reports that he paid his dues,
(Our report on his Union shows it was sound)
And our Social Psychology workers found
That he was popular with his mates and liked a drink.
The Press are convinced that he bought a paper every day
15 And that his reactions to advertisements were normal in every way.
Policies taken out in his name prove that he was fully insured,
And his Health-card shows he was once in hospital but left it cured.
Both Producers Research and High-Grade Living declare
He was fully sensible to the advantages of the Instalment Plan
20 And had everything necessary to the Modern Man,
A phonograph, a radio, a car, and a frigidaire.
Our researchers into Public Opinion are content
That he held the proper opinions for the time of year;
When there was peace, he was for peace; when there was war, he went.
25 He was married and added five children to the population,
Which our Eugenist says was the right number for a parent of his generation,
And our teachers report that he never interfered with their education.
Was he free? Was he happy? The question is absurd:
Had anything been wrong, we should certainly have heard.

Denise Levertov

(1923–   )

Mid-American Tragedy

They want to be their own old vision
of Mom and Dad. They want their dying son
to be eight years old again, not a gay man,
not ill, not dying. They have accepted him,
5 they would say if asked, unlike some who shut
errant sons out of house and heart,
and this makes them preen a little, secretly;
but enough of that, some voice within them
whispers, even more secretly, *he's our kid,*
10 *Mom and Dad are going to give him*
what all kids long for, a trip to Disney World,
what fun, the best Xmas ever.
And he, his wheelchair strung with bottles and tubes,
glass and metal glittering in winter sun,
15 shivers and sweats and tries to breathe as *Jingle Bells*
pervades the air and his mother, his father,
chatter and still won't talk, won't listen,
will never listen, never give him
the healing silence
20 in which they could have heard
his questions, his answers,
his life at last.

Imagery
19

SIMILES, METAPHORS, AND PERSONIFICATION

The three basic elements of any poem are the vision it embodies, the speaker who gives voice to the vision, and the language that creates voice and vision alike. (By stretching the terminology a bit, we could call them the three V's: vision, voice, and vocabulary.) In the preceding chapters, we examined the ways in which the language of a poem—its vocabulary, its connotations, its sounds—created and characterized the poem's speaker. Now it is time to look at the ways in which the language creates the vision.

Vision in literature always implies a shared vision. Originating in the writer's mind, the vision is first translated into words and then re-created in our minds, to be felt by us as it was felt by its writer. When we come to the end of a poem, therefore, the feeling we experience is likely to be a blend of recognition and surprise. We will have seen something familiar—perhaps even something of ourselves—as we have never seen it before.

There are two ways in which poets can go about creating this feeling. The first is to word their vision so precisely that we feel we are seeing things with a new closeness and clearness. This is the method chosen by Pound in "In a Station of the Metro" and Dickinson in "There's a Certain Slant of Light."

The second method relies on figures of speech or on unexpected comparisons to lead us into making connections we may not have made before. Pound also uses this method in "In a Station of the Metro," where human "faces in the crowd" are seen as "petals on a wet black bough," beauty and impersonality mingling. It is Dickinson's method, too, when she describes her "certain slant of light" as being one that "oppresses, like the weight/Of cathedral tunes."

This trick of mingling appeals to different senses in a single image—of describing a sound in terms of color, or a sight in terms of sound or feel—is called **synaesthesia.** Rather than trying to define a type of light in terms of its appearance, Dickinson compares it to a sound. But she speaks of both in terms of weight that presses down physically or spiritually. The word *cathedral,* meanwhile, not only defines the solemn, religious music that parallels the "slant of light," but also prepares us for the image of "heavenly hurt" introduced in the next line. Thus the poem weaves its pattern of imagery.

We have, then, already met poems that make use of both the literal and the figurative styles of imagery. To make sure the contrast is clear, however, let's look at two poems on one subject and see how the language works in each.

Walt Whitman

(1819–1892)

The Dalliance of the Eagles

Skirting the river road, (my forenoon walk, my rest,)
Skyward in air a sudden muffled sound, the dalliance of the eagles,
The rushing amorous contact high in space together,
The clinching interlocking claws, a living, fierce, gyrating wheel,
5   Four beating wings, two beaks, a swirling mass tight grappling,
In tumbling turning clustering loops, straight downward falling,
Till o'er the river pois'd, the twain yet one, a moment's lull,
A motionless still balance in the air, then parting, talons loosing,
Upward again on slow-firm pinions slanting, their separate diverse flight,
10 She hers, he his, pursuing.

Alfred, Lord Tennyson

(1809–1892)

The Eagle

He clasps the crag with crooked hands;
Close to the sun in lonely lands,
Ringed with the azure world, he stands.

The wrinkled sea beneath him crawls;
5   He watches from his mountain walls,
And like a thunderbolt he falls.

Obviously, these are very dissimilar poems. One, talking of a single eagle that remains unmoving throughout most of the poem, creates an atmosphere of space and solitude. The other, speaking of two eagles, seems a constant rush of motion. In part, it is the sound of the words the poets have chosen that creates these different atmospheres. Tennyson's words, lines, and sentences are all short, and the stop at the end of each line is strongly marked. Whitman uses longer lines, with less pronounced breaks between them; and his sentences are so involved and complex that they keep the reader's mind and voice in almost constant motion as dizzying as that of the eagles themselves. Yet the basic difference in the way these eagles are shown to us lies not in their motion or motionlessness, but rather in the imagery in which they are described.

If we go through each poem, noting carefully each descriptive term used, we will discover a marked contrast. Whitman relies heavily on adjectives, particularly on participles (adjectives formed from verbs). *Clinching, interlocking, living, gyrating, beating, swirling, grappling, tumbling, turning, clustering, falling—*

from these comes the poem's sense of action, as well as much of its power of description. The poet's stance is primarily that of the observer. Taking a walk, he has been startled first by the "sudden muffled sound" and then by the sight of the eagles; and he describes sight and sound alike as carefully and vividly as he can:

> The clinching interlocking claws, a living, fierce, gyrating
>   wheel,
> Four beating wings, two beaks, a swirling mass tight
>   grappling,
> In tumbling turning clustering loops, straight downward
>   falling.

Tennyson's fragment, too, is pure description. But its phrasing and its imagery come as much from the poet's imagination as from his powers of observation. Where Whitman uses no words that could not, in sober prose, be applied to an eagle, Tennyson uses almost none that could. His eagle is presented largely in terms that compare it to other things: an old man, grown crooked with age; an explorer in "lonely lands"; a thunderbolt. By calling our attention to these other things, he draws on our feelings about them (respect, for instance, or awe) and uses those feelings to influence our feelings about the eagle itself. Thus, instead of a bird's "clinching . . . claws," Tennyson's eagle has "crooked hands." He "stands"—which, to some readers, may sound more human than birdlike—and "watches," as men and birds both do. Later, he "falls"—an ambiguous verb. The landscape in which he is pictured is similarly humanized. The lands are "lonely," the sea is "wrinkled" and "crawls." There is exaggeration (or **hyperbole**) as well. The eagle's perch is "close to the sun"; the sky against which he is seen is an entire "azure world"; the eagle falls "like a thunderbolt." High and remote, yet somehow in his very remoteness human, Tennyson's eagle presents a striking image of a being in lofty isolation.

By linking disparate things, by forcing us to think of one thing in terms of another, poets make us see those things in new ways, creating new images, calling forth unexpected emotions, fostering new insights. With homely and familiar images, they bring strange things closer to us, while with exotic images they cast new light on everyday things. Concrete images give vivid life to abstract ideas whereas more abstract imagery suggests new significance for particular items or experiences. Poets can speak of their subjects in the most precise, closely fitting words they can find; or they can seek out unexpected startling terms that will call our own imaginations and creative impulses into play. Because it is so largely this choice of how language will be handled in any given poem that determines our sense of that poem, our first or final reaction to it—the totally different feelings that Whitman's torrent of precisely denotative adjectives and Tennyson's careful balance of connotations of humanity, space, and isolation provoke—it will be worth our while to examine some of the techniques that poets use in the creation of imagery. Let us look, therefore, at some of the commoner forms of imagery found in poetry. Because comparisons are often the result of figurative speech, we will start with figures that are forms of comparison: the explicit comparisons, the simile and the metaphor; and the implicit ones, implied metaphor and personification.

Simile

A **simile** is a comparison and is always stated as such. You will always find *like, as, so,* or some such word of comparison within it. Usually, the things it compares resemble each other in only one or two ways, differing in all other respects. An eagle and a thunderbolt are not really much alike; yet the fact that both go from the sky to the ground can allow Tennyson to declare that "like a thunderbolt he falls." In the differences between the two lies the simile's power. The fact that a thunderbolt is so much swifter, so much more powerful and dangerous than the eagle, lends a sense of speed and power and danger to the eagle's fall. A simile may be as brief as the traditional "red as blood," or it may be considerably more complicated, as in this example from "Tell All the Truth":

> As Lightning to the Children eased
> With explanation kind
> The Truth must dazzle gradually
> Or every man be blind—

Notice the use of similes in the following poem.

Langston Hughes

(1902–1967)

Harlem

What happens to a dream deferred?

Does it dry up
like a raisin in the sun?
Or fester like a sore—
5 And then run?
Does it stink like rotten meat?
Or crust and sugar over—
like a syrupy sweet?

Maybe it just sags
10 like a heavy load.

Or does it explode?

STUDY QUESTIONS

1. What relationship do the various similes have to each other and to the subject of the poem, as defined by the title and first line?
2. What has been done with the last simile? Why?

Metaphor and Implied Metaphor

Like similes, **metaphors** are direct comparisons of one object with another. In metaphors, however, the fusion between the two objects is more complete, for metaphor uses no "as" or "like" to separate the two things being compared. Instead, a metaphor simply declares that A "is" B; one element of the comparison becomes, for the moment at least, the other.

Some metaphors go even farther and omit the "is." They simply talk about A as if it were B, using terms appropriate to B. They may not even name B at all but rather let us guess what it is from the words being used. In this case, the metaphor becomes an **implied metaphor.**

Because a simile merely says that A is "like" B, it needs to find only one point or moment of similarity between two otherwise dissimilar objects in order to achieve its effect. (For example, the cherry that is "red as the blood" resembles blood in no other way.) Metaphors, in contrast, tend to make more detailed claims for closer likenesses between the subjects of their comparisons. Notice, for instance, how many points of similarity are suggested by the metaphors in the next two poems. Ask yourself, in each case, what points of comparison the metaphor makes openly or explicitly and what further points of comparison it suggests to you.

John Keats

(1795–1821)

On First Looking into Chapman's Homer

Much have I travelled in the realms of gold,
   And many goodly states and kingdoms seen;
   Round many western islands have I been
Which bards in fealty to Apollo hold.
5 Oft of one wide expanse had I been told
      That deep-browed Homer ruled as his demesne;
      Yet did I never breathe its pure serene
Till I heard Chapman speak out loud and bold:
Then felt I like some watcher of the skies
10   When a new planet swims into his ken;
Or like stout Cortez when with eagle eyes
      He stared at the Pacific—and all his men

Looked at each other with a wild surmise—
Silent, upon a peak in Darien.

STUDY QUESTIONS

1. The vocabulary in the first eight lines of this poem is taken mostly from the Middle Ages and its system of feudalism: *realms* for *kingdoms,* for example; *bards* for *poets; fealty* for the system under which a nobleman would rule part of a country, being himself ruled by a king or a greater nobleman; and *demesne* for the nobleman's domain, the part of the country he ruled. (*Oft* for *often, serene* for *air,* and *ken* for *knowledge* are also old words that are no longer in daily use.) Apollo, on the other hand, comes from classical mythology, and is the god of poets. (He's also the god of the sun, but that doesn't particularly enter into this poem.) Homer is an ancient Greek poet and Chapman a sixteenth-century English poet who translated Homer's *Iliad* into English verse. The question therefore arises: why should Keats use the language of the Middle Ages and the metaphor of traveling to talk about his joy in reading poetry and the great delight he felt when his discovery of Chapman's translation let him feel that he was really hearing Homer for the first time?

2. When Keats does discover Chapman's translation, two new similes occur to him that support the traveler metaphor. What is the first (ll. 9–10)? What sort of progression has been made: how does the new identity the poet feels resemble his earlier identity as traveler? How is it different? What sort of feelings go with each identity? (Note the phrase "a new planet"; why *new?*)

3. In lines 11–14, the second simile is set out. Whom does Keats feel like now? What kinds of feelings go with this third identity? How do they form a climax for the poem? (It was really Balboa, and not Cortez, who was the first European to see the Pacific Ocean. Does this make any difference to your enjoyment of the poem?)

Carl Sandburg

(1878–1967)

Fog

The fog comes
on little cat feet.
It sits looking
over harbor and city
5 on silent haunches
and then moves on.

Personification

Implied metaphors, being more compact and requiring the reader to share in their creation slightly more than regular metaphors do, are frequent in poetry. But one type appears so frequently that it has a name of its own. This is **personification,** the trick of talking about some nonhuman thing as if it were human. We saw personification used in the "crooked hands" of Tennyson's "Eagle."

The poems in the rest of this chapter are notable for their figures of speech. They can thus serve both as exercises in identifying metaphors, similes, and implied metaphors, and as poems illustrating how these figures of speech can help create tone and meaning in poetry. Read each of the poems through at least once. Then go through the poem and note the figures of speech you find in it. Identify each one: is it a simile, a metaphor, an implied metaphor, a personification? Decide what elements make up the comparison: what is being compared to what? And jot down your ideas on why the poet might have wanted his or her readers to think about that comparison.

When you have done this, read the poem through once more. Then look again at the figures of speech you have found. Decide how each relates to the subject of the poem, and how each contributes to your sense of the speaker's feelings toward that subject. Decide, too, how many subjects of comparison there are. Is each subject compared to one other thing, or is one subject compared to several things?

If one subject is compared to one other thing, is that comparison developed at any length? If it is, what does its development lend your sense of the poem and its progression?

If one subject is compared to more than one other thing, or if several subjects of comparison exist, how are the different images fitted together? Are unrelated images juxtaposed for you to fit into some total picture, or does the speaker suggest some relationship of similarity or contrast between them? How does the pattern thus created of related or juxtaposed images help create your sense of the speaker's vision, of the poem's meaning or movement?

Finally, read the poem through once again to see whether you are satisfied with the conclusions you have come to, or whether you think there are other things that should be said about the poem or its imagery.

This may sound like a very complicated procedure. But the method of reading through, looking closely, and reading through again allows you to give attention to details of technique without losing your grip on the poem as a whole. When dealing with relatively simple poems, it's a handy practice. When dealing with more complex poetry, it's essential.

William Wordsworth

(1770–1850)

Composed upon Westminster Bridge, September 3, 1802

Earth has not anything to show more fair:
Dull would he be of soul who could pass by
A sight so touching in its majesty;
This City now doth, like a garment, wear
5   The beauty of the morning; silent, bare,
Ships, towers, domes, theaters, and temples lie
Open unto the fields, and to the sky;
All bright and glittering in the smokeless air.
Never did sun more beautifully steep
10   In his first splendor, valley, rock, or hill;
Ne'er saw I, never felt, a calm so deep!
The river glideth at his own sweet will:
Dear God! the very houses seem asleep;
And all that mighty heart is lying still!

Emily Dickinson

(1830–1886)

I Like to See It Lap the Miles (#585)

I like to see it lap the Miles—
And lick the Valleys up—
And stop to feed itself at Tanks—
And then—prodigious step

5   Around a Pile of Mountains—
And supercilious peer
In Shanties—by the sides of Roads—
And then a Quarry pare

To fit its sides
10   And crawl between
Complaining all the while
In horrid—hooting stanza—
Then chase itself down Hill—

And neigh like Boanerges[1]—
15   Then—prompter than a Star

---

[1]Jesus' name for his apostles John and James; also used to refer to a loud-voiced preacher or speaker

Stop—docile and omnipotent
At its own stable door—

Nikki Giovanni

(1943–)

Woman

she wanted to be a blade
of grass amid the fields
but he wouldn't agree
to be the dandelion

5 she wanted to be a robin singing
through the leaves
but he refused to be
her tree

she spun herself into a web
10 and   looking for a place to rest
turned to him
but he stood straight
declining to be her corner

she tried to be a book
15 but he wouldn't read

she turned herself into a bulb
but he wouldn't let her grow

she decided to become
a woman
20 and though he still refused
to be a man
she decided it was all
right

Sylvia Plath

(1932–1963)

Metaphors

I'm a riddle in nine syllables,
An elephant, a ponderous house,
A melon strolling on two tendrils.

O red fruit, ivory, fine timbers!
5 This loaf's big with its yeasty rising.
Money's new-minted in this fat purse.
I'm a means, a stage, a cow in calf.
I've eaten a bag of green apples,
Boarded the train there's no getting off.

Most metaphors and similes have a certain timelessness to them. Wordsworth's vision of London asleep and Hughes's picture of energy turning angry in Harlem are both visions of something real and, therefore, enduring. In the following poem, however, the metaphorical vision is transitory and illusory. Nonetheless, it illuminates the speaker's view of the world. Note the movement of the imagery from metaphorical to literal within the poem. Consider how it expresses and develops the statement made by the poem's title. (Note particularly the "difficult balance" in the last line. What meanings does that phrase have here at the end of the poem?) Then discuss how the metaphor's statement and development create both the specific picture of the waking man and the wider vision that fills the speaker's mind.

Richard Wilbur

(1921–   )

Love Calls Us to the Things of This World

The eyes open to a cry of pulleys,
And spirited from sleep, the astounded soul
Hangs for a moment bodiless and simple
As false dawn.
5   Outside the open window
The morning air is all awash with angels.

Some are in bed-sheets, some are in blouses,
Some are in smocks: but truly there they are.
Now they are rising together in calm swells
10 Of halcyon feeling, filling whatever they wear
With the deep joy of their impersonal breathing;

Now they are flying in place, conveying
The terrible speed of their omnipresence, moving
And staying like white water; and now of a sudden
15 They swoon down into so rapt a quiet
That nobody seems to be there.
                    The soul shrinks

From all that it is about to remember,
From the punctual rape of every blessèd day,
20 And cries,

       "Oh, let there be nothing on earth but laundry,
Nothing but rosy hands in the rising steam
And clear dances done in the sight of heaven."

    Yet, as the sun acknowledges
25 With a warm look the world's hunks and colors,
The soul descends once more in bitter love
To accept the waking body, saying now
In a changed voice as the man yawns and rises,

    "Bring them down from their ruddy gallows;
30 Let there be clean linen for the backs of thieves;
Let lovers go fresh and sweet to be undone,
And the heaviest nuns walk in a pure floating
Of dark habits,
            keeping their difficult balance."

20

SYMBOL AND ALLEGORY

Similes and metaphors make their comparisons quickly and explicitly. They occupy a line or two; and then they are set, ready for further development, but equally ready to be superseded by another simile or metaphor. How the poet uses them, or how many are used within a poem, is up to the poet. The range of possibilities is wide.

Symbol and allegory, however, tend to dominate the poems in which they are used. Moreover, they usually stand alone: one symbol or allegory is usually the most any given poem can support.

Similes and metaphors are used to make us look more attentively at the poem's subject: at the beauty of an evening or early morning scene, at laundry on a clothesline, at a mirror. They appeal directly to our senses: "a cry of pulleys," a "cowling plated forehead." Often, they illuminate some larger question: "What happens to a dream deferred?" What does it mean to be a woman or a lover? Yet they illuminate the larger question by keeping our attention on the things they describe: the rotten meat and the clean laundry.

Symbols and allegories, on the other hand, urge us to look beyond the literal significance of the poem's statements or action. "The Tyger" does not call our attention to tigers so much as to the awesome qualities suggested.

When we meet with imagery that seems to be calling to us to look beyond the immediate event and its emotional ramifications, we may suspect we are dealing with symbol or allegory. But how are we to distinguish which we are dealing with?

An **allegory** always tells of an action. The events of that action should make sense literally but make more profound sense through a second, allegorical, interpretation. Usually that second interpretation will have a spiritual or a psychological significance; for allegories are particularly good at using physical actions to describe the workings of the human mind and spirit.

In allegory, then, we are given a story that presents a one-to-one correspondence between some physical action (most often an encounter of some kind) and some second action (usually psychological or spiritual), with each step in the literal tale corresponding to a parallel step on the allegorical level. **Symbolism** may likewise present us with a tale or an action. But it may equally well present us with a description of some unchanging being or object. And it is more likely to suggest several possible interpretations than it is to insist on a single one.

In "Ozymandias," for instance, the whole tale of the power and fall of the king is symbolic. But the most striking symbol within it is the broken statue with its vainly boastful inscription. (For many of us, it's the sight of that statue that leaps to mind when anyone says "Ozymandias." The full tale tends to come as an afterthought.)

And how do we explain the tale's symbolism? Does the king's fall symbolize the fall of the proud (which would give the poem a moral interpretation), the fall of tyranny (which would give it a political one), or merely the inevitable destruction by time of human lives and civilizations? May we not, in fact, read overtones of all three types of meaning into the traveler's tale? Certainly the tyrant, with his "sneer of cold command," seems unpleasant enough for us to rejoice in his overthrow. But the sculptor, he with "the hand that mocked" the sneer, is dead as well; and even his longer-enduring work is half destroyed. How do we feel about that? The picture the sonnet paints is straightforward enough; its tone and message are somewhat more complicated.

Some symbols are conventional; and these will suggest a single interpretation. "The Lamb," relying on the traditional association of the lamb as Christ, is an example of conventional symbolism in poetry. Alternatively, the poet may invent a symbol and provide its interpretation as well. In general, however, symbols in poetry ask the reader to interpret them. The interaction between poet and reader thus admits the greatest possible freedom of suggestion and response.

As you read the following poems, decide whether you think them better interpreted symbolically or allegorically. How would you discuss the poem's language, imagery, and progression to support your interpretation?

George Herbert

(1593–1633)

Love (III)

Love bade me welcome; yet my soul drew back,
    Guilty of dust and sin.
But quick-eyed Love, observing me grow slack
    From my first entrance in,
5 Drew nearer to me, sweetly questioning
    If I lacked anything.

"A guest," I answered, "worthy to be here."
    Love said, "You shall be he."
"I, the unkind, ungrateful? Ah my dear,
10   I cannot look on Thee."
Love took my hand, and smiling, did reply,
    "Who made the eyes but I?"

"Truth, Lord, but I have marred them; let my shame
    Go where it doth deserve."
15 "And know you not," says Love, "who bore the blame?"
    "My dear, then I will serve."
"You must sit down," says Love, "and taste my meat."
    So I did sit and eat.

Ralph Waldo Emerson

(1803–1882)

Days

Daughters of Time, the hypocritic Days,
Muffled and dumb like barefoot dervishes,
And marching single in an endless file,
Bring diadems and fagots in their hands.
5 To each they offer gifts after his will,
Bread, kingdoms, stars, and sky that holds them all.
I, in my pleached garden, watched the pomp,
Forgot my morning wishes, hastily
Took a few herbs and apples, and the Day
10 Turned and departed silent. I, too late,
Under her solemn fillet saw the scorn.

Edna St. Vincent Millay

(1892–1950)

First Fig

My candle burns at both ends;
   It will not last the night;
But ah, my foes, and oh, my friends—
   It gives a lovely light!

Stephen Crane

(1871–1900)

The Heart

In the desert
I saw a creature, naked, bestial,
Who, squatting on the ground,
Held his heart in his hands,
5 And ate of it.

I said, "Is it good, friend?"
"It is bitter—bitter," he answered;
"But I like it
Because it is bitter,
10 And because it is my heart."

Allen Ginsberg

(1926–   )

In back of the real

railroad yard in San Jose
   I wandered desolate
in front of a tank factory
   and sat on a bench
5 near the switchman's shack.

A flower lay on the hay on
   the asphalt highway
—the dread hay flower
   I thought—It had a
10 brittle black stem and

    corolla of yellowish dirty
spikes like Jesus' inchlong
    crown, and a soiled
dry center cotton tuft
15   like a used shaving brush
that's been lying under
    the garage for a year.

Yellow, yellow flower, and
    flower of industry,
20 tough spikey ugly flower,
    flower nonetheless,
with the form of the great yellow
    Rose in your brain!
This is the flower of the World.

Langston Hughes

(1902–1967)

Mother to Son

Well, son, I'll tell you:
Life for me ain't been no crystal stair.
It's had tacks in it,
And splinters,
5 And boards torn up,
And places with no carpet on the floor—
Bare.
But all the time
I'se been a-climbin' on,
10 And reachin' landin's,
And turnin' corners,
And sometimes goin' in the dark
Where there ain't been no light.
So boy, don't you turn back
15 Don't you set down on the steps
'Cause you finds it's kinder hard.
Don't you fall now—
For I'se still goin', honey,
I'se still climbin',
20 And life for me ain't been no crystal stair.

John Keats

(1795–1821)

Ode on a Grecian Urn

1

Thou still unravished bride of quietness,
   Thou foster-child of silence and slow time,
Sylvan historian, who canst thus express
   A flowery tale more sweetly than our rhyme:
5 What leaf-fringed legend haunts about thy shape
   Of deities or mortals, or of both,
      In Tempe or the dales of Arcady?[1]
   What men or gods are these? What maidens loath?
What mad pursuit? What struggle to escape?
10   What pipes and timbrels? What wild ecstasy?

2

Heard melodies are sweet, but those unheard
   Are sweeter; therefore, ye soft pipes, play on;
Not to the sensual ear, but, more endeared,
   Pipe to the spirit ditties of no tone:
15 Fair youth, beneath the trees, thou canst not leave
   Thy song, nor ever can those trees be bare;
      Bold Lover, never, never canst thou kiss,
Though winning near the goal—yet, do not grieve;
      She cannot fade, though thou hast not thy bliss,
20   Forever wilt thou love, and she be fair!

3

Ah, happy, happy boughs! that cannot shed
   Your leaves, nor ever bid the Spring adieu;
And, happy melodist, unwearièd,
   Forever piping songs forever new;
25 More happy love! more happy, happy love!
   Forever warm and still to be enjoyed,
      Forever panting, and forever young;
All breathing human passion far above,
   That leaves a heart high-sorrowful and cloyed,
30   A burning forehead, and a parching tongue.

---

[1]The vale of Tempe and Arcady (Arcadia) in Greece are symbolic of pastoral beauty.

4

Who are these coming to the sacrifice?
　　To what green altar, O mysterious priest,
Lead'st thou that heifer lowing at the skies,
　　And all her silken flanks with garlands dressed?
35　What little town by river or sea shore,
　　　Or mountain-built with peaceful citadel,
　　　　Is emptied of this folk, this pious morn?
And, little town, thy streets for evermore
　　Will silent be; and not a soul to tell
40　　　Why thou art desolate, can e'er return.

5

O Attic² shape! Fair attitude! with brede³
　　Of marble men and maidens overwrought,
With forest branches and the trodden weed;
　　Thou, silent form, dost tease us out of thought
45　As doth eternity: Cold Pastoral!
　　When old age shall this generation waste,
　　　Thou shalt remain, in midst of other woe
　　Than ours, a friend to man, to whom thou say'st,
"Beauty is truth, truth beauty,—that is all
50　　Ye know on earth, and all ye need to know."

William Blake

(1757–1827)

From **Songs of Innocence**

The Lamb

　　Little Lamb, who made thee?
　　　Dost thou know who made thee?
Gave thee life & bid thee feed,
By the stream & o'er the mead;
5　Gave thee clothing of delight,
Softest clothing wooly bright;
Gave thee such a tender voice,
Making all the vales rejoice!
　　Little Lamb who made thee?
10　　Dost thou know who made thee?

---

²Grecian, especially Athenian
³embroidery

Little Lamb I'll tell thee,
Little Lamb I'll tell thee!
He is callèd by thy name,
For he calls himself a Lamb:
15 He is meek & he is mild,
He became a little child:
I a child & thou a lamb,
We are callèd by his name.
Little Lamb God bless thee.
20 Little Lamb God bless thee.

From **Songs of Experience**

The Tyger

Tyger! Tyger! burning bright
In the forests of the night,
What immortal hand or eye
Could frame thy fearful symmetry?

5 In what distant deeps or skies
Burnt the fire of thine eyes?
On what wings dare he aspire?
What the hand, dare seize the fire?

And what shoulder, & what art,
10 Could twist the sinews of thy heart?
And when thy heart began to beat,
What dread hand? & what dread feet?

What the hammer? what the chain?
In what furnace was thy brain?
15 What the anvil? what dread grasp
Dare its deadly terrors clasp?

When the stars threw down their spears,
And water'd heaven with their tears,
Did he smile his work to see?
20 Did he who made the Lamb make thee?

Tyger! Tyger! burning bright
In the forests of the night,
What immortal hand or eye
Dare frame thy fearful symmetry?

21

CONCEITS AND ALLUSIONS

Metaphors and similes, because of their instant appeal, are usually the first types of figurative speech to catch our attention. Symbols and allegories, which develop as their poems progress, require more preparation from us if we are to enjoy them fully. They offer themselves only to those who are willing not only to read closely and well, but also to go beyond the poem's literal meaning into a realm of wider suggestion. Conceits and allusions may be brief or extensive in scope; but they are the most demanding figures of all, requiring the reader to be extremely alert and to have some outside knowledge in order to unravel them.

Conceits

A **conceit** could be defined as an outrageous metaphor, but a more traditional definition is a comparison between two highly dissimilar objects. Conceits are often developed at some length, revealing and weighing point after point of comparison or contrast between their two objects. In love poetry, they often grow out of Renaissance traditions that depict the man as a warrior and the woman as a walled town; he attacks, she defends herself or surrenders. Or the man might be a hunter and the woman a wild animal. Or she might be the warrior, wounding him with sharp looks or sharper words. Or, if she were kinder, she might be a treasure mine or a goddess of love. (The list could go on and on.) Some Renaissance poets take the conceits seriously; others play with them, making use of the surprise that can come from turning an expected cliché upside down.

With the metaphysical poets of the seventeenth century, the unexpected becomes a key ingredient in the conceit. The metaphysical poets used conceits not only in love poetry, but in religious poetry as well, thereby creating for both types of poetry conceits of unparalleled complexity and ingenuity. Physics, astronomy, navigation—any science, any intellectual endeavor—might yield a conceit that viewed the soul's progress and passions as parallels to the workings of the universe it inhabited. The resulting poetry tends to be remarkably tough intellectually (you read this poetry *very* slowly the first few times), but also remarkably free, self-assured, and optimistic in its visions.

Here is an example of conceits in metaphysical poetry. Note that there are two main clusters of imagery in the poem. The first turns on maps and voyages, the second on the image of Christ as "the second Adam." And note also that the two are connected by the concept of the soul's journey to salvation as an annihilation of time and space and by the physical image of the sick man, flat on his back in bed and sweating heavily with fever.

John Donne

(1572–1631)

Hymm to God My God, in My Sickness

Since I am coming to that holy room,
   Where, with thy choir of Saints for evermore,
I shall be made thy music; as I come
   I tune the instrument here at the door,
5   And what I must do then, think now before.

Whilst my physicians by their love are grown
   Cosmographers, and I their map, who lie
Flat on this bed, that by them may be shown
   That this is my Southwest discovery
10   *Per fretum febris,*[1] by these straits to die,

I joy, that in these straits, I see my west;[2]
   For, though their currents yield return to none,
What shall my west hurt me? As west and east
   In all flat maps (and I am one) are one,
15   So death doth touch the Resurrection.

Is the Pacific Sea my home? Or are
   The eastern riches? Is Jerusalem?
Anyan,[3] and Magellan, and Gibraltàr,
   All straits, and none but straits, are ways to them,
20   Whether where Japhet dwelt, or Cham, or Shem.[4]

We think that Paradise and Calvary,
   Christ's Cross, and Adam's tree, stood in one place;
Look Lord, and find both Adams met in me;
   As the first Adam's sweat surrounds my face,
25   May the last Adam's blood my soul embrace.

So, in his purple wrapped receive me, Lord,
   By these his thorns give me his other crown;
And as to others' souls I preached thy word,
   Be this my text, my sermon to mine own,
30   Therefore that he may raise, the Lord throws down.

---

[1]through the straits of fever
[2]my death
[3]modern Annam, then thought of as a strait between Asia and America
[4]sons of Noah, said to have settled Europe, Asia, and Africa after the flood

Allusions

Conceits ask that we bring some knowledge to our reading if we are to understand their implications. For example, we must understand the distortions of space involved in making a flat map represent a round world if we are to understand Donne's hymn. An **allusion** likewise asks us to bring some knowledge to our reading. For an allusion may be defined as a reference to some work of art or literature, or to some well-known person, event, or story. If we do not catch the reference, then we will miss the point of the allusion.

Here is a frequently anthologized Middle English poem that celebrates spring. Following that poem is a "celebration" of winter by a twentieth-century poet who, knowing of the earlier poem's popularity, felt free to burlesque it. Note that Pound's poem can stand on its own, and that it makes no direct reference to the lyric to which it alludes. But note also how much more effective its irascible tone becomes when set off in its reader's mind against the cheerfulness of its medieval model.

Anonymous—Middle English Lyric

Sumer Is Icumen In[5]

Sumer is icumen in,
   Lhude sing cuccu!
Groweth sed and bloweth med
   And springth the wude nu.
5   Sing cuccu!

Awe bleteth after lomb,
   Lhouth after calve cu,
Bulluc sterteth, bucke verteth;
   Murie sing cuccu!
10   Cuccu! cuccu!
Wel singes thu cuccu.
Ne swik thu naver nu!

Sing cuccu nu, Sing cuccu!
Sing cuccu, Sing cuccu nu!

---

[5] *Translation:*

Spring has come in,
   Loudly sing cuckoo!
Grows seed and blooms mead
   And springs the wood now.
     Sing cuckoo!

Ewe bleats after lamb,
   Lows after calf the cow,

Bullock starts, buck farts;
   Merrily sing cuckoo!
     Cuckoo! cuckoo!
Well sing thou cuckoo.
Cease thou never now!

Sing cuckoo now
     etc.

Ezra Pound

(1885–1972)

Ancient Music

Winter is icumen in,
Lhude sing Goddamm,
Raineth drop and staineth slop,
And how the wind doth ramm!
5   Sing : Goddamm.
Skiddeth bus and sloppeth us,
An ague hath my ham.
Freezeth river, turneth liver,
            Damn you, sing : Goddamm.
10 Goddamm, Goddamm, 'tis why I am, Goddamm,
            So 'gainst the winter's balm.
Sing goddamm, damm, sing Goddamm,
Sing goddamm, sing goddamm, DAMM.

　　　Discuss how the speakers of the following three poems use conceits or allusions to praise the women they love and to enlarge on the benefits of love. (You will want to concentrate on the poems' imagery; but note also the use of apostrophe, or direct address, and the different tones and logical progressions within each poem. Use the questions that follow each poem to help you.)

William Shakespeare

(1564–1616)

Sonnet 18

Shall I compare thee to a summer's day?
Thou art more lovely and more temperate:
Rough winds do shake the darling buds of May,
And summer's lease hath all too short a date:
5 Sometime too hot the eye of heaven shines,
And often is his gold complexion dimmed;
And every fair from fair sometime declines,
By chance or nature's changing course untrimmed:
But thy eternal summer shall not fade
10 Nor lose possession of that fair thou ow'st,[6]
Nor shall Death brag thou wand'rest in his shade,
When in eternal lines to time thou grow'st.

---

[6]ownest

So long as men can breathe or eyes can see,
So long lives this, and this gives life to thee.

STUDY QUESTIONS

This sonnet starts with a question relating to physical qualities–beauty and temperature—and ends up dealing with intangible ones. By what contrasts and what train of logic does it achieve this progression? (Note in particular the "summer's day" of line 1, "the eye of heaven" in line 5, and "eternal summer" in line 9. These phrases mark the starting points of three stages in the argument, with the last two lines marking the final stage. And be warned that "fair" has three meanings. It's a noun meaning "a lovely thing," an adjective meaning "lovely," and a noun meaning "beauty.")

Robert Frost

(1875–1963)

The Silken Tent

She is as in a field a silken tent
At midday when a sunny summer breeze
Has dried the dew and all its ropes relent,
So that in guys it gently sways at ease,
5 And its supporting central cedar pole,
That is its pinnacle to heavenward
And signifies the sureness of the soul,
Seems to owe naught to any single cord,
But strictly held by none, is loosely bound
10 By countless silken ties of love and thought
To everything on earth the compass round,
And only by one's going slightly taut
In the capriciousness of summer air
Is of the slightest bondage made aware.

John Donne

(1572–1631)

The Sun Rising

Busy old fool, unruly sun,
    Why dost thou thus
Through windows and through curtains call on us?

Must to thy motions lovers' seasons run?
5   Saucy, pedantic wretch, go chide
       Late schoolboys and sour 'prentices,
   Go tell court huntsmen that the king will ride,
   Call country ants to harvest offices.
Love, all alike, no season knows nor clime,
10 Nor hours, days, months, which are the rags of time.

       Thy beams, so reverend and strong
          Why shouldst thou think?
I could eclipse and cloud them with a wink,
But that I would not lose her sight so long.
15   If her eyes have not blinded thine,
          Look, and tomorrow late tell me
       Whether both th' Indias of spice and mine
       Be where thou left'st them, or lie here with me;
   Ask for those kings whom thou saw'st yesterday,
20 And thou shalt hear: All here in one bed lay.

       She's all states, and all princes I;
          Nothing else is.
Princes do but play us; compared to this,
All honor's mimic, all wealth alchemy.
25   Thou, sun, art half as happy as we,
          In that the world's contracted thus;
   Thine age asks ease, and since thy duties be
To warm the world, that's done in warming us.
Shine here to us, and thou art everywhere;
This bed thy center is, these walls thy sphere.

STUDY QUESTIONS

1. This poem falls into the category of **aubades,** or "dawn songs." What dramatic value does this placement in time give it?
2. Note that here again earthly riches are first equated with the woman's beauty and then devalued by it, and that time is forced to yield to timelessness. How does Donne's treatment of these conceits differ from those of Shakespeare and Frost?
3. In general, how would you compare this love poem with those two earlier ones?

The next two poems are spoken by discontented lovers. What could you say about the ways in which they use conceits or allusions to describe their predicaments or to convince themselves or their hearers that some change should be made?

Sir Philip Sidney

(1554–1586)

From **Astrophil and Stella**

Sonnet 31

With how sad steps, O moon,[7] thou climb'st the skies!
    How silently, and with how wan a face!
    What! may it be that even in heavenly place
    That busy archer his sharp arrows tries?
5 Sure, if that long-with-love-acquainted eyes
    Can judge of love, thou feel'st a lover's case;
    I read it in thy looks—thy languished grace
    To me, that feel the like, thy state descries.
Then, even of fellowship, O moon, tell me,
10   Is constant love deemed there but want of wit?
    Are beauties there as proud as here they be?
Do they above love to be loved, and yet
    Those lovers scorn whom that love doth possess?
    Do they call virtue there ungratefulness?

Andrew Marvell

(1621–1678)

To His Coy Mistress

Had we but world enough, and time,
This coyness, lady, were no crime.
We would sit down, and think which way
To walk, and pass our long love's day.
5 Thou by the Indian Ganges' side
Shouldst rubies find; I by the tide
Of Humber would complain. I would
Love you ten years before the Flood,
And you should, if you please, refuse
10 Till the conversion of the Jews.
My vegetable love should grow
Vaster than empires, and more slow;
An hundred years should go to praise
Thine eyes and on thy forehead gaze,
15 Two hundred to adore each breast,

---

[7]The technique of having the speaker seem to address someone or something within a poem is called **apostrophe.**

But thirty thousand to the rest:
An age at least to every part,
And the last age should show your heart.
For, lady, you deserve this state,
20 Nor would I love at lower rate.
    But at my back I always hear
Time's wingèd chariot hurrying near;
And yonder all before us lie
Deserts of vast eternity.
25 Thy beauty shall no more be found,
Nor in thy marble vault shall sound
My echoing song; then worms shall try
That long preserved virginity,
And your quaint honor turn to dust,
30 And into ashes all my lust.
The grave's a fine and private place,
But none, I think, do there embrace.
    Now, therefore, while the youthful hue
Sits on thy skin like morning dew,
35 And while thy willing soul transpires
At every pore with instant fires,
Now let us sport us while we may,
And now, like am'rous birds of prey,
Rather at once our time devour
40 Than languish in his slow-chapped power.
Let us roll all our strength and all
Our sweetness up into one ball,
And tear our pleasures with rough strife
Through the iron gates of life.
45 Thus, though we cannot make our sun
Stand still, yet we will make him run.

    Judith Ortiz Cofer's "The Latin Deli: An Ars Poetica" employs both a conceit and allusions. After you identify the central conceit, discuss the historical allusions that add poignancy to the poem.

Judith Ortiz Cofer

(1952–   )

The Latin Deli: An Ars Poetica

Presiding over a formica counter,
plastic Mother and Child magnetized

to the top of an ancient register,
the heady mix of smells from the open bins
5 of dried codfish, the green plantains
hanging in stalks like votive offerings,
she is the Patroness of Exiles,
a woman of no-age who was never pretty,
who spends her days selling canned memories
10 while listening to the Puerto Ricans complain
that it would be cheaper to fly to San Juan
than to buy a pound of Bustelo coffee here,
and to Cubans perfecting their speech
of a "glorious return" to Havana—where no one
15 has been allowed to die and nothing to change until then;
to Mexicans who pass through, talking lyrically
of *dólares* to be made in El Norte—
                              all wanting the comfort
of spoken Spanish, to gaze upon the family portrait
20 of her plain wide face, her ample bosom
resting on her plump arms, her look of maternal interest
as they speak to her and each other
of their dreams and their disillusions—
how she smiles understanding,
25 when they walk down the narrow aisles of her store
reading the labels of packages aloud, as if
they were the names of lost lovers: *Suspiros,*
Merengues, the stale candy of everyone's childhood,
                              She spends her days
30 slicing *jamón y queso* and wrapping it in wax paper
tied with string: plain ham and cheese
that would cost less at the A&P, but it would not satisfy
the hunger of the fragile old man lost in the folds
of his winter coat, who brings her lists of items
35 that he reads to her like poetry, or the others,
whose needs she must divine, conjuring up products
from places that now exist only in their hearts—
closed ports she must trade with.

STUDY QUESTIONS

1. Why is the poem subtitled "An Ars Poetica"—an "art of poetry"?
2. How does Ortiz Cofer equate food, language, and memory in the poem?
3. Discuss the poem's theme of exile.

22

PATTERNS OF IMAGERY

So far, we have spoken of different figures of speech in isolation. In practice, however, the various figures are almost always found in combination with each other. "Days," for instance, is an allegory. But the various gifts the Days carry are symbolic; and the phrase "morning wishes" is metaphorical. Moreover, just as form and meaning reinforce each other, so a poem's figures of speech reinforce each other to create the poem's overall patterns of meaning and imagery. When we discuss a poem, we may start by discussing some particularly striking aspect; and that may mean a particular use of imagery. But eventually we will want to talk of the complete poem; and that will mean talking of the patterns it contains.

The poems in the last chapter were heavily patterned. The Renaissance poems tended to be static, stating a position and then elaborating on it. The metaphysical poems showed more movement, following the speaker's mind through the ramifications of an idea or situation. The poems in this chapter will also display carefully worked-out patterns of imagery. And, as most of them are somewhat longer poems, the patterns will be even more complex. But these poems will also show a freer and more passionate movement, for they come either from the Romantic poetry of the nineteenth century or from twentieth-century poetry that was influenced by that movement. In the more melodious rhythms and harmonies of these poems, we find a vivid sense of immediacy, of unfolding memories or emotions, of minds and spirits caught up in vision and experience. Flowing sound and richly suggestive imagery create the sense of intense experience that was a trademark of the Romantic movement and that still provides some overtones of meaning to the common use of the word *romantic*.

As you read the following poems, be prepared for shifts of emotion as much as for shifts of thought. Note how these more modern poets create scenes, moods, and speakers through sound and imagery.

Percy Bysshe Shelley

(1792–1822)

Ode to the West Wind

1

O wild West Wind, thou breath of Autumn's being,
Thou, from whose unseen presence the leaves dead
Are driven, like ghosts from an enchanter fleeing,

Yellow, and black, and pale, and hectic red,
5 Pestilence-stricken multitudes: O thou,
Who chariotest to their dark wintry bed

The wingèd seeds, where they lie cold and low,
Each like a corpse within its grave, until
Thine azure sister of the Spring shall blow

10 Her clarion o'er the dreaming earth, and fill
(Driving sweet buds like flocks to feed in air)
With living hues and odors plain and hill:

Wild Spirit, which art moving everywhere;
Destroyer and preserver; hear, oh, hear!

2

15 Thou on whose stream, mid the steep sky's commotion,
Loose clouds like earth's decaying leaves are shed,
Shook from the tangled boughs of Heaven and Ocean,

Angels of rain and lightning: there are spread
On the blue surface of thine aery surge,
20 Like the bright hair uplifted from the head

Of some fierce Maenad,[1] even from the dim verge
Of the horizon to the zenith's height,
The locks of the approaching storm. Thou dirge

Of the dying year, to which this closing night
25 Will be the dome of a vast sepulcher,
Vaulted with all thy congregated might

Of vapors, from whose solid atmosphere
Black rain, and fire, and hail will burst: oh, hear!

---

[1]a female attendant of Dionysus

3

　　Thou who didst waken from his summer dreams
30　The blue Mediterranean, where he lay,
　　Lulled by the coil of his crystàlline streams,

　　Beside a pumice isle in Baiae's[2] bay,
　　And saw in sleep old palaces and towers
　　Quivering within the wave's intenser day,

35　All overgrown with azure moss and flowers
　　So sweet, the sense faints picturing them! Thou
　　For whose path the Atlantic's level powers

　　Cleave themselves into chasms, while far below
　　The sea-blooms and the oozy woods which wear
40　The sapless foliage of the ocean, know

　　Thy voice, and suddenly grow gray with fear,
　　And tremble and despoil themselves: oh, hear!

4

　　If I were a dead leaf thou mightest bear;
　　If I were a swift cloud to fly with thee;
45　A wave to pant beneath thy power, and share

　　The impulse of thy strength, only less free
　　Than thou, O uncontrollable! If even
　　I were as in my boyhood, and could be

　　The comrade of thy wanderings over Heaven,
50　As then, when to outstrip thy skiey speed
　　Scarce seem a vision; I would ne'er have striven

　　As thus with thee in prayer in my sore need.
　　Oh, lift me as a wave, a leaf, a cloud!
　　I fall upon the thorns of life! I bleed!

55　A heavy weight of hours has chained and bowed
　　One too like thee: tameless, and swift, and proud.

5

　　Make me thy lyre, even as the forest is:
　　What if my leaves are falling like its own!
　　The tumult of thy mighty harmonies

---

[2]ancient Roman resort whose submerged ruins can be seen north of Naples

60 Will take from both a deep, autumnal tone,
    Sweet though in sadness. Be thou, Spirit fierce,
    My spirit! be thou me, impetuous one!

    Drive my dead thoughts over the universe
    Like withered leaves to quicken a new birth!
65 And, by the incantation of this verse,

    Scatter, as from an unextinguished hearth
    Ashes and sparks, my words among mankind!
    Be through my lips to unawakened earth

    The trumpet of a prophecy! O Wind,
70 If Winter comes, can Spring be far behind?

John Keats

(1795–1821)

Ode to a Nightingale

1

My heart aches, and a drowsy numbness pains
   My sense, as though of hemlock I had drunk,
Or emptied some dull opiate to the drains
   One minute past, and Lethe-wards[3] had sunk:
5 'Tis not through envy of thy happy lot,
   But being too happy in thine happiness—
      That thou, light-wingèd Dryad of the trees,
         In some melodious plot
   Of beechen green, and shadows numberless,
10   Singest of summer in full-throated ease.

2

O, for a draught of vintage! that hath been
   Cooled a long age in the deep-delvèd earth,
Tasting of Flora[4] and the country green,
   Dance, and Provençal song, and sunburnt mirth!
15 O for a beaker full of the warm South,
   Full of the true, the blushful Hippocrene,[5]
      With beaded bubbles winking at the brim,
         And purple-stainèd mouth;

---

[3]toward the river Lethe, in the underworld
[4]goddess of flowers
[5]fountain of the Muses on Mt. Helicon

That I might drink, and leave the world unseen,
20   And with thee fade away into the forest dim:

3

Fade far away, dissolve, and quite forget
    What thou among the leaves hast never known,
The weariness, the fever, and the fret
    Here, where men sit and hear each other groan;
25 Where palsy shakes a few, sad, last gray hairs,
    Where youth grows pale, and spectre-thin, and dies,
        Where but to think is to be full of sorrow
            And leaden-eyed despairs,
Where Beauty cannot keep her lustrous eyes,
30   Or new Love pine at them beyond tomorrow.

4

Away! away! for I will fly to thee,
    Not charioted by Bacchus and his pards,[6]
But on the viewless wings of Poesy,
    Though the dull brain perplexes and retards:
35 Already with thee! tender is the night,
    And haply the Queen-Moon is on her throne,
        Clustered around by all her starry Fays;
            But here there is no light,
Save what from heaven is with the breezes blown
40   Through verdurous glooms and winding mossy ways.

5

I cannot see what flowers are at my feet,
    Nor what soft incense hangs upon the boughs,
But, in embalmèd darkness, guess each sweet
    Wherewith the seasonable month endows
45 The grass, the thicket, and the fruit-tree wild;
    White hawthorn, and the pastoral eglantine;
        Fast fading violets covered up in leaves;
            And mid-May's eldest child,
The coming musk-rose, full of dewy wine,
50   The murmurous haunt of flies on summer eves.

6

Darkling[7] I listen; and for many a time
    I have been half in love with easeful Death,

---

[6]leopards drawing the chariot of Bacchus, god of wine
[7]in the darkness

Called him soft names in many a musèd rhyme,
 To take into the air my quiet breath;
55 Now more than ever seems it rich to die,
 To cease upon the midnight with no pain,
  While thou art pouring forth thy soul abroad
   In such an ecstasy!
 Still wouldst thou sing, and I have ears in vain—
60 To thy high requiem become a sod.

7

Thou wast not born for death, immortal Bird!
 No hungry generations tread thee down;
The voice I hear this passing night was heard
 In ancient days by emperor and clown:
65 Perhaps the selfsame song that found a path
 Through the sad heart of Ruth, when, sick for home,
  She stood in tears amid the alien corn:
   The same that oft-times hath
 Charmed magic casements, opening on the foam
70 Of perilous seas, in faery lands forlorn.

8

Forlorn! the very word is like a bell
 To toll me back from thee to my sole self!
Adieu! the fancy cannot cheat so well
 As she is famed to do, deceiving elf.
75 Adieu! adieu! thy plaintive anthem fades
 Past the near meadows, over the still stream,
  Up the hill side; and now 'tis buried deep
   In the next valley-glades:
 Was it a vision, or a waking dream?
80 Fled is that music:—Do I wake or sleep?

Matthew Arnold

(1822–1888)

Dover Beach

The sea is calm tonight.
The tide is full, the moon lies fair
Upon the straits;—on the French coast the light
Gleams and is gone; the cliffs of England stand,
5 Glimmering and vast, out in the tranquil bay.
Come to the window, sweet is the night-air!

Only, from the long line of spray
Where the sea meets the moon-blanched land,
Listen! you hear the grating roar
10 Of pebbles which the waves draw back, and fling,
At their return, up the high strand,
Begin, and cease, and then again begin,
With tremulous cadence slow, and bring
The eternal note of sadness in.

15 Sophocles long ago
Heard it on the Aegean, and it brought
Into his mind the turbid ebb and flow
Of human misery; we
Find also in the sound a thought,
20 Hearing it by this distant northern sea.

The Sea of Faith
Was once, too, at the full, and round earth's shore
Lay like the folds of a bright girdle furled.
But now I only hear
25 Its melancholy, long, withdrawing roar,
Retreating, to the breath
Of the night-wind, down the vast edges drear
And naked shingles of the world.

Ah, love, let us be true
30 To one another! for the world, which seems
To lie before us like a land of dreams,
So various, so beautiful, so new,
Hath really neither joy, nor love, nor light,
Nor certitude, nor peace, nor help for pain;
35 And we are here as on a darkling plain
Swept with confused alarms of struggle and flight,
Where ignorant armies clash by night.

William Butler Yeats

(1865–1939)

Sailing to Byzantium

1

That is no country for old men. The young
In one another's arms, birds in the trees
—Those dying generations—at their song,
The salmon-falls, the mackerel-crowded seas,

5 Fish, flesh, or fowl, commend all summer long
  Whatever is begotten, born, and dies.
  Caught in that sensual music all neglect
  Monuments of unageing intellect.

2

   An aged man is but a paltry thing,
10 A tattered coat upon a stick, unless
   Soul clap its hands and sing, and louder sing
   For every tatter in its mortal dress,
   Nor is there singing school but studying
   Monuments of its own magnificence;
15 And therefore I have sailed the seas and come
   To the holy city of Byzantium.

3

   O sages standing in God's holy fire
   As in the gold mosaic of a wall,
   Come from the holy fire, perne in a gyre,
20 And be the singing-masters of my soul.
   Consume my heart away; sick with desire
   And fastened to a dying animal
   It knows not what it is; and gather me
   Into the artifice of eternity.

4

25 Once out of nature I shall never take
   My bodily form from any natural thing,
   But such a form as Grecian goldsmiths make
   Of hammered gold and gold enamelling
   To keep a drowsy Emperor awake;
30 Or set upon a golden bough to sing
   To lords and ladies of Byzantium
   Of what is past, or passing, or to come.

Dylan Thomas

(1914–1953)

Fern Hill

Now as I was young and easy under the apple boughs
About the lilting house and happy as the grass was green,
     The night above the dingle starry,

-Time let me hail and climb
5   Golden in the heydays of his eyes,
And honored among wagons I was prince of the apple towns
And once below a time I lordly had the trees and leaves
                Trail with daisies and barley
        Down the rivers of the windfall light.

10 And as I was green and carefree, famous among the barns
About the happy yard and singing as the farm was home,
                In the sun that is young once only,
                Time let me play and be
        Golden in the mercy of his means,
15 And green and golden I was huntsman and herdsman, the calves
Sang to my horn, the foxes on the hills barked clear and cold,
                And the sabbath rang slowly
        In the pebbles of the holy streams.

All the sun long it was running, it was lovely, the hay
20 Fields high as the house, the tunes from the chimneys, it was air
                And playing, lovely and watery
                And fire green as grass.
        And nightly under the simple stars
As I rode to sleep the owls were bearing the farm away,
25 All the moon long I heard, blessed among stables, the night-jars
                Flying with the ricks, and the horses
                Flashing into the dark.

And then to awake, and the farm, like a wanderer white
With the dew, come back, the cock on his shoulder: it was all
30   Shining, it was Adam and maiden,
                The sky gathered again
        And the sun grew round that very day.
So it must have been after the birth of the simple light
In the first, spinning place, the spellbound horses walking warm
35   Out of the whinnying green stable
                On to the fields of praise.

And honored among foxes and pheasants by the gay house
Under the new made clouds and happy as the heart was long,
                In the sun born over and over,
40   I ran my heedless ways,
                My wishes raced through the house high hay
And nothing I cared, at my sky blue trades, that time allows
In all his tuneful turning so few and such morning songs
                Before the children green and golden
45   Follow him out of grace,

Nothing I cared, in the lamb white days, that time would take me
Up to the swallow thronged loft by the shadow of my hand,
      In the moon that is always rising,
         Nor that riding to sleep
50   I should hear him fly with the high fields
And wake to the farm forever fled from the childless land.
Oh as I was young and easy in the mercy of his means,
       Time held me green and dying
      Though I sang in my chains like the sea.

Sound

23

METER AND ITS VARIATIONS

Sound in poetry is a function of two elements: the rhythm of a poem's lines, and the sounds of its words. Throughout our study of poetry, we have been aware of the important part sound and rhythm play in establishing our sense of a poem. But we have been more concerned with recognizing how the sounds of a given poem reinforce its ideas or emotions than with classifying the sounds themselves; and so we have not paused to build up a vocabulary of technical terms for meter and versification. Now it is time to learn that vocabulary, so that we may supplement our discussions of character and language in poetry with more detailed comments on the techniques of sound that reinforce them. Because rhythm is perhaps the most basic element of sound in a poem, and meter the most basic element of rhythm, we will start with meter.

Meter is the term used to describe the underlying rhythm of a poem, based on the number and the placement of stressed syllables in each line. In most poetry, these **stresses** will fall into a pattern and the pattern will have a particular name: **iambic pentameter,** for instance, to name one of the most common. When we learn to **scan** a poem, therefore, to find out the rhythm or meter in which it is written, these stresses and their patterns are what we will be looking at.

What do we mean by a **stress** or a **stressed syllable?** We mean that the word or syllable involved is one to which our voice will give greater emphasis than to its neighbors. Every word of more than one syllable in English has one accented, or stressed, syllable and one or more unaccented, or unstressed, ones. Thus in the word *human* we stress the first syllable: *hú - man;* in the word *humane* we stress the second: *hu - máne.* When we speak a sentence, these natural accents, or stresses, will be heard. Usually they will be joined by a second type of stress, one used for emphasis. If I say, "Is she coming?," for instance, and leave the strongest stress on the first syllable of *coming* ("Is she *coming?*"), there will be nothing startling in the sentence. If, however, I move the accent to the word *is* ("*Is* she coming?"), I sound doubtful or surprised that she'd come; while if I accent the word *she* ("Is *she* coming?") the stressed word suggests that "she" is the last person I would have expected (or perhaps wanted) to come. The emphasis may fall in an expected or an unexpected place. But it is sure to fall somewhere, because English is a heavily accented language; it sounds neither normal nor natural without the contrast of its stressed and unstressed syllables.

The number of stresses in a line of poetry, therefore, is the number of syllables on which our voice naturally tends to put a stronger emphasis. The emphasis must be natural; it must come either from the sound of the words themselves
or from the meaning and emphasis of the lines. Thus we must be able to find the
meter by reading naturally; we should not distort either the sense or the natural
rhythm of the lines to make them fit some preconceived meter.

So basic is this matter of stresses, in fact, that line lengths receive their
names according to the number of stressed syllables they contain. One simply
counts up the stressed syllables, translates the resulting number into Greek, and
adds the word *meter* to finish out the term, as follows:

Dimeter—two stresses per line:
Díe soón
Trimeter—three stresses:
Dóst thou knów who máde thee?
Tetrameter—four stresses:
Tell all the trúth but téll it slánt
Pentameter—five stresses:
Leáve me, O Lóve, which reáches bút to dúst
Hexameter—six stresses (also known as an **alexandrine**):
Which, líke a wóunded snáke, drágs its slow léngth alóng

By counting the number of stresses per line, we thus discover the skeleton of
a poem's rhythm. The question then becomes how those stresses are linked. In
accentual poetry, they are linked by **alliteration** or **assonance.** There will be
(usually) four stressed syllables per line; and two or three of them will start with
the same sound or contain the same vowel. Here is an example, from a poem you
will meet again at the chapter's end:

> Bitter breást-cares have Í abíded,
> Knówn on my kéel many a cáre's hold,
> And díre seá-súrge, and there I oft spént
> Narrow nightwatch nígh the ship's héad
> While she tóssed close to clíffs. Coldly afflicted,
> My féet were by fróst benúmbed.

The first line is marked by the alliteration of *bitter* and *breast* and the assonance
of *I* and *abided.* The second is similarly linked by the alliteration of the *k* sound
in *keel* and *care* and the assonance of the *o* sound in *known* and *hold.* But the
other lines are all marked by the alliteration of one sound each: *s* in the third
line, *n* in the fourth, *c* in the fifth, and *f* in the sixth. This is the patterning of Old
English poetry, a patterning used for several hundred years before the Norman
Conquest brought French influences and rhymed verse to England. Since that
time, accentual poetry has been relatively rare. One nineteenth-century poet,
Gerard Manley Hopkins, however, worked out an accentual style of his own,
which he called **sprung rhythm.** His style reflects the Old English influence in

its irregular placement of stresses and its marked use of alliteration and assonance.

Most English and American verse is **accentual syllabic.** This means that its rhythm depends not only on the number of stressed syllables, but also on the total number of syllables per line, and on the placement of the stresses within that totality. Tetrameter lines, for instance, vary in length from the four stressed syllables of "We real cool. We," to the eight syllables, half of them stressed, of "Tell all the truth but tell it slant," to the eleven or twelve syllables (every third syllable stressed) of "You left us in tatters, without shoes or socks,/Tired of digging potatoes and spudding up docks."

To define its various combinations of stressed and unstressed syllables, therefore, accentual-syllabic meters divide each line of poetry into **feet,** a **foot** consisting of one stressed syllable with its attendant unstressed syllables. Each type of foot—that is, each pattern of syllables—is given a name. An unstressed syllable followed by a stressed one, for instance (*the wórd*) is an **iamb;** two unstressed syllables followed by a stressed one (*that she heárd*) make an **anapest.** The meter of the poem thus consists of the *name of the foot* most frequently found in the poem joined to the basic *line length.* "There's a certain slant of light" thus becomes **iambic trimeter,** despite the fact that not all its feet are iambs and not all its lines have three feet.

With this background in mind, let us chart the types of feet most commonly found in English poetry. One of the most common **duple meters** is the **iambic,** which has two syllables, the second stressed:

Tell áll | the trúth | but téll | it slańt

The **trochaic** has two syllables, the first stressed:

Dóst thou | knów who | máde thee?

One of the two most common **triple meters** is the **anapestic,** with three syllables, the last stressed:

And thére | was my Ró- | land to béar | the whole weíght

The **dactylic** has three syllables, the first stressed:

Táking me | báck down the | vísta of | yéars, till I | sée

One should also know the **spondee,** a two-syllable foot with both syllables accented. The spondee is used only to lend particular emphasis or variety to poetry written in other meters; there is no "spondaic meter." The **amphibrach** is a three-syllable foot with the accent on the middle syllable. Unlike the spondee, the amphibrach can be used as a sustained meter; but it's not an easy meter to work with and isn't often used for an entire poem. The **monosyllabic foot** has one syllable, accented; Gwendolyn Brooks's "We Real Cool" is an example of this foot in action. The **paeon** is a four-syllable foot. It may be called first paeon, second paeon, third paeon, or fourth paeon, depending on whether the accented syllable comes first, second, third, or fourth. There may also be a secondary accent within the foot. Traditional ballads are often written in paeonic meters.

Meter, then, will create the basic rhythm of a poem, setting up a pattern to be repeated or varied with each line. Seldom does the pattern remain perfectly regular, because to hold too closely to a meter in spoken verse is to risk monotony and boredom.

A poet can avoid monotony by shifting stresses, so that a poem written in iambic meter will have some feet that are trochees and some that are spondees; by adding syllables, so that an iambic line will contain an occasional dactyl or anapest; or by dropping syllables, substituting a pause for the expected sound, or laying greater stress on the remaining syllables, as when a spondee is substituted for an anapest.

More importantly, poets vary their meters by making the sense of the poem, and the cadence of the speaker's voice, move in counterpoint to the rhythm:

> The sea is calm tonight.
> The tide is full, the moon lies fair
> Upon the straits;—on the French coast the light
> Gleams and is gone; the cliffs of England stand,
> Glimmering and vast, out in the tranquil bay.

The first statement fits the first line perfectly. But the next overlaps the second line, so that your voice cannot stop on "fair" but must continue with "Upon the straits." A pause, then, and the thought continues through that line and half of the next; then pauses more briefly, finishes the line with a slight pause, and comes to rest at the end of the fifth line. Because your voice stops at the end of them, the first and fifth lines are called **end-stopped lines.** Because the movement of thought and phrase forces your voice to continue past their ends, the second, third, and fourth lines are called **run-on lines.** Both end-stopped and run-on lines may contain internal pauses. We find one such pause after "full" in the second line, one after "straits" in the third," one after "gone" in the fourth, and one after "vast" in the fifth. These pauses are called **caesuras;** and their use and placement are vital in breaking the rhythms of poetry to create the sound of a speaking voice.

In contrast to "Dover Beach" (which you might want to reread in its entirety, to notice how flexible the lines are throughout), recall Blake's poems "The Lamb" and "The Tyger." Notice that many of their lines are end-stopped and that the regularity of the rhythm, with its procession of end-stopped lines and repeated questions, gives these poems almost the sound of incantations, sounds far removed from the wistful accents of Arnold's speaker. But notice, too, that even here, although each phrase is strongly separated from its fellows and heavily accented, the length of the phrases still varies, and caesuras and occasional run-on lines are still found:

> What the hammer? what the chain?
> In what furnace was thy brain?

What the anvil? what dread grasp
Dare its deadly terrors clasp?

We may notice, too, that Blake restricts himself to seven-syllable lines in "The Tyger," and to a patterned alternation between trimeter and tetrameter lines in "The Lamb," whereas Arnold varies his line lengths in "Dover Beach," the lines growing longer as the speaker warms to his topic. And, finally, we notice that all the lines quoted from Blake and Arnold end with stressed syllables. Your voice rises slightly to the stress at the end of these lines, and they are therefore said to have a **rising rhythm.** In contrast, lines that end on unstressed syllables—"O wild West Wind, thou breath of Autumn's being"—are said to have a **falling rhythm.** It's a small thing, but it can create subtle variations in tone.

These, then, are the basic meters of accentual-syllabic verse and the most common devices used to lend them variety. You will no doubt find many other devices at work as you continue your study of poetry. And you will also find that in much modern verse, such as that of Whitman and Cummings, the rules of accentual-syllabic verse have been replaced by the uncharted techniques and devices of **free verse.** Pauses and phrasings in free verse tend to be visual devices as well as rhythmic ones; line lengths and stress placement vary at the poet's will. Sounds are still being shaped with care, but the writers of free verse are being equally careful to avoid setting up rules to which critics can then bind them. In free verse, as in all verse, ultimately the total effect is the sole criterion.

Here are a modern translation of an Old English poem and an example of Hopkins's sprung rhythm. How would you compare and contrast the two types of verse?

Anonymous

(eighth century)

The Seafarer (modern version by Ezra Pound, 1912)

May I for my own self song's truth reckon,
Journey's jargon, how I in harsh days
Hardship endured oft.
Bitter breast-cares have I abided,
5 Known on my keel many a care's hold,
And dire sea-surge, and there I oft spent
Narrow nightwatch nigh the ship's head
While she tossed close to cliffs. Coldly afflicted,
My feet were by frost benumbed.
10 Chill its chains are; chafing signs
Hew my heart round and hunger begot.
Mere-weary mood. Lest man know not
That he on dry land loveliest liveth,

List how I, care-wretched, on ice-cold sea,
15 Weathered the winter, wretched outcast
Deprived of my kinsmen;
Hung with hard ice-flakes, where hail-scur flew,
There I heard naught save the harsh sea
And ice-cold wave, at whiles the swan cries,
20 Did for my games the gannet's clamor,
Sea-fowls' loudness was for me laughter,
The mews' singing all my mead-drink.
Storms, on the stone-cliffs beaten, fell on the stern
In icy feathers; full oft the eagle screamed
25 With spray on his pinion.
                                    Not any protector
May make merry man faring needy.
This he little believes, who aye in winsome life
Abides 'mid burghers some heavy business,
Wealthy and wine-flushed, how I weary oft
30 Must bide above brine.
Neareth nightshade, snoweth from north,
Frost froze the land, hail fell on earth then,
Corn of the coldest. Nathless there knocketh now
The heart's thought that I on high streams
35 The salt-wavy tumult traverse alone.
Moaneth alway my mind's lust
That I fare forth, that I afar hence
Seek out a foreign fastness.
For this there's no mood-lofty man over earth's midst,
40 Not though he be given his good, but will have in his youth greed;
Nor his deed to the daring, nor his king to the faithful
But shall have his sorrow for sea-fare
Whatever his lord will.
He hath not heart for harping, nor in ring-having
45 Nor winsomeness to wife, nor world's delight
Nor any whit else save the wave's slash,
Yet longing comes upon him to fare forth on the water.
Bosque taketh blossom, cometh beauty of berries,
Fields to fairness, land fares brisker,
50 All this admonisheth man eager of mood,
The heart turns to travel so that he then thinks
On flood-ways to be far departing.
Cuckoo calleth with gloomy crying,
He singeth summerward, bodeth sorrow,
55 The bitter heart's blood. Burgher knows not—
He the prosperous man—what some perform

Where wandering them widest draweth.
So that but now my heart burst from my breastlock,
My mood 'mid the mere-flood,
60 Over the whale's acre, would wander wide.
On earth's shelter cometh oft to me,
Eager and ready, the crying lone-flyer,
Whets for the whale-path the heart irresistibly,
O'er tracks of ocean; seeing that anyhow
65 My lord deems to me this dead life
On loan and on land, I believe not
That any earth-weal eternal standeth
Save there be somewhat calamitous
That, ere a man's tide go, turn it to twain.
70 Disease or oldness or sword-hate
Beats out the breath from doom-gripped body.
And for this, every earl whatever, for those speaking after—
Laud of the living, boasteth some last word,
That he will work ere he pass onward,
75 Frame on the fair earth 'gainst foes his malice,
Daring ado, . . .
So that all men shall honor him after
And his laud beyond them remain 'mid the English,
Aye, for ever, a lasting life's-blast,
80 Delight 'mid the doughty.
                        Days little durable,
And all arrogance of earthen riches,
There come now no kings nor Caesars
Nor gold-giving lords like those gone.
Howe'er in mirth most magnified,
85 Whoe'er lived in life most lordliest,
Drear all this excellence, delights undurable!
Waneth the watch, but the world holdeth.
Tomb hideth trouble. The blade is layed low.
Earthly glory ageth and seareth.
90 No man at all going the earth's gait,
But age fares against him, his face paleth,
Grey-haired he groaneth, knows gone companions,
Lordly men, are to earth o'ergiven,
Nor may he then the flesh-cover, whose life ceaseth,
95 Nor eat the sweet nor feel the sorry,
Nor stir hand nor think in mid heart,
And though he strew the grave with gold,
His born brothers, their buried bodies
Be an unlikely treasure hoard.

STUDY QUESTIONS

Notice the movement of the speaker's mood and thought. How does he characterize himself? What response does he seek from his audience?

Gerard Manley Hopkins

(1844–1889)

Felix Randal

Felix Randal the farrier, O he is dead then? my duty all ended
Who have watched his mould of man, big-boned and
      hardy-handsome
Pining, pining, till time when reason rambled in it and some
Fatal four disorders, fleshed there, all contended?

5 Sickness broke him. Impatient he cursed at first, but mended
Being anointed and all; though a heavenlier heart began some
Months earlier, since I had our sweet reprieve and ransom
Tendered to him. Ah well, God rest him all road ever he offended!

This seeing the sick endears them to us, us too it endears.
10 My tongue had taught thee comfort, touch had quenched thy tears,
Thy tears that touched my heart, child, Felix, poor Felix Randal;

How far from then forethought of, all thy more boisterous years,
When thou at the random grim forge, powerful amidst peers,
Didst fettle for the great grey drayhorse his bright and
      battering sandal!

STUDY QUESTIONS

1. Again, how does the speaker portray himself? How does he portray the blacksmith, Felix Randal?
2. Note the movement of the poem, from present to past. Why might Hopkins have chosen this organization for this poem?

Now read these two examples of accentual-syllabic verse. Note the metrical techniques that make the first sound like a song. The second is like the voice of a man arguing with himself.

Alfred, Lord Tennyson

(1809–1892)

The Splendor Falls on Castle Walls

The splendor falls on castle walls
    And snowy summits old in story:
The long light shakes across the lakes,
    And the wild cataract leaps in glory.
5 Blow, bugle, blow, set the wild echoes flying.
Blow, bugle; answer, echoes, dying, dying, dying.

    O hark, O hear! how thin and clear,
        And thinner, clearer, farther going!
    O sweet and far from cliff and scar
10   The horns of Elfland faintly blowing!
Blow, let us hear the purple glens replying:
Blow, bugle; answer, echoes, dying, dying, dying.

    O love, they die in yon rich sky,
        They faint on hill or field or river;
15   Our echoes roll from soul to soul,
        And grow for ever and for ever.
Blow, bugle, blow, set the wild echoes flying,
And answer, echoes, answer, dying, dying, dying.

STUDY QUESTIONS

1. What is the meter of the main part of the poem? What is the meter of the refrain? What has been achieved by combining the two?
2. What does Tennyson mean by the phrase "our echoes" (line 15)? How do these echoes differ from the other "echoes" of which the poem speaks?
3. Fairyland and fairy things are usually depicted in literature as being immortal and unchanging, in contrast to human affairs, which are transitory. Why does Tennyson reverse that contrast in this poem?
4. How do sound and imagery combine in this poem to reinforce the speaker's message?

George Herbert

(1593–1633)

The Collar[1]

I struck the board[2] and cried, "No more!
     I will abroad!
What, shall I ever sigh and pine?
My lines and life are free: free as the road,
5   Loose as the wind, as large as store.
     Shall I be still in suit?[3]
Have I no harvest but a thorn
To let me blood, and not restore
What I have lost with cordial[4] fruit?
10   Sure there was wine
Before my sighs did dry it; there was corn
    Before my tears did drown it.
Is the year only lost to me?
    Have I no bays[5] to crown it,
15 No flowers, no garlands gay? all blasted?
     All wasted?
Not so, my heart; but there is fruit,
    And thou hast hands.
Recover all thy sigh-blown age
20 On double pleasures. Leave thy cold dispute
Of what is fit and not. Forsake thy cage,
    Thy rope of sands,
Which petty thoughts have made and made to thee
    Good cable, to enforce and draw,
25   And be thy law,
While thou didst wink and wouldst not see.
     Away! take heed!
     I will abroad!
Call in thy death's-head there! Tie up thy fears!
30   He that forbears
    To suit and serve his need,
     Deserves his load."
But as I raved, and grew more fierce and wild

---

[1] the iron band encircling the neck of a prisoner or slave; also perhaps a pun on "choler" as "rebellious anger"
[2] dining table
[3] always petitioning
[4] restorative
[5] laurels

At every word,
35   Methought I heard one calling, "Child!"
And I replied, "My Lord."

STUDY QUESTIONS

Discuss how the movement of sound in "The Collar" helps create the sound of the speaker arguing with himself. (Note the addition of a second voice near the end of the poem. How do the speech of this second voice and the speaker's response to it bring the poem to its resolution?)

Finally, here are two examples of iambic pentameter by two masters of that meter. Note that even the use of the identical meter does not give these poems identical sounds. The rhythm of Shakespeare's sonnet, for all its basic regularity, is flexible and almost conversational; the rhythm of Milton's poem is as firm and regular as the marble tomb he uses as his poem's chief conceit. Read the two poems and then answer the following questions:

1. How does each poet handle his meter? How are phrasing and sentence structure fitted to the pentameter? How is the progression of the speaker's thought emphasized?
2. How does each poem's rhythm enhance or emphasize its imagery? Give examples.

William Shakespeare

(1564–1616)

Sonnet 29

When, in disgrace with Fortune and men's eyes,
I all alone beweep my outcast state,
And trouble deaf heaven with my bootless cries,
And look upon myself and curse my fate,
5   Wishing me like to one more rich in hope,
Featured like him, like him with friends possessed,
Desiring this man's art, and that man's scope,
With what I most enjoy contented least;
Yet in these thoughts myself almost despising,
10   Haply I think on thee, and then my state,
Like to the lark at break of day arising
From sullen earth, sings hymns at heaven's gate;
    For thy sweet love remembered such wealth brings
    That when I scorn to change my state with kings.

John Milton

(1608–1674)

On Shakespeare

What needs my Shakespeare for his honored bones
The labor of an age in pilèd stones?
Or that his hallowed reliques should be hid
Under a star-ypointing[6] pyramid?
5 Dear son of memory, great heir of fame,
What need'st thou such weak witness of they name?
Thou in our wonder and astonishment
Has built thyself a livelong monument.
For whilst, to the shame of slow-endeavoring art,
10 Thy easy numbers flow, and that each heart
Hath from the leaves of thy unvalued[7] book
Those Delphic[8] lines with deep impression took,
Then thou, our fancy of itself bereaving,
Dost make us marble with too much conceiving,[9]
15 And so sepùlchred in such pomp dost lie
That kings for such a tomb would wish to die.

STUDY QUESTIONS

Look back at the poems you have read in this book. Select several that you especially like. Analyze the meter in each, and consider the techniques by which it is varied. Then discuss how these metrical techniques enhance your enjoyment of each poem.

---

[6]Milton added the "y" for the sake of rhythm.
[7]invaluable
[8]inspired—as by the oracle at Delphi
[9]thinking

24

RHYME SCHEMES AND VERSE FORMS

Although rhyme is not found in all poetry written in English, it has been so important in the history of English and American verse that we often first divide poetry into two categories—rhymed and unrhymed—and then divide further from there. Accepting that categorization for the moment, we will note that unrhymed poems tend to fall into one of three major divisions: accentual verse, which has existed from Old English times and which we met in "The Seafarer" and "Felix Randal"; blank verse (unrhymed iambic pentameter), a sixteenth-century invention, of which Hamlet's soliloquies are classic examples; or free verse, sometimes called by the French name **vers libre,** a modern (and not always unrhymed) form that we met in the works of such diverse poets as Whitman, Cummings, Pound, and Levertov.

Rhymed Verse

Rhymed verse is harder to classify. There are so many ways of combining rhymed lines! Still, one can distinguish between those forms of rhymed verse that have a fixed total length (such as the **limerick,** with five lines; the **sonnet,** with fourteen; and the **villanelle,** with nineteen) and those that do not. Rhymed verse with no fixed length is usually composed of **stanzas.** Each stanza usually has a fixed length; but the number of stanzas, and hence the length of the poem as a whole, remain variable.

Underlying both types of rhymed verse, however, stand the basic combinations of rhyme. These embrace two-, three-, and four-line patterns, called the couplet, triplet, terza rima, and the quatrain. The **couplet** has two consecutive lines that rhyme:

> So long as men can breathe or eyes can see,
> So long lives this, and this gives life to thee.

The **tercet** or **triplet** has three lines that rhyme:

> He clasps the crag with crooked hands;
> Close to the sun in lonely lands,
> Ringed with the azure world, he stands.

The **terza rima** also has three lines, but only the first and last rhyme. When terza rima stanzas are linked together, the middle line of one stanza rhymes with the first and third lines of the stanza that follows.

> O wild West Wind, thou breath of Autumn's being,
> Thou, from whose unseen presence the leaves dead
> Are driven, like ghosts from an enchanter fleeing,
>
> Yellow, and black, and pale, and hectic red,
> Pestilence-stricken multitudes: O thou
> Who chariotest to their dark wintry bed

The **quatrain** has four lines joined by any one of the following rhyme schemes:

- Second and fourth lines rhyming (*abcb*):

> When I was one-and-twenty
>   I heard a wise man say,
> "Give crowns and pounds and guineas
>   But not your heart away;

- First and third, second and fourth lines rhyming (*abab*):

> She even thinks that up in heaven
> Her class lies late and snores,
> While poor black cherubs rise at seven
> To do celestial chores.

- First and fourth, second and third lines rhyming (*abba*):

> Earth hath not anything to show more fair!
> Dull would he be of soul who could pass by
> A sight so touching in its majesty.
> The city now doth, like a garment, wear

- First and second, third and fourth lines rhyming (*aabb*):

> "O 'Melia, my dear, this does everything crown!
> Who could have supposed I should meet you in Town?
> And whence such fair garments, such prosperi-ty?"—
> "O didn't you know I'd been ruined?" said she.

Any of these patterns can stand alone as a stanza, or patterns may be added to or combined to produce more complicated stanzas. For example, the first poem in this chapter, Robert Herrick's "The Night-Piece, To Julia," has two five-line stanzas consisting of two couplets and a final line rhyming with the first two lines. The next poem, Browning's "Home-Thoughts, from Abroad," combines couplets and *abab* quatrains into two stanzas of eight and twelve lines. The third poem, Sir Thomas Wyatt's "They Flee from Me," is written in **rime royale,** a seven-line stanza rhyming *ababbcc.*

Robert Herrick

(1591–1674)

The Night-Piece, to Julia

Her eyes the glowworm lend thee;
The shooting stars attend thee;
    And the elves also,
    Whose little eyes glow
5 Like the sparks of fire, befriend thee.

No will-o'-the-wisp mislight thee;
Nor snake or slowworm bite thee;
    But on, on thy way,
    Not making a stay,
10 Since ghost there's none to affright thee.

Let not the dark thee cumber;
What though the moon does slumber?
    The stars of the night
    Will lend thee their light,
15 Like tapers clear without number.

Then, Julia, let me woo thee,
Thus, thus to come unto me;
    And when I shall meet
    Thy silvery feet,
20 My soul I'll pour into thee.

Robert Browning

(1812–1889)

Home-Thoughts, from Abroad

1

Oh, to be in England
Now that April's there,
And whoever wakes in England
Sees, some morning, unaware,
5 That the lowest boughs and the brushwood sheaf
Round the elm-tree bole are in tiny leaf,
While the chaffinch sings on the orchard bough
In England—now!

2

And after April, when May follows,
10 And the whitethroat builds, and all the swallows!
Hark, where my blossomed pear-tree in the hedge
Leans to the field and scatters on the clover
Blossoms and dewdrops—at the bent spray's edge—
That's the wise thrush; he sings each song twice over,
15 Lest you should think he never could recapture
The first fine careless rapture!
And though the fields look rough with hoary dew,
All will be gay when noontide wakes anew
The buttercups, the little children's dower
20 —Far brighter than this gaudy melon-flower!

Sir Thomas Wyatt

(1503–1542)

They Flee from Me

They flee from me that sometime did me seek
    With naked foot stalking in my chamber.
I have seen them gentle tame and meek
    That now are wild and do not remember
5   That sometime they put themselves in danger
To take bread at my hand; and now they range
Busily seeking with a continual change.

Thankèd be Fortune, it hath been otherwise
    Twenty times better; but once in special,
10 In thin array after a pleasant guise,
    When her loose gown from her shoulders did fall,
    And she me caught in her arms long and small;
And therewithall sweetly did me kiss,
And softly said, "Dear heart, how like you this?"

15 It was no dream: I lay broad waking.
    But all is turned thorough my gentleness
Into a strange fashion of forsaking;
    And I have leave to go of her goodness,
    And she also to use newfangleness.
20 But since that I so kindely am served,
I fain would know what she hath deserved.

Limericks and Villanelles

Let us now look at two rhymed forms of fixed length: the limerick and the villanelle. (We will consider a third fixed-length form, the sonnet, in the next chapter.)

Limericks have five lines. The rhyme scheme is *aabba,* with all *a* lines having three feet, and all *b* lines two feet. The meter is usually anapestic.

Limericks are humorous verse, frequently employing puns, off-color humor, or deliberately tortured rhymes or rhythms. As one anonymous writer and critic remarks,

> The limerick packs laughs anatomical,
> Into space that is quite economical.
>   But the good ones I've seen
>   So seldom are clean,
> And the clean ones so seldom are comical.

More serious, but equally tightly controlled in form, is the **villanelle.** Entire lines, as well as rhyme sounds, are repeated in the villanelle to make up its prescribed pattern. Here is one of the finest twentieth-century villanelles. Analyze its form and discuss what the poet has done with it.

Dylan Thomas

(1914–1953)

Do Not Go Gentle into That Good Night

Do not go gentle into that good night,
Old age should burn and rave at close of day;
Rage, rage against the dying of the light.

Though wise men at their end know dark is right,
5 Because their words had forked no lightning they
Do not go gentle into that good night.

Good men, the last wave by, crying how bright
Their frail deeds might have danced in a green bay,
Rage, rage against the dying of the light.

10 Wild men who caught and sang the sun in flight,
And learn, too late, they grieved it on its way,
Do not go gentle into that good night.

Grave men, near death, who see with blinding sight
Blind eyes could blaze like meteors and be gay,
15 Rage, rage against the dying of the light.

And you, my father, there on the sad height,
Curse, bless, me now with your fierce tears, I pray.
Do not go gentle into that good night.
Rage, rage against the dying of the light.

Ballades, Ballads, and Odes

Three forms without fixed length are the **ballade, ballad,** and **ode.** The **ballade** was popular during the Middle Ages. It uses seven- or eight-line stanzas, usually in groups of three. Each stanza ends with the same line, the **refrain.** The ballade itself ends with a shorter stanza, the **envoy** or **envoi.** The envoy is addressed directly to the person for whom the ballade is being written. It, too, ends with the refrain.

In contrast to the tightly defined ballade, the term **ballad** (without the final *e*) may be used for poems that are, or can be, sung, and that have regular stanzas. Frequently, like the ballade, they make use of repeated lines or refrains. Note, in this next poem, how effectively the refrain works as its implication shifts a little in each stanza.

Lord Randal

"O where ha you been, Lord Randal, my son?
And where ha you been, my handsome young man?"
"I ha been at the greenwood; mother, mak my bed soon,
For I'm wearied wi hunting, and fain wad lie down."

5　"An wha met ye there, Lord Randal, my son?
An wha met you there, my handsome young man?"
"O I met wi my true-love; mother, mak my bed soon,
For I'm wearied wi huntin, and fain wad lie down."

"And what did she give you, Lord Randal, my son?
10　And what did she give you, my handsome young man?"
"Eels fried in a pan; mother, mak my bed soon,
For I'm wearied wi huntin, and fain wad lie down."

"And wha gat your leavins, Lord Randal, my son?
And wha gat your leavins, my handsome young man?"
15　"My hawks and my hounds; mother, mak my bed soon,
For I'm wearied wi hunting, and fain wad lie down."

"And what becam of them, Lord Randal, my son?
And what becam of them, my handsome young man?"
"They stretched their legs out and died; mother, mak my bed soon,
20　For I'm wearied wi huntin, and fain wad lie down."

"O I fear you are poisoned, Lord Randal, my son!
I fear you are poisoned, my handsome young man!"
"O yes, I am poisoned; mother, mak my bed soon,
For I'm sick at the heart, and I fain wad lie down."

25 "What d'ye leave to your mother, Lord Randal, my son?
What d'ye leave to your mother, my handsome young man?"
"Four and twenty milk kye[1]; mother, mak my bed soon,
For I'm sick at the heart, and I fain wad lie down."

"What d'ye leave to your sister, Lord Randal, my son?
30 What d'ye leave to your sister, my handsome young man?"
"My gold and my silver; mother, mak my bed soon,
For I'm sick at the heart, an I fain wad lie down."

"What d'ye leave to your brother, Lord Randal, my son?
What d'ye leave to your brother, my handsome young man?"
35 "My houses and my lands; mother, mak my bed soon,
For I'm sick at the heart, and I fain wad lie down."

"What d'ye leave to your true-love, Lord Randal, my son?
What d'ye leave to your true-love, my handsome young man?"
"I leave her hell and fire; mother, mak my bed soon,
40 For I'm sick at the heart, and I fain wad lie down."

Among the rhymed poetic forms, the **ode** is unique in leaving both the rhyme scheme and the length of each individual line to the poet's discretion. The one constant feature of odes in English poetry, in fact, is their elevated tone. In Keats's "Ode on a Grecian Urn" and "Ode to a Nightingale," and in Shelley's "Ode to the West Wind," we saw three different stanzaic patterns. Look back at these odes now (on pages 440, 454, and 456) and define their patterns. Note, too, that in each case the stanzaic form is constant throughout the ode. For this reason, these are sometimes called **Horatian odes.**

To conclude this chapter, we will read one further ode, this one of the type called the **irregular ode.** This particular ode, written by the early Romantic poet William Wordsworth, makes skillful use of rhyme and rhythm both. Yet, for all its careful contrivance, it maintains a remarkable freshness of tone, in keeping with its subject of early joys and maturer delights. Because it is an irregular ode, the stanzas in this poem vary among themselves, changing shape to follow the motions of the poet's mind. The basic meter remains iambic throughout, but line lengths and rhyme schemes shift constantly. The result is an unusual blend of patterning and fluidity that sometimes mutes its tone to a thoughtful expression of philosophy and sometimes rises to a hymn of joyful praise.

---

[1]cows

The ode deals with the relations between the human soul, nature, and immortality. In it, Wordsworth suggests not only that we know immortality after death, but that we know it before birth as well: "trailing clouds of glory do we come,/ From God, who is our home." The ode thus celebrates the heavenlike joy the young child sees in the natural world; and it laments the dulling of that joy that occurs when the child, responding to the novelty of his mundane existence, turns his mind more fully upon earthly things. Yet the final tone is not sorrow but a greater joy, as Wordsworth passes beyond mourning this early loss into celebrating the fully human joys and loves that are the gift of the mature soul.

As you read the ode, pay careful attention to the way Wordsworth develops this train of thought, and notice how the sound and shape of the stanzas convey the changing emotions the speaker feels.

William Wordsworth

(1770–1850)

Ode

Intimations of Immortality from Recollections of Early Childhood

The Child is father of the Man;
And I could wish my days to be
Bound each to each by natural piety.

1

There was a time when meadow, grove, and stream,
The earth, and every common sight,
    To me did seem
    Apparelled in celestial light,
5 The glory and the freshness of a dream.
It is not now as it hath been of yore;—
    Turn wheresoe'er I may,
      By night or day,
The things which I have seen I now can see no more.

2

10   The Rainbow comes and goes,
    And lovely is the Rose,
    The Moon doth with delight
Look round her when the heavens are bare;
    Waters on a starry night
15   Are beautiful and fair;
The sunshine is a glorious birth;

But yet I know, where'er I go,
That there hath past away a glory from the earth.

3

Now, while the birds thus sing a joyous song,
20   And while the young lambs bound
        As to the tabor's sound,
To me alone there came a thought of grief:
A timely utterance gave that thought relief,
      And I again am strong:
25 The cataracts blow their trumpets from the steep;
No more shall grief of mine the season wrong;
I hear the Echoes through the mountains throng,
The Winds come to me from the fields of sleep,
      And all the earth is gay;
30   Land and sea
    Give themselves up to jollity,
      And with the heart of May
Doth every Beast keep holiday;—
      Thou Child of Joy,
35 Shout round me, let me hear thy shouts, thou happy Shepherd-boy!

4

Ye blessèd Creatures, I have heard the call
    Ye to each other make; I see
The heavens laugh with you in your jubilee;
    My heart is at your festival,
40   My head hath its coronal,
The fulness of your bliss, I feel—I feel it all.
      Oh evil day! if I were sullen
      While Earth herself is adorning,
        This sweet May-morning,
45   And the Children are culling
        On every side,
      In a thousand valleys far and wide,
      Fresh flowers; while the sun shines warm,
And the Babe leaps up on his Mother's arm:—
50   I hear, I hear, with joy I hear!
      —But there's a Tree, of many, one,
A single Field which I have looked upon,
Both of them speak of something that is gone:
      The Pansy at my feet
55   Doth the same tale repeat:

Whither is fled the visionary gleam?
Where is it now, the glory and the dream?

5

Our birth is but a sleep and a forgetting:
The Soul that rises with us, our life's Star,
60   Hath had elsewhere its setting,
              And cometh from afar:
          Not in entire forgetfulness,
          And not in utter nakedness,
But trailing clouds of glory do we come
65   From God, who is our home:
Heaven lies about us in our infancy!
Shades of the prison-house begin to close
              Upon the growing Boy,
                   But He
70 Beholds the light, and whence it flows,
              He sees it in his joy;
The Youth, who daily farther from the east
              Must travel, still is Nature's Priest,
              And by the vision splendid
75   Is on his way attended;
At length the Man perceives it die away,
And fade into the light of common day.

6

Earth fills her lap with pleasures of her own;
Yearnings she hath in her own natural kind,
80 And, even with something of a Mother's mind,
              And no unworthy aim,
              The homely Nurse doth all she can
To make her Foster-child, her Inmate Man,
              Forget the glories he hath known,
85 And that imperial palace whence he came.

7

Behold the Child among his new-born blisses,
A six years' Darling of a pigmy size!
See, where 'mid work of his own hand he lies,
Fretted by sallies of his mother's kisses,
90 With light upon him from his father's eyes!
See, at his feet, some little plan or chart,
Some fragment from his dream of human life,
Shaped by himself with newly-learnèd art;

A wedding or a festival,
95   A mourning or a funeral;
            And this hath now his heart,
            And unto this he frames his song:
            Then will he fit his tongue
    To dialogues of business, love, or strife;
100   But it will not be long
            Ere this be thrown aside,
            And with new joy and pride
    The little Actor cons another part;
    Filling from time to time his "humorous stage"
105 With all the Persons, down to palsied Age,
    That Life brings with her in her equipage;
            As if his whole vocation
            Were endless imitation.

8

    Thou, whose exterior semblance doth belie
110   Thy Soul's immensity;
    Thou best Philosopher, who yet dost keep
    Thy heritage, thou Eye among the blind,
    That, deaf and silent, read'st the eternal deep,
    Haunted for ever by the eternal mind,—
115   Mighty Prophet! Seer blest!
            On whom those truths do rest,
    Which we are toiling all our lives to find,
    In darkness lost, the darkness of the grave;
    Thou, over whom thy Immortality
120 Broods like the Day, a Master o'er a Slave,
    A Presence which is not to be put by;
    Thou little Child, yet glorious in the might
    Of heaven-born freedom on thy being's height,
    Why with such earnest pains dost thou provoke
125 The years to bring the inevitable yoke,
    Thus blindly with thy blessedness at strife?
    Full soon thy Soul shall have her earthly freight,
    And custom lie upon thee with a weight,
    Heavy as frost, and deep almost as life!

9

130   O joy! that in our embers
            Is something that doth live,
            That nature yet remembers
            What was so fugitive!

The thought of our past years in me doth breed
135 Perpetual benediction: not indeed
For that which is most worthy to be blest;
Delight and liberty, the simple creed
Of Childhood, whether busy or at rest,
With new-fledged hope still fluttering in his breast:—
140   Not for these I raise
        The song of thanks and praise;
    But for those obstinate questionings
    Of sense and outward things,
    Falling from us, vanishings;
145   Blank misgivings of a Creature
Moving about in worlds not realised,
High instincts before which our mortal Nature
Did tremble like a guilty Thing surprised:
        But for those first affections,
150   Those shadowy recollections,
    Which, be they what they may,
Are yet the fountain-light of all our day,
Are yet a master-light of all our seeing;
    Uphold us, cherish, and have power to make
155 Our noisy years seem moments in the being
Of the eternal Silence: truths that wake,
            To perish never:
Which neither listlessness, nor mad endeavor,
            Nor Man nor Boy,
160 Nor all that is at enmity with joy,
    Can utterly abolish or destroy!
        Hence in a season of calm weather
        Though inland far we be,
Our Souls have sight of that immortal sea
165   Which brought us hither,
        Can in a moment travel thither,
And see the Children sport upon the shore,
And hear the mighty waters rolling evermore.

10

Then sing, ye Birds, sing, sing a joyous song!
170   And let the young Lambs bound
        As to the tabor's sound!
We in thought will join your throng,
        Ye that pipe and ye that play,
        Ye that through your hearts to-day
175   Feel the gladness of the May!

What though the radiance which was once so bright
Be now for ever taken from my sight,
   Though nothing can bring back the hour
Of splendor in the grass, of glory in the flower;
180   We will grieve not, rather find
     Strength in what remains behind;
     In the primal sympathy
     Which having been must ever be;
     In the soothing thoughts that spring
185   Out of human suffering;
     In the faith that looks through death,
In years that bring the philosophic mind.

11

And O, ye Fountains, Meadows, Hills, and Groves,
Forebode not any severing of our loves!
190 Yet in my heart of hearts I feel your might;
I only have relinquished one delight
To live beneath your more habitual sway.
I love the Brooks which down their channels fret,
Even more than when I tripped lightly as they;
195 The innocent brightness of a new-born Day
     Is lovely yet;
The Clouds that gather round the setting sun
Do take a sober coloring from an eye
That hath kept watch o'er man's mortality;
200 Another race hath been, and other palms are won.
Thanks to the human heart by which we live,
Thanks to its tenderness, its joys, and fears,
To me the meanest flower that blows can give
Thoughts that do often lie too deep for tears.

25

THE SONNET

Without a doubt, the most popular of the defined forms in English and American poetry is the **sonnet.** Sonnets are always fourteen lines long. Traditionally, they are divided into two main forms. The **Petrarchan sonnet** consists of an octet, rhymed *abba abba,* and a sestet, rhymed either *cdcdcd* or *cdecde;* and the **Shakespearean sonnet,** with three quatrains, usually rhymes *abab cdcd efef,* and a couplet at the end, *gg.* Less standard rhyme forms do, of course, exist. Notice, for example, the rhyme scheme in Cummings's "the Cambridge ladies who live in furnished souls," at the end of this chapter.

Of the two traditional forms, the Shakespearean usually seems the more emphatic. Because no sound needs to be used more than twice, it is also slightly easier to write. It was the favored form during the Renaissance. The Petrarchan sonnet, on the other hand, tends to have a somewhat smoother flow and often seems more graceful. It was therefore preferred by the Romantic poets of the nineteenth century.

The sonnet came into English as a love poem: we have read love sonnets by Shakespeare, Sidney, and Spenser. But the sonnet has proved capable of handling almost any subject and of expressing many moods and tones. Look back, for example, at "Ozymandias" (p. 420) and "Composed upon Westminster Bridge" (p. 430). And look, too, at the following examples of what can be done with the sonnet form.

William Shakespeare

(1564–1616)

Sonnet 116

Let me not to the marriage of true minds
Admit impediments. Love is not love
Which alters when it alteration finds,
Or bends with the remover to remove.
5 O no! it is an ever-fixèd mark
That looks on tempests and is never shaken;
It is the star to every wand'ring bark,
Whose worth's unknown, although his height be taken.
Love's not Time's fool, though rosy lips and cheeks
10 Within his bending sickle's compass come.

Love alters not with his brief hours and weeks,
But bears it out even to the edge of doom.
    If this be error, and upon me proved,
    I never writ, nor no man ever loved.

John Donne

(1572–1631)

Sonnet 10

Death, be not proud, though some have callèd thee
Mighty and dreadful, for thou art not so;
For those whom thou think'st thou dost overthrow
Die not, poor Death, nor yet canst thou kill me.
5 From rest and sleep, which but thy pictures be,
Much pleasure; then from thee much more must flow;
And soonest our best men with thee do go,
Rest of their bones and souls' delivery.
Thou'rt slave to fate, chance, kings, and desperate men,
10 And dost with poison, war, and sickness dwell;
And poppy or charms can make us sleep as well
And better than thy stroke. Why swell'st thou then?
One short sleep past, we wake eternally,
And Death shall be no more: Death, thou shalt die.

John Milton

(1608–1674)

On His Blindness

When I consider how my light is spent,
Ere half my days, in this dark world and wide,
And that one talent which is death to hide
Lodged with me useless, though my soul more bent
5 To serve therewith my Maker, and present
My true account, lest he returning chide,
"Doth God exact day labor, light denied?"
I fondly ask; but Patience, to prevent
That murmur, soon replies: "God doth not need
10 Either man's work or his own gifts; who best
Bear his mild yoke, they serve him best. His state
Is kingly: thousands at his bidding speed

And post o'er land and ocean without rest.
They also serve who only stand and wait."

Gerard Manley Hopkins

(1844–1889)

God's Grandeur

The world is charged with the grandeur of God.
    It will flame out, like shining from shook foil;[1]
    It gathers to a greatness, like the ooze of oil
Crushed. Why do men then now not reck his rod?[2]
5 Generations have trod, have trod, have trod;
    And all is seared with trade; bleared, smeared with toil;
    And wears man's smudge and shares man's smell: the soil
Is bare now, nor can foot feel, being shod.

And for all this, nature is never spent;
10   There lives the dearest freshness deep down things;
And though the last lights off the black West went
    Oh, morning, at the brown brink eastward, springs—
Because the Holy Ghost over the bent
    World broods with warm breast and with ah! bright wings.

Robert Frost

(1874–1963)

Design

I found a dimpled spider, fat and white,
On a white heal-all, holding up a moth
Like a white piece of rigid satin cloth—
Assorted characters of death and blight
5 Mixed ready to begin the morning right,
Like the ingredients of a witches' broth—
A snow-drop spider, a flower like a froth,
And dead wings carried like a paper kite.

What had that flower to do with being white,
10 The wayside blue and innocent heal-all?

---

[1] tinsel, goldfoil
[2] acknowledge his discipline

What brought the kindred spider to that height,
Then steered the white moth thither in the night?
What but design of darkness to appall?—
If design govern in a thing so small.

Edna St. Vincent Millay

(1892–1950)

Love Is Not All; It Is Not Meat Nor Drink

Love is not all; it is not meat nor drink
Nor slumber nor a roof against the rain;
Nor yet a floating spar to men that sink
And rise and sink and rise and sink again;
5 Love can not fill the thickened lung with breath,
Nor clean the blood, nor set the fractured bone;
Yet many a man is making friends with death
Even as I speak, for lack of love alone.
It well may be that in a difficult hour,
10 Pinned down by pain and moaning for release,
Or nagged by want past resolution's power,
I might be driven to sell your love for peace,
Or trade the memory of this night for food.
It well may be. I do not think I would.

Wilfred Owen

(1893–1918)

Anthem for Doomed Youth

What passing-bells for these who die as cattle?
  Only the monstrous anger of the guns.
  Only the stuttering rifles' rapid rattle
Can patter out their hasty orisons.
5 No mockeries now for them; no prayers nor bells,
  Nor any voice of mourning save the choirs—
The shrill, demented choirs of wailing shells;
  And bugles calling for them from sad shires.

What candles may be held to speed them all?
10 Not in the hands of boys, but in their eyes
Shall shine the holy glimmers of good-byes.
  The pallor of girls' brows shall be their pall;

Their flowers the tenderness of patient minds,
And each slow dusk a drawing-down of blinds.

E. E. Cummings

(1894–1963)

the Cambridge ladies who live in furnished souls

the Cambridge ladies who live in furnished souls
are unbeautiful and have comfortable minds
(also, with the church's protestant blessings
daughters, unscented shapeless spirited)
5 they believe in Christ and Longfellow, both dead,
are invariably interested in so many things—
at the present writing one still finds
delighted fingers knitting for the is it Poles?
perhaps. While permanent faces coyly bandy
10 scandal of Mrs. N and Professor D
. . . . the Cambridge ladies do not care, above
Cambridge if sometimes in its box of
sky lavender and cornerless, the
moon rattles like a fragment of angry candy

An Anthology of Poems

Anonymous—Middle English Lyric

Western Wind

Western wind, when will thou blow,
　The small rain down can rain?
Christ, if my love were in my arms
　And I in my bed again.

Christopher Marlowe

(1564–1593)

The Passionate Shepherd to His Love

Come live with me, and be my love,
And we will all the pleasures prove
That hills and valleys, dales and fields,
Woods, or steepy mountain yields.

5　And we will sit upon the rocks,
　Seeing the shepherds feed their flocks,
　By shallow rivers, to whose falls
　Melodious birds sing madrigals.

　And I will make thee beds of roses
10　And a thousand fragrant posies,
　A cap of flowers, and a kirtle
　Embroidered all with leaves of myrtle;

　A gown made of the finest wool,
　Which from our pretty lambs we pull,
15　Fair linèd slippers, for the cold,
　With buckles of the purest gold;

　A belt of straw and ivy-buds
　With coral clasps and amber studs.
　And if these pleasures may thee move,
20　Come live with me, and be my love.

　The shepherds' swains shall dance and sing
　For thy delight each May morning.
　If these delights thy mind may move,
　Then live with me, and be my love.

Sir Walter Raleigh

(1552?–1618)

The Nymph's Reply to the Shepherd

If all the world and love were young,
And truth in every shepherd's tongue,
These pretty pleasures might me move
To live with thee and be thy love.

5 Time drives the flocks from field to fold
When rivers rage and rocks grow cold,
And Philomel becometh dumb;
The rest complains of cares to come.

The flowers do fade, and wanton fields
10 To wayward winter reckoning yields;
A honey tongue, a heart of gall,
Is fancy's spring, but sorrow's fall.

Thy gowns, thy shoes, thy beds of roses,
Thy cap, thy kirtle, and thy posies
15 Soon break, soon wither, soon forgotten—
In folly ripe, in reason rotten.

Thy belt of straw and ivy buds,
Thy coral clasps and amber studs,
All these in me no means can move
20 To come to thee and be thy love.

But could youth last and love still breed,
Had joys no date nor age no need,
Then these delights my mind might move
To live with thee and be thy love.

William Shakespeare

(1564–1616)

Sonnet 55

Not marble nor the gilded monuments
Of princes shall outlive this powerful rime;
But you shall shine more bright in these contents
Than unswept stone, besmeared with sluttish time.
5 When wasteful war shall statues overturn,
And broils root out the work of masonry,

Nor Mars his sword nor war's quick fire shall burn
The living record of your memory.
'Gainst death and all oblivious enmity
10   Shall you pace forth; your praise shall still find room
Even in the eyes of all posterity
That wear this world out to the ending doom.
    So, till the Judgment that yourself arise,
    You live in this, and dwell in lovers' eyes.

John Donne

(1572–1631)

Sonnet 7

At the round earth's imagined corners, blow
Your trumpets, angels, and arise, arise
From death, you numberless infinities
Of souls, and to your scattered bodies go;
5   All whom the flood did, and fire shall o'erthrow;
All whom war, dearth, age, agues, tyrannies,
Despair, law, chance, hath slain, and you whose eyes
Shall behold God, and never taste death's woe.
But let them sleep, Lord, and me mourn a space,
10   For if above all these my sins abound,
'Tis late to ask abundance of thy grace
When we are there; here on this lowly ground
Teach me how to repent; for that's as good
As if thou hadst sealed my pardon with thy blood.

Edmund Waller

(1606–1687)

Go, Lovely Rose

    Go, lovely rose,
Tell her that wastes her time and me
    That now she knows,
When I resemble her to thee,
5   How sweet and fair she seems to be.

    Tell her that's young
And shuns to have her graces spied
    That hadst thou sprung

In deserts where no men abide,
10 Thou must have uncommended died.

    Small is the worth
Of beauty from the light retired;
    Bid her come forth,
Suffer herself to be desired,
15 And not blush so to be admired.

    Then die, that she
The common fate of all things rare
    May read in thee:
How small a part of time they share
20 That are so wondrous sweet and fair!

Sir John Suckling

(1609–1642)

The Constant Lover

Out upon it! I have loved
    Three whole days together;
And am like to love three more,
    If it prove fair weather!

5 Time shall moult away his wings,
    Ere he shall discover
In the whole wide world again
    Such a constant lover.

But the spite on't is, no praise
10   Is due at all to me:
Love with me had made no stays,
    Had it any been but she.

William Blake

(1757–1827)

London

I wander thro' each charter'd street,
Near where the charter'd Thames does flow,
And mark in every face I meet
Marks of weakness, marks of woe.

5 In every cry of every Man,
   In every Infant's cry of fear,
   In every voice, in every ban,
   The mind-forg'd manacles I hear.

   How the Chimney-sweeper's cry
10 Every blackning Church appalls;
   And the hapless Soldier's sigh
   Runs in blood down Palace walls.

   But most thro' midnight streets I hear
   How the youthful Harlot's curse
15 Blasts the new-born Infant's tear,
   And blights with plagues the Marriage hearse.

Samuel Taylor Coleridge

(1772–1834)

Kubla Khan

   In Xanadu did Kubla Khan
   A stately pleasure-dome decree:
   Where Alph, the sacred river, ran
   Through caverns measureless to man
5   Down to a sunless sea.
   So twice five miles of fertile ground
   With walls and towers were girdled round:
   And there were gardens bright with sinuous rills,
   Where blossomed many an incense-bearing tree;
10 And here were forests ancient as the hills,
   Enfolding sunny spots of greenery.

   But oh! that deep romantic chasm which slanted
   Down the green hill athwart a cedarn cover!
   A savage place! as holy and enchanted
15 As e'er beneath a waning moon was haunted
   By woman wailing for her demon-lover!
   And from this chasm, with ceaseless turmoil seething,
   As if this earth in fast thick pants were breathing,
   A mighty fountain momently was forced:
20 Amid whose swift half-intermitted burst
   Huge fragments vaulted like rebounding hail,
   Or chaffy grain beneath the thresher's flail:
   And 'mid these dancing rocks at once and ever
   It flung up momently the sacred river.

25 Five miles meandering with a mazy motion
Through wood and dale the sacred river ran,
Then reached the caverns measureless to man,

And sank in tumult to a lifeless ocean:
And 'mid this tumult Kubla heard from far
30 Ancestral voices prophesying war!

    The shadow of the dome of pleasure
    Floated midway on the waves;
    Where was heard the mingled measure
    From the fountain and the caves.

35 It was a miracle of rare device,
A sunny pleasure-dome with caves of ice!

    A damsel with a dulcimer
    In a vision once I saw:
    It was an Abyssinian maid,
40   And on her dulcimer she played,
    Singing of Mount Abora.
    Could I revive within me
    Her symphony and song,
    To such a deep delight 'twould win me,

45 That with music loud and long,
I would build that dome in air,
That sunny dome! those caves of ice!
And all who heard should see them there,
And all should cry, Beware! Beware!
50 His flashing eyes, his floating hair!
Weave a circle round him thrice,
And close your eyes with holy dread,
For he on honey-dew hath fed,
And drunk the milk of Paradise.

Alfred, Lord Tennyson

(1809–1892)

Ulysses

It little profits that an idle king,
By this still hearth, among these barren crags,
Matched with an aged wife, I mete and dole
Unequal laws unto a savage race,
5 That hoard, and sleep, and feed, and know not me.

I cannot rest from travel; I will drink
Life to the lees. All times I have enjoyed
Greatly, have suffered greatly, both with those
That loved me, and alone; on shore, and when
10 Through scudding drifts the rainy Hyades[1]
Vexed the dim sea: I am become a name;
For always roaming with a hungry heart
Much have I seen and known—cities of men
And manners, climates, councils, governments,
15 Myself not least, but honored of them all;
And drunk delight of battle with my peers,
Far on the ringing plains of windy Troy.
I am a part of all that I have met;
Yet all experience is an arch wherethrough
20 Gleams that untraveled world whose margin fades
For ever and for ever when I move.
How dull it is to pause, to make an end,
To rust unburnished, not to shine in use!
As though to breathe were life! Life piled on life
25 Were all too little, and of one to me
Little remains; but every hour is saved
From that eternal silence, something more,
A bringer of new things; and vile it were
For some three suns to store and hoard myself,
30 And this gray spirit yearning in desire
To follow knowledge like a sinking star,
Beyond the utmost bound of human thought.

This is my son, mine own Telemachus,
To whom I leave the scepter and the isle—
35 Well-loved of me, discerning to fulfil
This labor, by slow prudence to make mild
A rugged people, and through soft degrees
Subdue them to the useful and the good.
Most blameless is he, centered in the sphere
40 Of common duties, decent not to fail
In offices of tenderness, and pay
Meet adoration to my household gods,
When I am gone. He works his work, I mine.

There lies the port; the vessel puffs her sail;
45 There gloom the dark, broad seas. My mariners,

---

[1] a group of stars in the constellation Taurus, whose rise with the sun heralded the spring rains

Souls that have toiled, and wrought, and thought with me—
That ever with a frolic welcome took
The thunder and the sunshine, and opposed
Free hearts, free foreheads—you and I are old;
50 Old age hath yet his honor and his toil.
Death closes all; but something ere the end,
Some work of noble note, may yet be done,
Not unbecoming men that strove with Gods.
The lights begin to twinkle from the rocks:
55 The long day wanes: the slow moon climbs: the deep
Moans round with many voices. Come, my friends,
'Tis not too late to seek a newer world.
Push off, and sitting well in order smite
The sounding furrows; for my purpose holds
60 To sail beyond the sunset, and the baths
Of all the western stars, until I die.
It may be that the gulfs will wash us down;
It may be we shall touch the Happy Isles,
And see the great Achilles, whom we knew.
65 Though much is taken, much abides; and though
We are not now that strength which in old days
Moved earth and heaven, that which we are, we are;
One equal temper of heroic hearts,
Made weak by time and fate, but strong in will
70 To strive, to seek, to find, and not to yield.

Robert Browning

(1812–1889)

The Bishop Orders His Tomb at Saint Praxed's Church

Rome, 15—

Vanity, saith the preacher, vanity!
Draw round my bed: is Anselm keeping back?
Nephews[2]—sons mine . . . ah God, I know not! Well—
She, men would have to be your mother once,
5 Old Gandolf envied me, so fair she was!
What's done is done, and she is dead beside,
Dead long ago, and I am Bishop since,
And as she died so must we die ourselves,

---

[2]euphemism for illegitimate sons

And thence ye may perceive the world's a dream.
10 Life, how and what is it? As here I lie
In this state-chamber, dying by degrees,
Hours and long hours in the dead night, I ask
"Do I live, am I dead?" Peace, peace seems all.
Saint Praxed's ever was the church for peace;
15 And so, about this tomb of mine. I fought
With tooth and nail to save my niche, ye know:
—Old Gandolf cozened me, despite my care;
Shrewd was that snatch from out the corner South
He graced his carrion with, God curse the same!
20 Yet still my niche is not so cramped but thence
One sees the pulpit o' the epistle side,[3]
And somewhat of the choir, those silent seats,
And up into the aery dome where live
The angels, and a sunbeam's sure to lurk:
25 And I shall fill my slab of basalt there,
And 'neath my tabernacle take my rest,
With those nine columns round me, two and two,
The odd one at my feet where Anselm stands:
Peach-blossom marble all, the rare, the ripe
30 As fresh-poured red wine of a mighty pulse.
—Old Gandolf with his paltry onion-stone,
Put me where I may look at him! True peach,
Rosy and flawless: how I earned the prize!
Draw close: that conflagration of my church
35 —What then? So much was saved if aught were missed!
My sons, ye would not be my death? Go dig
The white-grape vineyard where the oil-press stood,
Drop water gently till the surface sink,
And if ye find . . . Ah God, I know not, I! . . .
40 Bedded in store of rotten fig-leaves soft,
And corded up in a tight olive-frail,
Some lump, ah God, of *lapis lazuli,*
Big as a Jew's head cut off at the nape,
Blue as a vein o'er the Madonna's breast . . .
45 Sons, all have I bequeathed you, villas, all,
That brave Frascati villa with its bath,
So, let the blue lump poise between my knees,
Like God the Father's globe on both his hands
Ye worship in the Jesu Church so gay,

---

[3]the right-hand side, as one faces the altar

50 For Gandolf shall not choose but see and burst!
    Swift as a weaver's shuttle fleet our years:
    Man goeth to the grave, and where is he?
    Did I say basalt for my slab, sons? Black—
    'Twas ever antique-black I meant! How else
55 Shall ye contrast my frieze to come beneath?
    The bas-relief in bronze ye promised me,
    Those Pans and Nymphs ye wot of, and perchance
    Some tripod,[4] thyrsus,[5] with a vase or so,
    The Saviour at his sermon on the mount,
60 Saint Praxed in a glory, and one Pan
    Ready to twitch the Nymph's last garment off,
    And Moses with the tables . . . but I know
    Ye mark me not! What do they whisper thee,
    Child of my bowels, Anselm? Ah, ye hope
65 To revel down my villas while I gasp
    Bricked o'er with beggar's moldy travertine
    Which Gandolf from his tomb-top chuckles at!
    Nay, boys, ye love me—all of jasper, then!
    'Tis jasper ye stand pledged to, lest I grieve
70 My bath must needs be left behind, alas!
    One block, pure green as a pistachio nut,
    There's plenty jasper somewhere in the world—
    And have I not Saint Praxed's ear to pray
    Horses for ye, and brown Greek manuscripts,
75 And mistresses with great smooth marbly limbs?
    —That's if ye carve my epitaph aright,
    Choice Latin, picked phrase, Tully's[6] every word,
    No gaudy ware like Gandolf's second line—
    Tully, my masters? Ulpian[7] serves his need!
80 And then how I shall lie through centuries,
    And hear the blessed mutter of the mass,
    And see God made and eaten all day long,
    And feel the steady candle-flame, and taste
    Good strong thick stupefying incense-smoke!
85 For as I lie here, hours of the dead night,
    Dying in state and by such slow degrees,
    I fold my arms as if they clasped a crook,

---

[4]three-legged stool used by the oracle at Delphi
[5]staff carried by Dionysus and his followers
[6]Marcus Tullius Cicero, master of Latin prose style
[7]Domitius Ulpianus, third-century Roman jurist, noted for bad prose

And stretch my feet forth straight as stone can point,
And let the bedclothes, for a mortcloth, drop
90 Into great laps and folds of sculptor's-work:
And as yon tapers dwindle, and strange thoughts
Grow, with a certain humming in my ears,
About the life before I lived this life,
And this life too, popes, cardinals, and priests,
95 Saint Praxed at his sermon on the mount,[8]
Your tall pale mother with her talking eyes,
And new-found agate urns as fresh as day,
And marble's language, Latin pure, discreet
—Aha, ELUCESCEBAT[9] quoth our friend?
100 No Tully, said I, Ulpian at the best!
Evil and brief hath been my pilgrimage.
All *lapis,* all, sons! Else I give the Pope
My villas! Will ye ever eat my heart?
Ever your eyes were as a lizard's quick,
105 They glitter like your mother's for my soul,
Or ye would heighten my impoverished frieze,
Piece out its starved design, and fill my vase
With grapes, and add a vizor and a Term,[1]
And to the tripod you would tie a lynx
110 That in his struggle throws the thyrsus down,
To comfort me on my entablature
Whereon I am to lie till I must ask
"Do I live, am I dead?" There, leave me, there!
For ye have stabbed me with ingratitude
115 To death—ye wish it—God, ye wish it! Stone—
Gritstone, a-crumble! Clammy squares which sweat
As if the corpse they keep were oozing through—
And no more *lapis* to delight the world!
Well go! I bless ye. Fewer tapers there,
120 But in a row: and, going, turn your backs
—Aye, like departing altar-ministrants,
And leave me in my church, the church for peace,
That I may watch at leisure if he leers—
Old Gandolf, at me, from his onion-stone,
125 As still he envied me, so fair she was!

---

[8]The bishop's failing mind attributes the Sermon on the Mount to Saint Praxed (a woman) instead of Christ.
[9]"He was illustrious," an example of Ulpian Latin
[1]a mask and bust on a pedestal

Walt Whitman

(1819–1892)

Out of the Cradle Endlessly Rocking

Out of the cradle endlessly rocking,
Out of the mocking-bird's throat, the musical shuttle,
Out of the Ninth-month midnight,
Over the sterile sands and the fields beyond, where the child leaving his bed
    wander'd alone, bareheaded, barefoot,
5 Down from the shower'd halo
Up from the mystic play of shadows twining and twisting as if they were alive,
Out from the patches of briers and blackberries,
From the memories of the bird that chanted to me,
From your memories sad brother, from the fitful risings and fallings I heard,
10 From under that yellow half-moon late-risen and swollen as if with tears,
From those beginning notes of yearning and love there in the mist,
From the thousand responses of my heart never to cease,
From the myriad thence-arous'd words,
From the word stronger and more delicious than any,
15 From such as now they start the scene revisiting,
As a flock, twittering, rising, or overhead passing,
Borne hither, ere all eludes me, hurriedly,
A man, yet by these tears a little boy again,
Throwing myself on the sand, confronting the waves,
20 I, chanter of pains and joys, uniter of here and hereafter,
Taking all hints to use them, but swiftly leaping beyond them,
A reminiscence sing.

Once Paumanok,[2]
When the lilac-scent was in the air and Fifth-month grass was growing,
25 Up this seashore in some briers,
Two feather'd guests from Alabama, two together,
And their nest, and four light-green eggs spotted with brown,
And every day the he-bird to and fro near at hand,
And every day the she-bird crouch'd on her nest, silent, with bright eyes,
30 And every day I, a curious boy, never too close, never disturbing them,
Cautiously peering, absorbing, translating.

Shine! shine! shine!
Pour down your warmth, great sun!
While we bask, we two together.

---

[2]the Indian name for Long Island

35 *Two together!*
   Winds blow south, or winds blow north,
   Day come white, or night come black,
   Home, or rivers and mountains from home,
   Singing all time, minding no time,
40 *While we two keep together.*

   Till of a sudden,
   May-be kill'd, unknown to her mate,
   One forenoon, the she-bird crouch'd not on the nest,
   Nor return'd that afternoon, nor the next,
45 Nor ever appear'd again.

   And thenceforward all summer in the sound of the sea,
   And at night under the full of the moon in calmer weather,
   Over the hoarse surging of the sea,
   Or flitting from brier to brier by day,
50 I saw, I heard at intervals the remaining one, the he-bird,
   The solitary guest from Alabama.

   Blow! blow! blow!
   Blow up sea-winds along Paumanok's shore;
   I wait and I wait till you blow my mate to me.

55 Yes, when the stars glisten'd,
   All night long on the prong of a moss-scallop'd stake,
   Down almost amid the slapping waves,
   Sat the lone singer wonderful causing tears.

   He call'd on his mate,
60 He pour'd forth the meanings which I of all men know.

   Yes my brother I know,
   The rest might not, but I have treasur'd every note,
   For more than once dimly down to the beach gliding,
   Silent, avoiding the moonbeams, blending myself with the shadows,
65 Recalling now the obscure shapes, the echoes, the sounds and sights
         after their sorts,
   The white arms out in the breakers tirelessly tossing,
   I, with bare feet, a child, the wind wafting my hair,
   Listen'd long and long.

   Listen'd to keep, to sing, now translating the notes,
70 Following you my brother.

   Soothe! soothe! soothe!
   Close on its wave soothes the wave behind,

And again another behind embracing and lapping, every one close,
But my love soothes not me, not me.

75   *Low hangs the moon, it rose late,*
   It is lagging—O I think it is heavy with love, with love.

O madly the sea pushes upon the land,
With love, with love.

O night! do I not see my love fluttering out among the breakers?
80   *What is that little black thing I see there in the white?*

Loud! loud! loud!
Loud I call to you, my love!
High and clear I shoot my voice over the waves,
Surely you must know who is here, is here,
85   *You must know who I am, my love.*

Low-hanging moon!
What is that dusky spot in your brown yellow?
O it is the shape, the shape of my mate!
O moon do not keep her from me any longer.

90   *Land! land! O land!*
   Whichever way I turn, O I think you could give me my mate back
      again if you only would,
   For I am almost sure I see her dimly whichever way I look.

O rising stars!
Perhaps the one I want so much will rise, will rise with some of you.

95   *O throat! O trembling throat!*
   Sound clearer through the atmosphere!
   Pierce the woods, the earth,
   Somewhere listening to catch you must be the one I want.

Shake out carols!
100   *Solitary here, the night's carols!*
   Carols of lonesome love! death's carols!
   Carols under that lagging, yellow, waning moon!
   O under that moon where she droops almost down into the sea!
   O reckless despairing carols.

105   *But soft! sink low!*
   Soft! let me just murmur,
   And do you wait a moment you husky-nois'd sea,
   For somewhere I believe I heard my mate responding to me,
   So faint, I must be still, be still to listen,
110   *But not altogether still, for then she might not come immediately to me.*

Hither my love!
Here I am! here!
With this just-sustain'd note I announce myself to you,
This gentle call is for you my love, for you.

115 *Do not be decoy'd elsewhere,*
That is the whistle of the wind, it is not my voice,
That is the fluttering, the fluttering of the spray,
Those are the shadows of leaves.

O darkness! O in vain!
120 *O I am very sick and sorrowful.*

O brown halo in the sky near the moon, drooping upon the sea!
O troubled reflection in the sea!
O throat! O throbbing heart!
And I singing uselessly, uselessly all the night.

125 *O past! O happy life! O songs of joy!*
In the air, in the woods, over fields,
Loved! loved! loved! loved! loved!
But my mate no more, no more with me!
We two together no more.

130 The aria sinking,
All else continuing, the stars shining,
The winds blowing, the notes of the bird continuous echoing,
With angry moans the fierce old mother incessantly moaning,
On the sands of Paumanok's shore gray and rustling,
135 The yellow half-moon enlarged, sagging down, drooping, the face of the sea
almost touching,
The boy ecstatic, with his bare feet the waves, with his hair the atmosphere
dallying,
The love in the heart long pent, now loose, now at last tumultuously
bursting,
The aria's meaning, the ears, the soul, swiftly depositing,
The strange tears down the cheeks coursing,
140 The colloquy there, the trio, each uttering,
The undertone, the savage old mother incessantly crying,
To the boy's soul's questions sullenly timing, some drown'd secret
hissing,
To the outsetting bard.

Demon or bird! (said the boy's soul,)
145 Is it indeed toward your mate you sing? or is it really to me?
For I, that was a child, my tongue's use sleeping, now I have heard you,
Now in a moment I know what I am for, I awake,

And already a thousand singers, a thousand songs, clearer, louder and more
    sorrowful than yours,
A thousand warbling echoes have started to life within me, never to die.

150 O you singer solitary, singing by yourself, projecting me,
    O solitary me listening, never more shall I cease perpetuating you,
    Never more shall I escape, never more the reverberations,
    Never more the cries of unsatisfied love be absent from me,
    Never again leave me to be the peaceful child I was before what there in the
        night,
155 By the sea under the yellow and sagging moon,
    The messenger there arous'd, the fire, the sweet hell within,
    The unknown want, the destiny of me.

    O give me the clew! (it lurks in the night here somewhere,)
    O if I am to have so much, let me have more!

160 A word then, (for I will conquer it,)
    The word final, superior to all,
    Subtle, sent up—what is it?—I listen;
    Are you whispering it, and have been all the time, you sea-waves?
    Is that it from your liquid rims and wet sands?

165 Whereto answering, the sea,
    Delaying not, hurrying not,
    Whisper'd me through the night, and very plainly before daybreak,
    Lisp'd to me the low and delicious word death,
    And again death, death, death, death,
170 Hissing melodious, neither like the bird nor like my arous'd child's heart,
    But edging near as privately for me rustling at my feet,
    Creeping thence steadily up to my ears and laving me softly all over,
    Death, death, death, death, death.

    Which I do not forget,
175 But fuse the song of my dusky demon and brother,
    That he sang to me in the moonlight on Paumanok's gray beach,
    With the thousand responsive songs at random,
    My own songs awaked from that hour,
    And with them the key, the word up from the waves,
180 The word of the sweetest song and all songs,
    That strong and delicious word which, creeping to my feet,
    (Or like some old crone rocking the cradle, swathed in sweet garments, bending
        aside,)
    The sea whisper'd me.

A. E. Housman

(1859–1936)

"Terence, This Is Stupid Stuff . . ."

"Terence, this is stupid stuff:
You eat your victuals fast enough;
There can't be much amiss, 'tis clear,
To see the rate you drink your beer.
5 But oh, good Lord, the verse you make,
It gives a chap the belly-ache.
The cow, the old cow, she is dead;
It sleeps well, the hornèd head:
We poor lads, 'tis our turn now
10 To hear such tunes as killed the cow.
Pretty friendship 'tis to rhyme
Your friends to death before their time
Moping melancholy mad:
Come, pipe a tune to dance to, lad."

15   Why, if 'tis dancing you would be,
There's brisker pipes than poetry.
Say, for what were hop-yards meant,
Or why was Burton built on Trent?[3]
Oh many a peer of England brews
20 Livelier liquor than the Muse,
And malt does more than Milton can
To justify God's ways to man.
Ale, man, ale's the stuff to drink
For fellows whom it hurts to think:
25 Look into the pewter pot
To see the world as the world's not.
And faith, 'tis pleasant till 'tis past:
The mischief is that 'twill not last.
Oh I have been to Ludlow fair
30 And left my necktie God knows where,
And carried half-way home, or near,
Pints and quarts of Ludlow beer:
Then the world seemed none so bad,
And I myself a sterling lad;
35 And down in lovely muck I've lain,

---

[3]a town noted for its breweries

Happy till I woke again.
Then I saw the morning sky:
Heigho, the tale was all a lie;
The world, it was the old world yet,
40 I was I, my things were wet,
And nothing now remained to do
But begin the game anew.

    Therefore, since the world has still
Much good, but much less good than ill,
45 And while the sun and moon endure
Luck's a chance, but trouble's sure,
I'd face it as a wise man would,
And train for ill and not for good.
'Tis true, the stuff I bring for sale
50 Is not so brisk a brew as ale:
Out of a stem that scored the hand
I wrung it in a weary land.
But take it: if the smack is sour,
The better for the embittered hour;
55 It should do good to heart and head
When your soul is in my soul's stead;
And I will friend you, if I may,
In the dark and cloudy day.

    There was a king reigned in the East:
60 There, when kings will sit to feast,
They get their fill before they think
With poisoned meat and poisoned drink.
He gathered all that springs to birth
From the many-venomed earth;
65 First a little, thence to more,
He sampled all her killing store;
An easy, smiling, seasoned sound,
Sate the king when healths went round.
They put arsenic in his meat
70 And stared aghast to watch him eat;
They poured strychnine in his cup
And shook to see him drink it up:
They shook, they stared as white's their shirt:
Them it was their poison hurt.
75 —I tell the tale that I heard told.
Mithridates,[4] he died old.

---

[4]king of Pontus in the first century B.C., who made himself immune to certain poisons by taking them frequently in small doses

A. E. Housman

(1859–1936)

To an Athlete Dying Young

The time you won your town the race
We chaired you through the market-place;
Man and boy stood cheering by,
And home we brought you shoulder-high.

5 To-day, the road all runners come,
Shoulder-high we bring you home,
And set you at your threshold down,
Townsman of a stiller town.

Smart lad, to slip betimes away
10 From fields where glory does not stay
And early though the laurel grows
It withers quicker than the rose.

Eyes the shady night has shut
Cannot see the record cut,
15 And silence sounds no worse than cheers
After earth has stopped the ears:

Now you will not swell the rout
Of lads that wore their honors out,
Runners whom renown outran
20 And the name died before the man.

So set, before its echoes fade,
The fleet foot on the sill of shade,
And hold to the low lintel up
The still-defended challenge-cup.

25 And round that early-laurelled head
Will flock to gaze the strengthless dead,
And find unwithered on its curls
The garland briefer than a girl's.

James Weldon Johnson

(1871–1938)

O Black and Unknown Bards

O black and unknown bards of long ago,
How came your lips to touch the sacred fire?
How, in your darkness, did you come to know
The power and beauty of the minstrel's lyre?
5 Who first from midst his bonds lifted his eyes?
Who first from out the still watch, lone and long,
Feeling the ancient faith of prophets rise
Within his dark-kept soul, burst into song?

Heart of what slave poured out such melody
10 As "Steal away to Jesus"? On its strains
His spirit must have nightly floated free,
Though still about his hands he felt his chains.
Who heard great "Jordan roll"? Whose starward eye
Saw chariot "swing low"? And who was he
15 That breathed that comforting, melodic sigh,
"Nobody knows de trouble I see"?

What merely living clod, what captive thing,
Could up toward God through all its darkness grope,
And find within its deadened heart to sing
20 These songs of sorrow, love and faith, and hope?
How did it catch that subtle undertone,
That note in music heard not with the ears?
How sound the elusive reed so seldom blown,
Which stirs the soul or melts the heart to tears?

25 Not that great German master[5] in his dream
Of harmonies that thundered amongst the stars
At the creation, ever heard a theme
Nobler than "Go down, Moses." Mark its bars,
How like a mighty trumpet-call they stir
30 The blood. Such are the notes that men have sung
Going to valorous deeds; such tones there were
That helped make history when Time was young.

There is a wide, wide wonder in it all,
That from degraded rest and servile toil
35 The fiery spirit of the seer should call

---

[5]Beethoven

These simple children of the sun and soil.
O black slave singers, gone, forgot, unfamed,
You—you alone, of all the long, long line
Of those who've sung untaught, unknown, unnamed,
40 Have stretched out upward, seeking the divine.

You sang not deeds of heroes or of kings;
No chant of bloody war, no exulting paean
Of arms-won triumphs; but your humble strings
You touched in chord with music empyrean.
45 You sang far better than you knew; the songs
That for your listeners' hungry hearts sufficed
Still live—but more than this to you belongs:
You sang a race from wood and stone to Christ.

Wallace Stevens

(1879–1955)

Thirteen Ways of Looking at a Blackbird

I

Among the twenty snowy mountains,
The only moving thing
Was the eye of the blackbird.

II

I was of three minds,
5 Like a tree
In which there are three blackbirds.

III

The blackbird whirled in the autumn winds.
It was a small part of the pantomime.

IV

A man and a woman
10 Are one.
A man and a woman and a blackbird
Are one.

V

I do not know which to prefer,
The beauty of inflections,
15 Or the beauty of innuendoes,

The blackbird whistling
Or just after.

VI

Icicles filled the long window
With barbaric glass.
20 The shadow of the blackbird
Crossed it, to and fro.
The mood
Traced in the shadow
An indecipherable cause.

VII

25 O thin men of Haddam[6]
Why do you imagine golden birds?
Do you not see how the blackbird
Walks around the feet
Of the women about you?

VIII

30 I know noble accents
And lucid, inescapable rhythms;
But I know, too,
That the blackbird is involved
In what I know.

IX

35 When the blackbird flew out of sight,
It marked the edge
Of one of many circles.

X

At the sight of blackbirds
Flying in a green light,
40 Even the bawds of euphony
Would cry out sharply.

XI

He rode over Connecticut
In a glass coach.
Once, a fear pierced him,

---

[6]A town in Connecticut; Stevens liked its name.

45 In that he mistook
The shadow of his equipage
For blackbirds.

XII

The river is moving.
The blackbird must be flying.

XIII

50 It was evening all afternoon.
It was snowing
And it was going to snow.
The blackbird sat
In the cedar-limbs.

William Butler Yeats

(1865–1939)

Leda and the Swan[7]

A sudden blow: the great wings beating still
Above the staggering girl, her thighs caressed
By the dark webs, her nape caught in his bill,
He holds her helpless breast upon his breast.

5 How can those terrified vague fingers push
The feathered glory from her loosening thighs?
And how can body, laid in that white rush,
But feel the strange heart beating where it lies?

A shudder in the loins engenders there
10 The broken wall, the burning roof and tower
And Agamemnon dead.
                              Being so caught up,
So mastered by the brute blood of the air,
Did she put on his knowledge with his power
15 Before the indifferent beak could let her drop?

---

[7]Zeus, in the form of a swan, violated *Leda,* who gave birth to Helen and Clytemnestra. Helen's flight with Paris to Troy, leaving her husband Menelaus, Agamemnon's brother, caused the war between the Greeks and the Trojans. Clytemnestra murdered her husband Agamemnon on his return from victory at Troy.

H. D. (Hilda Doolittle)

(1886–1961)

Heat

O wind, rend open the heat,
cut apart the heat,
rend it to tatters.

Fruit cannot drop
5 through this thick air—
fruit cannot fall into heat
that presses up and blunts
the points of pears
and rounds the grapes.

10 Cut the heat—
plough through it,
turning it on either side
of your path.

Marianne Moore

(1887–1972)

Poetry

I, too, dislike it: there are things that are important beyond all this fiddle.
    Reading it, however, with a perfect contempt for it, one discovers in
    it after all, a place for the genuine.
        Hands that can grasp, eyes
5   that can dilate, hair that can rise
            if it must, these things are important not because a

high-sounding interpretation can be put upon them but because they are
    useful. When they become so derivative as to become unintelligible,
    the same thing may be said for all of us, that we
10   do not admire what
        we cannot understand: the bat
            holding on upside down or in quest of something to

eat, elephants pushing, a wild horse taking a roll, a tireless wolf under
    a tree, the immovable critic twitching his skin like a horse that feels a flea, the
15   base-
        ball fan, the statistician—

nor is it valid
 to discriminate against "business documents and

school-books";[8] all these phenomena are important. One must make
  a distinction
 however: when dragged into prominence by half poets, the result
  is not poetry,
20 nor till the poets among us can be
  "literalists of
  the imagination"[9]—above
   insolence and triviality and can present

for inspection, "imaginary gardens with real toads in them," shall we have
25 it. In the meantime, if you demand on the one hand,
  the raw material of poetry in
   all its rawness and
   that which is on the other hand
    genuine, you are interested in poetry.

D. H. Lawrence

(1885–1930)

Piano

Softly, in the dusk, a woman is singing to me;
Taking me back down the vista of years, till I see
A child sitting under the piano, in the boom of the tingling strings
And pressing the small, poised feet of a mother who smiles as she sings.

5 In spite of myself, the insidious mastery of song
Betrays me back, till the heart of me weeps to belong
To the old Sunday evenings at home, with winter outside
And hymns in the cozy parlor, the tinkling piano our guide.

So now it is vain for the singer to burst into clamor
10 With the great black piano appassionato. The glamour
Of childish days is upon me, my manhood is cast
Down in the flood of remembrance, I weep like a child for the past.

---

[8]Moore's note cites the Diary of Tolstoy: "Poetry is everything with the exception of business documents and school books."
[9]from Yeats, *Ideas of Good and Evil*

T. S. Eliot

(1888–1965)

The Love Song of J. Alfred Prufrock

S'io credesse che mia risposta fosse
A persona che mai tornasse al mondo,
Questa fiamma staria senza piu scosse.
Ma perciocche giammai di questo fondo
Non torno vivo alcun, s'i'odo il vero,
Senza tema d'infamia ti rispondo.[1]

Let us go then, you and I,
When the evening is spread out against the sky
Like a patient etherized upon a table;
Let us go, through certain half-deserted streets,
5   The muttering retreats
Of restless nights in one-night cheap hotels
And sawdust restaurants with oyster-shells:
Streets that follow like a tedious argument
Of insidious intent
10 To lead you to an overwhelming question . . .

Oh, do not ask, "What is it?"
Let us go and make our visit.

In the room the women come and go
Talking of Michelangelo.

15 The yellow fog that rubs its back upon the window-panes
The yellow smoke that rubs its muzzle on the window panes
Licked its tongue into the corners of the evening,
Lingered upon the pools that stand in drains,
Let fall upon its back the soot that falls from chimneys,
20 Slipped by the terrace, made a sudden leap,
And seeing that it was a soft October night,
Curled once about the house, and fell asleep.

And indeed there will be time
For the yellow smoke that slides along the street,
25 Rubbing its back upon the window-panes;
There will be time, there will be time

---

[1]"If I thought that my response were given to one who would ever return to the world, this flame would move no more. But since never from this depth has man returned alive, if what I hear is true, without fear of infamy I answer thee." In Dante's *Inferno* these words are addressed to the poet by the spirit of Guido da Montefeltro.

To prepare a face to meet the faces that you meet;
There will be time to murder and create,
And time for all the works and days of hands
30 That lift and drop a question on your plate;
Time for you and time for me,
And time yet for a hundred indecisions,
And for a hundred visions and revisions,
Before the taking of a toast and tea.

35 In the room the women come and go
Talking of Michelangelo.

And indeed there will be time
To wonder, "Do I dare?" and, "Do I dare?"
Time to turn back and descend the stair,
40 With a bald spot in the middle of my hair—
[They will say: "How his hair is growing thin!"]
My morning coat, my collar mounting firmly to the chin,
My necktie rich and modest, but asserted by a simple pin—
[They will say: "But how his arms and legs are thin!"]
45 Do I dare
Disturb the universe?
In a minute there is time
For decisions and revisions which a minute will reverse.

For I have known them all already, known them all:
50 Have known the evenings, mornings, afternoons,
I have measured out my life with coffee spoons;
I know the voices dying with a dying fall
Beneath the music from a farther room.
        So how should I presume?

55 And I have known the eyes already, known them all—
The eyes that fix you in a formulated phrase,
And when I am formulated, sprawling on a pin,
When I am pinned and wriggling on the wall,
Then how should I begin
60 To spit out all the butt-ends of my days and ways?
        And how should I presume?

And I have known the arms already, known them all—
Arms that are braceleted and white and bare
[But in the lamplight, downed with light brown hair!]
65 Is it perfume from a dress
That makes me so digress?
Arms that lie along a table, or wrap about a shawl.

And should I then presume?
And how should I begin?

70 Shall I say, I have gone at dusk through narrow streets
And watched the smoke that rises from the pipes
Of lonely men in shirt-sleeves, leaning out of windows? . . .

I should have been a pair of ragged claws
Scuttling across the floors of silent seas.

75 And the afternoon, the evening, sleeps so peacefully!
Smoothed by long fingers,
Asleep . . . tired . . . or it malingers,
Stretched on the floor, here beside you and me.
Should I, after tea and cakes and ices,
80 Have the strength to force the moment to its crisis?
But though I have wept and fasted, wept and prayed,
Though I have seen my head [grown slightly bald] brought in upon a
    platter,
I am no prophet—and here's no great matter;
I have seen the moment of my greatness flicker,
85 And I have seen the eternal Footman hold my coat, and snicker,
And in short, I was afraid.

And would it have been worth it, after all,
After the cups, the marmalade, the tea,
Among the porcelain, among some talk of you and me,
90 Would it have been worth while,
To have bitten off the matter with a smile,
To have squeezed the universe into a ball
To roll it toward some overwhelming question,

To say: "I am Lazarus, come from the dead,
95 Come back to tell you all, I shall tell you all"—
If one, settling a pillow by her head,
    Should say: "That is not what I meant at all.
    That is not it, at all."

And would it have been worth it, after all,
100 Would it have been worth while,
After the sunsets and the dooryards and the sprinkled streets,
After the novels, after the teacups, after the skirts that trail along the floor—
And this, and so much more?—

It is impossible to say just what I mean!
105 But as if a magic lantern threw the nerves in patterns on a screen:
Would it have been worth while
If one, settling a pillow or throwing off a shawl,
And turning toward the window, should say:
     "That is not it at all,
110   That is not what I meant, at all."

No! I am not Prince Hamlet, nor was meant to be;
Am an attendant lord, one that will do
To swell a progress, start a scene or two,
Advise the prince; no doubt, an easy tool,
115 Deferential, glad to be of use,
Politic, cautious, and meticulous;
Full of high sentence, but a bit obtuse;
At times, indeed, almost ridiculous—
Almost, at times, the Fool.

120 I grow old . . . I grow old . . .
I shall wear the bottoms of my trousers rolled.

Shall I part my hair behind? Do I dare to eat a peach?
I shall wear white flannel trousers, and walk upon the beach.
I have heard the mermaids singing, each to each.

125 I do not think that they will sing to me.

I have seen them riding seaward on the waves
Combing the white hair of the waves blown back
When the wind blows the water white and black.

We have lingered in the chambers of the sea
130 By sea-girls wreathed with seaweed red and brown
Till human voices wake us, and we drown.

Archibald MacLeish

(1892–1982)

Ars Poetica

A poem should be palpable and mute
As a globed fruit,

Dumb
As old medallions to the thumb,

5 Silent as the sleeve-worn stone
Of casement ledges where the moss has grown—

A poem should be wordless
As the flight of birds.

A poem should be motionless in time
10 As the moon climbs,

Leaving, as the moon releases
Twig by twig the night-entangled trees,

Leaving, as the moon behind the winter leaves
Memory by memory the mind—

15 A poem should be motionless in time
As the moon climbs.

A poem should be equal to:
Not true.

For all the history of grief
20 An empty doorway and a maple leaf.

For love
The leaning grasses and two lights above the sea—

A poem should not mean
But be.

W. H. Auden

(1907–1973)

Musée des Beaux Arts[2]

About suffering they were never wrong,
The Old Masters: how well they understood
Its human position; how it takes place
While someone else is eating or opening a window or just walking dully along;
5 How, when the aged are reverently, passionately waiting
For the miraculous birth, there always must be
Children who did not specially want it to happen, skating
On a pond at the edge of the wood:
They never forgot
10 That even the dreadful martyrdom must run its course
Anyhow in a corner, some untidy spot

---

[2]the Museum of Fine Arts in Brussels, where Brueghel's *Landscape with the Fall of Icarus* hangs

Where the dogs go on with their doggy life and the torturer's horse
Scratches its innocent behind on a tree.

In Brueghel's *Icarus*,[3] for instance: how everything turns away
15 Quite leisurely from the disaster; the plowman may
Have heard the splash, the forsaken cry,
But for him it was not an important failure; the sun shone
As it had to on the white legs disappearing into the green
Water; and the expensive delicate ship that must have seen
20 Something amazing, a boy falling out of the sky,
Had somewhere to get to and sailed calmly on.

Allen Tate

(1899–1979)

The Wolves

There are wolves in the next room waiting
With heads bent low, thrust out, breathing
At nothing in the dark; between them and me
A white door patched with light from the hall
5 Where it seems never (so still is the house)
A man has walked from the front door to the stair.
It has all been forever. Beasts claw the floor.
I have brooded on angels and archfiends
But no man has ever sat where the next room's
10 Crowded with wolves, and for the honor of man
I affirm that never have I before. Now while
I have looked for the evening star at a cold window
And whistled when Arcturus spilt his light,
I've heard the wolves scuffle, and said: So this
15 Is man; so—what better conclusion is there—
The day will not follow night, and the heart
Of man has a little dignity, but less patience
Than a wolf's, and a duller sense that cannot
Smell its own mortality. (This and other
20 Meditations will be suited to other times
After dog silence howls his epitaph.)
Now remember courage, go to the door,
Open it and see whether coiled on the bed
Or cringing by the wall, a savage beast

---

[3]In Greek mythology Icarus falls into the sea and drowns when he flies too close to the sun on his wings of wax. In Brueghel's painting Icarus is an insignificant part of the picture.

25 Maybe with golden hair, with deep eyes
Like a bearded spider on a sunlit floor
Will snarl—and man can never be alone.

James Dickey

(1923–   )

The Heaven of Animals

Here they are. The soft eyes open.
If they have lived in a wood
It is a wood.
If they have lived on plains
5 It is grass rolling
Under their feet forever.

Having no souls, they have come,
Anyway, beyond their knowing.
Their instincts wholly bloom
10 And they rise.
The soft eyes open.

To match them, the landscape flowers,
Outdoing, desperately
Outdoing what is required:
15 The richest wood,
The deepest field.

For some of these,
It could not be the place
It is, without blood.
20 These hunt, as they have done
But with claws and teeth grown perfect,

More deadly than they can believe.
They stalk more silently,
And crouch on the limbs of trees,
25 And their descent
Upon the bright backs of their prey

May take years
In a sovereign floating of joy.
And those that are hunted
30 Know this as their life,
Their reward: to walk

Under such trees in full knowledge
Of what is in glory above them,
And to feel no fear,
35   But acceptance, compliance.
Fulfilling themselves without pain

At the cycle's center,
They tremble, they walk
Under the tree,
40   They fall, they are torn,
They rise, they walk again.

Gwendolyn Brooks

(1917–   )

The Bean Eaters

They eat beans mostly, this old yellow pair.
Dinner is a casual affair.
Plain chipware on a plain and creaking wood,
Tin flatware.

5   Two who are Mostly Good.
Two who have lived their day,
But keep on putting on their clothes
And putting things away.

And remembering . . .
10   Remembering, with twinklings and twinges,
As they lean over the beans in their rented back room that is full of beads and
      receipts and dolls and clothes, tobacco crumbs, vases and fringes.

Lawrence Ferlinghetti

(1919–   )

The pennycandystore beyond the El

The pennycandystore beyond the El
is where I first
                    fell in love
                              with unreality
5   Jellybeans glowed in the semi-gloom
of that september afternoon

A cat upon the counter moved among
$$\text{the licorice sticks}$$
$$\text{and tootsie rolls}$$
10 $\qquad$ and Oh Boy Gum

Outside the leaves were falling as they died

A wind had blown away the sun

A girl ran in
Her hair was rainy
15 Her breasts were breathless in the little room

Outside the leaves were falling
$$\text{and they cried}$$
$$\text{Too soon! too soon!}$$

Allen Ginsberg

(1926–   )

A Supermarket in California

What thoughts I have of you tonight, Walt Whitman, for I walked down the sidestreets under the trees with a headache self-conscious looking at the full moon.

In my hungry fatigue, and shopping for images, I went into the neon fruit
5 supermarket, dreaming of your enumerations!

What peaches and what penumbras! Whole families shopping at night! Aisles full of husbands! Wives in the avocados, babies in the tomatoes!—and you, Garcia Lorca,[4] what were you doing down by the watermelons?

10 I saw you, Walt Whitman, childless, lonely old grubber, poking among the meats in the refrigerator and eyeing the grocery boys.

I heard you asking questions of each: Who killed the pork chops? What price bananas? Are you my Angel?

I wandered in and out of the brilliant stacks of cans following you, and
15 followed in my imagination by the store detective.

We strode down the open corridors together in our solitary fancy tasting artichokes, possessing every frozen delicacy, and never passing the cashier.

Where are we going, Walt Whitman? The doors close in an hour. Which
20 way does your beard point tonight?

(I touch your book and dream of our odyssey in the supermarket and feel absurd.)

---

[4]Federico Garciá Lorca (1899–1936), Spanish poet and playwright. He was murdered at the start of the Spanish Civil War, and his works were suppressed by the Franco government.

Will we walk all night through solitary streets? The trees add shade to
shade, lights out in the houses, we'll both be lonely.

25   Will we stroll dreaming of the lost America of love past blue automobiles
in driveways, home to our silent cottage?

Ah, dear father, graybeard, lonely old courage-teacher, what America did
you have when Charon quit poling his ferry and you got out on a smoking bank
and stood watching the boat disappear on the black waters of Lethe?[5]

Anne Sexton

(1928–1974)

Welcome Morning

There is joy
in all:
in the hair I brush each morning,
in the Cannon towel, newly washed,
5   that I rub my body with each morning,
in the chapel of eggs I cook
each morning,
in the outcry from the kettle
that heats my coffee,
10   each morning,
in the spoon and the chair,
that cry "hello there, Anne"
each morning,
in the godhead of the table
15   that I set my silver, plate, cup upon,
each morning.

All this is God,
right here in my pea green house,
each morning
20   and I mean,
though often forget,
to give thanks,
to faint down by the kitchen table
in a prayer of rejoicing
25   as the holy birds at the kitchen window
peck into their marriage of seeds.

---

[5]Charon, in Greek myth, ferried the shades of the dead to Hades across Lethe, River of Forgetfulness.

So while I think of it,
let me paint a thank you on my palm
for this God, this laughter of the morning,
30 lest it go unspoken.

The Joy that isn't shared, I've heard,
dies young.

Ted Hughes

(1930–   )

Pike

Pike, three inches long, perfect
Pike in all parts, green tigering the gold.
Killers from the egg: the malevolent aged grin.
They dance on the surface among the flies.

5 Or move, stunned by their own grandeur,
Over a bed of emerald, silhouette
Of submarine delicacy and horror.
A hundred feet long in their world.

In ponds, under the heat-struck lily pads—
10 Gloom of their stillness:
Logged on last year's black leaves, watching upwards.
Or hung in an amber cavern of weeds

The jaw's hooked clamp and fangs
Not to be changed at this date;
15 A life subdued to its instrument;
The gills kneading quietly, and the pectorals.

Three we kept behind glass,
Jungled in weed: three inches, four,
And four and a half: fed fry to them—
20 Suddenly there were two. Finally one

With a sag belly and the grin it was born with.
And indeed they spare nobody.
Two, six pounds each, over two feet long,
High and dry and dead in the willow-herb—

25 One jammed past its gills down the other's gullet:
The outside eye stared: as a vice locks—
The same iron in this eye
Though its film shrank in death.

A pond I fished, fifty yards across,
30 Whose lilies and muscular tench
Had outlasted every visible stone
Of the monastery that planted them—

Stilled legendary depth:
It was as deep as England. It held
35 Pike too immense to stir, so immense and old
That past nightfall I dared not cast

But silently cast and fished
With the hair frozen on my head
For what might move, for what eye might move.
40 The still splashes on the dark pond,

Owls hushing the floating woods
Frail on my ear against the dream
Darkness beneath night's darkness had freed,
That rose slowly towards me, watching.

Amiri Baraka (LeRoi Jones)

(1934–   )

W. W.

Back home the black women are all beautiful,
and the white ones fall back, cutoff from 1000
years stacked booty, and Charles of the Ritz
where jooshladies turn into billy burke in blueglass
5 kicks. With wings, and jingly bew-teeful things.
The black women in Newark are fine. Even with all that grease
in their heads. I mean even the ones where the wigs
slide around, and they coming at you 75 degrees off course.
I could talk to them. Bring them around. To something.
10 Some kind of quick course, on the sidewalk, like Hey baby
why don't you take that thing off yo' haid. You look like
Miss Muffet in a runaway ugly machine. I mean. Like that.

Garrett Hongo

(1951–   )

Yellow Light

One arm hooked around the frayed strap
of a tar-black patent-leather purse,

the other cradling something for dinner:
fresh bunches of spinach from a J-Town *yaoya*,
5   sides of split Spanish mackerel from Alviso's,
maybe a loaf of Langendorf; she steps
off the hissing bus at Olympic and Fig,
begins the three-block climb up the hill,
passing gangs of schoolboys playing war,
10   Japs against Japs, Chicanas chalking sidewalks
with the holy double-yoked crosses of hopscotch,
and the Korean grocer's wife out for a stroll
around this neighborhood of Hawaiian apartments
just starting to steam with cooking
15   and the anger of young couples coming home
from work, yelling at kids, flicking on
TV sets for the Wednesday Night Fights.

If it were May, hydrangeas and jacaranda
flowers in the streetside trees would be
20   blooming through the smog of late spring.
Wisteria in Masuda's front yard would be
shaking out the long tresses of its purple hair.
Maybe mosquitoes, moths, a few orange butterflies
settling on the lattice of monkey flowers
25   tangled in chain-link fences by the trash.

But this is October, and Los Angeles
seethes like a billboard under twilight.
From used-car lots and the movie houses uptown,
long silver sticks of light probe the sky.
30   From the Miracle Mile, whole freeways away,
a brilliant fluorescence breaks out
and makes war with the dim squares
of yellow kitchen light winking on
in all the side streets of the Barrio.

35   She climbs up the two flights of flagstone
stairs to 201-B, the spikes of her high heels
clicking like kitchen knives on a cutting board,
props the groceries against the door,
fishes through memo pads, a compact,
40   empty packs of chewing gum, and finds her keys.

The moon then, cruising from behind
a screen of eucalyptus across the street,
covers everything, everything in sight,
in a heavy light like yellow onions.

Adrienne Rich

(1929–   )

Hunger

(For Audre Lorde)

1.

A fogged hill-scene on an enormous continent,
intimacy rigged with terrors,
a sequence of blurs the Chinese painter's ink-stick planned,
a scene of desolation comforted
5   by two human figures recklessly exposed,
leaning together in a sticklike boat
in the foreground. Maybe we look like this,
I don't know. I'm wondering
whether we even have what we think we have—
10 lighted windows signifying shelter,
a film of domesticity
over fragile roofs. I know I'm partly somewhere else—
huts strung across a drought-stretched land
not mine, dried breasts, mine and not mine, a mother
15 watching my children shrink with hunger.
I live in my Western skin,
my Western vision, torn
and flung to what I can't control or even fathom.
Quantify suffering, you could rule the world.

2.

20 They cán rule the world while they can persuade us
our pain belongs in some order.
Is death by famine worse than death by suicide,
than a life of famine and suicide, if a black lesbian dies,
if a white prostitute dies, if a woman genius
25 starves herself to feed others,
self-hatred battening on her body?
Something that kills us or leaves us half-alive
is raging under the name of an "act of god"
in Chad, in Niger, in the Upper Volta—
30 yes, that male god that acts on us and on our children,
that male State that acts on us and on our children
till our brains are blunted by malnutrition,
yet sharpened by the passion for survival,
our powers expended daily on the struggle

35 to hand a kind of life on to our children,
to change reality for our lovers
even in a single trembling drop of water.

3.

We can look at each other through both our lifetimes
like those two figures in the sticklike boat
40 flung together in the Chinese ink-scene;
even our intimacies are rigged with terror.
Quantify suffering? My guilt at least is open,
I stand convicted by all my convictions—
you, too. We shrink from touching
45 our power, we shrink away, we starve ourselves
and each other, we're scared shitless
of what it could be to take and use our love,
hose it on a city, on a world,
to wield and guide its spray, destroying
50 poisons, parasites, rats, viruses—
like the terrible mothers we long and dread to be.

4.

The decision to feed the world
is the real decision. No revolution
has chosen it. For that choice requires
55 that women shall be free.
I choke on the taste of bread in North America
but the taste of hunger in North America
is poisoning me. Yes, I'm alive to write these words,
to leaf through Kollwitz's women
60 huddling the stricken children into their stricken arms
the "mothers" drained of milk, the "survivors" driven
to self-abortion, self-starvation, to a vision
bitter, concrete, and wordless.
I'm alive to want more than life,
65 want it for others starving and unborn,
to name the deprivations boring
into my will, my affections, into the brains
of daughters, sisters, lovers caught in the crossfire
of terrorists of the mind.
70 In the black mirror of the subway window
hangs my own face, hollow with anger and desire.
Swathed in exhaustion, on the trampled newsprint,
a woman shields a dead child from the camera.
The passion to be inscribes her body.
75 Until we find each other, we are alone.

DRAMA

26

READING DRAMA

Analyzing Greek drama around 330 B.C., the philosopher Aristotle found each play to be composed of six parts: plot, character, thought, diction, spectacle, and music. Of these, he considered the plot—the putting together of diverse happenings to create a complete and unified action—to be the most important. Without plot, he says, there can be no play; for the chief purpose of drama is the acting-out of an action.

Characters come next in importance for Aristotle. Thought—by which he seems to mean not only the ideas expressed by the various speakers, but also their use of speech to sway the emotions of the audience—comes third. Diction, the choice of words, is fourth. Music and scenery, being pleasant and often impressive, but not essential, come last.

With the exception of music and spectacle, which apply only to plays in performance, Aristotle's categories are essentially the same categories we've been using in discussing fiction. The further we read in Aristotle, the more similarities we find: Aristotle warns would-be authors that their plots, to be complete, must have a natural beginning, middle, and end; that they must provide scope for their heroes to pass from happiness to unhappiness, or from unhappiness to happiness; and that they must be unified, containing nothing that could be taken away without leaving the drama incomplete.

In addition, Aristotle points out that the most important moments in the plot are those concerned with **reversals** and **recognition.** A reversal occurs when an action that is expected to have one result produces the opposite result instead. A recognition occurs when a character suddenly "recognizes" some fact or person, thus moving from a state of ignorance to a state of knowledge. In the best plays, the two events are joined and form the turning point of the play: the hero suddenly learns something of great personal importance, either by being informed of some facts by another character or by coming to a realization or insight himself. In either case, the result of the hero's enlightenment is a reversal, changing the course of the play's action and of the hero's life (from happiness to unhappiness or vice versa).

In discussing characterization, Aristotle reminds us that all characters must be people basically like ourselves, though some may be better and some worse. And again, he insists that consistency and probability are the two most important standards of judgment. The writer must make sure that the characters' actions are consistent with their natures, and that their natures remain consistent throughout the drama.

If we have not already discussed all of these ideas, at least we have no difficulty in applying them to the fiction we've read. To discuss consistency of character, for instance, we need only look at the narrator of "Bartleby the Scrivener," with his deep and basically kindly desire for tranquility in human relations and his persistent and misplaced faith in money as a means of attaining that tranquility, or at the narrator of "My Man Bovanne," with her caring nature and her strong concern for individual dignity. The basic elements of drama, then, are the same as those of fiction. It is the method of presentation that differs.

Fiction is the telling of tales. Its roots go back to the archetypal figure of the storyteller, rehearsing old legends and inventing new marvels for the listeners. The importance of voice in fiction, therefore, can hardly be overemphasized. Indeed, as fiction has become a more silent experience, writers seem to have attached increasing importance to the question of what voice would speak through their works. Listening to stories is still enjoyable. Any good story can be read aloud and be enjoyed the better for it. But our society seems to feel that listening to tales is a pleasure most proper for children and for those who cannot read to themselves. For most of us, therefore, fiction is something read silently and alone. It involves one book, one writer, one reader. We discuss stories in company, but we tend to read them in solitude.

Drama—in performance, at least—is wholly different. It is not written for one voice, but for many. It depends not on storytellers but on actors, men and women who impersonate their tale's characters not only in voice, but also in motion, gesture, and appearance, making them live for our eyes as well as our ears. Moreover, it is written for many viewers, for only in the midst of an audience can we appreciate fully the magic of drama. Laughing alone at a joke in print is enjoyable; being one laughing person among a hundred people can be hilarious.

Actors know this well. They know how fully they must bring their characters alive for their audience. They know, too, how dependent they are on the audience's response if they are to perform well. Many actors have declared that the best performances are those during which the emotions portrayed on stage are caught and sent back by the audience until audience and actors alike are caught up in the atmosphere they have created between them, and the illusion of the play becomes more real than the realities of the world outside. Similarly, many have said that acting in films, where no audience is present to reflect the emotional impact of the scene, is a more difficult and less enjoyable form of acting than acting on the stage. Playgoers and filmgoers, in their turn, agree that the experience of attending a live performance has an electric quality not to be found in viewing a film.

The fervor with which most of us discuss a really good play or film we've just seen, as opposed to the milder delight with which we discuss a really good book, testifies to the power of drama to move and delight us. A knowledge of the origins of drama, about which we shall speak in the next chapter, may help explain the intensity of our response. Within this course, however, we are readers rather than viewers of drama. And so the very power of drama in performance is likely to raise questions for us. "Here we are," we say, "with no stage, no actors—nothing but a playscript in front of us. What can we expect from this experience?"

Reading drama is certainly different from reading fiction. Drama generally gives us no narrator to describe scenes and characters, to comment on the significance of the action, to tie scenes together, or to provide a unifying viewpoint. Instead, drama gives us several characters, distinguished in the text only by their names, talking mostly to each other rather than to us, intent on their own affairs, entering and leaving the scene in bewildering succession.

If we were *watching* a play, we would recognize the characters by their appearance, mannerisms, and voices. Knowing the characters, we would then find it easy to follow the action. When we *read* a play, however, we must do without these visual clues—or rather, we must supply them for ourselves. We must use the text as the play's director would, judging from its words and from the actions they describe how the play would look and sound on stage.

Reading plays, in fact, gives our imagination free rein. How would I stage this scene? What sort of actor would I want for this role? What kind of stage setting would I use? What kind of camera work would I use in a film? Which would be my long shots, which my close-ups? What emotions would my filming be trying to capture?

Most of all, perhaps, you will think of the various characters as they are revealed in the text. What characteristics will each one exhibit? How will they carry themselves on stage? What tones of voice will they use in their speeches? How will they act toward each other?[1] The more clearly you can visualize the play's action and characters, the more readily the text will come alive for you.

Don't be afraid to experiment in your thinking. Actors, directors, and scene designers all allow themselves some freedom of interpretation when they put on a play. You can read for days about famous actors who have played Hamlet, each applying a very personal interpretation to emphasize one aspect or another of the prince's complex personality. Why should not we, as readers, enjoy the same freedom to visualize the play, interpreting and fitting together its parts to develop our vision of its conflicts and its meanings?

The text of a play will supply us with plenty of help. Because drama does depend so largely on the art of the actor, dramatists must create characters who can carry the play by their speeches and actions. Everything the actors (and readers) need must be contained in the speeches and stage directions. Here are some of the things we can look for:

We can look for characters who, like first-person narrators in fiction, reveal in their speech information about their habits, personalities, and thinking—

---

[1] A handy device for keeping track of a play's characters, in fact, is to "cast" the play for yourself with actors you'd enjoy watching in it. Then you can follow those actors through each scene, imagining how they would interpret the roles.

information they do not always know they are giving us. We can expect to be wiser than most of these characters, because we have the ability to stand apart from the action in which they participate, to see it fully or judge it objectively.

We can look for patterns in characterization and for conflicts between characters. We can look for characters who support each other and characters who oppose each other. We can expect to see strong characters opposed to weak ones, inflexible characters opposed to reasonable ones, good characters opposed to evil ones.

The speeches of the actors, therefore, set down in the play's text, will describe the play's characters for us, develop the action and conflict of the play, and contain the play's themes. The conflict between the ideas expressed in speeches will often be basic to the conflict of the play. Thus, in *Oedipus Rex,* much of the play's conflict centers around the question of whether it is wise or foolish for Oedipus to seek the truth about Laios's murder. And in *Hamlet,* the conflict between Hamlet and Claudius over who shall rule Denmark becomes almost secondary to the mental conflicts between Hamlet and the other characters (and within Hamlet himself) on the moral and practical issues arising from the political conflict.

Patterns of speech, characterization, and thought, then, are as important in drama as they are in fiction. Patterns of language and imagery, too, are important. Some plays, such as *A Doll's House,* try to imitate everyday speech patterns in their language. Other plays, such as *Hamlet* or *Oedipus Rex,* use the full power of poetry in their speeches. Dialogue in these plays can move in a few lines from the accents of everyday speech to those of extreme poetic passion, as the playwrights draw from the rhythms of poetry a capacity for dignity and grandeur and openness of expression that the limits of everyday speech deny them.

Patterns of imagery, too, can be used to great effect in these poetic plays. But imagery, as we have seen already in our work with fiction, is not restricted to poetry. Certainly, *Hamlet* is the richest in imagery of the eight plays presented here. But all make some use of imagery, such as the imagery of physical and mental blindness in *Oedipus Rex.*

Reading drama, therefore, can offer an intensification of the pleasure provided by reading fiction. More richly patterned in action, language, and characterization than most short stories, allowing its readers more scope for interpretation and for the visual imagination, drama offers us a chance to be actors, director, and audience in one.

27

GREEK TRAGEDY

Western drama is often said to have originated in ancient Greece. Certainly its two most outstanding forms, tragedy and comedy, began there.

About the beginnings of this drama, little is known, for few records have survived. We do know, however, that it began at festivals honoring Dionysus, or Bacchus, a god who was supposed to have taught people to cultivate grapes and make wine. Song and dance were the means by which this god was worshipped. At early festivals, choruses of fifty men dressed in tattered garments with wine-smeared faces or disguised as Dionysus's mythical companions, the satyrs, sang hymns praising the god's deeds while they half-danced, half-mimed his exploits. Eventually one man stepped out of the chorus and engaged his fellows in dialogue. Later still, the soloist began impersonating the god, thus dramatizing the events of which he was singing.

Sometime during this process, the content of the songs also shifted. Some still pertained to Dionysus, but some dealt with other, human, heroes. Although worshippers were reportedly shocked at the first introduction of the new tales, asking, "What has this to do with Dionysus?", the novelty soon became the rule. By 530 B.C., the performances were being called tragedies and were competing in Athens for an annual prize.

In the next hundred years, tragedy reached what Aristotle considered its full form. A second actor was added, and then a third. Episodes of dialogue among the actors, with the chorus occasionally joining in, became as important as the choric songs and dances with which they alternated. Painted backdrops, stage machinery, and special effects were introduced.

For all its developments, however, Greek drama remained a religious event. Plays were performed only at Dionysus's festivals; actors were considered his servants. Performances took place three times a year: twice at Athens, once at various rural festivals. The older of the Athenian festivals, the *Lenaea,* became the festival for comedy; but the *City Dionysia,* which drew visitors from all over Greece, was the festival for tragedy.

For this festival, three playwrights were chosen by Athenian authorities. Each was given a chorus and actors, who were paid and costumed by some rich citizen as a public service; each was allotted one day of the festival on which to perform. The performance would consist of three tragedies (sometimes on the same subject, sometimes not), followed by a satyr play, an obscene or satiric parody of some legendary event. At the end of the three days of playing, a jury of ten citizens, chosen by lot, judged the plays and awarded the prizes.[1] Any Athenian was welcome to attend these plays, which were held in a natural amphitheater that seated some 30,000 people. Because the theater was reported to be crowded at every performance, we may assume that virtually everybody who could attend, did.

All in all, drama in ancient Athens seems to have been regarded almost as a public possession. Looked on with a mixture of religious devotion, civic pride, and open enjoyment, it maintained a great and general popularity that seems to have declined only with the decline of Athens itself. And still the plays remained influential, both in themselves and in the theory of drama that Aristotle's comments on them provided. First the Romans copied them. Then, some 1500 years later, Renaissance playwrights took ideas from both Greek and Roman drama. We will discuss that development in the next chapter.

Tragedy and Comedy

Greek drama segregated its forms carefully. Tragedy dealt with the noble, the heroic, the sacrificial. In performance, three tragedies would be followed by a satyr play, which turned heroic figures into tricksters or clowns and often mocked the very legends that had supplied the day's tragedies. Comedy had its own festival, in which it could deal with the more practical aspirations of everyday people—good food, warm beds, and peaceful households and cities. The heroes of comedy battle such unheroic opponents as thieves, con men, unreasonable parents, and crooked politicians. Often, they must resort to trickery to outwit these unsavory sorts, who may very well be tricksters themselves. A happy ending is guaranteed.

Oedipus Rex and *Antigonê*

Oedipus Rex is, in many ways, the embodiment of Greek tragedy. It deals with a somewhat idealized, larger-than-life hero, a man caught in a dilemma between his ideals and his personal safety and fighting his way toward a terrifying knowledge. "Ah," cries the Shepherd in one climactic scene, "I am on the brink of dreadful speech." "And I of dreadful hearing," replies Oedipus. "Yet I must hear." This insistence on following through in a search, an action, the pursuit of an ideal has always attracted readers, perhaps because we all know how difficult that sort of courage is to sustain. It is the one force that is constant in tragedy.

The sad or terrible ending, incidentally, is not essential to tragedy. Some Greek tragedies end happily, in a reconciliation of their opposed forces, new

---

[1]Sophocles, the author of *Oedipus Rex*, held the all-time record of eighteen first prizes and is said never to have won less than second prize. Yet *Oedipus Rex* itself, which was praised by Aristotle and is still considered one of the finest of Greek tragedies, won only second prize when it was first produced.

knowledge having created new peace. The essentials of tragedy are the protagonist's own insistence on action or enlightenment and the ability of the play, however it ends, to arouse a sympathetic "fear and pity" (Aristotle's terms) in the audience as they watch the working-out of the hero's quest. *Oedipus Rex,* which begins on p. 547, clearly has these essentials.

Oedipus Rex gains much of its power from the unwavering intensity of its focus on the central character. But this focus, though not uncommon in tragedy, is also not essential to it. Many Greek tragedies have more than one central character. *The Trojan Women,* for example, has as heroines all the famous women who were caught up in the sack of Troy. *Antigonê,* which follows *Oedipus Rex* in this chapter, concentrates not so much on a single character as on the clash of wills between two characters. One of these characters is Kreon, Oedipus's uncle, now the ruler of Thebes; the other is Antigonê, Oedipus's daughter.

The action of *Antigonê* takes place some years after that of *Oedipus Rex.* In the time between the two plays, Oedipus's two sons have quarreled. In fact, just before *Antigonê* opens, one of the brothers (Polyneicês) has gathered a group of supporters and has attacked both his brother (Eteoclês) and the city of Thebes itself. In the battle, the two brothers have killed each other. Kreon, now ruling Thebes, has ordered a hero's funeral for Eteoclês, the defender of Thebes, but has refused burial to Polyneicês, Thebes's attacker. Antigonê's response to this proclamation, and Kreon's reaction to her response, form the action of the tragedy.

Throughout the play, Kreon's concern is for public welfare and order; he speaks most frequently as the voice of public authority, the defender of the public good. Antigonê's concern is for piety and for family ties. She speaks most often from her own conscience, as a private person. When she does speak of public matters, it is generally to contrast social law with divine law. Between these two forces of public and private good lies the play's tension. This is a play in which *thought,* Aristotle's third element of tragedy, is predominant. Yet, as with *Oedipus,* it is the strong-willed, dedicated nature of the antagonists that makes the play a true tragedy, not merely an argument. The issues involved are still argued; their expression here in tragedy is unique.

Oedipus Rex   SOPHOCLES

An English version by Dudley Fitts and Robert Fitzgerald

CHARACTERS

OEDIPUS, *King of Thebes, supposed son of Polybos and Meropê, King and Queen of Corinth*
IOKASTÊ, *wife of Oedipus and widow of the late King Laïos*
KREON, *brother of Iokastê, a prince of Thebes*
TEIRESIAS, *a blind seer who serves Apollo*
PRIEST
MESSENGER, *from Corinth*
SHEPHERD, *former servant of Laïos*
SECOND MESSENGER, *from the palace*
CHORUS OF THEBAN ELDERS
CHORAGOS, *leader of the Chorus*
ANTIGONÊ *and* ISMENÊ, *young daughters of Oedipus and Iokastê. They appear in the Exodos but do not speak.*
SUPPLIANTS, GUARDS, SERVANTS

THE SCENE. *Before the palace of* OEDIPUS, *King of Thebes. A central door and two lateral doors open onto a platform that runs the length of the façade. On the platform, right and left, are altars; and three steps lead down into the "orchestra" or chorus-ground. At the beginning of the action these steps are crowded by suppliants who have brought branches and chaplets of olive leaves and who sit in various attitudes of despair.* OEDIPUS *enters.*

Prologue

OEDIPUS   My children, generations of the living
In the line of Kadmos,[1] nursed at his ancient hearth:
Why have you strewn yourselves before these altars
In supplication, with your boughs and garlands?
5   The breath of incense rises from the city
With a sound of prayer and lamentation.
                                                        Children,
I would not have you speak through messengers,
And therefore I have come myself to hear you—
I, Oedipus, who bear the famous name.
10   (*to a* PRIEST) You, there, since you are eldest in the company,

---

[1]founder of Thebes

Speak for them all, tell me what preys upon you,
Whether you come in dread, or crave some blessing:
Tell me, and never doubt that I will help you
In every way I can; I should be heartless
15   Were I not moved to find you suppliant here.
   PRIEST   Great Oedipus, O powerful king of Thebes!
You see how all the ages of our people
Cling to your altar steps: here are boys
Who can barely stand alone, and here are priests
20   By weight of age, as I am a priest of God,
And young men chosen from those yet unmarried;
As for the others, all that multitude,
They wait with olive chaplets in the squares,
At the two shrines of Pallas, and where Apollo
25   Speaks in the glowing embers.
                          Your own eyes
Must tell you: Thebes is tossed on a murdering sea
And can not lift her head from the death surge.
A rust consumes the buds and fruits of the earth;
The herds are sick; children die unborn,
30   And labor is vain. The god of plague and pyre
Raids like detestable lightning through the city,
And all the house of Kadmos is laid waste,
All emptied, and all darkened: Death alone
Battens upon the misery of Thebes.

35   You are not one of the immortal gods, we know;
Yet we have come to you to make our prayer
As to the man surest in mortal ways
And wisest in the ways of God. You saved us
From the Sphinx, that flinty singer, and the tribute
40   We paid to her so long; yet you were never
Better informed than we, nor could we teach you:
A god's touch, it seems, enabled you to help us.

Therefore, O mighty power, we turn to you:
Find us our safety, find us a remedy,
45   Whether by counsel of the gods or of men.
A king of wisdom tested in the past
Can act in a time of troubles, and act well.
Noblest of men, restore
Life to your city! Think how all men call you
50   Liberator for your boldness long ago;
Ah, when your years of kingship are remembered,

Let them not say *We rose, but later fell*—
Keep the State from going down in the storm!
Once, years ago, with happy augury,
55 You brought us fortune; be the same again!
No man questions your power to rule the land:
But rule over men, not over a dead city!
Ships are only hulls, high walls are nothing,
When no life moves in the empty passageways.

60 OEDIPUS   Poor children! You may be sure I know
All that you longed for in your coming here.
I know that you are deathly sick; and yet,
Sick as you are, not one is as sick as I.
Each of you suffers in himself alone
65 His anguish, not another's; but my spirit
Groans for the city, for myself, for you.

I was not sleeping, you are not waking me.
No, I have been in tears for a long while
And in my restless thought walked many ways.
70 In all my search I found one remedy,
And I have adopted it: I have sent Kreon,
Son of Menoikeus, brother of the queen,
To Delphi, Apollo's place of revelation,
To learn there, if he can,
75 What act or pledge of mine may save the city.
I have counted the days, and now, this very day,
I am troubled, for he has overstayed his time.
What is he doing? He has been gone too long.
Yet whenever he comes back, I should do ill
80 Not to take any action the god orders.

PRIEST   It is a timely promise. At this instant
They tell me Kreon is here.

OEDIPUS   O Lord Apollo!
May his news be fair as his face is radiant!

PRIEST   Good news, I gather! he is crowned with bay,
85 The chaplet is thick with berries.

OEDIPUS   We shall soon know;
He is near enough to hear us now.

(*Enter* KREON.)

O prince:
Brother: son of Menoikeus:
What answer do you bring us from the god?

KREON   A strong one. I can tell you, great afflictions
90   Will turn out well, if they are taken well.
OEDIPUS   What was the oracle? These vague words
        Leave me still hanging between hope and fear.
KREON   Is it your pleasure to hear me with all these
        Gathered around us? I am prepared to speak,
95   But should we not go in?
OEDIPUS   Speak to them all,
        It is for them I suffer, more than for myself.
KREON   Then I will tell you what I heard at Delphi.
        In plain words
        The god commands us to expel from the land of Thebes
100   An old defilement we are sheltering.
        It is a deathly thing, beyond cure;
        We must not let it feed upon us longer.
OEDIPUS   What defilement? How shall we rid ourselves of it?
KREON   By exile or death, blood for blood. It was
105   Murder that brought the plague-wind on the city.
OEDIPUS   Murder of whom? Surely the god has named him?
KREON   My lord: Laïos once ruled this land,
        Before you came to govern us.
OEDIPUS   I know;
        I learned of him from others; I never saw him.
110 KREON   He was murdered; and Apollo commands us now
        To take revenge upon whoever killed him.
OEDIPUS   Upon whom? Where are they? Where shall we find a clue
        To solve that crime, after so many years?
KREON   Here in this land, he said. Search reveals
115   Things that escape an inattentive man.
OEDIPUS   Tell me: Was Laïos murdered in his house,
        Or in the fields, or in some foreign country?
KREON   He said he planned to make a pilgrimage.
        He did not come home again.
OEDIPUS   And was there no one,
120   No witness, no companion, to tell what happened?
KREON   They were all killed but one, and he got away
        So frightened that he could remember one thing only.
OEDIPUS   What was the one thing? One may be the key
        To everything, if we resolve to use it.
125 KREON   He said that a band of highwaymen attacked them,
        Outnumbered them, and overwhelmed the king.
OEDIPUS   Strange, that a highwayman should be so daring—
        Unless some faction here bribed him to do it.

KREON   We thought of that. But after Laïos' death
130   New troubles arose and we had no avenger.
    OEDIPUS   What troubles could prevent your hunting down
        the killers?
    KREON   The riddling Sphinx's song
        Made us deaf to all mysteries but her own.
    OEDIPUS   Then once more I must bring what is dark to light.
135   It is most fitting that Apollo shows,
        As you do, this compunction for the dead.
        You shall see how I stand by you, as I should,
        Avenging this country and the god as well,
        And not as though it were for some distant friend,
140   But for my own sake, to be rid of evil.
        Whoever killed King Laïos might—who knows?—
        Lay violent hands even on me—and soon.
        I act for the murdered king in my own interest.

        Come, then, my children: leave the altar steps,
145   Lift up your olive boughs!
                            One of you go
        And summon the people of Kadmos to gather here.
        I will do all that I can; you may tell them that.

(*Exit a* PAGE.)

        So, with the help of God,
        We shall be saved—or else indeed we are lost.
150   PRIEST   Let us rise, children. It was for this we came,
        And now the king has promised it.
        Phoibos[2] has sent us an oracle; may he descend
        Himself to save us and drive out the plague.

(*Exeunt* OEDIPUS *and* KREON *into the palace by the central door. The* PRIEST
and the SUPPLIANTS *disperse R and L. After a short pause the* CHORUS *enters the*
orchestra.)

------

[2]Apollo

Párodos[3]

Strophe I

CHORUS   What is God singing in his profound
Delphi of gold and shadow?
What oracle for Thebes, the sunwhipped city?
Fear unjoints me, the roots of my heart tremble.
5   Now I remember, O Healer, your power, and wonder:
Will you send doom like a sudden cloud, or weave it
Like nightfall of the past?
Speak to me, tell me, O
Child of golden Hope, immortal Voice.

Antistrophe I

10   Let me pray to Athenê, the immortal daughter of Zeus,
And to Artemis her sister
Who keeps her famous throne in the market ring,
And to Apollo, archer from distant heaven—
O gods, descend! Like three streams leap against
15   The fires of our grief, the fires of darkness;
Be swift to bring us rest!
As in the old time from the brilliant house
Of air you stepped to save us, come again!

Strophe 2

Now our afflictions have no end,
20   Now all our stricken host lies down
And no man fights off death with his mind;
The noble plowland bears no grain,
And groaning mothers can not bear—
See, how our lives like birds take wing,
25   Like sparks that fly when a fire soars,
To the shore of the god of evening.

---

[3]The song or ode chanted by the chorus on its entry. It is accompanied by dancing and music played on a flute. The chorus in this play represents elders of the city of Thebes. Chorus members remain onstage (on a level lower than the principal actors) for the remainder of the play. The choral odes and dances serve to separate one scene from another (there was no curtain in Greek theatre) as well as to comment on the action, reinforce the emotion, and interpret the situation. The chorus also performs dance movements during certain portions of the scenes themselves. *Strophe* and *antistrophe* are terms denoting the movement and counter-movement of the chorus from one side of its playing area to the other. When the chorus participates in dialogue with the other characters, its lines are spoken by the Choragos, its leader.

Antistrophe 2

> The plague burns on, it is pitiless,
> Though pallid children laden with death
> Lie unwept in the stony ways,
30 > And old gray women by every path
> Flock to the strand about the altars
> There to strike their breasts and cry
> Worship of Phoibos in wailing prayers:
> Be kind, God's golden child!

Strophe 3

35 > There are no swords in this attack by fire,
> No shields, but we are ringed with cries.
> Send the besieger plunging from our homes
> Into the vast sea-room of the Atlantic
> Or into the waves that foam eastward of Thrace—
40 > For the day ravages what the night spares—
> Destroy our enemy, lord of the thunder!
> Let him be riven by lightning from heaven!

Antistrophe 3

> Phoibos Apollo, stretch the sun's bowstring,
> That golden cord, until it sing for us,
45 > Flashing arrows in heaven!
> 　　　　　　　　　　　Artemis, Huntress,
> Race with flaring lights upon our mountains!
> O scarlet god, O golden-banded brow,
> O Theban Bacchos in a storm of Maenads,

(*Enter* OEDIPUS, *C.*)

> Whirl upon Death, that all the Undying hate!
50 > Come with blinding torches, come in joy!

Scene I

OEDIPUS　Is this your prayer? It may be answered. Come,
> Listen to me, act as the crisis demands,
> And you shall have relief from all these evils.

> Until now I was a stranger to this tale,
5 > As I had been a stranger to the crime.

Could I track down the murderer without a clue?
But now, friends,
As one who became a citizen after the murder,
I make this proclamation to all Thebans:

10 If any man knows by whose hand Laïos, son of Labdakos,
Met his death, I direct that man to tell me everything,
No matter what he fears for having so long withheld it.
Let it stand as promised that no further trouble
Will come to him, but he may leave the land in safety.

15 Moreover: If anyone knows the murderer to be foreign,
Let him not keep silent: he shall have his reward from me.
However, if he does conceal it; if any man
Fearing for his friend or for himself disobeys this edict,
Hear what I propose to do:

20 I solemnly forbid the people of this country,
Where power and throne are mine, ever to receive that man
Or speak to him, no matter who he is, or let him
Join in sacrifice, lustration, or in prayer.
I decree that he be driven from every house,
25 Being, as he is, corruption itself to us: the Delphic
Voice of Apollo has pronounced this revelation.
Thus I associate myself with the oracle
And take the side of the murdered king.

As for the criminal, I pray to God—
30 Whether it be a lurking thief, or one of a number—
I pray that that man's life be consumed in evil and wretchedness.
And as for me, this curse applies no less
If it should turn out that the culprit is my guest here,
Sharing my hearth.
                    You have heard the penalty.
35 I lay it on you now to attend to this
For my safe, for Apollo's, for the sick
Sterile city that heaven has abandoned.
Suppose the oracle had given you no command:
Should this defilement go uncleansed for ever?
40 You should have found the murderer: your king,
A noble king, had been destroyed!
                            Now I,
Having the power that he held before me,
Having his bed, begetting children there

Upon his wife, as he would have, had he lived—
45   Their son would have been my children's brother,
If Laïos had had luck in fatherhood!
(And now his bad fortune has struck him down)—
I say I take the son's part, just as though
I were his son, to press the fight for him
50   And see it won! I'll find the hand that brought
Death to Labdakos' and Polydoros' child,
Heir of Kadmos' and Agenor's line.[4]
And as for those who fail me,
May the gods deny them the fruit of the earth,
55   Fruit of the womb, and may they rot utterly!
Let them be wretched as we are wretched, and worse!

For you, for loyal Thebans, and for all
Who find my actions right, I pray the favor
Of justice, and of all the immortal gods.
60 CHORAGOS   Since I am under oath, my lord, I swear
I did not do the murder, I can not name
The murderer. Phoibos ordained the search;
Why did he not say who the culprit was?
OEDIPUS   An honest question. But no man in the world
65   Can make the gods do more than the gods will.
CHORAGOS   There is an alternative, I think—
OEDIPUS   Tell me.
Any or all, you must not fail to tell me.
CHORAGOS   A lord clairvoyant to the lord Apollo,
As we all know, is the skilled Teiresias.
70   One might learn much about this from him, Oedipus.
OEDIPUS   I am not wasting time:
Kreon spoke of this, and I have sent for him—
Twice, in fact; it is strange that he is not here.
CHORAGOS   The other matter—that old report—seems useless.
75 OEDIPUS   What was that? I am interested in all reports.
CHORAGOS   The king was said to have been killed by highwaymen.
OEDIPUS   I know. But we have no witnesses to that.
CHORAGOS   If the killer can feel a particle of dread,
Your curse will bring him out of hiding!
OEDIPUS   No.
80   The man who dared that act will fear no curse.

---

[4]father, grandfather, great-grandfather, and great-great-grandfather of Laïos

(*Enter the blind seer* TEIRESIAS, *led by a* PAGE.)

CHORAGOS   But there is one man who may detect the criminal.
　　　This is Teiresias, this is the holy prophet
　　　In whom, alone of all men, truth was born.
OEDIPUS   Teiresias: seer: student of mysteries,
85　　　Of all that's taught and all that no man tells,
　　　Secrets of Heaven and secrets of the earth:
　　　Blind though you are, you know the city lies
　　　Sick with plague; and from this plague, my lord,
　　　We find that you alone can guard or save us.

90　　　Possibly you did not hear the messengers?
　　　Apollo, when we sent to him,
　　　Sent us back word that this great pestilence
　　　Would lift, but only if we established clearly
　　　The identity of those who murdered Laïos.
95　　　They must be killed or exiled.
　　　　　　　　　　　　　Can you use
　　　Birdflight⁵ or any art of divination
　　　To purify yourself, and Thebes, and me
　　　From this contagion? We are in your hands.
　　　There is no fairer duty
100　　　Than that of helping others in distress.
TEIRESIAS   How dreadful knowledge of the truth can be
　　　When there's no help in truth! I knew this well,
　　　But did not act on it: else I should not have come.
OEDIPUS   What is troubling you? Why are your eyes so cold?
105 TEIRESIAS   Let me go home. Bear your own fate, and I'll
　　　Bear mine. It is better so: trust what I say.
OEDIPUS   What you say is ungracious and unhelpful
　　　To your native country. Do not refuse to speak.
TEIRESIAS   When it comes to speech, your own is neither temperate
110　　　Nor opportune. I wish to be more prudent.
OEDIPUS   In God's name, we all beg you—
TEIRESIAS   　　　　　　　　　You are all ignorant.
　　　No; I will never tell you what I know.
　　　Now it is my misery; then, it would be yours.
OEDIPUS   What! You do know something, and will not tell us?
115　　　You would betray us all and wreck the State?
TEIRESIAS   I do not intend to torture myself, or you.
　　　Why persist in asking? You will not persuade me.

---

⁵Prophets predicted the future or divined the unknown by observing the flight of birds.

OEDIPUS   What a wicked old man you are! You'd try a stone's
    Patience! Out with it! Have you no feeling at all?

120   TEIRESIAS   You call me unfeeling. If you could only see
    The nature of your own feelings . . .

OEDIPUS   Why,
    Who would not feel as I do? Who could endure
    Your arrogance toward the city?

TEIRESIAS   What does it matter?
    Whether I speak or not, it is bound to come.

125   OEDIPUS   Then, if "it" is bound to come, you are bound to tell me.

TEIRESIAS   No, I will not go on. Rage as you please.

OEDIPUS   Rage? Why not!
                    And I'll tell you what I think:
    You planned it, you had it done, you all but
    Killed him with your own hands; if you had eyes,

130   I'd say the crime was yours, and yours alone.

TEIRESIAS   So? I charge you, then,
    Abide by the proclamation you have made:
    From this day forth
    Never speak again to these men or to me;

135   You yourself are the pollution of this country.

OEDIPUS   You dare say that! Can you possibly think you have
    Some way of going free, after such insolence?

TEIRESIAS   I have gone free. It is the truth that sustains me.

OEDIPUS   Who taught you shamelessness? It was not your craft.

140   TEIRESIAS   You did. You made me speak. I did not want to.

OEDIPUS   Speak what? Let me hear it again more clearly.

TEIRESIAS   Was it not clear before? Are you tempting me?

OEDIPUS   I did not understand it. Say it again.

TEIRESIAS   I say that you are the murderer whom you seek.

145   OEDIPUS   Now twice you have spat out infamy. You'll pay for it!

TEIRESIAS   Would you care for more? Do you wish to be really angry?

OEDIPUS   Say what you will. Whatever you say is worthless.

TEIRESIAS   I say you live in hideous shame with those
    Most dear to you. You can not see the evil.

150   OEDIPUS   Can you go on babbling like this for ever?

TEIRESIAS   I can, if there is power in truth.

OEDIPUS   There is:
    But not for you, not for you,
    You sightless, witless, senseless, mad old man!

TEIRESIAS   You are the madman. There is no one here

155   Who will not curse you soon, as you curse me.

OEDIPUS   You child of total night! I would not touch you;
    Neither would any man who sees the sun.

TEIRESIAS   True: it is not from you my fate will come.
    That lies within Apollo's competence,
160   As it is his concern.
OEDIPUS   Tell me, who made
    These fine discoveries? Kreon? or someone else?
TEIRESIAS   Kreon is no threat. You weave your own doom.
OEDIPUS   Wealth, power, craft of statesmanship!
    Kingly position, everywhere admired!
165   What savage envy is stored up against these,
    If Kreon, whom I trusted, Kreon my friend,
    For this great office which the city once
    Put in my hands unsought—if for this power
    Kreon desires in secret to destroy me!

170   He has bought this decrepit fortune-teller, this
    Collector of dirty pennies, this prophet fraud—
    Why, he is no more clairvoyant than I am!
                           Tell us:
    Has your mystic mummery ever approached the truth?
    When that hellcat the Sphinx was performing here,
175   What help were you to these people?
    Her magic was not for the first man who came along:
    It demanded a real exorcist. Your birds—
    What good were they? or the gods, for the matter of that?
    But I came by,
180   Oedipus, the simple man, who knows nothing—
    I thought it out for myself, no birds helped me!
    And this is the man you think you can destroy,
    That you may be close to Kreon when he's king!
    Well, you and your friend Kreon, it seems to me,
185   Will suffer most. If you were not an old man,
    You would have paid already for your plot.
CHORAGOS   We can not see that his words or yours
    Have been spoken except in anger, Oedipus,
    And of anger we have no need. How to accomplish
190   The god's will best: that is what most concerns us.
TEIRESIAS   You are a king. But where argument's concerned
    I am your man, as much a king as you.
    I am not your servant, but Apollo's.
    I have no need of Kreon or Kreon's name.

195   Listen to me. You mock my blindness, do you?
    But I say that you, with both your eyes, are blind:
    You can not see the wretchedness of your life,

Nor in whose house you live, no, nor with whom.
Who are your father and mother? Can you tell me?
200   You do not even know the blind wrongs
That you have done them, on earth and in the world below.
But the double lash of your parents' curse will whip you
Out of this land some day, with only night
Upon your precious eyes.
205   Your cries then—where will they not be heard?
What fastness of Kithairon[6] will not echo them?
And that bridal-descant of yours—you'll know it then,
The song they sang when you came here to Thebes
And found your misguided berthing.
210   All this, and more, that you can not guess at now,
Will bring you to yourself among your children.

Be angry, then. Curse Kreon. Curse my words.
I tell you, no man that walks upon the earth
Shall be rooted out more horribly than you.
215 OEDIPUS   Am I to bear this from him?—Damnation
Take you! Out of this place! Out of my sight!
TEIRESIAS   I would not have come at all if you had not asked me.
OEDIPUS   Could I have told that you'd talk nonsense, that
You'd come here to make a fool of yourself, and of me?
220 TEIRESIAS   A fool? Your parents thought me sane enough.
OEDIPUS   My parents again!—Wait: who were my parents?
TEIRESIAS   This day will give you a father, and break your heart.
OEDIPUS   Your infantile riddles! Your damned abracadabra!
TEIRESIAS   You were a great man once at solving riddles.
225 OEDIPUS   Mock me with that if you like; you will find it true.
TEIRESIAS   It was true enough. It brought about your ruin.
OEDIPUS   But if it saved this town?
TEIRESIAS   (*to the* PAGE)   Boy, give me your hand.
OEDIPUS   Yes, boy; lead him away.
                      —While you are here
We can do nothing. Go; leave us in peace.
230 TEIRESIAS   I will go when I have said what I have to say.
How can you hurt me? And I tell you again:
The man you have been looking for all this time,
The damned man, the murderer of Laïos,
That man is in Thebes. To your mind he is foreign-born,
235   But it will soon be shown that he is a Theban,
A revelation that will fail to please.

---

[6]the mountain where Oedipus was taken to be exposed as an infant

A blind man,
Who has his eyes now; a penniless man, who is rich now;
And he will go tapping the strange earth with his staff.
To the children with whom he lives now he will be
240   Brother and father—the very same; to her
Who bore him, son and husband—the very same
Who came to his father's bed, wet with his father's blood.

Enough. Go think that over.
If later you find error in what I have said,
245   You may say that I have no skill in prophecy.

(*Exit* Teiresias, *led by his* Page. Oedipus *goes into the palace.*)

Ode I

Strophe I

CHORUS   The Delphic stone of prophecies
Remembers ancient regicide
And a still bloody hand.
That killer's hour of flight has come.
5   He must be stronger than riderless
Coursers of untiring wind,
For the son[7] of Zeus armed with his father's thunder
Leaps in lightning after him;
And the Furies hold his track, the sad Furies.

Antistrophe I

10   Holy Parnassos'[8] peak of snow
Flashes and blinds that secret man,
That all shall hunt him down:
Though he may roam the forest shade
Like a bull gone wild from pasture
15   To rage through glooms of stone.
Doom comes down on him; flight will not avail him;
For the world's heart calls him desolate,
And the immortal voices follow, for ever follow.

---

[7]Apollo   [8]mountain sacred to Apollo

Strophe 2

But now a wilder thing is heard
20   From the old man skilled at hearing Fate in the wing-beat of a bird.
Bewildered as a blown bird, my soul hovers and can not find
Foothold in this debate, or any reason or rest of mind.
But no man ever brought—none can bring
Proof of strife between Thebes' royal house,
25   Labdakos' line, and the son of Polybos;
And never until now has any man brought word
Of Laïos' dark death staining Oedipus the King.

Antistrophe 2

Divine Zeus and Apollo hold
Perfect intelligence alone of all tales ever told;
30   And well though this diviner works, he works in his own night;
No man can judge that rough unknown or trust in second sight,
For wisdom changes hands among the wise.
Shall I believe my great lord criminal
At a raging word that a blind old man let fall?
35   I saw him, when the carrion woman[9] faced him of old,
Prove his heroic mind. These evil words are lies.

Scene II

KREON   Men of Thebes:
I am told that heavy accusations
Have been brought against me by King Oedipus.

I am not the kind of man to bear this tamely.

5   If in these present difficulties
He holds me accountable for any harm to him
Through anything I have said or done—why, then,
I do not value life in this dishonor.
It is not as though this rumor touched upon
10   Some private indiscretion. The matter is grave.
The fact is that I am being called disloyal
To the State, to my fellow citizens, to my friends.
CHORAGOS   He may have spoken in anger, not from his mind.
KREON   But did you not hear him say I was the one
15   Who seduced the old prophet into lying?

---

[9]the Sphinx

CHORAGOS   The thing was said; I do not know how seriously.
KREON   But you were watching him! Were his eyes steady?
      Did he look like a man in his right mind?
CHORAGOS   I do not know.
      I can not judge the behavior of great men.
20   But here is the king himself.

(*Enter* OEDIPUS.)

OEDIPUS   So you dared come back.
      Why? How brazen of you to come to my house,
      You murderer!
                          Do you think I do not know
      That you plotted to kill me, plotted to steal my throne?
      Tell me, in God's name: am I coward, a fool,
25   That you should dream you could accomplish this?
      A fool who could not see your slippery game?
      A coward, not to fight back when I saw it?
      You are the fool, Kreon, are you not? hoping
      Without support or friends to get a throne?
30   Thrones may be won or bought: you could do neither.
KREON   Now listen to me. You have talked; let me talk, too.
      You can not judge unless you know the facts.
OEDIPUS   You speak well: there is one fact; but I find it hard
      To learn from the deadliest enemy I have.
35 KREON   That above all I must dispute with you.
OEDIPUS   That above all I will not hear you deny.
KREON   If you think there is anything good in being stubborn
      Against all reason, then I say you are wrong.
OEDIPUS   If you think a man can sin against his own kind
40   And not be punished for it, I say you are mad.
KREON   I agree. But tell me: What have I done to you?
OEDIPUS   You advised me to send for that wizard, did you not?
KREON   I did. I should do it again.
OEDIPUS   Very well. Now tell me:
      How long has it been since Laïos—
KREON   What of Laïos?
45 OEDIPUS   Since he vanished in that onset by the road?
KREON   It was long ago, a long time.
OEDIPUS   And this prophet,
      Was he practicing here then?
KREON   He was; and with honor, as now.
OEDIPUS   Did he speak of me at that time?

KREON He never did,
    At least, not when I was present.

OEDIPUS But . . . the enquiry?

50   I suppose you held one?

KREON We did, but we learned nothing.

OEDIPUS Why did the prophet not speak against me then?

KREON I do not know; and I am the kind of man
    Who holds his tongue when he has no facts to go on.

OEDIPUS There's one fact that you know, and you could tell it.

55 KREON What fact is that? If I know it, you shall have it.

OEDIPUS If he were not involved with you, he could not say
    That it was I who murdered Laïos.

KREON If he says that, you are the one that knows it!—
    But now it is my turn to question you.

60 OEDIPUS Put your questions. I am no murderer.

KREON First, then: You married my sister?

OEDIPUS I married your sister.

KREON And you rule the kingdom equally with her?

OEDIPUS Everything that she wants she has from me.

KREON And I am the third, equal to both of you?

65 OEDIPUS That is why I call you a bad friend.

KREON No. Reason it out, as I have done.
    Think of this first: Would any sane man prefer
    Power, with all a king's anxieties,
    To that same power and the grace of sleep?
70   Certainly not I.
    I have never longed for the king's power—only his rights.
    Would any wise man differ from me in this?
    As matters stand, I have my way in everything
    With your consent, and no responsibilities.
75   If I were king, I should be a slave to policy.

    How could I desire a scepter more
    Than what is now mine—untroubled influence?
    No, I have not gone mad; I need no honors,
    Except those with the perquisites I have now.
80   I am welcome everywhere; every man salutes me,
    And those who want your favor seek my ear,
    Since I know how to manage what they ask.
    Should I exchange this ease for that anxiety?
    Besides, no sober mind is treasonable.
85   I hate anarchy
    And never would deal with any man who likes it.
    Test what I have said. Go to the priestess

At Delphi, ask if I quoted her correctly.
And as for this other thing: if I am found
90   Guilty of treason with Teiresias,
Then sentence me to death. You have my word
It is a sentence I should cast my vote for—
But not without evidence!
                              You do wrong
When you take good men for bad, bad men for good.
95   A true friend thrown aside—why, life itself
Is not more precious!
                         In time you will know this well:
For time, and time alone, will show the just man,
Though scoundrels are discovered in a day.

CHORAGOS   This is well said, and a prudent man would ponder it.
100   Judgments too quickly formed are dangerous.

OEDIPUS   But is he not quick in his duplicity?
And shall I not be quick to parry him?
Would you have me stand still, hold my peace, and let
This man win everything, through my inaction?

105 KREON   And you want—what is it, then? To banish me?

OEDIPUS   No, not exile. It is your death I want,
So that all the world may see what treason means.

KREON   You will persist, then? You will not believe me?

OEDIPUS   How can I believe you?

KREON   Then you are a fool.

110 OEDIPUS   To save myself?

KREON   In justice, think of me.

OEDIPUS   You are evil incarnate.

KREON   But suppose that you are wrong?

OEDIPUS   Still I must rule.

KREON   But not if you rule badly.

OEDIPUS   O city, city!

KREON   It is my city, too!

CHORAGOS   Now, my lords, be still. I see the queen,
115   Iokastê, coming from her palace chambers;
And it is time she came, for the sake of you both.
This dreadful quarrel can be resolved through her.

(*Enter* IOKASTÊ.)

IOKASTÊ   Poor foolish men, what wicked din is this?
With Thebes sick to death, is it not shameful
120   That you should rake some private quarrel up?
(*to* OEDIPUS) Come into the house.

—And you, Kreon, go now:
　　Let us have no more of this tumult over nothing.
KREON　Nothing? No, sister: what your husband plans for me
　　Is one of two great evils: exile or death.
125 OEDIPUS　He is right.
　　　　　　　　　Why, woman I have caught him squarely
　　Plotting against my life.
KREON　　　　　　　No! Let me die
　　Accurst if ever I have wished you harm!
IOKASTÊ　Ah, believe it, Oedipus!
　　In the name of the gods, respect this oath of his
130　For my sake, for the sake of these people here!

Strophe 1

CHORAGOS　Open your mind to her, my lord. Be ruled by her, I beg you!
OEDIPUS　What would you have me do?
CHORAGOS　Respect Kreon's word. He has never spoken like a fool,
　　And now he has sworn an oath.
OEDIPUS　You know what you ask?
CHORAGOS　　　　　　　　　I do.
OEDIPUS　　　　　　　　　　　　Speak on, then.
135 CHORAGOS　A friend so sworn should not be baited so,
　　In blind malice, and without final proof.
OEDIPUS　You are aware, I hope, that what you say
　　Means death for me, or exile at the least.

Strophe 2

CHORAGOS　No, I swear by Helios, first in Heaven!
140　May I die friendless and accurst,
　　The worst of deaths, if ever I meant that!
　　　　　It is the withering fields
　　　　　　That hurt my sick heart:
　　　　　Must we bear all these ills,
145　　　　　　　And now your bad blood as well?
OEDIPUS　Then let him go. And let me die, if I must,
　　Or be driven by him in shame from the land of Thebes.
　　It is your unhappiness, and not his talk,
　　That touches me.
　　　　　　As for him—
150　Wherever he goes, hatred will follow him.
KREON　Ugly in yielding, as you were ugly in rage!
　　Natures like yours chiefly torment themselves.

OEDIPUS   Can you not go? Can you not leave me?
KREON   I can.
    You do not know me; but the city knows me,
155   And in its eyes I am just, if not in yours.

(*Exit* KREON.)

Antistrophe 1

CHORAGOS   Lady Iokastê, did you not ask the King to go to his chambers?
IOKASTÊ   First tell me what has happened.
CHORAGOS   There was suspicion without evidence; yet it rankled
    As even false charges will.
160   IOKASTÊ   On both sides?
CHORAGOS   On both.
IOKASTÊ   But what was said?
CHORAGOS   Oh let it rest, let it be done with!
    Have we not suffered enough?
OEDIPUS   You see to what your decency has brought you:
    You have made difficulties where my heart saw none.

Antistrophe 2

165   CHORAGOS   Oedipus, it is not once only I have told you—
    You must know I should count myself unwise
    To the point of madness, should I now forsake you—
        You, under whose hand,
          In the storm of another time,
170   Our dear land sailed out free.
        But now stand fast at the helm!
IOKASTÊ   In God's name, Oedipus, inform your wife as well:
    Why are you so set in this hard anger?
OEDIPUS   I will tell you, for none of these men deserves
175   My confidence as you do. It is Kreon's work,
    His treachery, his plotting against me.
IOKASTÊ   Go on, if you can make this clear to me.
OEDIPUS   He charges me with the murder of Laïos.
IOKASTÊ   Has he some knowledge? Or does he speak from hearsay?
180   OEDIPUS   He would not commit himself to such a charge,
    But he has brought in that damnable soothsayer
    To tell his story.
IOKASTÊ   Set your mind at rest.
    If it is a question of soothsayers, I tell you

That you will find no man whose craft gives knowledge
185   Of the unknowable.
                            Here is my proof:
An oracle was reported to Laïos once
(I will not say from Phoibos himself, but from
His appointed ministers, at any rate)
That his doom would be death at the hands of his own son—
190   His son, born of his flesh and of mine!

Now, you remember the story: Laïos was killed
By marauding strangers where three highways meet;
But his child had not been three days in this world
Before the king had pierced the baby's ankles
195   And left him to die on a lonely mountainside.

Thus, Apollo never caused that child
To kill his father, and it was not Laïos' fate
To die at the hands of his son, as he had feared.
This is what prophets and prophecies are worth!
200   Have no dread of them.
                            It is God himself
Who can show us what he wills, in his own way.
OEDIPUS   How strange a shadowy memory crossed my mind,
    Just now while you were speaking; it chilled my heart.
IOKASTÊ   What do you mean? What memory do you speak of?
205 OEDIPUS   If I understand you, Laïos was killed
    At a place where three roads meet.
IOKASTÊ   So it was said;
    We have no later story.
OEDIPUS   Where did it happen?
IOKASTÊ   Phokis, it is called: at a place where the Theban Way
    Divides into the roads toward Delphi and Daulia.
210 OEDIPUS   When?
IOKASTÊ   We had the news not long before you came
    And proved the right to your succession here.
OEDIPUS   Ah, what net has God been weaving for me?
IOKASTÊ   Oedipus! Why does this trouble you?
OEDIPUS   Do not ask me yet.
    First, tell me how Laïos looked, and tell me
215   How old he was.
IOKASTÊ   He was tall, his hair just touched
    With white; his form was not unlike your own.
OEDIPUS   I think that I myself may be accurst
    By my own ignorant edict.

IOKASTÊ   You speak strangely.
It makes me tremble to look at you, my king.
220 OEDIPUS   I am not sure that the blind man can not see.
But I should know better if you were to tell me—
IOKASTÊ   Anything—though I dread to hear you ask it.
OEDIPUS   Was the king lightly escorted, or did he ride
With a large company, as a ruler should?
225 IOKASTÊ   There were five men with him in all: one was a herald.
And a single chariot, which he was driving.
OEDIPUS   Alas, that makes it plain enough!
                                   But who—
Who told you how it happened?
IOKASTÊ   A household servant,
The only one to escape.
OEDIPUS   And is he still
230 A servant of ours?
IOKASTÊ   No; for when he came back at last
And found you enthroned in the place of the dead king,
He came to me, touched my hand with his, and begged
That I would send him away to the frontier district
Where only the shepherds go—
235 As far away from the city as I could send him.
I granted his prayer; for although the man was a slave,
He had earned more than this favor at my hands.
OEDIPUS   Can he be called back quickly?
IOKASTÊ   Easily.
But why?
OEDIPUS   I have taken too much upon myself
240 Without enquiry; therefore I wish to consult him.
IOKASTÊ   Then he shall come.
                          But am I not one also
To whom you might confide these fears of yours?
OEDIPUS   That is your right; it will not be denied you,
Now least of all; for I have reached a pitch
245 Of wild foreboding. Is there anyone
To whom I should sooner speak?

Polybos of Corinth is my father.
My mother is a Dorian: Meropê.
I grew up chief among the men of Corinth
250 Until a strange thing happened—
Not worth my passion, it may be, but strange.
At a feast, a drunken man maundering in his cups

Cries out that I am not my father's son![1]
I contained myself that night, though I felt anger

255   And a sinking heart. The next day I visited
My father and mother, and questioned them. They stormed,
Calling it all the slanderous rant of a fool;
And this relieved me. Yet the suspicion
Remained always aching in my mind;

260   I knew there was talk; I could not rest;
And finally, saying nothing to my parents,
I went to the shrine at Delphi.

The god dismissed my question without reply;
He spoke of other things.
                                  Some were clear,

265   Full of wretchedness, dreadful, unbearable:
As, that I should lie with my own mother, breed
Children from whom all men would turn their eyes;
And that I should be my father's murderer.

I heard all this, and fled. And from that day

270   Corinth to me was only in the stars
Descending in that quarter of the sky,
As I wandered farther and farther on my way
To a land where I should never see the evil
Sung by the oracle. And I came to this country

275   Where, so you say, King Laïos was killed.

I will tell you all that happened there, my lady.

There were three highways
Coming together at a place I passed;
And there a herald came towards me, and a chariot

280   Drawn by horses, with a man such as you describe
Seated in it. The groom leading the horses
Forced me off the road at his lord's command;
But as this charioteer lurched over towards me
I struck him in my rage. The old man saw me

285   And brought his double goad down upon my head
As I came abreast.
                              He was paid back, and more!
Swinging my club in this right hand I knocked him

---

[1]Oedipus perhaps interprets this as an allegation that he is a bastard, the son of Meropê but not of Polybos. The implication, at any rate, is that he is not of royal birth, not the legitimate heir to the throne of Corinth.

Out of his car, and he rolled on the ground.

I killed him.

I killed them all.

290 Now if that stranger and Laïos were—kin,
Where is a man more miserable than I?
More hated by the gods? Citizen and alien alike
Must never shelter me or speak to me—
I must be shunned by all.

And I myself

295 Pronounced this malediction upon myself!

Think of it: I have touched you with these hands,
These hands that killed your husband. What defilement!

Am I all evil, then? It must be so,
Since I must flee from Thebes, yet never again
300 See my own countrymen, my own country,
For fear of joining my mother in marriage
And killing Polybos, my father.

Ah,

If I was created so, born to this fate,
Who could deny the savagery of God?

305 O holy majesty of heavenly powers!
May I never see that day! Never!
Rather let me vanish from the race of men
Than know the abomination destined me!
CHORAGOS   We too, my lord, have felt dismay at this.
310 But there is hope: you have yet to hear the shepherd.
OEDIPUS   Indeed, I fear no other hope is left me.
IOKASTÊ   What do you hope from him when he comes?
OEDIPUS   This much:
If his account of the murder tallies with yours,
Then I am cleared.
IOKASTÊ   What was it that I said
315 Of such importance?
OEDIPUS   Why, "marauders," you said,
Killed the king, according to this man's story.
If he maintains that still, if there were several,
Clearly the guilt is not mine: I was alone.
But if he says one man, singlehanded, did it,
320 Then the evidence all points to me.

IOKASTÊ   You may be sure that he said there were several;
And can he call back that story now? He can not.
The whole city heard it as plainly as I.
But suppose he alters some detail of it:
325 He can not ever show that Laïos's death
Fulfilled the oracle: for Apollo said
My child was doomed to kill him; and my child—
Poor baby!—it was my child that died first.
No. From now on, where oracles are concerned,
330 I would not waste a second thought on any.
OEDIPUS   You may be right.
But come: let someone go
For the shepherd at once. This matter must be settled.
IOKASTÊ   I will send for him.
I would not wish to cross you in anything,
335 And surely not in this.—Let us go in.

(Exeunt into the palace.)

Ode II

Strophe I

CHORUS   Let me be reverent in the ways of right,
Lowly the paths I journey on;
Let all my words and actions keep
The laws of the pure universe
5 From highest Heaven handed down.
For Heaven is their bright nurse,
Those generations of the realms of light;
Ah, never of mortal kind were they begot,
Nor are they slaves of memory, lost in sleep:
10 Their Father is greater than Time, and ages not.

Antistrophe I

The tyrant is a child of Pride
Who drinks from his great sickening cup
Recklessness and vanity,
Until from his high crest headlong
15 He plummets to the dust of hope.
That strong man is not strong.
But let no fair ambition be denied;
May God protect the wrestler for the State

In government, in comely policy,
20 Who will fear God, and on His ordinance wait.

Strophe 2

Haughtiness and the high hand of disdain
Tempt and outrage God's holy law;
And any mortal who dares hold
No immortal Power in awe
25 Will be caught up in a net of pain:
The price for which his levity is sold.
Let each man take due earnings, then,
And keep his hands from holy things,
And from blasphemy stand apart—
30 Else the crackling blast of heaven
Blows on his head, and on his desperate heart.
Though fools will honor impious men,
In their cities no tragic poet sings.

Antistrophe 2

Shall we lose faith in Delphi's obscurities,
35 We who have heard the world's core
Discredited, and the sacred wood
Of Zeus at Elis praised no more?
The deeds and the strange prophecies
Must make a pattern yet to be understood.
40 Zeus, if indeed you are lord of all,
Throned in light over night and day,
Mirror this in your endless mind:
Our masters call the oracle
Words on the wind, and the Delphic vision blind!
45 Their hearts no longer know Apollo,
And reverence for the gods has died away.

Scene III

(*Enter* IOKASTÊ.)

IOKASTÊ   Princes of Thebes, it has occurred to me
To visit the altars of the gods, bearing
These branches as a suppliant, and this incense.
Our king is not himself: his noble soul
5 Is overwrought with fantasies of dread,
Else he would consider

The new prophecies in the light of the old.
He will listen to any voice that speaks disaster,
And my advice goes for nothing.

(*She approaches the altar, R.*)

                             To you, then, Apollo,
10   Lycéan lord, since you are nearest, I turn in prayer.
Receive these offerings, and grant us deliverance
From defilement. Our hearts are heavy with fear
When we see our leader distracted, as helpless sailors
Are terrified by the confusion of their helmsman.

(*Enter* MESSENGER.)

15 MESSENGER   Friends, no doubt you can direct me:
      Where shall I find the house of Oedipus,
      Or, better still, where is the king himself?
  CHORAGOS   It is this very place, stranger; he is inside.
      This is his wife and mother of his children.
20 MESSENGER   I wish her happiness in a happy house,
      Blest in all the fulfillment of her marriage.
  IOKASTÊ   I wish as much for you: your courtesy
      Deserves a like good fortune. But now, tell me:
      Why have you come? What have you to say to us?
25 MESSENGER   Good news, my lady, for your house and your husband.
  IOKASTÊ   What news? Who sent you here?
  MESSENGER   I am from Corinth.
      The news I bring ought to mean joy for you,
      Though it may be you will find some grief in it.
  IOKASTÊ   What is it? How can it touch us in both ways?
30 MESSENGER   The word is that the people of the Isthmus
      Intend to call Oedipus to be their king.
  IOKASTÊ   But old King Polybos—is he not reigning still?
  MESSENGER   No. Death holds him in his sepulchre.
  IOKASTÊ   What are you saying? Polybos is dead?
35 MESSENGER   If I am not telling the truth, may I die myself.
  IOKASTÊ (*to a* MAIDSERVANT)   Go in, go quickly; tell this to your master.

      O riddlers of God's will, where are you now!
      This was the man whom Oedipus, long ago,
      Feared so, fled so, in dread of destroying him—
40   But it was another fate by which he died.

(*Enter* OEDIPUS, *C.*)

OEDIPUS   Dearest Iokastê, why have you sent for me?

IOKASTÊ   Listen to what this man says, and then tell me
What has become of the solemn prophecies.

OEDIPUS   Who is this man? What is his news for me?

45 IOKASTÊ   He has come from Corinth to announce your father's death!

OEDIPUS   Is it true, stranger? Tell me in your own words.

MESSENGER   I can not say it more clearly: the king is dead.

OEDIPUS   Was it by treason? Or by an attack of illness?

MESSENGER   A little thing brings old men to their rest.

50 OEDIPUS   It was sickness, then?

MESSENGER   Yes, and his many years.

OEDIPUS   Ah!
Why should a man respect the Pythian hearth,[2] or
Give heed to the birds that jangle above his head?
They prophesied that I should kill Polybos,

55   Kill my own father; but he is dead and buried,
And I am here—I never touched him, never,
Unless he died of grief for my departure,
And thus, in a sense, through me. No. Polybos
Has packed the oracles off with him underground.

60   They are empty words.

IOKASTÊ   Had I not told you so?

OEDIPUS   You had; it was my faint heart that betrayed me.

IOKASTÊ   From now on never think of those things again.

OEDIPUS   And yet—must I not fear my mother's bed?

IOKASTÊ   Why should anyone in this world be afraid,

65   Since Fate rules us and nothing can be foreseen?
A man should live only for the present day.

Have no more fear of sleeping with your mother:
How many men, in dreams, have lain with their mothers!
No reasonable man is troubled by such things.

70 OEDIPUS   That is true; only—
If only my mother were not still alive!
But she is alive. I can not help my dread.

IOKASTÊ   Yet this news of your father's death is wonderful.

OEDIPUS   Wonderful. But I fear the living woman.

75 MESSENGER   Tell me, who is this woman that you fear?

OEDIPUS   It is Meropê, man; the wife of King Polybos.

MESSENGER   Meropê? Why should you be afraid of her?

OEDIPUS   An oracle of the gods, a dreadful saying.

MESSENGER   Can you tell me about it or are you sworn to silence?

---

[2]Delphi

80 OEDIPUS   I can tell you, and I will.
Apollo said through his prophet that I was the man
Who should marry his own mother, shed his father's blood
With his own hands. And so, for all these years
I have kept clear of Corinth, and no harm has come—
85   Though it would have been sweet to see my parents again.
MESSENGER   And is this the fear that drove you out of Corinth?
OEDIPUS   Would you have me kill my father?
MESSENGER   As for that
You must be reassured by the news I gave you.
OEDIPUS   If you could reassure me, I would reward you.
90 MESSENGER   I had that in mind, I will confess: I thought
I could count on you when you returned to Corinth.
OEDIPUS   No: I will never go near my parents again.
MESSENGER   Ah, son, you still do not know what you are doing—
OEDIPUS   What do you mean? In the name of God tell me!
95 MESSENGER   —if these are your reasons for not going home.
OEDIPUS   I tell you, I fear the oracle may come true.
MESSENGER   And guilt may come upon you through your parents?
OEDIPUS   That is the dread that is always in my heart.
MESSENGER   Can you not see that all your fears are groundless?
100 OEDIPUS   Groundless? Am I not my parents' son?
MESSENGER   Polybos was not your father.
OEDIPUS   Not my father?
MESSENGER   No more your father than the man speaking to you.
OEDIPUS   But you are nothing to me!
MESSENGER   Neither was he.
OEDIPUS   Then why did he call me son?
MESSENGER   I will tell you:
105   Long ago he had you from my hands, as a gift.
OEDIPUS   Then how could he love me so, if I was not his?
MESSENGER   He had no children, and his heart turned to you.
OEDIPUS   What of you? Did you buy me? Did you find me by chance?
MESSENGER   I came upon you in the woody vales of Kithairon.
110 OEDIPUS   And what were you doing there?
MESSENGER   Tending my flocks.
OEDIPUS   A wandering shepherd?
MESSENGER   But your savior, son, that day.
OEDIPUS   From what did you save me?
MESSENGER   Your ankles should tell you that.
OEDIPUS   Ah, stranger, why do you speak of that childhood pain?
MESSENGER   I pulled the skewer that pinned your feet together.
115 OEDIPUS   I have had the mark as long as I can remember.
MESSENGER   That was why you were given the name you bear.

OEDIPUS   God! Was it my father or my mother who did it?
    Tell me!
MESSENGER   I do not know. The man who gave you to me
    Can tell you better than I.
120 OEDIPUS   It was not you that found me, but another?
MESSENGER   It was another shepherd gave you to me.
OEDIPUS   Who was he? Can you tell me who he was?
MESSENGER   I think he was said to be one of Laïos' people.
OEDIPUS   You mean the Laïos who was king here years ago?
125 MESSENGER   Yes; King Laïos; and the man was one of his herdsmen.
OEDIPUS   Is he still alive? Can I see him?
MESSENGER   These men here
    Know best about such things.
OEDIPUS   Does anyone here
    Know this shepherd that he is talking about?
    Have you seen him in the fields, or in the town?
130   If you have, tell me. It is time things were made plain.
CHORAGOS   I think the man he means is that same shepherd
    You have already asked to see. Iokastê perhaps
    Could tell you something.
OEDIPUS   Do you know anything
    About him, Lady? Is he the man we have summoned?
135   Is that the man this shepherd means?
IOKASTÊ   Why think of him?
    Forget this herdsman. Forget it all.
    This talk is a waste of time.
OEDIPUS   How can you say that,
    When the clues to my true birth are in my hands?
IOKASTÊ   For God's love, let us have no more questioning!
140   Is your life nothing to you?
    My own is pain enough for me to bear.
OEDIPUS   You need not worry. Suppose my mother a slave,
    And born of slaves: no baseness can touch you.
IOKASTÊ   Listen to me, I beg you: do not do this thing!
145 OEDIPUS   I will not listen; the truth must be made known.
IOKASTÊ   Everything that I say is for your own good!
OEDIPUS   My own good
    Snaps my patience, then! I want none of it.
IOKASTÊ   You are fatally wrong! May you never learn who you are!
OEDIPUS   Go, one of you, and bring the shepherd here.
150   Let us leave this woman to brag of her royal name.
IOKASTÊ   Ah, miserable!
    That is the only word I have for you now.
    That is the only word I can ever have.

(*Exit into the palace.*)

CHORAGOS   Why has she left us, Oedipus? Why has she gone
155   In such a passion of sorrow? I fear this silence:
         Something dreadful may come of it.

OEDIPUS   Let it come!
         However base my birth, I must know about it.
         The Queen, like a woman, is perhaps ashamed
         To think of my low origin. But I
160   Am a child of Luck; I can not be dishonored.
         Luck is my mother; the passing months, my brothers,
         Have seen me rich and poor.
                                     If this is so,
         How could I wish that I were someone else?
165   How could I not be glad to know my birth?

Ode III

Strophe

CHORUS   If ever the coming time were known
         To my heart's pondering,
         Kithairon, now by Heaven I see the torches
         At the festival of the next full moon,
5   And see the dance, and hear the choir sing
         A grace to your gentle shade:
         Mountain where Oedipus was found,
         O mountain guard of a noble race!
         May the god[3] who heals us lend his aid,
10   And let that glory come to pass
         For our king's cradling-ground.

Antistrophe

Of the nymphs that flower beyond the years,
         Who bore you,[4] royal child,
         To Pan of the hills or the timberline Apollo,
15   Cold in delight where the upland clears,
         Or Hermês for whom Kyllenê's heights are piled?
         Or flushed as evening cloud,
         Great Dionysos, roamer of mountains,

---

[3]Apollo   [4]The chorus is suggesting that perhaps Oedipus is the son of one of the immortal nymphs and of a god—Pan, Apollo, Hermes, or Dionysos. The "sweet god-ravisher" (p. 60) is the presumed mother.

He—was it he who found you there,
20   And caught you up in his own proud
Arms from the sweet god-ravisher
Who laughed by the Muses' fountains?

Scene IV

OEDIPUS   Sirs: though I do not know the man,
I think I see him coming, this shepherd we want:
He is old, like our friend here, and the men
Bringing him seem to be servants of my house.
5   But you can tell, if you have ever seen him.

(*Enter* SHEPHERD *escorted by* SERVANTS.)

CHORAGOS   I know him, he was Laïos' man. You can trust him.
OEDIPUS   Tell me first, you from Corinth: is this the shepherd
We were discussing?
MESSENGER   This is the very man.
OEDIPUS (*to* SHEPHERD)   Come here. No, look at me. You must answer
10   Everything I ask.—You belonged to Laïos?
SHEPHERD   Yes: born his slave, brought up in his house.
OEDIPUS   Tell me: what kind of work did you do for him?
SHEPHERD   I was a shepherd of his, most of my life.
OEDIPUS   Where mainly did you go for pasturage?
15 SHEPHERD   Sometimes Kithairon, sometimes the hills near-by.
OEDIPUS   Do you remember ever seeing this man out there?
SHEPHERD   What would he be doing there? This man?
OEDIPUS   This man standing here. Have you ever seen him before?
SHEPHERD   No. At least, not to my recollection.
20 MESSENGER   And that is not strange, my lord. But I'll refresh
His memory: he must remember when we two
Spent three whole seasons together, March to September,
On Kithairon or thereabouts. He had two flocks;
I had one. Each autumn I'd drive mine home
25   And he would go back with his to Laïos' sheepfold.—
Is this not true, just as I have described it?
SHEPHERD   True, yes; but it was all so long ago.
MESSENGER   Well, then: do you remember, back in those days,
That you gave me a baby boy to bring up as my own?
30 SHEPHERD   What if I did? What are you trying to say?
MESSENGER   King Oedipus was once that little child.
SHEPHERD   Damn you, hold your tongue!

OEDIPUS   No more of that!
It is your tongue needs watching, not this man's.
SHEPHERD   My king, my master, what is it I have done wrong?
35 OEDIPUS   You have not answered his question about the boy.
SHEPHERD   He does not know . . . He is only making trouble . . .
OEDIPUS   Come, speak plainly, or it will go hard with you.
SHEPHERD   In God's name, do not torture an old man!
OEDIPUS   Come here, one of you; bind his arms behind him.
40 SHEPHERD   Unhappy king! What more do you wish to learn?
OEDIPUS   Did you give this man the child he speaks of?
SHEPHERD   I did.
And I would to God I had died that very day.
OEDIPUS   You will die now unless you speak the truth.
SHEPHERD   Yet if I speak the truth, I am worse than dead.
45 OEDIPUS (*to* ATTENDANT)   He intends to draw it out, apparently—
SHEPHERD   No! I have told you already that I gave him the boy.
OEDIPUS   Where did you get him? From your house? From somewhere else?
SHEPHERD   Not from mine, no. A man gave him to me.
OEDIPUS   Is that man here? Whose house did he belong to?
50 SHEPHERD   For God's love, my king, do not ask me any more!
OEDIPUS   You are a dead man if I have to ask you again.
SHEPHERD   Then . . . Then the child was from the palace of Laïos.
OEDIPUS   A slave child? or a child of his own line?
SHEPHERD   Ah, I am on the brink of dreadful speech!
55 OEDIPUS   And I of dreadful hearing. Yet I must hear.
SHEPHERD   If you must be told, then. . .
                                        They said it was Laïos' child;
But it is your wife who can tell you about that.
OEDIPUS   My wife!—Did she give it to you?
SHEPHERD   My lord, she did.
OEDIPUS   Do you know why?
SHEPHERD   I was told to get rid of it.
60 OEDIPUS   Oh heartless mother!
SHEPHERD   But in dread of prophecies . . .
OEDIPUS   Tell me.
SHEPHERD   It was said that the boy would kill his own father.
OEDIPUS   Then why did you give him over to this old man?
SHEPHERD   I pitied the baby, my king,
And I thought that this man would take him far away
65   To his own country.
                            He saved him—but for what a fate!
For if you are what this man says you are,
No man living is more wretched than Oedipus.

OEDIPUS   Ah God!
It was true!
All the prophecies!
—Now,
70   O Light, may I look on you for the last time!
I, Oedipus,
Oedipus, damned in his birth, in his marriage damned,
Damned in the blood he shed with his own hand!

(*He rushes into the palace.*)

Ode IV

Strophe I

CHORUS   Alas for the seed of men.
What measure shall I give these generations
That breathe on the void and are void
And exist and do not exist?
5   Who bears more weight of joy
Than mass of sunlight shifting in images,
Or who shall make his thought stay on
That down time drifts away?
Your splendor is all fallen.
10   O naked brow of wrath and tears,
O change of Oedipus!
I who saw your days call no man blest—
Your great days like ghosts gone.

Antistrophe I

That mind was a strong bow.
15   Deep, how deep you drew it then, hard archer,
At a dim fearful range,
And brought dear glory down!
You overcame the stranger[5]—
The virgin with her hooking lion claws—
20   And though death sang, stood like a tower
To make pale Thebes take heart.
Fortress against our sorrow!
True king, giver of laws,
Majestic Oedipus!

---

[5]the Sphinx

25   No prince in Thebes had ever such renown,
       No prince won such grace of power.

Strophe 2

       And now of all men ever known
       Most pitiful is this man's story:
       His fortunes are most changed, his state
30   Fallen to a low slave's
       Ground under bitter fate.
       O Oedipus, most royal one!
       The great door[6] that expelled you to the light
       Gave at night—ah, gave night to your glory:
35   As to the father, to the fathering son.
       All understood too late.
       How could that queen whom Laïos won,
       The garden that he harrowed at his height,
       Be silent when that act was done?

Antistrophe 2

40   But all eyes fail before time's eye,
       All actions come to justice there.
       Though never willed, though far down the deep past,
       Your bed, your dread sirings,
       Are brought to book at last.
45   Child by Laïos doomed to die,
       Then doomed to lose that fortunate little death,
       Would God you never took breath in this air
       That with my wailing lips I take to cry:
       For I weep the world's outcast.
50   I was blind, and now I can tell why:
       Asleep, for you had given ease of breath
       To Thebes, while the false years went by.

Exodos[7]

(*Enter, from the palace,* SECOND MESSENGER.)

SECOND MESSENGER   Elders of Thebes, most honored in this land,
       What horrors are yours to see and hear, what weight
       Of sorrow to be endured, if, true to your birth,
       You venerate the line of Labdakos!

---

[6]Iokastê's womb   [7]final scene

5   I think neither Istros nor Phasis, those great rivers,
Could purify this place of all the evil
It shelters now, or soon must bring to light—
Evil not done unconsciously, but willed.

The greatest griefs are those we cause ourselves.
10 CHORAGOS   Surely, friend, we have grief enough already;
What new sorrow do you mean?
SECOND MESSENGER   The queen is dead.
CHORAGOS   O miserable queen! But at whose hand?
SECOND MESSENGER   Her own.
The full horror of what happened you can not know,
For you did not see it; but I, who did, will tell you
15   As clearly as I can how she met her death.

When she had left us,
In passionate silence, passing through the court,
She ran to her apartment in the house,
Her hair clutched by the fingers of both hands.
20   She closed the doors behind her; then, by that bed
Where long ago the fatal son was conceived—
That son who should bring about his father's death—
We heard her call upon Laïos, dead so many years,
And heard her wail for the double fruit of her marriage,
25   A husband by her husband, children by her child.

Exactly how she died I do not know:
For Oedipus burst in moaning and would not let us
Keep vigil to the end: it was by him
As he stormed about the room that our eyes were caught.
30   From one to another of us he went, begging a sword,
Hunting the wife who was not his wife, the mother
Whose womb had carried his own children and himself.
I do not know: it was none of us aided him,
But surely one of the gods was in control!
35   For with a dreadful cry
He hurled his weight, as though wrenched out of himself,
At the twin doors: the bolts gave, and he rushed in.
And there we saw her hanging, her body swaying
From the cruel cord she had noosed about her neck.
40   A great sob broke from him, heartbreaking to hear,
As he loosed the rope and lowered her to the ground.

I would blot out from my mind what happened next!
For the king ripped from her gown the golden brooches

That were her ornament, and raised them, and plunged them down
45   Straight into his own eyeballs, crying, "No more,
No more shall you look on the misery about me,
The horrors of my own doing! Too long you have known
The faces of those whom I should never have seen,
Too long been blind to those for whom I was searching!
50   From this hour, go in darkness!" And as he spoke,
He struck at his eyes—not once, but many times;
And the blood spattered his beard,
Bursting from his ruined sockets like red hail.

So from the unhappiness of two this evil has sprung,
55   A curse on the man and woman alike. The old
Happiness of the house of Labdakos
Was happiness enough: where is it today?
It is all wailing and ruin, disgrace, death—all
The misery of mankind that has a name—
60   And it is wholly and for ever theirs.
CHORAGOS   Is he in agony still? Is there no rest for him?
SECOND MESSENGER   He is calling for someone to open the doors wide
So that all the children of Kadmos may look upon
His father's murderer, his mother's—no,
65   I can not say it!
                    And then he will leave Thebes,
Self-exiled, in order that the curse
Which he himself pronounced may depart from the house.
He is weak, and there is none to lead him,
So terrible is his suffering.
                    But you will see:
70   Look, the doors are opening; in a moment
You will see a thing that would crush a heart of stone.

(The central door is opened; OEDIPUS, *blinded, is led in.)*

CHORAGOS   Dreadful indeed for men to see.
Never have my own eyes
Looked on a sight so full of fear.

75   Oedipus!
What madness came upon you, what daemon
Leaped on your life with heavier
Punishment than a mortal man can bear?
No: I can not even
80   Look at you, poor ruined one.

And I would speak, question, ponder,
If I were able. No.
You make me shudder.
OEDIPUS   God. God.
85   Is there a sorrow greater?
Where shall I find harbor in this world?
My voice is hurled far on a dark wind.
What has God done to me?
CHORAGOS   Too terrible to think of, or to see.

Strophe 1

90 OEDIPUS   O cloud of night,
Never to be turned away: night coming on,
I can not tell how: night like a shroud!
My fair winds brought me here.
                                        O God. Again
The pain of the spikes where I had sight,
95   The flooding pain
Of memory, never to be gouged out.
CHORAGOS   This is not strange.
You suffer it all twice over, remorse in pain,
Pain in remorse.

Antistrophe 1

100 OEDIPUS   Ah dear friend
Are you faithful even yet, you alone?
Are you still standing near me, will you stay here,
Patient, to care for the blind?
                                        The blind man!
Yet even blind I know who it is attends me,
105   By the voice's tone—
Though my new darkness hide the comforter.
CHORAGOS   Oh fearful act!
What god was it drove you to rake black
Night across your eyes?

Strophe 2

110 OEDIPUS   Apollo. Apollo. Dear
Children, the god was Apollo.
He brought my sick, sick fate upon me.
But the blinding hand was my own!

How could I bear to see
115 When all my sight was horror everywhere?
CHORAGOS   Everywhere; that is true.
OEDIPUS   And now what is left?
Images? Love? A greeting even,
Sweet to the senses? Is there anything?
120 Ah, no, friends: lead me away.
Lead me away from Thebes.
                              Lead the great wreck
And hell of Oedipus, whom the gods hate.
CHORAGOS   Your misery, you are not blind to that.
Would God you had never found it out!

Antistrophe 2

125 OEDIPUS   Death take the man who unbound
My feet on that hillside
And delivered me from death to life! What life?
If only I had died,
This weight of monstrous doom
130 Could not have dragged me and my darlings down.
CHORAGOS   I would have wished the same.
OEDIPUS   Oh never to have come here
With my father's blood upon me! Never
To have been the man they call his mother's husband!
135 Oh accurst! Oh child of evil,
To have entered that wretched bed—
                              the selfsame one!
More primal than sin itself, this fell to me.
CHORAGOS   I do not know what words to offer you.
You were better dead than alive and blind.

140 OEDIPUS   Do not counsel me any more. This punishment
That I have laid upon myself is just.
If I had eyes,
I do not know how I could bear the sight
Of my father, when I came to the house of Death,
145 Or my mother: for I have sinned against them both
So vilely that I could not make my peace
By strangling my own life.
                              Or do you think my children,
Born as they were born, would be sweet to my eyes?
Ah never, never! Nor this town with its high walls,
150 Nor the holy images of the gods.

For I,

Thrice miserable!—Oedipus, noblest of all the line
Of Kadmos, have condemned myself to enjoy
These things no more, by my own malediction
Expelling that man whom the gods declared
155 To be a defilement in the house of Laïos.
After exposing the rankness of my own guilt,
How could I look men frankly in the eyes?
No, I swear it,
If I could have stifled my hearing at its source,
160 I would have done it and made all this body
A tight cell of misery, blank to light and sound:
So I should have been safe in my dark mind
Beyond external evil.

Ah Kithairon!

Why did you shelter me? When I was cast upon you,
165 Why did I not die? Then I should never
Have shown the world my execrable birth.

Ah Polybos! Corinth, city that I believed
The ancient seat of my ancestors: how fair
I seemed, your child! And all the while this evil
170 Was cancerous within me!

For I am sick

In my own being, sick in my origin.

O three roads, dark ravine, woodland and way
Where three roads met: you, drinking my father's blood,
My own blood, spilled by my own hand: can you remember
175 The unspeakable things I did there, and the things
I went on from there to do?

O marriage, marriage!

That act that engendered me, and again the act
Performed by the son in the same bed—

Ah, the net

Of incest, mingling fathers, brothers, sons,
180 With brides, wives, mothers: the last evil
That can be known by men: no tongue can say
How evil!

No. For the love of God, conceal me

Somewhere far from Thebes; or kill me; or hurl me
Into the sea, away from men's eyes for ever.

185 Come, lead me. You need not fear to touch me.
Of all men, I alone can bear this guilt.

(*Enter* KREON.)

CHORAGOS   Kreon is here now. As to what you ask,
    He may decide the course to take. He only
    Is left to protect the city in your place.
190 OEDIPUS   Alas, how can I speak to him? What right have I
    To beg his courtesy whom I have deeply wronged?
KREON   I have not come to mock you, Oedipus,
    Or to reproach you, either. (*to* ATTENDANTS)
                          —You, standing there:
    If you have lost all respect for man's dignity,
195   At least respect the flame of Lord Helios:
    Do not allow this pollution to show itself
    Openly here, an affront to the earth
    And Heaven's rain and the light of day. No, take him
    Into the house as quickly as you can.
200   For it is proper
    That only the close kindred see his grief.
OEDIPUS   I pray you in God's name, since your courtesy
    Ignores my dark expectation, visiting
    With mercy this man of all men most execrable:
205   Give me what I ask—for your good, not for mine.
KREON   And what is it that you turn to me begging for?
OEDIPUS   Drive me out of this country as quickly as may be
    To a place where no human voice can ever greet me.
KREON   I should have done that before now—only,
210   God's will had not been wholly revealed to me.
OEDIPUS   But his command is plain: the parricide
    Must be destroyed. I am that evil man.
KREON   That is the sense of it, yes; but as things are,
    We had best discover clearly what is to be done.
215 OEDIPUS   You would learn more about a man like me?
KREON   You are ready now to listen to the god.
OEDIPUS   I will listen. But it is to you
    That I must turn for help. I beg you, hear me.

    The woman in there—
220   Give her whatever funeral you think proper:
    She is your sister.
                  —But let me go, Kreon!
    Let me purge my father's Thebes of the pollution
    Of my living here, and go out to the wild hills,
    To Kithairon, that has won such fame with me,
225   The tomb my mother and father appointed for me,
    And let me die there, as they willed I should.

And yet I know
Death will not ever come to me through sickness
Or in any natural way: I have been preserved
230   For some unthinkable fate. But let that be.

As for my sons, you need not care for them.
They are men, they will find some way to live.
But my poor daughters, who have shared my table,
Who never before have been parted from their father—
235   Take care of them, Kreon; do this for me.

And will you let me touch them with my hands
A last time, and let us weep together?
Be kind, my lord,
Great prince, be kind!
                              Could I but touch them,
240   They would be mine again, as when I had my eyes.

(*Enter* ANTIGONÊ *and* ISMENÊ, *attended.*)

Ah, God!
Is it my dearest children I hear weeping?
Has Kreon pitied me and sent my daughters?
KREON   Yes, Oedipus: I knew that they were dear to you
245   In the old days, and know you must love them still.
OEDIPUS   My God bless you for this—and be a friendlier
Guardian to you than he has been to me!

Children, where are you?
Come quickly to my hands: they are your brother's—
250   Hands that have brought your father's once clear eyes
To this way of seeing—
                              Ah dearest ones,
I had neither sight nor knowledge then, your father
By the woman who was the source of his own life!
And I weep for you—having no strength to see you—,
255   I weep for you when I think of the bitterness
That men will visit upon you all your lives.
What homes, what festivals can you attend
Without being forced to depart again in tears?
And when you come to marriageable age,
260   Where is the man, my daughters, who would dare
Risk the bane that lies on all my children?
Is there any evil wanting? Your father killed
His father; sowed the womb of her who bore him;
Engendered you at the fount of his own existence!

265   That is what they will say of you.

                          Then, whom
    Can you ever marry? There are no bridegrooms for you,
    And your lives must wither away in sterile dreaming.

    O Kreon, son of Menoikeus!
    You are the only father my daughters have,
270   Since we, their parents, are both of us gone for ever.
    They are your own blood: you will not let them
    Fall into beggary and loneliness;
    You will keep them from the miseries that are mine!
    Take pity on them; see, they are only children,
275   Friendless except for you. Promise me this,
    Great prince, and give me your hand in token of it.

(KREON *clasps his right hand.*)

    Children:
    I could say much, if you could understand me,
    But as it is, I have only this prayer for you:
280   Live where you can, be as happy as you can—
    Happier, please God, than God has made your father.

KREON   Enough. You have wept enough. Now go within.

OEDIPUS   I must; but it is hard.

KREON   Time eases all things.

OEDIPUS   You know my mind, then?

KREON   Say what you desire.

285 OEDIPUS   Send me from Thebes!

KREON   God grant that I may!

OEDIPUS   But since God hates me . . .

KREON   No, he will grant your wish.

OEDIPUS   You promise?

KREON   I can not speak beyond my knowledge.

OEDIPUS   Then lead me in.

KREON   Come now, and leave your children.

OEDIPUS   No! Do not take them from me!

KREON   Think no longer
290   That you are in command here, but rather think
    How, when you were, you served your own destruction.

(*Exeunt into the house all but the* CHORUS; *the* CHORAGOS *chants directly to the audience.*)

CHORAGOS   Men of Thebes: look upon Oedipus.

This is the king who solved the famous riddle
And towered up, most powerful of men.
295 No mortal eyes but looked on him with envy,
Yet in the end ruin swept over him.

Let every man in mankind's frailty
Consider his last day; and let none
Presume on his good fortune until he find
300 Life, at his death, a memory without pain.

STUDY QUESTIONS

According to Aristotle, tragedies such as *Oedipus Rex* succeed by arousing pity and fear in their audiences—pity for the suffering the plays' heroes endure, fear that we might sometime face similar agonies. How does *Oedipus Rex* call forth these feelings? In thinking out your answer, you might want to consider the following questions:

1. What sort of person do you think Oedipus is? What are his strengths and weaknesses? How is he different from the other characters in the play?
2. What sorts of tensions are built up (for Oedipus, for the other characters, and for the audience) by the gradual unfolding of the truth about Laïos' murder and Oedipus's history?
3. How does your knowledge of the story of Oedipus, and hence your knowledge of how the play will end, affect your reaction to such scenes as those with Teiresias and the shepherds?
4. How are the images of sight and blindness used throughout the play?

Antigonê

SOPHOCLES

An English version by Dudley Fitts and Robert Fitzgerald

CHARACTERS

ANTIGONÊ
ISMENÊ
EURYDICÊ
KREON
HAIMON
TEIRESIAS
A SENTRY
A MESSENGER
CHORUS

SCENE. *Before the palace of* KREON, *King of Thebes. A central double door, and two lateral doors. A platform extends the length of the façade, and from this platform three steps lead down into the "orchestra," or chorus-ground.*

TIME. *Dawn of the day after the repulse of the Argive army from the assault on Thebes.*

Prologue

(ANTIGONÊ *and* ISMENÊ *enter from the central door of the palace.*)

ANTIGONÊ   Ismenê, dear sister,
　　You would think that we had already suffered enough
　　For the curse on Oedipus.
　　I cannot imagine any grief
5　　That you and I have not gone through. And now—
　　Have they told you of the new decree of our King Kreon?
ISMENÊ   I have heard nothing: I know
　　That two sisters lost two brothers, a double death
　　In a single hour; and I know that the Argive army
10　　Fled in the night; but beyond this, nothing.
ANTIGONÊ   I thought so. And that is why I wanted you
　　To come out here with me. There is something we must do.
ISMENÊ   Why do you speak so strangely?
ANTIGONÊ   Listen, Ismenê:
15　　Kreon buried our brother Eteoclês
　　With military honors, gave him a soldier's funeral,
　　And it was right that he should; but Polyneicês,

591

Who fought as bravely and died as miserably,—
They say that Kreon has sworn
20 No one shall bury him, no one mourn for him,
But his body must lie in the fields, a sweet treasure
For carrion birds to find as they search for food.
That is what they say, and our good Kreon is coming here
To announce it publicly; and the penalty—
25 Stoning to death in the public square!

                                                  There it is,
And now you can prove what you are:
A true sister, or a traitor to your family.
    ISMENÊ   Antigonê, you are mad! What could I possibly do?
30 ANTIGONÊ   You must decide whether you will help me or not.
    ISMENÊ   I do not understand you. Help you in what?
    ANTIGONÊ   Ismenê, I am going to bury him. Will you come?
    ISMENÊ   Bury him! You have just said the new law forbids it.
    ANTIGONÊ   He is my brother. And he is your brother, too.
35 ISMENÊ   But think of the danger! Think what Kreon will do!
    ANTIGONÊ   Kreon is not strong enough to stand in my way.
    ISMENÊ   Ah, sister!
Oedipus died, everyone hating him
For what his own search brought to light, his eyes
40 Ripped out by his own hand; and Iokastê died,
His mother and wife at once: she twisted the cords
That strangled her life; and our two brothers died,
Each killed by the other's sword. And we are left:
But oh, Antigonê,
45 Think how much more terrible than these
Our own death would be if we should go against Kreon
And do what he has forbidden! We are only women,
We cannot fight with men, Antigonê!
The law is strong, we must give in to the law
50 In this thing, and in worse. I beg the Dead
To forgive me, but I am helpless: I must yield
To those in authority. And I think it is dangerous business
To be always meddling.
    ANTIGONÊ   If that is what you think,
55 I should not want you, even if you asked to come.
You have made your choice, you can be what you want to be.
But I will bury him; and if I must die,
I say that this crime is holy: I shall lie down
With him in death, and I shall be as dear
60 To him as he to me.

It is the dead,
Not the living, who make the longest demands:
We die for ever . . .

You may do as you like,
65   Since apparently the laws of the gods mean nothing to you.
   ISMENÊ   They mean a great deal to me; but I have no strength
To break laws that were made for the public good.
   ANTIGONÊ   That must be your excuse, I suppose. But as for me,
I will bury the brother I love.
70 ISMENÊ   Antigonê,
I am so afraid for you!
   ANTIGONÊ   You need not be:
You have yourself to consider, after all.
   ISMENÊ   But no one must hear of this, you must tell no one!
75   I will keep it a secret, I promise!
   ANTIGONÊ   O tell it! Tell everyone!
Think how they'll hate you when it all comes out
If they learn that you knew about it all the time!
   ISMENÊ   So fiery! You should be cold with fear.
80 ANTIGONÊ   Perhaps. But I am doing only what I must.
   ISMENÊ   But can you do it? I say that you cannot.
   ANTIGONÊ   Very well: when my strength gives out,
I shall do no more.
   ISMENÊ   Impossible things should not be tried at all.
85 ANTIGONÊ   Go away, Ismenê:
I shall be hating you soon, and the dead will too,
For your words are hateful. Leave me my foolish plan:
I am not afraid of the danger; if it means death,
It will not be the worst of deaths—death without honor.
90 ISMENÊ   Go then, if you feel that you must.
You are unwise,
But a loyal friend indeed to those who love you.

(*Exit into the palace.* ANTIGONÊ *goes off, left. Enter the* CHORUS.)

Párodos

Strophe I

CHORUS   Now the long blade of the sun, lying
Level east to west, touches with glory
Thebes of the Seven Gates. Open, unlidded
Eye of golden day! O marching light

5   Across the eddy and rush of Dircê's stream,[1]
Striking the white shields of the enemy
Thrown headlong backward from the blaze of morning!
CHORAGOS[2]   Polyneicês their commander
Roused them with windy phrases,
10   He the wild eagle screaming
Insults above our land,
His wings their shields of snow,
His crest their marshalled helms.

Antistrophe 1

CHORUS   Against our seven gates in a yawning ring
15   The famished spears came onward in the night;
But before his jaws were sated with our blood,
Or pinefire took the garland of our towers,
He was thrown back; and as he turned, great Thebes—
No tender victim for his noisy power—
20   Rose like a dragon behind him, shouting war.
CHORAGOS   For God hates utterly
The bray of bragging tongues;
And when he beheld their smiling,
Their swagger of golden helms,
25   The frown of his thunder blasted
Their first man from our walls.

Strophe 2

CHORUS   We heard his shout of triumph high in the air
Turn to a scream; far out in a flaming arc
He fell with his windy torch, and the earth struck him.
30   And others storming in fury no less than his
Found shock of death in the dusty joy of battle.
CHORAGOS   Seven captains at seven gates
Yielded their clanging arms to the god
That bends the battle-line and breaks it.
35   These two only, brothers in blood,
Face to face in matchless rage,
Mirroring each the other's death,
Clashed in long combat.

---

[1]a stream to the west of Thebes   [2]the leader of the Chorus

Antistrophe 2

CHORUS   But now in the beautiful morning of victory
40   Let Thebes of the many chariots sing for joy!
With hearts for dancing we'll take leave of war:
Our temples shall be sweet with hymns of praise,
And the long nights shall echo with our chorus.

Scene I

CHORAGOS   But now at last our new King is coming:
Kreon of Thebes, Menoikeus' son.
In this auspicious dawn of his rein
What are the new complexities
5   That shifting Fate has woven for him?
What is his counsel? Why has he summoned
The old men to hear him?

(*Enter* KREON *from the palace, center. He addresses the* CHORUS *from the top step.*)

KREON   Gentlemen: I have the honor to inform you that our Ship of State,
which recent storms have threatened to destroy, has come safely to harbor at
10   last, guided by the merciful wisdom of Heaven. I have summoned you here
this morning because I know that I can depend upon you: your devotion to
King Laïos was absolute; you never hesitated in your duty to our late ruler
Oedipus; and when Oedipus died, your loyalty was transferred to his children. Unfortunately, as you know, his two sons, the princes Eteoclês and
15   Polyneicês, have killed each other in battle; and I, as the next in blood, have
succeeded to the full power of the throne.

   I am aware, of course, that no Ruler can expect complete loyalty from
his subjects until he has been tested in office. Nevertheless, I say to you at
the very outset that I have nothing but contempt for the kind of Governor
20   who is afraid, for whatever reason, to follow the course that he knows is best
for the State; and as for the man who sets private friendship above the public welfare,—I have no use for him, either. I call God to witness that if I saw
my country headed for ruin, I should not be afraid to speak out plainly; and
I need hardly remind you that I would never have any dealings with an en-
25   emy of the people. No one values friendship more highly than I; but we
must remember that friends made at the risk of wrecking our Ship are not
real friends at all.

   These are my principles, at any rate, and that is why I have made the following decision concerning the sons of Oedipus: Eteoclês, who died as a
30   man should die, fighting for his country, is to be buried with full military
honors, with all the ceremony that is usual when the greatest heroes die; but
his brother Polyneicês, who broke his exile to come back with fire and sword

against his native city and the shrines of his fathers' gods, whose one idea
was to spill the blood of his blood and sell his own people into slavery—
35   Polyneicês, I say, is to have no burial: no man is to touch him or say the least
prayer for him; he shall lie on the plain, unburied; and the birds and the
scavenging dogs can do with him whatever they like.

This is my command, and you can see the wisdom behind it. As long as
I am King, no traitor is going to be honored with the loyal man. But who-
40   ever shows by word and deed that he is on the side of the State,—he shall
have my respect while he is living and my reverence when he is dead.

CHORAGOS   If that is your will, Kreon son of Menoikeus,
You have the right to enforce it: we are yours.

KREON   That is my will. Take care that you do your part.

45 CHORAGOS   We are old men: let the younger ones carry it out.

KREON   I do not mean that: the sentries have been appointed.

CHORAGOS   Then what is it that you would have us do?

KREON   You will give no support to whoever breaks this law.

CHORAGOS   Only a crazy man is in love with death!

50 KREON   And death it is; yet money talks, and the wisest
Have sometimes been known to count a few coins too many.

(*Enter* SENTRY *from left.*)

SENTRY   I'll not say that I'm out of breath from running, King, because every
time I stopped to think about what I have to tell you, I felt like going back.
And all the time a voice kept saying, "You fool, don't you know you're walk-
55   ing straight into trouble?"; and then another voice: "Yes, but if you let somebody else get the news to Kreon first, it will be even worse than that for
you!" But good sense won out, at least I hope it was good sense, and here I
am with a story that makes no sense at all; but I'll tell it anyhow, because, as
they say, what's going to happen's going to happen and—

60 KREON   Come to the point. What have you to say?

SENTRY   I did not do it. I did not see who did it. You must not punish me for
what someone else has done.

KREON   A comprehensive defense! More effective, perhaps,
If I knew its purpose. Come: what is it?

65 SENTRY   A dreadful thing . . . I don't know how to put it—

KREON   Out with it!

SENTRY   Well, then;
The dead man—
                        Polyneicês—

(*Pause. The* SENTRY *is overcome, fumbles for words.* KREON *waits impassively.*)

70   out there—
                                                    someone,—

New dust on the slimy flesh!

(*Pause. No sign from* KREON.)

Someone has given it burial that way, and
    Gone . . .

(*Long pause.* KREON *finally speaks with deadly control.*)

75 KREON   And the man who dared do this?

SENTRY   I swear I

    Do not know! You must believe me!

                                Listen:

    The ground was dry, not a sign of digging, no,

80   Not a wheeltrack in the dust, no trace of anyone.

    It was when they relieved us this morning: and one of them,

    The corporal, pointed to it.

                          There it was,

    The strangest—

85   Look:

    The body, just mounded over with light dust: you see?

    Not buried really, but as if they'd covered it

    Just enough for the ghost's peace. And no sign

    Of dogs or any wild animal that had been there.

90   And then what a scene there was! Every man of us

    Accusing the other: we all proved the other man did it,

    We all had proof that we could not have done it.

    We were ready to take hot iron in our hands,

    Walk through fire, swear by all the gods,

95   *It was not I!*

    I do not know who it was, but it was not I!

(KREON's *rage has been mounting steadily, but the* SENTRY *is too intent upon his story to notice it.*)

    And then, when this came to nothing, someone said

    A thing that silenced us and made us stare

    Down at the ground: you had to be told the news,

100   And one of us had to do it! We threw the dice,

    And the bad luck fell to me. So here I am,

    No happier to be here than you are to have me:

    Nobody likes the man who brings bad news.

CHORAGOS   I have been wondering, King: can it be that the gods have done

105   this?

KREON (*furiously*)   Stop!

    Must you doddering wrecks

    Go out of your heads entirely? "The gods"!

    Intolerable!

110 The gods favor this corpse? Why? How had he served them?
Tried to loot their temples, burn their images,
Yes, and the whole State, and its laws with it!
Is it your senile opinion that the gods love to honor bad men?
A pious thought!—

115   No, from the very beginning
There have been those who have whispered together,
Stiff-necked anarchists, putting their heads together,
Scheming against me in alleys. These are the men,
And they have bribed my own guard to do this thing.

120 (*sententiously*) Money!
There's nothing in the world so demoralizing as money.
Down go your cities,
Homes gone, men gone, honest hearts corrupted,
Crookedness of all kinds, and all for money!

125 (*to* SENTRY)   But you—!
I swear by God and by the throne of God,
The man who has done this thing shall pay for it!
Find that man, bring him here to me, or your death
Will be the least of your problems: I'll string you up

130 Alive, and there will be certain ways to make you
Discover your employer before you die;
And the process may teach you a lesson you seem to have
     missed:
The dearest profit is sometimes all too dear:

135 That depends on the source. Do you understand me?
A fortune won is often misfortune.

SENTRY   King, may I speak?
KREON   Your very voice distresses me.
SENTRY   Are you sure that it is my voice, and not your conscience?
140 KREON   By God, he wants to analyze me now!
SENTRY   It is not what I say, but what has been done, that hurts you.
KREON   You talk too much.
SENTRY   Maybe; but I've done nothing.
KREON   Sold your soul for some silver: that's all you've done.
145 SENTRY   How dreadful it is when the right judge judges wrong!
KREON   Your figures of speech
May entertain you now; but unless you bring me the man,
You will get little profit from them in the end.

(*Exit* KREON *into the palace.*)

SENTRY   "Bring me the man"—!
150 I'd like nothing better than bringing him the man!

But bring him or not, you have seen the last of me here.
At any rate, I am safe!

(*Exit* SENTRY.)

Ode I

Strophe I

CHORUS   Numberless are the world's wonders, but none
    More wonderful than man; the stormgray sea
    Yields to his prows, the huge crests bear him high;
    Earth, holy and inexhaustible, is graven
5   With shining furrows where his plows have gone
    Year after year, the timeless labor of stallions.

Antistrophe I

    The lightboned birds and beasts that cling to cover,
    The lithe fish lighting their reaches of dim water,
    All are taken, tamed in the net of his mind;
10   The lion on the hill, the wild horse windy-maned,
    Resign to him; and his blunt yoke has broken
    The sultry shoulders of the mountain bull.

Strophe 2

    Words also, and thought as rapid as air,
    He fashions to his good use; statecraft is his,
15   And his the skill that deflects the arrows of snow,
    The spears of winter rain: from every wind
    He has made himself secure—from all but one:
    In the late wind of death he cannot stand.

Antistrophe 2

    O clear intelligence, force beyond all measure!
20   O fate of man, working both good and evil!
    When the laws are kept, how proudly his city stands!
    When the laws are broken, what of his city then?
    Never may the anárchic man find rest at my hearth,
    Never be it said that my thoughts are his thoughts.

Scene II

(*Reenter* SENTRY *leading* ANTIGONÊ.)

CHORAGOS   What does this mean? Surely this captive woman
    Is the Princess, Antigonê. Why should she be taken?
SENTRY   Here is the one who did it! We caught her
    In the very act of burying him.—Where is Kreon?
5 CHORAGOS   Just coming from the house.

(*Enter* KREON, *center.*)

KREON   What has happened?
    Why have you come back so soon?
SENTRY (*expansively*)   O King,
    A man should never be too sure of anything:
10   I would have sworn
    That you'd not see me here again: your anger
    Frightened me so, and the things you threatened me with;
    But how could I tell then
    That I'd be able to solve the case so soon?
15   No dice-throwing this time: I was only too glad to come!
    Here is this woman. She is the guilty one:
    We found her trying to bury him.
    Take her, then; question her; judge her as you will.
    I am through with the whole thing now, and glad of it.
20 KREON   But this is Antigonê! Why have you brought her here?
SENTRY   She was burying him, I tell you!
KREON (*severely*)   Is this the truth?
SENTRY   I saw her with my own eyes. Can I say more?
KREON   The details: come, tell me quickly!
25 SENTRY   It was like this:
    After those terrible threats of yours, King,
    We went back and brushed the dust away from the body.
    The flesh was soft by now, and stinking,
    So we sat on a hill to windward and kept guard.
30   No napping this time! We kept each other awake.
    But nothing happened until the white round sun
    Whirled in the center of the round sky over us:
    Then, suddenly,
    A storm of dust roared up from the earth, and the sky
35   Went out, the plain vanished with all its trees
    In the stinging dark. We closed our eyes and endured it.
    The whirlwind lasted a long time, but it passed;
    And then we looked, and there was Antigonê!

I have seen
40   A mother bird come back to a stripped nest, heard
Her crying bitterly a broken note or two
For the young ones stolen. Just so, when this girl
Found the bare corpse, and all her love's work wasted,
She wept, and cried on heaven to damn the hands
45   That had done this thing.
                      And then she brought more dust
And sprinkled wine three times for her brother's ghost.

We ran and took her at once. She was not afraid,
Not even when we charged her with what she had done.
50   She denied nothing.
                And this was a comfort to me,
And some uneasiness: for it is a good thing
To escape from death, but it is no great pleasure
To bring death to a friend.
55   Yet I always say
There is nothing so comfortable as your own safe skin!
KREON (*slowly, dangerously*)   And you, Antigonê,
You with your head hanging,—do you confess this thing?
ANTIGONÊ   I do. I deny nothing.
60 KREON (*to* SENTRY)   You may go.

(*Exit* SENTRY.)

(*to* ANTIGONÊ)   Tell me, tell me briefly:
Had you heard my proclamation touching this matter?
ANTIGONÊ   It was public. Could I help hearing it?
65 KREON   And yet you dared defy the law.
ANTIGONÊ   I dared.
It was not God's proclamation. That final Justice
That rules the world below makes no such laws.

Your edict, King, was strong,
70   But all your strength is weakness itself against
The immortal unrecorded laws of God.
They are not merely now: they were, and shall be,
Operative for ever, beyond man utterly.

I knew I must die, even without your decree:
75   I am only mortal. And if I must die
Now, before it is my time to die,
Surely this is no hardship: can anyone
Living, as I live, with evil all about me,
Think Death less than a friend? This death of mine

80   Is of no importance; but if I had left my brother
      Lying in death unburied, I should have suffered.
      Now I do not.
                         You smile at me. Ah Kreon,
      Think me a fool, if you like; but it may well be
85   That a fool convicts me of folly.
      CHORAGOS   Like father, like daughter: both headstrong,
            deaf to reason!
      She has never learned to yield:
      KREON   She has much to learn.
90   The inflexible heart breaks first, the toughest iron
      Cracks first, and the wildest horses bend their necks
      At the pull of the smallest curb.
                                      Pride? In a slave?
      This girl is guilty of a double insolence,
95   Breaking the given laws and boasting of it.
      Who is the man here,
      She or I, if this crime goes unpunished?
      Sister's child, or more than sister's child,
      Or closer yet in blood—she and her sister
100   Win bitter death for this!
      (*to* SERVANTS)   Go, some of you,
      Arrest Ismenê. I accuse her equally.
      Bring her: you will find her sniffling in the house there.

      Her mind's a traitor: crimes kept in the dark
105   Cry for light, and the guardian brain shudders;
      But how much worse than this
      Is brazen boasting of barefaced anarchy!
      ANTIGONÊ   Kreon, what more do you want than my death?
      KREON   Nothing.
110   That gives me everything.
      ANTIGONÊ   Then I beg you: kill me.
      This talking is a great weariness: your words
      Are distasteful to me, and I am sure that mine
      Seem so to you. And yet they should not seem so:
115   I should have praise and honor for what I have done.
      All these men here would praise me
      Were their lips not frozen shut with fear of you.
      (*bitterly*) Ah the good fortune of kings,
      Licensed to say and do whatever they please!
120 KREON   You are alone here in that opinion.
      ANTIGONÊ   No, they are with me. But they keep their tongues
            in leash.

KREON   Maybe. But you are guilty, and they are not.

ANTIGONÊ   There is no guilt in reverence for the dead.

125 KREON   But Eteoclês—was he not your brother too?

ANTIGONÊ   My brother too.

KREON   And you insult his memory?

ANTIGONÊ (*softly*)   The dead man would not say that I insult it.

KREON   He would: for you honor a traitor as much as him.

130 ANTIGONÊ   His own brother, traitor or not, and equal in blood.

KREON   He made war on his country. Eteoclês defended it.

ANTIGONÊ   Nevertheless, there are honors due all the dead.

KREON   But not the same for the wicked as for the just.

ANTIGONÊ   Ah Kreon, Kreon,

135   Which of us can say what the gods hold wicked?

KREON   An enemy is an enemy, even dead.

ANTIGONÊ   It is my nature to join in love, not hate.

KREON (*finally losing patience*)   Go join them then; if you must
        have your love,

140   Find it in hell!

CHORAGOS   But see, Ismenê comes:

(*Enter* ISMENÊ, *guarded.*)

     Those tears are sisterly, the cloud
     That shadows her eyes rains down gentle sorrow.

KREON   You too, Ismenê,

145   Snake in my ordered house, sucking my blood
     Stealthily—and all the time I never knew
     That these two sisters were aiming at my throne!

                           Ismenê

     Do you confess your share in this crime, or deny it?

150   Answer me.

ISMENÊ   Yes, if she will let me say so. I am guilty.

ANTIGONÊ (*coldly*)   No, Ismenê. You have no right to say so.
     You would not help me, and I will not have you help me.

ISMENÊ   But now I know what you meant; and I am here

155   To join you, to take my share of punishment.

ANTIGONÊ   The dead man and the gods who rule the dead
     Know whose act this was. Words are not friends.

ISMENÊ   Do you refuse me, Antigonê? I want to die with you:
     I too have a duty that I must discharge to the dead.

160 ANTIGONÊ   You shall not lessen my death by sharing it.

ISMENÊ   What do I care for life when you are dead?

ANTIGONÊ   Ask Kreon. You're always hanging on his opinions.

ISMENÊ   You are laughing at me. Why, Antigonê?

ANTIGONÊ   It's a joyless laughter, Ismenê.

165 ISMENÊ   But can I do nothing?

ANTIGONÊ   Yes. Save yourself. I shall not envy you.

There are those who will praise you; I shall have honor, too.

ISMENÊ   But we are equally guilty!

ANTIGONÊ   No more, Ismenê.

170   You are alive, but I belong to Death.

KREON (*to the* CHORUS)   Gentlemen, I beg you to observe these
    girls:

One has just now lost her mind; the other,

It seems, has never had a mind at all.

175 ISMENÊ   Grief teaches the steadiest minds to waver, King.

KREON   Yours certainly did, when you assumed guilt with the guilty!

ISMENÊ   But how could I go on living without her?

KREON   You are.

She is already dead.

180 ISMENÊ   But your own son's bride!

KREON   There are places enough for him to push his plow.

I want no wicked women for my sons!

ISMENÊ   O dearest Haimon, how your father wrongs you!

KREON   I've had enough of your childish talk of marriage!

185 CHORAGOS   Do you really intend to steal this girl from your son?

KREON   No; Death will do that for me.

CHORAGOS   Then she must die?

KREON (*ironically*)   You dazzle me.

                  —But enough of this talk!

190   (*to* GUARDS) You, there, take them away and guard them well:

For they are but women, and even brave men run

When they see Death coming.

(*Exeunt* ISMENÊ, ANTIGONÊ, *and* GUARDS.)

Ode II

Strophe I

CHORUS   Fortunate is the man who has never tasted God's
    vengeance!

Where once the anger of heaven has struck, that house is
    shaken

5   For ever: damnation rises behind each child

Like a wave cresting out of the black northeast,

When the long darkness under sea roars up

And bursts drumming death upon the windwhipped sand.

Antistrophe I

I have seen this gathering sorrow from time long past
10   Loom upon Oedipus' children: generation from generation
Takes the compulsive rage of the enemy god.
So lately this last flower of Oedipus' line
Drank the sunlight; but now a passionate word
And a handful of dust have closed up all its beauty.

Strophe 2

15   What mortal arrogance
     Transcends the wrath of Zeus?
Sleep cannot lull him nor the effortless long months
Of the timeless gods: but he is young for ever,
And his house is the shining day of high Olympos.
20   All that is and shall be,
      And all the past, is his.
No pride on earth is free of the curse of heaven.

Antistrophe 2

     The straying dreams of men
      May bring them ghosts of joy:
25   But as they drowse, the waking embers burn them;
Or they walk with fixed eyes, as blind men walk.
But the ancient wisdom speaks for our own time:
     Fate works most for woe
     With Folly's fairest show.
30   Man's little pleasure is the spring of sorrow.

Scene III

CHORAGOS   But here is Haimon, King, the last of all your sons.
    Is it grief for Antigonê that brings him here,
    And bitterness at being robbed of his bride?

(*Enter* HAIMON.)

KREON   We shall soon see, and no need of diviners.
5   —Son,
    You have heard my final judgment on that girl:
    Have you come here hating me, or have you come
    With deference and with love, whatever I do?

HAIMON   I am your son, father. You are my guide.
10   You make things clear for me, and I obey you.
No marriage means more to me than your continuing
     wisdom.
KREON   Good. That is the way to behave: subordinate
Everything else, my son, to your father's will.
15   This is what a man prays for, that he may get
Sons attentive and dutiful in his house,
Each one hating his father's enemies,
Honoring his father's friends. But if his sons
Fail him, if they turn out unprofitably,
20   What has he fathered but trouble for himself
And amusement for the malicious?
                         So you are right
Not to lose your head over this woman.
Your pleasure with her would soon grow cold, Haimon,
25   And then you'd have a hellcat in bed and elsewhere.
Let her find her husband in Hell!
Of all the people in this city, only she
Has had contempt for my law and broken it.

Do you want me to show myself weak before the people?
30   Or to break my sworn word? No, and I will not.
The woman dies.
I suppose she'll plead "family ties." Well, let her.
If I permit my own family to rebel,
How shall I earn the world's obedience?
35   Show me the man who keeps his house in hand,
He's fit for public authority.
                         I'll have no dealings
With lawbreakers, critics of the government:
Whoever is chosen to govern should be obeyed—
40   Must be obeyed, in all things, great and small,
Just and unjust! O Haimon,
The man who knows how to obey, and that man only,
Knows how to give commands when the time comes.
You can depend on him, no matter how fast
45   The spears come: he's a good soldier, he'll stick it out.

Anarchy, anarchy! Show me a greater evil!
This is why cities tumble and the great houses rain down,
This is what scatters armies!
No, no: good lives are made so by discipline.
50   We keep the laws then, and the lawmakers,
And no woman shall seduce us. If we must lose,
Let's lose to a man, at least! Is a woman stronger than we?

CHORAGOS   Unless time has rusted my wits,
What you say, King, is said with point and dignity.
55 HAIMON (*boyishly earnest*)   Father:
Reason is God's crowning gift to man, and you are right
To warn me against losing mine. I cannot say—
I hope that I shall never want to say!—that you
Have reasoned badly. Yet there are other men
60 Who can reason, too; and their opinions might be helpful.
You are not in a position to know everything
That people say or do, or what they feel:
Your temper terrifies—everyone
Will tell you only what you like to hear.
65 But I, at any rate, can listen; and I have heard them
Muttering and whispering in the dark about this girl.
They say no woman has ever, so unreasonably,
Died so shameful a death for a generous act:
"She covered her brother's body. Is this indecent?
70 She kept him from dogs and vultures. Is this a crime?
Death?—She should have all the honor that we can give her!"

This is the way they talk out there in the city.

You must believe me:
Nothing is closer to me than your happiness.
75 What could be closer? Must not any son
Value his father's fortune as his father does his?
I beg you, do not be unchangeable:
Do not believe that you alone can be right.
The man who thinks that,
80 The man who maintains that only he has the power
To reason correctly, the gift to speak, the soul—
A man like that, when you know him, turns out empty.

It is not reason never to yield to reason!

In flood time you can see how some trees bend,
85 And because they bend, even their twigs are safe,
While stubborn trees are torn up, roots and all.
And the same thing happens in sailing:
Make your sheet fast, never slacken,—and over you go,
Head over heels and under: and there's your voyage.
90 Forget you are angry! Let yourself be moved!
I know I am young; but please let me say this:
The ideal condition
Would be, I admit, that men should be right by instinct;
But since we are all too likely to go astray,
95 The reasonable thing is to learn from those who can teach.

CHORAGOS   You will do well to listen to him, King,
        If what he says is sensible. And you, Haimon,
        Must listen to your father.—Both speak well.
KREON   You consider it right for a man of my years
100   and experience
        To go to school to a boy?
HAIMON   It is not right
        If I am wrong. But if I am young, and right,
        What does my age matter?
105 KREON   You think it right to stand up for an anarchist?
HAIMON   Not at all. I pay no respect to criminals.
KREON   Then she is not a criminal?
HAIMON   The City would deny it, to a man.
KREON   And the City proposes to teach me how to rule?
110 HAIMON   Ah. Who is it that's talking like a boy now?
KREON   My voice is the one voice giving orders in this City!
HAIMON   It is no City if it takes orders from one voice.
KREON   The State is the King!
HAIMON   Yes, if the State is a desert.

(*Pause.*)

115 KREON   This boy, it seems, has sold out to a woman.
HAIMON   If you are a woman: my concern is only for you.
KREON   So? Your "concern"! In a public brawl with your
        father!
HAIMON   How about you, in a public brawl with justice?
120 KREON   With justice, when all that I do is within my rights?
HAIMON   You have no right to trample on God's right.
KREON (*completely out of control*)   Fool, adolescent fool! Taken
        in by a woman!
HAIMON   You'll never see me taken in by anything vile.
125 KREON   Every word you say is for her!
HAIMON (*quietly, darkly*)   And for you.
        And for me. And for the gods under the earth.
KREON   You'll never marry her while she lives.
HAIMON   Then she must die.—But her death will cause another.
130 KREON   Another?
        Have you lost your senses? Is this an open threat?
HAIMON   There is no threat in speaking to emptiness.
KREON   I swear you'll regret this superior tone of yours!
        You are the empty one!
135 HAIMON   If you were not my father,
        I'd say you were perverse.

KREON   You girlstruck fool, don't play at words with me!

HAIMON   I am sorry. You prefer silence.

KREON   Now, by God—!

140   I swear, by all the gods in heaven above us,
You'll watch it, I swear you shall!
(*to the* SERVANTS)   Bring her out!
Bring the woman out! Let her die before his eyes!
Here, this instant, with her bridegroom beside her!

145   HAIMON   Not here, no; she will not die here, King.
And you will never see my face again.
Go on raving as long as you've a friend to endure you.

(*Exit* HAIMON.)

CHORAGOS   Gone, gone.
Kreon, a young man in a rage is dangerous!

150   KREON   Let him do, or dream to do, more than a man can.
He shall not save these girls from death.

CHORAGOS   These girls?
You have sentenced them both?

KREON   No, you are right.

155   I will not kill the one whose hands are clean.

CHORAGOS   But Antigonê?

KREON (*somberly*)   I will carry her far away
Out there in the wilderness, and lock her
Living in a vault of stone. She shall have food,

160   As the custom is, to absolve the State of her death.
And there let her pray to the gods of hell:
They are her only gods:
Perhaps they will show her an escape from death,
Or she may learn,

165   though late,
That piety shown the dead is pity in vain.

(*Exit* KREON.)

Ode III

Strophe

CHORUS   Love, unconquerable
Waster of rich men, keeper
Of warm lights and all-night vigil
In the soft face of a girl:

5   Sea-wanderer, forest-visitor!

Even the pure Immortals cannot escape you,
And mortal man, in his one day's dusk,
Trembles before your glory.

Antistrophe

     Surely you swerve upon ruin
10   The just man's consenting heart,
     As here you have made bright anger
     Strike between father and son—
     And none has conquered but Love!
     A girl's glance working the will of heaven:
15   Pleasure to her alone who mocks us,
     Merciless Aphroditê.[3]

Scene IV

CHORAGOS (*as* ANTIGONÊ *enters guarded*)   But I can no longer
     stand in awe of this,
     Nor, seeing what I see, keep back my tears.
     Here is Antigonê, passing to that chamber
5   Where all find sleep at last.

Strophe I

ANTIGONÊ   Look upon me, friends, and pity me
     Turning back at the night's edge to say
     Good-by to the sun that shines for me no longer;
     Now sleepy Death
10   Summons me down to Acheron,[4] that cold shore:
     There is no bridesong there, nor any music.
CHORUS   Yet not unpraised, not without a kind of honor,
     You walk at last into the underworld;
     Untouched by sickness, broken by no sword.
15   What woman has ever found your way to death?

Antistrophe I

ANTIGONÊ   How often I have heard the story
20   of Niobê,[5]

---

[3]goddess of love   [4]a river in the underworld   [5]Niobê, the daughter of Tantalos, was turned into a stone on Mount Sipylus while bemoaning the destruction of her many children by Leto, the mother of Apollo.

Tantalos' wretched daughter, how the stone
Clung fast about her, ivy-close: and they say
25   The rain falls endlessly
And sifting soft snow; her tears are never done.
I feel the loneliness of her death in mine.
CHORUS   But she was born of heaven, and you
Are woman, woman-born. If her death is yours,
30   A mortal woman's, is this not for you
Glory in our world and in the world beyond?

Strophe 2

ANTIGONÊ   You laugh at me. Ah, friends, friends,
Can you not wait until I am dead? O Thebes,
O men many-charioted, in love with Fortune,
35   Dear springs of Dircê, sacred Theban grove,
Be witnesses for me, denied all pity,
Unjustly judged! and think a word of love
For her whose path turns
Under dark earth, where there are no more tears.
40 CHORUS   You have passed beyond human daring and come at last
Into a place of stone where Justice sits.
I cannot tell
What shape of your father's guilt appears in this.

Antistrophe 2

ANTIGONÊ   You have touched it at last:
45   that bridal bed
Unspeakable, horror of son and mother mingling:
Their crime, infection of all our family!
O Oedipus, father and brother!
Your marriage strikes from the grave to murder mine.
50   I have been a stranger here in my own land:
All my life
The blasphemy of my birth has followed me.
CHORUS   Reverence is a virtue, but strength
Lives in established law: that must prevail.
55   You have made your choice,
Your death is the doing of your conscious hand.

Epode

60 ANTIGONÊ   Then let me go, since all your words are bitter,
And the very light of the sun is cold to me.

Lead me to my vigil, where I must have
Neither love nor lamentation; no song, but silence.

(KREON *interrupts impatiently.*)

KREON   If dirges and planned lamentations could put off death,
Men would be singing for ever.
(*to the* SERVANTS)   Take her, go!
You know your orders: take her to the vault
65   And leave her alone there. And if she lives or dies,
That's her affair, not ours: our hands are clean.

ANTIGONÊ   O tomb, vaulted bride-bed in eternal rock,
Soon I shall be with my own again
Where Persephonê⁶ welcomes the thin ghosts
70   underground:
And I shall see my father again, and you, mother,
And dearest Polyneicês—
                            dearest indeed
To me, since it was my hand
75   That washed him clean and poured the ritual wine:
And my reward is death before my time!

And yet, as men's hearts know, I have done no wrong,
I have not sinned before God. Or if I have,
I shall know the truth in death. But if the guilt
80   Lies upon Kreon who judged me, then, I pray,
May his punishment equal my own.
CHORAGOS   O passionate heart,
Unyielding, tormented still by the same winds!
KREON   Her guards shall have good cause to regret their delaying.
85 ANTIGONÊ   Ah! That voice is like the voice of death!
KREON   I can give you no reason to think you are mistaken.
ANTIGONÊ   Thebes, and you my fathers' gods,
And rulers of Thebes, you see me now, the last
Unhappy daughter of a line of kings,
90   Your kings, led away to death. You will remember
What things I suffer, and at what men's hands,
Because I would not transgress the laws of heaven.
(*to the* GUARDS, *simply*) Come: let us wait no longer.

(*Exit* ANTIGONÊ, *left, guarded.*)

---

⁶queen of the underworld

Ode IV

Strophe I

CHORUS   All Danaê's[7] beauty was locked away
        In a brazen cell where the sunlight could not come:
        A small room still as any grave, enclosed her.
        Yet she was a princess too,
5   And Zeus in a rain of gold poured love upon her.
        O child, child,
        No power in wealth or war
        Or tough sea-blackened ships
        Can prevail against untiring Destiny!

Antistrophe I

10   And Dryas' son[8] also, that furious king,
        Bore the god's prisoning anger for his pride:
        Sealed up by Dionysos in deaf stone,
        His madness died among echoes.
        So at the last he learned what dreadful power
15   His tongue had mocked:
        For he had profaned the revels,
        And fired the wrath of the nine
        Implacable Sisters[9] that love the sound of the flute.

Strophe 2

        And old men tell a half-remembered tale
20   Of horror where a dark ledge splits the sea
        And a double surf beats on the gráy shóres:
        How a king's new woman,[1] sick
        With hatred for the queen he had imprisoned,
        Ripped out his two sons' eyes with her bloody hands
25   While grinning Arês[2] watched the shuttle plunge
        Four times: four blind wounds crying for revenge.

Antistrophe 2

30   Crying, tears and blood mingled.—Piteously born,
        Those sons whose mother was of heavenly birth!

---

[7]the mother of Perseus by Zeus, who visited her during her imprisonment in the form of a golden rain [8]Lycurgus, king of Thrace [9]the Muses [1]Eidothea, King Phineus' second wife, blinded her stepsons. [2]god of war

Her father was the god of the North Wind
35   And she was cradled by gales,
She raced with young colts on the glittering hills
And walked untrammeled in the open light:
But in her marriage deathless Fate found means
To build a tomb like yours for all her joy.

Scene V

(*Enter blind* Teiresias, *led by a boy. The opening speeches of* Teiresias *should be in singsong contrast to the realistic lines of* Kreon.)

TEIRESIAS   This is the way the blind man comes, Princes, Princes,
   Lock-step, two heads lit by the eyes of one.
KREON   What new thing have you to tell us, old Teiresias?
TEIRESIAS   I have much to tell you: listen to the prophet, Kreon.
5 KREON   I am not aware that I have ever failed to listen.
TEIRESIAS   Then you have done wisely, King, and ruled well.
KREON   I admit my debt to you. But what have you to say?
TEIRESIAS   This, Kreon: you stand once more on the edge of fate.
KREON   What do you mean? Your words are a kind of dread.
10 TEIRESIAS   Listen, Kreon:
   I was sitting in my chair of augury, at the place
   Where the birds gather about me. They were all a-chatter,
   As is their habit, when suddenly I heard
   A strange note in their jangling, a scream, a
15   Whirring fury; I knew that they were fighting,
   Tearing each other, dying
   In a whirlwind of wings clashing. And I was afraid.
   I began the rites of burnt-offering at the altar,
   But Hephaistos[3] failed me: instead of bright flame,
20   There was only the sputtering slime of the fat thigh-flesh
   Melting: the entrails dissolved in gray smoke,
   The bare bone burst from the welter. And no blaze!

   This was a sign from heaven. My boy described it,
   Seeing for me as I see for others.

25   I tell you, Kreon, you yourself have brought
   This new calamity upon us. Our hearths and altars
   Are stained with the corruption of dogs and carrion birds
   That glut themselves on the corpse of Oedipus' son.
   The gods are deaf when we pray to them, their fire

---

[3]god of fire

30 Recoils from our offering, their birds of omen
Have no cry of comfort, for they are gorged
With the thick blood of the dead.

O my son,
These are no trifles! Think: all men make mistakes,
35 But a good man yields when he knows his course is wrong,
And repairs the evil. The only crime is pride.

Give in to the dead man, then: do not fight with a corpse—
What glory is it to kill a man who is dead?
Think, I beg you:
40 It is for your own good that I speak as I do.
You should be able to yield for your own good.

KREON   It seems that prophets have made me their especial
province.
All my life long
45 I have been a kind of butt for the dull arrows
Of doddering fortune-tellers!

No, Teiresias:
If your birds—if the great eagles of God himself
Should carry him stinking bit by bit to heaven,
50 I would not yield. I am not afraid of pollution:
No man can defile the gods.

Do what you will,
Go into business, make money, speculate
In India gold or that synthetic gold from Sardis,
60 Get rich otherwise than by my consent to bury him.
Teiresias, it is a sorry thing when a wise man
Sells his wisdom, lets out his words for hire!

TEIRESIAS   Ah Kreon! Is there no man left in the world—

KREON   To do what?—Come, let's have the aphorism!

65 TEIRESIAS   No man who knows that wisdom outweighs any wealth?

KREON   As surely as bribes are baser than any baseness.

TEIRESIAS   You are sick, Kreon! You are deathly sick!

KREON   As you say: it is not my place to challenge a prophet.

TEIRESIAS   Yet you have said my prophecy is for sale.

70 KREON   The generation of prophets has always loved gold.

TEIRESIAS   The generation of kings has always loved brass.

KREON   You forget yourself! You are speaking to your King.

TEIRESIAS   I know it. You are a king because of me.

KREON   You have a certain skill; but you have sold out.

75 TEIRESIAS   King, you will drive me to words that—

KREON   Say them, say them!
Only remember: I will not pay you for them.

TEIRESIAS   No, you will find them too costly.

KREON   No doubt. Speak:

80   Whatever you say, you will not change my will.

TEIRESIAS   Then take this, and take it to heart!
The time is not far off when you shall pay back
Corpse for corpse, flesh of your own flesh.
You have thrust the child of this world into living night,

85   You have kept from the gods below the child that is theirs:
The one in a grave before her death, the other,
Dead, denied the grave. This is your crime:
And the Furies and the dark gods of Hell
Are swift with terrible punishment for you.

90   Do you want to buy me now, Kreon?

                                         Not many days,
And your house will be full of men and women weeping,
And curses will be hurled at you from far
Cities grieving for sons unburied, left to rot

95   Before the walls of Thebes.

These are my arrows, Kreon: they are all for you.

(*To* BOY.) But come, child: lead me home.
Let him waste his fine anger upon younger men.
Maybe he will learn at last

100   To control a wiser tongue in a better head.

(*Exit* TEIRESIAS.)

CHORAGOS   The old man has gone, King, but his words
Remain to plague us. I am old, too,
But I cannot remember that he was ever false.

KREON   That is true. . . . It troubles me.

105   Oh it is hard to give in! but it is worse
To risk everything for stubborn pride.

CHORAGOS   Kreon: take my advice.

KREON   What shall I do?

CHORAGOS   Go quickly: free Antigonê from her vault

110   And build a tomb for the body of Polyneicês.

KREON   You would have me do this!

CHORAGOS   Kreon, yes!
And it must be done at once: God moves
Swiftly to cancel the folly of stubborn men.

115   KREON   It is hard to deny the heart! But I
Will do it: I will not fight with destiny.

CHORAGOS   You must go yourself, you cannot leave it to others.
KREON   I will go.
                     —Bring axes, servants:
120   Come with me to the tomb. I buried her, I
       Will set her free.
                     Oh quickly!
       My mind misgives—
       The laws of the gods are mighty, and a man must serve them
125   To the last day of his life!

(*Exit* KREON.)

Paean⁴

Strophe I

CHORAGOS   God of many names
CHORUS   O Iacchos⁵
                                        son
       of Kadmeian Sémelê⁶
5   O born of the Thunder!
       Guardian of the West
                     Regent
       of Eleusis' plain
                     O Prince of maenad Thebes
10   and the Dragon Field by rippling Ismenós:⁷

Antistrophe I

CHORAGOS   God of many names
CHORUS   the flame of torches
       flares on our hills
                     the nymphs of Iacchos
15   dance at the spring of Castalia:⁸
       from the vine-close mountain
                              come ah come in ivy:
       Evohé evohé! sings through the streets of Thebes

---

⁴a hymn of praise   ⁵another name for Dionysos (Bacchus)   ⁶the daughter of Kadmos, the founder
of Thebes   ⁷a river east of Thebes. The ancestors of the Theban nobility sprang from dragon's teeth
sown by the Ismenós.   ⁸a spring on Mount Parnasos

Strophe 2

CHORAGOS   God of many names
20 CHORUS   Iacchos of Thebes
    heavenly Child
        of Sémelê bride of the Thunderer!
    The shadow of plague is upon us:
            come
25   with clement feet
        oh come from Parnasos
    down the long slopes
        across the lamenting water

Antistrophe 2

CHORAGOS   Iô Fire! Chorister of the throbbing stars!
30   O purest among the voices of the night!
    Thou son of God, blaze for us!
CHORUS   Come with choric rapture of circling Maenads[9]
    Who cry *Iô Iacche!*
        God of many names!

Exodos

(*Enter* MESSENGER *from left.*)

MESSENGER   Men of the line of Kadmos, you who live
    Near Amphion's citadel,[1]
        I cannot say
    Of any condition of human life "This is fixed,
5   This is clearly good, or bad." Fate raises up,
    And Fate casts down the happy and unhappy alike:
    No man can foretell his Fate.
        Take the case of Kreon:
    Kreon was happy once, as I count happiness:
10   Victorious in battle, sole governor of the land,
    Fortunate father of children nobly born.
    And now it has all gone from him! Who can say
    That a man is still alive when his life's joy fails?
    He is a walking dead man. Grant him rich,
15   Let him live like a king in his great house:

---

[9]the worshippers of Dionysos   [1]Amphion used the music of his magic lyre to lure stones to form a wall around Thebes.

If his pleasure is gone, I would not give
So much as the shadow of smoke for all he owns.

CHORAGOS   Your words hint at sorrow: what is your news for us?

MESSENGER   They are dead. The living are guilty of their death.

20 CHORAGOS   Who is guilty? Who is dead? Speak!

MESSENGER   Haimon.
Haimon is dead; and the hand that killed him
Is his own hand.

CHORAGOS   His father's? or his own?

25 MESSENGER   His own, driven mad by the murder his father had
       done.

CHORAGOS   Teiresias, Teiresias, how clearly you saw it all!

MESSENGER   This is my news: you must draw what conclusions
       you can from it.

30 CHORAGOS   But look: Eurydicê, our Queen:
Has she overheard us?

(*Enter* EURYDICÊ *from the palace, center.*)

EURYDICÊ   I have heard something, friends:
As I was unlocking the gate of Pallas'[2] shrine,
For I needed her help today, I heard a voice
35   Telling of some new sorrow. And I fainted
There at the temple all my maidens about me.
But speak again: whatever it is, I can bear it:
Grief and I are no strangers.

MESSENGER   Dearest Lady,
40   I will tell you plainly all that I have seen.
I shall not try to comfort you: what is the use,
Since comfort could lie only in what is not true?
The truth is always best.

                            I went with Kreon
45   To the outer plain where Polyneicês was lying,
No friend to pity him, his body shredded by dogs.
We made our prayers in that place to Hecatê
And Pluto,[3] that they would be merciful. And we bathed
The corpse with holy water, and we brought
50   Fresh-broken branches to burn what was left of it,
And upon the urn we heaped up a towering barrow
Of the earth of his own land.

                              When we were done, we ran
To the vault where Antigonê lay on her couch of stone.

---

[2]Pallas Athena, the goddess of wisdom   [3]*Hecatê . . . Pluto* the ruling deities of the underworld

55   One of the servants had gone ahead,
      And while he was yet far off he heard a voice
      Grieving within the chamber, and he came back
      And told Kreon. And as the King went closer,
      The air was full of wailing, the words lost,
60   And he begged us to make all haste. "Am I a prophet?"
      He said, weeping, "And must I walk this road,
      The saddest of all that I have gone before?
      My son's voice calls me on. Oh quickly, quickly!
      Look through the crevice there, and tell me
65   If it is Haimon, or some deception of the gods!"

      We obeyed; and in the cavern's farthest corner
      We saw her lying:
      She had made a noose of her fine linen veil
      And hanged herself. Haimon lay beside her,
70   His arms about her waist, lamenting her,
      His love lost under ground, crying out
      That his father had stolen her away from him.

      When Kreon saw him the tears rushed to his eyes
      And he called to him: "What have you done, child?
75   Speak to me.
      What are you thinking that makes your eyes so strange?
      O my son, my son, I come to you on my knees!"
      But Haimon spat in his face. He said not a word,
      Staring—
80   And suddenly drew his sword
      And lunged. Kreon shrank back, the blade missed; and the
         boy,
      Desperate against himself, drove it half its length
      Into his own side, and fell. And as he died
85   He gathered Antigonê close in his arms again,
      Choking, his blood bright red on her white cheek.
      And now he lies dead with the dead, and she is his
      At last, his bride in the house of the dead.

      (*Exit* EURYDICÊ *into the palace.*)

CHORAGOS   She has left us without a word. What can this mean?
90 MESSENGER   It troubles me, too; yet she knows what is best,
      Her grief is too great for public lamentation,
      And doubtless she has gone to her chamber to weep
      For her dead son, leading her maidens in his dirge.

      (*Pause.*)

CHORAGOS   It may be so: but I fear this deep silence.
95 MESSENGER   I will see what she is doing. I will go in.

(*Exit* MESSENGER *into the palace. Enter* KREON *with attendants, bearing* HAI-
MON'S *body.*)

CHORAGOS   But here is the king himself: oh look at him,
      Bearing his own damnation in his arms.
KREON   Nothing you say can touch me any more.
      My own blind heart has brought me
100   From darkness to final darkness. Here you see
      The father murdering, the murdered son—
      And all my civic wisdom!

      Haimon my son, so young, so young to die,
      I was the fool, not you; and you died for me.
105 CHORAGOS   That is the truth; but you were late in learning it.
KREON   This truth is hard to bear. Surely a god
      Has crushed me beneath the hugest weight of heaven,
      And driven me headlong a barbaric way
      To trample out the thing I held most dear.

110   The pains that men will take to come to pain!

(*Enter* MESSENGER *from the palace.*)

MESSENGER   The burden you carry in your hands is heavy,
      But it is not all: you will find more in your house.
KREON   What burden worse than this shall I find there?
MESSENGER   The Queen is dead.
115 KREON   O port of death, deaf world,
      Is there no pity for me? And you, Angel of evil,
      I was dead, and your words are death again.
      Is it true, boy? Can it be true?
      Is my wife dead? Has death bred death?
120 MESSENGER   You can see for yourself.

(*The doors are opened and the body of* EURYDICÊ *is disclosed within.*)

KREON   Oh pity!
      All true, all true, and more than I can bear!
      O my wife, my son!
MESSENGER   She stood before the altar, and her heart
125   Welcomed the knife her own hand guided,
      And a great cry burst from her lips for Megareus[4] dead,

---

[4]Megareus, brother of Haimon, had died in the assault on Thebes.

And for Haimon dead, her sons; and her last breath
Was a curse for their father, the murderer of her sons.
And she fell, and the dark flowed in through her closing eyes.

130 KREON   O God, I am sick with fear.
Are there no swords here? Has no one a blow for me?

MESSENGER   Her curse is upon you for the deaths of both.

KREON   It is right that it should be. I alone am guilty.
I know it, and I say it. Lead me in,

135   Quickly, friends.
I have neither life nor substance. Lead me in.

CHORAGOS   You are right, if there can be right in so much wrong.
The briefest way is best in a world of sorrow.

KREON   Let it come,

140   Let death come quickly, and be kind to me.
I would not ever see the sun again.

CHORAGOS   All that will come when it will; but we, meanwhile,
Have much to do. Leave the future to itself.

KREON   All my heart was in that prayer!

145 CHORAGOS   Then do not pray any more: the sky is deaf.

KREON   Lead me away. I have been rash and foolish.
I have killed my son and my wife.
I look for comfort; my comfort lies here dead.
Whatever my hands have touched has come to nothing.

150   Fate has brought all my pride to a thought of dust.

(*As* KREON *is being led into the house, the* CHORAGOS *advances and speaks directly to the audience.*)

CHORAGOS   There is no happiness where there is no wisdom;
No wisdom but in submission to the gods.
Big words are always punished,
And proud men in old age learn to be wise.

STUDY QUESTIONS

1. One might argue that in *Antigonê* each of the major characters undergoes his or her own moment of "recognition" and subsequent reversal of fortune. For instance, one can say that the play opens on Antigonê's recognition of Kreon's edict—both because she has just learned of the edict and because she here expresses her realization of how she must react to it and of what retaliation her reaction is likely to draw.
    a. Arguing along these lines, identify the scenes, events, and speeches that mark Kreon's recognition. What reversal would you say follows from it?

b. Would you also want to argue for recognitions for Haimon, Eurydicê, and Ismenê? If so, where would you place them, and what reversals would you say follow them?

c. Write an essay that (1) discusses each of these recognitions and their significance to the characters involved, and (2) demonstrates how the placement and cumulative effect of these several recognitions and reversals give the play its shape and dramatic impact. (Remember that you must define the structure and movement of the play as you see it, to ensure that you and your reader are working from the same basic understanding.)

2. How would you balance the claims of "thought" and "character" as the more important element in *Antigonê?* (In other words, is it the questions argued or the character and fate of the debaters that you feel provide the strongest source of the play's appeal?) Would either element alone suffice? Why or why not?

3. Antigonê and Kreon are, of course, the major antagonists in *Antigonê*. But each has another opponent as well. Ismenê argues against Antigonê's actions, and Haimon argues against Kreon. What do the presence and actions of these two characters add to the play?

28

HAMLET *AND ELIZABETHAN DRAMA*

Origins of English Drama

English drama can be traced back to two origins, one in tenth-century England and one in ancient Greece. The two beginnings differed greatly in style and content but did have one important thing in common: both formed parts of religious rituals.

Medieval Drama

Drama in medieval Europe seems to have begun as part of the Easter services. At some appropriate point during the Mass or the matins service, one or two men would unobtrusively position themselves near the altar or near some representation of a tomb. There, they would be approached by three other men, whose heads were covered to look like women and who moved slowly, as if seeking something. Singing in the Latin of the church service, the "angel" at the tomb would question the "women," "Whom seek you in the tomb, O followers of Christ?" The women would then sing the answer of the three Marys, "Jesus of Nazareth, who was crucified, O heavenly one." The angel then would sing again, "He is not here; he is risen, just as he foretold. Go, announce that he is risen from the tomb."

The dramatization might stop there, or it might continue with the showing of the empty tomb to the women, their song of joy, and the spreading of the good news to the disciples. In either case, the culmination of the drama would mark a return to the service itself with the singing of the Mass's *Ressurexi* ("I have risen") or the matins' final *Te deum, laudamus* ("We praise thee, Lord").

One medieval manuscript in particular emphasizes the closeness of the connection. It describes the singers of the *Te Deum* as rejoicing with the three women at Christ's triumph over death and commands that all the church bells be rung together as soon as the hymn of praise has begun. Drama and service thus celebrate the same event. The joy expressed by the women at the news of the resurrection is the same joy felt by the worshippers in the congregation.

Latin drama continued to develop within the church services. Manuscripts still survive, not only of Easter and Christmas plays but of plays dealing with prophets and saints as well. They show the plays growing longer and more elaborate than the early one just described, but they still emphasize the close ties between the plays and the services at which they are performed. Thus one Christmas pageant of the shepherds calls for many boys dressed as angels to sit in the roof of the church and sing in loud voices the angels' song, "Glory to God." But it also directs that, at the end of the pageant, the shepherds must return into the choir and there act as choir leaders for the Mass that follows.

By the fourteenth century, however, drama had also moved outside the church. There it was spoken almost wholly in the vernacular, though some bits of Latin, and a good deal of singing, remained. The plays were acted by laymen (including some professional actors) rather than by clerics, and they were developing modes of performance that might encompass up to three days of playing and involve most of the citizens of the towns where they were performed.

These were the Corpus Christi plays, also known as the "cycle plays" or the "mystery plays." Performed in celebration of Corpus Christi day, they comprised a series of pageants beginning with the creation of the world, proceeding through the history of the Old and New Testaments, and ending with the Last Judgment. Each pageant was performed on its own movable stage—its "pageant wagon." Mounted on four or six wheels, two stories high, the wagons provided facilities for some surprisingly complex stage effects and allowed each pageant to be presented several times at several different locations. One after another, the pageants would move through a town, usually stopping at three or four pre-arranged places to repeat their performances, so that everyone in town might see all of the twenty to fifty plays that made up the cycle.

The presentation of these cycles was undertaken by the towns themselves, with the town authorities ordering the performances. But the individual pageants were produced by the local trade and craft guilds. Ordinarily each guild would present one pageant, but sometimes several small guilds would team up to perform a single pageant or share the cost of a wagon that each could use. It is easy to imagine the competition this could produce, with each guild trying to outdo the next. But the plays were still religious in subject and import. They often spoke directly to the audience and always emphasized how the events they depicted pertained to each viewer's salvation.

Early English Dramatic Forms

As we suggested in the last chapter, Greek drama carefully labeled and segregated its forms. Tragedy dealt with noble persons and heroic actions. Comedy dealt with everyday affairs.

Medieval drama did not so carefully distinguish its forms. It had one central sacrificial subject: the death of Christ for the salvation of mankind. This sacrifice was always treated seriously; neither Christ nor Mary was ever burlesqued. But the world that Christ entered at his birth was the world of thin clothes and bad weather, of thieves and tricksters and con men, with the Devil himself, the arch-trickster, as Christ's opponent. It was, in short, the world of comedy. A drama that dealt with the history of humanity's fall and salvation would thus have to be both comic and tragic. There would be no way of separating the two.

Nor would medieval writers have wanted to separate them. Medieval art always seems to have preferred inclusiveness to exclusiveness. The great Gothic cathedrals themselves, with their profusion of sculpture and stained glass, would give their most prominent and most beautiful art to scenes of Christ, the Virgin, and the saints. But less prominent carvings would be likely to show small boys stealing apples, or people quarreling; while, in other places, comically or frighteningly grotesque demons would round out the portrayals.

A Corpus Christi cycle, therefore, would contain both serious and humorous elements. Some plays would be wholly serious; others would mix the serious with the comic. "The Sacrifice of Isaac," for instance, was always serious. The dilemma of the father, the emotions of the son as he realized what was happening, combined to produce plays that could virtually be described as tragedies with happy endings. "Noah's Flood," on the other hand, was usually given a comic treatment. (What would you do if your husband suddenly started building a giant boat in your front yard?) In some of the plays, Noah's wife thinks her husband has gone crazy. In others, she joins in the building until it is time to get on board, then rebels against leaving the world she knows and loves. In either case, a physical fight ensues before Noah can get her on board, and Noah's prophecies of doom are mixed with his complaints about marriage. Crucifixion plays, meanwhile, generally mixed the solemnity of the highest sacrifice with a certain amount of low comedy centering on the executioners. There was no thought of separating the two. Both were parts of the same event.

In this way, seeking to mirror life and to emphasize its mixture of noble and ignoble, sacred and mundane, the medieval drama provided Elizabethan playwrights a heritage of flexible, all-inclusive drama, capable at its best of seeing both sides of a subject at once, always insistent that both be recognized. By mixing this heritage with the more single-minded Greek tragic tradition, Elizabethan dramatists produced a tragic form of their own as rich and compelling as any that has existed.

In this chapter, we will study one of the most highly praised and frequently acted Elizabethan tragedies, Shakespeare's *Hamlet,* as well as one of his great "mature" comedies, *Much Ado About Nothing.*

Hamlet and *Oedipus Rex*

In many ways, *Hamlet* is similar to *Oedipus Rex.* Both were written at times when tragedy was just coming to its full maturity in their playwrights' cultures. Both were written by the most influential playwrights of their time. Both helped set the shape of tragedy for their own period's drama and for the drama of future ages.

Both plays have heroes who dominate the action, catching the audience's attention early in the play and holding their attention and their sympathy throughout. (Hamlet, in fact, can even address the audience in soliloquies and "asides" that no one on stage is meant to hear.) Princely in nature and position, both men seem born to rule. The heroes are somewhat alike in their situations, as well. Both must avenge their father's murder and thus remove a pollution from their land. To do so, however, they must first find out who the murderer is; and they must pursue their search among people who want the truth to remain hidden.

Here, however, the situations diverge. Oedipus' companions want to conceal the truth for Oedipus' own sake. Hamlet's opponent, Claudius, wants the truth to remain hidden because he is the murderer. The element of active, willed evil, which is absent from *Oedipus Rex*, is thus present in *Hamlet*. Hamlet must not only destroy his father's murderer but also do so before the murderer destroys him.

Hamlet, as we suggested earlier, is a play derived from both Greek and medieval drama. From Greek tragedy, it has taken the tragic hero—dominant, strong-willed, determined to accomplish his desires. It has also taken from Greek tragedy a certain elevation of tone and insistence on the dignity of human beings. From medieval drama, it has taken the medieval desire for inclusiveness and the medieval love of significant detail. *Hamlet* is much longer than *Oedipus Rex*. It has more characters, a more complex plot, and a generous amount of comedy.

Let us look at each of these elements in turn. Regarding characters, we notice that Oedipus is unique, but that Hamlet sees himself reflected in two other characters: first in Fortinbras, another son of a warrior king whose father has died and whose uncle has seized the throne, leaving him practically powerless; and later in Laertes, another son determined to avenge himself on his father's murderer. The deeds of Laertes and Fortinbras contrast with and comment on the actions of Hamlet himself, thus enriching our view of Hamlet and his dilemma. At the same time, the actions of the three men intertwine to create three of the play's major themes: fathers and sons, honor, and thought versus action.

Regarding plot, we can be sure that the affairs of three families will create a more complex plot than the affairs of one family. Thus critics sometimes speak of the Fortinbras "overplot" (which is mostly concerned with war and kingship) and the Laertes "underplot" (concerned with private family relationships) and how these two "subplots" complement the "main plot" (which deals with Hamlet's familial and princely concerns). But the English inclusiveness goes even beyond this, adding also a love story between Hamlet and Laertes' sister, Ophelia, a study of true versus false friendship in the persons of Horatio and Rosencrantz and Guildenstern, and a few comments on the contemporary theater by a troupe of strolling players. There are also glimpses of three purely comic characters: two gravediggers and one intolerably affected courtier. Again, all these themes and characters are interwoven to illuminate Hamlet's character and dilemma. (The gravediggers, for instance, who seem at first wildly irrelevant, ultimately serve to bring Hamlet to a new understanding of mortality, an understanding that is crucial to his ability to face his own death.)

In *Hamlet*, comedy is not separate from tragedy. Rather, it is used as a means to create a fuller awareness of tragedy. Hamlet himself is a master of comic wordplay. His first speech turns on a pun; and puns and bitter quips mark his speech to Claudius and his courtiers throughout the play. Many of these quips are spoken under the guise of pretended madness; and here the audience shares secrets with Hamlet. We know he is not really mad. But those on stage think he is. (The exception is Claudius, who suspects that Hamlet is not mad but who cannot reveal Hamlet's sanity without revealing his own crimes.) Pretending madness, therefore, Hamlet makes speeches that sound like nonsense to the courtiers but that we recognize as referring to his father's murder and his recognition of treachery in those around him. We are thus let into Hamlet's secrets and feelings as no single character in the play is let into them. Hamlet's use of jesting speech thus becomes not merely a weapon in his fight against Claudius but also a means of winning the sympathetic partnership of the audience. In comic speech and tragic soliloquy alike, Hamlet reveals himself to us. By the play's end, we know Hamlet as we know few other stage characters.

Adding to our sense of knowledge is the fact that Hamlet is a complex and changing character. In this he differs markedly from Oedipus, whose character remains firm and fixed until it changes so drastically in his final scene. The essentially fixed character is typical of Greek drama, which seems to have been more interested in the clash of character against character (or of character against fate) than it was in the changes within or the development of a single character. It is far less typical of Elizabethan tragedy.

This emphasis on Hamlet's developing character is an indication of the influence of medieval Christian drama, with its concern for salvation and the dangers and triumphs of the soul. English drama was secular drama by Shakespeare's time, being performed regularly by professional troupes for paying audiences. Concern for the soul, however, remained one of its major concerns. When Elizabethan dramatists wrote tragedies, therefore, they tended to make the hero's inner concerns—his passions, his temptations, his spiritual triumphs or defeats—the central focus of their plays. Even the ghost in *Hamlet*, coming to call for revenge, warns Hamlet to "taint not thy mind, nor let thy soul contrive/Against thy mother aught." Hamlet must avenge his father and free Denmark from the polluting rule of Claudius, but he must do so in a manner that will imperil neither his own nor his mother's salvation.

When the play opens, Hamlet is a bitter man. So far from being at peace with himself or his surroundings is he that he seems to have little chance of fulfilling the ghost's demands. So close does he come to flinging away his own soul in pursuit of Claudius, in fact, that some critics have refused to believe that Hamlet's speeches in Act III, Scene 3, mean what they say. In fact, they mean exactly what they say. Hamlet in this scene is on the brink of disaster.

In the next scene, the "closet scene," the unexpected happens. Hamlet is caught in the wrong, realizes it, and begins the painful process of returning from his bitterness and hatreds to a reconciliation with himself, his mother, and humanity in general. Throughout the rest of the play, we watch Hamlet's speeches on human nature become gentler, his attitude more compassionate; we hear a new acceptance of his fate, a new trust in providence, revealed. By the play's end, when Hamlet gets his one chance at Claudius, he is fully ready for the task and its consequences. And so the play ends in mingled loss and triumph: loss to Denmark and to us in the death of Hamlet, triumph that Hamlet has nobly achieved his purpose.

One final word must be said about the language of *Hamlet,* which is like the language of no other play we will read in this book. Seeking some meter in English that would match the beauty and dignity of the meters in which classical tragedy had been written, the sixteenth century dramatists had created **blank verse.** Blank verse does not rhyme. It usually has ten syllables to a line (though lines may be shorter or longer by a few syllables), and the second, fourth, sixth, eighth, and tenth syllables are generally accented more strongly than the rest. This meter was easily spoken. It was dignified and flexible. And it could slip neatly into prose (for comic scenes) or into rhymed couplets to mark a scene's end.

Blank verse was fairly new when Shakespeare began writing. In some of his early plays, it still sounds stiff and awkward. By the time he wrote *Hamlet,* however, Shakespeare was entering into a mastery of blank verse that no one has ever surpassed. The rhythms and imagery of Hamlet's language warn us of every change in his moods, from pretended madness to honest friendship to bitter passion. By the modulation of Hamlet's language, as well as by his actions, Shakespeare shows us the battle within Hamlet's soul.

If you can see *Hamlet*—live or on film—or if you can hear recordings of it, do so. If not, read as much of it aloud as you can. For readers unfamiliar with Shakespearean language, *Hamlet* is not an easy play to read. Nearly every word of it counts; so every word must be attended to. But the play is well worth the effort it takes, for it is truly one of the finest plays of all time.

Comedy and *Much Ado About Nothing*

In a typical tragedy, a thriving prince or king undergoes a "tragic fall" into the world of sorrow, suffering, and death. This reversal of fortune occurs partly because of fate, partly because of the ambitious schemes of evil men, and partly because of the protagonist's own character flaws. The protagonist, who had been integrated into his society, suddenly finds himself estranged from it. The only compensation for his suffering is the tragic knowledge he gains from his experience, and the resignation he usually displays before he dies.

In comedy, on the other hand, a different process takes place. Although the protagonists may have a high social standing at the beginning of the play, they are often blocked from full integration into their culture because they are experiencing difficulties in finding or wooing a mate. If death by murder or suicide is the distinguishing feature of tragedy, marriage is the unmistakable generic marker of comedy. Tragedy deals with the loneliness of being a morally sensitive being in a fallen world; comedy celebrates the universal pleasures of friendship, erotic love, and community—the bonds that constantly renew and sustain individuals even through their troubles.

Much Ado About Nothing fits this pattern perfectly. Its double wedding in Act V between Hero and Claudio and Beatrice and Benedick is a joyous celebration reconciling all the frustrations, tensions, and confusions of identity that make up its plot. But just as Shakespeare mixed comic elements into *Hamlet,* he darkened *Much Ado* with an Iago-like villain who threatens to turn the play into tragedy. Don Juan, Don Pedro's bastard brother, out of jealously over Claudio's friendship with Don Pedro, temporarily sets Claudio against Hero, Hero's father Leonato against both his daughter and Claudio, and Benedick against Claudio as well. These tensions are so extreme that even so great a dramatist as Shakespeare had trouble wrestling the tone of his play back toward comedy in Act V. Unlike the "happy" early comedies, such as *Two Gentlemen of Verona* or *The Taming of the Shrew,* such late comedies as *The Merchant of Venice, Much Ado,* and *Twelfth Night* reveal a more philosophical, even melancholic, comic imagination at work.

The two contrasting tonal elements in *Much Ado* are reflected in the contrasting love plots. Claudio and Hero's story is Italianate, both in its style and probable sources. It is driven by plot rather than by character, because the two lovers behave more like Petrarchan stereotypes than well-rounded protagonists. The sensational reversals in Claudio's attitude toward Hero—his passionate love; his instant belief in, despite little evidence of, her infidelity, his profession of grief when he finds he had falsely accused Hero, his strange willingness to marry the "dead" Hero's nonexistent cousin as a substitute—all seem designed to provide melodramatic scenes rather than to depict a realistic and consistent characterization. Leonato's hysterics at both Hero and Claudio, as well as Don Pedro's and Claudio's taunting of the old man when Leonato challenges them to a fight, are in the same dramatic vein. The real magic of the play, however, is in the rich and more realistic love-battle between Beatrice and Benedick. Their story is clearly in the English comic tradition of the war between the sexes. As wooden and "ideal" in the negative sense as are Hero and Claudio, Beatrice and Benedick are natural and earthy in their independence, their humor, their insecurity about committing themselves to each other. Their wordplay is some of the most delightful in all of Shakespeare. Their hard-won marriage—not Hero and Claudio's—is the great comic achievement and real cause for celebration of the play.

But we must not forget the other "English" aspect of this fine comedy—Constable Dogberry and his hapless band of Watchmen. Like the "rude mechanicals" who put on the unintentionally hilarious play for the king in *A Midsummer Night's Dream,* Dogberry and his men are delightful bumpkins who mangle their syntax, make fools of themselves in trying to impress their betters, and in the end bungle their way to success. Always the master of mixing the high and the low, Shakespeare makes us laugh at both Beatrice's and Benedick's learned puns and allusions and Dogberry's ironic, repeated insistence that the town clerk's record show "that I am an ass."

The Tragedy of Hamlet, Prince of Denmark

WILLIAM SHAKESPEARE

CHARACTERS

CLAUDIUS, *King of Denmark*
HAMLET, *son to the late King Hamlet, and nephew to the present King*
POLONIUS, *Lord Chamberlain*
HORATIO, *friend to Hamlet*
LAERTES, *son to Polonius*

VOLTEMAND
CORNELIUS
ROSENCRANTZ
GUILDENSTERN ⎬ *courtiers*
OSRIC
GENTLEMAN

MARCELLUS ⎬ *officers*
BARNARDO

FRANCISCO, *a soldier*
REYNALDO, *servant to Polonius*
FORTINBRAS, *Prince of Norway*
NORWEGIAN CAPTAIN
DOCTOR OF DIVINITY
PLAYERS
Two CLOWNS, *grave-diggers*
ENGLISH AMBASSADORS
GERTRUDE, *Queen of Denmark, and mother to Hamlet*
OPHELIA, *daughter to Polonius*
GHOST *of Hamlet's Father*
LORDS, LADIES, OFFICERS, SOLDIERS, SAILORS, MESSENGERS, *and* ATTENDANTS

SCENE: *Denmark*

Act I

Scene I

(*Enter* BARNARDO *and* FRANCISCO, *two sentinels* [*meeting*].)

BARNARDO   Who's there?
FRANCISCO   Nay, answer me. Stand and unfold yourself.

Words and passages enclosed in square brackets in the text are either emendations of the copy-text or additions to it.
I.i. Location: Elsinore; a guard-platform of the castle
2. **answer me:** *You* answer *me.* Francisco is on watch; Barnardo has come to relieve him.   **unfold yourself:** Make known who you are.

BARNARDO   Long live the King!

FRANCISCO   Barnardo.

5   BARNARDO   He.

FRANCISCO   You come most carefully upon your hour.

BARNARDO   'Tis now strook twelf. Get thee to bed, Francisco.

FRANCISCO   For this relief much thanks. 'Tis bitter cold,
   And I am sick at heart.

10   BARNARDO   Have you had quiet guard?

FRANCISCO   Not a mouse stirring.

BARNARDO   Well, good night.
   If you do meet Horatio and Marcellus,
   The rivals of my watch, bid them make haste.

(*Enter* HORATIO *and* MARCELLUS.)

15   FRANCISCO   I think I hear them. Stand ho! Who is there?

HORATIO   Friends to this ground.

MARCELLUS   And liegemen to the Dane.

FRANCISCO   Give you good night.

MARCELLUS   O, farewell, honest [soldier].

20   Who hath reliev'd you?

FRANCISCO   Barnardo hath my place.
   Give you good night.   (*Exit* FRANCISCO.)

MARCELLUS   Holla, Barnardo!

BARNARDO   Say—

25   What, is Horatio there?

HORATIO   A piece of him.

BARNARDO   Welcome, Horatio, welcome, good Marcellus.

HORATIO   What, has this thing appear'd again to-night?

BARNARDO   I have seen nothing.

30   MARCELLUS   Horatio says 'tis but our fantasy,
   And will not let belief take hold of him
   Touching this dreaded sight twice seen of us;
   Therefore I have entreated him along,
   With us to watch the minutes of this night,

35   That if again this apparition come,
   He may approve our eyes and speak to it.

HORATIO   Tush, tush, 'twill not appear.

BARNARDO   Sit down a while,
   And let us once again assail your ears,

---

3. **Long . . . King:** perhaps a password, perhaps simply an utterance to allow the voice to be recognized   7. **strook twelf:** struck twelve   9. **sick at heart:** in low spirits   14. **rivals:** partners
17. **liegemen . . . Dane:** loyal subjects to the king of Denmark   18. **Give:** God give
30. **fantasy:** imagination   36. **approve:** corroborate

40   That are so fortified against our story,
       What we have two nights seen.
HORATIO   Well, sit we down,
       And let us hear Barnardo speak of this.
BARNARDO   Last night of all,
45   When yond same star that's westward from the pole
       Had made his course t' illume that part of heaven
       Where now it burns, Marcellus and myself,
       The bell then beating one—

(*Enter* GHOST.)

MARCELLUS   Peace, break thee off! Look where it comes again!
50 BARNARDO   In the same figure like the King that's dead.
MARCELLUS   Thou art a scholar, speak to it, Horatio.
BARNARDO   Looks 'a not like the King? Mark it, Horatio.
HORATIO   Most like; it [harrows] me with fear and wonder.
BARNARDO   It would be spoke to.
55 MARCELLUS   Speak to it, Horatio.
HORATIO   What art thou that usurp'st this time of night,
       Together with that fair and warlike form
       In which the majesty of buried Denmark
       Did sometimes march? By heaven I charge thee speak!
60 MARCELLUS   It is offended.
BARNARDO   See, it stalks away!
HORATIO   Stay! Speak, speak, I charge thee speak!

(*Exit* GHOST.)

MARCELLUS   'Tis gone, and will not answer.
BARNARDO   How now, Horatio? you tremble and look pale.
65   Is not this something more than fantasy?
       What think you on't?
HORATIO   Before my God, I might not this believe
       Without the sensible and true avouch
       Of mine own eyes.
70 MARCELLUS   Is it not like the King?
HORATIO   As thou art to thyself.
       Such was the very armor he had on
       When he the ambitious Norway combated.

---

45. **pole:** pole star   46. **his:** its (the commonest form of the neuter possessive singular in Shakespeare's day)   50. **like:** in the likeness of   51. **a scholar:** one who knows how best to address it   52. **'a:** he   54. **It . . . to:** A ghost had to be spoken to before it could speak.   56. **usurp'st:** The ghost, a supernatural being, has invaded the realm of nature.   58. **majesty . . . Denmark:** late king of Denmark   59. **sometimes:** formerly   68. **sensible:** relating to the senses   **avouch:** guarantee   73. **Norway:** king of Norway

So frown'd he once when in an angry parle
75   He smote the sledded [Polacks] on the ice.
'Tis strange.
MARCELLUS   Thus twice before, and jump at this dead hour,
With martial stalk hath he gone by our watch.
HORATIO   In what particular thought to work I know not,
80   But in the gross and scope of mine opinion,
This bodes some strange eruption to our state.
MARCELLUS   Good row, sit down, and tell me, he that knows,
Why this same strict and most observant watch
So nightly toils the subject of the land,
85   And [why] such daily [cast] of brazen cannon,
And foreign mart for implements of war,
Why such impress of shipwrights, whose sore task
Does not divide the Sunday from the week,
What might be toward, that this sweaty haste
90   Doth make the night joint-laborer with the day:
Who is't that can inform me?
HORATIO   That can I,
At least the whisper goes so: our last king,
Whose image even but now appear'd to us,
95   Was, as you know, by Fortinbras of Norway,
Thereto prick'd on by a most emulate pride,
Dar'd to the combat; in which our valiant Hamlet
(For so this side of our known world esteem'd him)
Did slay this Fortinbras, who, by a seal'd compact
100   Well ratified by law and heraldy,
Did forfeit (with his life) all [those] his lands
Which he stood seiz'd of, to the conqueror;
Against the which a moi'ty competent
Was gaged by our king, which had [return'd]
105   To the inheritance of Fortinbras,
Had he been vanquisher; as by the same comart
And carriage of the article [design'd],
His fell to Hamlet. Now, sir, young Fortinbras,
Of unimproved mettle hot and full,

---

74. **parle:** parley   75. **sledded:** using sleds or sledges   **Polacks:** Poles   77. **jump:** precisely
79–80. **In . . . opinion:** while I have no precise theory about it, my general feeling is that; *gross* =
wholeness, totality; *scope* = range   81. **eruption:** upheaval   84. **toils:** causes to work   **subject:**
subjects   86. **foreign mart:** dealing with foreign markets   87. **impress:** forced service   89. **toward:**
in preparation   96. **emulate:** emulous, proceeding from rivalry   100. **law and heraldy:** heraldic
law (governing combat)   *Heraldy* is a variant of *heraldry.*   102. **seiz'd of:** possessed of
103. **moi'ty:** portion   **competent:** adequate, equivalent   104. **gaged:** pledged   **had:** would have
105. **inheritance:** possession   106. **comart:** bargain   107. **carriage:** tenor   **design'd:** drawn up
109. **unimproved:** untried (?) or not directed to any useful end (?)

110   Hath in the skirts of Norway here and there
       Shark'd up a list of lawless resolutes
       For food and diet to some enterprise
       That hath a stomach in't, which is no other,
       As it doth well appear unto our state,
115   But to recover of us, by strong hand
       And terms compulsatory, those foresaid lands
       So by his father lost; and this, I take it,
       Is the main motive of our preparations,
       The source of this our watch, and the chief head
120   Of this post-haste and romage in the land.
   BARNARDO   I think it be no other but e'en so.
       Well may it sort that this portentous figure
       Comes armed through our watch so like the King
       That was and is the question of these wars.
125 HORATIO   A mote it is to trouble the mind's eye.
       In the most high and palmy state of Rome,
       A little ere the mightiest Julius fell,
       The graves stood [tenantless] and the sheeted dead
       Did squeak and gibber in the Roman streets.
130   As stars with trains of fire, and dews of blood,
       Disasters in the sun; and the moist star
       Upon whose influence Neptune's empire stands
       Was sick almost to doomsday with eclipse.
       And even the like precurse of [fear'd] events,
135   As harbingers preceding still the fates
       And prologue to the omen coming on,
       Have heaven and earth together demonstrated
       Unto our climatures and countrymen.

(*Enter* GHOST.)

       But soft, behold! lo where it comes again!

(*It spreads his arms.*)

---

110. **skirts:** outlying territories   111. **Shark'd up:** gathered up hastily and indiscriminately   113. **stomach:** relish of danger (?) or demand for courage (?)   119. **head:** source   120. **romage:** rummage, bustling activity   122. **sort:** fit   **portentous:** ominous   129. One or more lines may have been lost between this line and the next.   131. **Disasters:** ominous signs   **moist star:** moon   132. **Neptune's empire stands:** the seas are dependent   133. **sick . . . doomsday:** almost totally darkened. When the Day of Judgment is imminent, says Matthew 24:29, "the moon shall not give her light."   **eclipse:** There were a solar and two total lunar eclipses visible in England in 1598; they caused gloomy speculation.   134. **precurse:** foreshadowing   135. **harbingers:** advance messengers   **still:** always   136. **omen:** the events portended   138. **climatures:** regions   139 s.d. (stage direction) **his:** its

140 I'll cross it though it blast me. Stay, illusion!
If thou hast any sound or use of voice,
Speak to me.
If there be any good thing to be done
That may to thee do ease, and grace to me,
145 Speak to me.
If thou art privy to thy country's fate,
Which happily foreknowing may avoid,
O speak!
Or if thou hast uphoarded in thy life
150 Extorted treasure in the womb of earth,
For which, they say, your spirits oft walk in death,
Speak of it, stay and speak!   (*The cock crows.*)   Stop it, Marcellus.
MARCELLUS   Shall I strike it with my partisan?
HORATIO   Do, if it will not stand.
155 BARNARDO   'Tis here!
HORATIO   'Tis here!

[*Exit* GHOST.]

MARCELLUS   'Tis gone!
We do it wrong, being so majestical,
To offer it the show of violence,
160 For it is as the air, invulnerable,
And our vain blows malicious mockery.
BARNARDO   It was about to speak when the cock crew.
HORATIO   And then it started like a guilty thing
Upon a fearful summons. I have heard
165 The cock, that is the trumpet to the morn,
Doth with his lofty and shrill-sounding throat
Awake the god of day, and at his warning,
Whether in sea or fire, in earth or air,
Th' extravagant and erring spirit hies
170 To his confine; and of the truth herein
This present object made probation.
MARCELLUS   It faded on the crowing of the cock.
Some say that ever 'gainst that season comes
Wherein our Saviour's birth is celebrated,
175 This bird of dawning singeth all night long,

---

140. **cross it:** cross its path, confront it directly   **blast:** wither (by supernatural means)
147. **happily:** haply, perhaps   151. **your:** Colloquial and impersonal; cf. I.v.183, IV.iii.23–25. Most editors adopt *you* from F1.   153. **partisan:** long-handled spear   161. **malicious mockery:** mockery of malice, empty pretenses of harming it.   165. **trumpet:** trumpeter   169. **extravagant:** wandering outside its proper bounds   **erring:** wandering abroad   **hies:** hastens   171. **object:** sight **probation:** proof   173. **'gainst:** just before

And then they say no spirit dare stir abroad,
The nights are wholesome, then no planets strike,
No fairy takes, nor witch hath power to charm,
So hallowed, and so gracious, is that time.

180 HORATIO   So have I heard and do in part believe it.
But look, the morn in russet mantle clad
Walks o'er the dew of yon high eastward hill.
Break we our watch up, and by my advice
Let us impart what we have seen to-night

185 Unto young Hamlet, for, upon my life,
This spirit, dumb to us, will speak to him.
Do you consent we shall acquaint him with it,
As needful in our loves, fitting our duty?

MARCELLUS   Let's do't, I pray, and I this morning know
190 Where we shall find him most convenient.

(*Exeunt.*)

[Scene II]

(*Flourish. Enter* CLAUDIUS, KING OF DENMARK, GERTRUDE THE QUEEN,
COUNCIL: *as* POLONIUS; *and his son* LAERTES, HAMLET, *cum aliis* [*including*
VOLTEMAND *and* CORNELIUS].)

KING   Though yet of Hamlet our dear brother's death
The memory be green, and that it us befitted
To bear our hearts in grief, and our whole kingdom
To be contracted in one brow of woe,

5 Yet so far hath discretion fought with nature
That we with wisest sorrow think on him
Together with remembrance of ourselves.
Therefore our sometime sister, now our queen,
Th' imperial jointress to this warlike state,

10 Have we, as 'twere with a defeated joy,
With an auspicious, and a dropping eye,
With mirth in funeral, and with dirge in marriage,
In equal scale weighing delight and dole,
Taken to wife; nor have we herein barr'd

---

177. **strike:** exert malevolent influence   178. **takes:** bewitches, charms   179. **gracious:** blessed
181. **russet:** coarse greyish-brown cloth

I.ii. Location: the castle
o.s.d. (opening stage direction) **Flourish:** trumpet fanfare   **cum aliis:** with others
2. **befitted:** would befit   4. **contracted in:** (1) reduced to; (2) knit or wrinkled in   **brow of woe:**
mournful brow   9. **jointress:** joint holder   10. **defeated:** impaired   11. **auspicious . . . dropping:**
cheerful . . . weeping

15   Your better wisdoms, which have freely gone
       With this affair along. For all, our thanks.
       Now follows that you know young Fortinbras,
       Holding a weak supposal of our worth,
       Or thinking by our late dear brother's death
20   Our state to be disjoint and out of frame,
       Co-leagued with this dream of his advantage,
       He hath not fail'd to pester us with message
       Importing the surrender of those lands
       Lost by his father, with all bands of law,
25   To our most valiant brother. So much for him.
       Now for ourself, and for this time of meeting,
       Thus much the business is: we have here writ
       To Norway, uncle of young Fortinbras—
       Who, impotent and bedred, scarcely hears
30   Of this his nephew's purpose—to suppress
       His further gait herein, in that the levies,
       The lists, and full proportions are all made
       Out of his subject; and we here dispatch
       You, good Cornelius, and you, Voltemand,
35   For bearers of this greeting to old Norway,
       Giving to you no further personal power
       To business with the King, more than the scope
       Of these delated articles allow.   [*Giving a paper.*]
       Farewell, and let your haste commend your duty.
40 CORNELIUS, VOLTEMAND   In that, and all things, will we show our duty.
    KING   We doubt it nothing; heartily farewell.

[*Exeunt* VOLTEMAND *and* CORNELIUS.]

       And now, Laertes, what's the news with you?
       You told us of some suit, what is't, Laertes?
       You cannot speak of reason to the Dane
45   And lose your voice. What wouldst thou beg, Laertes,
       That shall not be my offer, not thy asking?
       The head is not more native to the heart,
       The hand more instrumental to the mouth,

---

15. **freely:** fully, without reservation   17. **know:** be informed, learn   18. **supposal:** conjecture, estimate   21. **Co-leagued:** joined   22. **pester . . . message:** trouble me with persistent messages (the original sense of *pester* is "overcrowd")   23. **Importing:** having as import   24. **bands:** bonds, binding terms   29. **impotent and bedred:** feeble and bedridden   31. **gait:** proceeding   31–33. **in . . . subject:** since the troops are all drawn from his subjects   38. **delated:** extended, detailed (a variant of *dilated*)   41. **nothing:** not at all   45. **lose:** waste   47. **native:** closely related   48. **instrumental:** serviceable

Than is the throne of Denmark to thy father.
50 What wouldst thou have, Laertes?

LAERTES   My dread lord,
Your leave and favor to return to France,
From whence though willingly I came to Denmark
To show my duty in your coronation,
55 Yet now I must confess, that duty done,
My thoughts and wishes bend again toward France,
And bow them to your gracious leave and pardon.

KING   Have you your father's leave? What says Polonius?

POLONIUS   H'ath, my lord, wrung from me my slow leave
60 By laborsome petition, and at last
Upon his will I seal'd my hard consent.
I do beseech you give him leave to go.

KING   Take thy fair hour, Laertes, time be thine,
And thy best graces spend it at thy will!
65 But now, my cousin Hamlet, and my son—

HAMLET [*Aside.*]   A little more than kin, and less than kind.

KING   How is it that the clouds still hang on you?

HAMLET   Not so, my lord, I am too much in the sun.

QUEEN   Good Hamlet, cast thy nighted color off,
70 And let thine eye look like a friend on Denmark.
Do not for ever with thy vailed lids
Seek for thy noble father in the dust.
Thou know'st 'tis common, all that lives must die,
Passing through nature to eternity.

75 HAMLET   Ay, madam, it is common.

QUEEN   If it be,
Why seems it so particular with thee?

HAMLET   Seems, madam? nay, it is, I know not "seems."
'Tis not alone my inky cloak, [good] mother,
80 Nor customary suits of solemn black,
Nor windy suspiration of forc'd breath,
No, nor the fruitful river in the eye,
Nor the dejected havior of the visage,
Together with all forms, moods, [shapes] of grief,
85 That can [denote] me truly. These indeed seem,
For they are actions that a man might play,

---

52. **leave and favor:** gracious permission   57. **pardon:** permission to depart   59. **H'ath:** he hath   61. **hard:** reluctant   65. **cousin:** kinsman (used in familiar address to any collateral relative more distant than a brother or sister; here to a nephew)   66. **A little . . . kind:** closer than a nephew, since you are my mother's husband; yet more distant than a son, too (and not well disposed to you)   68. **sun:** with obvious quibble on *son*   71. **vailed:** downcast   73. **common:** general, universal   77. **particular:** individual, personal   82. **fruitful:** copious

But I have that within which passes show,
These but the trappings and the suits of woe.
KING   'Tis sweet and commendable in your nature, Hamlet,
90   To give these mourning duties to your father.
But you must know your father lost a father,
That father lost, lost his, and the survivor bound
In filial obligation for some term
To do obsequious sorrow. But to persever
95   In obstinate condolement is a course
Of impious stubbornness, 'tis unmanly grief,
It shows a will most incorrect to heaven,
A heart unfortified, or mind impatient,
An understanding simple and unschool'd:
100   For what we know must be, and is as common
As any the most vulgar thing to sense,
Why should we in our peevish opposition
Take it to heart? Fie, 'tis a fault to heaven,
A fault against the dead, a fault to nature,
105   To reason most absurd, whose common theme
Is death of fathers, and who still hath cried,
From the first corse till he that died to-day,
"This must be so." We pray you throw to earth
This unprevailing woe, and think of us
110   As of a father, for let the world take note
You are the most immediate to our throne,
And with no less nobility of love
Than that which dearest father bears his son
Do I impart toward you. For your intent
115   In going back to school in Wittenberg,
It is most retrograde to our desire,
And we beseech you bend you to remain
Here in the cheer and comfort of our eye,
Our chiefest courtier, cousin, and our son.
120 QUEEN   Let not thy mother lose her prayers, Hamlet,
I pray thee stay with us, go not to Wittenberg.
HAMLET   I shall in all my best obey you, madam.
KING   Why, 'tis a loving and a fair reply.
Be as ourself in Denmark. Madam, come.
125   This gentle and unforc'd accord of Hamlet
Sits smiling to my heart, in grace whereof,

---

94. **obsequious:** proper to obsequies   95. **condolement:** grief   97. **incorrect:** unsubmissive
101. **any ... sense:** what is perceived to be commonest   103. **to:** against   105. **absurd:** contrary
109. **unprevailing:** unavailing   113. **dearest:** most loving   114. **impart:** impart love

No jocund health that Denmark drinks to-day,
But the great cannon to the clouds shall tell,
And the King's rouse the heaven shall bruit again,
130   Respeaking earthly thunder. Come away.

(*Flourish. Exeunt all but* HAMLET.)

HAMLET   O that this too too sallied flesh would melt,
Thaw, and resolve itself into a dew!
Or that the Everlasting had not fix'd
His canon 'gainst [self-]slaughter! O God, God,
135   How [weary], stale, flat, and unprofitable
Seem to me all the uses of this world!
Fie on't, ah fie! 'tis an unweeded garden
That grows to seed, things rank and gross in nature
Possess it merely. That it should come [to this]!
140   But two months dead, nay, not so much, not two.
So excellent a king, that was to this
Hyperion to a satyr, so loving to my mother
That he might not beteem the winds of heaven
Visit her face too roughly. Heaven and earth,
145   Must I remember? Why, she should hang on him
As if increase of appetite had grown
By what it fed on, and yet, within a month—
Let me not think on't! Frailty, thy name is woman!—
A little month, or ere those shoes were old
150   With which she followed my poor father's body,
Like Niobe, all tears—why, she, [even she]—
O God, a beast that wants discourse of reason
Would have mourn'd longer—married with my uncle,
My father's brother, but no more like my father
155   Than I to Hercules. Within a month,
Ere yet the salt of most unrighteous tears
Had left the flushing in her galled eyes,
She married—O most wicked speed: to post
With such dexterity to incestious sheets,
160   It is not, nor it cannot come to good,
But break my heart, for I must hold my tongue.

---

129. **rouse:** bumper, drink   **bruit:** loudly declare   131. **sallied:** sullied.   Many editors prefer the F1 reading, *solid.*   134. **canon:** law   136. **uses:** customs   139. **merely:** utterly   141. **to:** in comparison with   142. **Hyperion:** the sun-god   143. **beteem:** allow   149. **or ere:** before   151. **Niobe:** She wept endlessly for her children, whom Apollo and Artemis had killed.   152. **wants . . . reason:** lacks the power of reason (which distinguishes men from beasts)   156. **unrighteous:** hypocritical 157. **flushing:** redness   **galled:** inflamed   159. **incestious:** incestuous. The marriage of a man to his brother's widow was so regarded until long after Shakespeare's day.

(*Enter* HORATIO, MARCELLUS *and* BARNARDO.)

HORATIO   Hail to your lordship!

HAMLET   I am glad to see you well.
    Horatio—or I do forget myself.

165 HORATIO   The same, my lord, and your poor servant ever.

HAMLET   Sir, my good friend—I'll change that name with you.
    And what make you from Wittenberg, Horatio?
    Marcellus.

MARCELLUS   My good lord.

170 HAMLET   I am very glad to see you.   [*to* BARNARDO]   Good even, sir.—
    But what, in faith, make you from Wittenberg?

HORATIO   A truant disposition, good my lord.

HAMLET   I would not hear your enemy say so,
    Nor shall you do my ear that violence
175 To make it truster of your own report
    Against yourself. I know you are no truant.
    But what is your affair in Elsinore?
    We'll teach you to drink [deep] ere you depart.

HORATIO   My lord, I came to see your father's funeral.

180 HAMLET   I prithee do not mock me, fellow studient,
    I think it was to [see] my mother's wedding.

HORATIO   Indeed, my lord, it followed hard upon.

HAMLET   Thrift, thrift, Horatio, the funeral bak'd-meats
    Did coldly furnish forth the marriage tables.
185 Would I had met my dearest foe in heaven
    Or ever I had seen that day, Horatio!
    My father—methinks I see my father.

HORATIO   Where, my lord?

HAMLET   In my mind's eye, Horatio.

190 HORATIO   I saw him once, 'a was a goodly king.

HAMLET   'A was a man, take him for all in all,
    I shall not look upon his like again.

HORATIO   My lord, I think I saw him yesternight.

HAMLET   Saw, who?

195 HORATIO   My lord, the King your father.

HAMLET   The King my father?

HORATIO   Season your admiration for a while
    With an attent ear, till I may deliver,
    Upon the witness of these gentlemen,
200 This marvel to you.

---

166. **change:** exchange   167. **what . . . from:** what are you doing away from
172. **truant disposition:** inclination to play truant   180. **studient:** student   184. **coldly:** when cold
185. **dearest:** most intensely hated   186. **Or:** ere, before   197. **Season:** temper
admiration: wonder   198. **deliver:** report

HAMLET   For God's love let me hear!

HORATIO   Two nights together had these gentlemen,
          Marcellus and Barnardo, on their watch,
          In the dead waste and middle of the night,
205   Been thus encount'red: a figure like your father,
          Armed at point exactly, cap-a-pe,
          Appears before them, and with solemn march
          Goes slow and stately by them; thrice he walk'd
          By their oppress'd and fear-surprised eyes
210   Within his truncheon's length, whilst they, distill'd
          Almost to jelly with the act of fear,
          Stand dumb and speak not to him. This to me
          In dreadful secrecy impart they did,
          And I with them the third night kept the watch,
215   Where, as they had delivered, both in time,
          Form of the thing, each word made true and good,
          The apparition comes. I knew your father,
          These hands are not more like.

HAMLET   But where was this?

220 MARCELLUS   My lord, upon the platform where we watch.

HAMLET   Did you not speak to it?

HORATIO   My lord, I did,
          But answer made it none. Yet once methought
          It lifted up it head and did address
225   Itself to motion like as it would speak;
          But even then the morning cock crew loud,
          And at the sound it shrunk in haste away
          And vanish'd from our sight.

HAMLET   'Tis very strange.

230 HORATIO   As I do live, my honor'd lord, 'tis true,
          And we did think it writ down in our duty
          To let you know of it.

HAMLET   Indeed, [indeed,] sirs. But this troubles me.
          Hold you the watch to-night?

235 [MARCELLUS, BARNARDO]   We do, my lord.

HAMLET   Arm'd, say you?

[MARCELLUS, BARNARDO]   Arm'd, my lord.

HAMLET   From top to toe?

[MARCELLUS, BARNARDO]   My lord, from head to foot.

---

204. **waste:** empty expanse   206. **at point exactly:** in every particular   **cap-a-pe:** from head to
foot   209. **fear-surprised:** overwhelmed by fear   210. **truncheon:** short staff carried as a symbol of
military command   211. **act:** action, operation   213. **dreadful:** held in awe, solemnly sworn
218. **are . . . like:** do not resemble each other more closely than the apparition resembled him
224. **it:** its   224–225. **address . . . motion:** begin to make a gesture

240   HAMLET   Then saw you not his face.

HORATIO   O yes, my lord, he wore his beaver up.

HAMLET   What, look'd he frowningly?

HORATIO   A countenance more
In sorrow than in anger.

245   HAMLET   Pale, or red?

HORATIO   Nay, very pale.

HAMLET   And fix'd his eyes upon you?

HORATIO   Most constantly.

HAMLET   I would I had been there.

250   HORATIO   It would have much amaz'd you.

HAMLET   Very like, [very like]. Stay'd it long?

HORATIO   While one with moderate haste might tell a hundredth.

BOTH [MARCELLUS, BARNARDO]   Longer, longer.

HORATIO   Not when I saw't.

255   HAMLET   His beard was grisl'd, no?

HORATIO   It was, as I have seen it in his life,
A sable silver'd.

HAMLET   I will watch to-night,
Perchance 'twill walk again.

260   HORATIO   I warr'nt it will.

HAMLET   If it assume my noble father's person,
I'll speak to it though hell itself should gape
And bid me hold my peace. I pray you all,
If you have hitherto conceal'd this sight,

265   Let it be tenable in your silence still,
And whatsomever else shall hap to-night,
Give it an understanding but no tongue.
I will requite your loves. So fare you well.
Upon the platform 'twixt aleven and twelf

270   I'll visit you.

ALL   Our duty to your honor.

HAMLET   Your loves, as mine to you; farewell.

(*Exeunt* [*all but* HAMLET].)

My father's spirit—in arms! All is not well,
I doubt some foul play. Would the night were come!

275   Till then sit still, my soul. [Foul] deeds will rise,
Though all the earth o'erwhelm them, to men's eyes.

(*Exit.*)

---

241. **beaver:** visor   252. **tell a hundreth:** count a hundred   255. **grisl'd:** grizzled, mixed with grey   265. **tenable:** held close   269. **aleven:** eleven   274. **doubt:** suspect

Of entrance to a quarrel, but being in,
Bear't that th' opposed may beware of thee.
Give every man thy ear, but few thy voice,
Take each man's censure, but reserve thy judgment.

75 Costly thy habit as thy purse can buy,
But not express'd in fancy, rich, not gaudy,
For the apparel oft proclaims the man,
And they in France of the best rank and station
[Are] of a most select and generous chief in that.

80 Neither a borrower nor a lender [be],
For [loan] oft loses both itself and friend,
And borrowing dulleth [th'] edge of husbandry.
This above all: to thine own self be true,
And it must follow, as the night the day,

85 Thou canst not then be false to any man.
Farewell, my blessing season this in thee!

LAERTES   Most humbly do I take my leave, my lord.

POLONIUS   The time invests you, go, your servants tend.

LAERTES   Farewell, Ophelia, and remember well

90 What I have said to you.

OPHELIA   'Tis in my memory lock'd,
And you yourself shall keep the key of it.

LAERTES   Farewell.   (*Exit* LAERTES.)

POLONIUS   What is't, Ophelia, he hath said to you?

95 OPHELIA   So please you, something touching the Lord Hamlet.

POLONIUS   Marry, well bethought.
'Tis told me, he hath very oft of late
Given private time to you, and you yourself
Have of your audience been most free and bounteous.

100 If it be so—as so 'tis put on me,
And that in way of caution—I must tell you,
You do not understand yourself so clearly
As it behooves my daughter and your honor.
What is between you? Give me up the truth.

105 OPHELIA   He hath, my lord, of late made many tenders
Of his affection to me.

POLONIUS   Affection, puh! You speak like a green girl,
Unsifted in such perilous circumstance.
Do you believe his tenders, as you call them?

110 OPHELIA   I do not know, my lord, what I should think.

---

72. **Bear't that:** manage it in such a way that   74. **Take:** listen to   **censure:** opinion   79. **generous:**
noble   **chief:** eminence (?) But the line is probably corrupt. Perhaps *of a* is intrusive, in which case
chief = chiefly.   82. **husbandry:** thrift   86. **season:** preserve (?) or ripen, make fruitful (?)
88. **invests:** besieges   **tend:** wait   96. **Marry:** indeed (originally the name of the Virgin Mary used
as an oath)   100. **put on:** told to   105. **tenders:** offers   108. **Unsifted:** untried

POLONIUS   Marry, I will teach you: think yourself a baby
          That you have ta'en these tenders for true pay,
          Which are not sterling. Tender yourself more dearly,
          Or (not to crack the wind of the poor phrase,
115   [Wringing] it thus) you'll tender me a fool.
OPHELIA   My lord, he hath importun'd me with love
          In honorable fashion.
POLONIUS   Ay, fashion you may call it. Go to, go to.
OPHELIA   And hath given countenance to his speech, my lord,
120   With almost all the holy vows of heaven.
POLONIUS   Ay, springes to catch woodcocks. I do know,
          When the blood burns, how prodigal the soul
          Lends the tongue vows. These blazes, daughter,
          Giving more light than heat, extinct in both
125   Even in their promise, as it is a-making,
          You must not take for fire. From this time
          Be something scanter of your maiden presence,
          Set your entreatments at a higher rate
          Than a command to parle. For Lord Hamlet,
130   Believe so much in him, that he is young,
          And with a larger teder may he walk
          Than may be given you. In few, Ophelia,
          Do not believe his vows, for they are brokers,
          Not of that dye which their investments show,
135   But mere [implorators] of unholy suits,
          Breathing like sanctified and pious bonds,
          The better to [beguile]. This is for all:
          I would not, in plain terms, from this time forth
          Have you so slander any moment leisure
140   As to give words or talk with the Lord Hamlet.
          Look to't, I charge you. Come your ways.
OPHELIA   I shall obey, my lord.

(*Exeunt.*)

---

112. **tenders:** with play on the sense "money offered in payment" (as in *legal tender*)   113. **Tender:** hold, value   115. **Wringing:** straining, forcing to the limit   **tender . . . fool:** (1) show me that you are a fool; (2) make me look like a fool; (3) present me with a (bastard) grandchild   118. **fashion:** See note on line 7.   119. **countenance:** authority   121. **springes:** snares   **woodcocks:** proverbially gullible birds   128–29. **Set . . . parle:** Place a higher value on your favors; do not grant interviews simply because he asks for them. Polonius uses a military figure: *entreatments* = negotiations for surrender; *parle* = parley, discuss terms.   130. **so . . . him:** no more than this with respect to him   131. **larger teder:** longer tether   133. **brokers:** procurers   134. **Not . . . show:** not of the color that their garments (*investments*) exhibit; not what they seem   135. **mere:** out-and-out   136. **bonds:** (lover's) vows or assurances. Many editors follow Theobald in reading *bawds*.   139. **slander:** disgrace   **moment:** momentary   141. **Come your ways:** come along

[Scene IV]

(*Enter* HAMLET, HORATIO, *and* MARCELLUS.)

HAMLET   The air bites shrowdly, it is very cold.

HORATIO   It is [a] nipping and an eager air.

HAMLET   What hour now?

HORATIO   I think it lacks of twelf.

5 MARCELLUS   No, it is strook.

HORATIO   Indeed? I heard it not. It then draws near the season
         Wherein the spirit held his wont to walk.

(*A flourish of trumpets, and two pieces goes off* [*within*].)

         What does this mean, my lord?

HAMLET   The King doth wake to-night and takes his rouse,

10   Keeps wassail, and the swagg'ring up-spring reels;
         And as he drains his draughts of Rhenish down,
         The kettle-drum and trumpet thus bray out
         The triumph of his pledge.

HORATIO   Is it a custom?

15 HAMLET   Ay, marry, is't,
         But to my mind, though I am native here
         And to the manner born, it is a custom
         More honor'd in the breach than the observance.
         This heavy-headed revel east and west

20   Makes us traduc'd and tax'd of other nations.
         They clip us drunkards, and with swinish phrase
         Soil our addition, and indeed it takes
         From our achievements, though perform'd at height,
         The pith and marrow of our attribute.

25   So, oft it chances in particular men,
         That for some vicious mole of nature in them,
         As in their birth, wherein they are not guilty
         (Since nature cannot choose his origin),
         By their o'ergrowth of some complexion

30   Oft breaking down the pales and forts of reason,

I.iv. Location: the guard-platform of the castle   1. **shrowdly:** shrewdly, wickedly   2. **eager:** sharp
7. s.d. **pieces:** cannon   9. **doth . . . rouse:** holds revels far into the night   10. **wassail:** carousal
up-spring: wild dance   11. **Rhenish:** Rhine wine   13. **triumph . . . pledge:** accomplishment of his
toast (by draining his cup at a single draught)   17. **manner:** custom (of carousing)   18. **More . . .**
observance: which it is more honorable to break than to observe   20. **tax'd of:** censured by
21. **clip:** clepe, call   22. **addition:** titles of honor   23. **at height:** most excellently   24. **attribute:**
reputation   25. **particular:** individual   26. **vicious . . . nature:** small natural blemish   28. **his:** its
29. **By . . . complexion:** by the excess of some one of the humors (which were thought to govern the
disposition)   30. **pales:** fences

Or by some habit, that too much o'er-leavens
The form of plausive manners—that these men,
Carrying, I say, the stamp of one defect,
Being nature's livery, or fortune's star,
35   His virtues else, be they as pure as grace,
As infinite as man may undergo,
Shall in the general censure take corruption
From that particular fault: the dram of [ev'l]
Doth all the noble substance of a doubt
40   To his own scandal.

(*Enter* GHOST.)

HORATIO   Look, my lord, it comes!
HAMLET   Angels and ministers of grace defend us!
    Be thou a spirit of health, or goblin damn'd,
    Bring with thee airs from heaven, or blasts from hell,
45   Be thy intents wicked, or charitable,
    Thou com'st in such a questionable shape
    That I will speak to thee. I'll call thee Hamlet,
    King, father, royal Dane. O, answer me!
    Let me not burst in ignorance, but tell
50   Why thy canoniz'd bones, hearsed in death,
    Have burst their cerements; why the sepulchre,
    Wherein we saw thee quietly [inurn'd,]
    Hath op'd his ponderous and marble jaws
    To cast thee up again. What may this mean,
55   That thou, dead corse, again in complete steel
    Revisits thus the glimpses of the moon,
    Making night hideous, and we fools of nature
    So horridly to shake our disposition
    With thoughts beyond the reaches of our souls?
60   Say why is this? wherefore? what should we do?

([GHOST] *beckons* [HAMLET].)

---

31. **o'er-leavens:** makes itself felt throughout (as leaven works in the whole mass of dough)
32. **plausive:** pleasing   34. **Being . . . star:** whether they were born with it, or got it by misfortune.
Star means "blemish."   36. **undergo:** carry the weight of, sustain   37. **general censure:** popular
opinion   38. **dram:** minute amount   **ev'l:** evil, with a pun on *eale*, "yeast" (cf. *o'er-leavens* in
line 31) 39. **of a doubt:** a famous crux, for which many emendations have been suggested, the most
widely accepted being Steevens' *often dout* (extinguish)   40. **To . . . scandal:** so that it all shares in
the disgrace   43. **of health:** wholesome, good   46. **questionable:** inviting talk   50. **canoniz'd:**
buried with the prescribed rites   51. **cerements:** grave-clothes   55. **complete steel:** full armor
56. **Revisits:** The *-s* ending in the second-person singular is common.   57. **fools of nature:** the children (or the dupes) of a purely natural order, baffled by the supernatural   58. **disposition:** nature

HORATIO   It beckons you to go away with it,
As if it some impartment did desire
To you alone.
MARCELLUS   Look with what courteous action
65   It waves you to a more removed ground,
But do not go with it.
HORATIO   No, by no means.
HAMLET   It will not speak, then I will follow it.
HORATIO   Do not, my lord.
70   HAMLET   Why, what should be the fear?
I do not set my life at a pin's fee,
And for my soul, what can it do to that,
Being a thing immortal as itself?
It waves me forth again, I'll follow it.
75   HORATIO   What if it tempt you toward the flood, my lord,
Or to the dreadful summit of the cliff
That beetles o'er his base into the sea,
And there assume some other horrible form
Which might deprive your sovereignty of reason,
80   And draw you into madness? Think of it.
The very place puts toys of desperation,
Without more motive, into every brain
That looks so many fadoms to the sea
And hears it roar beneath.
85   HAMLET   It waves me still.—
Go on, I'll follow thee.
MARCELLUS   You shall not go, my lord.
HAMLET   Hold off your hands.
HORATIO   Be rul'd, you shall not go.
90   HAMLET   My fate cries out,
And makes each petty artere in this body
As hardy as the Nemean lion's nerve.
Still am I call'd. Unhand me, gentlemen.
By heaven, I'll make a ghost of him that lets me!
95   I say away!—Go on, I'll follow thee.

(*Exeunt* GHOST *and* HAMLET.)

HORATIO   He waxes desperate with [imagination].
MARCELLUS   Let's follow. 'Tis not fit thus to obey him.

---

62. **impartment:** communication   71. **fee:** worth   79. **deprive . . . reason:** unseat reason from the rule of your mind   81. **toys of desperation:** fancies of desperate action, inclinations to jump off   83. **fadoms:** fathoms   91. **artere:** variant spelling of *artery;* here, ligament, sinew
92. **Nemean lion:** slain by Hercules as one of his twelve labors   **nerve:** sinew   94. **lets:** hinders

HORATIO   Have after. To what issue will this come?

MARCELLUS   Something is rotten in the state of Denmark.

100 HORATIO   Heaven will direct it.

MARCELLUS   Nay, let's follow him.

(*Exeunt.*)

[Scene V]

(*Enter* GHOST *and* HAMLET.)

HAMLET   Whither wilt thou lead me? Speak, I'll go no further.

GHOST   Mark me.

HAMLET   I will.

GHOST   My hour is almost come
     When I to sulph'rous and tormenting flames
     Must render up myself.

HAMLET   Alas, poor ghost!

5 GHOST   Pity me not, but lend thy serious hearing
     To what I shall unfold.

HAMLET   Speak, I am bound to hear.

GHOST   So art thou to revenge, when thou shalt hear.

HAMLET   What?

10 GHOST   I am thy father's spirit,
     Doom'd for a certain term to walk the night,
     And for the day confin'd to fast in fires,
     Till the foul crimes done in my days of nature
     Are burnt and purg'd away. But that I am forbid
15   To tell the secrets of my prison-house,
     I could a tale unfold whose lightest word
     Would harrow up thy soul, freeze thy young blood,
     Make thy two eyes like stars start from their spheres,
     Thy knotted and combined locks to part,
20   And each particular hair to stand an end,
     Like quills upon the fearful porpentine.
     But this eternal blazon must not be
     To ears of flesh and blood. List, list, O, list!
     If thou didst ever thy dear father love—

25 HAMLET   O God!

GHOST   Revenge his foul and most unnatural murther.

---

100. **it:** the issue

I.v. Location: on the battlements of the castle   12. **fast:** do penance   13. **crimes:** sins   18. **spheres:** eye-sockets; with allusion to the revolving spheres in which, according to the Ptolemaic astronomy, the stars were fixed   20. **an end:** on end   21. **fearful porpentine:** frightened porcupine
22. **eternal blazon:** revelation of eternal things

HAMLET Murther!

GHOST Murther most foul, as in the best it is,
But this most foul, strange, and unnatural.

30 HAMLET Haste me to know't, that I with wings as swift
As meditation, or the thoughts of love,
May sweep to my revenge.

GHOST   I find thee apt,
And duller shouldst thou be than the fat weed
35 That roots itself in ease on Lethe wharf,
Wouldst thou not stir in this. Now, Hamlet, hear:
'Tis given out that, sleeping in my orchard,
A serpent stung me, so the whole ear of Denmark
Is by a forged process of my death
40 Rankly abus'd; but know, thou noble youth,
The serpent that did sting thy father's life
Now wears his crown.

HAMLET   O my prophetic soul!
My uncle?

45 GHOST Ay, that incestuous, that adulterate beast,
With witchcraft of his wits, with traitorous gifts—
O wicked wit and gifts that have the power
So to seduce!—won to his shameful lust
The will of my most seeming virtuous queen.
50 O Hamlet, what [a] falling-off was there
From me, whose love was of that dignity
That it went hand in hand even with the vow
I made to her in marriage, and to decline
Upon a wretch whose natural gifts were poor
55 To those of mine!
But virtue, as it never will be moved,
Though lewdness court it in a shape of heaven,
So [lust], though to a radiant angel link'd,
Will [sate] itself in a celestial bed
60 And prey on garbage.
But soft, methinks I scent the morning air,
Brief let me be. Sleeping within my orchard,
My custom always of the afternoon,
Upon my secure hour thy uncle stole,
65 With juice of cursed hebona in a vial,
And in the porches of my ears did pour

---

31. **meditation:** thought   35. **Lethe:** river of Hades, the water of which made the drinker forget the past   **wharf:** bank   37. **orchard:** garden   39. **forged process:** false account   40. **abus'd:** deceived   45. **adulterate:** adulterous   57. **shape of heaven:** angelic form   64. **secure:** carefree   65. **hebona:** ebony (which Shakespeare, following a literary tradition, and perhaps also associating the word with *henbane,* thought the name of a poison)

The leprous distillment, whose effect
Holds such an enmity with blood of man
That swift as quicksilver it courses through
The natural gates and alleys of the body,
70   And with a sudden vigor it doth [posset]
And curd, like eager droppings into milk,
The thin and wholesome blood. So did it mine,
And a most instant tetter bark'd about,
Most lazar-like, with vile and loathsome crust
75   All my smooth body.
Thus was I, sleeping, by a brother's hand
Of life, of crown, of queen, at once dispatch'd,
Cut off even in the blossoms of my sin,
Unhous'led, disappointed, unanel'd,
80   No reck'ning made, but sent to my account
With all my imperfections on my head.
O, horrible, O, horrible, most horrible!
If thou hast nature in thee, bear it not,
Let not the royal bed of Denmark be
85   A couch for luxury and damned incest.
But howsomever thou pursues this act,
Taint not thy mind, nor let thy soul contrive
Against thy mother aught. Leave her to heaven,
And to those thorns that in her bosom lodge
90   To prick and sting her. Fare thee well at once!
The glow-worm shows the matin to be near,
And gins to pale his uneffectual fire.
Adieu, adieu, adieu! remember me.

[*Exit.*]

95   HAMLET   O all you host of heaven! O earth! What else?
And shall I couple hell? O fie, hold, hold, my heart,
And you, my sinows, grow not instant old,
But bear me [stiffly] up. Remember thee!
Ay, thou poor ghost, whiles memory holds a seat
100   In this distracted globe. Remember thee!
Yea, from the table of my memory
I'll wipe away all trivial fond records,

---

71. **posset:** curdle   72. **eager:** sour   74. **tetter:** scabby eruption   **bark'd:** formed a hard covering,
like bark on a tree   75. **lazar-like:** leperlike   78. **at once:** all at the same time   **dispatch'd:** deprived
80. **Unhous'led:** without the Eucharist   **disappointed:** without (spiritual) preparation   **unanel'd:**
unanointed, without extreme unction   84. **nature:** natural feeling   86. **luxury:** lust   92. **matin:**
morning   93. **gins:** begins   97. **sinows:** sinews   100. **globe:** head   101. **table:** writing tablet
102. **fond:** foolish

All saws of books, all forms, all pressures past
That youth and observation copied there,
105 And thy commandement all alone shall live
Within the book and volume of my brain,
Unmix'd with baser matter. Yes, by heaven!
O most pernicious woman!
O villain, villain, smiling, damned villain!
110 My tables—meet it is I set it down
That one may smile, and smile, and be a villain!
At least I am sure it may be so in Denmark.   [*He writes.*]
So, uncle, there you are. Now to my word:
It is "Adieu, adieu! remember me."
115 I have sworn't.
HORATIO [*Within.*]   My lord, my lord!
MARCELLUS [*Within.*]   Lord Hamlet!

(*Enter* HORATIO *and* MARCELLUS.)

HORATIO   Heavens secure him!
HAMLET   So be it!
120 MARCELLUS   Illo, ho, ho, my lord!
HAMLET   Hillo, ho, ho, boy! Come, [bird,] come.
MARCELLUS   How is't, my noble lord?
HORATIO   What news, my lord?
HAMLET   O, wonderful!
125 HORATIO   Good my lord, tell it.
HAMLET   No, you will reveal it.
HORATIO   Not I, my lord, by heaven.
MARCELLUS   Nor I, my lord.
HAMLET   How say you then, would heart of man once think it?—
130 But you'll be secret?
BOTH [HORATIO, MARCELLUS]   Ay, by heaven, [my lord].
HAMLET   There's never a villain dwelling in all Denmark
But he's an arrant knave.
HORATIO   There needs no ghost, my lord, come from the grave
135 To tell us this.
HAMLET   Why, right, you are in the right,
And so, without more circumstance at all,
I hold it fit that we shake hands and part,
You, as your business and desire shall point you,
140 For every man hath business and desire,

---

103. **saws:** wise sayings **forms:** shapes, images **pressures:** impressions 113. **word:** word of command from the Ghost 121. **Hillo . . . come:** Hamlet answers Marcellus' halloo with a falconer's cry 137. **circumstance:** ceremony

Such as it is, and for my own poor part,
        I will go pray.
HORATIO   These are but wild and whirling words, my lord.
HAMLET   I am sorry they offend you, heartily,
145   Yes, faith, heartily.
HORATIO   There's no offense, my lord.
HAMLET   Yes, by Saint Patrick, but there is, Horatio,
        And much offense too. Touching this vision here,
        It is an honest ghost, that let me tell you.
150   For your desire to know what is between us,
        O'ermaster't as you may. And now, good friends,
        As you are friends, scholars, and soldiers,
        Give me one poor request.
HORATIO   What is't, my lord, we will.
155 HAMLET   Never make known what you have seen tonight.
BOTH [HORATIO, MARCELLUS]   My lord, we will not.
HAMLET   Nay, but swear't.
HORATIO   In faith,
        My lord, not I.
160 MARCELLUS   Nor I, my lord, in faith.
HAMLET   Upon my sword.
MARCELLUS   We have sworn, my lord, already.
HAMLET   Indeed, upon my sword, indeed.

(GHOST *cries under the stage.*)

GHOST   Swear.
165 HAMLET   Ha, ha, boy, say'st thou so? Art thou there, truepenny?
        Come on, you hear this fellow in the cellarage,
        Consent to swear.
HORATIO   Propose the oath, my lord.
HAMLET   Never to speak of this that you have seen,
170   Swear by my sword.
GHOST [*beneath*]   Swear.
HAMLET   *Hic et ubique?* Then we'll shift our ground.
        Come hither, gentlemen,
        And lay your hands again upon my sword.
175   Swear by my sword
        Never to speak of this that you have heard.
GHOST [*beneath*]   Swear by his sword.
HAMLET   Well said, old mole, canst work i' th' earth so fast?
        A worthy pioner! Once more remove, good friends.

---

149. **honest:** true, genuine   154. **What is't:** whatever it is   161. **Upon my sword:** on the cross
formed by the hilt   165. **truepenny:** trusty fellow   172. **Hic et ubique:** here and everywhere
179. **pioner:** digger, miner (variant of *pioneer*)

180 HORATIO   O day and night, but this is wondrous strange!

HAMLET   And therefore as a stranger give it welcome.
       There are more things in heaven and earth, Horatio,
       Than are dreamt of in your philosophy.
       But come—

185   Here, as before, never, so help you mercy,
       How strange or odd some'er I bear myself—
       As I perchance hereafter shall think meet
       To put an antic disposition on—
       That you, at such times seeing me, never shall,

190   With arms encumb'red thus, or this headshake,
       Or by pronouncing of some doubtful phrase,
       As "Well, well, we know," or "We could, and if we would,"
       Or "If we list to speak," or "There be, and if they might,"
       Or such ambiguous giving out, to note

195   That you know aught of me—this do swear,
       So grace and mercy at your most need help you.

GHOST [*beneath*]   Swear.   [*They swear.*]

HAMLET   Rest, rest, perturbed spirit! So, gentlemen,
       With all my love I do commend me to you,

200   And what so poor a man as Hamlet is
       May do t' express his love and friending to you,
       God willing, shall not lack. Let us go in together,
       And still your fingers on your lips, I pray.
       The time is out of joint—O cursed spite,

205   That ever I was born to set it right!
       Nay, come, let's go together.

(*Exeunt.*)

Act II

Scene I

(*Enter old* POLONIUS *with his man* [REYNALDO].)

POLONIUS   Give him this money and these notes, Reynaldo.

REYNALDO   I will, my lord.

POLONIUS   You shall do marvell's wisely, good Reynaldo,
       Before you visit him, to make inquire
       Of his behavior.

---

181. **as . . . welcome:** give it the welcome due in courtesy to strangers   183. **your:** See note on I.i.151.
philosophy: natural philosophy, science   188. **put . . . on:** behave in some fantastic manner, act like a
madman   190. **encumb'red:** folded   192. **and if:** if   193. **list:** cared, had a mind   194. **note:** indicate   203. **still:** always   206. **Nay . . . together:** They are holding back to let him go first.

II.i. Location: Polonius's quarters in the castle   3. **marvell's:** marvellous(ly)

5 REYNALDO   My lord, I did intend it.

POLONIUS   Marry, well said, very well said. Look you, sir,
Inquire me first what Danskers are in Paris,
And how, and who, what means, and where they keep,
What company, at what expense; and finding

10   By this encompassment and drift of question
That they do know my son, come you more nearer
Than your particular demands will touch it.
Take you as 'twere some distant knowledge of him,
As thus, "I know his father and his friends,

15   And in part him." Do you mark this, Reynaldo?

REYNALDO   Ay, very well, my lord.

POLONIUS   "And in part him—but," you may say, "not well.
But if 't be he I mean, he's very wild,
Addicted so and so," and there put on him

20   What forgeries you please: marry, none so rank
As may dishonor him, take heed of that,
But, sir, such wanton, wild, and usual slips
As are companions and most known
To youth and liberty.

25 REYNALDO   As gaming, my lord.

POLONIUS   Ay, or drinking, fencing, swearing, quarreling,
Drabbing—you may go so far.

REYNALDO   My lord, that would dishonor him.

POLONIUS   Faith, as you may season it in the charge:

30   You must not put another scandal on him,
That he is open to incontinency—
That's not my meaning. But breathe his faults so quaintly
That they may seem the taints of liberty,
The flash and outbreak of a fiery mind,

35   A savageness in unreclaimed blood,
Of general assault.

REYNALDO   But, my good lord—

POLONIUS   Wherefore should you do this?

REYNALDO   Ay, my lord,

40   I would know that.

POLONIUS   Marry, sir, here's my drift,
And I believe it is a fetch of wit:

---

7. **Danskers:** Danes 8. **keep:** lodge 10. **encompassment:** circuitousness **drift of question:** directing of the conversation 12. **particular demands:** direct questions 20. **forgeries:** invented charges 22. **wanton:** sportive 27. **Drabbing:** whoring 29. **Faith:** Most editors read *Faith, no,* following F1; this makes easier sense. **season:** qualify, temper 31. **open to incontinency:** habitually profligate 32. **quaintly:** artfully 35. **unreclaimed:** untamed 36. **Of general assault:** to which young men are generally subject 42. **fetch of wit:** ingenious device

You laying these slight sallies on my son,
As 'twere a thing a little soil'd [wi' th'] working,
45   Mark you,
Your party in converse, him you would sound,
Having ever seen in the prenominate crimes
The youth you breathe of guilty, be assur'd
He closes with you in this consequence:
50   "Good sir," or so, or "friend," or "gentleman,"
According to the phrase or the addition
Of man and country.

REYNALDO   Very good, my lord.

POLONIUS   And then, sir, does 'a this—'a does—what was I about to say?
55   By the mass, I was about to say something.
Where did I leave?

REYNALDO   At "closes in the consequence."

POLONIUS   At "closes in the consequence," ay, marry.
He closes thus: "I know the gentleman.
60   I saw him yesterday, or th' other day,
Or then, or then, with such or such, and as you say,
There was 'a gaming, there o'ertook in 's rouse,
There falling out at tennis"; or, perchance,
"I saw him enter such a house of sale,"
65   *Videlicet*, a brothel, or so forth. See you now,
Your bait of falsehood take this carp of truth,
And thus do we of wisdom and of reach,
With windlasses and with assays of bias,
By indirections find directions out;
70   So by my former lecture and advice
Shall you my son. You have me, have you not?

REYNALDO   My lord, I have.

POLONIUS   God buy ye, fare ye well.

REYNALDO   Good my lord.

75 POLONIUS   Observe his inclination in yourself.

REYNALDO   I shall, my lord.

POLONIUS   And let him ply his music.

REYNALDO   Well, my lord.

---

42. **sallies:** sullies, blemishes   44. **soil'd . . . working:** shopworn   47. **Having:** if he has
prenominate crimes: aforementioned faults   49. **closes:** falls in   **in this consequence:** as follows
51. **addition:** style of address   62. **o'ertook in 's rouse:** overcome by drink   67. **reach:** capacity,
understanding   68. **windlasses:** roundabout methods   **assays of bias:** indirect attempts (a figure
from the game of bowls, in which the player must make allowance for the curving course his bowl
will take toward its mark)   69. **directions:** the way things are going   71. **have me:** understand me
73. **God buy ye:** good-bye (a contraction of *God be with you*)   75. **in:** by. Polonius asks him to observe Laertes directly, as well as making inquiries.   77. **let him ply:** see that he goes on with

POLONIUS   Farewell.

(*Exit* REYNALDO.)

(*Enter* OPHELIA.)

80
    How now, Ophelia, what's the matter?

OPHELIA   O my lord, my lord, I have been so affrighted!

POLONIUS   With what, i' th' name of God?

OPHELIA   My lord, as I was sewing in my closet,

85
    Lord Hamlet, with his doublet all unbrac'd,

    No hat upon his head, his stockins fouled,

    Ungart'red, and down-gyved to his ankle,

    Pale as his shirt, his knees knocking each other,

    And with a look so piteous in purport

90
    As if he had been loosed out of hell

    To speak of horrors—he comes before me.

POLONIUS   Mad for thy love?

OPHELIA   My lord, I do not know,

    But truly I do fear it.

95 POLONIUS   What said he?

OPHELIA   He took me by the wrist, and held me hard,

    Then goes he to the length of all his arm,

    And with his other hand thus o'er his brow,

    He falls to such perusal of my face

100
    As 'a would draw it. Long stay'd he so.

    At last, a little shaking of mine arm,

    And thrice his head thus waving up and down,

    He rais'd a sigh so piteous and profound

    As it did seem to shatter all his bulk

105
    And end his being. That done, he lets me go,

    And with his head over his shoulder turn'd,

    He seem'd to find his way without his eyes,

    For out a' doors he went without their helps,

    And to the last bended their light on me.

110 POLONIUS   Come, go with me. I will go seek the King.

    This is the very ecstasy of love,

    Whose violent property fordoes itself,

    And leads the will to desperate undertakings

    As oft as any passions under heaven

115
    That does afflict our natures. I am sorry—

    What, have you given him any hard words of late?

---

83. **closet:** private room   84. **unbrac'd:** unlaced   85. **stockins fouled:** stockings dirty
86. **down-gyved:** hanging down like fetters on a prisoner's legs   103. **bulk:** body   110. **ecstasy:**
madness   111. **property:** quality   **fordoes:** destroys

OPHELIA   No, my good lord, but as you did command
    I did repel his letters, and denied
    His access to me.
POLONIUS   That hath made him mad.
120   I am sorry that with better heed and judgment
    I had not coted him. I fear'd he did but trifle
    And meant to wrack thee, but beshrew my jealousy!
    By heaven, it is as proper to our age
    To cast beyond ourselves in our opinions,
125   As it is common for the younger sort
    To lack discretion. Come, go we to the King.
    This must be known, which, being kept close, might move
    More grief to hide, than hate to utter love.
    Come.

(*Exeunt.*)

[Scene II]

(*Flourish. Enter* KING *and* QUEEN, ROSENCRANTZ *and* GUILDENSTERN [*cum aliis*].)

KING   Welcome, dear Rosencrantz and Guildenstern!
    Moreover that we much did long to see you,
    The need we have to use you did provoke
    Our hasty sending. Something have you heard
5   Of Hamlet's transformation; so call it,
    Sith nor th' exterior nor the inward man
    Resembles that it was. What it should be,
    More than his father's death, that thus hath put him
    So much from th' understanding of himself,
10   I cannot dream of. I entreat you both
    That, being of so young days brought up with him,
    And sith so neighbored to his youth and havior,
    That you voutsafe your rest here in our court
    Some little time, so by your companies
15   To draw him on to pleasures, and to gather
    So much as from occasion you may glean,
    Whether aught to us unknown afflicts him thus,
    That, open'd, lies within our remedy.

---

121. **coted:** observed   122. **beshrow:** beshrew, plague take   **jealousy:** suspicious mind
123. **proper . . . age:** characteristic of men of my age   124. **cast beyond ourselves:** overshoot, go too
far (by way of caution)   127. **close:** secret   127–128. **move . . . love:** cause more grievous consequences by its concealment than we shall incur displeasure by making it known

II.ii. Location: the castle   2. **Moreover . . . you:** besides the fact that we wanted to see you for your
own sakes   6. **Sith:** since   11. **of:** from   13. **voutsafe your rest:** vouchsafe to remain

QUEEN   Good gentlemen, he hath much talk'd of you,
20   And sure I am two men there is not living
          To whom he more adheres. If it will please you
          To show us so much gentry and good will
          As to expend your time with us a while
          For the supply and profit of our hope,
25   Your visitation shall receive such thanks
          As fits a king's remembrance.
ROSENCRANTZ   Both your Majesties
          Might, by the sovereign power you have of us,
          Put your dread pleasures more into command
30   Than to entreaty.
GUILDENSTERN   But we both obey,
          And here give up ourselves, in the full bent,
          To lay our service freely at your feet,
          To be commanded.
35 KING   Thanks, Rosencrantz and gentle Guildenstern.
QUEEN   Thanks, Guildenstern and gentle Rosencrantz.
          And I beseech you instantly to visit
          My too much changed son. Go some of you
          And bring these gentlemen where Hamlet is.
40 GUILDENSTERN   Heavens make our presence and our practices
          Pleasant and helpful to him!
QUEEN   Ay, amen!

(*Exeunt* ROSENCRANTZ *and* GUILDENSTERN [*with some* ATTENDANTS].)

(*Enter* POLONIUS.)

POLONIUS   Th' embassadors from Norway, my good lord,
          Are joyfully return'd.
45 KING   Thou still hast been the father of good news.
POLONIUS   Have I, my lord? I assure my good liege
          I hold my duty as I hold my soul,
          Both to my God and to my gracious king;
          And I do think, or else this brain of mine
50   Hunts not the trail of policy so sure
          As it hath us'd to do, that I have found
          The very cause of Hamlet's lunacy.
KING   O, speak of that, that do I long to hear.

---

21. **more adheres:** is more attached   22. **gentry:** courtesy   24. **supply and profit:** support and
advancement   32. **in . . . bent:** to our utmost   43. **embassadors:** ambassadors
45. **still:** always   46. **liege:** sovereign   50. **policy:** statecraft

POLONIUS   Give first admittance to th' embassadors;
55   My news shall be the fruit to that great feast.
   KING   Thyself do grace to them, and bring them in.   [*Exit* POLONIUS.]
        He tells me, my dear Gertrude, he hath found
        The head and source of all your son's distemper.
   QUEEN   I doubt it is no other but the main,
60   His father's death and our [o'erhasty] marriage.

(*Enter* [POLONIUS *with* VOLTEMAND *and* CORNELIUS, *the*] EMBASSADORS.)

   KING   Well, we shall sift him.—Welcome, my good friends!
        Say, Voltemand, what from our brother Norway?
   VOLTEMAND   Most fair return of greetings and desires.
        Upon our first, he sent out to suppress
65   His nephew's levies, which to him appear'd
        To be a preparation 'gainst the Polack;
        But better look'd into, he truly found
        It was against your Highness. Whereat griev'd,
        That so his sickness, age, and impotence
70   Was falsely borne in hand, sends out arrests
        On Fortinbras, which he, in brief, obeys,
        Receives rebuke from Norway, and in fine,
        Makes vow before his uncle never more
        To give th' assay of arms against your Majesty.
75   Whereon old Norway, overcome with joy,
        Gives him threescore thousand crowns in annual fee,
        And his commission to employ those soldiers,
        So levied, as before, against the Polack,
        With an entreaty, herein further shown,   [*giving a paper*]
80   That it might please you to give quiet pass
        Through your dominions for this enterprise,
        On such regards of safety and allowance
        As therein are set down.
   KING   It likes us well,
85   And at our more considered time we'll read,
        Answer, and think upon this business.
        Mean time, we thank you for your well-took labor.
        Go to your rest, at night we'll feast together.
        Most welcome home!

---

55. **fruit:** dessert   58. **head:** synonymous with *source*   **distemper:** (mental) illness   59. **doubt:** suspect   **main:** main cause   64. **Upon our first:** at our first representation   68. **griev'd:** aggrieved, offended   70. **borne in hand:** taken advantage of   72. **in fine:** in the end   74. **assay:** trial   82. **On . . . allowance:** with such safeguards and provisos   84. **likes:** pleases   85. **consider'd:** suitable for consideration

(*Exeunt* EMBASSADORS [*and* ATTENDANTS].)

90 POLONIUS   This business is well ended.
My liege, and madam, to expostulate
What majesty should be, what duty is,
Why day is day, night night, and time is time,
Were nothing but to waste night, day, and time;
95   Therefore, [since] brevity is the soul of wit,
And tediousness the limbs and outward flourishes,
I will be brief. Your noble son is mad:
Mad call I it, for to define true madness,
What is't but to be nothing else but mad?
100   But let that go.
QUEEN   More matter with less art.
POLONIUS   Madam, I swear I use no art at all.
That he's mad, 'tis true, 'tis true 'tis pity,
And pity 'tis 'tis true—a foolish figure,
105   But farewell it, for I will use no art.
Mad let us grant him then, and now remains
That we find out the cause of this effect,
Or rather say, the cause of this defect,
For this effect defective comes by cause:
110   Thus it remains, and the remainder thus.
Perpend.
I have a daughter—have while she is mine—
Who in her duty and obedience, mark,
Hath given me this. Now gather, and surmise.

[*reads the salutation of the letter*]

115   "To the celestial and my soul's idol, the most beautified Ophelia"—
That's an ill phrase, a vile phrase, "beautified" is a vile phrase. But you shall
hear. Thus:
"In her excellent white bosom, these, etc."
QUEEN   Came this from Hamlet to her?
120 POLONIUS   Good madam, stay awhile. I will be faithful.

([*reads the*] *letter*)
          "Doubt thou the stars are fire,

---

91. **expostulate:** expound   95. **wit:** understanding, wisdom   101. **art:** rhetorical art
104. **figure:** figure of speech   109. **For . . . cause:** for this effect (which shows as a defect in Hamlet's
reason) is not merely accidental, and has a cause we may trace   111. **Perpend:** consider
115. **beautified:** beautiful (not an uncommon usage)

Doubt that the sun doth move,
Doubt truth to be a liar,
But never doubt I love.

125 O dear Ophelia, I am ill at these numbers. I have not art to reckon my
groans, but that I love thee best, O most best, believe it. Adieu.
   Thine evermore, most dear lady,
      whilst this machine is to him, Hamlet."
This in obedience hath my daughter shown me,
130 And more [above], hath his solicitings,
As they fell out by time, by means, and place,
All given to mine ear.

KING   But how hath she
Receiv'd his love?

135 POLONIUS   What do you think of me?
KING   As of a man faithful and honorable.
POLONIUS   I would fain prove so. But what might you think,
When I had seen this hot love on the wing—
As I perceiv'd it (I must tell you that)
140 Before my daughter told me—what might you,
Or my dear Majesty your queen here, think,
If I had play'd the desk or table-book,
Or given my heart a [winking,] mute and dumb,
Or look'd upon this love with idle sight,
145 What might you think? No, I went round to work,
And my young mistress thus I did bespeak:
"Lord Hamlet is a prince out of thy star;
This must not be"; and then I prescripts gave her,
That she should lock herself from [his] resort,
150 Admit no messengers, receive no tokens.
Which done, she took the fruits of my advice;
And he repell'd, a short tale to make,
Fell into a sadness, then into a fast,
Thence to a watch, thence into a weakness,
155 Thence to [a] lightness, and by this declension,
Into the madness wherein now he raves,
And all we mourn for.

---

124. **Doubt:** suspect   125. **ill . . . numbers:** bad at versifying   **reckon:** count (with a quibble on
numbers)   128. **machine:** body   130. **more above:** furthermore   137. **fain:** willingly, gladly
142. **play'd . . . table-book:** noted the matter secretly   143. **winking:** closing of the eyes
144. **idle sight:** noncomprehending eyes   145. **round:** straightforwardly   146. **bespeak:** address
147. **star:** sphere, lot in life   151. **took . . . of:** profited by, carried out   152. **repell'd:** repulsed
154. **watch:** sleeplessness   155. **lightness:** lightheadedness

KING   Do you think ['tis] this?

QUEEN   It may be, very like.

160   POLONIUS   Hath there been such a time—I would fain know that—
    That I have positively said, " 'Tis so,"
    When it prov'd otherwise?

KING   Not that I know.

POLONIUS [*points to his head and shoulder*]   Take this from this, if this be

165   otherwise.
    If circumstances lead me, I will find
    Where truth is hid, though it were hid indeed
    Within the centre.

KING   How may we try it further?

170   POLONIUS   You know sometimes he walks four hours together
    Here in the lobby.

QUEEN   So he does indeed.

POLONIUS   At such a time I'll loose my daughter to him.
    Be you and I behind an arras then,

175   Mark the encounter: if he love her not,
    And be not from his reason fall'n thereon,
    Let me be no assistant for a state,
    But keep a farm and carters.

KING   We will try it.

(*Enter* HAMLET [*reading on a book*].)

180   QUEEN   But look where sadly the poor wretch comes reading.

POLONIUS   Away, I do beseech you, both away.
    I'll board him presently.

(*Exeunt* KING *and* QUEEN.)
                   O, give me leave,
    How does my good Lord Hamlet?

185   HAMLET   Well, God-a-mercy.

POLONIUS   Do you know me, my lord?

HAMLET   Excellent well, you are a fishmonger.

POLONIUS   Not I, my lord.

HAMLET   Then I would you were so honest a man.

190   POLONIUS   Honest, my lord?

HAMLET   Ay, sir, to be honest, as this world goes, is to be one man pick'd out of
    ten thousand.

POLONIUS   That's very true, my lord.

---

168. **centre:** of the earth (which in the Ptolemaic system is also the centre of the universe)
174. **arras:** hanging tapestry 176. **thereon:** because of that 182. **board:** accost **presently:**
at once 185. **God-a-mercy:** thank you 187. **fishmonger:** Usually explained as slang for "bawd,"
but no evidence has been produced for such a usage in Shakespeare's day.

HAMLET   For if the sun breed maggots in a dead dog, being a good kissing car-
195   rion—Have you a daughter?
POLONIUS   I have, my lord.
HAMLET   Let her not walk i' th' sun. Conception is a blessing, but as your
daughter may conceive, friend, look to't.
POLONIUS [*aside*]   How say you by that? still harping on my daughter. Yet he
200   knew me not at first, 'a said I was a fishmonger. 'A is far gone. And truly in
my youth I suff'red much extremity for love—very near this. I'll speak to
him again.—What do you read, my lord?
HAMLET   Words, words, words.
POLONIUS   What is the matter, my lord?
205 HAMLET   Between who?
POLONIUS   I mean, the matter that you read, my lord.
HAMLET   Slanders, sir; for the satirical rogue says here that old men have grey
beards, that their faces are wrinkled, their eyes purging thick amber and
plumtree gum, and that they have a plentiful lack of wit, together with most
210   weak hams; all which, sir, though I most powerfully and potently believe, yet
I hold it not honesty to have it thus set down, for yourself, sir, shall grow old
as I am, if like a crab you could go backward.
POLONIUS [*aside*]   Though this be madness, yet there is method in't.—Will
you walk out of the air, my lord?
215 HAMLET   Into my grave.
POLONIUS   Indeed that's out of the air. [*aside*] How pregnant sometimes his
replies are! a happiness that often madness hits on, which reason and [san-
ity] could not so prosperously be deliver'd of. I will leave him, [and suddenly contrive the means of meeting between him] and my daughter.—My
220   lord, I will take my leave of you.
HAMLET   You cannot take from me any thing that I will not more willingly part
withal—except my life, except my life, except my life.
POLONIUS   Fare you well, my lord.
HAMLET   These tedious old fools!

(*Enter* GUILDENSTERN *and* ROSENCRANTZ.)

225 POLONIUS   You go to seek the Lord Hamlet, there he is.
ROSENCRANTZ [*to* POLONIUS]   God save you, sir!

[*Exit* POLONIUS.]

GUILDENSTERN   My honor'd lord!

194–95. **good kissing carrion:** flesh good enough for the sun to kiss   197. **Conception:** understanding (with following play on the sense "conceiving a child")   204. **matter:** subject; but Hamlet replies
as if he had understood Polonius to mean "cause for a quarrel."   211. **honesty:** a fitting thing
213. **method:** orderly arrangement, sequence of ideas   214. **out . . . air:** Outdoor air was thought to
be bad for invalids.   216. **pregnant:** apt   218–19. **suddenly:** at once

ROSENCRANTZ   My most dear lord!

HAMLET   My [excellent] good friends! How dost thou, Guildenstern? Ah,
230　　Rosencrantz! Good lads, how do you both?

ROSENCRANTZ   As the indifferent children of the earth.

GUILDENSTERN   Happy, in that we are not [over-]happy, on Fortune's [cap] we
　　are not the very button.

HAMLET   Nor the soles of her shoe?

235 ROSENCRANTZ   Neither, my lord.

HAMLET   Then you live about her waist, or in the middle of her favors?

GUILDENSTERN   Faith, her privates we.

HAMLET   In the secret parts of Fortune? O, most true, she is a strumpet. What
　　news?

240 ROSENCRANTZ   None, my lord, but the world's grown honest.

HAMLET   Then is doomsday near. But your news is not true. [Let me question
　　more in particular. What have you, my good friends, deserv'd at the hands
　　of Fortune, that she sends you to prison hither?

GUILDENSTERN   Prison, my lord?

245 HAMLET   Denmark's a prison.

ROSENCRANTZ   Then is the world one.

HAMLET   A goodly one, in which there are many confines, wards, and dun-
　　geons, Denmark being one o' th' worst.

ROSENCRANTZ   We think not so, my lord.

250 HAMLET   Why then 'tis none to you; for there is nothing either good or bad, but
　　thinking makes it so. To me it is a prison.

ROSENCRANTZ   Why then your ambition makes it one. 'Tis too narrow for your
　　mind.

HAMLET   O God, I could be bounded in a nutshell, and count myself a king of
255　　infinite space—were it not that I have bad dreams.

GUILDENSTERN   Which dreams indeed are ambition, for the very substance of
　　the ambitious is merely the shadow of a dream.

HAMLET   A dream itself is but a shadow.

ROSENCRANTZ   Truly, and I hold ambition of so airy and light a quality that it is
260　　but a shadow's shadow.

HAMLET   Then are our beggars bodies, and our monarchs and outstretch'd
　　heroes the beggars' shadows. Shall we to th' court? for, by my fay, I cannot
　　reason.

BOTH [ROSENCRANTZ, GUILDENSTERN]   We'll wait upon you.

265 HAMLET   No such matter. I will not sort you with the rest of my servants; for to
　　speak to you like an honest man, I am most dreadfully attended.] But in the
　　beaten way of friendship, what make you at Elsinore?

---

231. **indifferent:** average   237. **privates:** (1) intimate friends; (2) genitalia   238. **strumpet:** a common epithet for Fortune, because she grants favors to all men   247. **wards:** cells   261. **bodies:** not
shadows (since they lack ambition)   **outstretch'd:** with their ambition extended to the utmost (and
hence producing stretched-out or elongated shadows)   262. **fay:** faith   264. **wait upon you:** attend
you thither   265. **sort:** associate   266. **dreadfully:** execrably

ROSENCRANTZ   To visit you, my lord, no other occasion.

HAMLET   Beggar that I am, I am [even] poor in thanks—but I thank you, and
270   sure, dear friends, my thanks are too dear a halfpenny. Were you not sent
for? is it your own inclining? is it a free visitation? Come, come, deal justly
with me. Come, come—nay, speak.

GUILDENSTERN   What should we say, my lord?

HAMLET   Any thing but to th' purpose. You were sent for, and there is a kind of
275   confession in your looks, which your modesties have not craft enough to
color. I know the good King and Queen have sent for you.

ROSENCRANTZ   To what end, my lord?

HAMLET   That you must teach me. But let me conjure you, by the rights of our
fellowship, by the consonancy of our youth, by the obligation of our ever-
280   preserv'd love, and by what more dear a better proposer can charge you
withal, be even and direct with me, whether you were sent for or no!

ROSENCRANTZ [aside to GUILDENSTERN]   What say you?

HAMLET [aside]   Nay then I have an eye of you!—If you love me, hold not off.

GUILDENSTERN   My lord, we were sent for.

285   HAMLET   I will tell you why, so shall my anticipation prevent your discovery,
and your secrecy to the King and Queen moult no feather. I have of late—
but wherefore I know not—lost all my mirth, forgone all custom of exercises; and indeed it goes so heavily with my disposition, that this goodly
frame, the earth, seems to me a sterile promontory; this most excellent
290   canopy, the air, look you, this brave o'erhanging firmament, this majestical
roof fretted with golden fire, why, it appeareth nothing to me but a foul and
pestilent congregation of vapors. What [a] piece of work is a man, how noble in reason, how infinite in faculties, in form and moving, how express
and admirable in action, how like an angel in apprehension, how like a god!
295   the beauty of the world; the paragon of animals; and yet to me what is this
quintessence of dust? Man delights not me—nor women neither, though by
your smiling you seem to say so.

ROSENCRANTZ   My lord, there was no such stuff in my thoughts.

HAMLET   Why did ye laugh then, when I said, "Man delights not me"?

300   ROSENCRANTZ   To think, my lord, if you delight not in man, what lenten entertainment the players shall receive from you. We coted them on the way, and
hither are they coming to offer you service.

---

270. **too . . . halfpenny:** too expensive priced at a halfpenny; not worth much   271. **justly:** honestly
274. **but:** Ordinarily punctuated with a comma preceding, to give the sense "provided that it is"; but
Q2 has no comma, and Hamlet may intend, or include, the sense "except."   275. **modesties:** sense of
shame   279. **consonancy . . . youth:** similarity of our ages   280. **charge:** urge, adjure   **even:** frank,
honest (cf. modern "level with me")   283. **of:** on   285. **prevent your discovery:** forestall your disclosure (of what the king and queen have said to you in confidence)   286. **moult no feather:** not be
impaired in the least   287–88. **custom of exercises:** my usual athletic activities   290. **brave:** splendid   291. **fretted:** ornamented as with fretwork   292. **piece of work:** masterpiece   293–94. **how
infinite . . . god:** See the Textual Notes for the different punctuation in F1.   293. **express:** exact
296. **quintessence:** finest and purest extract   300–301. **lenten entertainment:** meagre reception
301. **coted:** outstripped

HAMLET   He that plays the king shall be welcome—his Majesty shall have tribute on me, the adventerous knight shall use his foil and target, the lover
305   shall not sigh gratis, the humorous man shall end his part in peace, [the
clown shall make those laugh whose lungs are [tickle] a' th' sere,] and the
lady shall say her mind freely, or the [blank] verse shall halt for't. What players are they?

ROSENCRANTZ   Even those you were wont to take such delight in, the tragedi-
310   ans of the city.

HAMLET   How chances it they travel? Their residence, both in reputation and
profit, was better both ways.

ROSENCRANTZ   I think their inhibition comes by the means of the late innovation.

315   HAMLET   Do they hold the same estimation they did when I was in the city? Are
they so follow'd?

ROSENCRANTZ   No indeed are they not.

[HAMLET   How comes it? do they grow rusty?

ROSENCRANTZ   Nay, their endeavor keeps in the wonted pace; but there is, sir,
320   an aery of children, little eyases, that cry out on the top of question, and are
most tyrannically clapp'd for't. These are now the fashion, and so [berattle]
the common stages—so they call them—that many wearing rapiers are
afraid of goose-quills and dare scarce come thither.

HAMLET   What, are they children? Who maintains 'em? How are they escoted?
325   Will they pursue the quality no longer than they can sing? Will they not say
afterwards, if they should grow themselves to common players (as it is

---

304. **on:** of, from   **adventerous:** adventurous, wandering in search of adventure   **foil and target:**
light fencing sword and small shield   305. **gratis:** without reward   **humorous:** dominated by some
eccentric trait (like the melancholy Jaques in *As You Like It*)   306. **tickle . . . sere:** easily made to
laugh (literally, describing a gun that goes off easily; *sere* = a catch in the gunlock; *tickle* = easily affected, highly sensitive to stimulus)   307. **halt:** limp, come off lamely (the verse will not scan if she
omits indecent words)   313. **inhibition:** hindrance (to playing in the city). The word could be used
of an official prohibition. See next note.   313–314. **innovation:** Shakespeare elsewhere uses this
word of a political uprising or revolt, and lines 313–314 are often explained as meaning that the
company had been forbidden to play in the city as the result of some disturbance. It is commonly
conjectured that the allusion is to the Essex rebellion of 1601, but it is known that Shakespeare's
company, though to some extent involved on account of the special performance of *Richard II* they
were commissioned to give on the eve of the rising, were not in fact punished by inhibition. A second
interpretation explains *innovation* as referring to the new theatrical vogue described in lines 320 ff.,
and conjectures that *inhibition* may allude to a Privy Council order of 1600 restricting the number of
London playhouses to two and the number of performances to two a week.   318–336. **How . . . too:**
This passage refers topically to the "War of the Theatres" between the child actors and their poet Jon-
son on the one side, and on the other the adults, with Dekker, Marston, and possibly Shakespeare as
spokesmen, in 1600–1601.   320. **aery:** nest   **eyases:** unfledged hawks   **cry . . . question:** cry
shrilly above others in controversy   321. **tyrannically:** outrageously   **berattle:** cry down, satirize
322. **common stages:** public theatres (the children played at the Blackfriars, a private theatre)
323. **goose-quills:** pens (of satirical playwrights)   324. **escoted:** supported   325. **quality:** profession (of acting)   **no . . . sing:** only until their voices change

[most like], if their means are [no] better), their writers do them wrong, to make them exclaim against their own succession?

ROSENCRANTZ   Faith, there has been much to do on both sides, and the nation

330   holds it no sin to tarre them to controversy. There was for a while no money bid for argument, unless the poet and the player went to cuffs in the question.

HAMLET   Is't possible?

GUILDENSTERN   O, there has been much throwing about of brains.

335   HAMLET   Do the boys carry it away?

ROSENCRANTZ   Ay, that they do, my lord—Hercules and his load too.]

HAMLET   It is not very strange, for my uncle is King of Denmark, and those that would make mouths at him while my father liv'd, give twenty, forty, fifty, a hundred ducats a-piece for his picture in little. 'Sblood, there is something

340   in this more than natural, if philosophy could find it out. (*a flourish [for the* PLAYERS])

GUILDENSTERN   There are the players.

HAMLET   Gentlemen, you are welcome to Elsinore. Your hands, come then: th' appurtenance of welcome is fashion and ceremony. Let me comply with you

345   in this garb, [lest my] extent to the players, which, I tell you, must show fairly outwards, should more appear like entertainment than yours. You are welcome; but my uncle-father and aunt-mother are deceiv'd.

GUILDENSTERN   In what, my dear lord?

HAMLET   I am but mad north-north-west. When the wind is southerly I know a

350   hawk from a hand-saw.

(*Enter* POLONIUS.)

POLONIUS   Well be with you, gentlemen!

HAMLET [*aside to them*]   Hark you, Guildenstern, and you too—at each ear a hearer—that great baby you see there is not yet out of his swaddling-clouts.

ROSENCRANTZ   Happily he is the second time come to them, for they say an old

355   man is twice a child.

HAMLET   I will prophesy, he comes to tell me of the players, mark it. [*aloud*] You say right, sir, a' Monday morning, 'twas then indeed.

POLONIUS   My lord, I have news to tell you.

---

328. **succession:** future   329. **to do:** ado   330. **tarre:** incite   331. **argument:** plot of a play 331–32. **in the question:** as part of the script   335. **carry it away:** win   336. **Hercules . . . too:** Hercules in the course of one of his twelve labors supported the world for Atlas; the children do better, for they carry away the world and Hercules as well. There is an allusion to the Globe playhouse, which reportedly had for its sign the figure of Hercules upholding the world.   338. **mouths:** derisive faces   339. **'Sblood:** by God's (Christ's) blood   344. **comply:** observe the formalities   345. **garb:** fashion, manner   **my extent:** the degree of courtesy I show   346. **more . . . yours:** seem to be a warmer reception than I have given you   350. **hawk, hand-saw:** both cutting tools; but also both birds, if *hand-saw* quibbles on *hernshaw,* "heron," a bird preyed upon by the hawk   353. **swaddling-clouts:** swaddling clothes   354. **Happily:** haply, perhaps   355. **twice:** for the second time

HAMLET   My lord, I have news to tell you. When Roscius was an actor in
360   Rome—
POLONIUS   The actors are come hither, my lord.
HAMLET   Buzz, buzz!
POLONIUS   Upon my honor—
HAMLET   "Then came each actor on his ass"—
365 POLONIUS   The best actors in the world, either for tragedy, comedy, history,
        pastoral, pastoral-comical, historical-pastoral, [tragical-historical, tragical-
        comical-historical-pastoral,] scene individable, or poem unlimited; Seneca
        cannot be too heavy, nor Plautus too light, for the law of writ and the lib-
        erty: these are the only men.
370 HAMLET   O Jephthah, judge of Israel, what a treasure hadst thou!
POLONIUS   What a treasure had he, my lord?
HAMLET   Why—
            "One fair daughter, and no more,
            The which he loved passing well."
375 POLONIUS [*aside*]   Still on my daughter.
HAMLET   Am I not i' th' right, old Jephthah?
POLONIUS   If you call me Jephthah, my lord, I have a daughter that I love pass-
        ing well.
HAMLET   Nay, that follows not.
380 POLONIUS   What follows then, my lord?
HAMLET   Why—
            "As by lot, God wot,"
    and then, you know,
            "It came to pass, as most like it was"—
385   the first row of the pious chanson will show you more, for look where my
        abridgment comes.

(*Enter the* PLAYERS, [*four or five*].)

    You are welcome, masters, welcome all. I am glad to see thee well. Welcome,
    good friends. O, old friend! why, thy face is valanc'd since I saw thee last;
    com'st thou to beard me in Denmark? What, my young lady and mistress!

---

359. **Roscius:** the most famous of Roman actors (died 62 B.C.). News about him would be stale news
indeed.   362. **Buzz:** exclamation of impatience at someone who tells news already known
367. **scene individable:** play observing the unity of place   **poem unlimited:** play ignoring rules
such as the three unities   **Seneca:** Roman writer of tragedies   368. **Plautus:** Roman writer of
comedies   368–69. **for . . . liberty:** for strict observance of the rules, or for freedom from them
(with possible allusion to the location of playhouses, which were not built in properties under city
jurisdiction, but in the "liberties"—land once monastic and now outside the jurisdiction of the city
authorities)   369. **only:** very best (a frequent use)   370. **Jephthah . . . Israel:** title of a ballad, from
which Hamlet goes on to quote. For the story of Jephthah and his daughter, see Judges 11.
385. **row:** stanza   **chanson:** song, ballad   386. **abridgment:** (1) interruption; (2) pastime
388. **valanc'd:** fringed, bearded   389. **beard:** confront boldly (with obvious pun)

390   by' lady, your ladyship is nearer to heaven than when I saw you last, by the
altitude of a chopine. Pray God your voice, like a piece of uncurrent gold, be
not crack'd within the ring. Masters, you are all welcome. We'll e'en to't like
[French] falc'ners—fly at any thing we see; we'll have a speech straight.
Come give us a taste of your quality, come, a passionate speech.

395   [1.] PLAYER   What speech, my good lord?

    HAMLET   I heard thee speak me a speech once, but it was never acted, or if it
was, not above once; for the play, I remember, pleas'd not the million, 'twas
caviary to the general, but it was—as I receiv'd it, and others, whose judgments in such matters cried in the top of mine—an excellent play, well di-
400   gested in the scenes, set down with as much modesty as cunning. I remember one said there were no sallets in the lines to make the matter savory, nor
no matter in the phrase that might indict the author of affection, but call'd
it an honest method, as wholesome as sweet, and by very much more handsome than fine. One speech in't I chiefly lov'd, 'twas Aeneas' [tale] to Dido,
405   and thereabout of it especially when he speaks of Priam's slaughter. If it live
in your memory, begin at this line—let me see, let me see:
"The rugged Pyrrhus, like th' Hyrcanian beast—"
'Tis not so, it begins with Pyrrhus:
"The rugged Pyrrhus, he whose sable arms,
410   Black as his purpose, did the night resemble
When he lay couched in th' ominous horse,
Hath now this dread and black complexion smear'd
With heraldy more dismal: head to foot
Now is he total gules, horridly trick'd
415   With blood of fathers, mothers, daughters, sons,
Bak'd and impasted with the parching streets,
That lend a tyrannous and a damned light
To their lord's murther. Roasted in wrath and fire,
And thus o'er-sized with coagulate gore,

---

390. **by' lady:** by Our Lady   391. **chopine:** thick-soled shoe   392. **crack'd . . . ring:** broken to the
point where you can no longer play female roles. A coin with a crack extending far enough in from
the edge to cross the circle surrounding the stamp of the sovereign's head was unacceptable in exchange (*uncurrent*).   393. **straight:** straightway   394. **quality:** professional skill   398. **caviary . . .
general:** caviare to the common people, too choice for the multitude   399. **cried . . . of:** were louder
than, carried more authority than   401. **sallets:** salads, spicy jokes   **savory:** zesty   402. **affection:**
affectation   404. **fine:** showily dressed (in language)   405. **Priam's slaughter:** the slaying of Priam
(at the fall of Troy)   407. **Pyrrhus:** another name for Neoptolemus, Achilles' son   **Hyrcanian
beast:** Hyrcania in the Caucasus was notorious for its tigers.   409. **sable arms:** The Greeks within
the Trojan horse had blackened their skin so as to be inconspicuous when they emerged at night.
413. **heraldy:** heraldry   **dismal:** ill-boding   414. **gules:** red (heraldic term)   **trick'd:** adorned
416. **Bak'd:** caked   **impasted:** crusted   **with . . . streets:** by the heat from the burning streets
419. **o'er-sized:** covered over as with a coat of sizing

420   With eyes like carbuncles, the hellish Pyrrhus
    Old grandsire Priam seeks."
    So proceed you.
 POLONIUS 'Fore God, my lord, well spoken, with good accent and good
    discretion.
425 [1.] PLAYER   "Anon he finds him
    Striking too short at Greeks. His antique sword,
    Rebellious to his arm, lies where it falls,
    Repugnant to command. Unequal match'd,
    Pyrrhus at Priam drives, in rage strikes wide,
430   But with the whiff and wind of his fell sword
    Th' unnerved father falls. [Then senseless Ilium,]
    Seeming to feel this blow, with flaming top
    Stoops to his base, and with a hideous crash
    Takes prisoner Pyrrhus' ear; for lo his sword,
435   Which was declining on the milky head
    Of reverent Priam, seem'd i' th' air to stick.
    So as a painted tyrant Pyrrhus stood
    [And,] like a neutral to his will and matter,
    Did nothing.
440   But as we often see, against some storm,
    A silence in the heavens, the rack stand still,
    The bold winds speechless, and the orb below
    As hush as death, anon the dreadful thunder
    Doth rend the region; so after Pyrrhus' pause,
445   A roused vengeance sets him new a-work,
    And never did the Cyclops' hammers fall
    On Mars's armor forg'd for proof eterne
    With less remorse than Pyrrhus' bleeding sword
    Now falls on Priam.
450   Out, out, thou strumpet Fortune! All you gods,
    In general synod take away her power!
    Break all the spokes and [fellies] from her wheel,
    And bowl the round nave down the hill of heaven
    As low as to the fiends!"
455 POLONIUS This is too long.

---

420. **carbuncles:** jewels believed to shine in the dark 428. **Repugnant:** resistant, hostile 430. **fell:** cruel 431. **unnerved:** drained of strength **senseless:** insensible **Ilium:** the citadel of Troy 436. **reverent:** reverend, aged 438. **like ... matter:** poised midway between intention and performance 440. **against:** just before 441. **rack:** cloud-mass 444. **region:** air 446. **Cyclops:** giants who worked in Vulcan's smithy, where armor was made for the gods 447. **proof eterne:** eternal endurance 448. **remorse:** pity 452. **fellies:** rims 453. **nave:** hub

HAMLET   It shall to the barber's with your beard. Prithee say on, he's for a jig
or a tale of bawdry, or he sleeps. Say on, come to Hecuba.
[1.] PLAYER   "But who, ah woe, had seen the mobled queen"—
HAMLET   "The mobled queen"?
460   POLONIUS   That's good, ["[mobled] queen" is good] .
[1.] PLAYER   "Run barefoot up and down, threat'ning the flames
With bisson rheum, a clout upon that head
Where late the diadem stood, and for a robe,
About her lank and all o'er-teemed loins,
465   A blanket, in the alarm of fear caught up—
Who this had seen, with tongue in venom steep'd,
'Gainst Fortune's state would treason have pronounc'd.
But if the gods themselves did see her then,
When she saw Pyrrhus make malicious sport
470   In mincing with his sword her [husband's] limbs,
The instant burst of clamor that she made,
Unless things mortal move them not at all,
Would have made milch the burning eyes of heaven,
And passion in the gods."
475   POLONIUS   Look whe'er he has not turn'd his color and has tears in 's eyes.
Prithee no more.
HAMLET   'Tis well, I'll have thee speak out the rest of this soon. Good my lord,
will you see the players well bestow'd? Do you hear, let them be well us'd, for
they are the abstract and brief chronicles of the time. After your death you
480   were better have a bad epitaph than their ill report while you live.
POLONIUS   My lord, I will use them according to their desert.
HAMLET   God's bodkin, man, much better: use every man after his desert, and
who shall scape whipping? Use them after your own honor and dignity—
the less they deserve, the more merit is in your bounty. Take them in.
485   POLONIUS   Come, sirs.

[*Exit.*]

HAMLET   Follow him, friends, we'll hear a play tomorrow.

[*Exeunt all the* PLAYERS *but the* FIRST.]

Dost thou hear me, old friend? Can you play "The Murther of Gonzago"?
[1.] PLAYER   Ay, my lord.

---

456. **jig:** song-and-dance entertainment performed after the main play   460. **mobled:** muffled
462. **bisson rheum:** blinding tears   **clout:** cloth   464. **o'er-teemed:** worn out by childbearing
467. **state:** rule, government   473. **milch:** moist (literally, milky)   474. **passion:** grief
475. **Look . . . not:** note how he has   478. **bestow'd:** lodged   **us'd:** treated   482. **God's bodkin:** by
God's (Christ's) little body

490 HAMLET   We'll ha't to-morrow night. You could for need study a speech of
some dozen lines, or sixteen lines, which I would set down and insert in't,
could you not?

[1.] PLAYER   Ay, my lord.

HAMLET   Very well. Follow that lord, and look you mock him not.

[*Exit* FIRST PLAYER.]

495   My good friends, I'll leave you [till] night. You are welcome to Elsinore.

ROSENCRANTZ   Good my lord!

HAMLET   Ay so, God buy to you.

(*Exeunt* [ROSENCRANTZ *and* GUILDENSTERN].)

                                                    Now I am alone.
500   O, what a rogue and peasant slave am I!
           Is it not monstrous that this player here,
           But in a fiction, in a dream of passion,
           Could force his soul so to his own conceit
           That from her working all the visage wann'd,
505   Tears in his eyes, distraction in his aspect,
           A broken voice, an' his whole function suiting
           With forms to his conceit? And all for nothing,
           For Hecuba!
           What's Hecuba to him, or he to [Hecuba],
510   That he should weep for her? What would he do
           Had he the motive and [the cue] for passion
           That I have? He would drown the stage with tears,
           And cleave the general ear with horrid speech,
           Make mad the guilty, and appall the free,
515   Confound the ignorant, and amaze indeed
           The very faculties of eyes and ears. Yet I,
           A dull and muddy-mettled rascal, peak
           Like John-a-dreams, unpregnant of my cause,
           And can say nothing; no, not for a king,
520   Upon whose property and most dear life
           A damn'd defeat was made. Am I a coward?
           Who calls me villain, breaks my pate across,

---

490. **for need:** if necessary   503. **conceit:** imaginative conception   506. **his whole function:** the
operation of his whole body   507. **forms:** actions, expressions   514. **free:** innocent   515. **amaze:**
confound   517. **muddy-mettled:** dull-spirited   **peak:** mope   518. **John-a-dreams:** a sleepy
fellow   **unpregnant of:** unquickened by   521. **defeat:** destruction

Plucks off my beard and blows it in my face,
Tweaks me by the nose, gives me the lie i' th' throat
525   As deep as to the lungs? Who does me this?
Hah, 'swounds, I should take it; for it cannot be
But I am pigeon-liver'd, and lack gall
To make oppression bitter, or ere this
I should 'a' fatted all the region kites
530   With this slave's offal. Bloody, bawdy villain!
Remorseless, treacherous, lecherous, kindless villain!
Why, what an ass am I! This is most brave,
That I, the son of a dear [father] murthered,
Prompted to my revenge by heaven and hell,
535   Must like a whore unpack my heart with words,
And fall a-cursing like a very drab,
A stallion. Fie upon't, foh!
About, my brains! Hum—I have heard
That guilty creatures sitting at a play
540   Have by the very cunning of the scene
Been strook so to the soul, that presently
They have proclaim'd their malefactions:
For murther, though it have no tongue, will speak
With most miraculous organ. I'll have these players
545   Play something like the murther of my father
Before mine uncle. I'll observe his looks,
I'll tent him to the quick. If 'a do blench,
I know my course. The spirit that I have seen
May be a [dev'l], and the [dev'l] hath power
550   T' assume a pleasing shape, yea, and perhaps,
Out of my weakness and my melancholy,
As he is very potent with such spirits,
Abuses me to damn me. I'll have grounds
More relative than this—the play's the thing
555   Wherein I'll catch the conscience of the King.

(*Exit.*)

524–25. **gives . . . lungs:** calls me a liar in the extremest degree   526. **'swounds:** by God's (Christ's) wounds   **should:** would certainly   527. **am . . . gall:** am constitutionally incapable of resentment. That doves were mild because they had no gall was a popular belief. 530. **offal:** entrails 531. **kindless:** unnatural   537. **stallion:** male whore. Most editors adopt the F1 reading *scullion,* "kitchen menial."   538. **About:** to work   541. **presently:** at once, then and there 547. **tent:** probe   **blench:** flinch   552. **spirits:** states of temperament   553. **Abuses:** deludes 554. **relative:** closely related (to fact), conclusive

Act III

Scene I

(*Enter* KING, QUEEN, POLONIUS, OPHELIA, ROSENCRANTZ, GUILDENSTERN, LORDS.)

KING   An' can you by no drift of conference
  Get from him why he puts on this confusion,
  Grating so harshly all his days of quiet
  With turbulent and dangerous lunacy?
5 ROSENCRANTZ   He does confess he feels himself distracted,
  But from what cause 'a will by no means speak.
GUILDENSTERN   Nor do we find him forward to be sounded,
  But with a crafty madness keeps aloof
  When we would bring him on to some confession
10   Of his true state.
QUEEN   Did he receive you well?
ROSENCRANTZ   Most like a gentleman.
GUILDENSTERN   But with much forcing of his disposition.
ROSENCRANTZ   Niggard of question, but of our demands
15   Most free in his reply.
QUEEN   Did you assay him
  To any pastime?
ROSENCRANTZ   Madam, it so fell out that certain players
  We o'erraught on the way; of these we told him,
20   And there did seem in him a kind of joy
  To hear of it. They are here about the court,
  And as I think, they have already order
  This night to play before him.
POLONIUS   'Tis most true,
25   And he beseech'd me to entreat your Majesties
  To hear and see the matter.
KING   With all my heart, and it doth much content me
  To hear him so inclin'd.
  Good gentlemen, give him a further edge,
30   And drive his purpose into these delights.
ROSENCRANTZ   We shall, my lord.

(*Exeunt* ROSENCRANTZ *and* GUILDENSTERN.)

III.i. Location: the castle   1. **An':** and   **drift of conference:** leading on of conversation
7. **forward:** readily willing   **sounded:** plumbed, probed   8. **crafty madness:** mad craftiness, the shrewdness that mad people sometimes exhibit   13. **disposition:** inclination   14. **question:** conversation   **demands:** questions   16. **assay:** attempt to win   19. **o'erraught:** passed (literally, overreached)   29. **edge:** stimulus   30. **into:** on to

KING   Sweet Gertrude, leave us two,
　　　For we have closely sent for Hamlet hither,
　　　That he, as 'twere by accident, may here
35　　Affront Ophelia. Her father and myself,
　　　We'll so bestow ourselves that, seeing unseen,
　　　We may of their encounter frankly judge,
　　　And gather by him, as he is behav'd,
　　　If't be th' affliction of his love or no
40　　That thus he suffers for.
QUEEN   I shall obey you.
　　　And for your part, Ophelia, I do wish
　　　That your good beauties be the happy cause
　　　Of Hamlet's wildness. So shall I hope your virtues
45　　Will bring him to his wonted way again,
　　　To both your honors.
OPHELIA   Madam, I wish it may.   [*Exit* QUEEN.]
POLONIUS   Ophelia, walk you here.—Gracious, so please you,
　　　We will bestow ourselves.   [*to* OPHELIA]   Read on this book,
50　　That show of such an exercise may color
　　　Your [loneliness]. We are oft to blame in this—
　　　'Tis too much prov'd—that with devotion's visage
　　　And pious action we do sugar o'er
　　　The devil himself.
55 KING   [*aside*]   O, 'tis too true!
　　　How smart a lash that speech doth give my conscience!
　　　The harlot's cheek, beautied with plast'ring art,
　　　Is not more ugly to the thing that helps it
　　　Than is my deed to my most painted word.
60　　O heavy burthen!
POLONIUS   I hear him coming. Withdraw, my lord.

[*Exeunt* KING *and* POLONIUS.]

(*Enter* HAMLET.)

HAMLET   To be, or not to be, that is the question:
　　　Whether 'tis nobler in the mind to suffer
　　　The slings and arrows of outrageous fortune,
65　　Or to take arms against a sea of troubles,
　　　And by opposing, end them. To die, to sleep—
　　　No more, and by a sleep to say we end

---

33. **closely:** privately   35. **Affront:** meet   37. **frankly:** freely   50. **exercise:** religious exercise (as the next sentence makes clear)   50–51. **color Your loneliness:** make your solitude seem natural   52. **too much prov'd:** too often proved true   53. **action:** demeanor   58. **to . . . it:** in comparison with the paint that makes it look beautiful   63. **suffer:** submit to, endure patiently

The heart-ache and the thousand natural shocks
That flesh is heir to; 'tis a consummation
70   Devoutly to be wish'd. To die, to sleep—
To sleep, perchance to dream—ay, there's the rub,
For in that sleep of death what dreams may come,
When we have shuffled off this mortal coil,
Must give us pause; there's the respect
75   That makes calamity of so long life:
For who would bear the whips and scorns of time,
Th' oppressor's wrong, the proud man's contumely,
The pangs of despis'd love, the law's delay,
The insolence of office, and the spurns
80   That patient merit of th' unworthy takes,
When he himself might his quietus make
With a bare bodkin; who would fardels bear,
To grunt and sweat under a weary life,
But that the dread of something after death,
85   The undiscover'd country, from whose bourn
No traveller returns, puzzles the will,
And makes us rather bear those ills we have,
Than fly to others that we know not of?
Thus conscience does make cowards [of us all],
90   And thus the native hue of resolution
Is sicklied o'er with the pale cast of thought,
And enterprises of great pitch and moment
With this regard their currents turn awry,
And lose the name of action.—Soft you now,
95   The fair Ophelia. Nymph, in thy orisons
Be all my sins rememb'red.

OPHELIA   Good my lord,
How does your honor for this many a day?
HAMLET   I humbly thank you, well, [well, well].
100 OPHELIA   My lord, I have remembrances of yours
That I have longed long to redeliver.
I pray you now receive them.

---

69. **consummation:** completion, end   71. **rub:** obstacle (a term from the game of bowls)
73. **shuffled off:** freed ourselves from   **this mortal coil:** the turmoil of this mortal life
74. **respect:** consideration   75. **of . . . life:** so long-lived   76. **time:** the world
81. **his quietus make:** write paid to his account   82. **bare bodkin:** mere dagger   **fardels:** burdens
85. **undiscover'd:** not disclosed to knowledge; about which men have no information   **bourn:**
boundary, region   86. **puzzles:** paralyzes   89. **conscience:** reflection (but with some of the modern
sense, too)   90. **native hue:** natural (ruddy) complexion   91. **pale cast:** pallor   **thought:** melancholy thought, brooding   92. **pitch:** loftiness (a term from falconry, signifying the highest point of a
hawk's flight   95. **orisons:** prayers

HAMLET   No, not I,
I never gave you aught.
105 OPHELIA   My honor'd lord, you know right well you did,
And with them words of so sweet breath compos'd
As made these things more rich. Their perfume lost,
Take these again, for to the noble mind
Rich gifts wax poor when givers prove unkind.
110   There, my lord.
HAMLET   Ha, ha! are you honest?
OPHELIA   My lord?
HAMLET   Are you fair?
OPHELIA   What means your lordship?
115 HAMLET   That if you be honest and fair, [your honesty] should admit no dis-
course to your beauty.
OPHELIA   Could beauty, my lord, have better commerce than with honesty?
HAMLET   Ay, truly, for the power of beauty will sooner transform honesty from
what it is to a bawd than the force of honesty can translate beauty into his
120   likeness. This was sometime a paradox, but now the time gives it proof. I did
love you once.
OPHELIA   Indeed, my lord, you made me believe so.
HAMLET   You should not have believ'd me, for virtue cannot so [inoculate] our
old stock but we shall relish of it. I lov'd you not.
125 OPHELIA   I was the more deceiv'd.
HAMLET   Get thee [to] a nunn'ry, why wouldst thou be a breeder of sinners? I
am myself indifferent honest, but yet I could accuse me of such things that
it were better my mother had not borne me: I am very proud, revengeful,
ambitious, with more offenses at my beck than I have thoughts to put them
130   in, imagination to give them shape, or time to act them in. What should
such fellows as I do crawling between earth and heaven? We are arrant
knaves, believe none of us. Go thy ways to a nunn'ry. Where's your father?
OPHELIA   At home, my lord.
HAMLET   Let the doors be shut upon him, that he may play the fool no where
135   but in 's own house. Farewell.
OPHELIA   O, help him, you sweet heavens!
HAMLET   If thou dost marry, I'll give thee this plague for thy dowry: be thou as
chaste as ice, as pure as snow, thou shalt not escape calumny. Get thee to a
nunn'ry, farewell. Or if thou wilt needs marry, marry a fool, for wise men
140   know well enough what monsters you make of them. To a nunn'ry, go, and
quickly too. Farewell.

---

111. **honest:** chaste   120. **sometime:** formerly   **paradox:** tenet contrary to accepted belief
123–124. **virtue . . . it:** Virtue, engrafted on our old stock (of viciousness), cannot so change the
nature of the plant that no trace of the original will remain.   127. **indifferent honest:** tolerably
virtuous   140. **monsters:** alluding to the notion that the husbands of unfaithful wives grew
horns   **you:** you women

OPHELIA   Heavenly powers, restore him!

HAMLET   I have heard of your paintings, well enough. God hath given you one
face, and you make yourselves another. You jig and amble, and you [lisp,]
145   you nickname God's creatures and make your wantonness [your] ignorance. Go to, I'll no more on't, it hath made me mad. I say we will have no
moe marriage. Those that are married already (all but one) shall live, the
rest shall keep as they are. To a nunn'ry, go.

(*Exit.*)

OPHELIA   O, what a noble mind is here o'erthrown!
150   The courtier's, soldier's, scholar's, eye, tongue, sword,
Th' expectation and rose of the fair state,
The glass of fashion and the mould of form,
Th' observ'd of all observers, quite, quite down!
And I, of ladies most deject and wretched,
155   That suck'd the honey of his [music] vows,
Now see [that] noble and most sovereign reason
Like sweet bells jangled out of time, and harsh;
That unmatch'd form and stature of blown youth
Blasted with ecstasy. O, woe is me
160   T' have seen what I have seen, see what I see!

[OPHELIA *withdraws.*]

(*Enter* KING *and* POLONIUS.)

KING   Love? his affections do not that way tend,
Nor what he spake, though it lack'd form a little,
Was not like madness. There's something in his soul
O'er which his melancholy sits on brood,
165   And I do doubt the hatch and the disclose
Will be some danger; which for to prevent,
I have in quick determination
Thus set it down: he shall with speed to England
For the demand of our neglected tribute.
170   Haply the seas, and countries different,
With variable objects, shall expel
This something-settled matter in his heart,

144–45. **You . . . creatures:** you walk and talk affectedly   145–46. **make . . . ignorance:** excuse your
affectation as ignorance   147. **moe:** more   151. **expectation:** hope   **rose:** ornament   **fair:** probably proleptic: "(the kingdom) made fair by his presence"   152. **glass:** mirror   **mould of form:** pattern of (courtly) behavior   153. **observ'd . . . observers:** Shakespeare uses *observe* to mean not only
"behold, mark attentively" but also "pay honor to".   158. **blown:** in full bloom   159. **Blasted:** withered   **ecstasy:** madness   161. **affections:** inclinations, feelings   165. **doubt:** fear   **disclose:** Synonymous with *hatch;* see also V.i.247.

Whereon his brains still beating puts him thus
From fashion of himself. What think you on't?
175 POLONIUS It shall do well; but yet do I believe
The origin and commencement of his grief
Sprung from neglected love. [OPHELIA *comes forward.*]
How now, Ophelia?
You need not tell us what Lord Hamlet said,
180 We heard it all. My lord, do as you please,
But if you hold it fit, after the play
Let his queen-mother all alone entreat him
To show his grief. Let her be round with him,
And I'll be plac'd (so please you) in the ear
185 Of all their conference. If she find him not,
To England send him, or confine him where
Your wisdom best shall think.
KING   It shall be so.
Madness in great ones must not [unwatch'd] go.

(*Exeunt.*)

[Scene II]

(*Enter* HAMLET *and three of the* PLAYERS.)

HAMLET   Speak the speech, I pray you, as I pronounc'd it to you, trippingly on
the tongue, but if you mouth it, as many of our players do, I had as live the
town-crier spoke my lines. Nor do not saw the air too much with your hand,
thus, but use all gently, for in the very torrent, tempest, and, as I may say,
5   whirlwind of your passion, you must acquire and beget a temperance that
may give it smoothness. O, it offends me to the soul to hear a robustious
periwig-pated fellow tear a passion to totters, to very rags, to spleet the ears
of the groundlings, who for the most part are capable of nothing but inexplicable dumb shows and noise. I would have such a fellow whipt for o'er-
10   doing Termagant, it out-Herods Herod, pray you avoid it.
[1.] PLAYER   I warrant your honor.
HAMLET   Be not too tame neither, but let your own discretion be your
tutor. Suit the action to the word, the word to the action, with this special

---

177. **neglected:** unrequited   183. **his grief:** what is troubling him   **round:** blunt, outspoken
185. **find him:** learn the truth about him.

III.ii. Location: the castle   2. **mouth:** pronounce with exaggerated distinctness or declamatory effect   **live:** lief, willingly   7. **totters:** tatters   **spleet:** split   8. **groundlings:** those who paid the lowest admission price and stood on the ground in the "yard" or pit of the theatre   **capable of:** able to
take in   10. **Termagant:** a supposed god of the Saracens, whose role in medieval drama, like that of
Herod (line 10), was noisy and violent

observance, that you o'erstep not the modesty of nature: for any thing so
15   o'erdone is from the purpose of playing, whose end, both at the first and
now, was and is, to hold as 'twere the mirror up to nature: to show virtue her
feature, scorn her own image, and the very age and body of the time his
form and pressure. Now this overdone, or come tardy off, though it makes
the unskillful laugh, cannot but make the judicious grieve; the censure of
20   which one must in your allowance o'erweigh a whole theatre of others. O,
there be players that I have seen play—and heard others [praise], and that
highly—not to speak it profanely, that, neither having th' accent of Christians nor the gait of Christian, pagan, nor man, have so strutted and bellow'd that I have thought some of Nature's journeymen had made men, and
25   not made them well, they imitated humanity so abominably.
[1.] PLAYER   I hope we have reform'd that indifferently with us, [sir].
HAMLET   O, reform it altogether. And let those that play your clowns speak no
more than is set down for them, for there be of them that will themselves
laugh to set on some quantity of barren spectators to laugh too, though in
30   the mean time some necessary question of the play be then to be consider'd.
That's villainous, and shows a most pitiful ambition in the fool that uses it.
Go make you ready.

[*Exeunt* PLAYERS.]

(*Enter* POLONIUS, GUILDENSTERN, *and* ROSENCRANTZ.)
How now, my lord? Will the King hear this piece of work?
POLONIUS   And the Queen too, and that presently.
35   HAMLET   Bid the players make haste.   [*Exit* POLONIUS.]
Will you two help to hasten them?
ROSENCRANTZ   Ay, my lord.   (*Exeunt they two.*)
HAMLET   What ho, Horatio!

(*Enter* HORATIO.)
HORATIO   Here, sweet lord, at your service.
40   HAMLET   Horatio, thou art e'en as just a man
As e'er my conversation cop'd withal.
HORATIO   O my dear lord—

---

14. **modesty:** moderation   15. **from:** contrary to   17. **scorn:** that which is worthy of scorn
18. **pressure:** impression (as of a seal), exact image   **tardy:** inadequately   19. **censure:** judgment
20. **which one:** (even) one of whom   **allowance:** estimation   22. **profanely:** irreverently
24–25. **some . . . abominably:** They were so unlike men that it seemed Nature had not made them
herself, but had delegated the task to mediocre assistants.   26. **indifferently:** pretty well
28. **of them:** some of them   31. **fool:** (1) stupid person; (2) actor playing a fool's role   33. **piece of
work:** masterpiece (said jocularly)   34. **presently:** at once   40. **thou . . . man:** you come as close to
being what a man should be (*just* = exact, precise)   41. **my . . . withal:** my association with people
has brought me into contact with

HAMLET   Nay, do not think I flatter,
For what advancement may I hope from thee
45   That no revenue hast but thy good spirits
To feed and clothe thee? Why should the poor be flatter'd?
No, let the candied tongue lick absurd pomp,
And crook the pregnant hinges of the knee
Where thrift may follow fawning. Dost thou hear?
50   Since my dear soul was mistress of her choice
And could of men distinguish her election,
Sh' hath seal'd thee for herself, for thou hast been
As one in suff'ring all that suffers nothing,
A man that Fortune's buffets and rewards
55   Hast ta'en with equal thanks; and blest are those
Whose blood and judgment are so well co-meddled,
That they are not a pipe for Fortune's finger
To sound what stop she please. Give me that man
That is not passion's slave, and I will wear him
60   In my heart's core, ay, in my heart of heart,
As I do thee. Something too much of this.
There is a play to-night before the King,
One scene of it comes near the circumstance
Which I have told thee of my father's death.
65   I prithee, when thou seest that act afoot,
Even with the very comment of thy soul
Observe my uncle. If his occulted guilt
Do not itself unkennel in one speech,
It is a damned ghost that we have seen,
70   And my imaginations are as foul
As Vulcan's stithy. Give him heedful note,
For I mine eyes will rivet to his face,
And after we will both our judgments join
In censure of his seeming.
75 HORATIO   Well, my lord.
If 'a steal aught the whilst this play is playing,
And scape [detecting], I will pay the theft.

([*Sound a flourish. Danish march.*] *Enter Trumpets and Kettle-drums,* KING,
QUEEN, POLONIUS, OPHELIA, [ROSENCRANTZ, GUILDENSTERN, *and other* LORDS
attendant, with his GUARD *carrying torches*].)

---

47. **candied:** sugared, flattering   **absurd:** tasteless (Latin sense)   48. **pregnant:** moving readily
49. **thrift:** thriving, profit   56. **blood:** passions   **co-meddled:** mixed, blended   60. **my heart of
heart:** the heart of my heart   66. **very … soul:** your most intense critical observation
67. **occulted:** hidden   68. **unkennel:** bring into the open   69. **damned ghost:** evil spirit, devil
71. **stithy:** forge   74. **censure … seeming:** reaching a verdict on his behavior

HAMLET   They are coming to the play. I must be idle; Get you a place.

KING   How fares our cousin Hamlet?

80 HAMLET   Excellent, i' faith, of the chameleon's dish: I eat the air, promise-cramm'd—you cannot feed capons so.

KING   I have nothing with this answer, Hamlet, these words are not mine.

HAMLET   No, nor mine now. [*to* POLONIUS] My lord, you play'd once i' th' university, you say?

85 POLONIUS   That did I, my lord, and was accounted a good actor.

HAMLET   What did you enact?

POLONIUS   I did enact Julius Caesar. I was kill'd i' th' Capitol; Brutus kill'd me.

HAMLET   It was a brute part of him to kill so capital a calf there. Be the players ready?

90 ROSENCRANTZ   Ay, my lord, they stay upon your patience.

QUEEN   Come hither, my dear Hamlet, sit by me.

HAMLET   No, good mother, here's metal more attractive.   [*lying down at* OPHELIA'*s feet*]

POLONIUS [*to the* KING]   O ho, do you mark that?

95 HAMLET   Lady, shall I lie in your lap?

OPHELIA   No, my lord.

[HAMLET   I mean, my head upon your lap?

OPHELIA   Ay, my lord.]

HAMLET   Do you think I meant country matters?

100 OPHELIA   I think nothing, my lord.

HAMLET   That's a fair thought to lie between maids' legs.

OPHELIA   What is, my lord?

HAMLET   Nothing.

OPHELIA   You are merry, my lord.

105 HAMLET   Who, I?

OPHELIA   Ay, my lord.

HAMLET   O God, your only jig-maker. What should a man do but be merry, for look you how cheerfully my mother looks, and my father died within 's two hours.

110 OPHELIA   Nay, 'tis twice two months, my lord.

HAMLET   So long? Nay then let the dev'l wear black, for I'll have a suit of sables. O heavens, die two months ago, and not forgotten yet? Then there's hope a great man's memory may outlive his life half a year, but, by'r lady, 'a must

---

78. **be idle:** act foolish, pretend to be crazy   79. **fares:** Hamlet takes up this word in another sense. 80. **chameleon's dish:** Chameleons were thought to feed on air. Hamlet says that he subsists on an equally nourishing diet, the promise of succession. There is probably a pun on *air/heir*. 82. **have nothing with:** do not understand   **mine:** an answer to my question   88. **part:** action 99. **country matters:** indecency   107. **only:** very best   **jig-maker:** one who composed or played in the farcical song-and-dance entertainments that followed plays   108. **'s:** this   111. **let . . . sables:** To the devil with my garments; after so long a time I am ready for the old man's garb of sables (fine fur).

115 build churches then, or else shall 'a suffer not thinking on, with the hobby-horse, whose epitaph is, "For O, for O, the hobby-horse is forgot."

(*The trumpets sounds. Dumb show follows.*)

(*Enter a King and a Queen [very lovingly], the Queen embracing him and he her. [She kneels and makes show of protestation unto him.] He takes her up and declines his head upon her neck. He lies him down upon a bank of flowers. She, seeing him asleep, leaves him. Anon come in another man, takes off his crown, kisses it, pours poison in the sleeper's ears, and leaves him. The Queen returns, finds the King dead, makes passionate action. The pois'ner with some three or four [mutes] come in again, seem to condole with her. The dead body is carried away. The pois'ner woos the Queen with gifts; she seems harsh [and unwilling] awhile, but in the end accepts love. [Exeunt.]*)

OPHELIA What means this, my lord?

HAMLET Marry, this' [miching] mallecho, it means mischief.

OPHELIA Belike this show imports the argument of the play.

(*Enter* PROLOGUE.)

HAMLET We shall know by this fellow. The players cannot keep [counsel],
120   they'll tell all.

OPHELIA Will 'a tell us what this show meant?

HAMLET Ay, or any show that you will show him. Be not you asham'd to show, he'll not shame to tell you what it means.

OPHELIA You are naught, you are naught. I'll mark the play.

125 PROLOGUE For us, and for our tragedy,
                Here stooping to your clemency,
                We beg your hearing patiently. [*Exit.*]

HAMLET Is this a prologue, or the posy of a ring?

OPHELIA 'Tis brief, my lord.

130 HAMLET As woman's love.

(*Enter [two* PLAYERS,] KING *and* QUEEN.)

[P.] KING Full thirty times hath Phoebus' cart gone round
                Neptune's salt wash and Tellus' orbed ground,
                And thirty dozen moons with borrowed sheen
                About the world have times twelve thirties been,

---

114. **not thinking on:** not being thought of, being forgotten   115. **For . . . forgot:** line from a popular ballad lamenting puritanical suppression of such country sports as the May-games, in which the hobby-horse, a character costumed to resemble a horse, traditionally appeared   117. **this' miching mallecho:** this is sneaking mischief   118. **argument:** subject, plot   119. **counsel:** secrets   122. **Be not you:** if you are not   124. **naught:** wicked   128. **posy . . . ring:** verse motto inscribed in a ring (necessarily short)   131. **Phoebus' cart:** the sun-god's chariot   132. **Tellus:** goddess of the earth

135   Since love our hearts and Hymen did our hands
       Unite comutual in most sacred bands.
   [P.] QUEEN   So many journeys may the sun and moon
       Make us again count o'er ere love be done!
       But woe is me, you are so sick of late,
140   So far from cheer and from [your] former state,
       That I distrust you. Yet though I distrust,
       Discomfort you, my lord, it nothing must,
       [For] women's fear and love hold quantity,
       In neither aught, or in extremity.
145   Now what my [love] is, proof hath made you know,
       And as my love is siz'd, my fear is so.
       Where love is great, the littlest doubts are fear;
       Where little fears grow great, great love grows there.
   [P.] KING   Faith, I must leave thee, love, and shortly too;
150   My operant powers their functions leave to do,
     ʹ And thou shalt live in this fair world behind,
       Honor'd, belov'd, and haply one as kind
       For husband shalt thou—
   [P.] QUEEN   O, confound the rest!
155   Such love must needs be treason in my breast.
       In second husband let me be accurs'd!
       None wed the second but who kill'd the first.
   HAMLET [*aside*]   That's wormwood!
   [P.] QUEEN   The instances that second marriage move
160   Are base respects of thrift, but none of love.
       A second time I kill my husband dead,
       When second husband kisses me in bed.
   [P.] KING   I do believe you think what now you speak,
       But what we do determine, oft we break.
165   Purpose is but the slave to memory,
       Of violent birth, but poor validity,
       Which now, the fruit unripe, sticks on the tree,
       But fall unshaken when they mellow be.
       Most necessary 'tis that we forget
170   To pay ourselves what to ourselves is debt.
       What to ourselves in passion we propose,
       The passion ending, doth the purpose lose.

---

135. **Hymen:** god of marriage   136. **bands:** bonds   141. **distrust:** fear for   143. **hold quantity:** are related in direct proportion   145. **proof:** experience   150. **operant:** active, vital   **leave to do:** cease to perform   154. **confound the rest:** May destruction befall what you are about to speak of—a second marriage on my part.   159. **instances:** motives   **move:** give rise to   160. **respects of thrift:** considerations of advantage   166. **validity:** strength, power to last   169–70. **Most . . . debt:** Such resolutions are debts we owe to ourselves, and it would be foolish to pay such debts.   171. **passion:** violent emotion

The violence of either grief or joy
Their own enactures with themselves destroy.
175   Where joy most revels, grief doth most lament;
Grief [joys], joy grieves, on slender accident.
This world is not for aye, nor 'tis not strange
That even our loves should with our fortunes change:
For 'tis a question left us yet to prove,
180   Whether love lead fortune, or else fortune love.
The great man down, you mark his favorite flies,
The poor advanc'd makes friends of enemies.
And hitherto doth love on fortune tend,
For who not needs shall never lack a friend,
185   And who in want a hollow friend doth try,
Directly seasons him his enemy.
But orderly to end where I begun,
Our wills and fates do so contrary run
That our devices still are overthrown,
190   Our thoughts are ours, their ends none of our own:
So think thou wilt no second husband wed,
But die thy thoughts when thy first lord is dead.
[P.] QUEEN   Nor earth to me give food, nor heaven light,
Sport and repose lock from me day and night,
195   To desperation turn my trust and hope,
[An] anchor's cheer in prison be my scope!
Each opposite that blanks the face of joy
Meet what I would have well and it destroy!
Both here and hence pursue me lasting strife,
200   If once I be a widow, ever I be a wife!
HAMLET   If she should break it now!
[P.] KING   'Tis deeply sworn. Sweet, leave me here a while,
My spirits grow dull, and fain I would beguile
The tedious day with sleep.   [*sleeps*]
205 [P.] QUEEN   Sleep rock thy brain,
And never come mischance between us twain!   (*Exit.*)
HAMLET   Madam, how like you this play?
QUEEN   The lady doth protest too much, methinks.
HAMLET   O but she'll keep her word.
210 KING   Have you heard the argument? is there no offense in't?
HAMLET   No, no, they do but jest, poison in jest—no offense i' th' world.

173–74. **The violence . . . destroy:** Both violent grief and violent joy fail of their intended acts because they destroy themselves by their very violence.   176. **slender accident:** slight occasion
186. **seasons:** ripens, converts into   189. **devices:** devisings, intentions   **still:** always
196. **anchor's cheer:** hermit's fare   **my scope:** the extent of my comforts   197. **blanks:** blanches, makes pale (a symptom of grief)   210. **offense:** offensive matter (but Hamlet quibbles on the sense "crime")   211. **jest:** pretend

KING   What do you call the play?

HAMLET   "The Mouse-trap." Marry, how? tropically: this play is the image of a
murther done in Vienna; Gonzago is the duke's name, his wife, Baptista. You

215   shall see anon. 'Tis a knavish piece of work, but what of that? Your Majesty,
and we that have free souls, it touches us not. Let the gall'd jade winch, our
withers are unwrung.

(*Enter* LUCIANUS.)

This is one Lucianus, nephew to the king.

OPHELIA   You are as good as a chorus, my lord.

220   HAMLET   I could interpret between you and your love, if I could see the pup-
pets dallying.

OPHELIA   You are keen, my lord, you are keen.

HAMLET   It would cost you a groaning to take off mine edge.

OPHELIA   Still better, and worse.

225   HAMLET   So you mistake your husbands. Begin, murtherer, leave thy damnable
faces and begin. Come, the croaking raven doth bellow for revenge.

LUCIANUS   Thoughts black, hands apt, drugs fit, and time agreeing,
[Confederate] season, else no creature seeing,
Thou mixture rank, of midnight weeds collected,

230   With Hecat's ban thrice blasted, thrice [infected],
Thy natural magic and dire property
On wholesome life usurps immediately.

[*pours the poison in his ears*]

HAMLET   'A poisons him i' th' garden for his estate. His name's Gonzago, the
story is extant, and written in very choice Italian. You shall see anon how the

235   murtherer gets the love of Gonzago's wife.

OPHELIA   The King rises.

[HAMLET   What, frighted with false fire?]

QUEEN   How fares my lord?

POLONIUS   Give o'er the play.

---

213. **tropically:** figuratively (with play on *tropically*—which is the reading of Q1—and probably
with allusion to the children's saying *marry trap*, meaning "now you're caught")   **image:** representation   216. **free souls:** clear consciences   **gall'd jade:** chafed horse   **winch:** wince   217. **withers:**
ridge between a horse's shoulders.   **unwrung:** not rubbed sore   219. **chorus:** one who explains the
forthcoming action   220–21. **I . . . dallying:** I could speak the dialogue between you and your lover
like a puppet-master (with an indecent jest).   222. **keen:** bitter, sharp   224. **better, and worse:**
more pointed and less decent   225. **So:** "for better, for worse," in the words of the marriage
service   **mistake:** mis-take, take wrongfully. Their vows, Hamlet suggests, prove false.   226. **faces:**
facial expressions   **the croaking . . . revenge:** misquoted from an old play, *The True Tragedy of
Richard III*   228. **Confederate season:** the time being my ally   230. **Hecat's ban:** the curse of
Hecate, goddess of witchcraft   237. **false fire:** a blank cartridge

240 KING   Give me some light. Away!

POLONIUS   Lights, lights, lights!

(*Exeunt all but* HAMLET *and* HORATIO.)

HAMLET   "Why, let the strooken deer go weep,
        The hart ungallèd play,
        For some must watch while some
245   must sleep,
        Thus runs the world away."
Would not this, sir, and a forest of feathers—if the rest of my fortunes turn
Turk with me—with [two] Provincial roses on my raz'd shoes, get me a
fellowship in a cry of players?

250 HORATIO   Half a share.

HAMLET   A whole one, I.
    "For thou dost know, O Damon dear,
        This realm dismantled was
        Of Jove himself, and now reigns here
255   A very, very"—pajock.

HORATIO   You might have rhym'd.

HAMLET   O good Horatio, I'll take the ghost's word for a thousand pound.
Didst perceive?

HORATIO   Very well, my lord.

260 HAMLET   Upon the talk of the pois'ning?

HORATIO   I did very well note him.

HAMLET   Ah, ha! Come, some music! Come, the recorders!
    For if the King like not the comedy,
    Why then belike he likes it not, perdy.
265 Come, some music!

(*Enter* ROSENCRANTZ *and* GUILDENSTERN.)

GUILDENSTERN   Good my lord, voutsafe me a word with you.

HAMLET   Sir, a whole history.

GUILDENSTERN   The King, sir—

HAMLET   Ay, sir, what of him?

270 GUILDENSTERN   Is in his retirement marvellous distemp'red.

HAMLET   With drink, sir?

---

242. **strooken:** struck, wounded   243. **ungalled:** unwounded   244. **watch:** stay awake
247. **feathers:** the plumes worn by tragic actors   248. **turn Turk:** go to the bad   **Provincial roses:** rosettes designed to look like a variety of French rose   **raz'd:** with decorating slashing
249. **fellowship:** partnership **cry:** company   253. **dismantled:** divested, deprived
255. **pajock:** peacock (substituting for the rhyme-word *ass*). The natural history of the time attributed many vicious qualities to the peacock.   264. **perdy:** assuredly (French *pardieu,* "by God")

GUILDENSTERN   No, my lord, with choler.

HAMLET   Your wisdom should show itself more richer to signify this to the doctor, for for me to put him to his purgation would perhaps plunge him
275   into more choler.

GUILDENSTERN   Good my lord, put your discourse into some frame, and [start] not so wildly from my affair.

HAMLET   I am tame, sir. Pronounce.

GUILDENSTERN   The Queen, your mother, in most great affliction of spirit,
280   hath sent me to you.

HAMLET   You are welcome.

GUILDENSTERN   Nay, good my lord, this courtesy is not of the right breed. If it shall please you to make me a wholesome answer, I will do your mother's commandement; if not, your pardon and my return shall be the end of [my]
285   business.

HAMLET   Sir, I cannot.

ROSENCRANTZ   What, my lord?

HAMLET   Make you a wholesome answer—my wit's diseas'd. But, sir, such answer as I can make, you shall command, or rather, as you say, my mother.
290   Therefore no more, but to the matter: my mother, you say—

ROSENCRANTZ   Then thus she says: your behavior hath strook her into amazement and admiration.

HAMLET   O wonderful son, that can so stonish a mother! But is there no sequel at the heels of this mother's admiration? Impart.

295 ROSENCRANTZ   She desires to speak with you in her closet ere you go to bed.

HAMLET   We shall obey, were she ten times our mother. Have you any further trade with us?

ROSENCRANTZ   My lord, you once did love me.

HAMLET   And do still, by these pickers and stealers.

300 ROSENCRANTZ   Good my lord, what is your cause of distemper? You do surely bar the door upon your own liberty if you deny your griefs to your friend.

HAMLET   Sir, I lack advancement.

ROSENCRANTZ   How can that be, when you have the voice of the King himself for your succession in Denmark?

305 HAMLET   Ay, sir, but "While the grass grows"—the proverb is something musty.

(*Enter the* PLAYERS *with recorders.*)

---

272. **choler:** anger (but Hamlet willfully takes up the word in the sense "biliousness")
274. **put . . . purgation:** prescribe for what's wrong with him   276. **frame:** logical structure
283. **wholesome:** sensible, rational   284. **pardon:** permission for departure
291–92. **amazement and admiration:** bewilderment and wonder   293. **stonish:** astound
295. **closet:** private room   299. **pickers and stealers:** hands, which, as the Catechism says, we must keep "from picking and stealing"   305. **proverb:** "While the grass grows, the steed starves."   305–306. **something musty:** somewhat stale

O, the recorders! Let me see one.—To withdraw with you—why do you go about to recover the wind of me, as if you would drive me into a toil?

GUILDENSTERN   O my lord, if my duty be too bold, my love is too unmannerly.

310 HAMLET   I do not well understand that. Will you play upon this pipe?

GUILDENSTERN   My lord, I cannot.

HAMLET   I pray you.

GUILDENSTERN   Believe me, I cannot.

HAMLET   I do beseech you.

315 GUILDENSTERN   I know no touch of it, my lord.

HAMLET   It is as easy as lying. Govern these ventages with your fingers and [thumbs], give it breath with your mouth, and it will discourse most eloquent music. Look you, these are the stops.

GUILDENSTERN   But these cannot I command to any utt'rance of harmony. I

320 have not the skill.

HAMLET   Why, look you now, how unworthy a thing you make of me! You would play upon me, you would seem to know my stops, you would pluck out the heart of my mystery, you would sound me from my lowest note to [the top of] my compass; and there is much music, excellent voice, in this

325 little organ, yet cannot you make it speak. 'Sblood, do you think I am easier to be play'd on than a pipe? Call me what instrument you will, though you fret me, [yet] you cannot play upon me.

(*Enter* POLONIUS.)

God bless you, sir.

POLONIUS   My lord, the Queen would speak with you, and presently.

330 HAMLET   Do you see yonder cloud that's almost in shape of a camel?

POLONIUS   By th' mass and 'tis, like a camel indeed.

HAMLET   Methinks it is like a weasel.

POLONIUS   It is back'd like a weasel.

HAMLET   Or like a whale.

335 POLONIUS   Very like a whale.

HAMLET   Then I will come to my mother by and by. [*aside*] They fool me to the top of my bent.—I will come by and by.

POLONIUS   I will say so. [*Exit.*]

HAMLET   "By and by" is easily said. Leave me, friends. [*Exeunt all but*

340 HAMLET.]

'Tis now the very witching time of night,
When churchyards yawn and hell itself [breathes] out
Contagion to this world. Now could I drink hot blood,

---

308. **recover the wind:** get to windward   **toil:** snare   316. **ventages:** stops   325. **organ:** instrument
327. **fret:** (1) finger (an instrument); (2) vex   329. **presently:** at once   336–337. **They . . . bent:**
They make me play the fool to the limit of my ability.   337. **by and by:** at once   341. **witching:**
when the powers of evil are at large

And do such [bitter business as the] day
345   Would quake to look on. Soft, now to my mother.
O heart, lose not thy nature! let not ever
The soul of Nero enter this firm bosom,
Let me be cruel, not unnatural;
I will speak [daggers] to her, but use none.
350   My tongue and soul in this be hypocrites—
How in my words somever she be shent,
To give them seals never my soul consent!

(*Exit.*)

[Scene III]

(*Enter* KING, ROSENCRANTZ, *and* GUILDENSTERN.)

KING   I like him not, nor stands it safe with us
To let his madness range. Therefore prepare you.
I your commission will forthwith dispatch,
And he to England shall along with you.
5   The terms of our estate may not endure
Hazard so near 's as doth hourly grow
Out of his brows.

GUILDENSTERN   We will ourselves provide.
Most holy and religious fear it is
10   To keep those many many bodies safe
That live and feed upon your Majesty.

ROSENCRANTZ   The single and peculiar life is bound
With all the strength and armor of the mind
To keep itself from noyance, but much more
15   That spirit upon whose weal depends and rests
The lives of many. The cess of majesty
Dies not alone, but like a gulf doth draw
What's near it with it. Or it is a massy wheel
Fix'd on the summit of the highest mount,
20   To whose [huge] spokes ten thousand lesser things
Are mortis'd and adjoin'd, which when it falls,
Each small annexment, petty consequence,

---

346. **nature:** natural affection, filial feeling   347. **Nero:** murderer of his mother   351. **shent:** rebuked   352. **give them seals:** confirm them by deeds

III.iii. Location: the castle   1. **him:** his state of mind, his behavior   3. **dispatch:** have drawn up
5. **terms:** conditions, nature   **our estate:** my position (as king)   7. **his brows:** the madness visible in his face (?)   9. **fear:** concern   12. **single and peculiar:** individual and private   14. **noyance:** injury   16. **cess:** cessation, death   17. **gulf:** whirlpool   21. **mortis'd:** fixed

Attends the boist'rous [ruin]. Never alone
Did the King sigh, but [with] a general groan.
25 KING   Arm you, I pray you, to this speedy viage,
For we will fetters put about this fear,
Which now goes too free-footed.
ROSENCRANTZ   We will haste us.

(*Exeunt* GENTLEMEN [ROSENCRANTZ *and* GUILDENSTERN].)

(*Enter* POLONIUS.)

POLONIUS   My lord, he's going to his mother's closet.
30   Behind the arras I'll convey myself
To hear the process. I'll warrant she'll tax him home,
And as you said, and wisely was it said,
'Tis meet that some more audience than a mother,
Since nature makes them partial, should o'erhear
35   The speech, of vantage. Fare you well, my liege,
I'll call upon you ere you go to bed,
And tell you what I know.
KING   Thanks, dear my lord.

(*Exit* [POLONIUS].)

O, my offense is rank, it smells to heaven,
40   It hath the primal eldest curse upon't,
A brother's murther. Pray can I not,
Though inclination be as sharp as will.
My stronger guilt defeats my strong intent,
And, like a man to double business bound,
45   I stand in pause where I shall first begin,
And both neglect. What if this cursed hand
Were thicker than itself with brother's blood,
Is there not rain enough in the sweet heavens
To wash it white as snow? Whereto serves mercy
50   But to confront the visage of offense?
And what's in prayer but this twofold force,
To be forestalled ere we come to fall,
Or [pardon'd] being down? then I'll look up.
My fault is past, but, O, what form of prayer
55   Can serve my turn? "Forgive me my foul murther"?

---

23. **Attends:** accompanies **ruin:** fall 25. **Arm:** prepare **viage:** voyage 26. **fear:** object of fear
31. **process:** course of the talk **tax him home:** take him severely to task 35. **of vantage:** from an
advantageous position (?) or in addition (?) 40. **primal eldest curse:** God's curse on Cain, who also
slew his brother 42. **Though . . . will:** though my desire is as strong as my resolve to do so
44. **bound:** committed 46. **neglect:** omit 49–50. **Whereto . . . offense:** what function has mercy
except when there has been sin

That cannot be, since I am still possess'd
Of those effects for which I did the murther:
My crown, mine own ambition, and my queen.
May one be pardon'd and retain th' offense?
60   In the corrupted currents of this world
Offense's gilded hand may [shove] by justice,
And oft 'tis seen the wicked prize itself
Buys out the law, but 'tis not so above:
There is no shuffling, there the action lies
65   In his true nature, and we ourselves compell'd,
Even to the teeth and forehead of our faults,
To give in evidence. What then? What rests?
Try what repentance can. What can it not?
Yet what can it, when one can not repent?
70   O wretched state! O bosom black as death!
O limed soul, that struggling to be free
Art more engag'd! Help, angels! Make assay,
Bow, stubborn knees, and heart, with strings of steel,
Be soft as sinews of the new-born babe!
75   All may be well.   [*He kneels.*]

(*Enter* HAMLET.)

HAMLET   Now might I do it [pat], now 'a is a-praying;
And now I'll do't—and so 'a goes to heaven,
And so am I [reveng'd]. That would be scann'd:
A villain kills my father, and for that
80   I, his sole son, do this same villain send
To heaven.
Why, this is [hire and salary], not revenge.
'A took my father grossly, full of bread,
With all his crimes broad blown, as flush as May,
85   And how his audit stands who knows save heaven?
But in our circumstance and course of thought
'Tis heavy with him. And am I then revenged,
To take him in the purging of his soul,
When he is fit and season'd for his passage?
90   No!

---

59. **th' offense:** the "effects" or fruits of the offense   60. **currents:** courses   61. **gilded:** bribing
62. **wicked prize:** rewards of vice   64. **shuffling:** evasion   **the action lies:** the charge comes for legal consideration   66. **Even . . . forehead:** fully recognizing their features, extenuating nothing   67. **rests:** remains   71. **limed:** caught (as in birdlime, a sticky substance used for catching birds)   72. **engag'd:** entangled   78. **would be scann'd:** must be carefully considered
83. **grossly:** in a gross state; not spiritually prepared   84. **crimes:** sins   **broad blown:** in full bloom   **flush:** lusty, vigorous   85. **audit:** account   86. **in . . . thought:** to the best of our knowledge and belief

Up, sword, and know thou a more horrid hent:
When he is drunk asleep, or in his rage,
Or in th' incestious pleasure of his bed,
At game a-swearing, or about some act
95   That has no relish of salvation in't—
Then trip him, that his heels may kick at heaven,
And that his soul may be as damn'd and black
As hell, whereto it goes. My mother stays,
This physic but prolongs thy sickly days.   (*Exit.*)
100   KING [*rising*]   My words fly up, my thoughts remain below:
Words without thoughts never to heaven go.

(*Exit.*)

[Scene IV]

(*Enter* [QUEEN] GERTRUDE *and* POLONIUS.)

POLONIUS   'A will come straight. Look you lay home to him.
Tell him his pranks have been too broad to bear with,
And that your Grace hath screen'd and stood between
Much heat and him. I'll silence me even here;
5   Pray you be round [with him].
QUEEN   I'll [warr'nt] you, fear me not. Withdraw,
I hear him coming.   [POLONIUS *hides behind the arras.*]

(*Enter* HAMLET.)

HAMLET   Now, mother, what's the matter?
QUEEN   Hamlet, thou hast thy father much offended.
10 HAMLET   Mother, you have my father much offended.
QUEEN   Come, come, you answer with an idle tongue.
HAMLET   Go, go, you question with a wicked tongue.
QUEEN   Why, how now, Hamlet?
HAMLET   What's the matter now?
15 QUEEN   Have you forgot me?
HAMLET   No, by the rood, not so:
You are the Queen, your husband's brother's wife,
And would it were not so, you are my mother.
QUEEN   Nay, then I'll set those to you that can speak.

---

91. **Up:** into the sheath   **know . . . hent:** be grasped at a more dreadful time   95. **relish:** trace
99. **physic:** (attempted) remedy, prayer.

III.iv. Location: the queen's closet in the castle   1. **lay . . . him:** reprove him severely   2. **broad:** un-
restrained   5. **round:** plain-spoken   6. **fear me not:** have no fears about my handling of the situation   11. **idle:** foolish   16. **rood:** cross

20 HAMLET   Come, come, and sit you down, you shall not boudge;
           You go not till I set you up a glass
           Where you may see the [inmost] part of you.
   QUEEN   What wilt thou do? Thou wilt not murther me?
           Help ho!
25 POLONIUS [*behind*]   What ho, help!
   HAMLET [*drawing*]   How now? A rat? Dead, for a ducat, dead!   [*Kills* POLO-
           NIUS *through the arras.*]
   POLONIUS [*behind*]   O, I am slain.
   QUEEN   O me, what hast thou done?
30 HAMLET   Nay, I know not, is it the King?
   QUEEN   O, what a rash and bloody deed is this!
   HAMLET   A bloody deed! almost as bad, good mother,
           As kill a king, and marry with his brother.
   QUEEN   As kill a king!
35 HAMLET   Ay, lady, it was my word.

   [*parts the arras and discovers* POLONIUS]

           Thou wretched, rash, intruding fool, farewell!
           I took thee for thy better. Take thy fortune;
           Thou find'st to be too busy is some danger.—
           Leave wringing of your hands. Peace, sit you down,
40   And let me wring your heart, for so I shall
           If it be made of penetrable stuff,
           If damned custom have not brass'd it so
           That it be proof and bulwark against sense.
   QUEEN   What have I done, that thou dar'st wag thy tongue
45   In noise so rude against me?
   HAMLET   Such an act
           That blurs the grace and blush of modesty,
           Calls virtue hypocrite, takes off the rose
           From the fair forehead of an innocent love
50   And sets a blister there, makes marriage vows
           As false as dicers' oaths, O, such a deed
           As from the body of contraction plucks
           The very soul, and sweet religion makes
           A rhapsody of words. Heaven's face does glow
55   O'er this solidity and compound mass

---

20. **boudge:** budge   26. **for a ducat:** I'll wager a ducat   38. **busy:** officious, meddlesome
42. **damned custom:** the habit of ill-doing   **brass'd:** hardened, literally, plated with brass
43. **proof:** armor   **sense:** feeling   50. **blister:** brand of shame   52. **contraction:** the making of
contracts, the assuming of solemn obligation   53. **religion:** sacred vows   54. **rhapsody:** miscella-
neous collection, jumble   **glow:** with anger   55. **this ... mass:** the earth; *compound* = compounded of the four elements

With heated visage, as against the doom;
Is thought-sick at the act.

QUEEN   Ay me, what act,
That roars so loud and thunders in the index?

60 HAMLET   Look here upon this picture, and on this,
The counterfeit presentment of two brothers.
See what a grace was seated on this brow:
Hyperion's curls, the front of Jove himself,
An eye like Mars, to threaten and command,

65 A station like the herald Mercury
New lighted on a [heaven-]kissing hill,
A combination and a form indeed,
Where every god did seem to set his seal
To give the world assurance of a man.

70 This was your husband. Look you now what follows:
Here is your husband, like a mildewed ear,
Blasting his wholesome brother. Have you eyes?
Could you not on this fair mountain leave to feed,
And batten on this moor? ha, have you eyes?

75 You cannot call it love, for at your age
The heyday in the blood is tame, it's humble,
And waits upon the judgment, and what judgment
Would step from this to this? Sense sure you have,
Else could you not have motion, but sure that sense

80 Is apoplex'd, for madness would not err,
Nor sense to ecstasy was ne'er so thrall'd
But it reserv'd some quantity of choice
To serve in such a difference. What devil was't
That thus hath cozen'd you at hoodman-blind?

85 Eyes without feeling, feeling without sight,
Ears without hands or eyes, smelling sans all,
Or but a sickly part of one true sense
Could not so mope. O shame, where is thy blush?
Rebellious hell,

90 If thou canst mutine in a matron's bones,
To flaming youth let virtue be as wax

---

56. **as . . . doom:** as if for Judgment Day   59. **index:** table of contents. The index was formerly placed at the beginning of a book.   61. **counterfeit presentment:** painted likenesses   63. **Hyperion's:** the sun-god's   **front:** forehead   65. **station:** bearing   71. **ear:** of grain   74. **batten:** gorge   76. **heyday:** excitement   78. **Sense:** sense perception, the five senses   80. **apoplex'd:** paralyzed   80–83. **madness . . . difference:** Madness itself could not go so far astray, nor were the senses ever so enslaved by lunacy that they did not retain the power to make so obvious a distinction.   84. **cozen'd:** cheated   **hoodman-blind:** blindman's bluff   86. **sans:** without   88. **mope:** be dazed   90. **mutine:** rebel

And melt in her own fire. Proclaim no shame
When the compulsive ardure gives the charge,
Since frost itself as actively doth burn,
95   And reason [panders] will.

QUEEN   O Hamlet, speak no more!
Thou turn'st my [eyes into my very] soul,
And there I see such black and [grained] spots
As will [not] leave their tinct.

100 HAMLET   Nay, but to live
In the rank sweat of an enseamed bed,
Stew'd in corruption, honeying and making love
Over the nasty sty!

QUEEN   O, speak to me no more!
105   These words like daggers enter in my ears.
No more, sweet Hamlet!

HAMLET   A murtherer and a villain!
A slave that is not twentith part the [tithe]
Of your precedent lord, a Vice of kings,
110   A cutpurse of the empire and the rule,
That from a shelf the precious diadem stole,
And put it in his pocket—

QUEEN   No more!

(*Enter* GHOST [*in his night-gown*].)

HAMLET   A king of shreds and patches—
115   Save me, and hover o'er me with your wings,
You heavenly guards! What would your gracious figure?

QUEEN   Alas, he's mad!

HAMLET   Do you not come your tardy son to chide,
That, laps'd in time and passion, lets go by
120   Th' important acting of your dread command?
O, say!

GHOST   Do not forget! This visitation
Is but to whet thy almost blunted purpose.
But look, amazement on thy mother sits,
125   O, step between her and her fighting soul.

92–95. **Proclaim . . . will:** Do not call it sin when the hot blood of youth is responsible for lechery, since here we see people of calmer age on fire for it; and reason acts as procurer for desire, instead of restraining it. *Ardure* = ardor 98. **grained:** fast-dyed, indelible 99. **leave their tinct:** lose their color 101. **enseamed:** greasy 108. **twentith:** twentieth 109. **precedent:** former **Vice:** buffoon (like the Vice of the morality plays) s.d. **night-gown:** dressing gown 114. **of . . . patches:** clownish (alluding to the motley worn by jesters) (?) or patched-up, beggarly (?) 119. **laps'd . . . passion:** "having suffered time to slip and passion to cool" (Johnson) 120. **important:** urgent 124. **amazement:** utter bewilderment

Conceit in weakest bodies strongest works,
Speak to her, Hamlet.
HAMLET   How is it with you, lady?
QUEEN   Alas, how is't with you,
130   That you do bend your eye on vacancy,
        And with th' incorporal air do hold discourse?
        Forth at your eyes your spirits wildly peep,
        And as the sleeping soldiers in th' alarm,
        Your bedded hair, like life in excrements,
135   Start up and stand an end. O gentle son,
        Upon the heat and flame of thy distemper
        Sprinkle cool patience. Whereon do you look?
HAMLET   On him, on him! look you how pale he glares!
        His form and cause conjoin'd, preaching to stones,
140   Would make them capable.—Do not look upon me,
        Lest with this piteous action you convert
        My stern effects, then what I have to do
        Will want true color—tears perchance for blood.
QUEEN   To whom do you speak this?
145 HAMLET   Do you see nothing there?
QUEEN   Nothing at all, yet all that is I see.
HAMLET   Nor did you nothing hear?
QUEEN   No, nothing but ourselves.
HAMLET   Why, look you there, look how it steals away!
150   My father, in his habit as he lived!
        Look where he goes, even now, out at the portal!

(*Exit* GHOST.)

QUEEN   This is the very coinage of your brain,
        This bodiless creation ecstasy
        Is very cunning in.
155 HAMLET   [Ecstasy?]
        My pulse as yours doth temperately keep time,
        And makes as healthful music. It is not madness
        That I have utt'red. Bring me to the test,
        And [I] the matter will reword, which madness
160   Would gambol from. Mother, for love of grace,
        Lay not that flattering unction to your soul,

---

126. **Conceit:** imagination   133. **in th' alarm:** when the call to arms is sounded   134. **excrements:**
outgrowths; here, hair (also used of nails)   135. **an end:** on end   137. **patience:** self-control
139. **His ... cause:** his appearance and what he has to say   140. **capable:** sensitive, recep-
tive   141. **convert:** alter   142. **effects:** (purposed) actions   143. **want true color:** lack its proper appearance   150. **habit:** dress   153. **ecstasy:** madness   160. **gambol:** start, jerk away
161. **flattering unction:** soothing ointment

That not your trespass but my madness speaks;
It will but skin and film the ulcerous place,
Whiles rank corruption, mining all within,
165   Infects unseen. Confess yourself to heaven,
Repent what's past, avoid what is to come,
And do not spread the compost on the weeds
To make them ranker. Forgive me this my virtue,
For in the fatness of these pursy times
170   Virtue itself of vice must pardon beg,
Yea, curb and woo for leave to do him good.
QUEEN   O Hamlet, thou hast cleft my heart in twain.
HAMLET   O, throw away the worser part of it,
And [live] the purer with the other half.
175   Good night, but go not to my uncle's bed—
Assume a virtue, if you have it not.
That monster custom, who all sense doth eat,
Of habits devil, is angel yet in this,
That to the use of actions fair and good
180   He likewise gives a frock or livery
That aptly is put on. Refrain [to-]night,
And that shall lend a kind of easiness
To the next abstinence, the next more easy;
For use almost can change the stamp of nature,
185   And either [. . . .] the devil or throw him out
With wondrous potency. Once more good night,
And when you are desirous to be blest,
I'll blessing beg of you. For this same lord,

[*pointing to* POLONIUS]

I do repent; but heaven hath pleas'd it so
190   To punish me with this, and this with me,
That I must be their scourge and minister.
I will bestow him, and will answer well
The death I gave him. So again good night.
I must be cruel only to be kind.

---

167. **compost:** manure   169. **pursy:** puffy, out of condition   171. **curb and woo:** bow and entreat
177. **all . . . eat:** wears away all natural feeling   178. **Of habits devil:** though it acts like a devil in establishing bad habits. Most editors read (in lines 171–178) *eat / Of habits evil*, following Theobald.
180–81. **frock . . . on:** a "habit" or customary garment, readily put on without need of any decision   184. **use:** habit   185. A word seems to be wanting after *either*.   187. **desirous . . . blest:** repentant   191. **scourge and minister:** the agent of heavenly justice against human crime. *Scourge* suggests a permissive cruelty (Tamburlaine was the "scourge of God"), but "woe to him by whom the offense cometh"; the scourge must suffer for the evil it performs.   192. **bestow:** dispose of **answer:** answer for

195   This bad begins and worse remains behind.
       One word more, good lady.
    QUEEN   What shall I do?
    HAMLET   Not this, by no means, that I bid you do:
       Let the bloat king tempt you again to bed,
200   Pinch wanton on your cheek, call you his mouse,
       And let him, for a pair of reechy kisses,
       Or paddling in your neck with his damn'd fingers,
       Make you to ravel all this matter out,
       That I essentially am not in madness,
205   But mad in craft. 'Twere good you let him know,
       For who that's but a queen, fair, sober, wise,
       Would from a paddock, from a bat, a gib,
       Such dear concernings hide? Who would do so?
       No, in despite of sense and secrecy,
210   Unpeg the basket on the house's top,
       Let the birds fly, and like the famous ape,
       To try conclusions in the basket creep,
       And break your own neck down.
    QUEEN   Be thou assur'd, if words be made of breath,
215   And breath of life, I have no life to breathe
       What thou hast said to me.
    HAMLET   I must to England, you know that?
    QUEEN   Alack,
       I had forgot. 'Tis so concluded on.
220 HAMLET   There's letters seal'd, and my two schoolfellows,
       Whom I will trust as I will adders fang'd,
       They bear the mandate, they must sweep my way
       And marshal me to knavery. Let it work,
       For 'tis the sport to have the enginer
225   Hoist with his own petar, an't shall go hard
       But I will delve one yard below their mines,
       And blow them at the moon. O, 'tis most sweet
       When in one line two crafts directly meet.
       This man shall set me packing;
230   I'll lug the guts into the neighbor room.
       Mother, good night indeed. This counsellor

---

195. **behind:** to come   201. **reechy:** filthy   207. **paddock:** toad   **gib:** tom-cat
208. **dear concernings:** matters of intense concern   210. **Unpeg the basket:** open the door of the
cage   211. **famous ape:** The actual story has been lost.   212. **conclusions:** experiments (to see
whether he too can fly if he enters the cage and then leaps out)   213. **down:** by the fall
223. **knavery:** some knavish scheme against me.   224. **enginer:** deviser of military "engines" or con-
trivances   225. **Hoist with:** blown up by   **petar:** petard, bomb   228. **crafts:** plots
229. **packing:** (1) taking on a load; (2) leaving in a hurry

Is now most still, most secret, and most grave,
Who was in life a foolish prating knave.
Come, sir, to draw toward an end with you.
235   Good night, mother.

(*Exeunt* [*severally,* HAMLET *tugging in* POLONIUS].)

Act IV

Scene I

(*Enter* KING *and* QUEEN *with* ROSENCRANTZ *and* GUILDENSTERN.)

KING   There's matter in these sighs, these profound heaves—
You must translate, 'tis fit we understand them.
Where is your son?
QUEEN   Bestow this place on us a little while.

[*Exeunt* ROSENCRANTZ *and* GUILDENSTERN.]

5   Ah, mine own lord, what have I seen to-night!
KING   What, Gertrude? How does Hamlet?
QUEEN   Mad as the sea and wind when both contend
Which is the mightier. In his lawless fit,
Behind the arras hearing something stir,
10   Whips out his rapier, cries, "A rat, a rat!"
And in this brainish apprehension kills
The unseen good old man.
KING   O heavy deed!
It had been so with us had we been there.
15   His liberty is full of threats to all,
To you yourself, to us, to every one.
Alas, how shall this bloody deed be answer'd?
It will be laid to us, whose providence
Should have kept short, restrain'd, and out of haunt
20   This mad young man; but so much was our love,
We would not understand what was most fit,
But like the owner of a foul disease,
To keep it from divulging, let it feed
Even on the pith of life. Where is he gone?
25   QUEEN   To draw apart the body he hath kill'd,
O'er whom his very madness, like some ore

---

234. **draw . . . end:** finish my conversation

IV.i. Location: the castle   11. **brainish apprehension:** crazy notion   17. **answer'd:** satisfactorily accounted for to the public   18. **providence:** foresight   19. **short:** on a short leash   **out of haunt:** away from other people   23. **divulging:** being revealed   26. **ore:** vein of gold

Among a mineral of metals base,
Shows itself pure: 'a weeps for what is done.

KING   O Gertrude, come away!
30   The sun no sooner shall the mountains touch,
But we will ship him hence, and this vile deed
We must with all our majesty and skill
Both countenance and excuse. Ho, Guildenstern!

(*Enter* ROSENCRANTZ *and* GUILDENSTERN.)

Friends both, go join you with some further aid:
35   Hamlet in madness hath Polonius slain,
And from his mother's closet hath he dragg'd him.
Go seek him out, speak fair, and bring the body
Into the chapel. I pray you haste in this.

[*Exeunt* ROSENCRANTZ *and* GUILDENSTERN.]

Come, Gertrude, we'll call up our wisest friends
40   And let them know both what we mean to do
And what's untimely done, [. . . .]
Whose whisper o'er the world's diameter,
As level as the cannon to his blank,
Transports his pois'ned shot, may miss our name,
45   And hit the woundless air. O, come away!
My soul is full of discord and dismay.

(*Exeunt.*)

[Scene II]

(*Enter* HAMLET.)

HAMLET   Safely stow'd.
[GENTLEMEN. (*Within.*)   Hamlet! Lord Hamlet!]
[HAMLET]   But soft, what noise? Who calls on Hamlet? O, here they come.

(*Enter* ROSENCRANTZ *and* [GUILDENSTERN].)

ROSENCRANTZ   What have you done, my lord, with the dead body?
5   HAMLET   [Compounded] it with dust, whereto 'tis kin.

---

27. **mineral:** mine   41. Some words are wanting at the end of the line. Capell's conjecture, *so, haply, slander,* probably indicates the intended sense of the passage.   43. **As level:** with aim as good **blank:** target   45. **woundless:** incapable of being hurt

IV.ii. Location: the castle

ROSENCRANTZ   Tell us where 'tis, that we may take it thence,
And bear it to the chapel.

HAMLET   Do not believe it.

ROSENCRANTZ   Believe what?

10 HAMLET   That I can keep your counsel and not mine own. Besides, to be demanded of a spunge, what replication should be made by the son of a king?

ROSENCRANTZ   Take you me for a spunge, my lord?

HAMLET   Ay, sir, that soaks up the King's countenance, his rewards, his authorities. But such officers do the King best service in the end: he keeps them, like

15 [an ape] an apple, in the corner of his jaw, first mouth'd, to be last swallow'd. When he needs what you have glean'd, it is but squeezing you, and,
spunge, you shall be dry again.

ROSENCRANTZ   I understand you not, my lord.

HAMLET   I am glad of it, a knavish speech sleeps in a foolish ear.

20 ROSENCRANTZ   My lord, you must tell us where the body is, and go with us to
the King.

HAMLET   The body is with the King, but the King is not with the body. The
King is a thing—

GUILDENSTERN   A thing, my lord?

25 HAMLET   Of nothing, bring me to him. [Hide fox, and all after.]

(*Exeunt.*)

[Scene III]

(*Enter* KING *and two or three.*)

KING   I have sent to seek him, and to find the body.
How dangerous is it that this man goes loose!
Yet must not we put the strong law on him.
He's lov'd of the distracted multitude,

5 Who like not in their judgment, but their eyes,
And where 'tis so, th' offender's scourge is weigh'd,
But never the offense. To bear all smooth and even,
This sudden sending him away must seem
Deliberate pause. Diseases desperate grown

10 By desperate appliance are reliev'd,
Or not at all.

10–11. **demanded of:** questioned by   11. **spunge:** sponge   **replication:** reply   13. **countenance:**
favor   19. **sleeps:** is meaningless   22. **The body . . . the body:** possibly alluding to the legal fiction
that the king's dignity is separate from his mortal body   25. **Of nothing:** of no account Cf. "Man is
like a thing of nought, his time passeth away like a shadow" (Psalm 144:4 in the Prayer Book version). "Hamlet at once insults the King and hints that his days are numbered" (Dover Wilson).
Hide . . . after: probably a cry in some game resembling hide-and-seek

IV.iii. Location: the castle   4. **distracted:** unstable   6. **scourge:** punishment   7. **bear:** manage
8–9. **must . . . pause:** must be represented as a maturely considered decision

(*Enter* ROSENCRANTZ.)

How now, what hath befall'n?

ROSENCRANTZ   Where the dead body is bestow'd, my lord,
We cannot get from him.

15 KING   But where is he?

ROSENCRANTZ   Without, my lord, guarded, to know your pleasure.

KING   Bring him before us.

ROSENCRANTZ   Ho, bring in the lord.

(*They* [HAMLET *and* GUILDENSTERN] *enter.*)

KING   Now, Hamlet, where's Polonius?

20 HAMLET   At supper.

KING   At supper? where?

HAMLET   Not where he eats, but where 'a is eaten; a certain convocation of
politic worms are e'en at him. Your worm is your only emperor for diet: we
fat all creatures else to fat us, and we fat ourselves for maggots; your fat king

25   and your lean beggar is but variable service, two dishes, but to one table—
that's the end.

KING   Alas, alas!

HAMLET   A man may fish with the worm that hath eat of a king, and eat of the
fish that hath fed of that worm.

30 KING   What dost thou mean by this?

HAMLET   Nothing but to show you how a king may go a progress through the
guts of a beggar.

KING   Where is Polonius?

HAMLET   In heaven, send thither to see; if your messenger find him not there,

35   seek him i' th' other place yourself. But if indeed you find him not within
this month, you shall nose him as you go up the stairs into the lobby.

KING [*to* ATTENDANTS]   Go seek him there.

HAMLET   'A will stay till you come.

[*Exeunt* ATTENDANTS.]

KING   Hamlet, this deed, for thine especial safety—

40   Which we do tender, as we dearly grieve
For that which thou hast done—must send thee hence
[With fiery quickness]; therefore prepare thyself,
The bark is ready, and the wind at help,
Th' associates tend, and every thing is bent

45   For England.

HAMLET   For England.

---

23. **politic:** crafty, prying; "such worms as might breed in a politician's corpse" (Dowden)   **e'en:**
even now   **for diet:** with respect to what it eats   25. **variable service:** different courses of a meal
31. **progress:** royal journey of state   40. **tender:** regard with tenderness, hold dear   **dearly:** with
intense feeling   43. **at help:** favorable   44. **Th':** thy   **tend:** await   **bent:** made ready

KING   Ay, Hamlet.

HAMLET   Good.

KING   So is it, if thou knew'st our purposes.

50 HAMLET   I see a cherub that sees them. But come, for England! Farewell, dear
        mother.

KING   Thy loving father, Hamlet.

HAMLET   My mother: father and mother is man and wife, man and wife is one
        flesh—so, my mother. Come, for England!   (*Exit.*)

55 KING   Follow him at foot, tempt him with speed aboard.
        Delay it not, I'll have him hence to-night.
        Away, for every thing is seal'd and done
        That else leans on th' affair. Pray you make haste.

[*Exeunt* ROSENCRANTZ *and* GUILDENSTERN.]

        And, England, if my love thou hold'st at aught—
60   As my great power thereof may give thee sense,
        Since yet thy cicatrice looks raw and red
        After the Danish sword, and thy free awe
        Pays homage to us—thou mayst not coldly set
        Our sovereign process, which imports at full,
65   By letters conguring to that effect,
        The present death of Hamlet. Do it, England,
        For like the hectic in my blood he rages,
        And thou must cure me. Till I know 'tis done,
        How e'er my haps, my joys [were] ne'er [begun].

(*Exit.*)

[Scene IV]

(*Enter* FORTINBRAS *with his army over the stage.*)

FORTINBRAS   Go, captain, from me greet the Danish king.
        Tell him that by his license Fortinbras
        Craves the conveyance of a promis'd march
        Over his kingdom. You know the rendezvous.
5   If that his Majesty would aught with us,
        We shall express our duty in his eye,
        And let him know so.

CAPTAIN   I will do't, my lord.

---

50. **I . . . them:** heaven sees them   55. **at foot:** at his heels, close behind   58. **leans on:** relates to
59. **England:** king of England   61. **cicatrice:** scar   62–63. **thy . . . Pays:** your fear makes you pay
voluntarily   63. **coldly set:** undervalue, disregard   64. **process:** command   65. **conguring to:** in
accord with   66. **present:** immediate   67. **hectic:** continuous fever   69. **haps:** fortunes

IV.iv. Location: the Danish coast, near the castle   3. **conveyance of:** escort for   6. **eye:** presence

FORTINBRAS   Go softly on.   [*Exeunt all but the* CAPTAIN.]

(*Enter* HAMLET, ROSENCRANTZ, [GUILDENSTERN,] *etc.*)

10 HAMLET   Good sir, whose powers are these?

CAPTAIN   They are of Norway, sir.

HAMLET   How purpos'd, sir, I pray you?

CAPTAIN   Against some part of Poland.

HAMLET   Who commands them, sir?

15 CAPTAIN   The nephew to old Norway, Fortinbras.

HAMLET   Goes it against the main of Poland, sir,
　　Or for some frontier?

CAPTAIN   Truly to speak, and with no addition,
　　We go to gain a little patch of ground
20　　That hath in it no profit but the name.
　　To pay five ducats, five, I would not farm it;
　　Nor will it yield to Norway or the Pole
　　A ranker rate, should it be sold in fee.

HAMLET   Why then the Polack never will defend it.

25 CAPTAIN   Yes, it is already garrison'd.

HAMLET   Two thousand souls and twenty thousand ducats
　　Will not debate the question of this straw.
　　This is th' imposthume of much wealth and peace,
　　That inward breaks, and shows no cause without
30　　Why the man dies. I humbly thank you, sir.

CAPTAIN   God buy you, sir.   [*Exit.*]

ROSENCRANTZ   Will't please you go, my lord?

HAMLET   I'll be with you straight—go a little before.

[*Exeunt all but* HAMLET.]

　　How all occasions do inform against me,
35　　And spur my dull revenge! What is a man,
　　If his chief good and market of his time
　　Be but to sleep and feed? a beast, no more.
　　Sure He that made us with such large discourse,
　　Looking before and after, gave us not
40　　That capability and godlike reason
　　To fust in us unus'd. Now whether it be
　　Bestial oblivion, or some craven scruple
　　Of thinking too precisely on th' event—

---

9. **softly:** slowly   10. **powers:** forces   16. **main:** main territory   21. **To pay:** for an annual rent of **farm:** lease   23. **ranker:** higher   **in fee:** outright   27. **Will not debate:** will scarcely be enough to fight out   28. **imposthume:** abscess   34. **inform against:** denounce, accuse   36. **market:** purchase, profit   38. **discourse:** reasoning power   41. **fust:** grow mouldy   42. **oblivion:** forgetfulness 43. **event:** outcome

A thought which quarter'd hath but one part wisdom
45 And ever three parts coward—I do not know
Why yet I live to say, "This thing's to do,"
Sith I have cause, and will, and strength, and means
To do't. Examples gross as earth exhort me:
Witness this army of such mass and charge,
50 Led by a delicate and tender prince,
Whose spirit with divine ambition puff'd
Makes mouths at the invisible event,
Exposing what is mortal and unsure
To all that fortune, death, and danger dare,
55 Even for an egg-shell. Rightly to be great
Is not to stir without great argument,
But greatly to find quarrel in a straw
When honor's at the stake. How stand I then,
That have a father kill'd, a mother stain'd,
60 Excitements of my reason and my blood,
And let all sleep, while to my shame I see
The imminent death of twenty thousand men,
That for a fantasy and trick of fame
Go to their graves like beds, fight for a plot
65 Whereon the numbers cannot try the cause,
Which is not tomb enough and continent
To hide the slain? O, from this time forth,
My thoughts be bloody, or be nothing worth!

(*Exit.*)

[Scene V]

(*Enter* HORATIO, [QUEEN] GERTRUDE, *and a* GENTLEMAN.)

QUEEN I will not speak with her.

GENTLEMAN She is importunate, indeed distract.
  Her mood will needs be pitied.

QUEEN   What would she have?

5 GENTLEMAN She speaks much of her father, says she hears
  There's tricks i' th' world, and hems, and beats her heart,
  Spurns enviously at straws, speaks things in doubt

---

48. **gross:** large, obvious 49. **mass and charge:** size and expense 52. **Makes mouths at:**
treats scornfully **invisible:** unforeseeable 56. **Is not to:** is *not* not to **argument:** cause
57. **greatly:** nobly 60. **Excitements of:** urgings by 63. **fantasy:** caprice **trick:** trifle
65. **Whereon . . . cause:** which isn't large enough to let the opposing armies engage upon it
66. **continent:** container

IV.v. Location: the castle 7. **Spurns . . . straws:** spitefully takes offense at trifles **in doubt:** obscurely

That carry but half sense. Her speech is nothing,
Yet the unshaped use of it doth move
10   The hearers to collection; they yawn at it,
And botch the words up fit to their own thoughts,
Which as her winks and nods and gestures yield them,
Indeed would make one think there might be thought,
Though nothing sure, yet much unhappily.
15 HORATIO   'Twere good she were spoken with, for she may strew
Dangerous conjectures in ill-breeding minds.
[QUEEN]   Let her come in.   [*Exit* GENTLEMAN.]
[*aside*] To my sick soul, as sin's true nature is,
Each toy seems prologue to some great amiss,
20   So full of artless jealousy is guilt,
It spills itself in fearing to be spilt.

(*Enter* OPHELIA [*distracted, with her hair down, playing on a lute*].)

OPHELIA   Where is the beauteous majesty of Denmark?
QUEEN   How now, Ophelia?
OPHELIA   "How should I your true-love   (*She sings.*)
25   know
          From another one?
          By his cockle hat and staff,
          And his sandal shoon."
QUEEN   Alas, sweet lady, what imports this song?
30 OPHELIA   Say you? Nay, pray you mark.
          "He is dead and gone, lady,   (*Song.*)
          He is dead and gone,
          At his head a grass-green turf,
          At his heels a stone."
35   O ho!
QUEEN   Nay, but, Ophelia—
OPHELIA   Pray you mark.   [*Sings.*]
          "White his shroud as the mountain snow"—

(*Enter* KING.)

---

8. **Her speech:** what she says   9. **unshaped use:** distracted manner   10. **collection:** attempts to
gather the meaning   **yawn at:** gape eagerly (as if to swallow). Most editors adopt the F1 reading *aim
at.*   11. **botch:** patch   12. **Which:** the words   13. **thought:** inferred, conjectured
16. **ill-breeding:** conceiving ill thoughts, prone to think the worst   19. **toy:** trifle   **amiss:** calamity
20. **artless jealousy:** uncontrolled suspicion   21. **spills:** destroys   24–25. These lines resemble a
passage in an earlier ballad beginning "As you came from the holy land / Of Walsingham." Probably
all the song fragments sung by Ophelia were familiar to the Globe audience, but only one other line
(187) is from a ballad still extant.   27. **cockle hat:** hat bearing a cockle shell, the badge of a pilgrim
to the shrine of St. James of Compostela in Spain   **staff:** another mark of a pilgrim   28. **shoon:**
shoes (already an archaic form in Shakespeare's day)

QUEEN   Alas, look here, my lord.

40   OPHELIA   "Larded all with sweet flowers,   (*Song.*)
                Which bewept to the ground did not go
                With true-love showers."

KING   How do you, pretty lady?

OPHELIA   Well, God dild you! They say the owl was a baker's daughter. Lord,
45   we know what we are, but know not what we may be. God be at your table!

KING   Conceit upon her father.

OPHELIA   Pray let's have no words of this, but when they ask you what it
        means, say you this:
                "To-morrow is Saint Valentine's   (*Song.*)
50   day,
                All in the morning betime,
                And I a maid at your window,
                To be your Valentine.

                "Then up he rose and donn'd his clo'es,
55   And dupp'd the chamber-door,
                Let in the maid, that out a maid
                Never departed more."

KING   Pretty Ophelia!

OPHELIA   Indeed without an oath I'll make an end on't.   [*Sings.*]
60   "By Gis, and by Saint Charity,
                Alack, and fie for shame!
                Young men will do't if they come to't,
                By Cock, they are to blame.

                "Quoth she, 'Before you tumbled me,
65   You promis'd me to wed.'"

                                                            (*He answers.*)

                " 'So would I 'a' done, by yonder sun,
                And thou hadst not come to my bed.'"

KING   How long hath she been thus?

OPHELIA   I hope all will be well. We must be patient, but I cannot choose but
70   weep to think they would lay him i' th' cold ground. My brother shall know
        of it, and so I thank you for your good counsel. Come, my coach! Good
        night, ladies, good night. Sweet ladies, good night, good night.   [*Exit.*]

KING   Follow her close, give her good watch, I pray you.   [*Exit* HORATIO.]
        O, this is the poison of deep grief, it springs
75   All from her father's death—and now behold!

---

40. **Larded:** adorned   41. **not:** contrary to the expected sense, and unmetrical; explained as Ophelia's alteration of the line to accord with the facts of Polonius' burial (see line 83)   44. **dild:** yield, reward   **owl:** alluding to the legend of a baker's daughter whom Jesus turned into an owl because she
did not respond generously to his request for bread   46. **Conceit:** fanciful brooding
55. **dupp'd:** opened   60. **Gis:** contraction of *Jesus*   63. **Cock:** corruption of *God*   67. **And:** if

O Gertrude, Gertrude,
When sorrows come, they come not single spies,
But in battalions: first, her father slain;
Next, your son gone, and he most violent author
80   Of his own just remove; the people muddied,
Thick and unwholesome in [their] thoughts and whispers
For good Polonius' death; and we have done but greenly
In hugger-mugger to inter him; poor Ophelia
Divided from herself and her fair judgment,
85   Without the which we are pictures, or mere beasts;
Last, and as much containing as all these,
Her brother is in secret come from France,
Feeds on this wonder, keeps himself in clouds,
And wants not buzzers to infect his ear
90   With pestilent speeches of his father's death,
Wherein necessity, of matter beggar'd,
Will nothing stick our person to arraign
In ear and ear. O my dear Gertrude, this,
Like to a murd'ring-piece, in many places
95   Gives me superfluous death.   (*a noise within*)
[QUEEN   Alack, what noise is this?]
KING   Attend!
Where is my Swissers? Let them guard the door.

(*Enter a* MESSENGER.)

What is the matter?
100 MESSENGER   Save yourself, my lord!
The ocean, overpeering of his list,
Eats not the flats with more impiteous haste
Than young Laertes, in a riotous head,
O'erbears your officers. The rabble call him lord,
105 And as the world were now but to begin,
Antiquity forgot, custom not known,
The ratifiers and props of every word,
[They] cry, "Choose we, Laertes shall be king!"
Caps, hands, and tongues applaud it to the clouds,
110 "Laertes shall be king, Laertes king!"   (*a noise within*)

---

77. **spies:** soldiers sent ahead of the main force to reconnoiter; scouts.   80. **muddied:** confused
82. **greenly:** unwisely   83. **In hugger-mugger:** secretly and hastily   88. **in clouds:** in cloudy surmise and suspicion (rather than the light of fact)   89. **wants:** lacks   **buzzers:** whispering informers
91. **of matter beggar'd:** destitute of facts   92. **nothing . . . arraign:** scruple not at all to charge me
with the crime   94. **murd'ring-piece:** cannon firing a scattering charge   98. **Swissers:** Swiss guards
101. **overpeering . . . list:** rising higher than its shores   103. **in . . . head:** with a rebellious force
105. **as:** as if   107. **word:** pledge, promise

QUEEN   How cheerfully on the false trail they cry!
    O, this is counter, you false Danish dogs!

(*Enter* LAERTES *with others.*)

KING   The doors are broke.
LAERTES   Where is this king? Sirs, stand you all without.
115   ALL   No, let's come in.
LAERTES   I pray you give me leave.
ALL   We will, we will.
LAERTES   I thank you, keep the door.   [*Exeunt* LAERTES' *followers.*]   O thou
    vile king,
120   Give me my father!
QUEEN   Calmly, good Laertes.
LAERTES   That drop of blood that's calm proclaims me bastard,
    Cries cuckold to my father, brands the harlot
    Even here between the chaste unsmirched brow
125   Of my true mother.
KING   What is the cause, Laertes,
    That thy rebellion looks so giant-like?
    Let him go, Gertrude, do not fear our person:
    There's such divinity doth hedge a king
130   That treason can but peep to what it would,
    Acts little of his will. Tell me, Laertes,
    Why thou art thus incens'd. Let him go, Gertrude.
    Speak, man.
LAERTES   Where is my father?
135   KING   Dead.
QUEEN   But not by him.
KING   Let him demand his fill.
LAERTES   How came he dead? I'll not be juggled with.
    To hell, allegiance! vows, to the blackest devil!
140   Conscience and grace, to the profoundest pit!
    I dare damnation. To this point I stand,
    That both the worlds I give to negligence,
    Let come what comes, only I'll be reveng'd
    Most throughly for my father.
145   KING   Who shall stay you?
LAERTES   My will, not all the world's:
    And for my means, I'll husband them so well,
    They shall go far with little.

---

112. **counter:** on the wrong scent (literally, following the scent backward)   128. **fear:** fear for
130. **would:** would like to do   142. **both . . . negligence:** I don't care what the consequences are in
this world or in the next.   144. **throughly:** thoroughly   146. **world's:** world's will

KING   Good Laertes,
150   If you desire to know the certainty
        Of your dear father, is't writ in your revenge
        That, swoopstake, you will draw both friend and foe,
        Winner and loser?
        LAERTES   None but his enemies.
155   KING   Will you know them then?
        LAERTES   To his good friends thus wide I'll ope my arms,
        And like the kind life-rend'ring pelican,
        Repast them with my blood.
        KING   Why, now you speak
160   Like a good child and a true gentleman.
        That I am guiltless of your father's death,
        And am most sensibly in grief for it,
        It shall as level to your judgment 'pear
        As day does to your eye.
165   (*a noise within:*)   "Let her come in!"
        LAERTES   How now, what noise is that?

        (*Enter* OPHELIA.)

        O heat, dry up my brains! tears seven times salt
        Burn out the sense and virtue of mine eye!
        By heaven, thy madness shall be paid with weight
170   [Till] our scale turn the beam. O rose of May!
        Dear maid, kind sister, sweet Ophelia!
        O heavens, is't possible a young maid's wits
        Should be as mortal as [an old] man's life?
        [Nature is fine in love, and where 'tis fine,
175   It sends some precious instance of itself
        After the thing it loves.]
        OPHELIA   "They bore him barefac'd on the   (*Song.*)
                            bier,
                        [Hey non nonny, nonny, hey nonny,]
180   And in his grave rain'd many a tear"—
        Fare you well, my dove!
        LAERTES   Hadst thou thy wits and didst persuade revenge,
        It could not move thus.

---

152. **swoopstake:** sweeping up everything without discrimination (modern *sweepstake*)
157. **pelican:** The female pelican was believed to draw blood from her own breast to nourish her
young.   160. **good child:** faithful son   162. **sensibly:** feelingly   163. **level:** plain   168. **virtue:** faculty
174. **fine in:** refined or spiritualized by   175. **instance:** proof, token. So delicate is Ophelia's love for
her father that her sanity has pursued him into the grave.   182. **persuade:** argue logically for

OPHELIA   You must sing, "A-down, a-down," and you call him a-down-a.
185   O how the wheel becomes it! It is the false steward, that stole his master's
daughter.
LAERTES   This nothing's more than matter.
OPHELIA   There's rosemary, that's for remembrance; pray you, love, remember.
And there is pansies, that's for thoughts.
190 LAERTES   A document in madness, thoughts and remembrance fitted.
OPHELIA   [*to* CLAUDIUS]   There's fennel for you, and columbines.   [*to*
GERTRUDE]   There's rue for you, and here's some for me; we may call it
herb of grace a' Sundays. You may wear your rue with a difference. There's a
daisy. I would give you some violets, but they wither'd all when my father
195   died. They say 'a made a good end—   [*sings*]
             "For bonny sweet Robin is all my joy."
LAERTES   Thought and afflictions, passion, hell itself,
She turns to favor and to prettiness.
OPHELIA   "And will 'a not come again?   (*Song.*)
200   And will 'a not come again?
                  No, no, he is dead,
                  Go to thy death-bed,
             He never will come again.

205   "His beard was as white as snow,
             [All] flaxen was his pole,
                  He is gone, he is gone,
                  And we cast away moan,
             God 'a' mercy on his soul!"
And of all Christians' souls, [I pray God]. God buy you.   [*Exit.*]
210 LAERTES   Do you [see] this, O God?
KING   Laertes, I must commune with your grief,
Or you deny me right. Go but apart,
Make choice of whom your wisest friends you will,
And they shall hear and judge 'twixt you and me.
215   If by direct or by collateral hand
They find us touch'd, we will our kingdom give,
Our crown, our life, and all that we call ours,
To you in satisfaction; but if not,
Be you content to lend your patience to us,

---

184. **and . . . a-down-a:** "if he indeed agrees that Polonius is 'a-down,' fallen low" (Dover Wilson)
185. **wheel:** refrain (?) or spinning-wheel, at which women sang ballads (?)   187. **matter:** lucid
speech   190. **A document in madness:** a lesson contained in mad talk   191. **fennel, columbines:**
symbols respectively of flattery and ingratitude   192. **rue:** symbolic of sorrow and repentance
193. **with a difference:** to represent a different cause of sorrow. *Difference* is a term from heraldry,
meaning a variation in a coat of arms made to distinguish different members of a family.
194. **daisy, violets:** symbolic respectively of dissembling and faithfulness. It is not clear who are
the recipients of these.   197. **Thought:** melancholy   198. **favor:** grace, charm   205. **flaxen:**
white   **pole:** poll, head   215. **collateral:** indirect   216. **touch'd:** guilty

220 And we shall jointly labor with your soul
   To give it due content.
LAERTES   Let this be so.
   His means of death, his obscure funeral—
   No trophy, sword, nor hatchment o'er his bones,
225 No noble rite nor formal ostentation—
   Cry to be heard, as 'twere from heaven to earth,
   That I must call't in question.
KING   So you shall,
   And where th' offense is, let the great axe fall.
230 I pray you go with me.

(*Exeunt.*)

[Scene VI]

(*Enter* HORATIO *and others.*)

HORATIO   What are they that would speak with me?
GENTLEMAN   Sea-faring men, sir. They say they have letters for you.
HORATIO   Let them come in.   [*Exit* GENTLEMAN.]
   I do not know from what part of the world
5   I should be greeted, if not from Lord Hamlet.

(*Enter* SAILORS.)

[1.] SAILOR   God bless you, sir.
HORATIO   Let him bless thee too.
[1.] SAILOR   'A shall, sir, and['t] please him. There's a letter for you, sir—it
   came from th' embassador that was bound for England—if your name be
10   Horatio, as I am let to know it is.
HORATIO [*reads*]   "Horatio, when thou shalt have overlook'd this, give these
   fellows some means to the King, they have letters for him. Ere we were two
   days old at sea, a pirate of very warlike appointment gave us chase. Finding
   ourselves too slow of sail, we put on a compell'd valor, and in the grapple I
15   boarded them. On the instant they got clear of our ship, so I alone became
   their prisoner. They have dealt with me like thieves of mercy, but they knew
   what they did: I am to do a [good] turn for them. Let the King have the letters I have sent, and repair thou to me with as much speed as thou wouldest
   fly death. I have words to speak in thine ear will make thee dumb, yet are
20   they much too light for the [bore] of the matter. These good fellows will

---

224. **trophy:** memorial   **hatchment:** heraldic memorial tablet   225. **formal ostentation:** fitting
and customary ceremony   227. **That:** so that

IV.vi. Location: the castle   16. **thieves of mercy:** merciful thieves   20. **bore:** calibre, size (gunnery
term)

bring thee where I am. Rosencrantz and Guildenstern hold their course for
England, of them I have much to tell thee. Farewell.

> [He] that thou knowest thine,
>
>   Hamlet."

Come, I will [give] you way for these your letters,
25   And do't the speedier that you may direct me
To him from whom you brought them.

(*Exeunt.*)

[Scene VII]

(*Enter* KING *and* LAERTES.)

KING   Now must your conscience my acquittance seal,
And you must put me in your heart for friend,
Sith you have heard, and with a knowing ear,
That he which hath your noble father slain
5   Pursued my life.
LAERTES   It well appears. But tell me
Why you [proceeded] not against these feats
So criminal and so capital in nature,
As by your safety, greatness, wisdom, all things else
10   You mainly were stirr'd up.
KING   O, for two special reasons,
Which may to you perhaps seem much unsinow'd,
But yet to me th' are strong. The Queen his mother
Lives almost by his looks, and for myself—
15   My virtue or my plague, be it either which—
She is so [conjunctive] to my life and soul,
That, as the star moves not but in his sphere,
I could not but by her. The other motive,
Why to a public count I might not go,
20   Is the great love the general gender bear him,
Who, dipping all his faults in their affection,
Work like the spring that turneth wood to stone,
Convert his gyves to graces, so that my arrows,
Too slightly timber'd for so [loud a wind],

IV.vii. Location: the castle   1. **my acquittance seal:** ratify my acquittal; i.e., acknowledge my innocence in Polonius's death.   7. **feats:** acts   9. **safety:** regard for your own safety   10. **mainly:** powerfully   12. **unsinow'd:** unsinewed, weak   15. **either which:** one or the other   16. **conjunctive:**
closely joined   17. **in his sphere:** by the movement of the sphere in which it is fixed (as the Ptolemaic astronomy taught)   19. **count:** reckoning   20. **the general gender:** everybody   23. **gyves:**
fetters

25 Would have reverted to my bow again,
But not where I have aim'd them.

LAERTES   And so have I a noble father lost,
A sister driven into desp'rate terms,
Whose worth, if praises may go back again,
30 Stood challenger on mount of all the age
For her perfections—but my revenge will come.

KING   Break not your sleeps for that. You must not think
That we are made of stuff so flat and dull
That we can let our beard be shook with danger
35 And think it pastime. You shortly shall hear more.
I lov'd your father, and we love ourself,
And that, I hope, will teach you to imagine—

(*Enter a* MESSENGER *with letters.*)

[How now? What news?
MESSENGER   Letters, my lord, from Hamlet:]
40 These to your Majesty, this to the Queen.

KING   From Hamlet? Who brought them?

MESSENGER   Sailors, my lord, they say, I saw them not.
They were given me by Claudio. He receiv'd them
Of him that brought them.

45 KING   Laertes, you shall hear them.
—Leave us.   [*Exit* MESSENGER.]
[*reads*] "High and mighty, You shall know I am set naked on your kingdom.
To-morrow shall I beg leave to see your kingly eyes, when I shall, first asking
you pardon thereunto, recount the occasion of my sudden [and more
50 strange] return.

                                                          [Hamlet.] "

What should this mean? Are all the rest come back?
Or is it some abuse, and no such thing?

LAERTES   Know you the hand?

KING   'Tis Hamlet's character. "Naked"!
55 And in a postscript here he says "alone."
Can you devise me?

LAERTES   I am lost in it, my lord. But let him come,
It warms the very sickness in my heart
That I [shall] live and tell him to his teeth,
60 "Thus didst thou."

---

28. **terms:** condition   29. **go back again:** refer to what she was before she went mad   30. **on mount:** preeminent   32. **for that:** for fear of losing your revenge   33. **flat:** spiritless   34. **let . . . shook:** To ruffle or tweak a man's beard was an act of insolent defiance that he could not disregard without loss of honor. Cf. II.ii.573.   **with:** by   47. **naked:** destitute   49. **pardon thereunto:** permission to do so   52. **abuse:** deceit   54. **character:** handwriting   56. **devise me:** explain it to me

KING   If it be so, Laertes—
          As how should it be so? how otherwise?—
          Will you be rul'd by me?

LAERTES   Ay, my lord,
65   So you will not o'errule me to a peace.

KING   To thine own peace. If he be now returned
          As [checking] at his voyage, and that he means
          No more to undertake it, I will work him
          To an exploit, now ripe in my device,
70   Under the which he shall not choose but fall;
          And for his death no wind of blame shall breathe,
          But even his mother shall uncharge the practice,
          And call it accident.

LAERTES   My lord, I will be rul'd,
75   The rather if you could devise it so
          That I might be the organ.

KING   It falls right.
          You have been talk'd of since your travel much,
          And that in Hamlet's hearing, for a quality
80   Wherein they say you shine. Your sum of parts
          Did not together pluck such envy from him
          As did that one, and that, in my regard,
          Of the unworthiest siege.

LAERTES   What part is that, my lord?

85 KING   A very riband in the cap of youth,
          Yet needful too, for youth no less becomes
          The light and careless livery that it wears
          Than settled age his sables and his weeds,
          Importing health and graveness. Two months since
90   Here was a gentleman of Normandy:
          I have seen myself, and serv'd against, the French,
          And they can well on horseback, but this gallant
          Had witchcraft in't, he grew unto his seat,
          And to such wondrous doing brought his horse,
95   As had he been incorps'd and demi-natur'd
          With the brave beast. So far he topp'd [my] thought,

---

62. **As . . . otherwise:** How can he have come back? Yet he obviously has.   65. **So:** provided that
67. **checking at:** turning from (like a falcon diverted from its quarry by other prey)
72. **uncharge the practice:** adjudge the plot no plot, fail to see the plot   76. **organ:** instrument,
agent   79. **quality:** skill   80. **Your . . . parts:** all your (other) accomplishments put together
83. **unworthiest:** least important (with no implication of unsuitableness)   **siege:** status, position
88. **weeds:** (characteristic) garb   89. **Importing . . . graveness:** signifying prosperity and dignity
92. **can . . . horseback:** are excellent riders   95. **incorps'd:** made one body   **demi-natur'd:** become
half of a composite animal

That I in forgery of shapes and tricks
Come short of what he did.

LAERTES   A Norman was't?

100 KING   A Norman.

LAERTES   Upon my life, Lamord.

KING   The very same.

LAERTES   I know him well. He is the brooch indeed
And gem of all the nation.

105 KING   He made confession of you,
And gave you such a masterly report
For art and exercise in your defense,
And for your rapier most especial,
That he cried out 'twould be a sight indeed

110 If one could match you. The scrimers of their nation
He swore had neither motion, guard, nor eye,
If you oppos'd them. Sir, this report of his
Did Hamlet so envenom with his envy
That he could nothing do but wish and beg

115 Your sudden coming o'er to play with you.
Now, out of this—

LAERTES   What out of this, my lord?

KING   Laertes, was your father dear to you?
Or are you like the painting of a sorrow,

120 A face without a heart?

LAERTES   Why ask you this?

KING   Not that I think you did not love your father,
But that I know love is begun by time,
And that I see, in passages of proof,

125 Time qualifies the spark and fire of it.
There lives within the very flame of love
A kind of week or snuff that will abate it,
And nothing is at a like goodness still,
For goodness, growing to a plurisy,

130 Dies in his own too much. That we would do,
We should do when we would; for this "would" changes,
And hath abatements and delays as many
As there are tongues, are hands, are accidents,

---

97. **forgery:** mere imagining   103. **brooch:** ornament (worn in the hat)   105. **made . . . you:** acknowledged your excellence   110. **scrimers:** fencers   115. **sudden:** speedy   123. **time:** a particular set of circumstances   124. **in . . . proof:** by the test of experience, by actual examples   125. **qualifies:** moderates   127. **week:** wick   128. **nothing . . . still:** nothing remains forever at the same pitch of perfection   129. **plurisy:** plethora (a variant spelling of *pleurisy,* which was erroneously related to *plus,* stem *plur,* "more, overmuch"   130. **too much:** excess

And then this "should" is like a spendthrift's sigh,
135   That hurts by easing. But to the quick of th' ulcer:
Hamlet comes back. What would you undertake
To show yourself indeed your father's son
More than in words?

LAERTES   To cut his throat i' th' church.
140 KING   No place indeed should murther sanctuarize,
Revenge should have no bounds. But, good Laertes,
Will you do this, keep close within your chamber.
Hamlet return'd shall know you are come home.
We'll put on those shall praise your excellence,
145   And set a double varnish on the fame
The Frenchman gave you, bring you in fine together,
And wager o'er your heads. He, being remiss,
Most generous, and free from all contriving,
Will not peruse the foils, so that with ease,
150   Or with a little shuffling, you may choose
A sword unbated, and in a [pass] of practice
Requite him for your father.

LAERTES   I will do't,
And for [that] purpose I'll anoint my sword.
155   I bought an unction of a mountebank,
So mortal that, but dip a knife in it,
Where it draws blood, no cataplasm so rare,
Collected from all simples that have virtue
Under the moon, can save the thing from death
160   That is but scratch'd withal. I'll touch my point
With this contagion, that if I gall him slightly,
It may be death.

KING   Let's further think of this,
Weigh what convenience both of time and means
165   May fit us to our shape. If this should fail,
And that our drift look through our bad performance,
'Twere better not assay'd; therefore this project
Should have a back or second, that might hold

---

134. **spendthrift's sigh:** A sigh was supposed to draw blood from the heart.   135. **hurts by easing:** injures us at the same time that it gives us relief   140. **sanctuarize:** offer asylum to   142. **Will . . . this:** if you want to undertake this   144. **put on those:** incite those who   145. **double varnish:** second coat of varnish   146. **in fine:** finally   147. **remiss:** careless, over-trustful   148. **generous:** noble-minded   **free . . . contriving:** innocent of sharp practices   149. **peruse:** examine   150. **shuffling:** cunning exchange   151. **unbated:** not blunted   **pass of practice:** tricky thrust   155. **unction:** ointment   **mountebank:** traveling quack-doctor   156. **mortal:** deadly   157. **cataplasm:** poultice   158. **simples:** medicinal herbs   **virtue:** curative power   161. **gall:** graze   165. **fit . . . shape:** suit our purposes best   166. **drift:** purpose   **look through:** become visible, be detected   168. **back or second:** a second plot in reserve for emergency

If this did blast in proof. Soft, let me see.
170 We'll make a solemn wager on your cunnings—
I ha't!
When in your motion you are hot and dry—
As make your bouts more violent to that end—
And that he calls for drink, I'll have preferr'd him
175 A chalice for the nonce, whereon but sipping,
If he by chance escape your venom'd stuck,
Our purpose may hold there. But stay, what noise?

(*Enter* QUEEN.)

QUEEN   One woe doth tread upon another's heel,
So fast they follow. Your sister's drown'd, Laertes.
180 LAERTES   Drown'd! O, where?
QUEEN   There is a willow grows askaunt the brook,
That shows his hoary leaves in the glassy stream,
Therewith fantastic garlands did she make
Of crow-flowers, nettles, daisies, and long purples
185 That liberal shepherds give a grosser name,
But our cull-cold maids do dead men's fingers call them.
There on the pendant boughs her crownet weeds
Clamb'ring to hang, an envious sliver broke,
When down her weedy trophies and herself
190 Fell in the weeping brook. Her clothes spread wide,
And mermaid-like awhile they bore her up,
Which time she chaunted snatches of old lauds,
As one incapable of her own distress,
Or like a creature native and indued
195 Unto that element. But long it could not be
Till that her garments, heavy with their drink,
Pull'd the poor wretch from her melodious lay
To muddy death.
LAERTES   Alas, then she is drown'd?
200 QUEEN   Drown'd, drown'd.
LAERTES   Too much of water hast thou, poor Ophelia,
And therefore I forbid my tears; but yet
It is our trick, Nature her custom holds,

---

169. **blast in proof:** blow up while being tried (an image from gunnery)   173. **As:** and you should
174. **preferr'd:** offered to. Most editors adopt the F1 reading *prepar'd.*   175. **nonce:** occasion
176. **stuck:** thrust (from *stoccado,* a fencing term)   181. **askaunt:** sideways over   182. **hoary:** grey-white   183. **Therewith:** with willow branches   184. **long purples:** wild orchids   185. **liberal:** free-spoken   186. **cull-cold:** chaste   187. **crownet:** made into coronets   188. **envious sliver:** malicious branch   192. **lauds:** hymns   193. **incapable:** insensible   194. **indued:** habituated   203. **It:** weeping   **trick:** natural way

Let shame say what it will; when these are gone,
205   The woman will be out. Adieu, my lord,
I have a speech a' fire that fain would blaze,
But that this folly drowns it.   (*Exit.*)

KING   Let's follow, Gertrude.
How much I had to do to calm his rage!
210   Now fear I this will give it start again,
Therefore let's follow.

(*Exeunt.*)

Act V

Scene I

(*Enter two* CLOWNS [*with spades and mattocks*].)

1. CLOWN   Is she to be buried in Christian burial when she willfully seeks her own salvation?

2. CLOWN   I tell thee she is, therefore make her grave straight. The crowner hath sate on her, and finds it Christian burial.

5 1. CLOWN   How can that be, unless she drown'd herself in her own defense?

2. CLOWN   Why, 'tis found so.

1. CLOWN   It must be [*se offendendo*], it cannot be else. For here lies the point: if I drown myself wittingly, it argues an act, and an act hath three branches— it is to act, to do, to perform; [argal], she drown'd herself wittingly.

10 2. CLOWN   Nay, but hear you, goodman delver—

1. CLOWN   Give me leave. Here lies the water; good. Here stands the man; good. If the man go to this water and drown himself, it is, will he, nill he, he goes, mark you that. But if the water come to him and drown him, he drowns not himself; argal, he that is not guilty of his own death shortens not his own
15   life.

2. CLOWN   But is this law?

1. CLOWN   Ay, marry, is't—crowner's quest law.

2. CLOWN   Will you ha' the truth an't? If this had not been a gentlewoman, she should have been buried out a' Christian burial.

20 1. CLOWN   Why, there thou say'st, and the more pity that great folk should have count'nance in this world to drown or hang themselves, more than their even-Christen. Come, my spade. There is no ancient gentlemen but

---

204. **these:** these tears   205. **The woman . . . out:** My womanish traits will be gone for good.

V.i. Location: a churchyard   o.s.d. **Clowns:** rustics   3. **straight:** immediately   **crowner:** coroner
7. **se offendendo:** blunder for *se defendendo,* "in self-defense"   9. **argal:** blunder for *ergo,* "therefore"
11–15. **Here . . . life:** Alluding to a very famous suicide case, that of Sir James Hales, a judge who drowned himself in 1554; it was long cited in the courts. The clown gives a garbled account of the defense summing-up and the verdict.   12. **nill he:** will he not   17. **quest:** inquest
22. **even-Christen:** fellow-Christians

gard'ners, ditchers, and grave-makers; they hold up Adam's profession.

2. CLOWN   Was he a gentleman?

25   1. CLOWN   'A was the first that ever bore arms.

[2. CLOWN   Why, he had none.

1. CLOWN   What, art a heathen? How dost thou understand the Scripture? The Scripture says Adam digg'd; could he dig without arms?] I'll put another question to thee. If thou answerest me not to the purpose, confess thyself—

30   2. CLOWN   Go to.

1. CLOWN   What is he that builds stronger than either the mason, the shipwright, or the carpenter?

2. CLOWN   The gallows-maker, for that outlives a thousand tenants.

1. CLOWN   I like thy wit well, in good faith. The gallows does well; but how does

35   it well? It does well to those that do ill. Now thou dost ill to say the gallows is built stronger than the church; argal, the gallows may do well to thee. To't again, come.

2. CLOWN   Who builds stronger than a mason, a shipwright, or a carpenter?

1. CLOWN   Ay, tell me that, and unyoke.

40   2. CLOWN   Marry, now I can tell.

1. CLOWN   To't.

2. CLOWN   Mass, I cannot tell.

(*Enter* HAMLET *and* HORATIO [*afar off*].)

1. CLOWN   Cudgel thy brains no more about it, for your dull ass will not mend his pace with beating, and when you are ask'd this question next, say "a

45   grave-maker": the houses he makes lasts till doomsday. Go get thee in, and fetch me a sup of liquor.

[*Exit* SECOND CLOWN. FIRST CLOWN *digs.*]

   "In youth when I did love, did love,   (*song*)
      Methought it was very sweet,
   To contract—O—the time for—a—my behove,

50   O, methought there—a—was nothing—a—meet."

HAMLET   Has this fellow no feeling of his business? 'a sings in grave-making.

HORATIO   Custom hath made it in him a property of easiness.

HAMLET   'Tis e'en so, the hand of little employment hath the daintier sense.

1. CLOWN   "But age with his stealing steps   (*song*)

55   Hath clawed me in his clutch,
         And hath shipped me into the land,
            As if I had never been such."

---

26. **none:** no coat of arms   39. **unyoke:** cease to labor, call it a day   42. **Mass:** by the mass
49. **contract . . . behove:** shorten, spend agreeably . . . advantage. The song, punctuated by the grunts of the clown as he digs, is a garbled version of a poem by Thomas Lord Vaux, entitled "The Aged Lover Renounceth Love."   52. **Custom:** habit   **a property of easiness:** a thing he can do with complete ease of mind   53. **daintier sense:** more delicate sensitivity

[*throws up a shovelful of earth with a skull in it*]

HAMLET   That skull had a tongue in it, and could sing once. How the knave
jowls it to the ground, as if 'twere Cain's jaw-bone, that did the first murder!
60   This might be the pate of a politician, which this ass now o'erreaches, one
that would circumvent God, might it not?

HORATIO   It might, my lord.

HAMLET   Or of a courtier, which could say, "Good morrow, sweet lord! How
dost thou, sweet lord?" This might be my Lord Such-a-one, that prais'd my
65   Lord Such-a-one's horse when 'a [meant] to beg it, might it not?

HORATIO   Ay, my lord.

HAMLET   Why, e'en so, and now my Lady Worm's, chopless, and knock'd about
the [mazzard] with a sexton's spade. Here's fine revolution, and we had the
trick to see't. Did these bones cost no more the breeding, but to play at log-
70   gats with them? Mine ache to think on't.

1. CLOWN   "A pickaxe and a spade, a spade,   (*song*)
                      For and a shrouding sheet:
                      O, a pit of clay for to be made
                      For such a guest is meet."

[*throws up another skull*]

75   HAMLET   There's another. Why may not that be the skull of a lawyer? Where be
his quiddities now, his quillities, his cases, his tenures, and his tricks? Why
does he suffer this mad knave now to knock him about the sconce with a
dirty shovel, and will not tell him of his action of battery? Hum! This fellow
might be in 's time a great buyer of land, with his statutes, his recognizances,
80   his fines, his double vouchers, his recoveries. [Is this the fine of his fines,
and the recovery of his recoveries,] to have his fine pate full of fine dirt? Will
[his] ˙vouchers vouch him no more of his purchases, and [double ones too],
than the length and breadth of a pair of indentures? The very conveyances
of his lands will scarcely lie in this box, and must th' inheritor himself have
85   no more, ha?

HORATIO   Not a jot more, my lord.

HAMLET   Is not parchment made of sheep-skins?

---

59. **jowls:** dashes   60. **politician:** schemer, intriguer   **o'erreaches:** gets the better of (with play
on the literal sense)   61. **circumvent God:** bypass God's law   67. **chopless:** lacking the lower
jaw   68. **mazzard:** head   **revolution:** change   **and:** if   69. **trick:** knack, ability   **Did . . . cost:**
were . . . worth   69–70. **loggats:** a game in which blocks of wood were thrown at a stake
76. **quiddities:** subtleties, quibbles   **quillities:** fine distinctions   **tenures:** titles to real estate
77. **sconce:** head   79. **statutes, recognizances:** bonds securing debts by attaching land and property
80. **fines, recoveries:** procedures for converting an entailed estate to freehold   **double vouchers:**
documents guaranteeing title to real estate, signed by two persons   **fine:** end
83. **pair of indentures:** legal document cut into two parts which fitted together on a serrated edge.
Perhaps Hamlet thus refers to the two rows of teeth in the skull, or to the bone sutures.
conveyances: documents relating to transfer of property   84. **this box:** the skull itself   **inheritor:**
owner

HORATIO   Ay, my lord, and of calves'-skins too.

HAMLET   They are sheep and calves which seek out assurance in that. I will
90   speak to this fellow. Whose grave's this, sirrah?

1. CLOWN   Mine, sir.   [*sings*]

> "[O], a pit of clay for to be made
> [For such a guest is meet]."

HAMLET   I think it be thine indeed, for thou liest in't.

95   1. CLOWN   You lie out on't, sir, and therefore 'tis not yours; for my part, I do not
lie in't, yet it is mine.

HAMLET   Thou dost lie in't, to be in't and say it is thine. 'Tis for the dead, not
for the quick; therefore thou liest.

1. CLOWN   'Tis a quick lie, sir, 'twill away again from me to you.

100   HAMLET   What man dost thou dig it for?

1. CLOWN   For no man, sir.

HAMLET   What woman then?

1. CLOWN   For none neither.

HAMLET   Who is to be buried in't?

105   1. CLOWN   One that was a woman, sir, but, rest her soul, she's dead.

HAMLET   How absolute the knave is! we must speak by the card, or equivocation will undo us. By the Lord, Horatio, this three years I have took note of
it: the age is grown so pick'd that the toe of the peasant comes so near the
heel of the courtier, he galls his kibe. How long hast thou been grave-maker?

110   1. CLOWN   Of [all] the days i' th' year, I came to't that day that our last king
Hamlet overcame Fortinbras.

HAMLET   How long is that since?

1. CLOWN   Cannot you tell that? Every fool can tell that. It was that very day
that young Hamlet was born—he that is mad, and sent into England.

115   HAMLET   Ay, marry, why was he sent into England?

1. CLOWN   Why, because 'a was mad. 'A shall recover his wits there, or if 'a do
not, 'tis no great matter there.

HAMLET   Why?

1. CLOWN   'Twill not be seen in him there, there the men are as mad as he.

120   HAMLET   How came he mad?

1. CLOWN   Very strangely, they say.

HAMLET   How strangely?

1. CLOWN   Faith, e'en with losing his wits.

HAMLET   Upon what ground?

125   1. CLOWN   Why, here in Denmark. I have been sexton here, man and boy, thirty
years.

HAMLET   How long will a man lie i' th' earth ere he rot?

---

90. **sirrah:** term of address to inferiors   106. **absolute:** positive   **by the card:** by the compass,
punctiliously   106–107. **equivocation:** ambiguity   108. **pick'd:** refined   109. **galls his kibe:** rubs
the courtier's chilblain

1. CLOWN   Faith, if 'a be not rotten before 'a die—as we have many pocky
corses, that will scarce hold the laying in—'a will last you some eight year or
130   nine year. A tanner will last you nine year.
HAMLET   Why he more than another?
1. CLOWN   Why, sir, his hide is so tann'd with his trade that 'a will keep out water a great while, and your water is a sore decayer of your whoreson dead
body. Here's a skull now hath lien you i' th' earth three and twenty years.
135   HAMLET   Whose was it?
1. CLOWN   A whoreson mad fellow's it was. Whose do you think it was?
HAMLET   Nay, I know not.
1. CLOWN   A pestilence on him for a mad rogue! 'a pour'd a flagon of Rhenish
on my head once. This same skull, sir, was, sir, Yorick's skull, the King's
140   jester.
HAMLET   This? [*takes the skull*]
1. CLOWN   E'en that.
HAMLET   Alas, poor Yorick! I knew him, Horatio, a fellow of infinite jest, of
most excellent fancy. He hath bore me on his back a thousand times, and
145   now how abhorr'd in my imagination it is! my gorge rises at it. Here hung
those lips that I have kiss'd I know not how oft. Where be your gibes now,
your gambols, your songs, your flashes of merriment, that were wont to set
the table on a roar? Not one now to mock your own grinning—quite chop-
fall'n. Now get you to my lady's [chamber], and tell her, let her paint an inch
150   thick, to this favor she must come; make her laugh at that. Prithee, Horatio,
tell me one thing.
HORATIO   What's that, my lord?
HAMLET   Dost thou think Alexander look'd a' this fashion i' th' earth?
HORATIO   E'en so.
155   HAMLET   And smelt so? pah!   [*puts down the skull*]
HORATIO   E'en so, my lord.
HAMLET   To what base uses we may return, Horatio! Why may not imagination
trace the noble dust of Alexander, till 'a find it stopping a bunghole?
HORATIO   'Twere to consider too curiously, to consider so.
160   HAMLET   No, faith, not a jot, but to follow him thither with modesty enough
and likelihood to lead it: Alexander died, Alexander was buried, Alexander
returneth to dust, the dust is earth, of earth we make loam, and why of that
loam whereto he was converted might they not stop a beer-barrel?
Imperious Caesar, dead and turn'd to clay,
165   Might stop a hole to keep the wind away.
O that that earth which kept the world in awe

---

128. **pocky:** rotten with venereal disease   129. **hold . . . in:** last out the burial   148–49. **chop-fall'n:**
(1) lacking the lower jaw; (2) downcast   150. **favor:** appearance   159. **curiously:** closely, minutely
160. **modesty:** moderation   162. **loam:** a mixture of moistened clay with sand, straw, etc.
164. **Imperious:** imperial

Should patch a wall t' expel the [winter's] flaw!
But soft, but soft awhile, here comes the King,

(*Enter* KING, QUEEN, LAERTES, *and* [*a* DOCTOR OF DIVINITY, *following*] *the corse,*
[*with* LORDS *attendant*].)

The Queen, the courtiers. Who is this they follow?
170   And with such maimed rites? This doth betoken
The corse they follow did with desp'rate hand
Foredo it own life. 'Twas of some estate.
Couch we a while and mark.   [*retiring with* HORATIO]

LAERTES   What ceremony else?

175 HAMLET   That is Laertes, a very noble youth. Mark.

LAERTES   What ceremony else?

DOCTOR   Her obsequies have been as far enlarg'd
As we have warranty. Her death was doubtful,
And but that great command o'ersways the order,
180   She should in ground unsanctified been lodg'd
Till the last trumpet; for charitable prayers,
[Shards,] flints, and pebbles should be thrown on her.
Yet here she is allow'd her virgin crants,
Her maiden strewments, and the bringing home
185   Of bell and burial.

LAERTES   Must there no more be done?

DOCTOR   No more be done:
We should profane the service of the dead
To sing a requiem and such rest to her
190   As to peace-parted souls.

LAERTES   Lay her i' th' earth,
And from her fair and unpolluted flesh
May violets spring! I tell thee, churlish priest,
A minist'ring angel shall my sister be
195   When thou liest howling.

HAMLET   What, the fair Ophelia!

QUEEN [*scattering flowers*]   Sweets to the sweet, farewell!
I hop'd thou shouldst have been my Hamlet's wife.
I thought thy bride-bed to have deck'd, sweet maid,
200   And not have strew'd thy grave.

---

167. **flaw:** gust   170. **maimed rites:** lack of customary ceremony   172. **Foredo:** fordo, destroy **it:** its **estate:** rank   173. **Couch we:** let us conceal ourselves   178. **doubtful:** the subject of an "open verdict"   179. **order:** customary procedure   180. **should:** would certainly   181. **for:** instead of   183. **crants:** garland   184. **maiden strewments:** flowers scattered on the grave of an unmarried girl   184–85. **bringing . . . burial:** burial in consecrated ground, with the bell tolling
189. **requiem:** dirge   197. **Sweets:** flowers

LAERTES   O, treble woe
    Fall ten times [treble] on that cursed head
    Whose wicked deed thy most ingenious sense
    Depriv'd thee of! Hold off the earth a while,
205   Till I have caught her once more in mine arms.

    [leaps in the grave]

    Now pile your dust upon the quick and dead,
    Till of this flat a mountain you have made
    T' o'ertop old Pelion, or the skyish head
    Of blue Olympus.
210 HAMLET *[coming forward]*   What is he whose grief
    Bears such an emphasis, whose phrase of sorrow
    Conjures the wand'ring stars and makes them stand
    Like wonder-wounded hearers? This is I,
    Hamlet the Dane!

    *[*HAMLET *leaps in after* LAERTES.*]*

215 LAERTES   The devil take thy soul!   *[grappling with him]*
HAMLET   Thou pray'st not well.
    I prithee take thy fingers from my throat.
    For though I am not splenitive [and] rash,
    Yet have I in me something dangerous,
220   Which let thy wisdom fear. Hold off thy hand!
KING   Pluck them asunder.
QUEEN   Hamlet, Hamlet!
ALL   Gentlemen!
HORATIO   Good my lord, be quiet.

    [The ATTENDANTS *part them, and they come out of the grave.]*

225 HAMLET   Why, I will fight with him upon this theme
    Until my eyelids will no longer wag.
QUEEN   O my son, what theme?
HAMLET   I lov'd Ophelia. Forty thousand brothers
    Could not with all their quantity of love
230   Make up my sum. What wilt thou do for her?
KING   O, he is mad, Laertes.
QUEEN   For love of God, forbear him.

---

203. **ingenious:** intelligent 208, 209. **Pelion, Olympus:** mountains in northeastern Greece
211. **emphasis, phrase:** rhetorical terms, here used in disparaging reference to Laertes' inflated language 212. **Conjures:** puts a spell upon **wand'ring stars:** planets 214. **the Dane:** This title normally signifies the king 218. **splenitive:** impetuous

HAMLET   'Swounds, show me what thou't do.
　　　Woo't weep, woo't fight, woo't fast, woo't tear thyself?
235　Woo't drink up eisel, eat a crocadile?
　　　I'll do't. Dost [thou] come here to whine?
　　　To outface me with leaping in her grave?
　　　Be buried quick with her, and so will I.
　　　And if thou prate of mountains, let them throw
240　Millions of acres on us, till our ground,
　　　Singeing his pate against the burning zone,
　　　Make Ossa like a wart! Nay, and thou'lt mouth,
　　　I'll rant as well as thou.
QUEEN　　　　　　　　　This is mere madness,
245　And [thus] a while the fit will work on him;
　　　Anon, as patient as the female dove,
　　　When that her golden couplets are disclosed,
　　　His silence will sit drooping.
HAMLET　　　　　　　　Hear you, sir,
250　What is the reason that you use me thus?
　　　I lov'd you ever. But it is no matter.
　　　Let Hercules himself do what he may,
　　　The cat will mew, and dog will have his day.

(*Exit* HAMLET.)

KING　I pray thee, good Horatio, wait upon him.

([*Exit*] HORATIO.)

255　[*to* LAERTES] Strengthen your patience in our last night's speech,
　　　We'll put the matter to the present push.—
　　　Good Gertrude, set some watch over your son.
　　　This grave shall have a living monument.
　　　An hour of quiet [shortly] shall we see,
260　Till then in patience our proceeding be.

(*Exeunt.*)

---

233. **thou't:** thou wilt   234-35. **Woo't:** wilt thou   235. **eisel:** vinegar   **crocadile:** crocodile
239. **if . . . mountains:** referring to lines 206–209   241. **burning zone:** sphere of the sun
242. **Ossa:** another mountain in Greece, near Pelion and Olympus   **mouth:** talk bombast (synonymous with *rant* in the next line)   244. **mere:** utter   246. **patient:** calm   247. **golden couplets:** pair
of baby birds, covered with yellow down   **disclosed:** hatched   252–53. **Let . . . day:** nobody can
prevent another from making the scenes he feels he has a right to   255. **in:** by recalling
256. **present push:** immediate test   258. **living:** enduring (?) or in the form of a lifelike effigy (?)

[Scene II]

(*Enter* HAMLET *and* HORATIO.)

HAMLET   So much for this, sir, now shall you see the other—
You do remember all the circumstance?
HORATIO   Remember it, my lord!
HAMLET   Sir, in my heart there was a kind of fighting
5   That would not let me sleep. [Methought] I lay
Worse than the mutines in the [bilboes]. Rashly—
And prais'd be rashness for it—let us know
Our indiscretion sometime serves us well
When our deep plots do pall, and that should learn us
10   There's a divinity that shapes our ends,
Rough-hew them how we will—
HORATIO   That is most certain.
HAMLET   Up from my cabin,
My sea-grown scarf'd about me, in the dark
15   Grop'd I to find out them, had my desire,
Finger'd their packet, and in fine withdrew
To mine own room again, making so bold,
My fears forgetting manners, to [unseal]
Their grand commission; where I found, Horatio—
20   Ah, royal knavery!—an exact command,
Larded with many several sorts of reasons,
Importing Denmark's health and England's too,
With, ho, such bugs and goblins in my life,
That, on the supervise, no leisure bated,
25   No, not to stay the grinding of the axe,
My head should be strook off.
HORATIO   Is't possible?
HAMLET   Here's the commission, read it at more leisure.
But wilt thou hear now how I did proceed?
30 HORATIO   I beseech you.
HAMLET   Being thus benetted round with [villainies],
Or I could make a prologue to my brains,

V.ii. Location: the castle   1. **see the other:** hear the other news I have to tell you (hinted at in the letter to Horatio, IV.vi.19–20)   6. **mutines:** mutineers (but the term *mutiny* was in Shakespeare's day used of almost any act of rebellion against authority)   **bilboes:** fetters attached to a heavy iron bar   **Rashly:** on impulse   7. **know:** recognize, acknowledge   9. **pall:** lose force, come to nothing   **learn:** teach   10. **shapes our ends:** gives final shape to our designs   11. **Rough-hew them:** block them out in initial form   16. **Finger'd:** filched, "pinched"   21. **Larded:** garnished   22. **Importing:** relating to   23. **bugs . . . life:** terrifying things in prospect if I were permitted to remain alive; *bugs* = bugaboos   24. **supervise:** perusal   **bated:** deducted (from the stipulated speediness)   25. **stay:** wait for   32. **Or:** before

They had begun the play. I sat me down,
Devis'd a new commission, wrote it fair.
35 I once did hold it, as our statists do,
A baseness to write fair, and labor'd much
How to forget that learning, but, sir, now
I did me yeman's service. Wilt thou know
Th' effect of what I wrote?
40 HORATIO   Ay, good my lord.
HAMLET   An earnest conjuration from the King,
As England was his faithful tributary,
As love between them like the palm might flourish,
As peace should still her wheaten garland wear
45 And stand a comma 'tween their amities,
And many such-like [as's] of great charge,
That on the view and knowing of these contents,
Without debatement further, more or less,
He should those bearers put to sudden death,
50 Not shriving time allow'd.
HORATIO   How was this seal'd?
HAMLET   Why, even in that was heaven ordinant.
I had my father's signet in my purse,
Which was the model of that Danish seal;
55 Folded the writ up in the form of th' other,
[Subscrib'd] it, gave't th' impression, plac'd it safely,
The changeling never known. Now the next day
Was our sea-fight, and what to this was sequent
Thou knowest already.
60 HORATIO   So Guildenstern and Rosencrantz go to't.
HAMLET   [Why, man, they did make love to this employment,]
They are not near my conscience. Their defeat
Does by their own insinuation grow.
'Tis dangerous when the baser nature comes
65 Between the pass and fell incensed points
Of mighty opposites.
HORATIO   Why, what a king is this!

---

34. **fair:** in a beautiful hand (such as a professional scribe would use)   35. **statists:** statesmen, public officials   36. **A baseness:** a skill befitting men of low rank   38. **yeman's:** yeoman's; solid, substantial   39. **effect:** purport, gist   45. **comma:** connective, link   46. **as's . . . charge:** (1) weighty clauses beginning with *as;* (2) asses with heavy loads   50. **shriving time:** time for confession and absolution   52. **ordinant:** in charge, guiding   54. **model:** small copy   56. **Subscrib'd:** signed   57. **changeling:** Hamlet's letter, substituted secretly for the genuine letter, as fairies substituted their children for human children   **never known:** never recognized as a substitution (unlike the fairies' changelings)   60. **go to't:** are going to their death   62. **defeat:** ruin, overthrow   63. **insinuation:** winding their way into the affair   64. **baser:** inferior   65. **pass:** thrust   **fell:** fierce

HAMLET   Does it not, think thee, stand me now upon—
He that hath kill'd my king and whor'd my mother,
70   Popp'd in between th' election and my hopes,
Thrown out his angle for my proper life,
And with such coz'nage—is't not perfect conscience
[To quit him with this arm? And is't not to be damn'd,
To let this canker of our nature come
75   In further evil?
HORATIO   It must be shortly known to him from England
What is the issue of the business there.
HAMLET   It will be short; the interim's mine,
And a man's life's no more than to say "one."
80   But I am very sorry, good Horatio,
That to Laertes I forgot myself,
For by the image of my cause I see
The portraiture of his. I'll [court] his favors.
But sure the bravery of his grief did put me
85   Into a tow'ring passion.
HORATIO   Peace, who comes here?]

(*Enter* [*young* OSRIC,] *a courtier.*)

OSRIC   Your lordship is right welcome back to Denmark.
HAMLET   I [humbly] thank you, sir.—Dost know this water-fly?
HORATIO   No, my good lord.
90   HAMLET   Thy state is the more gracious, for 'tis a vice to know him. He hath much land, and fertile; let a beast be lord of beasts, and his crib shall stand at the King's mess. 'Tis a chough, but, as I say, spacious in the possession of dirt.
OSRIC   Sweet lord, if your lordship were at leisure, I should impart a thing to
95   you from his Majesty.
HAMLET   I will receive it, sir, with all diligence of spirit. [Put] your bonnet to his right use, 'tis for the head.
OSRIC   I thank your lordship, it is very hot.
HAMLET   No, believe me, 'tis very cold, the wind is northerly.
100   OSRIC   It is indifferent cold, my lord, indeed.
HAMLET   But yet methinks it is very [sultry] and hot [for] my complexion.

---

68. **stand . . . upon:** rest upon me as a duty   70. **election:** as king of Denmark   71. **angle:** hook and line   **proper:** very   72. **coz'nage:** trickery   73. **quit him:** pay him back   74. **canker:** cancerous sore   74–75. **come In:** grow into   79. **a man's . . . more:** to kill a man takes no more time   **say "one."** Perhaps this is equivalent to "deliver one sword thrust"; see line 259 below, where Hamlet says "One" as he makes the first hit.   82. **image:** likeness   84. **bravery:** ostentatious expression   88. **water-fly:** tiny, vainly agitated creature   90. **gracious:** virtuous   91–92. **let . . . mess:** If a beast owned as many cattle as Osric, he could feast with the King.   92. **chough:** jackdaw, a bird that could be taught to speak   96. **bonnet:** hat   100. **indifferent:** somewhat   101. **complexion:** temperament

OSRIC Exceedingly, my lord, it is very sultry—as 'twere—I cannot tell how. My lord, his Majesty bade me signify to you that 'a has laid a great wager on your head. Sir, this is the matter—

105 HAMLET I beseech you remember.

[HAMLET *moves him to put on his hat.*]

OSRIC Nay, good my lord, for my ease, in good faith. Sir, here is newly come to court Laertes, believe me, an absolute [gentleman], full of most excellent differences, of very soft society, and great showing; indeed, to speak sellingly of him, he is the card or calendar of gentry; for you shall find in him the
110 continent of what part a gentleman would see.

HAMLET Sir, his definement suffers no perdition in you, though I know to divide him inventorially would dozy th' arithmetic of memory, and yet but yaw neither in respect of his quick sail; but in the verity of extolment, I take him to be a soul of great article, and his infusion of such dearth and
115 rareness as, to make true diction of him, his semblable is his mirror, and who else would trace him, his umbrage, nothing more.

OSRIC Your lordship speaks most infallibly of him.

HAMLET The concernancy, sir? Why do we wrap the gentleman in our more rawer breath?

120 OSRIC Sir?

HORATIO Is't not possible to understand in another tongue? You will to't, sir, really.

HAMLET What imports the nomination of this gentleman?

OSRIC Of Laertes?

125 HORATIO His purse is empty already: all 's golden words are spent.

HAMLET Of him, sir.

OSRIC I know you are not ignorant—

HAMLET I would you did, sir, yet, in faith, if you did, it would not much approve me. Well, sir?

130 OSRIC You are not ignorant of what excellence Laertes is—

---

106. **for my ease:** I am really more comfortable with my hat off (a polite insistence on maintaining ceremony). 107. **absolute:** complete, possessing every quality a gentleman should have 108. **differences:** distinguishing characteristics, personal qualities **soft:** agreeable **great showing:** splendid appearance **sellingly:** like a seller to a prospective buyer; in a fashion to do full justice. Most editors follow Q3 in reading *feelingly* = with exactitude, as he deserves. 109. **card or calendar:** chart or register, compendious guide **gentry:** gentlemanly behavior 109–110. **the continent . . . part:** one who contains every quality 111. **perdition:** loss 112. **dozy:** make dizzy 113. **yaw:** keep deviating erratically from its course (said of a ship) **neither:** for all that **in respect of:** compared with **in . . . extolment:** to praise him truly 114. **article:** scope (?) or importance (?) **infusion:** essence, quality **dearth:** scarceness 115. **make true diction:** speak truly **his semblable:** his only likeness or equal 116. **who . . . him:** anyone else who tries to follow him **umbrage:** shadow 118. **concernancy:** relevance 118–19. **more rawer breath:** words too crude to describe him properly 121. **in another tongue:** when someone else is the speaker 121–22. **You . . . really:** you can do it if you try 123. **nomination:** naming, mention 128–29. **approve:** commend

HAMLET   I dare not confess that, lest I should compare with him in excellence, but to know a man well were to know himself.

OSRIC   I mean, sir, for [his] weapon, but in the imputation laid on him by them, in his meed he's unfellow'd.

135 HAMLET   What's his weapon?

OSRIC   Rapier and dagger.

HAMLET   That's two of his weapons—but well.

OSRIC   The King, sir, hath wager'd with him six Barbary horses, against the which he has impawn'd, as I take it, six French rapiers and poniards, with
140   their assigns, as girdle, [hangers], and so. Three of the carriages, in faith, are very dear to fancy, very responsive to the hilts, most delicate carriages, and of very liberal conceit.

HAMLET   What call you the carriages?

HORATIO   I knew you must be edified by the margent ere you had done.

145 OSRIC   The [carriages], sir, are the hangers.

HAMLET   The phrase would be more germane to the matter if we could carry a cannon by our sides; I would it [might be] hangers till then. But on: six Barb'ry horses against six French swords, their assigns, and three liberal-conceited carriages; that's the French bet against the Danish. Why is this all
150   [impawn'd, as] you call it?

OSRIC   The King, sir, hath laid, sir, that in a dozen passes between yourself and him, he shall not exceed you three hits; he hath laid on twelve for nine; and it would come to immediate trial, if your lordship would vouchsafe the answer.

155 HAMLET   How if I answer no?

OSRIC   I mean, my lord, the opposition of your person in trial.

HAMLET   Sir, I will walk here in the hall. If it please his Majesty, it is the breathing time of day with me. Let the foils be brought, the gentleman willing, and the King hold his purpose, I will win for him and I can; if not, I will gain
160   nothing but my shame and the odd hits.

OSRIC   Shall I deliver you so?

HAMLET   To this effect, sir—after what flourish your nature will.

---

131. **compare . . . excellence:** seem to claim the same degree of excellence for myself
132. **but:** The sense seems to require *for.*   **himself:** oneself   133–34. **in . . . them:** in popular
estimation   134. **meed:** merit   139. **impawn'd:** staked   140. **assigns:** appurtenances
hangers: straps on which the swords hang from the girdle   **carriages:** properly, gun-carriages;
here used affectedly in place of *hangers*   141. **fancy:** taste   **very responsive to:** matching well
142. **liberal conceit:** elegant design   144. **must . . . margent:** would require enlightenment
from a marginal note   151. **laid:** wagered   152. **he . . . hits:** Laertes must win by at least eight to
four (if none of the "passes" or bouts are draws), since at seven to five he would be only two up.
he . . . nine: Not satisfactorily explained despite much discussion. One suggestion is that
Laertes has raised the odds against himself by wagering that out of twelve bouts he will win nine.
154. **answer:** encounter (as Hamlet's following quibble forces Osric to explain in his next speech)
157–58. **breathing . . . me:** my usual hour for exercise   162. **after what flourish:** with whatever
embellishment of language

OSRIC   I commend my duty to your lordship.

HAMLET   Yours. [*Exit* Osric.]   ['A]   does well to commend it himself,
165   there are no tongues else for 's turn.

HORATIO   This lapwing runs away with the shell on his head.

HAMLET   'A did [comply], sir, with his dug before 'a suck'd it. Thus has he, and
many more of the same breed that I know the drossy age dotes on, only got
the tune of the time, and out of an habit of encounter, a kind of [yesty] col-
170   lection, which carries them through and through the most [profound] and
[winnow'd] opinions, and do but blow them to their trial, the bubbles are
out.

(*Enter a* LORD.)

LORD   My lord, his Majesty commended him to you by young Osric, who
brings back to him that you attend him in the hall. He sends to know if your
175   pleasure hold to play with Laertes, or that you will take longer time.

HAMLET   I am constant to my purposes, they follow the King's pleasure. If his
fitness speaks, mine is ready; now or whensoever, provided I be so able as
now.

LORD   The King and Queen and all are coming down.

180   HAMLET   In happy time.

LORD   The Queen desires you to use some gentle entertainment to Laertes before you fall to play.

HAMLET   She well instructs me. [*Exit* LORD.]

HORATIO   You will lose, my lord.

185   HAMLET   I do not think so; since he went into France I have been in continual
practice. I shall win at the odds. Thou wouldst not think how ill all's here
about my heart—but it is no matter.

HORATIO   Nay, good my lord—

HAMLET   It is but foolery, but it is such a kind of [gain-]giving, as would per-
190   haps trouble a woman.

HORATIO   If your mind dislike any thing, obey it. I will forestall their repair
hither, and say you are not fit.

HAMLET   Not a whit, we defy augury. There is special providence in the fall of a
sparrow. If it be [now], 'tis not to come; if it be not to come, it will be now; if

---

163. **commend my duty:** offer my dutiful respects (but Hamlet picks up the phrase in the sense
"praise my manner of bowing")   166. **lapwing:** a foolish bird which upon hatching was
supposed to run with part of the eggshell still over its head. (Osric has put his hat on
at last.)   167. **comply . . . dug:** bow politely to his mother's nipple   168. **drossy:** worthless
169. **tune . . . time:** fashionable ways of talk   **habit of encounter:** mode of social intercourse
yesty: yeasty, frothy   169–70. **collection:** anthology of fine phrases   171. **winnow'd:** sifted, choice
opinions: judgments   **blow . . . trial:** test them by blowing on them; make even the least demanding trial of them   172. **out:** blown away (?) or at an end, done for (?)   176–77. **If . . . ready:** If this
is a good moment for him, it is for me also.   181. **gentle entertainment:** courteous greeting
189. **gain-giving:** misgiving   193–94. **special . . . sparrow:** See Matthew 10:29.

195   it be not now, yet it [will] come—the readiness is all. Since no man, of aught
      he leaves, knows what is't to leave betimes, let be.

(*A table prepar'd,* [*and flagons of wine on it. Enter*] *Trumpets, Drums, and Officers
with cushions, foils, daggers;* KING, QUEEN, LAERTES, [OSRIC,] *and all the State.*)

KING   Come, Hamlet, come, and take this hand from me.

[*The* KING *puts* LAERTES' *hand into* HAMLET'S.]

HAMLET   Give me your pardon, sir. I have done you wrong,
      But pardon't as you are a gentleman.
200   This presence knows,
      And you must needs have heard, how I am punish'd
      With a sore distraction. What I have done
      That might your nature, honor, and exception
      Roughly awake, I here proclaim was madness.
205   Was't Hamlet wrong'd Laertes? Never Hamlet!
      If Hamlet from himself be ta'en away,
      And when he's not himself does wrong Laertes,
      Then Hamlet does it not, Hamlet denies it.
      Who does it then? His madness. If't be so,
210   Hamlet is of the faction that is wronged,
      His madness is poor Hamlet's enemy.
      [Sir, in this audience,]
      Let my disclaiming from a purpos'd evil
      Free me so far in your most generous thoughts,
215   That I have shot my arrow o'er the house
      And hurt my brother.
LAERTES   I am satisfied in nature,
      Whose motive in this case should stir me most
      To my revenge, but in my terms of honor
220   I stand aloof, and will no reconcilement
      Till by some elder masters of known honor
      I have a voice and president of peace
      To [keep] my name ungor'd. But [till] that time
      I do receive your offer'd love like love,
225   And will not wrong it.

---

195. **of aught:** whatever   196. **knows . . . betimes:** knows what is the best time to leave it
s.d. **State:** nobles   200. **presence:** assembled court   201. **punish'd:** afflicted   203. **exception:**
objection   213. **my . . . evil:** my declaration that I intended no harm   214. **Free:** absolve
217. **in nature:** so far as my personal feelings are concerned   219. **in . . . honor:** as a man governed
by an established code of honor   222–23. **have . . . ungor'd:** can secure an opinion backed by
precedent that I can make peace with you without injury to my reputation

HAMLET   I embrace it freely,
   And will this brothers' wager frankly play.
   Give us the foils. [Come on.]
LAERTES   Come, one for me.
230 HAMLET   I'll be your foil, Laertes; in mine ignorance
   Your skill shall like a star i' th' darkest night
   Stick fiery off indeed.
LAERTES   You mock me, sir.
HAMLET   No, by this hand.
235 KING   Give them the foils, young Osric. Cousin Hamlet,
   You know the wager?
HAMLET   Very well, my lord.
   Your Grace has laid the odds a' th' weaker side.
KING   I do not fear it, I have seen you both;
240   But since he is [better'd], we have therefore odds.
LAERTES   This is too heavy; let me see another.
HAMLET   This likes me well. These foils have all a length?   [*Prepare to play.*]
OSRIC   Ay, my good lord.
KING   Set me the stoups of wine upon that table.
245   If Hamlet give the first or second hit,
   Or quit in answer of the third exchange,
   Let all the battlements their ord'nance fire.
   The King shall drink to Hamlet's better breath,
   And in the cup an [union] shall he throw,
250   Richer than that which four successive kings
   In Denmark's crown have worn. Give me the cups,
   And let the kettle to the trumpet speak,
   The trumpet to the cannoneer without,
   The cannons to the heavens, the heaven to earth,
255   "Now the King drinks to Hamlet." Come begin;

(*trumpets the while*)

   And you, the judges, bear a wary eye.
HAMLET   Come on, sir.
LAERTES   Come, my lord.

[*They play and* HAMLET *scores a hit.*]

---

227. **brothers':** amicable, as if between brothers   **frankly:** freely, without constraint
230. **foil:** thin sheet of metal placed behind a jewel to set it off   232. **Stick . . . off:** blaze out in contrast   238. **laid the odds:** wagered a higher stake (horses to rapiers)   240. **is better'd:** has perfected
his skill   **odds:** the arrangement that Laertes must take more bouts than Hamlet to win
242. **likes:** pleases   **a length:** the same length   244. **stoups:** tankards   246. **quit . . . exchange:** pays
back wins by Laertes in the first and second bouts by taking the third   249. **union:** an especially fine
pearl   252. **kettle:** kettle-drum

HAMLET   One.

260 LAERTES   No.

HAMLET   Judgment.

OSRIC   A hit, a very palpable hit.

LAERTES   Well, again.

KING   Stay, give me drink. Hamlet, this pearl is thine,

265   Here's to thy health! Give him the cup.

(*Drum, trumpets* [*sound*] *flourish. A piece goes off* [*within*].)

HAMLET   I'll play this bout first, set it by a while.

     Come.   [*They play again.*]   Another hit; what say you?

LAERTES   [*A touch, a touch,*] ˙I do confess't.

KING   Our son shall win.

270 QUEEN   He's fat, and scant of breath.

     Here, Hamlet, take my napkin, rub thy brows.

     The Queen carouses to thy fortune, Hamlet.

HAMLET   Good madam!

KING   Gertrude, do not drink.

275 QUEEN   I will, my lord, I pray you pardon me.

KING [*aside*]   It is the pois'ned cup, it is too late.

HAMLET   I dare not drink yet, madam; by and by.

QUEEN   Come, let me wipe thy face.

LAERTES   My lord, I'll hit him now.

280 KING   I do not think't.

LAERTES [*aside*]   And yet it is almost against my conscience.

HAMLET   Come, for the third, Laertes, you do but dally.

     I pray you pass with your best violence;

     I am sure you make a wanton of me.

285 LAERTES   Say you so? Come on.   [*They play.*]

OSRIC   Nothing, neither way.

LAERTES   Have at you now!

[LAERTES *wounds* HAMLET; *then, in scuffling, they change rapiers.*]

KING   Part them, they are incens'd.

290 HAMLET   Nay, come again.

[HAMLET *wounds* LAERTES. *The* QUEEN *falls.*]

OSRIC   Look to the Queen there ho!

HORATIO   They bleed on both sides. How is it, my lord?

OSRIC   How is't, Laertes?

LAERTES   Why, as a woodcock to mine own springe, Osric:

295   I am justly kill'd with mine own treachery.

---

270. **fat:** sweaty   272. **carouses:** drinks a toast   284. **make . . . me:** are holding back in order to let me win, as one does with a spoiled child (*wanton*)   294. **springe:** snare

HAMLET   How does the Queen?

KING   She sounds to see them bleed.

QUEEN   No, no, the drink, the drink—O my dear Hamlet—
The drink, the drink! I am pois'ned.   [*Dies.*]

300 HAMLET   O villainy! Ho, let the door be lock'd!
Treachery! Seek it out.

LAERTES   It is here, Hamlet. [Hamlet,] thou art slain.
No med'cine in the world can do thee good;
In thee there is not half an hour's life.

305   The treacherous instrument is in [thy] hand,
Unbated and envenom'd. The foul practice
Hath turn'd itself on me. Lo here I lie,
Never to rise again. Thy mother's pois'ned.
I can no more—the King, the King's to blame.

310 HAMLET   The point envenom'd too!
Then, venom, to thy work.   [*hurts the* KING]

ALL   Treason! treason!

KING   O, yet defend me, friends, I am but hurt.

HAMLET   Here, thou incestious, [murd'rous], damned Dane,

315   Drink [off] this potion! Is [thy union] here?
Follow my mother!   [KING *dies.*]

LAERTES   He is justly served,
It is a poison temper'd by himself.
Exchange forgiveness with me, noble Hamlet.

320   Mine and my father's death come not upon thee,
Nor thine on me!   [*dies*]

HAMLET   Heaven make thee free of it! I follow thee.
I am dead, Horatio. Wretched queen, adieu!
You that look pale, and tremble at this chance,

325   That are but mutes or audience to this act,
Had I but time—as this fell sergeant, Death,
Is strict in his arrest—O, I could tell you—
But let it be. Horatio, I am dead,
Thou livest. Report me and my cause aright

330   To the unsatisfied.

HORATIO   Never believe it;
I am more an antique Roman than a Dane.
Here's yet some liquor left.

HAMLET   As th' art a man,

335   Give me the cup. Let go! By heaven, I'll ha't!

---

297. **sounds:** swoons   306. **Unbated:** not blunted   **foul practice:** vile plot   s.d. **hurts:** wounds   318. **temper'd:** mixed   322. **make thee free:** absolve you   325. **mutes or audience:** silent spectators   326. **fell:** cruel   **sergeant:** sheriff's officer   332. **antique Roman:** one who will commit suicide on such an occasion

O God, Horatio, what a wounded name,
Things standing thus unknown, shall I leave behind me!
If thou didst ever hold me in thy heart,
Absent thee from felicity a while,
340   And in this harsh world draw thy breath in pain
To tell my story.   (*a march afar off* [*and a shot within*])
What warlike noise is this?

[OSRIC *goes to the door and returns.*]

OSRIC   Young Fortinbras, with conquest come from Poland,
To th' embassadors of England gives
345   This warlike volley.
HAMLET   O, I die, Horatio,
The potent poison quite o'er-crows my spirit.
I cannot live to hear the news from England,
But I do prophesy th' election lights
350   On Fortinbras, he has my dying voice.
So tell him, with th' occurrents more and less
Which have solicited—the rest is silence.   [*dies*]
HORATIO   Now cracks a noble heart. Good night, sweet prince,
And flights of angels sing thee to thy rest!

[*march within*]

355   Why does the drum come hither?

(*Enter* FORTINBRAS *with the* [ENGLISH] EMBASSADORS, [*with Drum, Colors, and*
ATTENDANTS].)

FORTINBRAS   Where is this sight?
HORATIO   What is it you would see?
If aught of woe or wonder, cease your search.
FORTINBRAS   This quarry cries on havoc. O proud death,
360   What feast is toward in thine eternal cell,
That thou so many princes at a shot
So bloodily hast strook?
[1.] EMBASSADOR   The sight is dismal,
And our affairs from England come too late.
365   The ears are senseless that should give us hearing,
To tell him his commandment is fulfill'd,
That Rosencrantz and Guildenstern are dead.
Where should we have our thanks?

---

347. **o'er-crows:** triumphs over (a term derived from cockfighting)   **spirit:** vital
energy   350. **voice:** vote   351. **occurrents:** occurrences   352. **solicited:** instigated
359. **This . . . havoc:** this heap of corpses proclaims a massacre   360. **toward:** in preparation

HORATIO   Not from his mouth,
370   Had it th' ability of life to thank you.
       He never gave commandement for their death.
       But since so jump upon this bloody question,
       You from the Polack wars, and you from England,
       Are here arrived, give order that these bodies
375   High on a stage be placed to the view,
       And let me speak to [th'] yet unknowing world
       How these things came about. So shall you hear
       Of carnal, bloody, and unnatural acts,
       Of accidental judgments, casual slaughters,
380   Of deaths put on by cunning and [forc'd] cause,
       And in this upshot, purposes mistook
       Fall'n on th' inventors' heads: all this can I
       Truly deliver.
FORTINBRAS   Let us haste to hear it,
385   And call the noblest to the audience.
       For me, with sorrow I embrace my fortune.
       I have some rights, of memory in this kingdom,
       Which now to claim my vantage doth invite me.
HORATIO   Of that I shall have also cause to speak,
390   And from his mouth whose voice will draw [on] more.
       But let this same be presently perform'd
       Even while men's minds are wild, lest more mischance
       On plots and errors happen.
FORTINBRAS   Let four captains
395   Bear Hamlet like a soldier to the stage,
       For he was likely, had he been put on,
       To have prov'd most royal; and for his passage,
       The soldiers' music and the rite of war
       Speak loudly for him.
400   Take up the bodies. Such a sight as this
       Becomes the field, but here shows much amiss.
       Go bid the soldiers shoot.

(*Exeunt* [*marching; after the which a peal of ordinance are shot off*].)

---

369. **his:** the king's   372. **jump:** precisely, pat   **question:** matter   375. **stage:** platform
379. **judgments:** retributions   **casual:** happening by chance   380. **put on:** instigated
387. **of memory:** unforgotten   388. **my vantage:** my opportune presence at a moment when the
throne is empty   390. **his . . . more:** the mouth of one (Hamlet) whose vote will induce others to
support your claim   391. **presently:** at once   392. **wild:** distraught   396. **put on:** put to the test
(by becoming king)   397. **passage:** death   401. **Becomes . . . amiss:** befits the battlefield, but appears very much out of place here

STUDY QUESTIONS

1. The climax in *Hamlet* extends over several scenes. Which ones do you think they are?
2. What states does Hamlet pass through within these scenes?
3. How do his actions after the climax contrast with his actions before it?
4. What changes in Hamlet's outlook, or in your reaction to him, begin during these climactic scenes and develop during the latter part of the play?
5. Choose some topic that shows how the climax functions as a turning point in *Hamlet* and develop it as fully as possible, making use of specific examples not only from the climactic scenes but from earlier and later scenes as well.

Much Ado About Nothing

WILLIAM SHAKESPEARE

CHARACTERS

DON PEDRO, *Prince of Arragon*
DON JOHN, *his bastard brother*
CLAUDIO, *a young lord of Florence*
BENEDICK, *a young lord of Padua*
LEONATO, *governor of Messina*
ANTONIO, *his brother*
BALTHASAR, *attendant on Don Pedro*
CONRADE ⎫
BORACHIO ⎭ *followers of Don John*
FRIAR FRANCIS
DOGBERRY, *a constable*
VERGES, *a headborough*
SEXTON
BOY
HERO, *daughter to Leonato*
BEATRICE, *niece to Leonato*
MARGARET ⎫
URSULA ⎭ *gentlewomen attending on Hero*
MESSENGERS, WATCH, LORD, ATTENDANTS, *etc.*

SCENE: *Messina*

Act I

Scene I

(*Enter* LEONATO, *governor of Messina,* HERO *his daughter, and* BEATRICE *his niece, with a* MESSENGER.)

LEONATO   I learn in this letter that Don [Pedro] of Arragon comes this night to Messina.

MESSENGER   He is very near by this, he was not three leagues off when I left him.

5   LEONATO   How many gentlemen have you lost in this action?

Words and passages enclosed in square brackets in the text above are either emendations of the copy-text or additions to it. The numbers in the footnotes are line numbers.
I.i. Location: Messina, before Leonato's house
5. **action:** battle

MESSENGER   But few of any sort, and none of name.

LEONATO   A victory is twice itself when the achiever brings home full numbers. I find here that Don [Pedro] hath bestow'd much honor on a young Florentine call'd Claudio.

10 MESSENGER   Much deserv'd on his part, and equally rememb'red by Don Pedro. He hath borne himself beyond the promise of his age, doing in the figure of a lamb the feats of a lion. He hath indeed better bett'red expectation than you must expect of me to tell you how.

LEONATO   He hath an uncle here in Messina will be very much glad of it.

15 MESSENGER   I have already deliver'd him letters, and there appears much joy in him, even so much that joy could not show itself modest enough without a badge of bitterness.

LEONATO   Did he break out into tears?

MESSENGER   In great measure.

20 LEONATO   A kind overflow of kindness. There are no faces truer than those that are so wash'd. How much better is it to weep at joy than to joy at weeping!

BEATRICE   I pray you, is Signior Mountanto return'd from the wars or no?

MESSENGER   I know none of that name, lady. There was none such in the army of any sort.

25 LEONATO   What is he that you ask for, niece?

HERO   My cousin means Signior Benedick of Padua.

MESSENGER   O, he's return'd, and as pleasant as ever he was.

BEATRICE   He set up his bills here in Messina, and challeng'd Cupid at the flight, and my uncle's fool, reading the challenge, subscrib'd for Cupid, and
30   challeng'd him at the burbolt. I pray you, how many hath he kill'd and eaten in these wars? But how many hath he kill'd? for indeed I promis'd to eat all of his killing.

LEONATO   Faith, niece, you tax Signior Benedick too much, but he'll be meet with you, I doubt it not.

35 MESSENGER   He hath done good service, lady, in these wars.

BEATRICE   You had musty victual, and he hath holp to eat it. He is a very valiant trencherman, he hath an excellent stomach.

---

6. **sort:** rank (so also in line 24)   **name:** reputation, prominence   12. **figure:** appearance
bett'red: surpassed   14. **will:** who will (a frequent construction)   16. **modest:** moderate
17. **badge of bitterness:** sign of sorrow. Leonato's next question translates these words into literal
terms.   20. **kind:** natural   22. **Mountanto:** from Italian *montanto,* a fencing term meaning an upward blow or thrust   27. **pleasant:** jocular   28. **bills:** public notices   28–29. **at the flight:** to an
archery contest. Perhaps she means that Benedick proclaimed himself immune to love.   29. **fool:**
jester. It has been suggested that perhaps Beatrice means herself, and is referring obliquely to an earlier romantic encounter with Benedick. See lines 44–46 and II.i.200–202.   **subscrib'd for:** made an
undertaking on behalf of   30. **burbolt:** bird-bolt, a blunt-headed arrow for shooting birds at short
distance. The bird-bolt was allowed to fools and children as being less dangerous than the barbed
long-distance arrow, and was frequently assigned to Cupid, perhaps because he was represented as a
child.   31–32. **promis'd . . . killing:** predicted that he wouldn't kill anyone   33. **tax:** take to task,
censure   **meet:** even, quits   36. **musty:** stale   **holp:** helped   37. **trencherman:** good eater
stomach: appetite

MESSENGER   And a good soldier too, lady.

BEATRICE   And a good soldier to a lady, but what is he to a lord?

40 MESSENGER   A lord to a lord, a man to a man, stuff'd with all honorable virtues.

BEATRICE   It is so indeed, he is no less than a stuff'd man. But for the stuffing—well, we are all mortal.

LEONATO   You must not, sir, mistake my niece. There is a kind of merry war be-

45   twixt Signior Benedick and her; they never meet but there's a skirmish of wit between them.

BEATRICE   Alas, he gets nothing by that. In our last conflict four of his five wits went halting off, and now is the whole man govern'd with one; so that if he have wit enough to keep himself warm, let him bear it for a difference be-

50   tween himself and his horse, for it is all the wealth that he hath left to be known a reasonable creature. Who is his companion now? he hath every month a new sworn brother.

MESSENGER   Is't possible?

BEATRICE   Very easily possible. He wears his faith but as the fashion of his hat:

55   it ever changes with the next block.

MESSENGER   I see, lady, the gentleman is not in your books.

BEATRICE   No, and he were, I would burn my study. But I pray you, who is his companion? Is there no young squarer now that will make a voyage with him to the devil?

60 MESSENGER   He is most in the company of the right noble Claudio.

BEATRICE   O Lord, he will hang upon him like a disease; he is sooner caught than the pestilence, and the taker runs presently mad. God help the noble Claudio! If he have caught the Benedick, it will cost him a thousand pound ere 'a be cur'd.

65 MESSENGER   I will hold friends with you, lady.

BEATRICE   Do, good friend.

LEONATO   You will never run mad, niece.

BEATRICE   No, not till a hot January.

MESSENGER   Don Pedro is approach'd.

(*Enter* DON PEDRO, CLAUDIO, BENEDICK, BALTHASAR, *and* [DON] JOHN *the Bastard.*)

---

39. **to:** in comparison with   42. **stuff'd man:** a dummy, not a real man   42–43. **for . . . mortal:** as for his character—well, we all have our faults   47. **five wits:** usually listed as memory, fantasy, judgment, imagination, and common wit   48. **halting:** limping   49. **wit . . . warm:** proverbial for minimal intelligence   **difference:** a variation in a coat of arms to distinguish a junior member or branch of a family from the chief line.   51. **known:** recognized as   52. **sworn brother:** friend with whom he has exchanged vows of lifelong fidelity   54. **faith:** loyalty   55. **block:** wooden mould for shaping hats; hence, fashion   56. **books:** good books, favor   57. **and:** if   58. **squarer:** quarreller   62. **presently:** immediately   64. **'a:** he   65. **hold friends:** keep on friendly terms (so as not to incur your wrath)   67. **run mad:** "catch the Benedick"

70 DON PEDRO   Good Signior Leonato, are you come to meet your trouble? The
       fashion of the world is to avoid cost, and you encounter it.
   LEONATO   Never came trouble to my house in the likeness of your Grace, for
       trouble being gone, comfort should remain; but when you depart from me,
       sorrow abides and happiness takes his leave.
75 DON PEDRO   You embrace your charge too willingly. I think this is your daugh-
       ter.
   LEONATO   Her mother hath many times told me so.
   BENEDICK   Were you in doubt, sir, that you ask'd her?
   LEONATO   Signior Benedick, no, for then were you a child.
80 DON PEDRO   You have it full, Benedick. We may guess by this what you are, be-
       ing a man. Truly the lady fathers herself. Be happy, lady, for you are like an
       honorable father.
   BENEDICK   If Signior Leonato be her father, she would not have his head on her
       shoulders for all Messina, as like him as she is.
85 BEATRICE   I wonder that you will still be talking, Signior Benedick, nobody
       marks you.
   BENEDICK   What, my dear Lady Disdain! are you yet living?
   BEATRICE   Is it possible disdain should die while she hath such meet food to
       feed it as Signior Benedick? Courtesy itself must convert to disdain, if you
90   come in her presence.
   BENEDICK   Then is courtesy a turncoat. But it is certain I am lov'd of all ladies,
       only you excepted; and I would I could find in my heart that I had not a
       hard heart, for truly I love none.
   BEATRICE   A dear happiness to women, they would else have been troubled
95   with a pernicious suitor. I thank God and my cold blood, I am of your
       humor for that: I had rather hear my dog bark at a crow than a man swear
       he loves me.
   BENEDICK   God keep your ladyship still in that mind! so some gentleman or
       other shall scape a predestinate scratch'd face.
100 BEATRICE   Scratching could not make it worse, and 'twere such a face as yours
       were.
   BENEDICK   Well, you are a rare parrot-teacher.
   BEATRICE   A bird of my tongue is better than a beast of yours.
   BENEDICK   I would my horse had the speed of your tongue, and so good a con-
105   tinuer. But keep your way a' God's name, I have done.

---

71. **cost:** expense   **encounter:** go to meet   75. **embrace your charge:** welcome your burden
80. **have it full:** are well answered, have got back as good as you gave   81. **fathers herself:** shows who
her father is (by her resemblance to him)   83. **his head:** with its marks of age   85. **still:** always
89. **convert:** change   94. **dear happiness:** great stroke of good fortune   96. **humor for that:** inclination in that respect   99. **scape:** escape   **predestinate:** foreordained, inevitable (for anyone who
marries Beatrice)   101. **were:** is (the verb has been attracted into the subjunctive by the preceding
'twere)   102. **rare:** excellent   **parrot-teacher:** one who says the same thing over and over
103. **A bird . . . yours:** A bird taught to speak like me would be better than an animal taught to speak
like you, for he would say nothing.   104–105. **so . . . continuer:** (were) so tireless

BEATRICE   You always end with a jade's trick, I know you of old.

DON PEDRO   That is the sum of all: Leonato—Signior Claudio and Signior Benedick—my dear friend Leonato hath invited you all. I tell him we shall stay here at the least a month, and he heartily prays some occasion may de-

110   tain us longer. I dare swear he is no hypocrite, but prays from his heart.

LEONATO   If you swear, my lord, you shall not be forsworn. [*to* DON JOHN] Let me bid you welcome, my lord, being reconcil'd to the Prince your brother: I owe you all duty.

DON JOHN   I thank you. I am not of many words, but I thank you.

115   LEONATO   Please it your Grace lead on?

DON PEDRO   Your hand, Leonato, we will go together.

(*Exeunt. Manent* BENEDICK *and* CLAUDIO.)

CLAUDIO   Benedick, didst thou note the daughter of Signior Leonato?

BENEDICK   I noted her not, but I look'd on her.

CLAUDIO   Is she not a modest young lady?

120   BENEDICK   Do you question me, as an honest man should do, for my simple true judgment? or would you have me speak after my custom, as being a profess'd tyrant to their sex?

CLAUDIO   No, I pray thee speak in sober judgment.

BENEDICK   Why, i' faith, methinks she's too low for a high praise, too brown for

125   a fair praise, and too little for a great praise; only this commendation I can afford her, that were she other than she is, she were unhandsome, and being no other but as she is, I do not like her.

CLAUDIO   Thou thinkest I am in sport. I pray thee tell me truly how thou lik'st her.

130   BENEDICK   Would you buy her, that you inquire after her?

CLAUDIO   Can the world buy such a jewel?

BENEDICK   Yea, and a case to put it into. But speak you this with a sad brow? or do you play the flouting Jack, to tell us Cupid is a good hare-finder and Vulcan a rare carpenter? Come, in what key shall a man take you to go in the

135   song?

CLAUDIO   In mine eye, she is the sweetest lady that ever I look'd on.

BENEDICK   I can see yet without spectacles, and I see no such matter. There's her cousin, and she were not possess'd with a fury, exceeds her as much in beauty as the first of May doth the last of December. But I hope you have no

140   intent to turn husband, have you?

---

106. **jade's trick:** A jade is an ill-conditioned horse, likely to drop out of a race before the end, as Benedick here lamely drops out of the contest of wits.   107. **That . . . all:** Don Pedro and Leonato have been conversing aside.   112. **being:** since you are   118. **noted her not:** didn't observe her in particular   122. **tyrant:** one pitiless and cruel   124. **low:** short   132. **sad:** serious
133. **flouting Jack:** mocking fellow   133–34. **to . . . carpenter:** by saying something as obviously wide of the truth as that Cupid has sharp eyes, or calling Vulcan a carpenter (Cupid was blind, Vulcan the blacksmith of the gods).   134–35. **go . . . song:** sing in harmony with you

CLAUDIO   I would scarce trust myself, though I had sworn the contrary, if Hero
would be my wife.

BENEDICK   Is't come to this? In faith, hath not the world one man but he will
wear his cap with suspicion? Shall I never see a bachelor of threescore again?
145   Go to, i' faith, and thou wilt needs thrust thy neck into a yoke, wear the print
of it, and sigh away Sundays. Look, Don Pedro is return'd to seek you.

(*Enter* DON PEDRO.)

DON PEDRO   What secret hath held you here, that you follow'd not to
Leonato's?

BENEDICK   I would your Grace would constrain me to tell.

150   DON PEDRO   I charge thee on thy allegiance.

BENEDICK   You hear, Count Claudio, I can be secret as a dumb man; I would
have you think so; but on my allegiance, mark you this, on my allegiance, he
is in love. With who? Now that is your Grace's part. Mark how short his answer is: with Hero, Leonato's short daughter.

155   CLAUDIO   If this were so, so were it utt'red.

BENEDICK   Like the old tale, my lord: "It is not so, nor 'twas not so, but indeed,
God forbid it should be so."

CLAUDIO   If my passion change not shortly, God forbid it should be otherwise.

DON PEDRO   Amen, if you love her, for the lady is very well worthy.

160   CLAUDIO   You speak this to fetch me in, my lord.

DON PEDRO   By my troth, I speak my thought.

CLAUDIO   And in faith, my lord, I spoke mine.

BENEDICK   And by my two faiths and troths, my lord, I spoke mine.

CLAUDIO   That I love her, I feel.

165   DON PEDRO   That she is worthy, I know.

BENEDICK   That I neither feel how she should be lov'd, nor know how she
should be worthy, is the opinion that fire cannot melt out of me; I will die in
it at the stake.

DON PEDRO   Thou wast ever an obstinate heretic in the despite of beauty.

170   CLAUDIO   And never could maintain his part but in the force of his will.

BENEDICK   That a woman conceiv'd me, I thank her; that she brought me up, I
likewise give her most humble thanks; but that I will have a rechate winded

---

144. **wear . . . suspicion:** an allusion to the popular jest that a cuckold (husband of an unfaithful
wife) grew horns   146. **Sundays:** the day a husband would be expected to spend with his wife
153. **part:** speaking part (namely, to ask "With who?")   155. **If . . . utt'red:** If it were true and I had
told him so in confidence, he would have violated my confidence in just this manner.   156. **old tale:**
Apparently some form of the Bluebeard story. In an eighteenth-century version cited by Furness, a
lady who has discovered the bodies of the victims describes her experience, under the fiction that
she is recalling a dream, and at intervals the murderer, who is among the listeners, interjects the
words here quoted.   160. **fetch me in:** trick me, take me in   169. **despite:** despising, contempt
170. **in . . . will:** by willful obstinacy (not by rational argument). Willful adherence to heterodox
opinion was the essential element of heresy.   172–73. **that . . . forehead:** that I should wear a cuckold's horns. A rechate (or recheat) is a series of notes sounded (*winded*) on the horn for calling the
hounds together.

in my forehead, or hang my bugle in an invisible baldrick, all women shall
pardon me. Because I will not do them the wrong to mistrust any, I will do
175   myself the right to trust none; and the fine is (for the which I may go the
finer), I will live a bachelor.

DON PEDRO   I shall see thee, ere I die, look pale with love.

BENEDICK   With anger, with sickness, or with hunger, my lord, not with love.
Prove that ever I lose more blood with love than I will get again with drink-
180   ing, pick out mine eyes with a ballad-maker's pen, and hang me up at the
door of a brothel-house for the sign of blind Cupid.

DON PEDRO   Well, if ever thou dost fall from this faith, thou wilt prove a notable argument.

BENEDICK   If I do, hang me in a bottle like a cat, and shoot at me, and he that
185   hits me, let him be clapp'd on the shoulder, and call'd Adam.

DON PEDRO   Well, as time shall try: "In time the savage bull doth bear the yoke."

BENEDICK   The savage bull may, but if ever the sensible Benedick bear it, pluck
off the bull's horns, and set them in my forehead, and let me be vildly
painted, and in such great letters as they write "Here is good horse to hire,"
190   let them signify under my sign, "Here you may see Benedick the married
man."

CLAUDIO   If this should ever happen, thou wouldst be horn-mad.

DON PEDRO   Nay, if Cupid have not spent all his quiver in Venice, thou wilt
quake for this shortly.

195 BENEDICK   I look for an earthquake too then.

DON PEDRO   Well, you will temporize with the hours. In the mean time, good
Signior Benedick, repair to Leonato's, commend me to him, and tell him I
will not fail him at supper, for indeed he hath made great preparation.

BENEDICK   I have almost matter enough in me for such an embassage, and so I
200   commit you—

CLAUDIO   To the tuition of God. From my house—if I had it—

DON PEDRO   The sixt of July. Your loving friend, Benedick.

---

173. **hang . . . baldrick:** carry my horn not in the usual place on the usual strap (*baldrick*) but where
no strap is seen (because none is present)—on my forehead   173–74. **shall pardon me:** must excuse
me from   175. **fine:** end   179. **Prove:** if you can show   179–80. **I . . . drinking:** It was a common
belief that sighing (characteristic of lovers) consumed the blood, but that wine generated fresh
blood.   180. **a ballad-maker's pen:** an instrument of satire   181. **sign:** Inns, shops, etc., were identified by painted signs.   182–83. **notable argument:** outstanding example in discussions of the
topic   184. **bottle:** wicker case. Sometimes a cat was suspended in such a container as a target for
archers.   185. **Adam:** probably an allusion to Adam Bell, an archer celebrated in ballads for his
skill   186. **try:** test, show   **In . . . yoke:** inaccurately quoted from Kyd's *The Spanish Tragedy*,
II.i.3   187. **sensible:** rational.   188. **vildly:** vilely, wretchedly   192. **horn-mad:** mad as a horned
beast, stark mad (with the common allusion to cuckold's horns)   193. **spent . . . quiver:** used up all
his arrows (with play following on *quiver* = tremble)   **Venice:** noted at the time for its licentious-
ness   195. **I . . . too:** it will take an earthquake as well   196. **temporize:** come to terms, compromise
197. **commend me:** present my compliments   199. **matter:** substance, intelligence
199–200. **and . . . you:** a conventional form of words which Claudio and Don Pedro jeer at by extending it into a stock complimentary closing for a letter   201. **tuition:** protection   202. **sixt:** sixth

BENEDICK   Nay, mock not, mock not. The body of your discourse is sometime
guarded with fragments, and the guards are but slightly basted on neither.
205   Ere you flout old ends any further, examine your conscience, and so I leave
you.

[*Exit.*]

CLAUDIO   My liege, your Highness now may do me good.
DON PEDRO   My love is thine to teach; teach it but how,
And thou shalt see how apt it is to learn
210   Any hard lesson that may do thee good.
CLAUDIO   Hath Leonato any son, my lord?
DON PEDRO   No child but Hero, she's his only heir.
Dost thou affect her, Claudio?
CLAUDIO   O my lord,
215   When you went onward on this ended action,
I look'd upon her with a soldier's eye,
That lik'd, but had a rougher task in hand
Than to drive liking to the name of love.
But now I am return'd, and that war-thoughts
220   Have left their places vacant, in their rooms
Come thronging soft and delicate desires,
All prompting me how fair young Hero is,
Saying I lik'd her ere I went to wars.
DON PEDRO   Thou wilt be like a lover presently,
225   And tire the hearer with a book of words.
If thou dost love fair Hero, cherish it,
And I will break with her, and with her father,
And thou shalt have her. Was't not to this end
That thou began'st to twist so fine a story?
230 CLAUDIO   How sweetly you do minister to love,
That know love's grief by his complexion!
But lest my liking might too sudden seem,
I would have salv'd it with a longer treatise.

---

204. **guarded with fragments:** trimmed with odds and ends (a metaphor from dressmaking, looking
back to *body* in the sense "bodice," and continued in *basted on;* but suggesting also that Don Pedro
can guard his serious concerns from exposure by talking inanities when it suits him)   **the guards
. . . neither:** the trimmings are very insecurely stitched on too (they have little connection with what
is being said)   205. **flout:** mock, jeer at   **old ends:** (1) old tags (= the *fragments* of line 286); (2)
conventional closings (of letters)   **examine your conscience:** consider whether you have ever been
guilty of the same thing   213. **affect:** love   215. **ended action:** campaign now ended   219. **now I:**
now that I   224. **presently:** any moment now   225. **book of words:** whole book of lover's set
speeches   227. **break with:** broach the subject to   229. **twist:** spin   231. **his complexion:** its outward appearance   233. **salv'd:** smoothed, put a better face on   **treatise:** discourse

DON PEDRO　What need the bridge much broader than the flood?
235　　　The fairest grant is the necessity.
　　　Look what will serve is fit: 'tis once, thou lovest,
　　　And I will fit thee with the remedy.
　　　I know we shall have revelling to-night;
　　　I will assume thy part in some disguise,
240　　　And tell fair Hero I am Claudio,
　　　And in her bosom I'll unclasp my heart,
　　　And take her hearing prisoner with the force
　　　And strong encounter of my amorous tale;
　　　Then after to her father will I break,
245　　　And the conclusion is, she shall be thine.
　　　In practice let us put it presently.

(*Exeunt.*)

[Scene II]

(*Enter* LEONATO *and an old man* [ANTONIO], *brother to* LEONATO, [*meeting*].)

LEONATO　How now, brother, where is my cousin, your son? Hath he provided this music?

ANTONIO　He is very busy about it. But, brother, I can tell you strange news that you yet dreamt not of.

5　LEONATO　Are they good?

ANTONIO　As the [event] stamps them, but they have a good cover; they show well outward. The Prince and Count Claudio, walking in a thick-pleach'd alley in mine orchard, were thus much overheard by a man of mine. The Prince discover'd to Claudio that he lov'd my niece your daughter, and
10　　　meant to acknowledge it this night in a dance; and if he found her accordant, he meant to take the present time by the top, and instantly break with you of it.

LEONATO　Hath the fellow any wit that told you this?

ANTONIO　A good sharp fellow. I will send for him, and question him yourself.

---

235. **The fairest . . . necessity:** The best gift is the one that fills the need of the occasion.
236. **Look what:** whatever　**'tis once:** the simple fact is　341. **in . . . unclasp:** to her private hearing I'll disclose the contents (*unclasp* = open the book) of.

I.ii. Location: Leonato's house
1. **cousin:** used of aunt, uncle, niece, or nephew, as well as of cousin in the modern sense
6. **event:** outcome　**stamps . . . cover:** Antonio uses the figure of news printed and bound in a book.
7–8. **thick-pleach'd alley:** walk bordered with bushes or small trees and overarched with their densely entwined boughs　8. **orchard:** garden　9. **discover'd:** revealed　10–11. **accordant:** consenting　11. **top:** forelock　13. **wit:** intelligence

15 LEONATO   No, no, we will hold it as a dream till it appear itself; but I will acquaint my daughter withal, that she may be the better prepar'd for an answer, if peradventure this be true. Go you and tell her of it.   [*Several persons cross the stage.*]   Cousins, you know what you have to do. O, I cry you
mercy, friend, go you with me, and I will use your skill. Good cousin, have a
20   care this busy time.

(*Exeunt.*)

[Scene III]

(*Enter* [DON] JOHN *the Bastard and* CONRADE, *his companion.*)

CONRADE   What the good-year, my lord, why are you thus out of measure sad?
DON JOHN   There is no measure in the occasion that breeds, therefore the sadness is without limit.
CONRADE   You should hear reason.
5 DON JOHN   And when I have heard it, what blessing brings it?
CONRADE   If not a present remedy, at least a patient sufferance.
DON JOHN   I wonder that thou (being, as thou say'st thou art, born under Saturn) goest about to apply a moral medicine to a mortifying mischief. I cannot hide what I am: I must be sad when I have cause, and smile at no man's
10   jests; eat when I have stomach, and wait for no man's leisure; sleep when I
am drowsy, and tend on no man's business; laugh when I am merry, and
claw no man in his humor.
CONRADE   Yea, but you must not make the full show of this till you may do it
without controlment. You have of late stood out against your brother, and
15   he hath ta'en you newly into his grace, where it is impossible you should
take true root but by the fair weather that you make yourself. It is needful
that you frame the season for your own harvest.
DON JOHN   I had rather be a canker in a hedge than a rose in his grace, and it
better fits my blood to be disdain'd of all than to fashion a carriage to rob
20   love from any. In this (though I cannot be said to be a flattering honest

---

15. **appear itself:** make itself evident (as a face)   16. **withal:** with it   18–19. **cry you mercy:** beg
your pardon

I.iii. Location: Leonato's house
1. **What the good-year:** an unexplained expletive   **out of measure:** immoderately
2. **breeds:** causes it   4. **hear:** listen to   6. **present:** immediate   **sufferance:** endurance
7–8. **born under Saturn:** born when the planet Saturn was predominant, hence supposedly
morose (cf. *saturnine*)   8. **goest . . . mischief:** dost endeavor to cure a deadly ill by means of
moralizing platitudes   11. **tend on:** attend to   12. **claw:** flatter, humor   **humor:** whims
14. **controlment:** restraint   **stood out:** rebelled   15. **grace:** favor   17. **frame:** create
18. **canker:** wild rose (considered a weed)   19. **blood:** mood, temper   **fashion a carriage:**
counterfeit a behavior

man) it must not be denied but I am a plain-dealing villain. I am trusted
with a muzzle, and enfranchis'd with a clog, therefore I have decreed not to
sing in my cage. If I had my mouth, I would bite; if I had my liberty, I would
do my liking. In the mean time let me be that I am, and seek not to alter me.

25 CONRADE   Can you make no use of your discontent?

DON JOHN   I make all use of it, for I use it only. Who comes here?

(*Enter* BORACHIO.)

What news Borachio?

BORACHIO   I came yonder from a great supper. The Prince your brother is roy-
ally entertain'd by Leonato, and I can give you intelligence of an intended
30   marriage.

DON JOHN   Will it serve for any model to build mischief on? What is he for a
fool that betroths himself to unquietness?

BORACHIO   Marry, it is your brother's right hand.

DON JOHN   Who, the most exquisite Claudio?

35 BORACHIO   Even he.

DON JOHN   A proper squire! And who, and who? which way looks he?

BORACHIO   Marry, one Hero, the daughter and heir of Leonato.

DON JOHN   A very forward March-chick! How came you to this?

BORACHIO   Being entertain'd for a perfumer, as I was smoking a musty room,
40   comes me the Prince and Claudio, hand in hand in sad conference. I whipt
me behind the arras, and there heard it agreed upon that the Prince should
woo Hero for himself, and having obtain'd her, give her to Count Claudio.

DON JOHN   Come, come, let us thither, this may prove food to my displeasure.
That young start-up hath all the glory of my overthrow. If I can cross him
45   any way, I bless myself every way. You are both sure, and will assist me?

CONRADE   To the death, my lord.

DON JOHN   Let us to the great supper, their cheer is the greater that I am sub-
du'd. Would the cook were a' my mind! Shall we go prove what's to be done?

BORACHIO   We'll wait upon your lordship.

(*Exeunt.*)

21–22. **trusted . . . muzzle:** trusted as a muzzled dog is trusted, not trusted at all
22. **enfranchis'd:** given my freedom   **clog:** a heavy block of wood attached to an animal to restrict
its movement   **decreed:** made up my mind   s.d. **Borachio:** Spanish *borracho* means "drunkard."
31–32. **What . . . fool:** what kind of fool is he   33. **Marry:** indeed (originally the name of the Virgin
Mary used as an oath)   36. **proper squire:** handsome young fellow (spoken sneeringly)
38. **forward:** precocious   **March-chick:** chick which has hatched prematurely   39. **entertain'd for:**
hired as   **smoking:** refreshing the air of (by burning some aromatic substance)   40. **sad:**
serious   41. **arras:** tapestry wall-hanging   43. **displeasure:** anger, hatred   44. **start-up:** upstart
cross: thwart (with following quibble on the sense "make the sign of the cross")   45. **sure:** loyal, to
be counted on   48. **prove:** try, discover   49. **wait upon:** attend

Act II

Scene I

(*Enter* LEONATO, [ANTONIO] *his brother,* HERO *his daughter, and* BEATRICE *his niece,* [MARGARET, URSULA,] *and a* KINSMAN.)

LEONATO   Was not Count John here at supper?

ANTONIO   I saw him not.

BEATRICE   How tartly that gentleman looks! I never can see him but I am heart-burn'd an hour after.

5 HERO   He is of a very melancholy disposition.

BEATRICE   He were an excellent man that were made just in the midway be-tween him and Benedick: the one is too like an image and says nothing, and the other too like my lady's eldest son, evermore tattling.

LEONATO   Then half Signior Benedick's tongue in Count John's mouth, and
10   half Count John's melancholy in Signior Benedick's face—

BEATRICE   With a good leg and a good foot, uncle, and money enough in his purse, such a man would win any woman in the world, if 'a could get her good will.

LEONATO   By my troth, niece, thou wilt never get thee a husband, if thou be so
15   shrewd of thy tongue.

ANTONIO   In faith, she's too curst.

BEATRICE   Too curst is more than curst. I shall lessen God's sending that way, for it is said, "God sends a curst cow short horns"—but to a cow too curst he sends none.

20 LEONATO   So, by being too curst, God will send you no horns.

BEATRICE   Just, if he send me no husband, for the which blessing I am at him upon my knees every morning and evening. Lord, I could not endure a hus-band with a beard on his face, I had rather lie in the woollen!

LEONATO   You may light on a husband that hath no beard.

25 BEATRICE   What should I do with him? dress him in my apparel and make him my waiting-gentlewoman? He that hath a beard is more than a youth, and he that hath no beard is less than a man; and he that is more than a youth is not for me, and he that is less than a man, I am not for him; therefore I will even take sixpense in earnest of the berrord, and lead his apes into hell.

30 LEONATO   Well then, go you into hell.

II.i. Location: Leonato's house
3. **tartly:** Modern idiom would require the adjective form.   3–4. **am heart-burn'd:** suffer from heartburn (caused by Don John's sour looks)   8. **my . . . son:** a spoiled child   15. **shrewd:** sharp, satirical   16. **curst:** ill-tempered; here, sharp-tongued; in line 18, vicious, savage   21. **Just:** pre-cisely, just so   **if . . . husband:** She implies that God, in sending her a husband, would also send horns—that her husband would certainly be a cuckold.   23. **in the woollen:** between woollen blan-kets, without sheets   29. **in earnest:** as advance payment   **berrord:** bear-ward, one who keeps and trains bears (and sometimes apes)   **lead . . . hell:** the proverbial fate of old maids

BEATRICE   No, but to the gate, and there will the devil meet me like an old
cuckold with horns on his head, and say, "Get you to heaven, Beatrice, get
you to heaven, here's no place for you maids." So deliver I up my apes, and
away to Saint Peter. For the heavens, he shows me where the bachelors sit,
35   and there live we as merry as the day is long.

ANTONIO [*to* HERO]   Well, niece, I trust you will be rul'd by your father.

BEATRICE   Yes, faith, it is my cousin's duty to make cur'sy and say, "Father, as it
please you." But yet for all that, cousin, let him be a handsome fellow, or else
make another cur'sy and say, "Father, as it please me."

40   LEONATO   Well, niece, I hope to see you one day fitted with a husband.

BEATRICE   Not till God make men of some other mettle than earth. Would it
not grieve a woman to be overmaster'd with a piece of valiant dust? to make
an account of her life to a clod of wayward marl? No, uncle, I'll none.
Adam's sons are my brethren, and truly I hold it a sin to match in my kinred.

45   LEONATO   Daughter, remember what I told you. If the Prince do solicit you in
that kind, you know your answer.

BEATRICE   The fault will be in the music, cousin, if you be not woo'd in good
time. If the Prince be too important, tell him there is measure in every
thing, and so dance out the answer. For hear me, Hero: wooing, wedding,
50   and repenting, is as a Scotch jig, a measure, and a cinquepace; the first suit
is hot and hasty, like a Scotch jib, and full as fantastical; the wedding,
mannerly-modest, as a measure, full of state and ancientry; and then comes
repentance, and with his bad legs falls into the cinquepace faster and faster,
till he sink into his grave.

55   LEONATO   Cousin, you apprehend passing shrewdly.

BEATRICE   I have a good eye, uncle, I can see a church by daylight.

LEONATO   The revellers are ent'ring, brother, make good room.   [*They put on their masks.*]

(*Enter Prince* [DON] PEDRO, CLAUDIO, *and* BENEDICK, *and* [DON] JOHN, [*and* BORACHIO *as maskers, with a Drum*].)

DON PEDRO   Lady, will you walk about with your friend?

HERO   So you walk softly, and look sweetly, and say nothing. I am yours for the
60   walk, and especially when I walk away.

DON PEDRO   With me in your company?

HERO   I may say so when I please.

---

34. **For the heavens:** so far as heaven is concerned   **bachelors:** unmarried persons of either
sex   37. **cur'sy:** curtsy   41. **mettle:** substance   43. **marl:** clay   44. **match...kinred:** marry within
the forbidden degrees of relationship; *kinred* = kindred   47–48. **in good time:** with propriety (with
obvious pun)   48. **important:** importunate, pressing   **measure:** (1) moderation; (2) slow, stately
dance   50. **cinquepace:** lively dance (trisyllabic)   51. **full:** fully, quite   52. **mannerly-modest:** be-
comingly moderate in tempo   **state and ancientry:** traditional stateliness   55. **apprehend passing
shrewdly:** perceive with unusual sharpness   s.d. **Drum:** drummer   58. **friend:** often used in the
sense "lover," and perhaps so here   59. **softly:** gently

DON PEDRO   And when please you to say so?

HERO   When I like your favor, for God defend the lute should be like the case!

65 DON PEDRO   My visor is Philemon's roof, within the house is Jove.

HERO   Why then your visor should be thatch'd.

DON PEDRO   Speak low if you speak love.

[They move aside.]

[BORACHIO]   Well, I would you did like me.

MARGARET   So would not I for your own sake, for I have many ill qualities.

70 [BORACHIO]   Which is one?

MARGARET   I say my prayers aloud.

[BORACHIO]   I love you the better; the hearers may cry amen.

MARGARET   God match me with a good dancer!

[BORACHIO]   Amen.

75 MARGARET   And God keep him out of my sight when the dance is done! Answer, clerk.

[BORACHIO]   No more words; the clerk is answer'd.

[They move aside.]

URSULA   I know you well enough, you are Signior Antonio.

ANTONIO   At a word, I am not.

80 URSULA   I know you by the waggling of your head.

ANTONIO   To tell you true, I counterfeit him.

URSULA   You could never do him so ill-well, unless you were the very man.
Here's his dry hand up and down. You are he, you are he.

ANTONIO   At a word, I am not.

85 URSULA   Come, come, do you think I do not know you by your excellent wit?
Can virtue hide itself? Go to, mum, you are he. Graces will appear, and
there's an end.

[They move aside.]

BEATRICE   Will you not tell me who told you so?

BENEDICK   No, you shall pardon me.

90 BEATRICE   Nor will you not tell me who you are?

BENEDICK   Not now.

---

64. **favor:** face   **God...case:** God forbid that your face should not be handsomer than your mask.
65. **visor:** mask   **Philemon's roof:** Philemon and his wife Baucis entertained Jove in their peasant
cottage, unaware of his identity (Ovid, *Metamorphoses,* viii).   66. **thatch'd:** (1) roofed with thatch
(as peasant cottages generally were); (2) bearded   69. **ill:** bad   75–76. **Answer, clerk:** say amen
(= so be it) again. It was the duty of the parish clerk to say the responses at church services.
79. **At:** in   82. **do ... ill-well:** imitate his imperfections so perfectly   83. **dry hand:** a sign of
age   **up and down:** exactly   86. **virtue:** excellence (of any kind)   **mum:** silence   87. **an end:** no
more to be said

BEATRICE   That I was disdainful, and that I had my good wit out of the "Hundred Merry Tales"—well, this was Signior Benedick that said so.

BENEDICK   What's he?

95   BEATRICE   I am sure you know him well enough.

BENEDICK   Not I, believe me.

BEATRICE   Did he never make you laugh?

BENEDICK   I pray you, what is he?

BEATRICE   Why, he is the Prince's jester, a very dull fool; only his gift is in devis-
100   ing impossible slanders. None but libertines delight in him, and the commendation is not in his wit, but in his villainy, for he both pleases men and angers them, and then they laugh at him and beat him. I am sure he is in the fleet; I would he had boarded me.

BENEDICK   When I know the gentleman, I'll tell him what you say.

105   BEATRICE   Do, do, he'll but break a comparison or two on me, which peradventure, not mark'd, or not laugh'd at, strikes him into melancholy, and then there's a partridge wing sav'd, for the fool will eat no supper that night. [*Music for the dance begins.*]   We must follow the leaders.

BENEDICK   In every good thing.

110   BEATRICE   Nay, if they lead to any ill, I will leave them at the next turning.

[*Dance.* [*Then*] *exeunt* [*all but* DON JOHN, BORACHIO, *and* CLAUDIO].)

DON JOHN   Sure my brother is amorous on Hero, and hath withdrawn her father to break with him about it. The ladies follow her, and but one visor remains.

BORACHIO   And that is Claudio. I know him by his bearing.

115   DON JOHN   Are not you Signior Benedick?

CLAUDIO   You know me well, I am he.

DON JOHN   Signior, you are very near my brother in his love. He is enamor'd on Hero. I pray you dissuade him from her, she is no equal for his birth. You may do the part of an honest man in it.

120   CLAUDIO   How know you he loves her?

DON JOHN   I heard him swear his affection.

BORACHIO   So did I too, and he swore he would marry her to-night.

DON JOHN   Come let us to the banquet.

(*Exeunt. Manet* CLAUDIO.)

92–93. **Hundred Merry Tales:** a popular collection of jests and tales, first published in 1526
99. **dull:** stupid   **only his gift:** his only talent   100. **impossible:** incredible   **libertines:** those who reject the customary restraints upon thought and behavior   101. **villainy:** satiric rudeness
103. **fleet:** company drifting about the room   **boarded:** come alongside (a ship) to attempt an attack on it; here, tried his wit on   105. **break a comparison:** crack a joke   108. **leaders:** of the dance
117. **very . . . love:** a very close friend of my brother's   123. **banquet:** light repast of sweets, fruit, and wine

CLAUDIO   Thus answer I in name of Benedick,
125   But hear these ill news with the ears of Claudio.
'Tis certain so, the Prince woos for himself.
Friendship is constant in all other things
Save in the office and affairs of love;
Therefore all hearts in love use their own tongues.
130   Let every eye negotiate for itself,
And trust no agent; for beauty is a witch
Against whose charms faith melteth into blood.
This is an accident of hourly proof,
Which I mistrusted not. Farewell therefore Hero!

(*Enter* BENEDICK.)

135   BENEDICK   Count Claudio?
CLAUDIO   Yea, the same.
BENEDICK   Come, will you go with me?
CLAUDIO   Whither?
BENEDICK   Even to the next willow, about your own business, County. What
140   fashion will you wear the garland of? about your neck, like an usurer's
chain? or under your arm, like a lieutenant's scarf? You must wear it one
way, for the Prince hath got your Hero.
CLAUDIO   I wish him joy of her.
BENEDICK   Why, that's spoken like an honest drovier; so they sell bullocks. But
145   did you think the Prince would have serv'd you thus?
CLAUDIO   I pray you leave me.
BENEDICK   Ho, now you strike like the blind man. 'Twas the boy that stole your
meat, and you'll beat the post.
CLAUDIO   If it will not be, I'll leave you.

(*Exit.*)

150   BENEDICK   Alas, poor hurt fowl, now will he creep into sedges. But that my
Lady Beatrice should know me, and not know me! The Prince's fool! hah, it
may be I go under that title because I am merry. Yea, but so I am apt to do
myself wrong. I am not so reputed. It is the base (though bitter) disposition

---

128. **office:** business   129. **all:** let all   132. **Against whose charms:** in the face of whose
spells   **blood:** passion   133. **accident ... proof:** occurrence of a sort that takes place every
hour   134. **mistrusted:** suspected   139. **next:** nearest   **willow:** the emblem of unrequited love
County: count   140. **garland:** of willow   141–42. **one way:** one way or another
144. **drovier:** drover, cattle dealer   147. **blind man:** The particular story has not been identified. In
the Spanish romance *Lazarillo de Tormes*, the hero steals a sausage from his master, a blind beggar,
and is so severely punished by him that, in revenge, he causes the blind man to jump against a stone
pillar.   148. **post:** pillar (but with a quibble on the sense "messenger")   150. **creep into sedges:** find
himself a hiding-place, as an injured bird seeks refuge in the rushes along a river bank
153. **base (though bitter):** low, yet capable of stinging its victim (?). The locution is not very natural,
and Johnson emended it to *base, the bitter*.

of Beatrice that puts the world into her person, and so gives me out. Well,
155   I'll be reveng'd as I may.

(*Enter the Prince* [Don Pedro].)

DON PEDRO   Now, signior, where's the Count? Did you see him?
BENEDICK   Troth, my lord, I have play'd the part of Lady Fame. I found him
here as melancholy as a lodge in a warren. I told him, and I think I told him
true, that your Grace had got the good will of this young lady, and I off'red
160   him my company to a willow-tree, either to make him a garland, as being
forsaken, or to bind him up a rod, as being worthy to be whipt.
DON PEDRO   To be whipt? What's his fault?
BENEDICK   The flat transgression of a schoolboy, who being overjoy'd with
finding a bird's nest, shows it his companion, and he steals it.
165 DON PEDRO   Wilt thou make a trust a transgression? The transgression is in the
stealer.
BENEDICK   Yet it had not been amiss the rod had been made, and the garland
too, for the garland he might have worn himself, and the rod he might have
bestow'd on you, who (as I take it) have stol'n his bird's nest.
170 DON PEDRO   I will but teach them to sing, and restore them to the owner.
BENEDICK   If their singing answer your saying, by my faith you say honestly.
DON PEDRO   The Lady Beatrice hath a quarrel to you. The gentleman that
danc'd with her told her she is much wrong'd by you.
BENEDICK   O, she misus'd me past the endurance of a block; an oak but with
175   one green leaf on it would have answer'd her. My very visor began to assume
life, and scold with her. She told me, not thinking I had been myself, that I
was the Prince's jester, that I was duller than a great thaw, huddling jest
upon jest with such impossible conveyance upon me that I stood like a man
at a mark, with a whole army shooting at me. She speaks poniards, and
180   every word stabs. If her breath were as terrible as her terminations, there
were no living near her, she would infect to the north star. I would not
marry her, though she were endow'd with all that Adam had left him before
he transgress'd. She would have made Hercules have turn'd spit, yea, and
have cleft his club to make the fire too. Come, talk not of her; you shall find

---

154. **puts . . . person:** assumes that everyone is of her opinion   **gives me out:** represents me
157. **Troth:** in truth   **Lady Fame:** Dame Rumor   158. **lodge . . . warren:** burrow in a rabbit warren.
Rabbits were proverbially melancholy.   163. **flat:** simple, silly   165. **a trust:** the placing of one's
trust in a person   169. **bestow'd:** used   170. **them:** the nestlings   171. **answer:** correspond
to   172. **to:** with   174. **misus'd:** abused   174–75. **but . . . it:** with the slightest vestige of life in it
177. **a great thaw:** when impassable roads would prevent the usual activities and pastimes
huddling: piling up   178. **impossible conveyance:** incredible adeptness   179. **at a mark:** set up as
a target   180. **terminations:** terms, words   181. **north star:** supposedly the remotest star
182. **left:** bestowed upon   183. **Hercules . . . spit:** Omphale forced the captive Hercules to put on
women's clothes and spin among her maids. Turning the spit was work of a far more menial order.

185   her the infernal Ate in good apparel. I would to God some scholar would conjure her, for certainly, while she is here, a man may live as quiet in hell as in a sanctuary, and people sin upon purpose, because they would go thither; so indeed all disquiet, horror, and perturbation follows her.

(*Enter* CLAUDIO *and* BEATRICE, [LEONATO *and* HERO].)

DON PEDRO   Look here she comes.

190 BENEDICK   Will your Grace command me any service to the world's end? I will go on the slightest arrand now to the Antipodes that you can devise to send me on; I will fetch you a toothpicker now from the furthest inch of Asia, bring you the length of Prester John's foot, fetch you a hair off the great Cham's beard, do you any embassage to the Pigmies, rather than hold three
195   words' conference with this harpy. You have no employment for me?

DON PEDRO   None, but to desire your good company.

BENEDICK   O God, sir, here's a dish I love not, I cannot endure my Lady Tongue.

(*Exit.*)

DON PEDRO   Come, lady, come, you have lost the heart of Signior Benedick.

200 BEATRICE   Indeed, my lord, he lent it me awhile, and I gave him use for it, a double heart for his single one. Marry, once before he won it of me with false dice, therefore your Grace may well say I have lost it.

DON PEDRO   You have put him down, lady, you have put him down.

BEATRICE   So I would not he should do me, my lord, lest I should prove the
205   mother of fools. I have brought Count Claudio, whom you sent me to seek.

DON PEDRO   Why, how now, Count, wherefore are you sad?

CLAUDIO   Not sad, my lord.

DON PEDRO   How then? sick?

CLAUDIO   Neither, my lord.

210 BEATRICE   The Count is neither sad, nor sick, nor merry, nor well; but civil count, civil as an orange, and something of that jealous complexion.

DON PEDRO   I' faith, lady, I think your blazon to be true, though I'll be sworn, if he be so, his conceit is false. Here, Claudio, I have woo'd in thy name, and

---

185. **Ate:** goddess of mischief and discord   **scholar:** one familiar with the Latin formulas for exorcising evil spirits   191. **arrand:** errand   193. **Prester John:** a legendary Far Eastern ruler who was both emperor and Christian priest (*Prester* is a shortened form of *Presbyter,* priest)   194. **Cham:** Khan of Tartary, ruler of the Mongols **Pigmies:** supposed to inhabit the mountains of India 195. **harpy:** creature of prey; literally, a mythical monster with the face and trunk of a woman and the wings and claws of a bird. In heraldry the harpy was assigned to one who had committed manslaughter (= Beatrice's crime!).   200. **use:** usury, interest   202. **false:** loaded   203. **put him down:** got the better of him (with following quibble by Beatrice)   210. **civil:** (1) grave, serious; (2) Seville (a homophone); oranges of Seville are bitter   211. **something:** somewhat, to some degree **jealous complexion:** yellow, the color associated with jealousy   212. **blazon:** description   213. **so:** jealous **conceit:** idea

fair Hero is won. I have broke with her father, and his good will obtain'd.
215   Name the day of marriage, and God give thee joy!

LEONATO   Count, take of me my daughter, and with her my fortunes. His Grace
hath made the match, and all grace say amen to it.

BEATRICE   Speak, Count, 'tis your cue.

CLAUDIO   Silence is the perfectest herald of joy; I were but little happy, if I could
220   say how much! Lady, as you are mine, I am yours. I give away myself for you,
and dote upon the exchange.

BEATRICE   Speak, cousin, or (if you cannot) stop his mouth with a kiss, and let
not him speak neither.

DON PEDRO   In faith, lady, you have a merry heart.

225 BEATRICE   Yea, my lord, I thank it—poor fool, it keeps on the windy side of
care. My cousin tells him in his ear that he is in her heart.

CLAUDIO   And so she doth, cousin.

BEATRICE   Good Lord, for alliance! Thus goes every one to the world but I, and
I am sunburnt. I may sit in a corner and cry "Heigh-ho for a husband!"

230 DON PEDRO   Lady Beatrice, I will get you one.

BEATRICE   I would rather have one of your father's getting. Hath your Grace
ne'er a brother like you? Your father got excellent husbands, if a maid could
come by them.

DON PEDRO   Will you have me, lady?

235 BEATRICE   No, my lord, unless I might have another for working-days. Your
Grace is too costly to wear every day. But I beseech your Grace pardon me, I
was born to speak all mirth and no matter.

DON PEDRO   Your silence most offends me, and to be merry best becomes you,
for out a' question, you were born in a merry hour.

240 BEATRICE   No, sure, my lord, my mother cried, but then there was a star danc'd,
and under that was I born. Cousins, God give you joy!

LEONATO   Niece, will you look to those things I told you of?

BEATRICE   I cry you mercy, uncle. By your Grace's pardon.

(*Exit* BEATRICE.)

DON PEDRO   By my troth, a pleasant-spirited lady.

245 LEONATO   There's little of the melancholy element in her, my lord. She is never
sad but when she sleeps, and not ever sad then, for I have heard my daughter
say, she hath often dreamt of unhappiness, and wak'd herself with laughing.

DON PEDRO   She cannot endure to hear tell of a husband.

LEONATO   O, by no means, she mocks all her wooers out of suit.

250 DON PEDRO   She were an excellent wife for Benedick.

---

217. **all grace:** the grace of God   219. **heralt:** herald   225. **windy:** windward, safe
228. **goes . . . world:** everyone gets married   229. **sunburnt:** unattractive   **Heigh-ho . . . husband:**
the title of a ballad   231. **getting:** begetting   237. **matter:** substance, sense   246. **ever:** always
247. **unhappiness:** "some amusing roguery or other" (Kittredge)   249. **suit:** courtship

LEONATO   O Lord, my lord, if they were but a week married, they would talk themselves mad.

DON PEDRO   County Claudio, when mean you to go to church?

CLAUDIO   To-morrow, my lord. Time goes on crutches till love have all his rites.

255   LEONATO   Not till Monday, my dear son, which is hence a just sevennight, and a time too brief too, to have all things answer my mind.

DON PEDRO   Come, you shake the head at so long a breathing, but I warrant thee, Claudio, the time shall not go dully by us. I will in the interim undertake one of Hercules' labors, which is, to bring Signior Benedick and the

260   Lady Beatrice into a mountain of affection th' one with th' other. I would fain have it a match, and I doubt not but to fashion it, if you three will but minister such assistance as I shall give you direction.

LEONATO   My lord, I am for you, though it cost me ten nights' watchings.

CLAUDIO   And I, my lord.

265   DON PEDRO   And you too, gentle Hero?

HERO   I will do any modest office, my lord, to help my cousin to a good husband.

DON PEDRO   And Benedick is not the unhopefullest husband that I know. Thus far can I praise him: he is of a noble strain, of approv'd valor, and confirm'd

270   honesty. I will teach you how to humor your cousin, that she shall fall in love with Benedick, and I, with your two helps, will so practice on Benedick that, in despite of his quick wit and his queasy stomach, he shall fall in love with Beatrice. If we can do this, Cupid is no longer an archer; his glory shall be ours, for we are the only love-gods. Go in with me, and I will tell you my

275   drift.

(*Exeunt.*)

[Scene II]

(*Enter* [DON] JOHN *and* BORACHIO.)

DON JOHN   It is so, the Count Claudio shall marry the daughter of Leonato.

BORACHIO   Yea, my lord, but I can cross it.

DON JOHN   Any bar, any cross, any impediment will be med'cinable to me. I am sick in displeasure to him, and whatsoever comes athwart his affection

5   ranges evenly with mine. How canst thou cross this marriage?

---

253. **go to church:** marry   255. **a just sevennight:** exactly a week   256. **answer my mind:** correspond with my wishes   257. **breathing:** interval, delay   262. **minister:** furnish, supply
263. **watchings:** lying awake   269. **approv'd:** tested   271. **practice on:** scheme against
272. **in despite of:** notwithstanding   **his queasy stomach:** his squeamishness about partaking of love   275. **drift:** intent

II.ii. Location: Leonato's house
1. **shall:** is going to   2. **cross:** thwart   3. **med'cinable:** medicinal, healing   4. **displeasure to:** anger against   **comes...affection:** goes contrary to his desires   5. **ranges evenly:** runs parallel

BORACHIO   Not honestly, my lord, but so covertly that no dishonesty shall appear in me.

DON JOHN   Show me briefly how.

BORACHIO   I think I told your lordship a year since, how much I am in the favor
10   of Margaret, the waiting-gentlewoman to Hero.

DON JOHN   I remember.

BORACHIO   I can, at any unseasonable instant of the night, appoint her to look out at her lady's chamber-window.

DON JOHN   What life is in that, to be the death of this marriage?

15 BORACHIO   The poison of that lies in you to temper. Go you to the Prince your brother; spare not to tell him that he hath wrong'd his honor in marrying the renown'd Claudio—whose estimation do you mightily hold up—to a contaminated stale, such a one as Hero.

DON JOHN   What proof shall I make of that?

20 BORACHIO   Proof enough to misuse the Prince, to vex Claudio, to undo Hero, and kill Leonato. Look you for any other issue?

DON JOHN   Only to despite them, I will endeavor any thing.

BORACHIO   Go then, find me a meet hour to draw Don Pedro and the Count Claudio alone, tell them that you know that Hero loves me, intend a kind of
25   zeal both to the Prince and Claudio—as in love of your brother's honor, who hath made this match, and his friend's reputation, who is thus like to be cozen'd with the semblance of a maid—that you have discover'd thus. They will scarcely believe this without trial. Offer them instances, which shall bear no less likelihood than to see me at her chamber-window, hear me
30   call Margaret Hero, hear Margaret term me Claudio; and bring them to see this the very night before the intended wedding—for in the mean time I will so fashion the matter that Hero shall be absent—and there shall appear such seeming truth of Hero's disloyalty, that jealousy shall be call'd assurance, and all the preparation overthrown.

35 DON JOHN   Grow this to what adverse issue it can, I will put it in practice. Be cunning in the working this, and thy fee is a thousand ducats.

BORACHIO   Be you constant in the accusation, and my cunning shall not shame me.

DON JOHN   I will presently go learn their day of marriage.

(*Exeunt.*)

---

8. **briefly:** quickly   15. **lies in:** depends upon   **temper:** mix   17. **estimation:** worth
18. **contaminated stale:** common prostitute   20. **misuse:** deceive   **vex:** torment   24. **intend:**
pretend   27. **cozen'd:** deceived   **semblance:** outward appearance   28. **instances:** proofs
30. **term me Claudio:** apparently a slip. Many editors emend to *Borachio* (following Theobald).
33. **jealousy:** suspicion   33–34. **assurance:** certainty   34. **preparation:** for the wedding
36. **ducats:** continental gold coins, variously valued (but Borachio's reward is clearly to be a large one)   39. **presently:** at once

[Scene III]

(*Enter* BENEDICK *alone.*)

BENEDICK   Boy!

[*Enter* BOY.]

BOY   Signior?

BENEDICK   In my chamber-window lies a book, bring it hither to me in the orchard.

5   BOY   I am here already, sir.

(*Exit.*)

BENEDICK   I know that, but I would have thee hence, and here again. I do much wonder that one man, seeing how much another man is a fool when he dedicates his behaviors to love, will, after he hath laugh'd at such shallow follies in others, become the argument of his own scorn by falling in love—and
10   such a man is Claudio. I have known when there was no music with him but the drum and the fife, and now had he rather hear the tabor and the pipe; I have known when he would have walk'd ten mile afoot to see a good armor, and now will he lie ten nights awake carving the fashion of a new doublet; he was wont to speak plain and to the purpose (like an honest man and a
15   soldier), and now is he turn'd ortography—his words are a very fantastical banquet, just so many strange dishes. May I be so converted and see with these eyes? I cannot tell; I think not. I will not be sworn but love may transform me to an oyster, but I'll take my oath on it, till he have made [an] oyster of me, he shall never make me such a fool. One woman is fair, yet I am
20   well; another is wise, yet I am well; another virtuous, yet I am well; but till all graces be in one woman, one woman shall not come in my grace. Rich she shall be, that's certain; wise, or I'll none; virtuous, or I'll never cheapen her; fair, or I'll never look on her; mild, or come not near me; noble, or not I for an angel; of good discourse, an excellent musician, and her hair shall be
25   of what color it please God. Hah! the Prince and Monsieur Love. I will hide me in the arbor.

[*Withdraws.*]

II.iii. Location: Leonato's garden
4. **orchard:** garden   5. **I . . . already:** I'll be back before you know I've gone.   9. **argument:** subject
11. **tabor:** small drum. The tabor and pipe were used for social merriment, in contrast to the martial drum and fife.   12. **armor:** suit of armor   13. **carving:** planning   **doublet:** close-fitting jacket
15. **turn'd ortography:** become a faddist in language   22. **I'll none:** I'll have none of her   **cheapen:** bargain for   24. **for an angel:** (1) though she be an angel; (2) for ten shillings (involving a play on *noble* as the name of another coin, worth two thirds as much as an angel)   24–25. **hair . . . God:** if she satisfies all these requirements, I won't stipulate what color her hair must be.

(*Enter Prince* [DON PEDRO], LEONATO, CLAUDIO. *Music* [*within*].)

DON PEDRO   Come, shall we hear this music?

CLAUDIO   Yea, my good lord. How still the evening is,
     As hush'd on purpose to grace harmony!

30 DON PEDRO   See you where Benedick hath hid himself?

CLAUDIO   O, very well, my lord. The music ended,
     We'll fit the [hid]-fox with a pennyworth.

(*Enter* BALTHASAR *with Music.*)

DON PEDRO   Come, Balthasar, we'll hear that song again.

BALTHASAR   O good my lord, tax not so bad a voice
35   To slander music any more than once.

DON PEDRO   It is the witness still of excellency
     To put a strange face on his own perfection.
     I pray thee sing, and let me woo no more.

BALTHASAR   Because you talk of wooing, I will sing;
40   Since many a wooer doth commence his suit
     To her he thinks not worthy, yet he woos,
     Yet he will swear he loves.

DON PEDRO   Nay, pray thee come,
     Or if thou wilt hold longer argument,
45   Do it in notes.

BALTHASAR   Note this before my notes:
     There's not a note of mine that's worth the noting.

DON PEDRO   Why, these are very crotchets that he speaks—
     Note notes, forsooth, and nothing.   [*Air.*]

50 BENEDICK   Now, divine air! now is his soul ravish'd! It is not strange that
     sheep's guts should hale souls out of men's bodies? Well, a horn for my
     money when all's done.

The Song

[BALTHASAR]   Sigh no more; ladies, sigh no more,
                     Men were deceivers ever,
55   One foot in sea, and one on shore,
                     To one thing constant never.

---

29. **grace harmony:** do honor to music   32. **hid-fox:** an allusion to a children's game; cf. *Hamlet,*
IV.ii.25: "Hide fox, and all after."   **pennyworth:** a good bargain, more than he bargained for   34.
tax: task   37. **To . . . on:** not to admit   38. **woo:** entreat   45. **notes:** musical notes
48. **crotchets:** (1) whims; (2) quarter notes in music   49. **nothing:** with homophonic pun on *noting*
51. **sheep's guts:** violin or lute strings   **hale:** draw, drag   **horn:** hunting horn (but an audience always alive to the cuckold jest would have found the remark comically incongruous in Benedick's
mouth)

Then sigh not so, but let them go,
    And be you blithe and bonny,
Converting all your sounds of woe
60   Into hey nonny nonny.
Sing no more ditties, sing no moe,
    Of dumps so dull and heavy;
The fraud of men was ever so,
    Since summer first was leavy.
65   Then sigh not so, etc.

DON PEDRO   By my troth, a good song.

BALTHASAR   And an ill singer, my lord.

DON PEDRO   Ha, no, no, faith, thou sing'st well enough for a shift.

BENEDICK   And he had been a dog that should have howl'd thus, they would
70   have hang'd him, and so I pray God his bad voice bode no mischief. I had as
    live have heard the night-raven, come what plague could have come after it.

DON PEDRO   Yea, marry, dost thou hear, Balthasar? I pray thee get us some ex-
    cellent music; for to-morrow night we would have it at the Lady Hero's
    chamber-window.

75 BALTHASAR   The best I can, my lord.

(*Exit* BALTHASAR.)

DON PEDRO   Do so, farewell. Come hither, Leonato. What was it you told me of
    to-day, that your niece Beatrice was in love with Signior Benedick?

CLAUDIO [*aside*]   O ay, stalk on, stalk on, the fowl sits.—I did never think that
    lady would have lov'd any man.

80 LEONATO   No, nor I neither, but most wonderful that she should so dote on
    Signior Benedick, whom she hath in all outward behaviors seem'd ever to
    abhor.

BENEDICK   Is't possible? Sits the wind in that corner?

LEONATO   By my troth, my lord, I cannot tell what to think of it but that she
85   loves him with an enrag'd affection; it is past the infinite of thought.

DON PEDRO   May be she doth but counterfeit.

CLAUDIO   Faith, like enough.

LEONATO   O God! counterfeit? There was never counterfeit of passion came so
    near the life of passion as she discovers it.

---

61. **moe:** more (in number)   62. **dumps:** mournful tunes   64. **leavy:** leafy   68. **for a shift:** to make
do   71. **live:** lief   **night-raven:** a bird, variously identified, whose cry presaged disaster
78. **stalk . . . sits:** walk stealthily, the bird has settled (in a bush)   83. **Sits . . . corner:** is that how the
wind blows   85. **enrag'd:** mad with passion   **infinite:** infinity, boundlessness
89. **discovers:** reveals

90 DON PEDRO Why, what effects of passion shows she?

CLAUDIO [*aside*] Bait the hook well, this fish will bite.

LEONATO What effects, my lord? She will sit you—you heard my daughter tell you how.

CLAUDIO She did indeed.

95 DON PEDRO How, how, I pray you? You amaze me, I would have thought her spirit had been invincible against all assaults of affection.

LEONATO I would have sworn it had, my lord, especially against Benedick.

BENEDICK I should think this a gull, but that the white-bearded fellow speaks it. Knavery cannot sure hide himself in such reverence.

100 CLAUDIO [*aside*] He hath ta'en th' infection. Hold it up.

DON PEDRO Hath she made her affection known to Benedick?

LEONATO No, and swears she never will. That's her torment.

CLAUDIO 'Tis true indeed, so your daughter says. "Shall I," says she, "that have so oft encount'red him with scorn, write to him that I love him?"

105 LEONATO This says she now when she is beginning to write to him, for she'll be up twenty times a night, and there will she sit in her smock till she have writ a sheet of paper. My daughter tells us all.

CLAUDIO Now you talk of a sheet of paper. I remember a pretty jest your daughter told [us of].

110 LEONATO O, when she had writ it, and was reading it over, she found "Benedick" and "Beatrice" between the sheet?

CLAUDIO That.

LEONATO O, she tore the letter into a thousand halfpence; rail'd at herself, that she should be so immodest to write to one that she knew would flout her. "I

115 measure him," says she, "by my own spirit, for I should flout him, if he writ to me, yea, though I love him, I should."

CLAUDIO Then down upon her knees she falls, weeps, sobs, beats her heart, tears her hair, prays, curses: "O sweet Benedick! God give me patience!"

LEONATO She doth indeed, my daughter says so; and the ecstasy hath so much

120 overborne her that my daughter is sometime afeard she will do a desperate outrage to herself. It is very true.

DON PEDRO It were good that Benedick knew of it by some other, if she will not discover it.

CLAUDIO To what end? he would make but a sport of it, and torment the poor

125 lady worse.

DON PEDRO And he should, it were an alms to hang him. She's an excellent sweet lady, and (out of all suspicion) she is virtuous.

---

92. **effects:** manifestations **sit you:** sit (a colloquialism) 98. **gull:** trick 100. **Hold it up:** keep it up 106. **smock:** undergarment 113. **halfpence:** very small bits 119. **ecstasy:** madness 121. **outrage:** act of violence 126. **alms:** good deed 127. **out of:** beyond

CLAUDIO   And she is exceeding wise.

DON PEDRO   In every thing but in loving Benedick.

130 LEONATO   O my lord, wisdom and blood combating in so tender a body, we
have ten proofs to one that blood hath the victory. I am sorry for her, as I
have just cause, being her uncle and her guardian.

DON PEDRO   I would she had bestow'd this dotage on me, I would have daff'd
all other respects, and made her half myself. I pray you tell Benedick of it,
135   and hear what 'a will say.

LEONATO   Were it good, think you?

CLAUDIO   Hero thinks surely she will die, for she says she will die if he love her
not, and she will die ere she make her love known, and she will die if he woo
her, rather than she will bate one breath of her accustom'd crossness.

140 DON PEDRO   She doth well. If she should make tender of her love, 'tis very possible he'll scorn it, for the man (as you know all) hath a contemptible spirit.

CLAUDIO   He is a very proper man.

DON PEDRO   He hath indeed a good outward happiness.

CLAUDIO   Before God, and in my mind, very wise.

145 DON PEDRO   He doth indeed show some sparks that are like wit.

CLAUDIO   And I take him to be valiant.

DON PEDRO   As Hector, I assure you, and in the managing of quarrels you may
say he is wise, for either he avoids them with great discretion, or undertakes
them with a most Christian-like fear.

150 LEONATO   If he do fear God, 'a must necessarily keep peace; if he break the
peace, he ought to enter into a quarrel with fear and trembling.

DON PEDRO   And so will he do, for the man doth fear God, howsoever it seems
not in him by some large jests he will make. Well, I am sorry for your niece.
Shall we go seek Benedick, and tell him of her love?

155 CLAUDIO   Never tell him, my lord. Let her wear it out with good counsel.

LEONATO   Nay, that's impossible, she may wear her heart out first.

DON PEDRO   Well, we will hear further of it by your daughter, let it cool the
while. I love Benedick well, and I could wish he would modestly examine
himself, to see how much he is unworthy so good a lady.

160 LEONATO   My lord, will you walk? Dinner is ready.

CLAUDIO [*aside*]   If he do not dote on her upon this, I will never trust my expectation.

DON PEDRO [*aside*]   Let there be the same net spread for her, and that must
your daughter and her gentlewomen carry. The sport will be, when they
165   hold one an opinion of another's dotage, and no such matter; that's the

---

130. **blood:** natural feeling   133. **dotage:** doting   **daff'd:** doffed, put aside   134. **respects:** considerations   **half myself:** my wife   139. **bate:** abate   **crossness:** perversity   140. **tender:** offer
141. **contemptible:** contemptuous   142. **proper:** handsome   143. **hath . . . happiness:** is fortunate
in his appearance   147. **Hector:** the greatest of the Trojan warriors   153. **large:** broad, indelicate
155. **good counsel:** giving herself good advice   160. **walk:** go   164. **carry:** undertake
165. **no such matter:** nothing of the kind exists

scene that I would see, which will be merely a dumb show. Let us send her to call him in to dinner.

[*Exeunt* Don Pedro, Claudio, *and* Leonato.]

BENEDICK [*coming forward*] This can be no trick: the conference was sadly borne; they have the truth of this from Hero; they seem to pity the lady. It
170 seems her affections have their full bent. Love me? why, it must be requited. I hear how I am censur'd; they say I will bear myself proudly, if I perceive the love come from her; they say too that she will rather die than give any sign of affection. I did never think to marry. I must not seem proud; happy are they that hear their detractions, and can put them to mending. They say
175 the lady is fair; 'tis a truth, I can bear them witness; and virtuous; 'tis so, I cannot reprove it; and wise, but for loving me; by my troth, it is no addition to her wit, nor no great argument of her folly, for I will be horribly in love with her. I may chance have some odd quirks and remnants of wit broken on me, because I have rail'd so long against marriage; but doth not the ap-
180 petite alter? A man loves the meat in his youth that he cannot endure in his age. Shall quips and sentences and these paper bullets of the brain awe a man from the career of his humor? No, the world must be peopled. When I said I would die a bachelor, I did not think I should live till I were married. Here comes Beatrice. By this day, she's a fair lady. I do spy some marks of
185 love in her.

(*Enter* Beatrice.)

BEATRICE Against my will I am sent to bid you come in to dinner.
BENEDICK Fair Beatrice, I thank you for your pains.
BEATRICE I took no more pains for those thanks than you take pains to thank me. If it had been painful, I would not have come.
190 BENEDICK You take pleasure in the message?
BEATRICE Yea, just so much as you may take upon a knive's point, and choke a daw withal. You have no stomach, signior, fare you well.

(*Exit.*)

BENEDICK Ha! "Against my will I am sent to bid you come in to dinner"— there's a double meaning in that. "I took no more pains for those thanks
195 than you took pains to thank me"—that's as much as to say, "Any pains that

---

166. **merely . . . show:** entirely pantomime (because with no occasion for satiric exchange they will have nothing to say) 168–169. **sadly borne:** seriously conducted 170. **have . . . bent:** are at full stretch 174. **their detractions:** unfavorable criticisms of themselves **put . . . mending:** i.e., apply themselves to correcting their faults 176. **reprove:** disprove, deny 178. **quirks:** jests
181. **sentences:** maxims **paper . . . brain:** verbal ammunition 182. **career . . . humor:** course of his inclination 192. **daw:** jackdaw **stomach:** appetite

I take for you is as easy as thanks." If I do not take pity of her, I am a villain;
if I do not love her, I am a Jew. I will go get her picture.

(*Exit.*)

Act III

Scene I

(*Enter* HERO *and two gentlewomen,* MARGARET *and* URSLEY.)

HERO   Good Margaret, run thee to the parlor,
    There shalt thou find my cousin Beatrice
    Proposing with the Prince and Claudio.
    Whisper her ear, and tell her I and Ursley
5   Walk in the orchard, and our whole discourse
    Is all of her. Say that thou overheardst us,
    And bid her steal into the pleached bower,
    Where honeysuckles, ripened by the sun,
    Forbid the sun to enter, like favorites
10   Made proud by princes, that advance their pride
    Against that power that bred it. There will she hide her,
    To listen our propose. This is thy office;
    Bear thee well in it, and leave us alone.
MARGARET   I'll make her come, I warrant you, presently.

[*Exit.*]

15 HERO   Now, Ursula, when Beatrice doth come,
    As we do trace this alley up and down,
    Our talk must only be of Benedick.
    When I do name him, let it be thy part
    To praise him more than ever man did merit.
20   My talk to thee must be how Benedick
    Is sick in love with Beatrice. Of this matter
    Is little Cupid's crafty arrow made,
    That only wounds by hearsay.

(*Enter* BEATRICE [*behind*].)

                    Now begin,
25   For look where Beatrice like a lapwing runs
    Close by the ground, to hear our conference.

III.i. Location: Leonato's garden
o.s.d. **Ursley:** variant form of *Ursula*   3. **Proposing:** talking   12. **listen our propose:** listen to our conversation   23. **only . . . hearsay:** wounds by hearsay only

URSULA   The pleasant'st angling is to see the fish
  Cut with her golden oars the silver stream,
  And greedily devour the treacherous bait;
30 So angle we for Beatrice, who even now
  Is couched in the woodbine coverture.
  Fear you not my part of the dialogue.
HERO   Then go we near her, that her ear lose nothing
  Of the false sweet bait that we lay for it.

[*They advance to the bower.*]

35 No, truly, Ursula, she is too disdainful,
  I know her spirits are as coy and wild
  As haggards of the rock.
URSULA   But are you sure
  That Benedick loves Beatrice so entirely?
40 HERO   So says the Prince and my new-trothed lord.
URSULA   And did they bid you tell her of it, madam?
HERO   They did entreat me to acquaint her of it,
  But I persuaded them, if they lov'd Benedick,
  To wish him wrastle with affection,
45 And never to let Beatrice know of it.
URSULA   Why did you so? Doth not the gentleman
  Deserve as full as fortunate a bed
  As ever Beatrice shall couch upon?
HERO   O god of love! I know he doth deserve
50 As much as may be yielded to a man;
  But nature never fram'd a woman's heart
  Of prouder stuff than that of Beatrice.
  Disdain and scorn ride sparkling in her eyes,
  Misprising what they look on, and her wit
55 Values itself so highly that to her
  All matter else seems weak. She cannot love,
  Nor take no shape nor project of affection,
  She is so self-endeared.
URSULA   Sure I think so,
60 And therefore certainly it were not good
  She knew his love, lest she'll make sport at it.
HERO   Why, you speak truth. I never yet saw man,
  How wise, how noble, young, how rarely featur'd,

---

31. **woodbine coverture:** honeysuckle bower   36. **coy:** shy   37. **haggards . . . rock:** mature female hawks snared in their mountain habitats, hence very difficult to tame   44. **wish him wrastle:** advise him to wrestle   47. **as full as:** fully as   54. **Misprising:** undervaluing, despising   56. **All matter else:** what anyone else has to say   57. **take . . . affection:** formulate any mental image or idea of what love is   58. **self-endeared:** full of self-love   63. **How:** however   **rarely featur'd:** excellent in face and form

But she would spell him backward. If fair-fac'd,
65   She would swear the gentleman should be her sister;
If black, why, Nature, drawing of an antic,
Made a foul blot; if tall, a lance ill-headed;
If low, an agot very vildly cut;
If speaking, why, a vane blown with all winds;
70   If silent, why, a block moved with none.
So turns she every man the wrong side out,
And never gives to truth and virtue that
Which simpleness and merit purchaseth.
URSULA   Sure, sure, such carping is not commendable.
75   HERO   No, not to be so odd, and from all fashions,
As Beatrice is, cannot be commendable.
But who dare tell her so? If I should speak,
She would mock me into air; O, she would laugh me
Out of myself, press me to death with wit.
80   Therefore let Benedick, like cover'd fire,
Consume away in sighs, waste inwardly.
It were a better death than die with mocks,
Which is as bad as die with tickling.
URSULA   Yet tell her of it, hear what she will say.
85   HERO   No, rather I will go to Benedick,
And counsel him to fight against his passion,
And truly I'll devise some honest slanders
To stain my cousin with. One doth not know
How much an ill word may empoison liking.
90   URSULA   O, do not do your cousin such a wrong.
She cannot be so much without true judgment—
Having so swift and excellent a wit
As she is priz'd to have—as to refuse
So rare a gentleman as Signior Benedick.
95   HERO   He is the only man of Italy,
Always excepted my dear Claudio.
URSULA   I pray you be not angry with me, madam,
Speaking my fancy: Signior Benedick,
For shape, for bearing, argument, and valor,
100   Goes foremost in report through Italy.

---

64. **spell him backward:** say the reverse of him, turn his merits into faults   66. **black:** dark
antic: grotesque figure   68. **agot:** agate; here, a small figure incised in agate for a seal or a ring
73. **simpleness:** sincerity   **purchaseth:** deserve   75. **from all fashions:** contrary to all accepted behavior   79. **press . . . death:** Accused felons who refused to plead either guilty or not guilty were
pressed to death by heavy weights.   81. **Consume . . . sighs:** an allusion to the belief that each sigh
cost the heart one drop of blood   87. **honest:** harmless   93. **priz'd:** esteemed   95. **only:** very best
99. **argument:** skills in conversation   100. **report:** reputation (so also *name*, line 101)

HERO Indeed he hath an excellent good name.
URSULA His excellence did earn it, ere he had it.
  Wh? are you married, madam?
HERO ?hy, every day to-morrow. Come go in,
105   I'll ?w thee some attires, and have thy counsel
  Wh? is the best to furnish me to-morrow.
URSUL?*side*] She's limed, I warrant you. We have caught her, madam.
HERO ?*le*] If it prove so, then loving goes by haps:
  S? Cupid kills with arrows, some with traps.

[*Exe* ?ERO *and* URSULA.]

110 BEA?[*coming forward*] What fire is in mine ears? Can this be true?
  ? I condemn'd for pride and scorn so much?
  ?empt, farewell, and maiden pride, adieu!
  ?lory lives behind the back of such.
  ?, Benedick, love on, I will requite thee,
  ?ing my wild heart to thy loving hand.
115 ?ou dost love, my kindness shall incite thee
  ?ind our loves up in a holy band;
  ?others say thou dost deserve, and I
  ?eve it better than reportingly.

? II]

?*Prince* [DON PEDRO], CLAUDIO, BENEDICK, *and* LEONATO.)

?EDRO I do but stay till your marriage be consummate, and then go I to-
?ard Arragon.
?IO I'll bring you thither, my lord, if you'll vouchsafe me.
?EDRO Nay, that would be as great a soil in the new gloss of your mar-
?iage as to show a child his new coat and forbid him to wear it. I will only

---

very day to-morrow: Tomorrow I shall be able to say that I am married every day.
?**imed:** caught, like a bird entangled in birdlime   108. **haps:** chance   110. **What . . . ears:** al-
?g to the folk belief that being talked about in one's absence causes one's ears to burn
?**No . . . such:** nothing good is said about such a person when his back is turned
?**Taming . . . hand:** Beatrice has been termed a "haggard" and now acknowledges the justness of
?pithet by her use of another image from falconry.   117. **band:** bond   119. **better than report-**
?**y:** on better evidence than mere rumor

?ii. Location: Leonato's house
?**bring:** escort   **vouchsafe:** allow

be bold with Benedick for his company, for from the crown of his head to
the sole of his foot, he is all mirth. He hath twice or thrice cut Cupid's bow-
string, and the little hangman dare not shoot at him. He hath a heart as
sound as a bell, and his tongue is the clapper, for what his heart thinks, his
10   tongue speaks.

BENEDICK   Gallants, I am not as I have been.

LEONATO   So say I, methinks you are sadder.

CLAUDIO   I hope he be in love.

DON PEDRO   Hang him, truant, there's no true drop of blood in him to truly
15   touch'd with love. If he be sad, he wants money.

BENEDICK   I have the toothache.

DON PEDRO   Draw it.

BENEDICK   Hang it!

CLAUDIO   You must hang it first, and draw it afterwards.

20 DON PEDRO   What? sigh for the toothache?

LEONATO   Where is but a humor or a worm.

BENEDICK   Well, every one [can] master a grief but he that has it.

CLAUDIO   Yet say I, he is in love.

DON PEDRO   There is no appearance of fancy in him, unless it be a fancy th
25   hath to strange disguises—as to be a Dutchman to-day, a Frenchma
morrow, or in the shape of two countries at once, as a German from
waist downward, all slops, and a Spaniard from the hip upward, no doub
Unless he have a fancy to this foolery, as it appears he hath, he is no fool
fancy, as you would have it appear he is.

30 CLAUDIO   If he be not in love with some woman, there is no believing old sig
'A brushes his hat a' mornings; what should that bode?

DON PEDRO   Hath any man seen him at the barber's?

CLAUDIO   No, but the barber's man hath been seen with him, and the old orna
ment of his cheek hath already stuff'd tennis-balls.

35 LEONATO   Indeed he looks younger than he did, by the loss of a beard.

DON PEDRO   Nay, 'a rubs himself with civet. Can you smell him out by that?

CLAUDIO   That's as much as to say, the sweet youth's in love.

[DON PEDRO]   The greatest note of it is his melancholy.

---

6. **be bold with:** take the liberty of asking   8. **hangman:** rogue (with play on Cupid as torturer, a
role played also by the public hangman)   12. **sadder:** more serious   14. **there's . . . him:** he hasn't
enough natural feeling   15. **wants:** lacks   16. **toothache:** Lovers were commonly supposed to suffer from toothaches, but Benedick may only be inventing an excuse for his changed appearance
18. **Hang it:** confound it   19. **hang . . . afterwards:** alluding to the execution of traitors, who were
hanged, cut down while still alive, drawn (disembowelled), and quartered   21. **humor . . . worm:**
Toothaches were supposedly caused by abnormal secretions or by actual worms in the teeth
24. **fancy:** love (with following quibble)   27. **slops:** loose breeches   **no doublet:** with his doublet
completely covered by a cloak   33–34. **old . . . cheek:** his beard   36. **civet:** perfume derived from
the civet cat   **smell him out:** discover his true nature (with obvious play on the literal sense)
37. **sweet:** with quibble on the sense "perfumed"   38. **greatest note:** most conspicuous mark

CLAUDIO   And when was he wont to wash his face?

40   DON PEDRO   Yea, or to paint himself? for the which I hear what they say of him.

CLAUDIO   Nay, but his jesting spirit, which is now crept into a lute-string, and now govern'd by stops.

DON PEDRO   Indeed that tells a heavy tale for him. Conclude, conclude, he is in love.

45   CLAUDIO   Nay, but I know who loves him.

DON PEDRO   That would I know too. I warrant one that knows him not.

CLAUDIO   Yes, and his ill conditions, and in despite of all, dies for him.

DON PEDRO   She shall be buried with her face upwards.

BENEDICK   Yet is this no charm for the toothache. Old signior, walk aside with
50   me, I have studied eight or nine wise words to speak to you, which these hobby-horses must not hear.

[*Exeunt* BENEDICK *and* LEONATO.]

DON PEDRO   For my life, to break with him about Beatrice.

CLAUDIO   'Tis even so. Hero and Margaret have by this play'd their parts with Beatrice, and then the two bears will not bite one another when they meet.

(*Enter* [DON] JOHN *the Bastard.*)

55   DON JOHN   My lord and brother, God save you!

DON PEDRO   Good den, brother.

DON JOHN   If your leisure serv'd, I would speak with you.

DON PEDRO   In private?

DON JOHN   If it please you, yet Count Claudio may hear, for what I would speak
60   of concerns him.

DON PEDRO   What's the matter?

DON JOHN [*to* CLAUDIO]   Means your lordship to be married to-morrow?

DON PEDRO   You know he does.

DON JOHN   I know not that, when he knows what I know.

65   CLAUDIO   If there be any impediment, I pray you discover it.

DON JOHN   You may think I love you not; let that appear hereafter, and aim better at me by that I now will manifest. For my brother, I think he holds you well, and in dearness of heart hath holp to effect your ensuing marriage— surely suit ill spent and labor ill bestow'd.

39, 40. **wash, paint:** with cosmetics   41. **now crept:** Some editors emend to *new-crept* (following Boas) in view of the second *now* in the sentence.   **lute-string:** the lute commonly provided the accompaniment for love songs   42. **govern'd by stops:** regulated by frets (on the fingerboard of the lute), subjected to restraints   47. **Yes:** she does know him   **ill conditions:** bad characteristics 48. **She . . . upwards:** sexual double-entendre, taking off from a quibble on Claudio's *dies* in the sense "experiences sexual climax"   51. **hobby-horses:** buffoons (from the name of a performer in the morris-dance whose costume and antics suggested a horse)   52. **For:** upon   56. **Good den:** good evening   65. **discover:** reveal   66–67. **aim better at:** judge better of   68. **well:** in high esteem   **dearness:** affection

DON PEDRO   Why, what's the matter?

70 DON JOHN   I came hither to tell you, and circumstances short'ned (for she has been too long a-talking of), the lady is disloyal.

CLAUDIO   Who, Hero?

DON JOHN   Even she—Leonato's Hero, your Hero, every man's Hero.

CLAUDIO   Disloyal?

75 DON JOHN   The word is too good to paint out her wickedness. I could say she were worse; think you of a worse title, and I will fit her to it. Wonder not till further warrant. Go but with me to-night, you shall see her chamber-window ent'red, even the night before her wedding-day. If you love her then, to-morrow wed her; but it would better fit your honor to change your

80   mind.

CLAUDIO   May this be so?

DON PEDRO   I will not think it.

DON JOHN   If you dare not trust that you see, confess not that you know. If you will follow me, I will show you enough, and when you have seen more, and

85   heard more, proceed accordingly.

CLAUDIO   If I see any thing to-night why I should not marry her, to-morrow in the congregation, where I should wed, there will I shame her.

DON PEDRO   And as I woo'd for thee to obtain her, I will join with thee to disgrace her.

90 DON JOHN   I will disparage her no farther till you are my witnesses. Bear it coldly but till midnight, and let the issue show itself.

DON PEDRO   O day untowardly turn'd!

CLAUDIO   O mischief strangely thwarting!

DON JOHN   O plague right well prevented! So, will you say when you have seen

95   the sequel.

[*Exeunt.*]

[Scene III]

(*Enter* DOGBERRY *and his compartner* [VERGES] *with the* WATCH.)

DOGBERRY   Are you good men and true?

VERGES   Yea, or else it were pity but they should suffer salvation, body and soul.

---

70. **circumstances short'ned:** without unnecessary details   70–71. **has . . . of:** is not worth even the short time we have spent in mentioning her   75. **paint out:** depict   77. **warrant:** proof (is shown)   83. **that:** what   91. **coldly:** calmly   92. **untowardly turn'd:** perversely altered

III.iii. Location: a street
1. **true:** loyal   2. **salvation:** blunder for *damnation.* Dogberry's and Verges' words frequently mean precisely the opposite of what the speaker intends; witness *allegiance* (line 4), *desartless* (line 6), *senseless* (line 15).

DOGBERRY   Nay, that were a punishment too good for them, if they should have any allegiance in them, being chosen for the Prince's watch.

5 VERGES   Well, give them their charge, neighbor Dogberry.

DOGBERRY   First, who think you the most desartless man to be constable?

1. WATCH   Hugh Oatcake, sir, or George Seacole, for they can write and read.

DOGBERRY   Come hither, neighbor Seacole. God hath blest you with a good name. To be a well-favor'd man is the gift of fortune, but to write and read

10 comes by nature.

2. WATCH   Both which, Master Constable—

DOGBERRY   You have: I knew it would be your answer. Well, for your favor, sir, why, give God thanks, and make no boast of it, and for your writing and reading, let that appear when there is no need of such vanity. You are

15 thought here to be the most senseless and fit man for the constable of the watch; therefore bear you the lanthorn. This is your charge: you shall comprehend all vagrom men; you are to bid any man stand, in the Prince's name.

2. WATCH   How if 'a will not stand?

20 DOGBERRY   Why then take no note of him, but let him go, and presently call the rest of the watch together, and thank God you are rid of a knave.

VERGES   If he will not stand when he is bidden, he is none of the Prince's subjects.

DOGBERRY   True, and they are to meddle with none but the Prince's subjects.

25 You shall also make no noise in the streets; for, for the watch to babble and to talk, is most tolerable, and not to be endur'd.

[2.] WATCH   We will rather sleep than talk, we know what belongs to a watch.

DOGBERRY   Why, you speak like an ancient and most quiet watchman, for I cannot see how sleeping should offend; only have a care that your bills be

30 not stol'n. Well, you are to call at all the alehouses, and bid those that are drunk get them to bed.

[2.] WATCH   How if they will not?

DOGBERRY   Why then let them alone till they are sober. If they make you not then the better answer, you may say they are not the men you took them for.

35 [2.] WATCH   Well, sir.

DOGBERRY   If you meet a thief, you may suspect him, by virtue of your office, to be no true man; and for such kind of men, the less you meddle or make with them, why, the more is for your honesty.

[2.] WATCH   If we know him to be a thief, shall we not lay hands on him?

---

9. **well-favor'd:** good-looking   12. **favor:** appearance   16. **lanthorn:** variant form of *lantern* (by popular etymology from the fact that lanterns often had sides made of transparent sheets of horn) 16–17. **comprehend:** apprehend   17. **vagrom:** vagrant   **stand:** stop   24. **meddle:** have to do 26. **tolerable:** *intolerable*   27. **belongs to:** are the duties of   29. **bills:** hooked blades fastened on long poles   33–34. **make . . . answer:** . . . don't then agree to go home   37. **true:** honest   38. **is:** it is

40 DOGBERRY   Truly by your office you may, but I think they that touch pitch will
be defil'd. The most peaceable way for you, if you do take a thief, is to let
him show himself what he is, and steal out of your company.

VERGES   You have been always call'd a merciful man, partner.

DOGBERRY   Truly, I would not hang a dog by my will, much more a man who
45   hath any honesty in him.

VERGES   If you hear a child cry in the night, you must call to the nurse and bid
her still it.

[2.] WATCH   How if the nurse be asleep and will not hear us?

DOGBERRY   Why then depart in peace, and let the child wake her with crying,
50   for the ewe that will not hear her lamb when it baes will never answer a calf
when he bleats.

VERGES   'Tis very true.

DOGBERRY   This is the end of the charge: you, constable, are to present the
Prince's own person. If you meet the Prince in the night, you may stay him.

55 VERGES   Nay, by'r lady, that I think 'a cannot.

DOGBERRY   Five shillings to one on't, with any man that knows the [statues], he
may stay him; marry, not without the Prince be willing, for indeed the
watch ought to offend no man, and it is an offense to stay a man against his
will.

60 VERGES   By'r lady, I think it be so.

DOGBERRY   Ha, ah ha! Well, masters, good night. And there be any matter of
weight chances, call up me. Keep your fellows' counsels and your own, and
good night. Come, neighbor.

[2.] WATCH   Well, masters, we hear our charge. Let us go sit here upon the
65   church-bench till two, and then all to bed.

DOGBERRY   One word more, honest neighbors. I pray you watch about Signior
Leonato's door, for the wedding being there to-morrow, there is a great coil
to-night. Adieu! Be vigitant, I beseech you.

(*Exeunt* [DOGBERRY *and* VERGES].)

(*Enter* BORACHIO *and* CONRADE.)

BORACHIO   What, Conrade!

70 [2.] WATCH [*aside*]   Peace, stir not.

BORACHIO   Conrade, I say!

CONRADE   Here, man, I am at thy elbow.

BORACHIO   Mass, and my elbow itch'd; I thought there would a scab follow.

CONRADE   I will owe thee an answer for that, and now forward with thy tale.

40–41. **they . . . defil'd:** a commonplace, derived from the Apocryphal book Ecclesiasticus (13:1)
44. **more:** for *less*   47. **still:** quiet   53. **present:** represent   56. **statues:** statutes   57. **without:** unless   67. **coil:** fuss, to-do   68. **vigitant:** vigilant   73. **Mass:** by the Mass   **scab:** scurvy fellow

75 BORACHIO   Stand thee close then under this penthouse, for it drizzles rain, and
I will, like a true drunkard, utter all to thee.

[2.] WATCH [*aside*]   Some treason, masters, yet stand close.

BORACHIO   Therefore know I have earn'd of Don John a thousand ducats.

CONRADE   Is it possible that any villainy should be so dear?

80 BORACHIO   Thou shouldst rather ask if it were possible any villainy should be
so rich; for when rich villains have need of poor ones, poor ones may make
what price they will.

CONRADE   I wonder at it.

BORACHIO   That shows thou art unconfirm'd. Thou knowest that the fashion of
85   a doublet, or a hat, or a cloak, is nothing to a man.

CONRADE   Yes, it is apparel.

BORACHIO   I mean the fashion.

CONRADE   Yes, the fashion is the fashion.

BORACHIO   Tush, I may as well say the fool's the fool. But seest thou not what a
90   deformed thief this fashion is?

[2.] WATCH [*aside*]   I know that Deformed; 'a has been a vile thief this seven
year; 'a goes up and down like a gentleman. I remember his name.

BORACHIO   Didst thou not hear somebody?

CONRADE   No, 'twas the vane on the house.

95 BORACHIO   Seest thou not, I say, what a deformed thief this fashion is, how gid-
dily 'a turns about all the hot-bloods between fourteen and five-and-thirty,
sometimes fashioning them like Pharaoh's soldiers in the reechy painting,
sometime like god Bel's priests in the old church-window, sometime like the
shaven Hercules in the smirch'd worm-eaten tapestry, where his codpiece
100   seems as massy as his club?

CONRADE   All this I see, and I see that the fashion wears out more apparel than
the man. But art not thou thyself giddy with the fashion too, that thou hast
shifted out of thy tale into telling me of the fashion?

BORACHIO   Not so neither, but know that I have to-night woo'd Margaret, the
105   Lady Hero's gentlewoman, by the name of Hero. She leans me out at her
mistress' chamber-window, bids me a thousand times good night—I tell
this tale vildly, I should first tell thee how the Prince, Claudio, and my

---

75. **penthouse:** a kind of porch structure, projecting from the main building   76. **like . . . all:** referring to the Latin tag "In vino veritas"   77. **stand close:** keep concealed   79. **dear:** costly
80. **villainy:** one wanting villainy to be committed   84. **unconfirm'd:** inexperienced
85. **is . . . man:** does not make the man   90. **deformed thief:** ill-formed thief (because fashion
assumes such fantastic shapes [lines 97–100] and robs men of their money by changing so often)   97. **reechy:** smoky, dirty   98. **Bel's priests:** an allusion to the Apocryphal story of Bel (Baal)
and the Dragon   99. **shaven Hercules:** This allusion has not been identified; probably the reference
is to the Omphale episode (see note to II.i.183).   **codpiece:** the bag-like flap at the front of men's
breeches   101–102. **fashion . . . man:** clothes are more often discarded because the fashion has
changed than because they are worn out   103. **shifted:** with a quibble on the meaning "changed
(clothing)"

master, planted and plac'd and possess'd by my master Don John, saw afar off in the orchard this amiable encounter.

110 CONRADE   And thought they Margaret was Hero?

BORACHIO   Two of them did, the Prince and Claudio, but the devil my master knew she was Margaret; and partly by his oaths, which first possess'd them, partly by the dark night, which did deceive them, but chiefly by my villainy, which did confirm any slander that Don John had made, away went Claudio

115   enrag'd; swore he would meet her as he was appointed next morning at the temple, and there, before the whole congregation, shame her with what he saw o'ernight, and send her home again without a husband.

[2.] WATCH   We charge you, in the Prince's name, stand!

[1.] WATCH   Call up the right Master Constable. We have here recover'd the

120   most dangerous piece of lechery that ever was known in the commonwealth.

[2.] WATCH   And one Deformed is one of them; I know him, 'a wears a lock.

CONRADE   Masters, masters—

[2.] WATCH   You'll be made bring Deformed forth, I warrant you.

125 CONRADE   Masters—

[2.] WATCH   Never speak, we charge you; let us obey you to go with us.

BORACHIO   We are like to prove a goodly commodity, being taken up of these men's bills.

CONRADE   A commodity in question, I warrant you. Come, we'll obey you.

(*Exeunt.*)

[Scene IV]

(*Enter* HERO *and* MARGARET *and* URSULA.)

HERO   Good Ursula, wake my cousin Beatrice, and desire her to rise.

URSULA   I will, lady.

HERO   And bid her come hither.

URSULA   Well.

[*Exit.*]

5 MARGARET   Troth, I think your other rebato were better.

HERO   No, pray thee, good Meg, I'll wear this.

---

108. **possess'd:** informed   109. **amiable:** loving   119. **right Master:** by mistaken analogy with such honorifics as "right honorable" and "right worshipful"   **recover'd:** for *discovered*   120. **lechery:** for *treachery* (?)   122. **lock:** a love-lock of hair   126. **obey:** He means *command*

127. **commodity:** goods   **taken up:** (1) taken on credit; (2) arrested   128. **bills:** (1) bonds; (2) pikes   129. **in question:** (1) questionable; (2) about to be tried at law

III.iv. Location: Hero's apartment in Leonato's house

4. **Well:** very well   5. **rebato:** stiff collar supporting a ruff

MARGARET   By my troth 's not so good, and I warrant your cousin will say so.

HERO   My cousin's a fool, and thou art another. I'll wear none but this.

MARGARET   I like the new tire within excellently, if the hair were a thought
10   browner; and your gown's a most rare fashion, i' faith. I saw the Duchess of
Milan's gown that they praise so.

HERO   O, that exceeds, they say.

MARGARET   By my troth 's but a night-gown [in] respect of yours: cloth a' gold
and cuts, and lac'd with silver, set with pearls, down sleeves, side sleeves, and
15   skirts, round underborne with a bluish tinsel; but for a fine, quaint, graceful, and excellent fashion, yours is worth ten on't.

HERO   God give me joy to wear it, for my heart is exceeding heavy.

MARGARET   'Twill be heavier soon by the weight of a man.

HERO   Fie upon thee, art not asham'd?

20   MARGARET   Of what, lady? of speaking honorably? Is not marriage honorable
in a beggar? Is not your lord honorable without marriage? I think you
would have me say, "saving your reverence, a husband." And bad thinking
do not wrest true speaking, I'll offend nobody. Is there any harm in "the
heavier for a husband"? None, I think, and it be the right husband and the
25   right wife; otherwise 'tis light, and not heavy. Ask my Lady Beatrice else,
here she comes.

(*Enter* BEATRICE.)

HERO   Good morrow, coz.

BEATRICE   Good morrow, sweet Hero.

HERO   Why, how now? Do you speak in the sick tune?

30   BEATRICE   I am out of all other tune, methinks.

MARGARET   Clap 's into "Light a' love"; that goes without a burden. Do you sing
it, and I'll dance it.

BEATRICE   Ye light a' love with your heels! then if your husband have stables
enough, you'll see he shall lack no barns.

35   MARGARET   O illegitimate construction! I scorn that with my heels.

BEATRICE   'Tis almost five a' clock, cousin, 'tis time you were ready. By my
troth, I am exceeding ill. Heigh-ho!

MARGARET   For a hawk, a horse, or a husband?

---

7. **'s:** it is   9. **tire:** headdress   **within:** in the inner room   12. **exceeds:** is beyond comparison
13. **night-gown:** dressing gown   **in respect of:** compared with   14. **cuts:** slashed openings, showing the fabric underneath   **lac'd:** trimmed   **down sleeves:** long tight sleeves   **side sleeves:** wide
ornamental sleeves hanging open from the shoulder   15. **round underborne:** lined around the bottom of the skirt   **quaint:** elegant   21. **in:** even in   22. **saving your reverence:** a phrase of apology
before an improper expression   **And bad:** if bawdy   23. **wrest:** twist, misinterpret   25. **light:** punning on the meaning "wanton"   **else:** if this isn't true   29. **sick tune:** voice of a sick person
31. **Clap 's:** let's shift   **Light a' love:** a popular song   **burden:** bass undersong (but with punning
reference to "weight of a man")   33. **Ye . . . heels:** you are light-heeled (slang for "unchaste")
34. **barns:** with pun on *bairns,* "children"   35. **with my heels:** contemptuously

BEATRICE   For the letter that begins them all, H.

40 MARGARET   Well, and you be not turn'd Turk, there's no more sailing by the star.

BEATRICE   What means the fool, trow?

MARGARET   Nothing I, but God send every one their heart's desire!

HERO   These gloves the Count sent me, they are an excellent perfume.

45 BEATRICE   I am stuff'd, cousin, I cannot smell.

MARGARET   A maid, and stuff'd! There's goodly catching of cold.

BEATRICE   O, God help me, God help me, how long have your profess'd apprehension?

MARGARET   Ever since you left it. Doth not my wit become me rarely?

50 BEATRICE   It is not seen enough, you should wear it in your cap. By my troth, I am sick.

MARGARET   Get you some of this distill'd *carduus benedictus,* and lay it to your heart; it is the only thing for a qualm.

HERO   There thou prick'st her with a thistle.

55 BEATRICE   *Benedictus!* why *benedictus?* You have some moral in this *benedictus.*

MARGARET   Moral? no, by my troth I have no moral meaning. I meant plain holy-thistle. You may think perchance that I think you are in love. Nay, by'r lady, I am not such a fool to think what I list, nor I list not to think what I can, nor indeed I cannot think, if I would think my heart out of thinking, that you are in love, or that you will be in love, or that you can be in love. Yet Benedick was such another, and now is he become a man. He swore he would never marry, and yet now in despite of his heart he eats his meat without grudging; and how you may be converted I know not, but methinks you look with your eyes as other women do.

65 BEATRICE   What pace is this that thy tongue keeps?

MARGARET   Not a false gallop.

(*Enter* URSULA.)

URSULA   Madam, withdraw, the Prince, the Count, Signior Benedick, Don John, and all the gallants of the town are come to fetch you to church.

HERO   Help to dress me, good coz, good Meg, good Ursula.

[*Exeunt.*]

---

39. **H:** with pun on *ache,* which was pronounced *aitch* in Shakespeare's day   40. **turn'd Turk:** abandoned your faith (which was that you would never fall in love)   40–41. **no . . . star:** no more navigating by the north star, no more trusting to anything   42. **trow:** I wonder   45. **I am stuff'd:** I have a cold (with bawdy pun by Margaret following)   47–48. **profess'd apprehension:** made wit your profession   50. **wear . . . cap:** as a fool does his coxcomb   52. **carduus benedictus:** blessed (or holy) thistle, a medicinal herb   55. **moral:** hidden meaning   58. **list:** please   61. **a man:** like other men   62–63. **eats . . . grudging:** has an appetite like any other man   66. **a false gallop:** (1) a canter; (2) running on untruthfully

[Scene V]

(*Enter* LEONATO *and the Constable* [DOGBERRY] *and the Headborough* [VERGES].)

LEONATO   What would you with me, honest neighbor?

DOGBERRY   Marry, sir, I would have some confidence with you that decerns you nearly.

LEONATO   Brief, I pray you, for you see it is a busy time with me.

5   DOGBERRY   Marry, this it is, sir.

VERGES   Yes, in truth it is, sir.

LEONATO   What is it, my good friends?

DOGBERRY   Goodman Verges, sir, speaks a little [off] the matter; an old man, sir, and his wits are not so blunt as, God help, I would desire they were, but

10   in faith, honest as the skin between his brows.

VERGES   Yes, I thank God I am as honest as any man living, that is an old man, and no honester than I.

DOGBERRY   Comparisons are odorous—*palabras*, neighbor Verges.

LEONATO   Neighbors, you are tedious.

15   DOGBERRY   It pleases your worship to say so, but we are the poor Duke's officers; but truly, for mine own part, if I were as tedious as a king, I could find in my heart to bestow it all of your worship.

LEONATO   All thy tediousness on me, ah?

DOGBERRY   Yea, and 'twere a thousand pound more than 'tis, for I hear as good

20   exclamation on your worship as of any man in the city, and though I be but a poor man, I am glad to hear it.

VERGES   And so am I.

LEONATO   I would fain know what you have to say.

VERGES   Marry, sir, our watch to-night, excepting your worship's presence, ha'

25   ta'en a couple of as arrant knaves as any in Messina.

DOGBERRY   A good old man, sir, he will be talking; as they say, "When the age is in, the wit is out." God help us, it is a world to see! Well said, i' faith, neighbor Verges. Well, God's a good man; and two men ride of a horse, one must ride behind. An honest soul, i' faith, sir, by my troth he is, as

---

III.v. Location: Leonato's house

o.s.d. **Headborough:** petty constable

2. **confidence:** for *conference*   **decerns:** for *concerns*   3. **nearly:** intimately   8. **Goodman:** regular title for one just below the rank of gentleman   10. **honest . . . brows:** a proverbial comparison   13. **odorous:** for *odious*   **palabras:** a shortening of Spanish *pocas palabras,* "few words"

15. **poor Duke's:** He intends *Duke's poor.*   17. **of:** on   19. **and:** even if   20. **exclamation:** *acclamation* (?). Dogberry's word is an unfortunate choice, since it normally meant "accusation" or "reproach."   24. **to-night:** last night   **excepting:** for *respecting.* Dogberry here intends a polite phrase meaning "If I may speak of such things without offending your worship," but he says something far different.   26–27. **When . . . out:** an adaptation of the proverb "When ale is in, wit is out"

27. **it . . . see:** a proverbial phrase equivalent to "It is wonderful to behold"; but Dogberry seems to mean "What a world we live in"   28. **God's . . . man:** God is good (proverbial)   **of a horse:** on one horse

30   ever broke bread; but God is to be worshipp'd; all men are not alike, alas, good neighbor!

LEONATO   Indeed, neighbor, he comes too short of you.

DOGBERRY   Gifts that God gives.

LEONATO   I must leave you.

35 DOGBERRY   One word, sir. Our watch, sir, have indeed comprehended two aspicious persons, and we would have them this morning examin'd before your worship.

LEONATO   Take their examination yourself, and bring it me. I am now in great haste, as it may appear unto you.

40 DOGBERRY   It shall be suffigance.

LEONATO   Drink some wine ere you go; fare you well.

[*Enter a* MESSENGER.]

MESSENGER   My lord, they stay for you to give your daughter to her husband.

LEONATO   I'll wait upon them, I am ready.

[*Exeunt* LEONATO *and* MESSENGER.]

DOGBERRY   Go, good partner, go, get you to Francis Seacole, bid him bring his
45   pen and inkhorn to the jail. We are now to examination these men.

VERGES   And we must do it wisely.

DOGBERRY   We will spare for no wit, I warrant you. Here's that shall drive some of them to a non-come; only get the learned writer to set down our excommunication, and meet me at the jail.

[*Exeunt.*]

Act IV

Scene I

(*Enter Prince* [DON PEDRO, DON JOHN *the*] *Bastard,* LEONATO, FRIAR [FRANCIS], CLAUDIO, BENEDICK, HERO, *and* BEATRICE [*with* ATTENDANTS].)

LEONATO   Come, Friar Francis, be brief—only to the plain form of marriage, and you shall recount their particular duties afterwards.

FRIAR FRANCIS   You come hither, my lord, to marry this lady.

CLAUDIO   No.

LEONATO   To be married to her. Friar, you come to marry her.

---

30. **God . . . worshipp'd:** We must praise God for whatever he sees fit to bestow (?).   35. **comprehended:** for *apprehended*   **aspicious:** for *suspicious*   40. **suffigance:** for *sufficient*   43. **wait upon:** attend   48. **non-come:** shortened form of *non compos mentis,* "not of sound mind," but Dogberry seems to intend *nonplus*   48–49. **excommunication:** *examination,* or (perhaps) *communication*

IV.i. Location: a church

FRIAR FRANCIS Lady, you come hither to be married to this count.

HERO I do.

FRIAR FRANCIS If either of you know any inward impediment why you should
not be conjoin'd, I charge you on your souls to utter it.

10 CLAUDIO Know you any, Hero?

HERO None, my lord.

FRIAR FRANCIS Know you any, Count?

LEONATO I dare make his answer, none.

CLAUDIO O, what men dare do! What men may do! What men daily do, not
15   knowing what they do!

BENEDICK How now! interjections? Why then, some be of laughing, as, ah, ha,
he!

CLAUDIO Stand thee by, friar. Father, be your leave,
    Will you with free and unconstrained soul
20   Give me this maid, your daughter?

LEONATO As freely, son, as God did give her me.

CLAUDIO And what have I to give you back whose worth
    May counterpoise this rich and precious gift?

DON PEDRO Nothing, unless you render her again.

25 CLAUDIO Sweet Prince, you learn me noble thankfulness.
    There, Leonato, take her back again.
    Give not this rotten orange to your friend,
    She's but the sign and semblance of her honor.
    Behold how like a maid she blushes here!
30   O, what authority and show of truth
    Can cunning sin cover itself withal!
    Comes not that blood as modest evidence
    To witness simple virtue? Would you not swear,
    All you that see her, that she were a maid,
35   By these exterior shows? But she is none:
    She knows the heat of a luxurious bed;
    Her blush is guiltiness, not modesty.

LEONATO What do you mean, my lord?

CLAUDIO   Not to be married,
40   Not to knit my soul to an approved wanton.

LEONATO Dear my lord, if you, in your own proof,
    Have vanquish'd the resistance of her youth,
    And made defeat of her virginity—

---

8. **inward:** secret, private   16–17. **some . . . he:** Grammars classified the interjections according to
the emotions they expressed; Benedick's sample is quoted from Lily's Latin grammar.
23. **counterpoise:** balance, be equivalent to   25. **learn:** teach   30. **authority:** authenticity
32. **modest evidence:** evidence of modesty   36. **luxurious:** lustful   40. **approved:** proved
41. **proof:** test or trial of her

CLAUDIO   I know what you would say. If I have known her,
45   You will say, she did embrace me as a husband,
And so extenuate the 'forehand sin.
No, Leonato,
I never tempted her with word too large,
But as a brother to his sister, show'd
50   Bashful sincerity and comely love.

HERO   And seem'd I ever otherwise to you?

CLAUDIO   Out on thee seeming! I will write against it:
You seem to me as Dian in her orb,
As chaste as is the bud ere it be blown;
55   But you are more intemperate in your blood
Than Venus, or those pamp'red animals
That rage in savage sensuality.

HERO   Is my lord well, that he doth speak so wide?

LEONATO   Sweet Prince, why speak not you?

60 DON PEDRO   What should I speak?
I stand dishonor'd, that have gone about
To link my dear friend to a common stale.

LEONATO   Are these things spoken, or do I but dream?

DON JOHN   Sir, they are spoken, and these things are true.

65 BENEDICK   This looks not like a nuptial.

HERO   "True"! O God!

CLAUDIO   Leonato, stand I here?
Is this the Prince? is this the Prince's brother?
Is this face Hero's? are our eyes our own?

70 LEONATO   All this is so, but what of this, my lord?

CLAUDIO   Let me but move one question to your daughter,
And by that fatherly and kindly power
That you have in her, bid her answer truly.

LEONATO   I charge thee do so, as thou art my child.

75 HERO   O God defend me, how am I beset!
What kind of catechizing call you this?

CLAUDIO   To make you answer truly to your name.

HERO   Is it not Hero? Who can blot that name
With any just reproach?

---

46. **extenuate:** lesson, excuse   **'forehand sin:** premarital sexual relations   48. **large:** broad, immodest   52. **thee seeming:** you in your mere appearance (of good)   53. **Dian:** Diana, emblematic of virginity   **orb:** sphere. Diana, in one of her aspects, was the moon-goddess.   54. **be blown:** open   58. **wide:** wide of the mark, far from the truth   61. **gone about:** endeavored   62. **stale:** whore   71. **move:** propose   72. **kindly:** natural   77. **answer . . . name:** tell truthfully by what name you should be called (?) or acknowledge that the name you have been called ("common stale") belongs to you (?)

80 CLAUDIO   Marry, that can Hero,
    Hero itself can blot out Hero's virtue.
    What man was he talk'd with you yesternight
    Out at your window betwixt twelve and one?
    Now if you are a maid, answer to this.
85 HERO   I talk'd with no man at that hour, my lord.
   DON PEDRO   Why then are you no maiden. Leonato,
    I am sorry you must hear. Upon mine honor,
    Myself, my brother, and this grieved count
    Did see her, hear her, at that hour last night
90   Talk with a ruffian at her chamber-window,
    Who hath indeed, most like a liberal villain,
    Confess'd the vile encounters they have had
    A thousand times in secret.
   DON JOHN   Fie, fie, they are not to be named, my lord,
95   Not to be spoke of;
    There is not chastity enough in language
    Without offense to utter them. Thus, pretty lady,
    I am sorry for thy much misgovernment.
   CLAUDIO   O Hero! what a Hero hadst thou been,
100   If half thy outward graces had been placed
    About thy thoughts and counsels of thy heart!
    But fare thee well, most foul, most fair! Farewell,
    Thou pure impiety and impious purity!
    For thee I'll lock up all the gates of love,
105   And on my eyelids shall conjecture hang,
    To turn all beauty into thoughts of harm,
    And never shall it more be gracious.
   LEONATO   Hath no man's dagger here a point for me?

[HERO *swoons.*]

   BEATRICE   Why, how now, cousin, wherefore sink you down?
110 DON JOHN   Come, let us go. These things, come thus to light,
    Smother her spirits up.

[*Exeunt* DON PEDRO, DON JOHN, *and* CLAUDIO.]

   BENEDICK   How doth the lady?

---

81. **Hero itself:** the name Hero (now the name of an unchaste woman)   88. **grieved:** aggrieved, wronged   91. **liberal:** gross, licentious   98. **much misgovernment:** great misconduct 101. **thoughts and counsels:** secret thoughts (hendiadys)   104. **For thee:** because of my experience with you   105. **conjecture:** suspicion   107. **be gracious:** seem beautiful   111. **spirits:** vital forces

BEATRICE   Dead, I think. Help, uncle!
        Hero, why, Hero! Uncle! Signior Benedick! Friar!
115 LEONATO   O Fate! take not away thy heavy hand,
        Death is the fairest cover for her shame
        That may be wish'd for.
        BEATRICE   How now, cousin Hero?
        FRIAR FRANCIS   Have comfort, lady.
120 LEONATO   Dost thou look up?
        FRIAR FRANCIS   Yea, wherefore should she not?
        LEONATO   Wherefore? why, doth not every earthly thing
        Cry shame upon her? could she here deny
        The story that is printed in her blood?
125   Do not live, Hero, do not ope thine eyes;
        For did I think thou wouldst not quickly die,
        Thought I thy spirits were stronger than thy shames,
        Myself would, on the rearward of reproaches,
        Strike at thy life. Griev'd I, I had but one?
130   Chid I for that at frugal nature's frame?
        O, one too much by thee! Why had I one?
        Why ever wast thou lovely in my eyes?
        Why had I not with charitable hand
        Took up a beggar's issue at my gates,
135   Who smirched thus and mir'd with infamy,
        I might have said, "No part of it is mine;
        This shame derives itself from unknown loins"?
        But mine, and mine I lov'd, and mine I prais'd,
        And mine that I was proud on, mine so much
140   That I myself was to myself not mine,
        Valuing of her—why, she, O she is fall'n
        Into a pit of ink, that the wide sea
        Hath drops too few to wash her clean again,
        And salt too little which may season give
145   To her foul tainted flesh!
        BENEDICK   Sir, sir, be patient.
        For my part I am so attir'd in wonder,
        I know not what to say.
        BEATRICE   O, on my soul, my cousin is belied!
150 BENEDICK   Lady, were you her bedfellow last night?
        BEATRICE   No, truly, not, although until last night,
        I have this twelvemonth been her bedfellow.

---

124. **blood:** blushes   127. **shames:** feelings of shame   128. **on . . . reproaches:** after reproaching
you   130. **frame:** design (with respect to the number of my offspring)   140. **I . . . mine:** that I was
nothing to myself   141. **Valuing of her:** since I valued her so exclusively   144. **season give:** act as a
preservative, as a restorative   147. **attir'd:** wrapped

LEONATO   Confirm'd, confirm'd! O, that is stronger made
Which was before barr'd up with ribs of iron!
155   Would the two princes lie, and Claudio lie,
Who lov'd her so, that speaking of her foulness,
Wash'd it with tears? Hence from her, let her die.
FRIAR FRANCIS   Hear me a little,
For I have only been silent so long,
160   And given way unto this course of fortune,
By noting of the lady. I have mark'd
A thousand blushing apparitions
To start into her face, a thousand innocent shames
In angel whiteness beat away those blushes,
165   And in her eye there hath appear'd a fire
To burn the errors that these princes hold
Against her maiden truth. Call me a fool,
Trust not my reading, nor my observations,
Which with experimental seal doth warrant
170   The tenure of my book; trust not my age,
My reverence, calling, nor divinity,
If this sweet lady lie not guiltless here
Under some biting error.
LEONATO   Friar, it cannot be.
175   Thou seest that all the grace that she hath left
Is that she will not add to her damnation
A sin of perjury; she not denies it.
Why seek'st thou then to cover with excuse
That which appears in proper nakedness?
180 FRIAR FRANCIS   Lady, what man is he you are accus'd of?
HERO   They know that do accuse me, I know none.
If I know more of any man alive
Than that which maiden modesty doth warrant,
Let all my sins lack mercy! O my father,
185   Prove you that any man with me convers'd
At hours unmeet, or that I yesternight
Maintain'd the change of words with any creature,
Refuse me, hate me, torture me to death!
FRIAR FRANCIS   There is some strange misprision in the princes.

159–61. **I . . . lady:** I have kept silence so long, allowing these events to take their free course, only because I have been occupied in observing the lady (?). The passage has difficulties and may be textually corrupt.   169–70. **experimental . . . book:** The seal of experience guarantees as genuine the conclusions I have drawn from my reading (of her face). *Tenure* = tenor, import   179. **proper:** its own   186. **unmeet:** improper   187. **change:** exchange   188. **Refuse:** renounce, cast off   189. **misprision:** misapprehension

190 BENEDICK   Two of them have the very bent of honor,
     And if their wisdoms be misled in this,
     The practice of it lives in John the Bastard,
     Whose spirits toil in frame of villainies.
    LEONATO   I know not. If they speak but truth of her,
195   These hands shall tear her; if they wrong her honor,
     The proudest of them shall well hear of it.
     Time hath not yet so dried this blood of mine,
     Nor age so eat up my invention,
     Nor fortune made such havoc of my means,
200   Nor my bad life reft me so much of friends,
     But they shall find, awak'd in such a kind,
     Both strength of limb, and policy of mind,
     Ability in means, and choice of friends,
     To quit me of them throughly.
205 FRIAR FRANCIS   Pause awhile,
     And let my counsel sway you in this case.
     Your daughter here the [princes] left for dead,
     Let her awhile be secretly kept in,
     And publish it that she is dead indeed.
210   Maintain a mourning ostentation,
     And on your family's old monument
     Hang mournful epitaphs, and do all rites
     That appertain unto a burial.
    LEONATO   What shall become of this? what will this do?
215 FRIAR FRANCIS   Marry, this well carried shall on her behalf
     Change slander to remorse; that is some good.
     But not for that dream I on this strange course,
     But on this travail look for greater birth:
     She dying, as it must be so maintain'd,
220   Upon the instant that she was accus'd,
     Shall be lamented, pitied, and excus'd
     Of every hearer; for it so falls out
     That what we have we prize not to the worth
     Whiles we enjoy it, but being lack'd and lost,
225   Why then we rack the value; then we find
     The virtue that possession would not show us
     Whiles it was ours. So will it fare with Claudio:

---

190. **the very bent of:** a perfect inclination toward   192. **practice:** plotting   193. **frame:** contriving
198. **eat:** eaten   **invention:** power of devising (retaliation); cf. *policy of mind,* line 202
201. **kind:** manner, degree   202. **policy of mind:** shrewdness in contriving   204. **quit . . .**
throughly: settle my account with them thoroughly   210. **mourning ostentation:** show of mourning   214. **become of:** result from   215. **carried:** managed   218. **travail:** labor (in the double sense
of "effort" and "pain of childbirth")   225. **rack:** stretch

When he shall hear she died upon his words,
Th' idea of her life shall sweetly creep
230   Into his study of imagination,
And every lovely organ of her life
Shall come apparell'd in more precious habit,
More moving, delicate, and full of life,
Into the eye and prospect of his soul,
235   Than when she liv'd indeed. Then shall he mourn,
If ever love had interest in his liver,
And wish he had not so accused her;
No, though he thought his accusation true.
Let this be so, and doubt not but success
240   Will fashion the event in better shape
Than I can lay it down in likelihood.
But if all aim but this be levell'd false,
The supposition of the lady's death
Will quench the wonder of her infamy.
245   And if it sort not well, you may conceal her,
As best befits her wounded reputation,
In some reclusive and religious life,
Out of all eyes, tongues, minds, and injuries.
BENEDICK   Signior Leonato, let the friar advise you,
250   And though you know my inwardness and love
Is very much unto the Prince and Claudio,
Yet, by mine honor, I will deal in this
As secretly and justly as your soul
Should with your body.
255 LEONATO   Being that I flow in grief,
The smallest twine may lead me.
FRIAR FRANCIS   'Tis well consented; presently away,
For to strange sores strangely they strain the cure.
Come, lady, die to live; this wedding-day
260   Perhaps is but prolong'd, have patience and endure.

(*Exit* [*with all but* BENEDICK *and* BEATRICE].)

---

228. **upon:** as a result of   230. **study of imagination:** imaginative study—i.e., musing, reverie
231. **organ . . . life:** aspect of her as she was when she lived   234. **prospect:** view   236. **interest in:**
any claim upon (a legal term)   **liver:** the supposed seat of the passion of love   239. **success:** the
happy working out (of my plan)   240. **event:** outcome   241. **lay . . . likelihood:** suggest its probable consequences   242. **if . . . false:** if we miss our aim in every other respect   245. **sort:** turn out
247. **reclusive:** retired, secluded (as a religious recluse)   248. **injuries:** insults   250. **inwardness
and love:** close friendship (hendiadys)   255. **Being that:** since **flow in:** am dissolved in (?) or am
afloat on (?)   258. **For . . . cure:** strange diseases require strange and desperate cures
260. **prolong'd:** postponed

BENEDICK   Lady Beatrice, have you wept all this while?

BEATRICE   Yea, and I will weep a while longer.

BENEDICK   I will not desire that.

BEATRICE   You have no reason, I do it freely.

265 BENEDICK   Surely I do believe your fair cousin is wrong'd.

BEATRICE   Ah, how much might the man deserve of me that would right her!

BENEDICK   Is there any way to show such friendship?

BEATRICE   A very even way, but no such friend.

BENEDICK   May a man do it?

270 BEATRICE   It is a man's office, but not yours.

BENEDICK   I do love nothing in the world so well as you—is not that strange?

BEATRICE   As strange as the thing I know not. It were as possible for me to say I lov'd nothing so well as you, but believe me not; and yet I lie not: I confess nothing, nor I deny nothing. I am sorry for my cousin.

275 BENEDICK   By my sword, Beatrice, thou lovest me.

BEATRICE   Do not swear and eat it.

BENEDICK   I will swear by it that you love me, and I will make him eat it that says I love not you.

BEATRICE   Will you not eat your word?

280 BENEDICK   With no sauce that can be devis'd to it. I protest I love thee.

BEATRICE   Why then God forgive me!

BENEDICK   What offense, sweet Beatrice?

BEATRICE   You have stay'd me in a happy hour, I was about to protest I lov'd you.

285 BENEDICK   And do it with all thy heart.

BEATRICE   I love you with so much of my heart that none is left to protest.

BENEDICK   Come, bid me do any thing for thee.

BEATRICE   Kill Claudio.

BENEDICK   Ha, not for the wide world.

290 BEATRICE   You kill me to deny it. Farewell.

BENEDICK   Tarry, sweet Beatrice.

BEATRICE   I am gone, though I am here; there is no love in you. Nay, I pray you let me go.

BENEDICK   Beatrice—

295 BEATRICE   In faith, I will go.

BENEDICK   We'll be friends first.

BEATRICE   You dare easier be friends with me than fight with mine enemy.

BENEDICK   Is Claudio thine enemy?

---

268. **even:** level, easy   272. **As strange:** as much a stranger (playing on Benedick's use of *strange*)   276. **eat it:** go back on your oath   280. **protest:** declare (but Beatrice pretends to take it in the sense of "object," as she uses it herself in line 286)   283. **in . . . hour:** at just the right moment, opportunely   290. **deny:** refuse   292. **am gone:** have left you (in spirit)

BEATRICE   Is 'a not approv'd in the height a villain, that hath slander'd, scorn'd,
300   dishonor'd my kinswoman? O that I were a man! What, bear her in hand
        until they come to take hands, and then with public accusation, uncover'd
        slander, unmitigated rancor—O God, that I were a man! I would eat his
        heart in the market-place.

BENEDICK   Hear me, Beatrice—
305 BEATRICE   Talk with a man out at a window! a proper saying!

BENEDICK   Nay, but, Beatrice—

BEATRICE   Sweet Hero, she is wrong'd, she is sland'red, she is undone.

BENEDICK   Beat—

BEATRICE   Princes and counties! Surely a princely testimony, a goodly count,
310   Count Comfect, a sweet gallant surely! O that I were a man for his sake! or
        that I had any friend would be a man for my sake! But manhood is melted
        into cur'sies, valor into compliment, and men are only turn'd into tongue,
        and trim ones too. He is now as valiant as Hercules that only tells a lie, and
        swears it. I cannot be a man with wishing, therefore I will die a woman with
315   grieving.

BENEDICK   Tarry, good Beatrice. By this hand, I love thee.

BEATRICE   Use it for my love some other way than swearing by it.

BENEDICK   Think you in your soul the Count Claudio hath wrong'd Hero?

BEATRICE   Yea, as sure as I have a thought or a soul.
320 BENEDICK   Enough, I am engag'd, I will challenge him. I will kiss your hand,
        and so I leave you. By this hand, Claudio shall render me a dear account. As
        you hear of me, so think of me. Go comfort your cousin. I must say she is
        dead; and so farewell.

[*Exeunt.*]

[Scene II]

(*Enter the Constables* [DOGBERRY *and* VERGES] *and the Town Clerk* [*or* SEXTON] *in gowns,* [*and the* WATCH *with* CONRADE *and*] BORACHIO.)

DOGBERRY   Is our whole dissembly appear'd?

VERGES   O, a stool and a cushion for the sexton.

SEXTON   Which be the malefactors?

---

299. **approv'd:** proved   **height:** highest degree   300. **bear . . . hand:** deceive her with false hopes
301. **uncover'd:** unconcealed, open   309. **counties:** counts   **count:** (1) the title; (2) legal indictment; (3) story   310. **Comfect:** comfit, sweetmeat   **for his sake:** to deal with him
313. **trim:** fine   320. **engag'd:** bound by a pledge   321. **render . . . account:** make a very costly set-
tlement with me

IV.ii. Location: a prison
o.s.d. **gowns:** robes of office   1. **dissembly:** for *assembly*

DOGBERRY   Marry, that am I and my partner.

5 VERGES   Nay, that's certain, we have the exhibition to examine.

SEXTON   But which are the offenders that are to be examin'd? Let them come before Master Constable.

DOGBERRY   Yea, marry, let them come before me. What is your name, friend?

BORACHIO   Borachio.

10 DOGBERRY   Pray write down Borachio. Yours, sirrah?

CONRADE   I am a gentleman, sir, and my name is Conrade.

DOGBERRY   Write down Master Gentleman Conrade. Masters, do you serve God?

BOTH [CONRADE, BORACHIO]   Yea, sir, we hope.

15 DOGBERRY   Write down, that they hope they serve God; and write God first, for God defend but God should go before such villains! Masters, it is prov'd already that you are little better than false knaves, and it will go near to be thought so shortly. How answer you for yourselves?

CONRADE   Marry, sir, we say we are none.

20 DOGBERRY   A marvellous witty fellow, I assure you, but I will go about with him. Come you hither, sirrah; a word in your ear, sir. I say to you, it is thought you are false knaves.

BORACHIO   Sir, I say to you, we are none.

DOGBERRY   Well, stand aside. 'Fore God, they are both in a tale. Have you writ 25 down, that they are none?

SEXTON   Master Constable, you go not the way to examine; you must call forth the watch that are their accusers.

DOGBERRY   Yea, marry, that's the eftest way; let the watch come forth. Masters, I charge you in the Prince's name accuse these men.

30 [1.] WATCH   This man said, sir, that Don John, the Prince's brother, was a villain.

DOGBERRY   Write down Prince John a villain. Why, this is flat perjury, to call a prince's brother villain.

BORACHIO   Master Constable—

DOGBERRY   Pray thee, fellow, peace. I do not like thy look, I promise thee.

35 SEXTON   What heard you him say else?

[2.] WATCH   Marry, that he had receiv'd a thousand ducats of Don John for accusing the Lady Hero wrongfully.

DOGBERRY   Flat burglary as ever was committed.

VERGES   Yea, by mass, that it is.

40 SEXTON   What else, fellow?

[1.] WATCH   And that Count Claudio did mean, upon his words, to disgrace Hero before the whole assembly, and not marry her.

---

5. **exhibition:** possibly for *commission*, but *exhibition* could mean "an allowance of money"; in either case, Verges blunders.   10. **sirrah:** form of address to inferiors   16. **defend:** forbid
20. **witty:** clever, cunning   **go about with:** outmaneuver   24. **in a tale:** agreed on the same lie
28. **eftest:** It is clear that he means something like "easiest" or "quickest" but not what word he may be mangling   41. **upon his words:** on the basis of his accusation

DOGBERRY   O villain! thou wilt be condemn'd into everlasting redemption for this.

45 SEXTON   What else?

[1. AND 2.] WATCH   This is all.

SEXTON   And this is more, masters, than you can deny. Prince John is this morning secretly stol'n away. Hero was in this manner accus'd, in this very manner refus'd, and upon the grief of this suddenly died. Master Constable,
50 let these men be bound, and brought to Leonato's. I will go before and show him their examination.

[*Exit.*]

[DOGBERRY]   Come let them be opinion'd.

VERGES   Let them be in the hands—

[CONRADE]   [Off,] coxcomb!

55 DOGBERRY   God's my life, where's the sexton? Let him write down the Prince's officer coxcomb. Come, bind them. Thou naughty varlet!

[CONRADE]   Away, you are an ass, you are an ass.

DOGBERRY   Dost thou not suspect my place? Dost thou not suspect my years? O that he were here to write me down as ass! But, masters, remember that I
60 am an ass; though it be not written down, yet forget not that I am an ass. No, thou villain, thou art full of piety, as shall be prov'd upon thee by good witness. I am a wise fellow, and which is more, an officer, and which is more, a householder, and which is more, as pretty a piece of flesh as any is in Messina, and one that knows the law, go to, and a rich fellow enough, go to,
65 and a fellow that hath had losses, and one that hath two gowns, and every thing handsome about him. Bring him away. O that I had been writ down an ass!

(*Exeunt.*)

Act V

Scene I

(*Enter* LEONATO *and his brother* [ANTONIO].)

ANTONIO   If you go on thus, you will kill yourself,
And 'tis not wisdom thus to second grief
Against yourself.

---

43. **redemption:** He means the opposite.   49. **refus'd:** renounced   52. **opinion'd:** for *pinioned*
55. **God's:** God save   56. **naughty:** wicked   58. **suspect:** for *respect*   61. **piety:** for *impiety*
63. **as . . . flesh:** as fine a fellow

V.i. Location: near Leonato's house
2. **second:** aid

LEONATO   I pray thee cease thy counsel,
5   Which falls into mine ears as profitless
    As water in a sieve. Give not me counsel,
    Nor let no comforter delight mine ear
    But such a one whose wrongs do suit with mine.
    Bring me a father that so lov'd his child,
10   Whose joy of her is overwhelm'd like mine,
    And bid him speak of patience;
    Measure his woe the length and breadth of mine,
    And let it answer every strain for strain,
    As thus for thus, and such a grief for such,
15   In every lineament, branch, shape, and form;
    If such a one will smile and stroke his beard,
    And, sorrow wag, cry "hem!" when he should groan,
    Patch grief with proverbs, make misfortune drunk
    With candle-wasters, bring him yet to me,
20   And I of him will gather patience.
    But there is no such man, for, brother, men
    Can counsel and speak comfort to that grief
    Which they themselves not feel, but tasting it,
    Their counsel turns to passion, which before
25   Would give preceptial med'cine to rage,
    Fetter strong madness in a silken thread,
    Charm ache with air, and agony with words.
    No, no, 'tis all men's office to speak patience
    To those that wring under the load of sorrow,
30   But no man's virtue nor sufficiency
    To be so moral when he shall endure
    The like himself. Therefore give me no counsel,
    My griefs cry louder than advertisement.
ANTONIO   Therein do men from children nothing differ.
35 LEONATO   I pray thee peace. I will be flesh and blood,
    For there was never yet philosopher
    That could endure the toothache patiently,
    However they have writ the style of gods,
    And made a push at chance and sufferance.

---

7. **delight:** try to please   8. **suit with:** match   12. **Measure his woe:** let his woe equal in its dimensions   13. **strain:** strong feeling   17. **And, sorrow wag:** and, letting sorrow go hang. Many editors emend to *Bid sorrow wag* (after Capell)—i.e., bid sorrow be off.   18. **drunk:** insensible
19. **candle-wasters:** those who sit up late over books; here, those who write moral treatises, and by extension, their good advice itself   25. **preceptial:** comprised of precepts   27. **air:** breath, words
29. **wring:** writhe   30. **sufficiency:** ability   31. **moral:** full of moral sentiments
33. **advertisement:** counsel   38. **style of gods:** language worthy of gods (who are above human suffering)   39. **a push at:** an onslaught against (?), or an expression of contempt toward (*push* being a common form of *pish*) (?), (an expression of contempt)   **sufferance:** suffering

40 ANTONIO   Yet bend not all the harm upon yourself;
    Make those that do offend you suffer too.
  LEONATO   There thou speak'st reason; nay, I will do so.
    My soul doth tell me Hero is belied,
    And that shall Claudio know; so shall the Prince,
45   And all of them that thus dishonor her.

(*Enter Prince* [DON PEDRO] *and* CLAUDIO.)

  ANTONIO   Here comes the Prince and Claudio hastily.
  DON PEDRO   Good den, good den.
  CLAUDIO   Good day to both of you.
  LEONATO   Hear you, my lords—
50 DON PEDRO   We have some haste, Leonato.
  LEONATO   Some haste, my lord! Well, fare you well, my lord.
    Are you so hasty now? well, all is one.
  DON PEDRO   Nay, do not quarrel with us, good old man.
  ANTONIO   If he could right himself with quarrelling,
55   Some of us would lie low.
  CLAUDIO   Who wrongs him?
  LEONATO   Marry, thou dost wrong me, thou dissembler, thou—
    Nay, never lay thy hand upon thy sword,
    I fear thee not.
60 CLAUDIO   Marry, beshrew my hand,
    If it should give your age such cause of fear.
    In faith, my hand meant nothing to my sword.
  LEONATO   Tush, tush, man, never fleer and jest at me;
    I speak not like a dotard nor a fool,
65   As under privilege of age to brag
    What I have done being young, or what would do
    Were I not old. Know, Claudio, to thy head,
    Thou hast so wrong'd mine innocent child and me
    That I am forc'd to lay my reverence by,
70   And with grey hairs and bruise of many days,
    Do challenge thee to trial of a man.
    I say thou hast belied mine innocent child!
    Thy slander hath gone through and through her heart,
    And she lies buried with her ancestors—
75   O, in a tomb where never scandal slept,
    Save this of hers, fram'd by thy villainy!
  CLAUDIO   My villainy?
  LEONATO   Thine, Claudio, thine, I say.

---

52. **all is one:** It does not matter. 55. **Some of us:** He means Don Pedro and Claudio.
60. **beshrew:** curse 62. **to:** in grasping 63. **fleer:** jeer 67. **head:** face 71. **trial . . . man:** text (or
combat) worthy of a man

DON PEDRO   You say not right, old man.

80 LEONATO   My lord, my lord,
    I'll prove it on his body, if he dare,
    Despite his nice fence and his active practice,
    His May of youth and bloom of lustihood.

CLAUDIO   Away, I will not have to do with you.

85 LEONATO   Canst thou so daff me? Thou hast kill'd my child.
    If thou kill'st me, boy, thou shalt kill a man.

ANTONIO   He shall kill two of us, and men indeed;
    But that's no matter, let him kill one first.
    Win me and wear me, let him answer me.

90   Come follow me, boy; come, sir boy, come follow me.
    Sir boy, I'll whip you from your foining fence,
    Nay, as I am a gentleman, I will.

LEONATO   Brother—

ANTONIO   Content yourself. God knows I lov'd my niece,

95   And she is dead, slander'd to death by villains,
    That dare as well answer a man indeed
    As I dare take a serpent by the tongue.
    Boys, apes, braggarts, Jacks, milksops!

LEONATO   Brother Anthony—

100 ANTONIO   Hold you content. What, man! I know them, yea,
    And what they weigh, even to the utmost scruple—
    Scambling, outfacing, fashion-monging boys,
    That lie and cog and flout, deprave and slander,
    Go anticly, and show outward hideousness,

105   And speak [off] half a dozen dang'rous words,
    How they might hurt their enemies—if they durst—
    And this is all.

LEONATO   But, brother Anthony—

ANTONIO   Come, 'tis no matter;

110   Do not you meddle, let me deal in this.

DON PEDRO   Gentlemen both, we will not wake your patience.
    My heart is sorry for your daughter's death;

---

82. **nice fence:** dextrous fencing (probably with a sneer in *nice* at the new Italian fashion of duelling with rapier and dagger in place of the older native half-sword and dagger; cf. line 92)

83. **lustihood:** bodily vigor   85. **daff:** doff, thrust aside   87. **men indeed:** true men (cf. line 96)

89. **Win . . . wear me:** If he wants to have me, he'll have to overcome me first (a proverbial phrase used as a summons to action).   **answer me:** meet me in response to my challenge

91. **foining:** thrusting   94. **Content yourself:** don't try to stop me   102. **Scambling:** contentious   **outfacing:** insolent   **fashion-monging:** following the fashions, foppish

103. **cog:** cheat   **deprave:** vilify   104. **Go anticly:** go about fantastically dressed   **outward hideousness:** a threatening appearance   105. **dang'rous:** arrogant, threatening   111. **wake your patience:** test your patience further, add to your troubles

But on my honor she was charg'd with nothing
But what was true, and very full of proof.
115 LEONATO   My lord, my lord—
DON PEDRO   I will not hear you.
LEONATO   No? Come, brother, away! I will be heard.
ANTONIO   And shall, or some of us will smart for it.

(*Exeunt ambo* [LEONATO *and* ANTONIO].)

(*Enter* BENEDICK.)

DON PEDRO   See, see, here comes the man we went to seek.
120 CLAUDIO   Now, signior, what news?
BENEDICK   Good day, my lord.
DON PEDRO   Welcome, signior, you are almost come to part almost a fray.
CLAUDIO   We had lik'd to have had our two noses snapp'd off with two old men without teeth.
125 DON PEDRO   Leonato and his brother. What think'st thou? Had we fought, I doubt we should have been too young for them.
BENEDICK   In a false quarrel there is no true valor. I came to seek you both.
CLAUDIO   We have been up and down to seek thee, for we are high-proof melancholy, and would fain have it beaten away. Wilt thou use thy wit?
130 BENEDICK   It is in my scabbard, shall I draw it?
DON PEDRO   Dost thou wear thy wit by thy side?
CLAUDIO   Never any did so, though very many have been beside their wit. I will bid thee draw, as we do the minstrels, draw to pleasure us.
DON PEDRO   As I am an honest man, he looks pale. Art thou sick, or angry?
135 CLAUDIO   What, courage, man! What though care kill'd a cat, thou hast mettle enough in thee to kill care.
BENEDICK   Sir, I shall meet your wit in the career, and you charge it against me. I pray you choose another subject.
CLAUDIO   Nay then give him another staff, this last was broke cross.
140 DON PEDRO   By this light, he changes more and more. I think he be angry indeed.
CLAUDIO   If he be, he knows how to turn his girdle.
BENEDICK   Shall I speak a word in your ear?
CLAUDIO   God bless me from a challenge!

---

s.d. **ambo:** both   126. **doubt:** fear   128. **high-proof:** at a high level of   132. **beside their wit:** out of their minds   133. **minstrels:** who are bidden to draw their bows across the strings of their instruments   137. **in the career:** at full speed (an expression from jousting)   **charge:** direct, level   139. **staff:** lance   **broke cross:** broken crosswise, athwart his opponent's shield. Claudio means that Benedick has performed wretchedly in this first exchange.   142. **he knows . . . girdle:** Proverbial, but of uncertain meaning; generally explained as meaning "it's up to him to get himself into a better frame of mind; I shall make no effort to placate him" (*girdle* = belt).

145 BENEDICK [*aside to* CLAUDIO]   You are a villain. I jest not; I will make it good
how you dare, with what you dare, and when you dare. Do me right, or I will
protest your cowardice. You have kill'd a sweet lady, and her death shall fall
heavy on you. Let me hear from you.

CLAUDIO   Well, I will meet you, so I may have good cheer.

150 DON PEDRO   What, a feast, a feast?

CLAUDIO   I' faith, I thank him, he hath bid me to a calve's-head and a capon, the
which if I do not carve most curiously, say my knife's naught. Shall I not
find a woodcock too?

BENEDICK   Sir, your wit ambles well, it goes easily.

155 DON PEDRO   I'll tell thee how Beatrice prais'd thy wit the other day. I said thou
hadst a fine wit. "True," said she, "a fine little one." "No," said I, "a great wit."
"Right," says she, "a great gross one." "Nay," said I, "a good wit." "Just," said
she, "it hurts nobody." "Nay," said I, "the gentleman is wise." "Certain," said
she, "a wise gentleman." "Nay," said I, "he hath the tongues." "That I believe,"

160 said she, "for he swore a thing to me on Monday night, which he forswore
on Tuesday morning. There's a double tongue, there's two tongues." Thus
did she an hour together trans-shape thy particular virtues, yet at last she
concluded with a sigh, thou wast the proper'st man in Italy.

CLAUDIO   For the which she wept heartily and said she car'd not.

165 DON PEDRO   Yea, that she did, but yet for all that, and if she did not hate him
deadly, she would love him dearly. The old man's daughter told us all.

CLAUDIO   All, all, and, moreover, God saw him when he was hid in the garden.

DON PEDRO   But when shall we set the savage bull's horns on the sensible
Benedick's head?

170 CLAUDIO   Yea, and text underneath, "Here dwells Benedick the married man"?

BENEDICK   Fare you well, boy, you know my mind. I will leave you now to your
gossip-like humor. You break jests as braggards do their blades, which, God
be thank'd, hurt not. My lord, for your many courtesies I thank you. I must
discontinue your company. Your brother the bastard is fled from Messina.

175 You have among you kill'd a sweet and innocent lady. For my Lord Lack-
beard there, he and I shall meet, and till then peace be with him.

[*Exit.*]

---

146. **Do me right:** give me satisfaction   147. **protest:** proclaim   149. **so . . . cheer:** so long
as I may have good cheer   151. **calve's-head, capon, woodcock:** types of stupidity
152. **curiously:** daintily   **naught:** worthless   154. **your . . . easily:** your wit moves smoothly like an
ambling horse (it shows no mettle or fire like a horse at the gallop).   157. **gross:** coarse
158. **hurts nobody:** has no bite   159. **a wise gentleman:** One of the established uses of this phrase
was in an ironic sense   **hath the tongues:** is a master of languages   162. **trans-shape:** distort
163. **proper'st:** handsomest   165. **and if:** if   166. **deadly:** mortally   167. **God . . . garden:** This reference to the action of III.i contains also an echo of Genesis 3:8.   168–70. **But . . . man:** Benedick is
put on notice that his lordly assertion at I.i.187–191 has not been forgotten.   172. **braggards:** brag-
garts, those better at boasting of their prowess than of demonstrating it

DON PEDRO He is in earnest.

CLAUDIO In most profound earnest, and I'll warrant you, for the love of Beatrice.

180 DON PEDRO And hath challeng'd thee?

CLAUDIO Most sincerely.

DON PEDRO What a pretty thing man is when he goes in his doublet and hose and leaves off his wit!

(*Enter Constables* [DOGBERRY *and* VERGES, *and the* WATCH *with*] CONRADE *and* BORACHIO.)

CLAUDIO He is then a giant to an ape, but then is an ape a doctor to such a
185 man.

DON PEDRO But soft you, let me be. Pluck up, my heart, and be sad. Did he not say my brother was fled?

DOGBERRY Come you, sir. If justice cannot tame you, she shall ne'er weigh more reasons in her balance. Nay, and you be a cursing hypocrite once, you
190 must be look'd to.

DON PEDRO How now? two of my brother's men bound? Borachio one!

CLAUDIO Hearken after their offense, my lord.

DON PEDRO Officers, what offense have these men done?

DOGBERRY Marry, sir, they have committed false report; moreover they have
195 spoken untruths; secondarily, they are slanders; sixt and lastly, they have belied a lady; thirdly, they have verified unjust things; and to conclude, they are lying knaves.

DON PEDRO First, I ask thee what they have done; thirdly, I ask thee what's their offense; sixt and lastly, why they are committed; and to conclude, what you
200 lay to their charge.

CLAUDIO Rightly reason'd, and in his own division, and by my troth there's one meaning well suited.

DON PEDRO Who have you offended, masters, that you are thus bound to your answer? This learned constable is too cunning to be understood. What's
205 your offense?

BORACHIO Sweet Prince, let me go no farther to mine answer: do you hear me, and let this count kill me. I have deceiv'd even your very eyes. What your wisdoms could not discover, these shallow fools have brought to light, who in the night overheard me confessing to this man how Don John your

---

182–183. **goes . . . wit:** forgets to put on his good sense along with his clothes 184. **a giant to:** much larger than (*to* = in comparison with) **doctor:** scholar, learned man 186. **soft you:** wait a minute **Pluck . . . heart:** collect yourself, my mind **sad:** serious 189. **reasons:** legal cases (Dogberry seems to have confused *reasons* and *causes*). Perhaps *reasons* quibbles on *raisins*, which it closely resembled in pronunciation. **balance:** scale 192. **Hearken after:** inquire into 195. **slanders:** slanderers 196. **verified:** affirmed as true (but perhaps a blunder for *testified*) 202. **well suited:** in several garbs 203–204. **bound . . . answer:** bound over for trial (perhaps with puns on *bound* in the senses "pinioned" and "on the way")

210 brother incens'd me to slander the Lady Hero, how you were brought into
the orchard, and saw me court Margaret in Hero's garments, how you dis-
grac'd her when you should marry her. My villainy they have upon record,
which I had rather seal with my death than repeat over to my shame. The
lady is dead upon mine and my master's false accusation; and briefly, I de-
215 sire nothing but the reward of a villain.

DON PEDRO   Runs not this speech like iron through your blood?

CLAUDIO   I have drunk poison whiles he utter'd it.

DON PEDRO   But did my brother set thee on to this?

BORACHIO   Yea, and paid me richly for the practice of it.

220 DON PEDRO   He is compos'd and fram'd of treachery,
And fled he is upon this villainy.

CLAUDIO   Sweet Hero, now thy image doth appear
In the rare semblance that I lov'd it first.

DOGBERRY   Come, bring away the plaintiffs. By this time our sexton hath re-
225 form'd Signior Leonato of the matter; and, masters, do not forget to specify,
when time and place shall serve, that I am an ass.

VERGES   Here, here comes Master Signior Leonato, and the sexton too.

(*Enter* LEONATO, *his brother* [ANTONIO], *and the* SEXTON.)

LEONATO   Which is the villain? Let me see his eyes,
That when I note another man like him
230 I may avoid him. Which of these is he?

BORACHIO   If you would know your wronger, look on me.

LEONATO   Art thou the slave that with thy breath hast kill'd
Mine innocent child?

BORACHIO   Yea, even I alone.

235 LEONATO   No, not so, villain, thou beliest thyself.
Here stand a pair of honorable men,
A third is fled, that had a hand in it.
I thank you, princes, for my daughter's death;
Record it with your high and worthy deeds.
240 'Twas bravely done, if you bethink you of it.

CLAUDIO   I know not how to pray your patience,
Yet I must speak. Choose your revenge yourself,
Impose me to what penance your invention
Can lay upon my sin; yet sinn'd I not,
245 But in mistaking.

---

210. **incens'd:** incited   212. **upon:** as a result of   219. **practice:** execution   224. **plaintiffs:** blunder
for *defendants*   224–25. **reform'd:** for *informed*   225. **specify:** for *testify* (?)   236. **honorable:** of
distinguished rank   243. **Impose:** subject

DON PEDRO   By my soul, nor I,
　　And yet, to satisfy this good old man,
　　I would bend under any heavy weight
　　That he'll enjoin me to.
250 LEONATO   I cannot bid you bid my daughter live—
　　That were impossible—but I pray you both,
　　Possess the people in Messina here
　　How innocent she died, and if your love
　　Can labor aught in sad invention,
255　　Hang her an epitaph upon her tomb,
　　And sing it to her bones, sing it to-night.
　　To-morrow morning come you to my house,
　　And since you could not be my son-in-law,
　　Be yet my nephew. My brother hath a daughter,
260　　Almost the copy of my child that's dead,
　　And she alone is heir to both of us.
　　Give her the right you should have giv'n her cousin,
　　And so dies my revenge.
　CLAUDIO   O noble sir!
265　　Your overkindness doth wring tears from me.
　　I do embrace your offer, and dispose
　　For henceforth of poor Claudio.
　LEONATO   To-morrow then I will expect your coming,
　　To-night I take my leave. This naughty man
270　　Shall face to face be brought to Margaret,
　　Who I believe was pack'd in all this wrong,
　　Hir'd to it by your brother.
　BORACHIO   No, by my soul she was not,
　　Nor knew not what she did when she spoke to me,
275　　But always hath been just and virtuous
　　In any thing that I do know by her.
　DOGBERRY   Moreover, sir, which indeed is not under white and black, this
　　plaintiff here, the offender, did call me ass. I beseech you let it be remem-
　　b'red in his punishment. And also, the watch heard them talk of one De-
280　　formed. They say he wears a key in his ear and a lock hanging by it, and bor-
　　rows money in God's name, the which he hath us'd so long and never paid
　　that now men grow hard-hearted and will lend nothing for God's sake. Pray
　　you examine him upon that point.

---

252. **Possess:** inform   261. **heir to both:** Antonio's son (mentioned in I.ii.1–2) has apparently been
forgotten.   262. **should:** were to   269. **naughty:** wicked   271. **pack'd:** involved as a conspirator
276. **by:** concerning   277. **under...black:** in writing   280. **key...it:** Dogberry's transmutation of
the *lock* of III.iii.122   281. **in God's name:** like a professional beggar (who commonly used this
phrase)   **us'd:** made a practice

LEONATO   I thank thee for thy care and honest pains.
285 DOGBERRY   Your worship speaks like a most thankful and reverent youth, and I
    praise God for you.
LEONATO   There's for thy pains.
DOGBERRY   God save the foundation!
LEONATO   Go, I discharge thee of thy prisoner, and I thank thee.
290 DOGBERRY   I leave an arrant knave with your worship, which I beseech your
    worship to correct yourself, for the example of others. God keep you wor-
    ship! I wish your worship well. God restore you to health! I humbly give you
    leave to depart, and if a merry meeting may be wish'd, God prohibit it!
    Come, neighbor.

[*Exeunt* DOGBERRY *and* VERGES.]

295 LEONATO   Until to-morrow morning, lords, farewell.
ANTONIO   Farewell, my lords, we look for you to-morrow.
DON PEDRO   We will not fail.
CLAUDIO   To-night I'll mourn with Hero.
LEONATO [*to the* WATCH]   Bring you these fellows on.
300   —We'll talk with Margaret,
    How her acquaintance grew with this lewd fellow.

(*Exeunt* [*severally*].)

[Scene II]

(*Enter* BENEDICK *and* MARGARET, [*meeting*].)

BENEDICK   Pray thee, sweet Mistress Margaret, deserve well at my hands by
    helping me to the speech of Beatrice.
MARGARET   Will you then write me a sonnet in praise of my beauty?
BENEDICK   In so high a style, Margaret, that no man living shall come over it,
5   for in most comely truth thou deservest it.
MARGARET   To have no man come over me? Why, shall I always keep below
    stairs?

---

285. **reverent:** Perhaps another blunder, but *reverent* was commonly used in the sense "reverend" (see V.iv.120).   288. **God . . . foundation:** a phrase used by those who received alms from a charitable foundation   290–91. **I . . . yourself:** Dogberry here makes use of locutions which, contrary to his intention, permit the interpretation that he is calling Leonato a knave and urging him to reform. 293. **prohibit:** one last example of Dogberry saying precisely the opposite of what he means
301. **lewd:** low, worthless

V.ii. Location: Leonato's orchard
4. **come over:** (1) exceed; (2) get across (pointing to a quibble on *style / stile* in line 6). Margaret then plays on a third sense, with characteristic ribaldry.   5. **in . . . comely truth:** (1) in good truth; (2) by virtue of your beauty   6. **keep:** dwell, stay   6–7. **below stairs:** in the servants' quarters

BENEDICK   Thy wit is as quick as the greyhound's mouth, it catches.

MARGARET   And yours as blunt as the fencer's foils, which hit, but hurt not.

10   BENEDICK   A most manly wit, Margaret, it will not hurt a woman. And so I pray thee call Beatrice; I give thee the bucklers.

MARGARET   Give us the swords, we have bucklers of our own.

BENEDICK   If you use them, Margaret, you must put in the pikes with a vice, and they are dangerous weapons for maids.

15   MARGARET   Well, I will call Beatrice to you, who I think hath legs.   (*Exit* MAR-GARET.)

BENEDICK   And therefore will come.   [*sings*]
              "The god of love,
              That sits above,
20   And knows me, and knows me,
                    How pitiful I deserve"—

I mean in singing; but in loving, Leander the good swimmer, Troilus the first employer of pandars, and a whole bookful of these quondam carpet-mongers, whose names yet run smoothly in the even road of a blank verse,
25   why, they were never so truly turn'd over and over as my poor self in love. Marry, I cannot show it in rhyme; I have tried. I can find out no rhyme to "lady" but "baby," an innocent rhyme; for "scorn," "horn," a hard rhyme; for "school," "fool," a babbling rhyme: very ominous endings. No, I was not born under a rhyming planet, nor I cannot woo in festival terms.

(*Enter* BEATRICE.)

30   Sweet Beatrice, wouldst thou come when I call'd thee?

BEATRICE   Yea, signior, and depart when you bid me.

BENEDICK   O, stay but till then!

BEATRICE   "Then" is spoken; fare you well now. And yet ere I go, let me go with that I came, which is, with knowing what hath pass'd between you and
35   Claudio.

BENEDICK   Only foul words—and thereupon I will kiss thee.

BEATRICE   Foul words is but foul wind, and foul wind is but foul breath, and foul breath is noisome; therefore I will depart unkiss'd.

---

11. **give . . . bucklers:** give up (*buckler* = a kind of shield)   13. **pikes:** spikes in the centre of a shield   **vice:** screw   18–20. The first lines of a contemporary song   21. **How . . . deserve:** how much I deserve pity (but Benedick twists the meaning to "how pitifully small my deserts are").   22. **Leander:** who swam the Hellespont nightly to see his love Hero   **Troilus:** whose union with Cressida was arranged by her uncle Pandarus   23. **quondam:** of former days   23–24. **carpet-mongers:** Knights who avoided military service were contemptuously called carpet knights. Benedick's use of the term for storied lovers of old implies that they were contemptible performers compared with himself.   27. **innocent:** childish   **hard:** (1) harsh, unpleasant (because associated with the idea of the cuckold's horn); (2) solid   29. **festival terms:** elevated language suitable for a special occasion   34. **that I came:** what I came for   38. **noisome:** ill-smelling

BENEDICK   Thou hast frighted the word out of his right sense, so forcible is thy
40   wit. But I must tell thee plainly, Claudio undergoes my challenge, and either
I must shortly hear from him, or I will subscribe him a coward. And I pray
thee now tell me, for which of my bad parts didst thou first fall in love with
me?

BEATRICE   For them all together, which maintain'd so politic a state of evil that
45   they will not admit any good part to intermingle with them. But for which
of my good parts did you first suffer love for me?

BENEDICK   Suffer love! a good epithite! I do suffer love indeed, for I love thee
against my will.

BEATRICE   In spite of your heart, I think. Alas, poor heart, if you spite it for my
50   sake, I will spite it for yours, for I will never love that which my friend hates.

BENEDICK   Thou and I are too wise to woo peaceably.

BEATRICE   It appears not in this confession; there's not one wise man among
twenty that will praise himself.

BENEDICK   An old, an old instance, Beatrice, that liv'd in the time of good
55   neighbors. If a man do not erect in this age his own tomb ere he dies, he
shall live no longer in monument than the bell rings and the widow weeps.

BEATRICE   And how long is that, think you?

BENEDICK   Question: why, an hour in clamor and a quarter in rheum; therefore
is it most expedient for the wise, if Don Worm (his conscience) find no im-
60   pediment to the contrary, to be the trumpet of his own virtues, as I am to
myself. So much for praising myself, who I myself will bear witness is
praiseworthy. And now tell me, how doth your cousin?

BEATRICE   Very ill.

BENEDICK   And how do you?

65   BEATRICE   Very ill too.

BENEDICK   Serve God, love me, and mend. There will I leave you too, for here
comes one in haste.

(*Enter* URSULA.)

URSULA   Madam, you must come to your uncle, yonder's old coil at home. It is
prov'd my Lady Hero hath been falsely accus'd, the Prince and Claudio
70   mightily abus'd, and Don John is the author of all, who is fled and gone.
Will you come presently?

---

39. **his right sense:** (1) its senses, its right mind; (2) its correct meaning   40. **undergoes:** is subject
to   41. **subscribe:** formally proclaim   44. **politic:** shrewdly managed   46. **suffer:** (1) experience;
(2) suffer from   47. **epithite:** epithet, expression   52. **It . . . confession:** Your wisdom is not shown
by this declaration that you are wise.   54. **instance:** proverb, maxim (that a wise man does not
praise himself)   54–55. **time . . . neighbors:** good old days when neighbors were willing to speak
well of one another   58. **Question:** that is the question   **clamor:** sound (of the bell)   **rheum:** tears
(of the widow)   59. **Don . . . conscience:** It was a commonplace to describe the conscience as a
gnawing worm.   60. **trumpet:** trumpeter   68. **old coil:** great confusion, much ado
70. **abus'd:** deceived   71. **presently:** immediately

BEATRICE   Will you go hear this news, signior?
BENEDICK   I will live in thy heart, die in thy lap, and be buried in thy eyes, and
moreover I will go with thee to thy uncle's.

(*Exeunt.*)

[Scene III]

(*Enter* CLAUDIO, *Prince* [DON PEDRO], *and three or four with tapers.*)

CLAUDIO   Is this the monument of Leonato?
[A] LORD   It is, my lord.
[CLAUDIO, *reading out of a scroll:*]

Epitaph

       "Done to death by slanderous tongues
       Was the Hero that here lies.
5   Death, in guerdon of her wrongs,
       Gives her fame which never dies.
       So the life that died with shame
       Lives in death with glorious fame."
       Hang thou there upon the tomb,

[*hangs up the scroll*]

10   Praising her when I am [dumb].
Now, music, sound, and sing your solemn hymn.

Song

       Pardon, goddess of the night,
       Those that slew thy virgin knight,
       For the which, with songs of woe,
15   Round about her tomb they go.
         Midnight, assist our moan,
         Help us to sigh and groan,
           Heavily, heavily.
       Graves, yawn and yield your dead,

---

73. **die:** used with the common sexual implication

V.iii. Location: a churchyard
5. **guerdon:** recompense   12. **goddess . . . night:** See note to IV.i.53.   18. **Heavily:** mournfully
19. **yield your dead:** so that they too may "assist our moan"

20 Till death be uttered,
Heavily, heavily.

[CLAUDIO]   Now, unto thy bones good night!
Yearly will I do this rite.
DON PEDRO   Good morrow, masters, put your torches out.
25 The wolves have preyed, and look, the gentle day,
Before the wheels of Phoebus, round about
Dapples the drowsy east with spots of grey.
Thanks to you all, and leave us. Fare you well.
CLAUDIO   Good morrow, masters—each his several way.
30 DON PEDRO   Come let us hence, and put on other weeds,
And then to Leonato's we will go.
CLAUDIO   And Hymen now with luckier issue speed's
Than this for whom we rend'red up this woe.

(*Exeunt.*)

[Scene IV]

(*Enter* LEONATO, BENEDICK, [BEATRICE,] MARGARET, URSULA, *old man* [ANTONIO], FRIAR [FRANCIS], HERO.)

FRIAR FRANCIS   Did I not tell you she was innocent?
LEONATO   So are the Prince and Claudio, who accus'd her
Upon the error that you heard debated.
But Margaret was in some fault for this,
5 Although against her will, as it appears
In the true course of all the question.
ANTONIO   Well, I am glad that all things sorts so well.
BENEDICK   And so am I, being else by faith enforc'd
To call young Claudio to a reckoning for it.
10 LEONATO   Well, daughter, and you gentlewoman all,
Withdraw into a chamber by yourselves,
And when I send for you, come hither masked.
The Prince and Claudio promis'd by this hour
To visit me. You know your office, brother:

---

20. **uttered:** fully expressed, adequately lamented   25. **have preyed:** have finished their night's preying   26. **Before . . . Phoebus:** preceding the chariot of the sun   30. **weeds:** clothes
32. **Hymen:** the god of marriage   **with . . . speed's:** favor us with better fortune

V.iv. Location: Leonato's house
3. **Upon:** because of   **debated:** publicly discussed   5. **against her will:** unintentionally
6. **question:** judicial examination   7. **sorts:** turn out   8. **faith:** his pledge to Beatrice   14. **office:** function, role

15   You must be father to your brother's daughter,
       And give her to young Claudio.

(*Exeunt* LADIES.)

ANTONIO   Which I will do with confirm'd countenance.
BENEDICK   Friar, I must entreat your pains, I think.
FRIAR FRANCIS   To do what, signior?
20 BENEDICK   To bind me, or undo me—one of them.
       Signior Leonato, truth it is, good signior,
       Your niece regards me with an eye of favor.
LEONATO   That eye my daughter lent her, 'tis most true.
BENEDICK   And I do with an eye of love requite her.
25 LEONATO   The sight whereof I think you had from me,
       From Claudio, and the Prince. But what's your will?
BENEDICK   Your answer, sir, is enigmatical,
       But for my will, my will is your good will
       May stand with ours, this day to be conjoin'd
30   In the state of honorable marriage,
       In which, good friar, I shall desire your help.
LEONATO   My heart is with your liking.
FRIAR FRANCIS   And my help.
       Here comes the Prince and Claudio.

(*Enter Prince* [DON PEDRO] *and* CLAUDIO *and two or three others.*)

35 DON PEDRO   Good morrow to this fair assembly.
LEONATO   Good morrow, Prince; good morrow, Claudio;
       We here attend you. Are you yet determined
       To-day to marry with my brother's daughter?
CLAUDIO   I'll hold my mind were she an Ethiope.
40 LEONATO   Call her forth, brother, here's the friar ready.   [*Exit* ANTONIO.]
DON PEDRO   Good morrow, Benedick. Why, what's the matter,
       That you have such a February face,
       So full of frost, of storm, and cloudiness?
CLAUDIO   I think he thinks upon the savage bull.
45   Tush, fear not, man, we'll tip thy horns with gold,
       And all Europa shall rejoice at thee,
       As once Europa did at lusty Jove,
       When he would play the noble beast in love.

---

17. **confirm'd:** steadfast, serious **countenance:** demeanor 20. **undo:** (1) ruin; (2) unbind
37. **yet:** still 44. **savage bull:** another reference to Benedick's complacent statement at I.i.187–191
46. **Europa:** Europe 47. **Europa:** a Phoenician princess whom Jove, in the form of a white bull, carried off from her native land

BENEDICK   Bull Jove, sir, had an amiable low,
50   And some such strange bull leapt your father's cow,
      And got a calf in that same noble feat
      Much like to you, for you have just his bleat.

(*Enter Brother* [ANTONIO], HERO, BEATRICE, MARGARET, URSULA, [*the ladies masked*].)

CLAUDIO   For this I owe you: here comes other reck'nings.
      Which is the lady I must seize upon?
55 [ANTONIO]   This same is she, and I do give you her.
CLAUDIO   Why then she's mine. Sweet, let me see your face.
LEONATO   No, that you shall not till you take her hand,
      Before this friar, and swear to marry her.
CLAUDIO   Give me your hand before this holy friar—
60   I am your husband if you like of me.
HERO [*unmasking*]   And when I liv'd, I was your other wife,
      And when you lov'd, you were my other husband.
CLAUDIO   Another Hero!
HERO   Nothing certainer:
65   One Hero died defil'd, but I do live,
      And surely as I live, I am a maid.
DON PEDRO   The former Hero! Hero that is dead!
LEONATO   She died, my lord, but whiles her slander liv'd.
FRIAR FRANCIS   All this amazement can I qualify,
70   When after that the holy rites are ended,
      I'll tell you largely of fair Hero's death.
      Mean time let wonder seem familiar,
      And to the chapel let us presently.
BENEDICK   Soft and fair, friar. Which is Beatrice?
75 BEATRICE [*unmasking*]   I answer to that name. What is your will?
BENEDICK   Do not you love me?
BEATRICE   Why, no, no more than reason.
BENEDICK   Why then your uncle and the Prince and Claudio
      Have been deceiv'd. They swore you did.
80 BEATRICE   Do not you love me?
BENEDICK   Troth, no, no more than reason.
BEATRICE   Why then my cousin, Margaret, and Ursula
      Are much deceiv'd, for they did swear you did.

---

49. **amiable low:** winning voice   53. **owe you:** will repay you later   **other reck'nings:** other accounts (that I must settle first)   60. **like of:** like, are willing to take   65. **defil'd:** disgraced, slandered   69. **qualify:** moderate   71. **largely:** fully, in detail   72. **let . . . familiar:** accept these amazing events as natural

BENEDICK   They swore that you were almost sick for me.

85 BEATRICE   They swore that you were well-nigh dead for me.

BENEDICK   'Tis no such matter. Then you do not love me?

BEATRICE   No, truly, but in friendly recompense.

LEONATO   Come, cousin, I am sure you love the gentleman.

CLAUDIO   And I'll be sworn upon't that he loves her,

90   For here's a paper written in his hand,
A halting sonnet of his own pure brain,
Fashion'd to Beatrice.

HERO   And here's another
Writ in my cousin's hand, stol'n from her pocket,

95   Containing her affection unto Benedick.

BENEDICK   A miracle! here's our own hands against our hearts. Come, I will
have thee, but by this light, I take thee for pity.

BEATRICE   I would not deny you, but by this good day, I yield upon great persuasion, and partly to save your life, for I was told you were in a consump-

100   tion.

[BENEDICK]   Peace, I will stop your mouth.   [*kissing her*]

DON PEDRO   How dost thou, Benedick the married man?

BENEDICK   I'll tell thee what, Prince: a college of wit-crackers cannot flout me
out of my humor. Dost thou think I care for a satire or an epigram? No, if a

105   man will be beaten with brains, 'a shall wear nothing handsome about him.
In brief, since I do purpose to marry, I will think nothing to any purpose
that the world can say against it, and therefore never flout at me for what I
have said against it; for man is a giddy thing, and this is my conclusion. For
thy part, Claudio, I did think to have beaten thee, but in that thou art like to

110   be my kinsman, live unbruis'd, and love my cousin.

CLAUDIO   I had well hop'd thou wouldst have denied Beatrice, that I might have
cudgell'd thee out of thy single life, to make thee a double-dealer, which out
of question thou wilt be, if my cousin do not look exceeding narrowly to
thee.

115 BENEDICK   Come, come, we are friends. Let's have a dance ere we are married,
that we may lighten our own hearts and our wives' heels.

LEONATO   We'll have dancing afterward.

---

96. **our . . . hearts:** our own written testimony to prove our hearts guilty as charged
102. **How . . man:** Cf. I.i.190–191   103. **college:** company, assemblage   **wit-crackers:** jokesters (cf.
crack a joke)   104–105. **if . . . him:** If a man is going to allow himself to be beaten up by wit, he will
never dare wear good clothes; i.e., if a man allows ridicule to dictate his actions, he will deprive himself of many desirable things.   108. **giddy:** fickle, changeable   **my conclusion:** the position I have
finally come to   112. **double-dealer:** (1) married man (cf. *single man*); (2) unfaithful husband   112–13. **out of question:** without doubt   113. **narrowly:** closely

BENEDICK   First, of my word; therefore play, music. Prince, thou art sad, get
thee a wife, get thee a wife. There is no staff more reverent than one tipp'd
120   with horn.

(*Enter* MESSENGER.)

MESSENGER   My lord, your brother John is ta'en in flight,
And brought with armed men back to Messina.

BENEDICK   Think not on him till to-morrow. I'll devise thee brave punish-
ments for him. Strike up, pipers.

(*Dance.* [*Exeunt.*])

STUDY QUESTIONS

1. One of the prevailing verbal motifs in the play is that of the mask. How do
the masks and mistaken identities contribute to the themes of *Much Ado
About Nothing?*

2. What are the two essential complications of the play? Is one more believable
than the other?

3. Discuss the role of Friar Francis, who comes up with the idea of pretending
Hero has died after she faints upon being humiliated by Claudio at their
aborted wedding ceremony. Is the Friar's counsel wise, or does it seem con-
trived so that Shakespeare can have his climactic "recognition" scene between Hero and Claudio in Act V?

4. Do you sense any problems in tone early in Act 5 between the play's potentially tragic and comic elements?

5. How does Benedick's final speech, in which he concludes that "man is a
giddy thing," serve to reconcile the play's darker elements with its essentially
comic vision?

---

118. **of:** on   119. **reverent:** reverend, honorable   120. **horn:** The cuckold joke once more
123. **brave:** capital, fine

29

REALISM

The late nineteenth and early twentieth centuries mark another period of notable theatrical growth and development throughout Europe—the age of realism. Realism was an international style, popular from Norway and Russia through England, Ireland, and America.

Realism was, of course, a literary style; but it was a style of production as well. Look, for instance, at the opening of *A Doll's House*. Not only does Ibsen carefully list the placement of the four doors and the furniture used in the action; he even details the "copperplate etchings on the walls" and the "deluxe editions" that are to fill the "small bookcase."

Note, too, that Ibsen speaks of the "rear wall," "left wall," and "right wall" of the room. To most of us, this seems quite natural. Of course a room has four walls. Of course three of them are shown onstage and the fourth is imagined to be at the front of the stage. Of course characters enter and exit through doors in these walls; how else does one enter or leave a room? In fact, however, this form of stage setting, known as the "box set," was a new form of stage setting. The box set was far more realistic than the older "wings"; but it was more cumbersome as well, requiring long intermissions between acts to allow for scene changes. Thus it may have helped to promote the popularity not only of realistic drama but also of the one-act play, which is often set in one scene and thus requires no change of scenery.

Realism in production, then, meant sets and costumes as like those of everyday life as possible. In playwriting, it meant plots, characters, and language drawn from everyday life, as well. (Comedy, as usual, retained the right of exaggeration in all these areas.)

In addition, realism implied a new approach to drama. The realistic play hoped to make two impacts on its audience. First, of course, it sought to make the audience sympathize with the plight of its characters. But it also strove to raise in the minds of its audience questions as to the rightness of some aspect of social order, and the desire to change what the dramatist perceived as evil or wrong.

From these goals came a new form of play known as the **realistic drama:** a serious play, usually on a domestic or semidomestic theme, featuring middle-class (or sometimes lower-class) characters, a contemporary setting, and a plot that questions some aspect or dictate of society.

Take, for example, *A Doll's House* by Henrik Ibsen, a Norwegian playwright who was one of the earliest and most admired of the realists. We see in *A Doll's*

House, one of Ibsen's most popular plays, the mixture of elements described above. The scene is unrelievedly domestic. Money and marriage (normally the concerns of comedy) are both major concerns in this play. Yet the movement within the play is more like that of tragedy, being, in general, "from happiness to unhappiness." Comedy usually ends in the making of a marriage. *A Doll's House* details the breakup of one. In line with the domesticity of the scene, we notice a new concern with detail: the clothes Nora wears, the ornaments she puts on her Christmas tree, the macaroons she eats or does not eat all reflect her struggle for self-identity. We see, too, her concern with upbringing: what effect has Nora's father had on her? What effect is she having on her own children? Finally, we observe how the domestic nature of the realistic drama heightens the disparity between what the play's main characters perceive and feel and what is perceived of them by those around them. The onlookers in *Œdipus Rex* and *Antigonê* recognize the magnitude of the struggles they are watching. The onlookers in *A Doll's House* see only a peaceful, prosperous, well-ordered household.

Today, *A Doll's House* is most frequently read as a complaint against the undervaluation and suppression of women. But strong arguments can be made for the theory that Ibsen is showing men and women as equal victims of society's insistence on "respectability." Notice, as you read this play, how the characters are grouped in this regard, how each sins and is sinned against. Consider, too, the ending, which is of a type impossible for both tragedy and comedy. What effect does it have on your response to the play?

Realism and Comedy

Comedy was a favorite form in the nineteenth century, both before and during the age of realism, if only because nineteenth-century theater and comedy are both strongly oriented toward middle-class characters and dilemmas. Nineteenth-century drama, following the theory that people are creatures of their society, saw its role as portraying and commenting on that society. Comedy, too, sees people in their roles as social beings, and has, since the ancient Greeks, been willing to comment on individuals and society alike.

Sometimes, comedy sets the folly of an individual against the good sense of society at large. At other times, a rebellious hero or heroine fights on the side of love and nature, against the follies of society. In either case, society is usually the victor. No matter how hard comic characters may struggle to escape the bonds of society—no matter what unusual methods they may use to outwit other characters or to solve some particular conflict between society's dictates and their own desires—at the play's end they return to the very society they've been fighting. The conflict has been solved, the goal or the marriage won; and society promises to go on exactly as it did before.

As we observed in *Much Ado About Nothing,* Shakespeare employs the comedy of setting an individual against the good sense of society by having Benedick proclaim himself a lifelong bachelor early in the play. There can be little doubt that in the world of comedy he will soon have to eat his words: in fact, much of our enjoyment comes from our anticipation of seeing this comic formula proceed to its inevitable conclusion, in which Benedick laughs at himself for having been wrong about love and happily marries Beatrice despite the teasing he gets from his friends.

All comedy is in a sense "realistic," because it deals with ordinary human folly, but there are degrees of comic realism. In *Much Ado,* Hero and Claudio are unrealistic stereotypes out of the Petrarchan tradition; Beatrice and Benedick, however, in their more complex and more believable characterization, look forward to the realistic comedy typical of modern drama.

Realism and Tragedy

Tragedy did not fare well during the nineteenth century, for several reasons. First, tragedy took kings and princes for its heroes, not members of the middle class. Second, it tended to insist that these kings and princes speak poetry, a speech form not well suited to discussion of everyday matters. Third, tragedy traditionally portrayed its heroes as people who have power over their societies: Oedipus, Hamlet, and Claudius are directly responsible for the physical and moral health of Thebes and of Denmark. And this characteristic of tragedy did not fit well with the trend of nineteenth-century drama to depict people as beings shaped by the society in which they had been born and reared. The thrust toward realism was thus antithetical to the grand tragedies of the classic and Renaissance styles; and attempts by nineteenth-century playwrights to reproduce some of that grandeur were generally failures.

Once realism was firmly established, however, the twentieth century could try variations on its theme; and some of these variations recreated tragedy as a newly effective form. Some of these new tragedies were written in poetry, but most were in prose—though in some few cases the prose is so artfully handled that it almost becomes poetry.

A Doll's House   HENRIK IBSEN

A translation by Otto Reinert

CHARACTERS

TORVALD HELMER, *a lawyer*
NORA, *his wife*
DR. RANK
MRS. LINDE
KROGSTAD
THE HELMERS' THREE SMALL CHILDREN
ANNE-MARIE, *the children's nurse*
A HOUSEMAID
A PORTER

SCENE. *The Helmers' living room.*

Act I

A pleasant, tastefully but not expensively furnished, living room. A door on the rear wall, right, leads to the front hall, another door, left, to HELMER's *study. Between the two doors a piano. A third door in the middle of the left wall; further front a window. Near the window a round table and a small couch. Towards the rear of the right wall a fourth door; further front a tile stove with a rocking chair and a couple of armchairs in front of it. Between the stove and the door a small table. Copperplate etchings on the walls. A whatnot with porcelain figurines and other small objects. A small bookcase with de luxe editions. A rug on the floor; fire in the stove. Winter day.*

The doorbell rings, then the sound of the front door opening. NORA, *dressed for outdoors, enters, humming cheerfully. She carries several packages, which she puts down on the table, right. She leaves the door to the front hall open; there a* PORTER *is seen holding a Christmas tree and a basket. He gives them to the* MAID *who has let them in.*

NORA   Be sure to hide the Christmas tree, Helene. The children mustn't see it before tonight when we've trimmed it. (*opens her purse; to the* PORTER:) How much?

PORTER   Fifty ore.

NORA   Here's a crown. No, keep the change. (*The* PORTER *thanks her, leaves.* NORA *closes the door. She keeps laughing quietly to herself as she takes off her coat, etc. She takes a bag of macaroons from her pocket and eats a couple. She walks cautiously over to the door to the study and listens.*) Yes, he's home. (*resumes her humming, walks over to the table, right*)

HELMER (*in his study*)   Is that my little lark twittering out there?

NORA (*opening some packages*)   That's right.

820

HELMER My squirrel bustling about?

NORA Yes.

HELMER When did squirrel come home?

NORA Just now. (*puts the bag of macaroons back in her pocket, wipes her mouth*) Come out here, Torvald. I want to show you what I've bought.

HELMER I'm busy! (*After a little while he opens the door and looks in, pen in hand.*) Bought, eh? All that? So little wastrel has been throwing money around again?

NORA Oh but Torvald, this Christmas we can be a little extravagant, can't we? It's the first Christmas we don't have to scrimp.

HELMER I don't know about that. We certainly don't have money to waste.

NORA Yes, Torvald, we do. A little, anyway. Just a tiny little bit? Now that you're going to get that big salary and make lots and lots of money.

HELMER Starting at New Year's, yes. But payday isn't till the end of the quarter.

NORA That doesn't matter. We can always borrow.

HELMER Nora! (*goes over to her and playfully pulls her ear*) There you go being irresponsible again. Suppose I borrowed a thousand crowns today and you spent it all for Christmas and on New Year's Eve a tile hit me in the head and laid me out cold.

NORA (*putting her hand over his mouth*) I won't have you say such horrid things.

HELMER But suppose it happened. Then what?

NORA If it did, I wouldn't care whether we owed money or not.

HELMER But what about the people I borrowed from?

NORA Who cares about them! They are strangers.

HELMER Nora, Nora, you *are* a woman! No, really! You know how I feel about that. No debts! A home in debt isn't a free home, and if it isn't free it isn't beautiful. We've managed nicely so far, you and I, and that's the way we'll go on. It won't be for much longer.

NORA (*walks over toward the stove*) All right, Torvald. Whatever you say.

HELMER (*follows her*) Come, come, my little songbird mustn't droop her wings. What's this? Can't have a pouty squirrel in the house, you know. (*takes out his wallet*) Nora, what do you think I have here?

NORA (*turns around quickly*) Money!

HELMER Here. (*gives her some bills*) Don't you think I know Christmas is expensive?

NORA (*counting*) Ten—twenty—thirty—forty. Thank you, thank you, Torvald. This helps a lot.

HELMER I certainly hope so.

NORA It does, it does. But I want to show you what I got. It was cheap, too. Look. New clothes for Ivar. And a sword. And a horse and trumpet for Bob. And a doll and a little bed for Emmy. It isn't any good, but it wouldn't last, anyway. And here's some dress material and scarves for the maids. I feel bad about old Anne-Marie, though. She really should be getting much more.

HELMER   And what's in here?

NORA (*cries*)   Not till tonight!

HELMER   I see. But now what does my little prodigal have in mind for herself?

NORA   Oh, nothing. I really don't care.

HELMER   Of course you do. Tell me what you'd like. Within reason.

NORA   Oh, I don't know. Really, I don't. The only thing—

HELMER   Well?

NORA (*fiddling with his buttons, without looking at him*)   If you really want to give me something, you might—you could—

HELMER   All right, let's have it.

NORA (*quickly*)   Some money, Torvald. Just as much as you think you can spare. Then I'll buy myself something one of these days.

HELMER   No, really Nora—

NORA   Oh yes, please, Torvald. Please? I'll wrap the money in pretty gold paper and hang it on the tree. Won't that be nice?

HELMER   What's the name for little birds that are always spending money?

NORA   Wastrels, I know. But please let's do it my way, Torvald. Then I'll have time to decide what I need most. Now that's sensible, isn't it?

HELMER (*smiling*)   Oh, very sensible. That is, if you really bought yourself something you could use. But it all disappears in the household expenses or you buy things you don't need. And then you come back to me for more.

NORA   Oh, but Torvald—

HELMER   That's the truth, dear little Nora, and you know it. (*puts his arm around her*) My wastrel is a little sweetheart, but she *does* go through an awful lot of money awfully fast. You've no idea how expensive it is for a man to keep a wastrel.

NORA   That's not fair, Torvald. I really save all I can.

HELMER (*laughs*)   Oh, I believe that. All you can. Meaning, exactly nothing!

NORA (*hums, smiles mysteriously*)   You don't know all the things we songbirds and squirrels need money for, Torvald.

HELMER   You know, you're funny. Just like your father. You're always looking for ways to get money, but as soon as you do it runs through your fingers and you can never say what you spent it for. Well, I guess I'll just have to take you the way you are. It's in your blood. Yes, that sort of thing is hereditary, Nora.

NORA   In that case, I wish I had inherited many of Daddy's qualities.

HELMER   And I don't want you any different from just what you are—my own sweet little songbird. Hey!—I think I just noticed something. Aren't you looking—what's the word?—a little—sly—?

NORA   I am?

HELMER   You definitely are. Look at me.

NORA (*looks at him*)   Well?

HELMER (*wagging a finger*)   Little sweet-tooth hasn't by any chance been on a rampage today, has she?

NORA   Of course not. Whatever makes you think that?

HELMER   A little detour by the pastryshop maybe?

NORA   No, I assure you, Torvald—

HELMER   Nibbled a little jam?

NORA   Certainly not!

HELMER   Munched a macaroon or two?

NORA   No, really, Torvald, I honestly—

HELMER   All right. Of course I was only joking.

NORA (*walks toward the table, right*)   You know I wouldn't do anything to displease you.

HELMER   I know. And I have your promise. (*over to her*) All right, keep your little Christmas secrets to yourself, Nora darling. They'll all come out tonight, I suppose, when we light the tree.

NORA   Did you remember to invite Rank?

HELMER   No, but there's no need to. He knows he'll have dinner with us. Anyway, I'll see him later this morning. I'll ask him then. I did order some good wine. Oh Nora, you've no idea how much I'm looking forward to tonight!

NORA   Me, too. And the children Torvald! They'll have such a good time!

HELMER   You know, it *is* nice to have a good, safe job and a comfortable income. Feels good just thinking about it. Don't you agree?

NORA   Oh, it's wonderful!

HELMER   Remember last Christmas? For three whole weeks you shut yourself up every evening till long after midnight making ornaments for the Christmas tree and I don't know what else. Some big surprise for all of us, anyway. I'll be damned if I've ever been so bored in my whole life!

NORA   I wasn't bored at all!

HELMER (*smiling*)   But you've got to admit you didn't have much to show for it in the end.

NORA   Oh, don't tease me again about that! Could I help it that the cat got in and tore up everything?

HELMER   Of course you couldn't, my poor little Nora. You just wanted to please the rest of us, and that's the important thing. But I *am* glad the hard times are behind us. Aren't you?

NORA   Oh yes. I think it's just wonderful.

HELMER   This year, I won't be bored and lonely. And you won't have to strain your dear eyes and your delicate little hands—

NORA (*claps her hands*)   No I won't, will I Torvald? Oh, how wonderful, how lovely, to hear you say that! (*puts her arm under his*) Let me tell you how I think we should arrange things, Torvald. Soon as Christmas is over—(*The doorbell rings.*) Someone's at the door. (*straightens things up a bit*) A caller, I suppose. Bother!

HELMER   Remember, I'm not home for visitors.

THE MAID (*in the door to the front hall*)   Ma'am, there's a lady here—

NORA   All right. Ask her to come in.

THE MAID (*to* HELMER)   And the Doctor just arrived.

HELMER   Is he in the study?

THE MAID   Yes, sir.

(HELMER *exits into his study.* THE MAID *shows* MRS. LINDE *in and closes the door behind her as she leaves.* MRS. LINDE *is in travel dress.*)

MRS. LINDE (*timid and a little hesitant*)   Good morning, Nora.

NORA (*uncertainly*)   Good morning.

MRS. LINDE   I don't believe you know who I am.

NORA   No—I'm not sure—Though I know I should—Of course! Kristine! It's you!

MRS. LINDE   Yes, it's me.

NORA   And I didn't even recognize you! I had no idea. (*in a lower voice*) You've changed, Kristine.

MRS. LINDE   I'm sure I have. It's been nine or ten long years.

NORA   Has it really been that long? Yes, you're right. I've been so happy these last eight years. And now you're here. Such a long trip in the middle of winter. How brave!

MRS. LINDE   I got in on the steamer this morning.

NORA   To have some fun over the holidays, of course. That's lovely. For we are going to have fun. But take off your coat! You aren't cold, are you? (*helps her*) There, now! Let's sit down here by the fire and just relax and talk. No, you sit there. I want the rocking chair. (*takes her hands*) And now you've got your old face back. It was just for a minute, right at first—Though you are a little more pale, Kristine. And maybe a little thinner.

MRS. LINDE   And much, much older, Nora.

NORA   Maybe a little older. Just a teeny-weeny bit, not much. (*interrupts herself, serious*) Oh, but how thoughtless of me, chatting away like this! Sweet, good Kristine, can you forgive me?

MRS. LINDE   Forgive you what, Nora?

NORA (*in a low voice*)   You poor dear, you lost your husband, didn't you?

MRS. LINDE   Three years ago, yes.

NORA   I know. I saw it in the paper. Oh please believe me, Kristine. I really meant to write you, but I never got around to it. Something was always coming up.

MRS. LINDE   Of course, Nora. I understand.

NORA   No, that wasn't very nice of me. You poor thing, all you must have been through. And he didn't leave you much, either, did he?

MRS. LINDE   No.

NORA   And no children?

MRS. LINDE   No.

NORA   Nothing at all, in other words?

MRS. LINDE   Not so much as a sense of loss—a grief to live on—

NORA (*incredulous*)   But Kristine, how can that *be?*

MRS. LINDE (*with a sad smile, strokes* NORA's *hair*)   That's the way it sometimes is, Nora.

NORA   All alone. How awful for you. I have three darling children. You can't see them right now, though; they're out with their nurse. But now you must tell me everything—

MRS. LINDE   No, no; I'd rather listen to you.

NORA   No, you begin. Today I won't be selfish. Today I'll think only of you. Except there's one thing I've just got to tell you first. Something marvelous that's happened to us just these last few days. You haven't heard, have you?

MRS. LINDE   No; tell me.

NORA   Just think. My husband's been made manager of the Mutual Bank.

MRS. LINDE   Your husband—! Oh, I'm so glad!

NORA   Yes, isn't that great? You see, private law practice is so uncertain, especially when you won't have anything to do with cases that aren't—you know—quite nice. And of course Torvald won't do that and I quite agree with him. Oh, you've no idea how delighted we are! He takes over at New Year's, and he'll be getting a big salary and all sorts of extras. From now on we'll be able to live in quite a different way—exactly as we like. Oh, Kristine! I feel so carefree and happy! It's lovely to have lots and lots of money and not have to worry about a thing! Don't you agree?

MRS. LINDE   It would be nice to have enough at any rate.

NORA   No, I don't mean just enough. I mean lots and lots!

MRS. LINDE (*smiles*)   Nora, Nora, when are you going to be sensible? In school you spent a great deal of money.

NORA (*quietly laughing*)   Yes, and Torvald says I still do. (*raises her finger at* MRS. LINDE) But "Nora, Nora" isn't so crazy as you all think. Believe me, we've had nothing to be extravagant with. We've both had to work.

MRS. LINDE   You too?

NORA   Yes. Oh, it's been little things, mostly—sewing, crocheting, embroidery— that sort of thing. (*casually*) And other things too. You know, of course, that Torvald left government service when we got married? There was no chance of promotion in his department, and of course he had to make more money than he had been making. So for the first few years he worked altogether too hard. He had to take jobs on the side and work night and day. It turned out to be too much for him. He became seriously ill. The doctors told him he needed to go south.

MRS. LINDE   That's right; you spent a year in Italy, didn't you?

NORA   Yes, we did. But you won't believe how hard it was to get away. Ivar had just been born. But of course we had to go. Oh, it was a wonderful trip. And it saved Torvald's life. But it took a lot of money, Kristine.

MRS. LINDE   I'm sure it did.

NORA   Twelve hundred specie dollars. Four thousand eight hundred crowns. That's a lot of money.

MRS. LINDE   Yes. So it's lucky you have it when something like that happens.

NORA   Well, actually we got the money from Daddy.

MRS. LINDE   I see. That was about the time your father died, I believe.

NORA   Yes, just about then. And I couldn't even go and take care of him. I was expecting little Ivar any day. And I had poor Torvald to look after, desperately sick and all. My dear, good Daddy! I never saw him again, Kristine. That's the saddest thing that's happened to me since I got married.

MRS. LINDE   I know you were very fond of him. But then you went to Italy?

NORA   Yes, for now we had the money, and the doctors urged us to go. So we left about a month later.

MRS. LINDE   And when you came back your husband was well again?

NORA   Healthy as a horse!

MRS. LINDE   But—the doctor?

NORA   What do you mean?

MRS. LINDE   I thought the maid said it was the doctor, that gentleman who came the same time I did.

NORA   Oh, that's Dr. Rank. He doesn't come as a doctor. He's our closest friend. He looks in at least once every day. No, Torvald hasn't been sick once since then. And the children are strong and healthy, too, and so am I. (*jumps up and claps her hands*) Oh God, Kristine! Isn't it wonderful to be alive and happy! Isn't it just lovely!—But now I'm being mean again, talking only about myself and my things. (*sits down on a footstool close to* MRS. LINDE *and puts her arm on her lap*) Please don't be angry with me! Tell me, is it really true that you didn't care for your husband? Then why did you marry him?

MRS. LINDE   Mother was still alive then, but she was bedridden and helpless. And I had my two younger brothers to look after. I didn't think I had the right to turn him down.

NORA   No, I suppose not. So he had money then?

MRS. LINDE   He was quite well off, I think. But it was an uncertain business, Nora. When he died, the whole thing collapsed and there was nothing left.

NORA   And then—?

MRS. LINDE   Well, I had to manage as best I could. With a little store and a little school and anything else I could think of. The last three years have been one long work day for me, Nora, without any rest. But now it's over. My poor mother doesn't need me any more. She's passed away. And the boys are on their own too. They've both got jobs and support themselves.

NORA   What a relief for you—

MRS. LINDE   No, not relief. Just a great emptiness. Nobody to live for any more. (*gets up restlessly*) That's why I couldn't stand it any longer in that little hole. Here in town it has to be easier to find something to keep me busy and occupy my thoughts. With a little luck I should be able to find a permanent job, something in an office—

NORA   Oh but Kristine, that's exhausting work, and you look worn out already. It would be much better for you to go to a resort.

MRS. LINDE (*walks over to the window*)   I don't have a Daddy who can give me the money, Nora.

NORA (*getting up*)   Oh, don't be angry with me.

MRS. LINDE (*over to her*)   Dear Nora, don't *you* be angry with *me*. That's the worst thing about my kind of situation: you become so bitter. You've nobody to work for, and yet you have to look out for yourself, somehow. You've got to keep on living, and so you become selfish. Do you know— when you told me about your husband's new position I was delighted not so much for your sake as for my own.

NORA   Why was that? Oh, I see. You think maybe Torvald can give you a job?

MRS. LINDE   That's what I had in mind.

NORA   And he will too, Kristine. Just leave it to me. I'll be ever so subtle about it. I'll think of something nice to tell him, something he'll like. Oh I so much want to help you.

MRS. LINDE   That's very good of you, Nora—making an effort like that for me. Especially since you've known so little trouble and hardship in your own life.

NORA   I—?—have known so little—?

MRS. LINDE (*smiling*)   Oh well, a little sewing or whatever it was. You're still a child, Nora.

NORA (*with a toss of her head, walks away*)   You shouldn't sound so superior.

MRS. LINDE   I shouldn't?

NORA   You're just like all the others. None of you think I'm good for anything really serious.

MRS. LINDE   Well, now—

NORA   That I've never been through anything difficult.

MRS. LINDE   But Nora! You just told me all your troubles!

NORA   That's nothing! (*lowers her voice*) I haven't told you about *it*.

MRS. LINDE   It? What's that? What do you mean?

NORA   You patronize me, Kristine, and that's not fair. You're proud that you worked so long and so hard for your mother.

MRS. LINDE   I don't think I patronize anyone. But it *is* true that I'm both proud and happy that I could make mother's last years comparatively easy.

NORA   And you're proud of all you did for your brothers.

MRS. LINDE   I think I have the right to be.

NORA   And so do I. But now I want to tell you something, Kristine. I have something to be proud and happy about too.

MRS. LINDE   I don't doubt that for a moment. But what exactly do you mean?

NORA   Not so loud! Torvald mustn't hear—not for anything in the world. Nobody must know about this, Kristine. Nobody but you.

MRS. LINDE   But what is it?

NORA   Come here. (*pulls her down on the couch beside her*) You see, I *do* have something to be proud and happy about. I've saved Torvald's life.

MRS. LINDE   Saved—? how do you mean—"saved"?

NORA   I told you about our trip to Italy. Torvald would have died if he hadn't gone.

MRS. LINDE   I understand that. And so your father gave you the money you needed.

NORA (*smiles*)   Yes, that's what Torvald and all the others think. But—

MRS. LINDE   But what?

NORA   Daddy didn't give us a penny. *I* raised that money.

MRS. LINDE   *You* did? That whole big amount?

NORA   Twelve hundred specie dollars. Four thousand eight hundred crowns. *Now* what do you say?

MRS. LINDE   But Nora, how could you? Did you win in the state lottery?

NORA (*contemptuously*)   State lottery! (*snorts*) What is so great about that?

MRS. LINDE   Where did it come from then?

NORA (*humming and smiling, enjoying her secret*)   Hmmm. Tra-la-la-la-la!

MRS. LINDE   You certainly couldn't have borrowed it.

NORA   Oh? And why not?

MRS. LINDE   A wife can't borrow money without her husband's consent.

NORA (*with a toss of her head*)   Oh, I don't know—take a wife with a little bit of a head for business—a wife who knows how to manage things—

MRS. LINDE   But Nora, I don't understand at all—

NORA   You don't have to. I didn't say I borrowed the money, did I? I could have gotten it some other way. (*leans back*) An admirer may have given it to me. When you're as tolerably good-looking as I am—

MRS. LINDE   Oh, you're crazy.

NORA   I think you're dying from curiosity, Kristine.

MRS. LINDE   I'm beginning to think you've done something very foolish, Nora.

NORA (*sits up*)   Is it foolish to save your husband's life?

MRS. LINDE   I say it's foolish to act behind his back.

NORA   But don't you see: he couldn't be told! You're missing the whole point, Kristine. We couldn't even let him know how seriously ill he was. The doctors came to *me* and told me his life was in danger, that nothing could save him but a stay in the south. Don't you think I tried to work on him? I told him how lovely it would be if I could go abroad like other young wives. I cried and begged. I said he'd better remember what condition I was in, that he had to be nice to me and do what I wanted. I even hinted he could borrow the money. But that almost made him angry with me. He told me I was being irresponsible and that it was his duty as my husband not to give in to my moods and whims—I think that's what he called it. All right, I said to myself, you've got to be saved somehow, and so I found a way—

MRS. LINDE   And your husband never learned from your father that the money didn't come from him?

NORA   Never. Daddy died that same week. I thought of telling him all about it and ask him not to say anything. But since he was so sick—It turned out I didn't have to—

MRS. LINDE   And you've never told your husband?

NORA   Of course not! Good heavens, how could I? He, with his strict principles! Besides, you know how men are. Torvald would find it embarrassing and humiliating to learn that he owed me anything. It would upset our whole relationship. Our happy, beautiful home would no longer be what it is.

MRS. LINDE   Aren't you ever going to tell him?

NORA   (*reflectively, half smiling*) Yes—one day, maybe. Many, many years from now, when I'm no longer young and pretty. Don't laugh! I mean when Torvald no longer feels about me the way he does now, when he no longer thinks it's fun when I dance for him and put on costumes and recite for him. Then it will be good to have something in reserve—(*interrupts herself*) Oh, I'm just being silly! That day will never come.—Well, now, Kristine, what do you think of my great secret? Don't you think I'm good for something too?—By the way, you wouldn't believe all the worry I've had because of it. It's been very hard to meet my obligations on schedule. You see, in business there's something called quarterly interest and something called installments on the principal, and those are terribly hard to come up with. I've had to save a little here and a little there, whenever I could. I couldn't use much of the housekeeping money, for Torvald has to eat well. And I couldn't use what I got for clothes for the children. They have to look nice, and I didn't think it would be right to spend less than I got—the sweet little things!

MRS. LINDE   Poor Nora! So you had to take it from your own allowance!

NORA   Yes, of course. After all, it was my affair. Every time Torvald gave me money for a new dress and things like that, I never used more than half of it. I always bought the cheapest, simplest things for myself. Thank God, everything looks good on me, so Torvald never noticed. But it was hard many times, Kristine, for it's fun to have pretty clothes. Don't you think?

MRS. LINDE   Certainly.

NORA   Anyway, I had other ways of making money too. Last winter I was lucky enough to get some copying work. So I locked the door and sat up writing every night till quite late. God! I often got so tired—! But it was great fun, too, working and making money. It was almost like being a man.

MRS. LINDE   But how much have you been able to pay off this way?

NORA   I couldn't tell you exactly. You see, it's very difficult to keep track of business like that. All I know is I have been paying off as much as I've been able to scrape together. Many times I just didn't know what to do. (*smiles*) Then I used to imagine a rich old gentleman had fallen in love with me—

MRS. LINDE   What! What old gentleman?

NORA   Phooey! And now he was dead and they were reading his will, and there it said in big letters, "All my money is to be paid in cash immediately to the charming Mrs. Nora Helmer."

MRS. LINDE   But dearest Nora—who *was* this old gentleman?

NORA   For heaven's sake, Kristine, don't you see? There *was* no old gentleman. He was just somebody I made up when I couldn't think of any way to raise the money. But never mind him. The old bore can be anyone he likes to for all I care. I have no use for him or his last will, for now I don't have a single worry in the world. (*jumps up*) Dear God, what a lovely thought this is! To be able to play and have fun with the children, to have everything nice and pretty in the house, just the way Torvald likes it! Not a care! And soon spring will be here, and the air will be blue and high. Maybe we can travel again. Maybe I'll see the ocean again! Oh, yes, yes!—it's wonderful to be alive and happy!

(*The doorbell rings.*)

MRS. LINDE (*getting up*)   There's the doorbell. Maybe I better be going.

NORA   No, please stay. I'm sure it's just someone for Torvald—

THE MAID (*in the hall door*)   Excuse me, ma'am. There's a gentleman here who'd like to see Mr. Helmer.

NORA   You mean the bank manager.

THE MAID   Sorry, ma'am; the bank manager. But I didn't know—since the Doctor is with him—

NORA   Who is the gentleman?

KROGSTAD (*appearing in the door*)   It's just me, Mrs. Helmer.

(MRS. LINDE *starts, looks, turns away toward the window.*)

NORA (*takes a step toward him, tense, in a low voice*)   You? What do you want? What do you want with my husband?

KROGSTAD   Bank business—in a way. I have a small job in the Mutual, and I understand your husband is going to be our new boss—

NORA   So, it's just—

KROGSTAD   Just routine business, ma'am. Nothing else.

NORA   All right. In that case, why don't you go through the door to the office.

(*Dismisses him casually as she closes the door. Walks over to the stove and tends the fire.*)

MRS. LINDE   Nora—who was that man?

NORA   His name's Krogstad. He's a lawyer.

MRS. LINDE   So it *was* him.

NORA   Do you know him?

MRS. LINDE   I used to—many years ago. For a while he clerked in our part of the country.

NORA   Right. He did.

MRS. LINDE   He has changed a great deal.

NORA   I believe he had a very unhappy marriage.

MRS. LINDE   And now he's a widower, isn't he?

NORA   With many children. There now; it's burning nicely again. (*closes the stove and moves the rocking chair a little to the side*)

MRS. LINDE   They say he's into all sorts of business.

NORA   Really? Maybe so. I wouldn't know. But let's not think about business. It's such a bore.

DR. RANK (*appears in the door to* HELMER'*s study*)   No. I don't want to be in the way. I'd rather talk to your wife a bit. (*closes the door and notices* MRS. LINDE) Oh, I beg your pardon. I believe I'm in the way here too.

NORA   No, not at all. (*introduces them*) Dr. Rank. Mrs. Linde.

RANK   Aha. A name often heard in this house. I believe I passed you on the stairs coming up.

MRS. LINDE   Yes. I'm afraid I climb stairs very slowly. They aren't good for me.

RANK   I see. A slight case of inner decay, perhaps?

MRS. LINDE   Overwork, rather.

RANK   Oh, is that all? And now you've come to town to relax at all the parties?

MRS. LINDE   I have come to look for a job.

RANK   A proven cure for overwork, I take it?

MRS. LINDE   One has to live, Doctor.

RANK   Yes, that seems to be the common opinion.

NORA   Come on, Dr. Rank—you want to live just as much as the rest of us.

RANK   Of course I do. Miserable as I am, I prefer to go on being tortured as long as possible. All my patients feel the same way. And that's true of the moral invalids too. Helmer is talking with a specimen right this minute.

MRS. LINDE (*in a low voice*)   Ah!

NORA   What do you mean?

RANK   Oh, this lawyer, Krogstad. You don't know him. The roots of his character are decayed. But even he began by saying something about having *to live*—as if it were a matter of the highest importance.

NORA   Oh? What did he want with Torvald?

RANK   I don't really know. All I heard was something about the bank.

NORA   I didn't know that Krog—that this Krogstad had anything to do with the Mutual Bank.

RANK   Yes, he seems to have some kind of job there. (*to* MRS. LINDE) I don't know if you are familiar in your part of the country with the kind of person who is always running around trying to sniff out cases of moral decrepitude and as soon as he finds one puts the individual under observation in some excellent position or other. All the healthy ones are left out in the cold.

MRS. LINDE   I should think it's the sick who need looking after the most.

RANK (*shrugs his shoulders*)   There we are. That's the attitude that turns society into a hospital.

(NORA, *absorbed in her own thoughts, suddenly starts giggling and clapping her hands.*)

RANK   What's so funny about that? Do you even know what society is?

NORA   What do I care about your stupid society! I laughed at something entirely different—something terribly amusing. Tell me, Dr. Rank—all the employees in the Mutual Bank, from now on they'll all be dependent on Torvald, right?

RANK   Is that what you find so enormously amusing?

NORA   (*smiles and hums*)   That's my business, that's my business! (*walks around*) Yes, I do think it's fun that we—that Torvald is going to have so much influence on so many people's lives. (*brings out the bag of macaroons*) Have a macaroon, Dr. Rank.

RANK   Well, well—macaroons. I thought they were banned around here.

NORA   Yes, but these were some that Kristine gave me.

MRS. LINDE   What! I?

NORA   That's all right. Don't look so scared. You couldn't know that Torvald won't let me have them. He's afraid they'll ruin my teeth. But who cares! Just once in a while—! Right, Dr. Rank? Have one! (*puts a macaroon into his mouth*) You too, Kristine. And one for me. A very small one. Or at most two. (*walks around again*) Yes, I really feel very, very happy. Now there's just one thing I'm dying to do.

RANK   Oh, and what's that?

NORA   Something I'm dying to say so Torvald could hear.

RANK   And why can't you?

NORA   I don't dare to, for it's not nice.

MRS. LINDE   Not nice?

RANK   In that case, I guess you'd better not. But surely to the two of us—? What is it you'd like to say for Helmer to hear?

NORA   I want to say, "Goddammit!"

RANK   Are you out of your mind!

MRS. LINDE   For heaven's sake, Nora!

RANK   Say it. Here he comes.

NORA (*hiding the macaroons*)   Shhh!

(HELMER *enters from his study, carrying his hat and overcoat.*)

NORA (*going to him*)   Well, dear, did you get rid of him?

HELMER   Yes, he just left.

NORA   Torvald, I want you to meet Kristine. She's just come to town.

HELMER   Kristine—? I'm sorry; I don't think—

NORA   Mrs. Linde, Torvald dear. Mrs. Kristine Linde.

HELMER   Ah, yes. A childhood friend of my wife's, I suppose.

MRS. LINDE   Yes, we've known each other for a long time.

NORA   Just think; she has come all this way just to see you.

HELMER   I'm not sure I understand—

MRS. LINDE   Well, not really—

NORA   You see, Kristine is an absolutely fantastic secretary, and she would so much like to work for a competent executive and learn more than she knows already—

HELMER   Very sensible, I'm sure, Mrs. Linde.

NORA   So when she heard about your appointment—there was a wire—she came here as fast as she could. How about it, Torvald? Couldn't you do something for Kristine? For my sake. Please?

HELMER   Quite possibly. I take it you're a widow, Mrs. Linde?

MRS. LINDE   Yes.

HELMER   And you've had office experience?

MRS. LINDE   Some—yes.

HELMER   In that case I think it's quite likely that I'll be able to find you a position.

NORA (*claps her hands*)   I knew it! I knew it!

HELMER   You've arrived at a most opportune time, Mrs. Linde.

MRS. LINDE   Oh, how can I ever thank you—

HELMER   Not at all, not at all. (*puts his coat on*) But today you'll have to excuse me—

RANK   Wait a minute; I'll come with you. (*gets his fur coat from the front hall, warms it by the stove*)

NORA   Don't be long, Torvald.

HELMER   An hour or so; no more.

NORA   Are you leaving, too, Kristine?

MRS. LINDE (*putting on her things*)   Yes, I'd better go and find a place to stay.

HELMER   Good. Then we'll be going the same way.

NORA (*helping her*)   I'm sorry this place is so small, but I don't think we very well could—

MRS. LINDE   Of course! Don't be silly, Nora. Goodbye, and thank you for everything.

NORA   Goodbye. We'll see you soon. You'll be back this evening, of course. And you too, Dr. Rank; right? If you feel well enough? Of course you will. Just wrap yourself up.

(*General small talk as all exit into the hall. Children's voices are heard on the stairs.*)

NORA   There they are! There they are! (*She runs and opens the door. The nurse* ANNE-MARIE *enters with the children.*)

NORA   Come in! Come in! (*bends over and kisses them*) Oh, you sweet, sweet darlings! Look at them, Kristine! Aren't they beautiful?

RANK   No standing around in the draft!

HELMER   Come along, Mrs. Linde. This place isn't fit for anyone but mothers right now.

(DR. RANK, HELMER, *and* MRS. LINDE *go down the stairs. The* NURSE *enters the living room with the children.* NORA *follows, closing the door behind her.*)

NORA   My, how nice you all look! Such red cheeks! Like apples and roses. (*The children all talk at the same time.*) You've had so much fun? I bet you have.

Oh, isn't that nice! You pulled both Emmy and Bob on your sleigh? Both at the same time? That's very good, Ivar. Oh, let me hold her for a minute, Anne-Marie. My sweet little doll baby! (*takes the smallest of the children from the* NURSE *and dances with her*) Yes, yes, of course; Mama'll dance with you too, Bob. What? You threw snowballs? Oh, I wish I'd been there! No, no; *I* want to take their clothes off, Anne-Marie. Please let me; I think it's so much fun. You go on in. You look frozen. There's hot coffee on the stove.

(*The* NURSE *exits into the room to the left.* NORA *takes the children's wraps off and throws them all around. They all keep telling her things at the same time.*)

NORA   Oh, really? A big dog ran after you? But it didn't bite you. Of course not. Dogs don't bite sweet little doll babies. Don't peek at the packages, Ivar! What's in them? Wouldn't you like to know! No, no; that's something terrible! Play? You want to play? What do you want to play? Okay, let's play hide-and-seek. Bob hides first. You want *me* to? All right. I'll go first.

(*Laughing and shouting,* NORA *and the children play in the living room and in the adjacent room, right. Finally,* NORA *hides herself under the table; the children rush in, look for her, can't find her. They hear her low giggle, run to the table, lift the rug that covers it, see her. General hilarity. She crawls out, pretends to scare them. New delight. In the meantime there has been a knock on the door between the living room and the front hall, but nobody has noticed. Now the door is opened halfway.* KROGSTAD *appears. He waits a little. The play goes on.*)

KROGSTAD   Pardon me, Mrs. Helmer—
NORA   (*with a muted cry turns around, jumps up*)   Ah! What do you want?
KROGSTAD   I'm sorry. The front door was open. Somebody must have forgotten to close it—
NORA   (*standing up*)   My husband isn't here, Mr. Krogstad.
KROGSTAD   I know.
NORA   So what do you want?
KROGSTAD   I'd like a word with you.
NORA   With—? (*to the children*) Go in to Anne-Marie. What? No, the strange man won't do anything bad to Mama. When he's gone we'll play some more.

(*She takes the children into the room to the left and closes the door.*)

NORA   (*tense, troubled*)   You want to speak with me?
KROGSTAD   Yes I do.
NORA   Today—? It isn't the first of the month yet.
KROGSTAD   No, it's Christmas Eve. It's up to you what kind of holiday you'll have.
NORA   What do you want? I can't possibly—
KROGSTAD   Let's not talk about that just yet. There's something else. You do have a few minutes, don't you?

NORA   Yes. Yes, of course. That is,—

KROGSTAD   Good. I was sitting in Olsen's restaurant when I saw your husband go by.

NORA   Yes—?

KROGSTAD   —with a lady.

NORA   What of it?

KROGSTAD   May I be so free as to ask: wasn't that lady Mrs. Linde?

NORA   Yes.

KROGSTAD   Just arrived in town?

NORA   Yes, today.

KROGSTAD   She's a good friend of yours, I understand?

NORA   Yes, she is. But I fail to see—

KROGSTAD   I used to know her myself.

NORA   I know that.

KROGSTAD   So you know about that. I thought as much. In that case, let me ask you a simple question. Is Mrs. Linde going to be employed in the bank?

NORA   What makes you think you have the right to cross-examine me like this, Mr. Krogstad—you, one of my husband's employees? But since you ask, I'll tell you. Yes, Mrs. Linde is going to be working in the bank. And it was I who recommended her, Mr. Krogstad. Now you know.

KROGSTAD   So I was right.

NORA   (*walks up and down*)   After all, one does have a little influence, you know. Just because you're a woman, it doesn't mean that—Really, Mr. Krogstad, people in a subordinate position should be careful not to offend someone who—oh well—

KROGSTAD   —has influence?

NORA   Exactly.

KROGSTAD (*changing his tone*)   Mrs. Helmer, I must ask you to be good enough to use your influence on my behalf.

NORA   What do you mean?

KROGSTAD   I want you to make sure that I am going to keep my subordinate position in the bank.

NORA   I don't understand. Who is going to take your position away from you?

KROGSTAD   There's no point in playing ignorant with me, Mrs. Helmer. I can very well appreciate that your friend would find it unpleasant to run into me. So now I know who I can thank for my dismissal.

NORA   But I assure you—

KROGSTAD   Never mind. Just want to say you still have time. I advise you to use your influence to prevent it.

NORA   But Mr. Krogstad, I don't have any influence—none at all.

KROGSTAD   No? I thought you just said—

NORA   Of course I didn't mean it that way. I! Whatever makes you think that I have any influence of that kind on my husband?

KROGSTAD   I went to law school with your husband. I have no reason to think that the bank manager is less susceptible than other husbands.

NORA   If you're going to insult my husband, I'll ask you to leave.

KROGSTAD   You're brave, Mrs. Helmer.

NORA   I'm not afraid of you any more. After New Year's I'll be out of this thing with you.

KROGSTAD (*more controlled*)   Listen, Mrs. Helmer. If necessary I'll fight as for my life to keep my little job in the bank.

NORA   So it seems.

KROGSTAD   It isn't just the money; that's really the smallest part of it. There is something else—Well, I guess I might as well tell you. It's like this. I'm sure you know, like everybody else, that some years ago I committed—an impropriety.

NORA   I believe I've heard it mentioned.

KROGSTAD   The case never came to court, but from that moment all doors were closed to me. So I took up the kind of business you know about. I had to do something, and I think I can say about myself that I have not been among the worst. But now I want to get out of all that. My sons are growing up. For their sake I must get back as much of my good name as I can. This job in the bank was like the first rung on the ladder. And now your husband wants to kick me down and leave me back in the mud again.

NORA   But I swear to you, Mr. Krogstad; it's not at all in my power to help you.

KROGSTAD   That's because you don't want to. But I have the means to force you.

NORA   You don't mean you're going to tell my husband I owe you money?

KROGSTAD   And if I did?

NORA   That would be a mean thing to do. (*almost crying*) That secret, which is my joy and my pride—for him to learn about it in such a coarse and ugly manner—to learn it from *you*—! It would be terribly unpleasant for me.

KROGSTAD   Just unpleasant?

NORA (*heatedly*)   But go ahead! Do it! It will be worse for you than for me. When my husband realizes what a bad person you are, you'll be sure to lose your job.

KROGSTAD   I asked you if it was just domestic unpleasantness you were afraid of?

NORA   When my husband finds out, of course he'll pay off the loan, and then we won't have anything more to do with you.

KROGSTAD (*stepping closer*)   Listen, Mrs. Helmer—either you have a very bad memory, or you don't know much about business. I think I had better straighten you out on a few things.

NORA   What do you mean?

KROGSTAD   When your husband was ill, you came to me to borrow twelve hundred dollars.

NORA   I knew nobody else.

KROGSTAD   I promised to get you the money—

NORA   And you did.

KROGSTAD   I promised to get you the money on certain conditions. At the time you were so anxious about your husband's health and so set on getting him away that I doubt very much that you paid much attention to the details of our transaction. That's why I remind you of them now. Anyway, I promised to get you the money if you would sign an I.O.U., which I drafted.

NORA   And which I signed.

KROGSTAD   Good. But below your signature I added a few lines, making your father security for the loan. Your father was supposed to put his signature to those lines.

NORA   Supposed to—? He did.

KROGSTAD   I had left the date blank. That is, your father was to date his own signature. You recall that, don't you, Mrs. Helmer?

NORA   I guess so—

KROGSTAD   I gave the note to you. You were to mail it to your father. Am I correct?

NORA   Yes.

KROGSTAD   And of course you did so right away, for no more than five or six days later you brought the paper back to me, signed by your father. Then I paid you the money.

NORA   Well? And haven't I been keeping up with the payments?

KROGSTAD   Fairly well, yes. But to get back to what we were talking about—those were difficult days for you, weren't they, Mrs. Helmer?

NORA   Yes, they were.

KROGSTAD   Your father was quite ill, I believe.

NORA   He was dying.

KROGSTAD   And died shortly afterwards?

NORA   That's right.

KROGSTAD   Tell me, Mrs. Helmer; do you happen to remember the date of your father's death? I mean the exact day of the month?

NORA   Daddy died on September 29.

KROGSTAD   Quite correct. I have ascertained that fact. That's why there is something peculiar about this (*takes out a piece of paper*), which I can't account for.

NORA   Peculiar? How? I don't understand—

KROGSTAD   It seems very peculiar, Mrs. Helmer, that your father signed this promissory note three days after his death.

NORA   How so? I don't see what—

KROGSTAD   Your father died on September 29. Now look. He has dated his signature October 2. Isn't that odd?

(NORA *remains silent.*)

KROGSTAD   Can you explain it?

(NORA *is still silent.*)

KROGSTAD   I also find it striking that the date and the month and the year are not in your father's handwriting but in a hand I think I recognize. Well, that might be explained. Your father may have forgotten to date his signature and somebody else may have done it here, guessing at the date before he had learned of your father's death. That's all right. It's only the signature itself that matters. And that is genuine, isn't it, Mrs. Helmer? Your father *did* put his name to this note?

NORA   (*after a brief silence tosses her head back and looks defiantly at him*)   No, he didn't. *I* wrote Daddy's name.

KROGSTAD   Mrs. Helmer—do you realize what a dangerous admission you just made?

NORA   Why? You'll get your money soon.

KROGSTAD   Let me ask you something. Why didn't you mail this note to your father?

NORA   Because it was impossible. Daddy was sick—you know that. If I had asked him to sign it, I would have had to tell him what the money was for. But I couldn't tell him, as sick as he was, that my husband's life was in danger. That was impossible. Surely you can see that.

KROGSTAD   Then it would have been better for you if you had given up your trip abroad.

NORA   No, that was impossible! That trip was to save my husband's life. I couldn't give it up.

KROGSTAD   But didn't you realize that what you did amounted to fraud against me?

NORA   I couldn't let that make any difference. I didn't care about you at all. I hated the way you made all those difficulties for me, even though you knew the danger my husband was in. I thought you were cold and unfeeling.

KROGSTAD   Mrs. Helmer, obviously you have no clear idea of what you have done. Let me tell you that what I did that time was no more and no worse. And it ruined my name and reputation.

NORA   You! Are you trying to tell me that you did something brave once in order to save your wife's life?

KROGSTAD   The law doesn't ask about motives.

NORA   Then it's a bad law.

KROGSTAD   Bad or not—if I produce this note in court you'll be judged according to the law.

NORA   I refuse to believe you. A daughter shouldn't have the right to spare her dying old father worry and anxiety? A wife shouldn't have the right to save her husband's life? I don't know the laws very well, but I'm sure that somewhere they make allowance for cases like that. And you, a lawyer, don't know that? I think you must be a bad lawyer, Mr. Krogstad.

KROGSTAD   That may be. But business—the kind of business you and I have with one another—don't you think I know something about that? Very well. Do what you like. But let me tell you this: if I'm going to be kicked out again, you'll keep me company. (*He bows and exits through the front hall.*)

NORA (*pauses thoughtfully; then, with a defiant toss of her head*)   Oh, nonsense! Trying to scare me like that! I'm not all that silly. (*starts picking up the children's clothes; soon stops*) But—? No! That's impossible! I did it for love!

THE CHILDREN (*in the door to the left*)   Mama, the strange man just left. We saw him.

NORA   Yes, yes; I know. But don't tell anybody about the strange man. Do you hear? Not even Daddy.

THE CHILDREN   We won't. But now you'll play with us again, won't you, Mama?

NORA   No, not right now.

THE CHILDREN   But Mama—you promised.

NORA   I know, but I can't just now. Go to your own room. I've so much to do. Be nice now, my little darlings. Do as I say. (*She nudges them gently into the other room and closes the door. She sits down on the couch, picks up a piece of embroidery, makes a few stitches, then stops.*) No! (*throws the embroidery down, goes to the hall door and calls out*) Helene! Bring the Christmas tree in here, please! (*goes to the table, left, opens the drawer, halts*) No—that's impossible!

THE MAID (*with the Christmas tree*)   Where do you want it, ma'am?

NORA   There. The middle of the floor.

THE MAID   You want anything else?

NORA   No, thanks. I have everything I need. (THE MAID *goes out.* NORA *starts trimming the tree.*) I want candles—and flowers—That awful man! Oh, nonsense! There's nothing wrong. This will be a lovely tree. I'll do everything you want me to, Torvald. I'll sing for you—dance for you—

(HELMER, *a bundle of papers under his arm, enters from outside.*)

NORA   Ah—you're back already?

HELMER   Yes. Has anybody been here?

NORA   Here? No.

HELMER   That's funny. I saw Krogstad leaving just now.

NORA   Oh? Oh yes, that's right. Krogstad was here for just a moment.

HELMER   I can tell from your face that he came to ask you to put in a word for him.

NORA   Yes.

HELMER   And it was supposed to be your own idea, wasn't it? You were not to tell me he'd been here. He asked you that too, didn't he?

NORA   Yes, Torvald, but—

NORA   Nora, Nora, how could you! Talk to a man like that and make him promises! And lying to me about it afterwards—!

NORA   Lying—?

HELMER   Didn't you say nobody had been here? (*shakes his finger at her*) My little songbird must never do that again. Songbirds are supposed to have clean beaks to chirp with—no false notes. (*puts his arms around her waist*) Isn't that so? Of course it is. (*lets her go*) And that's enough about that. (*sits down in front of the fireplace*) Ah, it's nice and warm in here. (*begins to leaf through his papers*)

NORA   (*busy with the tree; after a brief pause*)   Torvald.

HELMER   Yes.

NORA   I'm looking forward so much to the Stenborgs' costume party day after tomorrow.

HELMER   And I can't wait to find out what you're going to surprise me with.

NORA   Oh, that silly idea!

HELMER   Oh?

NORA   I can't think of anything. It all seems so foolish and pointless.

HELMER   Ah, my little Nora admits that?

NORA   (*behind his chair, her arms on the back of the chair*)   Are you very busy, Torvald?

HELMER   Well—

NORA   What are all those papers?

HELMER   Bank business.

NORA   Already?

HELMER   I've asked the board to give me the authority to make certain changes in organization and personnel. That's what I'll be doing over the holidays. I want it all settled before New Year's.

NORA   So that's why this poor Krogstad—

HELMER   Hm.

NORA   (*leisurely playing with the hair on his neck*)   If you weren't so busy, Torvald, I'd ask you for a great big favor.

HELMER   Let's hear it, anyway.

NORA   I don't know anyone with better taste than you, and I want so much to look nice at the party. Couldn't you sort of take charge of me, Torvald, and decide what I'll wear—Help me with my costume?

HELMER   Aha! Little Lady Obstinate is looking for someone to rescue her?

NORA   Yes, Torvald. I won't get anywhere without your help.

HELMER   All right. I'll think about it. We'll come up with something.

NORA   Oh, you *are* nice! (*goes back to the Christmas tree; a pause*) Those red flowers look so pretty.—Tell me, was it really all that bad what this Krogstad fellow did?

HELMER   He forged signatures. Do you have any idea what that means?

NORA   Couldn't it have been because he felt he had to?

HELMER   Yes, or like so many others he may simply have been thoughtless. I'm not so heartless as to condemn a man absolutely because of a single imprudent act.

NORA   Of course not, Torvald!

HELMER   People like him can redeem themselves morally by openly confessing their crime and taking their punishment.

NORA   Punishment—?

HELMER   But that was not the way Krogstad chose. He got out of it with tricks and evasions. That's what has corrupted him.

NORA   So you think that if—?

HELMER   Can't you imagine how a guilty person like that has to lie and fake and dissemble wherever he goes—putting on a mask before everybody he's close to, even his own wife and children. It's this thing with the children that's the worst part of it, Nora.

NORA   Why is that?

HELMER   Because when a man lives inside such a circle of stinking lies he brings infection into his own home and contaminates his whole family. With every breath of air his children inhale the germs of something ugly.

NORA (*moving closer behind him*)   Are you so sure of that?

HELMER   Of course I am. I have seen enough examples of that in my work. Nearly all young criminals have had mothers who lied.

NORA   Why mothers—particularly?

HELMER   Most often mothers. But of course fathers tend to have the same influence. Every lawyer knows that. And yet, for years this Krogstad has been poisoning his own children in an atmosphere of lies and deceit. That's why I call him a lost soul morally. (*reaches out for her hands*) And that's why my sweet little Nora must promise me never to take his side again. Let's shake on that.—What? What's this? Give me your hand. There! Now that's settled. I assure you, I would find it impossible to work in the same room with that man. I feel literally sick when I'm around people like that.

NORA (*withdraws her hand and goes to the other side of the Christmas tree*)   It's so hot in here. And I have so much to do.

HELMER (*gets up and collects his papers*)   Yes, and I really should try to get some of this reading done before dinner. I must think about your costume too. And maybe just possibly I'll have something to wrap in gilt paper and hang on the Christmas tree. (*puts his hand on her head*) Oh my adorable little songbird! (*enters his study and closes the door*)

NORA (*after a pause, in a low voice*)   It's all a lot of nonsense. It's not that way at all. It's impossible. It has to be impossible.

THE NURSE (*in the door, left*)   The little ones are asking ever so nicely if they can't come in and be with their mama.

NORA   No, no no! Don't let them in here! You stay with them, Anne-Marie.

THE NURSE   If you say so, ma'am. (*closes the door*)

NORA (*pale with terror*)   Corrupt my little children—! Poison my home—? (*Brief pause; she lifts her head.*) That's not true. Never. Never in a million years.

Act II

The same room. The Christmas tree is in the corner by the piano, stripped, shabby-looking, with burnt-down candles. NORA's outside clothes are on the couch. NORA is alone. She walks around restlessly. She stops by the couch and picks up her coat.

NORA (*drops the coat again*)   There's somebody now! (*goes to the door, listens*) No. Nobody. Of course not—not on Christmas. And not tomorrow either.[1]—But perhaps—(*opens the door and looks*) No, nothing in the mailbox. All empty. (*comes forward*) How silly I am! Of course he isn't serious. Nothing like that could happen. After all, I have three small children.

(*The NURSE enters from the room, left, carrying a big carton.*)

THE NURSE   Well, at last I found it—the box with your costume.

NORA   Thanks. Just put it on the table.

NURSE (*does so*)   But it's all a big mess, I'm afraid.

NORA   Oh, I wish I could tear the whole thing to little pieces!

NURSE   Heavens! It's not as bad as all that. It can be fixed all right. All it takes is a little patience.

NORA   I'll go over and get Mrs. Linde to help me.

NURSE   Going out again? In this awful weather? You'll catch a cold.

NORA   That might not be such a bad thing. How are the children?

NURSE   The poor little dears are playing with their presents, but—

NORA   Do they keep asking for me?

NURSE   Well, you know, they're used to being with their mamma.

NORA   I know. But Anne-Marie, from now on I can't be with them as much as before.

NURSE   Oh well. Little children get used to everything.

NORA   You think so? Do you think they'll forget their mamma if I were gone altogether?

NURSE   Goodness me—gone altogether?

NORA   Listen, Anne-Marie—something I've wondered about. How could you bring yourself to leave your children with strangers?

NURSE   But I had to, if I were to nurse you.

NORA   Yes, but how could you *want* to?

NURSE   When I could get such a nice place? When something like that happens to a poor young girl, she'd better be grateful for whatever she gets. For *he* didn't do a thing for me—the louse!

NORA   But your daughter has forgotten all about you, hasn't she?

NURSE   Oh no! Not at all! She wrote to me both when she was confirmed and when she got married.

NORA (*putting her arms around her neck*)   You dear old thing—you were a good mother to me when I was little.

---

[1] In Norway both December 25 and 26 are legal holidays.

NURSE   Poor little Nora had no one else, you know.

NORA   And if my little ones didn't, I know you'd—oh, I'm being silly! (*opens the carton*) Go in to them, please. I really should—. Tomorrow you'll see how pretty I'll be.

NURSE   I know. There won't be anybody at that party half as pretty as you, ma'am. (*goes out, left*)

NORA   (*begins to take clothes out of the carton; in a moment she throws it all down*)   If only I dared to go out. If only I knew nobody would come. That nothing would happen while I was gone.—How silly! Nobody'll come. Just don't think about it. Brush the muff. Beautiful gloves. Beautiful gloves. Forget it. Forget it. One, two, three, four, five, six—(*cries out*) There they are! (*moves toward the door, stops irresolutely*)

(MRS. LINDE *enters from the hall. She has already taken off her coat.*)

NORA   Oh, it's you, Kristine. There's no one else out there, is there? I'm so glad you're here.

MRS. LINDE   They told me you'd asked for me.

NORA   I just happened to walk by. I need your help with something—badly. Let's sit here on the couch. Look. Torvald and I are going to a costume party tomorrow night—at Consul Stenborg's upstairs—and Torvald wants me to go as a Neapolitan fisher girl and dance the tarantella. I learned it when we were on Capri.

MRS. LINDE   Well, well! So you'll be putting on a whole show?

NORA   Yes, Torvald thinks I should. Look, here's the costume. Torvald had it made for me while we were there. But it's all so torn and everything. I just don't know—

MRS. LINDE   Oh, that can be fixed. It's not that much. The trimmings have come loose in a few places. Do you have needle and thread? Ah, here we are. All set.

NORA   I really appreciate it, Kristine.

MRS. LINDE   (*sewing*)   So you'll be in disguise tomorrow night, eh? You know—I may come by for just a moment, just to look at you.—Oh dear. I haven't even thanked you for the nice evening last night.

NORA   (*gets up, moves around*)   Oh, I don't know. I don't think last night was as nice as it usually is.—You should have come to town a little earlier, Kristine.—Yes, Torvald knows how to make it nice and pretty around here.

MRS. LINDE   You too, I should think. After all, you're your father's daughter. By the way, is Dr. Rank always as depressed as he was last night?

NORA   No, last night was unusual. He's a very sick man, you know—very sick. Poor Rank, his spine is rotting away. Tuberculosis, I think. You see, his father was a nasty old man with mistresses and all that sort of thing. Rank has been sickly ever since he was a little boy.

MRS. LINDE   (*dropping her sewing to her lap*)   But dearest, Nora, where have you learned about things like that?

NORA (*still walking about*)   Oh, you know—with three children you sometimes get to talk with—other wives. Some of them know quite a bit about medicine. So you pick up a few things.

MRS. LINDE (*resumes her sewing; after a brief pause*)   Does Dr. Rank come here every day?

NORA   Every single day. He's Torvald's oldest and best friend, after all. And my friend too, for that matter. He's part of the family, almost.

MRS. LINDE   But tell me, is he quite sincere? I mean, isn't he the kind of man who likes to say nice things to people?

NORA   No, not at all. Rather the opposite, in fact. What makes you say that?

MRS. LINDE   When you introduced us yesterday, he told me he'd often heard my name mentioned in this house. But later on it was quite obvious that your husband really had no idea who I was. So how could Dr. Rank—?

NORA   You're right, Kristine, but I can explain that. You see, Torvald loves me so very much that he wants me all to himself. That's what he says. When we were first married he got almost jealous when I as much as mentioned anybody from back home that I was fond of. So of course I soon stopped doing that. But with Dr. Rank I often talk about home. You see, he likes to listen to me.

MRS. LINDE   Look here, Nora. In many ways you're still a child. After all, I'm quite a bit older than you and have had more experience. I want to give you a piece of advice. I think you should get out of this thing with Dr. Rank.

NORA   Get out of what thing?

MRS. LINDE   Several things in fact, if you want my opinion. Yesterday you said something about a rich admirer who was going to give you money—

NORA   One who doesn't exist, unfortunately. What of it?

MRS. LINDE   Does Dr. Rank have money?

NORA   Yes, he does.

MRS. LINDE   And no dependents?

MRS. LINDE   No. But—?

MRS. LINDE   And he comes here every day?

NORA   Yes, I told you that already.

MRS. LINDE   But how can that sensitive man be so tactless?

NORA   I haven't the slightest idea what you're talking about.

MRS. LINDE   Don't play games with me, Nora. Don't you think I know who you borrowed the twelve hundred dollars from?

NORA   Are you out of your mind! The very idea—! A friend of both of us who sees us every day—! What a dreadfully uncomfortable position that would be!

MRS. LINDE   So it really isn't Dr. Rank?

NORA   Most certainly not! I would never have dreamed of asking him—not for a moment. Anyway, he didn't have any money then. He inherited it afterwards.

MRS. LINDE   Well, I still think it may have been lucky for you, Nora dear.

NORA   The idea! It would never have occurred to me to ask Dr. Rank—. Though I'm sure that if I *did* ask him—

MRS. LINDE   But of course you wouldn't.

NORA   Of course not. I can't imagine that that would ever be necessary. But I am quite sure that if I told Dr. Rank—

MRS. LINDE   Behind your husband's back?

NORA   I must get out of—this other thing. That's also behind his back. I *must* get out of it.

MRS. LINDE   That's what I told you yesterday. But—

NORA (*walking up and down*)   A man manages these things so much better than a woman—

MRS. LINDE   One's husband, yes.

NORA   Silly, silly! (*stops*) When you've paid off all you owe, you get your I.O.U. back; right?

MRS. LINDE   Yes, of course.

NORA   And you can tear it into a hundred thousand little pieces and burn it—that dirty, filthy, paper!

MRS. LINDE (*looks hard at her, puts down her sewing, rises slowly*)   Nora—you're hiding something from me.

NORA   Can you tell?

MRS. LINDE   Something's happened to you, Nora, since yesterday morning. What is it?

NORA (*going to her*)   Kristine! (*listens*) Shhh. Torvald just came back. Listen. Why don't you go in to the children for a while. Torvald can't stand having sewing around. Get Anne-Marie to help you.

MRS. LINDE (*gathers some of the sewing things together*)   All right, but I'm not leaving here till you and I have talked.

(*She goes out left, as* HELMER *enters from the front hall.*)

NORA (*toward him*)   I have been waiting and waiting for you, Torvald.

HELMER   Was that the dressmaker?

NORA   No, it was Kristine. She's helping me with my costume. Oh Torvald, just wait till you see how nice I'll look!

HELMER   I told you. Pretty good idea I had, wasn't it?

NORA   Lovely! And wasn't it nice of me to go along with it?

HELMER (*his hands under her chin*)   Nice? To do what your husband tells you? All right, you little rascal; I know you didn't mean it that way. But don't let me interrupt you. I suppose you want to try it on.

NORA   And you'll be working?

HELMER   Yes. (*shows her a pile of papers*) Look. I've been down to the bank. (*is about to enter his study*)

NORA   Torvald.

HELMER (*halts*)   Yes?

NORA   What if your little squirrel asked you ever so nicely—

HELMER   For what?

NORA   Would you do it?

HELMER   Depends on what it is.

NORA   Squirrel would run around and do all sorts of fun tricks if you'd be nice and agreeable.

HELMER   All right. What is it?

NORA   Lark would chirp and twitter in all the rooms, up and down—

HELMER   So what? Lark does that anyway.

NORA   I'll be your elfmaid and dance for you in the moonlight, Torvald.

HELMER   Nora, don't tell me it's the same thing you mentioned this morning?

NORA   (*closer to him*)   Yes, Torvald. I beg you!

HELMER   You really have the nerve to bring that up again?

NORA   Yes. You've just got to do as I say. You *must* let Krogstad keep his job.

HELMER   My dear Nora. It's his job I intend to give to Mrs. Linde.

NORA   I know. And that's ever so nice of you. But can't you just fire somebody else?

HELMER   This is incredible! You just don't give up do you? Because you make some foolish promise, *I* am supposed to—!

NORA   That's not the reason, Torvald. It's for your own sake. That man writes for the worst newspapers. You've said so yourself. There's no telling what he may do to you. I'm scared to death of him.

HELMER   Ah, I understand. You're afraid because of what happened before.

NORA   What do you mean?

HELMER   You're thinking of your father, of course.

NORA   Yes. Yes, you're right. Remember the awful things they wrote about Daddy in the newspapers. I really think they might have forced him to resign if the ministry hadn't sent you to look into the charges and if you hadn't been so helpful and understanding.

HELMER   My dear little Nora, there is a world of difference between your father and me. Your father's official conduct was not above reproach. Mine is, and I intend for it to remain that way as long as I hold my position.

NORA   Oh, but you don't know what vicious people like that may think of. Oh, Torvald! Now all of us could be so happy together here in our own home, peaceful and carefree. Such a good life, Torvald, for you and me and the children! That's why I implore you—

HELMER   And it's exactly because you plead for him that you make it impossible for me to keep him. It's already common knowledge in the bank that I intend to let Krogstad go. If it gets out that the new manager has changed his mind because of his wife—

NORA   Yes? What then?

HELMER   No, of course, that wouldn't matter at all as long as little Mrs. Pighead here got her way! Do you want me to make myself look ridiculous before my whole staff—make people think I can be swayed by just anybody—by outsiders? Believe me, I would soon enough find out what the consequences would be! Besides, there's another thing that makes it absolutely impossible for Krogstad to stay on in the bank now that I'm in charge.

NORA   What's that?

HELMER   I suppose in a pinch I could overlook his moral shortcomings—

NORA   Yes, you could; couldn't you, Torvald?

HELMER   And I understand he's quite a good worker, too. But we've known each other for a long time. It's one of those imprudent relationships you get into when you're young that embarrass you for the rest of your life. I guess I might as well be frank with you: he and I are on a first name basis. And that tactless fellow never hides the fact even when other people are around. Rather, he seems to think it entitles him to be familiar with me. Every chance he gets he comes out with his damn "Torvald, Torvald." I'm telling you, I find it most awkward. He would make my position in the bank intolerable.

NORA   You don't really mean any of this, Torvald.

HELMER   Oh? I don't? And why not?

NORA   No, for it's all so petty.

HELMER   What! Petty? You think I'm being petty!

NORA   No, I *don't* think you are petty, Torvald dear. That's exactly why I—

HELMER   Never mind. You think my reasons are petty, so it follows that I must be petty too. Petty! Indeed! By God, I'll put an end to this right now! (*opens the door to the front hall and calls out*) Helene!

NORA   What are you doing?

HELMER   (*searching among his papers*)   Making a decision. (THE MAID *enters.*) Here. Take this letter. Go out with it right away. Find somebody to deliver it. But quick. The address is on the envelope. Wait. Here's money.

THE MAID   Very good sir. (*She takes the letter and goes out.*)

HELMER   (*collecting his papers*)   There now, little Mrs Obstinate!

NORA   (*breathless*)   Torvald—what was that letter?

HELMER   Krogstad's dismissal.

NORA   Call it back, Torvald! There's still time! Oh Torvald, please—call it back! For my sake, for your own sake, for the sake of the children! Listen to me, Torvald! Do it! You don't know what you're doing to all of us!

HELMER   Too late.

NORA   Yes. Too late.

HELMER   Dear Nora, I forgive you this fear you're in, although it really is an insult to me. Yes, it is! It's an insult to think that I am scared of a shabby scrivener's revenge. But I forgive you, for it's such a beautiful proof how much you love me. (*takes her in his arms*) And that's the way it should be, my sweet darling. Whatever happens, you'll see that when things get really rough I have both strength and courage. You'll find out that I am man enough to shoulder the whole burden.

NORA (*terrified*)　What do you mean by that?

HELMER　All of it, I tell you—

NORA (*composed*)　You'll never have to do that.

HELMER　Good. Then we'll share the burden, Nora—like husband and wife, the way it ought to be. (*caresses her*) Now are you satisfied? There, there, there. Not that look in your eyes—like a frightened dove. It's all your own foolish imagination.—Why don't you practice the tarantella—and your tambourine, too. I'll be in the inner office and close both doors, so I won't hear you. You can make as much noise as you like. (*turning in the doorway*) And when Rank comes, tell him where to find me. (*He nods to her, enters his study carrying his papers, and closes the door.*)

NORA (*transfixed by terror, whispers*)　He would do it. He'll do it. He'll do it in spite of the whole world.—No, this mustn't happen. Anything rather than that! There must be a way!—(*The doorbell rings.*) Dr. Rank! Anything rather than that! Anything—anything at all.

(*She passes her hand over her face, pulls herself together, and opens the door to the hall.* DR. RANK *is out there, hanging up his coat. Darkness begins to fall during the following scene.*)

NORA　Hello there, Dr. Rank. I recognized your ringing. Don't go in to Torvald yet. I think he's busy.

RANK　And you?

NORA (*as he enters and she closes the door behind him*)　You know I always have time for you.

RANK　Thanks. I'll make use of that as long as I can.

NORA　What do you mean by that—As long as you can?

RANK　Does that frighten you?

NORA　Well, it's a funny expression. As if something was going to happen.

RANK　Something is going to happen that I've long been expecting. But I admit I hadn't thought it would come quite so soon.

NORA (*seizes his arm*)　What is it you've found out? Dr. Rank—tell me!

RANK (*sits down by the stove*)　I'm going downhill fast. There's nothing to do about that.

NORA (*with audible relief*)　So it's *you*—

RANK　Who else? No point in lying to myself. I'm in worse shape than any of my other patients, Mrs. Helmer. These last few days I've been making up my inner status. Bankrupt. Chances are that within a month I'll be rotting up in the cemetery.

NORA　Shame on you! Talking that horrid way!

RANK　The thing itself is horrid—damn horrid. The worst of it, though, is all that other horror that comes first. There is only one more test I need to make. After that I'll have a pretty good idea when I'll start coming apart. There is something I want to say to you. Helmer's refined nature can't stand anything hideous. I don't want him in my sick room.

NORA Oh, but Dr. Rank—

RANK I don't want him there. Under no circumstances. I'll close my door to him. As soon as I have full certainty that the worst is about to begin I'll give you my card with a black cross on it. Then you'll know the last horror of destruction has started.

NORA Today you're really quite impossible. And I had hoped you'd be in a particularly good mood.

RANK With death on my hands? Paying for someone else's sins? Is there justice in that? And yet there isn't a single family that isn't ruled by the same law of ruthless retribution, in one way or another.

NORA (*puts her hands over her ears*) Poppycock! Be fun! Be fun!

RANK Well, yes. You may just as well laugh at the whole thing. My poor, innocent spine is suffering from my father's frolics as a young lieutenant.

NORA (*over by the table, left*) Right. He was addicted to asparagus and good liver paté, wasn't he?

RANK And truffles.

NORA Of course. Truffles. And oysters too, I think.

RANK And oysters. Obviously.

NORA And all the port and champagne that go with it. It's really too bad that goodies like that ruin your backbone.

RANK Particularly an unfortunate backbone that never enjoyed any of it.

NORA Ah yes, that's the saddest part of it all.

RANK (*looks searchingly at her*) Hm—

NORA (*after a brief pause*) Why did you smile just then?

RANK No, it was you that laughed.

NORA No, it was you that smiled, Dr. Rank!

RANK (*gets up*) You're more of a mischief-maker than I thought.

NORA I feel in the mood for mischief today.

RANK So it seems.

NORA (*with both her hands on his shoulders*) Dear, dear Dr. Rank, don't you go and die and leave Torvald and me.

RANK Oh, you won't miss me for very long. Those who go away are soon forgotten.

NORA (*with an anxious look*) Do you believe that?

RANK You'll make new friends, and then—

NORA Who'll make new friends?

RANK Both you and Helmer, once I'm gone. You yourself seem to have made a good start already. What was this Mrs. Linde doing here last night?

NORA Aha—Don't tell me you're jealous of poor Kristine?

RANK Yes, I am. She'll be my successor in this house. As soon as I have made my excuses, that woman is likely to—

NORA   Shh—not so loud. She's in there.

RANK   Today too? There you are!

NORA   She's mending my costume. My God, you really *are* unreasonable. (*sits down on the couch*) Now be nice, Dr. Rank. Tomorrow you'll see how beautifully I'll dance, and then you are to pretend I'm dancing just for you—and for Torvald too, of course. (*takes several items out of the carton*) Sit down, Dr. Rank; I want to show you something.

RANK (*sitting down*)   What?

NORA   Look.

RANK   Silk stockings.

NORA   Flesh-colored. Aren't they lovely? Now it's getting dark in here, but tomorrow—No, no. You only get to see the foot. Oh well, you might as well see all of it.

RANK   Hmm.

NORA   Why do you look so critical? Don't you think they'll fit?

RANK   That's something I can't possibly have a reasoned opinion about.

NORA (*looks at him for a moment*)   Shame on you. (*slaps his ear lightly with the stocking*) That's what you get. (*puts the things back in the carton*)

RANK   And what other treasures are you going to show me?

NORA   Nothing at all, because you're naughty. (*She hums a little and rummages in the carton.*)

RANK (*after a brief silence*)   When I sit here like this, talking confidently with you, I can't imagine—I can't possibly imagine what would have become of me if I hadn't had you and Helmer.

NORA (*smiles*)   Well, yes—I do believe you like being with us.

RANK (*in a lower voice, lost in thought*)   And then to have to go away from it all—

NORA   Nonsense. You are not going anywhere.

RANK (*as before*)   —and not to leave behind as much as a poor little token of gratitude, hardly a brief memory of someone missed, nothing but a vacant place that anyone can fill.

NORA   And what if I were to ask you—? No—

RANK   Ask me what?

NORA   For a great proof of your friendship—

RANK   Yes, yes—?

NORA   No, I mean—for an enormous favor—

RANK   Would you really for once make me as happy as all that?

NORA   But you don't even know what it is.

RANK   Well, then; tell me.

NORA   Oh, but I can't, Dr. Rank. It's altogether too much to ask—It's advice and help and a favor—

RANK   So much the better. I can't even begin to guess what it is you have in mind. So for heaven's sake tell me! Don't you trust me?

NORA   Yes, I trust you more than anyone else I know. You are my best and most faithful friend. I know that. So I will tell you. All right, Dr. Rank. There is something you can help me prevent. You know how much Torvald loves me—beyond all words. Never for a moment would he hesitate to give his life for me.

RANK (*leaning over to her*)　Nora—do you really think he's the only one—?

NORA (*with a slight start*)　Who—?

RANK　—would gladly give his life for you.

NORA (*heavily*)　I see.

RANK　I have sworn an oath to myself to tell you before I go. I'll never find a better occasion.—All right, Nora; now you know. And now you also know that you can confide in me more than in anyone else.

NORA (*gets up; in a calm, steady voice*)　Let me get by.

RANK (*makes room for her but remains seated*)　Nora—

NORA (*in the door to the front hall*)　Helene, bring the lamp in here, please. (*walks over to the stove*) Oh, dear Dr. Rank. That really wasn't very nice of you.

RANK (*gets up*)　That I have loved you as much as anybody—was that not nice?

NORA　No; not that. But that you told me. There was no need for that.

RANK　What do you mean? Have you known—?

(*The* MAID *enters with the lamp, puts it on the table, and goes out.*)

RANK　Nora—Mrs. Helmer—I'm asking you: did you know?

NORA　Oh, how can I tell what I knew and didn't know! I really can't say—But that you could be so awkward, Dr. Rank! Just when everything was so comfortable.

RANK　Well, anyway, now you know that I'm at your service with my life and soul. And now you must speak.

NORA (*looks at him*)　After what just happened?

RANK　I beg of you—let me know what it is.

NORA　There is nothing I can tell you now.

RANK　Yes, yes. You mustn't punish me this way. Please let me do for you whatever anyone *can* do.

NORA　Now there is nothing you can do. Besides, I don't think I really need any help, anyway. It's probably just my imagination. Of course that's all it is. I'm sure of it! (*sits down in the rocking chair, looks at him, smiles*) Well, well, well, Dr. Rank! What a fine gentleman you turned out to be! Aren't you ashamed of yourself, now that we have light?

RANK　No, not really. But perhaps I ought to leave—and not come back?

NORA　Don't be silly; of course not! You'll come here exactly as you have been doing. You know perfectly well that Torvald can't do without you.

RANK　Yes, but what about you?

NORA　Oh, I always think it's perfectly delightful when you come.

RANK　That's the very thing that misled me. You are a riddle to me. It has often seemed to me that you'd just as soon be with me as with Helmer.

NORA   Well, you see, there are people you love, and then there are other people you'd almost rather be with.

RANK   Yes, there is something in that.

NORA   When I lived at home with Daddy, of course I loved him most. But I always thought it was so much fun to sneak off down to the maids' room, for they never gave me good advice and they always talked about such fun things.

RANK   Aha! So it's *their* place I have taken.

NORA   (*jumps up and goes over to him*)   Oh dear, kind Dr. Rank, you know very well I didn't mean it that way. Can't you see that with Torvald it is the way it used to be with Daddy?

(*The* MAID *enters from the front hall.*)

THE MAID   Ma'am! (*whispers to her and gives her a caller's card*)

NORA   (*glances at the card*)   Ah! (*puts it in her pocket*)

RANK   Anything wrong?

NORA   No, no; not at all. It's nothing—just my new costume—

RANK   But your costume is lying right there!

NORA   Oh yes, that one. But this is another one. I ordered it. Torvald mustn't know—

RANK   Aha. So that's the great secret.

NORA   That's it. Why don't you go in to him, please. He's in the inner office. And keep him there for a while—

RANK   Don't worry. He won't get away. (*enters* HELMER'S *study*)

NORA   (*to the* MAID)   You say he's waiting in the kitchen?

THE MAID   Yes. He came up the back stairs.

NORA   But didn't you tell him there was somebody with me?

THE MAID   Yes, but he wouldn't listen.

NORA   He won't leave?

THE MAID   No, not till he's had a word with you, ma'am.

NORA   All right. But try not to make any noise. And, Helene—don't tell anyone he's here. It's supposed to be a surprise for my husband.

THE MAID   I understand, ma'am—(*She leaves.*)

NORA   The terrible is happening. It's happening, after all. No, no, no. It can't happen. It won't happen. (*She bolts the study door.*)

(*The* MAID *opens the front hall door for* KROGSTAD *and closes the door behind him. He wears a fur coat for traveling, boots, and a fur hat.*)

NORA   (*toward him*)   Keep your voice down. My husband's home.

KROGSTAD   That's all right.

NORA   What do you want?

KROGSTAD   To find out something.

NORA   Be quick, then. What is it?

KROGSTAD   I expect you know I've been fired.

NORA   I couldn't prevent it, Mr. Krogstad. I fought for you as long and as hard as I could but it didn't do any good.

KROGSTAD   Your husband doesn't love you any more than that? He knows what I can do to you, and yet he runs the risk—

NORA   Surely you didn't think I'd tell him?

KROGSTAD   No, I really didn't. It wouldn't be like Torvald Helmer to show that kind of guts—

NORA   Mr. Krogstad, I insist that you show respect for my husband.

KROGSTAD   By all means. All due respect. But since you're so anxious to keep this a secret, may I assume that you are a little better informed than yesterday about exactly what you have done?

NORA   Better than *you* could ever teach me.

KROGSTAD   Of course. Such a bad lawyer as I am—

NORA   What do you want of me?

KROGSTAD   I just wanted to find out how you are, Mrs. Helmer. I've been thinking about you all day. You see, even a bill collector, a pen pusher, a—anyway, someone like me—even he has a little of what they call a heart.

NORA   Then show it. Think of my little children.

KROGSTAD   Have you and your husband thought of mine? Never mind. All I want to tell you is that you don't need to take this business too seriously. I have no intention of bringing charges right away.

NORA   Oh no, you wouldn't; would you? I knew you wouldn't.

KROGSTAD   The whole thing can be settled quite amiably. Nobody else needs to know anything. It will be between the three of us.

NORA   My husband must never find out about this.

KROGSTAD   How are you going to prevent that? Maybe you can pay me the balance on the loan?

NORA   No, not right now.

KROGSTAD   Or do you have a way of raising the money one of these next few days?

NORA   None I intend to make use of.

KROGSTAD   It wouldn't do you any good, anyway. Even if you had the cash in your hand right this minute, I wouldn't give you your note back. It wouldn't make any difference *how* much money you offered me.

NORA   Then you'll have to tell me what you plan to use the note *for*.

KROGSTAD   Just keep it; that's all. Have it on hand, so to speak. I won't say a word to anybody else. So if you've been thinking about doing something desperate—

NORA   I have.

KROGSTAD   —like leaving house and home—

NORA   I have!

KROGSTAD   —or even something worse—

NORA   How did you know?

KROGSTAD —then: don't.

NORA How did you know I was thinking of *that?*

KROGSTAD Most of us do, right at first. I did, too, but when it came down to it I didn't have the courage—

NORA (*tonelessly*) Nor do I.

KROGSTAD (*relieved*) See what I mean? I thought so. You don't either.

NORA I don't. I don't.

KROGSTAD Besides, it would be very silly of you. Once that first domestic blowup is behind you—. Here in my pocket is a letter for your husband.

NORA Telling him everything?

KROGSTAD As delicately as possible.

NORA (*quickly*) He mustn't get that letter. Tear it up. I'll get you the money somehow.

KROGSTAD Excuse me, Mrs. Helmer, I thought I just told you—

NORA I'm not talking about the money I owe you. Just let me know how much money you want from my husband, and I'll get it for you.

KROGSTAD I want no money from your husband.

NORA Then, what *do* you want?

KROGSTAD I'll tell you, Mrs. Helmer. I want to rehabilitate myself; I want to get up in the world; and your husband is going to help me. For a year and a half I haven't done anything disreputable. All that time I have been struggling with the most miserable circumstances. I was content to work my way up step by step. Now I've been kicked out, and I'm no longer satisfied just getting my old job back. I want more than that; I want to get to the top. I'm being quite serious. I want the bank to take me back but in a higher position. I want your husband to create a new job for me—

NORA He'll never do that!

KROGSTAD He will. I know him. He won't dare not to. And once I'm back inside and he and I are working together, you'll see! Within a year I'll be the manager's right hand. It will be Nils Krogstad and not Torvald Helmer who'll be running the Mutual Bank!

NORA You'll never see that happen!

KROGSTAD Are you thinking of—?

NORA Now I *do* have the courage.

KROGSTAD You can't scare me. A fine, spoiled lady like you—

NORA You'll see, you'll see!

KROGSTAD Under the ice, perhaps? Down into that cold, black water? Then spring comes, and you float up again—hideous, can't be identified, hair all gone—

NORA You don't frighten me.

KROGSTAD Nor you me. One doesn't do that sort of thing, Mrs. Helmer. Besides, what good would it do? He'd still be in my power.

NORA Afterwards? When I'm no longer—?

KROGSTAD Aren't you forgetting that your reputation would be in my hands?

(NORA *stares at him, speechless.*)

KROGSTAD   All right; now I've told you what to expect. So don't do anything foolish. When Helmer gets my letter I expect to hear from him. And don't you forget that it's your husband himself who forces me to use such means again. That I'll never forgive him. Goodbye, Mrs. Helmer. (*goes out through the hall*)

NORA (*at the door, opens it a little, listens*)   He's going. And no letter. Of course not! That would be impossible. (*opens the door more*) What's he doing? He's still there. Doesn't go down. Having second thoughts—? Will he—?

(*The sound of a letter dropping into the mailbox. Then* KROGSTAD*'s steps are heard going down the stairs, gradually dying away.*)

NORA (*with a muted cry runs forward to the table by the couch; brief pause*)   In the mailbox. (*tiptoes back to the door to the front hall*) There it is. Torvald, Torvald—now we're lost!

MRS. LINDE (*enters from the left, carrying* NORA*'s Capri costume*)   There now. I think it's all fixed. Why don't we try it on you—

NORA (*in a low, hoarse voice*)   Kristine, come here.

MRS. LINDE   What's wrong with you? You look quite beside yourself.

NORA   Come over here. Do you see that letter? There, look—through the glass in the mailbox.

MRS. LINDE   Yes, yes; I see it.

NORA   That letter is from Krogstad.

MRS. LINDE   Nora—it was Krogstad who lent you the money!

NORA   Yes, and now Torvald will find out about it.

MRS. LINDE   Oh believe me, Nora. That's the best thing for both of you.

NORA   There's more to it than you know. I forged a signature—

MRS. LINDE   Oh my God—!

NORA   I just want to tell you this, Kristine, that you must be my witness.

MRS. LINDE   Witness? How? Witness to what?

NORA   If I lose my mind—and that could very well happen—

MRS. LINDE   Nora!

NORA   —or if something were to happen to me—something that made it impossible for me to be here—

MRS. LINDE   Nora, Nora! You're not yourself!

NORA   —and if someone were to take all the blame, assume the whole responsibility—Do you understand—?

MRS. LINDE   Yes, yes; but how can you think—!

NORA   Then you are to witness that that's not so, Kristine. I am not beside myself. I am perfectly rational, and what I'm telling you is that nobody else has known about this. I've done it all by myself, the whole thing. Just remember that.

MRS. LINDE   I will. But I don't understand any of it.

NORA   Oh, how could you! For it's the wonderful that's about to happen.

MRS. LINDE   The wonderful?

NORA   Yes, the wonderful. But it's so terrible, Kristine. It mustn't happen for anything in the whole world!

MRS. LINDE   I'm going over to talk to Krogstad right now.

NORA   No, don't. Don't go to him. He'll do something bad to you.

MRS. LINDE   There was a time when he would have done anything for me.

NORA   He!

MRS. LINDE   Where does he live?

NORA   Oh, I don't know—Yes, wait a minute—(*reaches into her pocket*)—here's his card.—But the letter, the letter—!

HELMER (*in his study, knocks on the door*)   Nora!

NORA (*cries out in fear*)   Oh, what is it? What do you want?

HELMER   That's all right. Nothing to be scared about. We're not coming in. For one thing, you've bolted the door, you know. Are you modeling your costume?

NORA   Yes, yes; I am. I'm going to be so pretty, Torvald.

MRS. LINDE (*having looked at the card*)   He lives just around the corner.

NORA   Yes, but it's no use. Nothing can save us now. The letter is in the mailbox.

MRS. LINDE   And your husband has the key?

NORA   Yes. He always keeps it with him.

MRS. LINDE   Krogstad must ask for his letter back, unread. He's got to think up some pretext or other—

NORA   But this is just the time of day when Torvald—

MRS. LINDE   Delay him. Go in to him. I'll be back as soon as I can. (*She hurries out through the hall door.*)

NORA (*walks over to* HELMER's *door, opens it, and peeks in*)   Torvald.

HELMER (*still offstage*)   Well, well! So now one's allowed in one's own living room again. Come on, Rank. Now we'll see—(*in the doorway*) But what's this?

NORA   What, Torvald dear?

HELMER   Rank prepared me for a splendid metamorphosis.

RANK (*in the doorway*)   That's how I understood it. Evidently I was mistaken.

NORA   Nobody gets to admire me in my costume before tomorrow.

HELMER   But, dearest Nora—you look all done in. Have you been practicing too hard?

NORA   No, I haven't practiced at all.

HELMER   But you'll have to, you know.

NORA   I know it, Torvald. I simply must. But I can't do a thing unless you help me. I have forgotten everything.

HELMER   Oh it will all come back. We'll work on it.

NORA   Oh yes, please, Torvald. You just have to help me. Promise? I am so nervous. That big party—. You mustn't do anything else tonight. Not a bit of business. Don't even touch a pen. Will you promise, Torvald?

HELMER   I promise. Tonight I'll be entirely at your service—you helpless little thing.—Just a moment, though. First I want to—(*goes to the door to the front hall*)

NORA   What are you doing out there?

HELMER   Just looking to see if there's any mail.

NORA   No, no! Don't, Torvald!

HELMER   Why not?

NORA   Torvald, I beg you. There is no mail.

HELMER   Let me just look, anyway. (*is about to go out*)

(NORA *by the piano, plays the first bars of the tarantella dance.*)

HELMER (*halts at the door*)   Aha!

NORA   I won't be able to dance tomorrow if I don't get to practice with you.

HELMER (*goes to her*)   Are you really all that scared, Nora dear?

NORA   Yes, so terribly scared. Let's try it right now. There's still time before we eat. Oh please, sit down and play for me, Torvald. Teach me, coach me, the way you always do.

HELMER   Of course I will, my darling, if that's what you want. (*sits down at the piano*)

(NORA *takes the tambourine out of the carton, as well as a long, many-colored shawl. She quickly drapes the shawl around herself, then leaps into the middle of the floor.*)

NORA   Play for me! I want to dance!

(HELMER *plays and* NORA *dances.* DR. RANK *stands by the piano behind* HELMER *and watches.*)

HELMER (*playing*)   Slow down, slow down!

NORA   Can't!

HELMER   Not so violent, Nora!

NORA   It has to be this way.

HELMER (*stops playing*)   No, no. This won't do at all.

NORA (*laughing, swinging her tambourine*)   What did I tell you?

RANK   Why don't you let me play?

HELMER (*getting up*)   Good idea. Then I can direct her better.

(RANK *sits down at the piano and starts playing.* NORA *dances more and more wildly.* HELMER *stands over by the stove, repeatedly correcting her. She doesn't seem to hear. Her hair comes loose and falls down over her shoulders. She doesn't notice but keeps on dancing.* MRS. LINDE *enters.*)

MRS. LINDE (*stops by the door, dumbfounded*)   Ah—!

NORA (*dancing*)   We're having such fun, Kristine!

HELMER   My dearest Nora, you're dancing as if it were a matter of life and death!

NORA   It is! It is!

HELMER   Rank, stop. This is sheer madness. Stop, I say!

(RANK *stops playing;* NORA *suddenly stops dancing.*)

HELMER (*goes over to her*)   If I hadn't seen it I wouldn't have believed it. You've forgotten every single thing I ever taught you.

NORA (*tosses away the tambourine*)   See? I told you.

HELMER   Well! You certainly need coaching.

NORA   Didn't I tell you I did? Now you've seen for yourself. I'll need your help till the very minute we're leaving for the party. Will you promise, Torvald?

HELMER   You can count on it.

NORA   You're not to think of anything except me—not tonight and not tomorrow. You're not to read any letters—not to look in the mailbox—

HELMER   Ah, I see. You're still afraid of that man.

NORA   Yes—yes, that too.

HELMER   Nora, I can tell from looking at you. There's a letter from him out there.

NORA   I don't know. I think so. But you're not to read it now. I don't want anything ugly to come between us before it's all over.

RANK (*to* HELMER *in a low voice*)   Better not argue with her.

HELMER (*throws his arm around her*)   The child shall have her way. But tomorrow night, when you've done your dance—

NORA   Then you'll be free.

THE MAID (*in the door, right*)   Dinner can be served any time, ma'am.

NORA   We want champagne, Helene.

THE MAID   Very good, ma'am. (*goes out*)

HELMER   Aha! Having a party, eh?

NORA   Champagne from now till sunrise! (*calls out*) And some macaroons, Helene. Lots!—just this once.

HELMER (*taking her hands*)   There, there—I don't like this wild—frenzy—Be my own sweet little lark again, the way you always are.

NORA   Oh, I will. But you go on in. You too, Dr. Rank. Kristine, please help me put up my hair.

RANK (*in a low voice to* HELMER *as they go out*)   You don't think she is—you know—expecting—?

HELMER   Oh no. Nothing like that. It's just this childish fear I was telling you about. (*They go out, right.*)

NORA   Well?

MRS. LINDE   Left town.

NORA   I saw it in your face.

MRS. LINDE   He'll be back tomorrow night. I left him a note.

NORA   You shouldn't have. I don't want you to try to stop anything. You see, it's a kind of ecstasy, too, this waiting for the wonderful.

MRS. LINDE   But what is it you're waiting *for*?

NORA   You wouldn't understand. Why don't you go in to the others. I'll be there in a minute.

(MRS. LINDE *enters the dining room, right.*)

NORA   (*stands still for a little while, as if collecting herself; she looks at her watch*)   Five o'clock. Seven hours till midnight. Twenty-four more hours till next midnight. Then the tarantella is over. Twenty-four plus seven— thirty-one more hours to live.

HELMER   (*in the door, right*)   What's happening to my little lark?

NORA   (*to him, with open arms*)   Here's your lark!

Act III

The same room. The table by the couch and the chairs around it have been moved to the middle of the floor. A lighted lamp is on the table. The door to the front hall is open. Dance music is heard from upstairs.

MRS. LINDE *is seated by the table, idly leafing through the pages of a book. She tries to read but seems unable to concentrate. Once or twice she turns her head in the direction of the door, anxiously listening.*

MRS. LINDE   (*looks at her watch*)   Not yet. It's almost too late. If only he hasn't— (*listens again*) Ah! There he is. (*She goes to the hall and opens the front door carefully. Quiet footsteps on the stairs. She whispers.*) Come in. There's nobody here.

KROGSTAD   (*in the door*)   I found your note when I got home. What's this all about?

MRS. LINDE   I've got to talk to you.

KROGSTAD   Oh? And it has to be here?

MRS. LINDE   It couldn't be at my place. My room doesn't have a separate entrance. Come in. We're quite alone. The maid is asleep and the Helmers are at a party upstairs.

KROGSTAD   (*entering*)   Really? The Helmers are dancing tonight, are they?

MRS. LINDE   And why not?

KROGSTAD   You're right. Why not, indeed.

MRS. LINDE   All right, Krogstad. Let's talk, you and I.

KROGSTAD   I didn't know we had anything to talk about.

MRS. LINDE   We have much to talk about.

KROGSTAD   I didn't think so.

MRS. LINDE   No, because you've never really understood me.

KROGSTAD   What was there to understand? What happened was perfectly commonplace. A heartless woman jilts a man when she gets a more attractive offer.

MRS. LINDE   Do you think I'm all that heartless? And do you think it was easy for me to break with you?

KROGSTAD   No?

MRS. LINDE   You really thought it was?

KROGSTAD   If it wasn't, why did you write the way you did that time?

MRS. LINDE   What else could I do? If I had to make a break, I also had the duty to destroy whatever feelings you had for me.

KROGSTAD (*clenching his hands*)   So that's the way it was. And you did—*that*—just for money!

MRS. LINDE   Don't forget I had a helpless mother and two small brothers. We couldn't wait for you, Krogstad. You know yourself how uncertain your prospects were then.

KROGSTAD   All right. But you still didn't have the right to throw me over for somebody else.

MRS. LINDE   I don't know. I have asked myself that question many times. Did I have that right?

KROGSTAD (*in a lower voice*)   When I lost you I lost my footing. Look at me now. A shipwrecked man on a raft.

MRS. LINDE   Rescue may be near.

KROGSTAD   It *was* near. Then you came between.

MRS. LINDE   I didn't know that, Krogstad. Only today did I find out it's your job I'm taking over in the bank.

KROGSTAD   I believe you when you say so. But now that you *do* know, aren't you going to step aside?

MRS. LINDE   No, for it wouldn't do you any good.

KROGSTAD   Whether it would or not—*I* would do it.

MRS. LINDE   I have learned common sense. Life and hard necessity have taught me that.

KROGSTAD   And life has taught me not to believe in pretty speeches.

MRS. LINDE   Then life has taught you a very sensible thing. But you do believe in actions, don't you?

KROGSTAD   How do you mean?

MRS. LINDE   You referred to yourself just now as a shipwrecked man.

KROGSTAD   It seems to me I had every reason to do so.

MRS. LINDE   And I am a shipwrecked woman. No one to grieve for, no one to care for.

KROGSTAD   You made your choice.

MRS. LINDE   I had no other choice that time.

KROGSTAD   Let's say you didn't. What then?

MRS. LINDE   Krogstad, how would it be if we two shipwrecked people got together?

KROGSTAD   What's this!

MRS. LINDE   Two on one wreck are better off than each on his own.

KROGSTAD   Kristine!

MRS. LINDE   Why do you think I came to town?

KROGSTAD   Surely not because of me?

MRS. LINDE   If I'm going to live at all I must work. All my life, for as long as I can remember, I have worked. That's been my one and only pleasure. But now that I'm all alone in the world I feel nothing but this terrible emptiness and desolation. There is no joy in working just for yourself. Krogstad—give me someone and something to work for.

KROGSTAD   I don't believe this. Only hysterical females go in for that kind of high-minded self-sacrifice.

MRS. LINDE   Did you ever know me to be hysterical?

KROGSTAD   You really could do this? Listen—do you know about my past? All of it?

MRS. LINDE   Yes, I do.

KROGSTAD   Do you also know what people think of me around here?

MRS. LINDE   A little while ago you sounded as if you thought that together with me you might have become a different person.

KROGSTAD   I'm sure of it.

MRS. LINDE   Couldn't that still be?

KROGSTAD   Kristine—do you know what you are doing? Yes, I see you do. And you think you have the courage—?

MRS. LINDE   I need someone to be a mother to, and your children need a mother. You and I need one another. Nils, I believe in you—in the real you. Together with you I dare to do anything.

KROGSTAD (*seizes her hands*)   Thanks, thanks, Kristine—Now I know I'll raise myself in the eyes of others—Ah, but I forget—!

MRS. LINDE (*listening*)   Shh!—there's the tarantella. You must go; hurry!

KROGSTAD   Why? What is it?

MRS. LINDE   Do you hear what they're playing up there? When that dance is over they'll be down.

KROGSTAD   All right. I'm leaving. The whole thing is pointless, anyway. Of course you don't know what I'm doing to the Helmers.

MRS. LINDE   Yes, Krogstad; I do know.

KROGSTAD   Still, you're brave enough—?

MRS. LINDE   I very well understand to what extremes despair can drive a man like you.

KROGSTAD   If only it could be undone!

MRS. LINDE   It could, for your letter is still out there in the mailbox.

KROGSTAD   Are you sure?

MRS. LINDE   Quite sure. But—

KROGSTAD (*looks searchingly at her*)   Maybe I'm beginning to understand. You want to save your friend at any cost. Be honest with me. That's it, isn't it?

MRS. LINDE   Krogstad, you may sell yourself once for somebody else's sake, but you don't do it twice.

KROGSTAD   I'll demand my letter back.

MRS. LINDE   No, no.

KROGSTAD   Yes, of course. I'll wait here till Helmer comes down. Then I'll ask him for my letter. I'll tell him it's just about my dismissal—that he shouldn't read it.

MRS. LINDE   No, Krogstad. You are not to ask for that letter back.

KROGSTAD   But tell me—wasn't that the real reason you wanted to meet me here?

MRS. LINDE   At first it was, because I was so frightened. But that was yesterday. Since then I have seen the most incredible things going on in this house. Helmer must learn the whole truth. This miserable secret must come out in the open; those two must come to a full understanding. They simply can't continue with all this concealment and evasion.

KROGSTAD   All right; if you want to take that chance. But there is one thing I *can* do, and I'll do that right now.

MRS. LINDE (*listening*)   But hurry! Go! The dance is over. We aren't safe another minute.

KROGSTAD   I'll be waiting for you downstairs.

MRS. LINDE   Yes, do. You must see me home.

KROGSTAD   I've never been so happy in my whole life. (*He leaves through the front door. The door between the living room and the front hall remains open.*)

MRS. LINDE (*straightens up the room a little and gets her things ready*)   What a change! Oh yes!—what a change! People to work for—to live for—a home to bring happiness to. I can't wait to get to work—! If only they'd come soon—(*listens*) Ah, there they are. Get my coat on—(*puts on her coat and hat*)

(HELMER's *and* NORA's *voices are heard outside. A key is turned in the lock, and* HELMER *almost forces* NORA *into the hall. She is dressed in her Italian costume, with a big black shawl over her shoulders. He is in evening dress under an open black cloak.*)

NORA (*in the door, still resisting*)   No, no, no! I don't want to! I want to go back upstairs. I don't want to leave so early.

HELMER   But dearest Nora—

NORA   Oh please, Torvald—please! I'm asking you as nicely as I can—just another hour!

HELMER   Not another minute, sweet. You know we agreed. There now. Get inside. You'll catch a cold out here. (*She still resists, but he guides her gently into the room.*)

MRS. LINDE   Good evening.

NORA   Kristine!

HELMER   Ah, Mrs. Linde. Still here?

MRS. LINDE   I know. I really should apologize, but I so much wanted to see Nora in her costume.

NORA   You've been waiting up for me?

MRS. LINDE Yes, unfortunately I didn't get here in time. You were already upstairs, but I just didn't feel like leaving till I had seen you.

HELMER (*removing* NORA*'s shawl*) Yes, do take a good look at her, Mrs. Linde. I think I may say she's worth looking at. Isn't she lovely?

MRS. LINDE She certainly is—

HELMER Isn't she a miracle of loveliness, though? That was the general opinion at the party, too. But dreadfully obstinate—that she is, the sweet little thing. What can we do about that? Will you believe it—I practically had to use force to get her away.

NORA Oh Torvald, you're going to be sorry you didn't give me even half an hour more.

HELMER See what I mean, Mrs. Linde? She dances the tarantella—she is a tremendous success—quite deservedly so, though perhaps her performance was a little too natural—I mean, more than could be reconciled with the rules of art. But all right! The point is: she's a success, a tremendous success. So should I let her stay after that? Weaken the effect? Of course not. So I take my lovely little Capri girl—I might say, my capricious little Capri girl—under my arm—a quick turn around the room—a graceful bow in all directions, and—as they say in the novels—the beautiful apparition is gone. A finale should always be done for effect, Mrs. Linde, but there doesn't seem to be any way of getting that into Nora's head. Poooh—! It's hot in here. (*throws his cloak down on a chair and opens the door to his room*) Why, it's dark in here! Of course. Excuse me—(*goes inside and lights a couple of candles*)

NORA (*in a hurried, breathless whisper*) Well?

MRS. LINDE (*in a low voice*) I have talked to him.

NORA And—?

MRS. LINDE Nora—you've got to tell your husband everything.

NORA (*no expression in her voice*) I knew it.

MRS. LINDE You have nothing to fear from Krogstad. But you must speak.

NORA I'll say nothing.

MRS. LINDE Then the letter will.

NORA Thank you, Kristine. Now I know what I have to do. Shh!

HELMER (*returning*) Well, Mrs. Linde, have you looked your fill?

MRS. LINDE Yes. And now I'll say goodnight.

HELMER So soon? Is that your knitting?

MRS. LINDE (*takes it*) Yes, thank you. I almost forgot.

HELMER So you knit, do you?

MRS. LINDE Oh yes.

HELMER You know—you ought to take up embroidery instead.

MRS. LINDE Oh? Why?

HELMER Because it's so much more beautiful. Look. You hold the embroidery so—in your left hand. Than with your right you move the needle—like this—in an easy, elongated arc—you see?

MRS. LINDE   Maybe you're right—

HELMER   Knitting, on the other hand, can never be anything but ugly. Look here: arms pressed close to the sides—the needles going up and down—there's something Chinese about it somehow—. That really was an excellent champagne they served us tonight.

MRS. LINDE   Well, goodnight! Nora. And don't be obstinate any more.

HELMER   Well said, Mrs. Linde!

MRS. LINDE   Goodnight, sir.

HELMER (*sees her to the front door*)   Goodnight, goodnight. I hope you'll get home all right? I'd be very glad to—but of course you don't have far to walk, do you? Goodnight, goodnight. (*She leaves. He closes the door behind her and returns to the living room.*) There! At last we got rid of her. She really is an incredible bore, that woman.

NORA   Aren't you very tired, Torvald?

HELMER   No, not in the least.

NORA   Not sleepy either?

HELMER   Not at all. Quite the opposite. I feel enormously—animated. How about you? Yes, you do look tired and sleepy.

NORA   Yes, I am very tired. Soon I'll be asleep.

HELMER   What did I tell you? I was right, wasn't I? Good thing I didn't let you stay any longer.

NORA   Everything you do is right.

HELMER (*kissing her forehead*)   Now my little lark is talking like a human being. But did you notice what splendid spirits Rank was in tonight?

NORA   Was he? I didn't notice. I didn't get to talk with him.

HELMER   Nor did I—hardly. But I haven't seen him in such a good mood for a long time. (*looks at her, comes closer to her*) Ah! It does feel good to be back in our own home again, to be quite alone with you—my young, lovely, ravishing woman!

NORA   Don't look at me like that, Torvald!

HELMER   Am I not to look at my most precious possession? All that loveliness that is mine, nobody's but mine, all of it mine.

NORA (*walks to the other side of the table*)   I won't have you talk to me like that tonight.

HELMER (*follows her*)   The Tarantella is still in your blood. I can tell. That only makes you all the more alluring. Listen! The guests are beginning to leave. (*softly*) Nora—soon the whole house will be quiet.

NORA   Yes, I hope so.

HELMER   Yes, don't you, my darling? Do you know—when I'm at a party with you, like tonight—do you know why I hardly ever talk to you, why I keep away from you, only look at you once in a while—a few stolen glances—do you know why I do that? It's because I pretend that you are my secret love, my young, secret bride-to-be, and nobody has the slightest suspicion that there is anything between us.

NORA Yes, I know. All your thoughts are with me.

HELMER Then when we're leaving and I lay your shawl around your delicate young shoulders—around that wonderful curve of your neck—then I imagine you're my young bride, that we're coming away from the wedding, that I am taking you to my home for the first time—that I am alone with you for the first time—quite alone with you, you young, trembling beauty! I have desired you all evening—there hasn't been a longing in me that hasn't been for you. When you were dancing the tarantella, chasing, inviting—my blood was on fire; I couldn't stand it any longer—that's why I brought you down so early—

NORA Leave me now, Torvald. Please! I don't want all this.

HELMER What do you mean? You're only playing your little teasing bird game with me; aren't you, Nora? Don't want to? I'm your husband, aren't I?

(*There is a knock on the front door.*)

NORA (*with a start*) Did you hear that—?

HELMER (*on his way to the hall*) Who is it?

RANK (*outside*) It's me. May I come in for a moment?

HELMER (*in a low voice, annoyed*) Oh, what does he want now? (*aloud*) Just a minute. (*opens the door*) Well! How good of you not to pass by our door.

RANK I thought I heard your voice, so I felt like saying hello. (*looks around*) Ah yes—this dear, familiar room. What a cozy, comfortable place you have here, you two.

HELMER Looked to me as if you were quite comfortable upstairs too.

RANK I certainly was. Why not? Why not enjoy all you can in this world? As much as you can for as long as you can, anyway. Excellent wine.

HELMER The champagne, particularly.

RANK You noticed that too? Incredible how much I managed to put away.

NORA Torvald drank a lot of champagne tonight, too.

RANK Did he?

NORA Yes, he did, and then he's always so much fun afterwards.

RANK Well, why not have some fun in the evening after a well spent day?

HELMER Well spent? I'm afraid I can't claim that.

RANK (*slapping him lightly on the shoulder*) But you see, I can!

NORA Dr. Rank, I believe you must have been conducting a scientific test today.

RANK Exactly.

HELMER What do you know—little Nora talking about scientific tests!

NORA May I congratulate you on the result?

RANK You may indeed.

NORA It was a good one?

RANK The best possible for both doctor and patient—certainty.

NORA (*a quick query*)   Certainty?

RANK   Absolute certainty. So why shouldn't I have myself an enjoyable evening afterwards?

NORA   I quite agree with you, Dr. Rank. You should.

HELMER   And so do I. If only you don't pay for it tomorrow.

RANK   Oh well—you get nothing for nothing in this world.

NORA   Dr. Rank—you are fond of costume parties, aren't you?

RANK   Yes, particularly when there is a reasonable number of amusing disguises.

NORA   Listen—what are the two of us going to be the next time?

HELMER   You frivolous little thing! Already thinking about the next party!

RANK   You and I? That's easy. You'll be Fortune's Child.

HELMER   Yes, but what is a fitting costume for that?

RANK   Let your wife appear just the way she always is.

HELMER   Beautiful. Very good indeed. But how about yourself? Don't you know what you'll go as?

RANK   Yes, my friend. I know precisely what I'll be.

HELMER   Yes?

RANK   At the next masquerade I'll be invisible.

HELMER   That's a funny idea.

RANK   There's a certain black hat—you've heard about the hat that makes you invisible, haven't you? You put that on, and nobody can see you.

HELMER (*suppressing a smile*)   I guess that's right.

RANK   But I'm forgetting what I came for. Helmer, give me a cigar—one of your dark Havanas.

HELMER   With the greatest pleasure. (*offers him his case*)

RANK (*takes one and cuts off the tip*)   Thanks.

NORA (*striking a match*)   Let me give you a light.

RANK   Thanks. (*She holds the match; he lights his cigar.*) And now goodbye!

HELMER   Goodbye, goodbye, my friend.

NORA   Sleep well, Dr. Rank.

RANK   I thank you.

NORA   Wish me the same.

RANK   You? Well, if you really want me to—. Sleep well. And thanks for the light. (*He nods to both of them and goes out.*)

HELMER (*in a low voice*)   He had had quite a bit to drink.

NORA (*absently*)   Maybe so.

(HELMER *takes out his keys and goes out into the hall.*)

NORA   Torvald—what are you doing out there?

HELMER   Emptying the mailbox. It is quite full. There wouldn't be room for the newspapers in the morning—

NORA   Are you going to work tonight?

HELMER   You know very well I won't.—Say! What's this? Somebody's been at the lock.

NORA   The lock—?

HELMER   Yes. Why, I wonder. I hate to think that any of the maids—. Here's a broken hairpin. It's one of yours. Nora.

NORA (*quickly*)   Then it must be one of the children.

HELMER   You better make damn sure they stop that. Hm, hm.—There! I got it open, finally. (*gathers up the mail, calls out to the kitchen*) Helene?—Oh Helene—turn out the light here in the hall, will you? (*He comes back into the living room and closes the door.*) Look how it's been piling up. (*shows her the bundle of letters, starts leafing through it*) What's this?

NORA (*by the window*)   The letter! Oh no, no, Torvald!

HELMER   Two calling cards—from Rank.

NORA   From Dr. Rank?

HELMER (*looking at them*)   "Doctor medicinae Rank." They were on top. He must have put them there when he left just now.

NORA   Anything written on them?

HELMER   A black cross above the name. What a macabre idea. Like announcing his own death.

NORA   That's what it is.

HELMER   Hm? You know about this? Has he said anything to you?

NORA   That card means he has said goodbye to us. He'll lock himself up to die.

HELMER   My poor friend. I knew of course he wouldn't be with me very long. But so soon—. And hiding himself away like a wounded animal—

NORA   When it has to be, it's better it happens without words. Don't you think so, Torvald?

HELMER (*walking up and down*)   He'd grown so close to us. I find it hard to think of him as gone. With his suffering and loneliness he was like a clouded background for our happy sunshine. Well, it may be better this way. For him, at any rate. (*stops*) And perhaps for us, too, Nora. For now we have nobody but each other. (*embraces her*) Oh you—my beloved wife! I feel I just can't hold you close enough. Do you know, Nora—many times I have wished some great danger threatened you, so I could risk my life and blood and everything—everything, for your sake.

NORA (*frees herself and says in a strong and firm voice*)   I think you should go and read your letters now, Torvald.

HELMER   No, no—not tonight. I want to be with you, my darling.

NORA   With the thought of your dying friend—?

HELMER   You are right. This has shaken both of us. Something not beautiful has come between us. Thoughts of death and dissolution. We must try to get over it—out of it. Till then—we'll each go to our own room.

NORA (*her arms around his neck*)   Torvald—goodnight! Goodnight!

HELMER (*kisses her forehead*)   Goodnight, my little songbird. Sleep well, Nora. Now I'll read my letters. (*He goes into his room, carrying the mail; closes the door.*)

NORA (*her eyes desperate, her hands groping, finds Helmer's black cloak and throws it around her; she whispers, quickly, brokenly, hoarsely*)   Never see him again. Never. Never. Never. (*puts her shawl over her head*) And never see the children again, either. Never; never.—The black, icy water—fathomless—this—! If only it was all over.—Now he has it. Now he's reading it. No, no; not yet. Torvald—goodbye—you—the children—

(*She is about to hurry through the hall, when* HELMER *flings open the door to his room and stands there with an open letter in his hand.*)

HELMER   Nora!

NORA (*cries out*)   Ah—!

HELMER   What is it? You know what's in this letter?

NORA   Yes, I do! Let me go! Let me out!

HELMER (*holds her back*)   Where do you think you're going?

NORA (*trying to tear herself loose from him*)   I won't let you save me, Torvald!

HELMER (*tumbles back*)   True! Is it true what he writes? Oh my God! No, no—this can't possibly be true.

NORA   It is true. I have loved you more than anything else in the whole world.

HELMER   Oh, don't give me any silly excuses.

NORA (*taking a step toward him*)   Torvald—!

HELMER   You wretch! What have you done!

NORA   Let me go. You are not to sacrifice yourself for me. You are not to take the blame.

HELMER   No more playacting. (*locks the door to the front hall*) You'll stay here and answer me. Do you understand what you have done? Answer me! Do you understand?

NORA (*gazes steadily at him with an increasingly frozen expression*)   Yes. Now I'm beginning to understand.

HELMER (*walking up and down*)   What a dreadful awakening. All these years—all these eight years—she, my pride and my joy—a hypocrite, a liar—oh worse! worse!—a criminal! Oh, the bottomless ugliness in all this! Damn! Damn! Damn!

(NORA, *silent, keeps gazing at him.*)

HELMER (*stops in front of her*)   I ought to have guessed that something like this would happen. I should have expected it. All your father's loose principles—Silence! You have inherited every one of your father's loose principles. No religion, no morals, no sense of duty—. Now I am being punished for my leniency with him. I did it for your sake, and this is how you pay me back.

NORA   Yes. This is how.

HELMER   You have ruined all my happiness. My whole future—that's what you have destroyed. Oh, it's terrible to think about. I am at the mercy of an unscrupulous man. He can do with me whatever he likes, demand anything of me, command me and dispose of me just as he pleases—I dare not say a word! To go down so miserably, to be destroyed—all because of an irresponsible woman!

NORA   When I am gone from the world, you'll be free.

HELMER   No noble gestures, please. Your father was always full of such phrases too. What good would it do me if you were gone from the world, as you put it? Not the slightest good at all. He could still make the whole thing public, and if he did, people would be likely to think I had been your accomplice. They might even think it was my idea—that it was I who urged you to do it! And for all this I have you to thank—you, whom I've borne on my hands through all the years of our marriage. *Now* do you understand what you've done to me?

NORA   (*with cold calm*)   Yes.

HELMER   I just can't get it into my head that this is happening; it's all so incredible. But we have to come to terms with it somehow. Take your shawl off. Take it off, I say! I have to satisfy him one way or another. The whole affair must be kept quiet at whatever cost.—And as far as you and I are concerned, nothing must seem to have changed. I'm talking about appearances, of course. You'll go on living here; that goes without saying. But I won't let you bring up the children; I dare not trust you with them.—Oh! Having to say this to one I have loved so much, and whom I still—! But all that is past. It's not a question of happiness any more but of hanging on to what can be salvaged—pieces, appearances—(*The doorbell rings.*)

HELMER   (*jumps*)   What's that? So late. Is the worst—? Has he—! Hide, Nora! Say you're sick.

(NORA *doesn't move.* HELMER *opens the door to the hall.*)

THE MAID   (*half dressed, out in the hall*)   A letter for your wife, sir.

HELMER   Give it to me. (*takes the letter and closes the door*) Yes, it's from him. But I won't let you have it. I'll read it myself.

NORA   Yes—you read it.

HELMER   (*by the lamp*)   I hardly dare. Perhaps we're lost, both you and I. No; I've got to know. (*tears the letter open, glances through it, looks at an enclosure; a cry of joy*) Nora!

(NORA *looks at him with a question in her eyes.*)

HELMER   Nora!—No, I must read it again.—Yes, yes; it is so! I'm saved! Nora, I'm saved!

NORA   And I?

HELMER   You too, of course; we're both saved, both you and I. Look! He's returning your note. He writes that he's sorry, he regrets, a happy turn in his life—oh, it doesn't matter what he writes. We're saved, Nora! Nobody can do anything to you now. Oh Nora, Nora—. No, I want to get rid of this disgusting thing first. Let me see—(*looks at the signature*) No, I don't want to see it. I don't want it to be more than a bad dream, the whole thing. (*tears up the note and both letters, throws the pieces in the stove, and watches them burn*) There! Now it's gone.—He wrote that ever since Christmas Eve—. Good God, Nora, these must have been three terrible days for you.

NORA   I have fought a hard fight these last three days.

HELMER   And been in agony and seen no other way out than—. No, we won't think of all that ugliness. We'll just rejoice and tell ourselves it's over, it's all over! Oh, listen to me, Nora. You don't seem to understand. It's over. What *is* it? Why do you look like that—that frozen expression on your face? Oh my poor little Nora, don't you think I know what it is? You can't make yourself believe that I have forgiven you. But I have, Nora; I swear to you, I have forgiven you for everything. Of course I know that what you did was for love of me.

NORA   That is true.

HELMER   You have loved me the way a wife ought to love her husband. You just didn't have the wisdom to judge the means. But do you think I love you any less because you don't know how to act on your own? Of course not. Just lean on me. I'll advise you; I'll guide you. I wouldn't be a man if I didn't find you twice as attractive because of your womanly helplessness. You mustn't pay any attention to the hard words I said to you right at first. It was just that first shock when I thought everything was collapsing all around me. I have forgiven you, Nora. I swear to you—I really have forgiven you.

NORA   I thank you for your forgiveness. (*She goes out through the door, right.*)

HELMER   No, stay—(*looks into the room she entered*) What are you doing in there?

NORA (*within*)   Getting out of my costume.

HELMER (*by the open door*)   Good, good. Try to calm down and compose yourself, my poor little frightened songbird. Rest safely; I have broad wings to cover you with. (*walks around near the door*) What a nice and cozy home we have, Nora. Here's shelter for you. Here I'll keep you safe like a hunted dove I have rescued from the hawk's talons. Believe me: I'll know how to quiet your beating heart. It will happen by and by, Nora; you'll see. Why, tomorrow you'll look at all this in quite a different light. And soon everything will be just the way it was before. I won't need to keep reassuring you that I have forgiven you; you'll feel it yourself. Did you really think I could have abandoned you, or even reproached you? Oh, you don't know a real man's heart, Nora. There is something unspeakably sweet and satisfactory for a man to know deep in himself that he has forgiven his wife—forgiven her in all the fullness of his honest heart. You see, that way she becomes his very own all over again—in a double sense, you might say. He has, so to speak, given her a second birth; it is as if she had become his wife and his child, both. From now on that's what you'll be to me, you lost and helpless creature. Don't worry about a thing, Nora. Only be frank with me, and I'll be your will and your conscience.—What's this? You're not in bed? You've changed your dress—!

NORA (*in an everyday dress*)   Yes, Torvald. I have changed my dress.

HELMER   But why—now—this late—?

NORA   I'm not going to sleep tonight.

HELMER   But my dear Nora—

NORA (*looks at her watch*)   It isn't all that late. Sit down here with me, Torvald. You and I have much to talk about. (*sits down at the table*)

HELMER   Nora—what is this all about? That rigid face—

NORA   Sit down. This will take a while. I have much to say to you.

HELMER (*sits down, facing her across the table*)   You worry me, Nora. I don't understand you.

NORA   No, that's just it. You don't understand me. And I have never understood you—not till tonight. No, don't interrupt me. Just listen to what I have to say.—This is a settling of accounts, Torvald.

HELMER   What do you mean by that?

NORA (*after a brief silence*)   Doesn't one thing strike you, now that we are sitting together like this?

HELMER   What would that be?

NORA   We have been married for eight years. Doesn't it occur to you that this is the first time that you and I, husband and wife, are having a serious talk?

HELMER   Well—serious—. What do you mean by that?

NORA   For eight whole years—longer, in fact—ever since we first met, we have never talked seriously to each other about a single serious thing.

HELMER   You mean I should forever have been telling you about worries you couldn't have helped me with anyway?

NORA   I am not talking about worries. I'm saying we have never tried seriously to get to the bottom of anything together.

HELMER   But dearest Nora, I hardly think that would have been something *you*—

NORA   That's the whole point. You have never understood me. Great wrong has been done to me, Torvald. First by Daddy and then by you.

HELMER   What! By us two? We who have loved you more deeply than anyone else?

NORA (*shakes her head*)   You never loved me—neither Daddy nor you. You only thought it was fun to be in love with me.

HELMER   But, Nora—what an expression to use!

NORA   That's the way it has been, Torvald. When I was home with Daddy, he told me all his opinions, and so they became my opinions too. If I disagreed with him I kept it to myself, for he wouldn't have liked that. He called me his little doll baby, and he played with me the way I played with my dolls. Then I came to your house—

HELMER What a way to talk about our marriage!

NORA (*imperturbably*) I mean that I passed from Daddy's hands into yours. You arranged everything according to your taste, and so I came to share it—or I pretended to; I'm not sure which. I think it was a little of both, now one and now the other. When I look back on it now, it seems to me I've been living here like a pauper—just a hand-to-mouth kind of existence. I have earned my keep by doing tricks for you, Torvald. But that's the way you wanted it. You have great sins against me to answer for, Daddy and you. It's your fault that nothing has become of me.

HELMER Nora, you're being both unreasonable and ungrateful. Haven't you been happy here?

NORA No, never. I thought I was, but I wasn't.

HELMER Not—not happy!

NORA No; just having fun. And you have always been very good to me. But our home has never been more than a playroom. I have been your doll wife here, just the way I used to be Daddy's doll child. And the children have been my dolls. I thought it was fun when you played with me, just as they thought it was fun when I played with them. That's been our marriage, Torvald.

HELMER There is something in what you are saying—exaggerated and hysterical though it is. But from now on things will be different. Playtime is over; it's time for growing up.

NORA Whose growing up—mine or the children's?

HELMER Both yours and the children's, Nora darling.

NORA Oh Torvald, you're not the man to bring me up to be the right kind of wife for you.

HELMER How can you say that?

NORA And I—? What qualifications do I have for bringing up the children?

HELMER Nora!

NORA You said so yourself a minute ago—that you didn't dare to trust me with them.

HELMER In the first flush of anger, yes. Surely, you're not going to count that.

NORA But you were quite right. I am *not* qualified. Something else has to come first. Somehow I have to grow up myself. And you are not the man to help me do that. That's a job I have to do by myself. And that's why I'm leaving you.

HELMER (*jumps up*) What did you say!

NORA I have to be by myself if I am to find out about myself and about all the other things too. So I can't stay here with you any longer.

HELMER Nora, Nora!

NORA I'm leaving now. I'm sure Kristine will put me up for tonight.

HELMER You're out of your mind! I won't let you! I forbid you!

NORA   You can't forbid me anything any more; it won't do any good. I'm taking my own things with me. I won't accept anything from you, either now or later.

HELMER   But this is madness!

NORA   Tomorrow I'm going home—I mean back to my old home town. It will be easier for me to find some kind of job there.

HELMER   Oh, you blind, inexperienced creature—!

NORA   I must see to it that I get experience, Torvald.

HELMER   Leaving your home, your husband, your children! Not a thought of what people will say!

NORA   I can't worry about that. All I know is that I have to leave.

HELMER   Oh, this is shocking! Betraying your most sacred duties like this!

NORA   And what do you consider my most sacred duties?

HELMER   Do I need to tell you that? They are your duties to your husband and your children.

NORA   I have other duties equally sacred.

HELMER   You do not. What duties would they be?

NORA   My duties to myself.

HELMER   You are a wife and a mother before you are anything else.

NORA   I don't believe that any more. I believe I am first of all a human being, just as much as you—or at any rate that I must try to become one. Oh, I know very well that most people agree with you, Torvald, and that it says something like that in all the books. But what people say and what the books say is no longer enough for me. I have to think about these things myself and see if I can't find the answers.

HELMER   You mean to tell me you don't know what your proper place in your own home is? Don't you have a reliable guide in such matters? Don't you have religion?

NORA   Oh but Torvald—I don't really know what religion is.

HELMER   What are you saying!

NORA   All I know is what the Reverend Hansen told me when he prepared me for confirmation. He said that religion was *this* and it was *that*. When I get by myself, away from here, I'll have to look into that, too. I have to decide if what the Reverend Hansen said was right, or anyway if it is right for *me*.

HELMER   Oh, this is unheard of in a young woman! If religion can't guide you, let me appeal to your conscience. For surely you have moral feelings? Or—answer me—maybe you don't?

NORA   Well, you see, Torvald, I don't really know what to say. I just don't know. I am confused about these things. All I know is that my ideas are quite different from yours. I have just found out that the laws are different from what I thought they were, but in no way can I get it into my head that those laws are right. A woman shouldn't have the right to spare her dying old father or save her husband's life! I just can't believe that.

HELMER   You speak like a child. You don't understand the society you live in.

NORA   No, I don't. But I want to find out about it. I have to make up my mind who is right, society or I.

HELMER   You are sick, Nora; you have a fever. I really don't think you are in your right mind.

NORA   I have never felt so clearheaded and sure of myself as I do tonight.

HELMER   And clearheaded and sure of yourself you're leaving your husband and children?

NORA   Yes.

HELMER   Then there is only one possible explanation.

NORA   What?

HELMER   You don't love me any more.

NORA   No, that's just it.

HELMER   Nora! Can you say that?

NORA   I am sorry, Torvald, for you have always been so good to me. But I can't help it. I don't love you any more.

HELMER   (*with forced composure*)   And this too is a clear and sure conviction?

NORA   Completely clear and sure. That's why I don't want to stay here any more.

HELMER   And are you ready to explain to me how I came to forfeit your love?

NORA   Certainly I am. It was tonight, when the wonderful didn't happen. That was when I realized you were not the man I thought you were.

HELMER   You have to explain. I don't understand.

NORA   I have waited patiently for eight years, for I wasn't such a fool that I thought the wonderful is something that happens any old day. Then this—thing—came crashing in on me, and then there wasn't a doubt in my mind that now—now comes the wonderful. When Krogstad's letter was in that mailbox, never for a moment did it even occur to me that you would submit to his conditions. I was so absolutely certain that you would say to him: make the whole thing public—tell everybody. And when that had happened—

HELMER   Yes, then what? When I had surrendered my wife to shame and disgrace—!

NORA   When that had happened, I was absolutely certain that you would stand up and take the blame and say, "I'm the guilty one."

HELMER   Nora!

NORA   You mean I never would have accepted such a sacrifice from you? Of course not. But what would my protests have counted against yours. *That* was the wonderful I was hoping for in terror. And to prevent that I was going to kill myself.

HELMER   I'd gladly work nights and days for you, Nora—endure sorrow and want for your sake. But nobody sacrifices his *honor* for his love.

NORA   A hundred thousand women have done so.

HELMER   Oh, you think and talk like a silly child.

NORA   All right. But you don't think and talk like the man I can live with. When you had gotten over your fright—not because of what threatened *me* but because of the risk to *you*—and the whole danger was past, then you acted as if nothing at all had happened. Once again I was your little songbird, your doll, just as before, only now you had to handle her even more carefully, because she was so frail and weak. (*rises*) Torvald—that moment I realized that I had been living here for eight years with a stranger and had borne him three children—Oh, I can't stand thinking about it! I feel like tearing myself to pieces!

HELMER   (*heavily*)   I see it, I see it. An abyss has opened up between us.—Oh but Nora—surely it can be filled?

NORA   The way I am now I am no wife for you.

HELMER   I have it in me to change.

NORA   Perhaps—if your doll is taken from you.

HELMER   To part—to part from you! No, no, Nora! I can't grasp that thought!

NORA   (*goes out, right*)   All the more reason why it has to be. (*She returns with her outdoor clothes and a small bag, which she sets down on the chair by the table.*)

HELMER   Nora, Nora! Not now! Wait till tomorrow.

NORA   (*putting on her coat*)   I can't spend the night in a stranger's rooms.

HELMER   But couldn't we live here together like brother and sister—?

NORA   (*tying on her hat*)   You know very well that wouldn't last long—. (*wraps her shawl around her*) Goodbye, Torvald. I don't want to see the children. I know I leave them in better hands than mine. The way I am now I can't be anything to them.

HELMER   But some day, Nora—some day—?

NORA   How can I tell? I have no idea what's going to become of me.

HELMER   But you're still my wife, both as you are now and as you will be.

NORA   Listen, Torvald—when a wife leaves her husband's house, the way I am doing now, I have heard he has no more legal responsibilities for her. At any rate, I now release you from all responsibility. You are not to feel yourself obliged to me for anything, and I have no obligations to you. There has to be full freedom on both sides. Here is your ring back. Now give me mine.

HELMER   Even this?

NORA   Even this.

HELMER   Here it is.

NORA   There. So now it's over. I'm putting the keys here. The maids know everything about the house—better than I. Tomorrow, after I'm gone, Kristine will come over and pack my things from home. I want them sent after me.

HELMER   Over! It's all over! Nora, will you never think of me?

NORA   I'm sure I'll often think of you and the children and this house.

HELMER   May I write to you, Nora?

NORA   No—never. I won't have that.

HELMER   But send you things—? You must let me.

NORA   Nothing, nothing.

HELMER   —help you, when you need help—?

NORA   I told you, no; I won't have it. I'll accept nothing from strangers.

HELMER   Nora—can I never again be more to you than a stranger?

NORA (*picks up her bag*)   Oh Torvald—then the most wonderful of all would have to happen—

HELMER   Tell me what that would be—!

NORA   For that to happen, both you and I would have to change so that—Oh Torvald, I no longer believe in the wonderful.

HELMER   But I *will* believe. Tell me! Change, so that—?

NORA   So that our living together would become a true marriage. Goodbye. (*She goes out through the hall.*)

HELMER (*sinks down on a chair near the door and covers his face with his hands*)   Nora! Nora! (*looks around him and gets up*) All empty. She's gone. (*with sudden hope*) The most wonderful—?!

(*From downstairs comes the sound of a heavy door slamming shut.*)

STUDY QUESTIONS

1. The action of *A Doll's House* centers on the development and the alterations of the relationships among Nora, Helmer, Krogstad, and Mrs. Linde. How does Ibsen portray these characters? How do their relationships illuminate their personalities and their actions? How do they emphasize the themes and social comments of the play?

2. Both Nora and Antigonê are women who place moral principles above legal values. What happens to each character in consequence, in terms of her play's plot? other characters' reactions to her action? her view of their reaction, and of herself?

3. Discuss the play's ending. Do you find it successful? What is its effect? What do you think is "the most wonderful of all"?

30

CONTEMPORARY DRAMA

By the middle of the twentieth century, new trends in drama were noticeable. Comedies, tragedies, and the hard-to-classify "dramas" alike often moved beyond realism into surrealism, beyond social comment to psychological portraiture. In stage settings, language, and refusal to follow a straightforward course of time, twentieth-century playwrights often pushed toward new forms of expression, hoping to evoke fresh responses from their audiences.

The study of humans as social beings, and of the way in which social pressures shape people, similarly modulates into the study of individual beings isolated in the midst of (often overwhelming) social demands. Thus spiritual (and sometimes physical) isolation remains an important theme in the three plays we study in this chapter: *The Glass Menagerie, A Raisin in the Sun,* and *Protest.* Yet, as we will see, these plays study isolation in no cold or clinical sense. Rather, they use the drama's traditional role as social critic to call for a more caring society, a society that can accommodate dreams and dreamers as well as the realistic and practical.

Isolation, depicted and set off by failed tenderness, is a notable theme in Tennessee Williams' *The Glass Menagerie.* Amanda lives half in a semiillusory past, half in a present of unpalatable truths that she ignores whenever possible; Laura is isolated by her physical disability and by her great shyness; and Tom has isolated himself from everything except his memories.

The play is performed as a series of remembered scenes, with Tom sometimes narrator and sometimes actor. This device allows for great differences in stagecraft between this play and the realistic plays against which it rebels. The episodic structure; the lyrical, beautifully modulated language that defines each character and differentiates each from his or her companions; the unrealistic stage setting, with its use of lighting and music to set moods and scenes; and the symbolic value of props such as the glass unicorn: all work together to create, in the narrator's words, "truth in the pleasant disguise of illusion."

In contrast to the experimental stagecraft of *The Glass Menagerie,* Lorraine Hansberry's *A Raisin in the Sun* reverts to an older form of stagecraft. The unity of place and action, the steady flow of time, parallel those of the eighteenth- and nineteenth-century "well-made play," while the play's emphasis on "the virtues of private life" are reminiscent of eighteenth-century sentimental comedy.[1] It is

---

[1] Oliver Goldsmith, in his 1773 "Essay on the Theatre," defined sentimental comedy as a form "in which the virtues of private life are exhibited, rather than the vices exposed; and the distresses rather than the faults of mankind make our interest in the piece."

perhaps not surprising that this should be so; like the rationalists of the eighteenth century, Hansberry unabashedly celebrates the spirit of humanity. (Asked by an interviewer, "You believe in a kind of increase in moral and philosophical strength by the use of reason, don't you?" she replied "Oh, yes. Yes. I don't think the time will ever come when we will dismiss the human spirit."[2])

This faith in the human spirit, whether rational, religious, or a blend of both, illumines *A Raisin in the Sun.* Where *The Glass Menagerie* looks primarily backwards, asking "how did these characters come to be this way?," *A Raisin in the Sun* looks primarily forward. Conflicts there certainly are within the play, both within the Younger family and between the Youngers and the outside world. But in each case the conflict is seen as a challenge for further growth. And though the play presents us with as open an ending as we have seen since *A Doll's House,* the ending is strongly optimistic. We may see further problems ahead for the Youngers as they move into a potentially hostile neighborhood, as Walter strives to learn to lead his family (and Lena to be a less assertive leader), as Beneatha chooses among her various potential roads to adulthood. But we have seen also the strengths and loves that will help them meet their challenges, and thrive by so doing.

A Raisin in the Sun is very much a black play. As such, it won immense acceptance and praise when it appeared in 1959, and placed Hansberry among the best twentieth-century dramatists. Paradoxically, the strength of the portrayal of what it means to be black allows the play to be something more, as well. As Hansberry herself said, "in order to create the universal, you must pay very great attention to the specific. . . . I think people, to the extent we accept them and believe them as who they're supposed to be, to that extent they can become everybody."[3] *Raisin* illustrates the truth of this belief. With a firm and unwavering insistence on the truth of her characters and their actions as a black Southside Chicago family in the 1950s, Hansberry has created not only a new Everyman, but a new Everywoman as well.

Whereas *The Glass Menagerie* and *A Raisin in the Sun* are American plays presenting concerns familiar to an American audience, Václav Havel's *The Protest* is set in communist Czechoslovakia before the disintegration of the Soviet Union and the subsequent establishment of democracies in eastern Europe. In 1968, after a "Prague Spring" of somewhat less oppressive government, Soviet troops took over the city and reinstituted a hard-line communist government and the practice of firing dissidents from their jobs or putting them in jail. Havel himself was imprisoned for writing subversive plays. After communism collapsed in 1989, Havel was elected president of Czechoslovakia. In 1993, however, his country split into its two ethnic components, the Czech Republic and Slovakia.

---

[2] *To Be Young, Gifted, and Black* (Prentice-Hall, 1969), pp. 185–86.
[3] *To Be Young, Gifted, and Black,* p. 114.

The Protest explores the moral complexities of living under a repressive government that controls the arts, the media, and most, if not all, significant jobs. What should the artist do under such circumstances? Become an outright opponent of the government like Vanek in Havel's play and risk losing opportunities for publication of his work, or even risk going to jail? Or should the artist do as Stanek does, and keep just quiet enough to hold onto his job, all the while chipping away at totalitarianism as best he can from inside the system? Vanek's moral dilemma is whether or not to sign a letter of protest in support of his daughter's lover, who has been imprisoned as a subversive. His long, at times idealistic, at times self-serving, analysis of whether or not he should sign the protest letter is the thematic center of this technically conventional but intellectually fascinating one-act play.

The Glass Menagerie TENNESSEE WILLIAMS

CHARACTERS

AMANDA WINGFIELD, *the mother.*

A little woman of great but confused vitality clinging frantically to another time and place. Her characterization must be carefully created, not copied from type. She is not paranoiac, but her life is paranoia. There is much to admire in **AMANDA,** *and as much to love and pity as there is to laugh at. Certainly she has endurance and a kind of heroism, and though her foolishness makes her unwittingly cruel at times, there is tenderness in her slight person.*

LAURA WINGFIELD, *her daughter.*

AMANDA, *having failed to establish contact with reality, continues to live vitally in her illusions, but* **LAURA'S** *situation is even graver. A childhood illness has left her crippled, one leg slightly shorter than the other, and held in a brace. This defect need not be more than suggested on the stage. Stemming from this,* **LAURA'S** *separation increases till she is like a piece of her own glass collection, too exquisitely fragile to move from the shelf.*

TOM WINGFIELD, *her son, and the narrator of the play.*

A poet with a job in a warehouse. His nature is not remorseless, but to escape from a trap he has to act without pity.

JIM O'CONNOR, *the gentleman caller.*

A nice, ordinary, young man.

SCENE: *An alley in St. Louis.*
PART I: *Preparation for a Gentleman Caller.*
PART II: *The Gentleman Calls.*
TIME: *Now and the Past.*

Scene I

The Wingfield apartment is in the rear of the building, one of those vast hive-like conglomerations of cellular living-units that flower as warty growths in overcrowded urban centers of lower middle-class population and are symptomatic of the impulse of this largest and fundamentally enslaved section of American society to avoid fluidity and differentiation and to exist and function as one interfused mass of automatism.

The apartment faces an alley and is entered by a fire-escape, a structure whose name is a touch of accidental poetic truth, for all of these huge buildings are always burning with the slow and implacable fires of human desperation. The fire-escape is included in the set—that is, the landing of it and steps descending from it.

The scene is memory and is therefore nonrealistic. Memory takes a lot of poetic license. It omits some details; others are exaggerated, according to the emotional value of the articles it touches, for memory is seated predominantly in the heart. The interior is therefore rather dim and poetic.

At the rise of the curtain, the audience is faced with the dark, grim rear wall of the Wingfield tenement. This building, which runs parallel to the footlights, is flanked on both sides by dark, narrow alleys which run into murky canyons of tangled clotheslines, garbage cans and the sinister latticework of neighboring fire-escapes. It is up and down these side alleys that exterior entrances and exits are made, during the play. At the end of TOM's opening commentary, the dark tenement wall slowly reveals (by means of a transparency) the interior of the ground floor Wingfield apartment.

Downstage is the living room, which also serves as a sleeping room for LAURA, the sofa unfolding to make her bed. Upstage, center, and divided by a wide arch or second proscenium with transparent faded portieres (or second curtain), is the dining room. In an old-fashioned what-not in the living room are seen scores of transparent glass animals. A blown-up photograph of the father hangs on the wall of the living room, facing the audience, to the left of the archway. It is the face of a very handsome young man in a doughboy's First World War cap. He is gallantly smiling, ineluctably smiling, as if to say, "I will be smiling forever."

The audience hears and sees the opening scene in the dining room through both the transparent fourth wall of the building and the transparent gauze portieres of the dining-room arch. It is during this revealing scene that the fourth wall slowly ascends, out of sight. This transparent exterior wall is not brought down again until the very end of the play, during TOM's final speech.

The narrator is an undisguised convention of the play. He takes whatever license with dramatic convention as is convenient to his purposes.

TOM enters dressed as a merchant sailor from alley, stage left, and strolls across the front of the stage to the fire-escape. There he stops and lights a cigarette. He addresses the audience.

TOM   Yes, I have tricks in my pocket, I have things up my sleeve. But I am the opposite of a stage magician. He gives you illusion that has the appearance of truth. I give you truth in the pleasant disguise of illusion. To begin with, I turn back time. I reverse it to that quaint period, the thirties, when the huge middle class of America was matriculating in a school for the blind. Their eyes had failed them, or they had failed their eyes, and so they were having their fingers pressed forcibly down by the fiery Braille alphabet of a dissolving economy. In Spain there was revolution. Here there was only shouting and confusion. In Spain there was Guernica. Here there were disturbances of labor, sometimes pretty violent, in otherwise peaceful cities such as Chicago, Cleveland, Saint Louis. . . . This is the social background of the play.

(Music.)

The play is memory. Being a memory play, it is dimly lighted, it is sentimental, it is not realistic. In memory everything seems to happen to music. That explains the fiddle in the wings. I am the narrator of the play, and also a character in it. The other characters are my mother, Amanda, my sister, Laura, and a gentleman caller who appears in the final scenes. He is the most realistic character in the play, being an emissary from a world of reality that we were somehow set apart from. But since I have a poet's weakness for symbols, I am using this character also as a symbol; he is the long delayed but always expected something that we live for. There is a fifth character in the play who doesn't appear except in this larger-than-life photograph over the mantel. This is our father who left us a long time ago. He was a telephone man who fell in love with long distances; he gave up his job with the telephone company and skipped the light fantastic out of town . . . The last we heard of him was a picture post-card from Mazatlan, on the Pacific coast of Mexico, containing a message of two words—"Hello—Goodbye!" and an address. I think the rest of the play will explain itself. . . .

(*Amanda's voice becomes audible through the portieres.*)

(*Legend on screen: "Où sont les neiges."*)

(*He divides the portieres and enters the upstage area.*

AMANDA *and* LAURA *are seated at a drop-leaf table. Eating is indicated by gestures without food or utensils.* AMANDA *faces the audience.* TOM *and* LAURA *are seated in profile.*

The interior has lit up softly and through the scrim we see AMANDA *and* LAURA *seated at the table in the upstage area.*)

AMANDA (*calling*) Tom?

TOM Yes, Mother.

AMANDA We can't say grace until you come to the table!

TOM Coming, Mother. (*He bows slightly and withdraws, reappearing a few moments later in his place at the table.*)

AMANDA (*to her son*) Honey, don't *push* with your *fingers*. If you have to push with something, the thing to push with is a crust of bread. And chew—chew! Animals have sections in their stomachs which enable them to digest food without mastication, but human beings are supposed to chew their food before they swallow it down. Eat food leisurely, son, and really enjoy it. A well-cooked meal has lots of delicate flavors that have to be held in the mouth for appreciation. So chew your food and give your salivary glands a chance to function!

(TOM *deliberately lays his imaginary fork down and pushes his chair back from the table.*)

TOM I haven't enjoyed one bite of this dinner because of your constant directions on how to eat it. It's you that makes me rush through meals with your hawk-like attention to every bite I take. Sickening—spoils my appetite—all this discussion of animals' secretion—salivary glands—mastication!

AMANDA (*lightly*) Temperament like a Metropolitan star! (*He rises and crosses downstage.*) You're not excused from the table.

TOM I am getting a cigarette.

AMANDA You smoke too much.

(Laura *rises.*)

LAURA   I'll bring in the blanc mange.

(*He remains standing with his cigarette by the portieres during the following.*)

AMANDA (*rising*)   No, sister, no, sister—you be the lady this time and I'll be the darky.
LAURA   I'm already up.
AMANDA   Resume your seat, little sister—I want you to stay fresh and pretty—for gentlemen callers!
LAURA   I'm not expecting any gentlemen callers.
AMANDA (*crossing out to kitchenette; airily*)   Sometimes they come when they are least expected! Why, I remember one Sunday afternoon in Blue Mountain—(*enters kitchenette*)
TOM   I know what's coming!
LAURA   Yes. But let her tell it.
TOM   Again?
LAURA   She loves to tell it.

(AMANDA *returns with bowl of dessert.*)

AMANDA   One Sunday afternoon in Blue Mountain—your mother received— seventeen!—gentlemen callers! Why, sometimes there weren't chairs enough to accommodate them all. We had to send the nigger over to bring in folding chairs from the parish house.
TOM (*remaining at portieres*)   How did you entertain those gentlemen callers?
AMANDA   I understood the art of conversation!
TOM   I bet you could talk.
AMANDA   Girls in those days *knew* how to talk, I can tell you.
TOM   Yes?

(*Image: Amanda as a girl on a porch greeting callers.*)

AMANDA   They knew how to entertain their gentlemen callers. It wasn't enough for a girl to be possessed of a pretty face and a graceful figure—although I wasn't slighted in either respect. She also needed to have a nimble wit and a tongue to meet all occasions.
TOM   What did you talk about?
AMANDA   Things of importance going on in the world! Never anything coarse or common or vulgar. (*She addresses* TOM *as though he were seated in the vacant chair at the table though he remains by portieres. He plays this scene as though he held the book.*) My callers were gentlemen—all! Among my callers were some of the most prominent young planters of the Mississippi Delta—planters and sons of planters!

(TOM *motions for music and a spot of light on* AMANDA. *Her eyes lift, her face glows, her voice becomes rich and elegiac.*)

(*Screen legend: "Où sont les neiges."*)

There was young Champ Laughlin who later became vice-president of the Delta Planters Bank. Hadley Stevenson who was drowned in Moon Lake and left his widow one hundred and fifty thousand in Government bonds. There were the Cutrere brothers, Wesley and Bates. Bates was one of my bright particular beaux! He got in a quarrel with that wild Wainright boy. They shot it out on the floor of Moon Lake Casino. Bates was shot through the stomach. Died in the ambulance on his way to Memphis. His widow was also well-provided for, came into eight or ten thousand acres, that's all. She married him on the rebound—never loved her—carried my picture on him the night he died! And there was that boy that every girl in the Delta had set her cap for! That beautiful, brilliant young Fitzhugh boy from Green County!

TOM   What did he leave his widow?

AMANDA   He never married! Gracious, you talk as though all of my old admirers had turned up their toes to the daisies!

TOM   Isn't this the first you mentioned that still survives?

AMANDA   That Fitzhugh boy went North and made a fortune—came to be known as the Wolf of Wall Street! He had the Midas touch, whatever he touched turned to gold! And I could have been Mrs. Duncan J. Fitzhugh, mind you! But—I picked your *father!*

LAURA (*rising*)   Mother, let me clear the table.

AMANDA   No, dear, you go in front and study your typewriter chart. Or practice your shorthand a little. Stay fresh and pretty—It's almost time for our gentlemen callers to start arriving. (*She flounces girlishly toward the kitchenette.*) How many do you suppose we're going to entertain this afternoon?

(TOM *throws down the paper and jumps up with a groan.*)

LAURA (*alone in the dining room*)   I don't believe we're going to receive any, Mother.

AMANDA (*reappearing, airily*)   What? No one—not one? You must be joking! (LAURA *nervously echoes her laugh. She slips in a fugitive manner through the half-open portieres and draws them gently behind her. A shaft of very clear light is thrown on her face against the faded tapestry of the curtains. Music: "The Glass Menagerie" under faintly; lightly.*) Not one gentleman caller? It can't be true! There must be a flood, there must have been a tornado!

LAURA   It isn't a flood, it's not a tornado, Mother. I'm just not popular like you were in Blue Mountain. . . . (TOM *utters another groan.* LAURA *glances at him with a faint, apologetic smile; her voice catching a little.*) Mother's afraid I'm going to be an old maid.

(*The scene dims out with "Glass Menagerie" music.*)

Scene II

(*"Laura, Haven't You Ever Liked Some Boy?"*)

On the dark stage the screen is lighted with the image of blue roses.
  Gradually LAURA's *figure becomes apparent and the screen goes out.*
  The music subsides.
  LAURA *is seated in the delicate ivory chair at the small clawfoot table.*
  She wears a dress of soft violet material for a kimono—her hair tied back from her forehead with a ribbon.
  She is washing and polishing her collection of glass.
  AMANDA *appears on the fire-escape steps. At the sound of her ascent,* LAURA *catches her breath, thrusts the bowl of ornaments away and seats herself stiffly before the diagram of the typewriter keyboard as though it held her spellbound. Something has happened to* AMANDA. *It is written in her face as she climbs to the landing: a look that is grim and hopeless and a little absurd.*
  She has on one of those cheap or imitation velvety-looking cloth coats with imitation fur collar. Her hat is five or six years old, one of those dreadful cloche hats that were worn in the late twenties and she is clasping an enormous black patent-leather pocket-book with nickel clasp and initials. This is her full-dress outfit, the one she usually wears to the D.A.R.
  Before entering she looks through the door.
  She purses her lips, opens her eyes wide, rolls them upward, and shakes her head.
  Then she slowly lets herself in the door. Seeing her mother's expression LAURA *touches her lips with a nervous gesture.*

LAURA   Hello, Mother, I was—(*She makes a nervous gesture toward the chart on the wall.* AMANDA *leans against the shut door and stares at* LAURA *with a martyred look.*)

AMANDA   Deception? Deception? (*She slowly removes her hat and gloves, continuing the swift suffering stare. She lets the hat and gloves fall on the floor—a bit of acting.*)

LAURA (*shakily*)   How was the D.A.R. meeting? (AMANDA *slowly opens her purse and removes a dainty white handkerchief which she shakes out delicately and delicately touches to her lips and nostrils.*) Didn't you go to the D.A.R. meeting, Mother?

AMANDA (*faintly, almost inaudibly*)   —No.—No. (*then more forcibly*) I did not have the strength—to go to the D.A.R. In fact, I did not have the courage! I wanted to find a hole in the ground and hide myself in it forever! (*She crosses slowly to the wall and removes the diagram of the typewriter keyboard. She holds it in front of her for a second, staring at it sweetly and sorrowfully—then bites her lips and tears it in two pieces.*)

LAURA (*faintly*)   Why did you do that, Mother? (AMANDA *repeats the same procedure with the chart of the Gregg Alphabet.*) Why are you—

AMANDA   Why? Why? How old are you, Laura?

LAURA   Mother, you know my age.

AMANDA   I thought that you were an adult; it seems that I was mistaken. (*She crosses slowly to the sofa and sinks down and stares at* LAURA.)

LAURA   Please don't stare at me, Mother.

(AMANDA *closes her eyes and lowers her head. Count ten.*)

AMANDA   What are we going to do, what is going to become of us, what is the future?

(*Count ten.*)

LAURA   Has something happened, Mother? (AMANDA *draws a long breath and takes out the handkerchief again; dabbing process.*) Mother, has—something happened?

AMANDA   I'll be all right in a minute. I'm just bewildered—(*Count five.*)—by life. . . .

LAURA   Mother, I wish that you would tell me what's happened.

AMANDA   As you know, I was supposed to be inducted into my office at the D.A.R. this afternoon. (IMAGE: A SWARM OF TYPEWRITERS.) But I stopped off at Rubicam's Business College to speak to your teachers about your having a cold and ask them what progress they thought you were making down there.

LAURA   Oh. . . .

AMANDA   I went to the typing instructor and introduced myself as your mother. She didn't know who you were. Wingfield, she said. We don't have any such student enrolled at the school! I assured her she did, that you had been going to classes since early in January. "I wonder," she said, "if you could be talking about that terribly shy little girl who dropped out of school after only a few days' attendance?" "No," I said, "Laura, my daughter, has been going to school every day for the past six weeks!" "Excuse me," she said. She took the attendance book out and there was your name, unmistakably printed, and all the dates you were absent until they decided that you had dropped out of school. I still said, "No, there must have been some mistake! There must have been some mix-up in the records!" And she said, "No—I remember her perfectly now. Her hand shook so that she couldn't hit the right keys! The first time we gave a speed-test, she broke down completely—was sick at the stomach and almost had to be carried into the wash-room! After that morning she never showed up any more. We phoned the house but never got any answer—while I was working at Famous and Barr, I suppose, demonstrating those—Oh!" I felt so weak I could barely keep on my feet! I had to sit down while they got me a glass of water! Fifty dollars' tuition, all of our plans—my hopes and ambitions for you—just gone up the spout, just gone up the spout like that. (LAURA *draws a long breath and gets awkwardly to her feet. She crosses to the victrola and winds it up.*) What are you doing?

LAURA   Oh! (*She releases the handle and returns to her seat.*)

AMANDA   Laura, where have you been going when you've gone out pretending that you were going to business college?

LAURA   I've just been going out walking.

AMANDA   That's not true.

LAURA   It is. I just went walking.

AMANDA   Walking? Walking? In winter? Deliberately courting pneumonia in that light coat? Where did you walk to, Laura?

LAURA   All sorts of places—mostly in the park.

AMANDA   Even after you'd started catching that cold?

LAURA   It was the lesser of two evils, Mother. (IMAGE: WINTER SCENE IN PARK.) I couldn't go back up. I—threw up—on the floor!

AMANDA   From half past seven till after five every day you mean to tell me you walked around in the park, because you wanted to make me think that you were still going to Rubicam's Business College?

LAURA   It wasn't as bad as it sounds. I went inside places to get warmed up.

AMANDA   Inside where?

LAURA   I went in the art museum and the bird-houses at the Zoo. I visited the penguins every day! Sometimes I did without lunch and went to the movies. Lately I've been spending most of my afternoons in the Jewel-box, that big glass house where they raise the tropical flowers.

AMANDA   You did all this to deceive me, just for the deception? (LAURA *looks down.*) Why?

LAURA   Mother, when you're disappointed, you get that awful suffering look on your face, like the picture of Jesus' mother in the museum!

AMANDA   Hush!

LAURA   I couldn't face it.

(*Pause. A whisper of strings.*)

(*Legend: "The crust of humility."*)

AMANDA   (*hopelessly fingering the huge pocketbook*)   So what are we going to do the rest of our lives? Stay home and watch the parades go by? Amuse ourselves with the glass menagerie, darling? Eternally play those worn-out phonograph records your father left as a painful reminder of him? We won't have a business career—we've given that up because it gave us nervous indigestion! (*laughs wearily*) What is there left but dependency all our lives? I know so well what becomes of unmarried women who aren't prepared to occupy a position. I've seen such pitiful cases in the South—barely tolerated spinsters living upon the grudging patronage of sister's husband or brother's wife!—stuck away in some little mouse-trap of a room—encouraged by one in-law to visit another—little birdlike women without any nest—eating the crust of humility all their life! Is that the future that we've mapped out for ourselves? I swear it's the only alternative I can think of! It isn't a very pleasant alternative, is it? Of course—some girls *do marry*. (LAURA *twists her hands nervously.*) Haven't you ever liked some boy?

LAURA   Yes. I liked one once. (*rises*) I came across his picture a while ago.

AMANDA (*with some interest*)   He gave you his picture?

LAURA   No, it's in the year-book.

AMANDA (*disappointed*)   Oh—a high-school boy.

(Screen image: Jim as a high-school hero bearing a silver cup.)

LAURA   Yes. His name was Jim. (LAURA *lifts the heavy annual from the claw-foot table.*) Here he is in *The Pirates of Penzance*.

AMANDA (*absently*)   The what?

LAURA   The operetta the senior class put on. He had a wonderful voice and we sat across the aisle from each other Mondays, Wednesdays and Fridays in the Aud. Here he is with the silver cup for debating! See his grin?

AMANDA (*absently*)   He must have had a jolly disposition.

LAURA   He used to call me—Blue Roses.

(Image: Blue roses.)

AMANDA   Why did he call you such a name as that?

AMANDA   When I had that attack of pleurosis—he asked me what was the matter when I came back. I said pleurosis—he thought that I said Blue Roses! So that's what he always called me after that. Whenever he saw me, he'd holler, "Hello, Blue Roses!" I didn't care for the girl that he went out with. Emily Meisenbach. Emily was the best-dressed girl at Soldan. She never struck me, though, as being sincere . . . It says in the Personal Section— they're engaged. That's—six years ago! They must be married by now.

AMANDA   Girls that aren't cut out for business careers usually wind up married to some nice man. (*gets up with a spark of revival*) Sister, that's what you'll do!

(LAURA *utters a startled, doubtful laugh. She reaches quickly for a piece of glass.*)

LAURA   But, Mother—

AMANDA   Yes? (*crossing to photograph*)

LAURA (*in a tone of frightened apology*)   I'm—crippled!

(Image: Screen.)

AMANDA   Nonsense! Laura, I've told you never, never to use that word. Why, you're not crippled, you just have a little defect—hardly noticeable, even! When people have some slight disadvantage like that, they cultivate other things to make up for it—develop charm—and vivacity—and—*charm!*

That's all you have to do! (*She turns again to the photograph.*) One thing your father had *plenty of*—was *charm!*

(Tom *motions to the fiddle in the wings.*)

(*The scene fades out with music.*)

Scene III

(*Legend on screen: "After the fiasco—"*)

Tom *speaks from the fire-escape landing.*

TOM   After the fiasco at Rubicam's Business College, the idea of getting a gentleman caller for Laura began to play a more important part in Mother's calculations. It became an obsession. Like some archetype of the universal unconscious, the image of the gentleman caller haunted our small apartment. . . . (IMAGE: YOUNG MAN AT DOOR WITH FLOWERS.) An evening at home rarely passed without some allusion to this image, this spectre, this hope. . . . Even when he wasn't mentioned, his presence hung in Mother's preoccupied look and in my sister's frightened, apologetic manner—hung like a sentence passed upon the Wingfields! Mother was a woman of action as well as words. She began to take logical steps in the planned direction. Late that winter and in the early spring—realizing that extra money would be needed to properly feather the nest and plume the bird—she conducted a vigorous campaign on the telephone, roping in subscribers to one of those magazines for matrons called *The Home-maker's Companion,* the type of journal that features the serialized sublimations of ladies of letters who think in terms of delicate cup-like breasts, slim, tapering waists, rich, creamy thighs, eyes like wood-smoke in autumn, fingers that soothe and caress like strains of music, bodies as powerful as Etruscan sculpture.

(*Screen image: Glamor magazine cover.*)

(AMANDA *enters with phone on long extension cord. She is spotted in the dim stage.*)

AMANDA   Ida Scott? This is Amanda Wingfield! We *missed* you at the D.A.R. last Monday! I said to myself: She's probably suffering with that sinus condition! How is that sinus condition? Horrors! Heaven have mercy!—You're a Christian martyr, yes, that's what you are, a Christian martyr! Well, I just now happened to notice that your subscription to the *Companion's* about to expire! Yes, it expires with the next issue, honey!—just when that wonderful new serial by Bessie Mae Hopper is getting off to such an exciting start. Oh, honey, it's something that you can't miss! You remember how *Gone With the Wind* took everybody by storm? You simply couldn't go out if you hadn't read it. All everybody *talked* was Scarlett O'Hara. Well, this is a book that critics already compare to *Gone With the Wind*. It's the *Gone With the Wind* of the post-World War generation!—What?—Burning?—Oh, honey, don't let them burn, go take a look in the oven and I'll hold the wire! Heavens—I think she's hung up!

(Dim out.)

(Legend on screen: "You think I'm in love with Continental Shoemakers?")

(Before the stage is lighted, the violent voices of TOM *and* AMANDA *are heard.*
They are quarreling behind the portieres. In front of them stands LAURA *with clenched hands and panicky expression.*
A clear pool of light on her figure throughout this scene.)

TOM   What in Christ's name am I—
AMANDA *(shrilly)*   Don't you use that—
TOM   Supposed to do!
AMANDA   Expression! Not in my—
TOM   Ohhh!
AMANDA   Presence! Have you gone out of your senses?
TOM   I have, that's true, *driven* out!
AMANDA   What is the matter with you, you—big—big—IDIOT!
TOM   Look—I've got *no thing,* no single thing—
AMANDA   Lower your voice!
TOM   In my life here that I can call my OWN! Everything is—
AMANDA   Stop that shouting!
TOM   Yesterday you confiscated my books! You had the nerve to—
AMANDA   I took that horrible novel back to the library—yes! That hideous book by that insane Mr. Lawrence. (TOM *laughs wildly.*) I cannot control the output of diseased minds or people who cater to them—(TOM *laughs still more wildly.*) BUT I WON'T ALLOW SUCH FILTH BROUGHT INTO MY HOUSE! No, no, no, no, no!
TOM   House, house! Who pays rent on it, who makes a slave of himself to—
AMANDA *(fairly screeching)*   Don't you DARE to—
TOM   No, no, I mustn't say things! *I've* got to just—
AMANDA   Let me tell you—
TOM   I don't want to hear any more! (*He tears the portieres open. The upstage area is lit with a turgid smoky red glow.*)

*(*AMANDA*'s hair is in metal curlers and she wears a very old bathrobe, much too large for her slight figure, a relic of the faithless Mr. Wingfield.*
An upright typewriter and a wild disarray of manuscripts is on the dropleaf table. The quarrel was probably precipitated by AMANDA*'s interruption of his creative labor. A chair lying overthrown on the floor.*
Their gesticulating shadows are cast on the ceiling by the fiery glow.)

AMANDA   You *will* hear more, you—

TOM   No, I won't hear more, I'm going out!

AMANDA   You come right back in—

TOM   Out, out out! Because I'm—

AMANDA   Come back here, Tom Wingfield! I'm not through talking to you!

TOM   Oh, go—

LAURA (*desperately*)   —Tom!

AMANDA   You're going to listen, and no more insolence from you! I'm at the end of my patience! (*He comes back toward her.*)

TOM   What do you think I'm at? Aren't I supposed to have any patience to reach the end of, Mother? I know, I know. It seems unimportant to you, what I'm *doing*—what I *want* to do—having a little *difference* between them! You don't think that—

AMANDA   I think you've been doing things that you're ashamed of. That's why you act like this. I don't believe that you go every night to the movies. Nobody goes to the movies night after night. Nobody in their right minds goes to the movies as often as you pretend to. People don't go to the movies at nearly midnight, and movies don't let out at two A.M. Come in stumbling. Muttering to yourself like a maniac! You get three hours sleep and then go to work. Oh, I can picture the way you're doing down there. Moping, doping, because you're in no condition.

TOM (*wildly*)   No, I'm in no condition!

AMANDA   What right have you got to jeopardize your job? Jeopardize the security of us all? How do you think we'd manage if you were—

TOM   Listen! You think I'm crazy *about* the *warehouse*? (*He bends fiercely toward her slight figure.*) You think I'm in love with the Continental Shoemakers? You think I want to spend fifty-five *years* down there in that—*celotex interior!* with—*fluorescent—tubes!* Look! I'd rather somebody picked up a crowbar and battered out my brains—than go back mornings! I *go!* Every time you come in yelling that God damn "*Rise and Shine!*" "*Rise and Shine!*" I say to myself "How *lucky dead* people are!" But I get up. I *go!* For sixty-five dollars a month I give up all that I dream of doing and being *ever!* And you say self—*self's* all I ever think of. Why, listen, if self is what I thought of, Mother, I'd be where he is—GONE! (*pointing to father's picture*) As far as the system of transportation reaches! (*He starts past her. She grabs his arm.*) Don't grab me, Mother!

AMANDA   Where are you going?

TOM   I'm going to the *movies!*

AMANDA   I don't believe that lie!

TOM (*crouching toward her, overtowering her tiny figure. She backs away, gasping.*)   I'm going to opium dens! Yes, opium dens, dens of vice and criminals' hangouts, Mother. I've joined the Hogan gang, I'm a hired assassin, I carry a tommy-gun in a violin case! I run a string of cat-houses in the Valley! They call me Killer, Killer Wingfield, I'm leading a double-life, a simple, honest warehouse worker by day, by night, a dynamic *czar* of the *underworld,*

Mother. I go to gambling casinos, I spin away fortunes on the roulette table! I wear a patch over one eye and a false mustache, sometimes I put on green whiskers. On those occasions they call me—*El Diablo!* Oh, I could tell you things to make you sleepless! My enemies plan to dynamite this place. They're going to blow us all sky-high some night! I'll be glad, very happy, and so will you! You'll go up, up on a broomstick, over Blue Mountain with seventeen gentlemen callers! You ugly—babbling old—*witch.* . . . (*He goes through a series of violent, clumsy movements, seizing his overcoat, lunging to the door, pulling it fiercely open. The women watch him, aghast. His arm catches in the sleeve of the coat as he struggles to pull it on. For a moment he is pinioned by the bulky garment. With an outraged groan he tears the coat off again, splitting the shoulders of it, and hurls it across the room. It strikes against the shelf of* LAURA'*s glass collection, there is a tinkle of shattering glass.* LAURA *cries out as if wounded.*)

(*Music legend: "The Glass Menagerie."*)

LAURA (*shrilly*) *My glass!*—menagerie. . . . (*She covers her face and turns away.*)

(*But* AMANDA *is still stunned and stupefied by the "ugly witch" so that she barely notices this occurrence. Now she recovers her speech.*)

AMANDA (*in an awful voice*) I won't speak to you—until you apologize! (*She crosses through portieres and draws them together behind her.* TOM *is left with* LAURA. LAURA *clings weakly to the mantel with her face averted.* TOM *stares at her stupidly for a moment. Then he crosses to shelf. Drops awkwardly to his knees to collect the fallen glass, glancing at* LAURA *as if he would speak but couldn't.*)

"*The Glass Menagerie*" steals in as

(*The scene dims out.*)

Scene IV

The interior is dark. Faint light in the alley.

A deep-voiced bell in a church is tolling the hour of five as the scene commences.

TOM *appears at the top of the alley. After each solemn boom of the bell in the tower, he shakes a little noise-maker or rattle as if to express the tiny spasm of man in contrast to the sustained power and dignity of the Almighty. This and the unsteadiness of his advance make it evident that he has been drinking.*

As he climbs the few steps to the fire-escape landing light steals up inside. LAURA *appears in night-dress, observing* TOM'*s empty bed in the front room.*

TOM *fishes in his pockets for the door-key, removing a motley assortment of articles in the search, including a perfect shower of movie-ticket stubs and an empty bottle. At last he finds the key, but just as he is about to insert it, it slips from his fingers. He strikes a match and crouches below the door.*

TOM (*bitterly*)   One crack—and it falls through!

(LAURA *opens the door.*)

LAURA   Tom! Tom, what are you doing?

TOM   Looking for a door-key.

LAURA   Where have you been all this time?

TOM   I have been to the movies.

LAURA   All this time at the movies?

TOM   There was a very long program. There was a Garbo picture and a Mickey Mouse and a travelogue and a newsreel and a preview of coming attractions. And there was an organ solo and a collection for the milk-fund—simultaneously—which ended up in a terrible fight between a fat lady and an usher!

LAURA (*innocently*)   Did you have to stay through everything?

TOM   Of course! And, oh, I forgot! There was a big stage show! The headliner on this stage show was Malvolio the Magician. He performed wonderful tricks, many of them, such as pouring water back and forth between pitchers. First it turned to wine and then it turned to beer and then it turned to whiskey. I know it was whiskey it finally turned into because he needed somebody to come up out of the audience to help him, and I came up—both shows! It was Kentucky Straight Bourbon. A very generous fellow, he gave souvenirs. (*He pulls from his back pocket a shimmering rainbow-colored scarf.*) He gave me this. This is his magic scarf. You can have it, Laura. You wave it over a canary cage and you get a bowl of gold-fish. You wave it over the gold-fish bowl and they fly away canaries. . . . But the wonderfullest trick of all was the coffin trick. We nailed him into a coffin and he got out of the coffin without removing one nail. (*He has come inside.*) There is a trick that would come in handy for me—get me out of this 2 by 4 situation! (*flops onto bed and starts removing shoes*)

LAURA   Tom—Shhh!

TOM   What you shushing me for?

LAURA   You'll wake up Mother.

TOM   Goody, goody! Pay 'er back for all those "Rise an' Shines." (*lies down, groaning*) You know it don't take much intelligence to get yourself into a nailed-up coffin, Laura. But who in hell ever got himself out of one without removing one nail?

(*As if in answer, the father's grinning photograph lights up.*)

(*Scene dims out.*)

(*Immediately following: The church bell is heard striking six. At the sixth stroke the alarm clock goes off in* AMANDA*'s room, and after a few moments we hear her calling: "Rise and Shine! Rise and Shine! Laura, go tell your brother to rise and shine!"*)

TOM (*sitting up slowly*)   I'll rise—but I won't shine.

(*The light increases.*)

AMANDA   Laura, tell your brother his coffee is ready.

(LAURA *slips into front room.*)

LAURA   Tom! it's nearly seven. Don't make Mother nervous. (*He stares at her stupidly, beseechingly.*) Tom, speak to Mother this morning. Make up with her, apologize, speak to her!

TOM   She won't to me. It's her that started not speaking.

LAURA   If you just say you're sorry she'll start speaking.

TOM   Her not speaking—is that such a tragedy?

LAURA   Please—please!

AMANDA (*calling from kitchenette*)   Laura, are you going to do what I asked you to do, or do I have to get dressed and go out myself?

LAURA   Going, going—soon as I get on my coat! (*She pulls on a shapeless felt hat with nervous, jerky movement, pleadingly glancing at* TOM. *Rushes awkwardly for coat. The coat is one of* AMANDA'S, *inaccurately made-over, the sleeves too short for* LAURA.) Butter and what else?

AMANDA (*entering upstage*)   Just butter. Tell them to charge it.

LAURA   Mother, they make such faces when I do that.

AMANDA   Sticks and stones may break my bones, but the expression on Mr. Garfinkel's face won't harm us! Tell your brother his coffee is getting cold.

LAURA (*at door*)   Do what I asked you, will you, will you, Tom?

(*He looks sullenly away.*)

AMANDA   Laura, go now or just don't go at all!

LAURA (*rushing out*)   Going—going! (*A second later she cries out.* TOMS *springs up and crosses to the door.* AMANDA *rushes anxiously in.* TOM *opens the door.*)

TOM   Laura?

LAURA   I'm all right. I slipped, but I'm all right.

AMANDA (*peering anxiously after her*)   If anyone breaks a leg on those fire-escape steps, the landlord ought to be sued for every cent he possesses! (*She shuts door, remembers she isn't speaking, and returns to other room.*)

(*As* TOM *enters listlessly for his coffee, she turns her back to him and stands rigidly facing the window on the gloomy gray vault of the areaway. Its light on her face with its aged but childish features is cruelly sharp, satirical as a Daumier print.*)

(*Music under: "Ave Maria."*)

(*TOM glances sheepishly but sullenly at her averted figure and slumps at the table. The coffee is scalding hot; he sips it and gasps and spits it back in the cup. At his gasp,* AMANDA *catches her breath and half turns. Then catches herself and turns back to window.*

TOM blows on his coffee, glancing sidewise at his mother. She clears her throat. TOM clears his. He starts to rise. Sinks back down again, scratches his head, clears his throat again. AMANDA *coughs.* TOM *raises his cup in both hands to blow on it, his eyes staring over the rim of it at his mother for several moments. Then he slowly sets the cup down and awkwardly and hesitantly rises from the chair.*)

TOM (*hoarsely*)   Mother. I—I apologize. Mother. (AMANDA *draws a quick, shuddering breath. Her face works grotesquely. She breaks into childlike tears.*) I'm sorry for what I said, for everything that I said, I didn't mean it.

AMANDA (*sobbingly*)   My devotion has made me a witch and so I make myself hateful to my children!

TOM   No, you *don't*.

AMANDA   I worry so much, don't sleep, it makes me nervous!

TOM (*gently*)   I understand that.

AMANDA   I've had to put up a solitary battle all these years. But you're my right-hand bower! Don't fall down, don't fail!

TOM (*gently*)   I try, Mother.

AMANDA (*with great enthusiasm*)   Try and you will SUCCEED! (*The notion makes her breathless.*) Why, you—you're just *full* of natural endowments! Both of my children—they're *unusual* children! Don't you think I know it? I'm so—*proud!* Happy and—feel I've—so much to be thankful for but— Promise me one thing, son!

TOM   What, Mother?

AMANDA   Promise, son, you'll—never be a drunkard!

TOM (*turns to her grinning*)   I will never be a drunkard, Mother.

AMANDA   That's what frightened me so, that you'd be drinking! Eat a bowl of Purina!

TOM   Just coffee, Mother.

AMANDA   Shredded wheat biscuit?

TOM   No. No, Mother, just coffee.

AMANDA   You can't put in a day's work on an empty stomach. You've got ten minutes—don't gulp! Drinking too-hot liquids makes cancer of the stomach. . . . Put cream in.

TOM   No, thank you.

AMANDA   To cool it.

TOM   No! No, thank you, I want it black.

AMANDA   I know, but it's not good for you. We have to do all that we can to build ourselves up. In these trying times we live in, all that we have to cling to is—each other. . . . That's why it's so important to—Tom, I—I sent out your sister so I could discuss something with you. If you hadn't spoken I would have spoken to you. (*sits down*)

TOM (*gently*)   What is it, Mother, that you want to discuss?

AMANDA   Laura!

(TOM *puts his cup down slowly.*)

(*Legend on screen: "Laura."*)

(Music: "The Glass Menagerie.")

TOM —Oh.—Laura . . .

AMANDA (*touching his sleeve*) You know how Laura is. So quiet but—still water runs deep! She notices things and I think she—broods about them. (TOM *looks up.*) A few days ago I came in and she was crying.

TOM What about?

AMANDA You.

TOM Me?

AMANDA She has an idea that you're not happy here.

TOM What gave her that idea?

AMANDA What gives her any idea? However, you do act strangely. I—I'm not criticizing, understand *that!* I know your ambitions do not lie in the warehouse, that like everybody in the whole wide world—you've had to—make sacrifices, but—Tom—Tom—life's not easy, it calls for—Spartan endurance! There's so many things in my heart that I cannot describe to you! I've never told you but I—*loved* your father. . . .

TOM (*gently*) I know that, Mother.

AMANDA And you—when I see you taking after his ways! Staying out late—and—well, you *had* been drinking the night you were in that—terrifying condition! Laura says that you hate the apartment and that you go out nights to get away from it! Is that true, Tom?

TOM No. You say there's so much in your heart that you can't describe to me. That's true of me, too. There's so much in my heart that I can't describe to *you!* So let's respect each other's—

AMANDA But, why—*why*, Tom—are you always so *restless?* Where do you go to, nights?

TOM I—go to the movies.

AMANDA Why do you go to the movies so much, Tom?

TOM I go to the movies because—I like adventure. Adventure is something I don't have much of at work, so I go to the movies.

AMANDA But, Tom, you go to the movies *entirely* too *much!*

TOM I like a lot of adventure.

(AMANDA *looks baffled, then hurt. As the familiar inquisition resumes he becomes hard and impatient again.* AMANDA *slips back into her querulous attitude toward him.*)

(Image on screen: Sailing vessel with Jolly Roger.)

AMANDA Most young men find adventure in their careers.

TOM Then most young men are not employed in a warehouse.

AMANDA The world is full of young men employed in warehouses and offices and factories.

TOM Do all of them find adventure in their careers?

AMANDA   They do or they do without it! Not everybody has a craze for adventure.

TOM   Man is by instinct a lover, a hunter, a fighter, and none of those instincts are given much play at the warehouse!

AMANDA   Man is by instinct! Don't quote instinct to me! Instinct is something that people have got away from! It belongs to animals! Christian adults don't want it!

TOM   What do Christian adults want, then, Mother?

AMANDA   Superior things! Things of the mind and the spirit! Only animals have to satisfy instincts! Surely your aims are somewhat higher than theirs! Than monkeys—pigs—

TOM   I reckon they're not.

AMANDA   You're joking. However, that isn't what I wanted to discuss.

TOM (*rising*)   I haven't much time.

AMANDA (*pushing his shoulders*)   Sit down.

TOM   You want me to punch in red at the warehouse, Mother?

AMANDA   You have five minutes. I want to talk about Laura.

(Legend: "Plans and provisions.")

TOM   All right! What about Laura?

AMANDA   We have to be making plans and provisions for her. She's older than you, two years, and nothing has happened. She just drifts along doing nothing. It frightens me terribly how she just drifts along.

TOM   I guess she's the type that people call home girls.

AMANDA   There's no such type, and if there is, it's a pity! That is unless the home is hers, with a husband!

TOM   What?

AMANDA   Oh, I can see the handwriting on the wall as plain as I see the nose in front of my face! It's terrifying! More and more you remind me of your father! He was out all hours without explanation—Then *left! Goodbye!* And me with a bag to hold. I saw that letter you got from the Merchant Marine. I know what you're dreaming of. I'm not standing here blindfolded. Very well, then. Then *do* it! But not till there's somebody to take your place.

TOM   What do you mean?

AMANDA   I mean that as soon as Laura has got somebody to take care of her, married, a home of her own, independent—why, then you'll be free to go wherever you please, on land, on sea, whichever way the wind blows! But until that time you've got to look out for your sister. I don't say me because I'm old and don't matter! I say for your sister because she's young and dependent. I put her in business college—a dismal failure! Frightened her so it made her sick to her stomach. I took her over to the Young People's League at the church. Another fiasco. She spoke to nobody, nobody spoke to her.

Now all she does is fool with those pieces of glass and play those worn-out records. What kind of life is that for a girl to lead?

TOM What can I do about it?

AMANDA Overcome selfishness! Self, self, self is all that you ever think of! (TOM *springs up and crosses to get his coat. It is ugly and bulky. He pulls on a cap with earmuffs.*) Where is your muffler? Put your wool muffler on! (*He snatches it angrily from the closet and tosses it around his neck and pulls both ends tight.*) Tom! I haven't said what I had in mind to ask you.

TOM I'm too late to—

AMANDA (*catching his arm—very importunately; then shyly:*) Down at the warehouse, aren't there some—nice young men?

TOM No!

AMANDA There *must* be—*some* . . .

TOM Mother—

(*Gesture.*)

AMANDA Find out one that's clean-living—doesn't drink and—ask him out for sister!

TOM What?

AMANDA For *sister!* To *meet!* Get *acquainted!*

TOM (*stamping to door*) Oh, my go-osh!

AMANDA Will you? (*He opens door; imploringly:*) Will you? (*He starts down.*) Will you? *Will* you, dear?

TOM (*calling back*) YES!

(AMANDA *closes the door hesitantly and with a troubled but faintly hopeful expression.*)

(*Screen image: Glamor magazine cover.*)

(*Spot* AMANDA *at phone.*)

AMANDA Ella Cartwright? This is Amanda Wingfield! How are you, honey? How is that kidney condition? (*Count five.*) Horrors! (*Count five.*) You're a Christian martyr, yes, honey, that's what you are, a Christian martyr! Well, I just happened to notice in my little red book that your subscription to the *Companion* has just run out! I knew that you wouldn't want to miss out on the wonderful serial starting in this new issue. It's by Bessie Mae Hopper, the first thing she's written since *Honeymoon for Three.* Wasn't that a strange and interesting story? Well, this one is even lovelier, I believe. It has a sophisticated society background. It's all about the horsey set on Long Island!

(*Fade out.*)

Scene V

(Legend on screen: "Annunciation.")

Fade with music.

It is early dusk of a spring evening. Supper has just been finished in the Wingfield apartment. AMANDA *and* LAURA *in light colored dresses are removing dishes from the table, in the up-stage area, which is shadowy, their movements formalized almost as a dance or ritual, their moving forms as pale and silent as moths.*

Tom, in white shirt and trousers, rises from the table and crosses toward the fire escape.

AMANDA *(as he passes her)*   Son, will you do me a favor?

TOM   What?

AMANDA   Comb your hair! You look so pretty when your hair is combed! (TOM *slouches on sofa with evening paper; enormous caption "Franco Triumphs."*) There is only one respect in which I would like you to emulate your father.

TOM   What respect is that?

AMANDA   The care he always took of his appearance. He never allowed himself to look untidy. (*He throws down the paper and crosses to fire escape.*) Where are you going?

TOM   I'm going out to smoke.

AMANDA   You smoke too much. A pack a day at fifteen cents a pack. How much would that amount to in a month? Thirty times fifteen is how much, Tom? Figure it out and you will be astounded at what you could save. Enough to give you a night-school course in accounting at Washington U! Just think what a wonderful thing that would be for you, son!

(TOM *is unmoved by the thought.*)

TOM   I'd rather smoke. (*He steps out on landing, letting the screen door slam.*)

AMANDA *(sharply)*   I know! That's the tragedy of it. . . . (*Alone, she turns to look at her husband's picture.*)

(Dance music: "All the world is waiting for the sunrise!")

TOM *(to the audience)*   Across the alley from us was the Paradise Dance Hall. On evenings in spring the windows and doors were open and the music came outdoors. Sometimes the lights were turned out except for a large glass sphere that hung from the ceiling. It would turn slowly about and filter the dusk with delicate rainbow colors. Then the orchestra played a waltz or a tango, something that had a slow and sensuous rhythm. Couples would come outside, to the relative privacy of the alley. You could see them kissing behind ash-pits and telephone poles. This was the compensation for lives that passed like mine, without any change or adventure. Adventure and change were imminent in this year. They were waiting around the corner for all these kids. Suspended in the mist over Berchtesgaden, caught in the folds of Chamberlain's umbrella—In Spain there was Guernica! But here there was only hot swing music and liquor, dance halls, bars, and movies, and sex that hung in the gloom like a chandelier and flooded the world with brief, deceptive rainbows. . . . All the world was waiting for bombardments!

(AMANDA *turns from the picture and comes outside.*)

AMANDA (*sighing*)   A fire-escape landing's a poor excuse for a porch. (*She spreads a newspaper on a step and sits down, gracefully and demurely as if she were settling into a swing on a Mississippi veranda.*) What are you looking at?

TOM   The moon.

AMANDA   Is there a moon this evening?

TOM   It's rising over Garfinkel's Delicatessen.

AMANDA   So it is! A little silver slipper of a moon. Have you made a wish on it yet?

TOM   Um-hum.

AMANDA   What did you wish for?

TOM   That's a secret.

AMANDA   A secret, huh? Well, I won't tell mine either. I will be just as mysterious as you.

TOM   I bet I can guess what yours is.

AMANDA   Is my head so transparent?

TOM   You're not a sphinx.

AMANDA   No, I don't have secrets. I'll tell you what I wished for on the moon. Success and happiness for my precious children! I wish for that whenever there's a moon, and when there isn't a moon, I wish for it, too.

TOM   I thought perhaps you wished for a gentleman caller.

AMANDA   Why do you say that?

TOM   Don't you remember asking me to fetch one?

AMANDA   I remember suggesting that it would be nice for your sister if you brought home some nice young man from the warehouse. I think I've made that suggestion more than once.

TOM   Yes, you have made it repeatedly.

AMANDA   Well?

TOM   We are going to have one.

AMANDA   *What?*

TOM   A gentleman caller!

(*The annunciation is celebrated with music.*)

(AMANDA *rises.*)

(*Image on screen: Caller with bouquet.*)

AMANDA   You mean you have asked some nice young man to come over?

TOM   Yep. I've asked him to dinner.

AMANDA   You really did?

TOM   I did!

AMANDA   You did, and did he—*accept?*

TOM   He did!

AMANDA   Well, well—well, well! That's—lovely!

TOM   I thought that you would be pleased.

AMANDA   It's definite, then?

TOM   Very definite.

AMANDA   Soon?

TOM   Very soon.

AMANDA   For heaven's sake, stop putting on and tell me some things, will you?

TOM   What things do you want me to tell you?

AMANDA   *Naturally* I would like to know when he's *coming!*

TOM   He's coming tomorrow.

AMANDA   *Tomorrow?*

TOM   Yep. Tomorrow.

AMANDA   But, Tom!

TOM   Yes, Mother?

AMANDA   Tomorrow gives me no time!

TOM   Time for what?

AMANDA   Preparations! Why didn't you phone me at once, as soon as you asked him, the minute that he accepted? Then, don't you see, I could have been getting ready!

TOM   You don't have to make any fuss.

AMANDA   Oh, Tom, Tom, Tom, of course I have to make a fuss! I want things nice, not sloppy! Not thrown together. I'll certainly have to do some fast thinking, won't I?

TOM   I don't see why you have to think at all.

AMANDA   You just don't know. We can't have a gentleman caller in a pig-sty! All my wedding silver has to be polished, the monogrammed table linen ought to be laundered! The windows have to be washed and fresh curtains put up. And how about clothes? We have to *wear* something, don't we?

TOM   Mother, this boy is no one to make a fuss over!

AMANDA   Do you realize he's the first young man we've introduced to your sister? It's terrible, dreadful, disgraceful that poor little sister has never received a single gentleman caller! Tom, come inside! (*She opens the screen door.*)

TOM   What for?

AMANDA   I want to ask you some things.

TOM   If you're going to make such a fuss, I'll call it off, I'll tell him not to come.

AMANDA   You certainly won't do anything of the kind. Nothing offends people worse than broken engagements. It simply means I'll have to work like a Turk! We won't be brilliant, but we'll pass inspection. Come on inside. (TOM *follows, groaning.*) Sit down.

TOM   Any particular place you would like me to sit?

AMANDA   Thank heavens I've got that new sofa! I'm also making payments on a floor lamp I'll have sent out! And put the chintz covers on, they'll brighten things up! Of course I'd hoped to have these walls re-papered. . . . What is the young man's name?

TOM   His name is O'Connor.

AMANDA   That, of course, means fish—tomorrow is Friday! I'll have that salmon loaf—with Durkee's dressing! What does he do? He works at the warehouse?

TOM   Of course! How else would I—

AMANDA   Tom, he—doesn't drink?

TOM   Why do you ask me that?

AMANDA   Your father *did!*

TOM   Don't get started on that!

AMANDA   He *does* drink, then?

TOM   Not that I know of!

AMANDA   Make sure, be certain! The last thing I want for my daughter's a boy who drinks!

TOM   Aren't you being a little premature? Mr. O'Connor has not yet appeared on the scene!

AMANDA   But will tomorrow. To meet your sister, and what do I know about this character? Nothing! Old maids are better off than wives of drunkards!

TOM   Oh, my God!

AMANDA   Be still!

TOM   (*leaning forward to whisper*)   Lots of fellows meet girls whom they don't marry!

AMANDA   Oh, talk sensibly, Tom—and don't be sarcastic! (*She has gotten a hairbrush.*)

TOM   What are you doing?

AMANDA   I'm brushing that cow-lick down! What is this young man's position at the warehouse?

TOM   (*submitting grimly to the brush and the interrogation*)   This young man's position is that of a shipping clerk, Mother.

AMANDA   Sounds to me like a fairly responsible job, the sort of a job *you* would be in if you just had more *get-up.* What is his salary? Have you got any idea?

TOM   I would judge it to be approximately eighty-five dollars a month.

AMANDA   Well—not princely, but—

TOM   Twenty more than I make.

AMANDA   Yes, how well I know! But for a family man, eighty-five dollars a month is not much more than you can just get by on. . . .

TOM   Yes, but Mr. O'Connor is not a family man.

AMANDA   He might be, mightn't he? Some time in the future?

TOM   I see. Plans and provisions.

AMANDA   You are the only young man that I know of who ignores the fact that the future becomes the present, the present the past, and the past turns into everlasting regret if you don't plan for it!

TOM   I will think that over and see what I can make of it.

AMANDA   Don't be supercilious with your mother! Tell me some more about this—what do you call him?

TOM   James D. O'Connor. The D. is for Delaney.

AMANDA   Irish on *both* sides! *Gracious!* And doesn't drink?

TOM   Shall I call him up and ask him right this minute?

AMANDA   The only way to find out about those things is to make discreet inquiries at the proper moment. When I was a girl in Blue Mountain and it was suspected that a young man drank, the girl whose attentions he had been receiving, if any girl *was*, would sometimes speak to the minister of his church, or rather her father would if her father was living, and sort of feel him out on the young man's character. That is the way such things are discreetly handled to keep a young woman from making a tragic mistake!

TOM   Then how did you happen to make a tragic mistake?

AMANDA   That innocent look of your father's had everyone fooled! He *smiled*—the world was *enchanted!* No girl can do worse than put herself at the mercy of a handsome appearance! I hope that Mr. O'Connor is not too good-looking.

TOM   No, he's not too good-looking. He's covered with freckles and hasn't too much of a nose.

AMANDA   He's not right-down homely, though?

TOM   Not right-down homely. Just medium homely. I'd say.

AMANDA   Character's what to look for in a man.

TOM   That's what I've always said, Mother.

AMANDA   You've never said anything of the kind and I suspect you would never give it a thought.

TOM   Don't be suspicious of me.

AMANDA   At least I hope he's the type that's up and coming.

TOM   I think he really goes in for self-improvement.

AMANDA   What reason have you to think so?

TOM   He goes to night school.

AMANDA (*beaming*)   Splendid! What does he do, I mean study?

TOM   Radio engineering and public speaking!

AMANDA   Then he has visions of being advanced in the world! Any young man who studies public speaking is aiming to have an executive job some day! And radio engineering? A thing for the future! Both of these facts are very illuminating. Those are the sort of things that a mother should know concerning any young man who comes to call on her daughter. Seriously or—not.

TOM   One little warning. He doesn't know about Laura. I didn't let on that we had dark ulterior motives. I just said, why don't you come have dinner with us? He said okay and that was the whole conversation.

AMANDA   I bet it was! You're eloquent as an oyster. However, he'll know about Laura when he gets here. When he sees how lovely and sweet and pretty she is, he'll thank his lucky stars he was asked to dinner.

TOM   Mother, you mustn't expect too much of Laura.

AMANDA   What do you mean?

TOM   Laura seems all those things to you and me because she's ours and we love her. We don't even notice she's crippled any more.

AMANDA   Don't say crippled! You know that I never allow that word to be used!

TOM   But face facts, Mother. She is and—that's not all—

AMANDA   What do you mean "not all"?

TOM   Laura is very different from other girls.

AMANDA   I think the difference is all to her advantage.

TOM   Not quite all—in the eyes of others—strangers—she's terribly shy and lives in a world of her own and those things make her seem a little peculiar to people outside the house.

AMANDA   Don't say peculiar.

TOM   Face the facts. She is.

(*The dance-hall music changes to a tango that has a minor and somewhat ominous tone.*)

AMANDA   In what was is she peculiar—may I ask?

TOM (*gently*)   She lives in a world of her own—a world of—little glass ornaments, Mother. . . . (*Gets up.* AMANDA *remains holding brush, looking at him, troubled.*) She plays old phonograph records and—that's about all—(*He glances at himself in the mirror and crosses to door.*)

AMANDA (*sharply*)   Where are you going?

TOM   I'm going to the movies. (*out screen door*)

AMANDA   Not to the movies, every night to the movies! (*follows quickly to screen door*) I don't believe you always go to the movies! (*He is gone.* AMANDA *looks worriedly after him for a moment. Then vitality and optimism return and she turns from the door, crossing to portieres.*) Laura! Laura! (LAURA *answers from kitchenette.*)

LAURA   Yes, Mother.

AMANDA   Let those dishes go and come in front! (LAURA *appears with dish towel; gaily:*) Laura, come here and make a wish on the moon!

LAURA (*entering*)   Moon—moon?

AMANDA   A little silver slipper of a moon. Look over your left shoulder, Laura, and make a wish! (LAURA *looks faintly puzzled as if called out of sleep.* AMANDA *seizes her shoulders and turns her at an angle by the door.*) No! Now, darling, *wish!*

LAURA   What shall I wish for, Mother?

AMANDA (*her voice trembling and her eyes suddenly filling with tears*)   Happiness! Good Fortune!

(*The violin rises and the stage dims out.*)

Scene VI

(Image: High school hero.)

TOM   And so the following evening I brought Jim home to dinner. I had known Jim slightly in high school. In high school Jim was a hero. He had tremendous Irish good nature and vitality with the scrubbed and polished look of white chinaware. He seemed to move in a continual spotlight. He was a star in basketball, captain of the debating club, president of the senior class and the glee club and he sang the male lead in the annual light operas. He was always running or bounding, never just walking. He seemed always at the point of defeating the law of gravity. He was shooting with such velocity through his adolescence that you would logically expect him to arrive at nothing short of the White House by the time he was thirty. But Jim apparently ran into more interference after his graduation from Soldan. His speed had definitely slowed. Six years after he left high school he was holding a job that wasn't much better than mine.

(Image: Clerk.)

He was the only one at the warehouse with whom I was on friendly terms. I was valuable to him as someone who could remember his former glory, who had seen him win basketball games and the silver cup in debating. He knew of my secret practice of retiring to a cabinet of the washroom to work on poems when business was slack in the warehouse. He called me Shakespeare. And while the other boys in the warehouse regarded me with suspicious hostility, Jim took a humorous attitude toward me. Gradually his attitude affected the others, their hostility wore off and they also began to smile at me as people smile at an oddly fashioned dog who trots across their path at some distance.

I knew that Jim and Laura had known each other at Soldan, and I had heard Laura speak admiringly of his voice. I didn't know if Jim remembered her or not. In high school Laura had been as unobtrusive as Jim had been astonishing. If he did remember Laura, it was not as my sister, for when I asked him to dinner, he grinned and said, "You know, Shakespeare, I never thought of you as having folks!"

He was about to discover that I did. . . .

(Light up stage.)

(Legend on screen: "The accent of a coming foot.")

Friday evening. It is about five o'clock of a late spring evening which comes "scattering poems in the sky."

A delicate lemony light is in the Wingfield apartment.

AMANDA *has worked like a Turk in preparation for the gentleman caller. The results are astonishing. The new floor lamp with its rose-silk shade is in place, a colored paper lantern* *conceals the broken light fixture in the ceiling, new billowing white curtains are at the windows, chintz covers are on chairs and sofa, a pair of new sofa pillows make their initial appearance.*

Open boxes and tissue paper are scattered on the floor.

LAURA *stands in the middle with lifted arms while* AMANDA *crouches before her, adjusting the hem of the new dress, devout and ritualistic. The dress is colored and designed by memory. The arrangement of* LAURA'S *hair is changed; it is softer and more becoming. A fragile, unearthly prettiness has come out in* LAURA: *she is like a piece of translucent glass touched by light, given a momentary radiance, not actual, not lasting.*

AMANDA (*impatiently*)   Why are you trembling?

LAURA   Mother, you've made me so nervous!

AMANDA   How have I made you nervous?

LAURA   By all this fuss! You make it seem so important!

AMANDA   I don't understand you, Laura. You couldn't be satisfied with just sitting home, and yet whenever I try to arrange something for you, you seem to resist it. (*She gets up.*) Now take a look at yourself. No, wait! Wait just a moment—I have an idea!

LAURA   What is it now?

(AMANDA *produces two powder puffs which she wraps in handkerchiefs and stuffs in* LAURA'S *bosom.*)

LAURA   Mother, what are you doing?

AMANDA   They call them "Gay Deceivers"!

LAURA   I won't wear them!

AMANDA   You will!

LAURA   Why should I?

AMANDA   Because, to be painfully honest, your chest is flat.

LAURA   You make it seem like we were setting a trap.

AMANDA   All pretty girls are a trap, a pretty trap, and men expect them to be. (*Legend: "A pretty trap."*) Now look at yourself, young lady. This is the prettiest you will ever be! I've got to fix myself now! You're going to be surprised by your mother's appearance! (*She crosses through portieres, humming gaily.*)

(LAURA *moves slowly to the long mirror and stares solemnly at herself.*

A wind blows the white curtains inward in a slow, graceful motion and with a faint, sorrowful sighing.)

AMANDA (*off stage*)   It isn't dark enough yet. (*She turns slowly before the mirror with a troubled look.*)

(*Legend on screen: "This is my sister: celebrate her with strings!" Music.*)

AMANDA (*laughing, off*)   I'm going to show you something. I'm going to make a spectacular appearance!

LAURA   What is it, mother?

AMANDA   Possess your soul in patience—you will see! Something I've resurrected from that old trunk! Styles haven't changed so terribly much after all. . . . (*She parts the portieres.*) Now just look at your mother! (*She wears a girlish frock of yellowed voile with a blue silk sash. She carries a bunch of jonquils—the legend of her youth is nearly revived; feverishly:*) This is the dress in which I led the cotillion. Won the cakewalk twice at Sunset Hill, wore one spring to the Governor's ball in Jackson! See how I sashayed around the ballroom, Laura? (*She raises her skirt and does a mincing step around the room.*) I wore it on Sundays for my gentlemen callers! I had it on the day I met your father—I had malaria fever all that spring. The change of climate from East Tennessee to the Delta—weakened resistance—I had a little temperature all the time—not enough to be serious—just enough to make me restless and giddy! Invitations poured in—parties all over the Delta!—"Stay in bed," said Mother, "you have fever!"—but I just wouldn't.—I took quinine but kept on going, going!—Evenings, dances!—Afternoons, long, long, rides! Picnics—lovely!—So lovely, that country in May.—All lacy with dogwood, literally flooded with jonquils!—That was the spring I had the craze for jonquils. Jonquils became an absolute obsession. Mother said, "Honey, there's no more room for jonquils." And still I kept bringing in more jonquils. Whenever, wherever I saw them, I'd say, "Stop! Stop! I see jonquils!" I made the young men help me gather the jonquils! It was a joke, Amanda and her jonquils! Finally there were no more vases to hold them, every available space was filled with jonquils. No vases to hold them? All right, I'll hold them myself! And then I—(*She stops in front of the picture. Music.*) met your father! Malaria fever and jonquils and then—this—boy. . . . (*She switches on the rose-colored lamp.*) I hope they get here before it starts to rain. (*She crosses upstage and places the jonquils in bowl on table.*) I gave your brother a little extra change so he and Mr. O'Connor could take the service car home.

LAURA (*with altered look*)   What did you say his name was?

AMANDA   O'Connor.

LAURA   What is his first name?

AMANDA   I don't remember. Oh, yes, I do. It was—Jim!

(LAURA *sways slightly and catches hold of a chair.*)

(*Legend on screen: "Not Jim!"*)

LAURA (*faintly*)   Not—Jim!

AMANDA   Yes, that was it, it was Jim! I've never known a Jim that wasn't nice!

(*Music: Ominous.*)

LAURA   Are you sure his name is Jim O'Connor?

AMANDA   Yes. Why?

LAURA   Is he the one that Tom used to know in high school?

AMANDA   He didn't say so. I think he just got to know him at the warehouse.

LAURA   There was a Jim O'Connor we both knew in high school—(*then, with effort:*) If that is the one that Tom is bringing to dinner—you'll have to excuse me, I won't come to the table.

AMANDA   What sort of nonsense is this?

LAURA   You asked me once if I'd ever liked a boy. Don't you remember I showed you this boy's picture?

AMANDA   You mean the boy you showed me in the year book?

LAURA   Yes, that boy.

AMANDA   Laura, Laura, were you in love with that boy?

LAURA   I don't know, Mother. All I know is I couldn't sit at the table if it was him!

AMANDA   It won't be him! It isn't the least bit likely. But whether it is or not, you will come to the table. You will not be excused.

LAURA   I'll have to be, Mother.

AMANDA   I don't intend to humor your silliness, Laura. I've had too much from you and your brother, both! So just sit down and compose yourself till they come. Tom has forgotten his key so you'll have to let them in, when they arrive.

LAURA (*panicky*)   Oh, Mother—*you* answer the door!

AMANDA (*lightly*)   I'll be in the kitchen—busy!

LAURA   Oh, Mother, please answer the door, don't make me do it!

AMANDA (*crossing into kitchenette*)   I've got to fix the dressing for the salmon. Fuss, fuss—silliness!—over a gentleman caller!

(*Door swings shut. LAURA is left alone.*)

(*Legend: "Terror!"*)

(*She utters a low moan and turns off the lamp—sits stiffly on the edge of the sofa, knotting her fingers together.*)

(*Legend on screen: "The opening of a door!"*)

(TOM *and* JIM *appear on the fire-escape steps and climb to landing. Hearing their approach,* LAURA *rises with a panicky gesture. She retreats to the portieres.*
    The doorbell. LAURA *catches her breath and touches her throat. Low drums.*)

AMANDA (*calling*)   Laura, sweetheart! The door!

(LAURA *stares at it without moving.*)

JIM   I think we just beat the rain.

TOM   Uh-huh. (*He rings again, nervously.* JIM *whistles and fishes for a cigarette.*)

AMANDA (*very, very gaily*)   Laura, that is your brother and Mr. O'Connor! Will you let them in, darling?

(LAURA *crosses toward kitchenette door.*)

LAURA (*breathlessly*)   Mother—you go to the door!

(AMANDA *steps out of kitchenette and stares furiously at* LAURA. *She points imperiously at the door.*)

LAURA   Please, please!

AMANDA (*in a fierce whisper*)   What is the matter with you, you silly thing?

LAURA (*desperately*)   Please, you answer it, *please!*

AMANDA   I told you I wasn't going to humor you, Laura. Why have you chosen this moment to lose your mind?

LAURA   Please, please, please, you go!

AMANDA   You'll have to go to the door because I can't!

LAURA (*despairingly*)   I can't either!

AMANDA   Why?

LAURA   I'm *sick!*

AMANDA   I'm sick, too—of your nonsense! Why can't you and your brother be normal people? Fantastic whims and behavior! (TOM *gives a long ring.*) Preposterous goings on! Can you give me one reason—(*calls out lyrically*) COMING! JUST ONE SECOND!—why should you be afraid to open a door? Now you answer it, Laura!

LAURA   Oh, oh, oh . . . (*She returns through the portieres. Darts to the victrola and winds it frantically and turns it on.*)

AMANDA   Laura Wingfield, you march right to that door!

LAURA   Yes—yes, Mother!

(*A faraway, scratchy rendition of "Dardanella" softens the air and gives her strength to move through it. She slips to the door and draws it cautiously open.*
    TOM *enters with the caller,* JIM O'CONNOR.)

TOM   Laura, this is Jim. Jim, this is my sister, Laura.

JIM (*stepping inside*)   I didn't know that Shakespeare had a sister!

LAURA (*retreating stiff and trembling from the door*)   How—how do you do?

JIM (*heartily extending his hand*)   Okay!

(LAURA *touches it hesitantly with hers.*)

JIM   Your hand's *cold*, Laura!

LAURA   Yes, well—I've been playing the victrola. . . .

JIM   Must have been playing classical music on it! You ought to play a little hot swing music to warm you up!

LAURA   Excuse me—I haven't finished playing the victrola. . . .

(*She turns awkwardly and hurries into the front room. She pauses a second by the victrola. Then catches her breath and darts through the portieres like a frightened deer.*)

JIM (*grinning*)   What was the matter?

TOM   Oh—with Laura? Laura is—terribly shy.

JIM   Shy, huh? It's unusual to meet a shy girl nowadays. I don't believe you ever mentioned you had a sister.

TOM   Well, now you know. I have one. Here is the *Post Dispatch*. You want a piece of it?

JIM   Uh-huh.

TOM   What piece? The comics?

JIM   Sports! (*glances at it*) Ole Dizzy Dean is on his bad behavior.

TOM (*disinterest*)   Yeah? (*lights cigarette and crosses back to fire-escape door*)

JIM   Where are *you* going?

TOM   I'm going out on the terrace.

JIM (*goes after him*)   You know, Shakespeare—I'm going to sell you a bill of goods!

TOM   What goods?

JIM   A course I'm taking.

TOM   Huh?

JIM   In public speaking! You and me, we're not the warehouse type.

TOM   Thanks—that's good news. But what has public speaking got to do with it?

JIM   It fits you for—executive positions!

TOM   Awww.

JIM   I tell you it's done a helluva lot for me.

(*Image: Executive at desk.*)

TOM   In what respect?

JIM   In every! Ask yourself what is the difference between you an' me and men in the office down front? Brains?—No!—Ability?—No! Then what? Just one little thing—

TOM   What is that one little thing?

JIM   Primarily it amounts to—social poise! Being able to square up to people and hold your own on any social level!

AMANDA (*off stage*)   Tom?

TOM   Yes, Mother?

AMANDA   Is that you and Mr. O'Connor?

TOM   Yes, Mother.

AMANDA   Well, you just make yourselves comfortable in there.

TOM   Yes, Mother.

AMANDA   Ask Mr. O'Connor if he would like to wash his hands.

JIM   Aw—no—no—thank you—I took care of that at the warehouse. Tom—

TOM   Yes?

JIM   Mr. Mendoza was speaking to me about you.

TOM   Favorably?

JIM   What do you think?

TOM   Well—

JIM   You're going to be out of a job if you don't wake up.

TOM   I am waking up—

JIM   You show no signs.

TOM   The signs are interior.

(Image on screen: The sailing vessel with Jolly Roger again.)

TOM   I'm planning to change. (*He leans over the rail speaking with quiet exhilaration. The incandescent marquees and signs of the first-run movie houses light his face from across the alley. He looks like a voyager.*) I'm right at the point of committing myself to a future that doesn't include the warehouse and Mr. Mendoza or even a night-school course in public speaking.

JIM   What are you gassing about?

TOM   I'm tired of the movies.

JIM   Movies!

TOM   Yes, movies! Look at them—(*a wave toward the marvels of Grand Avenue*) All of those glamorous people—having adventures—hogging it all, gobbling the whole thing up! You know what happens? People go to the *movies* instead of *moving!* Hollywood characters are supposed to have all the adventures for everybody in America, while everybody in America sits in a dark room and watches them have them! Yes, until there's a war. That's when adventure becomes available to the masses! *Everyone's* dish, not only Gable's! Then the people in the dark room come out of the dark room to have some adventures themselves—Goody, goody!—It's our turn now, to go to the South Sea Island—to make a safari—to be exotic, far-off!—But I'm not patient. I don't want to wait till then. I'm tired of the *movies* and I am *about* to move!

JIM (*incredulously*)   Move?

TOM   Yes.

JIM   When?

TOM   Soon!

JIM   Where? Where?

(Theme three music seems to answer the question, while Tom thinks it over. He searches among his pockets.)

TOM   I'm starting to boil inside. I know I seem dreamy, but inside—well, I'm boiling! Whenever I pick up a shoe, I shudder a little thinking how short life is and what I am doing!—Whatever that means. I know it doesn't mean shoes—except as something to wear on a traveler's feet! (*finds paper*) Look—

JIM   What?

TOM   I'm a member.

JIM (*reading*)   The Union of Merchant Seamen.

TOM   I paid my dues this month, instead of the light bill.

JIM   You will regret it when they turn the lights off.

TOM   I won't be here.

JIM   How about your mother?

TOM   I'm like my father. The bastard son of a bastard! See how he grins? And he's been absent going on sixteen years!

JIM   You're just talking, you drip. How does your mother feel about it?

TOM   Shhh!—Here comes Mother! Mother is not acquainted with my plans!

AMANDA (*enters portieres*)   Where are you all?

TOM   On the terrace, Mother.

(*They start inside. She advances to them.* TOM *is distinctly shocked at her appearance. Even* JIM *blinks a little. He is making his first contact with girlish Southern vivacity and in spite of the night-school course in public speaking is somewhat thrown off the beam by the unexpected outlay of social charm.*

Certain responses are attempted by JIM *but are swept aside by* AMANDA'*s gay laughter and chatter.* TOM *is embarrassed but after the first shock* JIM *reacts very warmly. Grins and chuckles, is altogether won over.*)

(*Image: Amanda as a girl.*)

AMANDA (*coyly smiling, shaking her girlish ringlets*) Well, well, well, so this is Mr. O'Connor. Introductions entirely unnecessary. I've heard so much about you from my boy. I finally said to him, Tom—good gracious!—why don't you bring this paragon to supper? I'd like to meet this nice young man at the warehouse!—Instead of just hearing him sing your praises so much! I don't know why my son is so stand-offish—that's not Southern behavior! Let's sit down and—I think we could stand a little more air in here! Tom, leave the door open. I felt a nice fresh breeze a moment ago. Where has it gone? Mmm, so warm already! And not quite summer, even. We're going to burn up when summer really gets started. However, we're having—we're having a very light supper. I think light things are better fo' this time of year. The same as light clothes are. Light clothes an' light food are what warm weather calls fo'. You know our blood gets so thick during th' winter—it takes a while fo' us to *adjust* ou'selves!—when the season changes . . . It's come so quick this year. I wasn't prepared. All of a sudden—heavens! Already summer!—I ran to the trunk an' pulled out this light dress—Terribly old! Historical almost! But feels so good—so good an' co-ol, y'know. . . .

TOM   Mother—

AMANDA   Yes, honey?

TOM   How about—supper?

AMANDA   Honey, you go ask Sister if supper is ready! You know that Sister is in full charge of supper! Tell her you hungry boys are waiting for it. (*to* JIM) Have you met Laura?

JIM   She—

AMANDA　Let you in? Oh, good, you've met already! It's rare for a girl as sweet an' pretty as Laura to be domestic! But Laura is, thank heavens, not only pretty but also very domestic. I'm not at all. I never was a bit. I never could make a thing but angel-food cake. Well, in the South we had so many servants. Gone, gone, gone. All vestige of gracious living! Gone completely! I wasn't prepared for what the future brought me. All of my gentlemen callers were sons of planters and so of course I assumed that I would be married to one and raise my family on a large piece of land with plenty of servants. But man proposes—and woman accepts the proposal!—To vary that old, old saying a little bit—I married no planter! I married a man who worked for the telephone company!—That gallantly smiling gentleman over there! (*points to the picture*) A telephone man who—fell in love with long-distance!—Now he travels and I don't even know where!—But what am I going on for about my—tribulations? Tell me yours—I hope you don't have any! Tom?

TOM (*returning*)　Yes, Mother?

AMANDA　Is supper nearly ready?

TOM　It looks to me like supper is on the table.

AMANDA　Let me look—(*She rises prettily and looks through portieres.*) Oh, lovely!—But where is Sister?

TOM　Laura is not feeling well and she says that she thinks she'd better not come to the table.

AMANDA　What?—Nonsense!—Laura? Oh, Laura!

LAURA (*off stage, faintly*)　Yes, Mother.

AMANDA　You really must come to the table. We won't be seated until you come to the table! Come in, Mr. O'Connor. You sit over there and I'll—Laura? Laura Wingfield! You're keeping us waiting, honey! We can't say grace until you come to the table!

(*The back door is pushed weakly open and* LAURA *comes in. She is obviously quite faint, her lips trembling, her eyes wide and staring. She moves unsteadily toward the table.*)

(*Legend: "Terror!"*)

(*Outside a summer storm is coming abruptly. The white curtains billow inward at the windows and there is a sorrowful murmur and deep blue dusk.*
　　LAURA *suddenly stumbles; she catches at a chair with a faint moan.*)

TOM　Laura!

AMANDA　Laura! (*There is a clap of thunder.*) (*Legend: "Ah!"*) (*despairingly:*) Why, Laura, you *are* sick, darling! Tom, help your sister into the living room, dear! Sit in the living room, Laura—rest on the sofa. Well! (*to the gentleman caller:*) Standing over the hot stove made her ill!—I told her that it was just too warm this evening, but—(TOM *comes back in.* LAURA *is on the sofa.*) Is Laura all right now?

TOM   Yes.

AMANDA   What *is* that? Rain? A nice cool rain has come up! (*She gives the gentleman caller a frightened look.*) I think we may—have grace—now . . . (TOM *looks at her stupidly.*) Tom, honey—you say grace!

TOM   Oh . . . "For these and all thy mercies—" (*They bow their heads,* AMANDA *stealing a nervous glance at* JIM. *In the living room* LAURA, *stretched on the sofa, clenches her hand to her lips, to hold back a shuddering sob.*) God's Holy Name be praised—

(*The scene dims out.*)

Scene VII

(*Legend: "A souvenir."*)

Half an hour later. Dinner is just being finished in the upstage area which is concealed by the drawn portieres.

As the curtain rises LAURA *is still huddled upon the sofa, her feet drawn under her, her head resting on a pale blue pillow, her eyes wide and mysteriously watchful. The new floor lamp with its shade of rose-colored silk gives a soft, becoming light to her face, bringing out the fragile, unearthly prettiness which usually escapes attention. There is a steady murmur of rain, but it is slackening and stops soon after the scene begins; the air outside becomes pale and luminous as the moon breaks out.*

A moment after the curtain rises, the lights in both rooms flicker and go out.

JIM   Hey, there, Mr. Light Bulb!

(AMANDA *laughs nervously.*)

(*Legend: "Suspension of a public service."*)

AMANDA   Where was Moses when the lights went out? Ha-ha. Do you know the answer to that one, Mr. O'Connor?

JIM   No, Ma'am, what's the answer?

AMANDA   In the dark! (JIM *laughs appreciably.*) Everybody sit still. I'll light the candles. Isn't it lucky we have them on the table? Where's a match? Which of you gentlemen can provide a match?

JIM   Here.

AMANDA   Thank you, sir.

JIM   Not at all, Ma'am!

AMANDA   I guess the fuse has burnt out. Mr. O'Connor, can you tell a burnt-out fuse? I know I can't and Tom is a total loss when it comes to mechanics. (*Sound: Getting up: voices recede a little to kitchenette.*) Oh, be careful you don't bump into something. We don't want our gentleman caller to break his neck. Now wouldn't that be a fine howdy-do?

JIM   Ha-ha! Where is the fuse-box?

AMANDA　Right here next to the stove. Can you see anything?

JIM　Just a minute.

AMANDA　Isn't electricity a mysterious thing? Wasn't it Benjamin Franklin who tied a key to a kite? We live in such a mysterious universe, don't we? Some people say that science clears up all mysteries for us. In my opinion it only creates more! Have you found it yet?

JIM　No, Ma'am. All these fuses look okay to me.

AMANDA　Tom!

TOM　Yes, Mother?

AMANDA　That light bill I gave you several days ago. The one I told you we got the notices about?

TOM　Oh.—Yeah.

(Legend: "Ha!")

AMANDA　You didn't neglect to pay it by any chance?

TOM　Why, I—

AMANDA　Didn't! I might have known it!

JIM　Shakespeare probably wrote a poem on that light bill, Mrs. Wingfield.

AMANDA　I might have known better than to trust him with it! There's such a high price for negligence in this world!

JIM　Maybe the poem will win a ten-dollar prize.

AMANDA　We'll just have to spend the remainder of the evening in the nineteenth century, before Mr. Edison made the Mazda lamp!

JIM　Candlelight is my favorite kind of light.

AMANDA　That shows you're romantic! But that's no excuse for Tom. Well, we got through dinner. Very considerate of them to let us get through dinner before they plunged us into everlasting darkness, wasn't it, Mr. O'Connor?

JIM　Ha-ha!

AMANDA　Tom, as a penalty for your carelessness you can help me with the dishes.

JIM　Let me give you a hand.

AMANDA　Indeed you will not!

JIM　I ought to be good for something.

AMANDA　Good for something? *(Her tone is rhapsodic.) You?* Why, Mr. O'Connor, nobody, *nobody's* given me this much entertainment in years—as you have!

JIM　Aw, now, Mrs. Wingfield!

AMANDA　I'm not exaggerating, not one bit! But Sister is all by her lonesome. You go keep her company in the parlor! I'll give you this lovely old candelabrum that used to be on the altar at the church of the Heavenly Rest. It was melted a little out of shape when the church burnt down. Lightning struck it one spring. Gypsy Jones was holding a revival at the time and he intimated that the church was destroyed because the Episcopalians gave card parties.

JIM   Ha-ha.

AMANDA   And how about coaxing Sister to drink a little wine? I think it would be good for her! Can you carry both at once?

JIM   Sure. I'm Superman!

AMANDA   Now, Thomas, get into this apron!

(*The door of kitchenette swings closed on* AMANDA's *gay laughter; the flickering light approaches the portieres.*

LAURA *sits up nervously as he enters. Her speech at first is low and breathless from the almost intolerable strain of being alone with a stranger.*)

(*The legend: "I don't suppose you remember me at all!"*)

(*In her first speeches in his scene, before* JIM's *warmth overcomes her paralyzing shyness,* LAURA's *voice is thin and breathless as though she has just run up a steep flight of stairs.*

JIM's *attitude is gently humorous. In playing this scene it should be stressed that while the incident is apparently unimportant, it is to* LAURA *the climax of her secret life.*)

JIM   Hello, there, Laura.

LAURA (*faintly*)   Hello. (*She clears her throat.*)

JIM   How are you feeling now? Better?

LAURA   Yes. Yes, thank you.

JIM   This is for you. A little dandelion wine. (*He extends it toward her with extravagant gallantry.*)

LAURA   Thank you.

JIM   Drink it—but don't get drunk! (*He laughs heartily.* LAURA *takes the glass uncertainly, laughs shyly.*) Where shall I set the candles?

LAURA   Oh—oh, anywhere . . .

JIM   How about here on the floor? Any objections?

LAURA   No.

JIM   I'll spread a newspaper under to catch the drippings. I like to sit on the floor. Mind if I do?

LAURA   Oh, no.

JIM   Give me a pillow?

LAURA   What?

JIM   A pillow!

LAURA   Oh . . . (*hands him one quickly*)

JIM   How about you? Don't you like to sit on the floor?

LAURA   Oh—yes.

JIM   Why don't you, then?

LAURA   I—will.

JIM   Take a pillow! (LAURA *does. Sits on the other side of the candelabrum.* JIM *crosses his legs and smiles engagingly at her.*) I can't hardly see you sitting way over there.

LAURA   I can—see you.

JIM   I know, but that's not fair, I'm in the limelight. (LAURA *moves her pillow closer.*) Good! Now I can see you! Comfortable?

LAURA   Yes.

JIM   So am I. Comfortable as a cow. Will you have some gum?

LAURA   No, thank you.

JIM   I think that I will indulge, with your permission. (*musingly unwraps it and holds it up*) Think of the fortune made by the guy that invented the first piece of chewing gum. Amazing, huh? The Wrigley Building is one of the sights of Chicago.—I saw it summer before last when I went up to the Century of Progress. Did you take in the Century of Progress?

LAURA   No, I didn't.

JIM   Well, it was quite a wonderful exposition. What impressed me most was the Hall of Science. Gives you an idea of what the future will be in America, even more wonderful than the present time is! (*pause; smiling at her:*) Your brother tells me you're shy. Is that right, Laura?

LAURA   I—don't know.

JIM   I judge you to be an old-fashioned type of girl. Well, I think that's a pretty good type to be. Hope you don't think I'm being too personal—do you?

LAURA   (*hastily, out of embarrassment*)   I believe I *will* take a piece of gum, if you—don't mind. (*clearing her throat*) Mr. O'Connor, have you—kept up with your singing?

JIM   Singing? Me?

LAURA   Yes, I remember what a beautiful voice you had.

JIM   When did you hear me sing?

(*Voice off stage in the pause.*)

VOICE (*off stage*)

> O blow, ye winds, heigh-ho,
> A-roving I will go!
> I'm off to my love
> With a boxing glove—
> Ten thousand miles away!

JIM   You say you've heard me sing?

LAURA   Oh, yes! Yes, very often . . . I—don't suppose you remember me—at all?

JIM   (*smiling doubtfully*)   You know I have an idea I've seen you before. I had that idea soon as you opened the door. It seemed almost like I was about to remember your name. But the name that I started to call you—wasn't a name! And so I stopped myself before I said it.

LAURA   Wasn't it—Blue Roses?

JIM   (*springs up, grinning*)   Blue Roses! My gosh, yes—Blue Roses! That's what I had on my tongue when you opened the door! Isn't it funny what tricks your memory plays? I didn't connect you with the high school somehow or other. But that's where it was; it was high school. I didn't even know you were Shakespeare's sister! Gosh, I'm sorry.

LAURA   I didn't expect you to. You—barely knew me!

JIM   But we did have a speaking acquaintance, huh?

LAURA   Yes, we—spoke to each other.

JIM   When did you recognize me?

LAURA   Oh, right away!

JIM   Soon as I came in the door?

LAURA   When I heard your name I thought it was probably you. I knew that Tom used to know you a little in high school. So when you came in the door—Well, then I was—sure.

JIM   Why didn't you *say* something, then?

LAURA   (*breathlessly*)   I didn't know what to say, I was—too surprised!

JIM   For goodness' sakes! You know, this sure is funny!

LAURA   Yes! Yes, isn't it, though . . .

JIM   Didn't we have a class in something together?

LAURA   Yes, we did.

JIM   What class was that?

LAURA   It was—singing—Chorus!

JIM   Aw!

LAURA   I sat across the aisle from you in the Aud.

JIM   Aw.

LAURA   Mondays, Wednesdays and Fridays.

JIM   Now I remember—you always came in late.

LAURA   Yes, it was so hard for me, getting upstairs. I had that brace on my leg—it clumped so loud!

JIM   I never heard any clumping.

LAURA   (*wincing at the recollection*)   To me it sounded like—thunder!

JIM   Well, well, well. I never even noticed.

LAURA   And everybody was seated before I came in. I had to walk in front of all those people. My seat was in the back row. I had to go clumping all the way up the aisle with everyone watching!

JIM   You shouldn't have been self-conscious.

LAURA   I know, but I was. It was always such a relief when the singing started.

JIM   Aw, yes. I've placed you now! I used to call you Blue Roses. How was it that I got started calling you that?

LAURA   I was out of school a little while with pleurosis. When I came back you asked me what was the matter. I said I had pleurosis—you thought I said Blue Roses. That's what you always called me after that!

JIM   I hope you didn't mind.

LAURA   Oh, no—I liked it. You see, I wasn't acquainted with many—people. . . .

JIM   As I remember you sort of stuck by yourself.

LAURA   I—I—never had much luck at—making friends.

JIM   I don't see why you wouldn't.

LAURA   Well, I—started out badly.

JIM   You mean being—

LAURA   Yes, it sort of—stood between me—

JIM   You shouldn't have let it!

LAURA   I know, but it did, and—

JIM   You were shy with people!

LAURA   I tried not to be but never could—

JIM   Overcome it?

LAURA   No, I—I never could!

JIM   I guess being shy is something you have to work out of kind of gradually.

LAURA (*sorrowfully*)   Yes—I guess it—

JIM   Takes time!

LAURA   Yes—

JIM   People are not so dreadful when you know them. That's what you have to remember! And everybody has problems, not just you, but practically everybody has got some problems. You think of yourself as having the only problems, as being the only one who is disappointed. But just look around you and you will see lots of people as disappointed as you are. For instance, I hoped when I was going to high school that I would be further along at this time, six years later, than I am now—You remember that wonderful write-up I had in *The Torch?*

LAURA   Yes! (*She rises and crosses to table.*)

JIM   It said I was bound to succeed in anything I went into! (LAURA *returns with the annual.*) Holy Jeez! *The Torch!* (*He accepts it reverently. They smile across it with mutual wonder.* LAURA *crouches beside him and they begin to turn through it.* LAURA'*s shyness is dissolving in his warmth.*)

LAURA   Here you are in *Pirates of Penzance!*

JIM (*wistfully*)   I sang the baritone lead in that operetta.

LAURA (*rapidly*)   So—*beautifully!*

JIM (*protesting*)   Aw—

LAURA   Yes, yes—beautifully—beautifully!

JIM   You heard me?

LAURA   All three times!

JIM   No!

LAURA   Yes!

JIM   All three performances?

LAURA (*looking down*)   Yes.

JIM   Why?

LAURA   I—wanted to ask you to—autograph my program.

JIM   Why didn't you ask me to?

LAURA   You were always surrounded by your own friends so much that I never had a chance to.

JIM   You should have just—

LAURA Well, I—thought you might think I was—

JIM Thought I might think you was—what?

LAURA Oh—

JIM (*with reflective relish*) I was beleaguered by females in those days.

LAURA You were terribly popular!

JIM Yeah—

LAURA You had such a—friendly way—

JIM I was spoiled in high school.

LAURA Everybody—liked you!

JIM Including you?

LAURA I—yes, I—I did, too—(*She gently closes the book in her lap.*)

JIM Well, well, well!—Give me that program, Laura. (*She hands it to him. He signs it with a flourish.*) There you are—better late than never!

LAURA Oh, I—what a—surprise!

JIM My signature isn't worth very much right now. But some day—maybe—it will increase in value! Being disappointed is one thing and being discouraged is something else. I am disappointed but I am not discouraged. I'm twenty-three years old. How old are you?

LAURA I'll be twenty-four in June.

JIM That's not old age!

LAURA No, but—

JIM You finished high school?

LAURA (*with difficulty*) I didn't go back.

JIM You mean you dropped out?

LAURA I made bad grades in my final examinations. (*She rises and replaces the book and the program; her voice strained:*) How is—Emily Meisenbach getting along?

JIM Oh, that kraut-head!

LAURA Why do you call her that?

JIM That's what she was.

LAURA You're not still—going with her?

JIM I never see her.

LAURA It said in the Personal Section that you were—engaged!

JIM I know, but I wasn't impressed by that—propaganda!

LAURA It wasn't—the truth?

JIM Only in Emily's optimistic opinion!

LAURA Oh—

(*Legend: "What have you done since high school?"*)

(JIM *lights a cigarette and leans indolently back on his elbows smiling at* LAURA *with a warmth and charm which lights her inwardly with altar candles. She remains by the table and turns in her hands a piece of glass to cover her tumult.*)

JIM (*after several reflective puffs on a cigarette*)   What have you done since high school? (*She seems not to hear him.*) Huh? (LAURA *looks up.*) I said what have you done since high school, Laura?

LAURA   Nothing much.

JIM   You must have been doing something these six long years.

LAURA   Yes.

JIM   Well, then, such as what?

LAURA   I took a business course at business college—

JIM   How did that work out?

LAURA   Well, not very—well—I had to drop out, it gave me—indigestion—

(JIM *laughs gently.*)

JIM   What are you doing now?

LAURA   I don't do anything—much. Oh, please don't think I sit around doing nothing! My glass collection takes up a good deal of my time. Glass is something you have to take good care of.

JIM   What did you say—about glass?

LAURA   Collection I said—I have one—(*She clears her throat and turns away again, acutely shy.*)

JIM (*abruptly*)   You know what I judge to be the trouble with you? Inferiority complex! Know what that is? That's what they call it when someone low-rates himself! I understand it because I had it, too. Although my case was not so aggravated as yours seems to be. I had it until I took up public speaking, developed my voice, and learned that I had an aptitude for science. Before that time I never thought of myself as being outstanding in any way whatsoever! Now I've never made a regular study of it, but I have a friend who says I can analyze people better than doctors that make a profession of it. I don't claim that to be necessarily true, but I can sure guess a person's psychology, Laura! (*takes out his gum*) Excuse me, Laura. I always take it out when the flavor is gone. I'll use this scrap of paper to wrap it in. I know how it is to get it stuck on a shoe. Yep—that's what I judge to be your principal trouble. A lack of confidence in yourself as a person. You don't have the proper amount of faith in yourself. I'm basing that fact on a number of your remarks and also on certain observations I've made. For instance that clumping you thought was so awful in high school. You say that you even dreaded to walk into class. You see what you did? You dropped out of school, you gave up an education because of a clump, which as far as I know was practically non-existent! A little physical defect is what you have. Hardly noticeable even! Magnified thousands of times by imagination! You know what my strong advice to you is? Think of yourself as *superior* in some way!

LAURA   In what way would I think?

JIM   Why, man alive, Laura! Just look about you a little. What do you see? A world full of common people! All of 'em born and all of 'em going to die!

Which of them has one-tenth of your good points! Or mine! Or anyone else's, as far as that goes—Gosh! Everybody excels in some one thing. Some in many! (*unconsciously glances at himself in the mirror*) All you've got to do is discover in *what*! Take me, for instance. (*He adjusts his tie at the mirror.*) My interest happens to lie in electro-dynamics. I'm taking a course in radio engineering at night school, Laura, on top of a fairly responsible job at the warehouse. I'm taking that course and studying public speaking.

LAURA Ohhhh.

JIM Because I believe in the future of television! (*turning back to her*) I wish to be ready to go up right along with it. Therefore I'm planning to get in on the ground floor. In fact, I've already made the right connections and all that remains is for the industry itself to get under way! Full steam—(*His eyes are starry.*) *Knowledge—Zzzzzp! Money—Zzzzzzp!—Power!* That's the cycle democracy is built on! (*His attitude is convincingly dynamic.* LAURA *stares at him, even her shyness eclipsed in her absolute wonder. He suddenly grins.*) I guess you think I think a lot of myself!

LAURA No—o-o-o, I—

JIM Now how about you? Isn't there something you take more interest in than anything else?

LAURA Well, I do—as I said—have my—glass collection—

(*A peal of girlish laughter from the kitchen.*)

JIM I'm not right sure I know what you're talking about. What kind of glass is it?

LAURA Little articles of it, they're ornaments mostly! Most of them are little animals made out of glass, the tiniest little animals in the world. Mother calls them a glass menagerie! Here's an example of one, if you'd like to see it! This one is one of the oldest. It's nearly thirteen. (*He stretches out his hand.*) (*Music: "The Glass Menagerie."*) Oh, be careful—if you breathe, it breaks!

JIM I'd better not take it. I'm pretty clumsy with things.

LAURA Go on, I trust you with him! (*places it in his palm*) There now—you're holding him gently! Hold him over the light, he loves the light! You see how the light shines through him?

JIM It sure does shine!

LAURA I shouldn't be partial, but he is my favorite one.

JIM What kind of thing is this one supposed to be?

LAURA Haven't you noticed the single horn on his forehead?

JIM A unicorn, huh?

LAURA Mmm-hmmm!

JIM Unicorns, aren't they extinct in the modern world?

LAURA I know!

JIM Poor little fellow, he must feel sort of lonesome.

LAURA (*smiling*)   Well, if he does he doesn't complain about it. He stays on a shelf with some horses that don't have horns and all of them seem to get along nicely together.

JIM   How do you know?

LAURA (*lightly*)   I haven't heard any arguments among them!

JIM (*grinning*)   No arguments, huh? Well, that's a pretty good sign! Where shall I set him?

LAURA   Put him on the table. They all like a change of scenery once in a while!

JIM (*stretching*)   Well, well, well, well—Look how big my shadow is when I stretch!

LAURA   Oh, oh, yes—it stretches across the ceiling!

JIM (*crossing to the door*)   I think it's stopped raining. (*opens fire-escape door*) Where does the music come from?

LAURA   From the Paradise Dance Hall across the alley.

JIM   How about cutting the rug a little, Miss Wingfield?

AMANDA   Oh, I—

JIM   Or is your program filled up? Let me have a look at it. (*grasps imaginary card*) Why, every dance is taken! I'll just have to scratch some out. (*Waltz music: "La Golondrina."*) Ahhh, a waltz! (*He executes some sweeping turns by himself, then holds his arms toward* LAURA.)

LAURA (*breathlessly*)   I—can't dance!

JIM   There you go, that inferiority stuff.

LAURA   I've never danced in my life!

JIM   Come on, try!

LAURA   Oh, but I'd step on you!

JIM   I'm not made out of glass.

LAURA   How—how—how do we start?

JIM   Just leave it to me. You hold your arms out a little.

LAURA   Like this?

JIM   A little big higher. Right. Now don't tighten up, that's the main thing about it—relax.

LAURA (*laughing breathlessly*)   It's hard not to.

JIM   Okay.

LAURA   I'm afraid you can't budge me.

JIM   What do you bet I can't? (*He swings her into motion.*)

LAURA   Goodness, yes, you can!

JIM   Let yourself go, now, Laura, just let yourself go.

LAURA   I'm—

JIM   Come on!

LAURA   Trying!

JIM   Not so stiff—Easy does it!

LAURA   I know but I'm—

JIM   Loosen th' backbone! There now, that's a lot better.

LAURA   Am I?

JIM Lots, lots better! (*He moves her about the room in a clumsy waltz.*)

LAURA Oh, my!

JIM Ha-ha!

LAURA Goodness, yes you can!

JIM Ha-ha-ha! (*They suddenly bump into the table.* JIM *stops.*) What did we hit on?

LAURA Table.

JIM Did something fall off it? I think—

LAURA Yes.

JIM I hope that it wasn't the little glass horse with the horn!

LAURA Yes.

JIM Aw, aw, aw. Is it broken?

LAURA Now it is just like all the other horses.

JIM It's lost its—

LAURA Horn! It doesn't matter. Maybe it's a blessing in disguise.

JIM You'll never forgive me. I bet that that was your favorite piece of glass.

LAURA I don't have favorites much. It's no tragedy, Freckles. Glass breaks so easily. No matter how careful you are. The traffic jars the shelves and things fall off them.

JIM Still I'm awfully sorry that I was the cause.

LAURA (*smiling*) I'll just imagine he had an operation. The horn was removed to make him feel less—freakish! (*They both laugh.*) Now he will feel more at home with the other horses, the ones that don't have horns . . .

JIM Ha-ha, that's very funny! (*suddenly serious:*) I'm glad to see that you have a sense of humor. You know—you're—well—very different! Surprisingly different from anyone else I know! (*His voice becomes soft and hesitant with a genuine feeling.*) Do you mind me telling you that? (LAURA *is abashed beyond speech.*) You make me feel sort of—I don't know how to put it! I'm usually pretty good at expressing things, but—This is something that I don't know how to say! (LAURA *touches her throat and clears it—turns the broken unicorn in her hands.*) (*even softer:*) Has anyone ever told you that you were pretty? (*Pause: Music*) (LAURA *looks up slowly, with wonder, and shakes her head.*) Well, you are! In a very different way from anyone else. And all the nicer because of the difference, too. (*His voice becomes low and husky.* LAURA *turns away, nearly faint with the novelty of her emotions.*) I wish that you were my sister. I'd teach you to have some confidence in yourself. The different people are not like other people, but being different is nothing to be ashamed of. Because other people are not such wonderful people. They're one hundred times one thousand. You're one times one! They walk all over the earth. You just stay here. They're common as—weeds, but—you—well, you're—*Blue Roses!*

(*Image on screen: Blue roses.*)

(*Music changes.*)

LAURA   But blue is wrong for—roses . . .

JIM   It's right for you—You're—pretty!

LAURA   In what respect am I pretty?

JIM   In all respects—believe me! Your eyes—your hair—are pretty! Your hands are pretty! (*He catches hold of her hand.*) You think I'm making this up because I'm invited to dinner and have to be nice. Oh, I could do that! I could put on an act for you, Laura, and say lots of things without being very sincere. But this time I am. I'm talking to you sincerely. I happened to notice you had this inferiority complex that keeps you from feeling comfortable with people. Somebody needs to build your confidence up and make you proud instead of shy and turning away and—blushing—Somebody ought to—Ought to—*kiss* you, Laura! (*His hand slips slowly up her arm to her shoulder.*) (*Music swells tumultuously.*) (*He suddenly turns her about and kisses her on the lips. When he releases her* LAURA *sinks on the sofa with a bright, dazed look.* JIM *backs away and fishes in his pocket for a cigarette.*) (*Legend on screen: "Souvenir."*) Stumble-john! (*He lights the cigarette, avoiding her look. There is a peal of girlish laughter from* AMANDA *in the kitchen.* LAURA *slowly raises and opens her hand. It still contains the little broken glass animal. She looks at it with a tender, bewildered expression.*) Stumble-john! I shouldn't have done that—That was way off the beam. You don't smoke, do you? (*She looks up, smiling, not hearing the question. He sits beside her a little gingerly. She looks at him speechlessly—waiting. He coughs decorously and moves a little farther aside as he considers the situation and senses her feelings, dimly, with perturbation; gently:*) Would you—care for a—mint? (*She doesn't seem to hear him but her look grows brighter even.*) Peppermint—Life Saver? My pocket's a regular drug store—wherever I go . . . (*He pops a mint in his mouth. Then gulps and decides to make a clean breast of it. He speaks slowly and gingerly.*) Laura, you know, if I had a sister like you, I'd do the same thing as Tom. I'd bring out fellows—introduce her to them. The right type of boys of a type to—appreciate her. Only—well—he made a mistake about me. Maybe I've got no call to be saying this. That may not have been the idea in having me over. But what if it was? There's nothing wrong about that. The only trouble is that in my case—I'm not in a situation to—do the right thing. I can't take down your number and say I'll phone. I can't call up next week and—ask for a date. I thought I had better explain the situation in case you misunderstood it and—hurt your feelings. . . . (*Pause. Slowly, very slowly,* LAURA'S *look changes, her eyes returning slowly from his to the ornament in her palm.*)

(AMANDA *utters another gay laugh in the kitchen.*)

LAURA (*faintly*)   You—won't—call again?

JIM   No, Laura, I can't. (*He rises from the sofa.*) As I was just explaining, I've—got strings on me, Laura, I've—been going steady! I go out all the time with a girl named Betty. She's a home-girl like you, and Catholic, and Irish, and in a great many ways we—get along fine. I met her last summer on a moonlight boat trip up the river to Alton, on the *Majestic*. Well—right away from the start it was—love! (*Legend: Love!*) (LAURA *sways slightly forward and grips the arm of the sofa. He fails to notice, now enrapt in his own comfortable being.*) Being in love has made a new man of me! (*Leaning stiffly forward, clutching the arm of the sofa,* LAURA *struggles visibly with her storm. But* JIM *is oblivious; she is a long way off.*) The power of love is really pretty tremendous! Love is something that—changes the whole world, Laura! (*The storm abates a little and* LAURA *leans back. He notices her again.*) It happened that Betty's aunt took sick, she got a wire and had to go to Centralia. So Tom—when he asked me to dinner—I naturally just accepted the invitation, not knowing that you—that he—that I—(*He stops awkwardly.*) Huh—I'm a stumble-john! (*He flops back on the sofa. The holy candles in the altar of* LAURA's *face have been snuffed out! There is a look of almost infinite desolation.* JIM *glances at her uneasily.*) I wish that you would— say something. (*She bites her lip which was trembling and then bravely smiles. She opens her hand again on the broken glass ornament. Then she gently takes his hand and raises it level with her own. She carefully places the unicorn in the palm of his hand, then pushes his fingers closed upon it.*) What are you—doing that for? You want me to have him?—Laura? (*She nods.*) What for?

LAURA   A—souvenir . . .

(*She rises unsteadily and crouches beside the victrola to wind it up.*)

(*Legend on screen: "Things have a way of turning out so badly."*)

(*Or image: "Gentleman caller waving goodbye!—gaily."*)

(*At this moment* AMANDA *rushes brightly back in the front room. She bears a pitcher of fruit punch in an old-fashioned cut-glass pitcher and a plate of macaroons. The plate has a gold border and poppies painted on it.*)

AMANDA   Well, well, well! Isn't the air delightful after the shower? I've made you children a little liquid refreshment. (*turns gaily to the gentleman caller*) Jim, do you know that song about lemonade?

> "Lemonade, lemonade
> Made in the shade and stirred with a spade—
> Good enough for any old maid!"

JIM (*uneasily*)   Ha-ha! No—I never heard it.
AMANDA   Why, Laura! You look so serious!
JIM   We were having a serious conversation.
AMANDA   Good! Now you're better acquainted!

JIM (*uncertainly*)   Ha-ha! Yes.

AMANDA   You modern young people are much more serious-minded than my generation. I was so gay as a girl!

JIM   You haven't changed, Mrs. Wingfield.

AMANDA   Tonight I'm rejuvenated! The gaiety of the occasion, Mr. O'Connor! (*She tosses her head with a peal of laughter, spills lemonade.*) Oooo! I'm baptizing myself!

JIM   Here—let me—

AMANDA (*setting the pitcher down*)   There now. I discovered we had some maraschino cherries. I dumped them in, juice and all!

JIM   You shouldn't have gone to that trouble, Mrs. Wingfield.

AMANDA   Trouble, trouble? Why it was loads of fun! Didn't you hear me cutting up in the kitchen? I bet your ears were burning! I told Tom how outdone with him I was for keeping you to himself so long a time! He should have brought you over much, much sooner! Well, now that you've found your way, I want you to be a very frequent caller! Not just occasional but all the time. Oh, we're going to have a lot of gay times together! I see them coming! Mmm, just breathe that air! So fresh, and the moon's so pretty! I'll skip back out—I know where my place is when young folks are having a—serious conversation!

JIM   Oh, don't go out, Mrs. Wingfield. The fact of the matter is I've got to be going.

AMANDA   Going, now? You're joking! Why, it's only the shank of the evening, Mr. O'Connor!

JIM   Well, you know how it is.

AMANDA   You mean you're a young workingman and have to keep workingmen's hours. We'll let you off early tonight. But only on the condition that next time you stay later. What's the best night for you? Isn't Saturday night the best night for you workingmen?

JIM   I have a couple of time-clocks to punch, Mrs. Wingfield. One at morning, another one at night!

AMANDA   My, but you *are* ambitious! You work at night, too?

JIM   No, Ma'am, not work but—Betty! (*He crosses deliberately to pick up his hat. The band at the Paradise Dance Hall goes into a tender waltz.*)

AMANDA   Betty? Betty? Who's—Betty! (*There is an ominous cracking sound in the sky.*)

JIM   Oh, just a girl. The girl I go steady with! (*He smiles charmingly. The sky falls.*)

(*Legend: "The sky falls."*)

AMANDA (*a long-drawn exhalation*)   Ohhhh . . . Is it a serious romance, Mr. O'Connor?

JIM   We're going to be married the second Sunday in June.

AMANDA   Ohhhh—how nice! Tom didn't mention that you were engaged to be married.

JIM   The cat's not out of the bag at the warehouse yet. You know how they are. They call you Romeo and stuff like that. (*He stops at the oval mirror to put on his hat. He carefully shapes the brim and the crown to give a discreetly dashing effect.*) It's been a wonderful evening, Mrs. Wingfield. I guess this is what they mean by Southern hospitality.

AMANDA   It really wasn't anything at all.

JIM   I hope it don't seem like I'm rushing off. But I promised Betty I'd pick her up at the Wabash depot, an' by the time I get my jalopy down there her train'll be in. Some women are pretty upset if you keep 'em waiting.

AMANDA   Yes, I know—The tyranny of women! (*extends her hand*) Goodbye, Mr. O'Connor. I wish you luck—and happiness—and success! All three of them, and so does Laura!—Don't you, Laura?

LAURA   Yes!

JIM (*taking her hand*)   Good-bye, Laura. I'm certainly going to treasure that souvenir. And don't you forget the good advice I gave you. (*raises his voice to a cheery shout*) So long, Shakespeare! Thanks again, ladies—Good night!

(*He grins and ducks jauntily out.*
   Still bravely grimacing, AMANDA *closes the door on the gentleman caller. Then she turns back to the room with a puzzled expression. She and* LAURA *don't dare to face each other.* LAURA *crouches beside the victrola to wind it.*)

AMANDA (*faintly*)   Things have a way of turning out so badly. I don't believe that I would play the victrola. Well, well—well—Our gentleman caller was engaged to be married! Tom!

TOM (*from back*)   Yes, Mother?

AMANDA   Come in here a minute. I want to tell you something awfully funny.

TOM (*enters with a macaroon and a glass of the lemonade*)   Has the gentleman caller gotten away already?

AMANDA   The gentleman caller has made an early departure. What a wonderful joke you played on us!

TOM   How do you mean?

AMANDA   You didn't mention that he was engaged to be married.

TOM   Jim? Engaged?

AMANDA   That's what he just informed us.

TOM   I'll be jiggered! I didn't know about that.

AMANDA   That seems very peculiar.

TOM   What's peculiar about it?

AMANDA   Didn't you call him your best friend down at the warehouse?

TOM   He is, but how did I know?

AMANDA   It seems extremely peculiar that you wouldn't know your best friend was going to be married!

TOM   The warehouse is where I work, not where I know things about people!

AMANDA   You don't know things anywhere! You live in a dream; you manufacture illusions! (*He crosses to door.*) Where are you going?

TOM   I'm going to the movies.

AMANDA   That's right, now that you've had us make such fools of ourselves. The effort, the preparations, all the expense! The new floor lamp, the rug, the clothes for Laura! All for what? To entertain some other girl's fiancé! Go to the movies, go! Don't think about us, a mother deserted, an unmarried sister who's crippled and has no job! Don't let anything interfere with your selfish pleasure! Just go, go, go—to the movies!

TOM   All right, I will! The more you shout about my selfishness to me the quicker I'll go, and I won't go to the movies!

AMANDA   Go, then! Then go to the moon—you selfish dreamer!

(TOM *smashes his glass on the floor. He plunges out on the fire-escape, slamming the door,* LAURA *screams—cut off by the door.*

Dance-hall music up. TOM *goes to the rail and grips it desperately, lifting his face in the chill white moonlight penetrating the narrow abyss of the alley.*)

(*Legend on screen: "And so good-bye . . ."*)

(TOM's *closing speech is timed with the interior pantomime. The interior scene is played as though viewed through soundproof glass.* AMANDA *appears to be making a comforting speech to* LAURA *who is huddled upon the sofa. Now that we cannot hear the mother's speech, her silliness is gone and she has dignity and tragic beauty.* LAURA's *dark hair hides her face until at the end of the speech she lifts it to smile at her mother.* AMANDA's *gestures are slow and graceful, almost dancelike, as she comforts the daughter. At the end of her speech she glances a moment at the father's picture—then withdraws through the portieres. At close of* TOM's *speech,* LAURA *blows out the candles, ending the play.*)

TOM   I didn't go to the moon, I went much further—for time is the longest distance between two places—Not long after that I was fired for writing a poem on the lid of a shoe-box. I left Saint Louis. I descended the steps of this fire-escape for a last time and followed, from then on, in my father's footsteps, attempting to find in motion what was lost in space—I traveled around a great deal. The cities swept about me like dead leaves, leaves that were brightly colored but torn away from the branches. I would have stopped, but I was pursued by something. It always came upon me unawares, taking me altogether by surprise. Perhaps it was a familiar bit of music. Perhaps it was only a piece of transparent glass—Perhaps I am walking along a street at night, in some strange city, before I have found companions. I pass the lighted window of a shop where perfume is sold. The window is filled with pieces of colored glass, tiny transparent bottles in delicate colors, like bits of a shattered rainbow. Then all at once my sister touches my shoulder. I turn around and look into her eyes . . . Oh, Laura, Laura, I tried to leave you behind me, but I am more faithful than I intended to be! I reach for a cigarette, I cross the street, I run into the movies or a bar, I buy a drink, I speak to the nearest stranger—anything that can blow your candles out! (LAURA *bends over the candles.*)—for nowadays the world is lit by lightning! Blow out your candles, Laura—and so good-bye. . . .

(*She blows the candles out.*)

(*The scene dissolves.*)

STUDY QUESTIONS

1. What elements of plot and characterization do you see in *The Glass Menagerie* that remind you of tragedy? of comedy? of realism? What elements will not fit into any of these categories?
2. Consider the play's characters. What strengths and weaknesses does each have? what illusions? What themes are associated with each? What development (if any) does each demonstrate in the play? How do the characterizations reinforce or contrast with each other?
3. Discuss the use Williams makes of the glass menagerie, and especially of the glass unicorn.
4. Discuss the use of candles as a symbol in the play.
5. Discuss the language of the play. How does it differ from the language of other plays you've read?
6. Discuss the device of having the play presented as a set of remembered scenes. How, in particular, does this affect the play's ending and our sense of any future the characters might have beyond the end of the play?

POSSIBLE ESSAY TOPIC

Discuss the relative importance of plot, character, and "thought" (both in terms of language and of symbolism) within *The Glass Menagerie*.

A Raisin in the Sun   LORRAINE HANSBERRY

To Mama: in gratitude for the dream

CHARACTERS

RUTH YOUNGER
TRAVIS YOUNGER
WALTER LEE YOUNGER (*Brother*)
BENEATHA YOUNGER
LENA YOUNGER (*Mama*)
JOSEPH ASAGAI
GEORGE MURCHISON
KARL LINDNER
BOBO
MOVING MEN

The action of the play is set in Chicago's Southside, sometime between World War II and the present.

ACT I

SCENE I
Friday morning.

SCENE II
The following morning.

ACT II

SCENE I
Later the same day.

SCENE II
Friday night, a few weeks later.

SCENE III
Saturday, moving day, one week later.

ACT III
An hour later.

> What happens to a dream deferred?
> Does it dry up
> Like a raisin in the sun?
> Or fester like a sore—

And then run?
Does it stink like rotten meat?
Or crust and sugar over—
Like a syrupy sweet?

Maybe it just sags
Like a heavy load.

Or does it explode?

Langston Hughes[1]

Act I

Scene I

The YOUNGER *living room would be a comfortable and well-ordered room if it were not for a number of indestructible contradictions to this state of being. Its furnishings are typical and undistinguished and their primary feature now is that they have clearly had to accommodate the living of too many people for too many years—and they are tired. Still, we can see that at some time, a time probably no longer remembered by the family (except perhaps for* MAMA), *the furnishings of this room were actually selected with care and love and even hope—and brought to this apartment and arranged with taste and pride.*

That was a long time ago. Now the once loved pattern of the couch upholstery has to fight to show itself from under acres of crocheted doilies and couch covers which have themselves finally come to be more important than the upholstery. And here a table or a chair has been moved to disguise the worn places in the carpet; but the carpet has fought back by showing its weariness, with depressing uniformity, elsewhere on its surface.

Weariness has, in fact, won in this room. Everything has been polished, washed, sat on, used, scrubbed too often. All pretenses but living itself have long since vanished from the very atmosphere of this room.

Moreover, a section of this room, for it is not really a room unto itself, though the landlord's lease would make it seem so, slopes backward to provide a small kitchen area, where the family prepares the meals that are eaten in the living room proper, which must also serve as dining room. The single window that has been provided for these "two" rooms is located in this kitchen area. The sole natural light the family may enjoy in the course of a day is only that which fights its way through this little window.

At left, a door leads to a bedroom which is shared by MAMA *and her daughter,* BENEATHA. *At right, opposite, is a second room (which in the beginning of the life of this apartment was probably a breakfast room), which serves as a bedroom for* WALTER *and his wife,* RUTH.

Time: Sometime between World War II and the present.

Place: Chicago's Southside.

At rise: It is morning dark in the living room. TRAVIS *is asleep on the make-down bed at center. An alarm clock sounds from within the bedroom at right, and presently* RUTH *enters*

---

[1]From "Dream Deferred." Copyright 1951 by Langston Hughes. Reprinted from *The Panther and the Lash* by Langston Hughes, by permission of Alfred A. Knopf, Inc.

from that room and closes the door behind her. She crosses sleepily toward the window. As she passes her sleeping son she reaches down and shakes him a little. At the window she raises the shade and a dusky Southside morning light comes in feebly. She fills a pot with water and puts it on to boil. She calls to the boy, between yawns, in a slightly muffled voice.

RUTH *is about thirty. We can see that she was a pretty girl, even exceptionally so, but now it is apparent that life has been little that she expected, and disappointment has already begun to hang in her face. In a few years, before thirty-five even, she will be known among her people as a "settled woman."*

She crosses to her son and gives him a good, final, rousing shake.

RUTH   Come on now, boy, it's seven thirty! (*Her son sits up at last, in a stupor of sleepiness.*) I say hurry up, Travis! You ain't the only person in the world got to use a bathroom! (*The child, a sturdy, handsome little boy of ten or eleven, drags himself out of the bed and almost blindly takes his towels and "today's clothes" from drawers and a closet and goes out to the bathroom, which is in an outside hall and which is shared by another family or families on the same floor.* RUTH *crosses to the bedroom door at right and opens it and calls in to her husband.*) Walter Lee! . . . It's after seven thirty! Lemme see you do some waking up in there now! (*She waits.*) You better get up from there, man! It's after seven thirty I tell you. (*She waits again.*) All right, you just go ahead and lay there and next thing you know Travis be finished and Mr. Johnson'll be in there and you'll be fussing and cussing round here like a mad man! And be late too! (*She waits, at the end of patience.*) Walter Lee—it's time for you to get up!

(*She waits another second and then starts to go into the bedroom, but is apparently satisfied that her husband has begun to get up. She stops, pulls the door to, and returns to the kitchen area. She wipes her face with a moist cloth and runs her fingers through her sleep-disheveled hair in a vain effort and ties an apron around her housecoat. The bedroom door at right opens and her husband stands in the doorway in his pajamas, which are rumpled and mismated. He is a lean, intense young man in his middle thirties, inclined to quick nervous movements and erratic speech habits—and always in his voice there is a quality of indictment.*)

WALTER   Is he out yet?

RUTH   What you mean *out?* He ain't hardly got in there good yet.

WALTER (*wandering in, still more oriented to sleep than to a new day*)   Well, what was you doing all that yelling for if I can't even get in there yet? (*stopping and thinking*) Check coming today?

RUTH   They *said* Saturday and this is just Friday and I hopes to God you ain't going to get up here first thing this morning and start talking to me 'bout no money—'cause I 'bout don't want to hear it.

WALTER   Something the matter with you this morning?

RUTH   No—I'm just sleepy as the devil. What kind of eggs you want?

WALTER   Not scrambled. (RUTH *starts to scramble eggs.*) Paper come? (RUTH *points impatiently to the rolled up* Tribune *on the table, and he gets it and*

spreads it out and vaguely reads the front page.) Set off another bomb yesterday.

RUTH (*maximum indifference*)   Did they?

WALTER (*looking up*)   What's the matter with you?

RUTH   Ain't nothing the matter with me. And don't keep asking me that this
morning.

WALTER   Ain't nobody bothering you. (*reading the news of the day absently
again*) Say Colonel McCormick is sick.

RUTH (*affecting tea-party interest*)   Is he now? Poor thing.

WALTER (*sighing and looking at his watch*)   Oh, me. (*He waits.*) Now what is that
boy doing in that bathroom all this time? He just going to have to start getting up earlier. I can't be being late to work on account of him fooling
around in there.

RUTH (*turning on him*)   Oh, no he ain't going to be getting up no earlier no
such thing! It ain't his fault that he can't get to bed no earlier nights 'cause
he got a bunch of crazy good-for-nothing clowns sitting up running their
mouths in what is supposed to be his bedroom after ten o'clock at night. . . .

WALTER   That's what you mad about, ain't it? The things I want to talk about
with my friends just couldn't be important in your mind, could they?

(*He rises and finds a cigarette in her handbag on the table and crosses to the little
window and looks out, smoking and deeply enjoying this first one.*)

RUTH (*almost matter of factly, a complaint too automatic to deserve emphasis*)
Why you always got to smoke before you eat in the morning?

WALTER (*at the window*)   Just look at 'em down there. . . . Running and racing
to work . . . (*he turns and faces his wife and watches her a moment at the
stove, and then, suddenly*) You look young this morning, baby.

RUTH (*indifferently*)   Yeah?

WALTER   Just for a second—stirring them eggs. It's gone now—just for a second
it was—you looked real young again. (*then, drily*) It's gone now—you look
like yourself again.

RUTH   Man, if you don't shut up and leave me alone.

WALTER (*looking out to the street again*)   First thing a man ought to learn in life
is not to make love to no colored woman first thing in the morning. You all
some evil people at eight o'clock in the morning.

(TRAVIS *appears in the hall doorway, almost fully dressed and quite wide awake
now, his towels and pajamas across his shoulders. He opens the door and signals for
his father to make the bathroom in a hurry.*)

TRAVIS (*watching the bathroom*)   Daddy, come on!

(WALTER *gets his bathroom utensils and flies out to the bathroom.*)

RUTH   Sit down and have your breakfast, Travis.

TRAVIS   Mama, this is Friday. (*gleefully*) Check coming tomorrow, huh?

RUTH   You get your mind off money and eat your breakfast.

TRAVIS (*eating*)   This is the morning we supposed to bring the fifty cents to school.

RUTH   Well, I ain't got no fifty cents this morning.

TRAVIS   Teacher say we have to.

RUTH   I don't care what teacher say. I ain't got it. Eat your breakfast, Travis.

TRAVIS   I *am* eating.

RUTH   Hush up now and just eat!

(*The boy gives her an exasperated look for her lack of understanding, and eats grudgingly.*)

TRAVIS   You think Grandmama would have it?

RUTH   No! And I want you to stop asking your grandmother for money, you hear me?

TRAVIS (*outraged*)   Gaaaleee! I don't ask her, she just gimme it sometimes!

RUTH   Travis Willard Younger—I got too much on me this morning to be—

TRAVIS   Maybe Daddy—

RUTH   *Travis!*

(*The boy hushes abruptly. They are both quiet and tense for several seconds.*)

TRAVIS (*presently*)   Could I maybe go carry some groceries in front of the supermarket for a little while after school then?

RUTH   Just hush, I said. (TRAVIS *jabs his spoon into his cereal bowl viciously, and rests his head in anger upon his fists.*) If you through eating, you can get over there and make up your bed.

(*The boy obeys stiffly and crosses the room, almost mechanically, to the bed and more or less carefully folds the covering. He carries the bedding into his mother's room and returns with his books and cap.*)

TRAVIS (*sulking and standing apart from her unnaturally*)   I'm gone.

RUTH (*looking up from the stove to inspect him automatically*)   Come *here*. (*He crosses to her and she studies his head.*) If you don't take this comb and fix this here head, you better! (TRAVIS *puts down his books with a great sigh of oppression, and crosses to the mirror. His mother mutters under her breath about his "slubbornness."*) 'Bout to march out of here with that head looking just like chickens slept in it! I just don't know where you get your slubborn ways. . . . And get your jacket, too. Looks chilly out this morning.

TRAVIS (*with conspicuously brushed hair and jacket*)   I'm gone.

RUTH   Get carfare and milk money—(*waving one finger*)—and not a single penny for no caps, you hear me?

TRAVIS (*with sullen politeness*)   Yes'm.

(*He turns in outrage to leave. His mother watches after him as in his frustration he approaches the door almost comically. When she speaks to him her voice has become a very gentle tease.*)

RUTH (*mocking; as she thinks he would say it*)   Oh, Mama makes me so mad sometimes, I don't know what to do! (*She waits and continues to his back as he stands stock-still in front of the door.*) I wouldn't kiss that woman good-bye for nothing in this world this morning! (*The boy finally turns around and rolls his eyes at her, knowing the mood has changed and he is vindicated; he does not, however, move toward her yet.*) Not for nothing in this world! (*She finally laughs aloud at him and holds out her arms to him and we see that it is a way between them, very old and practiced. He crosses to her and allows her to embrace him warmly but keeps his face fixed with masculine rigidity. She holds him back from her presently and looks at him and runs her fingers over the features of his face. With utter gentleness—*) Now—whose little old angry man are you?

TRAVIS (*the masculinity and gruffness start to fade at last*)   Aw gaalee— Mama . . .

RUTH (*mimicking*)   Aw—gaaaaalleeeee, Mama! (*She pushes him, with rough playfulness and finality, toward the door.*) Get on out of here or you going to be late.

TRAVIS (*in the face of love, new aggressiveness*)   Mama, could I *please* go carry groceries?

RUTH   Honey, it's starting to get so cold evenings.

WALTER (*coming in from the bathroom and drawing a make-believe gun from a make-believe holster and shooting at his son*)   What is it he wants to do?

RUTH   Go carry groceries after school at the supermarket.

WALTER   Well, let him go . . .

TRAVIS (*quickly, to the ally*)   I *have* to—she won't gimme the fifty cents. . . .

WALTER (*to his wife only*)   Why not?

RUTH (*simply, and with flavor*)   'Cause we don't have it.

WALTER (*to RUTH only*)   What you tell the boys things like that for? (*reaching down into his pants with a rather important gesture*) Here, son—

(*He hands the boy the coin, but his eyes are directed to his wife's. TRAVIS takes the money happily.*)

TRAVIS   Thanks, Daddy.

(*He starts out. RUTH watches both of them with murder in her eyes. WALTER stands and stares back at her with defiance, and suddenly reaches into his pocket again on an afterthought.*)

WALTER (*without even looking at his son, still staring hard at his wife*)   In fact, here's another fifty cents. . . . Buy yourself some fruit today—or take a taxi-cab to school or something!

TRAVIS   Whoopee—

(*He leaps up and clasps his father around the middle with his legs, and they face each other in mutual appreciation; slowly* WALTER LEE *peeks around the boy to catch the violent rays from his wife's eyes and draws his head back as if shot.*)

WALTER   You better get down now—and get to school, man.

TRAVIS (*at the door*)   O.K. Good-bye. (*He exits.*)

WALTER (*after him, pointing with pride*)   That's *my* boy. (*She looks at him with disgust and turns back to her work.*) You know what I was thinking 'bout in the bathroom this morning?

RUTH   No.

WALTER   How come you always try to be so pleasant!

RUTH   What is there to be pleasant 'bout!

WALTER   You want to know what I was thinking 'bout in the bathroom or not!

RUTH   I know what you thinking 'bout.

WALTER (*ignoring her*)   'Bout what me and Willy Harris was talking about last night.

RUTH (*immediately—a refrain*)   Willy Harris is a good-for-nothing loud mouth.

WALTER   Anybody who talks to me has got to be a good-for-nothing loud mouth, ain't he? And what you know about who is just a good-for-nothing loud mouth? Charlie Atkins was just a "good-for-nothing loud mouth" too, wasn't he! When he wanted me to go in the dry-cleaning business with him. And now—he's grossing a hundred thousand a year. A hundred thousand dollars a year! You still call *him* a loud mouth!

RUTH (*bitterly*)   Oh, Walter Lee. . . . (*She folds her head on her arms over the table.*)

WALTER (*rising and coming to her and standing over her*)   You tired, ain't you? Tired of everything. Me, the boy, the way we live—this beat-up hole—everything. Ain't you? (*She doesn't look up, doesn't answer.*) So tired—moaning and groaning all the time, but you wouldn't do nothing to help, would you? You couldn't be on my side that long for nothing, could you?

RUTH   Walter, please leave me alone.

WALTER   A man needs for a woman to back him up. . . .

RUTH   Walter—

WALTER   Mama would listen to you. You know she listen to you more than she do me and Bennie. She think more of you. All you have to do is just sit down with her when you drinking your coffee one morning and talking 'bout things like you do and—(*He sits down beside her and demonstrates graphically what he thinks her methods and tone should be.*)—you just sip your coffee, see, and say easy like that you been thinking 'bout that deal Walter Lee is so interested in, 'bout the store and all, and sip some more coffee, like what you saying ain't really that important to you—And the next thing you know, she be listening good and asking you questions and when I come home—I can tell her the details. This ain't no fly-by-night proposition, baby. I mean we figured it out, me and Willy and Bobo.

RUTH (*with a frown*)   Bobo?

WALTER   Yeah. You see, this little liquor store we got in mind cost seventy-five thousand and we figured the initial investment on the place be 'bout thirty thousand, see. That be ten thousand each. Course, there's a couple of hundred you got to pay so's you don't spend your life just waiting for them clowns to let your license get approved—

RUTH   You mean graft?

WALTER (*frowning impatiently*)   Don't call it that. See there, that just goes to show you what women understand about the world. Baby, don't *nothing* happen for you in this world 'less you pay *somebody* off!

RUTH   Walter, leave me alone! (*She raises her head and stares at him vigorously—then says, more quietly*) Eat your eggs, they gonna be cold.

WALTER (*straightening up from her and looking off*)   That's it. There you are. Man say to his woman: I got me a dream. His woman say: Eat your eggs. (*sadly, but gaining in power*) Man say: I got to take hold of this here world, baby! And a woman will say: Eat your eggs and go to work. (*passionately now*) Man say: I got to change my life, I'm choking to death, baby! And his woman say— (*in utter anguish as he brings his fists down on his thighs*)—Your eggs is getting cold!

RUTH (*softly*)   Walter, that ain't none of our money.

WALTER (*not listening at all or even looking at her*)   This morning, I was lookin' in the mirror and thinking about it. . . . I'm thirty-five years old; I been married eleven years and I got a boy who sleeps in the living room—(*very, very quietly*)—and all I got to give him is stories about how rich white people live. . . .

RUTH   Eat your eggs, Walter.

WALTER   *Damn my eggs . . . damn all the eggs that ever was!*

RUTH   Then go to work.

WALTER (*looking up at her*)   See—I'm trying to talk to you 'bout myself—(*shaking his head with the repetition*)—and all you can say is eat them eggs and go to work.

RUTH (*wearily*)   Honey, you never say nothing new. I listen to you every day, every night and every morning, and you never say nothing new. (*shrugging*) So you would rather *be* Mr. Arnold than be his chauffeur. So—I would *rather* be living in Buckingham Palace.

WALTER   That is just what is wrong with the colored woman in this world. . . . Don't understand about building their men up and making 'em feel like they somebody. Like they can do something.

RUTH (*drily, but to hurt*)   There *are* colored men who do things.

WALTER   No thanks to the colored woman.

RUTH   Well, being a colored woman, I guess I can't help myself none.

(*She rises and gets the ironing board and sets it up and attacks a huge pile of rough-dried clothes, sprinkling them in preparation for the ironing and then rolling them into tight fat balls.*)

WALTER (*mumbling*)   We one group of men tied to a race of women with small minds.

(*His sister* BENEATHA *enters. She is about twenty, as slim and intense as her brother. She is not as pretty as her sister-in-law, but her lean, almost intellectual face has a handsomeness of its own. She wears a bright-red flannel nightie, and her thick hair stands wildly about her head. Her speech is a mixture of many things; it is different from the rest of the family's insofar as education has permeated her sense of English—and perhaps the Midwest rather than the South has finally—at last—won out in her inflection; but not altogether, because over all of it is a soft slurring and transformed use of vowels which is the decided influence of the South-side. She passes through the room without looking at either* RUTH *or* WALTER *and goes to the outside door and looks, a little blindly, out to the bathroom. She sees that it has been lost to the Johnsons. She closes the door with a sleepy vengeance and crosses to the table and sits down a little defeated.*)

BENEATHA   I am going to start timing those people.

WALTER   You should get up earlier.

BENEATHA (*her face in her hands; she is still fighting the urge to go back to bed*)   Really—would you suggest dawn? Where's the paper?

WALTER (*pushing the paper across the table to her as he studies her almost clinically, as though he has never seen her before*)   You a horrible-looking chick at this hour.

BENEATHA (*drily*)   Good morning, everybody.

WALTER (*senselessly*)   How is school coming?

BENEATHA (*in the same spirit*)   Lovely. Lovely. And you know, biology is the greatest. (*looking up at him*) I dissected something that looked just like you yesterday.

WALTER   I just wondered if you've made up your mind and everything.

BENEATHA (*gaining in sharpness and impatience*)   And what did I answer yesterday morning—and the day before that?

RUTH (*from the ironing board, like someone disinterested and old*)   Don't be so nasty, Bennie.

BENEATHA (*still to her brother*)   And the day before that and the day before that!

WALTER (*defensively*)   I'm interested in you. Something wrong with that? Ain't many girls who decide—

WALTER *and* BENEATHA (*in unison*)   —"to be a doctor."

(*Silence.*)

WALTER   Have we figured out yet just exactly how much medical school is going to cost?

RUTH   Walter Lee, why don't you leave that girl alone and get out of here to work?

BENEATHA (*exits to the bathroom and bangs on the door*)   Come on out of there, please! (*She comes back into the room.*)

WALTER (*looking at his sister intently*)   You know the check is coming tomorrow.

BENEATHA (*turning on him with a sharpness all her own*)   That money belongs to Mama, Walter, and it's for her to decide how she wants to use it. I don't care if she wants to buy a house or a rocket ship or just nail it up somewhere and look at it. It's hers. Not ours—*hers.*

WALTER (*bitterly*)   Now ain't that fine! You just got your mother's interest at heart, ain't you, girl? You such a nice girl—but if Mama got that money she can always take a few thousand and help you through school too—can't she?

BENEATHA   I have never asked anyone around here to do anything for me!

WALTER   No! And the line between asking and just accepting when the time comes is big and wide—ain't it!

BENEATHA (*with fury*)   What do you want from me, Brother—that I quit school or just drop dead, which!

WALTER   I don't want nothing but for you to stop acting holy 'round here. Me and Ruth done made some sacrifices for you—why can't you do something for the family?

RUTH   Walter, don't be dragging me in it.

WALTER   You are in it—Don't you get up and go work in somebody's kitchen for the last three years to help put clothes on her back?

RUTH   Oh, Walter—that's not fair. . . .

WALTER   It ain't that nobody expects you to get on your knees and say thank you, Brother; thank you, Ruth; thank you, Mama—and thank you, Travis, for wearing the same pair of shoes for two semesters—

BENEATHA (*dropping to her knees*)   Well—I *do*—all right?—thank everybody . . . and forgive me for ever wanting to be anything at all . . . forgive me, forgive me!

RUTH   Please stop it! Your mama'll hear you.

WALTER   Who the hell told you you had to be a doctor? If you so crazy 'bout messing 'round with sick people—then go be a nurse like other women—or just get married and be quiet. . . .

BENEATHA   Well—you finally got it said. . . . It took you three years but you finally got it said. Walter, give up; leave me alone—it's Mama's money.

WALTER   *He was my father, too!*

BENEATHA   So what? He was mine, too—and Travis' grandfather—but the insurance money belongs to Mama. Picking on me is not going to make her give it to you to invest in any liquor stores—(*underbreath, dropping into a chair*)—and I for one say, God bless Mama for that!

WALTER (*to* RUTH)   See—did you hear? Did you hear!

RUTH   Honey, please go to work.

WALTER   Nobody in this house is ever going to understand me.

BENEATHA   Because you're a nut.

WALTER   Who's a nut?

BENEATHA   You—you are a nut. Thee is mad, boy.

WALTER (*looking at his wife and his sister from the door, very sadly*)   The world's most backward race of people, and that's a fact.

BENEATHA (*turning slowly in her chair*)   And then there are all those prophets who would lead us out of the wilderness—(WALTER *slams out of the house.*)—into the swamps!

RUTH   Bennie, why you always gotta be pickin' on your brother? Can't you be a little sweeter sometimes?

(*Door opens.* WALTER *walks in.*)

WALTER (*to* RUTH)   I need some money for carfare.

RUTH (*looks at him, then warms; teasing, but tenderly*)   Fifty cents? (*She goes to her bag and gets money.*) Here, take a taxi!

(WALTER *exits.* MAMA *enters. She is a woman in her early sixties, full-bodied and strong. She is one of those women of a certain grace and beauty who wear it so unobtrusively that it takes a while to notice. Her dark-brown face is surrounded by the total whiteness of her hair, and, being a woman who has adjusted to many things in life and overcome many more, her face is full of strength. She has, we can see, wit and faith of a kind that keep her eyes lit and full of interest and expectancy. She is, in a word, a beautiful woman. Her bearing is perhaps most like the noble bearing of the women of the Hereros of Southwest Africa—rather as if she imagines that as she walks she still bears a basket or a vessel upon her head. Her speech, on the other hand, is as careless as her carriage is precise—she is inclined to slur everything— but her voice is perhaps not so much quiet as simply soft.*)

MAMA   Who that 'round here slamming doors at this hour?

(*She crosses through the room, goes to the window, opens it, and brings in a feeble little plant growing doggedly in a small pot on the window sill. She feels the dirt and puts it back out.*)

RUTH   That was Walter Lee. He and Bennie was at it again.

MAMA   My children and they tempers. Lord, if this little old plant don't get more sun than it's been getting it ain't never going to see spring again. (*She turns from the window.*) What's the matter with you this morning, Ruth? You looks right peaked. You aiming to iron all them things? Leave some for me. I'll get to 'em this afternoon. Bennie honey, it's too drafty for you to be sitting 'round half dressed. Where's your robe?

BENEATHA   In the cleaners.

MAMA Well, go get mine and put it on.

BENEATHA I'm not cold, Mama, honest.

MAMA I know—but you so thin. . . .

BENEATHA (*irritably*) Mama, I'm not cold.

MAMA (*seeing the make-down bed as* TRAVIS *has left it*) Lord have mercy, look at that poor bed. Bless his heart—he tries, don't he? (*She moves to the bed* TRAVIS *has sloppily made up.*)

RUTH No—he don't half try at all 'cause he knows you going to come along behind him and fix everything. That's just how come he don't know how to do nothing right now—you done spoiled that boy so.

MAMA Well—he's a little boy. Ain't supposed to know 'bout housekeeping. My baby, that's what he is. What you fix for his breakfast this morning?

RUTH (*angrily*) I feed my son, Lena!

MAMA I ain't meddling—(*underbreath; busy bodyish*)—I just noticed all last week he had cold cereal, and when it starts getting this chilly in the fall a child ought to have some hot grits or something when he goes out in the cold—

RUTH (*furious*) I gave him hot oats—is that all right!

MAMA I ain't meddling. (*pause*) Put a lot of nice butter on it? (RUTH *shoots her an angry look and does not reply.*) He likes lots of butter.

RUTH (*exasperated*) Lena—

MAMA (*to* BENEATHA; MAMA *is inclined to wander conversationally sometimes*) What was you and your brother fussing 'bout this morning?

BENEATHA It's not important, Mama.

(*She gets up and goes to look out at the bathroom, which is apparently free, and she picks up her towels and rushes out.*)

MAMA What was they fighting about?

RUTH Now you know as well as I do.

MAMA (*shaking her head*) Brother still worrying his self sick about that money?

RUTH You know he is.

MAMA You had breakfast?

RUTH Some coffee.

MAMA Girl, you better start eating and looking after yourself better. You almost thin as Travis.

RUTH Lena—

MAMA Un-hunh?

RUTH What are you going to do with it?

MAMA Now don't you start, child. It's too early in the morning to be talking about money. It ain't Christian.

RUTH It's just that he got his heart set on that store—

MAMA You mean that liquor store that Willy Harris want him to invest in?

RUTH Yes—

MAMA   We ain't no business people, Ruth. We just plain working folks.

RUTH   Ain't nobody business people till they go into business. Walter Lee say colored people ain't never going to start getting ahead till they start gambling on some different kinds of things in the world—investments and things.

MAMA   What done got into you, girl? Walter Lee done finally sold you on investing.

RUTH   No. Mama, something is happening between Walter and me. I don't know what it is—but he needs something—something I can't give him any more. He needs this chance, Lena.

MAMA (*frowning deeply*)   But liquor, honey—

RUTH   Well—like Walter say—I spec people going to always be drinking themselves some liquor.

MAMA   Well—whether they drinks it or not ain't none of my business. But whether I go into business selling it to 'em *is,* and I don't want that on my ledger this late in life. (*stopping suddenly and studying her daughter-in-law*) Ruth Younger, what's the matter with you today? You look like you could fall over right there.

RUTH   I'm tired.

MAMA   Then you better stay home from work today.

RUTH   I can't stay home. She'd be calling up the agency and screaming at them, "My girl didn't come in today—send me somebody! My girl didn't come in!" Oh, she just have a fit. . . .

MAMA   Well, let her have it. I'll just call her up and say you got the flu—

RUTH (*laughing*)   Why the flu?

MAMA   'Cause it sounds respectable to 'em. Something white people get, too. They know 'bout the flu. Otherwise they think you been cut up or something when you tell 'em you sick.

RUTH   I got to go in. We need the money.

MAMA   Somebody would of thought my children done all but starved to death the way they talk about money here late. Child, we got a great big old check coming tomorrow.

RUTH (*sincerely, but also self-righteously*)   Now that's your money. It ain't got nothing to do with me. We all feel like that—Walter and Bennie and me—even Travis.

MAMA (*thoughtfully, and suddenly very far away*)   Ten thousand dollars—

RUTH   Sure is wonderful.

MAMA   Ten thousand dollars.

RUTH   You know what you should do, Miss Lena? You should take yourself a trip somewhere. To Europe or South America or someplace—

MAMA (*throwing up her hands at the thought*)   Oh, child!

RUTH   I'm serious. Just pack up and leave! Go on away and enjoy yourself some. Forget about the family and have yourself a ball for once in your life—

MAMA (*drily*) You sound like I'm just about ready to die. Who'd go with me? What I look like wandering 'round Europe by myself?

RUTH Shoot—these here rich white women do it all the time. They don't think nothing of packing up they suitcases and piling on one of them big steamships and—swoosh!—they gone, child.

MAMA Something always told me I wasn't no rich white woman.

RUTH Well—what are you going to do with it then?

MAMA I ain't rightly decided. (*thinking. She speaks now with emphasis.*) Some of it got to be put away for Beneatha and her schoolin'—and ain't nothing going to touch that part of it. Nothing. (*She waits several seconds, trying to make up her mind about something, and looks at* RUTH *a little tentatively before going on.*) Been thinking that we maybe could meet the notes on a little old two-story somewhere, with a yard where Travis could play in the summertime, if we use part of the insurance for a down payment and everybody kind of pitch in. I could maybe take on a little day work again, few days a week—

RUTH (*studying her mother-in-law furtively and concentrating on her ironing, anxious to encourage without seeming to*) Well, Lord knows, we've put enough rent into this here rat trap to pay for four houses by now. . . .

MAMA (*looking up at the words "rat trap" and then looking around and leaning back and sighing—in a suddenly reflective mood—*) "Rat trap"—yes, that's all it is. (*smiling*) I remember just as well the day me and Big Walter moved in here. Hadn't been married but two weeks and wasn't planning on living here no more than a year. (*She shakes her head at the dissolved dream.*) We was going to set away, little by little, don't you know, and buy a little place out in Morgan Park. We had even picked out the house. (*chuckling a little*) Looks right dumpy today. But Lord, child, you should know all the dreams I had 'bout buying that house and fixing it up and making me a little garden in the back—(*She waits and stops smiling.*) And didn't none of it happen. (*dropping her hands in a futile gesture*)

RUTH (*keeps her head down, ironing*) Yes, life can be a barrel of disappointments, sometimes.

MAMA Honey, Big Walter would come in here some nights back then and slump down on that couch there and just look at the rug, and look at me and look at the rug and then back at me—and I'd know he was down then . . . really down. (*After a second very long and thoughtful pause; she is seeing back to times that only she can see.*) And then, Lord, when I lost that baby—little Claude—I almost thought I was going to lose Big Walter too. Oh, that man grieved hisself! He was one man to love his children.

RUTH Ain't nothin' can tear at you like losin' your baby.

MAMA I guess that's how come that man finally worked hisself to death like he done. Like he was fighting his own war with this here world that took his baby from him.

RUTH He sure was a fine man, all right. I always liked Mr. Younger.

MAMA   Crazy 'bout his children! God knows there was plenty wrong with Walter Younger—hard-headed, mean, kind of wild with women—plenty wrong with him. But he sure loved his children. Always wanted them to have something—be something. That's where Brother gets all these notions, I reckon. Big Walter used to say, he'd get right wet in the eyes sometimes, lean his head back with the water standing in his eyes and say, "Seem like God didn't see fit to give the black man nothing but dreams—but He did give us children to make them dreams seem worth while." (*She smiles.*) He could talk like that, don't you know.

RUTH   Yes, he sure could. He was a good man, Mr. Younger.

MAMA   Yes, a fine man—just couldn't never catch up with his dreams, that's all.

(BENEATHA *comes in, brushing her hair and looking up to the ceiling, where the sound of a vacuum cleaner has started up.*)

BENEATHA   What could be so dirty on that woman's rugs that she has to vacuum them every single day?

RUTH   I wish certain young women 'round here who I could name would take inspiration about certain rugs in a certain apartment I could also mention.

BENEATHA   (*shrugging*)   How much cleaning can a house need, for Christ's sakes.

MAMA   (*not liking the Lord's name used thus*)   Bennie!

RUTH   Just listen to her—just listen!

BENEATHA   Oh, God!

MAMA   If you use the Lord's name just one more time—

BENEATHA   (*a bit of a whine*)   Oh, Mama—

RUTH   Fresh—just fresh as salt, this girl!

BENEATHA   (*drily*)   Well—if the salt loses its savor—

MAMA   Now that will do. I just ain't going to have you 'round here reciting the scriptures in vain—you hear me?

BENEATHA   How did I manage to get on everybody's wrong side by just walking into a room?

RUTH   If you weren't so fresh—

BENEATHA   Ruth, I'm twenty years old.

MAMA   What time you be home from school today?

BENEATHA   Kind of late. (*with enthusiasm*) Madeline is going to start my guitar lessons today.

(MAMA *and* RUTH *look up with the same expression.*)

MAMA   Your *what* kind of lessons?

BENEATHA   Guitar.

RUTH   Oh, Father!

MAMA   How come you done taken it in your mind to learn to play the guitar?

BENEATHA   I just want to, that's all.

MAMA (*smiling*) Lord, child, don't you know what to do with yourself? How long it going to be before you get tired of this now—like you got tired of that little play-acting group you joined last year? (*looking at* RUTH) And what was it the year before that?

RUTH The horseback-riding club for which she bought that fifty-five-dollar riding habit that's been hanging in the closet ever since!

MAMA (*to* BENEATHA) Why you got to flit so from one thing to another, baby?

BENEATHA (*sharply*) I just want to learn to play the guitar. Is there anything wrong with that?

MAMA Ain't nobody trying to stop you. I just wonders sometimes why you has to flit so from one thing to another all the time. You ain't never done nothing with all that camera equipment you brought home—

BENEATHA I don't flit! I—I experiment with different forms of expression—

RUTH Like riding a horse?

BENEATHA —People have to express themselves one way or another.

MAMA What is it you want to express?

BENEATHA (*angrily*) Me! (MAMA *and* RUTH *look at each other and burst into raucous laughter.*) Don't worry—I don't expect you to understand.

MAMA (*to change the subject*) Who you going out with tomorrow night?

BENEATHA (*with displeasure*) George Murchison again.

MAMA (*pleased*) Oh—you getting a little sweet on him?

RUTH You ask me, this child ain't sweet on nobody but herself—(*underbreath*) Express herself!

(*They laugh.*)

BENEATHA Oh—I like George all right, Mama. I mean I like him enough to go out with him and stuff, but—

RUTH (*for devilment*) What does *and stuff* mean?

BENEATHA Mind your own business.

MAMA Stop picking at her now, Ruth. (*a thoughtful pause, and then a suspicious sudden look at her daughter as she turns in her chair for emphasis*) What *does* it mean?

BENEATHA (*wearily*) Oh, I just mean I couldn't ever really be serious about George. He's—he's so shallow.

RUTH Shallow—what do you mean he's shallow? He's *rich*!

MAMA Hush, Ruth.

BENEATHA I know he's rich. He knows he's rich, too.

RUTH Well—what other qualities a man got to have to satisfy you, little girl?

BENEATHA You wouldn't even begin to understand. Anybody who married Walter could not possibly understand.

MAMA (*outraged*) What kind of way is that to talk about your brother?

BENEATHA Brother is a flip—let's face it.

MAMA (*to* RUTH, *helplessly*) What's a flip?

RUTH (*glad to add kindling*)   She's saying he's crazy.

BENEATHA   Not crazy. Brother isn't really crazy yet—he—he's an elaborate neurotic.

MAMA   Hush your mouth!

BENEATHA   As for George. Well. George looks good—he's got a beautiful car and he takes me to nice places and, as my sister-in-law says, he is probably the richest boy I will ever get to know and I even like him sometimes—but if the Youngers are sitting around waiting to see if their little Bennie is going to tie up the family with the Murchisons, they are wasting their time.

RUTH   You mean you wouldn't marry George Murchison if he asked you some-day? That pretty, rich thing? Honey, I knew you was odd—

BENEATHA   No I would not marry him if all I felt for him was what I feel now. Besides, George's family wouldn't really like it.

MAMA   Why not?

BENEATHA   Oh, Mama—The Murchisons are honest-to-God-real-*live*-rich col-ored people, and the only people in the world who are more snobbish than rich white people are rich colored people. I thought everybody knew that. I've met Mrs. Murchison. She's a scene!

MAMA   You must not dislike people 'cause they well off, honey.

BENEATHA   Why not? It makes just as much sense as disliking people 'cause they are poor, and lots of people do that.

RUTH (*a wisdom-of-the-ages manner; to* MAMA)   Well, she'll get over some of this—

BENEATHA   Get over it? What are you talking about, Ruth? Listen, I'm going to be a doctor. I'm not worried about who I'm going to marry yet—if I ever get married.

MAMA *and* RUTH   *If!*

MAMA   Now, Bennie—

BENEATHA   Oh, I probably will ... but first I'm going to be a doctor, and George, for one, still think's that's pretty funny. I couldn't be bothered with that, I am going to be a doctor and everybody around here better under-stand that!

MAMA (*kindly*)   'Course you going to be a doctor, honey, God willing.

BENEATHA (*drily*)   God hasn't got a thing to do with it.

MAMA   Beneatha—that just wasn't necessary.

BENEATHA   Well—neither is God. I get sick of hearing about God.

MAMA   Beneatha!

BENEATHA   I mean it! I'm just tired of hearing about God all the time. What has He got to do with anything? Does He pay tuition?

MAMA   You 'bout to get your fresh little jaw slapped!

RUTH   That's just what she needs, all right!

BENEATHA   Why? Why can't I say what I want to around here, like everybody else?

MAMA   It don't sound nice for a young girl to say things like that—you wasn't brought up that way. Me and your father went to trouble to get you and Brother to church every Sunday.

BENEATHA   Mama, you don't understand. It's all a matter of ideas, and God is just one idea I don't accept. It's not important, I am not going out and be immoral or commit crimes because I don't believe in God. I don't even think about it. It's just that I get tired of Him getting credit for all the things the human race achieves through its own stubborn effort. There simply is no blasted God—there is only man and it is he who makes miracles!

(MAMA *absorbs this speech, studies her daughter and rises slowly and crosses to* BE-NEATHA *and slaps her powerfully across the face. After, there is only silence and the daughter drops her eyes from her mother's face, and* MAMA *is very tall before her.*)

MAMA   Now—you say after me, in my mother's house there is still God. (*There is a long pause and* BENEATHA *stares at the floor wordlessly.* MAMA *repeats the phrase with precision and cool emotion.*) In my mother's house there is still God.

BENEATHA   In my mother's house there is still God.

(*A long pause.*)

MAMA (*walking away from* BENEATHA, *too disturbed for triumphant posture; stopping and turning back to her daughter*)   There are some ideas we ain't going to have in this house. Not long as I am at the head of this family.

BENEATHA   Yes, ma'am.

(MAMA *walks out of the room.*)

RUTH (*almost gently, with profound understanding*)   You think you a woman, Bennie—but you still a little girl. What you did was childish—so you got treated like a child.

BENEATHA   I see. (*quietly*) I also see that everybody thinks it's all right for Mama to be a tyrant. But all the tyranny in the world will never put a God in the heavens! (*She picks up her books and goes out.*)

RUTH (*goes to* MAMA's *door*)   She said she was sorry.

MAMA (*coming out, going to her plant*)   They frightens me, Ruth. My children.

RUTH   You got good children, Lena. They just a little off sometimes—but they're good.

MAMA   No—there's something come down between me and them that don't let us understand each other and I don't know what it is. One done almost lost his mind thinking 'bout money all the time and the other done commence to talk about things I can't seem to understand in no form or fashion. What is it that's changing, Ruth?

RUTH (*soothingly, older than her years*)   Now . . . you taking it all too seriously. You just got strong-willed children and it takes a strong woman like you to keep 'em in hand.

MAMA (*looking at her plant and sprinkling a little water on it*)   They spirited all right, my children. Got to admit they got spirit—Bennie and Walter. Like this old plant that ain't never had enough sunshine or nothing—and look at it. . . .

(*She has her back to* RUTH, *who has had to stop ironing and lean against something and put the back of her hand to her forehead.*)

RUTH (*trying to keep* MAMA *from noticing*)   You . . . sure . . . loves that little old thing, don't you? . . .

MAMA   Well, I always wanted me a garden like I used to see sometimes at the back of the houses down home. This plant is close as I ever got to having one. (*She looks out of the window as she replaces the plant.*) Lord, ain't nothing as dreary as the view from this window on a dreary day, is there? Why ain't you singing this morning, Ruth? Sing that "No Ways Tired." That song always lifts me up so—(*She turns at last to see that* RUTH *has slipped quietly into a chair, in a state of semiconsciousness.*) Ruth! Ruth honey—what's the matter with you . . . Ruth!

Curtain

Scene II

It is the following morning; a Saturday morning, and house cleaning is in progress at the YOUNGERS. *Furniture has been shoved hither and yon and* MAMA *is giving the kitchen-area walls a washing down.* BENEATHA, *in dungarees, with a handkerchief tied around her face, is spraying insecticide into the cracks in the walls. As they work, the radio is on and a Southside disc-jockey program is inappropriately filling the house with a rather exotic saxophone blues.* TRAVIS, *the sole idle one, is leaning on his arms, looking out of the window.*

TRAVIS   Grandmama, that stuff Bennie is using smells awful. Can I go downstairs, please?

MAMA   Did you get all them chores done already? I ain't see you doing much.

TRAVIS   Yes'm—finished early. Where did Mama go this morning?

MAMA (*looking at* BENEATHA)   She had to go on a little errand.

TRAVIS   Where?

MAMA   To tend to her business.

TRAVIS   Can I go outside then?

MAMA   Oh, I guess so. You better stay right in front of the house, though . . . and keep a good lookout for the postman.

TRAVIS   Yes'm. (*He starts out and decides to give his* AUNT BENEATHA *a good swat on the legs as he passes her.*) Leave them poor little old cockroaches alone, they ain't bothering you none.

(*He runs as she swings the spray gun at him both viciously and playfully.* WALTER *enters from the bedroom and goes to the phone.*)

MAMA   Look out there, girl, before you be spilling some of that stuff on that child!

TRAVIS (*teasing*)   That's right—look out now! (*He exits.*)

BENEATHA (*drily*)   I can't imagine that it would hurt him—it has never hurt the roaches.

MAMA   Well, little boys' hides ain't as tough as Southside roaches.

WALTER (*into phone*)   Hello—Let me talk to Willy Harris.

MAMA   You better get over there behind the bureau. I seen one marching out of there like Napoleon yesterday.

WALTER   Hello. Willy? It ain't come yet. It'll be here in a few minutes. Did the lawyer give you the papers?

BENEATHA   There's really only one way to get rid of them, Mama—

MAMA   How?

BENEATHA   Set fire to this building.

WALTER   Good. Good. I'll be right over.

BENEATHA   Where did Ruth go, Walter?

WALTER   I don't know. (*He exits abruptly.*)

BENEATHA   Mama, where did Ruth go?

MAMA (*looking at her with meaning*)   To the doctor, I think.

BENEATHA   The doctor? What's the matter? (*They exchange glances.*) You don't think—

MAMA (*with her sense of drama*)   Now I ain't saying what I think. But I ain't never been wrong 'bout a woman neither.

(*The phone rings.*)

BENEATHA (*at the phone*)   Hay-lo . . . (*pause, and a moment of recognition*) Well—when did you get back! . . . And how was it? . . . Of course I've missed you—in my way. . . . This morning? No . . . house cleaning and all that and Mama hates it if I let people come over when the house is like this. . . . You *have?* Well, that's different. . . . What is it—Oh, what the hell, come on over. . . . Right, see you then. (*She hangs up.*)

MAMA (*who has listened vigorously, as is her habit*)   Who is that you inviting over here with this house looking like this? You ain't got the pride you was born with!

BENEATHA   Asagai doesn't care how houses look, Mama—he's an intellectual.

MAMA   *Who?*

BENEATHA   Asagai—Joseph Asagai. He's an African boy I met on campus. He's been studying in Canada all summer.

MAMA   What's his name?

BENEATHA   Asagai, Joseph. Ah-sah-guy . . . He's from Nigeria.

MAMA   Oh, that's the little country that was founded by slaves way back. . . .

BENEATHA   No, Mama—that's Liberia.

MAMA   I don't think I never met no African before.

BENEATHA   Well, do me a favor and don't ask him a whole lot of ignorant questions about Africans. I mean, do they wear clothes and all that—

MAMA   Well, now, I guess if you think we so ignorant 'round here maybe you shouldn't bring your friends here—

BENEATHA   It's just that people ask such crazy things. All anyone seems to know about when it comes to Africa is Tarzan—

MAMA (*indignantly*)   Why should I know anything about Africa?

BENEATHA   Why do you give money at church for the missionary work?

MAMA   Well, that's to help save people.

BENEATHA   You mean to save them from *heathenism*—

MAMA (*innocently*)   Yes.

BENEATHA   I'm afraid they need more salvation from the British and the French.

(RUTH *comes in forlornly and pulls off her coat with dejection. They both turn to look at her.*)

RUTH (*dispiritedly*)   Well, I guess from all the happy faces—everybody knows.

BENEATHA   You pregnant?

MAMA   Lord have mercy, I sure hope it's a little old girl. Travis ought to have a sister.

(BENEATHA *and* RUTH *give her a hopeless look for this grandmotherly enthusiasm.*)

BENEATHA   How far along are you?

RUTH   Two months.

BENEATHA   Did you mean to? I mean did you plan it or was it an accident?

MAMA   What do you know about planning or not planning?

BENEATHA   Oh, Mama.

RUTH (*wearily*)   She's twenty years old, Lena.

BENEATHA   Did you plan it, Ruth?

RUTH   Mind your own business.

BENEATHA   It is my business—where is he going to live, on the *roof?* (*There is silence following the remark as the three women react to the sense of it.*) Gee—I didn't mean that, Ruth, honest. Gee, I don't feel like that at all. I—I think it is wonderful.

RUTH (*dully*)   Wonderful.

BENEATHA   Yes—really.

MAMA (*looking at* RUTH, *worried*)   Doctor say everything going to be all right?

RUTH (*far away*)   Yes—she says everything is going to be fine. . . .

MAMA (*immediately suspicious*)   "She"—What doctor you went to?

(RUTH *folds over, near hysteria.*)

MAMA (*worriedly hovering over* RUTH)   Ruth honey—what's the matter with you—you sick?

(RUTH *has her fists clenched on her thighs and is fighting hard to suppress a scream that seems to be rising in her.*)

BENEATHA   What's the matter with her, Mama?

MAMA (*working her fingers in* RUTH's *shoulder to relax her*)   She be all right. Women gets right depressed sometimes when they get her way. (*speaking softly, expertly, rapidly*) Now you just relax. That's right . . . just lean back, don't think 'bout nothing at all . . . nothing at all—

RUTH   I'm all right. . . .

(*The glassy-eyed look melts and then she collapses into a fit of heavy sobbing. The bell rings.*)

BENEATHA   Oh, my God—that must be Asagai.

MAMA (*to* RUTH)   Come on now, honey. You need to lie down and rest awhile . . . then have some nice hot food.

(*They exit,* RUTH's *weight on her mother-in-law.* BENEATHA, *herself profoundly disturbed, opens the door to admit a rather dramatic-looking young man with a large package.*)

ASAGAI   Hello, Alaiyo—

BENEATHA (*holding the door open and regarding him with pleasure*)   Hello . . . (*long pause*) Well—come in. And please excuse everything. My mother was very upset about my letting anyone come here with the place like this.

ASAGAI (*coming into the room*)   You look disturbed too. . . . Is something wrong?

BENEATHA (*still at the door, absently*)   Yes . . . we've all got acute ghetto-itus. (*She smiles and comes toward him, finding a cigarette and sitting.*) So—sit down! How was Canada?

ASAGAI (*a sophisticate*)   Canadian.

BENEATHA (*looking at him*)   I'm very glad you are back.

ASAGAI (*looking back at her in turn*)   Are you really?

BENEATHA   Yes—very.

ASAGAI   Why—you were quite glad when I went away. What happened?

BENEATHA   You went away.

ASAGAI   Ahhhhhhhh.

BENEATHA   Before—you wanted to be so serious before there was time.

ASAGAI   How much time must there be before one knows what one feels?

BENEATHA (*stalling this particular conversation, her hands pressed together in a deliberately childish gesture*)   What did you bring me?

ASAGAI (*handing her the package*)   Open it and see.

BENEATHA (*eagerly opening the package and drawing out some records and the colorful robes of a Nigerian woman*)   Oh, Asagai! . . . You got them for me! . . . How beautiful . . . and the records too! (*She lifts out the robes and runs to the mirror with them and holds the drapery up in front of herself.*)

ASAGAI (*coming to her at the mirror*)   I shall have to teach you how to drape it properly. (*He flings the material about her for the moment and stands back to look at her.*) Ah—Oh-pay-gay-day, oh-gbah-mu-shay. (*a Yoruba exclamation for admiration*) You wear it well . . . very well . . . mutilated hair and all.

BENEATHA (*turning suddenly*)   My hair—what's wrong with my hair?

ASAGAI (*shrugging*)   Were you born with it like that?

BENEATHA (*reaching up to touch it*)   No . . . of course not. (*She looks back to the mirror, disturbed.*)

ASAGAI (*smiling*)   How then?

BENEATHA   You know perfectly well how . . . as crinkly as yours . . . that's how.

ASAGAI   And it is ugly to you that way?

BENEATHA (*quickly*)   Oh, no—not ugly . . . (*more slowly, apologetically*) But it's so hard to manage when it's well—raw.

ASAGAI   And so to accommodate that—you mutilate it every week?

BENEATHA   It's not mutilation!

ASAGAI (*laughing aloud at her seriousness*)   Oh . . . please! I am only teasing you because you are so very serious about these things. (*He stands back from her and folds his arms across his chest as he watches her pulling at her hair and frowning in the mirror.*) Do you remember the first time you met me at school? . . . (*He laughs.*) You came up to me and said—and I thought you were the most serious little thing I had ever seen—you said: (*He imitates her.*) "Mr. Asagai—I want very much to talk with you. About Africa. You see, Mr. Asagai, I am looking for my *identity!*" (*He laughs.*)

BENEATHA (*turning to him, not laughing*)   Yes—(*Her face is quizzical, profoundly disturbed.*)

ASAGAI (*still teasing and reaching out and taking her face in his hands and turning her profile to him*)   Well . . . it is true that this is not so much a profile of a Hollywood queen as perhaps a queen of the Nile—(*a mock dismissal of the importance of the question*) But what does it matter? Assimilationism is so popular in your country.

BENEATHA (*wheeling, passionately, sharply*)   I am not an assimilationist!

ASAGAI (*the protest hangs in the room for a moment and* ASAGAI *studies her, his laughter fading*)   Such a serious one. (*There is a pause.*) So—you like the robes? You must take excellent care of them—they are from my sister's personal wardrobe.

BENEATHA (*with incredulity*) You—you sent all the way home—for me?

ASAGAI (*with charm*) For you—I would do much more. . . . Well, that is what I came for. I must go.

BENEATHA Will you call me Monday?

ASAGAI Yes . . . We have a great deal to talk about. I mean about identity and time and all that.

BENEATHA Time?

ASAGAI Yes. About how much time one needs to know what one feels.

BENEATHA You never understood that there is more than one kind of feeling which can exist between a man and a woman—or, at least, there should be.

ASAGAI (*shaking his head negatively but gently*) No. Between a man and a woman there need be only one kind of feeling. I have that for you. . . . Now even . . . right this moment. . . .

BENEATHA I know—and by itself—it won't do. I can find that anywhere.

ASAGAI For a woman it should be enough.

BENEATHA I know—because that's what it says in all the novels that men write. But it isn't. Go ahead and laugh—but I'm not interested in being someone's little episode in America or—(*with feminine vengeance*)—one of them! (ASAGAI *has burst into laughter again.*) That's funny as hell, huh!

ASAGAI It's just that every American girl I have known has said that to me. White—black—in this you are all the same. And the same speech, too!

BENEATHA (*angrily*) Yuk, yuk, yuk!

ASAGAI It's how you can be sure that the world's most liberated women are not liberated at all. You all talk about it too much!

(MAMA *enters and is immediately all social charm because of the presence of a guest.*)

BENEATHA Oh—Mama—this is Mr. Asagai.

MAMA How do you do?

ASAGAI (*total politeness to an elder*) How do you do, Mrs. Younger. Please forgive me for coming at such an outrageous hour on a Saturday.

MAMA Well, you are quite welcome. I just hope you understand that our house don't always look like this. (*chatterish*) You must come again. I would love to hear all about—(*not sure of the name*)—your country. I think it's so sad the way our American Negroes don't know nothing about Africa 'cept Tarzan and all that. And all that money they pour into these churches when they ought to be helping you people over there drive out them French and Englishmen done taken away your land.

(*The mother flashes a slightly superior look at her daughter upon completion of the recitation.*)

ASAGAI (*taken aback by this sudden and acutely unrelated expression of sympathy*) Yes . . . yes. . . .

MAMA (*smiling at him suddenly and relaxing and looking him over*)   How many miles is it from here to where you come from?

ASAGAI   Many thousands.

MAMA (*looking at him as she would* WALTER)   I bet you don't half look after yourself, being away from your mama either. I spec you better come 'round here from time to time and get yourself some decent home-cooked meals. . . .

ASAGAI (*moved*)   Thank you. Thank you very much. (*They are all quiet, then—*) Well . . . I must go. I will call you Monday, Alaiyo.

MAMA   What's that he call you?

ASAGAI   Oh—"Alaiyo." I hope you don't mind. It is what you would call a nickname, I think. It is a Yoruba word. I am a Yoruba.

MAMA (*looking at* BENEATHA)   I—I thought he was from—

ASAGAI (*understanding*)   Nigeria is my country. Yoruba is my tribal origin—

BENEATHA   You didn't tell us what Alaiyo means . . . for all I know, you might be calling me Little Idiot or something. . . .

ASAGAI   Well . . . let me see . . . I do not know how just to explain it. . . . The sense of a thing can be so different when it changes languages.

BENEATHA   You're evading.

ASAGAI   No—really it is difficult. . . . (*thinking*) It means . . . it means One for Whom Bread—Food—Is Not Enough. (*He looks at her.*) Is that all right?

BENEATHA (*understanding, softly*)   Thank you.

MAMA (*looking from one to the other and not understanding any of it*)   Well . . . that's nice. . . . You must come see us again—Mr.—

ASAGAI   Ah-sah-guy . . .

MAMA   Yes . . . Do come again.

ASAGAI   Good-bye. (*He exits.*)

MAMA (*after him*)   Lord, that's a pretty thing just went out here! (*insinuatingly, to her daughter*) Yes, I guess I see why we done commence to get so interested in Africa 'round here. Missionaries my aunt Jenny! (*She exits.*)

BENEATHA   Oh, Mama! . . .

(*She picks up the Nigerian dress and holds it up to her in front of the mirror again. She sets the headdress on haphazardly and then notices her hair again and clutches at it and then replaces the headdress and frowns at herself. Then she starts to wriggle in front of the mirror as she thinks a Nigerian woman might.* TRAVIS *enters and regards her.*)

TRAVIS   You cracking up?

BENEATHA   Shut up.

(*She pulls the headdress off and looks at herself in the mirror and clutches at her hair again and squinches her eyes as if trying to imagine something. Then, suddenly, she gets her raincoat and kerchief and hurriedly prepares for going out.*)

MAMA (*coming back into the room*)   She's resting now. Travis, baby, run next door and ask Miss Johnson to please let me have a little kitchen cleanser. This here can is empty as Jacob's kettle.

TRAVIS   I just come in.

MAMA   Do as you told. (*He exits and she looks at her daughter.*) Where you going?

BENEATHA (*halting at the door*)   To become a queen of the Nile!

(*She exits in a breathless blaze of glory.* RUTH *appears in the bedroom doorway.*)

MAMA   Who told you to get up?

RUTH   Ain't nothing wrong with me to be lying in no bed for. Where did Bennie go?

MAMA (*drumming her fingers*)   Far as I could make out—to Egypt. (RUTH *just looks at her.*) What time is it getting to?

RUTH   Ten twenty. And the mailman going to ring that bell this morning just like he done every morning for the last umpteen years.

(TRAVIS *comes in with the cleanser can.*)

TRAVIS   She say to tell you that she don't have much.

MAMA (*angrily*)   Lord, some people I could name sure is tight-fisted! (*directing her grandson*) Mark two cans of cleanser down on the list there. If she that hard up for kitchen cleanser, I sure don't want to forget to get her none!

RUTH   Lena—maybe the woman is just short on cleanser—

MAMA (*not listening*)   —Much baking powder as she done borrowed from me all these years, she could of done gone into the baking business!

(*The bell sounds suddenly and sharply and all three are stunned—serious and silent—mid-speech. In spite of all the other conversations and distractions of the morning, this is what they have been waiting for, even* TRAVIS, *who looks helplessly from his mother to his grandmother.* RUTH *is the first to come to life again.*)

RUTH (*to* TRAVIS)   *Get down them steps, boy!*

(TRAVIS *snaps to life and flies out to get the mail.*)

MAMA (*her eyes wide, her hand to her breast*)   You mean it done really come?

RUTH (*excitedly*)   Oh, Miss Lena!

MAMA (*collecting herself*)   Well . . . I don't know what we all so excited about 'round here for. We known it was coming for months.

RUTH   That's a whole lot different from having it come and being able to hold it in your hands . . . a piece of paper worth ten thousand dollars. . . . (TRAVIS *bursts back into the room. He holds the envelope high above his head, like a little dancer, his face is radiant and he is breathless. He moves to his grandmother with sudden slow ceremony and puts the envelope into her hands. She accepts it, and then merely holds it and looks at it.*) Come on! Open it . . . Lord have mercy, I wish Walter Lee was here!

TRAVIS Open it, Grandmama!

MAMA (*staring at it*) Now you all be quiet. It's just a check.

RUTH Open it. . . .

MAMA (*still staring at it*) Now don't act silly. . . . We ain't never been no people to act silly 'bout no money—

RUTH (*swiftly*) We ain't never had none before—*open it!*

(MAMA *finally makes a good strong tear and pulls out the thin blue slice of paper and inspects it closely. The boy and his mother study it raptly over* MAMA's *shoulders.*)

MAMA Travis! (*She is counting off with doubt.*) Is that the right number of zeros?

TRAVIS Yes'm . . . ten thousand dollars. Gaalee, Grandmama, you rich.

MAMA (*She holds the check away from her, still looking at it. Slowly her face sobers into a mask of unhappiness*) Ten thousand dollars. (*She hands it to* RUTH.) Put it away somewhere, Ruth. (*She does not look at* RUTH; *her eyes seem to be seeing something somewhere very far off.*) Ten thousand dollars they give you. Ten thousand dollars.

TRAVIS (*to his mother, sincerely*) What's the matter with Grandmama—don't she want to be rich?

RUTH (*distractedly*) You go out and play now, baby. (TRAVIS *exits.* MAMA *starts wiping dishes absently, humming intently to herself.* RUTH *turns to her, with kind exasperation.*) You're gone and got yourself upset.

MAMA (*not looking at her*) I spec if it wasn't for all you . . . I would just put that money away or give it to the church or something.

RUTH Now what kind of talk is that. Mr. Younger would just be plain mad if he could hear you talking foolish like that.

MAMA (*stopping and staring off*) Yes . . . he sure would. (*sighing*) We got enough to do with that money, all right. (*She halts then, and turns and looks at her daughter-in-law hard;* RUTH *avoids her eyes and* MAMA *wipes her hands with finality and starts to speak firmly to* RUTH.) Where did you go today, girl?

RUTH To the doctor.

MAMA (*impatiently*) Now, Ruth . . . you know better than that. Old Doctor Jones is strange enough in his way but there ain't nothing 'bout him make somebody slip and call him "she"—like you done this morning.

RUTH Well, that's what happened—my tongue slipped.

MAMA You went to see that woman, didn't you?

RUTH (*defensively, giving herself away*) What woman you talking about?

MAMA (*angrily*) That woman who—

(WALTER *enters in great excitement.*)

WALTER   Did it come?

MAMA (*quietly*)   Can't you give people a Christian greeting before you start asking about money?

WALTER (*to* RUTH)   Did it come? (RUTH *unfolds the check and lays it quietly before him, watching him intently with thoughts of her own.* WALTER *sits down and grasps it close and counts off the zeros.*) Ten thousand dollars—(*He turns suddenly, frantically to his mother and draws some papers out of his breast pocket.*) Mama—look. Old Willy Harris put everything on paper—

MAMA   Son—I think you ought to talk to your wife. . . . I'll go on out and leave you alone if you want—

WALTER   I can talk to her later—Mama, look—

MAMA   Son—

WALTER   WILL SOMEBODY PLEASE LISTEN TO ME TODAY!

MAMA (*quietly*)   I don't 'low no yellin' in this house, Walter Lee, and you know it—(WALTER *stares at them in frustration and starts to speak several times.*) And there ain't going to be no investing in no liquor stores. I don't aim to have to speak on that again.

(*A long pause.*)

WALTER   Oh—so you don't aim to have to speak on that again? So *you* have decided. . . . (*crumpling his papers*) Well, *you* tell that to my boy tonight when you put him to sleep on the living-room couch. . . . (*turning to* MAMA *and speaking directly to her*) Yeah—and tell it to my wife, Mama, tomorrow when she has to go out of here to look after somebody else's kids. And tell it to *me*, Mama, every time we need a new pair of curtains and I have to watch *you* go out and work in somebody's kitchen. Yeah, you tell me then!

(WALTER *starts out.*)

RUTH   Where you going?

WALTER   I'm going out!

RUTH   Where?

WALTER   Just out of this house somewhere—

RUTH (*getting her coat*)   I'll come too.

WALTER   I don't want you to come!

RUTH   I got something to talk to you about, Walter.

WALTER   That's too bad.

MAMA (*still quietly*)   Walter Lee—(*She waits and he finally turns and looks at her.*) Sit down.

WALTER   I'm a grown man, Mama.

MAMA   Ain't nobody said you wasn't grown. But you still in my house and my presence. And as long as you are—you'll talk to your wife civil. Now sit down.

RUTH (*suddenly*)   Oh, let him go on out and drink himself to death! He makes me sick to my stomach! (*She flings her coat against him.*)

WALTER (*violently*)   And you turn mine too, baby! (RUTH *goes into their bedroom and slams the door behind her.*) That was my greatest mistake—

MAMA (*still quietly*)   Walter, what is the matter with you?

WALTER   Matter with me? Ain't nothing the matter with *me!*

MAMA   Yes there is. Something eating you up like a crazy man. Something more than me not giving you this money. The past few years I been watching it happen to you. You get all nervous acting and kind of wild in the eyes—(WALTER *jumps up impatiently at her words.*) I said sit there now, I'm talking to you!

WALTER   Mama—I don't need no nagging at me today.

MAMA   Seem like you getting to a place where you always tied up in some kind of knot about something. But if anybody ask you 'bout it you just yell at 'em and bust out the house and go out and drink somewheres. Walter Lee, people can't live with that. Ruth's a good, patient girl in her way—but you getting to be too much. Boy, don't make the mistake of driving that girl away from you.

WALTER   Why—what she do for me?

MAMA   She loves you.

WALTER   Mama—I'm going out. I want to go off somewhere and be by myself for a while.

MAMA   I'm sorry 'bout your liquor store, son. It just wasn't the thing for us to do. That's what I want to tell you about—

WALTER   I got to go out, Mama—(*He rises.*)

MAMA   It's dangerous, son.

WALTER   What's dangerous?

MAMA   When a man goes outside his home to look for peace.

WALTER (*beseechingly*)   Then why can't there never be no peace in this house then?

MAMA   You done found it in some other house?

WALTER   No—there ain't no woman! Why do women always think there's a woman somewhere when a man gets restless. (*coming to her*) Mama—Mama—I want so many things. . . .

MAMA   Yes, son—

WALTER   I want so many things that they are driving me kind of crazy. . . . Mama—look at me.

MAMA   I'm looking at you. You a good-looking boy. You got a job, a nice wife, a fine boy and—

WALTER   A job. (*looks at her*) Mama, a job? I open and close car doors all day long. I drive a man around in his limousine and I say, "Yes, sir; no, sir; very good, sir; shall I take the Drive, sir?" Mama, that ain't no kind of job . . . that ain't nothing at all. (*very quietly*) Mama, I don't know if I can make you understand.

MAMA   Understand what, baby?

WALTER (*quietly*)   Sometimes it's like I can see the future stretched out in front of me—just plain as day. The future, Mama. Hanging over there at the edge of my days. Just waiting for me—a big, looming blank space—full of *nothing*. Just waiting for *me*. (*pause*) Mama—sometimes when I'm downtown and I pass them cool, quiet-looking restaurants where them white boys are sitting back and talking 'bout things . . . sitting there turning deals worth millions of dollars . . . sometimes I see guys don't look much older than me—

MAMA   Son—how come you talk so much 'bout money?

WALTER (*with immense passion*)   Because it is life, Mama!

MAMA (*quietly*)   Oh—(*very quietly*) So now it's life. Money is life. Once upon a time freedom used to be life—now it's money. I guess the world really do change. . . .

WALTER   No—it was always money, Mama. We just didn't know about it.

MAMA   No . . . something has changed. (*She looks at him.*) You something new, boy. In my time we was worried about not being lynched and getting to the North if we could and how to stay alive and still have a pinch of dignity too. . . . Now here come you and Beneatha—talking 'bout things we ain't never even thought about hardly, me and your daddy. You ain't satisfied or proud of nothing we done. I mean that you had a home; that we kept you out of trouble till you was grown; that you don't have to ride to work on the back of nobody's streetcar—You my children—but how different we done become.

WALTER   You just don't understand, Mama, you just don't understand.

MAMA   Son—do you know your wife is expecting another baby? (WALTER *stands, stunned, and absorbs what his mother has said.*) That's what she wanted to talk to you about. (WALTER *sinks down into a chair.*) This ain't for me to be telling—but you ought to know. (*She waits.*) I think Ruth is thinking 'bout getting rid of that child.

WALTER (*slowly understanding*)   No—no—Ruth wouldn't do that.

MAMA   When the world gets ugly enough—a woman will do anything for her family. *The part that's already living.*

WALTER   You don't know Ruth, Mama, if you think she would do that.

(RUTH *opens the bedroom door and stands there a little limp.*)

RUTH (*beaten*)   Yes I would too, Walter. (*pause*) I gave her a five-dollar down payment.

(*There is total silence as the man stares at his wife and the mother stares at her son.*)

MAMA (*presently*)   Well—(*tightly*) Well—son, I'm waiting to hear you say something. . . . I'm waiting to hear how you be your father's son. Be the man he was. . . . (*pause*) Your wife say she going to destroy your child. And I'm waiting to hear you talk like him and say we a people who give children life, not who destroys them—(*She rises.*) I'm waiting to see you stand up and look like your daddy and say we done give up one baby to poverty and that we ain't going to give up nary another one. . . . I'm waiting.

WALTER   Ruth—

MAMA   If you a son of mine, tell her! (WALTER *turns, looks at her and can say nothing. She continues, bitterly.*) You . . . you are a disgrace to your father's memory. Somebody get me my hat.

Curtain

Act II

Scene I

Time: Later the same day.

   At rise: RUTH *is ironing again. She has the radio going. Presently* BENEATHA'S *bedroom door opens and* RUTH'S *mouth falls and she puts down the iron in fascination.*

RUTH   What have we got on tonight!

BENEATHA (*emerging grandly from the doorway so that we can see her thoroughly robed in the costume* ASAGAI *brought*)   You are looking at what a well-dressed Nigerian woman wears—(*She parades for* RUTH, *her hair completely hidden by the headdress; she is coquettishly fanning herself with an ornate oriental fan, mistakenly more like Butterfly than any Nigerian that ever was.*) Isn't it beautiful? (*She promenades to the radio and, with an arrogant flourish, turns off the good loud blues that is playing.*) Enough of this assimilationist junk! (RUTH *follows her with her eyes as she goes to the phonograph and puts on a record and turns and waits ceremoniously for the music to come up. Then, with a shout—*) OCOMOGOSIAY!

(RUTH *jumps. The music comes up, a lovely Nigerian melody.* BENEATHA *listens, enraptured, her eyes far away—"back to the past." She begins to dance.* RUTH *is dumfounded.*)

RUTH   What kind of dance is that?

BENEATHA   A folk dance.

RUTH (*Pearl Bailey*)   What kind of folks do that, honey?

BENEATHA   It's from Nigeria. It's a dance of welcome.

RUTH   Who you welcoming?

BENEATHA   The men back to the village.

RUTH   Where they been?

BENEATHA   How should I know—out hunting or something. Anyway, they are coming back now. . . .

RUTH   Well, that's good.

BENEATHA (*with the record*)

> Alundi, alundi
> Alundi alunya
> Jop pu a jeepua
> Ang gu sooooooooooo
>
> Ai yai yae . . .
> Ayehaye—alundi . . .

(WALTER *comes in during this performance; he has obviously been drinking. He leans against the door heavily and watches his sister, at first with distaste. Then his eyes look off—"back to the past"—as he lifts both his fists to the roof, screaming.*)

WALTER YEAH . . . AND ETHIOPIA STRETCH FORTH HER HANDS AGAIN! . . .

RUTH (*drily, looking at him*) Yes—and Africa sure is claiming her own tonight. (*She gives them both up and starts ironing again.*)

WALTER (*all in a drunken, dramatic shout*) Shut up! . . . I'm digging them drums . . . them drums move me! . . . (*He makes his weaving way to his wife's face and leans in close to her.*) In my *heart of hearts*—(*he thumps his chest*)—I am much warrior!

RUTH (*without even looking up*) In your heart of hearts you are much drunkard.

WALTER (*coming away from her and starting to wander around the room, shouting.*) Me and Jomo . . . (*intently, in his sister's face. She has stopped dancing to watch him in this unknown mood.*) That's my man, Kenyatta. (*shouting and thumping his chest*) FLAMING SPEAR! HOT DAMN! (*He is suddenly in possession of an imaginary spear and actively spearing enemies all over the room.*) OCOMOGOSIAY . . . THE LION IS WAKING . . . OWIMOWEH! (*He pulls his shirt open and leaps up on a table and gestures with his spear. The bell rings.* RUTH *goes to answer.*)

BENEATHA (*to encourage* WALTER, *thoroughly caught up with this side of him*) OCOMOGOSIAY, FLAMING SPEAR!

WALTER (*on the table, very far gone, his eyes pure glass sheets; he sees what we cannot, that he is a leader of his people, a great chief, a descendant of Chaka, and that the hour to march has come*) Listen, my black broth—ers—

BENEATHA OCOMOGOSIAY!

WALTER —Do you hear the waters rushing against the shores of the coastlands—

BENEATHA OCOMOGOSIAY!

WALTER —Do you hear the screeching of the cocks in yonder hills beyond where the chiefs meet in council for the coming of the mighty war—

BENEATHA OCOMOGOSIAY!

WALTER —Do you hear the beating of the wings of the birds flying low over the mountains and the low places of our land—

(RUTH *opens the door.* GEORGE MURCHISON *enters.*)

BENEATHA   OCOMOGOSIAY!

WALTER   —Do you hear the singing of the women, singing the war songs of our fathers to the babies in the great houses . . . singing the sweet war songs? OH, DO YOU HEAR, MY BLACK BROTHERS!

BENEATHA (*completely gone*)   We hear you, Flaming Spear—

WALTER   Telling us to prepare for the greatness of the time—(*to* GEORGE) Black Brother! (*He extends his hand for the fraternal clasp.*)

GEORGE   Black Brother, hell!

RUTH (*having had enough, and embarrassed for the family*)   Beneatha, you got company—what's the matter with you? Walter Lee Younger, get down off that table and stop acting like a fool. . . .

(WALTER *comes down off the table suddenly and makes a quick exit to the bathroom.*)

RUTH   He's had a little to drink. . . . I don't know what her excuse is.

GEORGE (*to* BENEATHA)   Look honey, we're going *to* the theater—we're not going to be *in* it . . . so go change, huh?

RUTH   You expect this boy to go out with you looking like that?

BENEATHA (*looking at* GEORGE)   That's up to George. If he's ashamed of his heritage—

GEORGE   Oh, don't be so proud of yourself, Bennie—just because you look eccentric.

BENEATHA   How can something that's natural be eccentric?

GEORGE   That's what being eccentric means—being natural. Get dressed.

BENEATHA   I don't like that, George.

RUTH   Why must you and your brother make an argument out of everything people say?

BENEATHA   Because I hate assimilationist Negroes!

RUTH   Will somebody please tell me what assimila-whoever means!

GEORGE   Oh, it's just a college girl's way of calling people Uncle Toms—but that isn't what it means at all.

BENEATHA (*cutting* GEORGE *off and staring at him as she replies to* RUTH)   It means someone who is willing to give up his own culture and submerge himself completely in the dominant, and in this case, *oppressive* culture!

GEORGE   Oh, dear, dear, dear! Here we go! A lecture on the African past! On our Great West African Heritage! In one second we will hear all about the great Ashanti empires; the great Songhay civilizations; and the great sculpture of Bénin—and then some poetry in the Bantu—and the whole monologue will end with the word *heritage!* (*nastily*) Let's face it, baby, your heritage is nothing but a bunch of raggedy-assed spirituals and some grass huts!

BENEATHA   *Grass huts!* (RUTH *crosses to her and forcibly pushes her toward the bedroom.*) See there . . . you are standing there in your splendid ignorance talking about people who were the first to smelt iron on the face of the earth! (RUTH *is pushing her through the door.*) The Ashanti were performing surgical operations when the English—(RUTH *pulls the door to, with* BE- NEATHA *on the other side, and smiles graciously at* GEORGE. BENEATHA *opens the door and shouts the end of the sentence defiantly at* GEORGE.)—were still tattooing themselves with blue dragons. . . . (*She goes back inside.*)

RUTH   Have a seat, George. (*They both sit.* RUTH *folds her hands rather primly on her lap, determined to demonstrate the civilization of the family.*) Warm, ain't it? I mean for September. (*pause*) Just like they always say about Chicago weather: If it's too hot or cold for you, just wait a minute and it'll change. (*She smiles happily at this cliché of clichés.*) Everybody say it's got to do with them bombs and things they keep setting off. (*pause*) Would you like a nice cold beer?

GEORGE   No, thank you. I don't care for beer. (*He looks at his watch.*) I hope she hurries up.

RUTH   What time is the show?

GEORGE   It's an eight-thirty curtain. That's just Chicago, though. In New York standard curtain time is eight forty. (*He is rather proud of this knowledge.*)

RUTH (*properly appreciating it*)   You get to New York a lot?

GEORGE (*offhand*)   Few times a year.

RUTH   Oh—that's nice. I've never been to New York.

(WALTER *enters. We feel he has relieved himself, but the edge of unreality is still with him.*)

WALTER   New York ain't got nothing Chicago ain't. Just a bunch of hustling people all squeezed up together—being "Eastern." (*He turns his face into a screw of displeasure.*)

GEORGE   Oh—you've been?

WALTER   *Plenty* of times.

RUTH (*shocked at the lie*)   Walter Lee Younger!

WALTER (*staring her down*)   Plenty! (*pause*) What we got to drink in this house? Why don't you offer this man some refreshment? (*to* GEORGE) They don't know how to entertain people in this house, man.

GEORGE   Thank you—I don't really care for anything.

WALTER (*feeling his head; sobriety coming*)   Where's Mama?

RUTH   She ain't come back yet.

WALTER (*looking* MURCHISON *over from head to toe, scrutinizing his carefully casual tweed sports jacket over cashmere V-neck sweater over soft eyelet shirt and tie, and soft slacks, finished off with white buckskin shoes*)   Why all you college boys wear them fairyish-looking white shoes?

RUTH   Walter Lee!

(GEORGE MURCHISON *ignores the remark.*)

WALTER (*to* RUTH)   Well, they look crazy as hell—white shoes, cold as it is.

RUTH (*crushed*)   You have to excuse him—

WALTER   No he don't! Excuse me for what? What you always excusing me for! I'll excuse myself when I needs to be excused! (*a pause*) They look as funny as them black knee socks Beneatha wears out of here all the time.

RUTH   It's the college *style*, Walter.

WALTER   Style, hell. She looks like she got burnt legs or something!

RUTH   Oh, Walter—

WALTER (*an irritable mimic*)   Oh, Walter! Oh, Walter! (*to* MURCHISON) How's your old man making out? I understand you all going to buy that big hotel on the Drive? (*He finds a beer in the refrigerator, wanders over to* MURCHISON, *sipping and wiping his lips with the back of his hand, and straddling a chair backwards to talk to the other man.*) Shrewd move. Your old man is all right, man. (*tapping his head and half winking for emphasis*) I mean he knows how to operate. I mean he thinks *big,* you know what I mean, I mean for a *home,* you know? But I think he's kind of running out of ideas now. I'd like to talk to him. Listen, man, I got some plans that could turn this city upside down. I mean I think like he does. *Big.* Invest big, gamble big, hell, lose *big* if you have to, you know what I mean. It's hard to find a man on this whole Southside who understands my kind of thinking—you dig? (*He scrutinizes* MURCHISON *again, drinks his beer, squints his eyes and leans in close, confidential, man to man.*) Me and you ought to sit down and talk sometimes, man. Man, I got me some ideas. . . .

MURCHISON (*with boredom*)   Yeah—sometimes we'll have to do that, Walter.

WALTER (*understanding the indifference, and offended*)   Yeah—well, when you get the time, man. I know you a busy little boy.

RUTH   Walter, please—

WALTER (*bitterly, hurt*)   I know ain't nothing in this world as busy as you colored college boys with your fraternity pins and white shoes. . . .

RUTH (*covering her face with humiliation*)   Oh, Walter Lee—

WALTER   I see you all all the time—with the books tucked under your arms—going to your (*British A—a mimic*) "clahsses." And for what! What the hell you learning over there? Filling up your heads—(*counting off on his fingers*)—with the sociology and the psychology—but they teaching you how to be a man? How to take over and run the world? They teaching you how to run a rubber plantation or a steel mill? Naw—just to talk proper and read books and wear white shoes. . . .

GEORGE (*looking at him with distaste, a little above it all*)   You're all wacked up with bitterness, man.

WALTER (*intently, almost quietly, between the teeth, glaring at the boy*)   And you—ain't you bitter, man? Ain't you just about had it yet? Don't you see no stars gleaming that you can't reach out and grab? You happy?—You contented son-of-a-bitch—you happy? You got it made? Bitter? Man, I'm a volcano. Bitter? Here I am a giant—surrounded by ants! Ants who can't even understand what it is the giant is talking about.

RUTH (*passionately and suddenly*)   Oh, Walter—ain't you with nobody!

WALTER (*violently*)   No! 'Cause ain't nobody with me! Not even my own mother!

RUTH   Walter, that's a terrible thing to say!

(BENEATHA *enters, dressed for the evening in a cocktail dress and earrings.*)

GEORGE   Well—hey, you look great.

BENEATHA   Let's go, George. See you all later.

RUTH   Have a nice time.

GEORGE   Thanks. Good night. (*to* WALTER, *sarcastically*) Good night, *Prometheus.* (BENEATHA *and* GEORGE *exit.*)

WALTER (*to* RUTH)   Who is Prometheus?

RUTH   I don't know. Don't worry about it.

WALTER (*in a fury, pointing after* GEORGE)   See there—they get to a point where they can't insult you man to man—they got to talk about something ain't nobody never heard of!

RUTH   How do you know it was an insult? (*to humor him*) Maybe Prometheus is a nice fellow.

WALTER   Prometheus! I bet there ain't even no such thing! I bet that simpleminded clown—

RUTH   Walter—(*She stops what she is doing and looks at him.*)

WALTER (*yelling*)   Don't start!

RUTH   Start what?

WALTER   Your nagging! Where was I? Who was I with? How much money did I spend?

RUTH (*plaintively*)   Walter Lee—why don't we just try to talk about it. . . .

WALTER (*not listening*)   I been out talking with people who understand me. People who care about the things I got on my mind.

RUTH (*wearily*)   I guess that means people like Willy Harris.

WALTER   Yes, people like Willy Harris.

RUTH (*with a sudden flash of impatience*)   Why don't you all just hurry up and go into the banking business and stop talking about it!

WALTER   Why? You want to know why? 'Cause we all tied up in a race of people that don't know how to do nothing but moan, pray and have babies!

(*The line is too bitter even for him and he looks at her and sits down.*)

RUTH   Oh, Walter . . . (*softly*) Honey, why can't you stop fighting me?

WALTER (*without thinking*)   Who's fighting you? Who even cares about you?

(*This line begins the retardation of his mood.*)

RUTH   Well—(*She waits a long time, and then with resignation starts to put away her things.*) I guess I might as well go on to bed. . . . (*more or less to herself*) I don't know where we lost it . . . but we have. . . . (*then, to him*) I—I'm sorry about this new baby, Walter. I guess maybe I better go on and do what I started . . . I guess I just didn't realize how bad things was with us . . . I guess I just didn't really realize—(*She starts out to the bedroom and stops.*) You want some hot milk?

WALTER   Hot milk?

RUTH   Yes—hot milk.

WALTER   Why hot milk?

RUTH   'Cause after all that liquor you come home with you ought to have something hot in your stomach.

WALTER   I don't want no milk.

RUTH   You want some coffee then?

WALTER   No, I don't want no coffee. I don't want nothing hot to drink. (*almost plaintively*) Why you always trying to give me something to eat?

RUTH   (*standing and looking at him helplessly*)   What else can I give you, Walter Lee Younger?

(*She stands and looks at him and presently turns to go out again. He lifts his head and watches her going away from him in a new mood which began to emerge when he asked her "Who cares about you?"*)

WALTER   It's been rough, ain't it, baby? (*She hears and stops but does not turn around and he continues to her back.*) I guess between two people there ain't never as much understood as folks generally thinks there is. I mean like between me and you—(*She turns to face him.*) How we gets to the place where we scared to talk softness to each other. (*He waits, thinking hard himself.*) Why you think it got to be like that? (*He is thoughtful, almost as a child would be.*) Ruth, what is it gets into people ought to be close?

RUTH   I don't know, honey. I think about it a lot.

WALTER   On account of you and me, you mean? The way things are with us. The way something done come down between us.

RUTH   There ain't so much between us, Walter. . . . Not when you come to me and try to talk to me. Try to be with me . . . a little even.

WALTER   (*total honesty*)   Sometimes . . . sometimes . . . I don't even know how to try.

RUTH   Walter—

WALTER   Yes?

RUTH   (*coming to him, gently and with misgiving, but coming to him*)   Honey . . . life don't have to be like this. I mean sometimes people can do things so that things are better. . . . You remember how we used to talk when Travis was born . . . about the way we were going to live . . . the kind of house . . . (*She is stroking his head.*) Well, it's all starting to slip away from us. . . .

(MAMA *enters, and* WALTER *jumps up and shouts at her.*)

WALTER   Mama, where have you been?

MAMA   My—them steps is longer than they used to be. Whew! (*She sits down and ignores him.*) How you feeling this evening, Ruth?

(RUTH *shrugs, disturbed some at having been prematurely interrupted and watching her husband knowingly.*)

WALTER   Mama, where have you been all day?

MAMA (*still ignoring him and leaning on the table and changing to more comfortable shoes*)   Where's Travis?

RUTH   I let him go out earlier and he ain't come back yet. Boy, is he going to get it!

WALTER   Mama!

MAMA (*as if she has heard him for the first time*)   Yes, son?

WALTER   Where did you go this afternoon?

MAMA   I went downtown to tend to some business that I had to tend to.

WALTER   What kind of business?

MAMA   You know better than to question me like a child, Brother.

WALTER (*rising and bending over the table*)   Where were you, Mama? (*bringing his fists down and shouting*) Mama, you didn't go do something with that insurance money, something crazy?

(*The front door opens slowly, interrupting him, and* TRAVIS *peeks his head in, less than hopefully.*)

TRAVIS (*to his mother*)   Mama, I—

RUTH   "Mama I" nothing! You're going to get it, boy! Get on in that bedroom and get yourself ready!

TRAVIS   But I—

MAMA   Why don't you all never let the child explain hisself.

RUTH   Keep out of it now, Lena.

(MAMA *clamps her lips together, and* RUTH *advances toward her son menacingly.*)

RUTH   A thousand times I have told you not to go off like that—

MAMA (*holding out her arms to her grandson*)   Well—at least let me tell him something. I want him to be the first one to hear. . . . Come here, Travis. (*The boy obeys, gladly.*) Travis—(*She takes him by the shoulder and looks into his face.*)—you know that money we got in the mail this morning?

TRAVIS   Yes'm—

MAMA   Well—what do you think your grandmama gone and done with that money?

TRAVIS   I don't know, Grandmama.

MAMA (*putting her finger on his nose for emphasis*)   She went out and she bought you a house! (*The explosion comes from* WALTER *at the end of the revelation and he jumps up and turns away from all of them in a fury.* MAMA *continues, to* TRAVIS:) You glad about the house? It's going to be yours when you get to be a man.

TRAVIS   Yeah—I always wanted to live in a house.

MAMA   All right, gimme some sugar then—(TRAVIS *puts his arms around her neck as she watches her son over the boy's shoulder. Then, to* TRAVIS, *after the embrace:*) Now when you say your prayers tonight, you thank God and your grandfather—'cause it was him who give you the house—in his way.

RUTH (*taking the boy from* MAMA *and pushing him toward the bedroom*)   Now you get out of here and get ready for your beating.

TRAVIS   Aw, Mama—

RUTH   Get on in there—(*closing the door behind him and turning radiantly to her mother-in-law*) So you went and did it!

MAMA (*quietly, looking at her son with pain*)   Yes, I did.

RUTH (*raising both arms classically*)   Praise God! (*Looks at* WALTER *a moment, who says nothing. She crosses rapidly to her husband.*) Please, honey—let me be glad . . . you be glad too. (*She has laid her hands on his shoulders, but he shakes himself free of her roughly, without turning to face her.*) Oh, Walter . . . a home . . . a home . . . a home. (*She comes back to* MAMA.) Well—where is it? How big is it? How much it going to cost?

MAMA   Well—

RUTH   When we moving?

MAMA (*smiling at her*)   First of the month.

RUTH (*throwing back her head with jubilance*)   Praise God!

MAMA (*tentatively, still looking at her son's back turned against her and* RUTH)   It's—it's a nice house too. . . . (*She cannot help speaking directly to him. An imploring quality in her voice, her manner, makes her almost like a girl now.*) Three bedrooms—nice big one for you and Ruth. . . . Me and Beneatha still have to share our room, but Travis have one of his own—and (*with difficulty*) I figure if the—new baby—is a boy, we could get one of them double-decker outfits. . . . And there's a yard with a little patch of dirt where I could maybe get to grow me a few flowers. . . . And a nice big basement. . . .

RUTH   Walter honey, be glad—

MAMA (*still to his back, fingering things on the table*)   'Course I don't want to make it sound fancier than it is. . . . It's just a plain little old house—but it's made good and solid—and it will be *ours*. Walter Lee—it makes a difference in a man when he can walk on floors that belong to *him*. . . .

RUTH   Where is it?

MAMA (*frightened at this telling*)   Well—well—it's out there in Clybourne Park—

(RUTH's *radiance fades abruptly, and* WALTER *finally turns slowly to face his mother with incredulity and hostility.*)

RUTH   Where?

MAMA (*matter-of-factly*)   Four o six Clybourne Street, Clybourne Park.

RUTH   Clybourne Park? Mama, there ain't no colored people living in Clybourne Park.

MAMA (*almost idiotically*)   Well, I guess there's going to be some now.

WALTER (*bitterly*)   So that's the peace and comfort you went out and bought for us today!

MAMA (*raising her eyes to meet his finally*)   Son—I just tried to find the nicest place for the least amount of money for my family.

RUTH (*trying to recover from the shock*)   Well—well—'course I ain't one never been 'fraid of no crackers, mind you—but—well, wasn't there no other houses nowhere?

MAMA   Them houses they put up for colored in them areas way out all seem to cost twice as much as other houses. I did the best I could.

RUTH (*Struck senseless with the news, in its various degrees of goodness and trouble, she sits a moment, her fists propping her chin in thought, and then she starts to rise, bringing her fists down with vigor, the radiance spreading from cheek to cheek again.*)   Well—well!—All I can say is—if this is my time in life—my time—to say goodbye— (*And she builds with momentum as she starts to circle the room with an exuberant, almost tearfully happy release.*)—to these Goddamned cracking walls!— (*She pounds the walls.*) — and these marching roaches!— (*She wipes at an imaginary army of marching roaches.*)—and this cramped little closet which ain't now or never was no kitchen! . . . then I say it loud and good, Hallelujah! and good-bye misery. . . . I don't never want to see your ugly face again! (*She laughs joyously, having practically destroyed the apartment, and flings her arms up and lets them come down happily, slowly, reflectively, over her abdomen, aware for the first time perhaps that the life therein pulses with happiness and not despair.*) Lena?

MAMA (*moved, watching with happiness*)   Yes, honey?

RUTH (*looking off*)   Is there—is there a whole lot of sunlight?

MAMA (*understanding*)   Yes, child, there's a whole lot of sunlight.

(*Long pause.*)

RUTH (*collecting herself and going to the door of the room* TRAVIS *is in*) Well—I guess I better see 'bout Travis. (*to* MAMA) Lord, I sure don't feel like whipping nobody today! (*She exits.*)

MAMA (*the mother and son are left alone now and the mother waits a long time, considering deeply, before she speaks*)   Son—you—you understand what I done, don't you? (WALTER *is silent and sullen.*) I—I just seen my family falling apart today . . . just falling to pieces in front of my eyes. . . . We

couldn't of gone on like we was today. We was going backwards 'stead of for-
wards—talking 'bout killing babies and wishing each other was dead. . . .
When it gets like that in life—you just got to do something different, push
on out and do something bigger. . . . (*She waits.*) I wish you say something,
son . . . I wish you'd say how deep inside you you think I done the right
thing—

WALTER (*crossing slowly to his bedroom door and finally turning there and speaking measuredly*)   What you need me to say you done right for? *You* the head
of this family. You run our lives like you want to. It was your money and you
did what you wanted with it. So what you need for me to say it was all right
for? (*bitterly, to hurt her as deeply as he knows is possible*) So you butchered
up a dream of mine—you—who always talking 'bout your children's
dreams. . . .

MAMA   Walter Lee—

(*He just closes the door behind him.* MAMA *sits alone, thinking heavily.*)

Curtain

Scene II

Time: Friday night, a few weeks later.
   At rise: Packing crates mark the intention of the family to move. BENEATHA *and*
GEORGE *come in, presumably from an evening out again.*

GEORGE   O.K. . . . O.K., whatever you say. . . . (*They both sit on the couch. He
tries to kiss her. She moves away.*) Look, we've had a nice evening; let's not
spoil it, huh? . . .

(*He again turns her head and tries to nuzzle in and she turns away from him, not
with distaste but with momentary lack of interest; in a mood to pursue what they
were talking about.*)

BENEATHA   I'm *trying* to talk to you.

GEORGE   We always talk.

BENEATHA   Yes—and I love to talk.

GEORGE (*exasperated; rising*)   I know it and I don't mind it sometimes . . . I
want you to cut it out, see—The moody stuff. I mean. I don't like it. You're a
nice-looking girl . . . all over. That's all you need, honey, forget the atmosphere. Guys aren't going to go for the atmosphere—they're going to go for
what they see. Be glad for that. Drop the Garbo routine. It doesn't go with
you. As for myself, I want a nice—(*groping*)—simple (*thoughtfully*)—sophisticated girl . . . not a poet—O.K.?

(*She rebuffs him again and he starts to leave.*)

BENEATHA   Why are you angry?

GEORGE   Because this is stupid! I don't go out with you to discuss the nature of "quiet desperation" or to hear all about your thoughts—because the world will go on thinking what it thinks regardless—

BENEATHA   Then why read books? Why go to school?

GEORGE   (*with artificial patience, counting on his fingers*)   It's simple. You read books—to learn facts—to get grades—to pass the course—to get a degree. That's all—it has nothing to do with thoughts.

(*A long pause.*)

BENEATHA   I see. (*a longer pause as she looks at him*) Good night, George.

(GEORGE *looks at her a little oddly, and starts to exit. He meets* MAMA *coming in.*)

GEORGE   Oh—hello, Mrs. Younger.

MAMA   Hello, George, how you feeling?

GEORGE   Fine—fine, how are you?

MAMA   Oh, a little tired. You know them steps can get you after a day's work. You all have a nice time tonight?

GEORGE   Yes—a fine time. Well, good night.

MAMA   Good night. (*He exits.* MAMA *closes the door behind her.*) Hello, honey. What you sitting like that for?

BENEATHA   I'm just sitting.

MAMA   Didn't you have a nice time?

BENEATHA   No.

MAMA   No? What's the matter?

BENEATHA   Mama, George is a fool—honest. (*She rises.*)

MAMA   (*hustling around unloading the packages she has entered with; she stops*)   Is he, baby?

BENEATHA   Yes.

(BENEATHA *makes up* TRAVIS' *bed as she talks.*)

MAMA   You sure?

BENEATHA   Yes.

MAMA   Well—I guess you better not waste your time with no fools.

(BENEATHA *looks up at her mother, watching her put groceries in the refrigerator. Finally she gathers up her things and starts into the bedroom. At the door she stops and looks back at her mother.*)

BENEATHA   Mama—

MAMA   Yes, baby—

BENEATHA   Thank you.

MAMA   For what?

BENEATHA   For understanding me this time.

(*She exits quickly and the mother stands, smiling a little, looking at the place where* BENEATHA *just stood.* RUTH *enters.*)

RUTH   Now don't you fool with any of this stuff, Lena—
MAMA   Oh, I just thought I'd sort a few things out.

(*The phone rings.* RUTH *answers.*)

RUTH (*at the phone*)   Hello—Just a minute. (*goes to the door*) Walter, it's Mrs. Arnold. (*waits; goes back to the phone; tense*) Hello. Yes, this is his wife speaking . . . He's lying down now. Yes . . . well, he'll be in tomorrow. He's been very sick. Yes—I know we should have called, but we were so sure he'd be able to come in today. Yes—yes, I'm very sorry. Yes . . . Thank you very much. (*She hangs up.* WALTER *is standing in the doorway of the bedroom behind her.*) That was Mrs. Arnold.
WALTER (*indifferently*)   Was it?
RUTH   She said if you don't come in tomorrow that they are getting a new man. . . .
WALTER   Ain't that sad—ain't that crying sad.
RUTH   She said Mr. Arnold has had to take a cab for three days. . . . Walter, you ain't been to work for three days! (*This is a revelation to her.*) Where you been, Walter Lee Younger? (WALTER *looks at her and starts to laugh.*) You're going to lose your job.
WALTER   That's right . . .
RUTH   Oh, Walter, and with your mother working like a dog every day—
WALTER   That's sad too—Everything is sad.
MAMA   What you been doing for these three days, son?
WALTER   Mama—you don't know all the things a man what got leisure can find to do in this city. . . . What's this—Friday night? Well—Wednesday I borrowed Willy Harris' car and I went for a drive . . . just me and myself and I drove and drove . . . Way out . . . way past South Chicago, and I parked the car and I sat and looked at the steel mills all day long. I just sat in the car and looked at them big black chimneys for hours. Then I drove back and I went to the Green Hat. (*pause*) And Thursday—Thursday I borrowed the car again and I got in it and I pointed it the other way and I drove the other way—for hours—way, way up to Wisconsin, and I looked at the farms. I just drove and looked at the farms. Then I drove back and I went to the Green Hat. (*pause*) And today—today I didn't get the car. Today I just walked. All over the South side. And I looked at the Negroes and they looked at me and finally I just sat down on the curb at Thirty-ninth and South Parkway and I just sat there and watched the Negroes go by. And then I went to the Green Hat. You all sad? You all depressed? And you know where I am going right now—

(RUTH *goes out quietly.*)

MAMA   Oh, Big Walter, is this the harvest of our days?

WALTER   You know what I like about the Green Hat? (*He turns the radio on and a steamy, deep blues pours into the room.*) I like this little cat they got there who blows a sax. . . . He blows. He talks to me. He ain't but 'bout five feet tall and he's got a conked head and his eyes is always closed and he's all music—

MAMA (*rising and getting some papers out of her handbag*)   Walter—

WALTER   And there's this other guy who plays the piano . . . and they got a sound. I mean they can work on some music. . . . They got the best little combo in the world in the Green Hat. . . . You can just sit there and drink and listen to them three men play and you realize that don't nothing matter worth a damn, but just being there—

MAMA   I've helped do it to you, haven't I, son? Walter, I been wrong.

WALTER   Naw—you ain't never been wrong about nothing, Mama.

MAMA   Listen to me, now. I say I been wrong, son. That I been doing to you what the rest of the world been doing to you. (*She stops and he looks up slowly at her and she meets his eyes pleadingly.*) Walter—what you ain't never understood is that I ain't got nothing, don't own nothing, ain't never really wanted nothing that wasn't for you. There ain't nothing as precious to me. . . . There ain't nothing worth holding on to, money, dreams, nothing else—if it means—if it means it's going to destroy my boy. (*She puts her papers in front of him and he watches her without speaking or moving.*) I paid the man thirty-five hundred dollars down on the house. That leaves sixty-five hundred dollars. Monday morning I want you to take this money and take three thousand dollars and put it in a savings account for Beneatha's medical schooling. The rest you put in a checking account—with your name on it. And from now on any penny that come out of it or that go in it is for you to look after. For you to decide. (*She drops her hands a little helplessly.*) It ain't much, but it's all I got in the world and I'm putting it in your hands. I'm telling you to be the head of this family from now on like you supposed to be.

WALTER (*stares at the money*)   You trust me like that, Mama?

MAMA   I ain't never stop trusting you. Like I ain't never stop loving you.

(*She goes out, and* WALTER *sits looking at the money on the table as the music continues in its idiom, pulsing in the room. Finally, in a decisive gesture, he gets up, and, in mingled joy and desperation, picks up the money. At the same moment,* TRAVIS *enters for bed.*)

TRAVIS   What's the matter, Daddy? You drunk?

WALTER (*sweetly, more sweetly than we have ever known him*)   No, Daddy ain't drunk. Daddy ain't going to never be drunk again. . . .

TRAVIS   Well, good night, Daddy.

(*The Father has come from behind the couch and leans over, embracing his son.*)

WALTER   Son, I feel like talking to you tonight.

TRAVIS   About what?

WALTER   Oh, about a lot of things. About you and what kind of man you going to be when you grow up. . . . Son—son, what do you want to be when you grow up?

TRAVIS   A bus driver.

WALTER (*laughing a little*)   A what? Man, that ain't nothing to want to be!

TRAVIS   Why not?

WALTER   'Cause, man—it ain't big enough—you know what I mean.

TRAVIS   I don't know then. I can't make up my mind. Sometimes Mama asks me that too. And sometimes when I tell her I just want to be like you—she says she don't want me to be like that and sometimes she says she does. . . .

WALTER (*gathering him up in his arms*)   You know what, Travis? In seven years you going to be seventeen years old. And things is going to be very different with us in seven years, Travis. . . . One day when you are seventeen I'll come home—home from my office downtown somewhere—

TRAVIS   You don't work in no office, Daddy.

WALTER   No—but after tonight. After what your daddy gonna do tonight, there's going to be offices—a whole lot of offices. . . .

TRAVIS   What you gonna do tonight, Daddy?

WALTER   You wouldn't understand yet, son, but your daddy's gonna make a transaction . . . a business transaction that's going to change our lives. . . . That's how come one day when you 'bout seventeen years old I'll come home and I'll be pretty tired, you know what I mean, after a day of conferences and secretaries getting things wrong the way they do . . . 'cause an executive's life is hell, man—(*The more he talks, the farther away he gets.*) And I'll pull the car up on the driveway . . . just a plain black Chrysler, I think, with white walls—no—black tires. More elegant. Rich people don't have to be flashy . . . though I'll have to get something a little sportier for Ruth—maybe a Cadillac convertible to do her shopping in. . . . And I'll come up the steps to the house and the gardener will be clipping away at the hedges and he'll say, "Good evening, Mr. Younger." And I'll say, "Hello, Jefferson, how are you this evening?" And I'll go inside and Ruth will come downstairs and meet me at the door and we'll kiss each other and she'll take my arm and we'll go up to your room to see you sitting on the floor with the catalogues of all the great schools in America around you. . . . All the great schools in the world! And—and I'll say, all right son—it's your seventeenth birthday, what is it you've decided? . . . Just tell me, where you want to go to school and you'll *go*. Just tell me, what it is you want to be—and you'll *be* it . . . . Whatever you want to be—Yessir! (*He holds his arms open for* TRAVIS.) You just name it, son . . . (TRAVIS *leaps into them.*) and I hand you the world!

(WALTER's *voice has risen in pitch and hysterical promise and on the last line he lifts* TRAVIS *high.*)

Blackout

Scene III

Time: Saturday, moving day, one week later.

Before the curtain rises, RUTH's *voice, a strident, dramatic church alto cuts through the silence.*

It is, in the darkness a triumphant surge, a penetrating statement of expectation: "Oh, Lord, I don't feel no ways tired! Children, oh, glory hallelujah!"

As the curtain rises we see that RUTH *is alone in the living room, finishing up the family's packing. It is moving day. She is nailing crates and tying cartons.* BENEATHA *enters, carrying a guitar case, and watches her exuberant sister-in-law.*

RUTH Hey!

BENEATHA (*putting away the case*) Hi.

RUTH (*pointing at a package*) Honey—look in that package there and see what I found on sale this morning at the South Center. (RUTH *gets up and moves to the package and draws out some curtains.*) Lookahere—hand-turned hems!

BENEATHA How do you know the window size out there?

RUTH (*who hadn't thought of that*) Oh—Well, they bound to fit something in the whole house. Anyhow, they was too good a bargain to pass up. (RUTH *slaps her head, suddenly remembering something.*) Oh, Bennie—I meant to put a special note on that carton over there. That's your mamma's good china and she wants 'em to be very careful with it.

BENEATHA I'll do it.

(BENEATHA *finds a piece of paper and starts to draw large letters on it.*)

RUTH You know what I'm going to do soon as I get in that new house?

BENEATHA What?

RUTH Honey—I'm going to run me a tub of water up to here.... (*with her fingers practically up to her nostrils*) And I'm going to get in it—and I am going to sit ... and sit ... and sit in that hot water and the first person who knocks to tell *me* to hurry up and come out—

BENEATHA Gets shot at sunrise.

RUTH (*laughing happily*) You said it, sister! (*noticing how large* BENEATHA *is absent-mindedly making the note*) Honey, they ain't going to read that from no airplane.

BENEATHA (*laughing herself*) I guess I always think things have more emphasis if they are big, somehow.

RUTH (*looking up at her and smiling*)   You and your brother seem to have that as a philosophy of life. Lord, that man—done changed so 'round here. You know—you know what we did last night? Me and Walter Lee?

BENEATHA   What?

RUTH (*smiling to herself*)   We went to the movies. (*looking at* BENEATHA *to see if she understands*) We went to the movies. You know the last time me and Walter went to the movies together?

BENEATHA   No.

RUTH   Me neither. That's how long it been. (*smiling again*) But we went last night. The picture wasn't much good, but that didn't seem to matter. We went—and we held hands.

BENEATHA   Oh, Lord!

RUTH   We held hands—and you know what?

BENEATHA   What?

RUTH   When we come out of the show it was late and dark and all the stores and things was closed up . . . and it was kind of chilly and there wasn't many people on the streets . . . and we was still holding hands, me and Walter.

BENEATHA   You're killing me.

(WALTER *enters with a large package. His happiness is deep in him; he cannot keep still with his new-found exuberance. He is singing and wiggling and snapping his fingers. He puts his package in a corner and puts a phonograph record, which he has brought in with him, on the record player. As the music comes up he dances over to* RUTH *and tries to get her to dance with him. She gives in at last to his raunchiness and in a fit of giggling allows herself to be drawn into his mood and together they deliberately burlesque an old social dance of their youth.*)

BENEATHA (*regarding them a long time as they dance, then drawing in her breath for a deeply exaggerated comment which she does not particularly mean*)   Talk about—oldddddddddd-fashioneddddddd—Negroes!

WALTER (*stopping momentarily*)   What kind of Negroes?

(*He says this in fun. He is not angry with her today, nor with anyone. He starts to dance with his wife again.*)

BENEATHA   Old-fashioned.

WALTER (*as he dances with* RUTH)   You know, when these *New Negroes* have their convention—(*pointing at his sister*)—that is going to be the chairman of the Committee on Unending Agitation. (*He goes on dancing, then stops.*) Race, race, race! . . . Girl, I do believe you are the first person in the history of the entire human race to successfully brainwash yourself. (BENEATHA *breaks up and he goes on dancing. He stops again, enjoying his tease.*) Damn, even the N double A C P takes a holiday sometimes! (BENEATHA *and* RUTH *laugh. He dances with* RUTH *some more and starts to laugh and stops and pantomimes someone over an operating table.*) I can just see that chick someday looking down at some poor cat on an operating table before she starts to slice him, saying . . . (*pulling his sleeves back maliciously*) "By the way, what are your views on civil rights down there? . . ."

(*He laughs at her again and starts to dance happily. The bell sounds.*)

BENEATHA Sticks and stones may break my bones but . . . words will never hurt me!

(BENEATHA *goes to the door and opens it as* WALTER *and* RUTH *go on with the clowning.* BENEATHA *is somewhat surprised to see a quiet-looking middle-aged white man in a business suit holding his hat and a briefcase in his hand and consulting a small piece of paper.*)

MAN Uh—how do you do, miss. I am looking for a Mrs.—(*he looks at the slip of paper*) Mrs. Lena Younger?

BENEATHA (*smoothing her hair with slight embarrassment*) Oh—yes, that's my mother. Excuse me. (*She closes the door and turns to quiet the other two.*) Ruth! Brother! Somebody's here. (*Then she opens the door. The man casts a curious quick glance at all of them.*) Uh—come in please.

MAN (*coming in*) Thank you.

BENEATHA My mother isn't here just now. Is it business?

MAN Yes . . . well, of a sort.

WALTER (*freely, the Man of the House*) Have a seat. I'm Mrs. Younger's son. I look after most of her business matters.

(RUTH *and* BENEATHA *exchange amused glances.*)

MAN (*regarding* WALTER, *and sitting*) Well—my name is Karl Lindner . . .

WALTER (*stretching out his hand*) Walter Younger. This is my wife—(RUTH *nods politely.*)—and my sister.

LINDNER How do you do.

WALTER (*amiably, as he sits himself easily on a chair, leaning with interest forward on his knees and looking expectantly into the newcomer's face*) What can we do for you, Mr. Lindner!

LINDNER (*some minor shuffling of the hat and briefcase on his knees*) Well—I am a representative of the Clybourne Park Improvement Association—

WALTER (*pointing*) Why don't you sit your things on the floor?

LINDNER Oh—yes. Thank you. (*He slides the briefcase and hat under the chair.*) And as I was saying—I am from the Clybourne Park Improvement Association and we have had it brought to our attention at the last meeting that you people—or at least your mother—has bought a piece of residential property at—(*he digs for the slip of paper again*)—four o six Clybourne Street. . . .

WALTER That's right. Care for something to drink? Ruth, get Mr. Lindner a beer.

LINDNER (*upset for some reason*)   Oh—no, really. I mean thank you very much, but no thank you.

RUTH (*innocently*)   Some coffee?

LINDNER   Thank you, nothing at all.

(BENEATHA *is watching the man carefully.*)

LINDNER   Well, I don't know how much you folks know about our organization. (*He is a gentle man; thoughtful and somewhat labored in his manner.*) It is one of those community organizations set up to look after—oh, you know, things like block upkeep and special projects and we also have what we call our New Neighbors Orientation Committee. . . .

BENEATHA (*drily*)   Yes—and what do they do?

LINDNER (*turning a little to her and then returning the main force to* WALTER)   Well—it's what you might call a sort of welcoming committee, I guess. I mean they, we, I'm the chairman of the committee—go around and see the new people who move into the neighborhood and sort of give them the lowdown on the way we do things out in Clybourne Park.

BENEATHA (*with appreciation of the two meanings, which escape* RUTH *and* WALTER)   Uh-huh.

LINDNER   And we also have the category of what the association calls—(*He looks elsewhere.*)—uh—special community problems. . . .

BENEATHA   Yes—and what are some of those?

WALTER   Girl, let the man talk.

LINDNER (*with understated relief*)   Thank you. I would sort of like to explain this thing in my own way. I mean I want to explain to you in a certain way.

WALTER   Go ahead.

LINDNER   Yes. Well. I'm going to try to get right to the point. I'm sure we'll all appreciate that in the long run.

BENEATHA   Yes.

LINDNER   Well—

WALTER   Be still now!

LINDNER   Well—

RUTH (*still innocently*)   Would you like another chair—you don't look comfortable.

LINDNER (*more frustrated than annoyed*)   No, thank you very much. Please. Well—to get right to the point I—(*a great breath, and he is off at last*) I am sure you people must be aware of some of the incidents which have happened in various parts of the city when colored people have moved into certain areas—(BENEATHA *exhales heavily and starts tossing a piece of fruit up and down in the air.*) Well—because we have what I think is going to be a unique type of organization in American community life—not only do we deplore that kind of thing—but we are trying to do something about it. (BENEATHA *stops tossing and turns with a new and quizzical interest to the man.*) We feel—(*gaining confidence in his mission because of the interest in the faces of the people he is talking to*)—we feel that most of the trouble in this world, when you come right down to it—(*He hits his knee for emphasis.*)—most of the trouble exists because people just don't sit down and talk to each other.

RUTH (*nodding as she might in church, pleased with the remark*)   You can say that again, mister.

LINDNER (*more encouraged by such affirmation*)   That we don't try hard enough in this world to understand the other fellow's problem. The other guy's point of view.

RUTH   Now that's right.

(BENEATHA *and* WALTER *merely watch and listen with genuine interest.*)

LINDNER   Yes—that's the way we feel out in Clybourne Park. And that's why I was elected to come here this afternoon and talk to you people. Friendly like, you know, the way people should talk to each other and see if we couldn't find some way to work this thing out. As I say, the whole business is a matter of *caring* about the other fellow. Anybody can see that you are a nice family of folks, hard-working and honest I'm sure. (BENEATHA *frowns slightly, quizzically, her head tilted regarding him.*) Today everybody knows what it means to be on the outside of *something*. And of course, there is always somebody who is out to take the advantage of people who don't always understand.

WALTER   What do you mean?

LINDNER   Well—you see our community is made up of people who've worked hard as the dickens for years to build up that little community. They're not rich and fancy people; just hard-working, honest people who don't really have much but those little homes and a dream of the kind of community they want to raise their children in. Now, I don't say we are perfect and there is a lot wrong in some of the things they want. But you've got to admit that a man, right or wrong, has the right to want to have the neighborhood he lives in a certain kind of way. And at the moment the overwhelming majority of our people out there feel that people get along better, take more of a common interest in the life of the community, when they share a common background. I want you to believe me when I tell you that race prejudice simply doesn't enter into it. It is a matter of the people of Clybourne Park believing, rightly or wrongly, as I say, that for the happiness of all concerned that our Negro families are happier when they live in their *own* communities.

BENEATHA (*with a grand and bitter gesture*)   This, friends, is the Welcoming Committee!

WALTER (*dumbfounded, looking at* LINDNER)   Is this what you came marching all the way over here to tell us?

LINDNER   Well, now we've been having a fine conversation. I hope you'll hear me all the way through.

WALTER (*tightly*)   Go ahead, man.

LINDNER   You see—in the face of all things I have said, we are prepared to make your family a very generous offer. . . .

BENEATHA   Thirty pieces and not a coin less!

WALTER   Yeah?

LINDNER (*putting on his glasses and drawing a form out of the briefcase*)   Our association is prepared, through the collective effort of our people, to buy the house from you at a financial gain to your family.

RUTH   Lord have mercy, ain't this the living gall!

WALTER   All right, you through?

LINDNER   Well, I want to give you the exact terms of the financial arrangement—

WALTER   We don't want to hear no exact terms of no arrangements. I want to know if you got any more to tell us 'bout getting together?

LINDNER (*taking off his glasses*)   Well—I don't suppose that you feel. . . .

WALTER   Never mind how I feel—you got any more to say 'bout how people ought to sit down and talk to each other? . . . Get out of my house, man. (*He turns his back and walks to the door.*)

LINDNER (*looking around at the hostile faces and reaching and assembling his hat and briefcase*)   Well—I don't understand why you people are reacting this way. What do you think you are going to gain by moving into a neighborhood where you just aren't wanted and where some elements—well—people can get awful worked up when they feel that their whole way of life and everything they've ever worked for is threatened.

WALTER   Get out.

LINDNER (*at the door, holding a small card*)   Well—I'm sorry it went like this.

WALTER   Get out.

LINDNER (*almost sadly, regarding* WALTER)   You just can't force people to change their hearts, son.

(*He turns and puts his card on a table and exits.* WALTER *pushes the door to with stinging hatred, and stands looking at it.* RUTH *just sits and* BENEATHA *just stands. They say nothing.* MAMA *and* TRAVIS *enter.*)

MAMA   Well—this all the packing got done since I left out of here this morning. I testify before God that my children got all the energy of the dead. What time the moving men due?

BENEATHA   Four o'clock. You had a caller, Mama. (*She is smiling, teasingly.*)

MAMA   Sure enough—who?

BENEATHA (*her arms folded saucily*)   The Welcoming Committee.

(WALTER *and* RUTH *giggle.*)

MAMA (*innocently*)   Who?

BENEATHA   The Welcoming Committee. They said they're sure going to be glad to see you when you get there.

WALTER (*devilishly*)   Yeah, they said they can't hardly wait to see your face.

(*Laughter.*)

MAMA (*sensing their facetiousness*)   What's the matter with you all?

WALTER   Ain't nothing the matter with us. We just telling you 'bout the gentleman who came to see you this afternoon. From the Clybourne Park Improvement Association.

MAMA   What he want?

RUTH (*in the same mood as* BENEATHA *and* WALTER)   To welcome you, honey.

WALTER   He said they can't hardly wait. He said the one thing they don't have, that they just *dying* to have out there is a fine family of colored people! (*to* RUTH *and* BENEATHA) Ain't that right!

RUTH *and* BENEATHA (*mockingly*)   Yeah! He left his card in case—

(*They indicate the card, and* MAMA *picks it up and throws it on the floor—understanding and looking off as she draws her chair up to the table on which she has put her plant and some sticks and some cord.*)

MAMA   Father, give us strength. (*knowingly—and without fun*) Did he threaten us?

BENEATHA   Oh—Mama—they don't do it like that any more. He talked Brotherhood. He said everybody ought to learn how to sit down and hate each other with good Christian fellowship.

(*She and* WALTER *shake hands to ridicule the remark.*)

MAMA (*sadly*)   Lord, protect us. . . .

RUTH   You should hear the money those folks raised to buy the house from us. All we paid and then some.

BENEATHA   What they think we going to do—eat 'em?

RUTH   No, honey, marry 'em.

MAMA (*shaking her head*)   Lord, Lord, Lord. . . .

RUTH   Well—that's the way the crackers crumble. Joke.

BENEATHA (*laughingly noticing what her mother is doing*)   Mama, what are you doing?

MAMA   Fixing my plant so it won't get hurt none on the way. . . .

BENEATHA   Mama, you going to take *that* to the new house?

MAMA   Uh-huh—

BENEATHA   That raggedy-looking old thing?

MAMA (*stopping and looking at her*)   It expresses *me.*

RUTH (*with delight, to* BENEATHA)   So there, Miss Thing!

(WALTER *comes to* MAMA *suddenly and bends down behind her and squeezes her in his arms with all his strength. She is overwhelmed by the suddenness of it and, though delighted, her manner is like that of* RUTH *with* TRAVIS.)

MAMA   Look out now, boy! You make me mess up my thing here!

WALTER (*his face lit, he slips down on his knees beside her, his arms still around her*)   Mama . . . you know what it means to climb up in the chariot?

MAMA (*gruffly, very happy*)   Get on away from me now. . . .

RUTH (*near the gift-wrapped package, trying to catch* WALTER's *eye*)   Psst—

WALTER   What the old song say, Mama. . . .

RUTH   Walter—Now? (*She is pointing at the package.*)

WALTER (*speaking the lines, sweetly, playfully, in his mother's face*)

I got wings . . . you got wings . . .
All God's children got wings . . .

MAMA   Boy—get out of my face and do some work. . . .

WALTER

When I get to heaven gonna put on my wings.
Gonna fly all over God's heaven . . .

BENEATHA (*teasingly, from across the room*)   Everybody talking 'bout heaven ain't going there!

WALTER (*to* RUTH, *who is carrying the box across to them*)   I don't know, you think we ought to give her that. . . . Seems to me she ain't been very appreciative around here.

MAMA (*eyeing the box, which is obviously a gift*)   What is that?

WALTER (*taking it from* RUTH *and putting it on the table in front of* MAMA)   Well—what you all think? Should we give it to her?

RUTH   Oh—she was pretty good today.

MAMA   I'll good you—(*She turns her eyes to the box again.*)

BENEATHA   Open it, Mama.

(*She stands up, looks at it, turns and looks at all of them, and then presses her hands together and does not open the package.*)

WALTER (*sweetly*)   Open it, Mama. It's for you. (MAMA *looks in his eyes. It is the first present in her life without its being Christmas. Slowly she opens her package and lifts out, one by one, a brand-new sparkling set of gardening tools.* WALTER *continues, prodding:*) Ruth made up the note—read it . . .

MAMA (*picking up the card and adjusting her glasses*)   "To our own Mrs. Miniver—Love from Brother, Ruth and Beneatha." Ain't that lovely. . . .

TRAVIS (*tugging at his father's sleeve*)   Daddy, can I give her mine now?

WALTER   All right, son. (TRAVIS *flies to get his gift.*) Travis didn't want to go in with the rest of us, Mama. He got his own. (*somewhat amused*) We don't know what it is. . . .

TRAVIS (*racing back in the room with a large hatbox and putting it in front of his grandmother*)   Here!

MAMA   Lord have mercy, baby. You done gone and bought your grandmother a hat?

TRAVIS (*very proud*)   Open it!

(*She does and lifts out an elaborate, but very elaborate, wide gardening hat, and all the adults break up at the sight of it.*)

RUTH   Travis, honey, what is that?

TRAVIS (*who thinks it is beautiful and appropriate*)   It's a gardening hat! Like the ladies always have on in the magazines when they work in their gardens.

BENEATHA (*giggling fiercely*)   Travis—we were trying to make Mama Mrs. Miniver—not Scarlett O'Hara!

MAMA (*indignantly*)   What's the matter with you all! This here is a beautiful hat! (*absurdly*) I always wanted me one just like it!

(*She pops it on her head to prove it to her grandson, and the hat is ludicrous and considerably oversized.*)

RUTH   Hot dog! Go, Mama!

WALTER (*doubled over with laughter*)   I'm sorry, Mama—but you look like you ready to go out and chop you some cotton sure enough!

(*They all laugh except* MAMA, *out of deference to* TRAVIS' *feelings.*)

MAMA (*gathering the boy up to her*)   Bless your heart—this is the prettiest hat I ever owned—(WALTER, RUTH, *and* BENEATHA *chime in noisily, festively and insincerely congratulating* TRAVIS *on his gift.*) What are we all standing around here for? We ain't finished packin' yet. Bennie, you ain't packed one book.

(*The bell rings.*)

BENEATHA   That couldn't be the movers . . . it's not hardly two good yet—

(BENEATHA *goes into her room.* MAMA *starts for door.*)

WALTER (*turning, stiffening*)   Wait—wait—I'll get it. (*He stands and looks at the door.*)

MAMA   You expecting company, son?

WALTER (*just looking at the door*)   Yeah—yeah. . . .

(MAMA *looks at* RUTH, *and they exchange innocent and unfrightened glances.*)

MAMA (*not understanding*)   Well, let them in, son.

BENEATHA (*from her room*)   We need some more string.

MAMA   Travis—you run to the hardware and get me some string cord.

(MAMA *goes out and* WALTER *turns and looks at* RUTH. TRAVIS *goes to a dish for money.*)

RUTH   Why don't you answer the door, man?

WALTER (*suddenly bounding across the floor to her*)   'Cause sometimes it hard to let the future begin! (*stooping down in her face*)

> I got wings! You got wings!
> All God's children got wings!

(*He crosses to the door and throws it open. Standing there is a very slight little man in a not too prosperous business suit and with haunted frightened eyes and a hat pulled down tightly, brim up, around his forehead.* TRAVIS *passes between the men and exits.* WALTER *leans deep in the man's face, still in his jubilance.*)

> When I get to heaven gonna put on my wings.
> Gonna fly all over God's heaven . . .

(*The little man just stares at him.*)
> Heaven—

(*Suddenly he stops and looks past the little man into the empty hallway.*) Where's Willy, man?

BOBO   He ain't with me.

WALTER (*not disturbed*)   Oh—come on in. You know my wife.

BOBO (*dumbly, taking off his hat*)   Yes—h'you, Miss Ruth.

RUTH (*quietly, a mood apart from her husband already, seeing* BOBO)   Hello, Bobo.

WALTER   You right on time today. . . . Right on time. That's the way! (*He slaps* BOBO *on his back.*) Sit down . . . lemme hear.

(RUTH *stands stiffly and quietly in back of them, as though somehow she senses death, her eyes fixed on her husband.*)

BOBO (*his frightened eyes on the floor, his hat in his hands*)   Could I please get a drink of water, before I tell you about it, Walter Lee?

(WALTER *does not take his eyes off the man.* RUTH *goes blindly to the tap and gets a glass of water and brings it to* BOBO.)

WALTER   There ain't nothing wrong, is there?

BOBO   Lemme tell you—

WALTER   Man—didn't nothing go wrong?

BOBO   Lemme tell you—Walter Lee. (*looking at* RUTH *and talking to her more than to* WALTER) You know how it was. I got to tell you how it was. I mean first I got tell you how it was all the way . . . I mean about the money I put in, Walter Lee. . . .

WALTER (*with taut agitation*)   What about the money you put in?

BOBO   Well—it wasn't much as we told you—me and Willy—(*He stops.*) I'm sorry, Walter. I got a bad feeling about it. I got a real bad feeling about it. . . .

WALTER   Man, what you telling me about all this for? . . . Tell me what happened in Springfield. . . .

BOBO   Springfield.

RUTH (*like a dead woman*)   What was supposed to happen in Springfield?

BOBO (*to her*)   This deal that me and Walter went into with Willy—Me and Willy was going to go down to Springfield and spread some money 'round so's we wouldn't have to wait so long for the liquor license. . . . That's what we were going to do. Everybody said that was the way you had to do, you understand, Miss Ruth?

WALTER   Man—what happened down there?

BOBO (*a pitiful man, near tears*)   I'm trying to tell you, Walter.

WALTER (*screaming at him suddenly*)   THEN TELL ME, GOD-DAMMIT . . . WHAT'S THE MATTER WITH YOU?

BOBO   Man . . . I didn't go to no Springfield, yesterday.

WALTER (*halted, life hanging in the moment*)   Why not?

BOBO (*the long way, the hard way to tell*)   'Cause I didn't have no reasons to. . . .

WALTER   Man, what are you talking about!

BOBO   I'm talking about the fact that when I got to the train station yesterday morning—eight o'clock like we planned . . . Man—*Willy didn't never show up.*

WALTER   Why . . . where was he . . . where is he?

BOBO   That's what I'm trying to tell you . . . I don't know . . . I waited six hours . . . I called his house . . . and I waited . . . six hours . . . I waited in that train station six hours . . . (*breaking into tears*) That was all the extra money I had in the world. . . . (*looking up at* WALTER *with tears running down his face*) Man, *Willy is gone.*

WALTER   Gone, what you mean Willy is gone? Gone where? You mean he went by himself. You mean he went off to Springfield by himself—to take care of getting the license—(*turns and looks anxiously at* RUTH) You mean maybe he didn't want too many people in on the business down there? (*looks to* RUTH *again, as before*) You know Willy got his own ways. (*looks back to* BOBO) Maybe you was late yesterday and he just went on down there without you. Maybe—maybe—he's been callin' you at home tryin' to tell you what happened or something. Maybe—maybe—he just got sick. He's somewhere—he's got to be somewhere. We just got to find him—me and you got to find him. (*grabs* BOBO *senselessly by the collar and starts to shake him*) We got to!

BOBO (*in sudden angry, frightened agony*)   What's the matter with you, Walter! *When a cat take off with your money he don't leave you no maps!*

WALTER (*turning madly, as though he is looking for* WILLY *in the very room*) Willy! . . .Willy . . . don't do it. . . . Please don't do it . . . Man, not with that money . . . Man, please not with that money . . . Oh, God . . . Don't let it be true. . . . (*He is wandering around, crying out for* WILLY *and looking for him or perhaps for help from God.*) Man . . . I trusted you . . . Man, I put my life in your hands. . . . (*He starts to crumple down on the floor as* RUTH *just covers her face in horror.* MAMA *opens the door and comes into the room, with* BE-NEATHA *behind her.*) Man . . . (*He starts to pound the floor with his fists, sobbing wildly.*) *That money is made out of my father's flesh.* . . .

BOBO (*standing over him helplessly*) I'm sorry, Walter. . . . (*Only* WALTER's *sobs reply.* BOBO *puts on his hat.*) I had my life staked on this deal, too. . . . (*He exits.*)

MAMA (*to* WALTER) Son— (*She goes to him, bends down to him, talks to his bent head.*) Son . . . Is it gone? Son, I gave you sixty-five hundred dollars. Is it gone? All of it? Beneatha's money too?

WALTER (*lifting his head slowly*) Mama . . . I never . . . went to the bank at all. . . .

MAMA (*not wanting to believe him*) You mean . . . your sister's school money . . . you used that too . . . Walter? . . .

WALTER Yessss! . . . All of it. . . . It's all gone. . . .

(*There is total silence.* RUTH *stands with her face covered with her hands;* BE-NEATHA *leans forlornly against a wall, fingering a piece of red ribbon from the mother's gift.* MAMA *stops and looks at her son without recognition and then, quite without thinking about it, starts to beat him senselessly in the face.* BENEATHA *goes to them and stops it.*)

BENEATHA Mama!

(MAMA *stops and looks at both of her children and rises slowly and wanders vaguely, aimlessly away from them.*)

MAMA I seen . . . him . . . night after night . . . come in . . . and look at that rug . . . and then look at me . . . the red showing in his eyes . . . the veins moving in his head. . . . I seen him grow thin and old before he was forty . . . working and working and working like somebody's old horse . . . killing himself . . . and you—you give it all away in a day. . . .

BENEATHA Mama—

MAMA Oh, God. . . . (*She looks up to Him.*) Look down here—and show me the strength.

BENEATHA Mama—

MAMA (*plaintively*) Strength. . . .

BENEATHA (*plaintively*) Mama. . . .

MAMA Strength!

Curtain

Act III

An hour later.

> *At curtain, there is a sullen light of gloom in the living room, gray light not unlike that which began the first scene of Act I. At left we can see* **WALTER** *within his room, alone with himself. He is stretched out on the bed, his shirt out and open, his arms under his head. He does not smoke, he does not cry out, he merely lies there, looking up at the ceiling, much as if he were alone in the world.*
> *In the living room* **BENEATHA** *sits at the table, still surrounded by the now almost ominous packing crates. She sits looking off. We feel that this is a mood struck perhaps an hour before, and it lingers now, full of the empty sound of profound disappointment. We see on a line from her brother's bedroom the sameness of their attitudes. Presently the bell rings and* **BENEATHA** *rises without ambition or interest in answering. It is* **ASAGAI**, *smiling broadly, striding into the room with energy and happy expectation and conversation.*

ASAGAI I came over . . . I had some free time. I thought I might help with the packing. Ah, I like the look of packing crates! A household in preparation for a journey! It depresses some people . . . but for me . . . it is another feeling. Something full of the flow of life, do you understand? Movement, progress . . . It makes me think of Africa.

BENEATHA Africa!

ASAGAI What kind of a mood is this? Have I told you how deeply you move me?

BENEATHA He gave away the money, Asagai. . . .

ASAGAI Who gave away what money?

BENEATHA The insurance money. My brother gave it away.

ASAGAI Gave it away?

BENEATHA He made an investment! With a man even Travis wouldn't have trusted.

ASAGAI And it's gone?

BENEATHA Gone!

ASAGAI I'm very sorry. . . . And you, now?

BENEATHA Me? . . . Me? . . . Me I'm nothing. . . . Me. When I was very small . . . we used to take our sleds out in the wintertime and the only hills we had were the ice-covered stone steps of some houses down the street. And we used to fill them in with snow and make them smooth and slide down them all day . . . and it was very dangerous you know . . . far too steep . . . and sure enough one day a kid named Rufus came down too fast and hit the sidewalk . . . and we saw his face just split open right there in front of us. . . . And I remember standing there looking at his bloody open face thinking that was the end of Rufus. But the ambulance came and they took him to the hospital and they fixed the broken bones and they sewed it all up . . . and the next time I saw Rufus he just had a little line down the middle of his face. . . . I never got over that. . . .

(WALTER *sits up, listening on the bed. Throughout this scene it is important that we feel his reaction at all times, that he visibly respond to the words of his sister and* ASAGAI.)

ASAGAI   What?

BENEATHA   That was what one person could do for another, fix him up—sew up the problem, make him all right again. That was the most marvelous thing in the world. . . . I wanted to do that. I always thought it was the one concrete thing in the world that a human being could do. Fix up the sick, you know—and make them whole again. This was truly being God. . . .

ASAGAI   You wanted to be God?

BENEATHA   No—I wanted to cure. It used to be so important to me. I wanted to cure. It used to matter. I used to care. I mean about people and how their bodies hurt. . . .

ASAGAI   And you've stopped caring?

BENEATHA   Yes—I think so.

ASAGAI   Why?

(WALTER *rises, goes to the door of his room and is about to open it, then stops and stands listening, leaning on the door jamb.*)

BENEATHA   Because it doesn't seem deep enough, close enough to what ails mankind—I mean this thing of sewing up bodies or administering drugs. Don't you understand? It was a child's reaction to the world. I thought that doctors had the secret to all the hurts. . . . That's the way a child sees things—or an idealist.

ASAGAI   Children see things very well sometimes—and idealists even better.

BENEATHA   I know that's what you think. Because you are still where I left off—you still care. This is what you see for the world, for Africa. You with the dreams of the future will patch up all Africa—you are going to cure the Great Sore of colonialism with Independence—

ASAGAI   Yes!

BENEATHA   Yes—and you think that one word is the penicillin of the human spirit: "Independence!" But then what?

ASAGAI   That will be the problem for another time. First we must get there.

BENEATHA   And where does it end?

ASAGAI   End? Who even spoke of an end? To life? To living?

BENEATHA   An end to misery!

ASAGAI (*smiling*)   You sound like a French intellectual.

BENEATHA   No! I sound like a human being who just had her future taken right out of her hands! While I was sleeping in my bed in there, things were happening in this world that directly concerned me—and nobody asked me, consulted me—they just went out and did things—and changed my life. Don't you see there isn't any real progress, Asagai, there is only one large circle that we march in, around and around, each of us with our own little picture—in front of us—our own little mirage that we think is the future.

ASAGAI   That is the mistake.

BENEATHA   What?

ASAGAI   What you just said—about the circle. It isn't a circle—it is simply a long line—as in geometry, you know, one that reaches into infinity. And because we cannot see the end—we also cannot see how it changes. And it is very odd but those who see the changes are called "idealists"—and those who cannot, or refuse to think, they are the "realists." It is very strange, and amusing too, I think.

BENEATHA   You—you are almost religious.

ASAGAI   Yes . . . I think I have the religion of doing what is necessary in the world—and of worshipping man—because he is so marvelous, you see.

BENEATHA   Man is foul! And the human race deserves its misery!

ASAGAI   You see: *you* have become the religious one in the old sense. Already, and after such a small defeat, you are worshipping despair.

BENEATHA   From now on, I worship the truth—and the truth is that people are puny, small and selfish. . . .

ASAGAI   Truth? Why is it that you despairing ones always think that only you have the truth? I never thought to see *you* like that. You! Your brother made a stupid, childish mistake—and you are grateful to him. So that now you can give up the ailing human race on account of it. You talk about what good is struggle; what good is anything? Where are we all going? And why are we bothering?

BENEATHA   *And you cannot answer it!* All your talk and dreams about Africa and Independence. Independence and then what? What about all the crooks and petty thieves and just plain idiots who will come into power to steal and plunder the same as before—only now they will be black and do it in the name of the new Independence—You cannot answer that.

ASAGAI   (*shouting over her*)   *I live the answer!* (*pause*) In my village at home it is the exceptional man who can even read a newspaper . . . or who ever *sees* a book at all. I will go home and much of what I will have to say will seem strange to the people of my village. . . . But I will teach and work and things will happen, slowly and swiftly. At times it will seem that nothing changes at all . . . and then again . . . the sudden dramatic events which make history leap into the future. And then quiet again. Retrogression even. Guns, murder, revolution. And I even will have moments when I wonder if the quiet was not better than all that death and hatred. But I will look about my village at the illiteracy and disease and ignorance and I will not wonder long.

And perhaps . . . perhaps I will be a great man. . . . I mean perhaps I will hold on to the substance of truth and find my way always with the right course . . . and perhaps for it I will be butchered in my bed some night by the servants of the empire. . . .

BENEATHA   *The martyr!*

ASAGAI   . . . or perhaps I shall live to be a very old man, respected and esteemed in my new nation. . . . And perhaps I shall hold office and this is what I'm trying to tell you, Alaiyo; perhaps the things I believe now for my country will be wrong and outmoded, and I will not understand and do terrible things to have things my way or merely to keep my power. Don't you see that there will be young men and women, not British soldiers then, but my own black countrymen . . . to step out of the shadows some evening and slit my then useless throat? Don't you see they have always been there . . . that they always will be. And that such a thing as my own death will be an advance? They who might kill me even . . . actually replenish me!

BENEATHA   Oh, Asagai, I know all that.

ASAGAI   Good! Then stop moaning and groaning and tell me what you plan to do.

BENEATHA   Do?

ASAGAI   I have a bit of a suggestion.

BENEATHA   What?

ASAGAI (*rather quietly for him*)   That when it is all over—that you come home with me—

BENEATHA (*slapping herself on the forehead with exasperation born of misunderstanding*)   Oh—Asagai—at this moment you decide to be romantic!

ASAGAI (*quickly understanding and misunderstanding*)   My dear, young creature of the New World—I do not mean across the city—I mean across the ocean; home—to Africa.

BENEATHA (*slowly understanding and turning to him with murmured amazement*)   To—to Nigeria?

ASAGAI   Yes! . . . (*smiling and lifting his arms playfully*) Three hundred years later the African Prince rose up out of the seas and swept the maiden back across the middle passage over which her ancestors had come—

BENEATHA (*unable to play*)   Nigeria?

ASAGAI   Nigeria. Home. (*coming to her with genuine romantic flippancy*) I will show you our mountains and our stars; and give you cool drinks from gourds and teach you the old songs and the ways of our people—and, in time, we will pretend that—(*very softly*)—you have only been away for a day—

(*She turns her back to him, thinking. He swings her around and takes her full in his arms in a long embrace which proceeds to passion.*)

BENEATHA (*pulling away*)   You're getting me all mixed up—

ASAGAI   Why?

BENEATHA   Too many things—too many things have happened today. I must sit down and think. I don't know what I feel about anything right this minute. (*She promptly sits down and props her chin on her fist.*)

ASAGAI (*charmed*)   All right, I shall leave you. No—don't get up. (*touching her, gently, sweetly*) Just sit awhile and think. . . . Never be afraid to sit awhile and think. (*He goes to door and looks at her.*) How often I have looked at you and said, "Ah—so this is what the New World hath finally wrought. . . ."

(*He exits.* BENEATHA *sits on alone. Presently* WALTER *enters from his room and starts to rummage through things, feverishly looking for something. She looks up and turns in her seat.*)

BENEATHA (*hissingly*)   Yes—just look at what the New World hath wrought! . . . Just look! (*She gestures with bitter disgust.*) There he is! *Monsieur le petit bourgeois noir*—himself! There he is—Symbol of a Rising Class! Entrepreneur! Titan of the system! (WALTER *ignores her completely and continues frantically and destructively looking for something and hurling things to floor and tearing things out of their place in his search.* BENEATHA *ignores the eccentricity of his actions and goes on with the monologue of insult.*) Did you dream of yachts on Lake Michigan, Brother? Did you see yourself on that Great Day sitting down at the Conference Table, surrounded by all the mighty bald-headed men in America? All halted, waiting, breathless, waiting for your pronouncements on industry? Waiting for you—Chairman of the Board? (WALTER *finds what he is looking for—a small piece of white paper—and pushes it in his pocket and puts on his coat and rushes out without even having looked at her. She shouts after him.*) I look at you and I see the final triumph of stupidity in the world!

(*The door slams and she returns to just sitting again.* RUTH *comes quickly out of* MAMA'S *room.*)

RUTH   Who was that?

BENEATHA   Your husband.

RUTH   Where did he go?

BENEATHA   Who knows—maybe he has an appointment at U.S. Steel.

RUTH (*anxiously, with frightened eyes*)   You didn't say nothing bad to him, did you?

BENEATHA   Bad? Say anything bad to him? No—I told him he was a sweet boy and full of dreams and everything is strictly peachy keen, as the ofay kids say!

(MAMA *enters from her bedroom. She is lost, vague, trying to catch hold, to make some sense of her former command of the world, but it still eludes her. A sense of waste overwhelms her gait; a measure of apology rides on her shoulders. She goes to her plant, which has remained on the table, looks at it, picks it up and takes it to the window sill and sits it outside, and she stands and looks at it a long moment. Then she closes the window, straightens her body with effort and turns around to her children.)*

MAMA   Well—ain't it a mess in here, though? (*a false cheerfulness, a beginning of something*) I guess we all better stop moping around and get some work done. All this unpacking and everything we got to do. (RUTH *raises her head slowly in response to the sense of the line; and* BENEATHA *in similar manner turns very slowly to look at her mother.*) One of you all better call the moving people and tell 'em not to come.

RUTH   Tell 'em not to come?

MAMA   Of course, baby. Ain't no need in 'em coming all the way here and having to go back. They charges for that too. (*She sits down, fingers to her brow, thinking.*) Lord, ever since I was a little girl, I always remembers people saying, "Lena—Lena Eggleston, you aims too high all the time. You needs to slow down and see life a little more like it is. Just slow down some." That's what they always used to say down home—"Lord, that Lena Eggleston is a high-minded thing. She'll get her due one day!"

RUTH   No, Lena. . . .

MAMA   Me and Big Walter just didn't never learn right.

RUTH   Lena, no! We gotta go. Bennie—tell her. . . . (*She rises and crosses to* BE-NEATHA *with her arms outstretched.* BENEATHA *doesn't respond.*) Tell her we can still move . . . the notes ain't but a hundred and twenty-five a month. We got four grown people in this house—we can work. . . .

MAMA (*to herself*)   Just aimed too high all the time—

RUTH (*turning and going to* MAMA *fast—the words pouring out with urgency and desperation*)   Lena—I'll work. . . . I'll work twenty hours a day in all the kitchens in Chicago. . . . I'll strap my baby on my back if I have to and scrub all the floors in America and wash all the sheets in America if I have to—but we got to move. . . . We got to get out of here. . . .

(MAMA *reaches out absently and pats* RUTH's *hand.*)

MAMA   No—I see things differently now. Been thinking 'bout some of the things we could do to fix this place up some. I seen a second-hand bureau over on Maxwell Street just the other day that could fit right there. (*She points to where the new furniture might go.* RUTH *wanders away from her.*) Would need some new handles on it and then a little varnish and then it look like something brand-new. And—we can put up them new curtains in the kitchen. . . . Why this place be looking fine. Cheer us all up so that we forget trouble ever came. . . . (*to* RUTH) And you could get some nice screens to put up in your room round the baby's bassinet. . . . (*She looks at both of them, pleadingly.*) Sometimes you just got to know when to give up some things . . . and hold on to what you got.

(WALTER *enters from the outside, looking spent and leaning against the door, his coat hanging from him.*)

MAMA   Where you been, son?

WALTER (*breathing hard*)   Made a call.

MAMA   To who, son?

WALTER   To The Man.

MAMA   What man, baby?

WALTER   The Man, Mama. Don't you know who The Man is?

RUTH   Walter Lee?

WALTER   *The Man.* Like the guys in the streets say—The Man. Captain Boss—Mistuh Charley . . . Old Captain Please Mr. Bossman . . .

BENEATHA (*suddenly*)   Lindner!

WALTER   That's right! That's good. I told him to come right over.

BENEATHA (*fiercely, understanding*)   For what? What do you want to see him for!

WALTER (*looking at his sister*)   We going to do business with him.

MAMA   What you talking 'bout, son?

WALTER   Talking 'bout life, Mama. You all always telling me to see life like it is. Well—I laid in there on my back today . . . and I figured it out. Life just like it is. Who gets and who don't get. (*He sits down with his coat on and laughs.*) Mama, you know it's all divided up. Life is. Sure enough. Between the takers and the "tooken." (*He laughs.*) I've figured it out finally. (*He looks around at them.*) Yeah. Some of us always getting "tooken." (*He laughs.*) People like Willy Harris, they don't never get "tooken." And you know why the rest of us do? 'Cause we all mixed up. Mixed up bad. We get to looking 'round for the right and the wrong; and we worry about it and cry about it and stay up nights trying to figure out 'bout the wrong and the right of things all the time. . . . And all the time, man, them takers is out there operating, just taking and taking. Willy Harris? Shoot—Willy Harris don't even count. He don't even count in the big scheme of things. But I'll say one thing for old Willy Harris . . . he's taught me something. He's taught me to keep my eye on what counts in this world. Yeah—(*shouting out a little*) Thanks, Willy!

RUTH   What did you call that man for, Walter Lee?

WALTER   Called him to tell him to come on over to the show. Gonna put on a show for the man. Just what he wants to see. You see, Mama, the man came here today and he told us that them people out there where you want us to move—well they so upset they willing to pay us not to move out there. (*He laughs again.*) And—and oh, Mama—you would of been proud of the way me and Ruth and Bennie acted. We told him to get out . . . Lord have mercy! We told the man to get out. Oh, we was some proud folks this afternoon, yeah. (*He lights a cigarette.*) We were still full of that old-time stuff. . . .

RUTH (*coming toward him slowly*)   You talking 'bout taking them people's money to keep us from moving in that house?

WALTER   I ain't just talking 'bout it, baby—I'm telling you that's what's going to happen.

BENEATHA   Oh, God! Where is the bottom! Where is the real honest-to-God bottom so he can't go any farther!

WALTER   See—that's old stuff. You and that boy that was here today. You all want everybody to carry a flag and a spear and sing some marching songs, huh? You wanna spend your life looking into things and trying to find the right and the wrong part, huh? Yeah. You know what's going to happen to that boy someday—he'll find himself sitting in a dungeon, locked in forever—and the takers will have the key! Forget it, baby! There ain't no causes—there ain't nothing but taking in this world, and he who takes most is smartest—and it don't make a damn bit of difference *how*.

MAMA   You making something inside me cry, son. Some awful pain inside me.

WALTER   Don't cry, Mama. Understand. That white man is going to walk in that door able to write checks for more money than we ever had. It's important to him and I'm going to help him . . . I'm going to put on the show, Mama.

MAMA   Son—I come from five generations of people who was slaves and share-croppers—but ain't nobody in my family never let nobody pay 'em no money that was a way of telling us we wasn't fit to walk the earth. We ain't never been that poor. (*raising her eyes and looking at him*) We ain't never been that dead inside.

BENEATHA   Well—we are dead now. All the talk about dreams and sunlight that goes on in this house. All dead.

WALTER   What's the matter with you all! I didn't make this world! It was give to me this way! Hell, yes, I want me some yachts someday! Yes, I want to hang some real pearls 'round my wife's neck. Ain't she supposed to wear no pearls? Somebody tell me—tell me, who decides which women is suppose to wear pearls in this world. I tell you I am a *man*—and I think my wife should wear pearls in this world!

(*This last line hangs a good while and* WALTER *begins to move about the room. The word "Man" has penetrated his consciousness; he mumbles it to himself repeatedly between strange agitated pauses as he moves about.*)

MAMA   Baby, how you going to feel on the inside?

WALTER   Fine! . . . Going to feel fine . . . a man. . . .

MAMA   You won't have nothing left then, Walter Lee.

WALTER   (*coming to her*)   I'm going to feel fine, Mama. I'm going to look that son-of-a-bitch in the eyes and say—(*He falters.*)—and say, "All right, Mr. Lindner—(*He falters even more.*)—that's your neighborhood out there. You got the right to keep it like you want. You got the right to have it like you want. Just write the check and—the house is yours." And, and I am going to say—(*His voice almost breaks.*) And you—you people just put the money in my hand and you won't have to live next to this bunch of stinking niggers! . . . (*He straightens up and moves away from his mother, walking around the room.*) Maybe—maybe I'll just get down on my black knees. . . . (*He does so;* RUTH *and* BENNIE *and* MAMA *watch him in frozen horror.*) Captain, Mistuh, Bossman. (*He starts crying.*) A-hee-hee-hee! (*wringing his hands in profoundly anguished imitation*) Yassssssuh! Great White Father, just gi' ussen de money, fo' God's sake, and we's ain't gwine come out deh and dirty up yo' white folks neighborhood. . . .

(*He breaks down completely, then gets up and goes into the bedroom.*)

BENEATHA   That is not a man. That is nothing but a toothless rat.

MAMA   Yes—death done come in this here house. (*She is nodding, slowly, reflectively.*) Done come walking in my house. On the lips of my children. You what supposed to be my beginning again. You—what supposed to be my harvest. (*to* BENEATHA) You—you mourning your brother?

BENEATHA   He's no brother of mine.

MAMA   What you say?

BENEATHA   I said that that individual in that room is no brother of mine.

MAMA   That's what I thought you said. You feeling like you better than he is today? (BENEATHA *does not answer.*) Yes? What you tell him a minute ago? That he wasn't a man? Yes? You give him up for me? You done wrote his epitaph too—like the rest of the world? Well, who give you the privilege?

BENEATHA   Be on my side for once! You saw what he just did, Mama! You saw him—down on his knees. Wasn't it you who taught me—to despise any man who would do that. Do what he's going to do.

MAMA   Yes—I taught you that. Me and your daddy. But I thought I taught you something else too . . . I thought I taught you to love him.

BENEATHA   Love him? There is nothing left to love.

MAMA   There is always something left to love. And if you ain't learned that, you ain't learned nothing. (*looking at her*) Have you cried for that boy today? I don't mean for yourself and for the family 'cause we lost the money. I mean for him; what he been through and what it done to him. Child, when do you think is the time to love somebody the most; when they done good and made things easy for everybody? Well, then, you ain't through learning—because that ain't the time at all. It's when he's at his lowest and can't believe in hisself 'cause the world done whipped him so. When you starts measuring somebody, measure him right, child, measure him right. Make sure you done taken into account what hills and valleys he come through before he got to wherever he is.

(TRAVIS *bursts into the room at the end of the speech, leaving the door open.*)

TRAVIS   Grandmama—the moving men are downstairs! The truck just pulled up.

MAMA (*turning and looking at him*)   Are they, baby? They downstairs?

(*She sighs and sits.* LINDNER *appears in the doorway. He peers in and knocks lightly, to gain attention, and comes in. All turn to look at him.*)

LINDNER (*hat and briefcase in hand*)   Uh—hello . . .

(RUTH *crosses mechanically to the bedroom door and opens it and lets it swing open freely and slowly as the lights come up on* WALTER *within, still in his coat, sitting at the far corner of the room. He looks up and out through the room to* LINDNER.)

RUTH   He's here.

(*A long minute passes and* WALTER *slowly gets up.*)

LINDNER (*coming to the table with efficiency, putting his briefcase on the table and starting to unfold papers and unscrew fountain pens*)   Well, I certainly was glad to hear from you people. (WALTER *has begun the trek out of the room, slowly and awkwardly, rather like a small boy, passing the back of his sleeve across his mouth from time to time.*) Life can really be so much simpler than people let it be most of the time. Well—with whom do I negotiate? You, Mrs. Younger, or your son here? (MAMA *sits with her hands folded on her lap and her eyes closed as* WALTER *advances.* TRAVIS *goes close to* LINDNER *and looks at the papers curiously.*) Just some official papers, sonny.

RUTH   Travis, you go downstairs.

MAMA (*opening her eyes and looking into* WALTER'S)   No. Travis, you stay right here. And you make him understand what you doing, Walter Lee. You teach him good. Like Willy Harris taught you. You show where our five generations done come to. Go ahead, son—

WALTER (*looks down into his boy's eyes;* TRAVIS *grins up at him merrily and* WAL- TER *draws him beside him with his arm lightly around his shoulders*)   Well, Mr. Lindner. (BENEATHA *turns away.*) We called you—(*There is a profound, simple groping quality in his speech.*)—because, well, me and my fam- ily—(*He looks around and shifts from one foot to the other.*) Well—we are very plain people. . . .

LINDNER   Yes—

WALTER   I mean—I have worked as a chauffeur most of my life—and my wife here, she does domestic work in people's kitchens. So does my mother. I mean—we are plain people. . . .

LINDNER   Yes, Mr. Younger—

WALTER (*really like a small boy, looking down at his shoes and then up at the man*)   And—uh—well, my father, well, he was a laborer most of his life.

LINDNER (*absolutely confused*)   Uh, yes—

WALTER (*looking down at his toes once again*)   My father almost beat a man to death once because this man called him a bad name or something, you know what I mean?

LINDNER   No, I'm afraid I don't.

WALTER (*finally straightening up*)   Well, what I mean is that we come from people who had a lot of pride. I mean—we are very proud people. And that's my sister over there and she's going to be a doctor—and we are very proud—

LINDNER   Well—I am sure that is very nice, but—

WALTER (*starting to cry and facing the man eye to eye*)   What I am telling you is that we called you over here to tell you that we are very proud and that this is—this is my son, who makes the sixth generation of our family in this country, and that we have all thought about your offer and we have decided to move into our house because my father—my father—he earned it. (MAMA *has her eyes closed and is rocking back and forth as though she were in church, with her head nodding the amen yes.*) We don't want to make no trouble for nobody or fight no causes—but we will try to be good neighbors. That's all we got to say. (*He looks the man absolutely in the eyes.*) We don't want your money. (*He turns and walks away from the man.*)

LINDNER (*looking around at all of them*)   I take it then that you have decided to occupy.

BENEATHA   That's what the man said.

LINDNER (*to* MAMA *in her reverie*)   Then I would like to appeal to you, Mrs. Younger. You are older and wiser and understand things better I am sure . . .

MAMA (*rising*)   I am afraid you don't understand. My son said we was going to move and there ain't nothing left for me to say. (*shaking her head with double meaning*) You know how these young folks is nowadays, mister. Can't do a thing with 'em. Good-bye.

LINDNER (*folding up his materials*)   Well—if you are that final about it. . . . There is nothing left for me to say. (*He finishes. He is almost ignored by the family, who are concentrating on* WALTER LEE. *At the door* LINDNER *halts and looks around.*) I sure hope you people know what you're doing. (*He shakes his head and exits.*)

RUTH (*looking around and coming to life*)   Well, for God's sake—if the moving men are here—LET'S GET THE HELL OUT OF HERE!

MAMA (*into action*)   Ain't it the truth! Look at all this here mess. Ruth, put Travis' good jacket on him. . . . Walter Lee, fix your tie and tuck your shirt in, you look just like somebody's hoodlum. Lord have mercy, where is my plant? (*She flies to get it amid the general bustling of the family, who are deliberately trying to ignore the nobility of the past moment.*) You all start on down. . . . Travis child, don't go empty-handed. . . . Ruth, where did I put that box with my skillets in it? I want to be in charge of it myself. . . . I'm going to make us the biggest dinner we ever ate tonight. . . . Beneatha, what's the matter with them stockings? Pull them things up, girl. . . .

(*The family starts to file out as two moving men appear and begin to carry out the heavier pieces of furniture, bumping into the family as they move about.*)

BENEATHA   Mama, Asagai—asked me to marry him today and go to Africa—

MAMA (*in the middle of her getting-ready activity*)   He did? You ain't old enough to marry nobody—(*seeing the moving men lifting one of her chairs precariously*) Darling, that ain't no bale of cotton, please handle it so we can sit in it again. I had that chair twenty-five years. . . .

(*The movers sigh with exasperation and go on with their work.*)

BENEATHA (*girlishly and unreasonably trying to pursue the conversation*)   To go to Africa, Mama—be a doctor in Africa. . . .
MAMA (*distracted*)   Yes, baby—
WALTER   Africa! What he want you to go to Africa for?
BENEATHA   To practice there. . . .
WALTER   Girl, if you don't get all them silly ideas out of your head! You better marry yourself a man with some loot. . . .
BENEATHA (*angrily, precisely as in the first scene of the play*)   What have you got to do with who I marry!
WALTER   Plenty. Now I think George Murchison—

(*He and* BENEATHA *go out yelling at each other vigorously;* BENEATHA *is heard saying that she would not marry* GEORGE MURCHISON *if he were Adam and she were Eve, etc. The anger is loud and real till their voices diminish.* RUTH *stands at the door and turns to* MAMA *and smiles knowingly.*)

MAMA (*fixing her hat at last*)   Yeah—they something all right, my children. . . .
RUTH   Yeah—they're something. Let's go, Lena.
MAMA (*stalling, starting to look around at the house*)   Yes—I'm coming. Ruth—
RUTH   Yes?
MAMA (*quietly, woman to woman*)   He finally come into his manhood today, didn't he? Kind of like a rainbow after the rain. . . .
RUTH (*biting her lip lest her own pride explode in front of* MAMA)   Yes, Lena.

(WALTER's *voice calls for them raucously.*)

MAMA (*waving* RUTH *out vaguely*)   All right, honey—go on down. I be down directly.

(RUTH *hesitates, then exits.* MAMA *stands, at last alone in the living room, her plant on the table before her as the lights start to come down. She looks around at all the walls and ceilings and suddenly, despite herself, while the children call below, a great heaving thing rises in her and she puts her fist to her mouth, takes a final desperate look, pulls her coat about her, pats her hat and goes out. The lights dim down. The door opens and she comes back in, grabs her plant, and goes out for the last time.*)

Curtain

STUDY QUESTIONS

1. *A Raisin in the Sun* uses many comic devices in its plot: for instance, the young girl trying to choose between two suitors (shall she accept one, the other, or neither?), and the gullible man who, through obsession and folly, falls prey to a con man, a representative of vice. How are these two plots worked out in this play? How do they contrast with and support one another? What is their role in the play's overall plot?

2. Discuss the use of Lena's plant. What does it symbolize? How does it help emphasize Lena's role in the play?

POSSIBLE ESSAY TOPICS

1. Lorraine Hansberry wrote in a letter

   There is . . . a great deal to be fought in America—but, at the same time, there is so much that begs to be re-affirmed and cherished with sweet defiance. . . . There is simply no reason why dreams should dry up like raisins or prunes or anything else in America. If you will permit me to say so, I believe that we can impose beauty on our future . . ." (*To Be Young, Gifted, and Black*, p. 115).

   Discuss how *A Raisin in the Sun* dramatizes this thesis.

2. Discuss *A Raisin in the Sun* in conjunction with the Langston Hughes poems "Harlem" (from which the play got its title) and "Mother to Son" (p. 439) (from which Hansberry was considering a title, *The Crystal Stair*).

Protest

VÁCLAV HAVEL

Translated and adapted by Vera Blackwell

Stanek's ground-floor study in his house on the outskirts of Prague. The house is surrounded by a garden.

(*Doorbell. The front door is opened.*)

STANEK (*loud, cordial*)   Vanek!—Hello!

(*The front door is closed.*)

VANEK (*noncommittal*)   Hello, Mr. Stanek—

STANEK   Come in, come in! (*pause; sudden outburst of emotion*) Vanek! My dear fellow! (*pause; conversationally*) Did you have trouble finding it?

VANEK   Not really—

STANEK   Forgot to mention the flowering magnolias. That's how you know it's my house. Superb, aren't they?

VANEK   Yes—

STANEK   I managed to double their blossoms in less than three years, compared to the previous owner. Have you magnolias in your garden?

VANEK   No—

STANEK   You must have them! I'm going to find you two quality saplings and I'll come and plant them for you personally. (*crosses to the bar*) How about some brandy?

VANEK   I'd rather not, Mr. Stanek, if you don't mind—

STANEK   Come on, Vanek! Just a token one. Eh?

(*Two drinks are poured.*)

VANEK (*sighs*)

STANEK   Here we are. Well—here's to our reunion!

VANEK   Cheers—

(*Both drink.*)

VANEK (*shudders slightly, emits a soft groan*)

STANEK   I was afraid you weren't going to come.

VANEK   Why?

STANEK   Well, I mean, things got mixed up in an odd sort of way—What?— Won't you sit down?

VANEK (*sits down in an armchair, placing his briefcase on the floor beside him*)   Thanks—

STANEK (*sinks into an armchair opposite Vanek with a sigh*)   That's more like it! Peanuts?

1002

VANEK   No, thanks—

STANEK (*helps himself; munching*)   You haven't changed much in all these years, you know?

VANEK   Neither have you—

STANEK   Me? Come on! Getting on for fifty, going gray, aches and pains setting in—Not as we used to be, eh? And the present times don't make one feel any better either, what? When did we see each other last, actually?

VANEK   I don't know—

STANEK   Wasn't it at your last opening night?

VANEK   Could be—

STANEK   Seems like another age! We had a bit of an argument—

VANEK   Did we?

STANEK   You took me to task for my illusions and my over-optimism. Good Lord! How often since then I've had to admit to myself you were right! Of course, in those days I still believed that in spite of everything some of the ideals of my youth could be salvaged and I took you for an incorrigible pessimist.

VANEK   But I'm not a pessimist—

STANEK   You see, everything's turned around! (*short pause*) Are you—alone?

VANEK   How do you mean, alone?

STANEK   Well, isn't there somebody—you know—

VANEK   Following me?

STANEK   Not that I care! After all, it was me who rang you up, right?

VANEK   I haven't noticed anybody—

STANEK   By the way, suppose you want to shake them off one of these days, you know the best place to do it?

VANEK   No—

STANEK   A department store. You mingle with the crowd, then at a moment when they aren't looking you sneak into the loo and wait there for about two hours. They become convinced you managed to slip out through a side entrance and they give up. You must try it out sometime!

VANEK (*pause*)   Seems very peaceful here—

STANEK   That's why we moved here. It was simply impossible to go on writing near that railway station! We've been here three years, you know. Of course, my greatest joy is the garden. I'll show you around later—I'm afraid I'm going to boast a little—

VANEK   You do the gardening yourself?

STANEK   It's become my greatest private passion these days. Keep puttering about out there almost every day. Just now I've been rejuvenating the apricots. Developed my own method, you see, based on a mixture of natural and artificial fertilizers plus a special way of waxless grafting. You won't believe the results I get! I'll find some cuttings for you later on— (*opens a large silver box on coffee table between them*) Would you like a cigarette?

VANEK   Thanks—

(*clicking of lighter*)

VANEK (*exhales*)

STANEK (*sips his brandy.*)   Well now, Ferdinand, tell me—How *are* you?

VANEK   All right, thanks—

STANEK   Do they leave you alone—at least now and then?

VANEK   It depends—

STANEK (*short pause*)   And how was it in there?

VANEK   Where?

STANEK   Can our sort bear it at all?

VANEK   You mean prison? What else can one do?

STANEK   As far as I recall you used to be bothered by hemorrhoids. Must have been terrible, considering the hygiene in there.

VANEK   They gave me suppositories—

STANEK   You ought to have them operated on, you know. It so happens a friend of mine is our greatest hemorrhoids specialist. Works real miracles. I'll arrange it for you.

VANEK   Thanks—

STANEK (*short pause*)   You know, sometimes it all seems like a beautiful dream—all the exciting opening nights, private views, lectures, meetings— the endless discussions about literature and art! All the energy, the hopes, plans, activities, ideas—the wine-bars crowded with friends, the wild booze-ups, the madcap affrays in the small hours, the jolly girls dancing attendance on us! And the mountains of work we managed to get done, regardless!—That's all over now. It'll never come back!

(*Pause. They both drink.*)

STANEK   Did they beat you?

VANEK   No—

STANEK   Do they beat people up in there?

VANEK   Sometimes. But not the politicals—

STANEK   I thought about you a great deal!

VANEK   Thank you—

STANEK (*short pause*)   I bet in those days it never even occurred to you—

VANEK   What?

STANEK   How it'll all end up! I bet not even you had guessed that!

VANEK   Mmnn—

STANEK   It's disgusting, old boy, disgusting! The nation is governed by scum! And the people? Can this really be the same nation which not very long ago behaved so magnificently? All that horrible cringing, bowing and scraping! The selfishness, corruption and fear wherever you turn! Good Lord! What have they made of us, old boy? Can this really be us? Is this still ourselves at all?

VANEK   I don't believe things are as black as all that—

STANEK Forgive me, Ferdinand, but you don't happen to live in a normal environment. All you know are people who manage to resist this rot. You just keep on supporting and encouraging each other. You've no idea the sort of environment I've got to put up with! Makes you sick at your stomach!

VANEK You mean television?

STANEK In television, in the film studios—you name it.

VANEK There was a piece by you on the box the other day—

STANEK You can't imagine what an ordeal that was! First they kept blocking it for over a year, then they started changing it around—changed my whole opening and the entire closing sequence! You wouldn't believe the trifles they find objectionable these days! Nothing but sterility and intrigues, intrigues and sterility! How often I tell myself—wrap it up, chum, forget it, go hide somewhere—grow apricots—

VANEK I know what you mean—

STANEK The thing is though, one can't help wondering whether one's got the right to this sort of escape. Supposing even the little one might be able to accomplish today can, in spite of everything, help someone in some way, at least give him a bit of encouragement, uplift him a little—Let me bring you a pair of slippers.

VANEK Slippers? Why?

STANEK You can't be comfortable in those boots.

VANEK I'm all right—

STANEK Are you sure?

VANEK Yes. Really—

(*They both drink.*)

STANEK (*pause*) How about drugs? Did they give you any?

VANEK No—

STANEK No dubious injections?

VANEK Only some vitamin ones—

STANEK I bet there's some funny stuff in the food!

VANEK Just bromine against sex—

STANEK But surely they tried to break you down somehow!

VANEK Well—

STANEK If you'd rather not talk about it, it's all right with me.

VANEK Well, in a way, that's the whole point of pre-trial interrogations, isn't it? To take one down a peg or two—

STANEK And to make one talk!

VANEK Mmnn—

STANEK If they should haul me in for questioning—which sooner or later is bound to happen—you know what I'm going to do?

VANEK What?

STANEK   Simply not answer any of their questions! Refuse to talk to them at all! That's by far the best way. Least one can be quite sure one didn't say anything one ought not to have said!

VANEK   Mmnn—

STANEK   Anyway, you must have steel nerves to be able to bear it all and in addition to keep doing the things you do.

VANEK   Like what?

STANEK   Well, I mean all the protests, petitions, letters—the whole fight for human rights! I mean the things you and your friends keep on doing—

VANEK   I'm not doing so much—

STANEK   Now don't be too modest, Ferdinand! I follow everything that's going on! I know! If everybody did what you do the situation would be quite different! And that's a fact. It's extremely important there should be at least a few people here who aren't afraid to speak the truth aloud, to defend others, to call a spade a spade! What I'm going to say might sound a bit solemn perhaps, but frankly, the way I see it, you and your friends have taken on an almost superhuman task: to preserve and to carry the remains, the remnant of moral conscience through the present quagmire! The thread you're spinning may be thin, but—who knows—perhaps the hope of a moral rebirth of the nation hangs on it.

VANEK   You exaggerate—

STANEK   Well, that's how I see it, anyway.

VANEK   Surely our hope lies in all the decent people—

STANEK   But how many are there still around? How many?

VANEK   Enough—

STANEK   Are there? Even so, it's you and your friends who are the most exposed to view.

VANEK   And isn't that precisely what makes it easier for us?

STANEK   I wouldn't say so. The more you're exposed, the more responsibility you have towards all those who know about you, trust you, rely on you and look up to you, because to some extent you keep upholding their honor, too! (*gets up*) I'll get you those slippers!

VANEK   Please don't bother—

STANEK   I insist. I feel uncomfortable just looking at your boots.

(*Pause.* STANEK *returns with slippers.*)

VANEK (*sighs*)

STANEK   Here you are. Do take those ugly things off, I beg you. Let me— (*tries to take off* VANEK's *boots*) Won't you let me—Hold still—

VANEK (*embarrassed*)   No—please don't—no—I'll do it— (*struggles out of his boots, slips on slippers*) There—Nice, aren't they? Thank you very much.

STANEK   Good gracious, Ferdinand, what for?— (*hovering over* VANEK) Some more brandy?

VANEK   No more for me, thanks—

STANEK   Oh, come on. Give me your glass!

VANEK   I'm sorry, I'm not feeling too well—

STANEK   Lost the habit inside, is that it?

VANEK   Could be—But the point is—last night, you see—

STANEK   Ah, that's what it is. Had a drop too many, eh?

VANEK   Mmnn—

STANEK   I understand. (*returns to his chair*) By the way, you know the new wine-bar, "The Shaggy Dog"?

VANEK   No—

STANEK   You don't? Listen, the wine there comes straight from the cask, it's not expensive and usually it isn't crowded. Really charming spot, you know, thanks to a handful of fairly good artists who were permitted—believe it or not—to do the interior decoration. I can warmly recommend it to you. Lovely place. Where did you go, then?

VANEK   Well, we did a little pub-crawling, my friend Landovský and I—

STANEK   Oh, I see! You were with Landovský, were you? Well! In that case, I'm not at all surprised you came to a sticky end! He's a first class actor, but once he starts drinking—that's it! Surely you can take one more brandy! Right?

VANEK   (*Sighs.*)

(*Drinks poured. They both drink.*)

VANEK   (*shudders, emits a soft groan*)

STANEK   (*back in his armchair; short pause*)   Well, how are things otherwise? You do any writing?

VANEK   Trying to—

STANEK   A play?

VANEK   A one-actor—

STANEK   Another autobiographical one?

VANEK   More or less—

STANEK   My wife and I read the one about the brewery the other day. We thought it was very amusing.

VANEK   I'm glad—

STANEK   Unfortunately we were given a rather bad copy. Somewhat illegible.

VANEK   I'm sorry—

STANEK   It's a really brilliant little piece! I mean it! Only the ending seemed to me a bit muddy. The whole thing wants to be brought to a more straightforward conclusion, that's all. No problem. You can do it.

(*Pause. Both drink.* VANEK *shudders.*)

STANEK   Well, how are things? How about Pavel? Do you see him?

VANEK   Yes—

STANEK   Does he do any writing?

VANEK Just now he's finishing a one-actor, as well. It's supposed to be performed together with mine—

STANEK Wait a minute. You don't mean to tell me you two have teamed up also as authors!

VANEK More or less—

STANEK Well, well!—Frankly, Ferdinand, try as I may, I don't get it. I don't. I simply can't understand this alliance of yours. Is it quite genuine on your part? Is it?—Good heavens! Pavel! I don't know! Just remember the way he started! We both belong to the same generation, Pavel and I, we've both—so to speak—spanned a similar arc of development, but I don't mind telling you that what he did in those days—Well! It was a bit too strong even for me!—Still, I suppose it's your business. You know best what you're doing.

VANEK That's right—

(*Pause. Both drink.*)

STANEK Is your wife fond of gladioli?

VANEK I don't know. I think so—

STANEK You won't find many places with such a large selection as mine. I've got thirty-two shades, whereas at a common or garden nursery you'll be lucky to find six. Do you think your wife would like me to send her some bulbs?

VANEK I'm sure she would—

STANEK There's still time to plant them, you know. (*Pause.*) Ferdinand—

VANEK Yes?

STANEK Weren't you surprised when I suddenly rang you up?

VANEK A bit—

STANEK I thought so. After all, I happen to be among those who've still managed to keep their heads above water and I quite understand that—because of this—you might want to keep a certain distance from me.

VANEK No, not I—

STANEK Perhaps not you yourself, but I realize that some of your friends believe that anyone who's still got some chance today has either abdicated morally, or is unforgivably fooling himself.

VANEK I don't think so—

STANEK I wouldn't blame you if you did, because I know only too well the grounds from which such prejudice could grow. (*An embarrassed pause.*) Ferdinand—

VANEK Yes?

STANEK I realize what a high price you have to pay for what you're doing. But please don't think it's all that easy for a man who's either so lucky, or so unfortunate as to be still tolerated by the official apparatus, and who—at the same time—wishes to live at peace with his conscience.

VANEK I know what you mean—

STANEK   In some respects it may be even harder for him.

VANEK   I understand.

STANEK   Naturally, I didn't call you in order to justify myself! I don't really think there's any need. I called you, because I like you and I'd be sorry to see you sharing the prejudice which I assume exists among your friends.

VANEK   As far as I know nobody has ever said a bad word about you—

STANEK   Not even Pavel?

VANEK   No—

STANEK   (*embarrassed pause*)   Ferdinand—

VANEK   Yes?

STANEK   Excuse me— (*gets up; crosses to the tape recorder; switches it on; soft, nondescript background music under the following dialogue.* STANEK *returns to his chair.*) Ferdinand, does the name Javurek mean anything to you?

VANEK   Our pop bard? I know him very well—

STANEK   So I expect you know what happened to him.

VANEK   Of course. They locked him up for telling a story during one of his performances. The story about the copper who meets a penguin in the street—

STANEK   Ridiculous, isn't it? It was just an excuse, that's all. The fact is, they hate his guts because he sings the way he does. Good Lord! The whole thing is so cruel, so ludicrous, so base!

VANEK   And cowardly—

STANEK   Right! And cowardly! Look, I've been trying to do something for the lad. I mean, I know a few chaps at the town council and at the prosecutor's office, but you know how it is. Promises, promises! They all say they're going to look into it, but the moment your back is turned they drop it like a hot potato, so they don't get their fingers burnt! Sickening, the way everybody looks out for number one!

VANEK   Still, I think it's nice of you to have tried to do something—

STANEK   My dear Ferdinand, I'm really not the sort of man your friends obviously take me for! Peanuts?

VANEK   No, thanks—

STANEK   (*short pause*)   About Javurek—

VANEK   Yes?

STANEK   Since I didn't manage to accomplish anything through private intervention, it occurred to me perhaps it ought to be handled in a somewhat different way. You know what I mean. Simply write something—a protest or a petition? In fact, this is the main thing I wanted to discuss with you. Naturally, you're far more experienced in these matters than I. If this document contains a few fairly well-known signatures—like yours, for example—it's bound to be published somewhere abroad which might create some political pressure. Right? I mean, these things don't seem to impress them all that much, actually—but honestly, I don't see any other way to help the lad. Not to mention Annie—

VANEK   Annie?

STANEK   My daughter.

VANEK   Oh? Is that your daughter?

STANEK   That's right.

VANEK   Well, what about her?

STANEK   I thought you knew.

VANEK   Knew what?

STANEK   She's expecting. By Javurek—

VANEK   Oh, I see. That's why—

STANEK   Wait a minute! If you mean the case interests me merely because of family matters—

VANEK   I didn't mean that—

STANEK   But you just said—

VANEK   I only wanted to say, that's how you know about the case at all; you were explaining to me how you got to know about it. Frankly, I wouldn't have expected you to be familiar with the present pop scene. I'm sorry if it sounded as though I meant—

STANEK   I'd get involved in this case even if it was someone else expecting his child! No matter who—

VANEK   I know—

STANEK (*embarrassed pause*)   Well, what do you think about my idea of writing some sort of protest?

VANEK   Where did I leave my briefcase?

STANEK (*puzzled*)   By your chair—

VANEK   Oh, yes, of course— (*opens his briefcase, rummages inside, finds what he was looking for, hands the document to* STANEK) I guess this is the sort of thing you had in mind—

STANEK   What?

VANEK   Here—

STANEK (*grabs the document*)   What is it?

VANEK   Have a look—

STANEK (*glances at it*)   Good Lord! (*reads carefully, clearly surprised, getting excited; mumbles as he reads; finishes his reading, flabbergasted*) Well! Well, well! (*jumps up, begins to pace about in some agitation, the document in his hand*) Now isn't it marvelous! Marvelous!—That's a laugh, isn't it? Eh?— Good Lord! Here I was cudgeling my brains how to go about it, finally I take the plunge and consult you—and all this time you've had the whole thing wrapped up and ready! Isn't it marvelous? I knew I was doing the right thing when I turned to you! No question about it! (*sits down, glances at the document, slams it with his hand*) There! Precisely what I had in mind! Brief, to the point, fair, and yet emphatic. Manifestly the work of a professional! I'd be sweating over it for a whole day and I'd never come up with anything remotely like this!

VANEK (*mumbles in shy appreciation at the compliment*)

STANEK   Listen, just a small point—here at the end—do you think "wilfulness" is the right word to use? Couldn't one find a milder synonym, perhaps? Somehow seems a bit misplaced, you know. I mean, the whole text is composed in very measured, factual terms—and this word here suddenly sticks out, sounds much too emotional, wouldn't you agree? Otherwise it's absolutely perfect. Maybe the second paragraph is somewhat superfluous, in fact it's just a rehash of the first one. Except for the reference here to Javurek's impact on nonconformist youth. Excellent! Well done! This must stay. How about putting it at the end instead of your "wilfulness"? Wouldn't that do the trick?—But these are just my personal impressions. Good heavens! Why should you listen to what I have to say! On the whole the text is excellent and no doubt it's going to hit the mark. Let me say again, Ferdinand, how much I admire you. Your knack for expressing the fundamental points of an issue, while avoiding all needless abuse, is indeed rare in these parts!

VANEK   Come on—you don't really mean that—

STANEK   Great piece of work! Thank you for letting me see it. Here— (*hands the document back to* VANEK) You better put it back in your briefcase. (*drinks; short pause*) Anyway, it's good to know there's somebody around whom one can always turn to and rely on in a case like this.

VANEK   Good gracious, it's only natural, isn't it?

STANEK   It may seem so to you. But in the circles where I've to move such things aren't in the least natural! The natural response is much more likely to be the exact opposite. When a man gets into trouble everybody drops him as soon as possible, the lot of them. And out of fear for their own positions they try to convince all and sundry they've never had anything to do with him; on the contrary, they sized him up right away, they wouldn't have ever touched him with a barge pole! But why am I telling you all this, you know best the sort of thing that happens! Right? When you were in prison your long-time theatre pals held forth against you on the box. It was revolting!

VANEK   I'm not angry with them—

STANEK   But I am! And what's more I told them so. In no uncertain terms! You know, a man in my position learns to put up with a lot of things, but—if you'll forgive me—there are limits! I appreciate it might be awkward for you to blame the lads, as you happen to be the injured party. But listen to me, old boy. You've got to distance yourself from the affair, that's all! Just think! Once we, too, begin to tolerate this sort of muck—we're *de facto* assuming co-responsibility for the entire moral marasmus and indirectly contributing to its deeper penetration. Am I right?

VANEK   Mmnn—

STANEK   (*short pause*)   Have you sent it off yet?

VANEK   We're still collecting signatures—

STANEK   How many have you got so far?

VANEK   About fifty—

STANEK   Fifty? Not bad! (*short pause*) Well, never mind, I've just missed the boat, that's all.

VANEK   You haven't—

STANEK   But the thing's already in hand, isn't it?

VANEK   Yes, but it's still open—I mean—

STANEK   All right, but now it's sure to be sent off and published, right? By the way, I wouldn't give it to any of the agencies, if I were you. They'll only print a measly little news item which is bound to be overlooked. Better hand it over directly to one of the big European papers, so the whole text gets published, including all the signatures!

VANEK   I know—

STANEK   (*short pause*)   Do they already know about it?

VANEK   You mean the police?

STANEK   Yes.

VANEK   I don't think so. I suppose not—

STANEK   Look here, I don't want to give you any advice, but it seems to me you ought to wrap it up as soon as possible, else they'll get wind of what's going on and they'll find a way to stop it. Fifty signatures should be enough! Besides, what counts is not the number of signatures, but their significance.

VANEK   Each signature has its own significance!

STANEK   Absolutely, but as far as publicity abroad is concerned, it is essential that some well-known names are represented, right? Has Pavel signed?

VANEK   Yes—

STANEK   Good. His name—no matter what one may think of him personally— does mean something in the world today!

VANEK   No question—

STANEK   (*short pause*)   Listen, Ferdinand—

VANEK   Yes?

STANEK   There's one more thing I wanted to discuss with you. It's a bit delicate, though–

VANEK   Oh?

STANEK   Look here, I'm no millionaire, you know, but so far I've been able to manage—

VANEK   Good for you—

STANEK   Well, I was thinking—I mean—I'd like to—Look, a lot of your friends have lost their jobs. I was thinking—Would you be prepared to accept from me a certain sum of money?

VANEK   That's very nice of you! Some of my friends indeed find themselves in a bit of a spot. But there are problems, you know. I mean, one is never quite sure how to go about it. Those who most need help are often the most reluctant to accept—

STANEK   You won't be able to work miracles with what I can afford, but I expect there are situations when every penny counts. (*takes out his wallet, removes two banknotes, hesitates, adds a third, hands them to* VANEK) Here—please—a small offering.

VANEK   Thank you very much. Let me thank you for all my friends—

STANEK   Gracious, we've got to help each other out, don't we? Peanuts?

VANEK   Not for me—

STANEK   (*helps himself; munching*) Incidentally, there's no need for you to mention this little contribution comes from me. I don't wish to erect a monument to myself. I'm sure you've gathered that much by now, eh?

VANEK   Yes. Again many thanks—

STANEK   Well now, how about having a look at the garden?

VANEK   Mr. Stanek—

STANEK   Yes?

VANEK   We'd like to send it off tomorrow—

STANEK   What?

VANEK   The protest—

STANEK   Excellent! The sooner the better!

VANEK   So that today there's still—

STANEK   Today you should think about getting some sleep! That's the main thing! Don't forget you've a bit of a hangover after last night and tomorrow is going to be a hard day for you!

VANEK   I know. All I was going to say—

STANEK   Better go straight home and unplug the phone. Else Landovský rings you up again and heaven knows how you'll end up!

VANEK   Yes, I know. There're only a few signatures I've still got to collect—it won't take long. All I was going to say—I hope you'll agree with me—I mean, don't you think it would be helpful—As a matter of fact it would be sensational! After all, practically everybody's read your *Crash!*

STANEK   Oh, come on, Ferdinand! That was fifteen years ago!

VANEK   But it's never been forgotten!

STANEK   What do you mean—sensational?

VANEK   I'm sorry, I had the impression you'd actually like to—

STANEK   What?

VANEK   Participate—

STANEK   Participate? Wait a minute. Are you talking about the signatures? Is that what you're talking about?

VANEK   Yes—

STANEK   You mean I should—

VANEK   I'm sorry, but I had the impression—

STANEK   Good Lord! I'm going to have some more brandy. How about you?

VANEK   No, thanks—

STANEK   Suit yourself— (*crosses to bar, pours himself a drink; returns to his chair; drinks; pause*) Now that's a laugh, isn't it?

VANEK   What's a laugh?

STANEK   For heaven's sake, can't you see how absurd it is? Eh? I ask you over
hoping you might write something about Javurek's case, you come here and
produce a finished text and what's more, one furnished with fifty signatures! I'm bowled over like a little child, can't believe my eyes and ears, I
worry about ways to stop them from ruining your project—and all this time
it hasn't occurred to me to do the one simple, natural thing which I should
have done in the first place! I mean, at once sign the document myself! Well,
you must admit it's absurd!

VANEK   Mmnn—

STANEK   Listen, Ferdinand, isn't this a really terrifying testimony to the situation into which we've been brought? Isn't it? Just think: even I, though I
know it's rubbish, even I've got used to the idea that the signing of protests
is the business of local specialists, professionals in solidarity, dissidents!
While the rest of us—when we want to do something for the sake of ordinary human decency—automatically turn to you, as though you were a sort
of service establishment for moral matters. In other words, we're here simply to keep our mouths shut and to be rewarded by the relative peace and
quiet, whereas you're here to speak up for us and to be rewarded by kicks on
earth and glory in the heavens! Perverse, isn't it?

VANEK   Mmnn—

STANEK   Of course it is! And they've managed to bring things to such a point
that even a fairly intelligent and decent fellow—which, with your permission, I still think I am—is more or less ready to take this situation for
granted! As though it was quite normal, perfectly natural! Sickening, isn't it?
Sickening the depths we've reached! What do you say? Makes one puke, eh?

VANEK   Well—

STANEK   You think the nation can ever recover from all this?

VANEK   Hard to say—

STANEK   What can one do? What can one do? Well, seems clear, doesn't it? In
theory, that is. Everybody should start with himself. What? However! Is this
country inhabited only by Vaneks? It really doesn't seem that everybody can
become a fighter for human rights.

VANEK   Not everybody, no—

STANEK   Where is it?

VANEK   What?

STANEK   The list of signatures, of course.

VANEK (*embarrassed pause*)   Mr. Stanek—

STANEK   Yes?

VANEK   Forgive me, but—I'm sorry, I've suddenly a funny feeling that perhaps—

STANEK   What funny feeling?

VANEK   I don't know—I feel very embarrassed—Well, it seems to me perhaps I
wasn't being quite fair—

STANEK   In what way?

VANEK   Well, what I did—was a bit of a con trick—in a way—

STANEK   What are you talking about?

VANEK   I mean, first I let you talk, and only then I ask for your signature—I mean, after you're already sort of committed by what you've said before, you see—

STANEK   Are you suggesting that if I'd known you were collecting signatures for Javurek, I would never have started talking about him?

VANEK   No, that's not what I mean—

STANEK   Well, what do you mean?

VANEK   How shall I put it—

STANEK   Oh, come on! You mind I didn't organize the whole thing myself, is that it?

VANEK   No, that's not it—

STANEK   What is it then?

VANEK   Well, it seems to me it would've been a quite different matter if I'd come to you right away and asked for your signature. That way you would've had an option—

STANEK   And why didn't you come to me right away, actually? Was it because you'd simply written me off in advance?

VANEK   Well, I was thinking that in your position—

STANEK   Ah! There you are! You see? Now it's becoming clear what you really think of me, isn't it? You think that because now and then one of my pieces happens to be shown on the box, I'm no longer capable of the simplest act of solidarity!

VANEK   You misunderstand me—What I meant was—

STANEK   Let me tell you something, Ferdinand. (*drinks; short pause*) Look here, if I've—willy-nilly—got used to the perverse idea that common decency and morality are the exclusive domain of the dissidents—then you've—willy-nilly—got used to the idea as well! That's why it never crossed your mind that certain values might be more important to me than my present position. But suppose even I wanted to be finally a free man, suppose even I wished to renew my inner integrity and shake off the yoke of humiliation and shame? It never entered your head that I might've been actually waiting for this very moment for years, what? You simply placed me once and for all among those hopeless cases, among those whom it would be pointless to count on in any way. Right? And now that you found I'm not entirely indifferent to the fate of others—you made that slip about my signature! But you saw at once what happened, and so you began to apologize to me. Good God! Don't you realize how you humiliate me? What if all this time I'd been hoping for an opportunity to act, to do something that would again make a man of me, help me to be once more at peace with myself, help me to find again the free play of my imagination and my lost sense of humor, rid me of the need to escape my traumas by minding the apricots and the blooming magnolias! Suppose even I prefer to live in truth! What if I want to return from the world of custom-made literature and the proto-culture of the box to the world of art which isn't geared to serve anyone at all?

VANEK   I'm sorry—forgive me! I didn't mean to hurt your feelings—Wait a minute, I'll—Just a moment— (*rummages in his briefcase, extracts the list of signatures from among his papers, and hands it to* STANEK) Here you are, Mr. Stanek—

STANEK   What is it? The signatures?

VANEK   Yes—

STANEK   Ah! Good. (*peruses the list, mumbles, nods, gets up, begins to pace around*) Let me think aloud. May I?

VANEK   By all means—

STANEK (*halts, drinks, begins to pace again as he talks*)   I believe I've already covered the main points concerning the subjective side of the matter. If I sign the document, I'm going to regain—after years of being continually sick at my stomach—my self-esteem, my lost freedom, my honor, and perhaps even some regard among those close to me. I'll leave behind the insoluble dilemmas, forced on me by the conflict between my concern for my position and my conscience. I'll be able to face with equanimity Annie, myself, and even that lad when he comes back. It'll cost me my job. Though my job brings me no satisfaction—on the contrary, it brings me shame—nevertheless, it does support me and my family a great deal better than if I were to become a night watchman. It's more than likely that my son won't be permitted to continue his studies. On the other hand, I'm sure he's going to have more respect for me that way, than if his permission to study was bought by my refusal to sign the protest for Javurek. He happens to worship Javurek, as a matter of fact. He's crazy about him! (*sighs with some exasperation*) —Well then. This is the subjective side of the matter. Now how about the objective side? What happens when—among the signatures of a few well-known dissidents and a handful of Javurek's teenage friends—there suddenly crops up—to everybody's surprise and against all expectation—my signature? The signature of a man who hasn't been heard from regarding civic affairs for years! Well? What? Let's think about it. My co-signatories—as well as many of those who don't sign documents of this sort, but who nonetheless deep down side with those who do—are naturally going to welcome my signature with pleasure. The closed circle of habitual signers—whose signatures, by the way, are already beginning to lose their clout, because they cost practically nothing. I mean, the people in question have long since lost all ways and means by which they could actually pay for their signatures. Right? Well, this circle will be broken. A new name will appear, a name the value of which depends precisely on its previous absence. And of course, I may add, on the high price paid for its appearance! So much for the objective "plus" of my prospective signature. Now what about the authorities? My signature is going to surprise, annoy and upset them for the very reasons which will bring joy to the other signatories. I mean, because it'll make a breach in the barrier the authorities have been building around your lot for so long and with such effort. All right. Let's see about Javurek. Concerning his case, I very much doubt my participation would significantly influence its outcome. And if so, I'm afraid it's more than likely going to have a negative effect. The authorities will be anxious to prove they haven't been panicked. They'll want to show that a surprise of this sort can't make them lose their cool. Which brings us to the consideration of what they're going to do to me. Surely, my signature is bound to have a much more significant influence on what happens in my case. No doubt, they're going to punish me far more cruelly than you'd expect. The point being that my punishment will serve them as a warning signal to all those who might be tempted to follow my example in the future, choose freedom, and thus swell the ranks of the dissidents. You may be sure they'll want to teach them a lesson! Show them what the score is! Right? The thing is—well, let's face it—they're no longer worried all that much about dissident activities within the confines of the established ghetto. In some respects they even seem to prod them on here and there. But! What they're really afraid of is any semblance of a crack in the fence around the ghetto! That's what really scares them! So they'll want to exorcize the bogey of a prospective epidemic of dissent by an exemplary punishment of myself. They'll want to nip it in the bud, that's all. (*drinks; pause*) The last question I've got to ask myself is this: what sort of reaction to my signature can one expect among those who, in one way or another, have followed what you might call "the path of accommodation." I mean people who are, or ought to be, our main concern, because—I'm sure you'll agree—our hope for the future depends above all on whether or not it will be possible to awake them from their slumbers and to enlist them to take an active part in civic affairs. This is what really matters, isn't it? Well, I'm afraid that my signature is going to be received with absolute resentment by this crucial section of the populace. You know why? Because, as a matter of fact, these people secretly hate the dissidents. They've become their bad conscience, their living reproach! That's how they see the dissidents. And at the same time, they envy them their honor and their inner freedom, values which they themselves were denied by fate. This is why they never miss an opportunity to smear the dissidents. And precisely this opportunity is going to be offered to them by my signature. They're going to spread nasty rumors about you and your friends. They're going to say that you who have nothing more to lose—you who have long since landed at the bottom of the heap and, what's more, managed to make yourselves quite at home in there—are now trying to drag down to your own level an unfortunate man, a man who's so far been able to stay above the salt line. You're dragging him down—irresponsible as you are—without the slightest compunction, just for your own whim, just because you wish to irritate the authorities by creating a false impression that your ranks are being swelled! What do you care about losing him his job! Doesn't matter, does it? Or do you mean to suggest you'll find him a job down in the dump in which you yourselves exist? What? No—Ferdinand! I'm sorry. I'm afraid, I'm much too familiar with the way these people think! After all, I've got to live among them, day in day out. I know precisely what they're going to say. They'll say I'm your victim, shamelessly abused, misguided, led astray by your cynical appeal to my humanity! They'll say that in your ruthlessness you didn't shrink even from making use of my personal relationship to Javurek! And you know what? They're going to say that all the humane ideals you're constantly proclaiming have been tarnished by your treatment of me. That's the sort of reasoning one can expect from them! And I'm sure I don't have to tell you that the authorities are bound to support this inter-pretation, and to fan the coals as hard as they can! There are others, of course, somewhat more intelligent perhaps. These people might say that the extraordinary appearance of my signature among yours is actually counter-productive, in that it concentrates everybody's attention on my signature and away from the main issue concerning Javurek. They'll say it puts the whole protest in jeopardy, because one can't help asking oneself what was the purpose of the exercise: was it to help Javurek, or to parade a new-born dissident? I wouldn't be at all surprised if someone were to say that, as a matter of fact, Javurek was victimized by you and your friends. It might be suggested his personal tragedy only served you to further your ends—which are far removed from the fate of the unfortunate man. Furthermore, it'll be pointed out that by getting my signature you managed to dislodge me from the one area of operation—namely, backstage diplomacy, private interven-tion—where I've been so far able to maneuver and where I might have proved infinitely more helpful to Javurek in the end! I do hope you under-stand me, Ferdinand. I don't wish to exaggerate the importance of these opinions, nor am I prepared to become their slave. On the other hand, it seems to be in the interests of our case for me to take them into account. Af-ter all, it's a matter of a political decision and a good politician must con-sider all the issues which are likely to influence the end result of his action. Right? In these circumstances the question one must resolve is as follows: what do I prefer? Do I prefer the inner liberation which my signature is go-ing to bring me, a liberation paid for—as it now turns out—by a basically negative objective impact—or do I choose the other alternative. I mean, the more beneficial effect which the protest would have without my signature, yet paid for by my bitter awareness that I've again—who knows, perhaps for the last time—missed a chance to shake off the bonds of shameful compro-mises in which I've been choking for years? In other words, if I'm to act in-deed ethically—and I hope by now you've no doubt I want to do just that—which course should I take? Should I be guided by ruthless objective considerations, or by subjective inner feelings?

VANEK   Seems perfectly clear to me—

STANEK   And to me—

VANEK   So that you're going to—

STANEK   Unfortunately—

VANEK   Unfortunately?

STANEK   You thought I was—

VANEK   Forgive me, perhaps I didn't quite understand—

STANEK   I'm sorry if I've—

VANEK   Never mind—

STANEK   But I really believe—

VANEK   I know—

(STANEK *hands* VANEK *the list of signatures, crosses to the tape recorder, switches it off, returns to his chair, sits down.*)

VANEK (*puts papers back in his briefcase*)

(*Both drink.*)

VANEK (*shudders, emits a soft groan*)

STANEK (*embarrassed pause*)   Are you angry?

VANEK   No—

STANEK   You don't agree, though—

VANEK   I respect your reasoning—

STANEK   But what do you think?

VANEK   What should I think?

STANEK   That's obvious, isn't it?

VANEK   Is it?

STANEK   You think that when I saw all the signatures, I did, after all, get the wind up!

VANEK   I don't—

STANEK   I can see you do!

VANEK   I assure you—

STANEK   Why don't you level with me? Don't you realize that your benevolent hypocrisy is actually far more insulting than if you gave it to me straight?! Or do you mean I'm not even worthy of your comment?!

VANEK   But I told you, didn't I, I respect your reasoning—

STANEK   I'm not an idiot, Vanek!

VANEK   Of course not—

STANEK   I know precisely what's behind your "respect"!

VANEK   What is?

STANEK   A feeling of moral superiority!

VANEK   You're wrong—

STANEK   Only, I'm not quite sure if you—you of all people—have any right to feel so superior!

VANEK   What do you mean?

STANEK   You know very well what I mean!

VANEK   I don't—

STANEK   Shall I tell you?

VANEK   Please do—

STANEK (*emphatic*)   Well! As far as I know, in prison you talked more than you should have!

VANEK (*gasps, jumps up, wildly staring at* STANEK)

STANEK (*stares back in triumph*)   Right? (*short, tense pause*)

VANEK (*almost inaudible*)   What??

(*The telephone rings.*)

VANEK (*broken, sinks back in his chair*)

STANEK (*crosses to the phone, lifts the receiver*)   Hello—Yes—What?—Good Lord! You mean—Wait a minute—I see—I see—Where are you?—Yes, yes, of course—Absolutely!—Good!—You bet!—Sure—I'll be here waiting for you! Bye bye. (*replaces the receiver; pauses; returns to his chair, to* VANEK) You can go and burn it downstairs in the furnace!

VANEK   What?

STANEK   He's just walked into the canteen! To see Annie.

VANEK   Who did?

STANEK   Javurek! Who else?

VANEK (*jumps up*)   Javurek? You mean he was released? But that's wonderful! So your private intervention did work, after all! Just as well we didn't send off the protest a few days earlier! I'm sure they would've got their backs up and kept him inside!

STANEK (*pause. stares at* VANEK. *then suddenly cordial*)   My dear fellow, you mustn't fret! There's always the risk that you can do more harm than good by your activities! Right? Heavens, if you should worry about this sort of thing, you'd never be able to do anything at all! Come, let me get you those saplings—

End

STUDY QUESTIONS

1. What is the significance of all the small comforts, refreshments, and gifts— the slippers, the brandy, the money—that Stanek offers to Vanek?
2. What does Stanek's garden symbolize?
3. Discuss how the personal and the political are intertwined in the play.
4. How does Havel develop the theme of the great moral divide between simply talking about evil and actually doing something to oppose it?

POSSIBLE ESSAY TOPICS

1. Explore similarities between Stanek in *Protest* and Hamlet in Shakespeare's play.
2. Compare *A Raisin in the Sun* and *Protest* as plays about the psychological effects of living under various kinds of oppression.
3. Discuss Havel's idea of the paradoxical positive effects that may come out of living in a totalitarian state.

INDEX OF TERMS

INDEX OF AUTHORS AND TITLES

INDEX OF FIRST LINES